Profitability

Ratio	Formula	Page
Return on assets ratio	$\dfrac{\text{Net income}}{\text{Average total assets}}$	p. 60
Profit margin ratio	$\dfrac{\text{Net income}}{\text{Net sales}}$	p. 60
Gross profit rate	$\dfrac{\text{Gross profit}}{\text{Net sales}}$	p. 221
Operating expenses to sales ratio	$\dfrac{\text{Operating expenses}}{\text{Net sales}}$	p. 222
Average useful life of plant assets	$\dfrac{\text{Average cost of plant assets}}{\text{Depreciation expense}}$	p. 416
Average age of plant assets	$\dfrac{\text{Accumulated depreciation}}{\text{Depreciation expense}}$	p. 418
Asset turnover ratio	$\dfrac{\text{Net sales}}{\text{Average total assets}}$	p. 418
Payout ratio	$\dfrac{\text{Cash dividends declared on common stock}}{\text{Net income}}$	p. 533
Dividend yield	$\dfrac{\text{Cash dividends declared per share}}{\text{Stock price at year-end}}$	p. 533
Earnings per share	$\dfrac{\text{Net income} - \text{Preferred stock dividends}}{\text{Average common shares outstanding}}$	p. 534
Price-earnings ratio	$\dfrac{\text{Stock price per share}}{\text{Earnings per share}}$	p. 535
Return on common stockholders' equity	$\dfrac{\text{Net income} - \text{Preferred stock dividends}}{\text{Average common stockholders' equity}}$	p. 536
Cash return on sales ratio	$\dfrac{\text{Cash provided by operations}}{\text{Net sales}}$	p. 637

FINANCIAL ACCOUNTING

Tools for Business Decision Making

PAUL D. KIMMEL PhD, CPA
Associate Professor of Accounting
University of Wisconsin—Milwaukee

JERRY J. WEYGANDT PhD, CPA
Arthur Andersen Alumni Professor of Accounting
University of Wisconsin

DONALD E. KIESO PhD, CPA
KPMG Peat Marwick Emeritus Professor of Accountancy
Northern Illinois University

2ND
EDITION

JOHN WILEY & SONS, INC.
New York • Chichester • Weinheim
Brisbane • Singapore • Toronto

Dedicated to
our parents and our in-laws,
and to our families,
most especially our spouses,
      Merlynn
      Enid
      Donna

PUBLISHER: Susan Elbe
SENIOR DEVELOPMENT EDITOR: Nancy Perry
PRODUCTION SERVICES MANAGER: Jeanine Furino
SENIOR DESIGNER: Kevin Murphy
ILLUSTRATION EDITOR: Sandra Rigby
PRODUCTION MANAGEMENT SERVICES: Elm Street Publishing Services, Inc.
PHOTO EDITOR: Nicole Horlacher
COVER ART AND TEXT DESIGN: Kenny Beck
COVER DESIGN: Lynn Rogan

This book was set in New Aster by York Graphic Services and printed and bound by Von Hoffmann Press. The cover was printed by Von Hoffmann Press.

This book is printed on acid-free paper. ∞

ISBN 0-471-34774-4
Printed in the United States of America

10 9 8 7 6 5

ABOUT THE AUTHORS

Paul D. Kimmel, PhD, CPA, received his bachelor's degree from the University of Minnesota and his doctorate in accounting from the University of Wisconsin. He is an Associate Professor at the University of Wisconsin–Milwaukee. He has public accounting experience with Deloitte & Touche (Minneapolis). He is the recipient of the UWM School of Business Advisory Council Teaching Award, the Reggie Taite Excellence in Teaching Award, a three-time winner of the Outstanding Teaching Assistant Award at the University of Wisconsin, and a recipient of the Elijah Watts Sells Award for Honorary Distinction for his results on the CPA exam. He is a member of the American Accounting Association and has published articles in the *Accounting Review, Accounting Horizons, Issues in Accounting Education,* and the *Journal of Accounting Education* as well as other journals. His research interests include accounting for financial instruments and innovation in accounting education. He has published papers and given numerous talks on incorporating critical thinking into accounting education and helped prepare a catalog of critical thinking resources for the Federated Schools of Accountancy.

Jerry J. Weygandt, PhD, CPA, is Arthur Andersen Alumni Professor of Accounting at the University of Wisconsin–Madison. He holds a Ph.D. in accounting from the University of Illinois. Articles by Professor Weygandt have appeared in the *Accounting Review, Journal of Accounting Research,* the *Journal of Accountancy,* and other professional journals. These articles have examined such financial reporting issues as accounting for price-level adjustments, pensions, convertible securities, stock option contracts, and interim reports. He is a member of the American Accounting Association, the American Institute of Certified Public Accountants, and the Wisconsin Society of Certified Public Accountants. He has served on numerous committees of the American Accounting Association and as a member of the editorial board of the *Accounting Review.* In addition, he is actively involved with the American Institute of Certified Public Accountants and has been a member of the Accounting Standards Executive Committee (AcSEC) of that organization. He has served on the FASB task force that examined the reporting issues related to "accounting for income taxes" and is presently a trustee of the Financial Accounting Foundation. Professor Weygandt has received the Chancellor's Award for Excellence in Teaching; he also has served as President and Secretary-Treasurer of the American Accounting Association. Recently he received the Wisconsin Institute of CPAs' Outstanding Educator's Award and the Lifetime Achievement Award.

Donald E. Kieso, PhD, CPA, received his bachelor's degree from Aurora University and his doctorate in accounting from the University of Illinois. He has served as chairman of the Department of Accountancy and is currently the KPMG Peat Marwick Emeritus Professor of Accountancy at Northern Illinois University. He has public accounting experience with Price Waterhouse & Co. (San Francisco and Chicago) and Arthur Andersen & Co. (Chicago) and research experience with the Research Division of the American Institute of Certified Public Accountants (New York). He is a recipient of NIU's Teaching Excellence Award and four Golden Apple Teaching Awards. He has served as a member of the Board of Directors of the Illinois CPA Society, the AACSB's Accounting Accreditation Committee, the State of Illinois Comptroller's Commission, as Secretary-Treasurer of the Federation of Schools of Accountancy, and as Secretary-Treasurer of the American Accounting Association. Professor Kieso is serving as Chairman of the Board of Trustees and Executive Committee of Aurora University, the Boards of Directors of Castle BancGroup Inc. and Valley West Community Hospital, and as Secretary-Treasurer of The Sandwich Hospital Resolution Board. From 1989 to 1993 he served as a charter member of the national Accounting Education Change Commission. In 1988 he received the Outstanding Accounting Educator Award from the Illinois CPA Society; in 1992 he received the FSA's Joseph A. Silvoso Award of Merit and the NIU Foundation's Humanitarian Award for Service to Higher Education; and in 1995 he received a Distinguished Service Award from the Illinois CPA Society.

PREFACE

In recent years accounting education has seen numerous efforts to change the way accounting is taught. These efforts reflect the demands of an ever-changing business world, opportunities created by new instructional technologies, and an increased understanding of how students learn. In this book we have drawn from what we believe to be the most promising of these innovations. Our efforts were driven by a few key beliefs.

"Less is more." Our instructional objective is to provide students with an understanding of those concepts that are fundamental to the use of accounting. Most students will forget procedural details within a short period of time. On the other hand, concepts, if well taught, should be remembered for a lifetime. Concepts are especially important in a world where the details are constantly changing.

"Don't just sit there—do something." Students learn best when they are actively engaged. The overriding pedagogical objective of this book is to provide students with continual opportunities for active learning. One of the best tools for active learning is strategically placed questions. Our discussions are framed by questions, often beginning with rhetorical questions and ending with review questions. Even our selection of analytical devices, called Decision Toolkits, uses key questions to demonstrate the purpose of each.

"I'll believe it when I see it." Students will be most willing to commit time and energy to a topic when they believe that it is relevant to their future career. There is no better way to demonstrate relevance than to ground discussion in the real world. Consistent with this, we adopted a macro-approach: Chapters 1 and 2 show students how to use financial statements of real companies. By using high-profile companies such as Tootsie Roll, Microsoft, Nike, and Intel to frame our discussion of accounting issues, we demonstrate the relevance of accounting while teaching students about companies with which they have daily contact. As they become acquainted with the financial successes and failures of these companies, many students will begin to follow business news more closely, making their learning a dynamic, ongoing process. We also discuss small companies to highlight the challenges faced by small companies as they try to grow big.

"You need to make a decision." All business people must make decisions. Decision making involves critical evaluation and analysis of the information at hand, and this takes practice. We have integrated important analytical tools throughout the book. After each new decision tool is presented, we summarize the key features of that tool in a Decision Toolkit. At the end of each chapter we provide a comprehensive demonstration of an analysis of a real company using the decision tools presented in the chapter. The presentation of these tools throughout the book is logically sequenced to take full advantage of the tools presented in earlier chapters, culminating in a capstone analysis chapter.

"It's a small world." Rapid improvements to both information technology and transportation are resulting in a single global economy. The Internet has made it possible for even small businesses to sell their products virtually anywhere in the world. Few business decisions can be made without consideration to international factors. To heighten student awareness of international issues, we have increased references to international companies and issues and have added a new type of exercise, called A Global Focus, in each chapter.

KEY FEATURES OF EACH CHAPTER

Chapter 1, Introduction to Financial Statements
* Explains the purpose of each of the financial statements.
* Uses financial statements of a hypothetical company (to keep it simple), followed by those for a real company, **Tootsie Roll Industries** (to make it relevant).
* Presents accounting assumptions and principles.

Chapter 2, A Further Look at Financial Statements
* Discusses revenues, expenses, assets, and liabilities.
* Presents the classified balance sheet.
* Applies ratio analysis to real companies—**Best Buy** and **Circuit City** (current ratio, debt to total assets, return on assets, current cash debt coverage, and cash debt coverage).

Chapter 3, The Accounting Information System
* Covers transaction analysis—emphasizes fundamentals while avoiding unnecessary detail.

Chapter 4, Accrual Accounting Concepts
* Emphasizes difference between cash and accrual accounting.
* Discusses how some companies manage earnings through accrual practices.
* Presents minimal discussion of closing and worksheets; additional detail provided in an appendix.

Chapter 5, Merchandising Operations
* Introduces merchandising concepts using perpetual inventory approach.
* Presents the multiple-step income statement.
* Applies ratio analysis to real companies—**Kmart** and **Wal-Mart** (gross profit rate and operating expenses to sales ratio).

Chapter 6, Reporting and Analyzing Inventory
* Introduces the periodic inventory approach and compares it to perpetual.
* Covers cost flow assumptions and their implications for financial reporting. For simplification, emphasizes the periodic approach. Cost flow assumptions under perpetual inventory systems covered in an appendix.
* Applies ratio analysis to real companies—**Kmart** and **Wal-Mart** (inventory turnover).
* Discusses implications of LIFO reserve for real company—**Caterpillar Inc.**

Chapter 7, Internal Control and Cash
* Covers internal control concepts and implications of control failures.
* Presents bank reconciliation as a control device.
* Discusses cash management, including operating cycle, cash budgeting, ratio of cash to daily cash expenses, and free cash flow.

Chapter 8, Reporting and Analyzing Receivables
* Presents the basics of accounts and notes receivable, bad debt estimation, and interest calculations.
* Discusses receivables management, including: determining to whom to extend credit; establishing payment period; monitoring collections, evaluating the receivables balance; and accelerating receipts.
* Applies ratio analysis to a real company—**McKesson HBOC** (credit risk ratio and receivables turnover).

Chapter 9, Reporting and Analyzing Long-Lived Assets
* Covers the basics of plant assets and intangible assets.
* Discusses basics of buy or lease decision.
* Covers the implications of depreciation method choice; shows details of accelerated methods in appendix.
* Applies ratio analysis to real companies—**Southwest Airlines** and **AirTran.**
* Demonstrates implications of estimated useful life for intangible amortization to a real company—**Roberts Pharmaceuticals.**

Chapter 10, Reporting and Analyzing Liabilities
* Covers current liabilities: notes payable, sales taxes, payroll, unearned revenues, and current maturities of long-term debt.
* Covers long-term liabilities, including debt versus equity choice, bond pricing, and various types of bonds. For simplification, emphasizes straight-line amortization; effective interest method covered in an appendix.
* Includes present value discussion in an appendix.
* Discusses basics of contingent liabilities, lease obligations, and off-balance-sheet financing.
* Applies ratio analysis to real companies—**Ford** and **General Motors** (acid-test ratio, debt to total assets ratio, and times interest earned).

Chapter 11, Reporting and Analyzing Stockholders' Equity
* Presents pros and cons of corporate form of organization.
* Covers issues related to common and preferred stock, and reasons companies purchase treasury stock.
* Explains reasons for cash dividends, stock dividends, and stock splits and implications for analysis.
* Applies ratio analysis to real companies—**Nike** and **Reebok** (earnings per share, price-earnings ratio, return on common stockholders' equity, payout ratio, and dividend yield).

Chapter 12, Reporting and Analyzing Investments
* Explains why companies purchase investments.
* Presents alternative methods of accounting for investments.
* Discusses consolidation accounting at conceptual level.
* Analyzes implications of unrealized gains and losses of real company—**KeyCorp.**

Chapter 13, Statement of Cash Flows
* Explains purpose and usefulness of statement of cash flows.
* Splits chapter into two sections, allowing instructor to use either the indirect approach, the direct approach, or both.

- Employs two-year progression in examples, with first year looking at most basic items affecting cash flows, and second year looking at additional items.
- Applies ratio analysis to real companies—**Microsoft**, **Oracle**, **AMD**, and **Intel** (free cash flow, capital expenditure ratio, current cash debt coverage ratio, cash debt coverage ratio, and cash return on sales ratio).

Chapter 14, Financial Analysis: The Big Picture

- Capstone chapter—reinforces previous analytical tools and demonstrates their interrelationships, as well as presents new tools.
- Discusses "earnings power" and implications of discontinued operations, extraordinary items, accounting changes, nonrecurring charges, and comprehensive earnings.
- Demonstrates horizontal and vertical analysis.
- Applies comprehensive ratio analysis to real companies—**Kellogg** and **Quaker Oats**.

NEW IN THIS EDITION

The first edition was very well received. In the spirit of continuous improvement, we have made many changes in this edition. These changes come in response to suggestions made by reviewers, focus group participants, and comments from users. We sincerely appreciate your input.

Throughout the Book

- With this edition our "focus companies" are **Tootsie Roll Industries** and **Hershey Foods**. They were chosen because they had high name recognition with students, they operate primarily in a single industry, and they have relatively simple financial statements. Most importantly, the idea of evaluating candy companies seemed fun.
- In order to more closely tie the topic of each chapter to the real world, Review It questions relating to Tootsie Roll Industries have been added in every chapter.
- To enhance students' conceptual understanding of the impact of transactions, accounting equation analyses have been added in the margins next to each journal entry, beginning in Chapter 5.
- For those instructors wanting to incorporate technology in the course, most chapters now have problems that can be completed using General Ledger Software.
- Financial Reporting Problems and Comparative Analysis Problems in the Broadening Your Perspective section now cover Tootsie Roll Industries and Hershey Foods.
- We have enhanced relevance by adding many new references to real companies and many new brief exercises, exercises, and problems that use real-company data.
- To emphasize the global nature of today's business world, additional references to non-U.S. companies have been added, and a new Global Focus problem has been added in the Broadening Your Perspective section in every chapter.
- To ensure complete coverage of concepts, we have included 17 new Brief Exercises, 32 new Exercises, and 39 new Problems.

Chapter 1, Introduction to Financial Statements

- New feature story introducing Tootsie Roll Industries.
- Simpler financial statements used throughout the chapter.
- New Interpreting Financial Statements problem.

Chapter 2, A Further Look at Financial Statements

- Revised feature story to further emphasize the impact of the Internet by including actual Internet bulletin board postings about Best Buy Company.
- Updated data for Best Buy Company and Circuit City.
- New infographic on characteristics of useful information.
- New introduction to ratio analysis, with explanation of percentage, rate, and proportion.
- New infographic to illustrate liquidity, solvency, and profitability measures.
- New text discussion of Best Buy's recent dividend policy, drawn from Internet bulletin board.
- New excerpts from real-world companies to illustrate balance sheet classifications.
- Moved discussion of multiple-step income statement and nonoperating items to Chapter 5.
- Reorganized Section 2 to highlight balance sheet and to pull together ratio analysis tools in a section titled "Using the Financial Statements."
- New Business Insight about French attitudes regarding investing.
- New Interpreting Financial Statements problem.
- New Financial Analysis on the Web exercise.

Chapter 3, The Accounting Information System

- Expanded presentation and explanation of services on account (accounts payable).
- New Business Insight on Rhino Foods' efforts to motivate factory workers by teaching them the impact of transactions on financial statements.
- New Research Case.

Chapter 4, Accrual Accounting Concepts

- Four new Business Insights: on revenue recognition in the film industry; accrual accounting practices of New Zealand's government; Microsoft's use of an unearned revenue account to smooth earnings; and the speeding up of quarterly closings due to advances in information technology.
- New illustrations that provide additional explanation on closing entries and posting of closing entries.
- Expanded illustration in chapter appendix that provides additional explanation of the use of work sheets.

Chapter 5, Merchandising Operations

- Updated data for Wal-Mart and Kmart.
- New Before You Go On section added on the perpetual inventory system.
- Expanded discussion of multiple-step income statement and nonoperating activities—moved here from Chapter 2.

- Equation analyses added to margins, beginning in this chapter.
- New Research Case.

Chapter 6, Reporting and Analyzing Inventory

- Updated data for Caterpillar Corporation and Manitowoc Company.
- New comparison (text and illustration) of perpetual versus periodic inventory systems.
- Revised discussion of LIFO reserve; new illustration of adjustments to determine FIFO cost of goods sold.
- New Appendix 6A on inventory cost flow methods for perpetual systems (including a Demonstration Problem).
- New Research Case.

Chapter 7, Internal Control and Cash

- Two new Business Insights: on fraud at Bankers' Trust; and the practice of many banks of processing checks from biggest to smallest to maximize their fees on bounced checks.
- Many new end-of-chapter problems.
- New Research Case.
- Two new Financial Analysis on the Web exercises.
- New Ethics Case.

Chapter 8, Reporting and Analyzing Receivables

- Provided data for pharmaceutical giant McKesson HBOC and for Del Laboratories.
- Expanded coverage of direct write-off of uncollectible accounts.
- Reorganized presentation of direct write-off and allowance methods for uncollectible accounts.
- New infographics on managing receivables.
- Expanded discussion, with real-world example, of credit risk.
- Using the Decision Toolkit revised with pharmaceutical company data.
- Four new Business Insights: on Rite Aid's attempt to boost net income by dramatically increasing its allowances from its suppliers; Sears' increase in net income resulting from the reduction of its bad debt expense; international debt problems; and the failure of JWA Security Services due to poor receivables management.
- New Research Case.

Chapter 9, Reporting and Analyzing Long-Lived Assets

- Updated data on Southwest Airlines and AirTran.
- New Business Insight on the effect on Willamette Industries' net income of a change in depreciable life.
- New Research Case

Chapter 10, Reporting and Analyzing Liabilities

- Discussion of bond trading moved out of this chapter (and into investments chapter).
- Two new Business Insights: on lack of sales tax on Internet e-commerce; and Y2K contingent liabilities.
- New end-of-chapter appendix and related assignment materials on the effective-interest method.
- New end-of-chapter appendix and related assignment materials on accounting for long-term notes payable.
- New Research Case.
- New Interpreting Financial Statements problem.

Chapter 11, Reporting and Analyzing Stockholders' Equity

- Updated data for Nike and Reebok.
- New real financial statements (Amazon.com, Tektronix) in presentation section.
- New Business Insight on subchapter S corporations.
- New Research Case.

Chapter 12, Reporting and Analyzing Investments

- Terminology changed from "temporary investments" to "short-term investments."
- Added bond trading discussion.
- New Business Insight on the reporting of bonds in the financial press.
- New Research Case.
- Two new Financial Analysis on the Web exercises.

Chapter 13, Statement of Cash Flows

- Updated data for Microsoft, Oracle, Intel, and AMD.
- New Business Insight on use of cash flow numbers by analysts.
- New Research Case.
- New Interpreting Financial Statements problem.

Chapter 14, Financial Analysis: The Big Picture

- New feature story that emphasizes just how much the investment world has changed by telling the true story of a cabby who trades online while driving his cab.
- Updated all ratios and financial measures to reflect Kellogg's 1997 and 1998 results.
- Provided Kellogg's simplified financial statements to allow calculation of all ratios.
- Two new Financial Analysis on the Web exercises.

PROVEN PEDAGOGICAL FRAMEWORK

In this book we have used many proven pedagogical tools to help students learn accounting concepts and apply them to decision making in the business world. This pedagogical framework emphasizes the *processes* students undergo as they learn.

Learning How to Use the Text

A **Student Owner's Manual** begins the text to help students understand the value of the pedagogical framework and how to use it. After becoming familiar with the pedagogy, students can take a **learning styles quiz** (page xxiv) to help them identify how they learn best (visually, aurally, through reading and writing, kinesthetically, or through a combination of these styles). We then offer tips on in-class and at-home learning strategies, as well as help in identifying the text pedagogy that would be most useful to them for their learning style. Finally, Chapter 1 contains notes (printed in red) that explain each pedagogical element the first time it appears.

Understanding the Context

- **Study Objectives**, listed at the beginning of each chapter, form a learning framework throughout the text, with each objective repeated in the margin at the appropriate place in the main body of the chapter and again in the **Summary of Study Objectives**. Also, end-of-chapter assignment materials are linked to the Study Objectives.

- A **Chapter-Opening Vignette** presents a scenario that relates an actual business situation of a well-known company to the topic of the chapter. The vignette also serves as a recurrent example throughout the chapter. Most of the vignettes include the Internet address of the company cited in the story to encourage students to go on-line to get more information about these companies.

- A chapter **Preview** links the chapter-opening vignette to the major topics of the chapter. First, an introductory paragraph explains how the vignette relates to the topics to be discussed, and then a graphic outline of the chapter provides a "visual road map," useful for seeing the big picture as well as the connections between subtopics.

Learning the Material

- This book emphasizes the accounting experiences of **real companies throughout**, from chapter-opening vignettes to the chapter's last item of homework material. Details on these many features follow. In addition, every chapter uses **financial statements** from real companies. These specimen financial statements are easily identified by the company logo or related photo that appears near the statement heading.

- Continuing the real-world flavor of the book, **Business Insight** boxes in each chapter give students glimpses into how real companies make decisions using accounting information. The boxes, highlighted with striking photographs, focus on three different accounting perspectives—those of investors, managers, and international business.

- Color **illustrations** support and reinforce the concepts of the text. Infographics are a special type of illustration that help students visualize and apply accounting concepts to the real world. The infographics often portray important concepts in entertaining and memorable ways.

- **Before You Go On** sections occur at the end of each key topic and consist of two parts: **Review It** serves as a learning check within the chapter by asking students to stop and answer knowledge and comprehension questions about the material just covered. **Review It** questions marked with the Tootsie Roll icon send students to find information in Tootsie Roll Industries' 1998 annual report, which is packaged with new copies of the book and printed in Appendix A at the back of the book. These exercises help cement students' understanding of how topics covered in the chapter are reported in real-world financial statements. Answers appear at the end of the chapter. **Do It** is a brief demonstration problem that gives immediate practice using the material just covered. Solutions are provided to help students understand the reasoning involved in reaching an answer.

- **Accounting equation analyses** have been inserted in the margin next to key journal entries. This new feature reinforces students' understanding of the impact of an accounting transaction on the financial statements.

- **Helpful Hints** in the margins expand upon or help clarify concepts under discussion in the nearby text. This feature actually makes the book an Annotated Student Edition.

- **Alternative Terminology** notes in the margins present synonymous terms that students may come across in subsequent accounting courses and in business.

- Marginal **International Notes** provide a helpful and convenient way for instructors to begin to expose students to international issues in accounting, reporting, and decision making.

- Each chapter presents **decision tools** that are useful for analyzing the financial statement components discussed in that chapter. At the end of the text discussion relating to the decision tool, a **Decision Toolkit** summarizes the key features of that decision tool and reinforces its purpose. For example, Chapter 8 presents the receivables turnover ratio and average collection period as tools for use in analyzing receivables. At the end of that discussion the Toolkit you see at the top of page ix is shown.

- A **Using the Decision Toolkit** exercise, which follows the final Before You Go On section in the chapter, asks students to use the decision tools presented in that chapter. Students evaluate the financial situation of a real-world company, often using ratio analysis to do so. In most cases the company used in this analysis is a competitor of the example company in the chapter. For example, in Chapter 11, Nike was analyzed as the example company in the chapter discussion, so Reebok is analyzed in the Using the Decision Toolkit at the end of the chapter. Such comparisons expand and enrich the analysis and help focus student attention on comparative situations that flavor real-world decision making.

Putting It Together

- At the end of each chapter, between the body of the text and the homework materials, are several useful features for review and reference: a **Summary of Study Objectives** lists the main points of the chapter; the **Decision Toolkit—A Summary** presents in one place the decision tools used throughout the chapter; and a **Glossary** of important terms gives definitions with page references to the text.

- Next, a **Demonstration Problem** gives students another opportunity to refer to a detailed solution to a representative problem before they do homework assignments. **Problem-Solving Strategies** help establish a logic for approaching similar problems and assist students in understanding the solution.

DECISION TOOLKIT

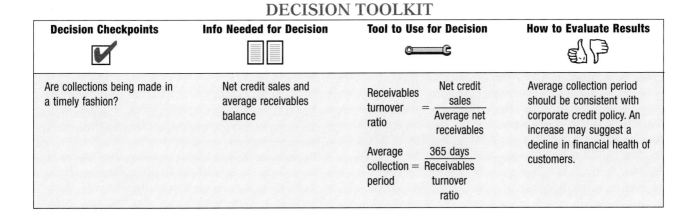

Decision Checkpoints	Info Needed for Decision	Tool to Use for Decision	How to Evaluate Results
Are collections being made in a timely fashion?	Net credit sales and average receivables balance	$\text{Receivables turnover ratio} = \dfrac{\text{Net credit sales}}{\text{Average net receivables}}$ $\text{Average collection period} = \dfrac{365 \text{ days}}{\text{Receivables turnover ratio}}$	Average collection period should be consistent with corporate credit policy. An increase may suggest a decline in financial health of customers.

Developing Skills Through Practice

Throughout the homework material, certain questions, exercises, and problems make use of the decision tools presented in the chapter. These are marked with the icon ⌐══════╝ . Others can be solved using the new **General Ledger Software**, available with this edition of the text. These are marked with the icon shown at left. The financial results of real companies are included in many exercises and problems; these are indicated by the company name shown in red.

- **Self-Study Questions** comprise a practice test to enable students to check their understanding of important concepts. These questions are keyed to the Study Objectives, so students can go back and review sections of the chapter in which they find they need further work.
- **Questions** provide a full review of chapter content and help students prepare for class discussions and testing situations.
- **Brief Exercises** build students' confidence and test their basic skills. Each Brief Exercise focuses on one of the Study Objectives.
- Each of the **Exercises** focuses on one or more of the Study Objectives. These tend to take a little longer to complete, and they present more of a challenge to students than Brief Exercises. The Exercises help instructors and students make a manageable transition to more challenging problems.
- **Problems** stress the applications of the concepts presented in the chapter. Two sets—**A** and **B**—have corresponding problems keyed to the same **Study Objectives**, thus giving instructors greater flexibility in assigning homework. Certain problems, marked with the icon ▭▭▭▶ , help build business writing skills.
- Each Brief Exercise, Exercise, and Problem has a **description of the concept** covered and is keyed to the Study Objectives.

Expanding and Applying Knowledge

Broadening Your Perspective is a unique section at the end of each chapter that offers a wealth of resources to help instructors and students pull together the learning for the chapter. This section offers problems and projects for those instructors who want to broaden the learning experience by bringing in more real-world decision making and critical thinking activities.

- **Financial Reporting and Analysis** problems use financial statements of real-world companies for further practice in understanding and interpreting financial reporting. A **Financial Reporting Problem** in each chapter directs students to study various aspects of the financial statements of Tootsie Roll Industries, Inc., which are printed in Chapter 1 (in simplified form) and in Appendix A (in full). A **Comparative Analysis Problem** offers the opportunity to compare and contrast the financial reporting of Tootsie Roll Industries, Inc., with a competitor, Hershey Foods Corporation. Since the ability to read and understand business publications is an asset over the span of one's career, **Research Cases** direct students to *The Wall Street Journal*, annual reports, or articles published in other popular business periodicals for further study and analysis of key topics. The **Interpreting Financial Statements** problems offer one or more minicases per chapter that ask students to read parts of financial statements of actual companies and use the decision tools presented in the chapter to interpret this information. New in this edition, **A Global Focus** problem asks students to apply concepts presented in the chapter to specific situations faced by actual international companies. **Financial Analysis on the Web** exercises guide students to Web sites from which they can mine and analyze information related to the chapter topic.
- **Critical Thinking** problems offer additional opportunities and activities. The **Group Decision Cases** help promote group collaboration and build decision-making skills by analyzing accounting information in a less structured situation. These cases require teams of students to evaluate a manager's decision or lead to a decision among alternative courses of action. They also give practice in building business communication skills. **Communication Activities** provide practice in written communication—a skill much in demand among employers. **Ethics Cases** describe typical ethical dilemmas and ask students to analyze the situation, identify the ethical issues involved, and decide on an appropriate course of action.

ACTIVE TEACHING AND LEARNING SUPPLEMENTARY MATERIAL

The supplementary material for students and instructors is driven by the same basic beliefs as the textbook, providing a consistent and well-integrated active learning system. This hands-on, real-world package guides *instructors* through the processes of active learning and gives them the tools to create an interactive learning environment. With its emphasis on activities, exercises, and the Internet, the package encourages *students* to take an active role in the course and prepares them for decision making in a real-world context.

Instructor's Active Teaching Aids

Financial Accounting Web Site at http://www.wiley.com/college/kimmel. As a resource and learning tool for instructors and students, the Financial Accounting Web Site serves as a launching pad to numerous activities, resources, and related sites. Available through the Web site are links to companies discussed in the text and Instructor's Manual, additional cases and problems for students, and items such as the Checklist of Key Figures and PowerPoint Presentations for download. This site also provides a link to the Business Extra Web Site discussed below. Visit this site often for updated and new materials.

Instructor's Resource System on CD-ROM. Responding to the changing needs of instructors and to developments in distance learning and electronic classrooms, the Supplement CD-ROM provides all the instructor support material in an electronic format that is easy to navigate and use. This CD-ROM contains all the print supplements, as well as the electronic ones, for use in the classroom, for printing out material, for uploading to your own Web site, or for downloading and modifying, thus giving you the flexibility to access and prepare the material based on your needs.

Solutions Manual. The Solutions Manual contains detailed solutions to all exercises and problems in the textbook and suggested answers to the questions and cases. Print is large and bold for easy readability in lecture settings, and instructors may duplicate any portion of the manual without paying a permissions fee. Each chapter includes an *assignment classification table*, which identifies end-of-chapter items by study objectives, and an *assignment characteristics table*, describing each problem and alternative problem and identifying difficulty level and estimated completion time. The Solutions Manual has been carefully verified by a team of independent accuracy checkers.

Solutions Transparencies. Packaged in an organizer box with chapter file folders, these transparencies feature detailed solutions to all exercises and problems in the textbook, and suggested answers to the Broadening Your Perspectives activities. They feature large, bold type for better projection and easy readability in large classroom settings.

Instructor's Manual. *Jessica Frazier, Eastern Kentucky University.* The Instructor's Manual is a comprehensive set of resources for preparing and presenting an active learning course. The Instructor's Manual discusses how to incorporate all the supplements, includes information on group and active learning, and has sample syllabi for use of the textbook. The Instructor's Manual also includes a series of discussions on how to incorporate ethics material, group activities, and communication activities in the course.

In addition to reading comprehension checks and short vocabulary and multiple-choice quizzes, each chapter also includes a number of activities and exercises designed to engage students in the learning process, including Research and Communication exercises, World Wide Web Research Exercises, Ethics Exercises, and International and Social Responsibility Exercises. The Web site for the text includes links for all Internet-based activities and exercises. Suggested solutions are provided where appropriate. Also included for each chapter are an *assignment classification table*; an *assignment characteristics table*; a *list of study objectives* in extra large, bold print for transparencies; and *suggestions for integrating supplements* into the classroom.

PowerPoint Presentation Material. *Ellen Sweatt, Georgia Perimeter College.* This PowerPoint lecture aid contains a combination of key concepts, images, and problems from the textbook for use in the classroom. Designed according to the organization of the material in the textbook, this series of electronic transparencies can be used to reinforce accounting principles visually and graphically.

Test Bank. *Lee Cannell, El Paso Community College.* Keeping assessment consistent with the focus of the text is the main objective of this comprehensive testing package. The Test Bank features over 3,000 questions with an emphasis on concepts, decision making, and a real-world environment. Actual financial statements have been used throughout the Test Bank to provide a relevant context for questions. All questions are classified according to study objectives and learning skills in tables at the beginning of each chapter, to make selection of exam questions easier. In addition to the examination material provided for each chapter, four comprehensive examinations covering four to five chapters are also included.

The Test Bank also includes a series of preprinted Achievement Tests for easy testing of major concepts. Each test covers two chapters from the textbook. In addition, a final exam covering all chapters in the text is included. The tests, easy to photocopy and distribute directly to students, consist of multiple-choice, matching, and true/false questions, and problems and exercises (computation and journal entries). Solutions are included at the end of each Achievement Test.

Computerized Test Bank. The Test Bank is also available for use with IBM and IBM true-compatibles running Windows 3.1 or higher. This Computerized Test Bank offers a number of valuable options that allow instructors to create multiple versions of the same test by scrambling questions; generate a large number of test questions randomly or manually; and modify and customize test questions by changing existing problems or adding your own.

Test Preparation Service. Simply call Wiley's special number (1-800-541-5602) with the questions you want on an examination. Wiley will provide a customized master exam within 24 hours. If you prefer, questions can be selected from a number of chapters.

Checklist of Key Figures. A list of key amounts for problems allows students to verify the accuracy of their answers as they work through the assignments. Available for download through our Web site at http://www.wiley.com/college/kimmel.

Nightly Business Report Video. To bring the relevance of financial accounting into the classroom, the authors have selected a series of video clips from the *Nightly Business Report,* related to some of the actual companies discussed in the text. Each of the segments is approximately 3–5 minutes long and can be used to introduce topics to the students, enhance lecture material, and provide real-world context for related concepts. An Instructor's Manual with suggestions for integrating the material into the classroom accompanies the video.

General Ledger Evaluator Disk. This program is a simple way to evaluate students' answers prepared using the General Ledger Software. It evaluates both the transactions that were posted and the ending balances for each of the accounts. The program also includes many reporting options, allowing instructors to print detailed or summary reports for a student or a class using a variety of sort sequences.

WebCT. Available to adopters of *Financial Accounting,* WebCT is an integrated set of course management tools that enable instructors to easily design, develop, and manage Web-based and Web-enhanced courses.

The Wiley *Financial Accounting* WebCT course is the WebCT shell, with all its course management features, filled with Wiley content; it is an on-line learning and resource guide for the student. This WebCT course allows the professor to present all or part of a course on-line and helps the student organize the course material, understand key concepts, and access additional on-line resources and tools. Your Wiley WebCT course can be customized by the instructor. Contact your Wiley representative for more information.

Technical Support. If you need assistance for any Wiley technology product, please contact Wiley at one of these addresses:

Tech support email: techhelp@wiley.com
Tech support hotline: (212) 850-6753
Tech support Web page: http://www.wiley.com/techsupport

Student Active Learning Aids

Student Workbook. The Student Workbook is a comprehensive review of accounting and a powerful tool for students to use in the classroom, guiding students through chapter content, tied to study objectives, and providing resources for use during lectures. This is an excellent resource when preparing for exams. The Student Workbook is also an active learning tool, providing students with opportunities to engage in the learning and decision-making process.

Each chapter of the Student Workbook includes study objectives and a chapter review consisting of 20–30 key points; a demonstration problem linked to study objectives in the textbook; true/false, multiple-choice, and matching questions related to key terms; and exercises linked to study objectives. Solutions to the exercises explain the hows and whys so students get immediate feedback. A chapter outline and blank working papers allow students space to take lecture notes and record problems worked in class.

Working Papers. *Dick Wasson, Southwestern College.* Working Papers are partially completed accounting forms for all end-of-chapter exercises, problems, and cases. A convenient resource for organizing and completing homework assignments, they demonstrate how to correctly set up solution formats and are directly tied to textbook assignments. Each page of the Working Papers has the problem number and company name, and space for students to write their name and course information, providing instructors with consistent forms to grade.

Take Note! This handy note-taking guide includes all the PowerPoint presentations printed out three to a page, with spaces next to them for you to take notes. Take Note! allows you to focus on the discussions at hand, instead of focusing on copying down slides projected in class.

General Ledger Software. The General Ledger Software (GLS) is one of the most exciting technology supplements accompanying the Second Edition. Available in a Windows or Network version, the GLS program allows students to solve selected end-of-chapter problems, which are identified by a diskette icon in the margin of the text.

- GLS is ideal for instructors who want their students to gain a hands-on feel for a computerized accounting system. The program demonstrates the immediate effects of each transaction, helping students understand the use of computers in a real-world accounting environment.
- GLS has the ability to modify the existing chart of accounts and beginning balances when creating new problems. This increases the instructor's flexibility in assigning alternate problems within the textbook. This feature also provides students with more opportunity to practice with computerized accounting systems.
- GLS is user-friendly and easy to use, with little start-up time. The Windows version is on two disks, plus a data disk.

Financial Accounting Tutor (FaCT)   *Dan Gode, New York University Stern School of Business*. FaCT is a self-paced CD-ROM tutorial designed to review financial accounting concepts. It uses simple examples that have been carefully crafted to introduce concepts gradually. Throughout, the program emphasizes the logic underlying the accounting process. FaCT uses interactive and graphical tools to enhance the learning process. Intuitive navigation and a powerful search mechanism allow you to easily follow the tutorial from start to finish or skip to the topics you want to complete. The discussions and examples are followed by brief, interactive problems that provide immediate feedback. Built-in tools, such as an on-line financial calculator, help solve the problems.

On-Line Business Survival Guide.   The journey of 1000 Web sites begins with one click, and this practical guide gets instructors and students on the road. The On-Line Business Survival Guide is a brief, clear introduction to using the World Wide Web as a business research tool. Starting with the basics, this manual covers everything students need to know to become master sleuths at finding critical information on the Internet. In addition, the guide provides a hands-on guide to using *The Wall Street Journal Interactive Edition*, as well as a discount offer for a subscription to *The Wall Street Journal Interactive* on-line.

Business Extra Web Site at http://www.wiley.com/college/ kimmel.   To complement the On-Line Business Survival Guide in Accounting, the Business Extra Web Site gives professors and students instant access to a wealth of current articles dealing with all aspects of financial accounting. The articles are organized by topic, and discussion questions follow each article. Students will find a password inside the On-Line Business Survival Guide that will give them access to the Business Extra Web Site.

Paul D. Kimmel
Milwaukee, Wisconsin

Jerry J. Weygandt
Madison, Wisconsin

Donald E. Kieso
DeKalb, Illinois

ACKNOWLEDGMENTS

During the course of development of *Financial Accounting*, the authors benefited greatly from the input of focus group participants, manuscript reviewers, ancillary authors, and proofers. The constructive suggestions and innovative ideas of the reviewers and the creativity and accuracy of the ancillary authors and checkers are greatly appreciated.

REVIEWERS AND FOCUS GROUP PARTICIPANTS FOR *FINANCIAL ACCOUNTING*, FIRST EDITION

Thomas G. Amyot, *College of Saint Rose*
Angela H. Bell, *Jacksonville State University*
G. Eddy Birrer, *Gonzaga University*
Sarah Ruth Brown, *University of North Alabama*
Judye Cadle, *Tarleton State University*
George M. Dow, *Valencia Community College–West*
Kathy J. Dow, *Salem State College*
Larry R. Falcetto, *Emporia State University*
Sheila D. Foster, *The Citadel*
Jessica J. Frazier, *Eastern Kentucky University*
David Gotlob, *Indiana University–Purdue University– Fort Wayne*
Leon J. Hanouille, *Syracuse University*

Carol Olson Houston, *San Diego State University*
Robert J. Kirsch, *Southern Connecticut State University*
Frank Korman, *Mountain View College*
Jerry G. Kreuze, *Western Michigan University*
P. Merle Maddocks, *University of Alabama–Huntsville*
Gale E. Newell, *Western Michigan University*
Franklin J. Plewa, *Idaho State University*
Marc A. Rubin, *Miami University*
Anne E. Selk, *University of Wisconsin–Green Bay*
William E. Smith, *Xavier University*
Teresa A. Speck, *St. Mary's University of Minnesota*
Linda G. Wade, *Tarleton State University*
Stuart K. Webster, *University of Wyoming*

REVIEWERS AND FOCUS GROUP PARTICIPANTS FOR *FINANCIAL ACCOUNTING*, SECOND EDITION

Dawn Addington, *Albuquerque TVI Community College*
Jon A. Booker, *Tennessee Technological University*
James Byrne, *Oregon State University*
Laura Claus, *Louisiana State University*
Leslie Cohen, *University of Arizona*
Larry R. Falcetto, *Emporia State University*
Emmett Griner, *Georgia State University*
Kenneth M. Hiltebeitel, *Villanova University*
Marianne L. James, *California State University–Los Angeles*
Christopher Jones, *George Washington University*
Susan Kattelus, *Eastern Michigan University*
Cindi Khanlarian, *University of North Carolina–Greensboro*
Keith Leeseberg, *Manatee Community College*
Alan Mayer-Sommer, *Georgetown University*

Noel McKeon, *Florida Community College*
John Purisky, *Salem State College*
Judith Resnick, *Borough of Manhattan Community College*
Christine Schalow, *California State University–San Bernardino*
Richard Schroeder, *University of North Carolina–Charlotte*
William Seltz, *University of Massachusetts*
Charles Stanley, *Baylor University*
Ron Stone, *California State University–Northridge*
Gary Stout, *California State University–Northridge*
Ellen Sweatt, *Georgia Perimeter College*
Allan Young, *DeVry Institute of Technology*
Michael F. van Breda, *Texas Christian University*

We have also benefited from suggestions made by the following people during discussions or through comments received via letters or email: Solochidi Ahiarah—Buffalo State College; Victoria Beard—University of North Dakota; Jim Christianson—Austin Community College; Janet Courts—San Bernadino Valley College; Helen Davis—Johnson and Wales University; Cheryl Dickerson—Western Washington University; Mary Emery—St. Olaf College; Scott Fargason—Louisiana State University; Judy Hora—University of San Diego; Jane Kaplan—Drexel University; John Lacey—California State University Long Beach; Jeff Ritter—St. Norbert College; Alfredo Salas—El Paso Community College; Mary Alice Seville—Oregon State University; Gary Stout—California State University–Northridge; Pamadda Tantral—Fairleigh Dickinson University; Frederick Weis—Claremont McKenna College.

ANCILLARY AUTHORS, CONTRIBUTORS, AND PROOFERS

Jack C. Borke, *University of Wisconsin–Platteville*—Solutions Manual Proofer and Technical Advisor
Lee Cannell, *El Paso Community College*—Test Bank Author and Solutions Manual Proofer
Jessica J. Frazier, *Eastern Kentucky University*—Instructor's Manual Author and Video Consultant
Larry R. Falcetto, *Emporia State University*—Solutions Manual Proofer and Technical Advisor
Ceil Fewox, *College of Charleston*—Study Guide Contributor

Marc Giullian, *Southwest Louisiana College*—Problem Material Contributor
Wayne Higley, *Buena Vista University*—Content Proofer and Technical Advisor
Ellen L. Sweatt, *Georgia Perimeter College*—PowerPoint Author
Dick Wasson, *Southwestern College*—Working Papers Contributor and Solutions Manual Proofer

We are especially grateful to Suzanne Sevalstad of the *University of Nevada–Las Vegas* and her students Renato Estacio, Ching-Ying Moore, Jeff Robson, and Ryan Small for their insightful comments on using this text for success in the financial accounting course.

We appreciate the exemplary support and professional commitment given us by our publisher Susan Elbe, development editors Ann Torbert and Nancy Perry, supplements editor Julie Kerr, vice-president of college production and manufacturing Ann Berlin, designer Kevin Murphy, illustration editor Anna Melhorn, photo editors Elaine Paoloni and Nicole Horlacher, production manager Jeanine Furino, and Ginger Yarrow, project editor at Elm Street Publishing Services.

We thank Tootsie Roll Industries and Hershey Foods Corporation for permitting us the use of their 1998 Annual Reports for our specimen financial statements and accompanying notes.

Suggestions and comments from users are encouraged and appreciated. Please feel free to e-mail any one of us at account@wiley.com.

Paul D. Kimmel / Jerry J. Weygandt / Donald E. Kieso

STUDENT TO STUDENT

Hello!

For many students, an introductory financial accounting class will be the first of many difficult challenges they will face in their academic career. With the proper use of this textbook, your probability of success in this course will be increased. A good idea is to preread the chapter or at least read the portion of the text that you will be covering in class that day. If you do this, often the professor will clarify points you were unsure of or reduce the number of questions that you may have on the material covered in that chapter.

This textbook has been designed in such a way as to facilitate the learning process for students. Each chapter begins with a situation from the real world. Companies such as Tootsie Roll, Wal-Mart, and Southwest Airlines are featured. Also, at the beginning of each chapter is a list of study objectives covering the key topics of the chapter.

Throughout the chapters there are Decision Toolkits. These toolkits are handy checkpoints that tell you how to put certain financial information to use in various business decisions. The toolkits describe what kind of information to use as well as how to interpret the results. In addition to the Decision Toolkits, scattered throughout the chapter are Before You Go On sections, which are small reviews of the material covered in each section. It is a good idea to make sure you comprehend the key material covered in the section before you move on to the next one. If you are still not sure you have a firm grasp of the material after using the Before You Go On materials, make a note of your question and ask your professor the next day in class.

Perhaps the most helpful aspect of this book is the material included at the end of each chapter. Each chapter contains a full summary of study objectives, a summary of the Decision Toolkits in the chapter, a glossary of new terms used, and a demonstration problem. In my experience, I have found that it is best to attempt to do the demonstration problem before I look at its solution; it is a good way to test your understanding of the material. There are also self-study questions, with answers, as well as many other questions, exercises, and problems. It is a good idea to attempt some of these materials as well, even if they aren't assigned as homework. Usually you will be able to get the answers from your instructor.

I hope that you have been able to pick up a few helpful study hints from this introduction. Ultimately, as with anything in life, what you get out of this class will largely depend on what you put into it.

Good luck, and I hope you enjoy this course as much as I did!

Jeff Robson

Jeff Robson
University of Nevada–Las Vegas

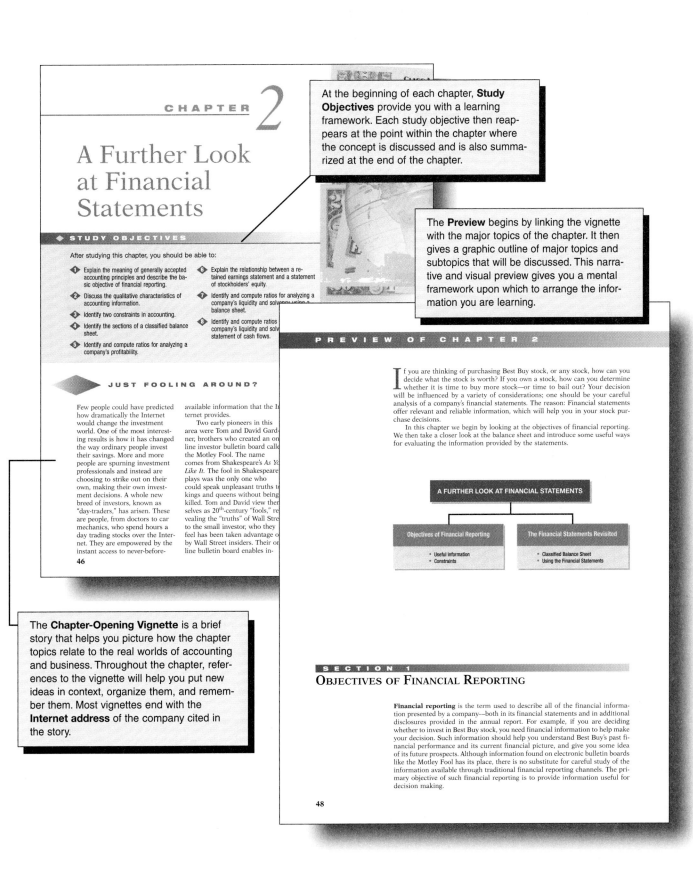

At the beginning of each chapter, **Study Objectives** provide you with a learning framework. Each study objective then reappears at the point within the chapter where the concept is discussed and is also summarized at the end of the chapter.

The **Preview** begins by linking the vignette with the major topics of the chapter. It then gives a graphic outline of major topics and subtopics that will be discussed. This narrative and visual preview gives you a mental framework upon which to arrange the information you are learning.

The **Chapter-Opening Vignette** is a brief story that helps you picture how the chapter topics relate to the real worlds of accounting and business. Throughout the chapter, references to the vignette will help you put new ideas in context, organize them, and remember them. Most vignettes end with the **Internet address** of the company cited in the story.

CHAPTER 2

A Further Look at Financial Statements

◆ STUDY OBJECTIVES

After studying this chapter, you should be able to:

1. Explain the meaning of generally accepted accounting principles and describe the basic objective of financial reporting.
2. Discuss the qualitative characteristics of accounting information.
3. Identify two constraints in accounting.
4. Identify the sections of a classified balance sheet.
5. Identify and compute ratios for analyzing a company's profitability.
6. Explain the relationship between a retained earnings statement and a statement of stockholders' equity.
7. Identify and compute ratios for analyzing a company's liquidity and solvency using a balance sheet.
8. Identify and compute ratios for analyzing a company's liquidity and solvency using a statement of cash flows.

◆ JUST FOOLING AROUND?

Few people could have predicted how dramatically the Internet would change the investment world. One of the most interesting results is how it has changed the way ordinary people invest their savings. More and more people are spurning investment professionals and instead are choosing to strike out on their own, making their own investment decisions. A whole new breed of investors, known as "day-traders," has arisen. These are people, from doctors to car mechanics, who spend hours a day trading stocks over the Internet. They are empowered by the instant access to never-before-

available information that the Internet provides.

Two early pioneers in this area were Tom and David Gardner, brothers who created an online investor bulletin board called the Motley Fool. The name comes from Shakespeare's *As You Like It*. The fool in Shakespeare's plays was the only one who could speak unpleasant truths to kings and queens without being killed. Tom and David view themselves as 20th-century "fools," revealing the "truths" of Wall Street to the small investor, who they feel has been taken advantage of by Wall Street insiders. Their online bulletin board enables in-

46

PREVIEW OF CHAPTER 2

If you are thinking of purchasing Best Buy stock, or any stock, how can you decide what the stock is worth? If you own a stock, how can you determine whether it is time to buy more stock—or time to bail out? Your decision will be influenced by a variety of considerations; one should be your careful analysis of a company's financial statements. The reason: Financial statements offer relevant and reliable information, which will help you in your stock purchase decisions.

In this chapter we begin by looking at the objectives of financial reporting. We then take a closer look at the balance sheet and introduce some useful ways for evaluating the information provided by the statements.

A FURTHER LOOK AT FINANCIAL STATEMENTS

Objectives of Financial Reporting	The Financial Statements Revisited
• Useful Information	• Classified Balance Sheet
• Constraints	• Using the Financial Statements

SECTION 1
OBJECTIVES OF FINANCIAL REPORTING

Financial reporting is the term used to describe all of the financial information presented by a company—both in its financial statements and in additional disclosures provided in the annual report. For example, if you are deciding whether to invest in Best Buy stock, you need financial information to help make your decision. Such information should help you understand Best Buy's past financial performance and its current financial picture, and give you some idea of its future prospects. Although information found on electronic bulletin boards like the Motley Fool has its place, there is no substitute for careful study of the information available through traditional financial reporting channels. The primary objective of such financial reporting is to provide information useful for decision making.

48

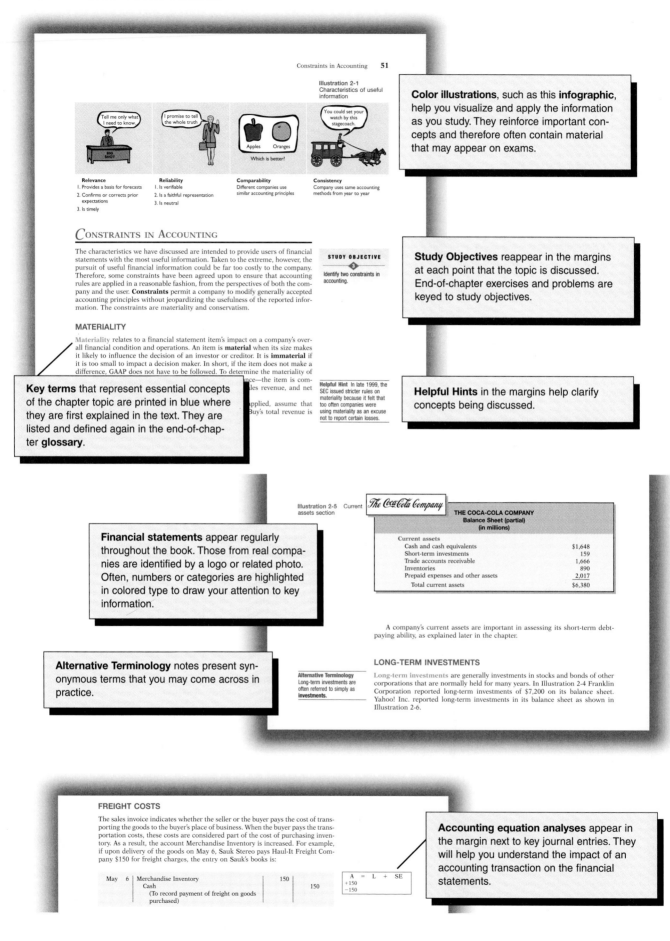

Illustration 2-1
Characteristics of useful
information

Color illustrations, such as this **infographic**, help you visualize and apply the information as you study. They reinforce important concepts and therefore often contain material that may appear on exams.

Relevance
1. Provides a basis for forecasts
2. Confirms or corrects prior expectations
3. Is timely

Reliability
1. Is verifiable
2. Is a faithful representation
3. Is neutral

Comparability
Different companies use similar accounting principles

Consistency
Company uses same accounting methods from year to year

CONSTRAINTS IN ACCOUNTING

The characteristics we have discussed are intended to provide users of financial statements with the most useful information. Taken to the extreme, however, the pursuit of useful financial information could be far too costly to the company. Therefore, some constraints have been agreed upon to ensure that accounting rules are applied in a reasonable fashion, from the perspectives of both the company and the user. **Constraints** permit a company to modify generally accepted accounting principles without jeopardizing the usefulness of the reported information. The constraints are materiality and conservatism.

MATERIALITY

Materiality relates to a financial statement item's impact on a company's overall financial condition and operations. An item is **material** when its size makes it likely to influence the decision of an investor or creditor. It is **immaterial** if it is too small to impact a decision maker. In short, if the item does not make a difference, GAAP does not have to be followed. To determine the materiality of

STUDY OBJECTIVE 3
Identify two constraints in accounting.

Study Objectives reappear in the margins at each point that the topic is discussed. End-of-chapter exercises and problems are keyed to study objectives.

Helpful Hint In late 1999, the SEC issued stricter rules on materiality because it felt that too often companies were using materiality as an excuse not to report certain losses.

Helpful Hints in the margins help clarify concepts being discussed.

Key terms that represent essential concepts of the chapter topic are printed in blue where they are first explained in the text. They are listed and defined again in the end-of-chapter **glossary**.

Illustration 2-5   Current assets section

The Coca-Cola Company

THE COCA-COLA COMPANY Balance Sheet (partial) (in millions)	
Current assets	
Cash and cash equivalents	$1,648
Short-term investments	159
Trade accounts receivable	1,666
Inventories	890
Prepaid expenses and other assets	2,017
Total current assets	$6,380

Financial statements appear regularly throughout the book. Those from real companies are identified by a logo or related photo. Often, numbers or categories are highlighted in colored type to draw your attention to key information.

A company's current assets are important in assessing its short-term debt-paying ability, as explained later in the chapter.

LONG-TERM INVESTMENTS

Alternative Terminology
Long-term investments are often referred to simply as **investments.**

Alternative Terminology notes present synonymous terms that you may come across in practice.

Long-term investments are generally investments in stocks and bonds of other corporations that are normally held for many years. In Illustration 2-4 Franklin Corporation reported long-term investments of $7,200 on its balance sheet. Yahoo! Inc. reported long-term investments in its balance sheet as shown in Illustration 2-6.

FREIGHT COSTS

The sales invoice indicates whether the seller or the buyer pays the cost of transporting the goods to the buyer's place of business. When the buyer pays the transportation costs, these costs are considered part of the cost of purchasing inventory. As a result, the account Merchandise Inventory is increased. For example, if upon delivery of the goods on May 6, Sauk Stereo pays Haul-It Freight Company $150 for freight charges, the entry on Sauk's books is:

Accounting equation analyses appear in the margin next to key journal entries. They will help you understand the impact of an accounting transaction on the financial statements.

May	6	Merchandise Inventory	150	
		Cash		150
		(To record payment of freight on goods purchased)		

A = L + SE
+150
−150

Business Insight examples give glimpses into how real companies make decisions using accounting information. Three different icons identify three different points of view—human silhouettes for *investor perspectives*, a city skyline for *management perspectives*, and a globe for *international perspectives*.

Each chapter presents **decision tools** that help business decision makers use financial statements. At the end of the text discussion, a **Decision Toolkit** summarizes the key features of a decision tool and reviews why and how you would use it.

Before You Go On sections follow each key topic. *Review It* questions prompt you to stop and review the key points you have just studied. If you cannot answer these questions, you should go back and read the section again. Brief *Do It* exercises ask you to put newly acquired knowledge to work in some form of financial statement preparation. They outline the **reasoning** necessary to complete the exercise and show a **solution**.

---

66 CHAPTER 2 A Further Look at Financial Statements

BUSINESS INSIGHT
Investor Perspective

Debt financing differs greatly across industries and companies. Here are some debt to total assets ratios for selected companies:

	Total Debt to Total Assets as a Percent
Callaway Golf Company	19%
Roberts Pharmaceutical	23%
Advanced Micro Devices	29%
Sears, Roebuck & Company	64%
Eastman Kodak Company	83%
General Motors Corporation	93%

DECISION TOOLKIT

Decision Checkpoints	Info Needed for Decision	Tool to Use for Decision	How to Evaluate Results
Can the company meet its near-term obligations?	Current assets and current liabilities	Current ratio = $\frac{\text{Current assets}}{\text{Current liabilities}}$	Higher ratio suggests favorable liquidity.
Can the company meet its long-term obligations?	Total debt and total assets	Debt to total assets ratio = $\frac{\text{Total liabilities}}{\text{Total assets}}$	Lower value suggests favorable solvency.

BEFORE YOU GO ON...

◆ **Review It**

1. What is liquidity? How can it be measured using a classified balance sheet?
2. What is solvency? How can it be measured using a classified balance sheet?

◆ **Do It**

Selected financial data for Drummond Company at December 31, 2001, are as follows: cash $60,000; receivables (net) $80,000; inventory $70,000; total assets $540,000; current liabilities $140,000; and total liabilities $270,000. Compute the current ratio and debt to total assets ratio.

Reasoning: The formula for the current ratio is: Current assets ÷ Current liabilities. The formula for the debt to total assets ratio is: Total liabilities ÷ Total assets.

Solution: The current ratio is 1.5:1 ($210,000 ÷ $140,000). The debt to total assets ratio is 50% ($270,000 ÷ $540,000).

STUDY OBJECTIVE

USING THE STATEMENT OF CASH FLOWS

As you learned in Chapter 1, the statement of cash flows provides financial insources and uses of a company's cash. Investors, creditors,
now what is happening to a company's most liquid rect, it is often said that "cash is king" because if a company
won't survive. To aid in the analysis of cash, the statement

The Classified Balance Sheet **57**

STOCKHOLDERS' EQUITY

Stockholders' equity is divided into two parts: common stock and retained earnings. Investments of assets in the business by the stockholders are recorded as common stock. Income retained for use in the business is recorded as retained earnings. These two parts are combined and reported as **stockholders' equity** on the balance sheet. In Illustration 2-4 Franklin reported common stock of $14,000 and retained earnings of $20,050.

Alternative Terminology
Common stock is sometimes called **capital stock.**

BEFORE YOU GO ON...

◆ **Review It**

1. What are the major sections in a classified balance sheet?
2. What is the primary determining factor to distinguish current assets from long-term assets?
3. What was Tootsie Roll's largest current asset at December 31, 1998? The answer to this question is provided on page 92.
4. Where is accumulated depreciation reported on the balance sheet?

◆ **Do It**

Baxter Hoffman recently received the following information related to Hoffman Corporation's December 31, 2001, balance sheet.

Prepaid expenses	$ 2,300	Inventory	$3,400
Cash	800	Accumulated depreciation	2,700
Property, plant, and equipment	10,700	Accounts receivable	1,100

Prepare the assets section of Hoffman Corporation's balance sheet.

Reasoning: Current assets are cash and other resources that are reasonably expected to be consumed in one year. Accumulated depreciation should be subtracted from property, plant, and equipment to determine net property, plant, and equipment.

Review It questions marked with the Tootsie Roll icon direct you to find information in Tootsie Roll Industries' 1998 Annual Report, packaged with new copies of the book and printed in Appendix A at the back of the book. These questions help you see how topics covered in the chapter are reported in real-world financial statements. Answers appear at the end of the chapter.

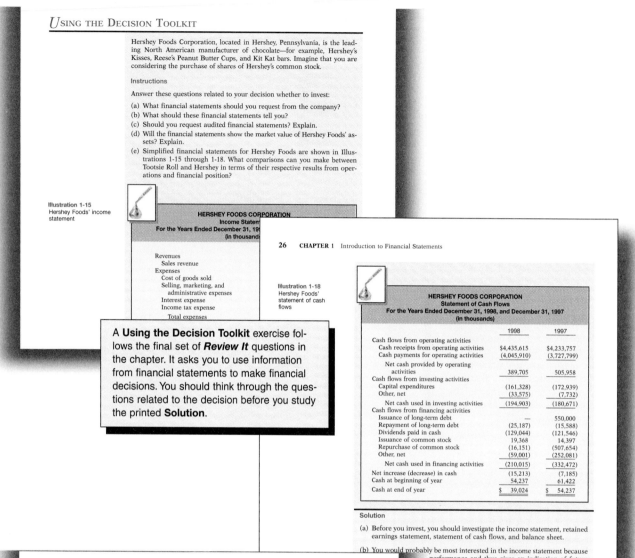

USING THE DECISION TOOLKIT

Hershey Foods Corporation, located in Hershey, Pennsylvania, is the leading North American manufacturer of chocolate—for example, Hershey's Kisses, Reese's Peanut Butter Cups, and Kit Kat bars. Imagine that you are considering the purchase of shares of Hershey's common stock.

Instructions

Answer these questions related to your decision whether to invest:

(a) What financial statements should you request from the company?
(b) What should these financial statements tell you?
(c) Should you request audited financial statements? Explain.
(d) Will the financial statements show the market value of Hershey Foods' assets? Explain.
(e) Simplified financial statements for Hershey Foods are shown in Illustrations 1-15 through 1-18. What comparisons can you make between Tootsie Roll and Hershey in terms of their respective results from operations and financial position?

Illustration 1-15
Hershey Foods' income statement

HERSHEY FOODS CORPORATION
Income Statem...
For the Years Ended December 31, 19...
(in thousand...

Revenues
Sales revenue
Expenses
Cost of goods sold
Selling, marketing, and
administrative expenses
Interest expense
Income tax expense
Total expenses

A **Using the Decision Toolkit** exercise follows the final set of *Review It* questions in the chapter. It asks you to use information from financial statements to make financial decisions. You should think through the questions related to the decision before you study the printed **Solution.**

26 **CHAPTER 1** Introduction to Financial Statements

Illustration 1-18
Hershey Foods'
statement of cash
flows

HERSHEY FOODS CORPORATION
Statement of Cash Flows
For the Years Ended December 31, 1998, and December 31, 1997
(in thousands)

	1998	1997
Cash flows from operating activities		
Cash receipts from operating activities	$4,435,615	$4,233,757
Cash payments for operating activities	(4,045,910)	(3,727,799)
Net cash provided by operating activities	389,705	505,958
Cash flows from investing activities		
Capital expenditures	(161,328)	(172,939)
Other, net	(33,575)	(7,732)
Net cash used in investing activities	(194,903)	(180,671)
Cash flows from financing activities		
Issuance of long-term debt	—	550,000
Repayment of long-term debt	(25,187)	(15,588)
Dividends paid in cash	(129,044)	(121,546)
Issuance of common stock	19,368	14,397
Repurchase of common stock	(16,151)	(507,654)
Other, net	(59,001)	(252,081)
Net cash used in financing activities	(210,015)	(332,472)
Net increase (decrease) in cash	(15,213)	(7,185)
Cash at beginning of year	54,237	61,422
Cash at end of year	$ 39,024	$ 54,237

Solution

(a) Before you invest, you should investigate the income statement, retained earnings statement, statement of cash flows, and balance sheet.

(b) You would probably be most interested in the income statement because ... performance and thus gives an indication of future ... retained earnings statement provides a record of the ... d history. The statement of cash flows reveals where ... tting and spending its cash. This is especially impor... / that wants to grow. Finally, the balance sheet reveals ...tween assets and liabilities.

...udited financial statements—statements that a CPA ...countant) has examined and expressed an opinion that ...sent fairly the financial position and results of opera-...ny. Investors and creditors should not make decisions ...udited financial statements.

SUMMARY OF STUDY OBJECTIVES

1 *Explain the meaning of generally accepted accounting principles and describe the basic objective of financial reporting.* Generally accepted accounting principles are a set of rules and practices recognized as a general guide for financial reporting purposes. The basic objective of financial reporting is to provide information that is useful for decision making.

2 *Discuss the qualitative characteristics of accounting information.* To be judged useful, information should possess these qualitative characteristics: relevance, reliability, comparability, and consistency.

3 *Identify two constraints in accounting.* The major constraints are materiality and conservatism.

4 *Identify the sections of a classified balance sheet.* In a classified balance sheet, assets are classified as current assets; long-term investments; property, plant, and equipment; or intangibles. Liabilities are classified as either current or long-term. There is also a stockholders' equity section, which shows common stock and retained earnings.

5 *Identify and compute ratios for analyzing a company's profitability.* Profitability ratios, such as profit margin and return on assets, measure different aspects of the operating success of a company for a given period of time.

6 *Explain the relationship between a retained earnings statement and a statement of stockholders' equity.* The retained earnings statement presents the factors that changed the retained earnings balance during the period. A statement of stockholders' equity presents the factors that changed stockholders' equity during the period, including those that changed retained earnings. Thus, a statement of stockholders' equity is more inclusive.

7 *Identify and compute ratios for analyzing a company's liquidity and solvency using a balance sheet.* Liquidity ratios, such as the current ratio, measure the short-term ability of a company to pay its maturing obligations and to meet unexpected needs for cash. Solvency ratios, such as the debt to total assets ratio, measure the ability of an enterprise to survive over a long period.

8 *Identify and compute ratios for analyzing a company's liquidity and solvency using a statement of cash flows.* The current cash debt coverage ratio measures a company's liquidity. The cash debt coverage ratio measures a company's solvency.

The **Summary of Study Objectives** relates the chapter summary to the study objectives located throughout the chapter. It gives you another opportunity to review as well as to see how all the key topics within the chapter are related.

Glossary **73**

DECISION TOOLKIT—A SUMMARY

Decision Checkpoints	Info Needed for Decision	Tool to Use for Decision	How to Evaluate Results
Is the company using its assets effectively?	Net income and average assets	Return on assets ratio $= \dfrac{\text{Net income}}{\text{Average total assets}}$	Higher value suggests favorable efficiency (use of assets).
Is the company maintaining an adequate margin between sales and expenses?	Net income and net sales	Profit margin ratio $= \dfrac{\text{Net income}}{\text{Net sales}}$	Higher value suggests favorable return on each dollar of sales.
Can the company meet its near-term obligations?	Current assets and current liabilities	Current ratio $= \dfrac{\text{Current assets}}{\text{Current liabilities}}$	Higher ratio suggests favorable liquidity.
Can the company meet its long-term obligations?	Total debt and total assets	Debt to total assets ratio $= \dfrac{\text{Total liabilities}}{\text{Total assets}}$	Lower value suggests favorable solvency.
Can the company meet its near-term obligations?	Current liabilities and cash provided by operating activities	Current cash debt coverage ratio $= \dfrac{\text{Cash provided by operations}}{\text{Average current liabilities}}$	A higher ratio indicates liquidity, that the company is generating cash sufficient to meet its near-term needs.
Can the company meet its long-term obligations?	Total liabilities and cash provided by operating activities	Cash debt coverage ratio $= \dfrac{\text{Cash provided by operations}}{\text{Average total liabilities}}$	A higher ratio indicates solvency, that the company is generating cash sufficient to meet its long-term needs.

> At the end of each chapter, **Decision Toolkit—A Summary** reviews the contexts and techniques useful for decision making that were covered in the chapter.

GLOSSARY

Cash debt coverage ratio A measure of solvency that is calculated as cash provided by operating activities divided by average total liabilities. (p. 68)

Classified balance sheet A balance sheet that contains a number of standard classifications or sections. (p. 52)

Comparability Ability to compare the accounting information of different companies because they use the same accounting principles. (p. 49)

Conservatism The approach of choosing an accounting method, when in doubt, that will least likely overstate assets and net income. (p. 51)

Consistency Use of the same accounting principles and

Current liabilities Obligations reasonably expected to be paid within the next year or operating cycle, whichever is longer. (p. 56)

Current ratio A measure used to evaluate a company's liquidity and short-term debt-paying ability, computed by dividing current assets by current liabilities. (p. 64)

Debt to total assets ratio Measures the percentage of total financing provided by creditors; computed by dividing total debt by total assets. (p. 65)

Financial Accounting Standards Board (FASB) A private organization that establishes generally accepted accounting principles. (p. 49)

> The **Glossary** defines all the terms and concepts introduced in the chapter.

DEMONSTRATION PROBLEM

Jeff Andringa, a former college hockey player, quit his job and started Ice Camp, a hockey camp for kids ages 8 to 18. Eventually he would like to open hockey camps nationwide. Jeff has asked you to help him prepare financial statements at the end of his first year of operations. He relates the following facts about his business activities.

In order to get the business off the ground, he decided to incorporate. He sold shares of common stock to a few close friends, as well as buying some of the shares himself. He initially raised $25,000 through the sale of these shares. In addition, the company took out a $10,000 loan at a local bank. A bus for transporting kids was purchased for $12,000 cash. Hockey goals and other miscellaneous equipment were purchased with $1,500 cash. The company earned camp tuition during the year of $100,000 but had collected only $80,000 of this amount. Thus, at the end of the year it was still owed $20,000. The company rents time at a local rink for $50 per hour. Total rink rental costs during the year were $8,000, insurance was $10,000, salary expense was $20,000, and administrative expenses totaled $9,000, all of which were paid in cash. The company incurred $800 in interest expense on the bank loan, which it still owed at the end of the year.

The company paid dividends during the year of $5,000 cash. The balance in the corporate bank account at December 31, 2001, was $49,500.

Instructions

Using the format of the Sierra Corporation statements in this chapter, prepare an income statement, retained earnings statement, balance sheet, and statement of cash flows. [*Hint:* Prepare the statements in the order stated to take advantage of the flow of information from one statement to the next, as shown in Illustration 1-4.]

> A **Demonstration Problem** is the final step before you begin homework. **Problem-Solving Strategies** in the margins give you tips about how to approach the problem, and the **Solution** demonstrates both the form and content of complete answers.

30 CHAPTER 1 Introduction to Financial Statements

Solution to Demonstration Problem

Problem-Solving Strategies

1. The income statement shows revenues and expenses for a period of time.
2. The retained earnings statement shows the changes in retained earnings for a period of time.
3. The balance sheet reports assets, liabilities, and stockholders' equity at a specific date.
4. The statement of cash flows reports sources and uses of cash from operating, investing, and financing activities for a period of time.

ICE CAMP
Income Statement
For the Year Ended December 31, 2001

Revenues		
Camp tuition revenue		$100,000
Expenses		
Salaries expense	$20,000	
Insurance expense	10,000	
Administrative expense	9,000	
Rink rental expense	8,000	
Interest expense	800	
Total expenses		47,800
Net income		$ 52,200

ICE CAMP
Retained Earnings Statement
For the Year Ended December 31, 2001

Retained earnings, January 1, 2001		$ 0
Add: Net income		52,200
		52,200
Less: Dividends		5,000
Retained earnings, December 31, 2001		$47,200

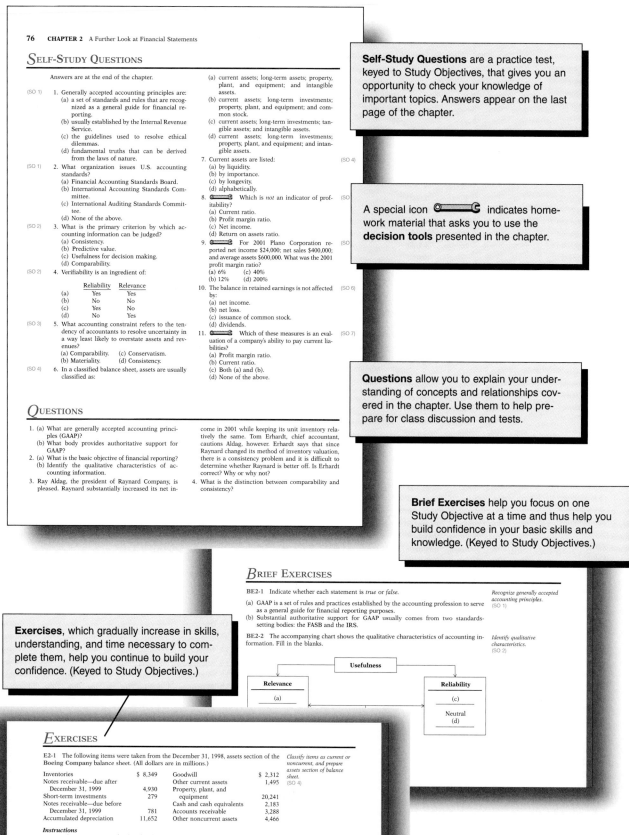

76   CHAPTER 2   A Further Look at Financial Statements

SELF-STUDY QUESTIONS

Answers are at the end of the chapter.

(SO 1) 1. Generally accepted accounting principles are:
   (a) a set of standards and rules that are recognized as a general guide for financial reporting.
   (b) usually established by the Internal Revenue Service.
   (c) the guidelines used to resolve ethical dilemmas.
   (d) fundamental truths that can be derived from the laws of nature.

(SO 1) 2. What organization issues U.S. accounting standards?
   (a) Financial Accounting Standards Board.
   (b) International Accounting Standards Committee.
   (c) International Auditing Standards Committee.
   (d) None of the above.

(SO 2) 3. What is the primary criterion by which accounting information can be judged?
   (a) Consistency.
   (b) Predictive value.
   (c) Usefulness for decision making.
   (d) Comparability.

(SO 2) 4. Verifiability is an ingredient of:

	Reliability	Relevance
(a)	Yes	Yes
(b)	No	No
(c)	Yes	No
(d)	No	Yes

(SO 3) 5. What accounting constraint refers to the tendency of accountants to resolve uncertainty in a way least likely to overstate assets and revenues?
   (a) Comparability.   (c) Conservatism.
   (b) Materiality.   (d) Consistency.

(SO 4) 6. In a classified balance sheet, assets are usually classified as:
   (a) current assets; long-term assets; property, plant, and equipment; and intangible assets.
   (b) current assets; long-term investments; property, plant, and equipment; and common stock.
   (c) current assets; long-term investments; tangible assets; and intangible assets.
   (d) current assets; long-term investments; property, plant, and equipment; and intangible assets.

(SO 4) 7. Current assets are listed:
   (a) by liquidity.
   (b) by importance.
   (c) by longevity.
   (d) alphabetically.

(SO 5) 8. ▭ Which is *not* an indicator of profitability?
   (a) Current ratio.
   (b) Profit margin ratio.
   (c) Net income.
   (d) Return on assets ratio.

(SO 5) 9. ▭ For 2001 Plano Corporation reported net income $24,000; net sales $400,000; and average assets $600,000. What was the 2001 profit margin ratio?
   (a) 6%   (c) 40%
   (b) 12%   (d) 200%

(SO 6) 10. The balance in retained earnings is not affected by:
   (a) net income.
   (b) net loss.
   (c) issuance of common stock.
   (d) dividends.

(SO 7) 11. ▭ Which of these measures is an evaluation of a company's ability to pay current liabilities?
   (a) Profit margin ratio.
   (b) Current ratio.
   (c) Both (a) and (b).
   (d) None of the above.

QUESTIONS

1. (a) What are generally accepted accounting principles (GAAP)?
   (b) What body provides authoritative support for GAAP?
2. (a) What is the basic objective of financial reporting?
   (b) Identify the qualitative characteristics of accounting information.
3. Ray Aldag, the president of Raynard Company, is pleased. Raynard substantially increased its net income in 2001 while keeping its unit inventory relatively the same. Tom Erhardt, chief accountant, cautions Aldag, however. Erhardt says that since Raynard changed its method of inventory valuation, there is a consistency problem and it is difficult to determine whether Raynard is better off. Is Erhardt correct? Why or why not?
4. What is the distinction between comparability and consistency?

BRIEF EXERCISES

BE2-1 Indicate whether each statement is *true* or *false*.

(a) GAAP is a set of rules and practices established by the accounting profession to serve as a general guide for financial reporting purposes.
(b) Substantial authoritative support for GAAP usually comes from two standards-setting bodies: the FASB and the IRS.

Recognize generally accepted accounting principles. (SO 1)

BE2-2 The accompanying chart shows the qualitative characteristics of accounting information. Fill in the blanks.

Identify qualitative characteristics. (SO 2)

EXERCISES

E2-1 The following items were taken from the December 31, 1998, assets section of the Boeing Company balance sheet. (All dollars are in millions.)

Classify items as current or noncurrent, and prepare assets section of balance sheet. (SO 4)

Inventories	$ 8,349	Goodwill	$ 2,312
Notes receivable—due after		Other current assets	1,495
December 31, 1999	4,930	Property, plant, and	
Short-term investments	279	equipment	20,241
Notes receivable—due before		Cash and cash equivalents	2,183
December 31, 1999	781	Accounts receivable	3,288
Accumulated depreciation	11,652	Other noncurrent assets	4,466

Instructions
Prepare the assets section of a classified balance sheet, listing the current assets in order of their liquidity.

Self-Study Questions are a practice test, keyed to Study Objectives, that gives you an opportunity to check your knowledge of important topics. Answers appear on the last page of the chapter.

A special icon ▭ indicates homework material that asks you to use the **decision tools** presented in the chapter.

Questions allow you to explain your understanding of concepts and relationships covered in the chapter. Use them to help prepare for class discussion and tests.

Brief Exercises help you focus on one Study Objective at a time and thus help you build confidence in your basic skills and knowledge. (Keyed to Study Objectives.)

Exercises, which gradually increase in skills, understanding, and time necessary to complete them, help you continue to build your confidence. (Keyed to Study Objectives.)

Problems: Set A

Each **Problem** helps you pull together and apply several concepts of the chapter. (Keyed to multiple Study Objectives.)

P2-1A The following items are taken from the 1998 balance sheet of Yahoo, Inc. (in thousands).   *Prepare a classified balance sheet.*
(SO 4)

Common stock	$523,020
Property and equipment, net	15,189
Accounts payable	6,302
Other assets	49,190
Long-term investments	90,266
Accounts receivable	24,831
Prepaid expenses and other current assets	8,909
Short-term investments	308,025
Retained earnings	13,190
Cash and cash equivalents	125,474
Long-term liabilities	5,691
Accrued expenses and other current liabilities	35,380
Unearned revenue—current	38,301

Instructions
Prepare a balance sheet for Yahoo! Inc. as of December 31, 1998.

Two sets of problems—**A** and **B**—are keyed to the same **Study Objectives** and provide additional opportunities to apply concepts learned in the chapter.

P2-2A These items are taken from the financial statements of Kidman Corporation for 2001:   *Prepare financial statements.*
(SO 4, 6)

Retained earnings (beginning of year)	$26,000
Utilities expense	1,700
Equipment	66,000
Accounts payable	13,300
Cash	13,600
Salaries payable	3,000
Common stock	13,000
Dividends	12,000
Service revenue	76,000
Prepaid insurance	3,500
Repair expense	1,800
Depreciation expense	2,600
Accounts receivable	13,500
Insurance expense	2,200
Salaries expense	35,000
Accumulated depreciation	20,600

---

84   **CHAPTER 2**   A Further Look at Financial Statements

Instructions
Compute these values and ratios for 2000 and 2001:
(a) Profit margin ratio.
(b) Return on assets ratio.
(c) Working capital.
(d) Current ratio.
(e) Debt to total assets ratio.
(f) Based on the ratios calculated, discuss briefly the improvement or lack thereof in financial position and operating results from 2000 to 2001 of Smashing Pumpkins Corporation.

Certain exercises or problems marked with an icon help you practice **written business communication**, a skill much in demand among employers.

Compute ratios and compare liquidity, solvency, and profitability for two companies.
(SO 5, 7)

P2-6A Selected financial data (in millions) of two intense competitors, Kmart and Wal-Mart, for 1998 are presented here:

	Kmart	Wal-Mart
Income Statement Data for Year		
Net sales	$33,674	$137,634
Cost of goods sold	26,319	108,725
Selling and administrative expenses	6,245	22,363
Interest expense	343	797
Other income (loss)	(19)	1,421
Income taxes	230	2,740
Net income	$ 518	$ 4,430
Balance Sheet Data (End of Year)		
Current assets	$ 7,830	$ 21,132
Noncurrent assets	6,336	28,864
Total assets	$14,166	$ 49,996
Current liabilities	$ 3,691	$ 16,762
Long-term debt	4,496	12,122
Total stockholders' equity	5,979	21,112
Total liabilities and stockholders' equity	$14,166	$ 49,996
Beginning-of-Year Balances		
Total assets	$13,558	$ 45,384

Instructions
For each company, compute these values and ratios:
(a) Working capital.
(b) Current ratio.
(c) Debt to total assets ratio.
(d) Return on assets ratio.
(e) Profit margin ratio.
(f) Compare the liquidity, solvency, and profitability of the two companies.

Homework material that can be solved using the **General Ledger Software** is marked with an icon.

Problems: Set B

Prepare a classified balance sheet.
(SO 4)

P2-1B The following items are taken from the 1998 balance sheet of Kellogg Company (in millions).

Common stock	$ 208.8
Other assets	666.2
Notes payable—current	620.4
Other current assets	215.7
Current maturities of long-term debt	1.1
Cash and cash equivalents	136.4
Other long-term liabilities	828.7
Retained earnings	681.0
Accounts payable	386.9

The financial results of real companies are included in many exercises and problems; these are indicated by the company name shown in red.

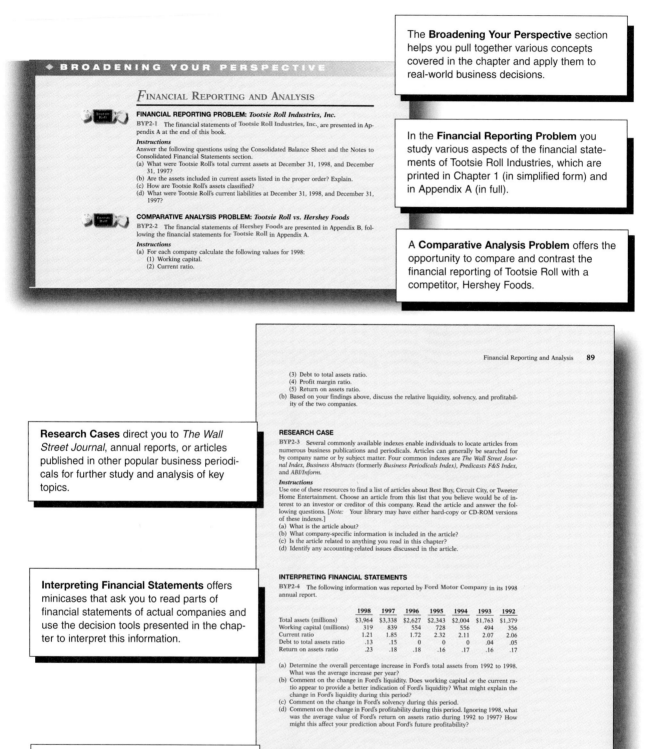

The **Broadening Your Perspective** section helps you pull together various concepts covered in the chapter and apply them to real-world business decisions.

◆ BROADENING YOUR PERSPECTIVE

*F*INANCIAL REPORTING AND ANALYSIS

FINANCIAL REPORTING PROBLEM: *Tootsie Roll Industries, Inc.*

BYP2-1 The financial statements of Tootsie Roll Industries, Inc., are presented in Appendix A at the end of this book.

Instructions
Answer the following questions using the Consolidated Balance Sheet and the Notes to Consolidated Financial Statements section.
(a) What were Tootsie Roll's total current assets at December 31, 1998, and December 31, 1997?
(b) Are the assets included in current assets listed in the proper order? Explain.
(c) How are Tootsie Roll's assets classified?
(d) What were Tootsie Roll's current liabilities at December 31, 1998, and December 31, 1997?

COMPARATIVE ANALYSIS PROBLEM: *Tootsie Roll vs. Hershey Foods*

BYP2-2 The financial statements of Hershey Foods are presented in Appendix B, following the financial statements for Tootsie Roll in Appendix A.

Instructions
(a) For each company calculate the following values for 1998:
    (1) Working capital.
    (2) Current ratio.

In the **Financial Reporting Problem** you study various aspects of the financial statements of Tootsie Roll Industries, which are printed in Chapter 1 (in simplified form) and in Appendix A (in full).

A **Comparative Analysis Problem** offers the opportunity to compare and contrast the financial reporting of Tootsie Roll with a competitor, Hershey Foods.

Financial Reporting and Analysis   **89**

(3) Debt to total assets ratio.
(4) Profit margin ratio.
(5) Return on assets ratio.
(b) Based on your findings above, discuss the relative liquidity, solvency, and profitability of the two companies.

Research Cases direct you to *The Wall Street Journal*, annual reports, or articles published in other popular business periodicals for further study and analysis of key topics.

RESEARCH CASE

BYP2-3 Several commonly available indexes enable individuals to locate articles from numerous business publications and periodicals. Articles can generally be searched for by company name or by subject matter. Four common indexes are *The Wall Street Journal Index, Business Abstracts* (formerly *Business Periodicals Index*), *Predicasts F&S Index,* and *ABI/Inform.*

Instructions
Use one of these resources to find a list of articles about Best Buy, Circuit City, or Tweeter Home Entertainment. Choose an article from this list that you believe would be of interest to an investor or creditor of this company. Read the article and answer the following questions. [*Note:* Your library may have either hard-copy or CD-ROM versions of these indexes.]
(a) What is the article about?
(b) What company-specific information is included in the article?
(c) Is the article related to anything you read in this chapter?
(d) Identify any accounting-related issues discussed in the article.

Interpreting Financial Statements offers minicases that ask you to read parts of financial statements of actual companies and use the decision tools presented in the chapter to interpret this information.

INTERPRETING FINANCIAL STATEMENTS

BYP2-4 The following information was reported by Ford Motor Company in its 1998 annual report.

	1998	1997	1996	1995	1994	1993	1992
Total assets (millions)	$3,964	$3,338	$2,627	$2,343	$2,004	$1,763	$1,379
Working capital (millions)	319	839	554	728	556	494	356
Current ratio	1.21	1.85	1.72	2.32	2.11	2.07	2.06
Debt to total assets ratio	.13	.15	0	0	0	.04	.05
Return on assets ratio	.23	.18	.18	.16	.17	.16	.17

(a) Determine the overall percentage increase in Ford's total assets from 1992 to 1998. What was the average increase per year?
(b) Comment on the change in Ford's liquidity. Does working capital or the current ratio appear to provide a better indication of Ford's liquidity? What might explain the change in Ford's liquidity during this period?
(c) Comment on the change in Ford's solvency during this period.
(d) Comment on the change in Ford's profitability during this period. Ignoring 1998, what was the average value of Ford's return on assets ratio during 1992 to 1997? How might this affect your prediction about Ford's future profitability?

A Global Focus asks you to apply concepts presented in the chapter to specific situations faced by actual foreign companies.

A GLOBAL FOCUS

BYP2-5 Mo och Comsjo AB (MoDo) is one of Europe's largest forest products companies. It has production facilities in Sweden, France, and Great Britain. Its headquarters is in Stockholm, Sweden. Its statements are presented in conformity with the standards issued by the Swedish Standards Board. Its financial statements are presented to be harmonized (that is, to have minimal difference in methods) with member countries of the European Union. The following balance sheet was taken from MoDo's 1998 annual report.

FINANCIAL ANALYSIS ON THE WEB

BYP2-6 *Purpose:* Identify summary liquidity, solvency, and profitability information about companies, and compare this information across companies in the same industry.

Address: http://biz.yahoo.com/i (or go to www.wiley.com/college/kimmel)

Steps:
1. Type in a company name, or use the index to find a company name. Perform instructions (a) and (b) below.
2. Click on the company's particular industry behind the heading "Industry." Perform instructions (c) and (d).

Instructions
Answer the following questions:
(a) What was the company's current ratio, debt to equity ratio (a variation of the debt to total assets ratio), profit margin ratio, and return on assets ratio?
(b) What is the company's industry?
(c) What is the name of a competitor? What is the competitor's current ratio, debt to equity ratio, profit margin ratio, and return on assets ratio?
(d) Based on these measures: Which company is more liquid? Which company is more solvent? Which company is more profitable?

BYP2-7 The opening story described the dramatic effect that investment bulletin boards are having on the investment world. This exercise will allow you to evaluate a bulletin board discussing a company of your choice.

Address: http://biz.yahoo.com/i (or go to www.wiley.com/college/kimmel)

Steps:
1. Type in a company name, or use the index to find a company name.
2. Choose **Msgs** (for messages).
3. Read the ten most recent messages.

Instructions
Answer the following questions:
(a) State the nature of each of these messages (e.g., offering advice, criticizing company, predicting future results, ridiculing other people who have posted messages).
(b) For those messages that expressed an opinion about the company, was evidence provided to support the opinion?
(c) What effect do you think it would have on bulletin board discussions if the participants provided their actual names? Do you think this would be a good policy?

> **Financial Analysis on the Web** exercises guide you to Web sites where you can find and analyze information related to the chapter topic.

CRITICAL THINKING

GROUP DECISION CASE

BYP2-8 As the accountant for J. Martinez Manufacturing Inc., you have been requested to develop some key ratios from the comparative financial statements. This information is to be used to convince creditors that J. Martinez Manufacturing Inc. is liquid, solvent, and profitable, and that it deserves their continued support. Lenders are particularly concerned about the company's ability to continue as a going concern.

These are the data requested and the computations developed from the financial statements:

> The **Group Decision Case** helps you build decision-making skills by analyzing accounting information in a less structured situation. These cases require teams of students to evaluate a manager's decision or lead to a decision among alternative courses of action. They also give practice in building business communication skills.

ial Statements

	2001	2000
rent ratio	3.1	2.1
rking capital	Up 22%	Down 7%
bt to total assets ratio	.60	.70
income	Up 32%	Down 8%
fit margin ratio	.05	.015
urn on assets ratio	.09	.04

facturing Inc. asks you to prepare brief comments stating how each of ports the argument that its financial health is improving. The company wishes to use these comments to support presentation of data to its creditors. With the class divided into groups, prepare the comments as requested, giving the implications and the limitations of each item separately, and then the collective inference that may be drawn from them about J. Martinez's financial well-being.

COMMUNICATION ACTIVITY

BYP2-9 L. R. Stanton is the chief executive officer of Hi-Tech Electronics. Stanton is an expert engineer but a novice in accounting.

Instructions
Write a letter to L. R. Stanton that explains (a) the three main types of ratios; (b) examples of each, how they are calculated, and what they measure; and (c) the bases for comparison in analyzing Hi-Tech's financial statements.

ETHICS CASE

BYP2-10 As the controller of Breathless Perfume Company, you discover a significant misstatement that overstated net income in the prior year's financial statements. The misleading financial statements are contained in the company's annual report, which was issued to banks and other creditors less than a month ago. After much thought about the consequences of telling the president, Eddy Kadu, about this misstatement, you gather your courage to inform him. Eddy says, "Hey! What they don't know won't hurt them. But, just so we set the record straight, we'll adjust this year's financial statements for last year's misstatement. We can absorb that misstatement better this year than last year anyway! Just don't make that kind of mistake again."

Instructions
(a) Who are the stakeholders in this situation?
(b) What are the ethical issues?
(c) What would you do as the controller?

> **Communication Activities** ask you to engage in real-world business situations via written communication.

> Through the **Ethics Cases**, you will reflect on typical ethical dilemmas and decide on an appropriate course of action.

> **Answers to Self-Study Questions** provide feedback on your understanding of concepts. **Answers to Review It** questions based on the Tootsie Roll financial statements appear here.

Answers to Self-Study Questions
1. a   2. a   3. c   4. c   5. c   6. d   7. a   8. a   9. a   10. c   11. b

Answer to Tootsie Roll Review It Question 3, p. 57
Tootsie Roll's largest current asset at December 31, 1998, was investments, at $83,176,000.

HOW DO YOU LEARN BEST?

Now that you have looked at your Owner's Manual, take time to find out how you learn best. This quiz was designed to help you find out something about your preferred learning method. Research on left brain/right brain differences and also on learning and personality differences suggests that each person has preferred ways to receive and communicate information. After taking the quiz, we will help you pinpoint the study aids in this text that will help you learn the material based on your learning style.

Circle the letter of the answer that best explains your preferences. If a single answer does not match your perception, please circle two or more choices. Leave blank any question that does not apply.

1. You are about to give directions to a person. She is staying in a hotel in town and wants to visit your house. She has a rental car. Would you
   V) draw a map on paper?
   R) write down the directions (without a map)?
   A) tell her the directions?
   K) pick her up at the hotel in your car?

2. You are staying in a hotel and have a rental car. You would like to visit friends whose address/location you do not know. Would you like them to
   V) draw you a map on paper?
   R) write down the directions (without a map)?
   A) tell you the directions by phone?
   K) pick you up at the hotel in their car?

3. You have just received a copy of your itinerary for a world trip. This is of interest to a friend. Would you
   A) call her immediately and tell her about it?
   R) send her a copy of the printed itinerary?
   V) show her on a map of the world?

4. You are going to cook a dessert as a special treat for your family. Do you
   K) cook something familiar without need for instructions?
   V) thumb through the cookbook looking for ideas from the pictures?
   R) refer to a specific cookbook where there is a good recipe?
   A) ask for advice from others?

5. A group of tourists has been assigned to you to find out about national parks. Would you
   K) drive them to a national park?
   R) give them a book on national parks?
   V) show them slides and photographs?
   A) give them a talk on national parks?

6. You are about to purchase a new stereo. Other than price, what would most influence your decision?
   A) A friend talking about it.
   K) Listening to it.
   R) Reading the details about it.
   V) Its distinctive, upscale appearance.

7. Recall a time in your life when you learned how to do something like playing a new board game. (Try to avoid choosing a very physical skill, e.g., riding a bike.) How did you learn best? By
   V) visual clues—pictures, diagrams, charts?
   A) listening to somebody explaining it?
   R) written instructions?
   K) doing it?

8. Which of these games do you prefer?
   V) *Pictionary*
   R) *Scrabble*
   K) Charades

9. You are about to learn to use a new program on a computer. Would you
   K) ask a friend to show you?
   R) read the manual that comes with the program?
   A) telephone a friend and ask questions about it?

10. You are not sure whether a word should be spelled "dependent" or "dependant." Do you
    R) look it up in the dictionary?
    V) see the word in your mind and choose the best way it looks?
    A) sound it out in your mind?
    K) write both versions down?

11. Apart from price, what would most influence your decision to buy a particular textbook?
    K) Using a friend's copy.
    R) Skimming parts of it.
    A) A friend talking about it.
    V) It looks OK.

12. A new movie has arrived in town. What would most influence your decision to go or not to go?
    A) Friends talked about it.
    R) You read a review of it.
    V) You saw a preview of it.

13. Do you prefer a lecturer/teacher who likes to use
    R) handouts and/or a textbook?
    V) flow diagrams, charts, slides?
    K) field trips, labs, practical sessions?
    A) discussion, guest speakers?

Results: To determine your learning preference, add up the number of individual Vs, As, Rs, and Ks you have circled. Take the letter you have the greatest number of and match it to the same letter in the Learning Styles Chart. Next to each letter in the chart are suggestions that will refer you to different learning aids throughout this text.

LEARNING STYLES CHART

V VISUAL

WHAT TO DO IN CLASS	WHAT TO DO WHEN STUDYING	TEXT FEATURES THAT MAY HELP YOU THE MOST	WHAT TO DO PRIOR TO AND DURING EXAMS
Underline. Use different colors. Use symbols, charts, arrangements on the page.	Use the "In Class" strategies. Reconstruct images in different ways. Redraw pages from memory. Replace words with symbols and initials.	**Vignettes** **Previews** **Infographics/Illustrations** **Accounting Equation Analysis in margin** **Photos** **Business Insights** **Decision Toolkits** **Key Terms in blue** **Words in bold** **Questions/Exercises/ Problems** **Financial Reporting and Analysis**	Recall the "pictures of the pages." Draw, use diagrams where appropriate. Practice turning visuals back into words.

A AURAL

WHAT TO DO IN CLASS	WHAT TO DO WHEN STUDYING	TEXT FEATURES THAT MAY HELP YOU THE MOST	WHAT TO DO PRIOR TO AND DURING EXAMS
Attend lectures and tutorials. Discuss topics with students. Explain new ideas to other people. Use a tape recorder. Describe overheads, pictures, and visuals to somebody not there. Leave space in your notes for later recall.	You may take poor notes because you prefer to listen. Therefore: Expand your notes. Put summarized notes on tape and listen. Read summarized notes out loud. Explain notes to another "aural" person.	**Infographics/Illustrations** **Business Insights** **Review It/Do It** **Summary of Study Objectives** **Glossary** **Demonstration Problem** **Self-Study Questions** **Questions/Exercises/ Problems** **Financial Reporting and Analysis** **Critical Thinking**	Listen to your "voices" and write them down. Speak your answers. Practice writing answers to old exam questions.

Source: Adapted from Neil D. Fleming and Colleen Mills, "Not Another Inventory, Rather a Catalyst for Reflections," *To Improve the Academy,* Volume II (1992), pp.137–155. Used by permission.

READING/WRITING

WHAT TO DO IN CLASS	WHAT TO DO WHEN STUDYING	TEXT FEATURES THAT MAY HELP YOU THE MOST	WHAT TO DO PRIOR TO AND DURING EXAMS
Use lists, headings. Use dictionaries and definitions. Use handouts and textbooks. Read. Use lecture notes.	Write out words again and again. Reread notes silently. Rewrite ideas into other words. Organize diagrams into statements.	**Study Objectives** **Previews** **Accounting Equation Analysis in margin** **Review It/Do It** **Using the Decision Toolkit** **Summary of Study Objectives** **Glossary** **Self-Study Questions** **Questions/Exercises/ Problems** **Writing Problems** **Financial Reporting and Analysis** **Critical Thinking**	Practice with multiple-choice questions. Write out lists. Write paragraphs, beginnings and endings.

KINESTHETIC

WHAT TO DO IN CLASS	WHAT TO DO WHEN STUDYING	TEXT FEATURES THAT MAY HELP YOU THE MOST	WHAT TO DO PRIOR TO AND DURING EXAMS
Use all your senses. Go to labs, take field trips. Use trial-and-error methods. Listen to real-life examples. Use hands-on approach.	You may take notes poorly because topics do not seem relevant. Therefore: Put examples in note summaries. Use pictures and photos to illustrate. Talk about notes with another "kinesthetic" person.	**Vignettes** **Previews** **Infographics/Illustrations** **Decision Toolkits** **Review It/Do It** **Using the Decision Toolkit** **Summary of Study Objectives** **Demonstration Problem** **Self-Study Questions** **Questions/Exercises/ Problems** **Financial Reporting and Analysis** **Critical Thinking**	Write practice answers. Role-play the exam situation.

BRIEF CONTENTS

CONTENTS

CHAPTER 14

Financial Analysis: The Big Picture 664
"Follow That Stock!" 664

APPENDIX A

APPENDIX B

APPENDIX C

Introduction to Financial Statements

◆ HAVE YOU HAD A TOOTSIE ROLL TODAY?

In an era when it seems the U.S. economy can do nothing but go up, and 25-year-old Internet millionaires are a dime a dozen, let us not forget those things that comprise the foundation of this great nation: ingenuity, perseverance, dedication, and Tootsie Rolls. That's right, Tootsie Rolls. What else can you think of that has consistently provided so much pleasure at so little cost? Although the price and recipe for Tootsie Rolls haven't changed much over the years, the company has changed a great deal.

Tootsie Rolls started off humbly in 1896 in a small New York City candy shop owned by Austrian immigrant Leo Hirshfield. The chocolatey, chewy candy's name came from his five-year-old daughter's nickname—"Tootsie." By 1905 the candies were being produced in a four-story factory, and by 1922 the company's stock was being traded on the New York Stock Exchange. During its long and steady route to becoming one of the premier U.S. candy companies, the company has continually had to build new and bigger facilities and has purchased other brands such as Blow Pops, Charms, Mason Dots, Junior

Mints, and Sugar Babies. The Chicago-based company produces more than 49 million Tootsie Rolls and 16 million Tootsie Pops *each day*.

Tootsie Rolls and Tootsie Pops have played an important role in American and world culture. They were included in World War II rations; they have been a favorite of celebrities such as Frank Sinatra, Sammy Davis Jr., and Rosie O'Donnell; and they have been at the center of one of science's most challenging questions: How many licks does it take to get to the Tootsie Roll center of a Tootsie Pop? The

answer varies: Licking machines created at Purdue University and the University of Michigan report an average of 364 and 411 licks respectively, but in studies using human lickers the answer ranges from 144 to 252. In a single year the company received 20,000 responses from children regarding this very important question. We recommend that you take a few minutes today away from your studies to determine your own results.

Source: Adapted from information on Tootsie Roll's Web page.

On the World Wide Web
Tootsie Roll Industries:
http://www.tootsie.com

Every **chapter-opening vignette** ends with the **Internet addresses** of the companies cited in the story to help you connect with these real businesses and explore them further.

The **Preview** describes the purpose of the chapter and outlines the major topics and subtopics you will find in it.

How do you start a business? How do you make it grow into a widely recognized brand name like Tootsie Roll? How do you determine whether your business is making or losing money? When you need to expand your operations, where do you get money to finance expansion—should you borrow, should you issue stock, should you use your own funds? How do you convince lenders to lend you money or investors to buy your stock? Success in business requires making countless decisions, and decisions require financial information.

The purpose of this chapter is to show you what role accounting plays in providing financial information. The content and organization of the chapter are as follows:

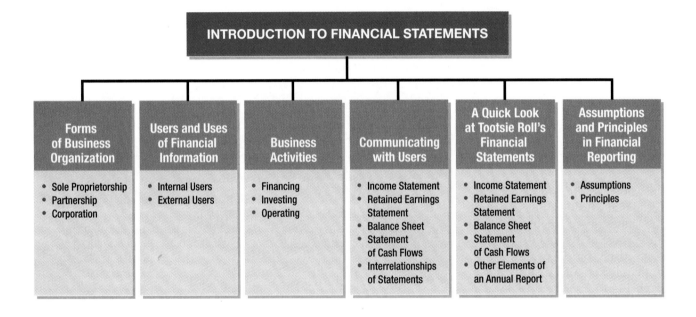

INTRODUCTION TO FINANCIAL STATEMENTS

Forms of Business Organization	Users and Uses of Financial Information	Business Activities	Communicating with Users	A Quick Look at Tootsie Roll's Financial Statements	Assumptions and Principles in Financial Reporting
• Sole Proprietorship • Partnership • Corporation	• Internal Users • External Users	• Financing • Investing • Operating	• Income Statement • Retained Earnings Statement • Balance Sheet • Statement of Cash Flows • Interrelationships of Statements	• Income Statement • Retained Earnings Statement • Balance Sheet • Statement of Cash Flows • Other Elements of an Annual Report	• Assumptions • Principles

FORMS OF BUSINESS ORGANIZATION

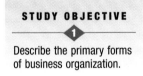

STUDY OBJECTIVE

1

Describe the primary forms of business organization.

Terms that represent essential concepts of the chapter topic are printed in blue where they are first explained in the text. They are listed and defined again in the **glossary** at the end of the chapter.

Suppose you graduate with a marketing degree and open your own marketing agency. One of your initial decisions is what organizational form your business will have. You have three choices—sole proprietorship, partnership, or corporation. A business owned by one person is a sole proprietorship. A business owned by more than one person is a partnership. A business organized as a separate legal entity owned by stockholders is a corporation. Illustration 1-1 highlights these three types of organizations and the advantages of each.

You will probably choose the sole proprietorship form for your marketing agency. It is **simple to set up** and **gives you control** over the business. Small owner-operated businesses such as barber shops, law offices, and auto repair shops are often sole proprietorships, as are farms and small retail stores.

Another possibility is for you to join forces with other individuals to form a partnership. Partnerships often are formed because one individual does not have **enough economic resources** to initiate or expand the business, or because

Illustrations like this one convey information in pictorial form to help you visualize and apply the ideas as you study.

Illustration 1-1   Forms of business organization

Sole Proprietorship

-Simple to establish
-Owner controlled
-Tax advantages

Partnership

-Simple to establish
-Shared control
-Broader skills and resources
-Tax advantages

Corporation

-Easier to transfer ownership
-Easier to raise funds
-No personal liability

partners bring unique skills or resources to the partnership. You and your partners should formalize your duties and contributions in a written partnership agreement. Partnerships are often used to organize retail and service-type businesses, including professional practices (lawyers, doctors, architects, and certified public accountants).

As a third alternative, you might organize as a corporation. As an investor in a corporation you receive shares of stock to indicate your ownership claim. Buying stock in a corporation is often more attractive than investing in a partnership because shares of stock are **easy to sell** (transfer ownership). Selling a proprietorship or partnership interest is much more involved. Also, individuals can become **stockholders** by investing relatively small amounts of money. Therefore, it is **easier for corporations to raise funds**. Successful corporations often have thousands of stockholders, and their stock is traded on organized stock exchanges like the New York Stock Exchange. Many businesses start as sole proprietorships or partnerships and eventually incorporate. For example, in 1896 Tootsie Roll was started as a sole proprietorship, but by 1919 it had incorporated.

Other factors to consider in deciding which organizational form to choose are **taxes and legal liability**. If you choose a sole proprietorship or partnership, you generally receive favorable tax treatment relative to a corporation. However, a disadvantage of proprietorships and partnerships is that proprietors and partners are personally liable for all debts of the business; corporate stockholders are not. In other words, corporate stockholders generally pay higher taxes but have no personal liability. We will discuss these issues in more depth in a later chapter.

Although the combined number of proprietorships and partnerships in the United States is more than five times the number of corporations, the revenue produced by corporations is eight times greater. Most of the largest enterprises in the United States—for example, Coca-Cola, Exxon, General Motors, Citigroup, and Microsoft—are corporations. Because the majority of U.S. business is transacted by corporations, the emphasis in this book is on the corporate form of organization.

Alternative Terminology
Stockholders are sometimes called **shareholders.**

Alternative Terminology notes present synonymous terms that you may come across in practice.

USERS AND USES OF FINANCIAL INFORMATION

The purpose of financial information is to provide inputs for decision making. Accounting is the information system that identifies, records, and communicates the economic events of an organization to interested users. Many people have an interest in knowing about the ongoing activities of the business. These people are **users** of accounting information. Users can be divided broadly into two groups: internal users and external users.

INTERNAL USERS

Internal users of accounting information are managers who plan, organize, and run a business. These include **marketing managers**, **production supervisors**, **finance directors**, **and company officers**. In running a business, managers must answer many important questions, as shown in Illustration 1-2.

Illustration 1-2

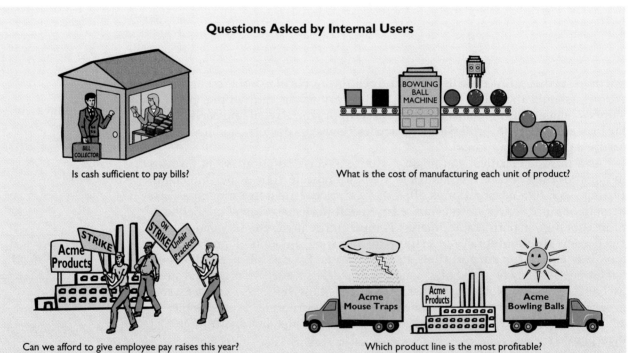

Questions Asked by Internal Users

Is cash sufficient to pay bills?

What is the cost of manufacturing each unit of product?

Can we afford to give employee pay raises this year?

Which product line is the most profitable?

To answer these and other questions, you need detailed information on a timely basis. For internal users, accounting provides internal reports, such as financial comparisons of operating alternatives, projections of income from new sales campaigns, and forecasts of cash needs for the next year. In addition, summarized financial information is presented in the form of financial statements.

EXTERNAL USERS

There are several types of **external users** of accounting information. **Investors** (owners) use accounting information to make decisions to buy, hold, or sell stock. **Creditors** such as suppliers and bankers use accounting information to evaluate the risks of granting credit or lending money. Some questions that may be asked by investors and creditors about a company are shown in Illustration 1-3.

Illustration 1-3

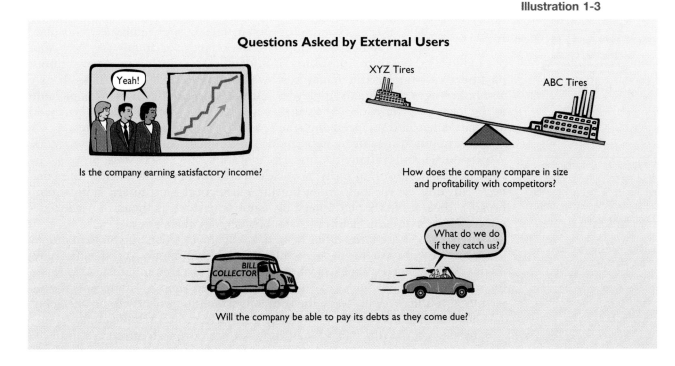

Questions Asked by External Users

Is the company earning satisfactory income?

How does the company compare in size and profitability with competitors?

Will the company be able to pay its debts as they come due?

The information needs and questions of other external users vary considerably. **Taxing authorities**, such as the Internal Revenue Service, want to know whether the company complies with the tax laws. **Regulatory agencies**, such as the Securities and Exchange Commission or the Federal Trade Commission, want to know whether the company is operating within prescribed rules. **Customers** are interested in whether a company will continue to honor product warranties and otherwise support its product lines. **Labor unions** want to know whether the owners have the ability to pay increased wages and benefits. **Economic planners** use accounting information to analyze and forecast economic activity.

BUSINESS ACTIVITIES

All businesses are involved in three types of activity—financing, investing, and operating. For example, the founder of Tootsie Roll needed financing to start and grow his business. Some of this **financing** came from personal savings, and some likely came from outside sources like banks. The cash obtained was then **invested** in the equipment necessary to run the business, such as mixing equipment and delivery vehicles. Once this equipment was in place, the founder could begin the **operating** activities of making and selling candy.

The **accounting information system** keeps track of the results of each of the various business activities—financing, investing, and operating. Let's look in more detail at each type of business activity.

STUDY OBJECTIVE

3

Explain the three principal types of business activity.

FINANCING ACTIVITIES

It takes money to make money. The two primary sources of outside funds for corporations are borrowing money and selling shares of stock.

For example, Tootsie Roll Industries may borrow money in a variety of ways. It can take out a loan at a bank, borrow directly from investors by issuing debt

Financing

Helpful Hints in the margins help clarify concepts being discussed.

securities called bonds, or borrow money from its suppliers by purchasing goods on credit. Persons or entities to whom Tootsie Roll owes money are its **creditors**. Amounts owed to creditors—in the form of debt and other obligations—are called liabilities. Specific names are given to different types of liabilities, depending on their source. Tootsie Roll, for instance, might purchase chocolate and corn syrup on credit from suppliers; the obligations to pay for these supplies are called **accounts payable**. Additionally, Tootsie Roll may have a **note payable** to a bank for the money borrowed to purchase delivery trucks. It may also have **wages payable** to employees, and **sales and real estate taxes payable** to the local government. Debt securities sold to investors and due to be repaid at a particular date some years in the future are called **bonds payable**.

A corporation may also obtain funds by selling shares of stock to investors. When Tootsie Roll initially became a corporation, the shares were probably issued to a small group of individuals who had an interest in starting the business. However, as the business grew, it became necessary to sell shares more broadly to obtain additional financing. Common stock is the term used to describe the total amount paid in by stockholders for the shares.

The claims of creditors differ from those of stockholders. If you loan money to a company, you are one of its creditors. In loaning money, you specify a payment schedule (for example, payment at the end of three months). As a creditor, you have a legal right to be paid at the agreed time. In the event of nonpayment, you may legally force the company to sell its property to pay its debts. The law requires that creditor claims be paid before ownership claims.

Owners, on the other hand, have no claim to corporate resources until the claims of creditors are satisfied. If you buy a company's stock instead of loaning it money, you have no right to expect any payments until all of its creditors are paid. However, many corporations make payments to stockholders on a regular basis as long as there is sufficient cash to cover expected payments to creditors. These payments to stockholders are called dividends.

INVESTING ACTIVITIES

Investing activities involve the purchase of those resources a company needs in order to operate. During the early stages of the company's life it must purchase many resources. For example, computers, delivery trucks, furniture, and buildings are resources obtained from investing activities. Resources owned by a business are called assets. Different types of assets are given different names. Tootsie Roll's mixing equipment is an asset referred to as **property**, **plant**, **and equipment**.

Many of the company's assets are purchased through investing activities. Others, however, result from operating activities. For example, if Tootsie Roll sells goods to a customer and does not receive cash immediately, then Tootsie Roll has a right to expect payment from that customer in the future. This right to receive money in the future is an asset called an **account receivable**.

Investing

Alternative Terminology Property, plant, and equipment is sometimes called **fixed assets.**

OPERATING ACTIVITIES

Once a business has the assets it needs to get started, it can begin its operations. Tootsie Roll is in the business of selling all things that smell, look, or taste like candy. It sells Tootsie Rolls, Tootsie Pops, Blow Pops, Caramel Apple Pops, Mason Dots, Mason Crows, Sugar Daddy, and Sugar Babies. In short, if it has anything to do with candy, Tootsie Roll sells it. We call the sale of these products revenues. In accounting language, revenues are the increase in assets arising from the sale of a product or service. For example, Tootsie Roll records revenue when it sells a candy product.

Revenues arise from different sources and are identified by various names depending on the nature of the business. For instance, Tootsie Roll's primary source of revenue is the sale of candy products. However, it also generates interest revenue on debt securities held as investments. Sources of revenue common to many businesses are **sales revenue**, **service revenue**, and **interest revenue**.

Before Tootsie Roll can sell a single Tootsie Roll, Tootsie Pop, or Blow Pop, it must purchase sugar, corn syrup, and other ingredients, mix these ingredients, process the mix, and wrap and ship the finished product. It also incurs costs like salaries, rents, and utilities. All of these costs, referred to as expenses, are necessary to sell the product. In accounting language, expenses are the cost of assets consumed or services used in the process of generating revenues.

Expenses take many forms and are identified by various names depending on the type of asset consumed or service used. For example, Tootsie Roll keeps track of these types of expenses: **cost of goods sold** (such as the cost of ingredients), **selling expenses** (such as the cost of salespersons' salaries), **marketing expenses** (such as the cost of advertising), **administrative expenses** (such as the salaries of administrative staff, and telephone and heat costs incurred at the corporate office), and **interest expense** (amounts of interest paid on various debts).

Tootsie Roll compares the revenues of a period with the expenses of that period to determine whether it earned a profit. When revenues exceed expenses, net income results. When expenses exceed revenues, a net loss results.

Operating

BEFORE YOU GO ON...

◆ Review It

1. What are the three forms of business organization and the advantages of each?
2. What are the two primary categories of users of financial information? Give examples of each.
3. What are the three types of business activity?
4. What are assets, liabilities, common stock, revenues, expenses, and net income?

◆ Do It

Classify each item as an asset, liability, common stock, revenue, or expense.

Cost of using property	Issuance of ownership shares
Service revenue	Truck purchased
Notes payable	Amounts owed to suppliers

Reasoning: Accounting classifies items by their economic characteristics. Proper classification of items is critical if accounting is to provide useful information.

Solution:

Cost of using property is classified as expense.

Service revenue is classified as revenue.

Notes payable are classified as liabilities.

Issuance of ownership shares is classified as common stock.

Truck purchased is classified as an asset.

Amounts owed to suppliers are classified as liabilities.

Review It questions at the end of major text sections prompt you to stop and review the key points you have just studied. Sometimes Review It questions stand alone; other times they are accompanied by practice exercises. The **Do It** exercises, like the one here, ask you to put newly acquired knowledge to work. They outline the reasoning necessary to complete the exercise and show a solution.

COMMUNICATING WITH USERS

Assets, liabilities, expenses, and revenues are of interest to users of accounting information. For business purposes, it is customary to arrange this information in the format of four different **financial statements**, which form the backbone

STUDY OBJECTIVE

4

Describe the content and purpose of each of the financial statements.

of financial accounting. To present a picture at a point in time of what your business owns (its assets) and what it owes (its liabilities), you would present a **balance sheet**. To show how successfully your business performed during a period of time, you would report its revenues and expenses in the **income statement**. To indicate how much of previous income was distributed to you and the other owners of your business in the form of dividends, and how much was retained in the business to allow for future growth, you would present a **retained earnings statement**. And finally, of particular interest to your bankers and other creditors, you would present a **statement of cash flows** to show where your business obtained cash during a period of time and how that cash was used.

To introduce you to these statements, we have prepared the financial statements for a marketing agency, Sierra Corporation, in Illustration 1-4 (on page 11). Take some time now to look at their general form and categories in preparation for the more detailed discussion that follows.

INCOME STATEMENT

Helpful Hint The heading of every income statement identifies the company, the type of statement, and the time period covered by the statement. Sometimes another line is added to indicate the unit of measure; when it is used, this fourth line usually indicates that the data are presented "in thousands" or "in millions."

The purpose of the income statement is to report the success or failure of the company's operations for a period of time. To indicate that Sierra's income statement reports the results of operations for a **period of time**, the income statement is dated "For the Month Ended October 31, 2001." The income statement lists the company's revenues followed by its expenses. Finally, the net income (or net loss) is determined by deducting expenses from revenues. This result is the famed "bottom line" often referred to in business.

Why are financial statement users interested in the bottom line? Investors buy and sell stock based on their beliefs about the future performance of a company. If you believe that Sierra will be even more successful in the future and that this success will translate into a higher stock price, you should buy Sierra's stock. Investors are interested in a company's past net income because it provides some information about future net income. Similarly, creditors also use the income statement to predict the future. When a bank loans money to a company, it does so with the belief that it will be repaid in the future. If it didn't think it was going to be repaid, it wouldn't loan the money. Therefore, prior to making the loan the bank loan officer will use the income statement as a source of information to predict whether the company will be profitable enough to repay its loan.

Note that the issuance of stock and dividend distributions are not used in determining net income. For example, $10,000 of cash received from issuing new stock was not treated as revenue by Sierra Corporation, and dividends paid of $500 were not regarded as a business expense.

Each chapter presents useful information about how decision makers use financial statements. **Decision Toolkits** summarize discussions of key decision-making contexts and techniques.

DECISION TOOLKIT

Decision Checkpoints	**Info Needed for Decision**	**Tool to Use for Decision**	**How to Evaluate Results**
Are the company's operations profitable?	Income statement	The income statement reports on the success or failure of the company's operations by reporting its revenues and expenses.	If the company's revenue exceeds its expenses, it will report net income; otherwise it will report a net loss.

SIERRA CORPORATION
Income Statement
For the Month Ended October 31, 2001

Revenues		
Service revenue		$10,600
Expenses		
Salaries expense	$5,200	
Supplies expense	1,500	
Rent expense	900	
Insurance expense	50	
Interest expense	50	
Depreciation expense	40	
Total expenses		7,740
Net income		$ 2,860

Illustration 1-4   Sierra Corporation's financial statements

Helpful Hint Note that final sums are double-underlined, and negative amounts are presented in parentheses.

SIERRA CORPORATION
Retained Earnings Statement
For the Month Ended October 31, 2001

Retained earnings, October 1	$ 0
Add: Net income	2,860
	2,860
Less: Dividends	500
Retained earnings, October 31	$2,360

SIERRA CORPORATION
Balance Sheet
October 31, 2001

Assets

Cash		$15,200
Accounts receivable		200
Advertising supplies		1,000
Prepaid insurance		550
Office equipment, net		4,960
Total assets		$ 21,910

Liabilities and Stockholders' Equity

Liabilities		
Notes payable	$ 5,000	
Accounts payable	2,500	
Interest payable	50	
Unearned revenue	800	
Salaries payable	1,200	
Total liabilities		$ 9,550
Stockholders' equity		
Common stock	10,000	
Retained earnings	2,360	
Total stockholders' equity		12,360
Total liabilities and stockholders' equity		$ 21,910

Helpful Hint The arrows in this illustration show interrelationships of the four financial statements.

SIERRA CORPORATION
Statement of Cash Flows
For the Month Ended October 31, 2001

Cash flows from operating activities		
Cash receipts from operating activities	$11,200	
Cash payments for operating activities	(5,500)	
Net cash provided by operating activities		$ 5,700
Cash flows from investing activities		
Purchased office equipment	(5,000)	
Net cash used by investing activities		(5,000)
Cash flows from financing activities		
Issuance of common stock	10,000	
Issued note payable	5,000	
Payment of dividend	(500)	
Net cash provided by financing activities		14,500
Net increase in cash		15,200
Cash at beginning of period		0
Cash at end of period		$15,200

RETAINED EARNINGS STATEMENT

If Sierra is profitable, at the end of each period it must decide what portion of profits to pay to shareholders in dividends. In theory it could pay all of its current-period profits, but few companies choose to do this. Why? Because they want to retain part of the profits to allow for further expansion. High-growth companies, for example, often choose to pay no dividends. **Retained earnings** is the net income retained in the corporation.

The **retained earnings statement** shows the amounts and causes of changes in retained earnings during the period. The time period is the same as that covered by the income statement. The beginning retained earnings amount is shown on the first line of the statement. Then net income is added and dividends are deducted to calculate the retained earnings at the end of the period. If a company has a net loss, it is deducted (rather than added) in the retained earnings statement.

By monitoring the retained earnings statement, users of financial statements learn a great deal about management's dividend payment philosophy. Some investors seek companies that pay high dividends. Others seek companies that pay lower dividends and instead reinvest to increase the company's growth potential. Lenders monitor their corporate customers' dividend payments because any money paid in dividends reduces a company's ability to repay its debts.

DECISION TOOLKIT

Decision Checkpoints	Info Needed for Decision	Tool to Use for Decision	How to Evaluate Results
What is the company's policy toward dividends and growth?	Retained earnings statement	How much of this year's income did the company pay out in dividends to shareholders?	A company striving for rapid growth will pay a low dividend.

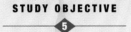
BALANCE SHEET

The **balance sheet** reports assets and claims to those assets at a specific **point** in time. These claims are subdivided into two categories: claims of creditors and claims of owners. As noted earlier, claims of creditors are called **liabilities.** Claims of owners are called **stockholders' equity**. This relationship is shown in equation form in Illustration 1-5. This equation is referred to as the **basic accounting equation.**

Illustration 1-5   Basic accounting equation

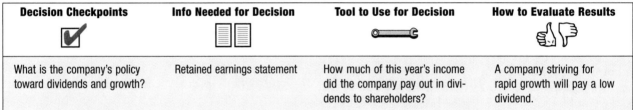

$$\text{Assets} = \text{Liabilities} + \text{Stockholders' Equity}$$

This relationship is where the name "balance sheet" comes from. Assets must be in balance with the claims to the assets.

As you can see from looking at Sierra's balance sheet in Illustration 1-4, assets are listed first, followed by liabilities and stockholders' equity. Stockholders' equity is comprised of two parts: (1) common stock and (2) retained earnings. As noted earlier, common stock results when the company sells new shares of stock. Retained earnings is the net income retained in the corporation. Sierra has common stock of $10,000 and retained earnings of $2,360, for total stockholders' equity of $12,360.

Creditors use the balance sheet as another source of information to determine the likelihood that they will be repaid. They carefully evaluate the nature of a company's assets and liabilities. For example, does the company have assets that could be easily sold to repay its debts? Managers use the balance sheet to determine whether inventory is adequate to support future sales and whether cash on hand is sufficient for immediate cash needs. Managers also look at the relationship between debt and stockholders' equity to determine whether they have the best proportion of debt and common stock financing.

DECISION TOOLKIT

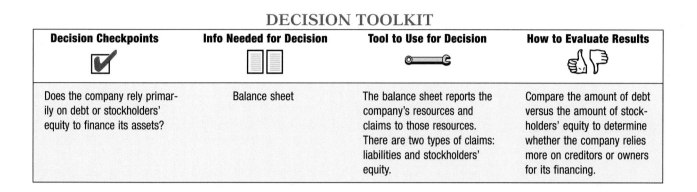

Decision Checkpoints	Info Needed for Decision	Tool to Use for Decision	How to Evaluate Results
Does the company rely primarily on debt or stockholders' equity to finance its assets?	Balance sheet	The balance sheet reports the company's resources and claims to those resources. There are two types of claims: liabilities and stockholders' equity.	Compare the amount of debt versus the amount of stockholders' equity to determine whether the company relies more on creditors or owners for its financing.

STATEMENT OF CASH FLOWS

The primary purpose of a statement of cash flows is to provide financial information about the cash receipts and cash payments of a business for a specific period of time. To help investors, creditors, and others in their analysis of a company's cash position, the statement of cash flows reports the cash effects of a company's: (1) operating activities, (2) investing activities, and (3) financing activities. In addition, the statement shows the net increase or decrease in cash during the period, and the cash amount at the end of the period.

Helpful Hint The heading of this statement identifies the company, the type of statement, and the time period covered by the statement.

Users are interested in the statement of cash flows because they want to know what is happening to a company's most important resource. The statement of cash flows provides answers to these simple but important questions:

Where did cash come from during the period?
How was cash used during the period?
What was the change in the cash balance during the period?

The statement of cash flows for Sierra, in Illustration 1-4, shows that cash increased $15,200 during the year. This increase resulted because operating activities (services to clients) increased cash $5,700, and financing activities increased cash $14,500. Investing activities used $5,000 of cash for the purchase of equipment.

DECISION TOOLKIT

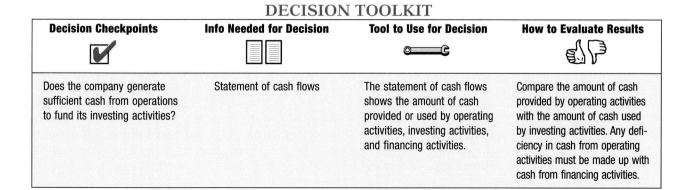

Decision Checkpoints	Info Needed for Decision	Tool to Use for Decision	How to Evaluate Results
Does the company generate sufficient cash from operations to fund its investing activities?	Statement of cash flows	The statement of cash flows shows the amount of cash provided or used by operating activities, investing activities, and financing activities.	Compare the amount of cash provided by operating activities with the amount of cash used by investing activities. Any deficiency in cash from operating activities must be made up with cash from financing activities.

INTERRELATIONSHIPS OF STATEMENTS

Because the results on some statements are used as inputs to other statements, the statements are interrelated. These interrelationships are evident in Sierra's statements in Illustration 1-4.

1. The retained earnings statement is dependent on the results of the income statement. Sierra reported net income of $2,860 for the period. This amount is added to the beginning amount of retained earnings as part of the process of determining ending retained earnings.
2. The balance sheet and retained earnings statement are interrelated because the ending amount of $2,360 on the retained earnings statement is reported as the retained earnings amount on the balance sheet.
3. The statement of cash flows and the balance sheet are also interrelated. The statement of cash flows shows how the cash account changed during the period by showing the amount of cash at the beginning of the period, the sources and uses of cash during the period, and the $15,200 of cash at the end of the period. The ending amount of cash shown on the statement of cash flows must agree with the amount of cash on the balance sheet.

Study these interrelationships carefully. To prepare financial statements you must understand the sequence in which these amounts are determined, and how each statement impacts the next.

BEFORE YOU GO ON . . .

◆ Review It

1. What questions might each of the following decision makers ask that could be answered by financial information: bank loan officer, stock investor, labor union president, and federal bank regulator?
2. What are the content and purpose of each statement: income statement, balance sheet, retained earnings statement, and statement of cash flows?
3. The accounting equation is: Assets = Liabilities + Stockholders' Equity. Tootsie Roll's financial statements are provided in Appendix A at the end of this book. Replacing words in the equation with dollar amounts, what is Tootsie Roll's accounting equation at December 31, 1998? The answer to this question is provided on page 45.

Review It questions marked with this **Tootsie Roll icon** require that you use Tootsie Roll's 1998 Annual Report in Appendix A at the back of the book.

◆ Do It

CSU Corporation began operations on January 1, 2001. The following information is available for CSU Corporation on December 31, 2001: service revenue $17,000; accounts receivable $4,000; accounts payable $2,000; building rental expense $9,000; notes payable $5,000; common stock $10,000; retained earnings ?; equipment $16,000; insurance expense $1,000; supplies $1,800; supplies expense $200; cash $2,000; dividends $0. Prepare an income statement, a retained earnings statement, and a balance sheet using this information.

Reasoning: An income statement reports the success or failure of a company's operations for a period of time. A retained earnings statement shows the amounts and causes of changes in retained earnings during the period. A balance sheet presents the assets and claims to those assets of a company at a specific point in time.

Solution:

CSU CORPORATION
Income Statement
For the Year Ended December 31, 2001

Revenues		
Service revenue		$17,000
Expenses		
Rent expense	$9,000	
Insurance expense	1,000	
Supplies expense	200	
Total expenses		10,200
Net income		$ 6,800

CSU CORPORATION
Retained Earnings Statement
For the Year Ended December 31, 2001

Retained earnings, January 1	$ 0
Add: Net income	6,800
	6,800
Less: Dividends	0
Retained earnings, December 31	$6,800

CSU CORPORATION
Balance Sheet
December 31, 2001

Assets

Cash	$ 2,000
Accounts receivable	4,000
Supplies	1,800
Equipment	16,000
Total assets	$23,800

Liabilities and Stockholders' Equity

Liabilities		
Accounts payable	$ 2,000	
Notes payable	5,000	
Total liabilities		$ 7,000
Stockholders' equity		
Common stock	10,000	
Retained earnings	6,800	
Total stockholders' equity		16,800
Total liabilities and stockholders' equity		$23,800

A Quick Look at Tootsie Roll's Financial Statements

The same relationships that you observed among the financial statements of Sierra Corporation are evident in the 1998 financial statements of Tootsie Roll Industries, Inc., which are presented in Illustrations 1-6 through 1-9. We have simplified the financial statements to assist your learning—but they may look complicated to you anyway. Do not be alarmed by their seeming complexity. (If you could already read and understand them, there would be little reason to take this course, except possibly to add a high grade to your transcript—which we hope you'll do anyway.) By the end of the book, you'll have a great deal of experience in reading and understanding financial statements such as these. **Tootsie Roll's actual financial statements are presented in Appendix A at the end of the book**.

Before we dive in, we need to explain two points:

1. Note that numbers are reported in thousands on Tootsie Roll's financial statements—that is, the last three 000s are omitted. Thus, Tootsie Roll's net income in 1998 is $67,526,000 not $67,526.

2. Tootsie Roll, like most companies, presents its financial statements for more than one year. Financial statements that report information for more than one period are called comparative statements. Comparative statements allow users to compare the financial position of the business at the end of an accounting period with that of previous periods.

Helpful Hint The percentage change in any amount from one year to the next is calculated as follows:

$$\frac{\text{Change during period}}{\text{Previous value}}$$

Thus, the percentage change in income is

$$\frac{\text{Change in income}}{\text{Previous year's income}}$$

INCOME STATEMENT

Tootsie Roll's income statement is presented in Illustration 1-6. It reports total revenues in 1998 of $393,457,000. It then subtracts four types of expenses—cost of goods sold; selling, marketing, and administrative expenses; amortization expense; and income tax expense—to arrive at net income of $67,526,000. This is an 11.3% increase over income for the previous year.

Illustration 1-6
Tootsie Roll's income statement

Financial statements of real companies, like these, are accompanied by either a company logo or an associated photograph.

TOOTSIE ROLL INDUSTRIES, INC.
Income Statements
For the Years Ended December 31, 1998, and December 31, 1997
(in thousands)

	1998	1997
Revenues		
Sales revenue	$388,659	$375,594
Other revenues	4,798	5,274
Total revenues	393,457	380,868
Expenses		
Cost of goods sold	187,617	188,313
Selling, marketing, and administrative expenses	97,071	94,488
Amortization expense	2,706	2,706
Income tax expense	38,537	34,679
Total expenses	325,931	320,186
Net income	$ 67,526	$ 60,682

RETAINED EARNINGS STATEMENT

Tootsie Roll presents information about its retained earnings in the retained earnings statement in Illustration 1-7. (Many companies present changes in retained earnings in a broader report called the Statement of Stockholders' Equity.) Find the line "Retained earnings, December 31, 1997." This number, $147,655,000, agrees with the retained earnings balance from the December 31, 1997, balance sheet.

As we proceed down the retained earnings statement, the next figure is net income of $67,526,000. Tootsie Roll distributed dividends of $61,998,000. The ending balance of retained earnings is $153,156,000 on December 31, 1998. Find this amount of retained earnings near the bottom of Tootsie Roll's balance sheet for December 31, 1998 (Illustration 1-8).

TOOTSIE ROLL INDUSTRIES, INC.
Retained Earnings Statements
For the Years Ended December 31, 1998, and December 31, 1997
(in thousands)

Retained earnings, December 31, 1996	$125,317
Add: Net income	60,682
	185,999
Less: Dividends	37,910
Other adjustments	434
Retained earnings, December 31, 1997	147,655
Add: Net income	67,526
	215,181
Less: Dividends	61,998
Other adjustments	27
Retained earnings, December 31, 1998	$153,156

Illustration 1-7
Tootsie Roll's retained earnings statement

BALANCE SHEET

As shown in its balance sheet in Illustration 1-8 (page 18), Tootsie Roll's assets include the kinds previously mentioned in our discussion of Sierra Corporation, such as cash, inventories, and property, plant, and equipment, plus other types of assets that we will discuss in later chapters, such as prepaid expenses. Tootsie Roll's total assets increased from $436,742,000 on December 31, 1997, to $487,423,000 on December 31, 1998. Its liabilities include accounts payable as well as items not yet discussed, such as postretirement health care and life insurance benefits payable.

You can see that Tootsie Roll relies far more on equity financing rather than on debt—it has over four times as much stockholders' equity as it has liabilities. As you learn more about financial statements we will discuss how to interpret the relationships and changes in financial statement items.

STATEMENT OF CASH FLOWS

Tootsie Roll's cash increased $20,311,000 during 1998. Tootsie Roll's balance sheet shows that cash was $60,433,000 at December 31, 1997, and $80,744,000 at December 31, 1998. The reasons for this increase can be determined by

Illustration 1-8
Tootsie Roll's balance
sheet

TOOTSIE ROLL INDUSTRIES, INC.
Balance Sheets
December 31, 1998, and December 31, 1997
(in thousands)

Assets

	1998	1997
Cash	$ 80,744	$ 60,433
Investments	83,176	81,847
Accounts receivable	19,110	18,636
Other receivables	3,324	4,683
Inventories	36,520	36,659
Prepaid expenses and other	5,665	4,703
Property, plant, and equipment, net	83,024	78,364
Other assets	175,860	151,417
Total assets	$487,423	$436,742

Liabilities and Stockholders' Equity

Liabilities

	1998	1997
Accounts payable	$ 12,450	$ 11,624
Dividends payable	2,514	1,930
Accrued liabilities	31,297	32,793
Income taxes payable	7,123	7,259
Postretirement health care and life insurance benefits payable	6,145	5,904
Industrial development bonds	7,500	7,500
Other liabilities	23,937	18,569
Total liabilities	90,966	85,579
Stockholders' equity		
Common stock	243,301	203,508
Retained earnings	153,156	147,655
Total stockholders' equity	396,457	351,163
Total liabilities and stockholders' equity	$487,423	$436,742

examining the statement of cash flows in Illustration 1-9 (page 19). Tootsie Roll generated $77,735,000 from its operating activities during 1998. Its investing activities included capital expenditures (purchases of property, plant, and equipment) as well as purchases and sales of investment securities. The net effect of its investment activities was an outflow of cash of $34,829,000. Its financing activities involved the issuance and repayment of notes payable, the repurchase of its own common stock, and the payment of cash dividends. In all, the net effect of the cash generated from its operating activities, less the cash used in its investing and financing activities, was an increase in cash of $20,311,000.

STUDY OBJECTIVE

◆ 6 ◆

Describe the components that supplement the financial statements in an annual report.

OTHER ELEMENTS OF AN ANNUAL REPORT

U.S. companies that are publicly traded must provide their shareholders with an annual report each year. The annual report always includes the financial statements introduced in this chapter. In addition, the annual report includes other important sources of information such as a management discussion and analysis section, notes to the financial statements, and an independent auditor's report. No analysis of a company's financial situation and prospects is complete without a review of each of these items.

TOOTSIE ROLL INDUSTRIES, INC.
Statement of Cash Flows
For the Years Ended December 31, 1998, and December 31, 1997
(in thousands)

	1998	1997
Cash flows from operating activities		
Cash receipts from operating activities	$389,102	$378,541
Cash payments for operating activities	(311,367)	(310,365)
Net cash provided by operating activities	77,735	68,176
Cash flows from investing activities		
Capital expenditures	(14,878)	(8,611)
Purchase of investment securities	(476,911)	(373,892)
Inflows from investment securities	456,960	350,805
Net cash used in investing activities	(34,829)	(31,698)
Cash flows from financing activities		
Issuance of notes payable	7,000	—
Repayment of notes payable	(7,000)	—
Repurchase of common stock	(13,445)	(14,401)
Dividends paid in cash	(9,150)	(7,303)
Net cash used in financing activities	(22,595)	(21,704)
Net increase in cash	20,311	14,774
Cash at beginning of year	60,433	45,659
Cash at end of year	$ 80,744	$ 60,433

Management Discussion and Analysis

The **management discussion and analysis (MD&A)** section covers three financial aspects of a company: its ability to pay near-term obligations, its ability to fund operations and expansion, and its results of operations. Management must highlight favorable or unfavorable trends and identify significant events and uncertainties that affect these three factors. This discussion obviously involves a number of subjective estimates and opinions. A brief excerpt from the MD&A section of Tootsie Roll's annual report is presented in Illustration 1-10.

TOOTSIE ROLL INDUSTRIES, INC.
Management's Discussion and Analysis
of Financial Condition and Results of Operations

Domestic sales growth was partially offset by declines in the sales of our Mexican subsidiary due to currency devaluations and difficult local market conditions.
Sales in our Canadian operation increased due to distribution gains, seasonal sales growth at Halloween, and a new product introduction. These increases were also partially offset by the effects of adverse currency translation.

Notes to the Financial Statements

Every set of financial statements is accompanied by explanatory notes and supporting schedules that are an integral part of the statements. The notes to the financial statements clarify information presented in the financial statements, as well as expand upon it where additional detail is needed. Information in the notes does not have to be quantifiable (numeric). Examples of notes are descriptions of the accounting policies and methods used in preparing the statements, explanations of uncertainties and contingencies, and statistics and details too voluminous to be included in the statements. The notes are essential to understanding a company's operating performance and financial position.

Illustration 1-11 is an excerpt from the notes to Tootsie Roll's financial statements. It describes the methods that Tootsie Roll uses to account for revenues.

Illustration 1-11
Notes to Tootsie Roll's financial statements

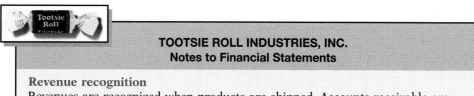

TOOTSIE ROLL INDUSTRIES, INC.
Notes to Financial Statements

Revenue recognition
Revenues are recognized when products are shipped. Accounts receivable are unsecured.

Auditor's Report

Another important source of information is the auditor's report. An **auditor** is an accounting professional who conducts an independent examination of the accounting data presented by a company. Only accountants who meet certain criteria, **Certified Public Accountants (CPAs)**, may perform audits. If the auditor is satisfied that the financial statements present fairly the financial position, results of operations, and cash flows in accordance with generally accepted accounting principles, then an **unqualified opinion** is expressed. If the auditor expresses anything other than an unqualified opinion, then the financial statements should be used only with caution. That is, without an unqualified opinion, we cannot have complete confidence that the financial statements give an accurate picture of the company's financial health.

Illustration 1-12 (page 21) is the auditor's report from Tootsie Roll's 1998 annual report. Tootsie Roll received an unqualified opinion from its auditor, PricewaterhouseCoopers.

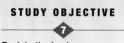
STUDY OBJECTIVE
7

Explain the basic assumptions and principles underlying financial statements.

ASSUMPTIONS AND PRINCIPLES IN FINANCIAL REPORTING

The Financial Accounting Standards Board (FASB) is the primary U.S. accounting standards body. To develop accounting standards, the FASB relies on some key assumptions and principles. It is helpful to look at some of these now

TOOTSIE ROLL INDUSTRIES, INC.
Auditor's Report

To the Board of Directors and Shareholders of Tootsie Roll Industries, Inc.

In our opinion, the accompanying consolidated statement of financial position and the related consolidated statement of earnings, comprehensive earnings and retained earnings and of cash flows present fairly, in all material respects, the financial position of Tootsie Roll Industries, Inc. and its subsidiaries at December 31, 1998 and 1997, and the results of their operations and their cash flows for each of the three years in the period ended December 31, 1998, in conformity with generally accepted accounting principles. These financial statements are the responsibility of the Company's management; our responsibility is to express an opinion on these financial statements based on our audits. We conducted our audits of these statements in accordance with generally accepted auditing standards which require that we plan and perform the audit to obtain reasonable assurance about whether the financial statements are free of material misstatement. An audit includes examining, on a test basis, evidence supporting the amounts and disclosures in the financial statements, assessing the accounting principles used and significant estimates made by management, and evaluating the overall financial statement presentation. We believe that our audits provide a reasonable basis for the opinion expressed above.

PricewaterhouseCoopers LLP

Chicago, Illinois
February 9, 1999

Illustration 1-12
Auditor's report on Tootsie Roll's financial statements

that we have begun to see how accounting can be used to convey financial information to decision makers. The assumptions and principles form a foundation for financial reporting that we will refer to throughout the book.

ASSUMPTIONS

Monetary Unit Assumption

First let's talk about the assumptions. In looking at Tootsie Roll's financial statements you will notice that everything is stated in terms of dollars. The **monetary unit assumption** requires that only those things that can be expressed in money are included in the accounting records. This might seem so obvious that it doesn't bear mentioning, but in fact it has important implications for financial reporting. Because the exchange of money is fundamental to business transactions, it makes sense that we measure a business in terms of money. However, it also means that certain important information needed by investors, creditors, and managers is not reported in the financial statements. For example, customer satisfaction is important to every business, but it is not easily quantified in dollar terms; thus it is not reported in the financial statements.

Economic Entity Assumption

The **economic entity assumption** states that every economic entity can be separately identified and accounted for. For example, suppose you are a stockholder in Tootsie Roll. The amount of cash you have in your personal bank account and the balance owed on your personal car loan are not reported in Tootsie Roll's balance sheet. The reason is that, for accounting purposes, you and Tootsie Roll are separate accounting entities. In order to accurately assess Tootsie Roll's performance and financial position, it is important that we not blur it with your personal transactions, or the transactions of any other company.

Business Insight examples provide interesting information about actual accounting situations in business.

BUSINESS INSIGHT
Management Perspective

A violation of the economic entity assumption contributed to the resignation of the chief executive of W. R. Grace and Company. Investors were angered to learn that company funds were allegedly used for personal medical care, a Manhattan apartment, and a personal chef for the company's chief executive. Funds were also used to support a hotel interest owned by the chief executive's son.

Source: New York Times, March 10, 1995.

Time Period Assumption

Next, notice that Tootsie Roll's income statement, retained earnings statement, and statement of cash flows all cover periods of one year, and the balance sheet is prepared at the end of each year. The time period assumption states that the life of a business can be divided into artificial time periods and that useful reports covering those periods can be prepared for the business. All companies report at least annually. Many also report at least every three months (quarterly) to stockholders, and many prepare monthly statements for internal purposes.

Going Concern Assumption

The going concern assumption states that the business will remain in operation for the foreseeable future. Of course many businesses do fail, but in general, it is reasonable to assume that the business will continue operating. The going concern assumption underlies much of what we do in accounting. To give you just one example, if going concern is not assumed, then plant assets should be stated at their liquidation value (selling price less cost of disposal), not at their cost. Only when liquidation of the business appears likely is the going concern assumption inappropriate.

These four accounting assumptions are shown graphically in Illustration 1-13.

PRINCIPLES

Cost Principle

All of the assets on Tootsie Roll's financial statements are recorded at the amount paid for them. The cost principle dictates that assets are recorded at their cost. This is true not only at the time the asset is purchased, but also over the time the asset is held. For example, if Tootsie Roll were to purchase some land for $30,000, it would initially be reported on the balance sheet at $30,000. But what would Tootsie Roll do if, by the end of the next year, the land had increased in value to $40,000? The answer is that under the cost principle the land would continue to be reported at $30,000.

The cost principle is often criticized as being irrelevant. Critics contend that market value would be more useful to financial decision makers. Proponents of the cost principle counter that cost is the best measure because it can be easily verified from transactions between two parties, while market value is often subjective.

Helpful Hint Recently, some accounting rules have been changed, requiring that certain investment securities be recorded at their market value.

Illustration 1-13
Accounting assumptions

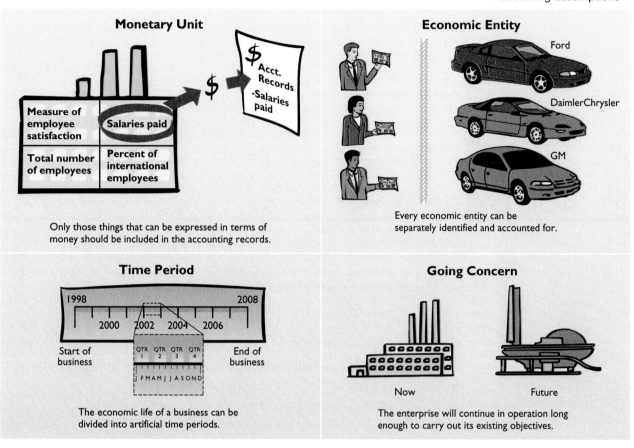

Full Disclosure Principle

Some important financial information is not easily reported on the face of the statements. For example, Tootsie Roll has debt outstanding. Investors and creditors would like to know the terms of the debt; that is, when does it mature, what is its interest rate, and is it renewable? Or Tootsie Roll might be sued by one of its customers. Investors and creditors might not know about this lawsuit. The full disclosure principle requires that all circumstances and events that would make a difference to financial statement users should be disclosed. If an important item cannot reasonably be reported directly in one of the four types of financial statements, then it should be discussed in notes that accompany the statements.

These two accounting principles are shown graphically in Illustration 1-14.

Illustration 1-14
Accounting principles

BEFORE YOU GO ON...

◆ **Review It**

1. What is the intent of the management discussion and analysis section in the annual report?
2. Why are notes to the financial statements necessary? What kinds of items are included in these notes?
3. What is the purpose of the auditor's report?
4. Describe the assumptions and principles of accounting addressed in this chapter.

USING THE DECISION TOOLKIT

Using the Decision Toolkit exercises, which follow the final set of Review It questions in the chapter, ask you to use information from financial statements to make financial decisions. We encourage you to think through the questions related to the decision before you study the solution.

Hershey Foods Corporation, located in Hershey, Pennsylvania, is the leading North American manufacturer of chocolate—for example, Hershey's Kisses, Reese's Peanut Butter Cups, and Kit Kat bars. Imagine that you are considering the purchase of shares of Hershey's common stock.

Instructions

Answer these questions related to your decision whether to invest:

(a) What financial statements should you request from the company?
(b) What should these financial statements tell you?
(c) Should you request audited financial statements? Explain.
(d) Will the financial statements show the market value of Hershey Foods' assets? Explain.
(e) Simplified financial statements for Hershey Foods are shown in Illustrations 1-15 through 1-18. What comparisons can you make between Tootsie Roll and Hershey in terms of their respective results from operations and financial position?

Illustration 1-15
Hershey Foods' income statement

HERSHEY FOODS CORPORATION **Income Statement** **For the Years Ended December 31, 1998, and December 31, 1997** **(in thousands)**		
	1998	1997
Revenues		
Sales revenue	$4,435,615	$4,302,236
Expenses		
Cost of goods sold	2,625,057	2,488,896
Selling, marketing, and administrative expenses	1,167,895	1,183,130
Interest expense	85,657	76,255
Income tax expense	216,118	217,704
Total expenses	4,094,727	3,965,985
Net income	$ 340,888	$ 336,251

HERSHEY FOODS CORPORATION
Retained Earnings Statement
For the Years Ended December 31, 1998, and December 31, 1997
(in thousands)

Retained earnings December 31, 1996	$ 938,639
Add: Net income	336,251
	1,274,890
Less: Dividends	121,546
Other adjustments	514,340
Retained earnings December 31, 1997	639,004
Add: Net income	340,888
	979,892
Less: Dividends	129,044
Other adjustments	18,492
Retained earnings December 31, 1998	$ 832,356

Illustration 1-16
Hershey Foods' retained earnings statement

HERSHEY FOODS CORPORATION
Balance Sheets
December 31, 1998, and December 31, 1997
(in thousands)

Assets	1998	1997
Cash	$ 39,024	$ 54,237
Accounts receivable	451,324	360,831
Inventories	493,249	505,525
Prepaid expenses and other	150,369	114,221
Property, plant, and equipment, net	1,648,058	1,648,237
Other assets	622,074	608,185
Total assets	$3,404,098	$3,291,236
Liabilities and Stockholders' Equity		
Liabilities		
Accounts payable	$ 156,937	$ 146,932
Accrued liabilities	294,415	371,545
Income taxes payable	17,475	19,692
Short-term debt and other	345,997	257,546
Long-term debt and liabilities	1,225,872	1,375,636
Other liabilities	321,101	267,079
Total liabilities	2,361,797	2,438,430
Stockholders' equity		
Common stock	209,945	213,802
Retained earnings	832,356	639,004
Total stockholders' equity	1,042,301	852,806
Total liabilities and stockholders' equity	$3,404,098	$3,291,236

Illustration 1-17
Hershey Foods' balance sheet

Illustration 1-18
Hershey Foods'
statement of cash
flows

HERSHEY FOODS CORPORATION
Statement of Cash Flows
For the Years Ended December 31, 1998, and December 31, 1997
(in thousands)

	1998	1997
Cash flows from operating activities		
Cash receipts from operating activities	$4,435,615	$4,233,757
Cash payments for operating activities	(4,045,910)	(3,727,799)
Net cash provided by operating activities	389,705	505,958
Cash flows from investing activities		
Capital expenditures	(161,328)	(172,939)
Other, net	(33,575)	(7,732)
Net cash used in investing activities	(194,903)	(180,671)
Cash flows from financing activities		
Issuance of long-term debt	—	550,000
Repayment of long-term debt	(25,187)	(15,588)
Dividends paid in cash	(129,044)	(121,546)
Issuance of common stock	19,368	14,397
Repurchase of common stock	(16,151)	(507,654)
Other, net	(59,001)	(252,081)
Net cash used in financing activities	(210,015)	(332,472)
Net increase (decrease) in cash	(15,213)	(7,185)
Cash at beginning of year	54,237	61,422
Cash at end of year	$ 39,024	$ 54,237

Solution

(a) Before you invest, you should investigate the income statement, retained earnings statement, statement of cash flows, and balance sheet.

(b) You would probably be most interested in the income statement because it tells about past performance and thus gives an indication of future performance. The retained earnings statement provides a record of the company's dividend history. The statement of cash flows reveals where the company is getting and spending its cash. This is especially important for a company that wants to grow. Finally, the balance sheet reveals the relationship between assets and liabilities.

(c) You would want audited financial statements—statements that a CPA (certified public accountant) has examined and expressed an opinion that the statements present fairly the financial position and results of operations of the company. Investors and creditors should not make decisions without studying audited financial statements.

(d) The financial statements will not show the market value of the company. As indicated, one important principle of accounting is the cost principle, which states that assets should be recorded at cost. Cost has an important advantage over other valuations: It is objective and reliable.

(e) Many interesting comparisons can be made between the two companies. Tootsie Roll is smaller, with total assets of $487,423,000 versus $3,404,098,000 for Hershey, and it has lower revenue—net sales of $388,659,000 versus $4,435,615,000 for Hershey. In addition, Tootsie Roll's cash provided by operating activities of $77,735,000 is less than Hershey's $389,705,000. While useful, these basic measures are not enough to determine whether one company is a better investment than the other. In later chapters you will learn tools that will allow you to compare the relative profitability and financial health of these and other companies.

SUMMARY OF STUDY OBJECTIVES

①▶Describe the primary forms of business organization. A sole proprietorship is a business owned by one person. A partnership is a business owned by two or more people. A corporation is a separate legal entity for which evidence of ownership is provided by shares of stock.

②▶Identify the users and uses of accounting information. Internal users are managers who need accounting information in planning, controlling, and evaluating business operations. The primary external users are investors and creditors. Investors (stockholders) use accounting information to help them decide whether to buy, hold, or sell shares of a company's stock. Creditors (suppliers and bankers) use accounting information to assess the risk of granting credit or loaning money to a business. Other groups who have an indirect interest in a business are taxing authorities, regulatory agencies, customers, labor unions, and economic planners.

③▶Explain the three principal types of business activity. Financing activities involve collecting the necessary funds to support the business. Investing activities involve acquiring the resources necessary to run the business. Operating activities involve putting the resources of the business into action to generate a profit.

④▶Describe the content and purpose of each of the financial statements. An income statement presents the revenues and expenses of a company for a specific period of time. A retained earnings statement summarizes the changes in retained earnings that have occurred for a specific period of time. A balance sheet reports the assets, liabilities, and stockholders' equity of a business at a specific date. A statement of cash flows summarizes information concerning the cash inflows (receipts) and outflows (payments) for a specific period of time.

⑤▶Explain the meaning of assets, liabilities, and stockholders' equity, and state the basic accounting equation. Assets are resources owned by a business. Liabilities are the debts and obligations of the business. Liabilities represent claims of creditors on the assets of the business. Stockholders' equity represents the claims of owners on the assets of the business. Stockholders' equity is composed of two parts: common stock and retained earnings. The basic accounting equation is: Assets = Liabilities + Stockholders' Equity.

⑥▶Describe the components that supplement the financial statements in an annual report. The management discussion and analysis provides management's interpretation of the company's results and financial position as well as a discussion of plans for the future. Notes to the financial statements provide additional explanation or detail to make the financial statements more informative. The auditor's report expresses an opinion as to whether the financial statements present fairly the company's results of operations and financial position.

⑦▶Explain the basic assumptions and principles underlying financial statements. The monetary unit assumption requires that only transaction data capable of being expressed in terms of money be included in the accounting records of the economic entity. The economic entity assumption states that economic events can be identified with a particular unit of accountability. The time period assumption states that the economic life of a business can be divided into artificial time periods and that meaningful accounting reports can be prepared for each period. The going concern assumption states that the enterprise will continue in operation long enough to carry out its existing objectives. The cost principle states that assets should be recorded at their cost. The full disclosure principle dictates that circumstances and events that matter to financial statement users must be disclosed.

DECISION TOOLKIT—A SUMMARY

Decision Checkpoints	Info Needed for Decision	Tool to Use for Decision	How to Evaluate Results
Are the company's operations profitable?	Income statement	The income statement reports on the sucess or failure of the company's operations by reporting its revenues and expenses.	If the company's revenue exceeds its expenses, it will report net income; otherwise it will report a net loss.
What is the company's policy toward dividends and growth?	Retained earnings statement	How much of this year's income did the company pay out in dividends to shareholders?	A company striving for rapid growth will pay a low dividend.
Does the company rely primarily on debt or stockholders' equity to finance its assets?	Balance sheet	The balance sheet reports the company's resources and claims to those resources. There are two types of claims: liabilities and stockholders' equity.	Compare the amount of debt versus the amount of stockholders' equity to determine whether the company relies more on creditors or owners for its financing.
Does the company generate sufficient cash from operations to fund its investing activities?	Statement of cash flows	The statement of cash flows shows the amount of cash provided or used by operating activities, investing activities, and financing activities.	Compare the amount of cash provided by operating activities with the amount of cash used by investing activities. Any deficiency in cash from operating activities must be made up with cash from financing activities.

GLOSSARY

Accounting The process of identifying, recording, and communicating the economic events of a business to interested users of the information. (p. 6)

Annual report A report prepared by corporate management that presents financial information including financial statements, notes, and the management discussion and analysis. (p. 18)

Assets Resources owned by a business. (p. 8)

Auditor's report A report prepared by an independent outside auditor stating the auditor's opinion as to the fairness of the presentation of the financial position and results of operations and their conformance with accepted accounting standards. (p. 20)

Balance sheet A financial statement that reports the assets, liabilities, and stockholders' equity at a specific date. (p. 12)

Basic accounting equation Assets = Liabilities + Stockholders' Equity. (p. 12)

Certified Public Accountant (CPA) An individual who has met certain criteria and is thus allowed to perform audits of corporations. (p. 20)

Common stock Stock representing the primary ownership interest in a corporation. In the balance sheet it represents the amount paid in by stockholders. (p. 8)

Comparative statements A presentation of the financial statements of a company for multiple years. (p. 16)

Corporation A business organized as a separate legal entity having ownership divided into transferable shares of stock. (p. 4)

Cost principle An accounting principle that states that assets should be recorded at their cost. (p. 22)

Dividends Distributions of cash or other assets from a corporation to its stockholders. (p. 8)

Economic entity assumption An assumption that economic events can be identified with a particular unit of accountability. (p. 21)

Expenses The cost of assets consumed or services used in ongoing operations to generate revenues. (p. 9)

Full disclosure principle Accounting principle that dictates that circumstances and events that make a difference to financial statement users should be disclosed. (p. 23)

Going concern assumption The assumption that the enterprise will continue in operation long enough to carry out its existing objectives and commitments. (p. 22)

Income statement A financial statement that presents the revenues and expenses and resulting net income or net loss of a company for a specific period of time. (p. 10)

Liabilities The debts and obligations of a business. Liabilities represent claims of creditors on the assets of a business. (p. 8)

Management discussion and analysis (MD&A) A section of the annual report that presents management's views on the company's short-term debt paying ability, expansion, financing, and results. (p. 19)

Monetary unit assumption An assumption stating that only transaction data that can be expressed in terms of money be included in the accounting records of the economic entity. (p. 21)

Net income The amount by which revenues exceed expenses. (p. 9)

Net loss The amount by which expenses exceed revenues. (p. 9)

Notes to the financial statements Notes that clarify information presented in the financial statements, as well as expand upon it where additional detail is needed. (p. 20)

Partnership A business owned by more than one person. (p. 4)

Retained earnings The amount of net income kept in the corporation for future use, not distributed to stockholders as dividends. (p. 12)

Retained earnings statement A financial statement that summarizes the changes in retained earnings for a specific period of time. (p. 12)

Revenues The assets that result from the sale of a product or service. (p. 8)

Sole proprietorship A business owned by one person. (p. 4)

Statement of cash flows A financial statement that provides information about the cash inflows (receipts) and cash outflows (payments) for a specific period of time. (p. 13)

Stockholders' equity The stockholders' claim on total assets. (p. 12)

Time period assumption An accounting assumption that the economic life of a business can be divided into artificial time periods. (p. 22)

DEMONSTRATION PROBLEM

Jeff Andringa, a former college hockey player, quit his job and started Ice Camp, a hockey camp for kids ages 8 to 18. Eventually he would like to open hockey camps nationwide. Jeff has asked you to help him prepare financial statements at the end of his first year of operations. He relates the following facts about his business activities.

In order to get the business off the ground, he decided to incorporate. He sold shares of common stock to a few close friends, as well as buying some of the shares himself. He initially raised $25,000 through the sale of these shares. In addition, the company took out a $10,000 loan at a local bank. A bus for transporting kids was purchased for $12,000 cash. Hockey goals and other miscellaneous equipment were purchased with $1,500 cash. The company earned camp tuition during the year of $100,000 but had collected only $80,000 of this amount. Thus, at the end of the year it was still owed $20,000. The company rents time at a local rink for $50 per hour. Total rink rental costs during the year were $8,000, insurance was $10,000, salary expense was $20,000, and administrative expenses totaled $9,000, all of which were paid in cash. The company incurred $800 in interest expense on the bank loan, which it still owed at the end of the year.

The company paid dividends during the year of $5,000 cash. The balance in the corporate bank account at December 31, 2001, was $49,500.

Instructions

Using the format of the Sierra Corporation statements in this chapter, prepare an income statement, retained earnings statement, balance sheet, and statement of cash flows. [*Hint:* Prepare the statements in the order stated to take advantage of the flow of information from one statement to the next, as shown in Illustration 1-4.]

Demonstration problems are a final review before you begin homework. **Problem-solving strategies** that appear in the margins give you tips about how to approach the problem, and the solution provided illustrates both the form and content of complete answers.

Solution to Demonstration Problem

ICE CAMP
Income Statement
For the Year Ended December 31, 2001

Revenues		
Camp tuition revenue		$100,000
Expenses		
Salaries expense	$20,000	
Insurance expense	10,000	
Administrative expense	9,000	
Rink rental expense	8,000	
Interest expense	800	
Total expenses		47,800
Net income		$ 52,200

ICE CAMP
Retained Earnings Statement
For the Year Ended December 31, 2001

Retained earnings, January 1, 2001	$ 0
Add: Net income	52,200
	52,200
Less: Dividends	5,000
Retained earnings, December 31, 2001	$47,200

ICE CAMP
Balance Sheet
December 31, 2001

Assets

Cash	$49,500
Accounts receivable	20,000
Bus	12,000
Equipment	1,500
Total assets	$83,000

Liabilities and Stockholders' Equity

Liabilities		
Bank loan payable	$10,000	
Interest payable	800	
Total liabilities		$10,800
Stockholders' equity		
Common stock	25,000	
Retained earnings	47,200	
Total stockholders' equity		72,200
Total liabilities and stockholders' equity		$83,000

ICE CAMP
Statement of Cash Flows
For the Year Ended December 31, 2001

Cash flows from operating activities	
Cash receipts from operating activities	$80,000
Cash payments for operating activities	(47,000)
Net cash provided by operating activities	33,000
Cash flows from investing activities	
Purchase of bus	(12,000)
Purchase of equipment	(1,500)
Net cash used by investing activities	(13,500)
Cash flows from financing activities	
Issuance of bank loan payable	10,000
Issuance of common stock	25,000
Dividends paid	(5,000)
Net cash provided by financing activities	30,000
Net increase in cash	49,500
Cash at beginning of period	0
Cash at end of period	$49,500

This would be a good time to return to the **Student Owner's Manual** at the beginning of the book (or look at it for the first time if you skipped it before) to read about the various types of homework materials that appear at the ends of chapters. Knowing the purpose of the different assignments will help you appreciate what each contributes to your accounting skills and competencies.

The tool icon ⌾━━━━⌇ indicates that an instructional activity employs one of the decision tools presented in the chapter. The pencil icon ▭▭▭▭▷ indicates that an instructional activity requires written communication by the student.

SELF-STUDY QUESTIONS

Answers are at the end of the chapter.

(SO 1) 1. Which is *not* one of the three forms of business organization?
(a) Sole proprietorship.
(b) Creditorship.
(c) Partnership.
(d) Corporation.

(SO 1) 2. Which is an advantage of corporations relative to partnerships and sole proprietorships?
(a) Lower taxes.
(b) Harder to transfer ownership.
(c) Reduced legal liability for investors.
(d) Most common form of organization.

(SO 3) 3. Which is *not* one of the three primary business activities?
(a) Financing.
(b) Operating.
(c) Advertising.
(d) Investing.

(SO 4) 4. Which statement about users of accounting information is *incorrect?*
(a) Management is considered an internal user.
(b) Taxing authorities are considered external users.
(c) Present creditors are considered external users.
(d) Regulatory authorities are considered internal users.

(SO 4) 5. Net income will result during a time period when:
(a) assets exceed liabilities.
(b) assets exceed revenues.
(c) expenses exceed revenues.
(d) revenues exceed expenses.

(SO 4) 6. ⌾━━━━⌇ What section of a cash flow statement indicates the cash spent on new equipment during the past accounting period?
(a) The investing section.
(b) The operating section.

(c) The financing section.
(d) The cash flow statement does not give this information.

(SO 4) 7. Which financial statement reports assets, liabilities, and stockholders' equity?
(a) Income statement.
(b) Retained earnings statement.
(c) Balance sheet.
(d) Statement of cash flows.

(SO 5) 8. As of December 31, 2001, Stoneland Corporation has assets of $3,500 and stockholders' equity of $2,000. What are the liabilities for Stoneland Corporation as of December 31, 2001?
(a) $1,500.   (c) $2,500.
(b) $1,000.   (d) $2,000.

(SO 6) 9. ◎▭▭ℂ The segment of a corporation's annual report that describes the corporation's accounting methods is the:
(a) notes to the financial statements.

(b) management discussion and analysis.
(c) auditor's report.
(d) income statement.

(SO 7) 10. The cost principle states that:
(a) assets should be recorded at cost and adjusted when the market value changes.
(b) activities of an entity should be kept separate and distinct from its owner.
(c) assets should be recorded at their cost.
(d) only transaction data capable of being expressed in terms of money should be included in the accounting records.

(SO 7) 11. Valuing assets at their market value rather than at their cost is inconsistent with the:
(a) time period assumption.
(b) economic entity assumption.
(c) cost principle.
(d) All of the above.

QUESTIONS

1. What are the three basic forms of business organizations?
2. What are the advantages to a business of being formed as a corporation? What are the disadvantages?
3. What are the advantages to a business of being formed as a partnership or sole proprietorship? What are the disadvantages?
4. "Accounting is ingrained in our society and is vital to our economic system." Do you agree? Explain.
5. Who are the internal users of accounting data? How does accounting provide relevant data to the internal users?
6. Who are the external users of accounting data? Give examples.
7. What are the three main types of business activity? Give examples of each activity.
8. Listed here are some items found in the financial statements of Ruth Weber, Inc. Indicate in which financial statement(s) each item would appear.
(a) Service revenue.   (d) Accounts receivable.
(b) Equipment.   (e) Common stock.
(c) Advertising expense. (f) Wages payable.
9. "A company's net income appears directly on the income statement and the retained earnings statement, and it is included indirectly in the company's balance sheet." Do you agree? Explain.
10. ◎▭▭ℂ What is the purpose of the statement of cash flows?
11. What are the three main categories of the statement of cash flows? Why do you think these categories were chosen?
12. What is retained earnings? What items increase the

balance in retained earnings? What items decrease the balance in retained earnings?
13. What is the basic accounting equation?
14. (a) Define the terms *assets, liabilities,* and *stockholders' equity.*
(b) What items affect stockholders' equity?
15. Which of these items are liabilities of Kool-Jewelry Stores?
(a) Cash.   (f) Equipment.
(b) Accounts payable.   (g) Salaries payable.
(c) Dividends.   (h) Service revenue.
(d) Accounts receivable. (i) Rent expense.
(e) Supplies.
16. How are each of the following financial statements interrelated? (a) Retained earnings statement and income statement. (b) Retained earnings statement and balance sheet. (c) Balance sheet and statement of cash flows.
17. ◎▭▭ℂ What is the purpose of the management discussion and analysis (MD&A)?
18. ◎▭▭ℂ Why is it important for financial statements to receive an unqualified auditor's opinion?
19. ◎▭▭ℂ What types of information are presented in the notes to the financial statements?
20. What purpose does the going concern assumption serve?
21. Sue Leonard is president of Better Books. She has no accounting background. Leonard cannot understand why market value is not used as the basis for accounting measurement and reporting. Explain what basis is used and why.
22. What is the importance of the economic entity assumption? Give an example of its violation.

BRIEF EXERCISES

BE1-1 Match each of the following forms of business organization with a set of characteristics: sole proprietorship (SP), partnership (P), corporation (C).
(a) _____ Shared control, tax advantages, increased skills and resources.
(b) _____ Simple to set up and maintains control with founder.
(c) _____ Easier to transfer ownership and raise funds, no personal liability.

Describe forms of business organization.
(SO 1)

BE1-2 Match each of the following types of evaluation with one of the listed users of accounting information.
1. Trying to determine whether the company complied with tax laws.
2. Trying to determine whether the company can pay its obligations.
3. Trying to determine whether a marketing proposal will be cost effective.
4. Trying to determine whether the company's net income will result in a stock price increase.
5. Trying to determine whether the company should employ debt or equity financing.
(a) _____ Investors in common stock.   (d) _____ Chief Financial Officer.
(b) _____ Marketing managers.   (e) _____ Internal Revenue Service.
(c) _____ Creditors.

Identify users of accounting information.
(SO 2)

BE1-3 Indicate in which part of the statement of cash flows each item would appear: operating activities (O), investing activities (I), or financing activities (F).
(a) Cash received from customers.
(b) Cash paid to stockholders (dividends).
(c) Cash received from issuing new common stock.
(d) Cash paid to suppliers.
(e) Cash paid to purchase a new office building.

Classify items by activity.
(SO 3, 4, 5)

BE1-4 Classify each of the following items as dividends (D), revenue (R), or expense (E).
(a) Costs incurred for advertising.
(b) Assets received for services performed.
(c) Costs incurred for insurance.
(d) Amounts paid to employees.
(e) Cash distributed to stockholders.
(f) Assets received in exchange for allowing the use of the company's building.
(g) Costs incurred for utilities used.

Classify various items.
(SO 4)

BE1-5 Presented below are three transactions. Determine whether each transaction affects common stock (C), dividends (D), revenue (R), expense (E), or does not affect stockholders' equity (NSE).
(a) Paid cash to purchase equipment.
(b) Received cash for services performed.
(c) Paid employee salaries.

Determine effect of transactions on stockholders' equity.
(SO 4)

BE1-6 In alphabetical order below are balance sheet items for Gidget Company at December 31, 2001. Prepare a balance sheet following the format of Illustration 1-4.

Prepare a balance sheet.
(SO 4)

Accounts payable	$90,000
Accounts receivable	81,000
Cash	40,500
Common stock	31,500

BE1-7 Eskimo Pie Corporation markets a broad range of frozen treats, including its famous Eskimo Pie ice cream bars. The following items were taken from a recent income statement and balance sheet. In each case identify whether the item would appear on the balance sheet (BS) or income statement (IS).
(a) _____ Income tax expense.
(b) _____ Inventories.
(c) _____ Accounts payable.
(d) _____ Retained earnings.
(e) _____ Property, plant, and equipment.
(f) _____ Net sales.
(g) _____ Cost of goods sold.
(h) _____ Common stock.
(i) _____ Receivables.
(j) _____ Interest expense.

Determine where items appear on financial statements.
(SO 4)

Determine proper financial statement.
(SO 4)

BE1-8 Indicate which statement you would examine to find each of the following items: income statement (I), balance sheet (B), retained earnings statement (R), or statement of cash flows (C).
(a) Revenue during the period.
(b) Supplies on hand at the end of the year.
(c) Cash received from issuing new bonds during the period.
(d) Total debts outstanding at the end of the period.

Use basic accounting equation.
(SO 5)

BE1-9 Use the basic accounting equation to answer these questions:
(a) The liabilities of Hogan Company are $90,000 and the stockholders' equity is $240,000. What is the amount of Hogan Company's total assets?
(b) The total assets of Potter Company are $170,000 and its stockholders' equity is $90,000. What is the amount of its total liabilities?
(c) The total assets of Barren Co. are $700,000 and its liabilities are equal to half of its total assets. What is the amount of Barren Co.'s stockholders' equity?

Use basic accounting equation.
(SO 5)

BE1-10 At the beginning of the year, Lamson Company had total assets of $700,000 and total liabilities of $500,000.
(a) If total assets increased $150,000 during the year and total liabilities decreased $80,000, what is the amount of stockholders' equity at the end of the year?
(b) During the year, total liabilities increased $100,000 and stockholders' equity decreased $70,000. What is the amount of total assets at the end of the year?
(c) If total assets decreased $90,000 and stockholders' equity increased $110,000 during the year, what is the amount of total liabilities at the end of the year?

Identify assets, liabilities, and stockholders' equity.
(SO 5)

BE1-11 Indicate whether each of these items is an asset (A), a liability (L), or part of stockholders' equity (SE).
(a) Accounts receivable.   (d) Office supplies.
(b) Salaries payable.   (e) Common stock.
(c) Equipment.   (f) Notes payable.

Determine required parts of annual report.
(SO 6)

BE1-12 Which is *not* a required part of an annual report of a publicly traded company?
(a) Statement of cash flows.
(b) Notes to the financial statements.
(c) Management discussion and analysis.
(d) All of these are required.

Define full disclosure principle.
(SO 7)

BE1-13 The full disclosure principle dictates that:
(a) financial statements should disclose all assets at their cost.
(b) financial statements should disclose only those events that can be measured in dollars.
(c) financial statements should disclose all events and circumstances that would matter to users of financial statements.
(d) financial statements should not be relied on unless an auditor has expressed an unqualified opinion on them.

*E*XERCISES

Match items with descriptions.
(SO 1, 2, 4, 6)

E1-1 Here is a list of words or phrases discussed in this chapter:
1. Corporation   5. Stockholder
2. Creditor   6. Common stock
3. Accounts receivable   7. Accounts payable
4. Partnership   8. Auditor's opinion

Instructions
Match each word or phrase with the best description of it.
_____ (a) An expression about whether financial statements are presented in a reasonable fashion.
_____ (b) A business enterprise that raises money by issuing shares of stock.
_____ (c) The portion of stockholders' equity that results from receiving cash from investors.
_____ (d) Obligations to suppliers of goods.
_____ (e) Amounts due from customers.

_____ (f) A party to whom a business owes money.
_____ (g) A party that invests in common stock.
_____ (h) A business that is owned jointly by two or more individuals but that does not issue stock.

E1-2 This information relates to Megan Co. for the year 2001:

Prepare income statement and retained earnings statement.
(SO 4)

Retained earnings, January 1, 2001	$57,000
Advertising expense	1,800
Dividends paid during 2001	7,000
Rent expense	10,400
Service revenue	61,000
Utilities expense	2,400
Salaries expense	28,000

Instructions
After analyzing the data, prepare an income statement and a retained earnings statement for the year ending December 31, 2001.

E1-3 Peter Kafka is the bookkeeper for Rake Company. Peter has been trying to get the balance sheet of Rake Company to balance. It finally balanced, but now he's not sure it is correct.

Correct an incorrectly prepared balance sheet.
(SO 4)

RAKE COMPANY
Balance Sheet
December 31, 2001

Assets		Liabilities and Stockholders' Equity	
Cash	$18,500	Accounts payable	$20,000
Supplies	8,000	Accounts receivable	(10,000)
Equipment	44,000	Common stock	40,000
Dividends	7,000	Retained earnings	27,500
Total assets	$77,500	Total liabilities and	
		stockholders' equity	$77,500

Instructions
Prepare a correct balance sheet.

E1-4 Bear Park Inc. is a public camping ground near the Lake Mead National Recreation Area. It has compiled the following financial information as of December 31, 2001:

Compute net income and prepare a balance sheet.
(SO 4)

Revenues during 2001: camping fees	$137,000	Dividends	$ 4,000
Revenues during 2001: general store	20,000	Notes payable	50,000
Accounts payable	11,000	Expenses during 2001	142,000
Cash on hand	10,500	Supplies on hand	2,500
Equipment	110,000	Common stock	40,000
		Retained earnings (1/1/2001)	11,000

Instructions
(a) Determine net income from Bear Park Inc. for 2001.
(b) Prepare a retained earnings statement and a balance sheet for Bear Park Inc. as of December 31, 2001.

E1-5 **Kellogg Company** is the world's leading producer of ready-to-eat cereal and a leading producer of grain-based convenience foods such as frozen waffles and cereal bars. The following items were taken from its 1998 income statement and balance sheet. (All dollars are in millions.)

Identify financial statement components and prepare an income statement.
(SO 4, 5)

_____	Retained earnings	$1,367.7	_____	Long-term debt	$1,614.5
_____	Cost of goods sold	3,282.6	_____	Inventories	451.4
_____	Selling and		_____	Net sales	6,762.1
	administrative expenses	2,513.9	_____	Accounts payable	386.9
_____	Cash	136.4	_____	Common stock	103.8
_____	Notes payable	620.4	_____	Income tax expenses	279.9
_____	Interest expense	119.5			
_____	Other expense	63.6			

Instructions

Perform each of the following:

(a) In each case identify whether the item is an asset (A), liability (L), stockholders' equity (SE), revenue (R), or expense (E).

(b) Prepare an income statement for Kellogg Company for the year ended December 31, 1998.

Prepare a retained earnings statement.
(SO 4)

E1-6 Presented here is information for Roger Peterson Inc. for 2001:

Retained earnings, January 1	$150,000
Revenue from legal services	395,000
Total expenses	195,000
Dividends	76,000

Instructions

Prepare the 2001 retained earnings statement for Roger Peterson Inc.

Interpret financial facts.
(SO 4)

E1-7 Consider each of the following independent situations.

(a) The retained earnings statement of Tone Kon Corporation shows dividends of $70,000, while net income for the year was $75,000.

(b) The statement of cash flows for Duchess Cruise Corporation shows that cash provided by operating activities was $10,000, cash used in investing activities was $110,000, and cash provided by financing activities was $130,000.

Instructions

For each company provide a brief discussion interpreting these financial facts. For example, you might discuss the company's financial health or its apparent growth philosophy.

Prepare a statement of cash flows.
(SO 4)

E1-8 This information is for Gilles Corporation for 2001:

Cash received from customers	$65,000
Cash dividends paid	4,000
Cash paid to suppliers	20,000
Cash paid for new equipment	50,000
Cash received from lenders	20,000

Instructions

Prepare the 2001 statement of cash flows for Gilles Corporation.

Calculate missing amounts.
(SO 4)

E1-9 Here are incomplete financial statements for Motzek, Inc.:

MOTZEK, INC.
Balance Sheet

Assets		Liabilities and Stockholders' Equity	
Cash	$ 5,000	Liabilities	
Inventory	10,000	Accounts payable	$ 5,000
Building	50,000	Stockholders' equity	
Total assets	$65,000	Common stock	(a)
		Retained earnings	(b)
		Total liabilities and stockholders' equity	$65,000

Income Statement

Revenues	$80,000
Cost of goods sold	(c)
Administrative expenses	10,000
Net income	$ (d)

Retained Earnings Statement

Beginning retained earnings	$10,000
Net income	(e)
Dividends	5,000
Ending retained earnings	$29,000

Instructions
Calculate the missing amounts.

E1-10 The following items were taken from the balance sheet of **NIKE, Inc.**

1. Cash	$ 108.6	7. Inventories	$1,396.6
2. Accounts receivable	1,674.4	8. Income taxes payable	28.9
3. Common stock	265.4	9. Property, plant, and equipment	1,153.1
4. Notes payable	480.2	10. Retained earnings	2,996.2
5. Other assets	1,064.7	11. Accounts payable	584.6
6. Other liabilities	1,042.1		

Classify items as assets, liabilities, and stockholders' equity and prepare accounting equation.
(SO 5)

Instructions
Perform each of the following:
(a) Classify each of these items as an asset, liability, or stockholders' equity. (All dollars are in millions.)
(b) Determine NIKE's accounting equation by calculating the value of total assets, total liabilities, and total stockholders' equity.

E1-11 The annual report provides financial information in a variety of formats including the following:

Management discussion and analysis (MD&A)
Financial statements
Notes to the financial statements
Auditor's opinion

Classify various items in an annual report.
(SO 6)

Instructions
For each of the following, state in what area of the annual report the item would be presented. If the item would probably not be found in an annual report, state "not disclosed."
(a) The total cumulative amount received from stockholders in exchange for common stock.
(b) An independent assessment concerning whether the financial statements present a fair depiction of the company's results and financial position.
(c) The interest rate the company is being charged on all outstanding debts.
(d) Total revenue from operating activities.
(e) Management's assessment of the company's results.
(f) The names and positions of all employees hired in the last year.

E1-12 Presented below are the assumptions and principles discussed in this chapter:
1. Full disclosure principle.   4. Time period assumption.
2. Going concern assumption.   5. Cost principle.
3. Monetary unit assumption.   6. Economic entity assumption.

Identify accounting assumptions and principles.
(SO 7)

Instructions
Identify by number the accounting assumption or principle that is described below. Do not use a number more than once.
_____ (a) Is the rationale for why plant assets are not reported at liquidation value. (*Note:* Do not use the cost principle.)
_____ (b) Indicates that personal and business record-keeping should be separately maintained.
_____ (c) Assumes that the dollar is the "measuring stick" used to report on financial performance.
_____ (d) Separates financial information into time periods for reporting purpose.
_____ (e) Indicates that market value changes subsequent to purchase are not recorded in the accounts.
_____ (f) Dictates that all circumstances and events that make a difference to financial statement users should be disclosed.

E1-13 Cheong Co. had three major business transactions during 2001:
(a) Merchandise inventory with a cost of $208,000 is reported at its market value of $260,000.
(b) The president of Cheong Co., Cheong Kong, purchased a truck for personal use and charged it to his expense account.

Identify the assumption or principle that has been violated.
(SO 7)

(c) Cheong Co. wanted to make its 2001 income look better, so it added 2 more weeks to the year (a 54-week year). Previous years were 52 weeks.

Instructions

In each situation, identify the assumption or principle that has been violated, if any, and discuss what should have been done.

PROBLEMS: SET A

Determine forms of business organization.
(SO 1)

P1-1A   Presented below are five independent situations.

(a) Three physics professors at MIT have formed a business to improve the speed of information transfer over the Internet for stock exchange transactions. Each has contributed an equal amount of cash and knowledge to the venture. Although their approach looks promising, they are concerned about the legal liabilities that their business might confront.

(b) Joe Robbins, a college student looking for summer employment, opened a bait shop in a small shed at a local marina.

(c) Robert Steven and Tom Cheng each owned separate shoe manufacturing businesses. They have decided to combine their businesses. They expect that within the coming year they will need significant funds to expand their operations.

(d) Darcy Becker, Ellen Sweatt, and Meg Dwyer recently graduated with marketing degrees. They have been friends since childhood. They have decided to start a consulting business focused on marketing sporting goods over the Internet.

(e) Anthony Troy wants to rent CD players and CDs in airports across the country. His idea is that customers will be able to rent equipment and CDs at one airport, listen to the CDs on their flights, and return the equipment and CDs at their destination airport. Of course, this will require a substantial investment in equipment and CDs, as well as employees and locations in each airport. Anthony has no savings or personal assets. He wants to maintain control over the business.

Instructions

In each case explain what form of organization the business is likely to take—sole proprietorship, partnership, or corporation. Give reasons for your choice.

Identify users and uses of financial statements.
(SO 2, 4)

P1-2A   Financial decisions often place heavier emphasis on one type of financial statement over the others. Consider each of the following hypothetical situations independently.

(a) **The North Face, Inc.** is considering extending credit to a new customer. The terms of the credit would require the customer to pay within 30 days of receipt of goods.

(b) An investor is considering purchasing common stock of **Amazon.com.** The investor plans to hold the investment for at least 5 years.

(c) **Chase Manhattan** is considering extending a loan to a small company. The company would be required to make interest payments at the end of each year for 5 years, and to repay the loan at the end of the fifth year.

(d) The president of **Campbell Soup** is trying to determine whether the company is generating enough cash to increase the amount of dividends paid to investors in this and future years, and still have enough cash to buy equipment as it is needed.

Instructions

In each situation, state whether the decision maker would be most likely to place primary emphasis on information provided by the income statement, balance sheet, or statement of cash flows. In each case provide a brief justification for your choice. Choose only one financial statement in each case.

Prepare an income statement, retained earnings statement, and balance sheet.
(SO 4, 5)

P1-3A   On June 1 One Planet Cosmetics Co. was started with an initial investment in the company of $26,200 cash. Here are the assets and liabilities of the company at June 30, and the revenues and expenses for the month of June, its first month of operations:

Cash	$ 6,000	Notes payable	$13,000
Accounts receivable	4,000	Accounts payable	1,300
Service revenue	7,500	Supplies expense	1,200
Cosmetic supplies	2,400	Gas and oil expense	900
Advertising expense	500	Utilities expense	300
Equipment	30,000		

The company issued no additional stock during June, but dividends of $2,700 were paid during the month.

Instructions
Prepare an income statement and a retained earnings statement for the month of June and a balance sheet at June 30, 2001.

P1-4A   Presented below is selected financial information for Gabelli Corporation for December 31, 2001:

Determine items included in a statement of cash flows and prepare the statement.
(SO 4, 5)

Inventory	$ 25,000
Cash paid to suppliers	90,000
Building	200,000
Common stock	50,000
Cash dividends paid	11,000
Cash paid to purchase equipment	15,000
Equipment	40,000
Revenues	100,000
Cash received from customers	120,000

Instructions
Determine which items should be included in a statement of cash flows and then prepare the statement for Gabelli Corporation.

P1-5A   Von Mises Corporation was formed on January 1, 2001. At December 31, 2001, Brandon Copple, the president and sole stockholder, decided to prepare a balance sheet, which appeared as follows:

Comment on proper accounting treatment and prepare a corrected balance sheet.
(SO 4, 5)

VON MISES CORPORATION
Balance Sheet
December 31, 2001

Assets		Liabilities and Stockholders' Equity	
Cash	$20,000	Accounts payable	$ 40,000
Accounts receivable	55,000	Notes payable	15,000
Inventory	30,000	Boat loan	10,000
Boat	15,000	Stockholders' equity	55,000

Brandon willingly admits that he is not an accountant by training. He is concerned that his balance sheet might not be correct. He has provided you with the following additional information:
1. The boat actually belongs to Brandon, not to Von Mises Corporation. However, because he thinks he might take customers out on the boat occasionally, he decided to list it as an asset of the company. To be consistent he also listed as a liability of the corporation his personal loan that he took out at the bank to buy the boat.
2. The inventory was originally purchased for $10,000, but due to a surge in demand Brandon now thinks he could sell it for $30,000. He thought it would be best to record it at $30,000.
3. Included in the accounts receivable balance is $10,000 that Brandon loaned to his brother 5 years ago. Brandon included this in the receivables of Von Mises Corporation so he wouldn't forget that his brother owes him money.

Instructions
(a) Comment on the proper accounting treatment of the three items above.
(b) Provide a corrected balance sheet for Von Mises Corporation. (*Hint:* To get the balance sheet to balance, adjust stockholders' equity.)

PROBLEMS: SET B

Determine form of business organization.
(SO 1)

P1-1B Presented below are five independent situations.

(a) Dawn Addington, a college student looking for summer employment, opened a vegetable stand along a busy local highway. Each morning she buys produce from local farmers, then sells it in the afternoon as people return home from work.

(b) Robert Steven and Phillip Cantor each owned separate swing-set manufacturing businesses. They have decided to combine their businesses and try to expand their reach beyond their local market. They expect that within the coming year they will need significant funds to expand their operations.

(c) Three chemistry professors at FIU have formed a business to employ bacteria to clean up toxic waste sites. Each has contributed an equal amount of cash and knowledge to the venture. The use of bacteria in this situation is experimental, and legal obligations could result.

(d) Jane Kaplan has run a successful, but small cooperative health food store for over 20 years. The increased sales of her own store have made her believe that the time is right to open a national chain of health food stores across the country. Of course, this will require a substantial investment in stores, inventory, and employees in each store. Jane has no savings or personal assets. She wants to maintain control over the business.

(e) Mary Emery and Richard Goedde recently graduated with graduate degrees in economics. They have decided to start a consulting business focused on teaching the basics of international economics to small business owners interested in international trade.

Instructions

In each case explain what form of organization the business is likely to take—sole proprietorship, partnership, or corporation. Give reasons for your choice.

Identify users and uses of financial statements.
(SO 2, 4)

P1-2B Financial decisions often place heavier emphasis on one type of financial statement over the others. Consider each of the following hypothetical situations independently.

(a) An investor is considering purchasing commmon stock of the **Bally Total Fitness** company. The investor plans to hold the investment for at least 3 years.

(b) **Boeing** is considering extending credit to a new customer. The terms of the credit would require the customer to pay within 60 days of receipt of goods.

(c) The president of **Northwest Airlines** is trying to determine whether the company is generating enough cash to increase the amount of dividends paid to investors in this and future years, and still have enough cash to buy new flight equipment as it is needed.

(d) **Bank of America** is considering extending a loan to a small company. The company would be required to make interest payments at the end of each year for 5 years, and to repay the loan at the end of the fifth year.

Instructions

In each of the situations above, state whether the decision maker would be most likely to place primary emphasis on information provided by the income statement, balance sheet, or statement of cash flows. In each case provide a brief justification for your choice. Choose only one financial statement in each case.

Prepare an income statement, retained earnings statement, and balance sheet.
(SO 4)

P1-3B Obscure Driving School was started on May 1 with an investment of $45,000 cash. Following are the assets and liabilities of the company on May 31, 2001, and the revenues and expenses for the month of May, its first month of operations.

Cash	$ 7,800	Notes payable	$30,000
Accounts receivable	11,200	Rent expense	1,200
Equipment	60,000	Repair expense	400
Service revenue	9,600	Fuel expense	3,400
Advertising expense	900	Insurance expense	400
Accounts payable	2,400		

No additional common stock was issued in May, but a dividend of $1,700 in cash was paid.

Instructions
Prepare an income statement and a retained earnings statement for the month of May and a balance sheet at May 31, 2001.

P1-4B   Presented below are selected financial statement items for Lincoln Corporation for December 31, 2001:

Determine items included in a statement of cash flows and prepare the statement.
(SO 4, 5)

Inventory	$ 55,000
Cash paid to suppliers	95,000
Building	400,000
Common stock	20,000
Cash dividends paid	8,000
Cash paid to purchase equipment	26,000
Equipment	40,000
Revenues	200,000
Cash received from customers	165,000

Instructions
Determine which items should be included in a statement of cash flows, and then prepare the statement for Lincoln Corporation.

P1-5B   Colorado Corporation was formed during 2000 by Pam Bollinger. Pam is the president and sole stockholder. At December 31, 2001, Pam prepared an income statement for Colorado Corporation. Pam is not an accountant, but she thinks she did a reasonable job preparing the income statement by looking at the financial statements of other companies. She has asked you for advice. Pam's income statement appears as follows:

Comment on proper accounting treatment and prepare a corrected income statement.
(SO 4)

COLORADO CORPORATION
Income Statement
For the Year Ended December 31, 2001

Accounts receivable	$10,000
Revenue	60,000
Rent expense	15,000
Insurance expense	5,000
Vacation expense	2,000
Net income	48,000

Pam has also provided you with these facts:
1. Included in the revenue account is $7,000 of revenue that the company earned and received payment for in 2000. She forgot to include it in the 2000 income statement, so she put it in this year's statement.
2. Pam operates her business out of the basement of her parents' home. They do not charge her anything, but she thinks that if she paid rent it would cost her about $15,000 per year. She therefore included $15,000 of rent expense in the statement.
3. To reward herself for a year of hard work, Pam went to Hawaii. She did not use company funds to pay for the trip, but she reported it as an expense on the income statement, since it was her job that made her need the vacation.

Instructions
(a) Comment on the proper accounting treatment of the three items above.
(b) Prepare a corrected income statement for Colorado Corporation.

FINANCIAL REPORTING AND ANALYSIS

FINANCIAL REPORTING PROBLEM: *Tootsie Roll Industries, Inc.*

BYP1-1 Simplified 1998 financial statements of **Tootsie Roll Industries, Inc.** are given in Illustrations 1-6 through 1-9.

Instructions
Refer to Tootsie Roll's financial statements to answer these questions:
(a) What were Tootsie Roll's total assets at December 31, 1998? At December 31, 1997?
(b) How much cash (and cash equivalents) did Tootsie Roll have on December 31, 1998?
(c) What amount of accounts payable did Tootsie Roll report on December 31, 1998? On December 31, 1997?
(d) What were Tootsie Roll's net sales in 1997? In 1998?
(e) What is the amount of the change in Tootsie Roll's net income from 1997 to 1998?
(f) The accounting equation is: Assets = Liabilities + Stockholders' Equity. Replacing the words in that equation with dollar amounts, give Tootsie Roll's accounting equation at December 31, 1998.

COMPARATIVE ANALYSIS PROBLEM: *Tootsie Roll vs. Hershey Foods*

BYP1-2 Simplified financial statements of **Hershey Foods Corporation** are presented in Illustrations 1-15 through 1-18, and **Tootsie Roll's** simplified financial statements are presented in Illustrations 1-6 through 1-9.

Instructions
(a) Based on the information in these financial statements, determine the following for each company.
    (1) Total assets at December 31, 1998.
    (2) Accounts receivable at December 31, 1998.
    (3) Net sales for 1998.
    (4) Net income for 1998.
(b) What conclusions concerning the two companies can you draw from these data?

RESEARCH CASE

BYP1-3 The June 28, 1999, issue of *The Wall Street Journal* includes an article (on page A10) by Teri Agins and Ann Davis entitled "Candie's Fires Ernst and Young as Auditor in Midst of Probe of Year-End Audit."

Instructions
Read the article and answer the following questions:
(a) What is the role of the auditor—that is, what does the auditor do, and who relies on the auditor?
(b) What was the cause of the dispute between Candie's Inc. and Ernst and Young?
(c) Suppose that you own stock in Candie's. What concerns might this article raise for you?

INTERPRETING FINANCIAL STATEMENTS

BYP1-4 **The North Face, Inc.** is one of the world's premier brands of high-performance outdoor apparel and equipment. Its products include high-performance outerwear, ski-wear, tents, sleeping bags, and backpacks. In 1997 the company's statement of cash flows reported the following (all dollars in thousands):

Cash used by operating activities	($18,388)
Cash used by investing activities	(16,886)
Cash provided by financing activities	31,470
Net decrease in cash	($ 3,804)

Additionally, the statement of cash flows reported that the cash used for investing activities was spent on the purchase of property, plant, and equipment, and that of the $31,470,000 provided by new financing, only $889,000 was provided by new common stock financing. All the rest came from new issues of debt.

Instructions
Use the information above to answer each of the following:
(a) If you were a creditor of The North Face, Inc. what reaction might you have to the above information?
(b) If you were an investor in the common stock of The North Face, Inc., what reaction might you have to the above information?
(c) If you were evaluating the company as either a creditor or a stockholder, what other information would you be interested in seeing?

A GLOBAL FOCUS

BYP1-5 Today companies must compete in a global economy. Both Tootsie Roll and Hershey must compete with **Nestlé**. Nestlé, a Swiss company, is the largest food company in the world. If you were interested in broadening your investment portfolio, you might consider investing in Nestlé. However, investing in international companies can pose some additional challenges. Consider the following excerpts from the notes to Nestlé's financial statements.

NESTLÉ
Notes to the Financial Statements (partial)

(a) The Group accounts comply with International Accounting Standards (IAS) issued by the International Accounting Standards Committee (IASC) and with the Standards Interpretations issued by the Standards Interpretation Committee of the IASC (SIC).

(b) The accounts have been prepared under the historical cost convention and on an accrual basis. All significant consolidated companies have a 31st December accounting year end. All disclosures required by the 4th and 7th European Union company law directives are provided.

(c) On consolidation, assets and liabilities of Group companies denominated in foreign currencies are translated into Swiss francs at year-end rates. Income and expense items are translated into Swiss francs at the annual average rates of exchange or, where known or determinable, at the rate on the date of the transaction for significant items.

Instructions
Discuss the implications of each of these items in terms of the effect it might have (positive or negative) on your ability to compare Nestlé to Tootsie Roll and Hershey Foods. (*Hint:* In preparing your answer review the discussion of principles and assumptions in financial reporting.)

FINANCIAL ANALYSIS ON THE WEB

BYP1-6 **Purpose:** Identify summary information about companies. This information includes basic descriptions of the company's location, activities, industry, financial health, and financial performance.

Address: http://biz.yahoo.com/i (or go to www.wiley.com/college/kimmel)

Steps:
1. Type in a company name, or use index to find company name.

2. Choose **Profile**. Perform instructions (a)–(c) below.
3. Choose **Industry** to identify competitors.
   Perform instructions (d)–(e) below.

Instructions
Answer the following questions:
(a) What was the company's net income? Over what period was this measured?
(b) What was the company's total sales? Over what period was this measured?
(c) What is the company's industry?
(d) What are the names of four companies in this industry?
(e) Choose one of the competitors. What is this competitor's name? What were its sales?
    What was its net income?

BYP1-7 *Purpose:* This exercise is an introduction to the "Big Five" Accounting firms.

Addresses:

Arthur Andersen	http://www.arthurandersen.com/
Deloitte & Touche	http://www.dttus.com/
Ernst & Young	http://www.ey.com/default.htm
KPMG Peat Marwick	http://www.us.kpmg.com/
PriceWaterhouseCoopers	http://www.pwcglobal.com/

Steps:
Go to the homepage of a firm that is of interest to you.

Instructions
Answer the following questions:
(a) Name two services provided by the firm.
(b) What is the firm's total annual revenue?
(c) How many clients does it service?
(d) How many people are employed by the firm?

CRITICAL THINKING

GROUP DECISION CASE

BYP1-8 **Kelly Services, Inc.** is a service company that provides personnel for temporary positions, primarily nontechnical. When a company requests assistance, Kelly matches the qualifications of its standby personnel with the requirements of the position. The companies pay Kelly Services; Kelly Services, in turn, pays the employees.

In a recent annual report, Kelly Services chronicled its contributions to community services over the past 30 years, or so. The following excerpts illustrate the variety of services provided:

1. KellyWeek, a Saint Patrick's Day customer appreciation event, originated in California. Kelly Services made donations of stationery, office decorations, and decals containing the company's name.
2. In support of Lady Bird Johnson's "Keep America Beautiful" campaign in the 1960s, the company donated, and its employees planted, gladiola gardens in cities across the United States.
3. The company initiated a holiday drawing in which thousands of customers throughout the United States and Canada nominate their favorite children's charities. Winning charities in the drawing receive a monetary donation from Kelly Services in the name of the customer.
4. KellyWeek was expanded by making donations of temporary help.
5. Kelly executives regularly volunteer their time and resources to serve as role models and mentors to youth in the Detroit area.

Instructions
With the class divided into groups, answer the following:
(a) The economic entity assumption requires that a company keep the personal expenses of its employees separate from business expenses. Which of the activities listed above were expenses of the business, and which were personal expenses of the employees?

Be specific. If part of the donation is business and part is personal, note which part is each.

(b) For those items that were company expenses, tell whether the expense was probably categorized as an advertising expense, employee wages expense, grounds maintenance expense, or charitable contribution expense. You may use any or all of the categories. Explain your answer.

COMMUNICATION ACTIVITY

BYP1-9   Amy Joan is the bookkeeper for Vermont Company, Inc. Amy has been trying to get the company's balance sheet to balance. She finally got it to balance, but she still isn't sure that it is correct.

VERMONT COMPANY, INC.
Balance Sheet
For the Month Ended December 31, 2001

Assets		Liabilities and Stockholders' Equity	
Equipment	$20,500	Common stock	$11,000
Cash	9,000	Accounts receivable	(3,000)
Supplies	2,000	Dividends	(2,000)
Accounts payable	(5,000)	Notes payable	10,500
Total assets	$26,500	Retained earnings	10,000
		Total liabilities and	
		stockholders' equity	$26,500

Instructions
Explain to Amy Joan in a memo (a) the purpose of a balance sheet, and (b) why this balance sheet is incorrect and what she should do to correct it.

ETHICS CASE

BYP1-10   The December 14, 1998, issue of *Forbes* magazine includes an article by Michael Ozanian entitled "Selective Accounting." It describes accounting practices by professional sports teams that result in lower reported income.

Instructions
Read the article and answer the following questions:

(a) What incentives do sports teams have to report lower income? Who is affected by their actions?

(b) What is the primary method used to report lower income? That is, what income statement item is affected the most by their methods?

(c) Are sports teams required to make their financial results available to the public?

(d) You will learn in this course that accounting requires many subjective choices between accounting rules. These choices will result in differing amounts being reported on a company's financial statements. Is it unethical to choose accounting methods that accomplish particular objectives—for example, to report higher or, in this case, lower net income?

Answers to Self-Study Questions
1. b   2. c   3. c   4. d   5. d   6. a   7. c   8. a   9. a   10. c   11. c

Answer to Tootsie Roll Review It Question 3, p. 14
Using dollar amounts, Tootsie Roll's accounting equation is:

Assets   =   Liabilities   + Stockholders' Equity

$487,423,000 = $90,966,000 + $396,457,000

A Further Look at Financial Statements

◆ STUDY OBJECTIVES

After studying this chapter, you should be able to:

1 Explain the meaning of generally accepted accounting principles and describe the basic objective of financial reporting.

2 Discuss the qualitative characteristics of accounting information.

3 Identify two constraints in accounting.

4 Identify the sections of a classified balance sheet.

5 Identify and compute ratios for analyzing a company's profitability.

6 Explain the relationship between a retained earnings statement and a statement of stockholders' equity.

7 Identify and compute ratios for analyzing a company's liquidity and solvency using a balance sheet.

8 Identify and compute ratios for analyzing a company's liquidity and solvency using a statement of cash flows.

◆ JUST FOOLING AROUND?

Few people could have predicted how dramatically the Internet would change the investment world. One of the most interesting results is how it has changed the way ordinary people invest their savings. More and more people are spurning investment professionals and instead are choosing to strike out on their own, making their own investment decisions. A whole new breed of investors, known as "day-traders," has arisen. These are people, from doctors to car mechanics, who spend hours a day trading stocks over the Internet. They are empowered by the instant access to never-before-

available information that the Internet provides.

Two early pioneers in this area were Tom and David Gardner, brothers who created an online investor bulletin board called the Motley Fool. The name comes from Shakespeare's *As You Like It*. The fool in Shakespeare's plays was the only one who could speak unpleasant truths to kings and queens without being killed. Tom and David view themselves as 20th-century "fools," revealing the "truths" of Wall Street to the small investor, who they feel has been taken advantage of by Wall Street insiders. Their online bulletin board enables in-

vestors to exchange information and insights about companies.

Critics of these bulletin boards contend that they are high-tech rumor mills. They suggest that because of the fervor created by bulletin board chatter, stock prices get bid up to unreasonable levels and people often pay prices that are far higher than the underlying worth of the company. One potentially troubling aspect of bulletin boards is that participants rarely give their real identities, instead using aliases. Consequently, there is little to stop people from putting misinformation on the board to influence a stock's price in the

direction they desire. For example, in April 1999 the stock of PairGain Technologies jumped 32% as a result of a bogus takeover rumor started on an investment bulletin board. Some observers are concerned that small investors—ironically, the very people the Gardner brothers are trying to help—will be hurt the most by misinformation and intentional scams.

To show how these bulletin boards work, suppose that in July 1997 you had $10,000 to invest. You were thinking about investing in Best Buy Company, the largest seller of electronic equipment in the United States. You scanned the Internet investment bulletin boards and found messages posted by two different investors. Here are excerpts from actual postings:

From "TMPVenus," June 14, 1997: "Where are the prospects for positive movement for this company? Poor margins, poor management, astronomical P/E!"

From "broachman," June 18, 1997: "I believe that this is a LONG TERM winner, and presently at a good price."

One says sell, and one says buy. Whom should you believe? If you had taken "broachman's" advice and purchased the stock in July 1997, by July 1999 the $10,000 you invested would have been worth over $200,000. Best Buy ended up being one of America's best-performing stocks during that two-year period.

Rather than getting swept away by rumors, investors must sort out the good information from the bad. One thing is certain—as information services such as the Motley Fool increase in number, gathering information will become even easier, and evaluating it will become the harder task.

On the World Wide Web
Motley Fool: http://www.fool.com.
Best Buy Company: http://www.bestbuy.com

47

I f you are thinking of purchasing Best Buy stock, or any stock, how can you decide what the stock is worth? If you own a stock, how can you determine whether it is time to buy more stock—or time to bail out? Your decision will be influenced by a variety of considerations; one should be your careful analysis of a company's financial statements. The reason: Financial statements offer relevant and reliable information, which will help you in your stock purchase decisions.

In this chapter we begin by looking at the objectives of financial reporting. We then take a closer look at the balance sheet and introduce some useful ways for evaluating the information provided by the statements.

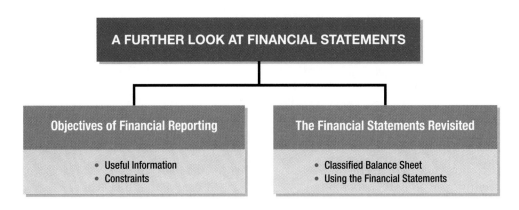

A FURTHER LOOK AT FINANCIAL STATEMENTS

Objectives of Financial Reporting
- Useful Information
- Constraints

The Financial Statements Revisited
- Classified Balance Sheet
- Using the Financial Statements

OBJECTIVES OF FINANCIAL REPORTING

Financial reporting is the term used to describe all of the financial information presented by a company—both in its financial statements and in additional disclosures provided in the annual report. For example, if you are deciding whether to invest in Best Buy stock, you need financial information to help make your decision. Such information should help you understand Best Buy's past financial performance and its current financial picture, and give you some idea of its future prospects. Although information found on electronic bulletin boards like the Motley Fool has its place, there is no substitute for careful study of the information available through traditional financial reporting channels. The primary objective of such financial reporting is to provide information useful for decision making.

CHARACTERISTICS OF USEFUL INFORMATION

How does a company like Best Buy decide on the amount and type of financial information to disclose? In what format should its financial information be presented? How should assets, liabilities, revenues, and expenses be measured? The answers to these questions are found in accounting rules that have substantial authoritative support and are recognized as a general guide for financial reporting purposes. These rules are referred to as generally accepted accounting principles (GAAP). They are determined by standard-setting bodies in consultation with the accounting profession and the business community.

The Securities and Exchange Commission (SEC) is the agency of the U.S. government that oversees U.S. financial markets and accounting standard-setting bodies. The primary accounting standard-setting body in the United States is the Financial Accounting Standards Board (FASB). The FASB's overriding criterion is that the accounting rules should generate the most **useful** financial information for making business decisions. To be useful, information should possess these qualitative characteristics: relevance, reliability, comparability, and consistency.

STUDY OBJECTIVE

1

Explain the meaning of GAAP and describe the basic objective of financial reporting.

RELEVANCE

Information of any sort is relevant if it would influence a decision. Accounting information is relevant if it would make a difference in a business decision. For example, when Best Buy issues financial statements, the information in the statements is considered relevant because it provides a basis for forecasting Best Buy's future earnings. Accounting information is also relevant to business decisions because it confirms or corrects prior expectations. Thus, Best Buy's financial statements help **predict** future events and **provide feedback** about prior expectations for the financial health of the company.

In addition, for accounting information to be relevant it must be **timely**. That is, it must be available to decision makers before it loses its capacity to influence decisions. If Best Buy reported its financial information only every five years, the information would have limited usefulness for decision-making purposes.

STUDY OBJECTIVE

2

Discuss the qualitative characteristics of accounting information.

RELIABILITY

Reliability of information means that the information can be depended on. To be reliable, accounting information must be **verifiable**—we must be able to prove that it is free of error. Also, the information must be a **faithful representation** of what it purports to be—it must be factual. If Best Buy's income statement reports sales of $20 billion when it actually had sales of $10 billion, then the statement is not a faithful representation of Best Buy's financial performance. Finally, accounting information must be **neutral**—it cannot be selected, prepared, or presented to favor one set of interested users over another. As noted in Chapter 1, to ensure reliability, certified public accountants audit financial statements.

COMPARABILITY AND CONSISTENCY

Comparability

Let's say that you and a friend kept track of your height each year as you were growing up. If you measured your height in feet and your friend measured hers in meters, it would be difficult to compare your heights. A conversion would be necessary. In accounting, comparability results when different companies use the same accounting principles.

At one level, U.S. accounting standards are fairly comparable because they are based on certain basic principles and assumptions. These principles and assumptions allow for some variation in methods, however. For example, there are a variety of ways to report inventory. Often these different methods result in different amounts of net income. To make comparison across companies easier, each company **must disclose** the accounting methods used. From the disclosures, the external user can determine whether the financial information is comparable and try to make adjustments. Unfortunately, converting the accounting numbers of companies that use different methods is not as easy as converting your height from feet to meters.

One factor that can affect the ability to compare two companies is their choice of accounting or fiscal year-end. Most companies choose December 31 as their fiscal year-end, although an increasing number of companies are choosing dates other than December 31. In the notes to its financial statements, Best Buy states that its accounting year-end is the Saturday nearest the end of February. This can create two problems for analysis. First, if Best Buy's competitors use a different year-end, then when you compare them, you are not comparing performance over the same period of time or financial position at the same point in time. Also, by not picking a particular date, the number of weeks in Best Buy's fiscal year will change. For example, its fiscal years 1998 and 1997 had 52 weeks, but fiscal year 1996 had 53 weeks.

BUSINESS INSIGHT
Management Perspective

Why do companies choose the particular year-ends that they do? For example, why doesn't every company use December 31 as the accounting year-end? Many companies choose to end their accounting year when inventory or operations are at a low. This is advantageous because compiling accounting information requires much time and effort by managers, so they would rather do it when they aren't as busy operating the business. Also, inventory is easier and less costly to count when it is low. Some companies whose year-ends differ from December 31 are Delta Air Lines, June 30; Walt Disney Productions, September 30; Kmart Corp., January 31; and Dunkin' Donuts, Inc., October 31.

Consistency

Users of accounting information also want to compare the same company's financial results over time. For example, to track Best Buy's net income over several years, you'd need to know that the same principles have been used from year to year; otherwise, you might be "comparing apples to oranges." **Consistency** means that a company uses the same accounting principles and methods from year to year. Thus, if a company selects one inventory accounting method in the first year of operations, it is expected to continue to use that same method in succeeding years. When financial information has been reported on a consistent basis, the financial statements permit meaningful analysis of trends within a company.

A company *can* change to a new method of accounting if management can justify that the new method produces more meaningful financial information. In the year in which the change occurs, the change must be disclosed in the notes to the financial statements so that users of the statements are aware of the lack of consistency.

The characteristics that make accounting information useful are summarized in Illustration 2-1.

Illustration 2-1
Characteristics of useful
information

Relevance
1. Provides a basis for forecasts
2. Confirms or corrects prior expectations
3. Is timely

Reliability
1. Is verifiable
2. Is a faithful representation
3. Is neutral

Comparability
Different companies use similar accounting principles

Consistency
Company uses same accounting methods from year to year

CONSTRAINTS IN ACCOUNTING

The characteristics we have discussed are intended to provide users of financial statements with the most useful information. Taken to the extreme, however, the pursuit of useful financial information could be far too costly to the company. Therefore, some constraints have been agreed upon to ensure that accounting rules are applied in a reasonable fashion, from the perspectives of both the company and the user. **Constraints** permit a company to modify generally accepted accounting principles without jeopardizing the usefulness of the reported information. The constraints are materiality and conservatism.

STUDY OBJECTIVE
❸
Identify two constraints in accounting.

MATERIALITY

Materiality relates to a financial statement item's impact on a company's overall financial condition and operations. An item is **material** when its size makes it likely to influence the decision of an investor or creditor. It is **immaterial** if it is too small to impact a decision maker. In short, if the item does not make a difference, GAAP does not have to be followed. To determine the materiality of an amount—that is, to determine its financial significance—the item is compared with such items as total assets, total liabilities, sales revenue, and net income.

To illustrate how the constraint of materiality is applied, assume that Best Buy made a $100 error in recording revenue. Best Buy's total revenue is $10 billion; thus a $100 error is not material.

Helpful Hint In late 1999, the SEC issued stricter rules on materiality because it felt that too often companies were using materiality as an excuse not to report certain losses.

CONSERVATISM

Conservatism in accounting means that when preparing financial statements, a company should choose the accounting method that will be least likely to overstate assets and income. It **does not mean understating assets or income**. Conservatism provides a guide in difficult situations, and the guide is a reasonable one: Do not overstate assets and income.

A common application of the conservatism constraint is in valuing inventories. Inventories are normally recorded at their cost. To be conservative, however, inventories are reported at market value if market value is below cost. This practice results in lower net income on the income statement and a lower stated amount of inventory on the balance sheet.

The two constraints are graphically depicted in Illustration 2-2.

Illustration 2-2
Accounting constraints

Materiality

For small amounts, GAAP does not have to be followed.

Conservatism

When in doubt, choose the solution that will be least likely to overstate assets and income.

BEFORE YOU GO ON...

◆ Review It

1. What are generally accepted accounting principles?
2. What is the basic objective of financial information?
3. What qualitative characteristics make accounting information useful?
4. What are the materiality constraint and the conservatism constraint?

SECTION 2
THE FINANCIAL STATEMENTS REVISITED

In Chapter 1 we introduced the four financial statements. In this section we review the statements and illustrate how these statements accomplish their intended objectives. We begin by introducing the classified balance sheet.

THE CLASSIFIED BALANCE SHEET

STUDY OBJECTIVE

Identify the sections of a classified balance sheet.

The balance sheet presents a snapshot of a company's financial position at a point in time. To improve users' understanding of a company's financial position, companies often group similar assets and similar liabilities together. This is useful because it tells you that items within a group have similar economic characteristics. A classified balance sheet generally contains the standard classifications listed in Illustration 2-3.

Illustration 2-3
Standard balance sheet classifications

Assets	Liabilities and Stockholders' Equity
Current assets	Current liabilities
Long-term investments	Long-term liabilities
Property, plant, and equipment	Stockholders' equity
Intangible assets	

These groupings help readers determine such things as (1) whether the company has enough assets to pay its debts as they come due and (2) the claims of short- and long-term creditors on the company's total assets. Many of these groupings can be seen in the balance sheet of Franklin Corporation shown in Illustration 2-4. Each of the groupings is explained next.

Illustration 2-4
Classified balance sheet
in report form

FRANKLIN CORPORATION
Balance Sheet
October 31, 2001

Assets

Current assets		
Cash	$ 6,600	
Short-term investments	2,000	
Accounts receivable	7,000	
Inventories	4,000	
Supplies	2,100	
Prepaid insurance	400	
Total current assets		$22,100
Long-term investments		
Investment in stock of Walters Corp.		7,200
Property, plant, and equipment		
Office equipment	24,000	
Less: Accumulated depreciation	5,000	19,000
Intangible assets		
Patents		3,100
Total assets		$51,400

Liabilities and Stockholders' Equity

Current liabilities		
Notes payable	$11,000	
Accounts payable	2,100	
Interest payable	450	
Unearned revenue	900	
Salaries payable	1,600	
Total current liabilities		$16,050
Long-term liabilities		
Notes payable		1,300
Total liabilities		17,350
Stockholders' equity		
Common stock	14,000	
Retained earnings	20,050	
Total stockholders' equity		34,050
Total liabilities and stockholders' equity		$51,400

CURRENT ASSETS

Current assets are assets that are expected to be converted to cash or used in the business within one year. In Illustration 2-4 Franklin Corporation had current assets of $22,100. For most businesses the cutoff for classification as current assets is one year from the balance sheet date. For example, accounts receivable are included in current assets because they will be converted to cash through collection within one year. Supplies is a current asset because we expect that it will be used in the business within one year. However, as noted in the Business Insight at the top of the next page, some businesses use a period longer than one year as the cutoff.

Management Perspective

Some companies use a period longer than one year to classify assets and liabilities as current because they have an operating cycle longer than one year. The **operating cycle** of a company is the average time that it takes to go from cash to cash in producing revenues. For example, if your business sells TVs, your operating cycle would be the average length of time it would take for you to purchase your inventory, sell it on account, and then collect cash from your customers. For most businesses this cycle takes less than a year, so they use a one-year cutoff. But, for some businesses, such as vineyards or airplane manufacturers, this period may be longer than a year. Except where noted, we will assume that one year is used to determine whether an asset or liability is current or long-term.

Common types of current assets are (1) cash, (2) marketable securities, such as U.S. government bonds held as a short-term investment, (3) receivables (notes receivable, accounts receivable, and interest receivable), (4) inventories, and (5) prepaid expenses (insurance and supplies). On the balance sheet, these items are listed in the order in which they are expected to be converted into cash. This arrangement is shown in Illustration 2-5 for The Coca-Cola Company.

Illustration 2-5 Current assets section

The Coca-Cola Company

THE COCA-COLA COMPANY
Balance Sheet (partial)
(in millions)

Current assets	
Cash and cash equivalents	$1,648
Short-term investments	159
Trade accounts receivable	1,666
Inventories	890
Prepaid expenses and other assets	2,017
Total current assets	$6,380

A company's current assets are important in assessing its short-term debt-paying ability, as explained later in the chapter.

LONG-TERM INVESTMENTS

Alternative Terminology
Long-term investments are often referred to simply as **investments.**

Long-term investments are generally investments in stocks and bonds of other corporations that are normally held for many years. In Illustration 2-4 Franklin Corporation reported long-term investments of $7,200 on its balance sheet. Yahoo! Inc. reported long-term investments in its balance sheet as shown in Illustration 2-6.

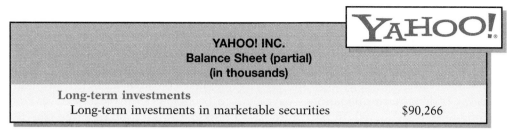

YAHOO! INC.
Balance Sheet (partial)
(in thousands)

Long-term investments
  Long-term investments in marketable securities $90,266

Illustration 2-6
Long-term investments
section

PROPERTY, PLANT, AND EQUIPMENT

Property, plant, and equipment are assets with relatively long useful lives that are used in operating the business. This category includes land, buildings, machinery and equipment, delivery equipment, and furniture. In Illustration 2-4 Franklin Corporation reported property, plant, and equipment of $24,000.

Depreciation is the practice of allocating the cost of assets to a number of years, rather than simply expensing the full purchase price of the asset in the year of purchase. Assets that the company depreciates should be reported on the balance sheet at cost less accumulated depreciation. In Illustration 2-4 Franklin Corporation reported accumulated depreciation of $5,000. The accumulated depreciation account shows the total amount of depreciation taken over the *life of the asset*. The use of an accumulated depreciation account is shown for Ben & Jerry's Homemade, Inc. in Illustration 2-7.

Alternative Terminology
Property, plant, and equipment is sometimes called **fixed assets.**

BEN & JERRY'S HOMEMADE, INC.
Balance Sheet (partial)
(in thousands)

Property, plant, and equipment
  Land and improvements $ 4,520
  Buildings   37,940
  Equipment and furniture   52,047
  Leasehold improvements   3,727
  Construction in process   2,058 $100,292
  Less: Accumulated depreciation   36,841
                                               $ 63,451

Illustration 2-7
Property, plant, and equipment section

INTANGIBLE ASSETS

Many companies have assets that cannot be seen yet often are very valuable. These assets are referred to as intangible assets. Intangible assets are noncurrent assets that do not have physical substance. They include patents, copyrights, and trademarks or trade names that give the company **exclusive right** of use for a specified period of time. Franklin Corporation reported intangible assets of $3,100. Illustration 2-8 shows how ski manufacturer K2, Inc. reported its intangible assets.

Helpful Hint Sometimes intangible assets are reported under a broader heading called **Other assets.**

K2, INC.
Balance Sheet (partial)
(in thousands)

Intangible assets
  Intangibles, principally goodwill, net $19,564

Illustration 2-8
Intangible assets section

CURRENT LIABILITIES

In the liabilities and stockholders' equity section of the balance sheet, the first grouping is current liabilities. Current liabilities are obligations that are to be paid within the coming year. Common examples are accounts payable, wages payable, bank loans payable, interest payable, taxes payable, and current maturities of long-term obligations (payments to be made within the next year on long-term obligations). In Illustration 2-4 Franklin Corporation reported five different types of current liabilities, for a total of $16,050.

Within the current liabilities section, notes payable is usually listed first, followed by accounts payable. Other items are then listed in any order. The current liabilities section adapted from the balance sheet of Gap Inc. is shown in Illustration 2-9.

Illustration 2-9 Current liabilities section

GAP INC.
Balance Sheet (partial)
(in thousands)

Current liabilities	
Notes payable	$ 90,690
Accounts payable	684,130
Accrued expenses and other current liabilities	655,770
Income taxes payable	122,513
Total current liabilities	$1,553,103

LONG-TERM LIABILITIES

Obligations expected to be paid after one year are classified as long-term liabilities. Liabilities in this category include bonds payable, mortgages payable, long-term notes payable, lease liabilities, and pension liabilities. Many companies report long-term debt maturing after one year as a single amount in the balance sheet and show the details of the debt in notes that accompany the financial statements. Others list the various types of long-term liabilities. In Illustration 2-4 Franklin Corporation reported long-term liabilities of $1,300. In its balance sheet, Northwest Airlines Corporation reported long-term liabilities as shown in Illustration 2-10.

Illustration 2-10 Long-term liabilities section

NORTHWEST AIRLINES
NORTHWEST AIRLINES CORPORATION
Balance Sheet (partial)
(in millions)

Long-term liabilities	
Long-term debt	$3,681.5
Long-term obligations under capital leases	597.3
Deferred credits and other liabilities	2,192.2
Total long-term liabilities	$6,471.0

STOCKHOLDERS' EQUITY

Alternative Terminology
Common stock is sometimes called **capital stock.**

Stockholders' equity is divided into two parts: common stock and retained earnings. Investments of assets in the business by the stockholders are recorded as common stock. Income retained for use in the business is recorded as retained earnings. These two parts are combined and reported as **stockholders' equity** on the balance sheet. In Illustration 2-4 Franklin reported common stock of $14,000 and retained earnings of $20,050.

BEFORE YOU GO ON...

◆ Review It

1. What are the major sections in a classified balance sheet?
2. What is the primary determining factor to distinguish current assets from long-term assets?
3. What was Tootsie Roll's largest current asset at December 31, 1998? The answer to this question is provided on page 92.
4. Where is accumulated depreciation reported on the balance sheet?

◆ Do It

Baxter Hoffman recently received the following information related to Hoffman Corporation's December 31, 2001, balance sheet.

Prepaid expenses	$ 2,300	Inventory	$3,400
Cash	800	Accumulated depreciation	2,700
Property, plant, and equipment	10,700	Accounts receivable	1,100

Prepare the assets section of Hoffman Corporation's balance sheet.

Reasoning: Current assets are cash and other resources that are reasonably expected to be consumed in one year. Accumulated depreciation should be subtracted from property, plant, and equipment to determine net property, plant, and equipment.

Solution:

HOFFMAN CORPORATION
Balance Sheet (partial)
December 31, 2001

Assets

Current assets		
Cash	$ 800	
Accounts receivable	1,100	
Inventory	3,400	
Prepaid expenses	2,300	
Total current assets		$ 7,600
Property, plant, and equipment	10,700	
Less: Accumulated depreciation	2,700	8,000
Total assets		$15,600

USING THE FINANCIAL STATEMENTS

In Chapter 1 we introduced the four financial statements. We discussed how these statements provide information about a company's performance and financial position. In this chapter we extend this discussion by showing you specific tools that can be used to analyze financial statements to make a more meaningful evaluation of a company.

RATIO ANALYSIS

Ratio analysis expresses the relationship among selected items of financial statement data. A *ratio* expresses the mathematical relationship between one quantity and another. The relationship is expressed in terms of either a percentage, a rate, or a simple proportion. To illustrate, Best Buy has current assets of $2,063 million and current liabilities of $1,387 million. The relationship between these accounts is determined by dividing current assets by current liabilities, to get 1.49. The alternative means of expression are:

Percentage: Current assets are 149% of current liabilities.
Rate: Current assets are 1.49 times as great as current liabilities.
Proportion: The relationship of current assets to liabilities is 1.49:1.

For analysis of the primary financial statements, ratios can be classified as follows:

Illustration 2-11
Financial ratio classifications

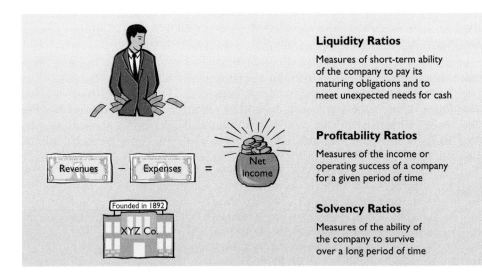

Liquidity Ratios

Measures of short-term ability of the company to pay its maturing obligations and to meet unexpected needs for cash

Profitability Ratios

Measures of the income or operating success of a company for a given period of time

Solvency Ratios

Measures of the ability of the company to survive over a long period of time

Ratios can provide clues to underlying conditions that may not be apparent from inspection of the individual components of a particular ratio. However, a single ratio by itself is not very meaningful. Accordingly, in this and the following chapters we will use:

1. **Intracompany comparisons** covering two years for the same company.
2. **Industry average comparisons** based on average ratios for particular industries.
3. **Intercompany comparisons** based on comparisons with a competitor in the same industry.

USING THE INCOME STATEMENT

STUDY OBJECTIVE
❺
Identify and compute ratios for analyzing a company's profitability.

Best Buy Company tries to generate a profit for its shareholders by selling electronics goods. The income statement reports how successful it is at generating a profit from its sales. The income statement reports the amount earned during the period—revenues—and the costs incurred during the period—expenses. An income statement for Best Buy is provided in Illustration 2-12.

Illustration 2-12
Best Buy's income statement

BEST BUY CO., INC.
Income Statements
For the Years Ended February 27, 1999, and February 28, 1998
(in thousands)

	1999	1998
Revenues		
Net sales and other revenue	$10,079,341	$8,358,212
Expenses		
Cost of goods sold	8,250,123	7,026,074
Selling, general, and administrative expenses	1,463,281	1,145,280
Interest expense, net	–0–	33,005
Income tax expense	141,500	59,400
Total expenses	9,854,904	8,263,759
Net income	$ 224,437	$ 94,453

From this income statement we can see that Best Buy's sales and net income both increased significantly during the year. Net income increased from $94,453,000 to $224,437,000. In order to increase net income the company needs its sales to increase more than its expenses. While this was the case for Best Buy during this period, this is not as easy as it sounds. The consumer electronics business is very competitive. New models are constantly arising, making old models obsolete. Buyers are fickle, and sales are very susceptible to economic swings. Best Buy's primary competitor is Circuit City. Circuit City reported net income of $142,924,000 for the year ended February 28, 1999.

To evaluate the profitability of Best Buy, we will use ratio analysis. Profitability ratios measure the operating success of a company for a given period of time. We will look at two examples of profitability ratios: return on assets and profit margin.

Return on Assets. An overall measure of profitability is the return on assets ratio. This ratio is computed by dividing net income by average assets. **(Average assets are commonly calculated by adding the beginning and ending values of assets and dividing by 2.)** The return on assets ratio indicates the amount of net income generated by each dollar invested in assets. Thus, the higher the return on assets, the more profitable the company. A simplified 1999 income statement for Best Buy was presented in Illustration 2-12. The 1999 and 1998 return on assets of Best Buy, Circuit City (a Best Buy competitor), and industry averages are presented in Illustration 2-13.

Illustration 2-13 Return
on assets ratio

$$\text{Return on Assets Ratio} = \frac{\text{Net Income}}{\text{Average Total Assets}}$$

	1999	1998
Best Buy ($ in millions)	$\frac{\$224}{(\$2,512 + \$2,056)/2^*} = 9.8\%$	$\frac{\$94}{(\$2,056 + \$1,734)/2^*} = 5.0\%$
Circuit City	4.3%	3.3%
Industry average	4.6%	2.9%

*Amounts used to calculate average assets are taken from Best Buy's balance sheet (Illustration 2-16). Total assets in 1997 were $1,734 million. Also note that amounts in the ratio calculations have been rounded.

We can evaluate Best Buy's 1998 and 1999 return on assets ratio in a number of ways. First we can compare it across time. That is, did its performance improve? The increase from 5.0% in 1998 to 9.8% in 1999 suggests strong improvement. The ratio tells us that in 1998 Best Buy generated 5 cents on every dollar invested in assets, and in 1999 it generated 9.8 cents on every dollar invested in assets. Then we can compare it to that of its main rival, Circuit City. In both years Best Buy's return on assets ratio was substantially better than that of Circuit City. Finally, we can compare it to industry averages. Again, in each year Best Buy's return on assets ratio exceeded that of the average firm in the industry. Thus, based on the return on assets ratio, Best Buy's profitability appears strong.

Profit Margin. The profit margin ratio measures the percentage of each dollar of sales that results in net income. It is computed by dividing net income by net sales (revenue) for the period. Businesses with high turnover, such as grocery stores (Safeway or Kroger) and discount stores (Kmart or Wal-Mart), generally experience low profit margins. Low-turnover businesses, such as jewelry stores (Tiffany & Co.) or airplane manufacturers (Boeing Aircraft), have high profit margins. Profit margins for Best Buy, Circuit City, and industry averages are shown in Illustration 2-14.

Illustration 2-14 Profit
margin ratio

$$\text{Profit Margin Ratio} = \frac{\text{Net Income}}{\text{Net Sales}}$$

	1999	1998
Best Buy ($ in millions)	$\frac{\$224}{\$10,079} = 2.2\%$	$\frac{\$94}{\$8,358} = 1.1\%$
Circuit City	1.3%	1.2%
Industry average	2.2%	1.6%

Best Buy's profit margin improved from 1.1% in 1998 to 2.2% in 1999. This means that in 1998 the company generated 1.1 cent on each dollar of sales, and in 1999 it generated 2.2 cents on each dollar of sales—a substantial improvement. But how does Best Buy compare to its competitors? Its profit margin ratio was lower than Circuit City's in 1998, but exceeded it in 1999. However, Best Buy's profit margin ratio was less than the industry average in 1998, and only equaled it in 1999. Thus, its profit margin ratio does not suggest exceptional profitability. In subsequent chapters you will learn more about evaluating a company's profitability, which will shed light on this seemingly conflicting information.

BUSINESS INSIGHT
International Perspective

The French know a lot about food and wine—but stocks are another matter. One observer went so far as to state, "Indeed, until recently the French widely derided people who invested in stocks as Anglo-Saxon speculators, greedy capitalists who deviously manipulated financial markets to line their pockets." But as stock markets (or as the French say, *les Bourses*) around the world hit record highs, many French are taking classes to learn more about how to invest. Many have a lot to learn. For example, Jacques Giraudou decided to take a class after he sustained a huge investment loss. He had purchased an investment in the Eurotunnel, which proceeded to lose 70 percent of its value over a two-year period. Only after two years did he realize that he had purchased stocks rather than bonds.

Source: Suzanne McGee, "The French Try to Demystify Investing," *The Wall Street Journal*, May 27, 1999, p. C1.

DECISION TOOLKIT

Decision Checkpoints	Info Needed for Decision	Tool to Use for Decision	How to Evaluate Results
Is the company using its assets effectively?	Net income and average assets	$\text{Return on assets ratio} = \dfrac{\text{Net income}}{\text{Average total assets}}$	Higher value suggests favorable efficiency (use of assets).
Is the company maintaining an adequate margin between sales and expenses?	Net income and net sales	$\text{Profit margin ratio} = \dfrac{\text{Net income}}{\text{Net sales}}$	Higher value suggests favorable return on each dollar of sales.

USING THE STATEMENT OF STOCKHOLDERS' EQUITY

STUDY OBJECTIVE

6

Explain the relationship between a retained earnings statement and a statement of stockholders' equity.

As discussed in Chapter 1, the retained earnings statement describes the changes in retained earnings during the year. This statement adds net income and then subtracts dividends from the beginning retained earnings to arrive at ending retained earnings.

Recall, however, that stockholders' equity is comprised of two parts: retained earnings and common stock. Therefore, the stockholders' equity of most companies is affected by factors other than just changes in retained earnings. For example, the company may issue or retire shares of common stock. Most companies, therefore, use what is called a **statement of stockholders' equity**, rather than a retained earnings statement, so that they can report **all changes** in stockholders' equity accounts. Illustration 2-15 is a simplified statement of stockholders' equity for Best Buy.

Illustration 2-15
Best Buy's statement of stockholders' equity

BEST BUY CO., INC. Statement of Stockholders' Equity (in thousands)		
	Common Stock	Retained Earnings
Balances at March 2, 1996	$240,676	$190,938
Issuance of common stock	4,953	
Net income		1,748
Balances at March 1, 1997	245,629	192,686
Issuance of common stock	24,978	
Net income		94,453
Balances at February 28, 1998	270,607	287,139
Issuance of common stock	281,951	
Net income		224,437
Balances at February 27, 1999	$552,558	$511,576

One observation that can be made from this financial statement is that Best Buy's common stock increased because of transactions in the company's own stock during this three-year period. Another observation from this financial statement is that Best Buy paid no dividends during the last three years. You might wonder why Best Buy paid no dividends during years when it was profitable. In fact, recently two Best Buy shareholders discussed this question about Best Buy's dividend policy on an investor bulletin board. Here are excerpts:

From "Katwoman," July 9, 1998: "Best Buy has a nice price increase. Earnings are on the way up. But why no dividends?"

From "AngryCandy," July 9, 1998: "I guess they feel they can make better use of the money by investing back in the business. They still view Best Buy as a rapidly growing company and would prefer to invest in expanding the infrastructure (building new stores, advertising, etc.) than in paying out dividends. . . . If Best Buy gets to the stage of 'stable, big company' with little room for expansion, then I'm sure you'll see them elect to pay out a dividend."

AngryCandy's response is an excellent explanation of the thought process that management goes through in deciding whether to pay a dividend. Management must evaluate what its cash needs are. If it has uses for cash that will increase the value of the company (for example, building a new, centralized warehouse), then it should retain cash in the company. However, if it has more cash than it has valuable opportunities, then it should distribute its excess cash as a dividend.

B E F O R E   Y O U   G O   O N . . .

◆ **Review It**

1. What are the three ways that ratios can be expressed?

2. What is the purpose of profitability ratios? Explain the return on assets ratio and the profit margin ratio.
3. What does a statement of stockholders' equity show?

USING A CLASSIFIED BALANCE SHEET

You can learn a lot about a company's financial health by also evaluating the relationship between its various assets and liabilities. A simplified balance sheet for Best Buy is provided in Illustration 2-16.

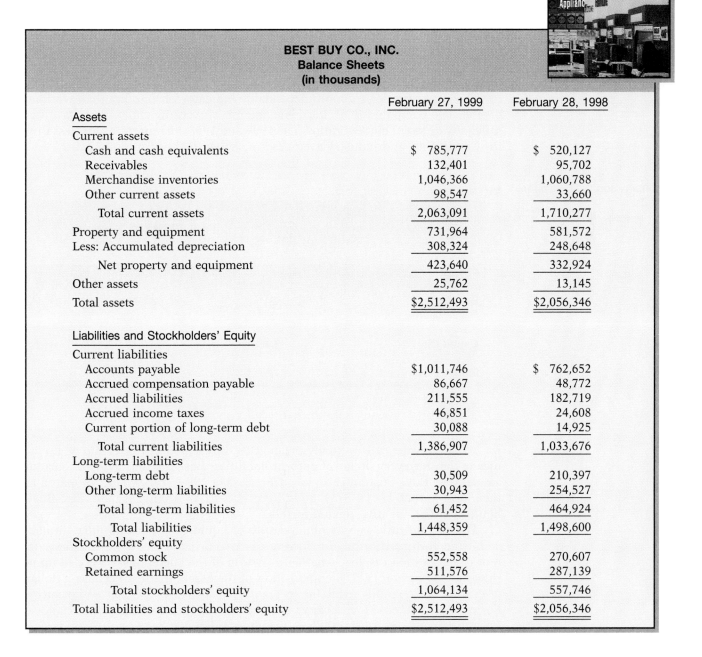

Illustration 2-16 Best Buy's balance sheet

BEST BUY CO., INC. Balance Sheets (in thousands)		
	February 27, 1999	February 28, 1998
Assets		
Current assets		
Cash and cash equivalents	$ 785,777	$ 520,127
Receivables	132,401	95,702
Merchandise inventories	1,046,366	1,060,788
Other current assets	98,547	33,660
Total current assets	2,063,091	1,710,277
Property and equipment	731,964	581,572
Less: Accumulated depreciation	308,324	248,648
Net property and equipment	423,640	332,924
Other assets	25,762	13,145
Total assets	$2,512,493	$2,056,346
Liabilities and Stockholders' Equity		
Current liabilities		
Accounts payable	$1,011,746	$ 762,652
Accrued compensation payable	86,667	48,772
Accrued liabilities	211,555	182,719
Accrued income taxes	46,851	24,608
Current portion of long-term debt	30,088	14,925
Total current liabilities	1,386,907	1,033,676
Long-term liabilities		
Long-term debt	30,509	210,397
Other long-term liabilities	30,943	254,527
Total long-term liabilities	61,452	464,924
Total liabilities	1,448,359	1,498,600
Stockholders' equity		
Common stock	552,558	270,607
Retained earnings	511,576	287,139
Total stockholders' equity	1,064,134	557,746
Total liabilities and stockholders' equity	$2,512,493	$2,056,346

Liquidity

Suppose you are a banker considering lending money to Best Buy, or you are a computer manufacturer interested in selling it computers. You would be concerned about Best Buy's liquidity—its ability to pay obligations that are expected to become due within the next year or operating cycle. You would look closely at the relationship of its current assets to current liabilities.

Working Capital.   One measure of liquidity is working capital, which is the difference between the amounts of current assets and current liabilities:

$$\text{Working capital} = \text{Current assets} - \text{Current liabilities}$$

When working capital is positive, there is greater likelihood that the company will pay its liabilities. When the reverse is true, short-term creditors may not be paid, and the company may ultimately be forced into bankruptcy. Best Buy had working capital in 1999 of $676,184,000 ($2,063,091,000 – $1,386,907,000).

Current Ratio.   Liquidity ratios measure the short-term ability of the enterprise to pay its maturing obligations and to meet unexpected needs for cash. One liquidity ratio is the current ratio, which is computed by dividing current assets by current liabilities.

The current ratio is a more dependable indicator of liquidity than working capital. Two companies with the same amount of working capital may have significantly different current ratios. The 1999 and 1998 current ratios for Best Buy, for Circuit City, and industry averages are shown in Illustration 2-17.

Illustration 2-17   Current ratio

$$\text{Current Ratio} = \frac{\text{Current Assets}}{\text{Current Liabilities}}$$

	1999	1998
Best Buy ($ in millions)	$\frac{\$2,063}{\$1,387} = 1.49:1$	$\frac{\$1,710}{\$1,034} = 1.65:1$
Circuit City	2.48:1	2.37:1
Industry average	1.87:1	2.13:1

What does the ratio actually mean? Best Buy's 1999 current ratio of 1.49:1 means that for every dollar of current liabilities, Best Buy has $1.49 of current assets. Best Buy's current ratio has decreased in 1999. Also, when compared to the industry average of 1.87:1, and Circuit City's 2.48:1 current ratio, Best Buy's liquidity should be investigated further.

The current ratio is only one measure of liquidity. It does not take into account the **composition** of the current assets. For example, a satisfactory current ratio does not disclose whether a portion of the current assets is tied up in slow-moving inventory. The composition of the assets matters because a dollar of cash is more readily available to pay the bills than is a dollar of inventory. For example, suppose a company's cash balance declined while its merchandise inventory increased substantially. If inventory increased because the company is having difficulty selling its products, then the current ratio might not fully reflect the reduction in the company's liquidity. In a later chapter you will learn additional ways to analyze a company's liquidity position.

Solvency

Now suppose that instead of being a short-term creditor, you are interested in either buying Best Buy's stock or extending the company a long-term loan. Long-term creditors and stockholders are interested in a company's long-run solvency—its ability to pay interest as it comes due and to repay the face value of the debt at maturity. Solvency ratios measure the ability of the enterprise to survive over a long period of time. The debt to total assets ratio is one source of information about long-term debt-paying ability.

Debt to Total Assets Ratio.   The debt to total assets ratio measures the percentage of assets financed by creditors rather than stockholders. Debt financing is more risky than equity financing because debt must be repaid at specific points in time, whether the company is performing well or not. Thus, the higher the percentage of debt financing, the riskier the company.

The debt to total assets ratio is computed by dividing total debt (both current and long-term liabilities) by total assets. The higher the percentage of total liabilities (debt) to total assets, the greater the risk that the company may be unable to pay its debts as they come due. The ratios of debt to total assets for Best Buy, for Circuit City, and industry averages are presented in Illustration 2-18.

Helpful Hint Some users evaluate solvency using a ratio of liabilities divided by stockholders' equity. The higher this ratio, the lower is a company's solvency.

Illustration 2-18   Debt to total assets ratio

Debt to Total Assets Ratio = $\dfrac{\text{Total Liabilities}}{\text{Total Assets}}$		
	1999	**1998**
Best Buy ($ in millions)	$\dfrac{\$1,448}{\$2,512} = 58\%$	$\dfrac{\$1,499}{\$2,056} = 73\%$
Circuit City	45%	46%
Industry average	52%	53%

The 1999 ratio of 58% means that $.58 of every dollar invested in assets by Best Buy has been provided by Best Buy's creditors. Best Buy's ratio exceeds the industry average of 52% and Circuit City's ratio of 45%. The higher the ratio, the lower the equity "buffer" available to creditors if the company becomes insolvent. Thus, from the creditors' point of view, a high ratio of debt to total assets is undesirable. Best Buy's solvency appears lower than that of Circuit City as well as the average company in the industry.

The adequacy of this ratio is often judged in the light of the company's earnings. Generally, companies with relatively stable earnings, such as public utilities, can support higher debt to total assets ratios than can cyclical companies with widely fluctuating earnings, such as many high-tech companies. In later chapters you will learn additional ways to evaluate solvency.

Investor Perspective

Debt financing differs greatly across industries and companies. Here are some debt to total assets ratios for selected companies:

	Total Debt to Total Assets as a Percent
Callaway Golf Company	19%
Roberts Pharmaceutical	23%
Advanced Micro Devices	29%
Sears, Roebuck & Company	64%
Eastman Kodak Company	83%
General Motors Corporation	93%

DECISION TOOLKIT

Decision Checkpoints	Info Needed for Decision	Tool to Use for Decision	How to Evaluate Results
Can the company meet its near-term obligations?	Current assets and current liabilities	$\text{Current ratio} = \dfrac{\text{Current assets}}{\text{Current liabilities}}$	Higher ratio suggests favorable liquidity.
Can the company meet its long-term obligations?	Total debt and total assets	$\dfrac{\text{Debt to total}}{\text{assets ratio}} = \dfrac{\text{Total liabilities}}{\text{Total assets}}$	Lower value suggests favorable solvency.

BEFORE YOU GO ON...

◆ Review It

1. What is liquidity? How can it be measured using a classified balance sheet?
2. What is solvency? How can it be measured using a classified balance sheet?

◆ Do It

Selected financial data for Drummond Company at December 31, 2001, are as follows: cash $60,000; receivables (net) $80,000; inventory $70,000; total assets $540,000; current liabilities $140,000; and total liabilities $270,000. Compute the current ratio and debt to total assets ratio.

Reasoning: The formula for the current ratio is: Current assets ÷ Current liabilities. The formula for the debt to total assets ratio is: Total liabilities ÷ Total assets.

Solution: The current ratio is 1.5:1 ($210,000 ÷ $140,000). The debt to total assets ratio is 50% ($270,000 ÷ $540,000).

STUDY OBJECTIVE

8

Identify and compute ratios for analyzing a company's liquidity and solvency using a statement of cash flows.

USING THE STATEMENT OF CASH FLOWS

As you learned in Chapter 1, the statement of cash flows provides financial information about the sources and uses of a company's cash. Investors, creditors, and others want to know what is happening to a company's most liquid resource—its cash. In fact, it is often said that "cash is king" because if a company can't generate cash, it won't survive. To aid in the analysis of cash, the statement of cash flows reports the cash effects of (1) a company's **operating activities**, (2) its **investing activities**, and (3) its **financing activities**.

Sources of cash matter. For example, you would feel much better about a company's health if you knew that its cash was generated from the operations of the business rather than borrowed. A cash flow statement provides this information. Similarly, net income does not tell you *how much* cash the firm generated from operations. The statement of cash flows can tell you that. In summary, neither the income statement nor the balance sheet can directly answer most of the important questions about cash, but the statement of cash flows does. A simplified statement of cash flows for Best Buy is provided in Illustration 2-19.

BEST BUY CO., INC. **Statement of Cash Flows** **(in thousands)**		
	For fiscal year ending	
	February 27, 1999	February 28, 1998
Cash flows provided by operating activities		
Cash receipts from operating activities	$10,041,207	$8,342,091
Cash payments for operating activities	9,378,776	7,891,648
Net cash provided (used) by operations	662,431	450,443
Cash flows provided by investing activities		
(Increase) decrease in property and plant	(165,698)	(72,063)
Other cash inflow (outflow)	(83,869)	49,764
Net cash provided (used) by investing	(249,567)	(22,299)
Cash flows provided by financing activities		
Issue of equity securities	18,182	14,869
Increase (decrease) in borrowing	(165,396)	(12,694)
Dividends, other distributions	0	0
Net cash provided (used) by financing	(147,214)	2,175
Net increase/(decrease) in cash or equivalents	265,650	430,319
Cash or equivalents at start of year	520,127	89,808
Cash or equivalents at year-end	$ 785,777	$ 520,127

Illustration 2-19
Best Buy's statement of cash flows

Different users have different reasons for being interested in the statement of cash flows. If you were a creditor of Best Buy (either short term or long term), you would be interested to know the source of its cash in recent years. This information would give you some indication of where it might get cash to pay you. If you have a long-term interest in Best Buy as a stockholder, you would look to the statement of cash flows for information regarding the company's ability to generate cash over the long run to meet its cash needs for growth.

Companies get cash from two sources: operating activities and financing activities. In the early years of a company's life it typically won't generate enough cash from operating activities to meet its investing needs, and so it will have to issue stock or borrow money. An established firm, however, will often be able to meet most of its cash needs with cash from operations. Best Buy's cash provided by operating activities in the previous three years was sufficient to meet its investing needs. For example, in 1999 cash provided by operating activities was $662,431,000, whereas cash spent on property, plant, and equipment was $165,658,000. However, as recently as 1997 its cash provided by operations was less than its purchases of property, plant, and equipment. In order to finance its investing activities, in 1997 Best Buy had to supplement its internally generated cash with cash from outside sources, by issuing new stock and by borrowing.

Earlier we introduced you to measures of liquidity and solvency. The statement of cash flows can also be used to calculate additional measures of liquidity and solvency. The **current cash debt coverage ratio** is a measure of liquidity that is calculated as cash provided by operating activities divided by average current liabilities. It indicates the company's ability to generate sufficient cash to meet its short-term needs. In general, a value below .40 times is considered cause for additional investigation of a company's liquidity.

The **cash debt coverage ratio** is a measure of solvency that is calculated as cash provided by operating activities divided by average total liabilities. It indicates the company's ability to generate sufficient cash to meet its long-term needs. Illustration 2-20 presents each of these measures for Best Buy and Circuit City. Industry measures are not available for these ratios. A general rule of thumb is that a ratio below .20 times is considered cause for additional investigation.

Illustration 2-20 Current cash debt coverage ratio and cash debt coverage ratio

Current Cash Debt Coverage Ratio = $\dfrac{\text{Cash Provided by Operations}}{\text{Average Current Liabilities}}$		
	1999	**1998**
Best Buy ($ in millions)	$\dfrac{\$662}{(\$1,387 + \$1,034)/2^*} = .55$ times	$\dfrac{\$450}{(\$1,034 + \$818)/2^*} = .49$ times
Circuit City	.27 times	.22 times

Cash Debt Coverage Ratio = $\dfrac{\text{Cash Provided by Operations}}{\text{Average Total Liabilities}}$		
	1999	**1998**
Best Buy ($ in millions)	$\dfrac{\$662}{(\$1,448 + \$1,499)/2^*} = .45$ times	$\dfrac{\$450}{(\$1,499 + \$1,296)/2^*} = .32$ times
Circuit City	.17 times	.13 times

*Amounts used to calculate average current liabilities and average total liabilities are taken from Best Buy's balance sheet (Illustration 2-16). Current liabilities at year-end 1997 were $818 million, and total liabilities at year-end 1997 were $1,066 million. Also note that amounts in the ratio calculations have been rounded.

We can use these measures to supplement our earlier measures to evaluate Best Buy's liquidity and solvency. Best Buy's current cash debt coverage ratio of .55 exceeds the recommended minimum level of .40, suggesting that its liquidity is adequate. On the other hand, Circuit City's value of .27 is less than the recommended level. Recall, however, that Circuit City's current ratio was quite high. The conflicting results of these two measures suggest that further evaluation of Circuit City's liquidity is warranted. For example, it is possible that Circuit City's current ratio was so high because it had accumulated obsolete inventory. This would result in a high current ratio, even though the inventory clearly was not very liquid.

Best Buy's cash debt coverage ratio of .45 is well in excess of the recommended minimum level of .2, suggesting that its solvency is also acceptable. Again, Circuit City's value falls short of the recommended level, leaving its solvency in doubt. We will investigate other measures of liquidity and solvency in later chapters.

DECISION TOOLKIT

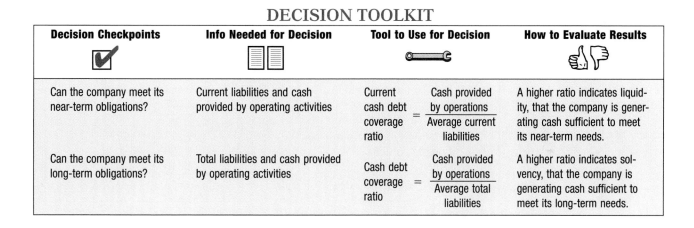

Decision Checkpoints	Info Needed for Decision	Tool to Use for Decision	How to Evaluate Results
Can the company meet its near-term obligations?	Current liabilities and cash provided by operating activities	$\text{Current cash debt coverage ratio} = \dfrac{\text{Cash provided by operations}}{\text{Average current liabilities}}$	A higher ratio indicates liquidity, that the company is generating cash sufficient to meet its near-term needs.
Can the company meet its long-term obligations?	Total liabilities and cash provided by operating activities	$\text{Cash debt coverage ratio} = \dfrac{\text{Cash provided by operations}}{\text{Average total liabilities}}$	A higher ratio indicates solvency, that the company is generating cash sufficient to meet its long-term needs.

BEFORE YOU GO ON...

◆ **Review It**

1. What information does the statement of cash flows provide that is not available in an income statement or a balance sheet?
2. What does the current cash debt coverage ratio measure? What does the cash debt coverage ratio measure?

*U*SING THE DECISION TOOLKIT

In the opening story we noted that Best Buy's stock price increased dramatically during 1998 and 1999. Tweeter Home Entertainment sells consumer electronic products from 52 stores on the East Coast. Its stock price also increased substantially during 1998 and 1999, going from a low of $10 per share to a high of over $40 per share. Was this increase justified? Let's look for ourselves: A simplified balance sheet and income statement for Tweeter Home Entertainment are presented in Illustrations 2-21 and 2-22.

Illustration 2-21
Tweeter Home Entertainment's balance sheet

TWEETER HOME ENTERTAINMENT GROUP Balance Sheets (in thousands)		
	September 30	
	1998	1997
Assets		
Current assets		
Cash and cash equivalents	$ 777	$ 1,157
Receivables	6,208	5,473
Inventories	38,362	31,160
Other current assets	2,189	2,043
Total current assets	47,536	39,833
Property, plant, and equipment, net	23,978	17,968
Other assets	20,129	20,887
Total assets	$91,643	$78,688
Liabilities and Stockholders' Equity		
Current liabilities		
Notes payable	$ 4,071	$ 4,949
Accounts payable	10,663	11,457
Accrued expenses	12,007	8,393
Other current liabilities	2,532	3,163
Total current liabilities	29,273	27,962
Long-term debt	5,250	30,888
Other liabilities	5,510	4,916
Total liabilities	40,033	63,766
Stockholders' equity	51,610	14,922
Total liabilities and stockholders' equity	$91,643	$78,688

Illustration 2-22
Tweeter Home Entertainment's income statement

TWEETER HOME ENTERTAINMENT GROUP Income Statements (in thousands)		
	Years ended September 30	
	1998	1997
Sales	$232,289	$132,525
Cost of sales	151,265	86,315
Operating expenses	68,952	44,157
Interest expense	2,753	1,808
Other expense	340	—
Income tax expense	3,724	99
Total expenses	227,034	132,379
Net income	$ 5,255	$ 146

Additional information: Tweeter's cash provided by operating activities was $4,429,000 in 1998 and negative $6,243 in 1997.

Instructions

Using these statements, answer the following questions:

1. Calculate the current ratio for Tweeter for 1998 and 1997 and the current cash debt coverage ratio for 1998, and discuss its liquidity position.
2. Calculate the debt to total assets ratio for Tweeter for 1998 and 1997 and the cash debt coverage ratio for 1998, and discuss its solvency.
3. Calculate the profit margin ratio and return on assets ratio for Tweeter for 1998, and discuss its profitability relative to Best Buy.
4. Best Buy's accounting year-end was February 27, 1999, whereas Tweeter's was September 30, 1998. How does the difference affect your ability to compare their profitability?

Solution

1. Current ratio:

    1998 ($47,536/$29,273) = 1.62   1997 ($39,833/$27,962) = 1.42

    Tweeter's liquidity improved from 1997 to 1998. In 1997 there was $1.42 of current assets available for every dollar of current liabilities. In 1998 there was $1.62. Tweeter's current ratio would be considered acceptable, but not strong. It is higher than that of Best Buy, but it is a much smaller company than Best Buy. Often, larger companies can get by with a lower current ratio.

    Current cash debt coverage ratio:

    $$1998 \quad \frac{\$4,429}{(\$29,273 + \$27,962)/2} = .15 \text{ times}$$

    A value above .40 times for this ratio is generally considered acceptable. This low measure, combined with Tweeter's marginal current ratio, might cause a creditor to investigate the company's liquidity further.

2. Debt to total assets ratio:

    1998 ($40,033/$91,643) = 44%   1997 ($63,766/$78,688) = 81%

    Based on the change in its ratio of debt to total assets, Tweeter's reliance on debt financing declined considerably from 1997 to 1998. The improvement in the value of this ratio suggests the company's solvency improved.

    Cash debt coverage ratio:

    $$1998 \quad \frac{\$4,429}{(\$40,033 + \$63,766)/2} = .085 \text{ times}$$

    Tweeter's value of .085 times is considerably lower than the generally acceptable level of .20 times. This would suggest that the company's solvency should be evaluated further.

3. Profit margin ratio: 1998 ($5,255/$232,289) = 2.3%

    $$\text{Return on assets:} \quad 1998 \; \frac{\$5,255}{(\$91,643 + \$78,688)/2} = 6.2\%$$

    Best Buy's profit margin ratio is 2.2% versus 2.3% for Tweeter. This means that on every dollar of sales, Best Buy generates 2.2 cents of net income while Tweeter generates 2.3 cents. Best Buy's return on assets ratio is 9.8%

versus 6.2% for Tweeter. This means that Best Buy generates 9.8 cents of net income for every dollar invested in assets, while Tweeter generates only 6.2 cents.

4. Best Buy's income statement covers five months not covered by Tweeter's. Suppose that the economy changed dramatically during this five-month period, either improving or declining. This change in the economy would be reflected in Best Buy's income statement but would not be reflected in Tweeter's income statement until the following September, thus reducing the usefulness of a comparison of the income statements of the two companies.

SUMMARY OF STUDY OBJECTIVES

1 *Explain the meaning of generally accepted accounting principles and describe the basic objective of financial reporting.* Generally accepted accounting principles are a set of rules and practices recognized as a general guide for financial reporting purposes. The basic objective of financial reporting is to provide information that is useful for decision making.

2 *Discuss the qualitative characteristics of accounting information.* To be judged useful, information should possess these qualitative characteristics: relevance, reliability, comparability, and consistency.

3 *Identify two constraints in accounting.* The major constraints are materiality and conservatism.

4 *Identify the sections of a classified balance sheet.* In a classified balance sheet, assets are classified as current assets; long-term investments; property, plant, and equipment; or intangibles. Liabilities are classified as either current or long-term. There is also a stockholders' equity section, which shows common stock and retained earnings.

5 *Identify and compute ratios for analyzing a company's profitability.* Profitability ratios, such as profit margin and return on assets, measure different aspects of the operating success of a company for a given period of time.

6 *Explain the relationship between a retained earnings statement and a statement of stockholders' equity.* The retained earnings statement presents the factors that changed the retained earnings balance during the period. A statement of stockholders' equity presents the factors that changed stockholders' equity during the period, including those that changed retained earnings. Thus, a statement of stockholders' equity is more inclusive.

7 *Identify and compute ratios for analyzing a company's liquidity and solvency using a balance sheet.* Liquidity ratios, such as the current ratio, measure the short-term ability of a company to pay its maturing obligations and to meet unexpected needs for cash. Solvency ratios, such as the debt to total assets ratio, measure the ability of an enterprise to survive over a long period.

8 *Identify and compute ratios for analyzing a company's liquidity and solvency using a statement of cash flows.* The current cash debt coverage ratio measures a company's liquidity. The cash debt coverage ratio measures a company's solvency.

DECISION TOOLKIT—A SUMMARY

Decision Checkpoints	Info Needed for Decision	Tool to Use for Decision	How to Evaluate Results
Is the company using its assets effectively?	Net income and average assets	$\text{Return on assets ratio} = \dfrac{\text{Net income}}{\text{Average total assets}}$	Higher value suggests favorable efficiency (use of assets).
Is the company maintaining an adequate margin between sales and expenses?	Net income and net sales	$\text{Profit margin ratio} = \dfrac{\text{Net income}}{\text{Net sales}}$	Higher value suggests favorable return on each dollar of sales.
Can the company meet its near-term obligations?	Current assets and current liabilities	$\text{Current ratio} = \dfrac{\text{Current assets}}{\text{Current liabilities}}$	Higher ratio suggests favorable liquidity.
Can the company meet its long-term obligations?	Total debt and total assets	$\text{Debt to total assets ratio} = \dfrac{\text{Total liabilities}}{\text{Total assets}}$	Lower value suggests favorable solvency.
Can the company meet its near-term obligations?	Current liabilities and cash provided by operating activities	$\text{Current cash debt coverage ratio} = \dfrac{\text{Cash provided by operations}}{\text{Average current liabilities}}$	A higher ratio indicates liquidity, that the company is generating cash sufficient to meet its near-term needs.
Can the company meet its long-term obligations?	Total liabilities and cash provided by operating activities	$\text{Cash debt coverage ratio} = \dfrac{\text{Cash provided by operations}}{\text{Average total liabilities}}$	A higher ratio indicates solvency, that the company is generating cash sufficient to meet its long-term needs.

GLOSSARY

Cash debt coverage ratio A measure of solvency that is calculated as cash provided by operating activities divided by average total liabilities. (p. 68)

Classified balance sheet A balance sheet that contains a number of standard classifications or sections. (p. 52)

Comparability Ability to compare the accounting information of different companies because they use the same accounting principles. (p. 49)

Conservatism The approach of choosing an accounting method, when in doubt, that will least likely overstate assets and net income. (p. 51)

Consistency Use of the same accounting principles and methods from year to year within a company. (p. 50)

Current assets Cash and other resources that are reasonably expected to be converted to cash or used in the business within one year or the operating cycle, whichever is longer. (p. 53)

Current cash debt coverage ratio A measure of liquidity that is calculated as cash provided by operating activities divided by average current liabilities. (p. 68)

Current liabilities Obligations reasonably expected to be paid within the next year or operating cycle, whichever is longer. (p. 56)

Current ratio A measure used to evaluate a company's liquidity and short-term debt-paying ability, computed by dividing current assets by current liabilities. (p. 64)

Debt to total assets ratio Measures the percentage of total financing provided by creditors; computed by dividing total debt by total assets. (p. 65)

Financial Accounting Standards Board (FASB) A private organization that establishes generally accepted accounting principles. (p. 49)

Generally accepted accounting principles (GAAP) A set of rules and practices, having substantial authoritative support, that are recognized as a general guide for financial reporting purposes. (p. 49)

Intangible assets Noncurrent assets that do not have physical substance. (p. 55)

Liquidity The ability of a company to pay obligations that are expected to become due within the next year or operating cycle. (p. 64)

Liquidity ratios Measures of the short-term ability of the enterprise to pay its maturing obligations and to meet unexpected needs for cash. (p. 64)

Long-term investments Generally, investments in stocks and bonds of other companies that are normally held for many years. (p. 54)

Long-term liabilities (Long-term debt) Obligations not expected to be paid within one year or the operating cycle. (p. 56)

Materiality The constraint of determining whether an item is large enough to likely influence the decision of an investor or creditor. (p. 51)

Operating cycle The average time required to go from cash to cash in producing revenues. (p. 54)

Profit margin ratio Measures the percentage of each dollar of sales that results in net income, computed by dividing net income by net sales. (p. 60)

Profitability ratios Measures of the income or operating success of an enterprise for a given period of time. (p. 59)

Property, plant, and equipment Assets of a relatively permanent nature that are being used in the business and are not intended for resale. (p. 55)

Ratio An expression of the mathematical relationship between one quantity and another; may be expressed as a percentage, a rate, or a proportion. (p. 58)

Ratio analysis A technique for evaluating financial statements that expresses the relationship among selected financial statement data. (p. 58)

Relevance The quality of information that indicates the information makes a difference in a decision. (p. 49)

Reliability The quality of information that gives assurance that it is free of error and bias. (p. 49)

Return on assets ratio An overall measure of profitability; computed by dividing net income by average assets. (p. 59)

Securities and Exchange Commission (SEC) The agency of the U.S. government that oversees U.S. financial markets and accounting standards-setting bodies. (p. 49)

Solvency The ability of a company to pay interest as it comes due and to repay the face value of debt at maturity. (p. 65)

Solvency ratios Measures of the ability of the enterprise to survive over a long period of time. (p. 65)

Statement of stockholders' equity A financial statement that presents the factors that caused stockholders' equity to change during the period, including those that caused retained earnings to change. (p. 61)

Working capital The difference between the amounts of current assets and current liabilities. (p. 64)

DEMONSTRATION PROBLEM

Listed here are items taken from the income statement and balance sheet of Circuit City Corporation for the year ended February 28, 1999. Certain items have been combined for simplification.

Long-term debt, excluding current installments	$ 426,585
Cash and cash equivalents	265,880
Selling, general, and administrative expenses	2,186,177
Common stock	637,654
Accounts payable	799,733
Prepaid expenses and other current assets	36,644
Property and equipment, net	1,005,773
Cost of goods sold	8,359,428
Current portion of long-term debt	2,707
Income taxes payable	9,764
Interest expense	28,319
Deferred revenue and other long-term liabilities	149,746
Retained earnings	1,267,476
Merchandise inventory	1,517,675
Net sales and operating revenues	10,804,447
Accounts and notes receivable, net	574,316
Income tax expense	87,599
Other assets	44,978
Accrued expenses and other current liabilities	143,585
Notes payable	8,016

Instructions

Prepare an income statement and a classified balance sheet using the items listed. No item should be used more than once.

Solution to Demonstration Problem

CIRCUIT CITY®
Price • Selection • Service

CIRCUIT CITY CORPORATION
Income Statement
For the Year Ended February 28, 1999
(in thousands)

Net sales and operating revenues		$10,804,447
Cost of goods sold	$8,359,428	
Selling, general, and administrative expenses	2,186,177	
Interest expense	28,319	
Income tax expense	87,599	
Total expenses		10,661,523
Net income		$ 142,924

CIRCUIT CITY CORPORATION
Balance Sheet
February 28, 1999
(in thousands)

Assets

Current assets		
Cash and cash equivalents	$ 265,880	
Accounts and notes receivable, net	574,316	
Merchandise inventory	1,517,675	
Prepaid expenses and other current assets	36,644	
Total current assets		$2,394,515
Property and equipment, net		1,005,773
Other assets		44,978
Total assets		$3,445,266

Liabilities and Stockholders' Equity

Current liabilities		
Notes payable	$ 8,016	
Current portion of long-term debt	2,707	
Accounts payable	799,733	
Accrued expenses and other current liabilities	143,585	
Income taxes payable	9,764	
Total current liabilities		$ 963,805
Long-term liabilities		
Long-term debt, excluding current installments	426,585	
Deferred revenue and other long-term liabilities	149,746	
Total liabilities		1,540,136
Stockholders' equity		
Common stock	637,654	
Retained earnings	1,267,476	
Total stockholders' equity		1,905,130
Total liabilities and stockholders' equity		$3,445,266

SELF-STUDY QUESTIONS

Answers are at the end of the chapter.

(SO 1)   1. Generally accepted accounting principles are:
   (a) a set of standards and rules that are recognized as a general guide for financial reporting.
   (b) usually established by the Internal Revenue Service.
   (c) the guidelines used to resolve ethical dilemmas.
   (d) fundamental truths that can be derived from the laws of nature.

(SO 1)   2. What organization issues U.S. accounting standards?
   (a) Financial Accounting Standards Board.
   (b) International Accounting Standards Committee.
   (c) International Auditing Standards Committee.
   (d) None of the above.

(SO 2)   3. What is the primary criterion by which accounting information can be judged?
   (a) Consistency.
   (b) Predictive value.
   (c) Usefulness for decision making.
   (d) Comparability.

(SO 2)   4. Verifiability is an ingredient of:

	Reliability	Relevance
(a)	Yes	Yes
(b)	No	No
(c)	Yes	No
(d)	No	Yes

(SO 3)   5. What accounting constraint refers to the tendency of accountants to resolve uncertainty in a way least likely to overstate assets and revenues?
   (a) Comparability.   (c) Conservatism.
   (b) Materiality.   (d) Consistency.

(SO 4)   6. In a classified balance sheet, assets are usually classified as:

   (a) current assets; long-term assets; property, plant, and equipment; and intangible assets.
   (b) current assets; long-term investments; property, plant, and equipment; and common stock.
   (c) current assets; long-term investments; tangible assets; and intangible assets.
   (d) current assets; long-term investments; property, plant, and equipment; and intangible assets.

(SO 4)   7. Current assets are listed:
   (a) by liquidity.
   (b) by importance.
   (c) by longevity.
   (d) alphabetically.

(SO 5)   8. Which is *not* an indicator of profitability?
   (a) Current ratio.
   (b) Profit margin ratio.
   (c) Net income.
   (d) Return on assets ratio.

(SO 5)   9. For 2001 Plano Corporation reported net income $24,000; net sales $400,000; and average assets $600,000. What was the 2001 profit margin ratio?
   (a) 6%   (c) 40%
   (b) 12%   (d) 200%

(SO 6)   10. The balance in retained earnings is not affected by:
   (a) net income.
   (b) net loss.
   (c) issuance of common stock.
   (d) dividends.

(SO 7)   11. Which of these measures is an evaluation of a company's ability to pay current liabilities?
   (a) Profit margin ratio.
   (b) Current ratio.
   (c) Both (a) and (b).
   (d) None of the above.

QUESTIONS

1. (a) What are generally accepted accounting principles (GAAP)?
   (b) What body provides authoritative support for GAAP?
2. (a) What is the basic objective of financial reporting?
   (b) Identify the qualitative characteristics of accounting information.
3. Ray Aldag, the president of Raynard Company, is pleased. Raynard substantially increased its net in-

come in 2001 while keeping its unit inventory relatively the same. Tom Erhardt, chief accountant, cautions Aldag, however. Erhardt says that since Raynard changed its method of inventory valuation, there is a consistency problem and it is difficult to determine whether Raynard is better off. Is Erhardt correct? Why or why not?
4. What is the distinction between comparability and consistency?

5. Describe the two constraints inherent in the presentation of accounting information.

6. Your roommate believes that international accounting standards are uniform throughout the world. Is your roommate correct? Explain.

7. What is meant by the term *operating cycle?*

8. Define current assets. What basis is used for ordering individual items within the current assets section?

9. Distinguish between long-term investments and property, plant, and equipment.

10. How do current liabilities differ from long-term liabilities?

11. Identify the two parts of stockholders' equity in a corporation and indicate the purpose of each.

12. ⊙━━C
(a) Tia Kim believes that the analysis of financial statements is directed at two characteristics of a company: liquidity and profitability. Is Tia correct? Explain.
(b) Are short-term creditors, long-term creditors, and stockholders primarily interested in the same characteristics of a company? Explain.

13. ⊙━━C Name ratios useful in assessing (a) liquidity, (b) solvency, and (c) profitability.

14. ⊙━━C Tony Robins is puzzled. His company had a profit margin ratio of 10% in 2001. He feels that this is an indication that the company is doing well. Joan Graham, his accountant, says that more information is needed to determine the firm's financial well-being. Who is correct? Why?

15. ⊙━━C What do these classes of ratios measure?
(a) Liquidity ratios.
(b) Profitability ratios.
(c) Solvency ratios.

16. ⊙━━C Holding all other factors constant, indicate whether each of the following signals generally good or bad news about a company.
(a) Increase in the profit margin ratio.
(b) Increase in the current ratio.
(c) Increase in the debt to total assets ratio.
(d) Decrease in the return on assets ratio.

17. ⊙━━C Which ratio or ratios from this chapter do you think should be of greatest interest to:
(a) a pension fund considering investing in a corporation's 20-year bonds?
(b) a bank contemplating a short-term loan?
(c) an investor in common stock?

BRIEF EXERCISES

BE2-1 Indicate whether each statement is *true* or *false*.

(a) GAAP is a set of rules and practices established by the accounting profession to serve as a general guide for financial reporting purposes.
(b) Substantial authoritative support for GAAP usually comes from two standards-setting bodies: the FASB and the IRS.

Recognize generally accepted accounting principles.
(SO 1)

BE2-2 The accompanying chart shows the qualitative characteristics of accounting information. Fill in the blanks.

Identify qualitative characteristics.
(SO 2)

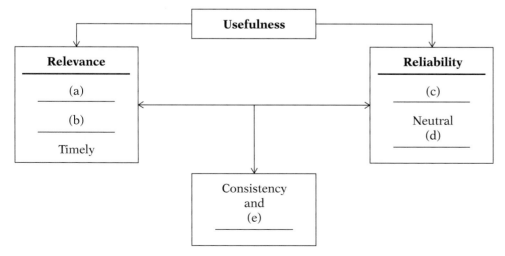

Identify qualitative characteristics.
(SO 2)

BE2-3 Given the *qualitative characteristics* of accounting established by the FASB's conceptual framework, complete each of the following statements.
(a) For information to be _____, it should have predictive or feedback value, and it must be presented on a timely basis.
(b) _____ is the quality of information that gives assurance that it is free of error and bias; it can be depended on.
(c) _____ means using the same accounting principles and methods from year to year within a company.

Identify qualitative characteristics.
(SO 2)

BE2-4 Here are some qualitative characteristics of accounting information:
1. Predictive value   3. Verifiable
2. Neutral   4. Timely

Match each qualitative characteristic to one of the following statements.
_____ (a) Accounting information should help users make predictions about the outcome of past, present, and future events.
_____ (b) Accounting information cannot be selected, prepared, or presented to favor one set of interested users over another.
_____ (c) Accounting information must be proved to be free of error and bias.
_____ (d) Accounting information must be available to decision makers before it loses its capacity to influence their decisions.

Identify constraints that have been violated.
(SO 3)

BE2-5 The Emelda Company uses these accounting practices:
(a) Inventory is reported at cost when market value is lower.
(b) Small tools are recorded as plant assets and depreciated.
(c) The income statement shows paper clips expense of $10.

Indicate the accounting constraint, if any, that has been violated by each practice.

Prepare the current assets section of a balance sheet.
(SO 4)

BE2-6 A list of financial statement items for Swann Company includes the following: accounts receivable $16,500; prepaid insurance $3,600; cash $18,400; supplies $5,200; and short-term investments $8,200. Prepare the current asset section of the balance sheet listing the items in the proper sequence.

Compute return on assets ratio and profit margin ratio.
(SO 5)

BE2-7 The following information (in thousands of dollars) is available for **The Limited** for 1998: Sales revenue $9,346,911; cost of goods sold $6,348,945; net income $2,053,646; total stockholders' equity $2,233,303; average total assets $4,425,235. Compute the return on assets ratio and profit margin ratio for The Limited for 1998.

Identify items affecting stockholders' equity.
(SO 6)

BE2-8 For each of the following events affecting the stockholders' equity of Seek Corporation, indicate whether the event would: increase retained earnings (IRE), decrease retained earnings (DRE), increase common stock (ICS), or decrease common stock (DCS).
_____ (a) Issued new shares of common stock.
_____ (b) Paid a cash dividend.
_____ (c) Reported net income of $75,000.
_____ (d) Repurchased its own shares of stock.

Calculate liquidity ratios.
(SO 7)

BE2-9 These selected condensed data are taken from a recent balance sheet of **Bob Evans Farms**:

Cash	$ 8,241,000
Short-term investments	1,947,000
Accounts receivable	12,545,000
Inventories	14,814,000
Other current assets	5,371,000
Total current assets	$42,918,000
Total current liabilities	$44,844,000

Additional information: Current liabilities at the beginning of the year were $38,242,000, and cash provided by operations for the current year was $58,297,200.

What are (a) the working capital, (b) the current ratio, and (c) the current cash debt coverage ratio?

EXERCISES

E2-1 The following items were taken from the December 31, 1998, assets section of the **Boeing Company** balance sheet. (All dollars are in millions.)

Classify items as current or noncurrent, and prepare assets section of balance sheet.
(SO 4)

Inventories	$ 8,349	Goodwill	$ 2,312
Notes receivable—due after		Other current assets	1,495
December 31, 1999	4,930	Property, plant, and	
Short-term investments	279	equipment	20,241
Notes receivable—due before		Cash and cash equivalents	2,183
December 31, 1999	781	Accounts receivable	3,288
Accumulated depreciation	11,652	Other noncurrent assets	4,466

Instructions
Prepare the assets section of a classified balance sheet, listing the current assets in order of their liquidity.

E2-2 These items are taken from the financial statements of Lumpy Lane Bowling Alley at December 31, 2001:

Prepare a classified balance sheet.
(SO 4)

Building	$105,800
Accounts receivable	14,520
Prepaid insurance	4,680
Cash	20,840
Equipment	82,400
Land	61,200
Insurance expense	780
Depreciation expense	5,360
Interest expense	2,600
Common stock	66,000
Retained earnings (January 1, 2001)	40,000
Accumulated depreciation—building	45,600
Accounts payable	12,480
Mortgage payable	93,600
Accumulated depreciation—equipment	18,720
Interest payable	3,600
Bowling revenues	18,180

Instructions
Prepare a classified balance sheet; assume that $13,600 of the mortgage payable will be paid in 2002.

E2-3 The following items were taken from the 1998 financial statements of **Texas Instruments**. (All dollars are in millions.)

Prepare a classified balance sheet.
(SO 4)

Long-term debt	$1,027	Loans payable in 1999	$ 267
Common stock	1,436	Cash	540
Prepaid expenses	75	Accumulated depreciation	3,006
Property, plant, and equipment	6,379	Accounts payable	1,582
Income taxes payable	193	Other noncurrent assets	467
Other current assets	583	Other noncurrent liabilities	1,500
Other current liabilities	154	Retained earnings	5,091
Long-term investments	2,564	Accounts receivable	1,343
Short-term investments	1,709	Inventories	596

Instructions
Prepare a classified balance sheet in good form as of December 31, 1998.

Prepare financial statements.
(SO 4, 6)

E2-4   These financial statement items are for Stasik Corporation at year-end, July 31, 2001:

Salaries expense	$54,700
Utilities expense	24,900
Equipment	15,900
Accounts payable	6,220
Commission revenue	61,100
Rent revenue	8,500
Unearned rent revenue	1,800
Common stock	16,000
Cash	21,940
Accounts receivable	8,780
Accumulated depreciation	5,400
Dividends	4,000
Depreciation expense	4,000
Retained earnings (beginning of the year)	35,200

Instructions
(a) Prepare an income statement and a retained earnings statement for the year. Stasik Corporation did not issue any new stock during the year.
(b) Prepare a classified balance sheet at July 31.

Compute profitability ratios.
(SO 5)

E2-5   Selected comparative statement data for Mediocre Products Company are presented here. All balance sheet data are as of December 31.

	2001	2000
Net sales	$900,000	$820,000
Cost of goods sold	480,000	400,000
Interest expense	7,000	5,000
Net income	61,000	48,000
Accounts receivable	120,000	100,000
Inventory	190,000	180,000
Total assets	800,000	500,000
Total common stockholders' equity	450,000	310,000

Instructions
(a) What is the profit margin ratio for 2001?
(b) Calculate the return on assets ratio for 2001.

Compute liquidity ratios and compare results.
(SO 7)

E2-6   **Nordstrom, Inc.,** operates department stores in numerous states. Selected financial statement data (in millions of dollars) for the year ended January 31, 1999, are as follows:

	End of Year	Beginning of Year
Cash and cash equivalents	$ 241	$ 25
Receivables (net)	587	664
Merchandise inventory	750	827
Other current assets	102	95
Total current assets	$1,680	$1,611
Total current liabilities	$ 769	$ 943

For the year, net sales were $5,028,000 and cost of goods sold was $3,345,000.

Instructions
(a) Compute the working capital and current ratio at the beginning of the year and at the end of the current year.
(b) Did Nordstrom's liquidity improve or worsen during the year?
(c) Using the data in the chapter, compare Nordstrom's liquidity with **Best Buy's**.

Compute and interpret solvency ratios.
(SO 7, 8)

E2-7   The following data were taken from the 1997 and 1998 financial statements of **Amazon.com.** (All dollars in thousands.)

	1998	**1997**
Current assets	$424,254	$137,709
Total assets	648,460	149,844
Current liabilities	161,575	44,551
Total liabilities	509,715	121,253
Total stockholders' equity	138,745	28,591
Cash provided by operating activities	31,035	687
Cash used in investing activities	261,777	125,677

Instructions

Perform each of the following:

(a) Calculate the debt to assets ratio for each year.

(b) Calculate the cash debt coverage ratio for each year. (Total liabilities at year-end 1996 were $4,870,000.)

(c) Discuss Amazon.com's solvency in 1998 versus 1997.

(d) Discuss Amazon.com's ability to finance its investment activities with cash provided by operating activities, and how any deficiency would be met.

PROBLEMS: SET A

P2-1A The following items are taken from the 1998 balance sheet of **Yahoo, Inc.** (in thousands).

Prepare a classified balance sheet.
(SO 4)

Common stock	$523,020
Property and equipment, net	15,189
Accounts payable	6,302
Other assets	49,190
Long-term investments	90,266
Accounts receivable	24,831
Prepaid expenses and other current assets	8,909
Short-term investments	308,025
Retained earnings	13,190
Cash and cash equivalents	125,474
Long-term liabilities	5,691
Accrued expenses and other current liabilities	35,380
Unearned revenue—current	38,301

Instructions

Prepare a balance sheet for Yahoo! Inc. as of December 31, 1998.

P2-2A These items are taken from the financial statements of Kidman Corporation for 2001:

Prepare financial statements.
(SO 4, 6)

Retained earnings (beginning of year)	$26,000
Utilities expense	1,700
Equipment	66,000
Accounts payable	13,300
Cash	13,600
Salaries payable	3,000
Common stock	13,000
Dividends	12,000
Service revenue	76,000
Prepaid insurance	3,500
Repair expense	1,800
Depreciation expense	2,600
Accounts receivable	13,500
Insurance expense	2,200
Salaries expense	35,000
Accumulated depreciation	20,600

Instructions

Prepare an income statement, a retained earnings statement, and a classified balance sheet for December 31, 2001.

Compute ratios; comment on relative profitability, liquidity, and solvency.
(SO 5, 7, 8)

P2-3A Comparative financial statement data for Fisher Corporation and Gisco Corporation, two competitors, appear below. All balance sheet data are as of December 31, 2001, and December 31, 2000.

	Fisher Corporation		Gisco Corporation	
	2001	**2000**	**2001**	**2000**
Net sales	$1,949,035		$539,038	
Cost of goods sold	1,280,490		338,006	
Operating expenses	302,275		79,000	
Interest expense	6,800		1,252	
Income tax expense	47,840		7,740	
Current assets	425,975	$412,410	190,336	$160,467
Plant assets (net)	521,310	500,000	139,728	125,812
Current liabilities	66,325	75,815	35,348	30,281
Long-term liabilities	108,500	90,000	29,620	25,000

Additional information: Cash provided by operations for 2001 was $162,594 for Fisher and $24,211 for Gisco.

Instructions

(a) Comment on the relative profitability of the companies by computing the return on assets ratios and the profit margin ratios for both companies.

(b) Comment on the relative liquidity of the companies by computing working capital, the current ratios, and the current cash debt coverage ratios for both companies.

(c) Comment on the relative solvency of the companies by computing the debt to total assets ratio and the cash debt coverage ratio for each.

Compute liquidity, solvency, and profitability ratios.
(SO 5, 7, 8)

P2-4A Here are the comparative statements of Eric Clapton Company:

ERIC CLAPTON COMPANY
Income Statement
For the Years Ended December 31

	2001	2000
Net sales	$2,218,500	$2,100,500
Cost of goods sold	1,005,500	996,000
Selling and administrative expense	906,000	879,000
Interest expense	98,000	79,000
Income tax expense	86,700	77,000
Net income	$ 122,300	$ 69,500

ERIC CLAPTON COMPANY
Balance Sheet
December 31

	2001	2000
Assets		
Current assets		
Cash	$ 60,100	$ 64,200
Short-term investments	54,000	50,000
Accounts receivable (net)	207,800	102,800
Inventory	123,000	115,500
Total current assets	444,900	332,500
Plant assets (net)	625,300	440,300
Total assets	$1,070,200	$772,800

Liabilities and Stockholders' Equity

Current liabilities		
Accounts payable	$ 200,000	$ 65,400
Income taxes payable	43,500	42,000
Total current liabilities	243,500	107,400
Bonds payable	210,000	200,000
Total liabilities	453,500	307,400
Stockholders' equity		
Common stock	330,000	300,000
Retained earnings	286,700	165,400
Total stockholders' equity	616,700	465,400
Total liabilities and stockholders' equity	$1,070,200	$772,800

Additional information: The cash provided by operating activities for 2001 was $190,800.

Instructions

Compute these values and ratios for 2001:
(a) Working capital.   (e) Cash debt coverage ratio.
(b) Current ratio.   (f) Profit margin ratio.
(c) Current cash debt coverage ratio.   (g) Return on assets ratio.
(d) Debt to total assets ratio.

P2-5A   Condensed balance sheet and income statement data for Smashing Pumpkins Corporation are presented here.

Compute and interpret liquidity, solvency, and profitability ratios.
(SO 5, 7)

SMASHING PUMPKINS CORPORATION
Balance Sheet
December 31

	2001	2000	1999
Assets			
Cash	$ 25,000	$ 20,000	$ 18,000
Receivables (net)	70,000	65,000	48,000
Other current assets	90,000	85,000	64,000
Long-term investments	75,000	70,000	45,000
Plant and equipment (net)	500,000	470,000	358,000
Total assets	$760,000	$710,000	$533,000
Liabilities and Stockholders' Equity			
Current liabilities	$ 75,000	$ 80,000	$ 70,000
Long-term debt	80,000	85,000	50,000
Common stock	340,000	300,000	300,000
Retained earnings	265,000	245,000	113,000
Total liabilities and stockholders' equity	$760,000	$710,000	$533,000

SMASHING PUMPKINS CORPORATION
Income Statement
For the Years Ended December 31

	2001	2000
Sales	$750,000	$670,000
Cost of goods sold	420,000	400,000
Operating expenses (including income taxes)	236,000	218,000
Net income	$ 94,000	$ 52,000

Instructions

Compute these values and ratios for 2000 and 2001:
(a) Profit margin ratio.
(b) Return on assets ratio.
(c) Working capital.
(d) Current ratio.
(e) Debt to total assets ratio.
(f) Based on the ratios calculated, discuss briefly the improvement or lack thereof in financial position and operating results from 2000 to 2001 of Smashing Pumpkins Corporation.

Compute ratios and compare liquidity, solvency, and profitability for two companies.
(SO 5, 7)

P2-6A Selected financial data (in millions) of two intense competitors, **Kmart** and **Wal-Mart**, for 1998 are presented here:

	Kmart	Wal-Mart
Income Statement Data for Year		
Net sales	$33,674	$137,634
Cost of goods sold	26,319	108,725
Selling and administrative expenses	6,245	22,363
Interest expense	343	797
Other income (loss)	(19)	1,421
Income taxes	230	2,740
Net income	$ 518	$ 4,430
Balance Sheet Data (End of Year)		
Current assets	$ 7,830	$ 21,132
Noncurrent assets	6,336	28,864
Total assets	$14,166	$ 49,996
Current liabilities	$ 3,691	$ 16,762
Long-term debt	4,496	12,122
Total stockholders' equity	5,979	21,112
Total liabilities and stockholders' equity	$14,166	$ 49,996
Beginning-of-Year Balances		
Total assets	$13,558	$ 45,384

Instructions

For each company, compute these values and ratios:
(a) Working capital.
(b) Current ratio.
(c) Debt to total assets ratio.
(d) Return on assets ratio.
(e) Profit margin ratio.
(f) Compare the liquidity, solvency, and profitability of the two companies.

PROBLEMS: SET B

Prepare a classified balance sheet.
(SO 4)

P2-1B The following items are taken from the 1998 balance sheet of **Kellogg Company** (in millions).

Common stock	$ 208.8
Other assets	666.2
Notes payable—current	620.4
Other current assets	215.7
Current maturities of long-term debt	1.1
Cash and cash equivalents	136.4
Other long-term liabilities	828.7
Retained earnings	681.0
Accounts payable	386.9

Other current liabilities	710.1
Accounts receivable	693.0
Property, net	2,888.8
Inventories	451.4
Long-term debt	1,614.5

Instructions
Prepare a balance sheet for Kellogg Company as of December 31, 1998.

P2-2B These items are taken from the financial statements of Crash Test Dummies Company:

Prepare financial statements.
(SO 4, 6)

Prepaid insurance	1,800
Equipment	31,000
Salaries expense	36,000
Utilities expense	2,100
Accumulated depreciation	8,600
Accounts payable	12,000
Cash	$ 6,200
Accounts receivable	7,500
Salaries payable	3,000
Common stock	5,900
Depreciation expense	5,300
Retained earnings (beginning)	14,000
Dividends	7,200
Service revenue	58,000
Repair expense	3,200
Insurance expense	1,200

Instructions
Prepare an income statement, a retained earnings statement, and a classified balance sheet for December 31, 2001.

P2-3B Comparative statement data for Nari Company and KJ Company, two competitors, are presented here. All balance sheet data are as of December 31, 2001, and December 31, 2000.

Compute ratios; comment on relative profitability, liquidity, and solvency.
(SO 5, 7, 8)

	Nari Company		KJ Company	
	2001	**2000**	**2001**	**2000**
Net sales	$450,000		$920,000	
Cost of goods sold	260,000		620,000	
Operating expenses	132,000		52,000	
Interest expense	3,000		10,000	
Income tax expense	11,000		65,000	
Current assets	180,000	$110,000	700,000	$550,000
Plant assets (net)	705,000	470,000	800,000	750,000
Current liabilities	60,000	52,000	250,000	275,000
Long-term liabilities	210,000	68,000	200,000	150,000

Additional information: Cash provided by operations for 2001 was $22,000 for Nari and $185,000 for KJ.

Instructions
(a) Comment on the relative profitability of the companies by computing the return on assets ratios and the profit margin ratios for both companies.
(b) Comment on the relative liquidity of the companies by computing working capital, the current ratios, and the current cash debt coverage ratios for both companies.
(c) Comment on the relative solvency of the companies by computing the debt to total assets ratio and the cash debt coverage ratio for each.

Compute liquidity, solvency, and profitability ratios.
(SO 5, 7, 8)

P2-4B The comparative statements of Helms Company are presented here:

HELMS COMPANY
Income Statement
For the Years Ended December 31

	2001	2000
Net sales	$690,000	$574,000
Cost of goods sold	420,000	335,600
Selling and administrative expense	143,880	149,760
Interest expense	7,920	7,200
Income tax expense	35,300	24,000
Net income	$ 82,900	$ 57,440

HELMS COMPANY
Balance Sheet
December 31

	2001	2000
Assets		
Current assets		
Cash	$ 23,100	$ 21,600
Short-term investments	34,800	33,000
Accounts receivable (net)	106,200	93,800
Inventory	182,400	64,000
Total current assets	346,500	212,400
Plant assets (net)	465,300	459,600
Total assets	$811,800	$672,000
Liabilities and Stockholders' Equity		
Current liabilities		
Accounts payable	$134,200	$132,000
Income taxes payable	25,300	24,000
Total current liabilities	159,500	156,000
Bonds payable	132,000	120,000
Total liabilities	291,500	276,000
Stockholders' equity		
Common stock	140,000	150,000
Retained earnings	380,300	246,000
Total stockholders' equity	520,300	396,000
Total liabilities and stockholders' equity	$811,800	$672,000

Additional information: Cash provided by operating activities was $82,300 for 2001.

Instructions
Compute these values and ratios for 2001:
(a) Current ratio.
(b) Working capital.
(c) Current cash debt coverage ratio.
(d) Debt to total assets ratio.
(e) Cash debt coverage ratio.
(f) Profit margin ratio.
(g) Return on assets ratio.

Compute and interpret liquidity, solvency, and profitability ratios.
(SO 5, 7)

P2-5B Condensed balance sheet and income statement data for Springsteen Corporation are presented at the top of the next page.

SPRINGSTEEN CORPORATION
Balance Sheet
December 31

	2001	2000	1999
Assets			
Cash	$ 50,000	$ 24,000	$ 20,000
Receivables (net)	90,000	65,000	32,000
Other current assets	80,000	75,000	62,000
Long-term investments	90,000	70,000	50,000
Plant and equipment (net)	550,000	420,000	310,000
Total assets	$860,000	$654,000	$474,000
Liabilities and Stockholders' Equity			
Current liabilities	$ 98,000	$ 75,000	$ 70,000
Long-term debt	97,000	75,000	65,000
Common stock	400,000	340,000	300,000
Retained earnings	265,000	164,000	39,000
Total liabilities and stockholders' equity	$860,000	$654,000	$474,000

SPRINGSTEEN CORPORATION
Income Statement
For the Years Ended December 31

	2001	2000
Sales	$660,000	$800,000
Cost of goods sold	420,000	400,000
Operating expenses (including income taxes)	194,000	237,000
Net income	$ 46,000	$163,000

Instructions

Compute these values and ratios for 2000 and 2001:
(a) Profit margin ratio.   (d) Current ratio.
(b) Return on assets ratio.   (e) Debt to total assets ratio.
(c) Working capital.

(f) Based on the ratios calculated, discuss briefly the improvement or lack thereof in the financial position and operating results from 2000 to 2001 of Springsteen.

P2-6B   Selected financial data (in millions) of two intense competitors, **Bethlehem Steel** and **USX**, in a recent year are presented here:

Compute ratios and compare liquidity, solvency, and profitability for two companies.
(SO 5, 7)

	Bethlehem Steel Corporation	USX Corporation
	Income Statement Data for Year	
Net sales	$4,478	$28,310
Cost of goods sold	3,883	20,712
Selling and administrative expense	371	5,839
Interest expense	62	279
Other income (loss)	(18)	(491)
Income tax expense	24	315
Net income	$ 120	$ 674

	Balance Sheet Data (End of Year)	
Current assets	$1,495	$ 4,206
Property, plant, and equipment (net)	2,656	12,929
Other assets	1,471	3,998
Total assets	$5,622	$21,133
Current liabilities	$ 985	$ 3,619
Long-term debt	3,147	11,109
Total stockholders' equity	1,490	6,405
Total liabilities and stockholders' equity	$5,622	$21,133
	Beginning-of-Year Balances	
Total assets	$4,803	$17,284

Instructions

For each company, compute these values and ratios:

(a) Working capital.
(b) Current ratio.
(c) Debt to total assets ratio.
(d) Return on assets ratio.
(e) Profit margin ratio.
(f) Compare the liquidity, profitability, and solvency of the two companies.

◆ **B R O A D E N I N G   Y O U R   P E R S P E C T I V E**

*F*INANCIAL REPORTING AND ANALYSIS

FINANCIAL REPORTING PROBLEM: *Tootsie Roll Industries, Inc.*

BYP2-1 The financial statements of Tootsie Roll Industries, Inc., are presented in Appendix A at the end of this book.

Instructions

Answer the following questions using the Consolidated Balance Sheet and the Notes to Consolidated Financial Statements section.

(a) What were Tootsie Roll's total current assets at December 31, 1998, and December 31, 1997?
(b) Are the assets included in current assets listed in the proper order? Explain.
(c) How are Tootsie Roll's assets classified?
(d) What were Tootsie Roll's current liabilities at December 31, 1998, and December 31, 1997?

COMPARATIVE ANALYSIS PROBLEM: *Tootsie Roll vs. Hershey Foods*

BYP2-2 The financial statements of Hershey Foods are presented in Appendix B, following the financial statements for Tootsie Roll in Appendix A.

Instructions

(a) For each company calculate the following values for 1998:
    (1) Working capital.
    (2) Current ratio.

(3) Debt to total assets ratio.

(4) Profit margin ratio.

(5) Return on assets ratio.

(b) Based on your findings above, discuss the relative liquidity, solvency, and profitability of the two companies.

RESEARCH CASE

BYP2-3   Several commonly available indexes enable individuals to locate articles from numerous business publications and periodicals. Articles can generally be searched for by company name or by subject matter. Four common indexes are *The Wall Street Journal Index*, *Business Abstracts* (formerly *Business Periodicals Index*), *Predicasts F&S Index*, and *ABI/Inform*.

Instructions

Use one of these resources to find a list of articles about Best Buy, Circuit City, or Tweeter Home Entertainment. Choose an article from this list that you believe would be of interest to an investor or creditor of this company. Read the article and answer the following questions. [*Note:*   Your library may have either hard-copy or CD-ROM versions of these indexes.]

(a) What is the article about?

(b) What company-specific information is included in the article?

(c) Is the article related to anything you read in this chapter?

(d) Identify any accounting-related issues discussed in the article.

INTERPRETING FINANCIAL STATEMENTS

BYP2-4   The following information was reported by **Ford Motor Company** in its 1998 annual report.

	1998	1997	1996	1995	1994	1993	1992
Total assets (millions)	$3,964	$3,338	$2,627	$2,343	$2,004	$1,763	$1,379
Working capital (millions)	319	839	554	728	556	494	356
Current ratio	1.21	1.85	1.72	2.32	2.11	2.07	2.06
Debt to total assets ratio	.13	.15	0	0	0	.04	.05
Return on assets ratio	.23	.18	.18	.16	.17	.16	.17

(a) Determine the overall percentage increase in Ford's total assets from 1992 to 1998. What was the average increase per year?

(b) Comment on the change in Ford's liquidity. Does working capital or the current ratio appear to provide a better indication of Ford's liquidity? What might explain the change in Ford's liquidity during this period?

(c) Comment on the change in Ford's solvency during this period.

(d) Comment on the change in Ford's profitability during this period. Ignoring 1998, what was the average value of Ford's return on assets ratio during 1992 to 1997? How might this affect your prediction about Ford's future profitability?

A GLOBAL FOCUS

BYP2-5   **Mo och Comsjo AB (MoDo)** is one of Europe's largest forest products companies. It has production facilities in Sweden, France, and Great Britain. Its headquarters is in Stockholm, Sweden. Its statements are presented in conformity with the standards issued by the Swedish Standards Board. Its financial statements are presented to be harmonized (that is, to have minimal difference in methods) with member countries of the European Union. The following balance sheet was taken from MoDo's 1998 annual report.

MODO
Consolidated Balance Sheet
at December 31
(Swedish kronor, in millions)

	1998	1997
Assets		
Fixed assets		
Intangible assets		
Goodwill, leases and similar rights	32	69
Tangible assets		
Forest land	4,585	4,560
Buildings, other land and land installations	2,565	2,049
Machinery and equipment	13,216	12,814
Fixed plants under construction and advance payments	341	128
	20,707	19,551
Financial assets		
Shares and participations		
Associate companies	89	129
Other shares and participations	59	48
Other long-term receivables	44	49
	192	226
	20,931	19,846
Current assets		
Inventories, etc.	3,648	3,620
Current receivables	4,614	4,600
Short-term placements	780	1,189
Cash in bank	461	447
	9,503	9,856
	30,434	29,702
Equity and Liabilities		
Equity		
Restricted equity		
Share capital	4,443	4,443
Restricted reserves	7,819	5,985
Non-restricted equity		
Non-restricted reserves	3,611	4,513
Profit for the year	2,504	1,434
	18,377	16,375
Minority Interests	5	5
Provisions		
Interest-bearing		
Pension provisions	135	1,544
Interest-free		
Tax provisions	3,228	3,815
Other provisions	240	239
	3,603	5,598
Liabilities		
Financial liabilities	4,249	3,961
Operating liabilities	4,200	3,763
	8,449	7,724
	30,434	29,702
Pledged assets	445	481
Contingent liabilities	233	182

Instructions

List all differences that you notice between MoDo's balance sheet presentation (format and terminology) and the presentation of U.S. companies shown in the chapter. For differences in terminology, list the corresponding terminology used by U.S. companies.

FINANCIAL ANALYSIS ON THE WEB

BYP2-6   *Purpose:*   Identify summary liquidity, solvency, and profitability information about companies, and compare this information across companies in the same industry.

Address: http://biz.yahoo.com/i (or go to www.wiley.com/college/kimmel)

Steps:

1. Type in a company name, or use the index to find a company name.
   Perform instructions (a) and (b) below.
2. Click on the company's particular industry behind the heading "Industry."
   Perform instructions (c) and (d).

Instructions

Answer the following questions:

(a) What was the company's current ratio, debt to equity ratio (a variation of the debt to total assets ratio), profit margin ratio, and return on assets ratio?
(b) What is the company's industry?
(c) What is the name of a competitor? What is the competitor's current ratio, debt to equity ratio, profit margin ratio, and return on assets ratio?
(d) Based on these measures: Which company is more liquid? Which company is more solvent? Which company is more profitable?

BYP2-7   The opening story described the dramatic effect that investment bulletin boards are having on the investment world. This exercise will allow you to evaluate a bulletin board discussing a company of your choice.

Address: http://biz.yahoo.com/i (or go to www.wiley.com/college/kimmel)

Steps:

1. Type in a company name, or use the index to find a company name.
2. Choose **Msgs** (for messages).
3. Read the ten most recent messages.

Instructions

Answer the following questions:

(a) State the nature of each of these messages (e.g., offering advice, criticizing company, predicting future results, ridiculing other people who have posted messages).
(b) For those messages that expressed an opinion about the company, was evidence provided to support the opinion?
(c) What effect do you think it would have on bulletin board discussions if the participants provided their actual names? Do you think this would be a good policy?

CRITICAL THINKING

GROUP DECISION CASE

BYP2-8   As the accountant for J. Martinez Manufacturing Inc., you have been requested to develop some key ratios from the comparative financial statements. This information is to be used to convince creditors that J. Martinez Manufacturing Inc. is liquid, solvent, and profitable, and that it deserves their continued support. Lenders are particularly concerned about the company's ability to continue as a going concern.

These are the data requested and the computations developed from the financial statements:

	2001	2000
Current ratio	3.1	2.1
Working capital	Up 22%	Down 7%
Debt to total assets ratio	.60	.70
Net income	Up 32%	Down 8%
Profit margin ratio	.05	.015
Return on assets ratio	.09	.04

Instructions

J. Martinez Manufacturing Inc. asks you to prepare brief comments stating how each of these items supports the argument that its financial health is improving. The company wishes to use these comments to support presentation of data to its creditors. With the class divided into groups, prepare the comments as requested, giving the implications and the limitations of each item separately, and then the collective inference that may be drawn from them about J. Martinez's financial well-being.

COMMUNICATION ACTIVITY

BYP2-9 L. R. Stanton is the chief executive officer of Hi-Tech Electronics. Stanton is an expert engineer but a novice in accounting.

Instructions

Write a letter to L. R. Stanton that explains (a) the three main types of ratios; (b) examples of each, how they are calculated, and what they measure; and (c) the bases for comparison in analyzing Hi-Tech's financial statements.

ETHICS CASE

BYP2-10 As the controller of Breathless Perfume Company, you discover a significant misstatement that overstated net income in the prior year's financial statements. The misleading financial statements are contained in the company's annual report, which was issued to banks and other creditors less than a month ago. After much thought about the consequences of telling the president, Eddy Kadu, about this misstatement, you gather your courage to inform him. Eddy says, "Hey! What they don't know won't hurt them. But, just so we set the record straight, we'll adjust this year's financial statements for last year's misstatement. We can absorb that misstatement better this year than last year anyway! Just don't make that kind of mistake again."

Instructions

(a) Who are the stakeholders in this situation?
(b) What are the ethical issues?
(c) What would you do as the controller?

Answers to Self-Study Questions

1. a   2. a   3. c   4. c   5. c   6. d   7. a   8. a   9. a   10. c   11. b

Answer to Tootsie Roll Review It Question 3, p. 57

Tootsie Roll's largest current asset at December 31, 1998, was investments, at $83,176,000.

CHAPTER *3*

The Accounting Information System

◆ STUDY OBJECTIVES

After studying this chapter, you should be able to:

1 Analyze the effect of business transactions on the basic accounting equation.

2 Explain what an account is and how it helps in the recording process.

3 Define debits and credits and explain how they are used to record business transactions.

4 Identify the basic steps in the recording process.

5 Explain what a journal is and how it helps in the recording process.

6 Explain what a ledger is and how it helps in the recording process.

7 Explain what posting is and how it helps in the recording process.

8 Explain the purposes of a trial balance.

◆ ACCIDENTS HAPPEN

How organized are you financially? Take a short quiz. Answer *yes* or *no* to each question:

• Is your wallet jammed full of gas station receipts from places you don't remember ever going?

• Does your wallet contain so many cash machine receipts that you've been declared a walking fire hazard?

• Is your wallet such a mess that it is often faster to fish for money in the crack of your car seat than to dig around in your wallet?

• Was Michael Jordan playing high school basketball the last time you balanced your checkbook?

• Have you ever been tempted to burn down your house so you don't have to try to find all of the forms, receipts, and records that you need to fill out your tax returns?

If you think it is hard to keep track of the many transactions that make up *your* life, imagine what it is like for a major corporation like Fidelity Investments. As the largest mutual fund management firm in the world, Fidelity manages more than $300 billion of investments. Millions of individuals have the bulk of their life savings invested in mutual funds. If you had your life savings invested at Fidelity Investments, you might be just slightly displeased if, when you called to find out your balance, the representative said, "You know, I kind of remember someone with a name like yours sending us some money—now what did we do with that?"

To ensure the accuracy of your balance and the security of your funds, Fidelity Investments, like all other companies large and small, relies on a sophisticated accounting information system. That's not to say that Fidelity or anybody else is error-free. In fact, if you've ever really messed up your checkbook register, you may take some comfort from one accountant's mistake at Fidelity Investments. The accountant failed to include a minus sign while doing a calculation, making what was actually a $1.3 billion loss look like a $1.3 billion gain—yes, *billion!* Fortunately, like most accounting errors, it was detected before any real harm was done.

No one expects that kind of mistake at a firm like Fidelity, which has sophisticated computer systems and top investment managers. In explaining the mistake to shareholders, a spokesperson wrote: "Some people have asked how, in this age of technology, such a mistake could be made. While many of our processes are computerized, accounting systems are complex and dictate that some steps must be handled manually by our managers and accountants, and people can make mistakes."

On the World Wide Web
Fidelity Investments:
http://www.fidelity.com

As indicated in the opening story, a reliable information system is a necessity for any company. The purpose of this chapter is to explain and illustrate the features of an accounting information system. The organization and content of the chapter are as follows:

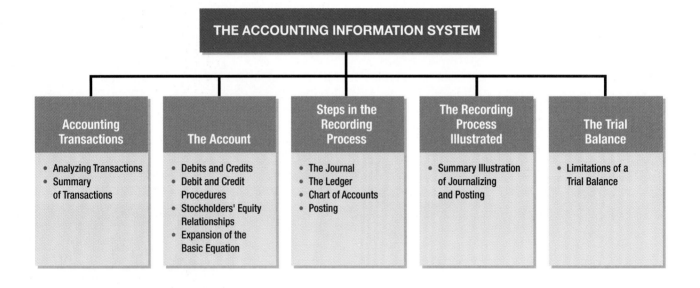

*T*HE ACCOUNTING INFORMATION SYSTEM

The system of collecting and processing transaction data and communicating financial information to interested parties is known as the **accounting information system**. Accounting information systems vary widely from one business to another. Factors that shape these systems include: the nature of the company's business, the types of transactions in which it engages, the size of the company, the volume of data to be handled, and the information demands that management and others place on the system.

In reading this chapter, it is important to note that most businesses of any size today use computerized accounting systems—sometimes referred to as electronic data processing (EDP) systems. These systems handle all the steps involved in the recording process, from initial data entry to preparation of the financial statements. In order to remain competitive, companies are continually updating and improving their accounting systems to provide accurate and timely data for decision making. For example, in its 1998 Annual Report, Tootsie Roll states that it has "upgraded our EDP systems to handle the vast data requirements we foresee as both we and the companies we do business with move forward in the 'information age.'"

In this chapter we focus on a manual accounting system because the accounting concepts and principles do not change whether a system is computerized or manual, and manual systems are easier to illustrate. You will note, however, that many of the problems in this and subsequent chapters can also be done using the computerized general ledger package that supplements this text.

ACCOUNTING TRANSACTIONS

To use an accounting information system to develop financial statements, you need to know which economic events to recognize (record). Not all events are recorded and reported in the financial statements. For example, suppose General Motors hired a new employee or purchased a new computer. Are these events entered in its accounting records? The first event would not be recorded, but the second event would. We call economic events that require recording in the financial statements accounting transactions.

An accounting transaction occurs when assets, liabilities, or stockholders' equity items change as a result of some economic event. The purchase of a computer by General Motors, the payment of rent by Microsoft, and the sale of advertising space by Sierra Corporation are examples of events that change a company's assets, liabilities, or stockholders' equity. Illustration 3-1 summarizes the decision process used to decide whether or not to record economic events.

Illustration 3-1   Transaction identification process

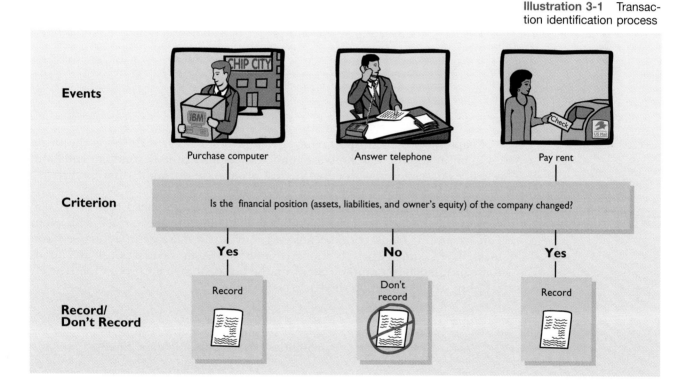

ANALYZING TRANSACTIONS

In Chapter 1 you learned the basic accounting equation:

STUDY OBJECTIVE

1

Analyze the effect of business transactions on the basic accounting equation.

In this chapter you will learn how to analyze transactions in terms of their effect on assets, liabilities, and stockholders' equity. **Transaction analysis** is the process of identifying the specific effects of economic events on the accounting equation.

The accounting equation must always balance. Therefore, each transaction has a dual (double-sided) effect on the equation. For example, if an individual asset is increased, there must be a corresponding:

Decrease in another asset, *or*

Increase in a specific liability, *or*

Increase in stockholders' equity.

It is quite possible that two or more items could be affected when an asset is increased. For example, if a company purchases a computer for $10,000 by paying $6,000 in cash and signing a note for $4,000, one asset (computer) increases $10,000, another asset (cash) decreases $6,000, and a liability (notes payable) increases $4,000. The result is that the accounting equation remains in balance—assets increased by a net $4,000 and liabilities increased by $4,000, as shown below:

Assets	=	Liabilities	+	Stockholders' Equity
+$10,000		+$4,000		
− 6,000				
$ 4,000		$4,000		

Chapter 1 presented the financial statements for Sierra Corporation for its first month. To illustrate how economic events affect the accounting equation, we will examine events affecting Sierra Corporation during its first month.

Event (1). Investment of Cash by Stockholders.   On October 1 cash of $10,000 is invested in the business in exchange for $10,000 of common stock. This event is an accounting transaction because it results in an increase in both assets and stockholders' equity. There is an increase of $10,000 in the asset Cash and an increase of $10,000 in Common Stock on the books of Sierra Corporation. The effect of this transaction on the basic equation is:

	Assets	=	Liabilities	+	Stockholders' Equity	
	Cash	=			Common Stock	
(1)	+$10,000	=			+$10,000	Issued stock

The equation is in balance. **The source of each change to stockholders' equity is noted to the right of the transaction.** In this case it was an issuance of common stock. Keeping track of the source of each change in stockholders' equity is essential for later accounting activities—in particular, the calculation of income.

Event (2). Note Issued in Exchange for Cash.   On October 1 Sierra issued a 3-month, 12%, $5,000 note payable to Castle Bank. This transaction results in an equal increase in assets and liabilities: Cash (an asset) increases $5,000, and Notes Payable (a liability) increases $5,000. The specific effect of this transaction and the cumulative effect of the first two transactions are:

	Assets	=	Liabilities	+	Stockholders' Equity
			Notes		Common
	Cash	=	Payable	+	Stock
Old Balance	$10,000				$10,000
(2)	+5,000		+$5,000		
New Balance	$15,000	=	$5,000	+	$10,000
			$15,000		

Observe that total assets are now $15,000, and stockholders' equity plus the new liability also total $15,000.

Event (3). Purchase of Office Equipment for Cash. On October 2 Sierra acquired office equipment by paying $5,000 cash to Superior Equipment Sales Co. This event is a transaction because an equal increase and decrease in Sierra's assets occur: Office Equipment (an asset) increases $5,000, and Cash (an asset) decreases $5,000:

	Assets			=	Liabilities	+	Stockholders' Equity
			Office		Notes		Common
	Cash	+	Equipment	=	Payable	+	Stock
Old Balance	$15,000				$5,000		$10,000
(3)	−5,000		+$5,000				
New Balance	$10,000	+	$5,000	=	$5,000	+	$10,000
		$15,000				$15,000	

The total assets are now $15,000, and stockholders' equity plus the liability also total $15,000.

Event (4). Receipt of Cash in Advance from Customer. On October 2 Sierra received a $1,200 cash advance from R. Knox, a client. This event is a transaction because cash (an asset) was received for advertising services that are expected to be completed by Sierra by December 31. However, **revenue should not be recorded until the work has been performed**. In the magazine and airline industries, customers are expected to prepay. These companies have a liability to the customer until the magazines are delivered or the flight is provided. As soon as the product or service is provided, revenue can be recorded. Since Sierra received cash prior to performance of the service, Sierra has a liability for the work due. Cash increases by $1,200, and a liability, Unearned Service Revenue (abbreviated as Unearned Revenue), increases by an equal amount.

	Assets			=	Liabilities			+	Stockholders' Equity
			Office		Notes		Unearned		Common
	Cash	+	Equipment	=	Payable	+	Revenue	+	Stock
Old Balance	$10,000		$5,000		$5,000				$10,000
(4)	+1,200						+$1,200		
New Balance	$11,200	+	$5,000	=	$5,000	+	$1,200	+	$10,000
		$16,200				$16,200			

Event (5). Services Rendered for Cash. On October 3 Sierra received $10,000 in cash from Copa Company for advertising services performed. This event is a transaction because Sierra received an asset (cash) in exchange for services. Advertising service is the principal revenue-producing activity of Sierra. **Revenue increases stockholders' equity**. Both assets and stockholders' equity are, then, increased by this transaction. Cash is increased $10,000, and Retained Earnings is increased $10,000. The new balances in the equation are:

		Assets		=	Liabilities	+		Stockholders' Equity	
			Office		Notes	Unearned	Common	Retained	
	Cash	+	Equipment	= Payable +	Revenue	+	Stock	+ Earnings	
Old Balance	$11,200		$5,000	$5,000	$1,200		$10,000		
(5)	+10,000							+$10,000	Service Revenue
New Balance	$21,200 +		$5,000	= $5,000 +	$1,200	+	$10,000 +	$10,000	
		$26,200				$26,200			

Often companies provide services "on account." That is, they provide service for which they are paid at a later date. Revenue, however, is earned when services are performed. Therefore, stockholders' equity would increase when services are performed, even though cash has not been recieved. Instead of receiving cash, the company receives a different type of asset, an account receivable. Accounts receivable represent the right to receive payment at a later date. Suppose that Sierra had provided these services on account rather than for cash. This event would be reported using the accounting equation as:

Assets	= Liabilities	+	Stockholders' Equity	
Accounts			Retained	
Receivable	=		Earnings	
+$10,000			+$10,000	Service Revenue

Later, when the $10,000 is collected from the customer, Accounts Receivable would decline by $10,000, and Cash would increase by $10,000.

	Assets	= Liabilities	+ Stockholders' Equity
	Accounts		
Cash	Receivable		
+$10,000	−$10,000		

Note that in this case, stockholders' equity is not affected by the collection of cash. Instead we record an exchange of one asset (Accounts Receivable) for a different asset (Cash).

Event (6). Payment of Rent. On October 3 Sierra Corporation paid its office rent for the month of October in cash, $900. Rent is an expense incurred by Sierra Corporation in its effort to generate revenues. **Expenses decrease stockholders' equity**. This rent payment is a transaction because it results in a decrease in cash. It is recorded by decreasing cash and decreasing stockholders' equity (specifically, Retained Earnings) to maintain the balance of the accounting equation. To record this transaction, Cash is decreased $900, and Retained Earnings is decreased $900. The effect of these payments on the accounting equation is:

		Assets		=	Liabilities		+	Stockholders' Equity		
			Office		Notes	Unearned		Common	Retained	
		Cash	+ Equipment	=	Payable	+ Revenue	+	Stock	+ Earnings	
(6)	Old Balance	$21,200	$5,000		$5,000	$1,200		$10,000	$10,000	
		−900							−900	**Rent Expense**
	New Balance	$20,300 +	$5,000	=	$5,000 +	$1,200	+	$10,000 +	$9,100	
			$25,300				$25,300			

Event (7). *Purchase of Insurance Policy in Cash.*

On October 4 Sierra paid $600 for a one-year insurance policy that will expire next year on September 30. This event is a transaction because one asset was exchanged for another. The asset Cash is decreased $600. The asset Prepaid Insurance is increased $600 because the payment extends to more than the current month. Payments of expenses that will benefit more than one accounting period are identified as prepaid expenses or prepayments. Note that the balance in total assets did not change; one asset account decreased by the same amount that another increased.

			Assets			=	Liabilities		+	Stockholders' Equity	
			Prepaid	Office		Notes	Unearned		Common	Retained	
		Cash	+ Insurance	+ Equipment	=	Payable	+ Revenue	+	Stock	+ Earnings	
(7)	Old Balance	$20,300		$5,000		$5,000	$1,200		$10,000	$9,100	
		−600	+$600								
	New Balance	$19,700 +	$600 +	$5,000	=	$5,000 +	$1,200	+	$10,000 +	$9,100	
			$25,300					$25,300			

Event (8). *Purchase of Supplies on Credit.*

On October 5 Sierra purchased an estimated three-month supply of advertising materials on account from Aero Supply for $2,500. Assets are increased by this transaction because supplies represent a resource that will be used in the process of providing services to customers. Liabilities are increased by the amount due Aero Supply. The asset Supplies is increased $2,500, and the liability Accounts Payable is increased by the same amount. The effect on the equation is:

				Assets			=		Liabilities		+	Stockholders' Equity	
				Prepaid	Office		Notes	Accounts	Unearned	Common		Retained	
		Cash	+ Supplies	+ Insurance	+ Equipment	=	Payable	+ Payable	+ Revenue	+	Stock	+	Earnings	
(8)	Old Balance	$19,700		$600	$5,000		$5,000		$1,200		$10,000		$9,100	
			+$2,500					+$2,500						
	New Balance	$19,700 +	$2,500 +	$600	+ $5,000	=	$5,000 +	$2,500 +	$1,200	+	$10,000 +		$9,100	
				$27,800					$27,800					

Event (9). *Hiring of New Employees.*

On October 9 Sierra hired four new employees to begin work on October 15. Each employee is to receive a weekly salary of $500 for a five-day work week, payable every two weeks. Employees are to receive their first paychecks on October 26. There is no effect on the accounting equation because the assets, liabilities, and stockholders' equity of the company have not changed. **An accounting transaction has not occurred**. At this point there is only an agreement that the employees will begin work on October 15. [See Event (11) for the first payment.]

Event (10). Payment of Dividend.   On October 20 Sierra paid a $500 dividend. Dividends are a distribution of net income and not an expense. A dividend transaction affects assets and stockholders' equity: Cash and Retained Earnings are decreased $500.

		Assets			=	Liabilities			+	Stockholders' Equity	
	Cash	+ Supplies	+ Prepaid Insurance	+ Office Equipment	=	Notes Payable	+ Accounts Payable	+ Unearned Revenue	+	Common Stock	+ Retained Earnings
Old Balance	$19,700	$2,500	$600	$5,000		$5,000	$2,500	$1,200		$10,000	$9,100
(10)	−500										−500 Dividends
New Balance	$19,200 +	$2,500 +	$600 +	$5,000	=	$5,000 +	$2,500 +	$1,200	+	$10,000 +	$8,600
			$27,300					$27,300			

Event (11). Payment of Cash for Employee Salaries.   Employees have worked two weeks, earning $4,000 in salaries, which were paid on October 26. Like the costs that were incurred for rent, salaries are an expense. Because they are a cost of generating revenues, they decrease stockholders' equity. This event involving employees is a transaction because assets and stockholders' equity are affected, each by an equal amount. Thus, Cash and Retained Earnings are each decreased $4,000.

		Assets			=	Liabilities			+	Stockholders' Equity	
	Cash	+ Supplies	+ Prepaid Insurance	+ Office Equipment	=	Notes Payable	+ Accounts Payable	+ Unearned Revenue	+	Common Stock	+ Retained Earnings
Old Balance	$19,200	$2,500	$600	$5,000		$5,000	$2,500	$1,200		$10,000	$8,600
(11)	−4,000										−4,000 Salaries
New Balance	$15,200 +	$2,500 +	$600 +	$5,000	=	$5,000 +	$2,500 +	$1,200	+	$10,000 +	$4,600 Expense
			$23,300					$23,300			

BUSINESS INSIGHT

Management Perspective

Many companies are finding that teaching their factory workers basic accounting skills can be a useful motivational tool. For example, Rhino Foods in Burlington, Vermont, uses a financial reporting game to motivate its production line employees. Employees are taught the costs of each element of the production process, from raw materials to machinery malfunctions, so that they will make decisions that will benefit the company. The employees' bonus checks (for managers as well as factory workers) are based on the results of the game. The owner, a former hockey coach, believes that his workers will work harder, and enjoy their work more, if they know what the score is.

SUMMARY OF TRANSACTIONS

The transactions of Sierra Corporation are summarized in Illustration 3-2 to show their cumulative effect on the basic accounting equation. The transaction number, the specific effects of the transaction, and the balances after each transaction are indicated. Remember that Event (9) did not result in a transaction, so no entry is included for that event. The illustration demonstrates three significant facts:

1. Each transaction is analyzed in terms of its effect on assets, liabilities, and stockholders' equity.
2. The two sides of the equation must always be equal.
3. The cause of each change in stockholders' equity must be indicated.

Illustration 3-2
Summary of transactions

	Cash	+ Supplies	+ Prepaid Insurance	+ Office Equipment	= Notes Payable	+ Accounts Payable	+ Unearned Revenue	+ Common Stock	+ Retained Earnings	
(1)	+$10,000				=			+$10,000		Issued stock
(2)	+5,000				+$5,000					
	15,000				= 5,000			+ 10,000		
(3)	−5,000			+$5,000						
	10,000			+ 5,000	= 5,000			+ 10,000		
(4)	+1,200						+$1,200			
	11,200			+ 5,000	= 5,000		+ 1,200	+ 10,000		
(5)	+10,000								+$10,000	Service Revenue
	21,200			+ 5,000	= 5,000		+ 1,200	+ 10,000	+ 10,000	
(6)	−900								−900	Rent Expense
	20,300			+ 5,000	= 5,000		+ 1,200	+ 10,000	+ 9,100	
(7)	−600		+$600							
	19,700	+	600	+ 5,000	= 5,000		+ 1,200	+ 10,000	+ 9,100	
(8)		+$2,500				+$2,500				
	19,700 +	2,500 +	600	+ 5,000	= 5,000 +	2,500 +	1,200	+ 10,000	+ 9,100	
(10)	−500								−500	Dividends
	19,200 +	2,500 +	600	+ 5,000	= 5,000 +	2,500 +	1,200	+ 10,000	+ 8,600	
(11)	−4,000								−4,000	Salaries Expense
	$15,200 +	$2,500 +	$600	+ $5,000	= $5,000 +	$2,500 +	$1,200	+ $10,000	+ $ 4,600	

$23,300 $23,300

DECISION TOOLKIT

Decision Checkpoints	Info Needed for Decision	Tool to Use for Decision	How to Evaluate Results
Has an accounting transaction occurred?	Details of the event	Accounting equation	Determine the effect, if any, on assets, liabilities, and stockholders' equity.

*T*HE ACCOUNT

Rather than using a tabular summary like the one in Illustration 3-2 for Sierra Corporation, an accounting information system uses accounts. An **account** is an individual accounting record of increases and decreases in a specific asset, liability, or stockholders' equity item. For example, Sierra Corporation has separate accounts for Cash, Accounts Receivable, Accounts Payable, Service Revenue, Salaries Expense, and so on. (Note that whenever we are referring to a specific account, we capitalize the name.)

STUDY OBJECTIVE

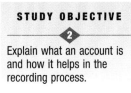

2

Explain what an account is and how it helps in the recording process.

In its simplest form, an account consists of three parts: (1) the title of the account, (2) a left or debit side, and (3) a right or credit side. Because the alignment of these parts of an account resembles the letter T, it is referred to as a **T account**. The basic form of an account is shown in Illustration 3-3.

Illustration 3-3 Basic form of account

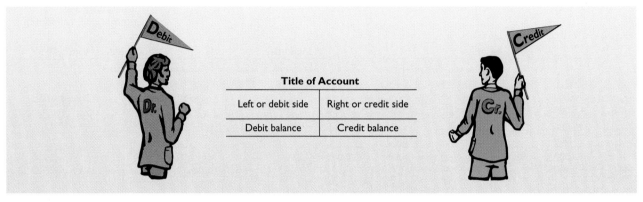

Title of Account	
Left or debit side	Right or credit side
Debit balance	Credit balance

This form of account is used often throughout this book to explain basic accounting relationships.

DEBITS AND CREDITS

STUDY OBJECTIVE

3

Define debits and credits and explain how they are used to record business transactions.

The term **debit** means left, and **credit** means right. They are commonly abbreviated as **Dr.** for debit and **Cr.** for credit. These terms are directional signals; they **do not** mean increase or decrease as is commonly thought. The terms *debit* and *credit* are used repeatedly in the recording process to describe where entries are made in accounts. For example, the act of entering an amount on the left side of an account is called **debiting** the account. Making an entry on the right side is **crediting** the account. When the totals of the two sides are compared, an account will have a **debit balance** if the total of the debit amounts exceeds the credits. Conversely, an account will have a **credit balance** if the credit amounts exceed the debits. Note the position of the debit or credit balances in Illustration 3-3.

The procedure of recording debits and credits in an account is shown in Illustration 3-4 for the transactions affecting the Cash account of Sierra Corporation. The data are taken from the Cash column of the tabular summary in Illustration 3-2.

Illustration 3-4 Tabular summary and account form for Sierra Corporation's Cash account

Tabular Summary		Account Form			
Cash			**Cash**		
$10,000		(Debits)	10,000	(Credits)	5,000
5,000			5,000		900
−5,000			1,200		600
1,200			10,000		500
10,000					4,000
−900					
−600		Balance	15,200		
−500		(Debit)			
−4,000					
$15,200					

Every positive item in the tabular summary represents a receipt of cash; every negative amount represents a payment of cash. **Notice that in the account form the increases in cash are recorded as debits, and the decreases in cash are recorded as credits.** Having increases on one side and decreases on the other reduces recording errors and helps in determining the totals of each side of the account as well as the balance in the account. The account balance, a debit of $15,200, indicates that Sierra Corporation had $15,200 more increases than decreases in cash. That is, since it started with a balance of zero, it has $15,200 in its Cash account.

DEBIT AND CREDIT PROCEDURES

Each transaction must affect two or more accounts to keep the basic accounting equation in balance. In other words, for each transaction, debits must equal credits. The equality of debits and credits provides the basis for the double-entry accounting system.

Under the universally used double-entry system, the dual (two-sided) effect of each transaction is recorded in appropriate accounts. This system provides a logical method for recording transactions. As was the case for the error in Fidelity's accounts, noted in the opening story, the double-entry system also offers a means of ensuring the accuracy of the recorded amounts. If every transaction is recorded with equal debits and credits, then the sum of all the debits to the accounts must equal the sum of all the credits. The double-entry system for determining the equality of the accounting equation is much more efficient than the plus/minus procedure used earlier. There, it was necessary after each transaction to compare total assets with total liabilities and stockholders' equity to determine the equality of the two sides of the accounting equation.

Dr./Cr. Procedures for Assets and Liabilities

In Illustration 3-4 for Sierra Corporation, increases in cash—an asset—were entered on the left side, and decreases in cash were entered on the right side. We know that both sides of the basic equation (Assets = Liabilities + Stockholders' Equity) must be equal. It therefore follows that increases and decreases in liabilities will have to be recorded *opposite from* increases and decreases in assets. Thus, increases in liabilities must be entered on the right or credit side, and decreases in liabilities must be entered on the left or debit side. The effects that debits and credits have on assets and liabilities are summarized in Illustration 3-5.

Debits	**Credits**
Increase assets	Decrease assets
Decrease liabilities	Increase liabilities

Illustration 3-5 Debit and credit effects—assets and liabilities

Asset accounts normally show debit balances. That is, debits to a specific asset account should exceed credits to that account. Likewise, liability accounts normally show credit balances. That is, credits to a liability account should exceed debits to that account. The normal balances may be diagrammed as in Illustration 3-6.

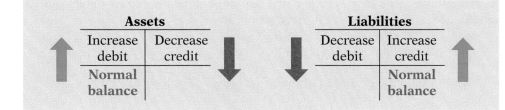

Illustration 3-6 Normal balances—assets and liabilities

Knowing which is the normal balance in an account may help when you are trying to trace errors. For example, a credit balance in an asset account such as Land or a debit balance in a liability account such as Wages Payable usually indicates errors in recording. Occasionally, however, an abnormal balance may be correct. The Cash account, for example, will have a credit balance when a company has overdrawn its bank balance (written a check that "bounced").

BUSINESS INSIGHT
Management Perspective

In automated accounting systems, the computer is programmed to flag violations of the normal balance and to print out error or exception reports. In manual systems, careful visual inspection of the accounts is required to detect normal balance problems.

Dr./Cr. Procedures for Stockholders' Equity

The five subdivisions of stockholders' equity are: common stock, retained earnings, dividends, revenues, and expenses. In a double-entry system, accounts are kept for each of these subdivisions.

Common Stock.   Common stock is issued in exchange for the stockholders' investment. The Common Stock account is increased by credits and decreased by debits. For example, when cash is invested in the business, Cash is debited and Common Stock is credited. The effects of debits and credits on the Common Stock account are shown in Illustration 3-7.

Illustration 3-7 Debit and credit effects—Common Stock

Debits	Credits
Decrease Common Stock	Increase Common Stock

The normal balance in the Common Stock account may be diagrammed as in Illustration 3-8.

Illustration 3-8 Normal balance—Common Stock

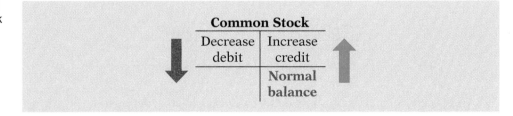

Retained Earnings.   Retained earnings is net income that is retained in the business. It represents the portion of stockholders' equity that has been accumulated through the profitable operation of the company. Retained Earnings is increased by credits (for example, net income) and decreased by debits (for example, net losses), as shown in Illustration 3-9.

Illustration 3-9 Debit and credit effects—Retained Earnings

Debits	Credits
Decrease Retained Earnings	Increase Retained Earnings

The normal balance for Retained Earnings may be diagrammed as in Illustration 3-10.

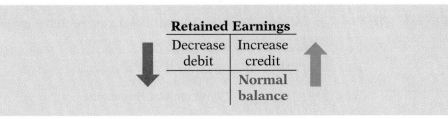

Illustration 3-10   Normal balance—Retained Earnings

Dividends.   A dividend is a distribution by a corporation to its stockholders in an amount proportional to each investor's percentage ownership. The most common form of distribution is a cash dividend. Dividends result in a reduction of the stockholders' claims on retained earnings. Because dividends reduce stockholders' equity, increases in the Dividends account are recorded with debits. As shown in Illustration 3-11, the Dividends account normally has a debit balance.

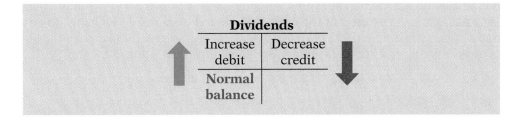

Illustration 3-11   Normal balance—Dividends

Revenues and Expenses.   When revenues are earned, stockholders' equity is increased. Accordingly, **the effect of debits and credits on revenue accounts is identical to their effect on stockholders' equity**. Revenue accounts are increased by credits and decreased by debits.

On the other hand, **expenses decrease stockholders' equity**. As a result, expenses are recorded by debits. Since expenses are the negative factor in the computation of net income and revenues are the positive factor, it is logical that the increase and decrease sides of expense accounts should be the reverse of revenue accounts. Thus, expense accounts are increased by debits and decreased by credits. The effects of debits and credits on revenues and expenses are shown in Illustration 3-12.

Debits	Credits
Decrease revenues	Increase revenues
Increase expenses	Decrease expenses

Illustration 3-12   Debit and credit effects— revenues and expenses

Credits to revenue accounts should exceed debits, and debits to expense accounts should exceed credits. Thus, revenue accounts normally show credit balances, and expense accounts normally show debit balances. The normal balances may be diagrammed as in Illustration 3-13.

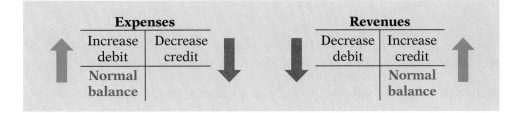

Illustration 3-13   Normal balances—revenues and expenses

BUSINESS INSIGHT
Investor Perspective

The Chicago Cubs baseball team has these major revenue and expense accounts:

Revenues	Expenses
Admissions (ticket sales)	Players' salaries
Concessions	Administrative salaries
Television and radio	Travel
Advertising	Ballpark maintenance

STOCKHOLDERS' EQUITY RELATIONSHIPS

As indicated in Chapters 1 and 2, common stock and retained earnings are reported in the stockholders' equity section of the balance sheet. Dividends are reported on the retained earnings statement. Revenues and expenses are reported on the income statement. Dividends, revenues, and expenses are eventually transferred to retained earnings at the end of the period. As a result, a change in any one of these three items affects stockholders' equity. The relationships of the accounts affecting stockholders' equity are shown in Illustration 3-14.

Illustration 3-14
Stockholders' equity relationships

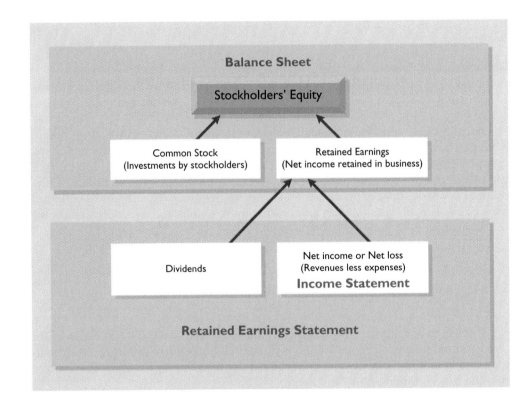

EXPANSION OF THE BASIC EQUATION

You have already learned the basic accounting equation. Illustration 3-15 expands this equation to show the accounts that make up stockholders' equity. In addition, the debit/credit rules and effects on each type of account are illustrated. **Study this diagram carefully**. It will help you understand the fundamentals of the double-entry system. Like the basic equation, the expanded basic equation must be in balance; total debits must equal total credits.

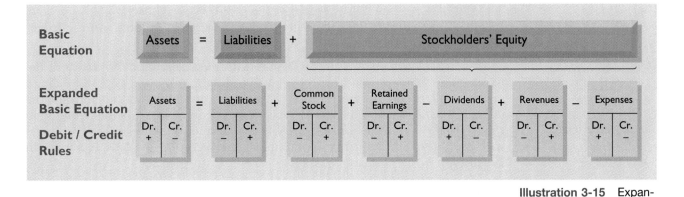

Basic Equation	Assets	=	Liabilities	+	Stockholders' Equity					

Expanded Basic Equation	Assets	=	Liabilities	+	Common Stock	+	Retained Earnings	−	Dividends	+	Revenues	−	Expenses
Debit / Credit Rules	Dr. +	Cr. −		Dr. −	Cr. +		Dr. −	Cr. +		Dr. −	Cr. +		Dr. +	Cr. −		Dr. −	Cr. +		Dr. +	Cr. −

Illustration 3-15 Expansion of the basic accounting equation

BEFORE YOU GO ON...

◆ **Review It**

1. What do the terms *debit* and *credit* mean?
2. What are the debit and credit effects on assets, liabilities, and stockholders' equity?
3. What are the debit and credit effects on revenues, expenses, and dividends?
4. What are the normal balances for the following accounts of Tootsie Roll Industries: Accounts Receivable; Income Taxes Payable; Sales; and Selling, Marketing, and Administrative Expense? The answer to this question is provided on page 147.

◆ **Do It**

Kate Browne, president of Hair It Is Inc., has just rented space in a shopping mall for the purpose of opening and operating a beauty salon. Long before opening day and before purchasing equipment, hiring assistants, and remodeling the space, Kate was strongly advised to set up a double-entry set of accounting records in which to record all of her business transactions.

Identify the balance sheet accounts that Hair It Is Inc. will likely need to record the transactions necessary to establish and open for business. Also, indicate whether the normal balance of each account is a debit or a credit.

Reasoning: To start the business, Hair It Is Inc. will need to have asset accounts for each different type of asset invested in the business. In addition, the corporation will need liability accounts for debts incurred by the business. Hair It Is Inc. will need only one stockholders' equity account for common stock when it begins the business. The other stockholders' equity accounts will be needed only after business has commenced.

Solution: Hair It Is Inc. would likely need the following accounts in which to record the transactions necessary to establish and ready the beauty salon for opening day: Cash (debit balance); Equipment (debit balance); Supplies (debit balance); Accounts Payable (credit balance); Notes Payable (credit balance), if the business borrows money; and Common Stock (credit balance).

STEPS IN THE RECORDING PROCESS

Although it is possible to enter transaction information directly into the accounts, few businesses do so. Practically every business uses these basic steps in the recording process:

1. Analyze each transaction in terms of its effect on the accounts.

STUDY OBJECTIVE

◆ 4

Identify the basic steps in the recording process.

2. Enter the transaction information in a journal.
3. Transfer the journal information to the appropriate accounts in the ledger (book of accounts).

The actual sequence of events begins with the transaction. Evidence of the transaction comes in the form of a **source document**, such as a sales slip, a check, a bill, or a cash register tape. This evidence is analyzed to determine the effect of the transaction on specific accounts. The transaction is then entered in the **journal**. Finally, the journal entry is transferred to the designated accounts in the **ledger**. The sequence of events in the recording process is shown in Illustration 3-16.

Illustration 3-16 The recording process

The basic steps in the recording process occur repeatedly in every business enterprise. The analysis of transactions has already been illustrated, and more examples of this step are given in this and later chapters. The other steps in the recording process are explained in the next sections.

STUDY OBJECTIVE

5

Explain what a journal is and how it helps in the recording process.

THE JOURNAL

Transactions are initially recorded in chronological order in a journal before they are transferred to the accounts. For each transaction the journal shows the debit and credit effects on specific accounts. Companies may use various kinds of journals, but every company has at least the most basic form of journal, a general journal. The journal makes three significant contributions to the recording process:

1. It discloses in one place the complete effect of a transaction.
2. It provides a chronological record of transactions.
3. It helps to prevent or locate errors because the debit and credit amounts for each entry can be readily compared.

Entering transaction data in the journal is known as journalizing. To illustrate the technique of journalizing, let's look at the first three transactions of Sierra Corporation. These transactions were: October 1, common stock was issued in exchange for $10,000 cash; October 1, $5,000 was borrowed by signing a note; October 2, office equipment was purchased for $5,000. In equation form, these transactions appeared in our earlier discussion as follows:

Assets	=	**Liabilities**	+	**Stockholders' Equity**
				Common
Cash	=			Stock
+$10,000				+$10,000 Issued stock

Assets	=	**Liabilities**	+	**Stockholders' Equity**
		Notes		
Cash	=	Payable		
+$5,000		+$5,000		

Assets		=	**Liabilities**	+	**Stockholders' Equity**
	Office				
Cash	Equipment				
−$5,000	+$5,000				

Separate journal entries are made for each transaction. A complete entry consists of: (1) the date of the transaction, (2) the accounts and amounts to be debited and credited, and (3) a brief explanation of the transaction. These transactions are journalized in Illustration 3-17.

	GENERAL JOURNAL		
Date	Account Titles and Explanation	Debit	Credit
2001			
Oct. 1	Cash	10,000	
	Common Stock		10,000
	(Invested cash in business)		
1	Cash	5,000	
	Notes Payable		5,000
	(Issued 3-month, 12% note payable for cash)		
2	Office Equipment	5,000	
	Cash		5,000
	(Purchased office equipment for cash)		

Illustration 3-17
Recording transactions in journal form

Note the following features of the journal entries:

1. The date of the transaction is entered in the Date column.
2. The account to be debited is entered first at the left. The account to be credited is then entered on the next line, indented under the line above. The indentation differentiates debits from credits and decreases the possibility of switching the debit and credit amounts.
3. The amounts for the debits are recorded in the Debit (left) column, and the amounts for the credits are recorded in the Credit (right) column.
4. A brief explanation of the transaction is given.

It is important to use correct and specific account titles in journalizing. Since most accounts are used in the financial statements, erroneous account titles lead to incorrect financial statements. Some flexibility exists initially in selecting account titles. The main criterion is that each title must appropriately describe the content of the account. For example, a company could use any of these account titles for recording the cost of delivery trucks: Delivery Equipment, Delivery Trucks, or Trucks. Once the company chooses the specific title to use, however, all subsequent transactions involving the account should be recorded under that account title.

BEFORE YOU GO ON...

◆ Review It

1. What is the correct sequence of steps in the recording process?
2. What contribution does the journal make to the recording process?
3. What are the standard form and content of a journal entry made in the general journal?

◆ Do It

The following events occurred during the first month of business of Hair It Is Inc., Kate Browne's beauty salon:

1. Issued common stock to shareholders in exchange for $20,000 cash.
2. Purchased $4,800 of equipment on account (to be paid in 30 days).
3. Interviewed three people for the position of beautician.

In what form (type of record) should the company record these three activities? Prepare the entries to record the transactions.

Reasoning: Kate should record the transactions in a journal, which is a chronological record of the transactions. The record should be a complete and accurate representation of the transactions' effects on the assets, liabilities, and stockholders' equity of her business.

Solution: Each transaction that is recorded is entered in the general journal. The three activities are recorded as follows:

1.	Cash		20,000	
		Common Stock		20,000
		(Issued stock for cash)		
2.	Equipment		4,800	
		Accounts Payable		4,800
		(Purchased equipment on account)		
3.		No entry because no transaction occurred.		

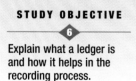

STUDY OBJECTIVE
6

Explain what a ledger is and how it helps in the recording process.

THE LEDGER

The entire group of accounts maintained by a company is referred to collectively as the **ledger**. The ledger keeps in one place all the information about changes in specific account balances.

Companies may use various kinds of ledgers, but every company has a general ledger. A **general ledger** contains all the assets, liabilities, and stockholders' equity accounts, as shown in Illustration 3-18. A business can use a loose-leaf binder or card file for the ledger, with each account kept on a separate sheet or card. Most businesses today, however, use a computerized accounting system. Whenever the term *ledger* is used in this textbook without additional specification, it will mean the general ledger.

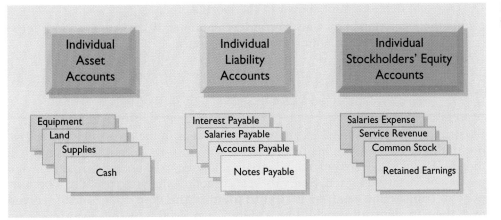

Illustration 3-18 The general ledger

CHART OF ACCOUNTS

The number and type of accounts used differ for each company, depending on the size, complexity, and type of business. For example, the number of accounts depends on the amount of detail desired by management. The management of one company may want one single account for all types of utility expense. Another may keep separate expense accounts for each type of utility expenditure, such as gas, electricity, and water. Similarly, a small corporation like Sierra Corporation will not have many accounts compared with a corporate giant like Ford Motor Company. Sierra may be able to manage and report its activities in 20 to 30 accounts, whereas Ford requires thousands of accounts to keep track of its worldwide activities.

Most companies list the accounts in a chart of accounts. The chart of accounts for Sierra Corporation is shown in Illustration 3-19. **Accounts shown in red are used in this chapter**; accounts shown in black are explained in later chapters. New accounts may be created as needed during the life of the business.

Illustration 3-19 Chart of accounts for Sierra Corporation

		SIERRA CORPORATION—Chart of Accounts		
Assets	**Liabilities**	**Stockholders' Equity**	**Revenues**	**Expenses**
Cash	Notes Payable	Common Stock	Service Revenue	Salaries Expense
Accounts Receivable	Accounts Payable	Retained Earnings		Supplies Expense
Advertising Supplies	Interest Payable	Dividends		Rent Expense
Prepaid Insurance	Unearned	Income Summary		Insurance Expense
Office Equipment	Service Revenue			Interest Expense
Accumulated Depreciation—	Salaries Payable			Depreciation Expense
Office Equipment				

POSTING

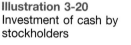

The procedure of transferring journal entries to ledger accounts is called post-ing. **This phase of the recording process accumulates the effects of jour-nalized transactions in the individual accounts.** Posting involves these steps:

1. In the ledger, enter in the appropriate columns of the debited account(s) the date and debit amount shown in the journal.
2. In the ledger, enter in the appropriate columns of the credited account(s) the date and credit amount shown in the journal.

THE RECORDING PROCESS ILLUSTRATED

Illustrations 3-20 through 3-30 show the basic steps in the recording process us-ing the October transactions of Sierra Corporation. Its accounting period is a month. A basic analysis and a debit–credit analysis precede the journalizing and posting of each transaction. Study these transaction analyses carefully. **The pur-pose of transaction analysis is first to identify the type of account involved and then to determine whether a debit or a credit to the account is re-quired.** You should always perform this type of analysis before preparing a jour-nal entry. Doing so will help you understand the journal entries discussed in this chapter as well as more complex journal entries to be described in later chapters.

Illustration 3-20
Investment of cash by stockholders

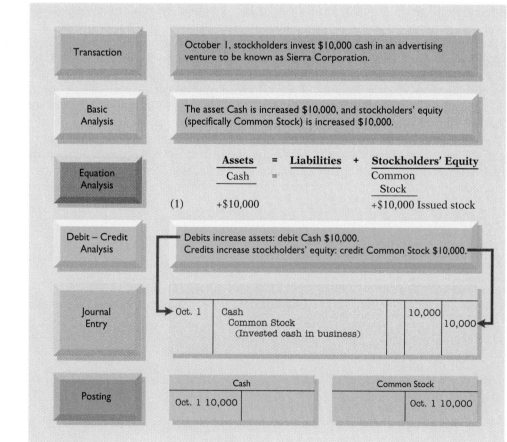

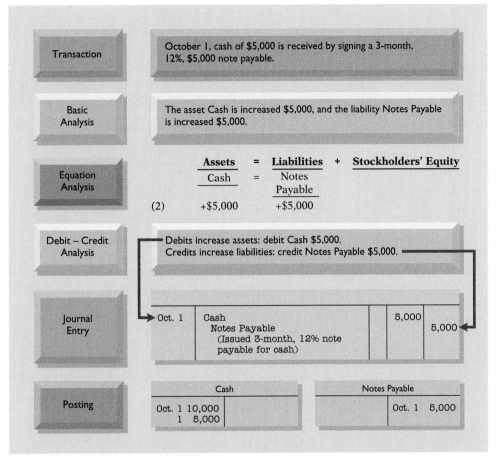

Illustration 3-21
Issue of note payable

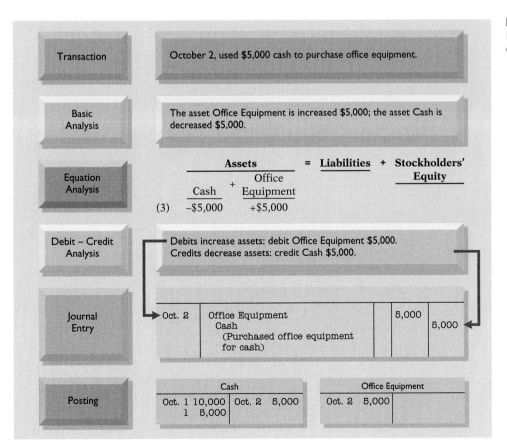

Illustration 3-22
Purchase of office
equipment

115

Illustration 3-23
Receipt of cash in advance from customer

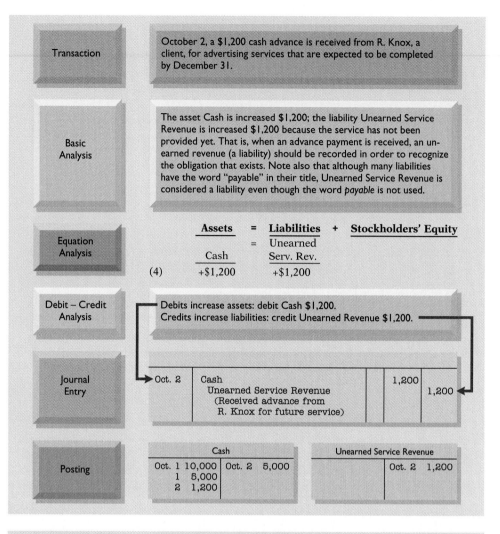

Transaction	October 2, a $1,200 cash advance is received from R. Knox, a client, for advertising services that are expected to be completed by December 31.
Basic Analysis	The asset Cash is increased $1,200; the liability Unearned Service Revenue is increased $1,200 because the service has not been provided yet. That is, when an advance payment is received, an unearned revenue (a liability) should be recorded in order to recognize the obligation that exists. Note also that although many liabilities have the word "payable" in their title, Unearned Service Revenue is considered a liability even though the word *payable* is not used.

Equation Analysis

	Assets	=	Liabilities	+	Stockholders' Equity
		=	Unearned		
	Cash		Serv. Rev.		
(4)	+$1,200		+$1,200		

Debit – Credit Analysis

Debits increase assets: debit Cash $1,200.
Credits increase liabilities: credit Unearned Revenue $1,200.

Journal Entry

Oct. 2	Cash	1,200	
	Unearned Service Revenue		1,200
	(Received advance from		
	R. Knox for future service)		

Posting

Cash				Unearned Service Revenue	
Oct. 1	10,000	Oct. 2	5,000	Oct. 2	1,200
1	5,000				
2	1,200				

Illustration 3-24
Services rendered for cash

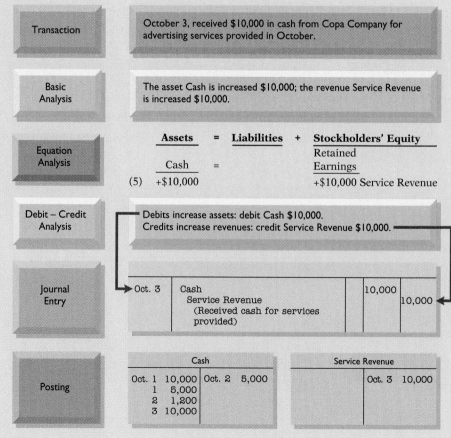

Transaction	October 3, received $10,000 in cash from Copa Company for advertising services provided in October.
Basic Analysis	The asset Cash is increased $10,000; the revenue Service Revenue is increased $10,000.

Equation Analysis

	Assets	=	Liabilities	+	Stockholders' Equity
					Retained
	Cash	=			Earnings
(5)	+$10,000				+$10,000 Service Revenue

Debit – Credit Analysis

Debits increase assets: debit Cash $10,000.
Credits increase revenues: credit Service Revenue $10,000.

Journal Entry

Oct. 3	Cash	10,000	
	Service Revenue		10,000
	(Received cash for services		
	provided)		

Posting

Cash				Service Revenue	
Oct. 1	10,000	Oct. 2	5,000	Oct. 3	10,000
1	5,000				
2	1,200				
3	10,000				

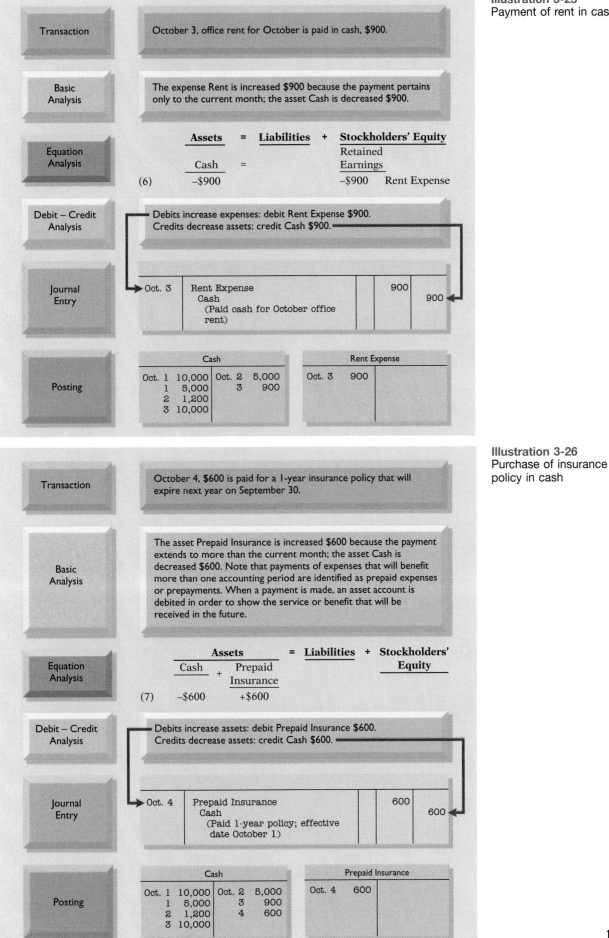

Illustration 3-25
Payment of rent in cash

Transaction	October 3, office rent for October is paid in cash, $900.
Basic Analysis	The expense Rent is increased $900 because the payment pertains only to the current month; the asset Cash is decreased $900.

Equation Analysis

	Assets	=	Liabilities	+	Stockholders' Equity
	Cash	=			Retained Earnings
(6)	−$900				−$900 Rent Expense

Debit − Credit Analysis

Debits increase expenses: debit Rent Expense $900.
Credits decrease assets: credit Cash $900.

Journal Entry

Oct. 3	Rent Expense	900	
	Cash		900
	(Paid cash for October office rent)		

Posting

Cash				Rent Expense	
Oct. 1	10,000	Oct. 2	5,000	Oct. 3	900
1	5,000	3	900		
2	1,200				
3	10,000				

Illustration 3-26
Purchase of insurance policy in cash

Transaction	October 4, $600 is paid for a 1-year insurance policy that will expire next year on September 30.
Basic Analysis	The asset Prepaid Insurance is increased $600 because the payment extends to more than the current month; the asset Cash is decreased $600. Note that payments of expenses that will benefit more than one accounting period are identified as prepaid expenses or prepayments. When a payment is made, an asset account is debited in order to show the service or benefit that will be received in the future.

Equation Analysis

	Assets		=	Liabilities	+	Stockholders' Equity
	Cash	+	Prepaid Insurance			
(7)	−$600		+$600			

Debit − Credit Analysis

Debits increase assets: debit Prepaid Insurance $600.
Credits decrease assets: credit Cash $600.

Journal Entry

Oct. 4	Prepaid Insurance	600	
	Cash		600
	(Paid 1-year policy; effective date October 1)		

Posting

Cash				Prepaid Insurance	
Oct. 1	10,000	Oct. 2	5,000	Oct. 4	600
1	5,000	3	900		
2	1,200	4	600		
3	10,000				

Illustration 3-27
Purchase of supplies
on credit

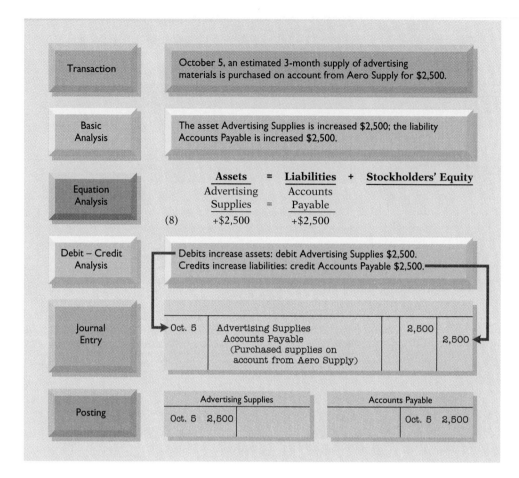

Transaction	October 5, an estimated 3-month supply of advertising materials is purchased on account from Aero Supply for $2,500.
Basic Analysis	The asset Advertising Supplies is increased $2,500; the liability Accounts Payable is increased $2,500.

Equation Analysis

	Assets	**=**	**Liabilities**	**+**	**Stockholders' Equity**
	Advertising Supplies	=	Accounts Payable		
(8)	+$2,500		+$2,500		

Debit – Credit Analysis	Debits increase assets: debit Advertising Supplies $2,500. Credits increase liabilities: credit Accounts Payable $2,500.

Journal Entry

Oct. 5	Advertising Supplies	2,500	
	Accounts Payable		2,500
	(Purchased supplies on account from Aero Supply)		

Posting

Advertising Supplies		Accounts Payable	
Oct. 5 2,500			Oct. 5 2,500

Illustration 3-28
Hiring of new employees

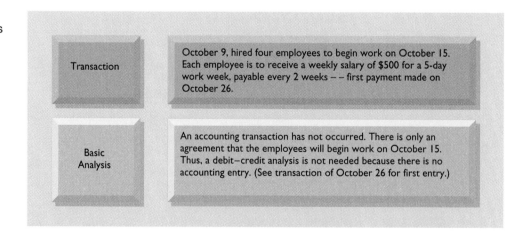

Transaction	October 9, hired four employees to begin work on October 15. Each employee is to receive a weekly salary of $500 for a 5-day work week, payable every 2 weeks – – first payment made on October 26.
Basic Analysis	An accounting transaction has not occurred. There is only an agreement that the employees will begin work on October 15. Thus, a debit–credit analysis is not needed because there is no accounting entry. (See transaction of October 26 for first entry.)

Illustration 3-29
Payment of dividend

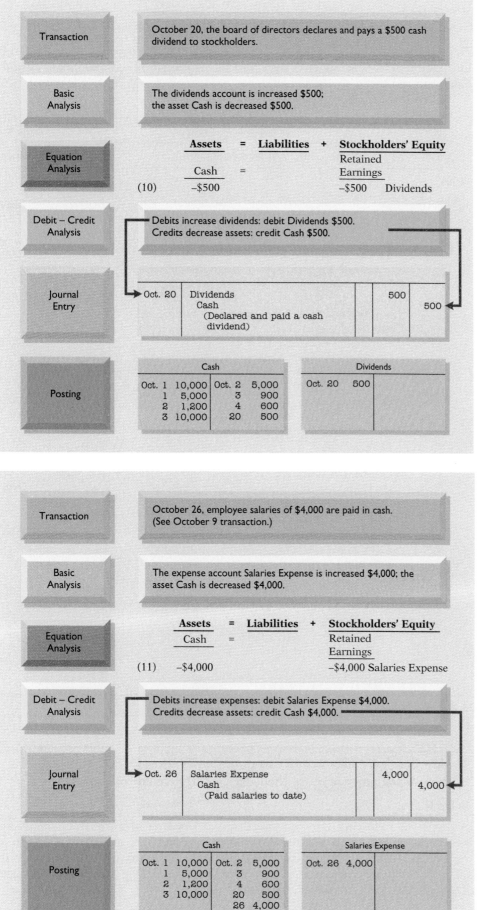

| Transaction | October 20, the board of directors declares and pays a $500 cash dividend to stockholders. |

| Basic Analysis | The dividends account is increased $500; the asset Cash is decreased $500. |

Equation Analysis

		Assets	=	**Liabilities**	+	**Stockholders' Equity**
		Cash	=			Retained Earnings
(10)		−$500				−$500 Dividends

| Debit – Credit Analysis | Debits increase dividends: debit Dividends $500. Credits decrease assets: credit Cash $500. |

Journal Entry

Oct. 20	Dividends		500	
	Cash			500
	(Declared and paid a cash dividend)			

Posting

Cash					Dividends	
Oct. 1	10,000	Oct. 2	5,000	Oct. 20	500	
1	5,000	3	900			
2	1,200	4	600			
3	10,000	20	500			

Illustration 3-30
Payment of cash for
employee salaries

| Transaction | October 26, employee salaries of $4,000 are paid in cash. (See October 9 transaction.) |

| Basic Analysis | The expense account Salaries Expense is increased $4,000; the asset Cash is decreased $4,000. |

Equation Analysis

		Assets	=	**Liabilities**	+	**Stockholders' Equity**
		Cash	=			Retained Earnings
(11)		−$4,000				−$4,000 Salaries Expense

| Debit – Credit Analysis | Debits increase expenses: debit Salaries Expense $4,000. Credits decrease assets: credit Cash $4,000. |

Journal Entry

Oct. 26	Salaries Expense		4,000	
	Cash			4,000
	(Paid salaries to date)			

Posting

Cash					Salaries Expense	
Oct. 1	10,000	Oct. 2	5,000	Oct. 26	4,000	
1	5,000	3	900			
2	1,200	4	600			
3	10,000	20	500			
		26	4,000			

119

SUMMARY ILLUSTRATION OF JOURNALIZING AND POSTING

The journal for Sierra Corporation for the month of October is summarized in Illustration 3-31. The ledger is shown in Illustration 3-32 with all balances highlighted in red.

Illustration 3-31
General journal for Sierra Corporation

Date		Account Titles and Explanation	Debit	Credit
GENERAL JOURNAL				
2001				
Oct.	1	Cash	10,000	
		Common Stock		10,000
		(Invested cash in business)		
	1	Cash	5,000	
		Notes Payable		5,000
		(Issued 3-month, 12% note payable for cash)		
	2	Office Equipment	5,000	
		Cash		5,000
		(Purchased office equipment for cash)		
	2	Cash	1,200	
		Unearned Service Revenue		1,200
		(Received advance from R. Knox for future service)		
	3	Cash	10,000	
		Service Revenue		10,000
		(Received cash for services rendered)		
	3	Rent Expense	900	
		Cash		900
		(Paid cash for October office rent)		
	4	Prepaid Insurance	600	
		Cash		600
		(Paid 1-year policy; effective date October 1)		
	5	Advertising Supplies	2,500	
		Accounts Payable		2,500
		(Purchased supplies on account from Aero Supply)		
	20	Dividends	500	
		Cash		500
		(Declared and paid a cash dividend)		
	26	Salaries Expense	4,000	
		Cash		4,000
		(Paid salaries to date)		

BEFORE YOU GO ON...

◆ **Review It**

1. How does journalizing differ from posting?
2. What is the purpose of (a) the ledger and (b) a chart of accounts?

◆ **Do It**

In the week following her successful grand opening of Hair It Is Inc., Kate Browne collected $2,280 in cash for hair styling services, and she paid $400 in wages and $92 for utilities. Kate recorded these transactions in a general journal and posted the entries to the general ledger. Explain the purpose and process of journalizing and posting these transactions.

GENERAL LEDGER

Illustration 3-32
General ledger for Sierra
Corporation

Cash					Unearned Service Revenue		
Oct. 1	10,000	Oct. 2	5,000			Oct. 2	1,200
1	5,000	3	900				
2	1,200	4	600			Bal.	1,200
3	10,000	20	500				
		26	4,000				
Bal.	15,200						

Advertising Supplies			Common Stock		
Oct. 5	2,500			Oct. 1	10,000
Bal.	2,500			Bal.	10,000

Prepaid Insurance			Dividends		
Oct. 4	600		Oct. 20	500	
Bal.	600		Bal.	500	

Office Equipment			Service Revenue		
Oct. 2	5,000			Oct. 3	10,000
Bal.	5,000			Bal.	10,000

Notes Payable			Salaries Expense		
		Oct. 1	5,000	Oct. 26	4,000	
		Bal.	5,000	Bal.	4,000	

Accounts Payable			Rent Expense		
		Oct. 5	2,500	Oct. 3	900	
		Bal.	2,500	Bal.	900	

Reasoning: Every business must keep track of its financial activities (receipts, payments, receivables, payables, etc.); journalizing does this. However, just recording every transaction in chronological order does not make the entries useful. To be useful, the entries need to be classified and summarized; posting the entries to specific ledger accounts does this.

Solution: The purpose of journalizing is to record every transaction in chronological order. Journalizing involves dating every transaction, measuring the dollar amount of each transaction, identifying or labeling each amount with account titles, and recording in a standard format equal debits and credits. Posting involves transferring the journalized debits and credits to specific accounts in the ledger.

THE TRIAL BALANCE

A **trial balance** is a list of accounts and their balances at a given time. Customarily, a trial balance is prepared at the end of an accounting period. The accounts are listed in the order in which they appear in the ledger. Debit balances are listed in the left column and credit balances in the right column. The totals of the two columns must be equal.

STUDY OBJECTIVE

8

Explain the purposes of a trial balance.

The primary purpose of a trial balance is to prove the mathematical equality of debits and credits after posting. Under the double-entry system this equality will occur when the sum of the debit account balances equals the sum of the credit account balances. A trial balance also uncovers errors in journalizing and posting. For example, a trial balance may well have allowed detection of the error at Fidelity Investments discussed in the opening story. In addition, a trial balance is useful in the preparation of financial statements, as explained in the next chapter.

These are the procedures for preparing a trial balance:

1. List the account titles and their balances.
2. Total the debit and credit columns.
3. Verify the equality of the two columns.

The trial balance prepared from the ledger of Sierra Corporation is presented in Illustration 3-33. Note that the total debits, $28,700, equal the total credits, $28,700.

Illustration 3-33 Sierra Corporation trial balance

SIERRA CORPORATION
Trial Balance
October 31, 2001

	Debit	Credit
Cash	$ 15,200	
Advertising Supplies	2,500	
Prepaid Insurance	600	
Office Equipment	5,000	
Notes Payable		$ 5,000
Accounts Payable		2,500
Unearned Service Revenue		1,200
Common Stock		10,000
Dividends	500	
Service Revenue		10,000
Salaries Expense	4,000	
Rent Expense	900	
	$28,700	$28,700

LIMITATIONS OF A TRIAL BALANCE

A trial balance does not prove that all transactions have been recorded or that the ledger is correct. Numerous errors may exist even though the trial balance columns agree. For example, the trial balance may balance even when any of the following occurs: (1) a transaction is not journalized, (2) a correct journal entry is not posted, (3) a journal entry is posted twice, (4) incorrect accounts are used in journalizing or posting, or (5) offsetting errors are made in recording the amount of a transaction. In other words, as long as equal debits and credits are posted, even to the wrong account or in the wrong amount, the total debits will equal the total credits. Nevertheless, despite its limitations, the trial balance is a useful screen for finding errors and is frequently used in practice.

BEFORE YOU GO ON...

◆ **Review It**

1. What is a trial balance, and how is it prepared?

2. What is the primary purpose of a trial balance?
3. What are the limitations of a trial balance?

DECISION TOOLKIT

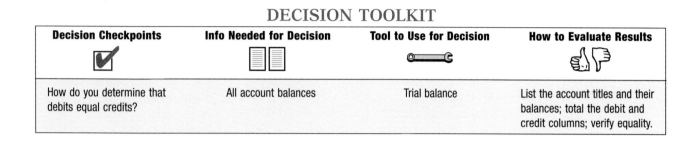

Decision Checkpoints	Info Needed for Decision	Tool to Use for Decision	How to Evaluate Results
How do you determine that debits equal credits?	All account balances	Trial balance	List the account titles and their balances; total the debit and credit columns; verify equality.

USING THE DECISION TOOLKIT

The Kansas Farmers' Vertically Integrated Cooperative, Inc. (K-VIC), was formed by over 200 northeast Kansas farmers in the late 1980s. Its purpose is to use raw materials, primarily grain and meat products grown by K-VIC's members, to process this material into end-user food products and to distribute the products nationally. Profits not needed for expansion or investment are returned to the members annually, on a pro-rata basis, according to the market value of the grain and meat products received from each farmer.

Assume that the following information was prepared for K-VIC's trial balance:

KANSAS FARMERS' VERTICALLY INTEGRATED COOPERATIVE, INC.
Trial Balance
December 31, 2001
(in thousands)

	Debit	Credit
Accounts Receivable	$ 712,000	
Accounts Payable		$ 37,000
Advertising and Promotion Payable		141,000
Buildings	365,000	
Cash	32,000	
Cost of Goods Sold	2,384,000	
Current Maturity of Long-Term Debt		12,000
Inventories	1,291,000	
Land	110,000	
Long-Term Debt		873,000
Machinery and Equipment	63,000	
Notes Payable to Members		495,000
Retained Earnings		822,000
Sales Revenue		3,741,000
Salaries and Wages Payable		62,000
Selling and Administrative Expense	651,000	
Trucking Expense	500,000	
	$6,108,000	$6,183,000

Because the trial balance is not in balance, you have checked with various people responsible for entering accounting data and have discovered the following:

1. The purchase of five new trucks, costing $7 million and paid for with cash, was not recorded.
2. A data entry clerk accidentally deleted the account name for an account with a credit balance of $472 million, so the amount was added to the Long-Term Debt account in the trial balance.
3. December cash sales revenue of $75 million was credited to the Sales Revenue account, but the other half of the entry was not made.
4. $50 million of selling expenses were mistakenly charged to Trucking Expense.

Instructions

Answer these questions:

(a) Which mistake or mistakes have caused the trial balance to be out of balance?
(b) Should all of the items be corrected? Explain.
(c) What is the name of the account the data entry clerk deleted?
(d) Make the necessary corrections and balance the trial balance.
(e) On your trial balance, write BAL beside the accounts that should be shown on the balance sheet and INC beside those that should be shown on the income statement.

Solution

(a) Only mistake 3 has caused the trial balance to be out of balance.
(b) All of the items should be corrected. The misclassification error (mistake 4) on the selling expense would not affect bottom line net income, but it does affect the amounts reported in the two expense accounts.
(c) There is no Common Stock account, so that must be the account that was deleted by the data entry clerk.
(d) and (e):

KANSAS FARMERS' VERTICALLY INTEGRATED COOPERATIVE, INC.
Trial Balance
December 31, 2001
(in thousands)

	Debit	Credit	
Accounts Receivable	$ 712,000		BAL
Accounts Payable		$ 37,000	BAL
Advertising and Promotion Payable		141,000	BAL
Buildings	365,000		BAL
Cash	100,000		BAL
Common Stock		472,000	BAL
Cost of Goods Sold	2,384,000		INC
Current Maturity of Long-Term Debt		12,000	BAL
Inventories	1,291,000		BAL
Land	110,000		BAL
Long-Term Debt		401,000	BAL
Machinery and Equipment	70,000		BAL

Notes Payable to Members	495,000	BAL
Retained Earnings	822,000	BAL
Sales Revenue	3,741,000	INC
Salaries and Wages Payable	62,000	BAL
Selling and Administrative Expense	701,000	INC
Trucking Expense	450,000	INC
	$6,183,000	$6,183,000

SUMMARY OF STUDY OBJECTIVES

1 *Analyze the effect of business transactions on the basic accounting equation.* Each business transaction must have a dual effect on the accounting equation. For example, if an individual asset is increased, there must be a corresponding (a) decrease in another asset, or (b) increase in a specific liability, or (c) increase in stockholders' equity.

2 *Explain what an account is and how it helps in the recording process.* An account is an individual accounting record of increases and decreases in specific asset, liability, and stockholders' equity items.

3 *Define debits and credits and explain how they are used to record business transactions.* The terms *debit* and *credit* are synonymous with *left* and *right*. Assets, dividends, and expenses are increased by debits and decreased by credits. Liabilities, common stock, retained earnings, and revenues are increased by credits and decreased by debits.

4 *Identify the basic steps in the recording process.* The basic steps in the recording process are: (a) analyze each transaction in terms of its effect on the accounts, (b) enter the transaction information in a journal, and (c) transfer the journal information to the appropriate accounts in the ledger.

5 *Explain what a journal is and how it helps in the recording process.* The initial accounting record of a transaction is entered in a journal before the data are entered in the accounts. A journal (a) discloses in one place the complete effect of a transaction, (b) provides a chronological record of transactions, and (c) prevents or locates errors because the debit and credit amounts for each entry can be readily compared.

6 *Explain what a ledger is and how it helps in the recording process.* The entire group of accounts maintained by a company is referred to collectively as a ledger. The ledger keeps in one place all the information about changes in specific account balances.

7 *Explain what posting is and how it helps in the recording process.* Posting is the procedure of transferring journal entries to the ledger accounts. This phase of the recording process accumulates the effects of journalized transactions in the individual accounts.

8 *Explain the purposes of a trial balance.* A trial balance is a list of accounts and their balances at a given time. The primary purpose of the trial balance is to prove the mathematical equality of debits and credits after posting. A trial balance also uncovers errors in journalizing and posting and is useful in preparing financial statements.

DECISION TOOLKIT—A SUMMARY

Decision Checkpoints	Info Needed for Decision	Tool to Use for Decision	How to Evaluate Results
Has an accounting transaction occurred?	Details of the event	Accounting equation	Determine the effect, if any, on assets, liabilities, and stockholders' equity.
How do you determine that debits equal credits?	All account balances	Trial balance	List the account titles and their balances; total the debit and credit columns; verify equality.

GLOSSARY

Account An individual accounting record of increases and decreases in specific asset, liability, and stockholders' equity items. (p. 103)

Accounting information system The system of collecting and processing transaction data and communicating financial information to interested parties. (p. 96)

Accounting transactions Events that require recording in the financial statements because they affect assets, liabilities, or stockholders' equity. (p. 97)

Chart of accounts A list of a company's accounts. (p. 113)

Credit The right side of an account. (p. 104)

Debit The left side of an account. (p. 104)

Double-entry system A system that records the dual effect of each transaction in appropriate accounts. (p. 105)

General journal The most basic form of journal. (p. 110)

General ledger A ledger that contains all asset, liability, and stockholders' equity accounts. (p. 112)

Journal An accounting record in which transactions are initially recorded in chronological order. (p. 110)

Journalizing The procedure of entering transaction data in the journal. (p. 110)

Ledger The group of accounts maintained by a company. (p. 112)

Posting The procedure of transferring journal entries to the ledger accounts. (p. 114)

T account The basic form of an account. (p. 104)

Trial balance A list of accounts and their balances at a given time. (p. 121)

DEMONSTRATION PROBLEM

Bob Sample and other student investors opened Campus Carpet Cleaning Inc. on September 1, 2001. During the first month of operations the following transactions occurred:

Sept. 1	Stockholders invested $20,000 cash in the business.
2	Paid $1,000 cash for store rent for the month of September.
3	Purchased industrial carpet-cleaning equipment for $25,000, paying $10,000 in cash and signing a $15,000 6-month, 12% note payable.
4	Paid $1,200 for 1-year accident insurance policy.
10	Received bill from the *Daily News* for advertising the opening of the cleaning service, $200.
15	Performed services on account for $6,200.
20	Declared and paid a $700 cash dividend to stockholders.
30	Received $5,000 from customers billed on September 15.

The chart of accounts for the company is the same as for Sierra Corporation except for the following: Cleaning Equipment and Advertising Expense.

Instructions

(a) Journalize the September transactions.
(b) Open ledger accounts and post the September transactions.
(c) Prepare a trial balance at September 30, 2001.

Problem-Solving Strategies

1. Make separate journal entries for each transaction.
2. Note that all debits precede all credit entries.
3. In journalizing, make sure debits equal credits.
4. In journalizing, use specific account titles taken from the chart of accounts.
5. Provide an appropriate explanation of each journal entry.
6. Arrange ledger in statement order, beginning with the balance sheet accounts.
7. Post in chronological order.
8. Prepare a trial balance, which lists accounts in the order in which they appear in the ledger.
9. List debit balances in the left column and credit balances in the right column.

Solution to Demonstration Problem

(a)

GENERAL JOURNAL

Date	Account Titles and Explanation	Debit	Credit
2001			
Sept. 1	Cash	20,000	
	Common Stock		20,000
	(Invested cash in business)		

2	Rent Expense		1,000	
	Cash			1,000
	(Paid September rent)			
3	Cleaning Equipment		25,000	
	Cash			10,000
	Notes Payable			15,000
	(Purchased cleaning equipment for cash			
	and 6-month, 12% note payable)			
4	Prepaid Insurance		1,200	
	Cash			1,200
	(Paid 1-year insurance policy)			
10	Advertising Expense		200	
	Accounts Payable			200
	(Received bill from *Daily News* for			
	advertising)			
15	Accounts Receivable		6,200	
	Service Revenue			6,200
	(To record credit sale)			
20	Dividends		700	
	Cash			700
	(Declared and paid a cash dividend)			
30	Cash		5,000	
	Accounts Receivable			5,000
	(To record collection of accounts receivable)			

(b)

GENERAL LEDGER

Cash

Sept. 1	20,000	Sept. 2	1,000		
30	5,000	3	10,000		
		4	1,200		
		20	700		
Bal.	12,100				

Common Stock

		Sept. 1	20,000
		Bal.	20,000

Accounts Receivable

Sept. 15	6,200	Sept. 30	5,000
Bal.	1,200		

Dividends

Sept. 20	700	
Bal.	700	

Prepaid Insurance

Sept. 4	1,200	
Bal.	1,200	

Service Revenue

	Sept. 30	6,200
	Bal.	6,200

Cleaning Equipment

Sept. 3	25,000	
Bal.	25,000	

Advertising Expense

Sept. 10	200	
Bal.	200	

Notes Payable

	Sept. 3	15,000
	Bal.	15,000

Rent Expense

Sept. 2	1,000	
Bal.	1,000	

Accounts Payable

	Sept. 10	200
	Bal.	200

(c)

CAMPUS CARPET CLEANING, INC.
Trial Balance
September 30, 2001

	Debit	Credit
Cash	$12,100	
Accounts Receivable	1,200	
Prepaid Insurance	1,200	
Cleaning Equipment	25,000	
Notes Payable		$15,000
Accounts Payable		200
Common Stock		20,000
Dividends	700	
Service Revenue		6,200
Advertising Expense	200	
Rent Expense	1,000	
	$41,400	$41,400

SELF-STUDY QUESTIONS

Answers are at the end of the chapter.

(SO 1)   1. The effects on the basic accounting equation of performing services for cash are to:
(a) increase assets and decrease stockholders' equity.
(b) increase assets and increase stockholders' equity.
(c) increase assets and increase liabilities.
(d) increase liabilities and increase stockholders' equity.

(SO 1)   2. Genesis Company buys a $900 machine on credit. This transaction will affect the:
(a) income statement only.
(b) balance sheet only.
(c) income statement and stockholders' equity statement only.
(d) income statement, stockholders' equity statement, and balance sheet.

(SO 2)   3. Which statement about an account is *true?*
(a) In its simplest form, an account consists of two parts.
(b) An account is an individual accounting record of increases and decreases in specific asset, liability, and stockholders' equity items.
(c) There are separate accounts for specific assets and liabilities but only one account for stockholders' equity items.
(d) The left side of an account is the credit or decrease side.

(SO 3)   4. Debits:
(a) increase both assets and liabilities.
(b) decrease both assets and liabilities.

(c) increase assets and decrease liabilities.
(d) decrease assets and increase liabilities.

(SO 3)   5. A revenue account:
(a) is increased by debits.
(b) is decreased by credits.
(c) has a normal balance of a debit.
(d) is increased by credits.

(SO 3)   6. Which accounts normally have debit balances?
(a) Assets, expenses, and revenues.
(b) Assets, expenses, and retained earnings.
(c) Assets, liabilities, and dividends.
(d) Assets, dividends, and expenses.

(SO 4)   7. Which is *not* part of the recording process?
(a) Analyzing transactions.
(b) Preparing a trial balance.
(c) Entering transactions in a journal.
(d) Posting transactions.

(SO 5)   8. Which of these statements about a journal is *false?*
(a) It contains only revenue and expense accounts.
(b) It provides a chronological record of transactions.
(c) It helps to locate errors because the debit and credit amounts for each entry can be readily compared.
(d) It discloses in one place the complete effect of a transaction.

(SO 6)   9. A ledger:
(a) contains only asset and liability accounts.
(b) should show accounts in alphabetical order.
(c) is a collection of the entire group of accounts maintained by a company.

(d) provides a chronological record of trans-actions.

(SO 7) 10. Posting:
(a) normally occurs before journalizing.
(b) transfers ledger transaction data to the journal.
(c) is an optional step in the recording process.
(d) transfers journal entries to ledger accounts.

(SO 8) 11. 〇━━━〇 A trial balance:
(a) is a list of accounts with their balances at a given time.
(b) proves the mathematical accuracy of jour-nalized transactions.

(c) will not balance if a correct journal entry is posted twice.
(d) proves that all transactions have been recorded.

12. 〇━━━〇 A trial balance will not balance if: (SO 8)
(a) a correct journal entry is posted twice.
(b) the purchase of supplies on account is deb-ited to Supplies and credited to Cash.
(c) a $100 cash dividend is debited to Dividends for $1,000 and credited to Cash for $100.
(d) a $450 payment on account is debited to Accounts Payable for $45 and credited to Cash for $45.

QUESTIONS

1. Describe the accounting information system and the steps in the recording process.

2. Can a business enter into a transaction that affects only the left side of the basic accounting equation? If so, give an example.

3. 〇━━━〇 Are the following events recorded in the accounting records? Explain your answer in each case.
(a) A major stockholder of the company dies.
(b) Supplies are purchased on account.
(c) An employee is fired.
(d) The company pays a cash dividend to its stock-holders.

4. Indicate how each business transaction affects the basic accounting equation.
(a) Paid cash for janitorial services.
(b) Purchased equipment for cash.
(c) Issued common stock to investors in exchange for cash.
(d) Paid an account payable in full.

5. Why is an account referred to as a T account?

6. The terms *debit* and *credit* mean "increase" and "de-crease," respectively. Do you agree? Explain.

7. Charles Thon, a fellow student, contends that the double-entry system means each transaction must be recorded twice. Is Charles correct? Explain.

8. Teresa Alvarez, a beginning accounting student, be-lieves debit balances are favorable and credit bal-ances are unfavorable. Is Teresa correct? Discuss.

9. State the rules of debit and credit as applied to (a) asset accounts, (b) liability accounts, and (c) the Common Stock account.

10. What is the normal balance for each of these ac-counts?
(a) Accounts Receivable.
(b) Cash.
(c) Dividends.
(d) Accounts Payable.
(e) Service Revenue.
(f) Salaries Expense.
(g) Common Stock.

11. Indicate whether each account is an asset, a liabil-ity, or a stockholders' equity account and whether it would have a normal debit or credit balance.
(a) Accounts Receivable.
(b) Accounts Payable.
(c) Equipment.
(d) Dividends.
(e) Supplies.

12. For the following transactions, indicate the account debited and the account credited.
(a) Supplies are purchased on account.
(b) Cash is received on signing a note payable.
(c) Employees are paid salaries in cash.

13. For each account listed here, indicate whether it gen-erally will have debit entries only, credit entries only, or both debit and credit entries.
(a) Cash.
(b) Accounts Receivable.
(c) Dividends.
(d) Accounts Payable.
(e) Salaries Expense.
(f) Service Revenue.

14. What are the basic steps in the recording process?

15. What are the advantages of using the journal in the recording process?

16. (a) When entering a transaction in the journal, should the debit or credit be written first?
(b) Which should be indented, the debit or the credit?

17. (a) Can accounting transaction debits and credits be recorded directly in the ledger accounts?
(b) What are the advantages of first recording trans-actions in the journal and then posting to the ledger?

18. Journalize these accounting transactions.
(a) Stockholders invested $9,000 in the business in exchange for common stock.
(b) Insurance of $800 is paid for the year.
(c) Supplies of $1,500 are purchased on account.
(d) Cash of $7,500 is received for services rendered.

19. (a) What is a ledger?
    (b) Why is a chart of accounts important?
20. What is a trial balance and what are its purposes?
21. Kap Shin is confused about how accounting information flows through the accounting system. He believes information flows in this order:
    (a) Debits and credits are posted to the ledger.
    (b) Accounting transaction occurs.
    (c) Information is entered in the journal.
    (d) Financial statements are prepared.
    (e) Trial balance is prepared.
    Indicate to Kap the proper flow of the information.

22. Two students are discussing the use of a trial balance. They wonder whether the following errors, each considered separately, would prevent the trial balance from balancing. What would you tell them?
    (a) The bookkeeper debited Cash for $600 and credited Wages Expense for $600 for payment of wages.
    (b) Cash collected on account was debited to Cash for $900, and Service Revenue was credited for $90.

BRIEF EXERCISES

Determine effect of transaction on basic accounting equation.
(SO 1)

BE3-1 Presented here are three economic events. On a sheet of paper, list the letters (a), (b), and (c) with columns for assets, liabilities, and stockholders' equity. In each column, indicate whether the event increased (+), decreased (−), or had no effect (NE) on assets, liabilities, and stockholders' equity.
(a) Purchased supplies on account.
(b) Received cash for providing a service.
(c) Expenses paid in cash.

Determine effect of transaction on basic accounting equation.
(SO 1)

BE3-2 Follow the same format as in BE3-1. Determine the effect on assets, liabilities, and stockholders' equity of the following three events:
(a) Issued common stock to investors in exchange for cash.
(b) Paid cash dividend to stockholders.
(c) Received cash from a customer who had previously been billed for services provided.

Indicate debit and credit effects.
(SO 3)

BE3-3 For each of the following accounts indicate the effect of a debit or a credit on the account and the normal balance.
(a) Accounts Payable.   (d) Accounts Receivable.
(b) Advertising Expense.   (e) Retained Earnings.
(c) Service Revenue.   (f) Dividends.

Identify accounts to be debited and credited.
(SO 3)

BE3-4 Transactions for the H. J. Oslo Company for the month of June are presented next. Identify the accounts to be debited and credited for each transaction.
    June 1 Issues common stock to investors in exchange for $2,500 cash.
          2 Buys equipment on account for $900.
          3 Pays $500 to landlord for June rent.
         12 Bills J. Kronsnoble $300 for welding work done.

Journalize transactions.
(SO 5)

BE3-5 Use the data in BE3-4 and journalize the transactions. (You may omit explanations.)

Identify steps in the recording process.
(SO 4)

BE3-6 Tage Shumway, a fellow student, is unclear about the basic steps in the recording process. Identify and briefly explain the steps in the order in which they occur.

Indicate basic debit–credit analysis.
(SO 4)

BE3-7 J. A. Norris Corporation has the following transactions during August of the current year. Indicate (a) the basic analysis and (b) the debit–credit analysis illustrated on pages 114–119.

    Aug. 1 Issues shares of common stock to investors in exchange for $5,000.
          4 Pays insurance in advance for 6 months, $1,800.
         16 Receives $900 from clients for services rendered.
         27 Pays secretary $500 salary.

Journalize transactions.
(SO 5)

BE3-8 Use the data in BE3-7 and journalize the transactions. (You may omit explanations.)

Post journal entries to T accounts.
(SO 7)

BE3-9 Selected transactions for Gonzales Company are presented in journal form (without explanations). Post the transactions to T accounts.

Date		Account Title	Debit	Credit
May	5	Accounts Receivable	3,200	
		Service Revenue		3,200
	12	Cash	2,400	
		Accounts Receivable		2,400
	15	Cash	2,000	
		Service Revenue		2,000

BE3-10   From the ledger balances below, prepare a trial balance for P. J. Carland Company at June 30, 2001. All account balances are normal.

Prepare a trial balance.
(SO 8)

Accounts Payable	$ 4,000	Service Revenue	$6,000
Cash	3,800	Accounts Receivable	3,000
Common Stock	20,000	Salaries Expense	4,000
Dividends	1,200	Rent Expense	1,000
Equipment	17,000		

BE3-11   An inexperienced bookkeeper prepared the following trial balance that does not balance. Prepare a correct trial balance, assuming all account balances are normal.

Prepare a corrected trial balance.
(SO 8)

GOMEZ COMPANY
Trial Balance
December 31, 2001

	Debit	Credit
Cash	$18,800	
Prepaid Insurance		$ 3,500
Accounts Payable		3,000
Unearned Revenue	2,200	
Common Stock		10,000
Retained Earnings		7,000
Dividends		4,500
Service Revenue		25,600
Salaries Expense	18,600	
Rent Expense		2,400
	$39,600	$56,000

EXERCISES

E3-1   Selected transactions for Speedy Lawn Care Company, Inc., are listed here:
1. Issued common stock to investors in exchange for cash received from investors.
2. Paid monthly rent.
3. Received cash from customers when service was rendered.
4. Billed customers for services performed.
5. Paid dividend to stockholders.
6. Incurred advertising expense on account.
7. Received cash from customers billed in (4).
8. Purchased additional equipment for cash.
9. Purchased equipment on account.

Analyze the effect of transactions.
(SO 1)

Instructions
Describe the effect of each transaction on assets, liabilities, and stockholders' equity. For example, the first answer is: (1) Increase in assets and increase in stockholders' equity.

E3-2   Sidhu Computer Company entered into these transactions during May 2001:
1. Purchased computer terminals for $29,000 from Digital Equipment on account.
2. Paid $4,000 cash for May rent on storage space.
3. Received $15,000 cash from customers for contracts billed in April.
4. Provided computer services to Brieske Construction Company for $3,000 cash.

Analyze the effect of transactions on assets, liabilities, and stockholders' equity.
(SO 1)

5. Paid Southern States Power Co. $11,000 cash for energy usage in May.
6. Stockholders invested an additional $22,000 in the business in exchange for common stock of the company.
7. Paid Digital Equipment for the terminals purchased in (1).
8. Incurred advertising expense for May of $1,000 on account.

Instructions
Indicate with the appropriate letter whether each of the transactions above results in:
(a) an increase in assets and a decrease in assets.
(b) an increase in assets and an increase in stockholders' equity.
(c) an increase in assets and an increase in liabilities.
(d) a decrease in assets and a decrease in stockholders' equity.
(e) a decrease in assets and a decrease in liabilities.
(f) an increase in liabilities and a decrease in stockholders' equity.
(g) an increase in stockholders' equity and a decrease in liabilities.

Analyze transactions and compute net income.
(SO 1)

E3-3 A tabular analysis of the transactions made during August, 2001 by Downtown Company during its first month of operations is shown below. Each increase and decrease in stockholders' equity is explained.

Cash	+	Accounts Receivable	+	Supplies	+	Office Equipment	=	Accounts Payable	+	Stockholders' Equity	
1. +$15,000										+$15,000	Issued common stock
2. −2,000						+$5,000		+$3,000			
3. −750				+$750							
4. +4,600		+$3,400								+8,000	Service Revenue
5. −1,500								−1,500			
6. −2,000										−2,000	Dividends
7. −650										−650	Rent Expense
8. +450		−450									
9. −2,900										−2,900	Salaries Expense
10.								+500		−500	Utilities Expense

Instructions
(a) Describe each transaction.
(b) Determine how much stockholders' equity increased for the month.
(c) Compute the net income for the month.

Prepare an income statement, retained earnings statement, and balance sheet.
(SO 1)

E3-4 The tabular analysis of transactions for Downtown Company is presented in E3-3.

Instructions
Prepare an income statement and a retained earnings statement for August and a balance sheet at August 31, 2001.

Identify debits, credits, and normal balances.
(SO 3)

E3-5 Selected transactions for Expensive Designs, an interior decorator corporation, in its first month of business, are as follows:
1. Issued stock to investors for $10,000 in cash.
2. Purchased used car for $5,000 cash for use in business.
3. Purchased supplies on account for $500.
4. Billed customers $1,800 for services performed.
5. Paid $200 cash for advertising start of business.
6. Received $700 cash from customers billed in transaction (4).
7. Paid creditor $300 cash on account.
8. Paid dividends of $400 cash to stockholders.

Instructions
For each transaction indicate (a) the basic type of account debited and credited (asset, liability, stockholders' equity); (b) the specific account debited and credited (Cash, Rent

Expense, Service Revenue, etc.); (c) whether the specific account is increased or decreased; and (d) the normal balance of the specific account. Use the following format, in which transaction 1 is given as an example:

	Account Debited				Account Credited			
Trans- action	(a) Basic Type	(b) Specific Account	(c) Effect	(d) Normal Balance	(a) Basic Type	(b) Specific Account	(c) Effect	(d) Normal Balance
1	Asset	Cash	Increase	Debit	Stock- holders' equity	Common Stock	Increase	Credit

E3-6 Data for Expensive Designs, interior decorator, are presented in E3-5.

Journalize transactions. *(SO 5)*

Instructions
Journalize the transactions. Do not provide explanations.

E3-7 This information relates to Verbos Real Estate Agency Corporation:

Analyze transactions and determine their effect on accounts. *(SO 3)*

Oct. 1 Stockholders invested $21,000 in exchange for common stock of the corporation.
2 Hires an administrative assistant.
3 Buys office furniture for $1,900, on account.
6 Sells a house and lot for B. Rollins; commissions due from Rollins, $6,200 (not paid by Rollins at this time).
10 Receives cash of $140 as commissions for renting an apartment for the owner of the apartment.
27 Pays $700 on account for the office furniture purchased on October 3.
30 Pays the administrative assistant $960 in salary for October.

Instructions
Prepare the debit–credit analysis for each transaction as illustrated on pages 114–119.

E3-8 Transaction data for Verbos Real Estate Agency are presented in E3-7.

Journalize transactions. *(SO 5)*

Instructions
Journalize the transactions. Do not provide explanations.

E3-9 Selected transactions from the journal of Red Hot Chili Peppers Inc. during its first month of operations are presented here:

Post journal entries and prepare a trial balance. *(SO 7, 8)*

Date	Account Titles	Debit	Credit
Aug. 1	Cash	1,600	
	Common Stock		1,600
10	Cash	2,400	
	Service Revenue		2,400
12	Office Equipment	6,000	
	Cash		1,000
	Notes Payable		5,000
25	Accounts Receivable	1,400	
	Service Revenue		1,400
31	Cash	600	
	Accounts Receivable		600

Instructions
(a) Post the transactions to T accounts.
(b) Prepare a trial balance at August 31, 2001.

Journalize transactions from T accounts and prepare a trial balance.
(SO 5, 8)

E3-10 These T accounts summarize the ledger of Crabgrass Landscaping Company Inc. at the end of the first month of operations:

Cash			
Apr. 1	9,000	Apr. 15	600
12	900	25	3,500
29	400		
30	800		

Unearned Revenue		
	Apr. 30	800

Accounts Receivable			
Apr. 7	2,400	Apr. 29	400

Common Stock		
	Apr. 1	9,000

Supplies	
Apr. 4	4,800

Service Revenue		
	Apr. 7	2,400
	Apr. 12	900

Accounts Payable			
Apr. 25	3,500	Apr. 4	4,800

Salaries Expense	
Apr. 15	600

Instructions
(a) Prepare in the order they occurred the journal entries (including explanations) that resulted in the amounts posted to the account.
(b) Prepare a trial balance at April 30, 2001.

Journalize transactions from T accounts and prepare a trial balance.
(SO 5, 8)

E3-11 Here is the ledger for Dave Matthews Co.:

Cash			
Oct. 1	4,000	Oct. 4	400
10	750	12	1,500
10	5,000	15	250
20	800	30	300
25	2,000	31	500

Common Stock		
	Oct. 1	4,000
	25	2,000

Accounts Receivable			
Oct. 6	800	Oct. 20	800
20	740		

Dividends		
Oct. 30	300		

Supplies			
Oct. 4	400	Oct. 31	180

Service Revenue		
	Oct. 6	800
	10	750
	20	740

Furniture	
Oct. 3	2,000

Store Wages Expense	
Oct. 31	500

Notes Payable		
	Oct. 10	5,000

Supplies Expense	
Oct. 31	180

Accounts Payable			
Oct. 12	1,500	Oct. 3	2,000

Rent Expense	
Oct. 15	250

Instructions

(a) Reproduce the journal entries for the transactions that occurred on October 1, 10, and 20 and provide explanations for each.

(b) Prepare a trial balance at October 31, 2001.

E3-12 Selected transactions for Dave Letterman Corporation during its first month in business are presented below:

Analyze transactions, prepare journal entries, and post transactions to T accounts.
(SO 1, 5, 7)

Sept. 1 Issued common stock in exchange for $15,000 cash received from investors.

　　 5 Purchased equipment for $10,000, paying $5,000 in cash and the balance on account.

　　 25 Paid $3,000 cash on balance owed for equipment.

　　 30 Paid $500 cash dividend.

Letterman's chart of accounts shows: Cash, Equipment, Accounts Payable, Common Stock, and Dividends.

Instructions

(a) Prepare a tabular analysis of the September transactions. The column headings should be: Cash + Equipment = Accounts Payable + Stockholders' Equity. For transactions affecting stockholders' equity, provide explanations in the right margin, as shown on page 103.

(b) Journalize the transactions. Do not provide explanations.

(c) Post the transactions to T accounts.

E3-13 The bookkeeper for Rosenberger's Equipment Repair Corporation made these errors in journalizing and posting:

Analyze errors and their effects on trial balance.
(SO 8)

1. A credit posting of $400 to Accounts Receivable was omitted.
2. A debit posting of $750 for Prepaid Insurance was debited to Insurance Expense.
3. A collection on account of $100 was journalized and posted as a debit to Cash $100 and a credit to Service Revenue $100.
4. A credit posting of $300 to Property Taxes Payable was made twice.
5. A cash purchase of supplies for $250 was journalized and posted as a debit to Supplies $25 and a credit to Cash $25.
6. A debit of $465 to Advertising Expense was posted as $456.

Instructions

For each error, indicate (a) whether the trial balance will balance; if the trial balance will not balance, indicate (b) the amount of the difference, and (c) the trial balance column that will have the larger total. Consider each error separately. Use the following form, in which error 1 is given as an example:

Error	(a) In Balance	(b) Difference	(c) Larger Column
1	No	$400	Debit

E3-14 The accounts in the ledger of Rocket Delivery Service contain the following balances on July 31, 2001:

Prepare a trial balance.
(SO 8)

Accounts Receivable	$13,642	Prepaid Insurance	$ 1,968
Accounts Payable	7,396	Repair Expense	961
Cash	?	Service Revenue	15,610
Delivery Equipment	59,360	Dividends	700
Gas and Oil Expense	758	Common Stock	40,000
Insurance Expense	523	Salaries Expense	4,428
Notes Payable	28,450	Salaries Payable	815
		Retained Earnings	4,636

Instructions

Prepare a trial balance with the accounts arranged as illustrated in the chapter, and fill in the missing amount for Cash.

PROBLEMS: SET A

Analyze transactions and compute net income.
(SO 1)

P3-1A On April 1 Matrix Travel Agency Inc. was established. These transactions were completed during the month:

1. Stockholders invested $20,000 cash in the company in exchange for common stock.
2. Paid $400 cash for April office rent.
3. Purchased office equipment for $2,500 cash.
4. Incurred $300 of advertising costs in the *Chicago Tribune,* on account.
5. Paid $600 cash for office supplies.
6. Earned $9,000 for services provided: Cash of $1,000 is received from customers, and the balance of $8,000 is billed to customers on account.
7. Paid $200 cash dividends.
8. Paid *Chicago Tribune* amount due in transaction (4).
9. Paid employees' salaries, $1,200.
10. Received $8,000 in cash from customers who have previously been billed in transaction (6).

Instructions
(a) Prepare a tabular analysis of the transactions using these column headings: Cash, Accounts Receivable, Supplies, Office Equipment, Accounts Payable, Common Stock, and Retained Earnings. Include margin explanations for any changes in Retained Earnings.
(b) From an analysis of the column Retained Earnings, compute the net income or net loss for April.

Analyze transactions and prepare financial statements.
(SO 1)

P3-2A Jessica Bell started her own consulting firm, Bell Consulting Inc., on May 1, 2001. The following transactions occurred during the month of May:

May 1 Stockholders invested $10,000 cash in the business.
    2 Paid $800 for office rent for the month.
    3 Purchased $500 of supplies on account.
    5 Paid $50 to advertise in the *County News.*
    9 Received $1,000 cash for services provided.
   12 Paid $200 cash dividend.
   15 Performed $3,000 of services on account.
   17 Paid $2,500 for employee salaries.
   20 Paid for the supplies purchased on account on May 3.
   23 Received a cash payment of $2,000 for services provided on account on May 15.
   26 Borrowed $5,000 from the bank on a note payable.
   29 Purchased office equipment for $2,400 on account.
   30 Paid $150 for utilities.

Instructions
(a) Show the effects of the previous transactions on the accounting equation using the following format:

		Assets				Liabilities		Stockholders' Equity	
Date	Cash +	Accounts Receivable +	Supplies +	Office Equipment =	Notes Payable +	Accounts Payable +	Common Stock +	Retained Earnings	

Include margin explanations for any changes in Retained Earnings.
(b) Prepare an income statement for the month of May.
(c) Prepare a balance sheet at May 31, 2001.

Analyze transactions and prepare an income statement, retained earnings statement, and balance sheet.
(SO 1)

P3-3A Ivan Izo created a corporation providing legal services, Ivan Izo Inc., on July 1, 2001. On July 31 the balance sheet showed: Cash $4,000; Accounts Receivable $1,500; Supplies $500; Office Equipment $5,000; Accounts Payable $4,200; Common Stock $6,500; and Retained Earnings $300. During August the following transactions occurred:

1. Collected $1,400 of accounts receivable.
2. Paid $2,700 cash on accounts payable.

3. Earned revenue of $6,400, of which $3,000 is collected in cash and the balance is due in September.
4. Purchased additional office equipment for $1,000, paying $400 in cash and the balance on account.
5. Paid salaries $1,500, rent for August $900, and advertising expenses $350.
6. Declared and paid a cash dividend of $550.
7. Received $2,000 from Standard Federal Bank; the money was borrowed on a 4-month note payable.
8. Incurred utility expenses for month on account, $250.

Instructions

(a) Prepare a tabular analysis of the August transactions beginning with July 31 balances. The column heading should be: Cash + Accounts Receivable + Supplies + Office Equipment = Notes Payable + Accounts Payable + Common Stock + Retained Earnings. Include margin explanations for any changes in Retained Earnings.
(b) Prepare an income statement for August, a retained earnings statement for August, and a classified balance sheet at August 31.

P3-4A Fantasy Miniature Golf and Driving Range Inc. was opened on March 1 by Jim Zarle. These selected events and transactions occurred during March:

Journalize a series of transactions.
(SO 3, 5)

Mar.	1	Stockholders invested $60,000 cash in the business in exchange for common stock of the corporation.
	3	Purchased Lee's Golf Land for $38,000 cash. The price consists of land $23,000, building $9,000, and equipment $6,000. (Record this in a single entry.)
	5	Advertised the opening of the driving range and miniature golf course, paying advertising expenses of $1,600 cash.
	6	Paid cash $1,480 for a 1-year insurance policy.
	10	Purchased golf clubs and other equipment for $1,600 from Tiger Company, payable in 30 days.
	18	Received golf fees of $800 in cash for golf fees earned.
	19	Sold 100 coupon books for $15.00 each in cash. Each book contains ten coupons that enable the holder to play one round of miniature golf or to hit one bucket of golf balls. [*Hint:* The revenue is not earned until the customers use the coupons.]
	25	Declared and paid a $500 cash dividend.
	30	Paid salaries of $600.
	30	Paid Tiger Company in full.
	31	Received $800 of fees in cash.

The company uses these accounts: Cash, Prepaid Insurance, Land, Buildings, Equipment, Accounts Payable, Unearned Golf Revenue, Common Stock, Retained Earnings, Dividends, Golf Revenue, Advertising Expense, and Salaries Expense.

Instructions

Journalize the March transactions, including explanations.

P3-5A Chambers Architects incorporated as licensed architects on April 1, 2001. During the first month of the operation of the business, these events and transactions occurred:

Journalize transactions, post, and prepare a trial balance.
(SO 3, 5, 6, 7, 8)

Apr.	1	Stockholders invested $13,000 cash in exchange for common stock of the corporation.
	1	Hired a secretary-receptionist at a salary of $300 per week, payable monthly.
	2	Paid office rent for the month, $700.
	3	Purchased architectural supplies on account from Halo Company, $1,500.
	10	Completed blueprints on a carport and billed client $900 for services.
	11	Received $500 cash advance from R. Welk for the design of a new home.
	20	Received $1,800 cash for services completed and delivered to P. Donahue.
	30	Paid secretary-receptionist for the month, $1,200.
	30	Paid $800 to Halo Company on account.

The company uses these accounts: Cash, Accounts Receivable, Supplies, Accounts Payable, Unearned Revenue, Common Stock, Service Revenue, Salaries Expense, and Rent Expense.

Instructions

(a) Journalize the transactions, including explanations.
(b) Post to the ledger T accounts.
(c) Prepare a trial balance on April 30, 2001.

Journalize transactions, post, and prepare a trial balance.
(SO 3, 5, 6, 7, 8)

P3-6A This is the trial balance of Dirty Laundry Corporation on September 30:

DIRTY LAUNDRY
Trial Balance
September 30, 2001

	Debit	Credit
Cash	$ 8,500	
Accounts Receivable	2,200	
Supplies	1,700	
Equipment	8,000	
Accounts Payable		$ 5,000
Unearned Revenue		700
Common Stock		14,700
	$20,400	$20,400

The October transactions were as follows:

Oct. 5 Received $900 cash from customers on account.
10 Billed customers for services performed, $3,500.
15 Paid employee salaries, $1,200.
17 Performed $600 of services for customers who paid in advance in August.
20 Paid $1,600 to creditors on account.
29 Paid a $500 cash dividend.
31 Paid utilities, $700.

Instructions

(a) Prepare a general ledger using T accounts. Enter the opening balances in the ledger accounts as of October 1. Provision should be made for these additional accounts: Dividends, Laundry Revenue, Salaries Expense, and Utilities Expense.
(b) Journalize the transactions, including explanations.
(c) Post to the ledger accounts.
(d) Prepare a trial balance on October 31, 2001.

Prepare a correct trial balance.
(SO 8)

P3-7A This trial balance of Salem Co. does not balance.

SALEM CO.
Trial Balance
June 30, 2001

	Debit	Credit
Cash		$ 2,840
Accounts Receivable	$ 3,231	
Supplies	800	
Equipment	3,000	
Accounts Payable		2,666
Unearned Revenue	1,200	
Common Stock		9,000
Dividends	800	
Service Revenue		2,380
Salaries Expense	3,400	
Office Expense	910	
	$13,341	$16,886

Each of the listed accounts has a normal balance per the general ledger. An examination of the ledger and journal reveals the following errors:

1. Cash received from a customer on account was debited for $570, and Accounts Receivable was credited for the same amount. The actual collection was for $750.
2. The purchase of a typewriter on account for $340 was recorded as a debit to Supplies for $340 and a credit to Accounts Payable for $340.
3. Services were performed on account for a client for $890. Accounts Receivable was debited for $890 and Service Revenue was credited for $89.
4. A debit posting to Salaries Expense of $600 was omitted.
5. A payment on account for $206 was credited to Cash for $206 and credited to Accounts Payable for $260.
6. Payment of a $400 cash dividend to Salem's stockholders was debited to Salaries Expense for $400 and credited to Cash for $400.

Instructions
Prepare the correct trial balance.

P3-8A The Oldies Theater Inc. was recently formed. It began operations in March 2001. The Oldies is unique in that it will show only triple features of sequential theme movies. As of February 28, the ledger of The Oldies showed: Cash $16,000; Land $42,000; Buildings (concession stand, projection room, ticket booth, and screen) $18,000; Equipment $16,000; Accounts Payable $12,000; and Common Stock $80,000. During the month of March the following events and transactions occurred:

Journalize transactions, post, and prepare a trial balance.
(SO 3, 5, 6, 7, 8)

Mar. 2 Acquired the three *Star Wars* movies (*Star Wars®*, *The Empire Strikes Back*, and *The Return of the Jedi*) to be shown for the first three weeks of March. The film rental was $12,000; $4,000 was paid in cash and $8,000 will be paid on March 10.
    3 Ordered the first three *Star Trek* movies to be shown the last 10 days of March. It will cost $400 per night.
    9 Received $8,500 cash from admissions.
  10 Paid balance due on *Star Wars* movies rental and $3,000 on February 28 accounts payable.
  11 Hired M. Brewer to operate concession stand. Brewer agrees to pay The Oldies Theater 15% of gross receipts, payable monthly.
  12 Paid advertising expenses $800.
  20 Received $7,200 cash from admissions.
  20 Received the *Star Trek* movies and paid rental fee of $4,000.
  31 Paid salaries of $3,800.
  31 Received statement from M. Brewer showing gross receipts from concessions of $8,000 and the balance due to The Oldies of $1,200 for March. Brewer paid half the balance due and will remit the remainder on April 5.
  31 Received $18,500 cash from admissions.

In addition to the accounts identified above, the chart of accounts includes: Accounts Receivable, Admission Revenue, Concession Revenue, Advertising Expense, Film Rental Expense, and Salaries Expense.

Instructions
(a) Using T accounts, enter the beginning balances to the ledger.
(b) Journalize the March transactions, including explanations.
(c) Post the March journal entries to the ledger.
(d) Prepare a trial balance on March 31, 2001.

PROBLEMS: SET B

P3-1B Rabbit Ears Repair Shop Inc. was started on May 1. Here is a summary of the May transactions:

Analyze transactions and compute net income.
(SO 1)

1. Stockholders invested $16,000 cash in the company in exchange for common stock.
2. Purchased equipment for $5,000 cash.

3. Paid $400 cash for May office rent.
4. Paid $500 cash for supplies.
5. Incurred $550 of advertising costs in the *Beacon News* on account.
6. Received $4,100 in cash from customers for repair service.
7. Declared and paid a $500 cash dividend.
8. Paid part-time employee salaries, $1,200.
9. Paid utility bills, $140.
10. Provided repair service on account to customers, $400.
11. Collected cash of $120 for services billed in transaction (10).

Instructions

(a) Prepare a tabular analysis of the transactions using these column headings: Cash, Accounts Receivable, Supplies, Equipment, Accounts Payable, Common Stock, and Retained Earnings. Revenue is called Service Revenue. Include margin explanations for any changes in Retained Earnings.

(b) From an analysis of the column Retained Earnings, compute the net income or net loss for May.

Analyze transactions and prepare financial statements.
(SO 1)

P3-2B   Peter Alex started his own delivery service, Alex Deliveries Inc., on June 1, 2001. The following transactions occurred during the month of June:

June	1	Stockholders invested $15,000 cash in the business.
	2	Purchased a used van for deliveries for $10,000. Alex paid $2,000 cash and signed a note payable for the remaining balance.
	3	Paid $500 for office rent for the month.
	5	Performed $1,000 of services on account.
	9	Paid $200 in cash dividends.
	12	Purchased supplies for $150 on account.
	15	Received a cash payment of $750 for services provided on June 5.
	17	Purchased gasoline for $100 on account.
	20	Received a cash payment of $1,500 for services provided.
	23	Made a cash payment of $500 on the note payable.
	26	Paid $250 for utilities.
	29	Paid for the gasoline purchased on account on June 17.
	30	Paid $500 for employee salaries.

Instructions

(a) Show the effects of the previous transactions on the accounting equation using the following format:

		Assets				Liabilities		Stockholders' Equity	
Date	Cash	+ Accounts Receivable	+ Supplies	+ Delivery Van	=	Notes Payable	+ Accounts Payable	+ Common Stock	+ Retained Earnings

Include margin explanations for any changes in Retained Earnings.

(b) Prepare an income statement for the month of June.

(c) Prepare a balance sheet at June 30, 2001.

Analyze transactions and prepare an income statement, retained earnings statement, and balance sheet.
(SO 1)

P3-3B   Donna Corso opened Corso Company, a veterinary business in Hills, Iowa, on August 1, 2001. On August 31 the balance sheet showed: Cash $9,000; Accounts Receivable $1,700; Supplies $600; Office Equipment $6,000; Accounts Payable $3,600; Common Stock $13,000; and Retained Earnings $700. During September the following transactions occurred:

1. Paid $3,100 cash on accounts payable.
2. Collected $1,300 of accounts receivable.
3. Purchased additional office equipment for $4,100, paying $800 in cash and the balance on account.

4. Earned revenue of $8,900, of which $2,500 is paid in cash and the balance is due in October.
5. Declared and paid a $600 cash dividend.
6. Paid salaries $700, rent for September $900, and advertising expense $300.
7. Incurred utility expenses for month on account, $170.
8. Received $7,000 from Hilldale Bank; the money was borrowed on a 6-month note payable.

Instructions

(a) Prepare a tabular analysis of the September transactions beginning with August 31 balances. The column headings should be: Cash + Accounts Receivable + Supplies + Office Equipment = Notes Payable + Accounts Payable + Common Stock + Retained Earnings. Include margin explanations for any changes in Retained Earnings.
(b) Prepare an income statement for September, a retained earnings statement for September, and a classified balance sheet at September 30, 2001.

P3-4B   Gold Rush Park was started on April 1 by Neil Young. These selected events and transactions occurred during April:

Journalize a series of transactions.
(SO 3, 5)

Apr.   1   Stockholders invested $60,000 cash in the business in exchange for common stock.
  4   Purchased land costing $30,000 for cash.
  8   Incurred advertising expense of $1,800 on account.
  11   Paid salaries to employees, $1,700.
  12   Hired park manager at a salary of $4,000 per month, effective May 1.
  13   Paid $3,000 for a 1-year insurance policy.
  17   Paid $600 cash dividends.
  20   Received $5,700 in cash for admission fees.
  25   Sold 100 coupon books for $25 each. Each book contains ten coupons that entitle the holder to one admission to the park. [*Hint*: The revenue is not earned until the coupons are used.]
  30   Received $7,900 in cash admission fees.
  30   Paid $700 on account for advertising incurred on April 8.

The company uses the following accounts: Cash, Prepaid Insurance, Land, Accounts Payable, Unearned Admissions, Common Stock, Dividends, Admission Revenue, Advertising Expense, and Salaries Expense.

Instructions

Journalize the April transactions, including explanations.

P3-5B   Roger Miller incorporated Skeptical Accountants, an accounting practice, on May 1, 2001. During the first month of operations of his business, these events and transactions occurred:

Journalize transactions, post, and prepare a trial balance.
(SO 3, 5, 6, 7, 8)

May   1   Stockholders invested $52,000 cash in exchange for common stock of the corporation.
  2   Hired a secretary-receptionist at a salary of $1,000 per month.
  3   Purchased $1,200 of supplies on account from Read Supply Company.
  7   Paid office rent of $900 for the month.
  11   Completed a tax assignment and billed client $1,100 for services provided.
  12   Received $4,500 advance on a management consulting engagement.
  17   Received cash of $1,200 for services completed for H. Arnold Co.
  31   Paid secretary-receptionist $1,000 salary for the month.
  31   Paid 40% of balance due Read Supply Company.

The company uses the following chart of accounts: Cash, Accounts Receivable, Supplies, Accounts Payable, Unearned Revenue, Common Stock, Service Revenue, Salaries Expense, and Rent Expense.

Instructions

(a) Journalize the transactions, including explanations.
(b) Post to the ledger T accounts.
(c) Prepare a trial balance on May 31, 2001.

Journalize transactions, post, and prepare a trial balance.
(SO 3, 5, 6, 7, 8)

P3-6B The trial balance of Bellingham Dry Cleaners on June 30 is given here:

BELLINGHAM DRY CLEANERS
Trial Balance
June 30, 2001

	Debit	Credit
Cash	$12,532	
Accounts Receivable	10,536	
Supplies	4,844	
Equipment	25,950	
Accounts Payable		$15,878
Unearned Revenue		1,730
Common Stock		36,254
	$53,862	$53,862

The July transactions were as follows:

July	8	Collected $4,936 in cash on June 30 accounts receivable.
	9	Paid employee salaries, $2,100.
	11	Received $4,925 in cash for services provided.
	14	Paid June 30 creditors $10,750 on account.
	17	Purchased supplies on account, $554.
	22	Billed customers for services provided, $4,700.
	30	Paid employee salaries $3,114, utilities $1,584, and repairs $492.
	31	Paid $500 cash dividend.

Instructions
(a) Prepare a general ledger using T accounts. Enter the opening balances in the ledger accounts as of July 1. Provision should be made for the following additional accounts: Dividends, Dry Cleaning Revenue, Repair Expense, Salaries Expense, and Utilities Expense.
(b) Journalize the transactions.
(c) Post to the ledger accounts.
(d) Prepare a trial balance on July 31, 2001.

Prepare a correct trial balance.
(SO 8)

P3-7B This trial balance of Eau Claire Company does not balance.

EAU CLAIRE COMPANY
Trial Balance
May 31, 2001

	Debit	Credit
Cash	$ 5,850	
Accounts Receivable		$ 2,750
Prepaid Insurance	700	
Equipment	8,000	
Accounts Payable		4,500
Property Taxes Payable	560	
Common Stock		5,700
Retained Earnings		6,000
Service Revenue	6,690	
Salaries Expense	4,200	
Advertising Expense		1,100
Property Tax Expense	800	
	$26,800	$20,050

Your review of the ledger reveals that each account has a normal balance. You also discover the following errors:

1. The totals of the debit sides of Prepaid Insurance, Accounts Payable, and Property Tax Expense were each understated $100.
2. Transposition errors were made in Accounts Receivable and Service Revenue. Based on postings made, the correct balances were $2,570 and $6,960, respectively.
3. A debit posting to Salaries Expense of $200 was omitted.
4. A $700 cash dividend was debited to Common Stock for $700 and credited to Cash for $700.
5. A $420 purchase of supplies on account was debited to Equipment for $420 and credited to Cash for $420.
6. A cash payment of $250 for advertising was debited to Advertising Expense for $25 and credited to Cash for $25.
7. A collection from a customer for $210 was debited to Cash for $210 and credited to Accounts Payable for $210.

Instructions

Prepare the correct trial balance. [*Note:* The chart of accounts also includes the following: Dividends, Supplies, and Supplies Expense.]

P3-8B   Lights Out Theater Inc. was recently formed. All facilities were completed on March 31. On April 1, the ledger showed: Cash $6,000; Land $10,000; Buildings (concession stand, projection room, ticket booth, and screen) $8,000; Equipment $6,000; Accounts Payable $2,000; Mortgage Payable $8,000; and Common Stock $20,000. During April, the following events and transactions occurred:

Journalize transactions, post, and prepare a trial balance.
(SO 3, 5, 6, 7, 8)

Apr. 2   Paid film rental of $800 on first movie.
  3   Ordered two additional films at $700 each.
  9   Received $3,800 cash from admissions.
  10   Made $2,000 payment on mortgage and $1,000 on accounts payable.
  11   Hired R. Thoms to operate concession stand. Thoms agrees to pay Lights Out Theater 17% of gross receipts, payable monthly.
  12   Paid advertising expenses, $300.
  20   Received one of the films ordered on April 3 and was billed $500. The film will be shown in April.
  25   Received $3,200 cash from admissions.
  29   Paid salaries, $1,600.
  30   Received statement from R. Thoms showing gross receipts of $1,000 and the balance due to Lights Out Theater of $170 for April. Thoms paid half of the balance due and will remit the remainder on May 5.
  30   Prepaid $700 rental on special film to be run in May.

In addition to the accounts identified above, the chart of accounts shows: Accounts Receivable, Prepaid Rentals, Admission Revenue, Concession Revenue, Advertising Expense, Film Rental Expense, Salaries Expense.

Instructions

(a) Enter the beginning balances in the ledger T accounts as of April 1.
(b) Journalize the April transactions, including explanations.
(c) Post the April journal entries to the ledger T accounts.
(d) Prepare a trial balance on April 30, 2001.

*F*INANCIAL REPORTING AND ANALYSIS

FINANCIAL REPORTING PROBLEM: *Tootsie Roll Industries*

BYP3-1   The financial statements of **Tootsie Roll** in Appendix A at the back of this book contain the following selected accounts, all in thousands of dollars:

Common Stock	$ 22,527
Accounts Payable	12,450
Accounts Receivable	19,110
Selling, Marketing, and Administrative Expense	97,071
Prepaid Expenses	3,081
Property, Plant, and Equipment (net)	83,024
Net Sales	388,659

Instructions
(a) What is the increase and decrease side for each account? What is the normal balance for each account?
(b) Identify the probable other account in the transaction and the effect on that account when:
   (1) Accounts Receivable is decreased.
   (2) Accounts Payable is decreased.
   (3) Prepaid Expenses is increased.
(c) Identify the other account(s) that ordinarily would be involved when:
   (1) Interest Expense is increased.
   (2) Property, Plant, and Equipment is increased.

COMPARATIVE ANALYSIS PROBLEM: *Tootsie Roll vs. Hershey Foods*

BYP3-2   The financial statements of **Hershey Foods** are presented in Appendix B, following the financial statements for **Tootsie Roll** in Appendix A.

Instructions
(a) Based on the information contained in these financial statements, determine the normal balance for:

Tootsie Roll Industries	**Hershey Foods**
(1) Accounts Receivable	(1) Inventories
(2) Property, Plant, and Equipment	(2) Provision for Income Taxes
(3) Accounts Payable	(3) Accrued Liabilities
(4) Retained Earnings	(4) Common Stock
(5) Net Sales	(5) Interest Expense

(b) Identify the other account ordinarily involved when:
   (1) Accounts Receivable is increased.
   (2) Notes Payable is decreased.
   (3) Machinery is increased.
   (4) Interest Income is increased.

RESEARCH CASE

BYP3-3   The North American Industry Classification System (NAICS), a new classification system for organizing economic data, has recently replaced the separate standard classification systems previously used by Canada, the United States, and Mexico. NAICS provides a common standard framework for the collection of economic and financial data for all three nations.

Instructions
At your library, find the *NAICS Manual*, and answer the following:

(a) The NAICS numbering system uses five levels of detail to identify company activities. What do the first two digits identify? The fourth digit? The sixth digit?

(b) Identify the sector, subsector, industry group, NAICS industry, and U.S. industry represented by the code 513322.

INTERPRETING FINANCIAL STATEMENTS

BYP3-4   Chieftain International, Inc., is an oil and natural gas exploration and production company. A recent balance sheet reported $208 million in assets with only $4.6 million in liabilities, all of which were short-term accounts payable.

During the year, Chieftain expanded its holdings of oil and gas rights, drilled 37 new wells, and invested in expensive 3-D seismic technology. The company generated $19 million cash from operating activities and paid no dividends. It had a cash balance of $102 million at the end of the year.

Instructions

(a) Name at least two advantages to Chieftain from having no long-term debt. Can you think of disadvantages?

(b) What are some of the advantages to Chieftain from having this large a cash balance? What is a disadvantage?

(c) Why do you suppose Chieftain has the $4.6 million balance in accounts payable, since it appears that it could have made all its purchases for cash?

A GLOBAL FOCUS

BYP3-5   Doman Industries Ltd., whose products are sold in 30 countries worldwide, is an integrated Canadian forest products company.

Doman sells the majority of its lumber products in the United States, and a significant amount of its pulp products in Asia. Doman also has loans from other countries. For example, on June 18, 1999, the Company borrowed US$160 million at an annual interest rate of 12%. Doman must repay this loan, and interest, in U.S. dollars.

One of the challenges global companies face is to make themselves attractive to investors from other countries. This is difficult to do when different accounting rules in different countries blur the real impact of earnings. For example, in 1998 Doman reported a loss of $2.3 million, using Canadian accounting rules. Had it reported under U.S. accounting rules, its loss would have been $12.1 million.

Many companies that want to be more easily compared with U.S. and other global competitors have switched to U.S. accounting principles. Canadian National Railway, Corel, Cott, Inco, and the Thomson Corporation are but a few examples of large Canadian companies whose financial statements are now presented in U.S. dollars, which adhere to U.S. GAAP, or are reconciled to U.S. GAAP.

Instructions

(a) Identify advantages and disadvantages that companies should consider when switching to U.S. reporting standards.

(b) Suppose you wish to compare Doman Industries to a U.S.-based competitor. Do you believe the use of country-specific accounting policies would hinder your comparison? If so, explain how.

(c) Suppose you wish to compare Doman Industries to a Canadian-based competitor. If the companies chose to apply generally acceptable Canadian accounting policies differently, how could this affect your comparison of their financial results?

(d) Do you see any significant distinction between comparing statements prepared using generally accepted accounting principles of different countries and comparing statements prepared using generally accepted accounting principles of the same country (e.g. U.S.) but that apply the principles differently?

FINANCIAL ANALYSIS ON THE WEB

BYP3-6   *Purpose:* This exercise will familiarize you with skill requirements, job descriptions, and salaries for accounting careers.

Address: http://www.cob.ohio-state.edu/dept/fin/jobs/account.htm (or go to www.wiley.com/college/kimmel)

Steps: Go to the site shown above.

Instructions

Answer the following questions:

(a) What are the three broad areas of accounting?

(b) List four skills required in these areas.

(c) How do these areas differ in required skills?

(d) Explain one of the key job functions in accounting.

(e) Based on the *Smart Money* survey, what is the salary range for a junior staff accountant with Deloitte & Touche?

CRITICAL THINKING

GROUP DECISION CASE

BYP3-7 Lucy Lars operates Lucy Riding Academy, Inc. The academy's primary sources of revenue are riding fees and lesson fees, which are provided on a cash basis. Lucy also boards horses for owners, who are billed monthly for boarding fees. In a few cases, boarders pay in advance of expected use. For its revenue transactions, the academy maintains these accounts: Cash, Accounts Receivable, Unearned Revenue, Riding Revenue, Lesson Revenue, and Boarding Revenue.

The academy owns ten horses, a stable, a riding corral, riding equipment, and office equipment. These assets are accounted for in accounts Horses, Building, Riding Corral, Riding Equipment, and Office Equipment.

The academy employs stable helpers and an office employee, who receive weekly salaries. At the end of each month, the mail usually brings bills for advertising, utilities, and veterinary service. Other expenses include feed for the horses and insurance. For its expenses, the academy maintains the following accounts: Hay and Feed Supplies, Prepaid Insurance, Accounts Payable, Salaries Expense, Advertising Expense, Utilities Expense, Veterinary Expense, Hay and Feed Expense, and Insurance Expense.

Lucy Lars's sole source of personal income is dividends from the academy. Thus, the corporation declares and pays periodic dividends. To record stockholders' equity in the business and dividends, two accounts are maintained: Common Stock and Dividends.

During the first month of operations an inexperienced bookkeeper was employed. Lucy Lars asks you to review the following eight entries of the 50 entries made during the month. In each case, the explanation for the entry is correct.

May 1	Cash	15,000	
	Common Stock		15,000
	(Issued common stock in exchange for $15,000 cash)		
5	Cash	250	
	Riding Revenue		250
	(Received $250 cash for lesson fees)		
7	Cash	500	
	Boarding Revenue		500
	(Received $500 for boarding of horses beginning June 1)		
9	Hay and Feed Expense	1,700	
	Cash		1,700
	(Purchased estimated 5 months' supply of feed and hay for $1,700 on account)		
14	Riding Equipment	80	
	Cash		800
	(Purchased desk and other office equipment for $800 cash)		
15	Salaries Expense	400	
	Cash		400
	(Issued check to Lucy Lars for personal use)		
20	Cash	145	
	Riding Revenue		154
	(Received $154 cash for riding fees)		

May 31	Veterinary Expense	75	
	Accounts Payable		75
	(Received bill of $75 from veterinarian for services provided)		

Instructions

With the class divided into groups, answer the following:

(a) For each journal entry that is correct, so state. For each journal entry that is incorrect, prepare the entry that should have been made by the bookkeeper.

(b) Which of the incorrect entries would prevent the trial balance from balancing?

(c) What was the correct net income for May, assuming the bookkeeper originally reported net income of $4,500 after posting all 50 entries?

(d) What was the correct cash balance at May 31, assuming the bookkeeper reported a balance of $12,475 after posting all 50 entries?

COMMUNICATION ACTIVITY

BYP3-8   Milly Maid Company offers home cleaning service. Two recurring transactions for the company are billing customers for services provided and paying employee salaries. For example, on March 15 bills totaling $6,000 were sent to customers, and $2,000 was paid in salaries to employees.

Instructions

Write a memorandum to your instructor that explains and illustrates the steps in the recording process for each of the March 15 transactions. Use the format illustrated in the text under the heading "The Recording Process Illustrated" (p. 114).

ETHICS CASE

BYP3-9   Mary Vonesh is the assistant chief accountant at Staples Company, a manufacturer of computer chips and cellular phones. The company presently has total sales of $20 million. It is the end of the first quarter and Mary is hurriedly trying to prepare a general ledger trial balance so that quarterly financial statements can be prepared and released to management and the regulatory agencies. The total credits on the trial balance exceed the debits by $1,000. In order to meet the 4 P.M. deadline, Mary decides to force the debits and credits into balance by adding the amount of the difference to the Equipment account. She chose Equipment because it is one of the larger account balances; percentage-wise it will be the least misstated. Mary plugs the difference! She believes that the difference is quite small and will not affect anyone's decisions. She wishes that she had another few days to find the error but realizes that the financial statements are already late.

Instructions

(a) Who are the stakeholders in this situation?

(b) What ethical issues are involved?

(c) What are Mary's alternatives?

Answers to Self-Study Questions

1. b   2. b   3. b   4. c   5. d   6. d   7. b   8. a   9. c   10. d   11. a   12. c

Answer to Tootsie Roll Review It Question 4, p. 109

Accounts Receivable—debit; Income Taxes Payable—credit; Sales—credit; Selling, Marketing, and Administrative Expense—debit.

Accrual Accounting Concepts

CLA...
COMMON
PAR V...
$1 PER S...
NUMBER
A
CUSIP 9

◆ STUDY OBJECTIVES

After studying this chapter, you should be able to:

1 Explain the revenue recognition principle and the matching principle.

2 Differentiate between the cash basis and the accrual basis of accounting.

3 Explain why adjusting entries are needed and identify the major types of adjusting entries.

4 Prepare adjusting entries for prepayments.

5 Prepare adjusting entries for accruals.

6 Describe the nature and purpose of the adjusted trial balance.

7 Explain the purpose of closing entries.

8 Describe the required steps in the accounting cycle.

◆ TIMING IS EVERYTHING

A few simple truths:

Truth 1: Net income = Revenues − Expenses

Truth 2: In general, more net income is better than less.

Truth 3: To increase net income you must increase reported revenue or decrease reported expense.

Truth 4: Timing is everything.

So far you have learned some nice orderly rules about how to keep track of corporate transactions. Guess what? It isn't that nice and neat. In fact, it is often difficult to determine in what period some revenues and expenses should be reported. There are rules that give guidance, but occasionally these rules are overlooked, misinterpreted, or even intentionally ignored. Consider the following examples:

- Cambridge Biotech Corp., which develops vaccines and diagnostic tests for humans and animals, said that it reported revenue from transactions that "don't appear to be bona fide."
- Media Vision Technology Inc., a maker of sound and animation equipment for computers, was accused of operating a "phantom" warehouse to hide inventory for returned products already recorded as sales.
- Policy Management Systems Corp., which makes insurance software, said that it reported some sales before contracts were signed or products delivered.
- Penguin USA, a book publisher, said that it understated expenses in a number of years because it failed to report expenses for discounts given to customers for paying early.

In each case, accrual accounting concepts were violated. That is, revenues or expenses were not recorded in the proper period, which had a substantial impact on reported income.

Why might management want to report revenues or expenses in the wrong period? One *Wall Street Journal* article states that high-tech firms have intense pressure to report higher earnings every year. If actual perfor-

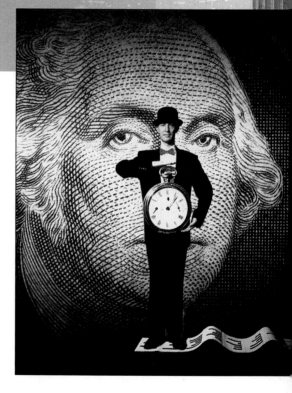

mance falls short of expectations, management might be tempted to bend the rules. An accounting expert suggests that investors and auditors should be suspicious of sharp increases in monthly sales at the end of each quarter or big jumps in fourth-quarter sales. Such events don't always mean management is cheating, but they are certainly worth investigating.[1]

[1]Based on Lee Burton, "Tech Concerns Fudge Figures to Buoy Stocks," *The Wall Street Journal,* May 19, 1994, p. B1.

As indicated in the opening story, making adjustments properly is important and necessary. To do otherwise leads to a misstatement of revenues and expenses. In this chapter we introduce you to the accrual accounting concepts that make such adjustments possible.

The organization and content of the chapter are as follows:

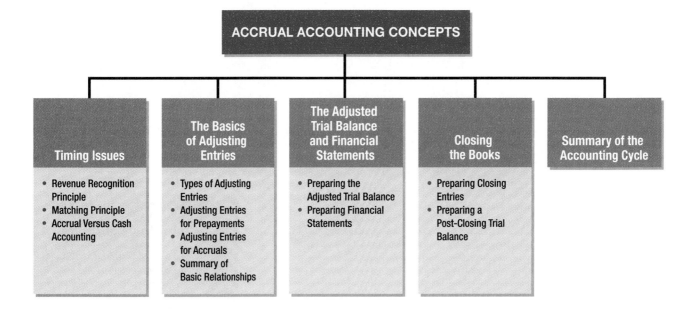

ACCRUAL ACCOUNTING CONCEPTS

Timing Issues	The Basics of Adjusting Entries	The Adjusted Trial Balance and Financial Statements	Closing the Books	Summary of the Accounting Cycle
• Revenue Recognition Principle • Matching Principle • Accrual Versus Cash Accounting	• Types of Adjusting Entries • Adjusting Entries for Prepayments • Adjusting Entries for Accruals • Summary of Basic Relationships	• Preparing the Adjusted Trial Balance • Preparing Financial Statements	• Preparing Closing Entries • Preparing a Post-Closing Trial Balance	

*T*IMING ISSUES

STUDY OBJECTIVE

1

Explain the revenue recognition principle and the matching principle.

Consider this story:

A grocery store owner from the old country kept his accounts payable on a spindle, accounts receivable on a note pad, and cash in a cigar box. His daughter, having just passed the CPA exam, chided her father: "I don't understand how you can run your business this way. How do you know what your profits are?"

"Well," the father replied, "when I got off the boat 40 years ago, I had nothing but the pants I was wearing. Today your brother is a doctor, your sister is a college professor, and you are a CPA. Your mother and I have a nice car, a well-furnished house, and a lake home. We have a good business and everything is paid for. So, you add all that together, subtract the pants, and there's your profit."

Although the old grocer may be correct in his evaluation of how to calculate income over his lifetime, most businesses need more immediate feedback about how well they are doing. For example, management usually wants monthly reports on financial results, most large corporations are required to present quarterly and annual financial statements to stockholders, and the Internal Revenue Service requires all businesses to file annual tax returns. Consequently, **accounting divides the economic life of a business into artificial time peri-**

ods. As indicated in Chapter 1, this is the time period assumption. **Accounting time periods are generally a month, a quarter, or a year**.

Helpful Hint An accounting time period that is one year long is called a fiscal year.

Many business transactions affect more than one of these arbitrary time periods. For example, a new building purchased by Citicorp or a new airplane purchased by Delta Air Lines will be used for many years. It doesn't make good sense to expense the full amount of the building or the airplane at the time it is purchased because each will be used for many subsequent periods. Therefore, it is necessary to determine the impact of each transaction on specific accounting periods.

Determining the amount of revenues and expenses to be reported in a given accounting period can be difficult. Proper reporting requires a thorough understanding of the nature of the company's business. Accountants have developed two principles to use as guidelines as part of generally accepted accounting principles (GAAP): the revenue recognition principle and the matching principle.

THE REVENUE RECOGNITION PRINCIPLE

The revenue recognition principle dictates that revenue should be recognized in the accounting period in which it is earned. In a service company, revenue is considered to be earned at the time the service is performed. To illustrate, assume a dry cleaning business cleans clothing on June 30, but customers do not claim and pay for their clothes until the first week of July. Under the revenue recognition principle, revenue is earned in June when the service is performed, not in July when the cash is received. At June 30 the dry cleaner would report a receivable on its balance sheet and revenue in its income statement for the service performed.

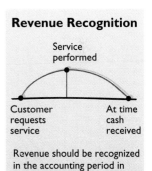

Revenue Recognition

Service performed

Customer requests service — At time cash received

Revenue should be recognized in the accounting period in which it is earned (generally when service is performed).

Improper application of the revenue recognition principle can have devastating consequences for investors. For example, the stock price of outdoor equipment manufacturer The North Face plunged when it announced that $9 million of sales from a previous period were being reversed because it had repurchased goods from a customer. This raised the question of whether a sale should have been recorded in the first place. Recently, investors also lost money because of improper revenue recognition at McKesson HBOC and Cendant Corporation.

DECISION TOOLKIT

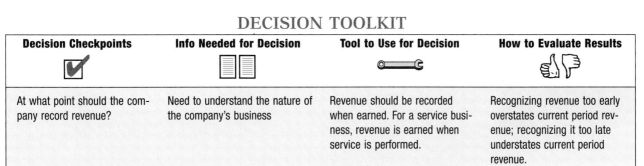

Decision Checkpoints	Info Needed for Decision	Tool to Use for Decision	How to Evaluate Results
At what point should the company record revenue?	Need to understand the nature of the company's business	Revenue should be recorded when earned. For a service business, revenue is earned when service is performed.	Recognizing revenue too early overstates current period revenue; recognizing it too late understates current period revenue.

THE MATCHING PRINCIPLE

In recognizing expenses, a simple rule is followed: "Let the expenses follow the revenues." Thus, expense recognition is tied to revenue recognition. Applied to the preceding example, this means that the salary expense incurred in performing the cleaning service on June 30 should be reported in the same period in which the service revenue is recognized. The critical issue in expense recognition is determining when the expense makes its contribution to revenue. This may or may not be the same period in which the expense is paid. If the salary incurred on June 30 is not paid until July, the dry cleaner would report salaries payable on its June 30 balance sheet. The practice of expense recognition is referred to as the match-

ing principle because it dictates that efforts (expenses) be matched with accomplishments (revenues). These relationships are shown in Illustration 4-1.

Illustration 4-1 GAAP relationships in revenue and expense recognition

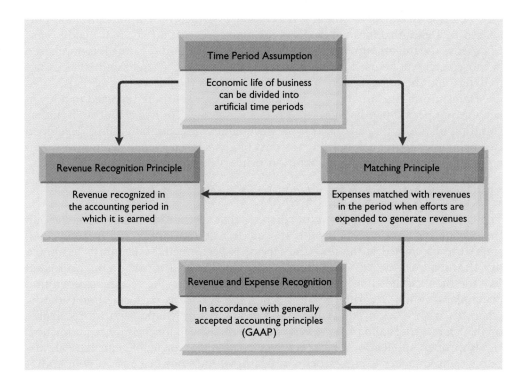

Time Period Assumption

Economic life of business can be divided into artificial time periods

Revenue Recognition Principle

Revenue recognized in the accounting period in which it is earned

Matching Principle

Expenses matched with revenues in the period when efforts are expended to generate revenues

Revenue and Expense Recognition

In accordance with generally accepted accounting principles (GAAP)

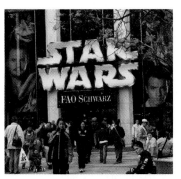

BUSINESS INSIGHT

Management Perspective

Suppose you are a filmmaker like George Lucas and spend $11 million to produce a film such as *StarWars*. Over what period should the cost be expensed? It should be expensed over the economic life of the film. But what is its economic life? The filmmaker must estimate how much revenue will be earned from box office sales, video sales, television, and games and toys—a period that could be less than a year or more than 20 years, as is the case for Twentieth Century Fox's *StarWars*. Originally released in 1977, and rereleased in 1997, domestic revenues total nearly $500 million for *StarWars* and continue to grow. This situation demonstrates the difficulty of properly matching expenses to revenues.

Source: StarTrek Newsletter, 22.

DECISION TOOLKIT

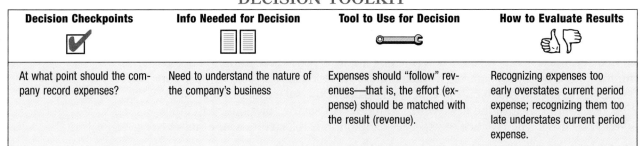

Decision Checkpoints	Info Needed for Decision	Tool to Use for Decision	How to Evaluate Results
At what point should the company record expenses?	Need to understand the nature of the company's business	Expenses should "follow" revenues—that is, the effort (expense) should be matched with the result (revenue).	Recognizing expenses too early overstates current period expense; recognizing them too late understates current period expense.

ACCRUAL VERSUS CASH BASIS OF ACCOUNTING

Application of the revenue recognition and matching principles results in accrual basis accounting. Accrual basis accounting means that transactions that change a company's financial statements are recorded **in the periods in which the events occur**, rather than in the periods in which the company receives or pays cash. For example, **using the accrual basis to determine net income means recognizing revenues when earned rather than when the cash is received, and recognizing expenses when incurred rather than when paid**.

Under cash basis accounting, **revenue is recorded only when the cash is received, and an expense is recorded only when cash is paid. An income statement presented under the cash basis of accounting does not satisfy generally accepted accounting principles**. Why? Because it fails to record revenue that has been earned but for which the cash has not been received, thus violating the revenue recognition principle. In addition, expenses are also not matched with earned revenues, and therefore the matching principle is violated. Accountants are sometimes asked to convert cash-based records to the accrual basis. As you might expect, extensive adjustments to the accounting records are required for this task.

Illustration 4-2 shows the relationship between accrual-based numbers and cash-based numbers, using a simple example. Suppose that you own a painting company and you paint a large building during year 1. In year 1 you incurred and paid total expenses of $50,000, which includes the cost of the paint and your employees' salaries. Now assume that you billed your customer $80,000 at the end of year 1, but you weren't paid until year 2. On an accrual basis, you would report the revenue during the period earned—year 1—and the expenses would be matched to the period in which the revenues were earned. Thus, your net income for year 1 would be $30,000, and no revenue or expense from this project would be reported in year 2. The $30,000 of income reported for year 1 provides a useful indication of the profitability of your efforts during that period. If, instead, you were reporting on a cash basis, you would report expenses of $50,000 in year 1 and revenues of $80,000 in year 2. Net income for year 1 would be a loss of $50,000, while net income for year 2 would be $80,000. The cash basis measures are not very informative about the results of your efforts during year 1 or year 2.

STUDY OBJECTIVE

2

Differentiate between the cash basis and the accrual basis of accounting.

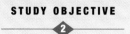 **International Note**

Although different accounting standards are often used by companies in other countries, the accrual basis of accounting is central to all of these standards.

Illustration 4-2 Accrual versus cash basis accounting

	Year 1	Year 2
Activity	Purchased paint, painted building, paid employees	Received payment for work done in year 1
Accrual basis	Revenue $80,000 Expense 50,000 Net income $30,000	Revenue $ 0 Expense 0 Net income $ 0
Cash basis	Revenue $ 0 Expense 50,000 Net loss $(50,000)	Revenue $80,000 Expense 0 Net income $80,000

Although most companies use the accrual basis of accounting, some small companies use the cash basis because they have few receivables and payables. For these companies, the cash basis might approximate the accrual basis.

BUSINESS INSIGHT
International Perspective

Many Americans are frustrated with the confusion surrounding such important debates as the savings and loan bailout, Social Security reform, and tax cuts. How can people looking at the same numbers come up with such drastically different conclusions? One cause of this problem is that the United States government essentially uses a cash basis accounting system rather than an accrual system. In fact, nearly all governments worldwide use a cash basis system. One exception is New Zealand. Since 1989 New Zealand has employed accrual accounting. The reason for this change was to make departmental managers more aware of the costs of various programs (such as the pension plans of government employees) and of the value of government assets, such as buildings and parks. Maybe U.S. political debates would be less murky if the government adopted accrual accounting concepts.

BEFORE YOU GO ON...

◆ Review It

1. What are the revenue recognition and matching principles?
2. What are the differences between the cash and accrual bases of accounting?

THE BASICS OF ADJUSTING ENTRIES

STUDY OBJECTIVE

3

Explain why adjusting entries are needed and identify the major types of adjusting entries.

In order for revenues to be recorded in the period in which they are earned, and for expenses to be recognized in the period in which they are incurred, adjusting entries are made to revenue and expense accounts at the end of the accounting period. In short, **adjusting entries are needed to ensure that the revenue recognition and matching principles are followed**.

The use of adjusting entries makes it possible to produce accurate financial statements at the end of the accounting period. Thus, the balance sheet reports appropriate assets, liabilities, and stockholders' equity at the statement date, and the income statement shows the proper net income (or loss) for the period. Adjusting entries are necessary because the trial balance—the first pulling together of the transaction data—may not contain up-to-date and complete data. This is true for these reasons:

1. Some events are not journalized daily because it would not be useful or efficient to do so. Examples are the use of supplies and the earning of wages by employees.
2. Some costs are not journalized during the accounting period because these costs expire with the passage of time rather than as a result of recurring daily transactions. Examples of such costs are building and equipment deterioration and rent and insurance.
3. Some items may be unrecorded. An example is a utility service bill that will not be received until the next accounting period.

Adjusting entries are required every time financial statements are prepared. An essential starting point is an analysis of each account in the trial balance to determine whether it is complete and up to date for financial statement purposes.

TYPES OF ADJUSTING ENTRIES

Adjusting entries can be classified as either prepayments or accruals. Each of these classes has two subcategories as shown in Illustration 4-3.

Prepayments:

1. **Prepaid expenses:** Expenses paid in cash and recorded as assets before they are used or consumed.
2. **Unearned revenues:** Cash received and recorded as liabilities before revenue is earned.

Accruals:

1. **Accrued revenues:** Revenues earned but not yet received in cash or recorded.
2. **Accrued expenses:** Expenses incurred but not yet paid in cash or recorded.

Illustration 4-3
Categories of adjusting entries

Specific examples and explanations of each type of adjustment are given in subsequent sections. Each example is based on the October 31 trial balance of Sierra Corporation, from Chapter 3, reproduced in Illustration 4-4. Note that Retained Earnings has been added to this trial balance with a zero balance. We will explain its use later.

Illustration 4-4
Trial balance

SIERRA CORPORATION Trial Balance October 31, 2001	Debit	Credit
Cash	$15,200	
Advertising Supplies	2,500	
Prepaid Insurance	600	
Office Equipment	5,000	
Notes Payable		$ 5,000
Accounts Payable		2,500
Unearned Service Revenue		1,200
Common Stock		10,000
Retained Earnings		0
Dividends	500	
Service Revenue		10,000
Salaries Expense	4,000	
Rent Expense	900	
	$28,700	$28,700

It will be assumed that Sierra Corporation uses an accounting period of one month. Thus, monthly adjusting entries will be made. The entries will be dated October 31.

ADJUSTING ENTRIES FOR PREPAYMENTS

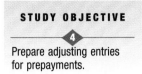

STUDY OBJECTIVE

◆ 4

Prepare adjusting entries for prepayments.

Prepayments are either prepaid expenses or unearned revenues. Adjusting entries for prepayments are required at the statement date to record the portion of the prepayment that represents the expense incurred or the revenue earned in the current accounting period. Adjusting entries for prepayments are graphically depicted in Illustration 4-5.

Illustration 4-5
Adjusting entries for prepayments

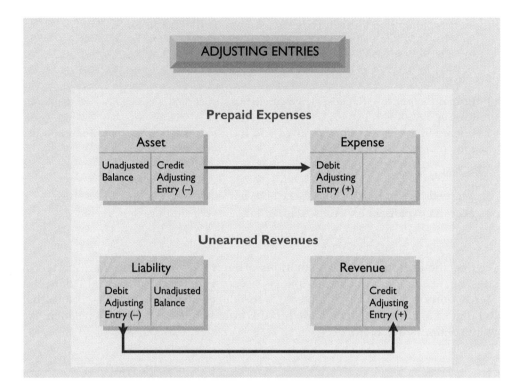

Prepaid Expenses

Payments of expenses that will benefit more than one accounting period are called prepaid expenses or prepayments. When such a cost is incurred, an asset account is increased (debited) to show the service or benefit that will be received in the future. Examples of common prepayments are insurance, supplies, advertising, and rent. In addition, prepayments are made when buildings and equipment are purchased.

   Prepaid expenses expire either with the passage of time (e.g., rent and insurance) or through use (e.g., supplies). The expiration of these costs does not require daily entries, which would be impractical and unnecessary. Accordingly, we postpone the recognition of such cost expirations until financial statements are prepared. At each statement date, adjusting entries are made to record the expenses applicable to the current accounting period and to show the remaining amounts in the asset accounts. Prior to adjustment, assets are overstated and expenses are understated. Therefore, **an adjusting entry for prepaid expenses results in an increase (a debit) to an expense account and a decrease (a credit) to an asset account.**

Supplies.   The purchase of supplies, such as paper and envelopes, results in an increase (a debit) to an asset account. During the accounting period, supplies are used. Rather than record supplies expense as the supplies are used, supplies expense is recognized at the **end** of the accounting period. At the end of the accounting period the company must count the remaining supplies. The difference between the unadjusted balance in the Supplies (asset) account and the actual cost of supplies on hand represents the supplies used (expense) for that period.

Recall from the facts presented in Chapter 3 that Sierra Corporation purchased advertising supplies costing $2,500 on October 5. The payment was recorded by increasing (debiting) the asset Advertising Supplies, and this account shows a balance of $2,500 in the October 31 trial balance. An inventory count at the close of business on October 31 reveals that $1,000 of supplies are still on hand. Thus, the cost of supplies used is $1,500 ($2,500 − $1,000). This use of supplies decreases an asset, Advertising Supplies, and decreases stockholders' equity by increasing an expense account, Advertising Supplies Expense. The use of supplies affects the accounting equation in the following way:

$$\underline{\textbf{Assets}} \quad = \quad \underline{\textbf{Liabilities}} \quad + \quad \underline{\textbf{Stockholders' Equity}}$$
$$-\$1,500 \qquad\qquad\qquad\qquad\qquad -\$1,500$$

Supplies

Oct.5

Supplies purchased; record asset

Oct.31

Supplies used; record supplies expense

Thus, the following entry is made:

Oct.	31	Advertising Supplies Expense	1,500	
		Advertising Supplies		1,500
		(To record supplies used)		

After the adjusting entry is posted, the two supplies accounts, in T account form, are as in Illustration 4-6.

Advertising Supplies			**Advertising Supplies Expense**	
Oct. 5	2,500	Oct. 31 **Adj. 1,500**	Oct. 31 **Adj. 1,500**	
Oct. 31	Bal. 1,000		Oct. 31 Bal. 1,500	

Illustration 4-6 Supplies accounts after adjustment

The asset account Advertising Supplies now shows a balance of $1,000, which is equal to the cost of supplies on hand at the statement date. In addition, Advertising Supplies Expense shows a balance of $1,500, which equals the cost of supplies used in October. **If the adjusting entry is not made, October expenses will be understated and net income overstated by $1,500. Moreover, both assets and stockholders' equity will be overstated by $1,500 on the October 31 balance sheet**.

BUSINESS INSIGHT
Management Perspective

The costs of advertising on radio, television, and magazines for burgers, bleaches, athletic shoes, and such products are sometimes considered prepayments. As a manager for Procter & Gamble noted, "If we run a long ad campaign for soap and bleach, we sometimes report the costs as prepayments if we think we'll receive sales benefits from the campaign down the road." Presently it is a judgment call whether these costs should be prepayments or expenses in the current period. Developing guidelines consistent with the matching principle is difficult. The issue is important because the outlays for advertising can be substantial. Recent big spenders: Sears, Roebuck spent $1.28 billion, Nike $978 million, Kellogg $695 million, and McDonald's $503 million.

Insurance

Oct.4

Insurance purchased;
record asset

Insurance Policy			
Oct $50	Nov $50	Dec $50	Jan $50
Feb $50	March $50	April $50	May $50
June $50	July $50	Aug $50	Sept $50
I YEAR $600			

Oct.31

Insurance expired;
record insurance expense

Insurance.   Companies purchase insurance to protect themselves from losses due to fire, theft, and unforeseen events. Insurance must be paid in advance, often for more than one year. Insurance payments (premiums) made in advance are normally recorded in the asset account Prepaid Insurance. At the financial statement date it is necessary to increase (debit) Insurance Expense and decrease (credit) Prepaid Insurance for the cost of insurance that has expired during the period.

On October 4 Sierra Corporation paid $600 for a one-year fire insurance policy. Coverage began on October 1. The payment was recorded by increasing (debiting) Prepaid Insurance when it was paid. This account shows a balance of $600 in the October 31 trial balance. An analysis of the policy reveals that $50 ($600/12) of insurance expires each month. The expiration of Prepaid Insurance would have the following impact on the accounting equation in October (and each of the next 11 months):

Assets	=	Liabilities	+	Stockholders' Equity
−$50				−$50

Thus, the following adjusting entry is made:

Oct.	31	Insurance Expense	50	
		Prepaid Insurance		50
		(To record insurance expired)		

After the adjusting entry is posted, the accounts appear as in Illustration 4-7.

Illustration 4-7
Insurance accounts after adjustment

Prepaid Insurance				Insurance Expense		
Oct. 4	600	Oct. 31	**Adj. 50**	Oct. 31	**Adj. 50**	
Oct. 31	Bal. 550			Oct. 31	Bal. 50	

The asset Prepaid Insurance shows a balance of $550, which represents the cost that applies to the remaining 11 months of coverage. At the same time the balance in Insurance Expense is equal to the insurance cost that was used in October. If this adjustment is not made, October expenses would be understated by $50 and net income overstated by $50. Moreover, as the accounting equation shows, both assets and stockholders' equity will be overstated by $50 on the October 31 balance sheet.

Depreciation.   A company typically owns a variety of assets that have long lives, such as buildings, equipment, and motor vehicles. The term of service is referred to as the useful life of the asset. Because a building is expected to provide service for many years, it is recorded as an asset, rather than an expense, on the date it is acquired. As explained in Chapter 1, such assets are recorded **at cost,** as required by the cost principle. According to the matching principle, a portion of this cost should then be reported as an expense during each period of the asset's useful life. Depreciation is the process of allocating the cost of an asset to expense over its useful life.

Need for Adjustment.   From an accounting standpoint, the acquisition of long-lived assets is essentially a long-term prepayment for services. The need for making periodic adjusting entries for depreciation is therefore the same as described before for other prepaid expenses—that is, to recognize the cost that has been used (an expense) during the period and to report the unused cost (an asset) at the end of the period. One point is very important to understand: **Depreciation is an allocation concept**, **not a valuation concept**. That is, we depreciate an asset **to allocate its cost to the periods in which we use it. We are not attempting to reflect the actual change in the value of the asset.**

For Sierra Corporation, assume that depreciation on the office equipment is estimated to be $480 a year, or $40 per month. This would have the following impact on the accounting equation:

$$\underline{\text{Assets}} \quad = \quad \underline{\text{Liabilities}} \quad + \quad \underline{\text{Stockholders' Equity}}$$
$$-\$40 \qquad\qquad\qquad\qquad\qquad\qquad -\$40$$

Accordingly, depreciation for October is recognized by this adjusting entry:

Oct. 31	Depreciation Expense	40	
	Accumulated Depreciation—Office		
	Equipment		40
	(To record monthly depreciation)		

After the adjusting entry is posted, the accounts appear as in Illustration 4-8.

Office Equipment

| Oct. 2 | 5,000 | |
| Oct. 31 | Bal. 5,000 | |

Accumulated Depreciation— Office Equipment

| | Oct. 31 | **Adj. 40** |
| | Oct. 31 | Bal. 40 |

Depreciation Expense

| Oct. 31 | **Adj. 40** | |
| Oct. 31 | Bal. 40 | |

Depreciation

Oct.2

Office equipment purchased; record asset

Office Equipment			
Oct	Nov	Dec	Jan
$40	$40	$40	$40
Feb	March	April	May
$40	$40	$40	$40
June	July	Aug	Sept
$40	$40	$40	$40
Depreciation = $480/year			

Oct.31

Depreciation recognized; record depreciation expense

Illustration 4-8
Accounts after adjustment for depreciation

The balance in the Accumulated Depreciation account will increase $40 each month.

Statement Presentation. Accumulated Depreciation—Office Equipment is a contra asset account, which means that it is offset against Office Equipment on the balance sheet, and its normal balance is a credit. This account is used instead of decreasing (crediting) Office Equipment in order to disclose *both* the original cost of the equipment and the total cost that has expired to date. In the balance sheet, Accumulated Depreciation—Office Equipment is deducted from the related asset account as shown in Illustration 4-9.

Office equipment	$5,000
Less: Accumulated depreciation—office equipment	40
	$4,960

Illustration 4-9 Balance sheet presentation of accumulated depreciation

The difference between the cost of any depreciable asset and its related accumulated depreciation is referred to as the book value of that asset. In Illustration 4-9, the book value of the equipment at the balance sheet date is $4,960. The book value and the market value of the asset are generally two different values. As noted earlier, depreciation is not a matter of valuation, but a means of cost allocation.

Note also that depreciation expense identifies the portion of an asset's cost that has expired in October. The accounting equation shows that, as in the case of other prepaid adjustments, the omission of this adjusting entry would cause total assets, total stockholders' equity, and net income to be overstated and depreciation expense to be understated.

Alternative Terminology
Book value is also referred to as **carrying value.**

Unearned Revenues

Cash received before revenue is earned is recorded by increasing (crediting) a liability account called unearned revenues. Items like rent, magazine sub-

Unearned Revenues

Oct. 2

Cash is received in advance; liability is recorded

Oct. 31

Some service has been provided; some revenue is recorded

scriptions, and customer deposits for future service may result in unearned revenues. Airlines such as United, American, and Delta, for instance, treat receipts from the sale of tickets as unearned revenue until the flight service is provided. Unearned revenues are the opposite of prepaid expenses. Indeed, unearned revenue on the books of one company is likely to be a prepayment on the books of the company that has made the advance payment. For example, if identical accounting periods are assumed, a landlord will have unearned rent revenue when a tenant has prepaid rent.

When payment is received for services to be provided in a future accounting period, an unearned revenue (a liability) account should be credited to recognize the obligation that exists. Unearned revenues are subsequently earned by providing service to a customer. During the accounting period it is not practical to make daily entries as the revenue is earned. Instead, we delay recognition of earned revenue until the adjustment process. Then an adjusting entry is made to record the revenue that has been earned during the period and to show the liability that remains at the end of the accounting period. Typically, prior to adjustment, liabilities are overstated and revenues are understated. Therefore, **the adjusting entry for unearned revenues results in a decrease (a debit) to a liability account and an increase (a credit) to a revenue account**.

Sierra Corporation received $1,200 on October 2 from R. Knox for advertising services expected to be completed by December 31. The payment was credited to Unearned Revenue, and this liability account shows a balance of $1,200 in the October 31 trial balance. From an evaluation of the work performed by Sierra for Knox during October, it is determined that $400 has been earned in October. This would affect the accounting equation in the following way:

Assets	=	Liabilities	+	Stockholders' Equity
		−$400		+$400

The following adjusting entry is made:

Oct.	31	Unearned Service Revenue	400	
		Service Revenue		400
		(To record revenue earned)		

After the adjusting entry is posted, the accounts appear as in Illustration 4-10.

Illustration 4-10 Service revenue accounts after adjustment

Unearned Service Revenue				Service Revenue		
Oct. 31 **Adj. 400**	Oct. 2	1,200			Oct. 3	10,000
					31 **Adj. 400**	
	Oct. 31 **Bal. 800**				Oct. 31 Bal. 10,400	

The liability Unearned Service Revenue now shows a balance of $800, which represents the remaining advertising services expected to be performed in the future. At the same time, Service Revenue shows total revenue earned in October of $10,400. **If this adjustment is not made, revenues and net income will be understated by $400 in the income statement. Moreover, liabilities will be overstated and stockholders' equity will be understated by $400 on the October 31 balance sheet.**

BUSINESS INSIGHT
Investor Perspective

Companies would rather report steadily increasing profits than fluctuating profits. To "smooth" earnings, companies sometimes shift the reporting of revenues or expenses between periods. Some analysts have suggested that Microsoft uses its Unearned Revenue account for this purpose. Microsoft says that it reports as unearned revenue a portion of cash received for software sold in order to reflect costs to deliver upgrades and customer support in future years for software that was shipped during the current year. But critics contend that Microsoft intentionally overstates this amount—salting away unearned revenue that can be reported as revenue in some future period when the company's sales don't meet expectations. Microsoft is not alone in its efforts to smooth earnings. In fact, one prominent Chief Executive Officer bellowed, "The number 1 job of management is to smooth out earnings." In an effort to improve the accuracy of financial information, the Securities and Exchange Commission has made the reduction of income smoothing practices a top priority.

BEFORE YOU GO ON...

◆ Review It

1. What are the four types of adjusting entries?
2. What is the effect on assets, stockholders' equity, expenses, and net income if a prepaid expense adjusting entry is not made?
3. What is the effect on liabilities, stockholders' equity, revenues, and net income if an unearned revenue adjusting entry is not made?

◆ Do It

The ledger of Hammond, Inc., on March 31, 2001, includes these selected accounts before adjusting entries are prepared:

	Debit	Credit
Prepaid Insurance	$ 3,600	
Office Supplies	2,800	
Office Equipment	25,000	
Accumulated Depreciation—Office Equipment		$5,000
Unearned Service Revenue		9,200

An analysis of the accounts shows the following:

1. Insurance expires at the rate of $100 per month.
2. Supplies on hand total $800.
3. The office equipment depreciates $200 a month.
4. One-half of the unearned service revenue was earned in March.

Prepare the adjusting entries for the month of March.

Reasoning: In order for revenues to be recorded in the period in which they are earned and for expenses to be recognized in the period in which they are incurred, adjusting entries are made at the *end* of the accounting period. Adjusting entries for prepayments are required at the statement date. They record the portion of the prepayment that represents the expense incurred or the revenue earned in the current accounting period. The failure to adjust for the prepayment would lead to an overstatement of the asset or liability and a related understatement of the expense or revenue.

Solution:

1. Insurance Expense	100	
Prepaid Insurance		100
(To record insurance expired)		
2. Office Supplies Expense	2,000	
Office Supplies		2,000
(To record supplies used)		
3. Depreciation Expense	200	
Accumulated Depreciation—Office Equipment		200
(To record monthly depreciation)		
4. Unearned Service Revenue	4,600	
Service Revenue		4,600
(To record revenue earned)		

ADJUSTING ENTRIES FOR ACCRUALS

STUDY OBJECTIVE

◆ 5 ◆

Prepare adjusting entries for accruals.

The second category of adjusting entries is **accruals**. Adjusting entries for accruals are required in order to record revenues earned and expenses incurred in the current accounting period that have not been recognized through daily entries and thus are not yet reflected in the accounts. Prior to an accrual adjustment, the revenue account (and the related asset account) or the expense account (and the related liability account) are understated. Thus, the adjusting entry for accruals will **increase both a balance sheet and an income statement account**. Adjusting entries for accruals are graphically depicted in Illustration 4-11.

Illustration 4-11 Adjusting entries for accruals

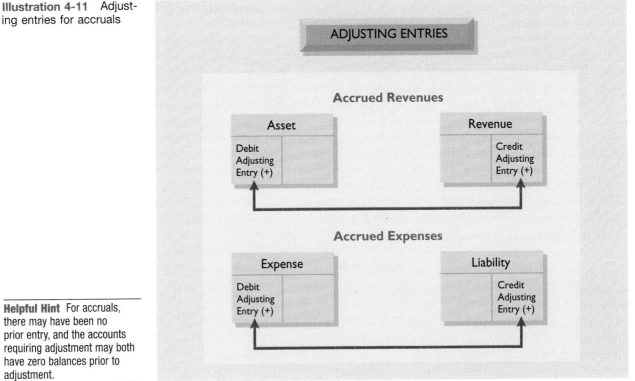

Helpful Hint For accruals, there may have been no prior entry, and the accounts requiring adjustment may both have zero balances prior to adjustment.

Accrued Revenues

Revenues earned but not yet received in cash or recorded at the statement date are accrued revenues. Accrued revenues may accumulate (accrue) with the passing of time, as in the case of interest revenue. Or they may result from services that have been performed but neither billed nor collected, as in the case of commissions and fees. The former are unrecorded because the earning of interest does not involve daily transactions. The latter may be unrecorded because only a portion of the total service has been provided and the clients won't be billed until the service has been completed.

An adjusting entry is required to show the receivable that exists at the balance sheet date and to record the revenue that has been earned during the period. Prior to adjustment both assets and revenues are understated. Accordingly, **an adjusting entry for accrued revenues results in an increase (a debit) to an asset account and an increase (a credit) to a revenue account**.

In October Sierra Corporation earned $200 for advertising services that were not billed to clients before October 31. Because these services have not been billed, they have not been recorded. Assets and stockholders' equity would be affected as follows:

Assets	=	Liabilities	+	Stockholders' Equity
+$200				+$200

Thus, the following adjusting entry is made:

Oct.	31	Accounts Receivable	200	
		Service Revenue		200
		(To accrue revenue earned but not billed or collected)		

After the adjusting entry is posted, the accounts appear as in Illustration 4-12.

Accrued Revenues

Oct.31

Revenue and receivable are recorded for unbilled services

Nov.

Cash is received; receivable is reduced

Accounts Receivable		**Service Revenue**	
Oct. 31 **Adj. 200**			Oct. 3 10,000
			31 400
			31 **Adj. 200**
Oct. 31 Bal. 200			Oct. 31 Bal. 10,600

Illustration 4-12
Receivable and revenue accounts after accrual adjustments

The asset Accounts Receivable shows that $200 is owed by clients at the balance sheet date. The balance of $10,600 in Service Revenue represents the total revenue earned during the month ($10,000 + $400 + $200). **If the adjusting entry is not made**, **assets and stockholders' equity on the balance sheet**, **and revenues and net income on the income statement will be understated**.

In the next accounting period, the clients will be billed. When this occurs, the entry to record the billing should recognize that $200 of revenue earned in October has already been recorded in the October 31 adjusting entry. To illustrate, assume that bills totaling $3,000 are mailed to clients on November 10. Of this amount, $200 represents revenue earned in October and recorded as Service Revenue in the October 31 adjusting entry. The remaining $2,800 represents revenue earned in November. Assets and stockholders' equity would be affected as follows:

Assets	=	Liabilities	+	Stockholders' Equity
+$2,800				+$2,800

Thus, the following entry is made:

Nov. 10	Accounts Receivable	2,800	
	Service Revenue		2,800
	(To record revenue earned)		

This entry records the amount of revenue earned between November 1 and November 10. The subsequent collection of cash from clients (including the $200 earned in October) will be recorded with an increase (a debit) to Cash and a decrease (a credit) to Accounts Receivable.

Accrued Expenses

Expenses incurred but not yet paid or recorded at the statement date are called accrued expenses. Interest, rent, taxes, and salaries are common examples of accrued expenses. Accrued expenses result from the same factors as accrued revenues. In fact, an accrued expense on the books of one company is an accrued revenue to another company. For example, the $200 accrual of service revenue by Sierra Corporation is an accrued expense to the client that received the service.

Adjustments for accrued expenses are necessary to record the obligations that exist at the balance sheet date and to recognize the expenses that apply to the current accounting period. Prior to adjustment, both liabilities and expenses are understated. Therefore, **an adjusting entry for accrued expenses results in an increase (a debit) to an expense account and an increase (a credit) to a liability account**.

Accrued Interest. Sierra Corporation signed a three-month note payable in the amount of $5,000 on October 1. The note requires interest at an annual rate of 12%. The amount of the interest accumulation is determined by three factors: (1) the face value of the note, (2) the interest rate, which is always expressed as an annual rate, and (3) the length of time the note is outstanding. In this instance, the total interest due on the $5,000 note at its due date three months in the future is $150 ($5,000 $\times$ 12% $\times \frac{3}{12}$), or $50 for one month. The formula for computing interest and its application to Sierra Corporation for the month of October are shown in Illustration 4-13.

Illustration 4-13
Formula for computing interest

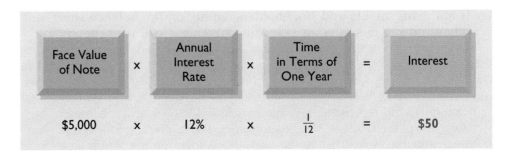

Note that the time period is expressed as a fraction of a year. The accrual of interest at October 31 would have the following impact on the accounting equation:

Assets	=	**Liabilities**	+	**Stockholders' Equity**
		+$50		−$50

This would be reflected in an accrued expense adjusting entry at October 31 as follows:

Oct. 31	Interest Expense	50	
	Interest Payable		50
	(To accrue interest on notes payable)		

After this adjusting entry is posted, the accounts appear as in Illustration 4-14.

Interest Expense		**Interest Payable**	
Oct. 31 **Adj. 50**			Oct. 31 **Adj. 50**
Oct. 31 Bal. 50			Oct. 31 Bal. 50

Illustration 4-14   Interest accounts after adjustment

Interest Expense shows the interest charges for the month of October. The amount of interest owed at the statement date is shown in Interest Payable. It will not be paid until the note comes due at the end of three months. The Interest Payable account is used, instead of crediting Notes Payable, to disclose the two different types of obligations—interest and principal—in the accounts and statements. **If this adjusting entry is not made, liabilities and interest expense will be understated, and net income and stockholders' equity will be overstated.**

Accrued Salaries.   Some types of expenses, such as employee salaries and commissions, are paid for after the services have been performed. At Sierra Corporation, salaries were last paid on October 26; the next payment of salaries will not occur until November 9. As shown in the calendar, three working days remain in October (October 29–31).

At October 31 the salaries for these days represent an accrued expense and a related liability to Sierra. The employees receive total salaries of $2,000 for a five-day work week, or $400 per day. Thus, accrued salaries at October 31 are $1,200 ($400 × 3). This accrual increases a liability, Salaries Payable, and an expense account, Salaries Expense, and has the following impact on the accounting equation:

$$\underline{\textbf{Assets}} \quad = \quad \underline{\textbf{Liabilities}} \quad + \quad \underline{\textbf{Stockholders' Equity}}$$
$$+\$1,200 \qquad\qquad -\$1,200$$

The adjusting entry is:

Oct.	31	Salaries Expense	1,200	
		Salaries Payable		1,200
		(To record accrued salaries)		

After this adjusting entry is posted, the accounts are as in Illustration 4-15.

Illustration 4-15 Salary accounts after adjustment

Salaries Expense			**Salaries Payable**	
Oct. 26	4,000		Oct. 31	Adj. **1,200**
31	Adj. **1,200**			
Oct. 31	Bal. 5,200		Oct. 31	Bal. 1,200

After this adjustment, the balance in Salaries Expense of $5,200 (13 days × $400) is the actual salary expense for October. The balance in Salaries Payable of $1,200 is the amount of the liability for salaries owed as of October 31. **If the $1,200 adjustment for salaries is not recorded, Sierra's expenses will be understated $1,200 and its liabilities will be understated $1,200.**

At Sierra Corporation, salaries are payable every two weeks. Consequently, the next payday is November 9, when total salaries of $4,000 will again be paid. The payment consists of $1,200 of salaries payable at October 31 plus $2,800 of salaries expense for November (7 working days as shown in the November calendar × $400). Therefore, the following entry is made on November 9:

Nov.	9	Salaries Payable	1,200	
		Salaries Expense	2,800	
		Cash		4,000
		(To record November 9 payroll)		

This entry eliminates the liability for Salaries Payable that was recorded in the October 31 adjusting entry and records the proper amount of Salaries Expense for the period between November 1 and November 9.

BEFORE YOU GO ON...

◆ Review It

1. What is the effect on assets, stockholders' equity, revenues, and net income if an accrued revenue adjusting entry is not made?

2. What is the effect on liabilities, stockholders' equity, expenses, and net income if an accrued expense adjusting entry is not made?

3. What was the amount of Tootsie Roll's 1998 depreciation expense? (*Hint:* The amount is reported in the notes to the financial statements.) The answer to this question is provided on page 203.

◆ Do It

Micro Computer Services Inc. began operations on August 1, 2001. At the end of August 2001, management attempted to prepare monthly financial statements. This information relates to August:

1. At August 31 the company owed its employees $800 in salaries that will be paid on September 1.

2. On August 1 the company borrowed $30,000 from a local bank on a 15-year mortgage. The annual interest rate is 10%.

3. Revenue earned but unrecorded for August totaled $1,100.

Prepare the adjusting entries needed at August 31, 2001.

Reasoning: Adjusting entries for accruals are required to record revenues earned and expenses incurred in the current accounting period that have not been recognized through daily entries. An adjusting entry for accruals will increase both a balance sheet and an income statement account.

Solution:

1. Salaries Expense	800	
Salaries Payable		800
(To record accrued salaries)		
2. Interest Expense	250	
Interest Payable		250
(To record accrued interest:		
$30,000 \times 10\% \times \frac{1}{12} = \$250$)		
3. Accounts Receivable	1,100	
Service Revenue		1,100
(To accrue revenue earned		
but not billed or collected)		

SUMMARY OF BASIC RELATIONSHIPS

Pertinent data on each of the four basic types of adjusting entries are summarized in Illustration 4-16. Take some time to study and analyze the adjusting entries. Be sure to note that **each adjusting entry affects one balance sheet account and one income statement account**.

Illustration 4-16
Summary of adjusting entries

Type of Adjustment	Accounts Before Adjustment	Adjusting Entry
Prepaid expenses	Assets overstated Expenses understated	Dr. Expenses Cr. Assets
Unearned revenues	Liabilities overstated Revenues understated	Dr. Liabilities Cr. Revenues
Accrued revenues	Assets understated Revenues understated	Dr. Assets Cr. Revenues
Accrued expenses	Expenses understated Liabilities understated	Dr. Expenses Cr. Liabilities

The journalizing and posting of adjusting entries for Sierra Corporation on October 31 are shown in Illustrations 4-17 and 4-18. When reviewing the general ledger in Illustration 4-18, note that the adjustments are highlighted in color.

Illustration 4-17
General journal showing adjusting entries

	GENERAL JOURNAL			
Date	Account Titles and Explanation		Debit	Credit
2001	Adjusting Entries			
Oct. 31	Advertising Supplies Expense		1,500	
	Advertising Supplies			1,500
	(To record supplies used)			
31	Insurance Expense		50	
	Prepaid Insurance			50
	(To record insurance expired)			
31	Depreciation Expense		40	
	Accumulated Depreciation—Office Equipment			40
	(To record monthly depreciation)			
31	Unearned Service Revenue		400	
	Service Revenue			400
	(To record revenue earned)			
31	Accounts Receivable		200	
	Service Revenue			200
	(To accrue revenue earned but not billed or collected)			
31	Interest Expense		50	
	Interest Payable			50
	(To accrue interest on notes payable)			
31	Salaries Expense		1,200	
	Salaries Payable			1,200
	(To record accrued salaries)			

Cash

Oct.	1	10,000	Oct.	2	5,000
	1	5,000		3	900
	2	1,200		4	600
	3	10,000		20	500
				26	4,000
Oct. 31	Bal. 15,200				

Accounts Receivable

Oct. 31	200	
Oct. 31	Bal. 200	

Advertising Supplies

Oct.	5	2,500	Oct. 31	1,500
Oct. 31	Bal. 1,000			

Prepaid Insurance

Oct.	4	600	Oct. 31	50
Oct. 31	Bal. 550			

Office Equipment

Oct.	2	5,000
Oct. 31	Bal. 5,000	

Accumulated Depreciation—
Office Equipment

	Oct. 31	40
	Oct. 31	Bal. 40

Notes Payable

	Oct. 1	5,000
	Oct. 31	Bal. 5,000

Accounts Payable

	Oct. 5	2,500
	Oct. 31	Bal. 2,500

Interest Payable

	Oct. 31	50
	Oct. 31	Bal. 50

Unearned Service Revenue

Oct. 31	400	Oct.	2	1,200
		Oct. 31	Bal. 800	

Salaries Payable

	Oct. 31	1,200
	Oct. 31	Bal. 1,200

Common Stock

	Oct. 1	10,000
	Oct. 31	Bal. 10,000

Retained Earnings

	Oct. 31	Bal. 0

Dividends

Oct. 20	500	
Oct. 31	Bal. 500	

Service Revenue

	Oct. 3	10,000
	31	400
	31	200
	Oct. 31	Bal. 10,600

Salaries Expense

Oct. 26	4,000	
	31	1,200
Oct. 31	Bal. 5,200	

Advertising Supplies Expense

Oct. 31	1,500	
Oct. 31	Bal. 1,500	

Rent Expense

Oct.	3	900
Oct. 31	Bal. 900	

Insurance Expense

Oct. 31	50	
Oct. 31	Bal. 50	

Interest Expense

Oct. 31	50	
Oct. 31	Bal. 50	

Depreciation Expense

Oct. 31	40	
Oct. 31	Bal. 40	

Illustration 4-18
General ledger after
adjustments

*T*HE ADJUSTED TRIAL BALANCE AND FINANCIAL STATEMENTS

STUDY OBJECTIVE

◆ 6 ◆

Describe the nature and purpose of the adjusted trial balance.

After all adjusting entries have been journalized and posted, another trial balance is prepared from the ledger accounts. This trial balance is called an **adjusted trial balance**. It shows the balances of all accounts, including those that have been adjusted, at the end of the accounting period. The purpose of an adjusted trial balance is to **prove the equality** of the total debit balances and the total credit balances in the ledger after all adjustments have been made. Because the accounts contain all data that are needed for financial statements, the adjusted trial balance is the primary basis for the preparation of financial statements.

PREPARING THE ADJUSTED TRIAL BALANCE

The adjusted trial balance for Sierra Corporation presented in Illustration 4-19 has been prepared from the ledger accounts in Illustration 4-18. To facilitate the comparison of account balances, the trial balance data, labeled "Before Adjustment" (presented earlier in Illustration 4-4), are shown alongside the adjusted data, labeled "After Adjustment." In addition, the amounts affected by the adjusting entries are highlighted in color in the "After Adjustment" columns.

Illustration 4-19 Trial balance and adjusted trial balance compared

SIERRA CORPORATION
Trial Balances
October 31, 2001

	Before Adjustment		After Adjustment	
	Dr.	Cr.	Dr.	Cr.
Cash	$15,200		$ 15,200	
Accounts Receivable			200	
Advertising Supplies	2,500		1,000	
Prepaid Insurance	600		550	
Office Equipment	5,000		5,000	
Accumulated Depreciation— Office Equipment				$ 40
Notes Payable		$ 5,000		5,000
Accounts Payable		2,500		2,500
Interest Payable				50
Unearned Service Revenue		1,200		800
Salaries Payable				1,200
Common Stock		10,000		10,000
Retained Earnings		0		0
Dividends	500		500	
Service Revenue		10,000		10,600
Salaries Expense	4,000		5,200	
Advertising Supplies Expense			1,500	
Rent Expense	900		900	
Insurance Expense			50	
Interest Expense			50	
Depreciation Expense			40	
	$28,700	$28,700	$30,190	$30,190

PREPARING FINANCIAL STATEMENTS

Financial statements can be prepared directly from an adjusted trial balance. The interrelationships of data in the adjusted trial balance of Sierra Corporation are presented in Illustrations 4-20 and 4-21. As Illustration 4-20 shows, the income statement is prepared from the revenue and expense accounts. Similarly, the retained earnings statement is derived from the retained earnings account, dividends account, and the net income (or net loss) shown in the income statement. As shown in Illustration 4-21, the balance sheet is then prepared from the asset and liability accounts and the ending retained earnings as reported in the retained earnings statement.

Illustration 4-20
Preparation of the income statement and retained earnings statement from the adjusted trial balance

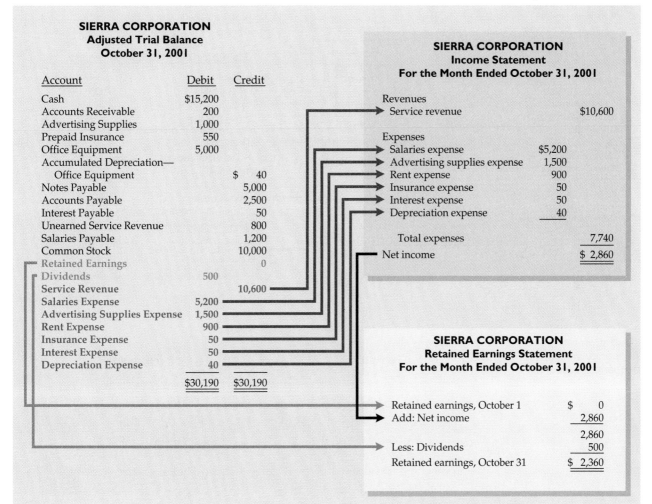

CLOSING THE BOOKS

In previous chapters you learned that revenue and expense accounts and the dividends account are subdivisions of retained earnings, which is reported in the stockholders' equity section of the balance sheet. Because revenues, expenses, and dividends relate to only a given accounting period, they are considered tem-porary accounts. In contrast, all balance sheet accounts are considered per-manent accounts because their balances are carried forward into future accounting periods. Illustration 4-22 identifies the accounts in each category.

Alternative Terminology
Temporary accounts are sometimes called **nominal accounts,** and permanent accounts are sometimes called **real accounts.**

Illustration 4-21   Preparation of the balance
sheet from the adjusted trial balance

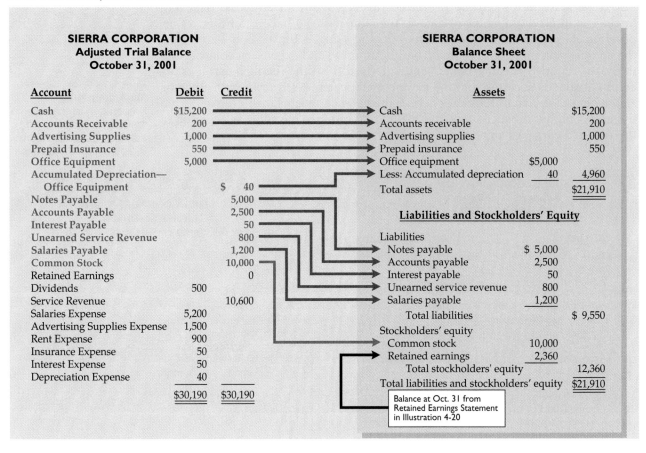

Illustration 4-22
Temporary versus
permanent accounts

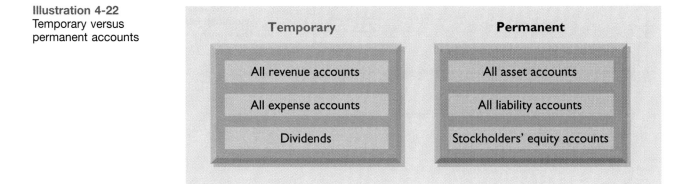

STUDY OBJECTIVE
_____ 7 _____
Explain the purpose of closing entries.

PREPARING CLOSING ENTRIES

At the end of the accounting period, the temporary account balances are transferred to the permanent stockholders' equity account—Retained Earnings—
through the preparation of closing entries. **Closing entries** formally recognize
in the ledger the transfer of net income (or net loss) and dividends to retained
earnings, which will be shown in the retained earnings statement. For example,

notice that in Illustration 4-21 Retained Earnings has an adjusted balance of zero. This is because it was Sierra's first year of operations. Retained Earnings started with a balance of zero, and net income has not yet been calculated and closed out to Retained Earnings. Therefore, the adjusted balance is still zero. Similarly, the zero balance does not yet reflect dividends declared during the period, since that account has not yet been closed out either.

In addition to updating Retained Earnings to its correct ending balance, closing entries produce a **zero balance in each temporary account**. As a result, these accounts are ready to accumulate data about revenues, expenses, and dividends in the next accounting period separate from the data in the prior periods. Permanent accounts are not closed.

When closing entries are prepared, each income statement account could be closed directly to Retained Earnings. However, to do so would result in excessive detail in the retained earnings account. Accordingly, the revenue and expense accounts are closed to another temporary account, Income Summary, and only the resulting net income or net loss is transferred from this account to Retained Earnings. The closing entries for Sierra Corporation are shown in Illustration 4-23.

Illustration 4-23
Closing entries journalized

Date	Account Titles and Explanation	Debit	Credit
	General Journal		
	Closing Entries		
	(1)		
2001			
Oct. 31	Service Revenue	10,600	
	Income Summary		10,600
	(To close revenue account)		
	(2)		
31	Income Summary	7,740	
	Salaries Expense		5,200
	Advertising Supplies Expense		1,500
	Rent Expense		900
	Insurance Expense		50
	Interest Expense		50
	Depreciation Expense		40
	(To close expense accounts)		
	(3)		
31	Income Summary	2,860	
	Retained Earnings		2,860
	(To close net income to retained earnings)		
	(4)		
31	Retained Earnings	500	
	Dividends		500
	(To close dividends to retained earnings)		

Helpful Hint Income Summary is a very descriptive title: total revenues are closed to Income Summary, total expenses are closed to Income Summary, and the balance in the Income Summary is a net income or net loss.

The closing process for Sierra Corporation's closing entries is diagrammed in Illustration 4-24.

Illustration 4-24
Posting of closing entries

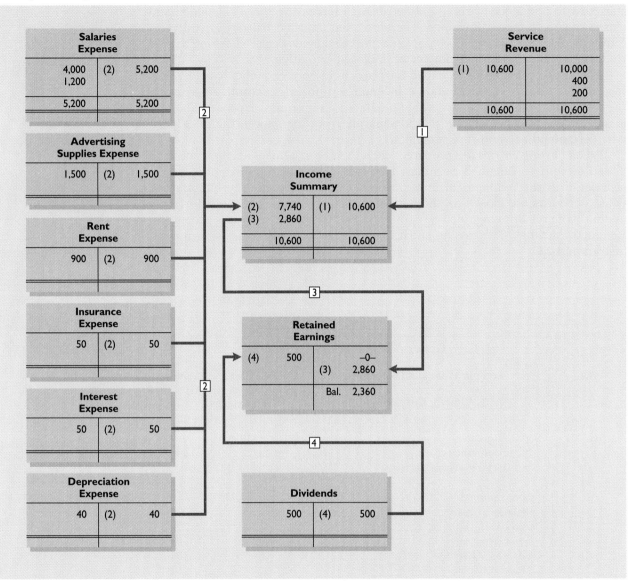

PREPARING A POST-CLOSING TRIAL BALANCE

After all closing entries are journalized and posted, another trial balance, called a **post-closing trial balance**, is prepared from the ledger. A post-closing trial balance is a list of all permanent accounts and their balances after closing entries are journalized and posted. **The purpose of this trial balance is to prove the equality of the permanent account balances that are carried forward into the next accounting period.** Since all temporary accounts will have zero balances, **the post-closing trial balance will contain only permanent—balance sheet—accounts.**

Management Perspective

Until Sam Walton had opened 20 Wal-Mart stores, he used what he called the "ESP method" of closing the books. ESP was a pretty basic method: If the books didn't balance, Walton calculated the amount by which they were off and entered that amount under the heading ESP—which stood for "Error Some Place." As Walton noted, "It really sped things along when it came time to close those books."

Source: Sam Walton, *Made in America* (New York: Doubleday Publishing Company, 1992), p. 53.

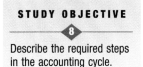

SUMMARY OF THE ACCOUNTING CYCLE

STUDY OBJECTIVE
8
Describe the required steps in the accounting cycle.

The required steps in the accounting cycle are shown graphically in Illustration 4-25. You can see that the cycle begins with the analysis of business trans-

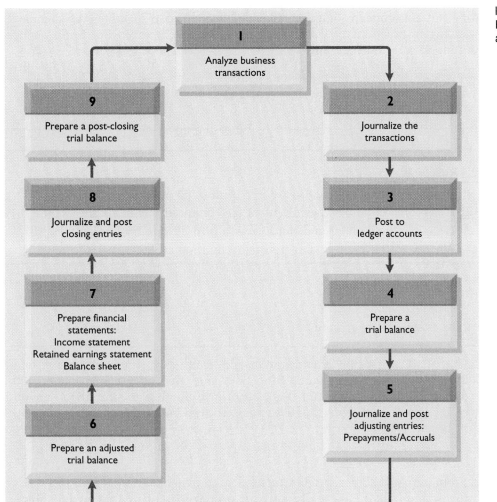

Illustration 4-25
Required steps in the accounting cycle

Helpful Hint Some accountants prefer to reverse certain adjusting entries at the beginning of a new accounting period. A *reversing entry* is made at the beginning of the next accounting period and is the exact opposite of the adjusting entry made in the previous period.

actions and ends with the preparation of a post-closing trial balance. The steps in the cycle are performed in sequence and are repeated in each accounting period.

Steps 1–3 may occur daily during the accounting period, as explained in Chapter 3. Steps 4–7 are performed on a periodic basis, such as monthly, quarterly, or annually. Steps 8 and 9, closing entries and a post-closing trial balance, are usually prepared only at the end of a company's **annual** accounting period.

BUSINESS INSIGHT

Management Perspective

Technology has dramatically changed the accounting process. When Larry Carter became chief financial officer of Cisco Systems, closing the quarterly accounts would take up to ten days. Within four years he got it down to two days and halved the cost of finance, to 1% of sales. Now he is aiming to be able to do a "virtual close"—closing within a day on any day in the quarter. This is not just showing off. Knowing exactly where you are all of the time, says Mr. Carter, allows you to respond faster than your competitors. But it also means that the 600 people who used to spend ten days a quarter tracking transactions can now be more usefully employed on things such as mining data for business intelligence.

Source: Excerpted from "Business and the Internet," *The Economist*, June 26, 1999, p. 12.

BEFORE YOU GO ON...

◆ Review It

1. How do permanent accounts differ from temporary accounts?
2. What four different types of entries are required in closing the books?
3. What are the content and purpose of a post-closing trial balance?
4. What are the required steps in the accounting cycle?

*U*SING THE *D*ECISION *T*OOLKIT

Humana Corporation provides managed health care services to more than 2 million people. Headquartered in Louisville, Kentucky, it has over 16,300 employees in 14 states and the District of Columbia. A simplified version of Humana's December 31, 1998, adjusted trial balance is shown at the top of the next page.

Instructions

From the trial balance, prepare an income statement, retained earnings statement, and balance sheet. **Be sure to prepare them in that order**, since **each statement depends on information determined in the preceding statement.**

HUMANA CORPORATION
Trial Balance
December 31, 1998
(in millions)

Account	Dr.	Cr.
Cash	$ 913	
Short-Term Investments	1,594	
Receivables	276	
Other Current Assets	336	
Property and Equipment, Net	433	
Long-Term Investments	305	
Other Long-Term Assets	1,639	
Medical Costs Payable		$ 484
Accounts Payable		1,865
Other Current Liabilities		294
Long-Term Debt		1,165
Common Stock		935
Dividends	0	
Retained Earnings		624
Revenues		9,781
Medical Cost Expense	8,041	
Selling, General, and Administrative Expense	1,328	
Depreciation Expense	128	
Other Expenses	34	
Interest Expense	47	
Income Tax Expense	74	
	$15,148	$15,148

Solution

HUMANA CORPORATION
Income Statement
For the Year Ended December 31, 1998
(in millions)

Revenues		$9,781
Medical cost expense	$8,041	
Selling, general, and administrative expense	1,328	
Depreciation expense	128	
Interest expense	47	
Other expenses	34	
Income tax expense	74	9,652
Net income		$ 129

HUMANA CORPORATION
Retained Earnings Statement
For the Year Ended December 31, 1998
(in millions)

Beginning retained earnings	$624
Add: Net income	129
Less: Dividends	0
Ending retained earnings	$753

HUMANA.

HUMANA CORPORATION
Balance Sheet
December 31, 1998
(in millions)

Assets

Current assets		
Cash	$ 913	
Short-term investments	1,594	
Receivables	276	
Other current assets	336	
Total current assets		$3,119
Long-term investments		305
Property and equipment, net		433
Other long-term assets		1,639
Total assets		$5,496

Liabilities and Stockholders' Equity

Liabilities		
Current liabilities		
Medical costs payable	$ 484	
Accounts payable	1,865	
Other current liabilities	294	
Total current liabilities		$2,643
Long-term debt		1,165
Total liabilities		3,808
Stockholders' equity		
Common stock	935	
Retained earnings	753	
Total stockholders' equity		1,688
Total liabilities and stockholders' equity		$5,496

SUMMARY OF STUDY OBJECTIVES

1 Explain the revenue recognition principle and the matching principle. The revenue recognition principle dictates that revenue be recognized in the accounting period in which it is earned. The matching principle dictates that expenses be recognized when they make their contribution to revenues.

2 Differentiate between the cash basis and the accrual basis of accounting. Accrual-based accounting means that events that change a company's financial statements are recorded in the periods in which the events occur. Under the cash basis, events are recorded only in the periods in which the company receives or pays cash.

3 Explain why adjusting entries are needed and identify the major types of adjusting entries. Adjusting entries are made at the end of an accounting period. They ensure that revenues are recorded in the period in which they are earned and that expenses are recognized in the period in which they are incurred. The major types of adjusting entries are prepaid expenses, unearned revenues, accrued revenues, and accrued expenses.

4 Prepare adjusting entries for prepayments. Prepayments are either prepaid expenses or unearned revenues. Adjusting entries for prepayments are required at the statement date to record the portion of the prepayment that represents the expense incurred or the revenue earned in the current accounting period.

5 Prepare adjusting entries for accruals. Accruals are either accrued revenues or accrued expenses. Adjusting entries for accruals are required to record revenues earned and expenses incurred in the current accounting period that have not been recognized through daily entries.

6 ▸ *Describe the nature and purpose of the adjusted trial balance.* An adjusted trial balance is a trial balance that shows the balances of all accounts, including those that have been adjusted, at the end of an accounting period. The purpose of an adjusted trial balance is to show the effects of all financial events that have occurred during the accounting period.

7 ▸ *Explain the purpose of closing entries.* One purpose of closing entries is to transfer the results of operations for the period to Retained Earnings. A second purpose is that, to begin a new period, all temporary accounts (revenue accounts, expense accounts, and div-

idends) must start with a zero balance. To accomplish this, all temporary accounts are "closed" at the end of an accounting period. Separate entries are made to close revenues and expenses to Income Summary, Income Summary to Retained Earnings, and Dividends to Retained Earnings. Only temporary accounts are closed.

8 ▸ *Describe the required steps in the accounting cycle.* The required steps in the accounting cycle are: (a) analyze business transactions, (b) journalize the transactions, (c) post to ledger accounts, (d) prepare a trial balance, (e) journalize and post adjusting entries, (f) prepare an adjusted trial balance, (g) prepare financial statements, (h) journalize and post closing entries, and (i) prepare a post-closing trial balance.

DECISION TOOLKIT—A SUMMARY

Decision Checkpoints	Info Needed for Decision	Tool to Use for Decision	How to Evaluate Results
At what point should the company record revenue?	Need to understand the nature of the company's business	Revenue should be recorded when earned. For a service business, revenue is earned when service is performed.	Recognizing revenue too early overstates current period revenue; recognizing it too late understates current period revenue.
At what point should the company record expenses?	Need to understand the nature of the company's business	Expenses should "follow" revenues—that is, the effort (expense) should be matched with the result (revenue).	Recognizing expenses too early overstates current period expense; recognizing expenses too late understates current period expense.

APPENDIX

ADJUSTING ENTRIES IN AN AUTOMATED WORLD—USING A WORK SHEET

In the previous discussion we used T accounts and trial balances to arrive at the amounts used to prepare financial statements. Accountants frequently use a device known as a work sheet to determine these amounts. A **work sheet** is a multiple-column form that may be used in the adjustment process and in preparing financial statements. Work sheets can be prepared manually, but today most are prepared on computer spreadsheets. As its name suggests, the work sheet is a working tool or a supplementary device for the accountant. **A work sheet is not a permanent accounting record**; it is neither a journal nor a part of the general ledger. The work sheet is merely a device used to make it easier to prepare adjusting entries and the financial statements. In small companies that have relatively few accounts and adjustments, a work sheet may not be needed. In large companies with numerous accounts and many adjustments, it is almost indispensable.

STUDY OBJECTIVE

9

Describe the purpose and the basic form of a work sheet.

The basic form of a work sheet is shown in Illustration 4A-1. Note the headings. The work sheet starts with two columns for the Trial Balance. The next two columns record all Adjustments. Next is the Adjusted Trial Balance. The last two sets of columns correspond to the Income Statement and the Balance Sheet. All items listed in the Adjusted Trial Balance columns are recorded in either the Income Statement or the Balance Sheet columns.

Illustration 4A-1 Form and procedure for a work sheet

SIERRA CORPORATION
Work Sheet
For the Month Ended October 31, 2001

Account Titles	Trial Balance Dr.	Trial Balance Cr.	Adjustments Dr.	Adjustments Cr.	Adjusted Trial Balance Dr.	Adjusted Trial Balance Cr.	Income Statement Dr.	Income Statement Cr.	Balance Sheet Dr.	Balance Sheet Cr.
Cash	15,200				15,200				15,200	
Advertising Supplies	2,500			(a) 1,500	1,000				1,000	
Prepaid Insurance	600			(b) 50	550				550	
Office Equipment	5,000				5,000				5,000	
Notes Payable		5,000				5,000				5,000
Accounts Payable		2,500				2,500				2,500
Unearned Service Revenue		1,200	(d) 400			800				800
Common Stock		10,000				10,000				10,000
Retained Earnings		–0–				–0–				–0–
Dividends	500				500				500	
Service Revenue		10,000		(d) 400		10,600		10,600		
				(e) 200						
Salaries Expense	4,000		(g) 1,200		5,200		5,200			
Rent Expense	900				900		900			
Totals	28,700	28,700								
Advertising Supplies Expense			(a) 1,500		1,500		1,500			
Insurance Expense			(b) 50		50		50			
Accum. Depreciation—Office Equipment				(c) 40		40				40
Depreciation Expense			(c) 40		40		40			
Interest Expense			(f) 50		50		50			
Accounts Receivable			(e) 200		200				200	
Interest Payable				(f) 50		50				50
Salaries Payable				(g) 1,200		1,200				1,200
Totals			3,440	3,440	30,190	30,190	7,740	10,600	22,450	19,590
Net Income							2,860			2,860
Totals							10,600	10,600	22,450	22,450

1. Prepare a trial balance on the work sheet

2. Enter adjustment data

3. Enter adjusted balances

4. Extend adjusted balances to appropriate statement columns

5. Total the statement columns, compute net income (or net loss), and complete work sheet

SUMMARY OF STUDY OBJECTIVE FOR APPENDIX

9 *Describe the purpose and the basic form of a work sheet.* The work sheet is a device used to make it easier to prepare adjusting entries and the financial statements. It is often prepared on a computer spreadsheet. The sets of columns of the work sheet are, from left to right, the unadjusted trial balance, adjustments, adjusted trial balance, income statement, and balance sheet.

GLOSSARY

Accrual basis accounting Accounting basis in which transactions that change a company's financial statements are recorded in the periods in which the events occur, rather than in the periods in which the company receives or pays cash. (p. 153)

Accrued expenses Expenses incurred but not yet paid in cash or recorded. (p. 164)

Accrued revenues Revenues earned but not yet received in cash or recorded. (p. 163)

Adjusted trial balance A list of accounts and their balances after all adjustments have been made. (p. 170)

Adjusting entries Entries made at the end of an accounting period to ensure that the revenue recognition and matching principles are followed. (p. 154)

Book value The difference between the cost of a depreciable asset and its related accumulated depreciation. (p. 159)

Cash basis accounting An accounting basis in which revenue is recorded only when cash is received, and an expense is recorded only when cash is paid. (p. 153)

Closing entries Entries at the end of an accounting period to transfer the balances of temporary accounts to a permanent stockholders' equity account, Retained Earnings. (p. 172)

Contra asset account An account that is offset against an asset account on the balance sheet. (p. 159)

Depreciation The process of allocating the cost of an asset to expense over its useful life. (p. 158)

Fiscal year An accounting period that is one year long. (p. 151)

Income Summary A temporary account used in closing revenue and expense accounts. (p. 173)

Matching principle The principle that dictates that efforts (expenses) be matched with accomplishments (revenues). (p. 151)

Permanent accounts Balance sheet accounts whose balances are carried forward to the next accounting period. (p. 171)

Post-closing trial balance A list of permanent accounts and their balances after closing entries have been journalized and posted. (p. 174)

Prepaid expenses (Prepayments) Expenses paid in cash and recorded as assets before they are used or consumed. (p. 156)

Revenue recognition principle The principle that revenue be recognized in the accounting period in which it is earned. (p. 151)

Reversing entry An entry made at the beginning of the next accounting period; the exact opposite of the adjusting entry made in the previous period. (p. 176)

Temporary accounts Revenue, expense, and dividend accounts whose balances are transferred to Retained Earnings at the end of an accounting period. (p. 171)

Time period assumption An assumption that the economic life of a business can be divided into artificial time periods. (p. 151)

Unearned revenues Cash received before revenues were earned and recorded as liabilities until they are earned. (p. 159)

Useful life The length of service of a productive facility. (p. 158)

Work sheet A multiple-column form that may be used in the adjustment process and in preparing financial statements. (p. 179)

DEMONSTRATION PROBLEM

Terry Thomas and a group of investors incorporate the Green Thumb Lawn Care Corporation on April 1. At April 30 the trial balance shows the following balances for selected accounts:

Prepaid Insurance	$ 3,600
Equipment	28,000
Notes Payable	20,000
Unearned Service Revenue	4,200
Service Revenue	1,800

Analysis reveals the following additional data pertaining to these accounts:
1. Prepaid insurance is the cost of a 2-year insurance policy, effective April 1.
2. Depreciation on the equipment is $500 per month.
3. The note payable is dated April 1. It is a 6-month, 12% note.
4. Seven customers paid for the company's 6 months' lawn service package of $600 beginning in April. These customers were serviced in April.
5. Lawn services performed for other customers but not billed at April 30 totaled $1,500.

Instructions
Prepare the adjusting entries for the month of April. Show computations.

Problem-Solving Strategies

1. Note that adjustments are being made for 1 month.
2. Make computations carefully.
3. Select account titles carefully.
4. Make sure debits are made first and credits are indented.
5. Check that debits equal credits for each entry.

Solution to Demonstration Problem

GENERAL JOURNAL

Date	Account Titles and Explanation	Debit	Credit
	Adjusting Entries		
Apr. 30	Insurance Expense	150	
	Prepaid Insurance		150
	(To record insurance expired:		
	$3,600 ÷ 24 = $150 per month)		
30	Depreciation Expense	500	
	Accumulated Depreciation—Equipment		500
	(To record monthly depreciation)		
30	Interest Expense	200	
	Interest Payable		200
	(To accrue interest on notes payable:		
	$20,000 × 12% × $\frac{1}{12}$ = $200)		
30	Unearned Service Revenue	700	
	Service Revenue		700
	(To record revenue earned: $600 ÷ 6 = $100;		
	$100 per month × 7 = $700)		
30	Accounts Receivable	1,500	
	Service Revenue		1,500
	(To accrue revenue earned but not billed or		
	collected)		

SELF-STUDY QUESTIONS

Answers are at the end of this chapter.

(SO 1)   1. What is the time period assumption?
       (a) Revenue should be recognized in the accounting period in which it is earned.
       (b) Expenses should be matched with revenues.
       (c) The economic life of a business can be divided into artificial time periods.
       (d) The fiscal year should correspond with the calendar year.

(SO 1)   2. Which principle dictates that efforts (expenses) be recorded with accomplishments (revenues)?
       (a) Matching principle.
       (b) Cost principle.
       (c) Periodicity principle.
       (d) Revenue recognition principle.

(SO 3)   3. Adjusting entries are made to ensure that:
       (a) expenses are recognized in the period in which they are incurred.
       (b) revenues are recorded in the period in which they are earned.
       (c) balance sheet and income statement accounts have correct balances at the end of an accounting period.
       (d) All of the above.

(SO 4, 5)   4. Each of the following is a major type (or category) of adjusting entry *except:*
       (a) prepaid expenses.
       (b) accrued revenues.
       (c) accrued expenses.
       (d) earned expenses.

(SO 5)   5. The trial balance shows Supplies $1,350 and Supplies Expense $0. If $600 of supplies are on hand at the end of the period, the adjusting entry is:
       (a) Supplies   600
            Supplies Expense   600
       (b) Supplies   750
            Supplies Expense   750
       (c) Supplies Expense   750
            Supplies   750
       (d) Supplies Expense   600
            Supplies   600

(SO 4)   6. Adjustments for unearned revenues:
       (a) decrease liabilities and increase revenues.
       (b) increase liabilities and increase revenues.
       (c) increase assets and increase revenues.
       (d) decrease revenues and decrease assets.

(SO 5)   7. Adjustments for accrued revenues:
       (a) increase assets and increase liabilities.
       (b) increase assets and increase revenues.
       (c) decrease assets and decrease revenues.
       (d) decrease liabilities and increase revenues.

(SO 5)   8. Kathy Kiska earned a salary of $400 for the last week of September. She will be paid on October 1. The adjusting entry for Kathy's employer at September 30 is:

(a) No entry is required.

(b) Salaries Expense | 400 |
Salaries Payable | | 400

(c) Salaries Expense | 400 |
Cash | | 400

(d) Salaries Payable | 400 |
Cash | | 400

(SO 6) 9. Which statement is *incorrect* concerning the adjusted trial balance?

(a) An adjusted trial balance proves the equality of the total debit balances and the total credit balances in the ledger after all adjustments are made.

(b) The adjusted trial balance provides the primary basis for the preparation of financial statements.

(c) The adjusted trial balance lists the account balances segregated by assets and liabilities.

(d) The adjusted trial balance is prepared after the adjusting entries have been journalized and posted.

(SO 3) 10. ⊙▬▬ℂ Which one of these statements about the accrual basis of accounting is *false?*

(a) Events that change a company's financial statements are recorded in the periods in which the events occur.

(b) Revenue is recognized in the period in which it is earned.

(c) This basis is in accord with generally accepted accounting principles.

(d) Revenue is recorded only when cash is received, and expense is recorded only when cash is paid.

11. Which account will have a zero balance after closing entries have been journalized and posted? (SO 7)

(a) Service Revenue.

(b) Advertising Supplies.

(c) Prepaid Insurance.

(d) Accumulated Depreciation.

12. Which types of accounts will appear in the post-closing trial balance? (SO 7)

(a) Permanent accounts.

(b) Temporary accounts.

(c) Accounts shown in the income statement columns of a work sheet.

(d) None of the above.

13. All of the following are required steps in the accounting cycle *except:* (SO 8)

(a) journalizing and posting closing entries.

(b) preparing an adjusted trial balance.

(c) preparing a post-closing trial balance.

(d) preparing a work sheet.

Note: All asterisked Questions, Exercises, and Problems relate to material in the appendix to the chapter.

QUESTIONS

1. (a) How does the time period assumption affect an accountant's analysis of accounting transactions?
   (b) Explain the term *fiscal year.*

2. Identify and state two generally accepted accounting principles that relate to adjusting the accounts.

3. ⊙▬▬ℂ Tony Galego, a lawyer, accepts a legal engagement in March, performs the work in April, and is paid in May. If Galego's law firm prepares monthly financial statements, when should it recognize revenue from this engagement? Why?

4. ⊙▬▬ℂ In completing the engagement in question 3, Galego incurs $2,000 of expenses in March, $2,500 in April, and none in May. How much expense should be deducted from revenues in the month the revenue is recognized? Why?

5. "Adjusting entries are required by the cost principle of accounting." Do you agree? Explain.

6. Why may the financial information in a trial balance not be up to date and complete?

7. Distinguish between the two categories of adjusting entries, and identify the types of adjustments applicable to each category.

8. What accounts are debited and credited in a prepaid expense adjusting entry?

9. "Depreciation is a process of valuation that results in the reporting of the fair market value of the asset." Do you agree? Explain.

10. Explain the differences between depreciation expense and accumulated depreciation.

11. Cher Company purchased equipment for $12,000. By the current balance sheet date, $7,000 had been depreciated. Indicate the balance sheet presentation of the data.

12. What accounts are debited and credited in an unearned revenue adjusting entry?

13. ⊙▬▬ℂ A company fails to recognize revenue earned but not yet received. Which of the following accounts are involved in the adjusting entry: (a) asset, (b) liability, (c) revenue, or (d) expense? For the accounts selected, indicate whether they would be debited or credited in the entry.

14. ⊙▬▬ℂ A company fails to recognize an expense incurred but not paid. Indicate which of the following accounts is debited and which is credited in the

adjusting entry: (a) asset, (b) liability, (c) revenue, or (d) expense.

15. ▣▬▬◀ A company makes an accrued revenue adjusting entry for $900 and an accrued expense adjusting entry for $600. How much was net income understated prior to these entries? Explain.

16. On January 9 a company pays $5,000 for salaries, of which $1,700 was reported as Salaries Payable on December 31. Give the entry to record the payment.

17. For each of the following items before adjustment, indicate the type of adjusting entry—prepaid expense, unearned revenue, accrued revenue, and accrued expense—that is needed to correct the misstatement. If an item could result in more than one type of adjusting entry, indicate each of the types.
    (a) Assets are understated.
    (b) Liabilities are overstated.
    (c) Liabilities are understated.
    (d) Expenses are understated.
    (e) Assets are overstated.
    (f) Revenue is understated.

18. One-half of the adjusting entry is given below. Indicate the account title for the other half of the entry.
    (a) Salaries Expense is debited.
    (b) Depreciation Expense is debited.
    (c) Interest Payable is credited.
    (d) Supplies is credited.
    (e) Accounts Receivable is debited.
    (f) Unearned Service Revenue is debited.

19. "An adjusting entry may affect more than one balance sheet or income statement account." Do you agree? Why or why not?

20. Why is it possible to prepare financial statements directly from an adjusted trial balance?

21. ▣▬▬◀
    (a) What information do accrual basis financial statements provide that cash basis statements do not?
    (b) What information do cash basis financial statements provide that accrual basis statements do not?

22. What is the relationship, if any, between the amount shown in the adjusted trial balance column for an account and that account's ledger balance?

23. Identify the account(s) debited and credited in each of the four closing entries, assuming the company has net income for the year.

24. Describe the nature of the Income Summary account, and identify the types of summary data that may be posted to this account.

25. What items are disclosed on a post-closing trial balance, and what is the purpose of this work paper?

26. Which of these accounts would not appear in the post-closing trial balance? Interest Payable, Equipment, Depreciation Expense, Dividends, Unearned Service Revenue, Accumulated Depreciation—Equipment, and Service Revenue.

27. Indicate, in the sequence in which they are made, the three required steps in the accounting cycle that involve journalizing.

28. Identify, in the sequence in which they are prepared, the three trial balances that are required in the accounting cycle.

*29. What is the purpose of a work sheet?

*30. What is the basic form of a work sheet?

BRIEF EXERCISES

Identify impact of transactions on cash and retained earnings.
(SO 2)

BE4-1 Transactions that affect earnings do not necessarily affect cash.

Instructions
Identify the effect, if any, that each of the following transactions would have upon cash and retained earnings. The first transaction has been completed as an example.

	Cash	Retained Earnings
(a) Purchased supplies for cash.	$-100	$ 0
(b) Recorded an adjusting entry to record use of $50 of the above supplies.		
(c) Made sales of $1,000, all on account.		
(d) Received $800 from customers in payment of their accounts.		
(e) Purchased capital asset for cash, $2,500.		
(f) Recorded depreciation of building for period used, $1,000.		

BE4-2 The ledger of Lena Company includes the following accounts. Explain why each account may require adjustment.
(a) Prepaid Insurance.
(b) Depreciation Expense.
(c) Unearned Service Revenue.
(d) Interest Payable.

Indicate why adjusting entries are needed.
(SO 3)

BE4-3 Riko Company accumulates the following adjustment data at December 31. Indicate (1) the type of adjustment (prepaid expense, accrued revenues, and so on) and (2) the status of the accounts before adjustment (overstated or understated).
(a) Supplies of $600 are on hand. Supplies account shows $1,900 balance.
(b) Service Revenues earned but unbilled total $900.
(c) Interest of $200 has accumulated on a note payable.
(d) Rent collected in advance totaling $800 has been earned.

Identify the major types of adjusting entries.
(SO 3)

BE4-4 Sain Advertising Company's trial balance at December 31 shows Advertising Supplies $9,700 and Advertising Supplies Expense $0. On December 31 there are $1,500 of supplies on hand. Prepare the adjusting entry at December 31 and, using T accounts, enter the balances in the accounts, post the adjusting entry, and indicate the adjusted balance in each account.

Prepare adjusting entry for supplies.
(SO 4)

BE4-5 At the end of its first year, the trial balance of Shah Company shows Equipment $25,000 and zero balances in Accumulated Depreciation—Equipment and Depreciation Expense. Depreciation for the year is estimated to be $3,000. Prepare the adjusting entry for depreciation at December 31, post the adjustments to T accounts, and indicate the balance sheet presentation of the equipment at December 31.

Prepare adjusting entry for depreciation.
(SO 4)

BE4-6 On July 1, 2001, Bere Co. pays $15,000 to Marla Insurance Co. for a 3-year insurance contract. Both companies have fiscal years ending December 31. For Bere Co. journalize and post the entry on July 1 and the adjusting entry on December 31.

Prepare adjusting entry for prepaid expense.
(SO 4)

BE4-7 Using the data in BE4-6, journalize and post the entry on July 1 and the adjusting entry on December 31 for Marla Insurance Co. Marla uses the accounts Unearned Insurance Revenue and Insurance Revenue.

Prepare adjusting entry for unearned revenue.
(SO 4)

BE4-8 The bookkeeper for DeVoe Company asks you to prepare the following accrued adjusting entries at December 31:
(a) Interest on notes payable of $400 is accrued.
(b) Service revenue earned but unbilled totals $1,400.
(c) Salaries of $700 earned by employees have not been recorded.
Use these account titles: Service Revenue, Accounts Receivable, Interest Expense, Interest Payable, Salaries Expense, and Salaries Payable.

Prepare adjusting entries for accruals.
(SO 5)

BE4-9 The trial balance of Hoi Company includes the following balance sheet accounts. Identify the accounts that might require adjustment. For each account that requires adjustment, indicate (1) the type of adjusting entry (prepaid expenses, unearned revenues, accrued revenues, and accrued expenses) and (2) the related account in the adjusting entry.
(a) Accounts Receivable.
(b) Prepaid Insurance.
(c) Equipment.
(d) Accumulated Depreciation—Equipment.
(e) Notes Payable.
(f) Interest Payable.
(g) Unearned Service Revenue.

Analyze accounts in an adjusted trial balance.
(SO 6)

BE4-10 The adjusted trial balance of Lumas Corporation at December 31, 2001, includes the following accounts: Retained Earnings $15,600; Dividends $6,000; Service Revenue $35,400; Salaries Expense $13,000; Insurance Expense $2,000; Rent Expense $4,000; Supplies Expense $1,500; and Depreciation Expense $1,000. Prepare an income statement for the year.

Prepare an income statement from an adjusted trial balance.
(SO 6)

BE4-11 Partial adjusted trial balance data for Lumas Corporation are presented in BE4-10. The balance in Retained Earnings is the balance as of January 1. Prepare a statement of retained earnings for the year assuming net income is $14,000.

Prepare a retained earnings statement from an adjusted trial balance.
(SO 6)

Identify financial statement for selected accounts.
(SO 6)

BE4-12 The following selected accounts appear in the adjusted trial balance for Khanna Company. Indicate the financial statement on which each balance would be reported.
(a) Accumulated Depreciation.   (e) Service Revenue.
(b) Depreciation Expense.   (f) Supplies.
(c) Retained Earnings.   (g) Accounts Payable.
(d) Dividends.

Identify post-closing trial-balance accounts.
(SO 7)

BE4-13 Using the data in BE4-12, identify the accounts that would be included in a post-closing trial balance.

List required steps in the accounting cycle sequence.
(SO 8)

BE4-14 The required steps in the accounting cycle are listed in random order below. List the steps in proper sequence.
(a) Prepare a post-closing trial balance.
(b) Prepare an adjusted trial balance.
(c) Analyze business transactions.
(d) Prepare a trial balance.
(e) Journalize the transactions.
(f) Journalize and post closing entries.
(g) Prepare financial statements.
(h) Journalize and post adjusting entries.
(i) Post to ledger accounts.

*E*XERCISES

Identify accounting assumptions, principles, and constraints.
(SO 1)

E4-1 These are the assumptions, principles, and constraints discussed in this and previous chapters:
1. Economic entity assumption.
2. Matching principle.
3. Monetary unit assumption.
4. Time period assumption.
5. Cost principle.
6. Materiality.
7. Full disclosure principle.
8. Going concern assumption.
9. Revenue recognition principle.
10. Conservatism.

Instructions
Identify by number the accounting assumption, principle, or constraint that describes each situation below. Do not use a number more than once.
_____ (a) Is the rationale for why plant assets are not reported at liquidation value. (Do not use the cost principle.)
_____ (b) Indicates that personal and business record-keeping should be separately maintained.
_____ (c) Ensures that all relevant financial information is reported.
_____ (d) Assumes that the dollar is the "measuring stick" used to report on financial performance.
_____ (e) Requires that accounting standards be followed for all *significant* items.
_____ (f) Separates financial information into time periods for reporting purpose.
_____ (g) Requires recognition of expenses in the same period as related revenues.
_____ (h) Indicates that market value changes subsequent to purchase are not recorded in the accounts.

Identify the violated assumption, principle, or constraint.
(SO 1)

E4-2 Here are some accounting reporting situations:
(a) Tercek Company recognizes revenue at the end of the production cycle but before sale. The price of the product, as well as the amount that can be sold, is not certain.
(b) Bonilla Company is in its fifth year of operation and has yet to issue financial statements. (Do not use the full disclosure principle.)
(c) Barton, Inc. is carrying inventory at its current market value of $100,000. Inventory had an original cost of $110,000.

(d) Ravine Hospital Supply Corporation reports only current assets and current liabilities on its balance sheet. Property, plant, and equipment and bonds payable are reported as current assets and current liabilities, respectively. Liquidation of the company is unlikely.

(e) Watts Company has inventory on hand that cost $400,000. Watts reports inventory on its balance sheet at its current market value of $425,000.

(f) Steph Wolfson, president of the Classic Music Company, bought a computer for her personal use. She paid for the computer by using company funds and debited the "computers" account.

Instructions
For each situation, list the assumption, principle, or constraint that has been violated, if any. Some of these assumptions, principles, and constraints were presented in earlier chapters. List only one answer for each situation.

E4-3 In its first year of operations, Brisson Company earned $26,000 in services revenue, $4,000 of which was on account and still outstanding at year-end. The remaining $22,000 was received in cash from customers.

Determine cash basis and accrual basis earnings.
(SO 2)

The company incurred operating expenses of $15,000. Of these expenses $13,500 were paid in cash; $1,500 was still owed on account at year-end. In addition, Brisson prepaid $2,500 for insurance coverage that would not be used until the second year of operations.

Instructions
(a) Calculate the first year's net earnings under the cash basis of accounting, and calculate the first year's net earnings under the accrual basis of accounting.
(b) Which basis of accounting (cash or accrual) provides more useful information for decision makers?

E4-4 Rafael Company accumulates the following adjustment data at December 31:
(a) Service Revenue earned but unbilled totals $600.
(b) Store supplies of $300 are on hand. Supplies account shows $2,300 balance.
(c) Utility expenses of $225 are unpaid.
(d) Service revenue of $260 collected in advance has been earned.
(e) Salaries of $800 are unpaid.
(f) Prepaid insurance totaling $350 has expired.

Identify types of adjustments and accounts before adjustment.
(SO 3, 4, 5)

Instructions
For each item indicate (1) the type of adjustment (prepaid expense, unearned revenue, accrued revenue, or accrued expense) and (2) the accounts before adjustment (overstatement or understatement).

E4-5 The ledger of Convenient Rental Agency on March 31 of the current year includes these selected accounts before adjusting entries have been prepared:

Prepare adjusting entries from selected account data.
(SO 4, 5)

	Debits	Credits
Prepaid Insurance	$ 3,600	
Supplies	2,800	
Equipment	25,000	
Accumulated Depreciation—Equipment		$ 8,400
Notes Payable		20,000
Unearned Rent Revenue		9,300
Rent Revenue		60,000
Interest Expense	0	
Wage Expense	14,000	

An analysis of the accounts shows the following:
1. The equipment depreciates $250 per month.
2. One-third of the unearned rent revenue was earned during the quarter.
3. Interest of $500 is accrued on the notes payable.
4. Supplies on hand total $850.
5. Insurance expires at the rate of $300 per month.

Instructions
Prepare the adjusting entries at March 31, assuming that adjusting entries are made quarterly. Additional accounts are: Depreciation Expense, Insurance Expense, Interest Payable, and Supplies Expense.

Prepare adjusting entries.
(SO 4, 5)

E4-6   Brian Brunn, D.D.S., opened an incorporated dental practice on January 1, 2001. During the first month of operations the following transactions occurred:
1. Performed services for patients who had dental plan insurance. At January 31, $750 of such services was earned but not yet billed to the insurance companies.
2. Utility expenses incurred but not paid prior to January 31 totaled $520.
3. Purchased dental equipment on January 1 for $80,000, paying $20,000 in cash and signing a $60,000, 3-year note payable (Interest is paid each December 31). The equipment depreciates $400 per month. Interest is $500 per month.
4. Purchased a 1-year malpractice insurance policy on January 1 for $12,000.
5. Purchased $1,600 of dental supplies. On January 31 determined that $500 of supplies were on hand.

Instructions
Prepare the adjusting entries on January 31. Account titles are: Accumulated Depreciation—Dental Equipment, Depreciation Expense, Service Revenue, Accounts Receivable, Insurance Expense, Interest Expense, Interest Payable, Prepaid Insurance, Supplies, Supplies Expense, Utilities Expense, and Utilities Payable.

Prepare adjusting entries.
(SO 4, 5)

E4-7   The trial balance for Sierra Corporation is shown in Illustration 4-4. In lieu of the adjusting entries shown in the text at October 31, assume the following adjustment data:
1. Advertising supplies on hand at October 31 total $1,400.
2. Expired insurance for the month is $100.
3. Depreciation for the month is $50.
4. Unearned service revenue earned in October totals $600.
5. Revenue earned but unbilled at October 31 is $300.
6. Interest accrued at October 31 is $70.
7. Accrued salaries at October 31 are $1,500.

Instructions
Prepare the adjusting entries for these items.

Prepare a correct income statement.
(SO 1, 4, 5, 6)

E4-8   The income statement of Garstka Co. for the month of July shows net income of $1,400 based on Service Revenue $5,500; Wages Expense $2,300; Supplies Expense $1,200; and Utilities Expense $600. In reviewing the statement, you discover the following:
1. Insurance expired during July of $300 was omitted.
2. Supplies expense includes $400 of supplies that are still on hand at July 31.
3. Depreciation on equipment of $150 was omitted.
4. Accrued but unpaid wages at July 31 of $300 were not included.
5. Revenue earned but unrecorded totaled $750.

Instructions
Prepare a correct income statement for July 2001.

Analyze adjusted data.
(SO 1, 4, 5, 6)

E4-9   This is a partial adjusted trial balance of Kaffen Company:

KAFFEN COMPANY
Adjusted Trial Balance
January 31, 2001

	Debit	Credit
Supplies	$ 700	
Prepaid Insurance	2,400	
Salaries Payable		$ 800
Unearned Service Revenue		750
Supplies Expense	950	
Insurance Expense	400	
Salaries Expense	1,800	
Service Revenue		2,000

Instructions
Answer these questions, assuming the year begins January 1:
(a) If the amount in Supplies Expense is the January 31 adjusting entry, and $850 of supplies was purchased in January, what was the balance in Supplies on January 1?

(b) If the amount in Insurance Expense is the January 31 adjusting entry, and the original insurance premium was for 1 year, what was the total premium and when was the policy purchased?

(c) If $2,500 of salaries was paid in January, what was the balance in Salaries Payable at December 31, 2000?

(d) If $1,600 was received in January for services performed in January, what was the balance in Unearned Service Revenue at December 31, 2000?

E4-10 Selected accounts of Snowmass Company are shown here:

Journalize basic transactions and adjusting entries.
(SO 4, 5, 6)

Supplies Expense		
July 31	500	

Salaries Payable		
	July 31	1,200

Salaries Expense		
July 15	1,200	
31	1,200	

Service Revenue		
	July 14	3,000
	31	900
	31	500

Supplies			
July 1	Bal. 1,100	July 31	500
10	200		

Accounts Receivable		
July 31	500	

Unearned Service Revenue			
July 31	900	July 1	Bal. 1,500
		20	700

Instructions

After analyzing the accounts, journalize (a) the July transactions and (b) the adjusting entries that were made on July 31. [*Hint:* July transactions were for cash.]

E4-11 The trial balances shown below are before and after adjustment for Digital Company at the end of its fiscal year:

Prepare adjusting entries from analysis of trial balances.
(SO 4, 5, 6)

DIGITAL COMPANY
Trial Balance
August 31, 2001

	Before Adjustment		After Adjustment	
	Dr.	Cr.	Dr.	Cr.
Cash	$10,400		$10,400	
Accounts Receivable	8,800		9,400	
Office Supplies	2,300		700	
Prepaid Insurance	4,000		2,500	
Office Equipment	14,000		14,000	
Accumulated Depreciation—Office Equipment		$ 3,600		$ 4,800
Accounts Payable		5,800		5,800
Salaries Payable		0		1,100
Unearned Rent Revenue		1,500		700
Common Stock		10,000		10,000
Retained Earnings		5,600		5,600
Service Revenue		34,000		34,600
Rent Revenue		11,000		11,800
Salaries Expense	17,000		18,100	
Office Supplies Expense	0		1,600	
Rent Expense	15,000		15,000	
Insurance Expense	0		1,500	
Depreciation Expense	0		1,200	
	$71,500	$71,500	$74,400	$74,400

Instructions
Prepare the adjusting entries that were made.

Prepare financial statements from adjusted trial balance.
(SO 6)

E4-12 The adjusted trial balance for Digital Company is given in E4-11.

Instructions
Prepare the income and retained earnings statements for the year and the balance sheet at August 31.

Prepare closing entries.
(SO 7)

E4-13 The adjusted trial balance for Digital Company is given in E4-11.

Instructions
Prepare the closing entries for the temporary accounts at December 31.

PROBLEMS: SET A

Identify accounting assumptions, principles, and constraints.
(SO 1)

P4-1A Presented below are the assumptions, principles, and constraints used in this and previous chapters.

1. Economic entity assumption.
2. Going concern assumption.
3. Monetary unit assumption.
4. Time period assumption.
5. Full disclosure principle.
6. Revenue recognition principle.
7. Matching principle.
8. Cost principle.
9. Materiality.
10. Conservatism.

Instructions
Identify by number the accounting assumption, principle, or constraint that describes each of these situations. Do not use a number more than once.

_____ (a) Repair tools are expensed when purchased. (Do not use conservatism.)
_____ (b) Allocates expenses to revenues in proper period.
_____ (c) Assumes that the dollar is the measuring stick used to report financial information.
_____ (d) Separates financial information into time periods for reporting purposes.
_____ (e) Market value changes subsequent to purchase are not recorded in the accounts. (Do not use the revenue recognition principle.)
_____ (f) Indicates that personal and business record keeping should be separately maintained.
_____ (g) Ensures that all relevant financial information is reported.
_____ (h) Lower of cost or market is used to value inventories.

Prepare adjusting entries, post to ledger accounts, and prepare adjusted trial balance.
(SO 4, 5, 6)

P4-2A Han Solo started his own consulting firm, Solo Company, on June 1, 2001. The trial balance at June 30 is as follows:

SOLO COMPANY
Trial Balance
June 30, 2001

	Debit	Credit
Cash	$ 7,750	
Accounts Receivable	6,000	
Prepaid Insurance	2,400	
Supplies	2,000	
Office Equipment	15,000	
Accounts Payable		$ 4,500
Unearned Service Revenue		4,000
Common Stock		21,750
Service Revenue		7,900
Salaries Expense	4,000	
Rent Expense	1,000	
	$38,150	$38,150

In addition to those accounts listed on the trial balance, the chart of accounts for Solo Company also contains the following accounts: Accumulated Depreciation—Office Equipment, Utilities Payable, Salaries Payable, Depreciation Expense, Insurance Expense, Utilities Expense, and Supplies Expense.

Other data:

1. Supplies on hand at June 30 total $1,300.
2. A utility bill for $150 has not been recorded and will not be paid until next month.
3. The insurance policy is for a year.
4. $2,500 of unearned service revenue has been earned at the end of the month.
5. Salaries of $1,500 are accrued at June 30.
6. The office equipment has a 5-year life with no salvage value and is being depreciated at $250 per month for 60 months.
7. Invoices representing $3,000 of services performed during the month have not been recorded as of June 30.

Instructions
(a) Prepare the adjusting entries for the month of June.
(b) Post the adjusting entries to the ledger accounts. Enter the totals from the trial balance as beginning account balances. Use T accounts.
(c) Prepare an adjusted trial balance at June 30, 2001.

P4-3A The Palpatine Hotel opened for business on May 1, 2001. Here is its trial balance before adjustment on May 31:

Prepare adjusting entries, adjusted trial balance, and financial statements.
(SO 4, 5, 6)

PALPATINE HOTEL
Trial Balance
May 31, 2001

	Debit	Credit
Cash	$ 2,500	
Prepaid Insurance	1,800	
Supplies	1,900	
Land	15,000	
Lodge	70,000	
Furniture	16,800	
Accounts Payable		$ 4,700
Unearned Rent Revenue		3,600
Mortgage Payable		35,000
Common Stock		60,000
Rent Revenue		9,200
Salaries Expense	3,000	
Utilities Expense	1,000	
Advertising Expense	500	
	$112,500	$112,500

Other data:
1. Insurance expires at the rate of $200 per month.
2. An inventory of supplies shows $1,200 of unused supplies on May 31.
3. Annual depreciation is $3,600 on the lodge and $3,000 on furniture.
4. The mortgage interest rate is 12%. (The mortgage was taken out on May 1.)
5. Unearned rent of $1,500 has been earned.
6. Salaries of $300 are accrued and unpaid at May 31.

Instructions
(a) Journalize the adjusting entries on May 31.
(b) Prepare a ledger using T accounts. Enter the trial balance amounts and post the adjusting entries.
(c) Prepare an adjusted trial balance on May 31.
(d) Prepare an income statement and a retained earnings statement for the month of May and a balance sheet at May 31.
(e) Identify which accounts should be closed on May 31.

Prepare adjusting entries, and financial statements; identify accounts to be closed.
(SO 4, 5, 6, 7)

P4-4A Yoda Inc. was organized on July 1, 2001. Quarterly financial statements are prepared. The trial balance and adjusted trial balance on September 30 are shown here:

YODA INC.
Trial Balance
September 30, 2001

	Unadjusted		Adjusted	
	Dr.	Cr.	Dr.	Cr.
Cash	$ 6,700		$ 6,700	
Accounts Receivable	400		1,000	
Prepaid Rent	1,500		900	
Supplies	1,200		1,000	
Equipment	15,000		15,000	
Accumulated Depreciation—Equipment				$ 350
Notes Payable		$ 5,000		5,000
Accounts Payable		1,510		1,510
Salaries Payable				400
Interest Payable				50
Unearned Rent Revenue		900		600
Common Stock		14,000		14,000
Retained Earnings		0		0
Dividends	600		600	
Commission Revenue		14,000		14,600
Rent Revenue		400		700
Salaries Expense	9,000		9,400	
Rent Expense	900		1,500	
Depreciation Expense			350	
Supplies Expense			200	
Utilities Expense	510		510	
Interest Expense			50	
	$35,810	$35,810	$37,210	$37,210

Instructions
(a) Journalize the adjusting entries that were made.
(b) Prepare an income statement and a retained earnings statement for the 3 months ending September 30 and a balance sheet at September 30.
(c) Identify which accounts should be closed on September 30.
(d) If the note bears interest at 12%, how many months has it been outstanding?

Prepare adjusting entries.
(SO 4, 5)

P4-5A A review of the ledger of Ewoks Company at December 31, 2001, produces these data pertaining to the preparation of annual adjusting entries:
1. Prepaid Insurance $12,300: The company has separate insurance policies on its buildings and its motor vehicles. Policy B4564 on the building was purchased on July 1, 2000, for $9,000. The policy has a term of 3 years. Policy A2958 on the vehicles was purchased on January 1, 2001, for $4,800. This policy has a term of 2 years.
2. Unearned Subscription Revenue $49,000: The company began selling magazine subscriptions on October 1, 2001 on an annual basis. The selling price of a subscription is $50. A review of subscription contracts reveals the following:

Subscription Start Date	Number of Subscriptions
October 1	200
November 1	300
December 1	480
	980

3. Notes Payable, $40,000: This balance consists of a note for 6 months at an annual interest rate of 9%, dated September 1.

4. Salaries Payable $0: There are eight salaried employees. Salaries are paid every Friday for the current week. Five employees receive a salary of $600 each per week, and three employees earn $700 each per week. December 31 is a Wednesday. Employees do not work weekends. All employees worked the last 3 days of December.

Instructions
Prepare the adjusting entries at December 31, 2001.

P4-6A   On November 1, 2001, the following were the account balances of Naboo Equipment Repair:

Journalize transactions and follow through accounting cycle to preparation of financial statements.
(SO 4, 5, 6)

	Debits		**Credits**
Cash	$ 2,790	Accumulated Depreciation	$ 500
Accounts Receivable	2,510	Accounts Payable	2,100
Supplies	1,000	Unearned Service Revenue	400
Store Equipment	10,000	Salaries Payable	500
		Common Stock	10,000
		Retained Earnings	2,800
	$16,300		$16,300

During November the following summary transactions were completed:

Nov. 8 Paid $1,100 for salaries due employees, of which $600 is for November and $500 is for October.
     10 Received $1,200 cash from customers on account.
     12 Received $1,400 cash for services performed in November.
     15 Purchased store equipment on account $3,000.
     17 Purchased supplies on account $1,500.
     20 Paid creditors on account $2,500.
     22 Paid November rent $300.
     25 Paid salaries $1,000.
     27 Performed services on account and billed customers for services provided $900.
     29 Received $550 from customers for future service.

Adjustment data:
1. Supplies on hand are valued at $1,600.
2. Accrued salaries payable are $500.
3. Depreciation for the month is $120.
4. Unearned service revenue of $300 is earned.

Instructions
(a) Enter the November 1 balances in the ledger accounts. (Use T accounts.)
(b) Journalize the November transactions.
(c) Post to the ledger accounts. Use Service Revenue, Depreciation Expense, Supplies Expense, Salaries Expense, and Rent Expense.
(d) Prepare a trial balance at November 30.
(e) Journalize and post adjusting entries.
(f) Prepare an adjusted trial balance.
(g) Prepare an income statement and a retained earnings statement for November and a balance sheet at November 30.

P4-7A   Brett Farve opened Corellian Window Washing Inc. on July 1, 2001. During July the following transactions were completed.

Complete all steps in accounting cycle.
(SO 4, 5, 6, 7, 8)

July 1 Issued $9,000 of common stock for $9,000 cash.
     1 Purchased used truck for $6,000, paying $3,000 cash and the balance on account.
     3 Purchased cleaning supplies for $900 on account.
     5 Paid $1,200 cash on 1-year insurance policy effective July 1.
     12 Billed customers $2,500 for cleaning services.
     18 Paid $1,000 cash on amount owed on truck and $500 on amount owed on cleaning supplies.
     20 Paid $1,200 cash for employee salaries.

21   Collected $1,400 cash from customers billed on July 12.
25   Billed customers $2,000 for cleaning services.
31   Paid gas and oil for month on truck $200.
31   Declared and paid $600 cash dividend.

The chart of accounts for Corellian Window Washing contains the following accounts: Cash, Accounts Receivable, Cleaning Supplies, Prepaid Insurance, Equipment, Accumulated Depreciation—Equipment, Accounts Payable, Salaries Payable, Common Stock, Retained Earnings, Dividends, Income Summary, Service Revenue, Gas & Oil Expense, Cleaning Supplies Expense, Depreciation Expense, Insurance Expense, Salaries Expense.

Instructions
(a) Journalize the July transactions.
(b) Post to the ledger accounts. (Use T accounts.)
(c) Prepare a trial balance at July 31.
(d) Journalize the following adjustments.
    (1) Services provided but unbilled and uncollected at July 31 were $1,100.
    (2) Depreciation on equipment for the month was $200.
    (3) One-twelfth of the insurance expired.
    (4) An inventory count shows $600 of cleaning supplies on hand at July 31.
    (5) Accrued but unpaid employee salaries were $400.
(e) Post adjusting entries to the T accounts.
(f) Prepare an adjusted trial balance.
(g) Prepare the income statement and a retained earnings statement for July and a classified balance sheet at July 31.
(h) Journalize and post closing entries and complete the closing process.
(i) Prepare a post-closing trial balance at July 31.

Problems: Set B

Identify accounting assumptions, principles, and constraints.
(SO 1)

P4-1B   Presented here are the assumptions, principles, and constraints used in this and previous chapters:

1. Economic entity assumption.
2. Materiality.
3. Monetary unit assumption.
4. Time period assumption.
5. Matching principle.
6. Revenue recognition principle.
7. Full disclosure principle.
8. Cost principle.
9. Going concern assumption.
10. Conservatism.

Instructions
Identify by number the accounting assumption, principle, or constraint that describes each of these situations. Do not use a number more than once.
_____ (a) Assets are not stated at their liquidation value. (Do not use the cost principle.)
_____ (b) The death of the president is not recorded in the accounts.
_____ (c) Pencil sharpeners are expensed when purchased.
_____ (d) An allowance for doubtful accounts is established. (Do not use conservatism.)
_____ (e) Each entity is kept as a unit distinct from its owner or owners.
_____ (f) Reporting must be done at defined intervals.
_____ (g) Revenue is recorded at the point of sale.
_____ (h) When in doubt, it is better to understate rather than overstate net income.
_____ (i) All important information related to inventories is presented in the footnotes or in the financial statements.

P4-2B   Julie Brown started her own consulting firm, Astromech Consulting, on May 1, 2001. The trial balance at May 31 is as follows:

Prepare adjusting entries, post to ledger accounts, and prepare an adjusted trial balance.
(SO 4, 5, 6)

ASTROMECH CONSULTING
Trial Balance
May 31, 2001

	Debit	Credit
Cash	$ 6,500	
Accounts Receivable	4,000	
Prepaid Insurance	3,600	
Supplies	1,500	
Office Furniture	12,000	
Accounts Payable		$ 3,500
Unearned Service Revenue		3,000
Common Stock		19,100
Service Revenue		6,000
Salaries Expense	3,000	
Rent Expense	1,000	
	$31,600	$31,600

In addition to those accounts listed on the trial balance, the chart of accounts for Astromech Consulting also contains the following accounts: Accumulated Depreciation—Office Furniture, Travel Payable, Salaries Payable, Depreciation Expense, Insurance Expense, Travel Expense, and Supplies Expense.

Other data:
1. $500 of supplies have been used during the month.
2. Travel costs incurred but not paid are $200.
3. The insurance policy is for 2 years.
4. $1,000 of the balance in the Unearned Service Revenue account remains unearned at the end of the month.
5. May 31 is a Wednesday and employees are paid on Fridays. Astromech Consulting has two employees that are paid $500 each for a 5-day work week.
6. The office furniture has a 5-year life with no salvage value and is being depreciated at $200 per month for 60 months.
7. Invoices representing $2,000 of services performed during the month have not been recorded as of May 31.

Instructions
(a) Prepare the adjusting entries for the month of May.
(b) Post the adjusting entries to the ledger accounts. Enter the totals from the trial balance as beginning account balances. Use T accounts.
(c) Prepare an adjusted trial balance at May 31, 2001.

P4-3B   Obi-Wan Resort opened for business on June 1 with eight air-conditioned units. Its trial balance before adjustment on August 31 is presented here:

Prepare adjusting entries, adjusted trial balance, and financial statements.
(SO 4, 5, 6)

OBI-WAN RESORT
Trial Balance
August 31, 2001

	Debit	Credit
Cash	$ 19,600	
Prepaid Insurance	5,400	
Supplies	3,300	
Land	25,000	
Cottages	125,000	
Furniture	26,000	
Accounts Payable		$ 6,500
Unearned Rent Revenue		6,800
Mortgage Payable		80,000
Common Stock		100,000
Dividends	5,000	
Rent Revenue		80,000
Salaries Expense	51,000	
Utilities Expense	9,400	
Repair Expense	3,600	
	$273,300	$273,300

Other data:
1. Insurance expires at the rate of $300 per month.
2. An inventory count on August 31 shows $900 of supplies on hand.
3. Annual depreciation is $4,800 on cottages and $2,400 on furniture.
4. Unearned rent of $5,000 was earned prior to August 31.
5. Salaries of $400 were unpaid at August 31.
6. Rentals of $800 were due from tenants at August 31. (Use Accounts Receivable.)
7. The mortgage interest rate is 12% per year. (The mortgage was taken out August 1.)

Instructions
(a) Journalize the adjusting entries on August 31 for the 3-month period June 1–August 31.
(b) Prepare a ledger using T accounts. Enter the trial balance amounts and post the adjusting entries.
(c) Prepare an adjusted trial balance on August 31.
(d) Prepare an income statement and a retained earnings statement for the 3 months ended August 31 and a balance sheet as of August 31.
(e) Identify which accounts should be closed on August 31.

Prepare adjusting entries and financial statements; identify accounts to be closed.
(SO 4, 5, 6, 7)

P4-4B R2–D2 Advertising Agency was founded by Thomas Grant in January 1997. Presented here are both the adjusted and unadjusted trial balances as of December 31, 2001.

R2–D2 ADVERTISING AGENCY
Trial Balance
December 31, 2001

	Unadjusted		Adjusted	
	Dr.	Cr.	Dr.	Cr.
Cash	$ 11,000		$ 11,000	
Accounts Receivable	20,000		21,500	
Art Supplies	8,400		5,000	
Prepaid Insurance	3,350		2,500	
Printing Equipment	60,000		60,000	
Accumulated Depreciation		$ 28,000		$ 35,000
Accounts Payable		5,000		5,000
Interest Payable		0		150
Notes Payable		5,000		5,000
Unearned Advertising Revenue		7,000		5,600
Salaries Payable		0		1,300
Common Stock		20,000		20,000

Retained Earnings		5,500	5,500
Dividends	12,000	12,000	
Advertising Revenue		58,600	61,500
Salaries Expense	10,000	11,300	
Insurance Expense		850	
Interest Expense	350	500	
Depreciation Expense		7,000	
Art Supplies Expense		3,400	
Rent Expense	4,000	4,000	
	$129,100	$129,100	$139,050 $139,050

Instructions
(a) Journalize the annual adjusting entries that were made.
(b) Prepare an income statement and a retained earnings statement for the year ended December 31, and a balance sheet at December 31.
(c) Identify which accounts should be closed on December 31.
(d) If the note has been outstanding 3 months, what is the annual interest rate on that note?
(e) If the company paid $13,500 in salaries in 2001, what was the balance in Salaries Payable on December 31, 2000?

P4-5B   A review of the ledger of Greenberg Company at December 31, 2001, produces the following data pertaining to the preparation of annual adjusting entries:

Prepare adjusting entries.
(SO 4, 5)

1. Salaries Payable $0: There are eight salaried employees. Salaries are paid every Friday for the current week. Five employees receive a salary of $700 each per week, and three employees earn $500 each per week. December 31 is a Tuesday. Employees do not work weekends. All employees worked the last 2 days of December.
2. Unearned Rent Revenue $369,000: The company began subleasing office space in its new building on November 1. Each tenant is required to make a $5,000 security deposit that is not refundable until occupancy is terminated. At December 31 the company had the following rental contracts that are paid in full for the entire term of the lease:

Date	Term (in months)	Monthly Rent	Number of Leases
Nov. 1	6	$4,000	5
Dec. 1	6	8,500	4

3. Prepaid Advertising $13,200: This balance consists of payments on two advertising contracts. The contracts provide for monthly advertising in two trade magazines. The terms of the contracts are as follows:

Contract	Date	Amount	Number of Magazine Issues
A650	May 1	$6,000	12
B974	Sept. 1	7,200	24

The first advertisement runs in the month in which the contract is signed.
4. Notes Payable $80,000: This balance consists of a note for 1 year at an annual interest rate of 12%, dated June 1, 2001.

Instructions
Prepare the adjusting entries at December 31, 2001. Show all computations.

P4-6B   On September 1, 2001, the following were the account balances of Rijo Equipment Repair:

Journalize transactions and follow through accounting cycle to preparation of financial statements.
(SO 4, 5, 6)

	Debits		**Credits**
Cash	$ 4,880	Accumulated Depreciation	$ 1,500
Accounts Receivable	3,520	Accounts Payable	3,400
Supplies	1,000	Unearned Service Revenue	400
Store Equipment	15,000	Salaries Payable	500
	$24,400	Common Stock	10,000
		Retained Earnings	8,600
			$24,400

During September the following summary transactions were completed:

Sept. 8 Paid $1,100 for salaries due employees, of which $600 is for September and $500 is for August.
10 Received $1,200 cash from customers on account.
12 Received $3,400 cash for services performed in September.
15 Purchased store equipment on account $3,000.
17 Purchased supplies on account $1,500.
20 Paid creditors $4,500 on account.
22 Paid September rent $500.
25 Paid salaries $1,050.
27 Performed services on account and billed customers for services rendered $700.
29 Received $650 from customers for future service.

Adjustment data:
1. Supplies on hand $1,800.
2. Accrued salaries payable $400.
3. Depreciation $200 per month.
4. Unearned service revenue of $350 earned.

Instructions
(a) Enter the September 1 balances in the ledger T accounts.
(b) Journalize the September transactions.
(c) Post to the ledger T accounts. Use Service Revenue, Depreciation Expense, Supplies Expense, Salaries Expense, and Rent Expense.
(d) Prepare a trial balance at September 30.
(e) Journalize and post adjusting entries.
(f) Prepare an adjusted trial balance.
(g) Prepare an income statement and a retained earnings statement for September and a balance sheet at September 30.

Complete all steps in accounting cycle.
(SO 4, 5, 6, 7, 8)

P4-7B Ewok-Ackbar opened Ewok's Carpet Cleaners on March 1. During March, the following transactions were completed.

Mar. 1 Issued $10,000 of common stock for $10,000 cash.
1 Purchased used truck for $6,000, paying $4,000 cash and the balance on account.
3 Purchased cleaning supplies for $1,200 on account.
5 Paid $1,800 cash on 1-year insurance policy effective March 1.
14 Billed customers $2,800 for cleaning services.
18 Paid $1,500 cash on amount owed on truck and $500 on amount owed on cleaning supplies.
20 Paid $1,500 cash for employee salaries.
21 Collected $1,600 cash from customers billed on July 14.
28 Billed customers $3,500 for cleaning services.
31 Paid gas and oil for month on truck $200.
31 Declared and paid a $900 cash dividend.

The chart of accounts for Ewok's Carpet Cleaners contains the following accounts: Cash, Accounts Receivable, Cleaning Supplies, Prepaid Insurance, Equipment, Accumulated Depreciation—Equipment, Accounts Payable, Salaries Payable, Common Stock, Retained Earnings, Dividends, Income Summary, Service Revenue, Gas & Oil Expense, Cleaning Supplies Expense, Depreciation Expense, Insurance Expense, Salaries Expense.

Instructions
(a) Journalize the March transactions.
(b) Post to the ledger accounts. (Use T accounts.)
(c) Prepare a trial balance at March 31.
(d) Journalize the following adjustments.
 1. Earned but unbilled revenue at March 31 was $600.
 2. Depreciation on equipment for the month was $250.

3. One-twelfth of the insurance expired.

4. An inventory count shows $400 of cleaning supplies on hand at March 31.

5. Accrued but unpaid employee salaries were $500.

(e) Post adjusting entries to the T accounts.

(f) Prepare an adjusted trial balance.

(g) Prepare the income statement and a retained earnings statement for March and a classified balance sheet at March 31.

(h) Journalize and post closing entries and complete the closing process.

(i) Prepare a post-closing trial balance at July 31.

◆ BROADENING YOUR PERSPECTIVE

*F*INANCIAL *R*EPORTING AND *A*NALYSIS

FINANCIAL REPORTING PROBLEM: *Tootsie Roll Industries, Inc.*

BYP4-1 The financial statements of Tootsie Roll are presented in Appendix A at the end of this book.

Instructions

(a) Using the consolidated income statement and balance sheet, identify items that may result in adjusting entries for prepayments.

(b) Using the consolidated income statement, identify two items that may result in adjusting entries for accruals.

(c) What was the amount of depreciation expense for 1998 and 1997? (You will need to examine the notes to the financial statements.) Where was accumulated depreciation reported?

(d) What was the cash paid for income taxes during 1998, reported at the bottom of the Consolidated Statement of Cash Flows? What was income tax expense (provision for income taxes) for 1998? Where is the remainder presumably reported in the balance sheet?

COMPARATIVE ANALYSIS PROBLEM: *Tootsie Roll vs. Hershey Foods*

BYP4-2 The financial statements of Hershey Foods are presented in Appendix B, following the financial statements for Tootsie Roll in Appendix A.

Instructions

(a) Identify two accounts on Hershey Foods' balance sheet that provide evidence that Hershey uses accrual accounting. In each case, identify the income statement account that would be affected by the adjustment process.

(b) Identify two accounts on Tootsie Roll's balance sheet that provide evidence that Tootsie Roll uses accrual accounting (different from the two you listed for Hershey). In each case, identify the income statement account that would be affected by the adjustment process.

RESEARCH CASE

BYP4-3 The March 1995 issue of *Management Review* includes an article by Barbara Ettorre entitled "How Motorola Closes Its Books in Two Days."

Instructions

Read the article and answer the following questions:

(a) How often does Motorola close its books? How long did the process used to take?

(b) What was the major change Motorola initiated to shorten the closing process?

(c) What incentive does Motorola offer to ensure accurate and timely information?

(d) In a given year, how many journal entry lines does Motorola process?

(e) Provide an example of an external force that prevents Motorola from closing faster than a day and a half.

(f) According to Motorola's corporate vice-president and controller, how do external users of financial statements perceive companies that release information early?

INTERPRETING FINANCIAL STATEMENTS

BYP4-4 **Case Corporation,** based in Racine, Wisconsin, manufactures farm tractors, farm equipment, and light- and medium-sized construction equipment. The company's products are distributed through both independent and company-owned distributing companies, which are located throughout the world. Case Corporation's 1998 partial income statement is shown below.

CASE

CASE CORPORATION Income Statement (partial) For the Year Ended 1998 (in millions)		
Revenues		
Net sales	$5,738	
Interest income and other	279	
		$6,017
Cost and expenses		
Cost of goods sold	4,700	
Selling, general, and administrative	747	
Research, development, and engineering	224	
Interest expense	240	
		5,911
Income from operations before taxes		$ 106

Assume that this partial income statement was prepared before all adjusting entries had been made, and that the internal audit staff identified the following items that require adjustments:

1. Depreciation on the administrative offices of $13 million needs to be recorded.
2. A physical inventory determined that $1 million in office supplies had been used in 1998.
3. $4 million in salaries have been earned but not recorded. Half of this amount is for the salaries of engineering staff; the other half is for the administrative staff.
4. $3 million in insurance premiums were prepaid on May 1 and expired by year end.
5. $7 million in prepaid rent has expired at year-end.
6. Cost of goods sold of $2 million was recorded in error as interest expense.

Instructions

(a) Make the adjusting entries required. Use standard account titles.
(b) Which of the entries is not a routine adjusting entry? Explain your answer.
(c) For each of the accounts in these adjusting entries that will be posted to Case's general ledger, tell which item on the income statement will be increased or decreased.
(d) Recast the partial income statement based on the adjusting entries prepared.

A GLOBAL FOCUS

BYP4-5 **Hoescht Marion Roussel (HMR)** is one of the world's largest research-based pharmaceutical companies. It is headquartered in Frankfurt, Germany. It conducts research in Germany, France, and the United States. Its financial statements are based on the International Accounting Standards of the International Accounting Standards Committee.

Instructions
Answer each of the following questions.

1. The statement of cash flows reports interest paid during 1998 of $344 million, while the income statement reports interest expense of $721 million. What might explain this difference? Give an example of the journal entry that you would expect to see that would cause this difference (ignore amounts).
2. Among its liabilities, the company reports provisions for litigation and environmental protection. What types of litigation and environmental protection costs might this company incur? What are the possible points in time that litigation costs might be expensed? At what point do you think these costs should be expensed on the income statement in order to provide proper matching of revenues and expenses? What challenges to matching does litigation present?
3. The notes to the company's financial statements state that the company records revenues "at the time of shipment of products or performance of services." Is this consistent with the revenue recognition practices described in this chapter? What considerations might you want to take into account in determining whether this is the appropriate approach to recognize revenues?

FINANCIAL ANALYSIS ON THE WEB

BYP4-6 *Purpose:* Using "Edgar Database" to locate and identify common corporate filings required by the SEC forms and their definitions.

Address: http://www.sec.gov/index.html (or go to www.wiley.com/college/kimmel)

Steps:
1. Choose **EDGAR Database**.
2. Choose **EDGAR Form Definitions**.

Instructions
Describe the following:
(a) Prospectus.   (d) 10K.
(b) Schedule 14A.   (e) 10Q.
(c) Forms 3, 4, and 5.

CRITICAL THINKING

GROUP DECISION CASE

BYP4-7 Holiday Travel Court was organized on April 1, 2000, by Alice Adare. Alice is a good manager but a poor accountant. From the trial balance prepared by a part-time bookkeeper, Alice prepared the following income statement for the quarter that ended March 31, 2001:

HOLIDAY TRAVEL COURT
Income Statement
For the Quarter Ended March 31, 2001

Revenues		
Rental revenues		$95,000
Operating expenses		
Advertising	$ 5,200	
Wages	29,800	
Utilities	900	
Depreciation	800	
Repairs	4,000	
Total operating expenses		40,700
Net income		$54,300

CHAPTER 5

Merchandising Operations

◆ STUDY OBJECTIVES

After studying this chapter, you should be able to:

1. Identify the differences between a service enterprise and a merchandising company.

2. Explain the recording of purchases under a perpetual inventory system.

3. Explain the recording of sales revenues under a perpetual inventory system.

4. Distinguish between a single-step and a multiple-step income statement.

5. Explain the factors affecting profitability.

◆ WHO DOESN'T SHOP AT WAL-MART?

In his book *The End of Work*, Jeremy Rifkin notes that until the 20th century the word *consumption* evoked negative images; to be labeled a "consumer" was an insult. (In fact, one of the deadliest diseases in history was often referred to as "consumption.") Twentieth-century merchants realized, however, that in order to prosper, they had to convince people of the need for things not previously needed. For example, General Motors made annual changes in its cars so that people would be discontented with the cars they already owned. Thus began consumerism.

Today consumption describes the U.S. lifestyle in a nutshell. We consume twice as much today per person as we did at the end of World War II. The amount of U.S. retail space per person is vastly greater than that of any other country. It appears that we live to shop.

The first great retail giant was Sears, Roebuck. It started as a catalog company enabling people in rural areas to buy things by mail. For decades it was the uncontested merchandising leader. But in recent years Sears lost its edge. It didn't recognize changes in consumer shopping patterns and tastes. First it was outdone by the "blue-light special," but Kmart's time at the top was short-lived. Today the king of the shopping cart is Wal-Mart.

Wal-Mart had only 18 stores as recently as 1970. A key cause of its incredible growth is its amazing system of inventory control and distribution. Wal-Mart has a management information system that employs six satellite channels. After a decade of annual increases in earnings of 25%, the Walton family, which owns 40% of Wal-Mart, is among the wealthiest in the nation. As Wal-Mart glimmered, the fortunes of both Sears and Kmart tarnished, though each tried to remake its image and identity.

For a few years in the 1990s Wal-Mart's profit increases, while still a healthy 12% annually, came down to earth. The company experienced less than stellar results from some of its international holdings and stores in large cities. But in fiscal year 1999 Wal-Mart posted a 25% increase in net income, pummeling its competitors, to firmly establish its title as the largest satisfier of basic (and perhaps not so basic) human needs.

It would appear things have never looked better at Wal-Mart. On the other hand, a recent *Wall Street Journal* article entitled "How to Sell More to Those Who Think It's Cool to Be Frugal" suggests that consumerism as a way of life might be dying. Don't bet your wide-screen TV on it, though.

Wal-Mart, Kmart, and Sears are called merchandising companies because they buy and sell merchandise rather than perform services as their primary source of revenue. Merchandising companies that purchase and sell directly to consumers are called **retailers**. Merchandising companies that sell to retailers are known as **wholesalers**. For example, retailer Walgreens might buy goods from wholesaler McKesson HBOC; retailer Office Depot might buy office supplies from wholesaler United Stationers.

Merchandising is one of the largest and most influential industries in the United States. Understanding the financial statements of these companies is important. The content and organization of the chapter are as follows:

MERCHANDISING OPERATIONS				
Merchandising Operations	**Recording Purchases of Merchandise**	**Recording Sales of Merchandise**	**Income Statement Presentation**	**Evaluating Profitability**
• Operating Cycles • Inventory Systems	• Purchase Returns and Allowances • Freight Costs • Purchase Discounts	• Sales Returns and Allowances • Sales Discounts	• Sales Revenues • Gross Profit • Operating Expenses • Nonoperating Activities	• Gross Profit Rate • Operating Expenses to Sales Ratio

Merchandising Operations

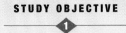

STUDY OBJECTIVE

1

Identify the differences between a service enterprise and a merchandising company.

The primary source of revenues for merchandising companies is the sale of merchandise, often referred to simply as sales revenue or **sales**. Expenses for a merchandising company are divided into two categories: the cost of goods sold and operating expenses.

The cost of goods sold is the total cost of merchandise sold during the period. This expense is directly related to the revenue recognized from the sale of goods. The income measurement process for a merchandising company is shown in Illustration 5-1. The items in the two blue boxes are unique to a merchandising company; they are not used by a service company.

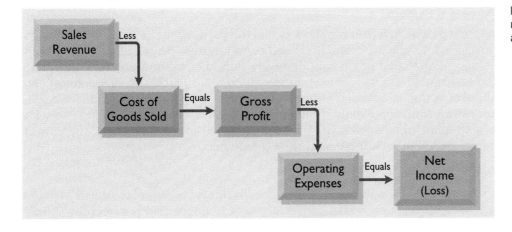

Illustration 5-1 Income measurement process for a merchandising company

OPERATING CYCLES

The operating cycle of a merchandising company ordinarily is longer than that of a service company. The purchase of merchandise inventory and its eventual sale lengthen the cycle. The operating cycles of service and merchandising companies are contrasted in Illustration 5-2. Note that the added asset account for a merchandising company is the Merchandise Inventory account.

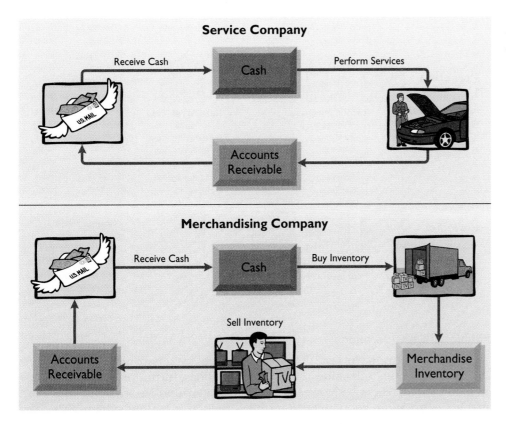

Illustration 5-2 Operating cycles for a service company and a merchandising company

INVENTORY SYSTEMS

A merchandising company keeps track of its inventory to determine what is available for sale and what has been sold. One of two systems is used to account for inventory: a **perpetual inventory system** or a **periodic inventory system**.

Perpetual System

In a **perpetual inventory system**, detailed records of the cost of each inventory purchase and sale are maintained and continuously—perpetually—show the inventory that should be on hand for every item. For example, a Ford dealership has separate inventory records for each automobile, truck, and van on its lot and showroom floor. Similarly, with the use of bar codes and optical scanners, a grocery store can keep a daily running record of every box of cereal and every jar of jelly that it buys and sells. Under a perpetual inventory system, the cost of goods sold is **determined each time a sale occurs**.

Periodic System

In a **periodic inventory system**, detailed inventory records of the goods on hand are not kept throughout the period. The cost of goods sold is **determined only at the end of the accounting period**—that is, periodically—when a physical inventory count is taken to determine the cost of goods on hand. To determine the cost of goods sold under a periodic inventory system, the following steps are necessary: (1) Determine the cost of goods on hand at the beginning of the accounting period; (2) add to it the cost of goods purchased; and (3) subtract the cost of goods on hand at the end of the accounting period.

Illustration 5-3 graphically compares the sequence of activities and the timing of the cost of goods sold computation under the two inventory systems.

Illustration 5-3
Comparing periodic and perpetual inventory systems

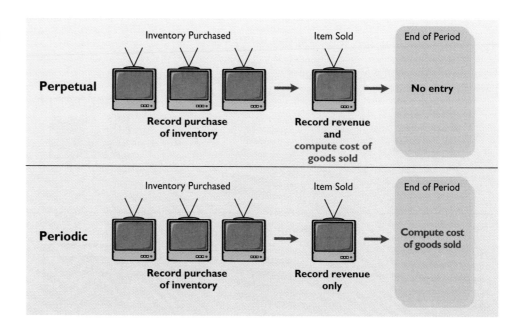

Additional Considerations

Perpetual systems have traditionally been used by companies that sell merchandise with high unit values, such as automobiles, furniture, and major home appliances. The recent widespread use of computers and electronic scanners has enabled many more companies to install perpetual inventory systems. The perpetual inventory system is so named because the accounting records continuously—perpetually—show the quantity and cost of the inventory that should be on hand at any time.

A perpetual inventory system provides better control over inventories than a periodic system. Since the inventory records show the quantities that should be on hand, the goods can be counted at any time to see whether the amount of goods actually on hand agrees with the inventory records. Any shortages uncovered can be investigated immediately. Although a perpetual inventory system requires additional clerical work and additional cost to maintain the subsidiary records, a computerized system can minimize this cost. As noted in the opening story, much of Wal-Mart's success is attributed to its sophisticated inventory system.

Some businesses find it either unnecessary or uneconomical to invest in a computerized perpetual inventory system. Many small merchandising businesses, in particular, find that a perpetual inventory system costs more than it is worth. Managers of these businesses can control their merchandise and manage day-to-day operations without detailed inventory records by using a periodic inventory system.

Because the perpetual inventory system is growing in popularity and use, we illustrate it in this chapter. The periodic system, still widely used, is described in the next chapter.

BUSINESS INSIGHT
Investor Perspective

Investors are often eager to invest in a company that has a hot new product. However, when snowboard maker Morrow Snowboards, Inc., issued shares of stock to the public for the first time, some investors expressed reluctance to invest in Morrow because of a number of accounting control problems. To reduce investor concerns, Morrow implemented a perpetual inventory system to improve its control over inventory. In addition, it stated that it would perform a physical inventory count every quarter until it felt that the perpetual inventory system was reliable.

RECORDING PURCHASES OF MERCHANDISE

Purchases of inventory may be made for cash or on account (credit). Purchases are normally recorded when the goods are received from the seller. Every purchase should be supported by business documents that provide written evidence of the transaction. Each cash purchase should be supported by a canceled check or a cash register receipt indicating the items purchased and amounts paid. Cash purchases are recorded by an increase in Merchandise Inventory and a decrease in Cash.

Each credit purchase should be supported by a **purchase invoice**, which indicates the total purchase price and other relevant information. However, the purchaser does not prepare a separate purchase invoice. Instead, the copy of the sales invoice sent by the seller is used by the buyer as a purchase invoice. In Illustration 5-4 (page 210), for example, the sales invoice prepared by PW Audio Supply, Inc. (the seller) is used as a purchase invoice by Sauk Stereo (the buyer).

The associated entry for Sauk Stereo for the invoice from PW Audio Supply is:

STUDY OBJECTIVE

2

Explain the recording of purchases under a perpetual inventory system.

In the margins next to key journal entries are **equation analyses** that summarize the effects of the transaction on the three elements of the accounting equation.

May	4	Merchandise Inventory	3,800	
		Accounts Payable		3,800
		(To record goods purchased on account from PW Audio Supply)		

A	=	L	+	SE
+3,800		+3,800		

Illustration 5-4 Sales invoice used as purchase invoice by Sauk Stereo

Helpful Hint To better understand the contents of this invoice, identify these items:
1. Seller
2. Invoice date
3. Purchaser
4. Salesperson
5. Credit terms
6. Freight terms
7. Goods sold: catalog number, description, quantity, price per unit
8. Total invoice amount

INVOICE NO. 731

PW AUDIO SUPPLY, INC.
27 CIRCLE DRIVE
HARDING, MICHIGAN 48281

SOLD TO

Firm Name ___ Sauk Stereo

Attention of ___ James Hoover, Purchasing Agent

Address ___ 125 Main Street

Chelsea   Illinois   60915
City   State   Zip

Date 5/4/01	Salesperson Malone	Terms 2/10, n/30	Freight Paid by Buyer		
Catalog No.	Description		Quantity	Price	Amount
X572Y9820	Printed Circuit Board-prototype		1	2,300	$2,300
A2547Z45	Production Model Circuits		5	300	1,500

IMPORTANT: ALL RETURNS MUST BE MADE WITHIN 10 DAYS   **TOTAL** $3,800

Under the perpetual inventory system, purchases of merchandise for sale are recorded in the Merchandise Inventory account. Thus, Wal-Mart would increase (debit) Merchandise Inventory for clothing, sporting goods, and anything else purchased for resale to customers. Not all purchases are debited to Merchandise Inventory, however. Purchases of assets acquired for use and not for resale, such as supplies, equipment, and similar items, are recorded as increases to specific asset accounts rather than to Merchandise Inventory. For example, Wal-Mart would increase Supplies to record the purchase of materials used to make shelf signs or for cash register receipt paper.

PURCHASE RETURNS AND ALLOWANCES

A purchaser may be dissatisfied with the merchandise received because the goods are damaged or defective, of inferior quality, or do not meet the purchaser's specifications. In such cases, the purchaser may return the goods to the seller for credit if the sale was made on credit, or for a cash refund if the purchase was for cash. This transaction is known as a **purchase return**. Alternatively, the purchaser may choose to keep the merchandise if the seller is willing to grant an allowance (deduction) from the purchase price. This transaction is known as a **purchase allowance**.

Assume that Sauk Stereo returned goods costing $300 to PW Audio Supply on May 8. The entry by Sauk Stereo for the returned merchandise is:

May	8	Accounts Payable	300	
		Merchandise Inventory		300
		(To record return of goods received from PW Audio Supply)		

A	=	L	+	SE
−300		−300		

Because Sauk Stereo increased Merchandise Inventory when the goods were received, Merchandise Inventory is decreased when Sauk returns the goods.

FREIGHT COSTS

The sales invoice indicates whether the seller or the buyer pays the cost of transporting the goods to the buyer's place of business. When the buyer pays the transportation costs, these costs are considered part of the cost of purchasing inventory. As a result, the account Merchandise Inventory is increased. For example, if upon delivery of the goods on May 6, Sauk Stereo pays Haul-It Freight Company $150 for freight charges, the entry on Sauk's books is:

May	9	Merchandise Inventory	150	
		Cash		150
		(To record payment of freight on goods purchased)		

A	=	L	+	SE
+150				
−150				

In contrast, **freight costs incurred by the seller on outgoing merchandise are an operating expense to the seller**. These costs increase an expense account titled Freight-out or Delivery Expense. For example, if the freight terms on the invoice in Illustration 5-4 had required that PW Audio Supply pay the $150 freight charges, the entry by PW Audio would be:

May	4	Freight-out	150	
		Cash		150
		(To record payment of freight on goods sold)		

A	=	L	+	SE
−150				−150

When the freight charges are paid by the seller, the seller will usually establish a higher invoice price for the goods, to cover the expense of shipping.

PURCHASE DISCOUNTS

The credit terms of a purchase on account may permit the buyer to claim a cash discount for prompt payment. The buyer calls this cash discount a purchase discount. This incentive offers advantages to both parties: The purchaser saves money, and the seller is able to shorten the operating cycle by converting the accounts receivable into cash earlier.

The **credit terms** specify the amount of the cash discount and time period during which it is offered. They also indicate the length of time in which the purchaser is expected to pay the full invoice price. In the sales invoice in Illustration 5-4, credit terms are 2/10, n/30, which is read "two-ten, net thirty." This means that a 2% cash discount may be taken on the invoice price, less ("net of") any returns or allowances, if payment is made within 10 days of the invoice date (the **discount period**); otherwise, the invoice price, less any returns or allowances, is due 30 days from the invoice date. Alternatively, the discount period may extend to a specified number of days following the month in which the sale occurs. For example, 1/10 EOM (end of month) means that a 1% discount is available if the invoice is paid within the first 10 days of the next month.

Helpful Hint The term *net* in "net 30" means the remaining amount due after subtracting any sales returns and allowances and partial payments.

When the seller elects not to offer a cash discount for prompt payment, credit terms will specify only the maximum time period for paying the balance due. For example, the time period may be stated as n/30, n/60, or n/10 EOM, meaning, respectively, that the net amount must be paid in 30 days, 60 days, or within the first 10 days of the next month.

When an invoice is paid within the discount period, the amount of the discount decreases Merchandise Inventory because inventory is recorded at its cost and, by paying within the discount period, the merchandiser has reduced its cost. To illustrate, assume Sauk Stereo pays the balance due of $3,500 (gross invoice price of $3,800 less purchase returns and allowances of $300) on May 14, the last day of the discount period. The cash discount is $70 ($3,500 × 2%), and the amount of cash paid by Sauk Stereo is $3,430 ($3,500 − $70). The entry to record the May 14 payment by Sauk Stereo is:

A	=	L	+	SE
−3,430		−3,500		
		−70		

May	14	Accounts Payable	3,500	
		Cash		3,430
		Merchandise Inventory		70
		(To record payment within discount period)		

If Sauk Stereo failed to take the discount and instead made full payment on June 3, Sauk's entry is:

A	=	L	+	SE
−3,500		−3,500		

June	3	Accounts Payable	3,500	
		Cash		3,500
		(To record payment with no discount taken)		

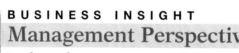

BUSINESS INSIGHT
Management Perspective

In the early 1990s, Sears wielded its retail clout by telling its suppliers that, rather than pay its obligations in the standard 30-day period, it would now pay in 60 days. This practice is often adopted by firms that are experiencing financial distress from a shortage of cash. A Sears spokesperson insisted, however, that Sears did not have cash problems but, rather, was simply utilizing "vendor-financed inventory methods to improve its return on investment." Supplier trade groups have been outspoken critics of Sears' policy and have suggested that consumers will be the ultimate victims, because the financing costs will eventually be passed on to them.

Source: The Wall Street Journal, August 15, 1991.

Helpful Hint So as not to miss purchase discounts, unpaid invoices should be filed by due dates. This procedure helps the purchaser remember the discount date, prevents early payment of bills, and maximizes the time that cash can be used for other purposes.

A merchandising company usually should take all available discounts. Passing up the discount may be viewed as **paying interest** for use of the money. For example, if Sauk Stereo passed up the discount, it would be like paying an interest rate of 2% for the use of $3,500 for 20 days. This is the equivalent of an annual interest rate of approximately 36.5% (2% × 365/20). Obviously, it would be better for Sauk Stereo to borrow at prevailing bank interest rates of 8% to 12% than to lose the discount.

◆ **Review It**

1. How does the measurement of net income in a merchandising company differ from that in a service enterprise?
2. In what ways is a perpetual inventory system different from a periodic system?
3. Under the perpetual inventory system, what entries are made to record purchases, purchase returns and allowances, purchase discounts, and freight costs?

RECORDING SALES OF MERCHANDISE

Sales revenues, like service revenues, are recorded when earned in order to comply with the revenue recognition principle. Typically, sales revenues are earned when the goods are transferred from the seller to the buyer. At this point the sales transaction is completed and the sales price is established.

Sales may be made on credit or for cash. Every sales transaction should be supported by a **business document** that provides written evidence of the sale. **Cash register tapes** provide evidence of cash sales. A sales invoice, like the one that was shown in Illustration 5-4 (page 210), provides support for a credit sale. The original copy of the invoice goes to the customer, and a copy is kept by the seller for use in recording the sale. The invoice shows the date of sale, customer name, total sales price, and other relevant information.

Two entries are made for each sale. The first entry records the sale: Assuming a cash sale, Cash is increased by a debit, and Sales is increased by a credit at the selling (invoice) price of the goods. The second entry records the cost of the merchandise sold: Cost of Goods Sold is increased by a debit, and Merchandise Inventory is decreased by a credit for the cost of those goods. For example, assume that on May 4 PW Audio Supply has cash sales of $2,200 from merchandise having a cost of $1,400. The entries to record the day's cash sales are as follows:

> **STUDY OBJECTIVE**
> **3**
> Explain the recording of sales revenues under a perpetual inventory system.

May	4	Cash	2,200	
		Sales		2,200
		(To record daily cash sales)		
	4	Cost of Goods Sold	1,400	
		Merchandise Inventory		1,400
		(To record cost of merchandise sold for cash)		

A	=	L	+	SE
+2,200				+2,200

A	=	L	+	SE
−1,400				−1,400

For credit sales (1) Accounts Receivable is increased and Sales is increased, and (2) Cost of Goods Sold is increased and Merchandise Inventory is decreased. As a result, the Merchandise Inventory account will show at all times the amount of inventory that should be on hand. To illustrate a credit sales transaction, PW Audio Supply's sale of $3,800 on May 4 to Sauk Stereo (see Illustration 5-4, page 210) is recorded as follows (assume the merchandise cost PW Audio Supply $2,400):

A	=	L	+	SE
+3,800				+3,800

A	=	L	+	SE
−2,400				−2,400

May	4	Accounts Receivable		3,800	
		Sales			3,800
		(To record credit sale to Sauk Stereo per invoice #731)			
	4	Cost of Goods Sold		2,400	
		Merchandise Inventory			2,400
		(To record cost of merchandise sold on invoice #731 to Sauk Stereo)			

Helpful Hint The Sales account is credited only for sales of goods held for resale. Sales of assets not held for resale, such as equipment or land, are credited directly to the asset account.

For internal decision-making purposes, merchandising companies may use more than one sales account. For example, PW Audio Supply may decide to keep separate sales accounts for its sales of TV sets, videocassette recorders, and microwave ovens. By using separate sales accounts for major product lines, rather than a single combined sales account, company management can monitor sales trends more closely and respond in a more appropriate strategic fashion to changes in sales patterns. For example, if TV sales are increasing while microwave oven sales are decreasing, the company should reevaluate both its advertising and pricing policies on each of these items to ensure they are optimal. On its income statement presented to outside investors a merchandising company would normally provide only a single sales figure—the sum of all of its individual sales accounts. This is done for two reasons. First, providing detail on all of its individual sales accounts would add considerable length to its income statement. Second, companies do not want their competitors to know the details of their operating results.

SALES RETURNS AND ALLOWANCES

We now look at the "flipside" of purchase returns and allowances, which are recorded as **sales returns and allowances** on the books of the seller. PW Audio Supply's entries to record credit for returned goods involve (1) an increase in Sales Returns and Allowances and a decrease in Accounts Receivable at the $300 selling price, and (2) an increase in Merchandise Inventory (assume a $140 cost) and a decrease in Cost of Goods Sold as follows:

A	=	L	+	SE
−300				−300

A	=	L	+	SE
+140				+140

May	8	Sales Returns and Allowances		300	
		Accounts Receivable			300
		(To record credit granted to Sauk Stereo for returned goods)			
	8	Merchandise Inventory		140	
		Cost of Goods Sold			140
		(To record cost of goods returned)			

Helpful Hint Remember that the increases, decreases, and normal balances of contra accounts are the opposite of the accounts to which they correspond.

Sales Returns and Allowances is a contra revenue account to Sales. The normal balance of Sales Returns and Allowances is a debit. A contra account is used, instead of debiting Sales, to disclose in the accounts and in the income statement the amount of sales returns and allowances. Disclosure of this information is important to management. Excessive returns and allowances suggest inferior merchandise, inefficiencies in filling orders, errors in billing customers, and mistakes in delivery or shipment of goods. Moreover, a decrease (debit) recorded directly to Sales would obscure the relative importance of sales returns and allowances as a percentage of sales. It also could distort comparisons between total sales in different accounting periods.

BUSINESS INSIGHT
Investor Perspective

How high is too high? Returns can become so high that it is questionable whether sales revenue should have been recognized in the first place. An example of high returns is Florafax International Inc., a floral supply company, which was alleged to have shipped its product without customer authorization on ten holiday occasions, including 8,562 shipments of flowers to customers for Mother's Day and 6,575 for Secretary's Day. The return rate on these shipments went as high as 69% of sales. As one employee noted: "Products went out the front door and came in the back door."

SALES DISCOUNTS

As mentioned in our discussion of purchase transactions, the seller may offer the customer a cash discount—called by the seller a *sales discount*—for the prompt payment of the balance due. Like a purchase discount, a sales discount is based on the invoice price less returns and allowances, if any. The Sales Discounts account is increased (debited) for discounts that are taken. The entry by PW Audio Supply to record the cash receipt on May 14 from Sauk Stereo within the discount period is

May 14	Cash	3,430	
	Sales Discounts	70	
	Accounts Receivable		3,500
	(To record collection within 2/10, n/30		
	discount period from Sauk Stereo)		

A	=	L	+	SE
+3,430				−70
−3,500				

Like Sales Returns and Allowances, Sales Discounts is a **contra revenue account** to Sales. Its normal balance is a debit. This account is used, instead of debiting sales, to disclose the amount of cash discounts taken by customers. If the discount is not taken, PW Audio Supply increases Cash for $3,500 and decreases Accounts Receivable for the same amount at the date of collection.

BEFORE YOU GO ON...

◆ **Review It**

1. Under a perpetual inventory system, what are the two entries that must be recorded at the time of each sale?
2. Why is it important to use the Sales Returns and Allowances account, rather than simply reducing the Sales account, when goods are returned?

◆ **Do It**

On September 5, De La Hoya Company buys merchandise on account from Junot Diaz Company. The selling price of the goods is $1,500, and the cost to Diaz

Company was $800. On September 8 defective goods with a selling price of $200 and a cost of $80 are returned. Record the transaction on the books of both companies.

Reasoning: Under a perpetual inventory system the purchaser will record goods at cost. The seller will record both the sale and the cost of goods sold at the time of the sale. When goods are returned the purchaser will directly reduce Merchandise Inventory, but the seller records the return in a contra account, Sales Returns and Allowances.

Solution:

De La Hoya Company

Sept.	5	Merchandise Inventory	1,500	
		Accounts Payable		1,500
		(To record goods purchased on account)		
Sept.	8	Accounts Payable	200	
		Merchandise Inventory		200
		(To record return of defective goods)		

Junot Diaz Company

Sept.	5	Accounts Receivable	1,500	
		Sales		1,500
		(To record credit sale)		
	5	Cost of Goods Sold	800	
		Merchandise Inventory		800
		(To record cost of goods sold on account)		
Sept.	8	Sales Returns and Allowances	200	
		Accounts Receivable		200
		(To record credit granted for receipt of returned goods)		
	8	Merchandise Inventory	80	
		Cost of Goods Sold		80
		(To record cost of goods returned)		

INCOME STATEMENT PRESENTATION

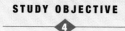

STUDY OBJECTIVE

4

Distinguish between a single-step and a multiple-step income statement.

Two forms of the income statement are widely used by companies. One is the **single-step income statement**. The statement is so named because only one step, subtracting total expenses from total revenues, is required in determining net income (or net loss). In a single-step statement, all data are classified into two categories: (1) **revenues**, which include both operating revenues and non-operating revenues and gains (for example, interest revenue and gain on sale of equipment); and (2) **expenses**, which include cost of goods sold, operating expenses, and nonoperating expenses and losses (for example, interest expense, loss on sale of equipment, or income tax expense). The single-step income statement is the form we have used thus far in the text. A single-step statement for Wal-Mart is shown in Illustration 5-5.

WAL-MART STORES, INC.
Income Statement
(in millions)

	For the years ended January 31	
	1999	1998
Revenues		
Net sales	$137,634	$117,958
Other revenues, net	1,421	1,263
	139,055	119,221
Expenses		
Cost of goods sold	108,725	93,438
Selling, general, and administrative		
expenses	22,363	19,358
Interest expense	797	784
Income taxes	2,740	2,115
	134,625	115,695
Net income	$ 4,430	$ 3,526

Illustration 5-5
Single-step income statement

There are two primary reasons for using the single-step form: (1) A company does not realize any type of profit or income until total revenues exceed total expenses, so it makes sense to divide the statement into these two categories. (2) The form is simple and easy to read.

A second form of the income statement is the **multiple-step income statement**. The multiple-step income statement is often considered more useful because it highlights the components of net income. The Wal-Mart income statement in Illustration 5-6 is an example.

WAL-MART STORES, INC.
Income Statement
(in millions)

	For the years ended January 31	
	1999	1998
Net sales	$137,634	$117,958
Cost of goods sold	108,725	93,438
Gross profit	28,909	24,520
Operating expenses		
Selling, general, and administrative		
expenses	22,363	19,358
Income from operations	6,546	5,162
Other revenues and gains		
Other revenues, net	1,421	1,263
Other expenses and losses		
Interest expense	797	784
Income before income taxes	7,170	5,641
Income tax expense	2,740	2,115
Net income	$ 4,430	$ 3,526

Illustration 5-6
Multiple-step income statement

The multiple-step income statement has three important line items: gross profit, income from operations, and net income. They are determined as follows: (1) Cost of goods sold is subtracted from sales to determine gross profit. (2) Operating expenses are deducted from gross profit to determine income from operations. (3) The results of activities not related to operations are added or subtracted to determine net income. You should note that income tax expense is reported in a separate section of the income statement before net income. The following discussion provides additional information about the components of a multiple-step income statement.

SALES REVENUES

The income statement for a merchandising company typically presents gross sales revenues for the period and provides details about deductions from that total amount. As contra revenue accounts, sales returns and allowances and sales discounts are deducted from sales in the income statement to arrive at net sales. The sales revenues section of the income statement for PW Audio Supply is shown in Illustration 5-7.

Illustration 5-7 Statement presentation of sales revenues section

PW AUDIO SUPPLY, INC. Income Statement (partial)		
Sales revenues		
Sales		$ 480,000
Less: Sales returns and allowances	$12,000	
Sales discounts	8,000	20,000
Net sales		$460,000

GROSS PROFIT

Alternative Terminology
Gross profit is sometimes referred to as **gross margin**.

Cost of goods sold is deducted from sales revenue to determine gross profit. As shown in Illustration 5-6, Wal-Mart had a gross profit of $28,909,000,000 in fiscal year 1999. Sales revenue used for this computation is **net sales**, which takes into account sales returns and allowances and sales discounts. On the basis of the sales data presented in Illustration 5-7 (net sales of $460,000) and the cost of goods sold (assume a balance of $316,000), the gross profit for PW Audio Supply is $144,000, computed as follows:

Net sales	$ 460,000
Cost of goods sold	316,000
Gross profit	**$144,000**

It is important to understand what gross profit is—and what it is not. Gross profit represents the **merchandising profit** of a company. It is *not* a measure of the overall profit of a company because operating expenses have not been deducted. Nevertheless, the amount and trend of gross profit are closely watched by management and other interested parties. Comparisons of current gross profit with past amounts and rates and with those in the industry indicate the effectiveness of a company's purchasing and pricing policies.

OPERATING EXPENSES

Operating expenses are the next component in measuring net income for a merchandising company. At Wal-Mart, operating expenses were $22,363,000,000 in fiscal year 1999. These expenses are similar in merchandising and service enterprises. At PW Audio Supply, operating expenses were $114,000. The firm's income from operations is determined by subtracting operating expenses from gross profit. Thus, income from operations is $30,000 as shown below:

Gross profit	$144,000
Operating expenses	114,000
Income from operations	$ 30,000

Subgrouping of Operating Expenses

Sometimes, operating expenses are subdivided into selling expenses and administrative expenses (as shown in the income statement in Illustration 5-9 on page 220). **Selling expenses** are those associated with making sales. They include advertising expenses as well as expenses of completing the sale, such as delivery and shipping expenses. **Administrative expenses** relate to general operating activities such as human resources management, accounting, and store security.

Alternative Terminology
Administrative expenses are sometimes called **general expenses**.

NONOPERATING ACTIVITIES

Nonoperating activities consist of various revenues and expenses and gains and losses that are unrelated to the company's main line of operations. When nonoperating items are included, the label **Income from operations** (or Operating income) precedes them. This label clearly identifies the results of the company's normal operations, an amount determined by subtracting cost of goods sold and operating expenses from net sales. The results of nonoperating activities are shown in the categories **Other revenues and gains** and **Other expenses and losses**. Examples of each are listed in Illustration 5-8.

Other Revenues and Gains	Other Expenses and Losses
Interest revenue from notes receivable and marketable securities	Interest expense on notes and loans payable
Dividend revenue from investments in capital stock	Casualty losses from recurring causes, such as vandalism and accidents
Rent revenue from subleasing a portion of the store	Loss from the sale or abandonment of property, plant, and equipment
Gain from the sale of property, plant, and equipment	Loss from strikes by employees and suppliers

Illustration 5-8 Other items of nonoperating activities

The distinction between operating and nonoperating activities is crucial to many external users of financial data. Operating income is viewed as sustainable, and many nonoperating activities are viewed as nonrecurring. Therefore, when forecasting next year's income, analysts put the most weight on this year's operating income, and less weight on this year's nonoperating activities.

BUSINESS INSIGHT
Investor Perspective

It was once reported that a large cinema chain in North America was selling some of its assets and counting the gains as part of operating income. As a result, operating losses were being offset by these gains. Because of unfavorable press reaction to this practice, the company revised its financial statements. By not counting its nonrecurring items as part of operating income, the company changed its first-quarter results from $24.9 million operating income to a $22.6 million loss. Although the net income figure didn't change, investors were able to see that income was derived from selling *assets* rather than from selling *movie tickets*. Thus, with this new information, investors were able to make a more informed decision about the company's earnings.

The nonoperating activities are reported in the income statement immediately after the operating activities. Included among these activities in Illustration 5-6 for Wal-Mart is net interest expense of $797,000,000 for fiscal year 1999. The amount remaining, after adding the operating and nonoperating sections together, is Wal-Mart's net income of $4,430,000,000. Note that the net incomes in Illustrations 5-5 and 5-6 are the same. The difference in the two income statements is the amount of detail displayed and the order presented.

In Illustration 5-9 we have provided the multiple-step income statement of a hypothetical company. This statement provides more detail than that of Wal-Mart.

For homework problems, the multiple-step form of the income statement should be used unless the requirements state otherwise

Illustration 5-9 Multiple-step income statement

Helpful Hint What is and is not disclosed?
1. Did company sell on credit? Yes, it had sales discounts.
2. Did company take all purchase discounts? Don't know; purchase discounts taken are not reported.

Calculation of gross profit

Calculation of income from operations

Results of activities not related to operations

PW AUDIO SUPPLY
Income Statement
For the Year Ended December 31, 2001

Sales revenues			
Sales			$480,000
Less: Sales returns and allowances		$12,000	
Sales discounts		8,000	20,000
Net sales			460,000
Cost of goods sold			316,000
Gross profit			144,000
Operating expenses			
Selling expenses			
Store salaries expense		45,000	
Advertising expense		16,000	
Depreciation expense—store equipment		8,000	
Freight-out		7,000	
Total selling expenses		76,000	
Administrative expenses			
Salaries expense		19,000	
Utilities expense		17,000	
Insurance expense		2,000	
Total administrative expenses		38,000	
Total operating expenses			114,000
Income from operations			30,000
Other revenues and gains			
Interest revenue		3,000	
Gain on sale of equipment		600	
		3,600	
Other expenses and losses			
Interest expense		1,800	
Casualty loss from vandalism		200	
		2,000	
			1,600
Income before income taxes			31,600
Income tax expense			10,100
Net income			$ 21,500

BEFORE YOU GO ON...

◆ Review It

1. Under the perpetual inventory system, what entries are made to record sales, sales returns and allowances, and sales discounts?

2. How are sales and contra revenue accounts reported in the income statement?

3. What is the significance of gross profit?

4. What title does Tootsie Roll use for gross profit? By what percentage did its gross profit increase in 1998? The answer to this question is provided on p. 242.

EVALUATING PROFITABILITY

GROSS PROFIT RATE

A company's gross profit may be expressed as a **percentage** by dividing the amount of gross profit by net sales; this is referred to as the gross profit rate. For PW Audio Supply the gross profit rate is 31.3% ($144,000 ÷ $460,000). The gross profit *rate* is generally considered to be more informative than the gross profit *amount* because it expresses a more meaningful (qualitative) relationship between gross profit and net sales. For example, a gross profit amount of $1,000,000 may sound impressive. But if it was the result of sales of $100,000,000, the company's gross profit rate was only 1%. A 1% gross profit rate is acceptable in only a few industries.

A decline in a company's gross profit rate might have several causes. The company may have begun to sell products with a lower "markup"—for example, budget blue jeans versus designer blue jeans. Increased competition may have resulted in a lower selling price. Or, the company may be forced to pay higher prices to its suppliers without being able to pass these costs on to its customers. The gross profit rates for Wal-Mart and Kmart are presented in Illustration 5-10.

STUDY OBJECTIVE

5

Explain the factors affecting profitability.

Illustration 5-10   Gross profit rate

Gross Profit Rate = $\dfrac{\text{Gross Profit}}{\text{Net Sales}}$			
($ in millions)	1999	1998	
Wal-Mart	$\dfrac{\$28,909}{\$137,634} = 21.0\%$	$\dfrac{\$24,520}{\$117,958} = 20.8\%$	
Kmart	21.8%	21.8%	

Kmart's gross profit rate was 21.8% in both years. In its Management Discussion and Analysis, Kmart explained that "the impact of its competitive pricing strategy and growth in lower margined sales categories, such as consumables, was offset by improved margins resulting from increased import and private label goods." At first glance it might be surprising that Wal-Mart has a lower gross profit rate than Kmart. It is likely, however, that this can be explained by the fact that grocery products are becoming an increasing component of Wal-Mart's sales. Grocery products tend to have very low gross profit rates. Also, Wal-Mart is expanding its warehouse-style sales in its Sam's Club stores, which are a low-margin, high-volume operation.

BUSINESS INSIGHT
Management Perspective

Gross profit rates vary across retailers. In a recent year The Limited reported a gross profit rate of 32%; J. C. Penney, 26%; Best Buy, 18%; and Circuit City, 23%. Gross profit is critical. "If you don't have someone monitoring it," says one business consultant, "you are asking for instant death." A decline should trigger a search for the cause. The drop could be due to an increase in cost of goods sold or a decrease in sales revenue, either of which needs prompt attention. The change may be temporary and easily reversed, or it may signal the beginning of a bad trend.

DECISION TOOLKIT

Decision Checkpoints	Info Needed for Decision	Tool to Use for Decision	How to Evaluate Results
☑	▤▤	⚲	👍👎
Is the price of goods keeping pace with changes in the cost of inventory?	Gross profit and net sales	$\text{Gross profit rate} = \dfrac{\text{Gross profit}}{\text{Net sales}}$	Higher ratio suggests the average margin between selling price and inventory cost is increasing. Too high a margin may result in lost sales.

OPERATING EXPENSES TO SALES RATIO

A useful measure of operating expenses is the operating expenses to sales ratio. In recent years many companies have improved the efficiency of their operations, thus reducing the ratio of operating expenses to sales. As a consequence, they have increased their profitability. The record profits of many companies in the 1990s were achieved as much by reducing costs as by increasing revenues. The use of computers and changes in organizational structure have brought added efficiency. For example, one study of a thousand companies that successfully reengineered their warehouse operations by employing new technologies found savings on labor costs averaging 25%. Epson Computers, for example, reported space savings of 50%, labor savings of 43%, and operating cost savings of 25% on their warehouses. Operating costs have been reduced to such low levels for so many companies that many investors believe further improvements in corporate profits from cost reductions will be difficult to accomplish.

The ratios of operating expenses to sales for Wal-Mart and Kmart are presented in Illustration 5-11. The ratios suggest that Wal-Mart is better at controlling its operating costs than is Kmart: In 1999 Wal-Mart incurred 16.2 cents of operating costs for every sales dollar; Kmart incurred 18.5 cents per sales dollar. One reason Wal-Mart has been so successful is that it has had a very lean organizational structure, with highly effective information systems that allow it to adapt rapidly to changing conditions.

Illustration 5-11
Operating expenses to
sales ratio

Operating Expenses to Sales Ratio $= \dfrac{\text{Operating Expenses}}{\text{Net Sales}}$		
($ in millions)	**1999**	**1998**
Wal-Mart	$\dfrac{\$22,363}{\$137,634} = 16.2\%$	$\dfrac{\$19,358}{\$117,958} = 16.4\%$
Kmart	18.5%	19.1%

BUSINESS INSIGHT
Investor Perspective

In this chapter we have compared the gross profit rates and operating expenses to sales ratios of Kmart and Wal-Mart—two fierce competitors in the retail wars. Although such comparisons are vital to an analysis of either of these companies, we must now alert you to one problem often encountered in such comparisons: Companies do not always classify expenses in the same way. Kmart includes buying and occupancy costs in cost of goods sold, whereas Wal-Mart includes these expenses in the operating expense line item. Thus, in comparing ratios for these two companies, we should recognize that at least some of the difference in the value of the ratios is due simply to this difference in classification. Since neither company provides sufficient detail in its notes to enable us to adjust the figures to similar presentation, we can at best make a rough comparison.

BEFORE YOU GO ON...

◆ Review It

1. How is the gross profit rate calculated? What might cause it to decline?
2. What effect does improved efficiency of operations have on the operating expenses to sales ratio?

DECISION TOOLKIT

Decision Checkpoints	Info Needed for Decision	Tool to Use for Decision	How to Evaluate Results
✔	▤▤	⌐╍╍╾	👍👎
Is management controlling operating costs?	Net sales and operating expenses	Operating expenses to sales ratio $= \dfrac{\text{Operating expenses}}{\text{Net sales}}$	Higher value should be investigated to determine whether cost cutting is necessary.

USING THE DECISION TOOLKIT

Sears is currently the number 2 retailer in the United States behind Wal-Mart. Sears has enacted many changes trying to turn itself around. In 1992 it shocked and disappointed many loyal customers by closing its catalog business. In 1993 Sears closed 113 stores and eliminated 50,000 jobs. Although Sears wants to surpass Wal-Mart, it is aiming for a different niche. It is directing itself more toward clothing and "hard-line" items rather than toward being a discounter. The following financial data are available for Sears:

	Year ended	
($ in millions)	1/02/99	1/02/98
Net income	$ 1,048	$ 1,188
Beginning total assets	38,700	36,167
Ending total assets	37,675	38,700
Sales	41,322	41,296
Cost of goods sold	27,257	26,779
Operating expenses	8,318	8,322

Instructions

Using the basic facts in the table, evaluate the following components of Sears' profitability for the years ended January 2, 1999 and 1998:

Return on assets ratio
Profit margin ratio
Gross profit rate
Operating expenses to sales ratio

How do Sears' gross profit rate and operating expenses to sales ratio compare to those of Wal-Mart and Kmart?

Solution

	Year ended	
($ in millions)	1/02/99	1/02/98
Return on assets ratio	$\dfrac{\$1,048}{(\$37,675 + \$38,700)/2} = 2.7\%$	$\dfrac{\$1,188}{(\$38,700 + \$36,167)/2} = 3.2\%$
Profit margin ratio	$\dfrac{\$1,048}{\$41,322} = 2.5\%$	$\dfrac{\$1,188}{\$41,296} = 2.9\%$
Gross profit rate	$\dfrac{\$41,322 - \$27,257}{\$41,322} = 34.0\%$	$\dfrac{\$41,296 - \$26,779}{\$41,296} = 35.2\%$
Operating expenses to sales ratio	$\dfrac{\$8,318}{\$41,322} = 20.1\%$	$\dfrac{\$8,322}{\$41,296} = 20.2\%$

The return on assets ratio for Sears declined from 1998 to 1999—from 3.2% to 2.7%. This decline was the result of a number of factors. The profit margin ratio (income per dollar of sales) declined from 2.9% to 2.5%. The gross profit rate also declined, from 35.2% to 34.0%. The one positive element was that the operating expenses incurred per dollar of sales declined very slightly, an indication that Sears is becoming more efficient. However, this reduction in costs was not enough to overcome the other negative factors.

Sears' 1999 gross profit rate of 34.0% exceeds that of both Wal-Mart (21%) and Kmart (21.8%), suggesting that it can command a higher markup on its goods. However, Sears' ratio of operating expenses to sales of 20.1% suggests that it is not able to control its costs as well as Wal-Mart (16.2%) and Kmart (18.5%).

SUMMARY OF STUDY OBJECTIVES

1 *Identify the differences between a service enterprise and a merchandising company.* Because of the presence of inventory, a merchandising company has sales revenue, cost of goods sold, and gross profit. To account for inventory, a merchandising company must choose between a perpetual inventory system and a periodic inventory system.

2 *Explain the recording of purchases under a perpetual inventory system.* The Merchandise Inventory account is debited for all purchases of merchandise and for freight costs, and it is credited for purchase discounts and purchase returns and allowances.

3 *Explain the recording of sales revenues under a perpetual inventory system.* When inventory is sold, Accounts Receivable (or Cash) is debited and Sales is credited for the selling price of the merchandise. At the same time, Cost of Goods Sold is debited and

Merchandise Inventory is credited for the cost of inventory items sold. When sales revenues are recorded, entries are required for (a) cash and credit sales, (b) sales returns and allowances, and (c) sales discounts.

4 *Distinguish between a single-step and a multiple-step income statement.* In a single-step income statement, all data are classified under two categories, revenues or expenses, and net income is determined in one step. A multiple-step income statement shows numerous steps in determining net income, including results of nonoperating activities.

5 *Explain the factors affecting profitability.* Profitability is affected by gross profit, as measured by the gross profit rate, and by management's ability to control costs, as measured by the ratio of operating expenses to sales.

DECISION TOOLKIT—A SUMMARY

Decision Checkpoints	Info Needed for Decision	Tool to Use for Decision	How to Evaluate Results
Is the price of goods keeping pace with changes in the cost of inventory?	Gross profit and net sales	$$\text{Gross profit rate} = \frac{\text{Gross profit}}{\text{Net sales}}$$	Higher ratio suggests the average margin between selling price and inventory cost is increasing. Too high a margin may result in lost sales.
Is management controlling operating costs?	Net sales and operating expenses	$$\text{Operating expenses to sales ratio} = \frac{\text{Operating expenses}}{\text{Net sales}}$$	Higher value should be investigated to determine whether cost cutting is necessary.

GLOSSARY

Contra revenue account An account that is offset against a revenue account on the income statement. (p. 214)

Cost of goods sold The total cost of merchandise sold during the period. (p. 206)

Gross profit The excess of net sales over the cost of goods sold. (p. 218)

Gross profit rate Gross profit expressed as a percentage by dividing the amount of gross profit by net sales. (p. 221)

Net sales Sales less sales returns and allowances and sales discounts. (p. 218)

Operating expenses to sales ratio A measure that indicates whether a company is controlling operating expenses relative to each dollar of sales. (p. 222)

Periodic inventory system An inventory system in which detailed records are not maintained and the cost of goods sold is determined only at the end of an accounting period. (p. 208)

Perpetual inventory system A detailed inventory system in which the cost of each inventory item is maintained and the records continuously show the inventory that should be on hand. (p. 208)

Purchase discount A cash discount claimed by a buyer for prompt payment of a balance due. (p. 211)

Purchase invoice A document that supports each credit purchase. (p. 209)

Sales discount A reduction given by a seller for prompt payment of a credit sale. (p. 215)

Sales invoice A document that provides support for credit sales. (p. 213)

Sales revenue Primary source of revenue in a merchandising company. (p. 206)

DEMONSTRATION PROBLEM

The adjusted trial balance for the year ended December 31, 2001, for Dykstra Company is shown below.

DYKSTRA COMPANY
Adjusted Trial Balance
For the Year Ended December 31, 2001

	Dr.	Cr.
Cash	$ 14,500	
Accounts Receivable	11,100	
Merchandise Inventory	29,000	
Prepaid Insurance	2,500	
Store Equipment	95,000	
Accumulated Depreciation		$ 18,000
Notes Payable		25,000
Accounts Payable		10,600
Common Stock		70,000
Retained Earnings		11,000
Dividends	12,000	
Sales		536,800
Sales Returns and Allowances	6,700	
Sales Discounts	5,000	
Cost of Goods Sold	363,400	
Freight-out	7,600	
Advertising Expense	12,000	
Store Salaries Expense	56,000	
Utilities Expense	18,000	
Rent Expense	24,000	
Depreciation Expense	9,000	
Insurance Expense	4,500	
Interest Expense	3,600	
Interest Revenue		2,500
	$673,900	$673,900

Instructions

Prepare an income statement assuming Dykstra Company does not use subgroupings for operating expenses.

Solution to Demonstration Problem

DYKSTRA COMPANY
Income Statement
For the Year Ended December 31, 2001

Sales revenues		
Sales		$536,800
Less: Sales returns and allowances	$ 6,700	
Sales discounts	5,000	11,700
Net sales		525,100
Cost of goods sold		363,400
Gross profit		161,700
Operating expenses		
Store salaries expense	56,000	
Rent expense	24,000	
Utilities expense	18,000	
Advertising expense	12,000	
Depreciation expense	9,000	
Freight-out	7,600	
Insurance expense	4,500	
Total operating expenses		131,100
Income from operations		30,600
Other revenues and gains		
Interest revenue	2,500	
Other expenses and losses		
Interest expense	3,600	1,100
Net income		$ 29,500

Problem-Solving Strategies

1. In preparing the income statement, remember that the key components are net sales, cost of goods sold, gross profit, total operating expenses, and net income (loss). These components are reported in the right-hand column of the income statement.

2. Nonoperating items follow income from operations.

SELF-STUDY QUESTIONS

Answers are at the end of the chapter.

(SO 2) 1. Which of the following statements about a periodic inventory system is true?
  (a) Cost of goods sold is determined only at the end of the accounting period.
  (b) Detailed records of the cost of each inventory purchase and sale are maintained continuously.
  (c) The periodic system provides better control over inventories than a perpetual system.
  (d) The increased use of computerized systems has increased the use of the periodic system.

(SO 2) 2. Which of the following items does *not* result in an adjustment in the merchandise inventory account under a perpetual system?
  (a) A purchase of merchandise.
  (b) A return of merchandise inventory to the supplier.
  (c) Payment of freight costs for goods shipped to a customer.
  (d) Payment of freight costs for goods received from a supplier.

(SO 3) 3. Which sales accounts normally have a debit balance?
  (a) Sales discounts.
  (b) Sales returns and allowances.

  (c) Both (a) and (b).
  (d) Neither (a) nor (b).

(SO 3) 4. A credit sale of $750 is made on June 13, terms 2/10, n/30, on which a return of $50 is granted on June 16. What amount is received as payment in full on June 23?
  (a) $700.   (c) $685.
  (b) $686.   (d) $650.

(SO 4) 5. Gross profit will result if:
  (a) operating expenses are less than net income.
  (b) sales revenues are greater than operating expenses.
  (c) sales revenues are greater than cost of goods sold.
  (d) operating expenses are greater than cost of goods sold.

(SO 4) 6. If sales revenues are $400,000, cost of goods sold is $310,000, and operating expenses are $60,000, what is the gross profit?
  (a) $30,000.   (c) $340,000.
  (b) $90,000.   (d) $400,000.

(SO 4) 7. The income statement for a merchandising company shows each of these features *except:*
  (a) gross profit.
  (b) cost of goods sold.
  (c) a sales revenue section.
  (d) All of these are present.

(SO 5) 8. ◖▭◗ Which of the following would *not* affect the operating expenses to sales ratio? (Assume sales remains constant.)
   (a) An increase in advertising expense.
   (b) A decrease in depreciation expense.
   (c) An increase in cost of goods sold.
   (d) A decrease in insurance expense.

(SO 5) 9. ◖▭◗ The gross profit *rate* is equal to:
   (a) net income divided by sales.
   (b) cost of goods sold divided by sales.
   (c) sales minus cost of goods sold, divided by net sales.
   (d) sales minus cost of goods sold, divided by cost of goods sold.

10. ◖▭◗ Which factor would *not* affect the (SO 5) gross profit rate?
   (a) An increase in the cost of heating the store.
   (b) An increase in the sale of luxury items.
   (c) An increase in the use of "discount pricing" to sell merchandise.
   (d) An increase in the price of inventory items.

QUESTIONS

1. (a) "The steps in the accounting cycle for a merchandising company are different from the steps in the accounting cycle for a service enterprise." Do you agree or disagree?
   (b) Is the measurement of net income in a merchandising company conceptually the same as in a service enterprise? Explain.

2. How do the components of revenues and expenses differ between a merchandising company and a service enterprise?

3. (a) Explain the income measurement process in a merchandising company.
   (b) How does income measurement differ between a merchandising company and a service company?

4. Chuck Rudy Co. has sales revenue of $ 100,000, cost of goods sold of $70,000, and operating expenses of $20,000. What is its gross profit?

5. Joan Hollins believes revenues from credit sales may be earned before they are collected in cash. Do you agree? Explain.

6. (a) What is the primary source document for recording (1) cash sales and (2) credit sales?
   (b) Using XXs for amounts, give the journal entry for each of the transactions in part (a).

7. A credit sale is made on July 10 for $900, terms 2/10, n/30. On July 12, $100 of goods are returned for credit. Give the journal entry on July 19 to record the receipt of the balance due within the discount period.

8. Goods costing $1,600 are purchased on account on July 15 with credit terms of 2/10, n/30. On July 18 a $100 credit memo is received from the supplier for damaged goods. Give the journal entry on July 24 to record payment of the balance due within the discount period.

9. Anna Ford Company reports net sales of $800,000, gross profit of $580,000, and net income of $300,000. What are its operating expenses?

10. Identify the distinguishing features of an income statement for a merchandising company.

11. Why is the normal operating cycle for a merchandising company likely to be longer than for a service company?

12. What merchandising account(s) will appear in the post-closing trial balance?

13. What types of businesses are most likely to use a perpetual inventory system?

14. ◖▭◗ What two ratios measure factors that affect profitability?

15. ◖▭◗ What factors affect a company's gross profit rate—that is, what can cause the gross profit rate to increase and what can cause it to decrease?

BRIEF EXERCISES

Compute missing amounts in determining net income.
(SO 4)

BE5-1 Presented here are the components in Sang Nam Company's income statement. Determine the missing amounts.

	Sales	Cost of Goods Sold	Gross Profit	Operating Expenses	Net Income
	$ 75,000	(b)	$ 43,500	(d)	$10,800
	$108,000	$65,000	(c)	(e)	$29,500
	(a)	$71,900	$109,600	$39,500	(f)

Journalize perpetual inventory entries.
(SO 2, 3)

BE5-2 Keo Company buys merchandise on account from Mayo Company. The selling price of the goods is $900 and the cost of goods is $600. Both companies use perpetual inventory systems. Journalize the transactions on the books of both companies.

BE5-3 Prepare the journal entries to record the following transactions on H. Hunt Company's books using a perpetual inventory system.
(a) On March 2 H. Hunt Company sold $900,000 of merchandise to B. Streisand Company, terms 2/10, n/30. The cost of the merchandise sold was $600,000.
(b) On March 6 B. Streisand Company returned $130,000 of the merchandise purchased on March 2 because it was defective. The cost of the merchandise returned was $80,000.
(c) On March 12 H. Hunt Company received the balance due from B. Streisand Company.

Journalize sales transactions.
(SO 3)

BE5-4 From the information in BE5-3, prepare the journal entries to record these transactions on B. Streisand Company's books under a perpetual inventory system.

Journalize purchase transactions.
(SO 2)

BE5-5 A. Cosby Company provides this information for the month ended October 31, 2001: sales on credit $300,000; cash sales $100,000; sales discounts $5,000; and sales returns and allowances $20,000. Prepare the sales revenues section of the income statement based on this information.

Prepare sales revenue section of income statement.
(SO 4)

BE5-6 Explain where each of these items would appear on a multiple-step income statement: gain on sale of equipment, cost of goods sold, depreciation expense, and sales returns and allowances.

Identify placement of items on a multiple-step income statement.
(SO 4)

BE5-7 Paisley Corporation reported net sales of $250,000, cost of goods sold of $100,000, operating expenses of $50,000, net income of $80,000, beginning total assets of $500,000, and ending total assets of $600,000. Calculate each of these values:
(a) Return on assets ratio.   (c) Gross profit rate.
(b) Profit margin ratio.   (d) Operating expenses to sales ratio.

Calculate profitability ratios.
(SO 5)

BE5-8 Ry Corporation reported net sales $550,000; cost of goods sold $300,000; operating expenses $150,000; and net income $70,000. Calculate these values:
(a) Profit margin ratio.   (c) Operating expenses to sales ratio.
(b) Gross profit rate.

Calculate profitability ratios.
(SO 5)

EXERCISES

E5-1 The following transactions are for Pippen Company:
1. On December 3 Pippen Company sold $480,000 of merchandise to Barkley Co., terms 2/10, n/30. The cost of the merchandise sold was $320,000.
2. On December 8 Barkley Co. was granted an allowance of $20,000 for merchandise purchased on December 3.
3. On December 13 Pippen Company received the balance due from Barkley Co.

Journalize sales transactions.
(SO 3)

Instructions
(a) Prepare the journal entries to record these transactions on the books of Pippen Company.
(b) Assume that Pippen Company received the balance due from Barkley Co. on January 2 of the following year instead of December 13. Prepare the journal entry to record the receipt of payment on January 2.

E5-2 On September 1 College Office Supply had an inventory of 30 deluxe pocket calculators at a cost of $20 each. The company uses a perpetual inventory system. During September these transactions occurred:

Journalize perpetual inventory entries.
(SO 2, 3)

Sept. 6   Purchased 80 calculators at $19 each from Digital Co. for cash.
     9   Paid freight of $80 on calculators purchased from Digital Co.
    10   Returned two calculators to Digital Co. for $40 credit (including refund of freight cost) because they did not meet specifications.
    12   Sold 26 calculators costing $20 (including freight) for $30 each to Campus Book Store, terms n/30.
    14   Granted credit of $30 to Campus Book Store for the return of one calculator that was not ordered.
    20   Sold 30 calculators costing $20 for $30 each to Varsity Card Shop, terms n/30.

Instructions
Journalize the September transactions.

Journalize purchase transactions.
(SO 2)

E5-3 This information relates to Hans Olaf Co.:
1. On April 5 purchased merchandise from D. DeVito Company for $18,000, terms 2/10, n/30.
2. On April 6 paid freight costs of $900 on merchandise purchased from D. DeVito.
3. On April 7 purchased equipment on account for $26,000.
4. On April 8 returned damaged merchandise to D. DeVito Company and was granted a $3,000 allowance.
5. On April 15 paid the amount due to D. DeVito Company in full.

Instructions
(a) Prepare the journal entries to record the transactions listed above on the books of Hans Olaf Co.
(b) Assume that Hans Olaf Co. paid the balance due to D. DeVito Company on May 4 instead of April 15. Prepare the journal entry to record this payment.

Journalize purchase transactions.
(SO 2)

E5-4 On June 10 Arcadian Company purchased $6,000 of merchandise from Duvall Company, terms 2/10, n/30. Arcadian pays the freight costs of $300 on June 11. Damaged goods totaling $300 are returned to Duvall for credit on June 12. On June 19 Arcadian Company pays Duvall Company in full, less the purchase discount. Both companies use a perpetual inventory system.

Instructions
(a) Prepare separate entries for each transaction on the books of Arcadian Company.
(b) Prepare separate entries for each transaction for Duvall Company. The merchandise purchased by Arcadian on June 10 cost Duvall $3,000, and the goods returned cost Duvall $150.

E5-5 Presented is information related to Gonzales Co. for the month of January 2001:

Prepare an income statement and calculate profitability ratios.
(SO 4, 5)

Cost of goods sold	$208,000	Rent expense	$ 20,000
Freight-out	7,000	Sales discounts	8,000
Insurance expense	12,000	Sales returns and allowances	13,000
Salary expense	61,000	Sales	350,000

Instructions
(a) Prepare an income statement using the format presented on page 220. Operating expenses should not be segregated into selling and administrative expenses.
(b) Calculate these values: profit margin ratio, gross profit rate, and operating expenses to sales ratio.

E5-6 Financial information is presented here for two companies:

Compute missing amounts and calculate profitability ratios.
(SO 4, 5)

	Young Company	Rice Company
Sales	$90,000	?
Sales returns	?	$ 5,000
Net sales	81,000	95,000
Cost of goods sold	56,000	?
Gross profit	?	38,000
Operating expenses	15,000	?
Net income	?	15,000

Instructions
(a) Fill in the missing amounts. Show all computations.
(b) Calculate the profit margin ratio, gross profit rate, and operating expenses to sales ratio for each company.

E5-7 In its income statement for the year ended December 31, 2001, Violin Company reported the following condensed data:

Prepare multiple-step income statement and calculate profitability ratios.
(SO 4, 5)

Administrative expenses	$435,000	Selling expenses	$690,000
Cost of goods sold	989,000	Loss on sale of equipment	10,000
Interest expense	70,000	Net sales	2,350,000
Interest revenue	45,000		

Instructions

(a) Prepare a multiple-step income statement.
(b) Calculate the profit margin ratio, gross profit rate, and operating expenses to sales ratio.

E5-8 The adjusted trial balance of Cecilie Company shows these data pertaining to sales at the end of its fiscal year, October 31, 2001: Sales $900,000; Freight-out $12,000; Sales Returns and Allowances $14,000; and Sales Discounts $12,000.

Prepare sales revenue section of income statement.
(SO 4)

Instructions

Prepare the sales revenues section of the income statement.

PROBLEMS: SET A

P5-1A Hummingbird Hardware Store completed the following merchandising transactions in the month of May. At the beginning of May, Hummingbird's ledger showed Cash of $5,000 and Common Stock of $5,000.

Journalize, post, prepare partial income statement, and calculate ratios.
(SO 2, 3, 4, 5)

May 1 Purchased merchandise on account from Depot Wholesale Supply for $6,000, terms 2/10, n/30.
2 Sold merchandise on account for $4,500, terms 2/10, n/30. The cost of the merchandise sold was $3,000.
5 Received credit from Depot Wholesale Supply for merchandise returned $200.
9 Received collections in full, less discounts, from customers billed on sales of $4,500 on May 2.
10 Paid Depot Wholesale Supply in full, less discount.
11 Purchased supplies for cash $900.
12 Purchased merchandise for cash $2,400.
15 Received refund for poor-quality merchandise from supplier on cash purchase $230.
17 Purchased merchandise from Harlow Distributors for $1,900, terms 2/10, n/30.
19 Paid freight on May 17 purchase $250.
24 Sold merchandise for cash $6,200. The cost of the merchandise sold was $4,340.
25 Purchased merchandise from Horicon Inc. for $1,000, terms 2/10, n/30.
27 Paid Harlow Distributors in full, less discount.
29 Made refunds to cash customers for defective merchandise $100. The returned merchandise had cost $70.
31 Sold merchandise on account for $1,600, terms n/30. The cost of the merchandise sold was $1,120.

Hummingbird Hardware's chart of accounts includes Cash, Accounts Receivable, Merchandise Inventory, Supplies, Accounts Payable, Common Stock, Sales, Sales Returns and Allowances, Sales Discounts, and Cost of Goods Sold.

Instructions

(a) Journalize the transactions using a perpetual inventory system.
(b) Post the transactions to T accounts. Be sure to enter the beginning cash and common stock balances.
(c) Prepare an income statement through gross profit for the month of May.
(d) Calculate the profit margin ratio and the gross profit rate. (Assume operating expenses were $1,500.)

P5-2A Dazzle Book Warehouse distributes hardback books to retail stores and extends credit terms of 2/10, n/30 to all of its customers. During the month of June the following merchandising transactions occurred.

Journalize purchase and sale transactions under a perpetual inventory system.
(SO 2, 3)

June 1 Purchased 130 books on account for $5 each from Reader's World Publishers, terms 1/10, n/30. Also made a cash payment of $50 for the freight on this date.

3 Sold 140 books on account to the Book Nook for $10 each.

6 Received $50 credit for 10 books returned to Reader's World Publishers.

9 Paid Reader's World Publishers in full.

15 Received payment in full from the Book Nook.

17 Sold 120 books on account to Read-A-Lot Bookstore for $10 each.

20 Purchased 120 books on account for $5 each from Read More Publishers, terms 2/15, n/30.

24 Received payment in full from Read-A-Lot Bookstore.

26 Paid Read More Publishers in full.

28 Sold 110 books on account to Readers Bookstore for $10 each.

30 Granted Readers Bookstore $150 credit for 15 books returned costing $75.

Instructions

Journalize the transactions for the month of June for Dazzle Book Warehouse, using a perpetual inventory system. Assume the cost of each book sold was $5.

Prepare financial statements and calculate profitability ratios.

(SO 4, 5)

P5-3A Rowbuck Department Store is located in midtown Metropolis. During the past several years, net income has been declining because suburban shopping centers have been attracting business away from city areas. At the end of the company's fiscal year on November 30, 2001, these accounts appeared in its adjusted trial balance:

Accounts Payable	$ 27,310
Accounts Receivable	11,770
Accumulated Depreciation—Delivery Equipment	19,680
Accumulated Depreciation—Store Equipment	41,800
Cash	8,000
Common Stock	30,000
Cost of Goods Sold	633,220
Delivery Expense	8,200
Delivery Equipment	57,000
Depreciation Expense—Delivery Equipment	4,000
Depreciation Expense—Store Equipment	9,500
Dividends	12,000
Insurance Expense	9,000
Interest Expense	8,000
Interest Revenue	5,000
Merchandise Inventory	36,200
Notes Payable	46,000
Prepaid Insurance	4,500
Property Tax Expense	3,500
Rent Expense	29,000
Retained Earnings	14,200
Salaries Expense	110,000
Sales	910,000
Sales Commissions Expense	14,000
Sales Commissions Payable	6,000
Sales Returns and Allowances	10,000
Store Equipment	125,000
Property Taxes Payable	3,500
Utilities Expense	10,600

Additional data: Notes payable are due in 2005.

Instructions

(a) Prepare a multiple-step income statement, a retained earnings statement, and a classified balance sheet. (Do not separate operating expenses into selling and administrative categories.)

(b) Calculate the return on assets ratio, profit margin ratio, gross profit rate, and operating expenses to sales ratio. Assume that total assets at the beginning of the year were $160,000.

P5-4A   At the beginning of the current season on April 1, the ledger of Watry's Pro Shop showed Cash $2,500; Merchandise Inventory $3,500; and Common Stock $6,000. The following transactions were completed during April 2001:

Journalize, post, and prepare trial balance and partial income statement.
(SO 2, 3, 4)

Apr.		
	5	Purchased golf bags, clubs, and balls on account from Balata Co. $1,700, terms 2/10, n/60.
	7	Paid freight on Balata purchase $80.
	9	Received credit from Balata Co. for merchandise returned $200.
	10	Sold merchandise on account to members $900, terms n/30. The merchandise sold had a cost of $630.
	12	Purchased golf shoes, sweaters, and other accessories on account from Arrow Sportswear $660, terms 1/10, n/30.
	14	Paid Balata Co. in full.
	17	Received credit from Arrow Sportswear for merchandise returned $60.
	20	Made sales on account to members $700, terms n/30. The cost of the merchandise sold was $490.
	21	Paid Arrow Sportswear in full.
	27	Granted an allowance to members for clothing that did not fit properly $60.
	30	Received payments on account from members $1,100.

The chart of accounts for the pro shop includes Cash, Accounts Receivable, Merchandise Inventory, Accounts Payable, Common Stock, Sales, Sales Returns and Allowances, and Cost of Goods Sold.

Instructions
(a) Journalize the April transactions using a perpetual inventory system.
(b) Using T accounts, enter the beginning balances in the ledger accounts and post the April transactions.
(c) Prepare a trial balance on April 30, 2001.
(d) Prepare an income statement through gross profit.

P5-5A   An inexperienced accountant prepared this condensed income statement for Horizon Company, a retail firm that has been in business for a number of years.

Prepare a correct multiple-step income statement.
(SO 4)

HORIZON COMPANY
Income Statement
For the Year Ended December 31, 2001

Revenues	
Net sales	$840,000
Other revenues	24,000
	864,000
Cost of goods sold	555,000
Gross profit	309,000
Operating expenses	
Selling expenses	104,000
Administrative expenses	89,000
	193,000
Net earnings	$116,000

As an experienced, knowledgeable accountant, you review the statement and determine the following facts:
1. Net sales consist of sales $900,000, less delivery expense on merchandise sold $30,000, and sales returns and allowances $30,000.
2. Other revenues consist of sales discounts $16,000 and rent revenue $8,000.
3. Selling expenses consist of salespersons' salaries $80,000; depreciation on accounting equipment $8,000; advertising $10,000; and sales commissions $6,000. The commissions represent commissions paid. At December 31, $4,000 of commissions have been earned by salespersons but have not been paid.
4. Administrative expenses consist of office salaries $37,000; dividends $14,000; utilities $12,000; interest expense $2,000; and rent expense $24,000, which includes prepayments totaling $6,000 for the first quarter of 2002.

Journalize, post, and prepare adjusted trial balance and financial statements.
(SO 4)

Instructions
Prepare a correct detailed multiple-step income statement.

P5-6A The trial balance of A-Whole-Lot-of-Stuff Wholesale Company contained the accounts shown at December 31, the end of the company's fiscal year:

A-WHOLE-LOT-OF-STUFF WHOLESALE COMPANY
Trial Balance
December 31, 2001

	Debit	Credit
Cash	$ 33,400	
Accounts Receivable	37,600	
Merchandise Inventory	110,000	
Land	92,000	
Buildings	197,000	
Accumulated Depreciation—Buildings		$ 57,000
Equipment	83,500	
Accumulated Depreciation—Equipment		42,400
Notes Payable		50,000
Accounts Payable		37,500
Common Stock		200,000
Retained Earnings		67,800
Dividends	10,000	
Sales		922,100
Sales Discounts	4,600	
Cost of Goods Sold	709,900	
Salaries Expense	69,800	
Utilities Expense	9,400	
Repair Expense	8,900	
Gas and Oil Expense	7,200	
Insurance Expense	3,500	
	$1,376,800	$1,376,800

Adjustment data:
1. Depreciation is $10,000 on buildings and $9,000 on equipment. (Both are administrative expenses.)
2. Interest of $7,000 is due and unpaid on notes payable at December 31.

Other data: $15,000 of the notes payable are payable next year.

Instructions
(a) Journalize the adjusting entries.
(b) Create T accounts for all accounts used in part (a). Enter the trial balance amounts into the T accounts and post the adjusting entries.
(c) Prepare an adjusted trial balance.
(d) Prepare a multiple-step income statement and a retained earnings statement for the year, and a classified balance sheet at December 31, 2001.

PROBLEMS: SET B

Journalize, post, prepare partial income statement, and calculate ratios.
(SO 2, 3, 4, 5)

P5-1B Maggie Zine Distributing Company completed these merchandising transactions in the month of April. At the beginning of April, the ledger of Maggie Zine showed Cash of $9,000 and Common Stock of $9,000.

Apr. 2 Purchased merchandise on account from Kentucky Supply Co. $5,900, terms 2/10, n/30.
4 Sold merchandise on account $5,000, terms 2/10, n/30. The cost of the merchandise sold was $4,000.

5   Paid $200 freight on April 4 sale.
6   Received credit from Kentucky Supply Co. for merchandise returned $300.
11 Paid Kentucky Supply Co. in full, less discount.
13 Received collections in full, less discounts, from customers billed on April 4.
14 Purchased merchandise for cash $4,400.
16 Received refund from supplier on cash purchase of April 14, $500.
18 Purchased merchandise from Pigeon Distributors $4,200, terms 2/10, n/30.
20 Paid freight on April 18 purchase $100.
23 Sold merchandise for cash $7,400. The cost of the merchandise sold was
     $6,120.
26 Purchased merchandise for cash $2,300.
27 Paid Pigeon Distributors in full, less discount.
29 Made refunds to cash customers for defective merchandise $90. The returned
     merchandise had a cost of $70.
30 Sold merchandise on account $3,700, terms n/30. The cost of the merchan-
     dise sold was $3,000.

Maggie Zine Distributing Company's chart of accounts includes Cash, Accounts Receivable, Merchandise Inventory, Accounts Payable, Common Stock, Sales, Sales Returns and
Allowances, Sales Discounts, Cost of Goods Sold, and Freight-out.

Instructions
(a) Journalize the transactions.
(b) Post the transactions to T accounts. Be sure to enter the beginning cash and com-
    mon stock balances.
(c) Prepare the income statement through gross profit for the month of April.
(d) Calculate the profit margin ratio and the gross profit rate. (Assume operating ex-
    penses were $900.)

P5-2B Travel Warehouse distributes suitcases to retail stores and extends credit terms
of 1/10, n/30 to all of its customers. During the month of July the following merchandising transactions occurred.

*Journalize purchase and sale
transactions under a
perpetual inventory system.*
(SO 2, 3)

July 1   Purchased 50 suitcases on account for $30 each from Suitcase Manufactur-
          ers, terms 1/15, n/30.
      3   Sold 40 suitcases on account to Luggage World for $50 each.
      9   Paid Suitcase Manufacturers in full.
      12 Received payment in full from Luggage World.
      17 Sold 30 suitcases on account to The Travel Spot for $50 each.
      18 Purchased 60 suitcases on account for $30 each from Vacation Manufactur-
          ers, terms 2/10, n/30. Also made a cash payment of $100 for freight on this
          date.
      20 Received $300 credit for 10 suitcases returned to Vacation Manufacturers.
      21 Received payment in full from The Travel Spot.
      22 Sold 40 suitcases on account to Vacations-Are-Us for $50 each.
      30 Paid Vacation Manufacturers in full.
      31 Granted Vacations-Are-Us $250 credit for 5 suitcases returned costing $150.

Instructions
Journalize the transactions for the month of July for Travel Warehouse, using a perpetual inventory system. Assume the cost of each suitcase sold was $30.

P5-3B Al Falfa Department Store is located near the Village Shopping Mall. At the end
of the company's fiscal year on December 31, 2001, the following accounts appeared in
its adjusted trial balance:

*Prepare financial statements
and calculate profitability
ratios.*
(SO 4, 5)

Accounts Payable	$ 79,300
Accounts Receivable	50,300
Accumulated Depreciation—Building	52,500
Accumulated Depreciation—Equipment	42,900
Building	190,000
Cash	33,000

Common Stock	150,000
Cost of Goods Sold	412,700
Depreciation Expense—Building	10,400
Depreciation Expense—Equipment	13,300
Dividends	28,000
Equipment	100,000
Insurance Expense	7,200
Interest Expense	11,000
Interest Payable	8,000
Interest Revenue	4,000
Merchandise Inventory	75,000
Mortgage Payable	80,000
Office Salaries Expense	32,000
Prepaid Insurance	2,400
Property Taxes Payable	4,800
Property Taxes Expense	4,800
Retained Earnings	26,600
Sales Salaries Expense	76,000
Sales	628,000
Sales Commissions Expense	14,500
Sales Commissions Payable	3,500
Sales Returns and Allowances	8,000
Utilities Expense	11,000

Additional data: $20,000 of the mortgage payable is due for payment next year.

Instructions

(a) Prepare a multiple-step income statement, a retained earnings statement, and a classified balance sheet.

(b) Calculate the return on assets ratio, profit margin ratio, gross profit rate, and operating expenses to sales ratio. Assume total assets at the beginning of the year were $320,000.

Journalize, post, and prepare trial balance and partial income statement.
(SO 2, 3, 4)

P5-4B At the beginning of the current season, the ledger of Star-Struck Tennis Shop showed Cash $2,500; Merchandise Inventory $1,700; and Common Stock $4,200. The following transactions were completed during April:

Apr. 4 Purchased racquets and balls from Robert Co. $840, terms 3/10, n/30.
   6 Paid freight on Robert Co. purchase $40.
   8 Sold merchandise to members $900, terms n/30. The merchandise sold cost $600.
   10 Received credit of $40 from Robert Co. for a damaged racquet that was returned.
   11 Purchased tennis shoes from Niki Sports for cash $300.
   13 Paid Robert Co. in full.
   14 Purchased tennis shirts and shorts from Martina's Sportswear $500, terms 2/10, n/60.
   15 Received cash refund of $50 from Niki Sports for damaged merchandise that was returned.
   17 Paid freight on Martina's Sportswear purchase $30.
   18 Sold merchandise to members $900, terms n/30. The cost of the merchandise sold was $530.
   20 Received $500 in cash from members in settlement of their accounts.
   21 Paid Martina's Sportswear in full.
   27 Granted an allowance of $30 to members for tennis clothing that did not fit properly.
   30 Received cash payments on account from members $500.

The chart of accounts for the tennis shop includes Cash, Accounts Receivable, Merchandise Inventory, Accounts Payable, Common Stock, Sales, Sales Returns and Allowances, and Cost of Goods Sold.

Instructions
(a) Journalize the April transactions.
(b) Using T accounts, enter the beginning balances in the ledger accounts and post the April transactions.
(c) Prepare a trial balance on April 30, 2001.
(d) Prepare an income statement through gross profit.

P5-5B A part-time bookkeeper prepared this income statement for Sima Nan Company for the year ending December 31, 2001:

Prepare a correct multiple-step income statement.
(SO 4)

SIMA NAN COMPANY
Income Statement
December 31, 2001

Revenues		
Sales		$702,000
Less: Freight-out	$10,000	
Sales discounts	11,300	21,300
Net sales		680,700
Other revenues (net)		1,300
Total revenues		682,000
Expenses		
Cost of goods sold		470,000
Selling expenses		100,000
Administrative expenses		50,000
Dividends		12,000
Total expenses		632,000
Net income		$ 50,000

As an experienced, knowledgeable accountant, you review the statement and determine the following facts:
1. Sales include $10,000 of deposits from customers for future sales orders.
2. Other revenues contain two items: interest expense $4,000 and interest revenue $5,300.
3. Selling expenses consist of sales salaries $76,000, advertising $10,000, depreciation on store equipment $7,500, and sales commissions expense $6,500.
4. Administrative expenses consist of office salaries $19,000; utilities expense $8,000; rent expense $16,000; and insurance expense $7,000. Insurance expense includes $1,200 of insurance applicable to 2002.

Instructions
Prepare a correct detailed multiple-step income statement.

P5-6B The trial balance of Shakira Fashion Center contained the following accounts at November 30, the end of the company's fiscal year:

Journalize, post, and prepare adjusted trial balance and financial statements.
(SO 4)

SHAKIRA FASHION CENTER
Trial Balance
November 30, 2001

	Debit	Credit
Cash	$ 36,700	
Accounts Receivable	33,700	
Merchandise Inventory	45,000	
Store Supplies	5,500	
Store Equipment	85,000	
Accumulated Depreciation—Store Equipment		$ 38,000
Delivery Equipment	38,000	
Accumulated Depreciation—Delivery Equipment		6,000
Notes Payable		41,000

Accounts Payable		48,500
Common Stock		80,000
Retained Earnings		30,000
Dividends	12,000	
Sales		747,200
Sales Returns and Allowances	4,200	
Cost of Goods Sold	507,400	
Salaries Expense	130,000	
Advertising Expense	26,400	
Utilities Expense	14,000	
Repair Expense	12,100	
Delivery Expense	16,700	
Rent Expense	24,000	
	$990,700	$990,700

Adjustment data:
1. Store supplies on hand total $3,500.
2. Depreciation is $9,000 on the store equipment and $7,000 on the delivery equipment.
3. Interest of $11,000 is accrued on notes payable at November 30.

Other data: $30,000 of notes payable are due for payment next year.

Instructions
(a) Journalize the adjusting entries.
(b) Prepare T accounts for all accounts used in part (a). Enter the trial balance into the T accounts and post the adjusting entries.
(c) Prepare an adjusted trial balance.
(d) Prepare a multiple-step income statement and a retained earnings statement for the year, and a classified balance sheet at November 30, 2001.

◆ **B R O A D E N I N G   Y O U R   P E R S P E C T I V E**

*F*INANCIAL REPORTING AND ANALYSIS

FINANCIAL REPORTING PROBLEM: *Tootsie Roll Industries, Inc.*

BYP5-1   The financial statements for **Tootsie Roll Industries** are presented in Appendix A at the end of this book.

Instructions
Answer these questions using the Consolidated Income Statement:
(a) What was the percentage change in sales and in net income from 1997 to 1998?
(b) What was the profit margin ratio in each of the 3 years? Comment on the trend.
(c) What was Tootsie Roll's gross profit rate in each of the 3 years? Comment on the trend.
(d) What was the operating expenses to sales ratio in each of the 3 years? Comment on any trend in this percentage.

COMPARATIVE ANALYSIS PROBLEM: *Tootsie Roll vs. Hershey Foods*

BYP5-2   The financial statements of **Hershey Foods** are presented in Appendix B, following the financial statements for **Tootsie Roll** in Appendix A.

Instructions

(a) Based on the information contained in these financial statements, determine the following values for each company:
   (1) Profit margin ratio for 1998.
   (2) Gross profit for 1998.
   (3) Gross profit rate for 1998.
   (4) Operating income for 1998.
   (5) Percentage change in operating income from 1997 to 1998.
   (6) Operating expenses to sales ratio for 1998.
(b) What conclusions concerning the relative profitability of the two companies can be drawn from these data?

RESEARCH CASE

BYP5-3   The May 1998 issue of the *Journal of Accountancy* includes an article by Randall W. Luecke and David T. Meeting entitled "How Companies Report Income."

Instructions

Read the article and answer the following questions:
(a) What two major income reporting concepts have been used by business accountants at different times over the years? Define and differentiate these two income reporting concepts.
(b) The article states, "The pendulum of income reporting is again changing direction." Which way is the pendulum swinging?
(c) What recent pronouncement pushed income reporting in the new direction?
(d) What items are included in Other Comprehensive Income?
(e) What are three ways companies have to display comprehensive income?

INTERPRETING FINANCIAL STATEMENTS

BYP5-4   Bob Evans Farms, Inc., operates 315 restaurants in 19 states and produces fresh and fully cooked sausage products, fresh salads, and related products distributed to grocery stores in the Midwest, Southwest, and Southeast. For a recent 3-year period Bob Evans Farms reported the following selected income statement data (in millions of dollars):

	1999	1998	1997
Sales	$968.5	$886.8	$822.2
Cost of goods sold	275.9	271.4	265.5
Selling and administrative expenses	566.5	509.3	470.4
Net income	57.6	45.7	36.1
Total assets	590.4	579.9	564.1

In his letters to stockholders, the chief executive officer (CEO) expressed great enthusiasm for the company's future. Here is an excerpt from that letter:

Bob Evans Farms is uniquely positioned as a trusted brand name in both the restaurant and grocery store sectors, providing us with numerous growth opportunities. Our principal long-term goal is to capitalize on that potential for the benefit of our stockholders.

Instructions

(a) Compute the percentage change in sales and in net income from 1997 to 1999.
(b) What contribution, if any, did the company's gross profit rate make to the improved earnings?
(c) Compute the ratio of operating expenses to sales for each of the 3 years. Comment on any trend in this percentage.
(d) What was Bob Evans' profit margin ratio in each of the 3 years? Comment on any trend in this percentage.

(e) The CEO's letter also stated that the company's "same-store sales" have increased by 5% in each of the last 2 years. What effect would you expect this change to have on return on assets? Calculate the company's return on assets for 1998 and 1999 to see if it reflects the increase in same-store sales.

(f) Based on the trends in these ratios, does the CEO's optimism seem appropriate?

A GLOBAL FOCUS

BYP5-5 In August 1999 it was announced that two giant French retailers, **Carrefour SA** and **Promodes SA**, would merge. A headline in *The Wall Street Journal* blared, "French Retailers Create New Wal-Mart Rival." While **Wal-Mart**'s total sales would still exceed those of the combined company, Wal-Mart's international sales are far less than those of the combined company. This is a serious concern for Wal-Mart, since its primary opportunity for future growth lies outside of the United States.

Below are basic financial data for the combined corporation (in French francs) and Wal-Mart (in U.S. dollars). Even though their results are presented in different currencies, by employing ratios we can make some basic comparisons.

	Carrefour/ Promodes (in billions)	Wal-Mart (in billions)
Sales	Fr 298.0	$137.6
Cost of goods sold	274.0	108.7
Operating expenses	9.6	22.4
Net income	5.5	4.4
Total assets	155.0	50.0
Average total assets	140.4	47.7
Current assets	63.5	21.1
Current liabilities	85.8	16.8
Total liabilities	114.2	28.9

Instructions

Compare the two companies by answering the following:

(a) Calculate the gross profit rate and operating expense to sales ratio for each of the companies, and discuss their relative abilities to control cost of goods sold and operating expenses.

(b) Calculate the return on assets ratio and profit margin ratio, and discuss their relative profitability.

(c) Calculate the current ratio and debt to total assets ratios for the two companies, and discuss their relative liquidity and solvency.

(d) What concerns might you have in relying on this comparison?

FINANCIAL ANALYSIS ON THE WEB

BYP5-6 *Purpose:* No financial decision maker should ever rely solely on the financial information reported in the annual report to make decisions. It is important to keep abreast of financial news. This activity demonstrates how to search for financial news on the Web.

Address: http://biz.yahoo.com/i (or go to www.wiley.com/college/kimmel)

Steps:

1. Type in either Wal-Mart or Kmart.
2. Choose **News**.
3. Select an article that sounds interesting to you and that would be relevant to an investor in these companies.

Instructions

(a) What was the source of the article? (For example, Reuters, Businesswire, Prnewswire.)

(b) Pretend that you are a personal financial planner and that one of your clients owns stock in the company. Write a brief memo to your client summarizing the article and explaining the implications of the article for their investment.

CRITICAL THINKING

GROUP DECISION CASE

BYP5-7   Three years ago Kathy Webb and her brother-in-law John Utley opened FedCo Department Store. For the first 2 years, business was good, but the following condensed income results for 2001 were disappointing:

FEDCO DEPARTMENT STORE
Income Statement
For the Year Ended December 31, 2001

Net sales		$700,000
Cost of goods sold		546,000
Gross profit		154,000
Operating expenses		
Selling expenses	$100,000	
Administrative expenses	25,000	
		125,000
Net income		$ 29,000

Kathy believes the problem lies in the relatively low gross profit rate (gross profit divided by net sales) of 22%. John believes the problem is that operating expenses are too high. Kathy thinks the gross profit rate can be improved by making two changes: (1) Increase average selling prices by 17%; this increase is expected to lower sales volume so that total sales will increase only 6%. (2) Buy merchandise in larger quantities and take all purchase discounts; these changes are expected to increase the gross profit rate by 3%. Kathy does not anticipate that these changes will have any effect on operating expenses.

John thinks expenses can be cut by making these two changes: (1) Cut 2001 sales salaries of $60,000 in half and give sales personnel a commission of 2% of net sales. (2) Reduce store deliveries to one day per week rather than twice a week; this change will reduce 2001 delivery expenses of $30,000 by 40%. John feels that these changes will not have any effect on net sales.

Kathy and John come to you for help in deciding the best way to improve net income.

Instructions
With the class divided into groups, answer the following:
(a) Prepare a condensed income statement for 2002 assuming (1) Kathy's changes are implemented and (2) John's ideas are adopted.
(b) What is your recommendation to Kathy and John?
(c) Prepare a condensed income statement for 2002 assuming both sets of proposed changes are made.
(d) Discuss the impact that other factors might have. For example, would increasing the quantity of inventory increase costs? Would a salary cut affect employee morale? Would decreased morale affect sales? Would decreased store deliveries decrease customer satisfaction? What other suggestions might be considered?

COMMUNICATION ACTIVITY

BYP5-8   The following situation is presented in chronological order:
1. Dexter decides to buy a surfboard.
2. He calls Surfing USA Co. to inquire about their surfboards.
3. Two days later he requests Surfing USA Co. to make him a surfboard.
4. Three days later Surfing USA Co. sends him a purchase order to fill out.
5. He sends back the purchase order.
6. Surfing USA Co. receives the completed purchase order.
7. Surfing USA Co. completes the surfboard.

CHAPTER 6

Reporting and Analyzing Inventory

STUDY OBJECTIVES

After studying this chapter, you should be able to:

1. Explain the recording of purchases and sales of inventory under a periodic inventory system.

2. Explain how to determine cost of goods sold under a periodic inventory system.

3. Describe the steps in determining inventory quantities.

4. Identify the unique features of the income statement for a merchandising company under a periodic inventory system.

5. Explain the basis of accounting for inventories and apply the inventory cost flow methods under a periodic inventory system.

6. Explain the financial statement and tax effects of each of the inventory cost flow assumptions.

7. Explain the lower of cost or market basis of accounting for inventories.

8. Compute and interpret the inventory turnover ratio.

9. Describe the LIFO reserve and explain its importance for comparing results of different companies.

◆ WHERE IS THAT SPARE BULLDOZER BLADE?

Let's talk inventory—big, bulldozer-size inventory. Caterpillar Inc. is the world's largest manufacturer of construction and mining equipment, diesel and natural gas engines, and industrial gas turbines. It sells its products in over 200 countries, making it one of the most successful U.S. exporters. More than 70% of its productive assets are located domestically, while nearly 50% of its sales are foreign.

During the 1980s Caterpillar's profitability suffered, but today it enjoys record sales, profits, and growth. A big part of this turnaround can be attributed to effective management of its inventory. Imagine what a bulldozer costs. Now imagine what it costs Caterpillar to have too many bulldozers sitting around in inventory—a situation the company definitely wants to avoid. Conversely, Caterpillar must make sure it has enough inventory to meet demand.

Between 1991 and 1998 Caterpillar's sales increased by 100%, while its inventory increased by only 50%. To achieve this dramatic reduction in the amount of resources tied up in inventory, while continuing to meet customers' needs, Caterpillar used a two-pronged approach. First, it completed a factory modernization program in 1993, which dramatically increased its production efficiency. The program reduced the amount of inventory being processed at any one time by 60% and also reduced by an incredible 75% the time it takes to manufacture a part.

Second, Caterpillar dramatically improved its parts distribution system. It ships more than 100,000 items daily from its 23 distribution centers strategically located around the world (10 million square feet of warehouse space—remember, we're talking bulldozers). The company can virtually guarantee that it can get any part to anywhere in the world within 24 hours. Although this network services 550,000 part numbers, 99.7% of orders are filled immediately or shipped within hours. In fact, Caterpillar's distribution system is so advanced that it created a subsidiary, Caterpillar Logistics Services, Inc., that warehouses and distributes other companies' products. This subsidiary distributes products as diverse as running shoes, computer software, and auto parts all around the world. In short, how Caterpillar manages and accounts for its inventory goes a long way in explaining how profitable it is.

On the World Wide Web
Caterpillar Inc.:
http://www.cat.com

In the previous chapter, we discussed the accounting for merchandise inventory using a perpetual inventory system. In this chapter, we explain the periodic inventory system and methods used to calculate the cost of inventory on hand at the balance sheet date. We conclude by illustrating methods for analyzing inventory.

The content and organization of this chapter are as follows:

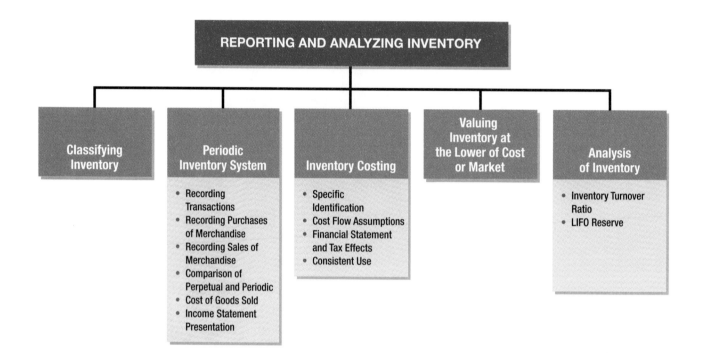

CLASSIFYING INVENTORY

How a company classifies its inventory depends on whether the firm is a merchandiser or a manufacturer. In a **merchandising** company, such as those described in Chapter 5, inventory consists of many different items. For example, in a grocery store, canned goods, dairy products, meats, and produce are just a few of the inventory items on hand. These items have two common characteristics: (1) they are owned by the company, and (2) they are in a form ready for sale to customers in the ordinary course of business. Thus, only one inventory classification, **merchandise inventory**, is needed to describe the many different items that make up the total inventory.

In a **manufacturing** company, some inventory may not yet be ready for sale. As a result, inventory is usually classified into three categories: finished goods, work in process, and raw materials. Finished goods inventory is manufactured items that are completed and ready for sale. Work in process is that portion of manufactured inventory that has been placed into the production process but is not yet complete. Raw materials are the basic goods that will be used in production but have not yet been placed into production. For example, Caterpillar classifies earth-moving tractors completed and ready for sale as **finished goods**. The tractors on the assembly line in various stages of production are classified

Helpful Hint Regardless of the classification, all inventories are reported under Current Assets on the balance sheet.

as **work in process**. The steel, glass, tires, and other components that are on hand waiting to be used in the production of tractors are identified as **raw materials**.

By observing the levels and changes in the levels of these three inventory types, financial statement users can gain insight into management's production plans. For example, low levels of raw materials and high levels of finished goods suggest that management believes it has enough inventory on hand, and production will be slowing down—perhaps in anticipation of a recession. On the other hand, high levels of raw materials and low levels of finished goods probably indicate that management is planning to step up production.

The accounting concepts discussed in this chapter apply to the inventory classifications of both merchandising and manufacturing companies. Our focus here is on merchandise inventory.

PERIODIC INVENTORY SYSTEM

As described in Chapter 5, one of two basic systems of accounting for inventories may be used: (1) the perpetual inventory system or (2) the periodic inventory system. In Chapter 5 we focused on the characteristics of the perpetual inventory system. In this chapter we discuss and illustrate the **periodic inventory system**. One key difference between the two systems is the point at which cost of goods sold is computed. For a visual reminder of this difference, you may want to refer back to Illustration 5-3 on page 208.

RECORDING MERCHANDISE TRANSACTIONS

STUDY OBJECTIVE

◆ 1 ◆

Explain the recording of purchases and sales of inventory under a periodic inventory system.

In a periodic inventory system, revenues from the sale of merchandise are recorded when sales are made, just as in a perpetual system. Unlike the perpetual system, however, **no attempt is made on the date of sale to record the cost of the merchandise sold.** Instead, a physical inventory count is taken at the **end of the period** to determine (1) the cost of the merchandise then on hand and (2) the cost of the goods sold during the period. And, under a periodic system, purchases of merchandise are recorded in the Purchases account rather than the Merchandise Inventory account. Also, in a periodic system, purchase returns and allowances, purchase discounts, and freight costs on purchases are recorded in separate accounts.

To illustrate the recording of merchandise transactions under a periodic inventory system, we will use purchase/sale transactions between PW Audio Supply, Inc. and Sauk Stereo, as illustrated for the perpetual inventory system in Chapter 5.

RECORDING PURCHASES OF MERCHANDISE

On the basis of the sales invoice (Illustration 5-4, shown on page 210) and receipt of the merchandise ordered from PW Audio Supply, Sauk Stereo records the $3,800 purchase as follows:

May 4	Purchases	3,800	
	Accounts Payable		3,800
	(To record goods purchased on account, terms 2/10, n/30)		

A	=	L	+	SE
		+3,800		−3,800

Purchases is a temporary account whose normal balance is a debit.

Purchase Returns and Allowances

Because $300 of merchandise received from PW Audio Supply is inoperable, Sauk Stereo returns the goods and prepares the following entry to recognize the return:

A	=	L	+	SE
		−300		+300

May	8	Accounts Payable	300	
		Purchase Returns and Allowances		300
		(To record return of inoperable goods purchased from PW Audio Supply)		

Purchase Returns and Allowances is a temporary account whose normal balance is a credit.

Freight Costs

When the purchaser directly incurs the freight costs, the account Freight-in (or Transportation-in) is debited. For example, if upon delivery of the goods on May 6, Sauk pays Haul-It Freight Company $150 for freight charges on its purchase from PW Audio Supply, the entry on Sauk's books is:

A	=	L	+	SE
−150				−150

May	9	Freight-in (Transportation-in)	150	
		Cash		150
		(To record payment of freight on goods purchased)		

Like Purchases, Freight-in is a temporary account whose normal balance is a debit. **Freight-in is part of cost of goods purchased**. The reason is that cost of goods purchased should include any freight charges necessary to bring the goods to the purchaser. Freight costs are not subject to a purchase discount. Purchase discounts apply on the invoice cost of the merchandise.

Purchase Discounts

On May 14 Sauk Stereo pays the balance due on account to PW Audio Supply, taking the 2% cash discount allowed by PW Audio for payment within 10 days. The payment and discount are recorded by Sauk Stereo as follows:

A	=	L	+	SE
−3,430		−3,500		+70

May	14	Accounts Payable ($3,800 − $300)	3,500	
		Purchase Discounts ($3,500 × .02)		70
		Cash		3,430
		(To record payment to PW Audio Supply within the discount period)		

Purchase Discounts is a temporary account whose normal balance is a credit.

RECORDING SALES OF MERCHANDISE

The sale of $3,800 of merchandise to Sauk Stereo on May 4 (sales invoice No. 731, Illustration 5-4) is recorded by the seller, PW Audio Supply, as follows:

A	=	L	+	SE
+3,800				+3,800

May	4	Accounts Receivable	3,800	
		Sales		3,800
		(To record credit sales per invoice #731 to Sauk Stereo)		

Sales Returns and Allowances

To record the returned goods received from Sauk Stereo on May 8, PW Audio Supply records the $300 sales return as follows:

May 8	Sales Returns and Allowances	300	
	Accounts Receivable		300
	(To record return of goods from Sauk Stereo)		

A	=	L	+	SE
−300				−300

Sales Discounts

On May 15, PW Audio Supply receives payment of $3,430 on account from Sauk Stereo. PW Audio honors the 2% cash discount and records the payment of Sauk's account receivable in full as follows:

May 15	Cash	3,430	
	Sales Discounts ($3,500 × .02)	70	
	Accounts Receivable ($3,800 − $300)		3,500
	(To record collection from Sauk Stereo within 2/10, n/30 discount period)		

A	=	L	+	SE
+3,430				−70
−3,500				

COMPARISON OF ENTRIES—PERPETUAL vs. PERIODIC

The periodic inventory system entries above are shown in Illustration 6-1 next to those that were illustrated in Chapter 5 (pages 209–215) under the perpetual inventory system for both Sauk Stereo and PW Audio Supply.

Illustration 6-1 Comparison of journal entries under perpetual and periodic inventory systems

ENTRIES ON SAUK STEREO'S BOOKS

	Transaction	Perpetual Inventory System		Periodic Inventory System	
May 4	Purchase of merchandise on credit.	Merchandise Inventory 3,800 　Accounts Payable	3,800	Purchases 3,800 　Accounts Payable	3,800
May 8	Purchase returns and allowances.	Accounts Payable 300 　Merchandise Inventory	300	Accounts Payable 300 　Purchase Returns 　and Allowances	300
May 9	Freight costs on purchases.	Merchandise Inventory 150 　Cash	150	Freight-in 150 　Cash	150
May 14	Payment on account with a discount.	Accounts Payable 3,500 　Cash 　Merchandise Inventory	3,430 70	Accounts Payable 3,500 　Cash 　Purchase Discounts	3,430 70

ENTRIES ON PW AUDIO SUPPLY'S BOOKS

	Transaction	Perpetual Inventory System		Periodic Inventory System	
May 4	Sale of merchandise on credit.	Accounts Receivable 3,800 　Sales Revenue	3,800	Accounts Receivable 3,800 　Sales Revenue	3,800
		Cost of Goods Sold 2,400 　Merchandise Inventory	2,400	No entry for cost of goods sold	
May 8	Return of merchandise sold.	Sales Returns and Allowances 300 　Accounts Receivable	300	Sales Returns and Allowances 300 　Accounts Receivable	300
		Merchandise Inventory 140 　Cost of Goods Sold	140	No entry	
May 15	Cash received on account with a discount.	Cash 3,430 Sales Discounts 70 　Accounts Receivable	3,500	Cash 3,430 Sales Discounts 70 　Accounts Receivable	3,500

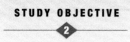

STUDY OBJECTIVE

◆ 2

Explain how to determine cost of goods sold under a periodic inventory system.

COST OF GOODS SOLD

Under a periodic inventory system, a running account of the changes in inventory is not recorded when either purchases or sales transactions occur. Neither the daily amount of inventory of merchandise on hand nor the cost of goods sold is known. To determine the cost of goods sold under a periodic inventory system, it is necessary to (1) record purchases of merchandise (as shown on the previous page), (2) determine the cost of goods purchased, and (3) determine the cost of goods on hand at the beginning and end of the accounting period. The cost of goods on hand must be determined by (a) a physical inventory count and (b) an application of the cost to the items counted in the inventory.

Determining Cost of Goods Purchased

Under a periodic inventory system, various accounts, such as purchases, freight-in, purchase discounts, and purchase returns and allowances, are used to record the cost of goods purchased. (A perpetual system uses only one account, Merchandise Inventory.) These accounts, with their impact on cost of goods purchased, are listed in Illustration 6-2.

Illustration 6-2 Accounts used to record purchases of inventory

Item	Periodic Account Title	Debit or Credit Entry	Effect on Cost of Goods Purchased
Invoice price	Purchases	Debit	Increase
Freight charges paid by purchaser	Freight-in	Debit	Increase
Purchase discounts taken by purchaser	Purchase Discounts	Credit	Decrease
Purchase returns and allowances granted by seller	Purchase Returns and Allowances	Credit	Decrease

To determine cost of goods purchased we begin with **gross** purchases. This amount is then adjusted for any savings resulting from purchase discounts or any reductions due to the return of unwanted goods. The result is net purchases. Because freight charges are a necessary cost incurred to acquire inventory, **freight-in** is added to net purchases to arrive at cost of goods purchased. To summarize:

1. The accounts with credit balances (Purchase Returns and Allowances and Purchase Discounts) are subtracted from Purchases to get **net purchases**.
2. Freight-in is added to net purchases to arrive at **cost of goods purchased**.

To illustrate, assume that PW Audio Supply shows these balances for the accounts above: Purchases $325,000; Purchase Returns and Allowances $10,400; Purchase Discounts $6,800; and Freight-in $12,200. Net purchases and cost of goods purchased are $307,800 and $320,000, as computed in Illustration 6-3.

Illustration 6-3 Computation of net purchases and cost of goods purchased

Purchases		$ 325,000
(1) Less: Purchase returns and allowances	$10,400	
Purchase discounts	6,800	17,200
Net purchases		307,800
(2) Add: Freight-in		12,200
Cost of goods purchased		**$320,000**

All four of the accounts used in the periodic system are temporary accounts. They are used to determine cost of goods sold. Therefore, the balances in these accounts are reduced to zero at the end of each accounting period (i.e., annually).

Determining Inventory Quantities

Companies that use a periodic inventory system take a physical inventory to determine the inventory on hand at the balance sheet date and to compute cost of goods sold. Even businesses that use a perpetual inventory system take a physical inventory. They do so to check the accuracy of the "book inventory" and to determine the amount of inventory shortage or shrinkage due to wasted raw materials, shoplifting, or employee theft.

Determining inventory quantities involves two steps: (1) taking a physical inventory of goods on hand and (2) determining the ownership of goods.

Taking a Physical Inventory. Taking a physical inventory involves actually counting, weighing, or measuring each kind of inventory on hand. In many companies, taking an inventory is a formidable task. Retailers such as Kmart, True Value Hardware, or Home Depot have thousands of different inventory items. An inventory count is generally more accurate when goods are not being sold or received during the counting. Consequently, companies often "take inventory" when the business is closed or when business is slow. Many retailers close early on a chosen day in January—after the holiday sales and returns, when inventories are at their lowest level—to count inventory. Recall from Chapter 5 that both Wal-Mart and Kmart had year-ends of January 31. Under a periodic inventory system, the physical inventory is taken at the end of the accounting period.

After the physical inventory is taken, the quantity of each kind of inventory is listed on **inventory summary sheets**. To assure the accuracy of the summary sheets, the listing should be verified by a second employee or supervisor. Subsequently, unit costs will be applied to the quantities to determine a total cost of the inventory (which is the topic of later sections). Although taking the physical inventory may seem mechanical, an accurate inventory count is important to help companies avoid the negative consequences of poor inventory taking—incorrect financial statements and incorrect income tax returns.

Describe the steps in determining inventory quantities.

BUSINESS INSIGHT
Management Perspective

Failure to observe internal control procedures over inventory contributed to the Great Salad Oil Swindle. In this case, management intentionally overstated its salad oil inventory, which was stored in large holding tanks. Three procedures contributed to overstating the oil inventory: (1) Water added to the bottom of the holding tanks caused the oil to float to the top. Inventory-taking crews who viewed the holding tanks from the top observed only salad oil, when, in fact, as much as 37 out of 40 feet of many of the holding tanks contained water. (2) The company's inventory records listed more holding tanks than it actually had. The company repainted numbers on the tanks after inventory crews examined them, so the crews counted the same tanks twice. (3) Underground pipes pumped oil from one holding tank to another during the inventory taking; therefore, the same salad oil was counted more than once. Although the salad oil swindle was unusual, it demonstrates the complexities involved in assuring that inventory is properly counted.

Determining Ownership of Goods. To determine ownership of goods, two questions must be answered: Do all of the goods included in the count belong to the company? Does the company own any goods that were not included in the count?

Goods in Transit. A complication in determining ownership is goods in transit (on board a truck, train, ship, or plane) at the end of the period. The company may have purchased goods that have not yet been received, or it may have sold goods that have not yet been delivered. To arrive at an accurate count, ownership of these goods must be determined.

Goods in transit should be included in the inventory of the company that has legal title to the goods. Legal title is determined by the terms of the sale, as shown in Illustration 6-4 and described below:

Illustration 6-4 Terms of sale

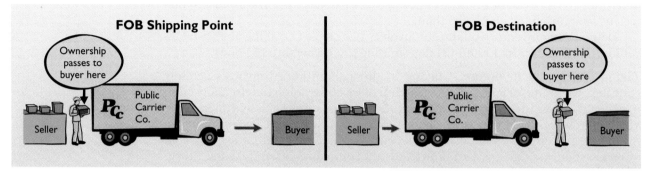

1. When the terms are **FOB (free on board) shipping point**, ownership of the goods passes to the buyer when the public carrier accepts the goods from the seller.

2. When the terms are **FOB destination**, ownership of the goods remains with the seller until the goods reach the buyer.

Consigned Goods. In some lines of business, it is customary to hold the goods of other parties and try to sell the goods for them for a fee, but without taking ownership of the goods. These are called consigned goods. For example, you might have a used car that you would like to sell. If you take the item to a dealer, the dealer might be willing to put the car on its lot and charge you a commission if it is sold. But under this agreement the dealer **would not take ownership** of the car, which would still belong to you. Therefore, if an inventory count were taken, the car would not be included in the dealer's inventory. Many car, boat, and antique dealers sell goods on consignment to keep their inventory costs down and to avoid the risk of purchasing an item that they won't be able to sell. Today even some manufacturers are arranging consignment agreements with their suppliers in order to keep their inventory levels low.

Computing Cost of Goods Sold

We have now reached the point where we can compute cost of goods sold. Doing so involves two steps:

1. Add the cost of goods purchased to the cost of goods on hand at the beginning of the period (beginning inventory) to obtain the cost of goods available for sale.

2. Subtract the cost of goods on hand at the end of the period (ending inventory) from the cost of goods available for sale to arrive at the **cost of goods sold**.

For PW Audio Supply the cost of goods available for sale and the cost of goods sold are $356,000 and $316,000, respectively. The beginning and ending inventory are assumed to be $36,000 and $40,000, respectively. The computation of cost of goods available for sale and cost of goods sold is shown in Illustration 6-5.

Illustration 6-5 Computation of cost of goods available for sale and cost of goods sold

Beginning inventory		$ 36,000
(1) Add: Cost of goods purchased		320,000
Cost of goods available for sale		356,000
(2) Less: Ending inventory		40,000
Cost of goods sold		$316,000

INCOME STATEMENT PRESENTATION

The income statement for a merchandising company is the same whether a periodic or perpetual inventory system is used, except for the cost of goods sold section. **Under a periodic inventory system**, **the cost of goods sold section generally contains more detail**. An income statement for PW Audio Supply, using a periodic inventory system, is shown in Illustration 6-6.

STUDY OBJECTIVE

4

Identify the unique features of the income statement for a merchandising company under a periodic inventory system.

Illustration 6-6 Income statement for a merchandising company using a periodic inventory system

PW AUDIO SUPPLY Income Statement For the Year Ended December 31, 2001			
Sales revenues			
Sales			$480,000
Less: Sales returns and allowances		$ 12,000	
Sales discounts		8,000	20,000
Net sales			460,000
Cost of goods sold			
Inventory, January 1		36,000	
Purchases		$325,000	
Less: Purchases returns and			
allowances	$10,400		
Purchase discounts	6,800	17,200	
Net purchases		307,800	
Add: Freight-in		12,200	
Cost of goods purchased		320,000	
Cost of goods available for sale		356,000	
Inventory, December 31		40,000	
Cost of goods sold			316,000
Gross profit			144,000
Operating expenses			114,000
Net income			$ 30,000

Helpful Hint The far right column identifies the major subdivisions of the income statement. The next column identifies the primary items that make up cost of goods sold of $316,000; in addition, contra revenue items of $20,000 are reported. The third column explains cost of goods purchased of $320,000. The fourth column reports contra purchase items of $17,200.

The use of the periodic inventory system does not affect the content of the balance sheet. As under the perpetual system, merchandise inventory is reported at the same amount in the current assets section.

In the remainder of this chapter we address additional issues related to inventory costing. To simplify our presentation, we assume a periodic inventory accounting system.

BEFORE YOU GO ON...

◆ **Review It**

1. Discuss the three steps in determining cost of goods sold in a periodic inventory system.
2. What accounts are used in determining the cost of goods purchased?
3. In what ways is a perpetual inventory system different from a periodic inventory system?

◆ **Do It**

Aerosmith Company's accounting records show the following at year-end: Purchase Discounts $3,400; Freight-in $6,100; Sales $240,000; Purchases $162,500;

Beginning Inventory $18,000; Ending Inventory $20,000; Sales Discounts $10,000; Purchase Returns $5,200; and Operating Expenses $57,000. Compute these amounts for Aerosmith Company:

(a) Net sales.   (d) Gross profit.
(b) Cost of goods purchased.   (e) Net income.
(c) Cost of goods sold.

Reasoning: To compute the required amounts, it is important to know the relationships in measuring net income for a merchandising company. For example, it is necessary to know the difference between sales and net sales, goods available for sale and cost of goods sold, and gross profit and net income.

Solution:
(a) Net sales: Sales − Sales discounts
         $240,000 − $10,000 = $230,000
(b) Cost of goods purchased:
     Purchases − Purchase returns − Purchase discounts + Freight-in
     $162,500 − $5,200 − $3,400 + $6,100 = $160,000
(c) Cost of goods sold:
     Beginning inventory + Cost of goods purchased − Ending inventory
     $18,000 + $160,000 − $20,000 = $158,000
(d) Gross profit: Net sales − Cost of goods sold
         $230,000 − $158,000 = $72,000
(e) Net income: Gross profit − Operating expenses
         $72,000 − $57,000 = $15,000

*I*NVENTORY COSTING

STUDY OBJECTIVE

5

Explain the basis of accounting for inventories and apply the inventory cost flow methods under a periodic inventory system.

Purchases, purchase discounts, purchase returns and allowances, and freight-in are all costs included in the cost of goods available for sale. Cost of goods available for sale must be allocated between cost of goods sold and ending inventory at the end of the accounting period. First, the costs assignable to the ending inventory are determined. Second, the cost of the ending inventory is subtracted from the cost of goods available for sale to determine the cost of goods sold. (Refer back to Illustration 6-5 to see this computation.)

Determining ending inventory can be complicated if the units on hand for a specific item of inventory have been purchased at different prices. Assume, for example, that Crivitz TV Company purchases three 46-inch TVs at costs of $700, $750, and $800. During the year, two sets are sold at $1,200 each. Ending inventory might be $700, $750, or $800, and corresponding cost of goods sold might be $1,550 ($750 + $800), $1,500 ($700 + $800), or $1,450 ($700 + $750), respectively, depending on how Crivitz measures the cost flows of the inventory purchased and sold. In this section we discuss alternative inventory costing methods.

SPECIFIC IDENTIFICATION

If we determine that the TV in Crivitz's inventory is the one originally purchased for $750, then the ending inventory is $750 and cost of goods sold is $1,500 ($700 + $800). If Crivitz can positively identify which particular units were sold and which are still in ending inventory, it can use the **specific identification method** of inventory costing (see Illustration 6-7). In this case ending inventory and cost of goods sold are easily and accurately determined.

Specific identification is possible when a company sells a limited variety of high-unit-cost items that can be identified clearly from the time of purchase through the time of sale. Examples of such companies are automobile dealer-

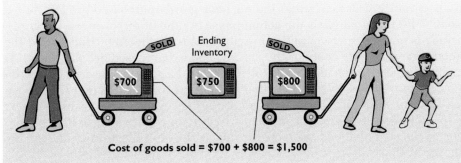

Cost of goods sold = $700 + $800 = $1,500

ships (cars, trucks, and vans), music stores (pianos and organs), and antique shops (tables and cabinets).

But what if we cannot specifically identify particular inventory units? For example, drug, grocery, and hardware stores sell thousands of relatively low-unit-cost items of inventory. These items are often indistinguishable from one another, making it impossible or impractical to track each item's cost. In that case, we must make assumptions, called **cost flow assumptions**, about which units were sold.

COST FLOW ASSUMPTIONS

Because specific identification is often impractical, other cost flow methods are allowed. These differ from specific identification in that they **assume** flows of costs that may be unrelated to the physical flow of goods. There are three assumed cost flow methods:

1. First-in, first-out (FIFO)
2. Last-in, first-out (LIFO)
3. Average cost

There is no accounting requirement that the cost flow assumption be consistent with the physical movement of the goods. The selection of the appropriate cost flow method is made by management.

To illustrate these three inventory cost flow methods, we will assume that Houston Electronics uses a periodic inventory system and has the information shown in Illustration 6-8 for its Astro condenser.

Illustration 6-8 Cost of goods available for sale

HOUSTON ELECTRONICS Astro Condensers				
Date	Explanation	Units	Unit Cost	Total Cost
Jan. 1	Beginning inventory	100	$10	$ 1,000
Apr. 15	Purchase	200	11	2,200
Aug. 24	Purchase	300	12	3,600
Nov. 27	Purchase	400	13	5,200
	Total	1,000		$12,000

The company had a total of 1,000 units available that it could have sold during the period. The total cost of these units was $12,000. A physical inventory at the end of the year determined that during the year 550 units were sold and 450 units were in inventory at December 31. The question then is how to determine what prices to use to value the goods sold and the ending inventory. The sum of the cost allocated to the units sold plus the cost of the units in inventory must add up to $12,000, the total cost of all goods available for sale.

First-In, First-Out (FIFO)

The **FIFO method** assumes that the **earliest goods** purchased are the first to be sold. FIFO often parallels the actual physical flow of merchandise because it generally is good business practice to sell the oldest units first. Under the FIFO method, therefore, the **costs** of the earliest goods purchased are the first to be recognized as cost of goods sold. (Note that this does not necessarily mean that the oldest units *are* sold first, but that the costs of the oldest units are recognized first. In a bin of picture hangers at the hardware store, for example, no one really knows, nor would it matter, which hangers are sold first.) The allocation of the cost of goods available for sale at Houston Electronics under FIFO is shown in Illustration 6-9.

Illustration 6-9
Allocation of costs—
FIFO method

Helpful Hint Note the sequencing of the allocation: (1) compute ending inventory and (2) determine cost of goods sold.

Helpful Hint The calculation of FIFO **ending inventory** is based on the LISH assumption (last in still here).

COST OF GOODS AVAILABLE FOR SALE				
Date	Explanation	Units	Unit Cost	Total Cost
Jan. 1	Beginning inventory	100	$10	$ 1,000
Apr. 15	Purchase	200	11	2,200
Aug. 24	Purchase	300	12	3,600
Nov. 27	Purchase	400	13	5,200
	Total	1,000		$12,000

STEP 1: ENDING INVENTORY

Date	Units	Unit Cost	Total Cost
Nov. 27	400	$13	$ 5,200
Aug. 24	50	12	600
Total	450		$5,800

STEP 2: COST OF GOODS SOLD

Cost of goods available for sale	$12,000
Less: Ending inventory	5,800
Cost of goods sold	$ 6,200

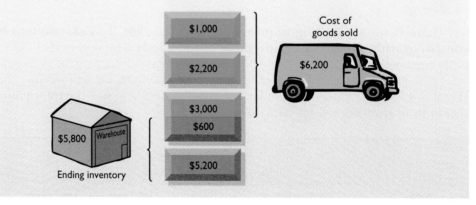

Note that under FIFO, since it is assumed that the first goods purchased were the first goods sold, ending inventory is based on the prices of the most recent units purchased. That is, **under FIFO, the cost of the ending inventory is obtained by taking the unit cost of the most recent purchase and working backward until all units of inventory have been costed (LISH–last in still here).** In this example, the 450 units of ending inventory must be priced using the most recent prices. The last purchase was 400 units at $13 on November 27. The remaining 50 units are priced at the price of the second most recent purchase, $12, on August 24. Next, cost of goods sold is calculated by subtracting the cost of the units **not sold** (ending inventory) from the cost of all goods available for sale.

Illustration 6-10 demonstrates that cost of goods sold can also be calculated by pricing the 550 units sold using the prices of the first 550 units acquired. Note that of the 300 units purchased on August 24, only 250 units are assumed sold. This agrees with our calculation of the cost of ending inventory, where 50 of these units were assumed unsold and thus included in ending inventory.

Date	Units	Unit Cost	Total Cost
Jan. 1	100	$10	$1,000
Apr. 15	200	11	2,200
Aug. 24	250	12	3,000
Total	550		$6,200

Illustration 6-10 Proof of cost of goods sold

Last-In, First-Out (LIFO)

The **LIFO method** assumes that the **latest goods** purchased are the first to be sold. LIFO seldom coincides with the actual physical flow of inventory. (Exceptions include goods stored in piles, such as coal or hay, where goods are removed from the top of the pile as sold.) Under the LIFO method, the **costs** of the latest goods purchased are the first to be recognized as cost of goods sold. The allocation of the cost of goods available for sale at Houston Electronics under LIFO is shown in Illustration 6-11.

Illustration 6-11 Allocation of costs— LIFO method

COST OF GOODS AVAILABLE FOR SALE				
Date	Explanation	Units	Unit Cost	Total Cost
Jan. 1	Beginning inventory	100	$10	$ 1,000
Apr. 15	Purchase	200	11	2,200
Aug. 24	Purchase	300	12	3,600
Nov. 27	Purchase	400	13	5,200
	Total	1,000		$12,000

STEP 1: ENDING INVENTORY

Date	Units	Unit Cost	Total Cost
Jan. 1	100	$10	$ 1,000
Apr. 15	200	11	2,200
Aug. 24	150	12	1,800
Total	450		$5,000

STEP 2: COST OF GOODS SOLD

Cost of goods available for sale	$12,000
Less: Ending inventory	5,000
Cost of goods sold	$ 7,000

Helpful Hint The calculation of LIFO **ending inventory** is based on the FISH assumption (first in still here).

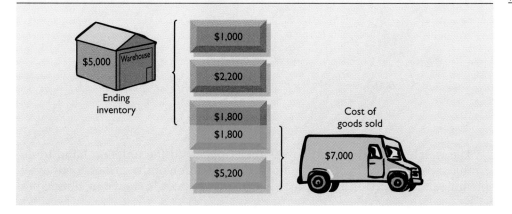

Under LIFO, since it is assumed that the first goods sold were those that were most recently purchased, ending inventory is based on the prices of the oldest units purchased. That is, **under LIFO, the cost of the ending inventory is obtained by taking the unit cost of the earliest goods available for sale and working forward until all units of inventory have been costed (FISH—first in still here)**. In this example, the 450 units of ending inventory must be priced using the earliest prices. The first purchase was 100 units at $10 in the January 1 beginning inventory. Then 200 units were purchased at $11. The remaining 150 units needed are priced at $12 per unit (August 24 purchase). Next, cost of goods sold is calculated by subtracting the cost of the units **not sold** (ending inventory) from the cost of all goods available for sale.

Illustration 6-12 demonstrates that cost of goods sold can also be calculated by pricing the 550 units sold using the prices of the last 550 units acquired. Note that of the 300 units purchased on August 24, only 150 units are assumed sold. This agrees with our calculation of the cost of ending inventory, where 150 of these units were assumed unsold and thus included in ending inventory.

Illustration 6-12 Proof of cost of goods sold

Date	Units	Unit Cost	Total Cost
Nov. 27	400	$13	$5,200
Aug. 24	150	12	1,800
Total	550		$7,000

Under a periodic inventory system, which we are using here, **all goods purchased during the period are assumed to be available for the first sale, regardless of the date of purchase**.

Average Cost

The average cost method allocates the cost of goods available for sale on the basis of the weighted average unit cost incurred. The average cost method assumes that goods are similar in nature. The formula and a sample computation of the weighted average unit cost are given in Illustration 6-13.

Illustration 6-13 Formula for weighted average unit cost

The weighted average unit cost is then applied to the units on hand to determine the cost of the ending inventory. The allocation of the cost of goods available for sale at Houston Electronics using average cost is shown in Illustration 6-14.

Illustration 6-14
Allocation of costs—
average cost method

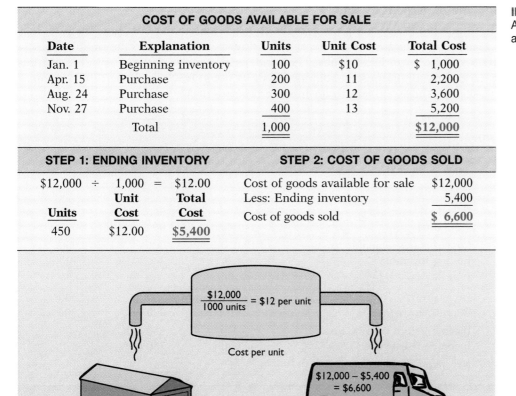

COST OF GOODS AVAILABLE FOR SALE

Date	Explanation	Units	Unit Cost	Total Cost
Jan. 1	Beginning inventory	100	$10	$ 1,000
Apr. 15	Purchase	200	11	2,200
Aug. 24	Purchase	300	12	3,600
Nov. 27	Purchase	400	13	5,200
	Total	1,000		$12,000

STEP 1: ENDING INVENTORY	STEP 2: COST OF GOODS SOLD

$12,000 ÷ 1,000 = $12.00

Units	Unit Cost	Total Cost
450	$12.00	$5,400

Cost of goods available for sale	$12,000
Less: Ending inventory	5,400
Cost of goods sold	$ 6,600

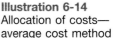

We can verify the cost of goods sold under this method by multiplying the units sold by the weighted average unit cost ($550 \times \$12 = \$6,600$). Note that this method does not use the average of the unit costs. That average is $11.50 ($\$10 + \$11 + \$12 + \$13 = \$46; \$46 \div 4$). The average cost method instead uses the average **weighted** by the quantities purchased at each unit cost.

FINANCIAL STATEMENT AND TAX EFFECTS OF COST FLOW METHODS

Each of the three assumed cost flow methods is acceptable for use. For example, Black and Decker Manufacturing Company and Wendy's International currently use the FIFO method of inventory costing. Campbell Soup Company, Krogers, and Walgreen Drugs use LIFO for part or all of their inventory. Bristol-Myers, Starbucks, and Motorola use the average cost method. Indeed, a company may also use more than one cost flow method at the same time. Del Monte Corporation, for example, uses LIFO for domestic inventories and FIFO for foreign inventories. Illustration 6-15 shows the use of the three cost flow methods in the 600 largest U.S. companies. The reasons companies adopt different inventory cost flow methods are varied, but they usually involve one of three factors:

1. Income statement effects
2. Balance sheet effects
3. Tax effects

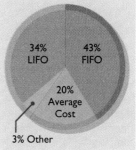

Illustration 6-15 Use of cost flow methods in major U.S. companies

Income Statement Effects

To understand why companies might choose a particular cost flow method, let's examine the effects of the different cost flow assumptions on the financial statements of Houston Electronics. The condensed income statements in Illustration 6-16 assume that Houston sold its 550 units for $11,500, had operating expenses of $2,000, and is subject to an income tax rate of 30%.

Illustration 6-16   Comparative effects of cost flow methods

HOUSTON ELECTRONICS Condensed Income Statements			
	FIFO	LIFO	Average Cost
Sales	$11,500	$11,500	$11,500
Beginning inventory	1,000	1,000	1,000
Purchases	11,000	11,000	11,000
Cost of goods available for sale	12,000	12,000	12,000
Ending inventory	5,800	5,000	5,400
Cost of goods sold	6,200	7,000	6,600
Gross profit	5,300	4,500	4,900
Operating expenses	2,000	2,000	2,000
Income before income taxes	3,300	2,500	2,900
Income tax expense (30%)	990	750	870
Net income	$ 2,310	$ 1,750	$ 2,030

Although the cost of goods available for sale ($12,000) is the same under each of the three inventory cost flow methods, both the ending inventories and costs of goods sold are different. This difference is due to the unit costs that are allocated to cost of goods sold and to ending inventory. Each dollar of difference in ending inventory results in a corresponding dollar difference in income before income taxes. For Houston, an $800 difference exists between FIFO and LIFO cost of goods sold.

Helpful Hint Managers of different companies in the same industry may reach different conclusions as to the most appropriate inventory method.

In periods of changing prices, the cost flow assumption can have a significant impact on income and on evaluations based on income. In most instances, prices are rising (inflation). In a period of inflation, FIFO produces a higher net income because the lower unit costs of the first units purchased are matched against revenues. In a period of rising prices (as is the case here for Houston), FIFO reports the highest net income ($2,310) and LIFO the lowest ($1,750); average cost falls in the middle ($2,030). If prices are falling, the results from the use of FIFO and LIFO are reversed: FIFO will report the lowest net income and LIFO the highest. To management, higher net income is an advantage: It causes external users to view the company more favorably. In addition, if management bonuses are based on net income, FIFO will provide the basis for higher bonuses.

Some argue that the use of LIFO in a period of inflation enables the company to avoid reporting **paper** or **phantom profit** as economic gain. To illustrate, assume that Kralik Company buys 200 units of a product at $20 per unit on January 10 and 200 more on December 31 at $24 each. During the year, 200 units are sold at $30 each. The results under FIFO and LIFO are shown in Illustration 6-17.

Illustration 6-17
Income statement effects compared

	FIFO	**LIFO**
Sales (200 × $30)	$6,000	$6,000
Cost of goods sold	4,000 (200 × $20)	4,800 (200 × $24)
Gross profit	$2,000	$1,200

Under LIFO, Kralik Company has recovered the current replacement cost ($4,800) of the units sold. Thus, the gross profit in economic terms is real. However, under FIFO, the company has recovered only the January 10 cost ($4,000). To replace the units sold, it must reinvest $800 (200 × $4) of the gross profit. Thus, $800 of the gross profit is said to be phantom or illusory. As a result, reported net income is also overstated in real terms.

Balance Sheet Effects

A major advantage of the FIFO method is that in a period of inflation, the costs allocated to ending inventory will approximate their current cost. For example, for Houston, 400 of the 450 units in the ending inventory are costed under FIFO at the higher November 27 unit cost of $13.

Conversely, a major shortcoming of the LIFO method is that in a period of inflation, the costs allocated to ending inventory may be significantly understated in terms of current cost. This is true for Houston, where the cost of the ending inventory includes the $10 unit cost of the beginning inventory. The understatement becomes greater over prolonged periods of inflation if the inventory includes goods purchased in one or more prior accounting periods.

Tax Effects

We have seen that both inventory on the balance sheet and net income on the income statement are higher when FIFO is used in a period of inflation. Yet, many companies have switched to LIFO. The reason is that LIFO results in the lowest income taxes (because of lower net income) during times of rising prices. For example, at Houston Electronics, income taxes are $750 under LIFO, compared to $990 under FIFO. The tax saving of $240 makes more cash available for use in the business.

DECISION TOOLKIT

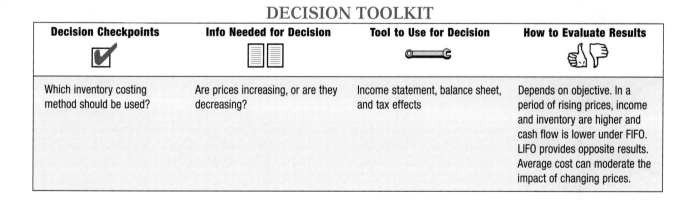

Decision Checkpoints	Info Needed for Decision	Tool to Use for Decision	How to Evaluate Results
Which inventory costing method should be used?	Are prices increasing, or are they decreasing?	Income statement, balance sheet, and tax effects	Depends on objective. In a period of rising prices, income and inventory are higher and cash flow is lower under FIFO. LIFO provides opposite results. Average cost can moderate the impact of changing prices.

BUSINESS INSIGHT
Management Perspective

Most small firms use the FIFO method. But fears of rising inflation often cause many firms to switch to LIFO. For example, Chicago Heights Steel Co. in Illinois boosted cash "by 5% to 10% by lowering income taxes" when it switched to LIFO. Electronic games distributor Atlas Distributing Inc. in Chicago considered a switch "because the costs of our games, made in Japan, are rising 15% a year," says Joseph Serpico, treasurer. When inflation heats up, "the number of companies electing LIFO will rise dramatically," says William Spiro of BDO Seidman, New York.

USING INVENTORY COST FLOW METHODS CONSISTENTLY

Whatever cost flow method a company chooses, it should be used consistently from one accounting period to another. Consistent application enhances the comparability of financial statements over successive time periods. In contrast, using the FIFO method one year and the LIFO method the next year would make it difficult to compare the net incomes of the two years.

Helpful Hint As you learned in Chapter 2, consistency and comparability are important characteristics of accounting information.

Although consistent application is preferred, it does not mean that a company may *never* change its method of inventory costing. When a company adopts a different method, the change and its effects on net income should be disclosed in the financial statements. A typical disclosure is shown in Illustration 6-18, using information from recent financial statements of the Quaker Oats Company.

Illustration 6-18
Disclosure of change in cost flow method

QUAKER OATS COMPANY
Notes to the Financial Statements

Note 1: Effective July 1, the Company adopted the LIFO cost flow assumption for valuing the majority of U.S. Grocery Products inventories. The Company believes that the use of the LIFO method better matches current costs with current revenues. The effect of this change on the current year was to decrease net income by $16.0 million.

BUSINESS INSIGHT

International Perspective

U.S. companies typically choose between LIFO and FIFO. Many choose LIFO because it reduces inventory profits and taxes. However, in many foreign countries LIFO is not allowed. International regulators recently considered rules that would ban LIFO entirely and force companies to use FIFO. This proposed rule was defeated, but the issue is almost certain to reappear.

The issue is sensitive. As John Wulff, controller for Union Carbide, noted, "We were in support of the international effort up until the proposal to eliminate LIFO." Wulff says that if Union Carbide had been suddenly forced to switch from LIFO to FIFO recently, its reported $632 million pretax income would have jumped by $300 million. That would have increased Carbide's income tax bill by as much as $120 million.

Do you believe that accounting principles and rules should be the same around the world?

VALUING INVENTORY AT THE LOWER OF COST OR MARKET

STUDY OBJECTIVE
7
Explain the lower of cost or market basis of accounting for inventories.

The value of the inventory of companies selling high-technology or fashion goods can drop very quickly due to changes in technology or changes in fashions. These circumstances sometimes call for inventory valuation methods other than those presented so far. For example, suppose you are the owner of a retail store that sells Compaq computers. Imagine that during the recent 12-month period, the cost of the computers dropped $300 per unit. At the end of your fiscal year, you have some of these computers in inventory. Do you think your inventory should be stated at cost, in accordance with the cost principle, or at its lower replacement cost?

As you probably reasoned, this situation requires a departure from the cost basis of accounting. When the value of inventory is lower than its cost, the inventory is written down to its market value. This is done by valuing the inventory at the lower of cost or market (LCM) in the period in which the price decline occurs. LCM is an example of the accounting concept of conservatism, which means that the best choice among accounting alternatives is the method that is least likely to overstate assets and net income.

LCM is applied to the items in inventory after one of the cost flow methods (specific identification, FIFO, LIFO, or average cost) has been used to determine cost. Under the LCM basis, market is defined as current replacement cost, not selling price. For a merchandising company, market is the cost of purchasing the same goods at the present time from the usual suppliers in the usual quantities. Current replacement cost is used because a decline in the replacement cost of an item usually leads to a decline in the selling price of the item.

BEFORE YOU GO ON...

◆ Review It

1. What factors should be considered by management in selecting an inventory cost flow method?
2. What inventory cost flow method does Tootsie Roll Industries use for U.S. inventories? What method does it use for foreign inventories? (*Hint:* You will need to examine the notes for Tootsie Roll's financial statements.) The answer to these questions is provided on p. 297.

3. Which inventory cost flow method produces the highest net income in a period of rising prices? The lowest income taxes?
4. When should inventory be reported at a value other than cost?

◆ Do It

The accounting records of Shumway Ag Implement show these data:

Beginning inventory	4,000 units at $3
Purchases	6,000 units at $4
Sales	5,000 units at $12

Determine the cost of goods sold during the period under a periodic inventory system using (a) the FIFO method, (b) the LIFO method, and (c) the average cost method.

Reasoning: Because the units of inventory on hand and available for sale may have been purchased at different prices, a systematic method must be adopted to allocate the costs between the goods sold and the goods on hand (ending inventory).

Solution:

(a) FIFO: (4,000 @ $3) + (1,000 @ $4) = $12,000 + $4,000 = $16,000
(b) LIFO: 5,000 @ $4 = $20,000
(c) Average cost: [(4,000 @ $3) + (6,000 @ $4)] ÷ 10,000
     = ($12,000 + $24,000) ÷ 10,000
     = $3.60 per unit; 5,000 @ $3.60 = $18,000

ANALYSIS OF INVENTORY

For companies that sell goods, managing inventory levels can be one of the most critical tasks. Having too much inventory on hand costs the company money in storage costs, interest cost (on funds tied up in inventory), and costs associated with the obsolescence of technical goods (e.g., computer chips) or shifts in fashion for products like clothes. But having too little inventory on hand results in lost sales. In this section we discuss some issues related to evaluating inventory levels.

INVENTORY TURNOVER RATIO

STUDY OBJECTIVE

◆ 8 ◆

Compute and interpret the inventory turnover ratio.

The inventory turnover ratio is calculated as cost of goods sold divided by average inventory. Its complement, days in inventory, indicates the average age of the inventory. It is calculated as 365 days divided by the inventory turnover ratio. Both measures indicate how quickly a company sells its goods—how many times the inventory "turns over" (is sold) during the year. High inventory turnover or low days in inventory indicates the company is tying up little of its funds in inventory—that it has a minimal amount of inventory on hand at any one time. Although minimizing the funds tied up in inventory is efficient, too high an inventory turnover ratio may indicate that the company is losing sales opportunities because of inventory shortages. For example, in August 1999 investment analysts suggested that Office Depot had gone too far in reducing its inventory—they said they were seeing too many empty shelves. Thus, management should closely monitor this ratio to achieve the best balance between too much and too little inventory.

In Chapter 5 we discussed the increasingly competitive environment of retailers like Wal-Mart and Kmart. We noted that Wal-Mart has implemented many technological innovations to improve the efficiency of its operations. Illustration 6-19 presents the inventory turnover ratios and days in inventory for Wal-Mart and Kmart, using data from the financial statements of those corporations for 1999 and 1998.

Illustration 6-19 Inventory turnover ratio and days in inventory

$$\text{Inventory Turnover Ratio} = \frac{\text{Cost of Goods Sold}}{\text{Average Inventory}}$$

$$\text{Days in Inventory} = \frac{365}{\text{Inventory Turnover Ratio}}$$

($ in millions)		1999	1998
Wal-Mart	Inventory turnover ratio	$\frac{\$108,725}{(\$17,076 + \$16,497)/2} = 6.5$ times	$\frac{\$93,438}{(\$16,497 + \$15,897)/2} = 5.8$ times
	Days in inventory	$\frac{365 \text{ days}}{6.5} = 56.2$ days	$\frac{365 \text{ days}}{5.8} = 62.9$ days
Kmart	Inventory turnover ratio	4.1 times	4.0 times
	Days in inventory	89.0 days	91.3 days

The calculations in Illustration 6-19 show that Wal-Mart turns its inventory more frequently than Kmart (6.5 times for Wal-Mart versus 4.1 times for Kmart). Consequently, the average time an item spends on a Wal-Mart shelf is shorter (56.2 days for Wal-Mart versus 89.0 days for Kmart). This suggests that Wal-Mart is more efficient than Kmart in its inventory management. Note also that Wal-Mart's inventory turnover, which was already substantially better than Kmart's in 1998, improved in 1999. Wal-Mart's sophisticated inventory tracking and distribution system allows it to keep minimum amounts of inventory on hand, while still keeping the shelves full of what customers are looking for. In contrast, even though its inventory turnover is lower than that of Wal-Mart, Kmart has been criticized for inventory outages. However, recent improvements in Kmart's inventory tracking and distribution systems have resulted in significant improvements. It recently achieved 97% inventory stock availability, although it still had not met its goal of 98%.

BUSINESS INSIGHT
Management Perspective

As noted in the opening story, in recent years many companies, including Caterpillar, have adopted inventory management techniques to reduce the amount of inventory they have on hand. These practices are referred to as "just-in-time" inventory, or JIT. A recent *Wall Street Journal* story noted, however, that sometimes these practices can cause hardship for companies. Drops in supply and surges in the prices of oil, natural gas, corn, wheat, and coffee have left many companies that are reliant on these raw materials scrambling to find enough goods to meet their needs. By having only small amounts of inventory on hand, these companies subject themselves to much more price and supply volatility than if they held large inventories.

To reduce such volatility, many companies enter into "hedges"—financial transactions that act as a sort of insurance against big price changes. Even with hedges such as futures contracts, many times companies have to pass higher prices of commodities for raw materials on to the consumer.

Source: Aaron Lucchetti, "Low Inventories Add to Unpredictability," *The Wall Street Journal,* March 10, 1997, p. C1.

DECISION TOOLKIT

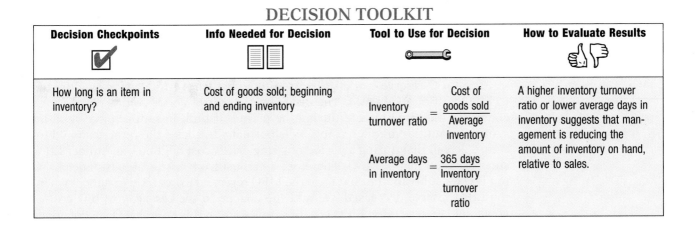

Decision Checkpoints	Info Needed for Decision	Tool to Use for Decision	How to Evaluate Results
How long is an item in inventory?	Cost of goods sold; beginning and ending inventory	$\text{Inventory turnover ratio} = \dfrac{\text{Cost of goods sold}}{\text{Average inventory}}$ $\text{Average days in inventory} = \dfrac{365 \text{ days}}{\text{Inventory turnover ratio}}$	A higher inventory turnover ratio or lower average days in inventory suggests that management is reducing the amount of inventory on hand, relative to sales.

STUDY OBJECTIVE

9

Describe the LIFO reserve and explain its importance for comparing results of different companies.

ANALYSTS' ADJUSTMENTS FOR LIFO RESERVE

Earlier we noted that using LIFO rather than FIFO can result in significant differences in the results reported in the balance sheet and the income statement. With increasing prices, FIFO will result in higher income than LIFO. On the balance sheet, FIFO will result in higher reported inventory. The financial statement differences of using LIFO normally increase the longer a company uses LIFO.

Using different inventory cost flow assumptions complicates analysts' attempts to compare the results of companies that use different inventory methods. Fortunately, companies using LIFO are required to report the amount that inventory would increase (or occasionally decrease) if the company had instead been using FIFO. This amount is referred to as the LIFO reserve. Reporting the LIFO reserve enables analysts to make adjustments to compare companies that use different cost flow methods.

Illustration 6-20 presents an excerpt from the notes to Caterpillar's 1998 financial statements that discloses and discusses Caterpillar's LIFO reserve.

Illustration 6-20
Caterpillar LIFO reserve

CATERPILLAR INC.
Notes to the Financial Statements

Inventories: Inventories are valued principally by the LIFO (last-in, first-out) method. If the FIFO (first-in, first-out) method had been in use, inventories would have been $1,978 million and $2,067 million higher than reported at December 31, 1998 and 1997, respectively.

Caterpillar has used LIFO for nearly 50 years. Thus, the cumulative difference between LIFO and FIFO reflected in the inventory account is very large. In fact, the 1998 LIFO reserve of $1,978 million is nearly as large as the 1998 LIFO inventory of $2,842 million. Such a huge difference would clearly distort any comparisons you might try to make with one of Caterpillar's competitors that used FIFO.

To adjust Caterpillar's inventory balance we add the LIFO reserve to reported inventory, as shown in Illustration 6-21. That is, if Caterpillar had used FIFO all along, its inventory would be $4,820 million, rather than $2,842 million.

Illustration 6-21
Conversion of inventory from LIFO to FIFO

	(in millions)
1998 inventory using LIFO	$2,842
1998 LIFO reserve	1,978
1998 inventory assuming FIFO	**$4,820**

The LIFO reserve can also be used to adjust from LIFO cost of goods sold to FIFO cost of goods sold. The difference in cost of goods sold is equal to the change in the LIFO reserve during the period. If both inventory prices and inventory quantities are increasing, as is normally the case, the reserve should increase. Recall that during a period of rising prices cost of goods sold under LIFO should exceed that of FIFO. Therefore, to adjust from cost of goods under LIFO to FIFO we **subtract** the change in the LIFO reserve. However, in instances where the LIFO reserve decreased, we **add** the change in the reserve to LIFO cost of goods sold to determine FIFO cost of goods sold. In this case, FIFO cost of goods sold would actually exceed LIFO cost of goods sold. These relationships are depicted in Illustration 6-22.

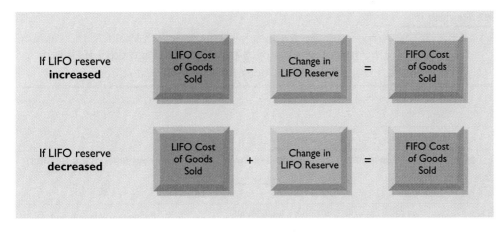

Illustration 6-22
Adjustments to determine
FIFO cost of goods sold

Caterpillar's LIFO reserve decreased by $89 million during 1998 (from $2,067 to $1,978). To determine Caterpillar's cost of goods sold under FIFO, we add the $89 million change in the LIFO reserve to the LIFO cost of goods sold, as shown in Illustration 6-23.

Illustration 6-23
Conversion of cost of
goods sold from LIFO to
FIFO

	(in millions)
1998 cost of goods sold using LIFO	$15,031
1998 decrease in LIFO reserve	89
1998 cost of goods sold assuming FIFO	**$15,120**

Now we will consider the effect that the LIFO reserve has on two ratios commonly used by analysts, the current ratio (discussed in Chapter 2) and the inventory turnover ratio. Illustration 6-24 calculates the value of these ratios under both the LIFO and FIFO cost flow assumptions.

Illustration 6-24 Impact
of LIFO reserve on ratios

($ in millions)	LIFO	FIFO
Current ratio	$\dfrac{\$11,459}{\$7,945} = 1.4 : 1$	$\dfrac{\$11,459 + \$1,978}{\$7,945} = 1.7 : 1$
Inventory turnover ratio	$\dfrac{\$15,031}{(\$2,842 + \$2,603)/2} = \dfrac{5.5}{\text{times}}$	$\dfrac{\$15,120}{(\$4,820 + \$3,870)/2} = \dfrac{3.5}{\text{times}}$

Additional information: Current assets $11,459; current liabilities $7,945; 1997 LIFO inventory $2,603; 1996 FIFO inventory $3,870.

As shown in Illustration 6-24, if Caterpillar uses FIFO, its current ratio is 1.7:1 rather than 1.4:1. Thus, Caterpillar's liquidity appears stronger if a FIFO assumption is used in valuing inventories. At the same time, Caterpillar's inventory turnover actually looks worse under FIFO than under LIFO, dropping from 5.5 times for LIFO to 3.5 times using the FIFO assumption. The reason: LIFO reports low inventory amounts, which cause inventory turnover to be overstated. Case Corporation, a competitor of Caterpillar, uses FIFO to account for its inventory. This illustration clearly demonstrates that comparing Caterpillar to Case Corporation without converting Caterpillar's inventory to FIFO would lead to distortions and potentially erroneous decisions.

BEFORE YOU GO ON...

◆ Review It

1. What is the purpose of the inventory turnover ratio? What is the relationship between the inventory turnover ratio and average days in inventory?
2. What is the LIFO reserve? What does it tell a financial statement user?

DECISION TOOLKIT

Decision Checkpoints	Info Needed for Decision	Tool to Use for Decision	How to Evaluate Results
What is the impact of LIFO on the company's reported inventory?	LIFO reserve, cost of goods sold, ending inventory	Inventory adjustment $$\text{LIFO inventory} + \text{LIFO reserve} = \text{FIFO inventory}$$ Cost of goods sold adjustment $$\text{LIFO cost of goods sold} + \text{Change in LIFO reserve} = \text{FIFO cost of goods sold}$$	If these adjustments are material, they can significantly affect such measures as the current ratio and the inventory turnover ratio.

USING THE DECISION TOOLKIT

Manitowoc Company is located in Manitowoc, Wisconsin. In recent years it has acquired a number of businesses in varying industries in order to dampen the impact of economic cycles on its results. As a consequence, today it operates in three separate lines of business: food service equipment (commercial refrigerators, freezers, and ice cube makers), cranes and related products (such as truck-mounted cranes), and marine operations (which repairs Great Lakes freshwater and saltwater ships). For 1998 the company reported net income of $51.4 million. Here is the inventory note taken from the 1998 financial statements.

MANITOWOC COMPANY
Notes to the Financial Statements

Inventories: The components of inventories are summarized at December 31 as follows (in thousands):

	1998	1997
Components		
Raw materials	$ 32,564	$ 25,881
Work in process	27,882	22,331
Finished goods	42,304	27,972
Total inventories at FIFO cost	102,750	76,184
Excess of FIFO cost over LIFO value	(20,772)	(21,483)
Total inventories	$ 81,978	$ 54,701

Inventory is carried at the lower of cost or market using the first-in, first-out (FIFO) method for 47% and 60% of total inventory for 1998 and 1997, respectively. The remainder of the inventory is costed using the last-in, first-out (LIFO) method.

Additional facts:

1998 Current liabilities	$198,112
1998 Current assets (as originally reported)	$190,877
1998 Cost of goods sold	$499,201

Instructions

Answer these questions:

1. Why does the company report its inventory in three components?
2. Why might the company use two methods (LIFO and FIFO) to account for its inventory?
3. Perform each of the following:
   (a) Calculate the inventory turnover ratio and average days in inventory using the LIFO inventory.
   (b) Show the conversion of the 1998 LIFO inventory values to FIFO values.
   (c) Calculate the 1998 current ratio using LIFO and the current ratio using FIFO. Discuss the difference.
   (d) Calculate the 1998 cost of goods sold assuming FIFO.
   (e) Calculate the inventory turnover ratio assuming FIFO, and compare it to your results from part (a).

Solution

1. Manitowoc Company is a manufacturer, so it purchases raw materials and makes them into finished products. At the end of each period, it has some goods that have been started but are not yet complete, referred to as work in process. By reporting all three components of inventory, the company reveals important information about its inventory position. For example, if amounts of raw materials have increased significantly compared to the previous year, we might assume the company is planning to step up production. On the other hand, if levels of finished goods have increased relative to last year and raw materials have declined, we might conclude that sales are slowing down—that the company has too much inventory on hand and is cutting back production.

2. Companies are free to choose different cost flow assumptions for different types of inventory. A company might choose to use FIFO for a product that is expected to decrease in price over time. One common reason for choosing a method other than LIFO is that many foreign countries do not allow LIFO; thus, the company cannot use LIFO for its foreign operations.

3. (a)
$$\frac{\text{Inventory turnover}}{\text{ratio}} = \frac{\text{Cost of goods sold}}{\text{Average inventory}} = \frac{\$499,201}{(\$81,978 + \$54,701)/2} = 7.3$$

$$\frac{\text{Average days in}}{\text{inventory}} = \frac{365}{\text{Inventory turnover ratio}} = \frac{365}{7.3} = 50.0 \text{ days}$$

(b) Conversion from LIFO to FIFO values

	1998	1997
LIFO inventory	$ 81,978	$54,701
LIFO reserve	20,772	21,483
FIFO inventory	$102,750	$76,184

(c) Current ratio

	LIFO	FIFO
$\dfrac{\text{Current assets}}{\text{Current liabilities}}=$	$\dfrac{\$190,877}{\$198,112}=.96:1$	$\dfrac{\$190,877 + \$20,772}{\$198,112}=1.07:1$

This represents an 11% increase in the current ratio $(1.07 - .96)/.96$.

(d) Note that the LIFO reserve actually declined by $711. Thus, the change in the LIFO reserve would be added (rather than subtracted as in the case of an increase in the LIFO reserve) to LIFO cost of goods sold to determine FIFO cost of goods sold (see Illustration 6-22 on page 267). Thus, in the case of a liquidation of inventory, cost of goods sold under FIFO actually exceeds that of LIFO.

1998 LIFO cost of goods sold	$499,201
Change in LIFO reserve ($20,772 − $21,483)	711
1998 FIFO cost of goods sold	$499,912

(e) $\dfrac{\text{Inventory turnover}}{\text{ratio}} = \dfrac{\text{Cost of goods sold}}{\text{Average inventory}} = \dfrac{\$499,912}{(\$102,750 + \$76,184)/2} = 5.6$

$\dfrac{\text{Average days in}}{\text{inventory}} = \dfrac{365}{\text{Inventory turnover ratio}} = \dfrac{365}{5.6} = 65.2 \text{ days}$

The inventory turnover under LIFO is substantially higher than that under FIFO, even though the cost of goods sold is higher under FIFO. The LIFO inventory turnover is overstated because it matches a numerator calculated with current prices with a denominator calculated with old prices. The FIFO inventory turnover is considered a better measure, since the impact of the price mismatch is less severe.

SUMMARY OF STUDY OBJECTIVES

1 *Explain the recording of purchases and sales of inventory under a periodic inventory system.* In records of purchases, entries are required for (a) cash and credit purchases, (b) purchase returns and allowances, (c) purchase discounts, and (d) freight costs. In records of sales, entries are required for (a) cash and credit sales, (b) sales returns and allowances, and (c) sales discounts.

2 *Explain how to determine cost of goods sold under a periodic inventory system.* The steps in determining cost of goods sold are (a) recording the purchase of merchandise, (b) determining the cost of goods purchased, and (c) determining the cost of goods on hand at the beginning and end of the accounting period.

3 *Describe the steps in determining inventory quantities.* The steps are (1) taking a physical inventory of goods on hand and (2) determining the ownership of goods in transit or on consignment.

4 *Identify the unique features of the income statement for a merchandising company under a periodic inventory system.* The income statement for a merchandising company contains three features not found in a service enterprise's income statement: sales revenue, cost of goods sold, and a gross profit line. The cost of goods sold section generally shows more detail under a periodic than a perpetual inventory system by reporting beginning and ending inventories, net purchases, and total goods available for sale.

5 *Explain the basis of accounting for inventories and apply the inventory cost flow methods under a periodic inventory system.* The primary basis of accounting for inventories is cost. Cost includes all expenditures necessary to acquire goods and place them in condition ready for sale. Cost of goods available for sale includes (a) cost of beginning inventory and (b) cost of goods purchased. The inventory cost flow methods are: specific identification and three assumed cost flow methods—FIFO, LIFO, and average cost.

6 *Explain the financial statement and tax effects of each of the inventory cost flow assumptions.* The cost of goods available for sale may be allocated to cost of goods sold and ending inventory by specific identification or by a method based on an assumed cost flow. When prices are rising, the first-in, first-out (FIFO) method results in lower cost of goods sold and higher net income than the average cost and the last-in, first-out (LIFO) methods. The reverse is true when prices are falling. In the balance sheet, FIFO results in an ending inventory that is closest to current value, whereas the inventory under LIFO is the farthest from current value. LIFO results in the lowest income taxes (because of lower net income).

7 *Explain the lower of cost or market basis of accounting for inventories.* The lower of cost or market (LCM) basis may be used when the current replacement cost (market) is less than cost. Under LCM, the loss is recognized in the period in which the price decline occurs.

8 *Compute and interpret the inventory turnover ratio.* The inventory turnover ratio is calculated as cost of goods sold divided by average inventory. It can be converted to average days in inventory by dividing 365 days by the inventory turnover ratio. A higher turnover ratio or lower average days in inventory suggests that management is trying to keep inventory levels low relative to its sales level.

9 *Describe the LIFO reserve and explain its importance for comparing results of different companies.* The LIFO reserve represents the difference between ending inventory using LIFO and ending inventory if FIFO were employed instead. For some companies this difference can be significant, and ignoring it can lead to inappropriate conclusions when using the current ratio or inventory turnover ratio.

DECISION TOOLKIT—A SUMMARY

Decision Checkpoints	Info Needed for Decision	Tool to Use for Decision	How to Evaluate Results
Which inventory costing method should be used?	Are prices increasing, or are they decreasing?	Income statement, balance sheet, and tax effects	Depends on objective. In a period of rising prices, income and inventory are higher and cash flow is lower under FIFO. LIFO provides opposite results. Average cost can moderate the impact of changing prices.
How long is an item in inventory?	Cost of goods sold; beginning and ending inventory	$\text{Inventory turnover ratio} = \dfrac{\text{Cost of goods sold}}{\text{Average inventory}}$ $\text{Average days in inventory} = \dfrac{365 \text{ days}}{\text{Inventory turnover ratio}}$	A higher inventory turnover ratio or lower average days in inventory suggests that management is reducing the amount of inventory on hand, relative to sales.
What is the impact of LIFO on the company's reported inventory?	LIFO reserve, cost of goods sold, ending inventory	Inventory adjustment $\text{LIFO inventory} + \text{LIFO reserve} = \text{FIFO inventory}$ Cost of goods sold adjustment $\text{LIFO cost of goods sold} + \text{Change in LIFO reserve} = \text{FIFO cost of goods sold}$	If these adjustments are material, they can significantly affect such measures as the current ratio and the inventory turnover ratio.

> ### A P P E N D I X   6 A
> # INVENTORY COST FLOW METHODS IN PERPETUAL INVENTORY SYSTEMS

STUDY OBJECTIVE

◆ 10 ◆

Apply the inventory cost flow methods to perpetual inventory records.

Each of the inventory cost flow methods described in the chapter for a periodic inventory system may be used in a perpetual inventory system. To illustrate the application of the three assumed cost flow methods (FIFO, LIFO, and average cost), we will use the data shown below and in this chapter for Houston Electronic's Astro Condenser.

Illustration 6A-1
Inventoriable units and costs

	HOUSTON ELECTRONICS Astro Condensers				
Date	**Explanation**	**Units**	**Unit Cost**	**Total Cost**	**Balance in Units**
1/1	Beginning inventory	100	$10	$ 1,000	100
4/15	Purchases	200	11	2,200	300
8/24	Purchases	300	12	3,600	600
9/10	Sale	550			50
11/27	Purchases	400	13	5,200	450
				$12,000	

FIRST-IN, FIRST-OUT (FIFO)

Under FIFO, the cost of the earliest goods on hand **prior to each sale** is charged to cost of goods sold. Therefore, the cost of goods sold on September 10 consists of the units on hand January 1 and the units purchased April 15 and August 24. The inventory on a FIFO method perpetual system is shown in Illustration 6A-2.

Illustration 6A-2
Perpetual system—FIFO

Date	Purchases	Sales	Balance
January 1			(100 @ $10) $1,000
April 15	(200 @ $11) $2,200		(100 @ $10)⎱ $3,200 (200 @ $11)⎰
August 24	(300 @ $12) $3,600		(100 @ $10)⎱ (200 @ $11)⎱ $6,800 (300 @ $12)⎰
September 10		(100 @ $10) (200 @ $11) (250 @ $12) $6,200	(50 @ $12) $ 600
November 27	(400 @ $13) $5,200		(50 @ $12)⎱ $5,800 (400 @ $13)⎰

The ending inventory in this situation is $5,800, and the cost of goods sold is $6,200 [(100 @ $10) + (200 @ $11) + (250 @ $12)].

The results under FIFO in a perpetual system are the **same as in a periodic system** (see Illustration 6-9 on page 256 where, similarly, the ending inventory is $5,800 and cost of goods sold is $6,200). Regardless of the system, the first costs in are the costs assigned to cost of goods sold.

LAST-IN, FIRST-OUT (LIFO)

Under the LIFO method using a perpetual system, the cost of the most recent purchase prior to sale is allocated to the units sold. Therefore, the cost of the goods sold on September 10 consists of all the units from the August 24 and April 15 purchases and 50 of the units in beginning inventory. The ending inventory on a LIFO method is computed in Illustration 6A-3.

Date	Purchases		Sales	Balance	
January 1				(100 @ $10)	$1,000
April 15	(200 @ $11)	$2,200		(100 @ $10)⎫ (200 @ $11)⎭	$3,200
August 24	(300 @ $12)	$3,600		(100 @ $10)⎫ (200 @ $11)⎬ (300 @ $12)⎭	$6,800
September 10			(300 @ $12) (200 @ $11) (50 @ $10)	(50 @ $10)	$ 500
			$6,300		
November 27	(400 @ $13)	$5,200		(50 @ $10)⎫ (400 @ $13)⎭	$5,700

Illustration 6A-3
Perpetual system—LIFO

The use of LIFO in a perpetual system will usually produce cost allocations that differ from using LIFO in a periodic system. In a perpetual system, the latest units incurred prior to each sale are allocated to cost of goods sold. In contrast, in a periodic system, the latest units incurred during the period are allocated to cost of goods sold. Thus, when a purchase is made after the last sale, the LIFO periodic system will apply this purchase to the previous sale. See Illustration 6-12 on page 258 where the proof shows the 400 units at $13 purchased on November 27 applied to the sale of 550 units on September 10.

As shown above under the LIFO perpetual system, the 400 units at $13 purchased on November 27 are all applied to the ending inventory.

The ending inventory in this LIFO perpetual illustration is $5,700 and cost of goods sold is $6,300, as compared to the LIFO periodic illustration where the ending inventory is $5,000 and cost of goods sold is $7,000.

AVERAGE COST

The average cost method in a perpetual inventory system is called the **moving average method**. Under this method a new average is computed **after each purchase**. The average cost is computed by dividing the cost of goods available for sale by the units on hand. The average cost is then applied to: (1) the units sold, to determine the cost of goods sold, and (2) the remaining units on hand, to determine the ending inventory amount. The application of the average cost method by Houston Electronics is shown in Illustration 6A-4.

Date	Purchases		Sales	Balance	
January 1				(100 @ $10)	$1,000
April 15	(200 @ $11)	$2,200		(300 @ $10.667)	$3,200
August 24	(300 @ $12)	$3,600		(600 @ $11.333)	$6,800
September 10			(550 @ $11.333)	(50 @ $11.333)	$ 567
			$6,233		
November 27	(400 @ $13)	$5,200		(450 @ $12.816)	$5,767

Illustration 6A-4
Perpetual system—average cost method

As indicated above, **a new average is computed each time a purchase is made**. On April 15, after 200 units are purchased for $2,200, a total of 300 units costing $3,200 ($1,000 + $2,200) are on hand. The average unit cost is $10.667 ($3,200 ÷ 300). On August 24, after 300 units are purchased for $3,600, a total of 600 units costing $6,800 ($1,000 + $2,200 + $3,600) are on hand at an average cost per unit of $11.333 ($6,800 ÷ 600). This unit cost of $11.333 is used in costing sales until another purchase is made, when a new unit cost is computed. Accordingly, the unit cost of the 550 units sold on September 10 is $11.333, and the total cost of goods sold is $6,233. On November 27, following the purchase of 400 units for $5,200, there are 450 units on hand costing $5,767 ($567 + $5,200) with a new average cost of $12.816 ($5,767 ÷ 450).

This moving average cost under the perpetual inventory system should be compared to Illustration 6-14 on page 259 showing the weighted average method under a periodic inventory system.

DEMONSTRATION PROBLEM FOR APPENDIX 6A

The Demonstration Problem on pages 278–279 shows cost of goods sold computations under a periodic inventory system. Here, we assume that Englehart Company uses a perpetual inventory system and has the same inventory, purchases, and sales data for the month of March as shown there:

Inventory, March 1	200 units @ $4.00	$ 800
Purchases		
March 10	500 units @ $4.50	2,250
March 20	400 units @ $4.75	1,900
March 30	300 units @ $5.00	1,500
Sales		
March 15	500 units	
March 25	400 units	

The physical inventory count on March 31 shows 500 units on hand.

Instructions

Under a **perpetual inventory system**, determine the cost of inventory on hand at March 31 and the cost of goods sold for March under the (a) first-in, first-out (FIFO) method; (b) last-in, first-out (LIFO) method; and (c) average cost method.

Problem-Solving Strategies

1. For FIFO, the latest costs are allocated to inventory.
2. For LIFO, the earliest costs are allocated to inventory.
3. For average costs, use a weighted average for periodic and a moving average for perpetual.
4. Remember, the costs allocated to cost of goods sold can be proved.
5. Total puchases are the same under all three cost flow methods.

Solution to Demonstration Problem

The cost of goods available for sale is $6,450:

Inventory	200 units @ $4.00	$ 800
Purchases		
March 10	500 units @ $4.50	2,250
March 20	400 units @ $4.75	1,900
March 30	300 units @ $5.00	1,500
Total cost of goods available for sale		$6,450

Under a **perpetual inventory system**, the cost of goods sold under each cost flow method is as follows:

FIFO Method

Date	Purchases	Sales	Balance
March 1			(200 @ $4.00) $ 800
March 10	(500 @ $4.50) $2,250		(200 @ $4.00) (500 @ $4.50) } $3,050
March 15		(200 @ $4.00) (300 @ $4.50) ———— $2,150	(200 @ $4.50) $ 900

March 20   (400 @ $4.75) $1,900 $\left.\begin{array}{l}(200 @ \$4.50) \\ (400 @ \$4.75)\end{array}\right\}$ $2,800

March 25   (200 @ $4.50)
                                                   (200 @ $4.75)   (200 @ $4.75) $ 950
                                                   —————————
                                                       $1,850

March 30   (300 @ $5.00) $1,500 $\left.\begin{array}{l}(200 @ \$4.75) \\ (300 @ \$5.00)\end{array}\right\}$ $2,450

Ending inventory $2,450. Cost of goods sold: $6,450 − $2,450 = $4,000

LIFO Method

Date	Purchases	Sales	Balance	
March 1			(200 @ $4.00)	$ 800
March 10	(500 @ $4.50) $2,250		$\left.\begin{array}{l}(200 @ \$4.00) \\ (500 @ \$4.50)\end{array}\right\}$	$3,050
March 15		(500 @ $4.50) $2,250	(200 @ $4.00)	$ 800
March 20	(400 @ $4.75) $1,900		$\left.\begin{array}{l}(200 @ \$4.00) \\ (200 @ \$4.75)\end{array}\right\}$	$2,700
March 25		(400 @ $4.75) $1,900	(200 @ $4.00)	$ 800
March 30	(300 @ $5.00) $1,500		$\left.\begin{array}{l}(200 @ \$4.00) \\ (300 @ \$5.00)\end{array}\right\}$	$2,300

Ending inventory $2,300. Cost of goods sold: $6,450 − $2,300 = $4,150

Moving Average Cost Method

Date	Purchases	Sales	Balance	
March 1			(200 @ $4.00)	$ 800
March 10	(500 @ $4.50) $2,250		(700 @ $4.357)	$3,050
March 15		(500 @ $4.357) $2,179	(200 @ $4.357)	$ 871
March 20	(400 @ $4.75) $1,900		(600 @ $4.618)	$2,771
March 25		(400 @ $4.618) $1,847	(200 @ $4.618)	$ 924
March 30	(300 @ $5.00) $1,500		(500 @ $4.848)	$2,424

Ending inventory $2,424. Cost of goods sold: $6,450 − $2,424 = $4,026

SUMMARY OF STUDY OBJECTIVE FOR APPENDIX 6A

10 *Apply the inventory cost flow methods to perpetual inventory records.* Under FIFO, the cost of the earliest goods on hand prior to each sale is charged to cost of goods sold. Under LIFO, the cost of the most recent purchase prior to sale is charged to cost of goods sold. Under the average cost method, a new average cost is computed after each purchase.

A P P E N D I X   6 B

INVENTORY ERRORS

Unfortunately, errors occasionally occur in accounting for inventory. In some cases, errors are caused by failure to count or price the inventory correctly. In other cases, errors occur because proper recognition is not given to the transfer of legal title to goods that are in transit. When errors occur, they affect both the income statement and the balance sheet.

STUDY OBJECTIVE
11
Indicate the effects of inventory errors on the financial statements.

INCOME STATEMENT EFFECTS

As you know, both the beginning and ending inventories appear in the income statement. The ending inventory of one period automatically becomes the beginning inventory of the next period. Inventory errors affect the determination of cost of goods sold and net income in two periods.

The effects on cost of goods sold can be determined by entering incorrect data in the formula in Illustration 6B-1 and then substituting the correct data.

Illustration 6B-1
Formula for cost of goods sold

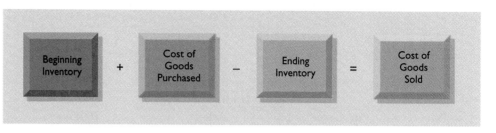

If beginning inventory is understated, cost of goods sold will be understated. On the other hand, understating ending inventory will overstate cost of goods sold. The effects of inventory errors on the current year's income statement are shown in Illustration 6B-2.

Illustration 6B-2   Effects of inventory errors on current year's income statement

Inventory Error	Cost of Goods Sold	Net Income
Understate beginning inventory	Understated	Overstated
Overstate beginning inventory	Overstated	Understated
Understate ending inventory	Overstated	Understated
Overstate ending inventory	Understated	Overstated

An error in the ending inventory of the current period will have a **reverse effect on net income of the next accounting period**. This is shown in Illustration 6B-3. Note that the understatement of ending inventory in 2000 results in an understatement of beginning inventory in 2001 and an overstatement of net income in 2001.

Illustration 6B-3   Effects of inventory errors on two years' income statements

		SAMPLE COMPANY			
		Condensed Income Statement			
	2000		2001		
	Incorrect	Correct	Incorrect	Correct	
Sales	$80,000	$80,000	$90,000	$90,000	
Beginning inventory	$20,000	$20,000	$12,000	$15,000	
Cost of goods purchased	40,000	40,000	68,000	68,000	
Cost of goods available for sale	60,000	60,000	80,000	83,000	
Ending inventory	12,000	15,000	23,000	23,000	
Cost of goods sold	48,000	45,000	57,000	60,000	
Gross profit	32,000	35,000	33,000	30,000	
Operating expenses	10,000	10,000	20,000	20,000	
Net income	$22,000	$25,000	$13,000	$10,000	

$(3,000)
Net income
understated

$3,000
Net income
overstated

The errors cancel. Thus the combined total income for the 2-year period is correct.

Over the two years, total net income is correct because the errors offset each other. Notice that total income using incorrect data is $35,000 ($22,000 + $13,000), which is the same as the total income of $35,000 ($25,000 + $10,000) using correct data. Also note in this example that an error in the beginning inventory does not result in a corresponding error in the ending inventory for that period. The correctness of the ending inventory depends entirely on the accuracy of taking and costing the inventory at the balance sheet date under the periodic inventory system.

BUSINESS INSIGHT
Investor Perspective
Inventory fraud increases during recessions. Such fraud includes pricing inventory at amounts in excess of its actual value, or claiming to have inventory when no inventory exists. Inventory fraud is usually done to overstate ending inventory, thereby understating cost of goods sold and creating higher income.

BALANCE SHEET EFFECTS

The effect of ending inventory errors on the balance sheet can be determined by using the basic accounting equation: Assets = Liabilities + Stockholders' equity. Errors in the ending inventory have the effects shown in Illustration 6B-4.

Ending Inventory Error	Assets	Liabilities	Stockholders' Equity
Overstated	Overstated	No effect	Overstated
Understated	Understated	No effect	Understated

Illustration 6B-4 Effects of ending inventory errors on balance sheet

The effect of an error in ending inventory on the subsequent period was shown in Illustration 6B-3. Recall that if the error is not corrected, the combined total net income for the two periods would be correct. Thus, total stockholders' equity reported on the balance sheet at the end of 2001 will also be correct.

SUMMARY OF STUDY OBJECTIVE FOR APPENDIX 6B

Indicate the effects of inventory errors on the financial statements. In the income statement of the current year: (a) an error in beginning inventory will have a reverse effect on net income (overstatement of inventory results in understatement of net income, and vice versa) and (b) an error in ending inventory will have a similar effect on net income (e.g., overstatement of inventory results in overstatement of net income). If ending inventory errors are not corrected in the following period, their effect on net income for that period is reversed, and total net income for the two years will be correct. In the balance sheet, ending inventory errors will have the same effect on total assets and total stockholders' equity and no effect on liabilities.

GLOSSARY

Average cost method An inventory costing method that uses the weighted average unit cost to allocate the cost of goods available for sale to ending inventory and cost of goods sold. (p. 258)

Consigned goods Goods held for sale by one party (the consignee) although ownership of the goods is retained by another party (the consignor). (p. 252)

Cost of goods available for sale The sum of the beginning merchandise inventory and the cost of goods purchased. (p. 252)

Cost of goods purchased The sum of net purchases and freight-in. (p. 250)

Cost of goods sold The total cost of merchandise sold during the period, determined by subtracting ending inventory from the cost of goods available for sale. (p. 250)

Current replacement cost The current cost to replace an inventory item. (p. 263)

Days in inventory Measure of the average number of days inventory is held; calculated as 365 divided by inventory turnover ratio. (p. 264)

Finished goods inventory Manufactured items that are completed and ready for sale. (p. 246)

First-in, first-out (FIFO) method An inventory costing method that assumes that the costs of the earliest goods purchased are the first to be recognized as cost of goods sold. (p. 256)

FOB destination Freight terms indicating that the goods are placed free on board at the buyer's place of business, and the seller pays the freight cost; goods belong to the seller while in transit. (p. 252)

FOB shipping point Freight terms indicating that the goods are placed free on board the carrier by the seller, and the buyer pays the freight cost; goods belong to the buyer while in transit. (p. 252)

Inventory turnover ratio A ratio that measures the number of times on average the inventory sold during the period; computed by dividing cost of goods sold by the average inventory during the period. (p. 264)

Last-in, first-out (LIFO) method An inventory costing method that assumes that the costs of the latest units purchased are the first to be allocated to cost of goods sold. (p. 257)

LIFO reserve For a company using LIFO, the difference between inventory reported using LIFO and inventory using FIFO. (p. 266)

Lower of cost or market (LCM) basis (inventories) A basis whereby inventory is stated at the lower of cost or market (current replacement cost). (p. 263)

Net purchases Purchases less purchase returns and allowances and purchase discounts. (p. 250)

Periodic inventory system An inventory system in which inventoriable costs are allocated to ending inventory and cost of goods sold at the end of the period. Cost of goods sold is computed at the end of the period by subtracting the ending inventory (costs are assigned to a physical count of items on hand) from the cost of goods available for sale. (p. 247)

Raw materials Basic goods that will be used in production but have not yet been placed in production. (p. 246)

Specific identification method An actual physical flow costing method in which items still in inventory are specifically costed to arrive at the total cost of the ending inventory. (p. 254)

Weighted average unit cost Average cost that is weighted by the number of units purchased at each unit cost. (p. 258)

Work in process That portion of manufactured inventory that has begun the production process but is not yet complete. (p. 246)

DEMONSTRATION PROBLEM

Englehart Company has the following inventory, purchases, and sales data for the month of March:

Inventory, March 1	200 units @ $4.00	$ 800
Purchases		
March 10	500 units @ $4.50	2,250
March 20	400 units @ $4.75	1,900
March 30	300 units @ $5.00	1,500
Sales		
March 15	500 units	
March 25	400 units	

The physical inventory count on March 31 shows 500 units on hand.

Instructions

Under a **periodic inventory system**, determine the cost of inventory on hand at March 31 and the cost of goods sold for March under (a) the first-in, first-out (FIFO) method; (b) the last-in, first-out (LIFO) method; and (c) the average cost method.

Solution to Demonstration Problem

The cost of goods available for sale is $6,450:

Inventory	200 units @ $4.00	$ 800
Purchases		
March 10	500 units @ $4.50	2,250
March 20	400 units @ $4.75	1,900
March 30	300 units @ $5.00	1,500
Total cost of goods available for sale		$6,450

(a) **FIFO Method**

Ending inventory:

Date	Units	Unit Cost	Total Cost	
Mar. 30	300	$5.00	$1,500	
Mar. 20	200	4.75	950	$2,450

Cost of goods sold: $6,450 − $2,450 = $4,000

(b) **LIFO Method**

Ending inventory:

Date	Units	Unit Cost	Total Cost	
Mar. 1	200	$4.00	$ 800	
Mar. 10	300	4.50	1,350	$2,150

Cost of goods sold: $6,450 − $2,150 = $4,300

(c) **Weighted Average Cost Method**

Weighted average unit cost: $6,450 ÷ 1,400 = $4.607
Ending inventory: 500 × $4.607 = $2,303.50

Cost of goods sold: $6,450 − $2,303.50 = $4,146.50

Note: All Questions, Exercises, and Problems marked with an asterisk relate to material in the appendixes to the chapter.

SELF-STUDY QUESTIONS

Answers are at the end of the chapter.

(SO 1) 1. When goods are purchased for resale by a company using a periodic inventory system:
(a) purchases on account are debited to Merchandise Inventory.
(b) purchases on account are debited to Purchases.
(c) purchase returns are debited to Purchase Returns and Allowances.
(d) freight costs are debited to Purchases.

(SO 2)   2. In determining cost of goods sold:
    (a) purchase discounts are deducted from net purchases.
    (b) freight-out is added to net purchases.
    (c) purchase returns and allowances are deducted from net purchases.
    (d) freight-in is added to net purchases.

(SO 2)   3. If beginning inventory is $60,000, cost of goods purchased is $380,000, and ending inventory is $50,000, what is cost of goods sold?
    (a) $390,000.   (c) $330,000.
    (b) $370,000.   (d) $420,000.

(SO 3)   4. Which of the following should *not* be included in the physical inventory of a company?
    (a) Goods held on consignment from another company.
    (b) Goods shipped on consignment to another company.
    (c) Goods in transit from another company shipped FOB shipping point.
    (d) All of the above should be included.

(SO 5)   5. Kam Company has the following units and costs:

	Units	Unit Cost
Inventory, Jan. 1	8,000	$11
Purchase, June 19	13,000	12
Purchase, Nov. 8	5,000	13

If 9,000 units are on hand at December 31, what is the cost of the ending inventory under FIFO?
    (a) $99,000.   (c) $113,000.
    (b) $108,000.   (d) $117,000.

(SO 5)   6. From the data in question 5, what is the cost of the ending inventory under LIFO?
    (a) $113,000.   (c) $99,000.
    (b) $108,000.   (d) $100,000.

(SO 6)   7. In periods of rising prices, LIFO will produce:
    (a) higher net income than FIFO.
    (b) the same net income as FIFO.
    (c) lower net income than FIFO.
    (d) higher net income than average costing.

(SO 6)   8. Considerations that affect the selection of an inventory costing method do *not* include:
    (a) tax effects.
    (b) balance sheet effects.
    (c) income statement effects.
    (d) perpetual versus periodic inventory system.

(SO 7)   9. The lower of cost or market rule for inventory is an example of the application of:
    (a) the conservatism constraint.
    (b) the historical cost principle.
    (c) the materiality constraint.
    (d) the economic entity assumption.

(SO 8)   10. Which of these would cause the inventory turnover ratio to increase the most?
    (a) Increasing the amount of inventory on hand.
    (b) Keeping the amount of inventory on hand constant but increasing sales.
    (c) Keeping the amount of inventory on hand constant but decreasing sales.
    (d) Decreasing the amount of inventory on hand and increasing sales.

(SO 10)   *11. In a perpetual inventory system,
    (a) LIFO cost of goods sold will be the same as in a periodic inventory system.
    (b) average costs are based entirely on unit-cost simple averages.
    (c) a new average is computed under the average cost method after each sale.
    (d) FIFO cost of goods sold will be the same as in a periodic inventory system.

(SO 11)   *12. Fran Company's ending inventory is understated by $4,000. The effects of this error on the current year's cost of goods sold and net income, respectively, are:
    (a) understated and overstated.
    (b) overstated and understated.
    (c) overstated and overstated.
    (d) understated and understated.

QUESTIONS

1. Goods costing $1,600 are purchased on account on July 15 with credit terms of 2/10, n/30. On July 18 a $100 credit memo is received from the supplier for damaged goods. Give the journal entry on July 24 to record payment of the balance due within the discount period assuming a periodic inventory system.

2. Identify the accounts that are added to or deducted from purchases to determine the cost of goods purchased. For each account, indicate (a) whether it is added or deducted and (b) its normal balance.

3. In the following cases, use a periodic inventory system to identify the item(s) designated by the letters X and Y.
    (a) Purchases $- X - Y =$ Net purchases.
    (b) Cost of goods purchased $-$ Net purchases $= X$.
    (c) Beginning inventory $+ X =$ Cost of goods available for sale.
    (d) Cost of goods available for sale $-$ Cost of goods sold $= X$.

4. "The key to successful business operations is effective inventory management." Do you agree? Explain.

5. An item must possess two characteristics to be classified as inventory. What are these two characteristics?

6. Your friend Tom Wetzel has been hired to help take the physical inventory in Casey's Hardware Store. Explain to Tom Wetzel what this job will entail.

7. (a) Janine Company ships merchandise to Laura Corporation on December 30. The merchandise reaches the buyer on January 5. Indicate the terms of sale that will result in the goods being included in (1) Janine's December 31 inventory and (2) Laura's December 31 inventory.

   (b) Under what circumstances should Janine Company include consigned goods in its inventory?

8. Mary Ann's Hat Shop received a shipment of hats for which it paid the wholesaler $2,940. The price of the hats was $3,000, but Mary Ann's was given a $60 cash discount and required to pay freight charges of $70. In addition, Mary Ann's paid $100 to cover the travel expenses of an employee who negotiated the purchase of the hats. What amount should Mary Ann's include in inventory? Why?

9. What is the primary basis of accounting for inventories? What is the major objective in accounting for inventories?

10. Identify the distinguishing features of an income statement for a merchandising company.

11. Dave Wier believes that the allocation of cost of goods available for sale should be based on the actual physical flow of the goods. Explain to Dave why this may be both impractical and inappropriate.

12. What are the major advantage and major disadvantage of the specific identification method of inventory costing?

13. "The selection of an inventory cost flow method is a decision made by accountants." Do you agree? Explain. Once a method has been selected, what accounting requirement applies?

14. Which assumed inventory cost flow method:
   (a) usually parallels the actual physical flow of merchandise?
   (b) assumes that goods available for sale during an accounting period are similar in nature?
   (c) assumes that the latest units purchased are the first to be sold?

15. In a period of rising prices, the inventory reported in Plato Company's balance sheet is close to the current cost of the inventory, whereas York Company's inventory is considerably below its current cost. Identify the inventory cost flow method used by each company. Which company probably has been reporting the higher gross profit?

16. Shaunna Corporation has been using the FIFO cost flow method during a prolonged period of inflation. During the same time period, Shaunna has been paying out all of its net income as dividends. What adverse effects may result from this policy?

17. Lucy Ritter is studying for the next accounting midterm examination. What should Lucy know about (a) departing from the cost basis of accounting for inventories and (b) the meaning of "market" in the lower of cost or market method?

18. Rock Music Center has five CD players on hand at the balance sheet date that cost $400 each. The current replacement cost is $320 per unit. Under the lower of cost or market basis of accounting for inventories, what value should be reported for the CD players on the balance sheet? Why?

19. What cost flow assumption may be used under the lower of cost or market basis of accounting for inventories?

20. Why is it inappropriate for a company to include freight-out expense in the Cost of Goods Sold account?

21. Maureen & Nathan Company's balance sheet shows Inventories $162,800. What additional disclosures should be made?

22. Under what circumstances might the inventory turnover ratio be too high; that is, what possible negative consequences might occur?

23. What is the LIFO reserve? What are the consequences of ignoring a large LIFO reserve when analyzing a company?

*24. "When perpetual inventory records are kept, the results under the FIFO and LIFO methods are the same as they would be in a periodic inventory system." Do you agree? Explain.

*25. How does the average method of inventory costing differ between a perpetual inventory system and a periodic inventory system?

*26. Mila Company discovers in 2001 that its ending inventory at December 31, 2000, was $5,000 understated. What effect will this error have on (a) 2000 net income, (b) 2001 net income, and (c) the combined net income for the 2 years?

BRIEF EXERCISES

BE6-1 Prepare the journal entries to record these transactions on H. Hunt Company's books using a periodic inventory system.
(a) On March 2, H. Hunt Company purchased $900,000 of merchandise from B. Streisand Company, terms 2/10, n/30.

Journalize purchase transactions.
(SO 1)

(b) On March 6 H. Hunt Company returned $130,000 of the merchandise purchased on March 2 because it was defective.

(c) On March 12 H. Hunt Company paid the balance due to B. Streisand Company.

Compute net purchases and cost of goods purchased.
(SO 2)

BE6-2 Assume that K. Bassing Company uses a periodic inventory system and has these account balances: Purchases $400,000; Purchase Returns and Allowances $11,000; Purchase Discounts $8,000; and Freight-in $16,000. Determine net purchases and cost of goods purchased.

Compute cost of goods sold and gross profit.
(SO 2, 3)

BE6-3 Assume the same information as in BE6-2 and also that K. Bassing Company has beginning inventory of $60,000, ending inventory of $90,000, and net sales of $630,000. Determine the amounts to be reported for cost of goods sold and gross profit.

Identify items to be included in taking a physical inventory.
(SO 3)

BE6-4 Ginger Helgeson Company identifies the following items for possible inclusion in the physical inventory. Indicate whether each item should be included or excluded from the inventory taking.

(a) Goods shipped on consignment by Helgeson to another company.

(b) Goods in transit from a supplier shipped FOB destination.

(c) Goods sold but being held for customer pickup.

(d) Goods held on consignment from another company.

Identify the components of cost of goods available for sale.
(SO 3)

BE6-5 The ledger of Wharton Company includes these items: Freight-in, Purchase Returns and Allowances, Purchases, Sales Discounts, and Purchase Discounts. Identify which items are included in calculating cost of goods available for sale.

Compute ending inventory using FIFO and LIFO.
(SO 5)

BE6-6 In its first month of operations, Quilt Company made three purchases of merchandise in the following sequence: (1) 300 units at $6, (2) 400 units at $7, and (3) 500 units at $9. Assuming there are 400 units on hand, compute the cost of the ending inventory under (a) the FIFO method and (b) the LIFO method. Quilt uses a periodic inventory system.

Compute the ending inventory using average costs.
(SO 5)

BE6-7 Data for Quilt Company are presented in BE6-6. Compute the cost of the ending inventory under the average cost method, assuming there are 400 units on hand.

Determine the LCM valuation.
(SO 7)

BE6-8 Hawkeye Appliance Center accumulates the following cost and market data at December 31:

Inventory Categories	Cost Data	Market Data
Cameras	$12,000	$10,200
Camcorders	9,000	9,500
VCRs	14,000	12,800

Compute the lower of cost or market valuation for Hawkeye's total inventory.

Compute inventory turnover ratio and days in inventory.
(SO 8)

BE6-9 At December 31, 1998, the following information (in thousands) was available for sunglasses manufacturer **Oakley, Inc.**: ending inventory $35,548; beginning inventory $26,200; cost of goods sold $86,134; and sales revenue $231,934. Calculate the inventory turnover ratio and days in inventory for Oakley, Inc.

Determine ending inventory and cost of goods sold using LIFO reserve.
(SO 9)

BE6-10 **Winnebago Industries, Inc.** is a leading manufacturer of motor homes. Winnebago reported ending inventory at December 31, 1998, of $55,433,000 under the LIFO inventory method. In the notes to its financial statements, Winnebago reported a LIFO reserve of $17,742,000 at January 1, 1998, and $17,426,000 at December 31, 1998. Cost of goods sold for 1998 was $450,934,000. What would Winnebago Industries' ending inventory and cost of goods sold have been for 1998 if it had used FIFO?

Apply cost flow methods to records.
(SO 10)

*BE6-11 Spain Department Store uses a perpetual inventory system. Data for product E2–D2 include the following purchases:

Date	Number of Units	Unit Price
May 7	50	$10
July 28	30	15

On June 1 Spain sold 30 units, and on August 27, 33 more units. Compute the cost of goods sold using (1) FIFO, (2) LIFO, and (3) average cost.

*BE6-12   Creole Company reports net income of $90,000 in 2001. However, ending inventory was understated by $7,000. What is the correct net income for 2001? What effect, if any, will this error have on total assets as reported in the balance sheet at December 31, 2001?

Determine correct financial statement amount.
(SO 11)

EXERCISES

E6-1   This information relates to Hans Olaf Co.:
1. On April 5 purchased merchandise from D. DeVito Company for $18,000, terms 2/10, net/30, FOB shipping point.
2. On April 6 paid freight costs of $900 on merchandise purchased from D. DeVito Company.
3. On April 7 purchased equipment on account for $26,000.
4. On April 8 returned damaged merchandise to D. DeVito Company and was granted a $3,000 allowance.
5. On April 15 paid the amount due to D. DeVito Company in full.

Journalize purchase transactions.
(SO 1)

Instructions
(a) Prepare the journal entries to record these transactions on the books of Hans Olaf Co. using a periodic inventory system.
(b) Assume that Hans Olaf Co. paid the balance due to D. DeVito Company on May 4 instead of April 15. Prepare the journal entry to record this payment.

E6-2   The trial balance of G. Garbo Company at the end of its fiscal year, August 31, 2001, includes these accounts: Merchandise Inventory $17,200; Purchases $142,400; Sales $190,000; Freight-in $4,000; Sales Returns and Allowances $3,000; Freight-out $1,000; and Purchase Returns and Allowances $2,000. The ending merchandise inventory is $26,000.

Prepare cost of goods sold section.
(SO 2)

Instructions
Prepare a cost of goods sold section for the year ending August 31.

E6-3   Below is a series of cost of goods sold sections for companies X, F, L, and S.

Prepare cost of goods sold section.
(SO 2)

	X	F	L	S
Beginning inventory	250	120	1,000	(j)
Purchases	1,500	1,080	(g)	43,590
Purchase returns and allowances	40	(d)	290	(k)
Net purchases	(a)	1,030	7,210	42,090
Freight-in	110	(e)	(h)	2,240
Cost of goods purchased	(b)	1,230	7,940	(l)
Cost of goods available for sale	1,820	1,350	(i)	49,530
Ending inventory	310	(f)	1,450	6,230
Cost of goods sold	(c)	1,230	7,490	43,300

Instructions
Fill in the lettered blanks to complete the cost of goods sold sections.

E6-4   First Bank and Trust is considering giving Novotna Company a loan. Before doing so, they decide that further discussions with Novotna's accountant may be desirable. One area of particular concern is the inventory account, which has a year-end balance of $295,000. Discussions with the accountant reveal the following:
1. Novotna sold goods costing $35,000 to Moghul Company FOB shipping point on December 28. The goods are not expected to arrive in India until January 12. The goods were not included in the physical inventory because they were not in the warehouse.

Determine the correct inventory amount.
(SO 3)

2. The physical count of the inventory did not include goods costing $95,000 that were shipped to Novotna FOB destination on December 27 and were still in transit at year-end.

3. Novotna received goods costing $25,000 on January 2. The goods were shipped FOB shipping point on December 26 by Cellar Co. The goods were not included in the physical count.

4. Novotna sold goods costing $40,000 to Sterling of Canada FOB destination on December 30. The goods were received in Canada on January 8. They were not included in Novotna's physical inventory.

5. Novotna received goods costing $44,000 on January 2 that were shipped FOB destination on December 29. The shipment was a rush order that was supposed to arrive December 31. This purchase was included in the ending inventory of $295,000.

Instructions
Determine the correct inventory amount on December 31.

Prepare an income statement.
(SO 4)

E6-5   Presented here is information related to Baja Co. for the month of January 2001:

Freight-in	$ 10,000
Rent expense	20,000
Freight-out	7,000
Salary expense	61,000
Insurance expense	12,000
Sales discounts	8,000
Purchases	200,000
Sales returns and allowances	13,000
Purchase discounts	3,000
Sales	312,000
Purchase returns and allowances	6,000

Beginning merchandise inventory was $42,000, and ending inventory was $63,000.

Instructions
Prepare an income statement using the format presented on page 253. Operating expenses should not be divided into selling and administrative expenses.

Compute inventory and cost of goods sold using FIFO and LIFO.
(SO 5)

E6-6   Powder! sells a snowboard, Xpert, that is popular with snowboard enthusiasts. Below is information relating to Powder!'s purchases of Xpert snowboards during September. During the same month, 124 Xpert snowboards were sold. Powder! uses a periodic inventory system.

Date	Explanation	Units	Unit Cost	Total Cost
Sept. 1	Inventory	26	$ 97	$ 2,522
Sept. 12	Purchases	45	102	4,590
Sept. 19	Purchases	28	104	2,912
Sept. 26	Purchases	40	105	4,200
	Totals	139		$14,224

Instructions
(a) Compute the ending inventory at September 30 using the FIFO and LIFO methods. Prove the amount allocated to cost of goods sold under each method.
(b) For both FIFO and LIFO, calculate the sum of ending inventory and cost of goods sold. What do you notice about the answers you found for each method?

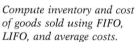

Compute inventory and cost of goods sold using FIFO, LIFO, and average costs.
(SO 5)

E6-7   In June, Dakota Company reports the following for the month of June:

Date	Explanation	Units	Unit Cost	Total Cost
June 1	Inventory	200	$5	$1,000
12	Purchase	300	6	1,800
23	Purchase	500	7	3,500
30	Inventory	180		

Instructions

(a) Compute cost of the ending inventory and the cost of goods sold under (1) FIFO, (2) LIFO, and (3) average cost.

(b) Which costing method gives the highest ending inventory and the highest cost of goods sold? Why?

(c) How do the average cost values for ending inventory and cost of goods sold relate to ending inventory and cost of goods sold for FIFO and LIFO?

(d) Explain why the average cost is not $6.

E6-8 This information is available for **PepsiCo, Inc.** for 1996, 1997, and 1998:

(in millions)	**1996**	**1997**	**1998**
Beginning inventory	$ 1,051	$ 853	$ 732
Ending inventory	853	732	1,016
Cost of goods sold	8,452	8,525	9,330
Sales	20,337	20,917	22,348

Instructions

Calculate the inventory turnover ratio, days in inventory, and gross profit rate (from Chapter 5) for PepsiCo., Inc. for 1996, 1997, and 1998. Comment on any trends.

E6-9 Deere & Company is a global manufacturer and distributor of agricultural, construction, and forestry equipment. It reported the following information in its 1998 annual report:

(in millions)	**1998**
Inventories (LIFO)	$ 1,287
Current assets	14,638
Current liabilities	8,763
LIFO reserve	1,050

Instructions

(a) Compute Deere's current ratio using the 1998 data as presented, and then again after adjusting for the LIFO reserve.

(b) Comment on how ignoring the LIFO reserve might affect your evaluation of Deere's liquidity.

*E6-10 Information about Powder! is presented in E6-6. Additional data regarding Powder!'s sales of Xpert snowboards are provided below. Assume that Powder! uses a perpetual inventory system.

Date		**Units**	**Unit Price**	**Total Cost**
Sept. 5	Sale	12	$199	$ 2,388
Sept. 16	Sale	50	199	9,950
Sept. 29	Sale	62	209	12,958
	Totals	124		$25,296

Instructions

(a) Compute ending inventory at September 30 using FIFO, LIFO, and average cost.

(b) Compare ending inventory using a perpetual inventory system to ending inventory using a periodic inventory system (from E6-6).

(c) Which inventory cost flow method (FIFO, LIFO) gives the same ending inventory value under both periodic and perpetual? Which method gives different ending inventory values?

*E6-11 Seles Hardware reported cost of goods sold as follows:

	2001	**2002**
Beginning inventory	$ 20,000	$ 30,000
Cost of goods purchased	150,000	175,000
Cost of goods available for sale	170,000	205,000
Ending inventory	30,000	35,000
Cost of goods sold	$140,000	$170,000

Seles made two errors:
1. 2001 ending inventory was overstated by $4,000.
2. 2002 ending inventory was understated by $3,000.

Instructions
Compute the correct cost of goods sold for each year.

Prepare correct income statements.
(SO 11)

*E6-12   Aruba Company reported these income statement data for a 2-year period:

	2001	2002
Sales	$210,000	$250,000
Beginning inventory	32,000	40,000
Cost of goods purchased	173,000	202,000
Cost of goods available for sale	205,000	242,000
Ending inventory	40,000	52,000
Cost of goods sold	165,000	190,000
Gross profit	$ 45,000	$ 60,000

Aruba Company uses a periodic inventory system. The inventories at January 1, 2001, and December 31, 2002, are correct. However, the ending inventory at December 31, 2001, is overstated by $6,000.

Instructions
(a) Prepare correct income statement data for the 2 years.
(b) What is the cumulative effect of the inventory error on total gross profit for the 2 years?
(c) Explain in a letter to the president of Aruba Company what has happened—that is, the nature of the error and its effect on the financial statements.

PROBLEMS: SET A

Journalize, post, and prepare trial balance and partial income statement.
(SO 1, 2, 4)

P6-1A   At the beginning of the current season on April 1, the ledger of Murdoch's Pro Shop showed Cash $2,500; Merchandise Inventory $3,500; and Common Stock $6,000. These transactions occurred during April 2001:

Apr. 5   Purchased golf bags, clubs, and balls on account from Balata Co. $2,600, FOB shipping point, terms 2/10, n/60.
      7   Paid freight on Balata Co. purchases $80.
      9   Received credit from Balata Co. for merchandise returned $100.
     10   Sold merchandise on account to members $1,200, terms n/30.
     12   Purchased golf shoes, sweaters, and other accessories on account from Arrow Sportswear $660, terms 1/10, n/30.
     14   Paid Balata Co. in full.
     17   Received credit from Arrow Sportswear for merchandise returned $60.
     20   Made sales on account to members $900, terms n/30.
     21   Paid Arrow Sportswear in full.
     27   Granted credit to members for clothing that did not fit $30.
     30   Made cash sales $600.
     30   Received payments on account from members $1,100.

The chart of accounts for the pro shop includes Cash, Accounts Receivable, Merchandise Inventory, Accounts Payable, Common Stock, Sales, Sales Returns and Allowances, Purchases, Purchase Returns and Allowances, Purchase Discounts, and Freight-in.

Instructions
(a) Journalize the April transactions using a periodic inventory system.
(b) Using T accounts, enter the beginning balances in the ledger accounts and post the April transactions.
(c) Prepare a trial balance on April 30, 2001.
(d) Prepare an income statement through Gross Profit, assuming merchandise inventory on hand at April 30 is $4,200.

P6-2A   Parking Lot City Department Store is located in midtown Metropolis. At the end of the company's fiscal year on November 30, 2001, the following accounts appeared in its adjusted trial balance:

Prepare a multiple-step income statement.
(SO 2, 4)

Accounts Payable	$ 35,310
Accounts Receivable	13,770
Accumulated Depreciation—Delivery Equipment	19,680
Accumulated Depreciation—Store Equipment	41,800
Cash	8,000
Delivery Expense	8,200
Delivery Equipment	57,000
Depreciation Expense—Delivery Equipment	4,000
Depreciation Expense—Store Equipment	9,500
Freight-in	5,060
Common Stock	70,000
Retained Earnings	17,200
Dividends	12,000
Insurance Expense	9,000
Merchandise Inventory	34,360
Notes Payable	46,000
Prepaid Insurance	4,500
Property Tax Expense	3,500
Purchases	630,000
Purchase Discounts	7,000
Purchase Returns and Allowances	3,000
Rent Expense	19,000
Salaries Expense	140,000
Sales	960,000
Sales Commissions Expense	12,000
Sales Commissions Payable	8,000
Sales Returns and Allowances	10,000
Store Equipment	125,000
Property Taxes Payable	3,500
Utilities Expense	20,600

Additional facts:
1. Merchandise inventory at November 30, 2001, is $36,200.
2. Note that Parking Lot City Department Store uses a periodic system.

Instructions
Prepare an income statement for the year ended November 30, 2001.

P6-3A   Apocalypse Distribution markets CDs of the performing artist Harrilyn Hannson. At the beginning of March, Apocalypse had in beginning inventory 1,500 Hannson CDs with a unit cost of $7. During March Apocalypse made the following purchases of Hannson CDs:

Determine cost of goods sold and ending inventory using FIFO, LIFO, and average cost.
(SO 5, 6)

March 5	3,500 @ $8	March 21	4,000 @ $10
March 13	5,500 @ $9	March 26	1,500 @ $11

During March 13,500 units were sold. Apocalypse uses a periodic inventory system.

Instructions
(a) Determine the cost of goods available for sale.
(b) Determine (1) the ending inventory and (2) the cost of goods sold under each of the assumed cost flow methods (FIFO, LIFO, and average cost). Prove the accuracy of the cost of goods sold under the FIFO and LIFO methods.
(c) Which cost flow method results in (1) the highest inventory amount for the balance sheet and (2) the highest cost of goods sold for the income statement?

Compute ending inventory, prepare income statements, and answer questions using FIFO and LIFO.
(SO 5, 6)

P6-4A The management of Zucchini Inc. asks your help in determining the comparative effects of the FIFO and LIFO inventory cost flow methods. For 2001 the accounting records show these data:

Inventory, January 1 (10,000 units)	$ 35,000
Cost of 120,000 units purchased	502,000
Selling price of 95,000 units sold	665,000
Operating expenses	120,000

Units purchased consisted of 40,000 units at $4.00 on May 10; 60,000 units at $4.20 on August 15; and 20,000 units at $4.50 on November 20. Income taxes are 28%.

Instructions
(a) Prepare comparative condensed income statements for 2001 under FIFO and LIFO. (Show computations of ending inventory.)

(b) Answer the following questions for management in the form of a business letter:
   1. Which inventory cost flow method produces the most meaningful inventory amount for the balance sheet? Why?
   2. Which inventory cost flow method produces the most meaningful net income? Why?
   3. Which inventory cost flow method is most likely to approximate the actual physical flow of the goods? Why?
   4. How much more cash will be available for management under LIFO than under FIFO? Why?
   5. How much of the gross profit under FIFO is illusionary in comparison with the gross profit under LIFO?

Compute inventory turnover ratio, days in inventory, and current ratio based on LIFO and after adjusting for LIFO reserve.
(SO 8, 9)

P6-5A This information is available for the Automotive and Electronics Divisions of **General Motors Corporation** for 1998. General Motors uses the LIFO inventory method.

(in millions)	**1998**
Beginning inventory	$ 12,102
Ending inventory	12,207
Beginning LIFO reserve	2,268
Ending LIFO reserve	2,295
Current assets	44,363
Current liabilities	47,806
Cost of goods sold	117,973
Sales	140,433

Instructions
Calculate the inventory turnover ratio, days in inventory, and current ratio for General Motors Corporation for 1998 as follows:
(a) Based on LIFO.
(b) After adjusting for the LIFO reserve.
(c) Comment on any difference between parts (a) and (b).

Determine ending inventory under a perpetual inventory system.
(SO 10)

*P6-6A Save-Mart Center began operations on July 1. It uses a perpetual inventory system. During July the company had the following purchases and sales:

	Purchases		
Date	**Units**	**Unit Cost**	**Sales Units**
July 1	5	$90	
July 6			3
July 11	4	$99	
July 14			3
July 21	3	$106	
July 27			4

Instructions
(a) Determine the ending inventory under a perpetual inventory system using (1) FIFO, (2) average cost, and (3) LIFO.
(b) Which costing method produces the highest ending inventory valuation?

Problems: Set B

P6-1B   At the beginning of the current season, the ledger of Kicked-Back Tennis Shop showed Cash $2,500; Merchandise Inventory $1,700; and Common Stock $4,200. These transactions were completed during April 2001:

Journalize, post, and prepare trial balance and partial income statement.
(SO 1, 2, 4)

Apr.	4	Purchased racquets and balls from Robert Co. $940, FOB shipping point, terms 3/10, n/30.
	6	Paid freight on Robert Co. purchase $40.
	8	Sold merchandise to members $900, terms n/30.
	10	Received credit of $40 from Robert Co. for a damaged racquet that was returned.
	11	Purchased tennis shoes from Niki Sports for cash $600.
	13	Paid Robert Co. in full.
	14	Purchased tennis shirts and shorts from Martina's Sportswear $500, FOB shipping point, terms 2/10, n/60.
	15	Received cash refund of $50 from Niki Sports for damaged merchandise that was returned.
	17	Paid freight on Martina's Sportswear purchase $30.
	18	Sold merchandise to members $800, terms n/30.
	20	Received $500 in cash from members in settlement of their accounts.
	21	Paid Martina's Sportswear in full.
	27	Granted credit of $30 to members for tennis clothing that did not fit.
	30	Sold merchandise to members $900, terms n/30.
	30	Received cash payments on account from members, $500.

The chart of accounts for the tennis shop includes Cash, Accounts Receivable, Merchandise Inventory, Accounts Payable, Common Stock, Sales, Sales Returns and Allowances, Purchases, Purchase Returns and Allowances, Purchase Discounts, and Freight-in.

Instructions
(a) Journalize the April transactions using a periodic inventory system.
(b) Using T accounts, enter the beginning balances in the ledger accounts and post the April transactions.
(c) Prepare a trial balance on April 30, 2001.
(d) Prepare an income statement through Gross Profit, assuming merchandise inventory on hand at April 30 is $1,800.

P6-2B   High-Point Department Store is located near the Village Shopping Mall. At the end of the company's fiscal year on December 31, 2001, these accounts appeared in its adjusted trial balance:

Prepare a multiple-step income statement.
(SO 2, 4)

Accounts Payable	$ 89,300
Accounts Receivable	50,300
Accumulated Depreciation—Building	52,500
Accumulated Depreciation—Equipment	42,900
Building	190,000
Cash	23,000
Depreciation Expense—Building	10,400
Depreciation Expense—Equipment	13,300
Equipment	110,000
Freight-in	5,600
Insurance Expense	7,200
Merchandise Inventory	40,500
Mortgage Payable	80,000
Office Salaries Expense	32,000
Prepaid Insurance	2,400
Property Taxes Payable	4,800
Purchases	442,000
Purchase Discounts	12,000
Purchase Returns and Allowances	6,400
Sales Salaries Expense	76,000

Sales	718,000
Sales Commissions Expense	14,500
Sales Commissions Payable	3,500
Sales Returns and Allowances	8,000
Common Stock	150,000
Retained Earnings	27,600
Dividends	28,000
Property Taxes Expense	6,800
Utilities Expense	11,000

Additional facts:
1. Merchandise inventory on December 31, 2001, is $75,000.
2. Note that High-Point Department Store uses a periodic system.

Instructions
Prepare an income statement for the year ended December 31, 2001.

Determine cost of goods sold and ending inventory using FIFO, LIFO, and average cost with analysis.
(SO 5, 6)

P6-3B Heartland Distribution markets CDs of the performing artist Brooks Straight. At the beginning of October, Heartland had in beginning inventory 1,000 Straight CDs with a unit cost of $5. During October Heartland made the following purchases of Straight CDs:

Oct. 3	3,500 @ $6		Oct. 19	3,000 @ $8
Oct. 9	4,000 @ $7		Oct. 25	2,000 @ $9

During October 11,000 units were sold. Heartland uses a periodic inventory system.

Instructions
(a) Determine the cost of goods available for sale.
(b) Determine (1) the ending inventory and (2) the cost of goods sold under each of the assumed cost flow methods (FIFO, LIFO, and average cost). Prove the accuracy of the cost of goods sold under the FIFO and LIFO methods.
(c) Which cost flow method results in (1) the highest inventory amount for the balance sheet and (2) the highest cost of goods sold for the income statement?

Compute ending inventory, prepare income statements, and answer questions using FIFO and LIFO.
(SO 5, 6)

P6-4B The management of Real Novelty Inc. is reevaluating the appropriateness of using its present inventory cost flow method, which is average cost. The company requests your help in determining the results of operations for 2001 if either the FIFO or the LIFO method had been used. For 2001 the accounting records show these data:

Inventories		**Purchases and Sales**	
Beginning (15,000 units)	$34,000	Total net sales (225,000 units)	$865,000
Ending (20,000 units)		Total cost of goods purchased	
		(230,000 units)	578,500

Purchases were made quarterly as follows:

Quarter	Units	Unit Cost	Total Cost
1	60,000	$2.30	$138,000
2	50,000	2.50	125,000
3	50,000	2.60	130,000
4	70,000	2.65	185,500
	230,000		$578,500

Operating expenses were $147,000, and the company's income tax rate is 32%.

Instructions
(a) Prepare comparative condensed income statements for 2001 under FIFO and LIFO. (Show computations of ending inventory.)
(b) Answer the following questions for management in business-letter form:
   1. Which cost flow method (FIFO or LIFO) produces the more meaningful inventory amount for the balance sheet? Why?

2. Which cost flow method (FIFO or LIFO) produces the more meaningful net income? Why?

3. Which cost flow method (FIFO or LIFO) is more likely to approximate the actual physical flow of goods? Why?

4. How much more cash will be available for management under LIFO than under FIFO? Why?

5. Will gross profit under the average cost method be higher or lower than FIFO? Than LIFO? [*Note:* It is not necessary to quantify your answer.]

P6-5B **Ag-Chem Equipment Co. Inc.,** headquartered in Minnetonka, Minnesota, manufactures a full line of equipment that is used to apply fertilizer. Many of these systems are computer controlled. This information is available for Ag-Chem for 1998. Ag-Chem uses the LIFO inventory method.

Compute inventory turnover ratio, days in inventory, and current ratio based on LIFO and after adjusting for LIFO reserve.

(SO 8, 9)

(in thousands)	**1998**
Beginning inventory	$ 99,894
Ending inventory	101,751
Beginning LIFO reserve	12,454
Ending LIFO reserve	12,006
Current assets	134,045
Current liabilities	57,871
Cost of goods sold	234,959
Sales	322,122

Instructions

Calculate the inventory turnover ratio, days in inventory, and current ratio for Ag-Chem for 1998 as follows:

(a) Based on LIFO.

(b) After adjusting for the LIFO reserve.

(c) Comment on any difference between parts (a) and (b).

◆ BROADENING YOUR PERSPECTIVE

*F*INANCIAL REPORTING AND ANALYSIS

FINANCIAL REPORTING PROBLEM: *Tootsie Roll Industries, Inc.*

BYP6-1 The notes that accompany a company's financial statements provide informative details that would clutter the amounts and descriptions presented in the statements. Refer to the financial statements of **Tootsie Roll** and the accompanying Notes to Consolidated Financial Statements in Appendix A.

Instructions

Answer the following questions. (Give the amounts in thousands of dollars, as shown in Tootsie Roll's annual report.)

(a) What did Tootsie Roll report for the amount of inventories in its Consolidated Balance Sheet at December 31, 1998? At December 31, 1997?

(b) Compute the dollar amount of change and the percentage change in inventories between 1997 and 1998. Compute inventory as a percentage of current assets for 1998.

(c) What are the cost of goods sold reported by Tootsie Roll for 1998, 1997, and 1996? Compute the ratio of cost of goods sold to net sales in 1998.

COMPARATIVE ANALYSIS PROBLEM: *Tootsie Roll vs. Hershey Foods*

BYP6-2 The financial statements of **Hershey Foods** are presented in Appendix B, following the financial statements for **Tootsie Roll** in Appendix A.

Instructions

(a) Based on the information in the financial statements, compute these 1998 values for each company. (Do not adjust for the LIFO reserve.)
1. Inventory turnover ratio.
2. Days in inventory.
(b) What conclusions concerning the management of the inventory can be drawn from these data?

RESEARCH CASE

BYP6-3 The March 5, 1999, issue of *Industry Week* contains an article by Doug Bartholomew entitled "What's Really Driving Apple's Recovery."

Instructions

Read the article and answer the following inventory-related questions:

(a) What were Timothy D. Cook's twin goals upon being hired as senior vice president at **Apple Computer Inc.**?
(b) What did Cook say was the primary cause of Apple Computer's huge $1 billion loss in 1997?
(c) What was Apple's inventory turnover in 1997, and what were its competitors' inventory turnover ratios?
(d) What improvements relative to inventory turnover did Cook accomplish by the end of 1998 at Apple Computer?

INTERPRETING FINANCIAL STATEMENTS

BYP6-4 Snowboarding is a rapidly growing sport in the United States. In 1995 **Morrow Snowboards** announced it would sell shares of stock to the public. In its prospectus (an information-filled document that must be provided by every publicly traded U.S. company the first time it issues shares to the public), Morrow disclosed the following information:

MORROW SNOWBOARDS
Prospectus

Uncertain Ability to Manage Growth: Since inception, the Company has experienced rapid growth in its sales, production, and employee base. These increases have placed significant demands on the Company's management, working capital, and financial and management control systems. The Company's independent auditors used management letters in connection with their audit of the fiscal years ended December 31, 1993 and 1994, and the 9-month period ended September 30, 1995, that identified certain significant deficiencies in the Company's accounting systems, procedures, and controls. To address these growth issues, the Company has, in the past 18 months, relocated its facilities and expanded production capacity, implemented a number of financial accounting control systems, and hired experienced finance, accounting, manufacturing, and marketing personnel. In the accounting area, the Company has begun implementing or improving a perpetual inventory system, a cost accounting system, written accounting policies and procedures, and a comprehensive annual capital expenditure budget. Until the Company develops a reliable perpetual inventory system, it intends to perform physical inventories on a quarterly basis. Although the Company is continuously evaluating and improving its facilities, management, and financial control systems, there can be no assurance that such improvements will meet the demands of future growth. Any inadequacies in these areas could have a material adverse effect on the Company's business, financial condition, and results of operations.

Instructions

(a) What implications does this disclosure have for someone interested in investing in Morrow Snowboards?

(b) Do you think that the price of Morrow's stock will suffer because of these admitted deficiencies in its internal controls, including its controls over inventory?

(c) Why do you think Morrow decided to disclose this negative information?

(d) List the steps that Morrow has taken to improve its control systems.

(e) Do you think that these weaknesses are unusual for a rapidly growing company?

BYP6-5 Nike and **Reebok** compete head-to-head in the sport shoe and sport apparel business. For both companies, inventory is a significant portion of total assets. The following information was taken from each company's financial statements and notes to those financial statements.

NIKE, INC.
Notes to the Financial Statements

Inventory. Inventories are stated at the lower of cost or market. Cost is determined using the last-in, first-out (LIFO) method for substantially all U.S. inventories. International inventories are valued on a first-in, first-out (FIFO) basis.

Inventories by major classification are as follows (in thousands):

	May 31	
	1998	**1997**
Finished goods	$1,303.8	$1,248.4
Work in process	34.7	50.2
Raw materials	58.1	40.0

Other information for Nike (in thousands):

	May 31	
	1998	**1997**
Inventory	$1,396.6	$1,338.6
Cost of goods sold	6,065.5	5,503.0

REEBOK INTERNATIONAL, LTD.
Notes to the Financial Statements

Inventory. Inventory, substantially all finished goods, is recorded at the lower of cost (first-in, first-out method) or market.

Other information for Reebok (in thousands):

	December 31	
	1998	**1997**
Inventory	$ 535.5	$ 563.7
Cost of goods sold	2,037.5	2,294.0

Instructions

Address each of these questions on how these two companies manage inventory:

(a) What challenges of inventory management face Nike and Reebok in the international sport apparel industry?

(b) What inventory cost flow assumptions does each company use? Why might Nike use a different approach for U.S. operations than for international operations? What are the implications of their respective cost flow assumptions for their financial statements?

(c) Nike provides more detail regarding the nature of its inventory (e.g., raw materials, work in process, and finished goods) than does Reebok. How might this additional information be useful in evaluating Nike?

(d) Calculate and interpret the inventory turnover ratio and days in inventory for each company. Comment on how the use of different cost flow methods by the two companies affects your ability to compare their ratios.

A GLOBAL FOCUS

BYP6-6 **Fuji Photo Film Company** is a Japanese manufacturer of photographic products. Its U.S. counterpart, and arch rival, is **Eastman Kodak.** Together the two dominate the global market for film. The following information was extracted from the financial statements of the two companies.

FUJI PHOTO FILM
Notes to the Financial Statements

Summary of significant accounting policies

The Company and its domestic subsidiaries maintain their records and prepare their financial statements in accordance with accounting practices generally accepted in Japan. . . . Certain reclassifications and adjustments, including those relating to tax effects of temporary differences and the accrual of certain expenses, have been incorporated in the accompanying consolidated financial statements to conform with accounting principles generally accepted in the United States.

Inventories

Inventories are valued at the lower of cost or market, cost being determined generally by the moving-average method, except that the cost of the principal raw materials is determined by the last-in, first-out method.

Note 6. Inventories

Inventories at March 31, 1998 and 1997, consisted of the following:

	(millions of yen)		(thousands of U.S. dollars)
	1998	1997	1998
Finished goods	¥135,795	¥123,010	$1,028,750
Work in process	51,001	48,867	386,371
Raw materials and supplies	55,525	46,959	420,644
	¥242,321	¥218,836	$1,835,765

EASTMAN KODAK COMPANY
Notes to the Financial Statements

Inventories
Inventories are valued at cost, which is not in excess of market. The cost of most inventories in the U.S. is determined by the "last-in, first-out" (LIFO) method.

Note 3. Inventories

	(in millions)	
	1998	1997
At FIFO or average cost (approximates current cost)		
Finished goods	$ 907	$ 788
Work in process	569	538
Raw materials and supplies	439	460
	1,915	1,786
LIFO reserve	(491)	(534)
Total	$1,424	$1,252

Inventories valued on the LIFO method are approximately 57% and 56% of total inventories in 1998 and 1997, respectively.

Additional information:

	Fuji Photo Film (yen)	Eastman Kodak (dollars)
1998 Cost of goods sold (millions)	735,953	7,293

Instructions
Answer each of the following questions.
(a) Why do you suppose that Fuji makes adjustments to its accounts so that they conform with U.S. accounting principles when it reports its results?
(b) What are the 1998 inventory turnover ratios and average days in inventory of the two companies (ignoring the LIFO reserve)?
(c) What are the 1998 inventory turnover ratios and average days in inventory of the two companies, adjusting for the LIFO reserve, if given? Do you encounter any problems when making this comparison?
(d) Calculate as a percentage of total inventory the portion that each of the components of 1998 inventory (raw materials, work in process, and finished goods) represents. Comment on your findings. (Use FIFO for Kodak.)

FINANCIAL ANALYSIS ON THE WEB

BYP6-7 *Purpose:* Use a company's annual report to identify the inventory method used and analyze the effects on the income statement and balance sheet.

Address: http://www.cisco.com (or go to www.wiley.com/college/kimmel)

Steps:
1. From Cisco System's homepage, choose **Investor information.**
2. Choose **View the Annual Report.**
3. Use the financial statements and related notes to the financial statements to answer the questions below.

Instructions
Answer the following questions:
(a) At Cisco's fiscal year-end, what was the net inventory on the balance sheet?
(b) How has its inventory changed from the previous fiscal year-end?
(c) What percentage of the inventory was finished goods? Find this answer in the notes to the financial statements.
(d) What inventory method does Cisco use?

CRITICAL THINKING

GROUP DECISION CASE

BYP6-8 **Morton International, Inc.,** headquartered in Chicago, Illinois, manufactures specialty chemicals, automobile airbags, and salt. Recently, its specialty chemicals business was reorganized, and three manufacturing plants were closed. Profits were generally high, however, mostly because of an improved product mix. The automotive airbag business did very well, with sales more than 30% higher than the previous year. However, toward the end of the year, questions were being raised about the safety of airbags, and this put the future of this business in some jeopardy. The salt business had dramatically increased volume because of the demand for ice-control salt due to an unusually severe winter in the northeastern United States. However, ice-control salt has a low profit margin, and so profits were up only modestly.

The current assets portion of Morton International's balance sheet for the year-ended June 30, 1998 follows.

MORTON INTERNATIONAL, INC.	
Balance Sheet (partial)	
June 30, 1998	
(in millions)	
Current assets	
Cash and cash equivalents	$ 138.0
Receivables, less allowance of $10.8	468.6
Inventories	381.0
Other current assets	125.4
Total current assets	$1,113.0

Assume that the following transactions occurred during June and July of 1998:
1. Office supplies were shipped to Morton by Office Max, FOB destination. The goods were shipped June 29 and received June 30.
2. Morton purchased specialty plastic from Uniroyal Technology for use in airbag manufacture. The goods were shipped FOB shipping point July 1, and were received by Morton July 4.
3. Ford Motor Company purchased 10,000 airbags to be used in the manufacture of new cars. These were shipped FOB shipping point June 30, and were received by Ford July 2.
4. Bassett Furniture shipped office furniture to Morton, FOB destination, June 29. The goods were received July 3.
5. Inland Specialty Chemical shipped Morton chemicals that Morton uses in the manufacture of airbags and other items. The goods were sent FOB shipping point June 29, and were received July 1.
6. Morton purchased new automobiles for its executives from General Motors. The cars were shipped FOB destination June 19, and were received July 2.
7. Morton shipped salt to New York State Public Works, FOB Chicago, June 29. The shipment arrived in Chicago June 30 and in New York July 2.
8. Morton purchased steel, to be used in expanding its manufacturing plant, from Inland Steel, FOB Dallas. The steel was shipped June 30, arrived in Dallas July 2, and at Morton's plant July 6.
9. Morton shipped packaged salt to Associated Wholesale Grocers FOB Kansas City. The salt was shipped June 30, arrived in Kansas City July 1, and at Associated Wholesale Grocers' warehouse July 2.

Instructions

With the class divided into groups, answer the following:

(a) Which items would be owned by Morton International as of June 30, 1998?

(b) Which transactions involve Morton's inventory account?

COMMUNICATION ACTIVITIES

BYP6-9   In a discussion of dramatic increases in coffee bean prices, a recent *Wall Street Journal* article noted the following fact about **Starbucks**:

> Before this year's bean-price hike, Starbucks added several defenses that analysts say could help it maintain earnings and revenue. The company last year began accounting for its coffee-bean purchases by taking the average price of all beans in inventory.

> *Source:* Aaron Lucchetti, "Crowded Coffee Market May Keep a Lid on Starbucks After Price Rise Hurt Stock," *The Wall Street Journal,* June 4, 1997, p. C1.

Prior to this change the company was using FIFO.

Instructions

Your client, the CEO of Hot Cup Coffee, Inc., read this article and sent you an e-mail message requesting that you explain why Starbucks might have taken this action. Your response should explain what impact this change in accounting method has on earnings, why the company might want to do this, and any possible disadvantages of such a change.

*BYP6-10   You are the controller of Small Toys Inc. Joy Small, the president, recently mentioned to you that she found an error in the 2000 financial statements which she believes has corrected itself. She determined, in discussions with the purchasing department, that 2000 ending inventory was overstated by $1 million. Joy says that the 2001 ending inventory is correct, and she assumes that 2001 income is correct. Joy says to you, "What happened has happened—there's no point in worrying about it anymore."

Instructions

You conclude that Joy is incorrect. Write a brief, tactful memo to her, clarifying the situation.

ETHICS CASE

BYP6-11   Lonergan Wholesale Corp. uses the LIFO cost flow method. In the current year, profit at Lonergan is running unusually high. The corporate tax rate is also high this year, but it is scheduled to decline significantly next year. In an effort to lower the current year's net income and to take advantage of the changing income tax rate, the president of Lonergan Wholesale instructs the plant accountant to recommend to the purchasing department a large purchase of inventory for delivery 3 days before the end of the year. The price of the inventory to be purchased has doubled during the year, and the purchase will represent a major portion of the ending inventory value.

Instructions

(a) What is the effect of this transaction on this year's and next year's income statement and income tax expense? Why?

(b) If Lonergan Wholesale had been using the FIFO method of inventory costing, would the president give the same directive?

(c) Should the plant accountant order the inventory purchase to lower income? What are the ethical implications of this order?

Answers to Self-Study Questions

1. b   2. d   3. a   4. a   5. c   6. d   7. c   8. d   9. a   10. d
*11. d   *12. b

Answer to Tootsie Roll Review It Question 2, p. 263

Tootsie Roll uses LIFO for U.S. inventories and FIFO for foreign inventories.

CHAPTER 7

Internal Control and Cash

◆ STUDY OBJECTIVES

After studying this chapter, you should be able to:

1 Identify the principles of internal control.

2 Explain the applications of internal control to cash receipts.

3 Explain the applications of internal control to cash disbursements.

4 Prepare a bank reconciliation.

5 Explain the reporting of cash.

6 Discuss the basic principles of cash management.

7 Identify the primary elements of a cash budget.

8 Identify and interpret measures that evaluate the adequacy of cash.

◆ IT TAKES A THIEF

HAVE YOU SEEN THIS MAN? Fifty years old, thinning brown hair, hump on back, bulbous red nose with prominent veins, and wart on upper lip, goes by the name David Shelton—and at least 14 other names. David Shelton is good at what he does. He's a thief who specializes in inside jobs. It's believed that in seven recent years, while working as a bookkeeper for small businesses, he stole at least $600,000.

Ask Celia Imperiale. She hired Mr. Shelton after he responded to an employment ad she placed for a bookkeeper. His resume boasted 20 years of experience with two different employers. He had been with his "current" employer since 1981. When Ms. Imperiale called the number of this "current" employer, she

was greeted by a woman who answered with the corporate name and then was transferred to the owner of the company. The owner gave a glowing recommendation. Ms. Imperiale also tried to call the previous employer, but she couldn't find a listing. Since it had been more than 12 years since Mr. Shelton had worked there, she didn't worry about it. But the "current" reference was phony. The phone number that Ms. Imperiale called belonged to a room at a low-rent motel. The glowing reference was given by Mr. Shelton's accomplice.

Mr. Shelton was a reasonably good employee, giving Ms. Imperiale no cause for concern until the day her auditor showed up—which by coincidence was the day after the last time she saw Mr. Shelton. Mr. Shelton

had stolen $44,000, mainly by pocketing cash receipts from Ms. Imperiale's three stores. He filled out a proper bank deposit slip, which she always checked. But on his way to the bank he made out a new deposit slip for 10% less than the total; then he deposited 90% and kept 10% for himself. He hid his theft by manipulating the accounting records and by not paying the company's state and federal taxes as they came due. At previous companies Mr. Shelton had pocketed money by creating phony suppliers who billed his employer for work never done. He then made out a check to the phony company and sent it to a bank account that he controlled under another phony name.

Mr. Shelton was careful to leave little evidence. He drove

nondescript cars, which he parked far away from where he both worked and lived. He didn't attend corporate social functions and was never in corporate pictures. When he left Ms. Imperiale's company, he stole all of his personnel files. Ms. Imperiale is probably still paying off the loan she had to take out to pay the back taxes that Mr. Shelton didn't pay.

Postscript: David Shelton (whose real name is Donald Peterson) was apprehended when a small business owner recognized him as one of his employees after reading about him in a *Wall Street Journal* article.

C ash is the lifeblood of any company. Large and small companies alike must guard it carefully. Even companies that are in every other way successful can go bankrupt if they fail to manage cash. Managers must know both how to use cash efficiently and how to protect it. Due to its liquid nature, cash is the easiest asset to steal. As the opening story suggests, a particularly difficult problem arises when a company has a dishonest employee.

In this chapter you will learn ways to reduce the risk of theft of cash and other assets, how to report cash in the financial statements, and how to manage cash through the course of the company's operating cycle. The content and organization of the chapter are as follows:

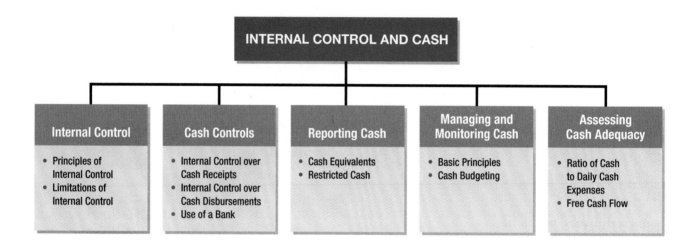

INTERNAL CONTROL AND CASH

Internal Control	Cash Controls	Reporting Cash	Managing and Monitoring Cash	Assessing Cash Adequacy
• Principles of Internal Control • Limitations of Internal Control	• Internal Control over Cash Receipts • Internal Control over Cash Disbursements • Use of a Bank	• Cash Equivalents • Restricted Cash	• Basic Principles • Cash Budgeting	• Ratio of Cash to Daily Cash Expenses • Free Cash Flow

*I*NTERNAL CONTROL

In a 1998 survey of certified fraud examiners, 66% reported that fraud had become "significantly worse" during the previous five-year period, while only 7% said it had diminished. Survey findings such as these, as well as situations such as the one described in the opening story, emphasize the need for a good system of internal control.

Internal control consists of all the related methods and measures adopted within a business to:

1. **Safeguard its assets** from employee theft, robbery, and unauthorized use; and

2. **Enhance the accuracy and reliability of its accounting records** by reducing the risk of errors (unintentional mistakes) and irregularities (intentional mistakes and misrepresentations) in the accounting process.

All major U.S. corporations are required to maintain an adequate system of internal control. Companies that fail to comply are subject to fines, and company officers may be imprisoned.

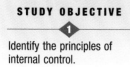

STUDY OBJECTIVE

1

Identify the principles of internal control.

PRINCIPLES OF INTERNAL CONTROL

To safeguard assets and enhance the accuracy and reliability of its accounting records, a company follows internal control principles. The specific control measures used vary with the size and nature of the business and with management's control philosophy. However, the six principles listed in Illustration 7-1 apply to most enterprises. Each principle is explained in the following sections.

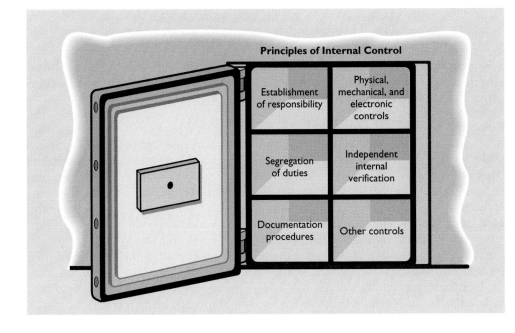

Principles of Internal Control

Establishment of responsibility	Physical, mechanical, and electronic controls
Segregation of duties	Independent internal verification
Documentation procedures	Other controls

Illustration 7-1 Principles of internal control

Establishment of Responsibility

An essential characteristic of internal control is the assignment of responsibility to specific individuals. **Control is most effective when only one person is responsible for a given task**. To illustrate, assume that the cash on hand at the end of the day in a Safeway supermarket is $10 short of the cash rung up on the cash register. If only one person has operated the register, responsibility for the shortage can be assessed quickly. If two or more individuals have worked the register, it may be impossible to determine who is responsible for the error unless each person is assigned a separate cash drawer and register key.

Establishing responsibility includes the authorization and approval of transactions. The vice-president of sales should have the authority to establish policies for making credit sales. These policies ordinarily will require written credit department approval of credit sales.

It's your shift now. I'm turning in my cash drawer and heading home.

Transfer of cash drawers

BUSINESS INSIGHT
Investor Perspective

Poor internal controls can cost a company money even if no theft occurs. For example, it was recently reported that the share prices of two companies, Morrow Snowboards and Home Theater Products, suffered because their auditors said that the firms had inadequate internal controls. The stock prices fell because investors and creditors are uncomfortable investing in companies that don't have good internal controls. In addition, companies can even be fined for having poor internal controls. German multinational corporation Metallgesellschaft was recently fined by the Commodities Futures Trading Commission for material inadequacies in internal control systems at some of its U.S. subsidiaries.

Segregation of Duties

Segregation of duties is indispensable in a system of internal control. There are two common applications of this principle:

1. The responsibility for related activities should be assigned to different individuals.
2. The responsibility for keeping the records for an asset should be separate from the physical custody of that asset.

The rationale for segregation of duties is that the work of one employee should, without a duplication of effort, provide a reliable basis for evaluating the work of another employee.

Related Activities. Related activities should be assigned to different individuals in both the purchasing and selling areas. **When one individual is responsible for all of the related activities, the potential for errors and irregularities is increased.** *Related purchasing activities* include ordering merchandise, receiving goods, and paying (or authorizing payment) for merchandise. In purchasing, for example, orders could be placed with friends or with suppliers who give kickbacks. In addition, payment might be authorized without a careful review of the invoice or, even worse, fictitious invoices might be approved for payment. When the responsibilities for ordering, receiving, and paying are assigned to different individuals, the risk of such abuses is minimized.

Similarly, *related sales activities* should be assigned to different individuals. Related sales activities include making a sale, shipping (or delivering) the goods to the customer, and billing the customer. When one person is responsible for these related sales transactions, a salesperson could make sales at unauthorized prices to increase sales commissions, a shipping clerk could ship goods to himself, or a billing clerk could understate the amount billed for sales made to friends and relatives. These abuses are less likely to occur when salespersons make the sale, shipping department employees ship the goods on the basis of the sales order, and billing department employees prepare the sales invoice after comparing the sales order with the report of goods shipped.

Accountability for Assets. If accounting is to provide a valid basis of accountability for an asset, the accountant (as record keeper) should have neither physical custody of the asset nor access to it. Moreover, the custodian of the asset should not maintain or have access to the accounting records. **The custodian of the asset is not likely to convert the asset to personal use if one employee maintains the record of the asset that should be on hand and a different employee has physical custody of the asset.** The separation of accounting responsibility from the custody of assets is especially important for cash and inventories because these assets are very vulnerable to unauthorized use or misappropriation. The segregation of duties is shown in Illustration 7-2.

Illustration 7-2
The segregation of duties (accountability for assets) principle

Accounting Employee A
Maintains cash balances per books

Segregation of Duties (Accountability for assets)

Assistant Cashier B
Maintains custody of cash on hand

BUSINESS INSIGHT

Management Perspective

A former electronic data processing employee of Texaco, Inc., and his wife were indicted for stealing thousands of dollars from the company in an accounts payable-type fraud. The employee instructed Texaco's computer to pay his wife rent for land she allegedly leased to Texaco by assigning her an alphanumeric code as a lessor and then ordering that payments be made. The lesson here is simple: *Never* allow the same person to both authorize and pay for goods and services. Doing otherwise violates the segregation of duties principle of internal control.

Documentation Procedures

Documents provide evidence that transactions and events have occurred. For example, the shipping document indicates that the goods have been shipped, and the sales invoice indicates that the customer has been billed for the goods. By adding signatures (or initials) to the documents, the individual(s) responsible for the transaction or event can be identified.

Procedures should be established for documents. First, whenever possible, **documents should be prenumbered and all documents should be accounted for**. Prenumbering helps to prevent a transaction from being recorded more than once or, conversely, to prevent the transactions from not being recorded. Second, documents that are **source documents for accounting entries should be promptly forwarded to the accounting department to help ensure timely recording of the transaction and event**. This control measure contributes directly to the accuracy and reliability of the accounting records.

Helpful Hint An important corollary to prenumbering is that voided documents be kept until all documents are accounted for.

Physical, Mechanical, and Electronic Controls

Use of physical, mechanical, and electronic controls is essential. Physical controls relate primarily to the safeguarding of assets. Mechanical and electronic controls safeguard assets and enhance the accuracy and reliability of the accounting records. Examples of these controls are shown in Illustration 7-3.

Illustration 7-3
Physical, mechanical, and electronic controls

Physical Controls

Safes, vaults, and safety deposit boxes for cash and business papers

Locked warehouses and storage cabinets for inventories and records

Computer facilities with pass key access

Mechanical and Electronic Controls

Alarms to prevent break-ins

Television monitors and garment sensors to deter theft

Time clocks for recording time worked

A crucial consideration in programming computerized systems is building in controls that limit unauthorized or unintentional tampering. Entire books and movies have been produced with computer system tampering as a major theme. Most programmers would agree that tamper-proofing and debugging programs are the most difficult and time-consuming phases of their jobs. Program controls built into the computer prevent intentional or unintentional errors or unauthorized access. To prevent unauthorized access, the computer system may require that passwords be entered and random personal questions be correctly answered before system access is allowed. Once access has been allowed, other program controls identify data having a value higher or lower than a predetermined amount (limit checks), validate computations (math checks), and detect improper processing order (sequence checks).

Independent Internal Verification

Most systems of internal control provide for independent internal verification. This principle involves the review, comparison, and reconciliation of data prepared by employees. Three measures are recommended to obtain maximum benefit from independent internal verification:

1. The verification should be made periodically or on a surprise basis.
2. The verification should be done by an employee who is independent of the personnel responsible for the information.
3. Discrepancies and exceptions should be reported to a management level that can take appropriate corrective action.

Independent internal verification is especially useful in comparing recorded accountability with existing assets. The reconciliation of the cash register tape with the cash in the register is an example. Another common example is the reconciliation by an independent person of the cash balance per books with the cash balance per bank. The relationship between this principle and the segregation of duties principle is shown graphically in Illustration 7-4.

Illustration 7-4
Comparison of segregation of duties principle with independent internal verification principle

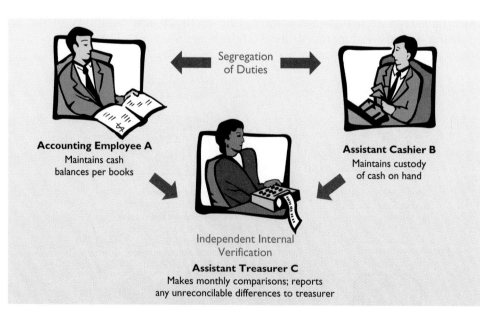

Segregation of Duties

Accounting Employee A
Maintains cash balances per books

Assistant Cashier B
Maintains custody of cash on hand

Independent Internal Verification
Assistant Treasurer C
Makes monthly comparisons; reports any unreconcilable differences to treasurer

In large companies, independent internal verification is often assigned to internal auditors. Internal auditors are employees of the company who evaluate on a continuous basis the effectiveness of the company's system of internal control. They periodically review the activities of departments and individuals to determine whether prescribed internal controls are being followed. The importance of this function is illustrated by the number of internal auditors employed by companies. In a recent year, AT&T had 350 internal auditors, Exxon had 395, and IBM had 142.

BUSINESS INSIGHT
International Perspective

Recently Sumitomo Corporation became the fifth Japanese company to announce a huge loss, this time $1.8 billion, due to a single copper trader. Some are blaming Japanese culture because it encourages group harmony over confrontation and thus may contribute to poor internal controls. For example, good controls require that both parties to a copper trade send a confirmation slip to management to verify all trades. In Japan the counterparty to the trade often sends the confirmation slip to the trader, who then forwards it to management. Thus, it is possible for the trader to change the confirmation slip. An unethical trader could create fictitious trades to hide losses for an extended period of time.

Source: Adapted from Sheryl Wudunn, "Big New Loss Makes Japan Look Inward," *New York Times,* June 17, 1996, p. D1.

Other Controls

Here are two other control measures:

1. **Bonding of employees who handle cash**. Bonding involves obtaining insurance protection against misappropriation of assets by dishonest employees. This measure contributes to the safeguarding of cash in two ways: First, the insurance company carefully screens all individuals before adding them to the policy and may reject risky applicants. Second, bonded employees know that the insurance company will vigorously prosecute all offenders.
2. **Rotating employees' duties and requiring employees to take vacations**. These measures are designed to deter employees from attempting any thefts, since they will not be able to permanently conceal their improper actions. Many bank embezzlements, for example, have been discovered when the perpetrator has been on vacation or assigned to a new position.

DECISION TOOLKIT

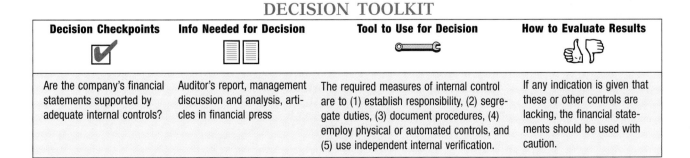

Decision Checkpoints	Info Needed for Decision	Tool to Use for Decision	How to Evaluate Results
Are the company's financial statements supported by adequate internal controls?	Auditor's report, management discussion and analysis, articles in financial press	The required measures of internal control are to (1) establish responsibility, (2) segregate duties, (3) document procedures, (4) employ physical or automated controls, and (5) use independent internal verification.	If any indication is given that these or other controls are lacking, the financial statements should be used with caution.

LIMITATIONS OF INTERNAL CONTROL

A company's system of internal control is generally designed to provide **reasonable assurance** that assets are properly safeguarded and that the accounting records are reliable. **The concept of reasonable assurance rests on the premise that the costs of establishing control procedures should not exceed their expected benefit.** To illustrate, consider shoplifting losses in retail stores. Such losses could be completely eliminated by having a security guard stop and search customers as they leave the store. Store managers have concluded, however, that the negative effects of this procedure cannot be justified. Instead, stores have attempted to "control" shoplifting losses by less costly procedures such as: (1) posting signs saying, "We reserve the right to inspect all packages" and "All shoplifters will be prosecuted," (2) using hidden TV cameras and store detectives to monitor customer activity, and (3) using sensor equipment at exits.

The **human element** is an important factor in every system of internal control. A good system can become ineffective as a result of employee fatigue, carelessness, or indifference. For example, a receiving clerk may not bother to count goods received or may just "fudge" the counts. Occasionally, two or more individuals may work together to get around prescribed controls. Such **collusion** can significantly impair the effectiveness of a system because it eliminates the protection anticipated from segregation of duties. If a supervisor and a cashier collaborate to understate cash receipts, the system of internal control may be subverted (at least in the short run). No system of internal control is perfect.

The size of the business may impose limitations on internal control. In a small company, for example, it may be difficult to apply the principles of segregation of duties and independent internal verification because of the small number of employees.

It has been suggested that the most important and inexpensive measure any business can take to reduce employee theft and fraud is to conduct thorough background checks. Two tips: (1) Check to see whether job applicants actually graduated from the schools they list. (2) Never use the telephone numbers for previous employers given on the reference sheet; always look them up yourself.

BUSINESS INSIGHT
Management Perspective

A study by the Association of Certified Fraud Examiners suggests that businesses with fewer than 100 employees are most at risk for employee theft. Also, the average loss per incident for small companies—$126,000—was actually higher than the average loss for larger companies. The high degree of trust often found in small companies makes them more vulnerable to dishonest employees. One employee intentionally asked the owner to sign checks only when the owner was extremely busy. The employee would slip in one check that was made out to himself and the owner didn't notice because he was preoccupied with other matters.

Source: J. R. Emshwiller, "Small Business Is the Biggest Victim of Theft by Employees, Survey Shows," *The Wall Street Journal,* October 2, 1995, p. B2.

BEFORE YOU GO ON...

◆ Review It

1. What are the two primary objectives of internal control?
2. Identify and describe the principles of internal control.
3. What are the limitations of internal control?

◆ Do It

Li Song owns a small retail store. Li wants to establish good internal control procedures but is confused about the difference between segregation of duties and independent internal verification. Explain the differences to Li.

Reasoning: In order to help Li, you need to thoroughly understand each principle. From this knowledge and a study of Illustration 7-4, you should be able to explain the differences between the two principles.

Solution: Segregation of duties pertains to the assignment of responsibility so that (1) the work of one employee will check the work of another employee and (2) the custody of assets is separated from the records that keep track of the assets. Segregation of duties occurs daily in using assets and in executing and recording transactions. In contrast, independent internal verification involves reviewing, comparing, and reconciling data prepared by one or several employees. Independent internal verification occurs after the fact, as in reconciling cash register totals at the end of the day with cash on hand.

CASH CONTROLS

Just as cash is the beginning of a company's operating cycle, it is usually the starting point for a company's system of internal control. Cash is the one asset that is readily convertible into any other type of asset; it is easily concealed and transported; and it is highly desired. Because of these characteristics, cash is the asset most susceptible to improper diversion and use. Moreover, because of the large volume of cash transactions, numerous errors may occur in executing and recording cash transactions. To safeguard cash and to assure the accuracy of the accounting records for cash, effective internal control over cash is imperative.

Cash consists of coins, currency (paper money), checks, money orders, and money on hand or on deposit in a bank or similar depository. The general rule is that if the bank will accept it for deposit, it is cash. The application of internal control principles to cash receipts and cash disbursements is explained in the next sections.

🌐 International Note

Other countries also have control problems. For example, a judge in France has issued a 36-page book detailing many of the scams that are widespread, such as kickbacks in public-works contracts, the skimming of development aid money to Africa, and bribes on arms sales.

INTERNAL CONTROL OVER CASH RECEIPTS

Cash receipts result from a variety of sources: cash sales; collections on account from customers; the receipt of interest, rents, and dividends; investments by owners; bank loans; and proceeds from the sale of noncurrent assets. The internal control principles explained earlier apply to cash receipts transactions as shown in Illustration 7-5 (at the top of the next page). As might be expected, companies vary considerably in how they apply these principles.

STUDY OBJECTIVE

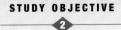

Explain the applications of internal control to cash receipts.

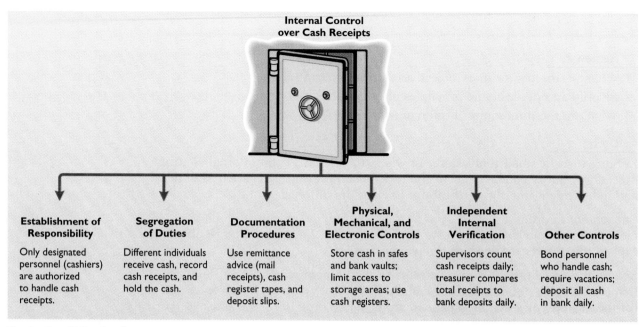

Internal Control over Cash Receipts

Establishment of Responsibility	Segregation of Duties	Documentation Procedures	Physical, Mechanical, and Electronic Controls	Independent Internal Verification	Other Controls
Only designated personnel (cashiers) are authorized to handle cash receipts.	Different individuals receive cash, record cash receipts, and hold the cash.	Use remittance advice (mail receipts), cash register tapes, and deposit slips.	Store cash in safes and bank vaults; limit access to storage areas; use cash registers.	Supervisors count cash receipts daily; treasurer compares total receipts to bank deposits daily.	Bond personnel who handle cash; require vacations; deposit all cash in bank daily.

Illustration 7-5 Application of internal control principles to cash receipts

BUSINESS INSIGHT

Management Perspective

John Patterson, a young Ohio merchant, couldn't understand why his retail business didn't show a profit. Patterson suspected pilferage and sloppy bookkeeping by store clerks. Frustrated, he placed an order with a Dayton, Ohio, company for two rudimentary cash registers. A year later Patterson's store was in the black.

"What is a good thing for this little store is a good thing for every retail store in the world," he observed. A few months later, in 1884, John Patterson and his brother, Frank, bought the tiny cash register maker for $6,500.

In the following 37 years, John Patterson built National Cash Register Co. into a corporate giant. Patterson died in 1922, the year in which NCR sold its two millionth cash register. Imagine how surprised the Patterson brothers would be to see how technology has changed the cash register. One thing hasn't changed, though; the cash register is still a critical component of internal control.

Source: The Wall Street Journal, January 28, 1989.

STUDY OBJECTIVE

3

Explain the applications of internal control to cash disbursements.

INTERNAL CONTROL OVER CASH DISBURSEMENTS

Cash is disbursed for a variety of reasons, such as to pay expenses and liabilities or to purchase assets. **Generally, internal control over cash disbursements is more effective when payments are made by check, rather than by cash, except for incidental amounts that are paid out of petty cash.** Payment is made by check generally only after specified control procedures have been followed. In addition, the "paid" check provides proof of payment. The principles of internal control apply to cash disbursements as shown in Illustration 7-6.

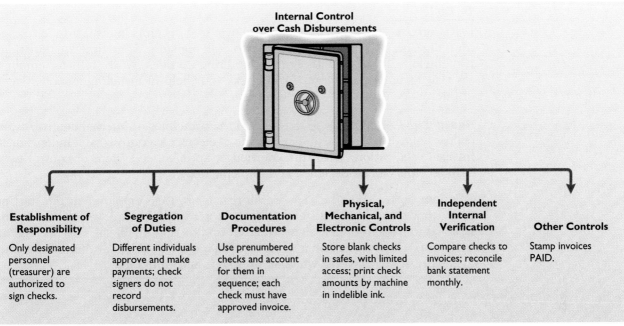

Illustration 7-6 Application of internal control principles to cash disbursements

Electronic Funds Transfer (EFT) System

To account for and control cash is an expensive and time-consuming process. For example, the cost to process a check through a bank system ranges from $.55 to $1.00 per check and is increasing. It is not surprising, therefore, that new approaches are being developed to transfer funds among parties without the use of paper (deposit tickets, checks, etc.). Such procedures, called **electronic funds transfers (EFT)**, are disbursement systems that use wire, telephone, telegraph, or computer to transfer cash from one location to another. Use of EFT is quite common. For example, many employees receive no formal payroll checks from their employers, which instead send magnetic tapes to the appropriate banks for deposit. Regular payments such as those for house, car, or utilities are frequently made by EFT.

Petty Cash Fund

As you learned earlier in the chapter, better internal control over cash disbursements is possible when payments are made by check. However, using checks to pay such small amounts as those for postage due, employee working lunches, and taxi fares is both impractical and a nuisance. A common way of handling such payments, while maintaining satisfactory control, is to use a petty cash fund. A **petty cash fund** is a cash fund used to pay relatively small amounts. Information regarding the operation of a petty cash fund is provided in the appendix at the end of this chapter.

BEFORE YOU GO ON...

◆ Review It

1. How do the principles of internal control apply to cash receipts?
2. How do the principles of internal control apply to cash disbursements?
3. What is the purpose of a petty cash fund?

◆ **Do It**

L. R. Cortez is concerned about control over cash receipts in his fast-food restaurant, Big Cheese. The restaurant has two cash registers. At no time do more than two employees take customer orders and ring up sales. Work shifts for employees range from 4 to 8 hours. Cortez asks your help in installing a good system of internal control over cash receipts.

Reasoning: Cortez needs to understand the principles of internal control, especially establishing responsibility, the use of electronic controls, and independent internal verification. With this knowledge, an effective system of control over cash receipts can be designed and implemented.

Solution: Cortez should assign a cash register to each employee at the start of each work shift, with register totals set at zero. Each employee should be instructed to use only the assigned register and to ring up all sales. At the end of each work shift, Cortez or a supervisor/manager should total the register and make a cash count to see whether all cash is accounted for.

USE OF A BANK

The use of a bank contributes significantly to good internal control over cash. A company can safeguard its cash by using a bank as a depository and clearinghouse for checks received and checks written. The use of a bank minimizes the amount of currency that must be kept on hand. In addition, it facilitates the control of cash because a double record is maintained of all bank transactions—one by the business and the other by the bank. The asset account Cash maintained by the company is the reciprocal of the bank's liability account for that company. It should be possible to **reconcile these accounts**—make them agree—at any time.

Many companies have more than one bank account. For efficiency of operations and better control, national retailers like Wal-Mart and Kmart may have regional bank accounts. Similarly, a company such as Exxon with more than 150,000 employees may have a payroll bank account as well as one or more general bank accounts. In addition, a company may maintain several bank accounts in order to have more than one source for obtaining short-term loans when needed.

Bank Statements

Each month, the company receives from the bank a bank statement showing its bank transactions and balances. For example, the statement for W. A. Laird Company in Illustration 7-7 shows (1) checks paid and other debits that reduce the balance in the depositor's account, (2) deposits and other credits that increase the balance in the depositor's account, and (3) the account balance after each day's transactions. Remember that bank statements are prepared from the *bank's* perspective. Therefore, every deposit received from W. A. Laird Company by the National Bank and Trust is *credited* by the bank to W. A. Laird Company. The reverse occurs when the bank "pays" a check issued by W. A. Laird Company on its checking account balance: Payment reduces the bank's liability and is therefore *debited* to Laird's account with the bank.

All paid checks are listed in numerical sequence on the bank statement along with the date the check was paid and its amount. Upon paying a check, the bank stamps the check "paid"; a paid check is sometimes referred to as a **canceled** check. In addition, the bank includes with the bank statement memoranda explaining other debits and credits made by the bank to the depositor's account.

Helpful Hint Essentially, the bank statement is a copy of the bank's records sent to the customer for periodic review.

Illustration 7-7 Bank statement

National Bank & Trust
Midland, Michigan 48654   Member FDIC

ACCOUNT STATEMENT

W. A. LAIRD COMPANY
77 WEST CENTRAL AVENUE
MIDLAND, MICHIGAN 48654

Statement Date/Credit Line Closing Date

April 30, 2001

457923

ACCOUNT NUMBER

Balance Last Statement	Deposits and Credits		Checks and Debits		Balance This Statement
	No.	Total Amount	No.	Total Amount	
13,256.90	20	34,805.10	26	32,154.55	15,907.45

CHECKS AND DEBITS			DEPOSITS AND CREDITS		DAILY BALANCE	
Date	No.	Amount	Date	Amount	Date	Amount
4-2	435	644.95	4-2	4,276.85	4-2	16,888.80
4-5	436	3,260.00	4-3	2,137.50	4-3	18,249.65
4-4	437	1,185.79	4-5	1,350.47	4-4	17,063.86
4-3	438	776.65	4-7	982.46	4-5	15,154.33
4-8	439	1,781.70	4-8	1,320.28	4-7	14,648.89
4-7	440	1,487.90	4-9 CM	1,035.00	4-8	11,767.47
4-8	441	2,420.00	4-11	2,720.00	4-9	12,802.47
4-11	442	1,585.60	4-12	757.41	4-11	13,936.87
4-12	443	1,226.00	4-13	1,218.56	4-12	13,468.28
4-29	NSF	425.60	4-27	1,545.57	4-27	13,005.45
4-29	459	1,080.30	4-29	2,929.45	4-29	14,429.00
4-30	DM	30.00	4-30	2,128.60	4-30	15,907.45
4-30	461	620.15				

Symbols: **CM** Credit Memo   **EC** Error Correction   **NSF** Not Sufficient Funds

DM Debit Memo   **INT** Interest Earned   **SC** Service Charge

Reconcile Your Account Promptly

A debit memorandum is used by the bank when a previously deposited customer's check "bounces" because of insufficient funds. In such a case, the check is marked **NSF** (not sufficient funds) by the customer's bank and is returned to the depositor's bank. The bank then debits (decreases) the depositor's account, as shown by the symbol NSF on the bank statement in Illustration 7-7, and sends the NSF check and debit memorandum to the depositor as notification of the charge. The NSF check creates an account receivable for the depositor and reduces cash in the bank account.

BUSINESS INSIGHT
Management Perspective

Banks charge fees for bounced checks. That is, if you overdraw a business or personal account, you may pay as much as $30 for each bad check. What you might not know is that many banks process checks from largest to smallest, in order to maximize the number of bounced checks, and therefore to maximize the revenue they earn from bounced checks. Overdrawing your account could cost you much more than you might think.

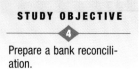

STUDY OBJECTIVE

4

Prepare a bank reconciliation.

Reconciling the Bank Account

Because the bank and the company maintain independent records of the company's checking account, you might assume that the respective balances will always agree. In fact, the two balances are seldom the same at any given time. Therefore it is necessary to make the balance per books agree with the balance per bank—a process called **reconciling the bank account**. The lack of agreement between the balances has two causes:

1. **Time lags** that prevent one of the parties from recording the transaction in the same period.
2. **Errors** by either party in recording transactions.

Time lags occur frequently. For example, several days may elapse between the time a company pays by check and the date the check is paid by the bank. Similarly, when a company uses the bank's night depository to make its deposits, there will be a difference of one day between the time the receipts are recorded by the company and the time they are recorded by the bank. A time lag also occurs whenever the bank mails a debit or credit memorandum to the company.

BUSINESS INSIGHT
Management Perspective

Some firms have used time lags to their advantage. For example, E. F. Hutton managers at one time overdrew their accounts by astronomical amounts—on some days the overdrafts totaled $1 billion—creating interest-free loans they could invest. The loans lasted as long as it took for the covering checks to be collected. Although not technically illegal at the time, Hutton's actions were wrong because it did not have bank permission to do so.

The incidence of errors depends on the effectiveness of the internal controls maintained by the company and the bank. Bank errors are infrequent. However, either party could inadvertently record a $450 check as $45 or $540. In addition, the bank might mistakenly charge a check drawn by C. D. Berg to the account of C. D. Burg.

Reconciliation Procedure. In reconciling the bank account, it is customary to reconcile the balance per books and balance per bank to their adjusted (correct or true) cash balances. **To obtain maximum benefit from a bank reconciliation, the reconciliation should be prepared by an employee who has no other responsibilities pertaining to cash**. When the internal control principle of independent internal verification is not followed in preparing the reconciliation, cash embezzlements may escape unnoticed. For example, in the opening story, a bank reconciliation by someone other than Mr. Shelton might have exposed his embezzlement.

The reconciliation schedule is divided into two sections, as shown in Illustration 7-8. The starting point in preparing the reconciliation is to enter the balance per bank statement and balance per books on the schedule. The following steps should reveal all the reconciling items that cause the difference between the two balances:

Helpful Hint Deposits in transit and outstanding checks are reconciling items because of time lags.

1. Compare the individual deposits on the bank statement with the deposits in transit from the preceding bank reconciliation and with the deposits per company records or copies of duplicate deposit slips. Deposits recorded by the depositor that have not been recorded by the bank represent deposits in transit and are added to the balance per bank.

Illustration 7-8 Bank reconciliation procedures

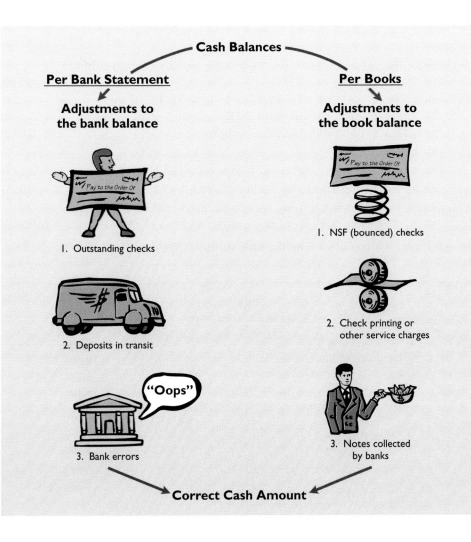

2. Compare the paid checks shown on the bank statement or the paid checks returned with the bank statement with (a) checks outstanding from the preceding bank reconciliation and (b) checks issued by the company as recorded in the cash payments journal. Issued checks recorded by the company that have not been paid by the bank represent outstanding checks that are deducted from the balance per the bank.

3. Note any **errors** discovered in the foregoing steps and list them in the appropriate section of the reconciliation schedule. For example, if a paid check correctly written by the company for $195 was mistakenly recorded by the company for $159, the error of $36 is deducted from the balance per books. All errors made by the depositor are reconciling items in determining the adjusted cash balance per books. In contrast, all errors made by the bank are reconciling items in determining the adjusted cash balance per the bank.

4. Trace **bank memoranda** to the depositor's records. Any unrecorded memoranda should be listed in the appropriate section of the reconciliation schedule. For example, a $5 debit memorandum for bank service charges is deducted from the balance per books, and a $32 credit memorandum for interest earned is added to the balance per books.

Bank Reconciliation Illustrated.   The bank statement for Laird Company was shown in Illustration 7-7. It shows a balance per bank of $15,907.45 on April 30, 2001. On this date the balance of cash per books is $11,589.45. From the foregoing steps, the following reconciling items are determined:

Helpful Hint Note in the bank statement that checks No. 459 and 461 have been paid but check No. 460 is not listed. Thus, this check is outstanding. If a complete bank statement were provided, checks No. 453 and 457 would also not be listed. The amounts for these three checks are obtained from the company's cash payments records.

1. **Deposits in transit:** April 30 deposit (received by bank on May 1). $2,201.40

2. **Outstanding checks:** No. 453: $3,000.00; No. 457: $1,401.30; No. 460: $1,502.70.   5,904.00

3. **Errors:** Check No. 443 was correctly written by Laird for $1,226.00 and was correctly paid by the bank. However, it was recorded for $1,262.00 by Laird Company.   36.00

4. **Bank memoranda:**

   (a) Debit—NSF check from J. R. Baron for $425.60   425.60

   (b) Debit—Printing company checks charge, $30.00   30.00

   (c) Credit—Collection of note receivable for $1,000 plus interest earned $50, less bank collection fee $15.00   1,035.00

The bank reconciliation is shown in Illustration 7-9.

Illustration 7-9   Bank reconciliation

Helpful Hint The terms *adjusted balance, true cash balance,* and *correct cash balance* may be used interchangeably.

W. A. LAIRD COMPANY
Bank Reconciliation
April 30, 2001

Cash balance per bank statement		$ 15,907.45
Add: Deposits in transit		2,201.40
		18,108.85
Less: Outstanding checks		
No. 453	$3,000.00	
No. 457	1,401.30	
No. 460	1,502.70	5,904.00
Adjusted cash balance per bank		$12,204.85
Cash balance per books		$ 11,589.45
Add: Collection of note receivable for $1,000 plus interest earned $50, less collection fee $15	$1,035.00	
Error in recording check No. 443	36.00	1,071.00
		12,660.45
Less: NSF check	425.60	
Bank service charge	30.00	455.60
Adjusted cash balance per books		$12,204.85

BUSINESS INSIGHT
Management Perspective

If a bank account becomes dormant, and the rightful owner can't be found, the bank is supposed to turn the money over to the state in which the account is located. During the mid-1990s however, Banker's Trust instead began to treat unclaimed funds as revenue. Officials in various states that Banker's Trust operates in became suspicious when the unclaimed funds they received from the bank declined dramatically relative to prior years. The state of New York determined that it was owed at least $41 million. In a similar case, the Bank of America agreed to pay California $187.5 million. Auditors stated that the banks hid the abuse by moving the money around very quickly between accounts, making detection through reconciliation more difficult.

Entries from Bank Reconciliation.   Each reconciling item used to determine the **adjusted cash balance per books** should be recorded by the depositor. If these items are not journalized and posted, the Cash account will not show the correct balance. The adjusting entries for the Laird Company bank reconciliation on April 30 are as follows:

Collection of Note Receivable.   This entry involves four accounts. Assuming that the interest of $50 has not been recorded and the collection fee is charged to Miscellaneous Expense, the entry is:

Apr. 30	Cash	1,035.00	
	Miscellaneous Expense	15.00	
	Notes Receivable		1,000.00
	Interest Revenue		50.00
	(To record collection of notes receivable by bank)		

A	=	L	+	SE
+1,035.00				−15.00
−1,000.00				+50.00

Book Error.   An examination of the cash disbursements journal shows that check No. 443 was a payment on account to Andrea Company, a supplier. The correcting entry is:

Apr. 30	Cash	36.00	
	Accounts Payable—Andrea Company		36.00
	(To correct error in recording check No. 443)		

A	=	L	+	SE
+36.00		+36.00		

NSF Check.   As indicated earlier, an NSF check becomes an accounts receivable to the depositor. The entry is:

Apr. 30	Accounts Receivable—J. R. Baron	425.60	
	Cash		425.60
	(To record NSF check)		

A	=	L	+	SE
+425.60				
−425.60				

Bank Service Charges.   Check printing charges (DM) and other bank service charges (SC) are debited to Miscellaneous Expense because they are usually nominal in amount. The entry is:

Apr. 30	Miscellaneous Expense	30.00	
	Cash		30.00
	(To record charge for printing company checks)		

A	=	L	+	SE
−30.00				−30.00

The foregoing entries could also be combined into one compound entry.

After the entries are posted, the cash account will appear as in Illustration 7-10. The adjusted cash balance in the ledger should agree with the adjusted cash balance per books in the bank reconciliation in Illustration 7-9.

Cash

Apr. 30 Bal.	$11,589.45	Apr. 30	$425.60
30	1,035.00	30	30.00
30	36.00		
Apr. 30 Bal.	$12,204.85		

Illustration 7-10
Adjusted balance in cash account

What entries does the bank make? If any bank errors are discovered in preparing the reconciliation, the bank should be notified so it can make the necessary corrections on its records. The bank does not make any entries for deposits in transit or outstanding checks. Only when these items reach the bank will the bank record these items.

BEFORE YOU GO ON...

◆ Review It

1. Why is it necessary to reconcile a bank account?
2. What steps are involved in the reconciliation procedure?
3. What information is included in a bank reconciliation?

◆ Do It

Sally Kist owns Linen Kist Fabrics. Sally asks you to explain how the following reconciling items should be treated in reconciling the bank account at December 31: (1) a debit memorandum for an NSF check, (2) a credit memorandum for a note collected by the bank, (3) outstanding checks, and (4) a deposit in transit.

Reasoning: Sally needs to understand that one cause of reconciling items is time lags. Items (1) and (2) are reconciling items because Linen Kist Fabrics has not yet recorded the memoranda. Items (3) and (4) are reconciling items because the bank has not recorded the transactions.

Solution: In reconciling the bank account, the reconciling items are treated by Linen Kist Fabrics as follows:

NSF check: Deducted from balance per books.
Collection of note: Added to balance per books.
Outstanding checks: Deducted from balance per bank.
Deposit in transit: Added to balance per bank.

REPORTING CASH

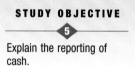

STUDY OBJECTIVE

5

Explain the reporting of cash.

Cash is reported in two different statements: the balance sheet and the statement of cash flows. The balance sheet reports the amount of cash available at a given point in time. The statement of cash flows shows the sources and uses of cash during a period of time. The cash flow statement was introduced in Chapters 1 and 2 and will be discussed in much detail in Chapter 13. In this section we discuss some important points regarding the presentation of cash in the balance sheet.

When presented in a balance sheet, cash on hand, cash in banks, and petty cash are often combined and reported simply as **Cash**. Because it is the most liquid asset owned by the company, cash is listed first in the current asset section of the balance sheet.

CASH EQUIVALENTS

Many companies use the designation "Cash and cash equivalents" in reporting cash, as shown in Illustration 7-11 for Avis Rent A Car, Inc. **Cash equivalents** are short-term, highly liquid investments that are both:

1. Readily convertible to known amounts of cash, and
2. So near their maturity that their market value is relatively insensitive to changes in interest rates.

Examples of cash equivalents are Treasury bills, commercial paper (short-term corporate notes), and money market funds. All typically are purchased with cash that is in excess of immediate needs.

AVIS RENT A CAR, INC.
Balance Sheets (partial)
December 31
(in thousands)

Assets	1998	1997
Current assets		
Cash and cash equivalents	$ 29,751	$ 44,899
Restricted cash	133,284	106,984
Accounts receivable, net	360,574	359,463
Prepaid expenses	42,083	47,360
Total current assets	$565,692	$558,706

Illustration 7-11
Balance sheet presentation of cash

Occasionally a company will have a net negative balance in its account at a bank. In this case, the negative balance should be reported among current liabilities. For example, in 1998 farm equipment manufacturer Ag-Chem reported "Checks outstanding in excess of cash balances" of $2,145,000 among its current liabilities.

RESTRICTED CASH

A company may have cash that is not available for general use but rather is restricted for a special purpose. For example, landfill companies are often required to maintain a fund of restricted cash to ensure they will have adequate resources to cover closing and clean-up costs at the end of a landfill site's useful life. Cash restricted in use should be reported separately on the balance sheet as **restricted cash**. If the restricted cash is expected to be used within the next year, the amount should be reported as a current asset. When this is not the case, the restricted funds should be reported as a noncurrent asset. An example of the presentation of restricted cash is provided by the financial statements of Avis Rent A Car in Illustration 7-11. The company is required to maintain restricted cash as part of some of its debt and lease agreements, and as part of its insurance program. The company does not have access to these funds for general use, and so they must be reported separately, rather than as part of cash and cash equivalents.

DECISION TOOLKIT

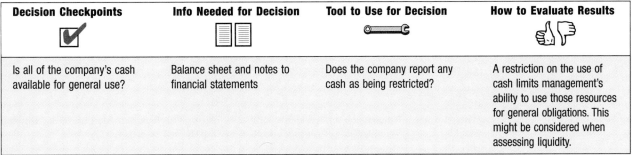

Decision Checkpoints	Info Needed for Decision	Tool to Use for Decision	How to Evaluate Results
Is all of the company's cash available for general use?	Balance sheet and notes to financial statements	Does the company report any cash as being restricted?	A restriction on the use of cash limits management's ability to use those resources for general obligations. This might be considered when assessing liquidity.

MANAGING AND MONITORING CASH

Many companies struggle, not because they can't generate sales, but because they can't manage their cash. A real-life example of this is a clothing manufacturing company owned by Sharon McCollick. McCollick gave up a stable, high-paying marketing job with Intel Corporation to start her own company. Soon she had more orders from stores such as J. C. Penney Co. and Dayton Hudson Corporation than she could fill. Yet she found herself on the brink of financial disaster, owing three mortgage payments on her house and $2,000 to the IRS. Her company could generate sales, but it wasn't collecting cash fast enough to support its operations. The bottom line is that a business must have cash.[1]

To understand cash management, consider the operating cycle of Sharon McCollick's clothing manufacturing company. To begin it must purchase cloth. Let's assume that it purchases the cloth on credit provided by the supplier, so the company owes its supplier money. Next, employees convert the cloth to clothing. Now the company also owes its employees money. Next, it sells the clothing to retailers, on credit. McCollick's company has no money to repay suppliers or employees until its customers pay it. In a manufacturing operation there may be a significant lag between the original purchase of raw materials and the ultimate receipt of cash from customers. Managing the often precarious balance created by the ebb and flow of cash during the operating cycle is one of a company's greatest challenges. The objective is to ensure that a company has sufficient cash to meet payments as they come due, yet minimize the amount of non-revenue-generating cash on hand.

A merchandising company's operating cycle is generally shorter than a manufacturing company's, depending on how long the inventory is held for sale. The cash to cash operating cycle of a merchandising operation is shown graphically in Illustration 7-12.

Illustration 7-12
Operating cycle of a
merchandising company

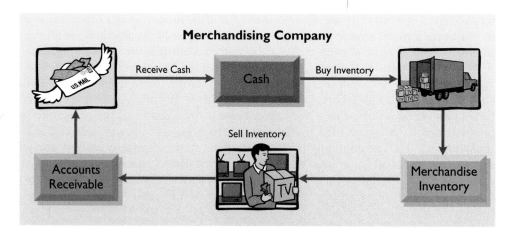

BASIC PRINCIPLES OF CASH MANAGEMENT

STUDY OBJECTIVE

6

Discuss the basic principles of cash management.

Management of cash is the responsibility of the company treasurer. Any company can improve its chances of having adequate cash by following five basic principles of cash management:

---

[1]Adapted from T. Petzinger, Jr., "The Front Lines—Sharon McCollick Got Mad and Tore Down a Bank's Barriers," *The Wall Street Journal,* May 19, 1995, p. B1.

1. **Increase the speed of collection on receivables**. Money owed Sharon McCollick by her customers is money that she can't use. The more quickly customers pay her, the more quickly she can use those funds. Thus, rather than have an average collection period of 30 days, she may want an average collection period of 15 days. However, any attempt to force her customers to pay earlier must be carefully weighed against the possibility that she may anger or alienate customers. Perhaps her competitors are willing to provide a 30-day grace period. As noted in Chapter 5, one common way to encourage customers to pay more quickly is to offer cash discounts for early payment under such terms as 2/10, n/30.

2. **Keep inventory levels low**. Maintaining a large inventory of cloth and finished clothing is costly. It requires that large amounts of cash be tied up, as well as warehouse space. Increasingly, firms are using techniques to reduce the inventory on hand, thus conserving their cash. Of course, if Sharon McCollick has inadequate inventory, she will lose sales. The proper level of inventory is an important decision.

3. **Delay payment of liabilities**. By keeping track of when her bills are due, Sharon McCollick's company can avoid paying bills too early. Let's say her supplier allows 30 days for payment. If she pays in 10 days, she has lost the use of cash for 20 days. Therefore, she should use the full payment period but should not "stretch" payment past the point that could damage her credit rating (and future borrowing ability). Sharon McCollick's company also should conserve cash by taking cash discounts offered by suppliers, when possible.

4. **Plan the timing of major expenditures**. To maintain operations or to grow, all companies must make major expenditures, which normally require some form of outside financing. In order to increase the likelihood of obtaining outside financing, the timing of major expenditures should be carefully considered in light of the company's operating cycle. If at all possible, the expenditure should be made when the company normally has excess cash—usually during the off-season.

5. **Invest idle cash**. Cash on hand earns nothing. An important part of the treasurer's job is to ensure that any excess cash is invested, even if it is only overnight. Many businesses, such as Sharon McCollick's clothing company, are seasonal. During her slow season, when she has excess cash, she should invest it. To avoid a cash crisis, however, it is very important that these investments be highly liquid and risk-free. A *liquid investment* is one with a market in which someone is always willing to buy or sell the investment. A *risk-free investment* means there is no concern that the party will default on its promise to pay its principal and interest. For example, using excess cash to purchase stock in a small company because you heard that it was probably going to increase in value in the near term is totally inappropriate. First, the stock of small companies is often illiquid. Second, if the stock suddenly decreases in value, you might be forced to sell the stock at a loss in order to pay your bills as they come due. The most common form of liquid investments is interest-paying U.S. government securities.

These five principles of cash management are summarized in Illustration 7-13 (on the next page).

International Note

International sales complicate cash management. For example, if Nike must repay a Japanese supplier 30 days from today in Japanese yen, it will be concerned about how the exchange rate of U.S. dollars for yen might change during those 30 days. Often corporate treasurers make investments known as *hedges* to lock in an exchange rate to reduce the company's exposure to exchange rate fluctuation.

Illustration 7-13   Five principles of sound cash management

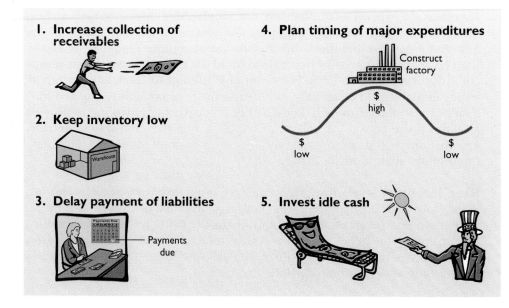

1. **Increase collection of receivables**

2. **Keep inventory low**

3. **Delay payment of liabilities**

Payments due

4. **Plan timing of major expenditures**

Construct factory

$ high

$ low $ low

5. **Invest idle cash**

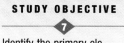

STUDY OBJECTIVE

7

Identify the primary elements of a cash budget.

CASH BUDGETING

Because cash is so vital to a company, **planning the company's cash needs** is a key business activity. It enables the company to plan ahead to cover possible cash shortfalls and to make investments of idle funds. The cash budget shows anticipated cash flows, usually over a one- to two-year period. In this section we introduce the basics of cash budgeting. More advanced discussion of cash budgets and budgets in general is provided in managerial accounting texts.

As shown in Illustration 7-14, the cash budget contains three sections—cash receipts, cash disbursements, and financing—and the beginning and ending cash balances.

Illustration 7-14   Basic form of a cash budget

ANY COMPANY Cash Budget	
Beginning cash balance	$X,XXX
Add: **Cash receipts** (itemized)	X,XXX
Total available cash	X,XXX
Less: **Cash disbursements** (itemized)	X,XXX
Excess (deficiency) of available cash over cash disbursements	X,XXX
Financing needed	X,XXX
Ending cash balance	$X,XXX

The **Cash receipts** section includes expected receipts from the company's principal source(s) of revenue, such as cash sales and collections from customers on credit sales. This section also shows anticipated receipts of interest and dividends, and proceeds from planned sales of investments, plant assets, and the company's capital stock.

The **Cash disbursements** section shows expected payments for direct materials, direct labor, manufacturing overhead, and selling and administrative expenses. This section also includes projected payments for income taxes, dividends, investments, and plant assets.

The **Financing** section shows expected borrowings and the repayment of the borrowed funds plus interest. This entry is needed when there is a cash deficiency or when the cash balance is less than management's minimum required balance.

Data in the cash budget must be prepared in sequence because the ending cash balance of one period becomes the beginning cash balance for the next period. Data for preparing the cash budget are obtained from other budgets and from information provided by management. In practice, cash budgets are often prepared for the year on a monthly basis.

To minimize detail, we will assume that Hayes Company prepares an annual cash budget by quarters. Preparing a cash budget requires making some assumptions. For example, the cash budget for Hayes Company is based on the company's assumptions regarding collection of accounts receivable, sales of securities, payments for materials and salaries, and purchases of property, plant, and equipment. The accuracy of the cash budget is very dependent on the accuracy of these assumptions.

The cash budget for Hayes Company is shown in Illustration 7-15. The budget indicates that $3,000 of financing will be needed in the second quarter to maintain a minimum cash balance of $15,000. Since there is an excess of available cash over disbursements of $22,500 at the end of the third quarter, the borrowing is repaid in this quarter plus $100 interest.

Illustration 7-15 Cash budget

HAYES COMPANY Cash Budget For the Year Ending December 31, 2001				
	Quarter			
	1	2	3	4
Beginning cash balance	$ 38,000	$ 25,500	$ 15,000	$ 19,400
Add: **Cash receipts**				
Collections from customers	168,000	198,000	228,000	258,000
Sale of securities	2,000	0	0	0
Total receipts	170,000	198,000	228,000	258,000
Total available cash	208,000	223,500	243,000	277,400
Less: **Cash disbursements**				
Materials	23,200	27,200	31,200	35,200
Salaries	62,000	72,000	82,000	92,000
Selling and administrative expenses (excluding depreciation)	94,300	99,300	104,300	109,300
Purchase of truck	0	10,000	0	0
Income tax expense	3,000	3,000	3,000	3,000
Total disbursements	182,500	211,500	220,500	239,500
Excess (deficiency) of available cash over disbursements	25,500	12,000	22,500	37,900
Financing				
Borrowings	0	3,000	0	0
Repayments—plus $100 interest	0	0	3,100	0
Ending cash balance	$ 25,500	$ 15,000	$ 19,400	$ 37,900

A cash budget contributes to more effective cash management. For example, it can show when additional financing will be necessary well before the actual need arises. Conversely, it can indicate when excess cash will be available for investments or other purposes.

DECISION TOOLKIT

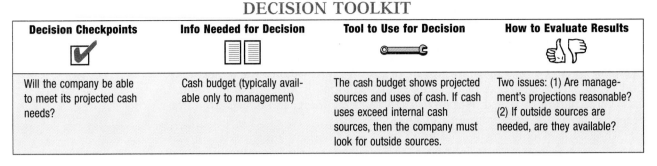

Decision Checkpoints	Info Needed for Decision	Tool to Use for Decision	How to Evaluate Results
Will the company be able to meet its projected cash needs?	Cash budget (typically available only to management)	The cash budget shows projected sources and uses of cash. If cash uses exceed internal cash sources, then the company must look for outside sources.	Two issues: (1) Are management's projections reasonable? (2) If outside sources are needed, are they available?

BEFORE YOU GO ON...

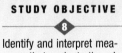

◆ Review It

1. What are the five principal elements of sound cash management?
2. What are the three sections of the cash budget?
3. What was Tootsie Roll's balance in cash and cash equivalents at December 31, 1998? Did it report any restricted cash? How did Tootsie Roll define cash equivalents? The answer to these questions is provided on p. 351.

◆ Do It

Martian Company's management wants to maintain a minimum monthly cash balance of $15,000. At the beginning of March the cash balance is $16,500; expected cash receipts for March are $210,000; and cash disbursements are expected to be $220,000. How much cash, if any, must be borrowed to maintain the desired minimum monthly balance?

Reasoning: The best way to answer this question is to insert the dollar data into the basic form of the cash budget.

Solution:

Beginning cash balance	$ 16,500
Add: Cash receipts for March	210,000
Total available cash	226,500
Less: Cash disbursements for March	220,000
Excess of available cash over cash disbursements	6,500
Financing	**8,500**
Ending cash balance	$ 15,000

To maintain the desired minimum cash balance of $15,000, Martian Company must borrow $8,500 of cash.

ASSESSING CASH ADEQUACY

In evaluating a company's cash management practices we are interested in whether the amount of cash it has on hand is adequate. This can be evaluated using the ratio of cash to daily cash expenses. We also want to know whether the company can generate enough cash internally to meet its projected needs. This can be evaluated using a measure known as free cash flow.

RATIO OF CASH TO DAILY CASH EXPENSES

Company managers as well as outside investors closely monitor a company's cash position. Announcement of a projected cash shortfall, such as that made by rapidly growing Internet-access provider EarthLink in August 1997, can send shock waves through a company's stock price. One measure of the adequacy of cash is the ratio of cash to daily cash expenses. In this ratio, "cash" includes cash plus cash equivalents. It computes the number of days of cash expenses the cash on hand can cover. Cash expenses per day can be approximated by subtracting depreciation (a noncash expense) from total expenses and dividing by 365 days. (Note that this is a rough approximation that ignores many other accrual adjustments.) Dividing the balance in cash and cash equivalents by average daily cash expenses, as shown in Illustration 7-16, gives the number of days the company can operate without an additional infusion of cash.

Illustration 7-16 Ratio of cash to daily cash expenses

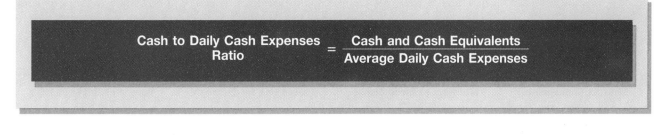

A computation of free cash flow for Elle Company is shown below:

FREE CASH FLOW

Another important measure that helps investors and management understand a company's solvency and overall financial strength is free cash flow analysis. This analysis starts with net cash provided by operating activities and ends with free cash flow, which is calculated as cash provided by operations less capital expenditures and cash dividends (Illustration 7-17).

Illustration 7-17 Free cash flow

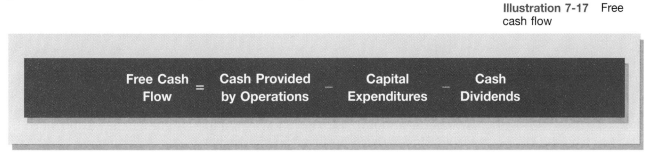

A computation of free cash flow for Elle Company is shown below:

Illustration 7-18 Computation of free cash flow

ELLE COMPANY		
Free Cash Flow Analysis		
Cash provided by operations		$250,000
Less: Capital expenditures	$80,000	
Dividends paid	50,000	130,000
Free cash flow		$120,000

Free cash flow is the amount of discretionary cash flow a company has for purchasing additional investments, paying its debts, or adding to its liquidity. It provides an assessment of a company's solvency and financial flexibility. For example, the information for Elle Company shows that it has a positive and substantial net cash provided by operating activities of $250,000. Capital spending is deducted first. Dividends are then deducted to arrive at free cash flow. Although a company can cut its dividend, it will do so only in a financial emergency. Elle has more than sufficient cash flow to meet its dividend payments and, therefore, appears to have satisfactory solvency.

A company that has significant free cash flow also has financial flexibility. In other words, Elle has discretionary cash flow to add to its liquidity, retire debt, or increase capital spending. If it finds additional investments that are profitable, it can increase its spending without putting its dividend or basic capital spending in jeopardy. Companies that have substantial free cash flow can take advantage of profitable investments even in tough times. In addition, companies with substantial free cash flow do not have to worry about survival in poor economic times. In fact, they often fare better in poor economic times because they can take advantage of opportunities that other companies cannot.

DECISION TOOLKIT

Decision Checkpoints	Info Needed for Decision	Tool to Use for Decision	How to Evaluate Results
Does the company have adequate cash to meet its daily needs?	Cash and cash equivalents, average daily expenses	$\text{Cash to daily cash expenses ratio} = \dfrac{\text{Cash and cash equivalents}}{\text{Average daily cash expenses}}$	A low measure should be investigated. If this measure is low, additional financing may be necessary.
Does the company have any discretionary cash available?	Net cash provided by operating activities, capital expenditures, and cash dividends	$\text{Free cash flow} = \text{Cash provided by operations minus capital expenditures and cash dividends}$	Free cash flow allows a company to buy additional investments, reduce its debts, or add to its liquidity. The greater the free cash flow, the greater its options.

Each of these measures is applied to the Harley-Davidson Corporation, as shown in Illustration 7-19. The following financial information was provided in the 1998 Harley-Davidson financial statements:

HARLEY-DAVIDSON CORPORATION
Selected Financial Information
(in millions)

	1998	1997
Sales	$2,064	$1,763
Total expenses	1,850	1,589
Depreciation	87	70
Cash and cash equivalents	165	147
Cash from operations	318	310
Cash paid for capital expenditures	183	186
Cash paid for dividends	24	21

($ in millions)	1998	1997
Cash to daily cash expenses ratio	$\dfrac{\$165}{(\$1,850 - \$87)/365} = 34.2 \text{ days}$	$\dfrac{\$147}{(\$1,589 - \$70)/365} = 35.3 \text{ days}$
Free cash flow	$318 - $183 - $24 = $111	$310 - $186 - $21 = $103

Illustration 7-19   Cash adequacy measures for Harley-Davidson

Harley-Davidson had a strong cash position in both years. The ratio of cash to daily cash expenses indicates that at the end of 1998 its cash was sufficient to meet the needs of 34.2 days of normal activity; in 1997 its cash balance would cover 35.3 days of activity.

The computation of Harley's free cash flow shows that in 1998 Harley generated positive free cash flow of $111,000,000. In 1998 Harley's operating activities generated sufficient cash to cover capital expenditures and dividend payments, and gave management additional flexibility to increase capital expenditures or dividend payments or to retire its own stock or debt. Harley's cash to daily cash expenses ratio suggests that its cash on hand is very adequate. Its free cash flow suggests it can generate cash from internal operations to meet projected needs and to grow.

BEFORE YOU GO ON...

◆ Review It

1. What is the formula for the cash to daily cash expenses ratio? What does it tell management about the company's cash position?
2. How is free cash flow computed?

USING THE DECISION TOOLKIT

Presented below is hypothetical financial information for the Mattel Corporation. Included in this information is financial statement data from the year ended December 31, 2000, which should be used to calculate free cash flow and the cash to daily cash expenses ratio.

Selected Financial Information
Year Ended December 31, 2000
(in millions)

Net cash provided by operations	$325
Capital expenditures	162
Dividends paid	80
Total expenses	680
Depreciation expense	40
Cash balance	506

Also provided is projected data which is management's best estimate of its sources and uses of cash during 2001. This information should be used to prepare a cash budget for 2001.

Projected Sources and Uses of Cash
(in millions)

Beginning cash balance	$506
Cash receipts from sales	355
Cash receipts from sale of short-term investments	20
Cash payments for inventory	357
Cash payments for selling and administrative expense	201
Cash payments for property, plant, and equipment	45
Cash payments for taxes	17

Mattel Corporation's management believes it should maintain a balance of $400 million cash.

Instructions

(a) Using the hypothetical projected sources and uses of cash information presented above, prepare a cash budget for 2001 for the Mattel Corporation.
(b) Using the year 2000 selected financial information presented above, calculate the cash to daily cash expenses ratio and free cash flow.
(c) Comment on Mattel's cash adequacy, and discuss steps that might be taken to improve its cash position.

Solution

(a)

MATTEL CORPORATION
Cash Budget
For the Year 2001
(in millions)

Beginning cash balance		$506
Add: Cash receipts		
From sales of product	$355	
From sale of short-term investments	20	375
Total cash available		881
Less: Cash disbursements		
Payments for inventory	357	
Payments for selling and administrative costs	201	
Payments for taxes	17	575
Excess of available cash over cash disbursements		306
Financing needed		94
Ending cash balance		$400

(b) To calculate the cash to daily cash expenses ratio, first approximate average daily cash expenses using total expenses minus depreciation expense divided by 365. The average daily cash expenses (in millions) is calculated as: $(\$680 - \$40)/365 = \$1.753$. Next, the cash to daily cash expenses ratio is calculated as: $\$506/\$1.753 = 288.6$ days. This ratio suggests the company will have cash sufficient to cover 289 days of normal expenses.

The company's free cash flow is calculated by subtracting cash paid for dividends and capital expenditures from cash provided by operating activities:

**Free Cash Flow Analysis
(in millions)**

Cash provided by operations		$325
Less: Capital expenditures	$162	
Dividends paid	80	242
Free cash flow in 2000		$ 83

(c) Mattel's cash position appears adequate. It has enough cash on hand to cover 289 days, and its year 2000 free cash flow was sufficient to cover its needs and provided additional cash for expansion, dividends, or other uses. For 2001 it is projecting a cash shortfall. This is not necessarily of concern, but it should be investigated. Given that its primary line of business is toys, and that most toys are sold during December, we would expect Mattel's cash position to vary significantly during the course of the year. After Christmas it probably has a lot of excess cash, and earlier in the year, when it is making and selling its product but has not yet been paid, it may need to borrow to meet any temporary cash shortfalls.

In the event that Mattel's management is concerned with its cash position, it could take the following steps: (1) Offer its customers cash discounts for early payment, such as 2/10, n/30. (2) Implement inventory management techniques to reduce the need for large inventories of such things as the plastics used to make its toys. (3) Carefully time payments to suppliers by keeping track of when payments are due, so as not to pay too early. (4) If it has plans for major expenditures, time those expenditures to coincide with its seasonal period of excess cash.

SUMMARY OF STUDY OBJECTIVES

❶Identify the principles of internal control. The principles of internal control are establishment of responsibility; segregation of duties; documentation procedures; physical, mechanical, and electronic controls; independent internal verification; and other controls.

❷Explain the applications of internal control to cash receipts. Internal controls over cash receipts include: (a) designating only personnel such as cashiers to handle cash; (b) assigning the duties of receiving cash, recording cash, and having custody of cash to different individuals; (c) obtaining remittance advices for mail receipts, cash register tapes for over-the-counter receipts, and deposit slips for bank deposits; (d) using company safes and bank vaults to store cash with access limited to authorized personnel, and using cash registers in executing over-the-counter receipts; (e) making independent daily counts of register receipts and daily comparisons of total receipts with total deposits; and (f) bonding personnel who handle cash and requiring them to take vacations.

❸Explain the applications of internal control to cash disbursements. Internal controls over cash disbursements include: (a) having only specified individuals such as the treasurer authorized to sign checks; (b) assigning the duties of approving items for payment, paying the items, and recording the payment to different individuals; (c) using prenumbered checks and accounting for all checks, with each check supported by an approved invoice; (d) storing blank checks in a safe or vault with access restricted to authorized personnel, and using a checkwriter to imprint amounts on checks; (e) comparing each check with the approved invoice before issuing the check, and making monthly reconciliations of bank and book balances; and (f) after payment, stamping each approved invoice "paid."

❹Prepare a bank reconciliation. In reconciling the bank account, it is customary to reconcile the balance per books and the balance per bank to their adjusted balance. The steps in determining the reconciling items are to ascertain deposits in transit, outstanding checks, errors by the depositor or the bank, and unrecorded bank memoranda.

❺Explain the reporting of cash. Cash is listed first in the current assets section of the balance sheet. In some cases, cash is reported together with cash equivalents. Cash restricted for a special purpose is reported separately as a current asset or as a noncurrent asset depending on when the cash is expected to be used.

❻Discuss the basic principles of cash management. The basic principles of cash management include: (a) Increase collection of receivables, (b) keep inventory levels low, (c) delay payment of liabilities, (d) plan timing of major expenditures, and (e) invest idle cash.

❼Identify the primary elements of a cash budget. The three main elements of a cash budget are the cash receipts section, cash disbursements section, and financing section.

8 *Identify and interpret measures that evaluate the adequacy of cash.* The cash to daily cash expenses ratio indicates how many days of expenditures the current cash resources will cover. The computation of free cash flow reveals the amount of discretionary cash available.

DECISION TOOLKIT—A SUMMARY

Decision Checkpoints	Info Needed for Decision	Tool to Use for Decision	How to Evaluate Results
Are the company's financial statements supported by adequate internal controls?	Auditor's report, management discussion and analysis, articles in financial press	The required measures of internal control are to (1) establish responsibility, (2) segregate duties, (3) document procedures, (4) employ physical or automated controls, and (5) use independent internal verification.	If any indication is given that these or other controls are lacking, the financial statements should be used with caution.
Is all of the company's cash available for general use?	Balance sheet and notes to financial statements	Does the company report any cash as being restricted?	A restriction on the use of cash limits management's ability to use those resources for general obligations. This might be considered when assessing liquidity.
Will the company be able to meet its projected cash needs?	Cash budget (typically available only to management)	The cash budget shows projected sources and uses of cash. If cash uses exceed internal cash sources, then the company must look for outside sources.	Two issues: (1) Are management's projections reasonable? (2) If outside sources are needed, are they available?
Does the company have adequate cash to meet its daily needs?	Cash and cash equivalents, average daily expenses	$$\text{Cash to daily cash expenses ratio} = \frac{\text{Cash and cash equivalents}}{\text{Average daily cash expenses}}$$	A low measure should be investigated. If this measure is low, additional financing may be necessary.
Does the company have any discretionary cash available?	Net cash provided by operating activities, capital expenditures, and cash dividends	$$\text{Free cash flow} = \text{Cash provided by operations minus capital expenditures and cash dividends}$$	Free cash flow allows a company to buy additional investments, reduce its debts, or add to its liquidity. The greater the free cash flow, the greater its options.

APPENDIX

OPERATION OF THE PETTY CASH FUND

STUDY OBJECTIVE

9

Explain the operation of a petty cash fund.

The operation of a petty cash fund involves (1) establishing the fund, (2) making payments from the fund, and (3) replenishing the fund.

ESTABLISHING THE PETTY CASH FUND

Two essential steps in establishing a petty cash fund are appointing a petty cash custodian who will be responsible for the fund and determining the size of the fund. Ordinarily, the amount is expected to cover anticipated disbursements for a three- to four-week period. When the fund is established, a check payable to the petty cash custodian is issued for the stipulated amount. If Laird Company decides to establish a $100 fund on March 1, the entry in general journal form is:

Mar.	1	Petty Cash	100.00	
		Cash		100.00
		(To establish a petty cash fund)		

A	=	L	+	SE
+100				
−100				

The check is then cashed and the proceeds are placed in a locked petty cash box or drawer. Most petty cash funds are established on a fixed amount basis. Moreover, no additional entries will be made to the Petty Cash account unless the stipulated amount of the fund is changed. For example, if Laird Company decides on July 1 to increase the size of the fund to $250, it would debit Petty Cash $150 and credit Cash $150.

Helpful Hint Petty cash funds are authorized and legitimate. In contrast, "slush" funds are unauthorized and hidden (under the table).

MAKING PAYMENTS FROM PETTY CASH

The custodian of the petty cash fund has the authority to make payments from the fund that conform to prescribed management policies. Usually management limits the size of expenditures that may be made and does not permit use of the fund for certain types of transactions (such as making short-term loans to employees). Each payment from the fund must be documented on a prenumbered petty cash receipt (or petty cash voucher). The signatures of both the custodian and the individual receiving payment are required on the receipt. If other supporting documents such as a freight bill or invoice are available, they should be attached to the petty cash receipt.

Helpful Hint From the standpoint of internal control, the receipt satisfies two principles: (1) establishing responsibility (signature of custodian) and (2) documentation procedures.

The receipts are kept in the petty cash box until the fund is replenished. As a result, the sum of the petty cash receipts and money in the fund should equal the established total at all times. This means that surprise counts can be made at any time by an independent person, such as an internal auditor, to determine whether the fund is being maintained intact.

No accounting entry is made to record a payment at the time it is taken from petty cash. It is considered both inexpedient and unnecessary to do so. Instead, the accounting effects of each payment are recognized when the fund is replenished.

REPLENISHING THE PETTY CASH FUND

When the money in the petty cash fund reaches a minimum level, the fund is replenished. The request for reimbursement is initiated by the petty cash custodian. This individual prepares a schedule (or summary) of the payments that have been made and sends the schedule, supported by petty cash receipts and other documentation, to the treasurer's office. The receipts and supporting documents are examined in the treasurer's office to verify that they were proper payments from the fund. The treasurer then approves the request and a check is prepared to restore the fund to its established amount. At the same time, all supporting documentation is stamped "paid" so that it cannot be submitted again for payment.

Helpful Hint Replenishing involves three internal control procedures: segregation of duties, documentation procedures, and independent internal verification.

To illustrate, assume that on March 15 the petty cash custodian requests a check for $87. The fund contains $13 cash and petty cash receipts for postage $44, supplies $38, and miscellaneous expenses $5. The entry, in general journal form, to record the check is:

A	=	L	+	SE
+38				−44
−87				−5

Mar. 15	Postage Expense	44	
	Supplies	38	
	Miscellaneous Expense	5	
	Cash		87
	(To replenish petty cash fund)		

Note that the Petty Cash account is not affected by the reimbursement entry. Replenishment changes the composition of the fund by replacing the petty cash receipts with cash, but it does not change the balance in the fund.

Occasionally, in replenishing a petty cash fund it may be necessary to recognize a cash shortage or overage. To illustrate, assume in the preceding example that the custodian had only $12 in cash in the fund plus the receipts as listed. The request for reimbursement would therefore be for $88, and the following entry would be made:

A	=	L	+	SE
+38				−44
−88				−5
				−1

Mar. 15	Postage Expense	44	
	Supplies	38	
	Miscellaneous Expense	5	
	Cash Over and Short	1	
	Cash		88
	(To replenish petty cash fund)		

Conversely, if the custodian had $14 in cash, the reimbursement request would be for $86, and Cash Over and Short would be credited for $1. A debit balance in Cash Over and Short is reported in the income statement as miscellaneous expense; a credit balance is reported as miscellaneous revenue. Cash Over and Short is closed to Income Summary at the end of the year.

A petty cash fund should be replenished **at the end of the accounting period, regardless of the cash in the fund**. Replenishment at this time is necessary in order to recognize the effects of the petty cash payments on the financial statements.

Internal control over a petty cash fund is strengthened by (1) having a supervisor make surprise counts of the fund to ascertain whether the paid vouchers and fund cash equal the designated amount and (2) canceling or mutilating the paid vouchers so they cannot be resubmitted for reimbursement.

SUMMARY OF STUDY OBJECTIVE FOR APPENDIX

9 ▶ Explain the operation of a petty cash fund. In operating a petty cash fund, a company establishes the fund by appointing a custodian and determining the size of the fund. Payments from the fund are made for documented expenditures, and the fund is replenished as needed. The fund is replenished at least at the end of each accounting period, and accounting entries to record payments are made at that time.

GLOSSARY

Bank statement A statement received monthly from the bank that shows the depositor's bank transactions and balances. (p. 310)

Cash Resources that consist of coins, currency, checks, money orders, and money on hand or on deposit in a bank or similar depository. (p. 307)

Cash budget A projection of anticipated cash flows, usually over a one- to two-year period. (p. 320)

Cash equivalents Highly liquid investments, with maturities of three months or less when purchased, that can be converted to a specific amount of cash. (p. 316)

Deposits in transit Deposits recorded by the depositor that have not been recorded by the bank. (p. 312)

Electronic funds transfer (EFT) A disbursement system that uses wire, telephone, telegraph, or computer to transfer cash from one location to another. (p. 309)

Free cash flow A measure that computes the amount of discretionary cash available by subtracting capital expenditures and cash dividends from net cash provided by operating activities. (p. 323)

Internal auditors Company employees who evaluate on a continuous basis the effectiveness of the company's system of internal control. (p. 304)

Internal control The plan of organization and all the related methods and measures adopted within a business to safeguard its assets and enhance the accuracy and reliability of its accounting records. (p. 300)

NSF check A check that is not paid by a bank because of insufficient funds in a customer's bank account. (p. 311)

Outstanding checks Checks issued and recorded by a company that have not been paid by the bank. (p. 313)

Petty cash fund A cash fund used to pay relatively small amounts. (p. 309)

Ratio of cash to daily cash expenses A measure that indicates the number of days of expenses available cash can cover. Calculated as cash and cash equivalents divided by average daily expenses. (p. 323)

Restricted cash Cash that is not available for general use, but instead is restricted for a particular purpose. (p. 317)

Treasurer Employee responsible for the management of a company's cash. (p. 318)

DEMONSTRATION PROBLEM

Trillo Company's bank statement for May 2001 shows these data:

Balance May 1	$12,650	Balance May 31	$14,280
Debit memorandum:		Credit memorandum:	
NSF check	175	Collection of note receivable	505

The cash balance per books at May 31 is $13,319. Your review of the data reveals the following:

1. The NSF check was from Hup Co., a customer.
2. The note collected by the bank was a $500, 3-month, 12% note. The bank charged a $10 collection fee. No interest has been accrued.
3. Outstanding checks at May 31 total $2,410.
4. Deposits in transit at May 31 total $1,752.
5. A Trillo Company check for $352 dated May 10 cleared the bank on May 25. This check, which was a payment on account, was journalized for $325.

Instructions

(a) Prepare a bank reconciliation at May 31.
(b) Journalize the entries required by the reconciliation.

Solution to Demonstration Problem

(a)

Cash balance per bank statement		$14,280
Add: Deposits in transit		1,752
		16,032
Less: Outstanding checks		2,410
Adjusted cash balance per bank		$13,622
Cash balance per books		$13,319
Add: Collection of note receivable $500,		
plus $15 interest less collection fee $10		505
		13,824
Less: NSF check	$175	
Error in recording check	27	202
Adjusted cash balance per books		$13,622

Problem-Solving Strategies

1. Follow the four steps used in reconciling items (pp. 312–313).
2. Work carefully to minimize mathematical errors in the reconciliation.
3. All entries are based on reconciling items per books.
4. Make sure the cash ledger balance after posting the reconciling entries agrees with the adjusted cash balance per books.

(b)

May	31	Cash	505	
		Miscellaneous Expense	10	
		Notes Receivable		500
		Interest Revenue		15
		(To record collection of note by bank)		
	31	Accounts Receivable—Hup Co.	175	
		Cash		175
		(To record NSF check from Hup Co.)		
	31	Accounts Payable	27	
		Cash		27
		(To correct error in recording check)		

Note: All Questions, Exercises, and Problems marked with an asterisk relate to material in the appendix to the chapter.

SELF-STUDY QUESTIONS

Answers are at the end of the chapter.

(SO 1) 1. Internal control is used in a business to enhance the accuracy and reliability of its accounting records and to:
(a) safeguard its assets.
(b) prevent fraud.
(c) produce correct financial statements.
(d) deter employee dishonesty.

(SO 1) 2. ⊙━━━━⊂ The principles of internal control do *not* include:
(a) establishment of responsibility.
(b) documentation procedures.
(c) management responsibility.
(d) independent internal verification.

(SO 1) 3. Physical controls do *not* include:
(a) safes and vaults to store cash.
(b) independent bank reconciliations.
(c) locked warehouses for inventories.
(d) bank safety deposit boxes for important papers.

(SO 2) 4. Permitting only designated personnel such as cashiers to handle cash receipts is an application of the principle of:
(a) segregation of duties.
(b) establishment of responsibility.
(c) independent internal verification.
(d) other controls.

(SO 3) 5. The use of prenumbered checks in disbursing cash is an application of the principle of:
(a) establishment of responsibility.
(b) segregation of duties.
(c) physical, mechanical, and electronic controls.
(d) documentation procedures.

(SO 3) 6. The control features of a bank account do *not* include:
(a) having bank auditors verify the correctness of the bank balance per books.
(b) minimizing the amount of cash that must be kept on hand.
(c) providing a double record of all bank transactions.
(d) safeguarding cash by using a bank as a depository.

7. In a bank reconciliation, deposits in transit are: (SO 4)
(a) deducted from the book balance.
(b) added to the book balance.
(c) added to the bank balance.
(d) deducted from the bank balance.

8. Which of the following items in a cash drawer (SO 5) at November 30 is *not* cash?
(a) Money orders.
(b) Coins and currency.
(c) A customer check dated December 1.
(d) A customer check dated November 28.

9. ⊙━━━━⊂ Which of the following is *not* one of (SO 6) the sections of a cash budget?
(a) Cash receipts section.
(b) Cash disbursements section.
(c) Financing section.
(d) Cash from operations section.

10. ⊙━━━━⊂ Which statement correctly describes (SO 5) the reporting of cash?
(a) Cash cannot be combined with cash equivalents.
(b) Restricted cash funds may be combined with Cash.
(c) Cash is listed first in the current assets section.
(d) Restricted cash funds cannot be reported as a current asset.

*11. A check is written to replenish a $100 petty cash (SO 9) fund when the fund contains receipts of $94 and $3 in cash. In recording the check:
(a) Cash Over and Short should be debited for $3.
(b) Petty Cash should be debited for $94.
(c) Cash should be credited for $94.
(d) Petty Cash should be credited for $3.

QUESTIONS

1. ⚒ "Internal control is concerned only with enhancing the accuracy of the accounting records." Do you agree? Explain.

2. What principles of internal control apply to most business enterprises?

3. In the corner grocery store, all sales clerks make change out of one cash register drawer. Is this a violation of internal control? Why?

4. J. Duma is reviewing the principle of segregation of duties. What are the two common applications of this principle?

5. How do documentation procedures contribute to good internal control?

6. What internal control objectives are met by physical, mechanical, and electronic controls?

7. (a) Explain the control principle of independent internal verification.
   (b) What practices are important in applying this principle?

8. As the company accountant, explain these ideas to the management of Cobo Company:
   (a) The concept of reasonable assurance in internal control.
   (b) The importance of the human factor in internal control.

9. Midwest Inc. owns these assets at the balance sheet date:

Cash in bank—savings account	$ 5,000
Cash on hand	850
Cash refund due from the IRS	1,000
Checking account balance	12,000
Postdated checks	500

   What amount should be reported as Cash in the balance sheet?

10. What principle(s) of internal control is (are) involved in making daily cash counts of over-the-counter receipts?

11. Dent Department Stores has just installed new electronic cash registers in its stores. How do cash registers improve internal control over cash receipts?

12. At Allen Wholesale Company two mail clerks open all mail receipts. How does this strengthen internal control?

13. "To have maximum effective internal control over cash disbursements, all payments should be made by check." Is this true? Explain.

14. Handy Company's internal controls over cash disbursements provide for the treasurer to sign checks imprinted by a checkwriter after comparing the check with the approved invoice. Identify the internal control principles that are present in these controls.

15. How do these principles apply to cash disbursements:
    (a) Physical, mechanical, and electronic controls?
    (b) Other controls?

16. What is the essential feature of an electronic funds transfer (EFT) procedure?

17. "The use of a bank contributes significantly to good internal control over cash." Is this true? Why?

18. Paul Pascal is confused about the lack of agreement between the cash balance per books and the balance per bank. Explain the causes for the lack of agreement to Paul, and give an example of each cause.

19. ⚒ Describe the basic principles of cash management.

20. Mary Mora asks your help concerning an NSF check. Explain to Mary (a) what an NSF check is, (b) how it is treated in a bank reconciliation, and (c) whether it will require an adjusting entry on the company's books.

21. ⚒
    (a) "Cash equivalents are the same as cash." Do you agree? Explain.
    (b) How should restricted cash funds be reported on the balance sheet?

22. ⚒ What measures may be computed to evaluate the adequacy of cash?

*23. (a) Identify the three activities that pertain to a petty cash fund, and indicate an internal control principle that is applicable to each activity.
    (b) When are journal entries required in the operation of a petty cash fund?

BRIEF EXERCISES

BE7-1 Gina Milan is the new owner of Liberty Parking. She has heard about internal control but is not clear about its importance for her business. Explain to Gina the two purposes of internal control, and give her one application of each purpose for Liberty Parking.

⚒ *Explain the importance of internal control.* (SO 1)

BE7-2 The internal control procedures in Marion Company make the following provisions. Identify the principles of internal control that are being followed in each case.
(a) Employees who have physical custody of assets do not have access to the accounting records.
(b) Each month the assets on hand are compared to the accounting records by an internal auditor.
(c) A prenumbered shipping document is prepared for each shipment of goods to customers.

Identify internal control principles. (SO 1)

Identify the internal control principles applicable to cash receipts.
(SO 2)

BE7-3   Tene Company has the following internal control procedures over cash receipts. Identify the internal control principle that is applicable to each procedure.
(a) All over-the-counter receipts are registered on cash registers.
(b) All cashiers are bonded.
(c) Daily cash counts are made by cashier department supervisors.
(d) The duties of receiving cash, recording cash, and having custody of cash are assigned to different individuals.
(e) Only cashiers may operate cash registers.

Identify the internal control principles applicable to cash disbursements.
(SO 3)

BE7-4   Hills Company has the following internal control procedures over cash disbursements. Identify the internal control principle that is applicable to each procedure.
(a) Company checks are prenumbered.
(b) The bank statement is reconciled monthly by an internal auditor.
(c) Blank checks are stored in a safe in the treasurer's office.
(d) Only the treasurer or assistant treasurer may sign checks.
(e) Check signers are not allowed to record cash disbursement transactions.

Identify the control features of a bank account. (SO 3)

BE7-5   T. J. Boad is uncertain about the control features of a bank account. Explain the control benefits of (a) a check and (b) a bank statement.

Indicate location of reconciling items in a bank reconciliation.
(SO 4)

BE7-6   The following reconciling items are applicable to the bank reconciliation for Ashley Co. Indicate how each item should be shown on a bank reconciliation.
(a) Outstanding checks.
(b) Bank debit memorandum for service charge.
(c) Bank credit memorandum for collecting a note for the depositor.
(d) Deposit in transit.

Identify reconciling items that require adjusting entries.
(SO 4)

BE7-7   Using the data in BE7-6, indicate (a) the items that will result in an adjustment to the depositor's records and (b) why the other items do not require adjustment.

Prepare partial bank reconciliation. (SO 4)

BE7-8   At July 31 Dana Company has this bank information: cash balance per bank $7,420; outstanding checks $762; deposits in transit $1,700; and a bank service charge $20. Determine the adjusted cash balance per bank at July 31.

Explain the statement presentation of cash balances.
(SO 5)

BE7-9   Tijuana Company has these cash balances: cash in bank $12,742; payroll bank account $6,000; and plant expansion fund cash $25,000. Explain how each balance should be reported on the balance sheet.

Prepare a cash budget.
(SO 6)

BE7-10   The following information is available for Marais Company for the month of January: expected cash receipts $60,000; expected cash disbursements $65,000; cash balance on January 1 $12,000. Management wishes to maintain a minimum cash balance of $10,000. Prepare a basic cash budget for the month of January.

Compute free cash flow.
(SO 8)

BE7-11   Kellogg Company's 1998 annual report disclosed the following financial information: net income $503 million; cash dividends $375 million; cash provided by operating activities $720 million; and capital expenditures $374 million. Compute Kellogg Company's free cash flow for 1998.

Compute cash to daily cash expenses ratio.
(SO 8)

BE7-12   Einstein/Noah Bagel Corp.'s 1998 annual report disclosed the following financial information (in thousands): total expenses $575,846; depreciation, depletion, and amortization $34,777; and cash and cash equivalents $3,766. Compute the company's cash to daily cash expenses ratio.

Prepare entry to replenish a petty cash fund.
(SO 9)

*BE7-13**   On March 20 Gimbal's petty cash fund of $100 is replenished when the fund contains $12 in cash and receipts for postage $52, supplies $26, and travel expense $10. Prepare the journal entry to record the replenishment of the petty cash fund.

EXERCISES

Identify the principles of internal control.
(SO 1)

E7-1   Galenti's Pizza operates strictly on a carryout basis. Customers pick up their orders at a counter where a clerk exchanges the pizza for cash. While at the counter, the customer can see other employees making the pizzas and the large ovens in which the pizzas are baked.

Instructions

Identify the six principles of internal control and give an example of each principle that you might observe when picking up your pizza. [*Note:* It may not be possible to observe all the principles.]

E7-2 The following control procedures are used in Seymor Company for over-the-counter cash receipts:

1. Cashiers are experienced; thus, they are not bonded.
2. All over-the-counter receipts are registered by three clerks who share a cash register with a single cash drawer.
3. To minimize the risk of robbery, cash in excess of $100 is stored in an unlocked attaché case in the stock room until it is deposited in the bank.
4. At the end of each day the total receipts are counted by the cashier on duty and reconciled to the cash register total.
5. The company accountant makes the bank deposit and then records the day's receipts.

List internal control weaknesses over cash receipts and suggest improvements.
(SO 1, 2)

Instructions

(a) For each procedure, explain the weakness in internal control and identify the control principle that is violated.
(b) For each weakness, suggest a change in procedure that will result in good internal control.

E7-3 The following control procedures are used in Hilga's Boutique Shoppe for cash disbursements:

1. Each week Hilga leaves 100 company checks in an unmarked envelope on a shelf behind the cash register.
2. The store manager personally approves all payments before signing and issuing checks.
3. The company checks are unnumbered.
4. After payment, bills are "filed" in a paid invoice folder.
5. The company accountant prepares the bank reconciliation and reports any discrepancies to the owner.

List internal control weaknesses for cash disbursements and suggest improvements.
(SO 1, 3)

Instructions

(a) For each procedure, explain the weakness in internal control and identify the internal control principle that is violated.
(b) For each weakness, suggest a change in the procedure that will result in good internal control.

E7-4 At Vermont Company checks are not prenumbered because both the purchasing agent and the treasurer are authorized to issue checks. Each signer has access to unissued checks kept in an unlocked file cabinet. The purchasing agent pays all bills pertaining to goods purchased for resale. Prior to payment, the purchasing agent determines that the goods have been received and verifies the mathematical accuracy of the vendor's invoice. After payment, the invoice is filed by vendor and the purchasing agent records the payment in the cash disbursements journal. The treasurer pays all other bills following approval by authorized employees. After payment, the treasurer stamps all bills "paid," files them by payment date, and records the checks in the cash disbursements journal. Vermont Company maintains one checking account that is reconciled by the treasurer.

Identify internal control weaknesses for cash disbursements and suggest improvements.
(SO 3)

Instructions

(a) List the weaknesses in internal control over cash disbursements.
(b) ▮▮▮▭⟩ Write a memo indicating your recommendations for improving company procedures.

E7-5 Alana Davis is unable to reconcile the bank balance at January 31. Alana's reconciliation is shown here:

Prepare bank reconciliation and adjusting entries.
(SO 4)

Cash balance per bank	$3,660.20
Add: NSF check	430.00
Less: Bank service charge	25.00
Adjusted balance per bank	$4,065.20
Cash balance per books	$3,975.20
Less: Deposits in transit	590.00
Add: Outstanding checks	730.00
Adjusted balance per books	$4,115.20

Instructions

(a) Prepare a correct bank reconciliation.

(b) Journalize the entries required by the reconciliation.

Determine outstanding checks.
(SO 4)

E7-6 At April 30 the bank reconciliation of Bossa Nova Company shows three outstanding checks: No. 254 $650, No. 255 $720, and No. 257 $410. The May bank statement and the May cash payments journal are given here:

Bank Statement Checks Paid		
Date	Check No.	Amount
5/4	254	$650
5/2	257	410
5/17	258	159
5/12	259	275
5/20	261	500
5/29	263	480
5/30	262	750

Cash Payments Journal Checks Issued		
Date	Check No.	Amount
5/2	258	$159
5/5	259	275
5/10	260	925
5/15	261	500
5/22	262	750
5/24	263	480
5/29	264	360

Instructions

Using step 2 in the reconciliation procedure (see page 313), list the outstanding checks at May 31.

Prepare bank reconciliation and adjusting entries.
(SO 4)

E7-7 The following information pertains to Cody Camera Company:

1. Cash balance per bank, July 31, $7,263.
2. July bank service charge not recorded by the depositor $15.
3. Cash balance per books, July 31, $7,190.
4. Deposits in transit, July 31, $1,700.
5. Note for $1,000 collected for Cody in July by the bank, plus interest $36 less fee $20. The collection has not been recorded by Cody, and no interest has been accrued.
6. Outstanding checks, July 31, $772.

Instructions

(a) Prepare a bank reconciliation at July 31.

(b) Journalize the adjusting entries at July 31 on the books of Cody Camera Company.

Prepare bank reconciliation and adjusting entries.
(SO 4)

E7-8 This information relates to the Cash account in the ledger of Mawmeg Company:

Balance September 1—$17,150; Cash deposited—$64,000
Balance September 30—$17,404; Checks written—$63,746

The September bank statement shows a balance of $16,422 at September 30 and the following memoranda:

Credits		Debits	
Collection of $1,800 note plus interest $30	$1,830	NSF check: J. Hower	$410
Interest earned on checking account	45	Safety deposit box rent	30

At September 30 deposits in transit were $4,800 and outstanding checks totaled $2,383.

Instructions

(a) Prepare the bank reconciliation at September 30.

(b) Prepare the adjusting entries at September 30, assuming (1) the NSF check was from a customer on account, and (2) no interest had been accrued on the note.

Compute deposits in transit and outstanding checks for two bank reconciliations.
(SO 4)

E7-9 The cash records of Blue Diamond Company show the following:

1. The June 30 bank reconciliation indicated that deposits in transit total $750. During July the general ledger account Cash shows deposits of $15,750, but the bank statement indicates that only $15,600 in deposits were received during the month.
2. The June 30 bank reconciliation also reported outstanding checks of $920. During the month of July, Blue Diamond Company books show that $17,200 of checks were issued, yet the bank statement showed that $16,400 of checks cleared the bank in July.

3. In September deposits per bank statement totaled $26,700, deposits per books were $25,400, and deposits in transit at September 30 were $2,400.
4. In September cash disbursements per books were $23,700, checks clearing the bank were $24,000, and outstanding checks at September 30 were $2,100.

There were no bank debit or credit memoranda, and no errors were made by either the bank or Blue Diamond Company.

Instructions

Answer these questions:
(a) In situation 1, what were the deposits in transit at July 31?
(b) In situation 2, what were the outstanding checks at July 31?
(c) In situation 3, what were the deposits in transit at August 31?
(d) In situation 4, what were the outstanding checks at August 31?

E7-10 Hanover Company expects to have a cash balance of $46,000 on January 1, 2001. These are the relevant monthly budget data for the first 2 months of 2001:
1. Collections from customers: January $70,000; February $155,000.
2. Payments to suppliers: January $40,000; February $75,000.
3. Direct labor: January $30,000; February $40,000. Wages are paid in the month they are incurred.
4. Manufacturing overhead: January $21,000; February $30,000. These costs include depreciation of $1,000 per month. All other overhead costs are paid as incurred.
5. Selling and administrative expenses: January $14,000; February $18,000. These costs are exclusive of depreciation. They are paid as incurred.
6. Sales of marketable securities in January are expected to realize $7,000 in cash. Hanover Company has a line of credit at a local bank that enables it to borrow up to $25,000. The company wants to maintain a minimum monthly cash balance of $20,000.

Prepare cash budget for two months.
(SO 7)

Instructions

Prepare a cash budget for January and February.

E7-11 Texas Instruments Inc. reported the following financial data in its 1998 annual report: net income $407 million; cash and cash equivalents $540 million; total expenses (not including depreciation) $6,909 million; net cash provided by operating activities $1,251 million; dividends paid, $133 million; and capital expenditures $1,031 million. Compute and comment on the following two measures of cash adequacy: (1) cash to daily cash expenses ratio and (2) free cash flow.

Compute and comment on cash to daily cash expenses ratio and free cash flow.
(SO 8)

*****E7-12** During October, Kadloc Company experiences the following transactions in establishing a petty cash fund.

Prepare journal entries for a petty cash fund.
(SO 9)

Oct. 1 An imprest fund is established with a check for $100 issued to the petty cash custodian.

   31 A count of the petty cash fund disclosed the following items:

Currency	$6.00
Coins	.40
Expenditure receipts (vouchers):	
Office supplies	$28.10
Telephone and FAX	16.40
Postage	41.30
Freight-out	6.80

   31 A check was written to reimburse the fund and increase the fund to $200.

Instructions

Journalize the entries in October that pertain to the petty cash fund.

*****E7-13** ABM Company maintains a petty cash fund for small expenditures. These transactions occurred during the month of August.

Journalize and post petty cash fund transactions.
(SO 9)

Aug. 1 Established the petty cash fund by writing a check on Metro Bank for $200.

   15 Replenished the petty cash fund by writing a check for $188.00. On this date, the fund consisted of $12.00 in cash and these petty cash receipts: freight-out $74.40, entertainment expense $43.00, postage expense $33.00, and miscellaneous expense $38.00.

16 Increased the amount of the petty cash fund to $400 by writing a check for $200.

31 Replenished the petty cash fund by writing a check for $283.00. On this date, the fund consisted of $117 in cash and these petty cash receipts: postage expense $145.00, entertainment expense $90.60, and freight-out $45.40.

Instructions

(a) Journalize the petty cash transactions.

(b) Post to the Petty Cash account.

(c) What internal control features exist in a petty cash fund?

PROBLEMS: SET A

Identify internal control weaknesses over cash receipts.
(SO 1, 2)

P7-1A   Burlington Theater is in the Burlington Mall. A cashier's booth is located near the entrance to the theater. Two cashiers are employed. One works from 1:00 to 5:00 P.M., the other from 5:00 to 9:00 P.M. Each cashier is bonded. The cashiers receive cash from customers and operate a machine that ejects serially numbered tickets. The rolls of tickets are inserted and locked into the machine by the theater manager at the beginning of each cashier's shift.

After purchasing a ticket, the customer takes the ticket to a doorperson stationed at the entrance of the theater lobby some 60 feet from the cashier's booth. The doorperson tears the ticket in half, admits the customer, and returns the ticket stub to the customer. The other half of the ticket is dropped into a locked box by the doorperson.

At the end of each cashier's shift, the theater manager removes the ticket rolls from the machine and makes a cash count. The cash count sheet is initialed by the cashier. At the end of the day, the manager deposits the receipts in total in a bank night deposit vault located in the mall. In addition, the manager sends copies of the deposit slip and the initialed cash count sheets to the theater company treasurer for verification and to the company's accounting department. Receipts from the first shift are stored in a safe located in the manager's office.

Instructions

(a) Identify the internal control principles and their application to the cash receipts transactions of Burlington Theater.

(b) If the doorperson and cashier decided to collaborate to misappropriate cash, what actions might they take?

Identify internal control weaknesses in cash receipts and cash disbursements.
(SO 1, 2, 3)

P7-2A   Cedar Grove Middle School wants to raise money for a new sound system for its auditorium. The primary fund-raising event is a dance at which the famous disc jockey Obnoxious Al will play classic and not-so-classic dance tunes. Roger DeMaster, the music and theater instructor, has been given the responsibility for coordinating the fund-raising efforts. This is Roger's first experience with fund-raising. He decides to put the eighth-grade choir in charge of the event; he will be a relatively passive observer.

Roger had 500 unnumbered tickets printed for the dance. He left the tickets in a box on his desk and told the choir students to take as many tickets as they thought they could sell for $5 each. In order to ensure that no extra tickets would be floating around, he told them to dispose of any unsold tickets. When the students received payment for the tickets, they were to bring the cash back to Roger, and he would put it in a locked box in this desk drawer.

Some of the students were responsible for decorating the gymnasium for the dance. Roger gave each of them a key to the money box and told them that if they took money out to purchase materials, they should put a note in the box saying how much they took and what it was used for. After two weeks the money box appeared to be getting full, so Roger asked Steve Stevens to count the money, prepare a deposit slip, and deposit the money in a bank account Roger had opened.

The day of the dance, Roger wrote a check from the account to pay Obnoxious Al. The DJ said, however, that he accepted only cash and did not give receipts. So Roger took $200 out of the cash box and gave it to Al. At the dance Roger had Sara Billings working at the entrance to the gymnasium, collecting tickets from students and selling tickets to those who had not pre-purchased them. Roger estimated that 400 students attended the dance.

The following day Roger closed out the bank account, which had $250 in it, and gave that amount plus the $180 in the cash box to Principal Skinner. Principal Skinner seemed surprised that, after generating roughly $2,000 in sales, the dance netted only $430 in cash. Roger did not know how to respond.

Instructions
Identify as many internal control weaknesses as you can in this scenario, and suggest how each could be addressed.

P7-3A On July 31, 2001, Grace Company had a cash balance per books of $6,815.30. The statement from Tri-County Bank on that date showed a balance of $7,695.80. A comparison of the bank statement with the cash account revealed the following facts:

Prepare bank reconciliation and adjusting entries.
(SO 4)

1. The bank service charge for July was $25.
2. The bank collected a note receivable of $1,800 for Grace Company on July 15, plus $68 of interest. The bank made a $10 charge for the collection. Grace has not accrued any interest on the note.
3. The July 31 receipts of $1,819.60 were not included in the bank deposits for July. These receipts were deposited by the company in a night deposit vault on July 31.
4. Company check No. 2480 issued to J. Brokaw, a creditor, for $492 that cleared the bank in July was incorrectly entered in the cash payments journal on July 10 for $429.
5. Checks outstanding on July 31 totaled $1,480.10.
6. On July 31 the bank statement showed an NSF charge of $550 for a check received by the company from R. Close, a customer, on account.

Instructions
(a) Prepare the bank reconciliation as of July 31.
(b) Prepare the necessary adjusting entries at July 31.

P7-4A The bank portion of the bank reconciliation for Zurich Company at October 31, 2001, is shown here:

Prepare bank reconciliation and adjusting entries from detailed data.
(SO 4)

ZURICH COMPANY
Bank Reconciliation
October 31, 2001

Cash balance per bank		$12,367.90
Add: Deposits in transit		1,530.20
		13,898.10
Less: Outstanding checks		

Check Number	Check Amount	
2451	$1,260.40	
2470	720.10	
2471	844.50	
2472	426.80	
2474	1,050.00	4,301.80

Adjusted cash balance per bank	$ 9,596.30

The adjusted cash balance per bank agreed with the cash balance per books at October 31. The November bank statement showed the following checks and deposits:

Bank Statement

	Checks			Deposits	
Date	Number	Amount	Date		Amount
11-1	2470	$ 720.10	11-1		$ 1,530.20
11-2	2471	844.50	11-4		1,211.60
11-5	2474	1,050.00	11-8		990.10
11-4	2475	1,640.70	11-13		2,575.00
11-8	2476	2,830.00	11-18		1,472.70
11-10	2477	600.00	11-21		2,945.00
11-15	2479	1,750.00	11-25		2,567.30
11-18	2480	1,330.00	11-28		1,650.00
11-27	2481	695.40	11-30		1,186.00
11-30	2483	575.50	Total		$16,127.90
11-29	2486	900.00			
	Total	$12,936.20			

The cash records per books for November showed the following:

Cash Payments Journal

Date	Number	Amount	Date	Number	Amount
11-1	2475	$1,640.70	11-20	2483	$ 575.50
11-2	2476	2,830.00	11-22	2484	829.50
11-2	2477	600.00	11-23	2485	974.80
11-4	2478	538.20	11-24	2486	900.00
11-8	2479	1,570.00	11-29	2487	398.00
11-10	2480	1,330.00	11-30	2488	800.00
11-15	2481	695.40	Total		$14,294.10
11-18	2482	612.00			

Cash Receipts Journal

Date	Amount
11-3	$ 1,211.60
11-7	990.10
11-12	2,575.00
11-17	1,472.70
11-20	2,954.00
11-24	2,567.30
11-27	1,650.00
11-29	1,186.00
11-30	1,225.00
Total	$15,831.70

The bank statement contained two bank memoranda:
1. A credit of $1,905.00 for the collection of an $1,800 note for Zurich Company plus interest of $120 and less a collection fee of $15. Zurich Company has not accrued any interest on the note.
2. A debit for the printing of additional company checks $70.00.

At November 30 the cash balance per books was $11,133.90 and the cash balance per bank statement was $17,394.60. The bank did not make any errors, but two errors were made by Zurich Company.

Instructions
(a) Using the four steps in the reconciliation procedure described on pages 312–313, prepare a bank reconciliation at November 30.
(b) Prepare the adjusting entries based on the reconciliation. [*Note:* The correction of any errors pertaining to recording checks should be made to Accounts Payable. The correction of any errors relating to recording cash receipts should be made to Accounts Receivable.]

Prepare a bank reconciliation and adjusting entries.
(SO 4)

P7-5A Agricultural Genetics Company of Emporia, Kansas, spreads herbicides and applies liquid fertilizer for local farmers. On May 31, 2001, the company's cash account per its general ledger showed a balance of $6,781.50.

The bank statement from Emporia State Bank on that date showed the following balance:

EMPORIA STATE BANK

Checks and Debits	Deposits and Credits	Daily Balance
XXX	XXX	5-31 6,804.60

A comparison of the details on the bank statement with the details in the cash account revealed the following facts:

1. The statement included a debit memo of $40 for the printing of additional company checks.
2. Cash sales of $836.15 on May 12 were deposited in the bank. The cash receipts journal entry and the deposit slip were incorrectly made for $846.15. The bank credited Agricultural Genetics Company for the correct amount.
3. Outstanding checks at May 31 totaled $276.25, and deposits in transit were $936.15.
4. On May 18, the company issued check No. 1181 for $685 to L. Kingston, on account. The check, which cleared the bank in May, was incorrectly journalized and posted by Agricultural Genetics Company for $658.
5. A $2,000 note receivable was collected by the bank for Agricultural Genetics Company on May 31 plus $80 interest. The bank charged a collection fee of $20. No interest has been accrued on the note.
6. Included with the cancelled checks was a check issued by Teller Company to P. Jonet for $600 that was incorrectly charged to Agricultural Genetics Company by the bank.
7. On May 31, the bank statement showed an NSF charge of $700 for a check issued by Pete Dell, a customer, to Agricultural Genetics Company on account.

Instructions
(a) Prepare the bank reconciliation at May 31, 2001.
(b) Prepare the necessary adjusting entries for Agricultural Genetics Company at May 31, 2001.

P7-6A Pokemon Company prepares monthly cash budgets. Here are relevant data from operating budgets for 2001:

Prepare cash budget for two months.
(SO 7)

	January	February
Sales	$380,000	$420,000
Direct materials purchases	100,000	110,000
Direct labor	80,000	95,000
Manufacturing overhead	60,000	75,000
Selling and administrative expenses	75,000	85,000

All sales are on account. Collections are expected to be 50% in the month of sale, 30% in the first month following the sale, and 20% in the second month following the sale. Forty percent (40%) of direct materials purchases are paid in cash in the month of purchase, and the balance due is paid in the month following the purchase. All other items above are paid in the month incurred. Depreciation has been excluded from manufacturing overhead and selling and administrative expenses.

Other data are listed here:
1. Credit sales—November 2000, $200,000; December 2000, $280,000.
2. Purchases of direct materials—December 2000, $90,000.
3. Other receipts—January: collection of December 31, 2000, interest receivable $3,000; February: proceeds from sale of securities $5,000.
4. Other disbursements—February: payment of $30,000 for land.
The company's cash balance on January 1, 2001, is expected to be $60,000. The company wants to maintain a minimum cash balance of $55,000.

Instructions
(a) Prepare schedules for (1) expected collections from customers and (2) expected payments for direct materials purchases.
(b) Prepare a cash budget for January and February.

P7-7A Wizards and Dragons Company is a very profitable small business. It has not, however, given much consideration to internal control. For example, in an attempt to keep clerical and office expenses to a minimum, the company has combined the jobs of

Prepare comprehensive bank reconciliation with internal control deficiencies.
(SO 1, 2, 3, 4)

cashier and bookkeeper. As a result, Rob Rowe handles all cash receipts, keeps the accounting records, and prepares the monthly bank reconciliations.

The balance per the bank statement on October 31, 2001, was $18,380. Outstanding checks were: No. 62 for $126.75, No. 183 for $150, No. 284 for $253.25, No. 862 for $190.71, No. 863 for $226.80, and No. 864 for $165.28. Included with the statement was a credit memorandum of $200 indicating the collection of a note receivable for Wizards and Dragons Company by the bank on October 25. This memorandum has not been recorded by Wizards and Dragons Company.

The company's ledger showed one cash account with a balance of $21,892.72. The balance included undeposited cash on hand. Because of the lack of internal controls, Rowe took for personal use all of the undeposited receipts in excess of $3,795.51. He then prepared the following bank reconciliation in an effort to conceal his theft of cash:

Cash balance per books, October 31		$21,892.72
Add: Outstanding checks		
No. 862	$190.71	
No. 863	226.80	
No. 864	165.28	482.79
		22,375.51
Less: Undeposited receipts		3,795.51
Unadjusted balance per bank, October 31		18,580.00
Less: Bank credit memorandum		200.00
Cash balance per bank statement, October 31		$18,380.00

Instructions
(a) Prepare a correct bank reconciliation. [*Hint:* Deduct the amount of the theft from the adjusted balance per books.]
(b) Indicate the three ways that Rowe attempted to conceal the theft and the dollar amount involved in each method.
(c) What principles of internal control were violated in this case?

PROBLEMS: SET B

Identify internal control principles over cash disbursements.
(SO 1, 3)

P7-1B Rabbit Ears Pet Food Company recently changed its system of internal control over cash disbursements. The system includes the following features:

Instead of being unnumbered and manually prepared, all checks must now be prenumbered and written by using the new checkwriter purchased by the company. Before a check can be issued, each invoice must have the approval of Cindy Morris, the purchasing agent, and Ray Mills, the receiving department supervisor. Checks must be signed by either Frank Malone, the treasurer, or Mary Arno, the assistant treasurer. Before signing a check, the signer is expected to compare the amounts of the check with the amounts on the invoice.

After signing a check, the signer stamps the invoice "paid" and inserts within the stamp, the date, check number, and amount of the check. The "paid" invoice is then sent to the accounting department for recording.

Blank checks are stored in a safe in the treasurer's office. The combination to the safe is known by only the treasurer and assistant treasurer. Each month the bank statement is reconciled with the bank balance per books by the assistant chief accountant.

Instructions
Identify the internal control principles and their application to cash disbursements of Rabbit Ears Pet Food Company.

Identify internal control weaknesses in cash receipts.
(SO 1, 2)

P7-2B The board of trustees of a local church is concerned about the internal accounting controls pertaining to the offering collections made at weekly services. They ask you to serve on a three-person audit team with the internal auditor of the university and a CPA who had just joined the church. At a meeting of the audit team and the board of trustees you learn the following:

1. The church's board of trustees has delegated responsibility for the financial management and audit of the financial records to the finance committee. This group prepares the annual budget and approves major disbursements but is not involved in collections or recordkeeping. No audit has been made in recent years because the same trusted employee has kept church records and served as financial secretary for 15 years. The church does not carry any fidelity insurance.
2. The collection at the weekly service is taken by a team of ushers who volunteer to serve for 1 month. The ushers take the collection plates to a basement office at the rear of the church. They hand their plates to the head usher and return to the church service. After all plates have been turned in, the head usher counts the cash received. The head usher then places the cash in the church safe along with a notation of the amount counted. The head usher volunteers to serve for 3 months.
3. The next morning the financial secretary opens the safe and recounts the collection. The secretary withholds $150–$200 in cash, depending on the cash expenditures expected for the week, and deposits the remainder of the collections in the bank. To facilitate the deposit, church members who contribute by check are asked to make their checks payable to "Cash."
4. Each month the financial secretary reconciles the bank statement and submits a copy of the reconciliation to the board of trustees. The reconciliations have rarely contained any bank errors and have never shown any errors per books.

Instructions
(a) Indicate the weaknesses in internal accounting control in the handling of collections.
(b) List the improvements in internal control procedures that you plan to make at the next meeting of the audit team for (1) the ushers, (2) the head usher, (3) the financial secretary, and (4) the finance committee.
(c) What church policies should be changed to improve internal control?

P7-3B On May 31, 2001, Interactive Company had a cash balance per books of $5,681.50. The bank statement from Community Bank on that date showed a balance of $7,784.60. A comparison of the statement with the cash account revealed the following facts:

Prepare bank reconciliation and adjusting entries.
(SO 4)

1. The statement included a debit memo of $60 for the printing of additional company checks.
2. Cash sales of $836.15 on May 12 were deposited in the bank. The cash receipts journal entry and the deposit slip were incorrectly made for $846.15. The bank credited Interactive Company for the correct amount.
3. Outstanding checks at May 31 totaled $1,276.25, and deposits in transit were $836.15.
4. On May 18 the company issued check No. 1181 for $685 to M. Helms, on account. The check, which cleared the bank in May, was incorrectly journalized and posted by Interactive Company for $658.
5. A $3,000 note receivable was collected by the bank for Interactive Company on May 31 plus $80 interest. The bank charged a collection fee of $20. No interest has been accrued on the note.
6. Included with the cancelled checks was a check issued by Teller Company to P. Jonet for $600 that was incorrectly charged to Interactive Company by the bank.
7. On May 31 the bank statement showed an NSF charge of $700 for a check issued by W. Hoad, a customer, to Interactive Company on account.

Instructions
(a) Prepare the bank reconciliation as of May 31, 2001.
(b) Prepare the necessary adjusting entries at May 31, 2001.

P7-4B The bank portion of the bank reconciliation for Kona Company at November 30, 2001, is shown here:

Prepare bank reconciliation and adjusting entries from detailed data.
(SO 4)

KONA COMPANY
Bank Reconciliation
November 30, 2001

Cash balance per bank	$14,367.90
Add: Deposits in transit	2,530.20
	16,898.10

Less: Outstanding checks

Check Number	Check Amount	
3451	$2,260.40	
3470	720.10	
3471	844.50	
3472	1,426.80	
3474	1,050.00	6,301.80
Adjusted cash balance per bank		$10,596.30

The adjusted cash balance per bank agreed with the cash balance per books at November 30. The December bank statement showed the following checks and deposits:

Bank Statement

	Checks			Deposits	
Date	Number	Amount	Date	Amount	
12-1	3451	$ 2,260.40	12-1	$ 2,530.20	
12-2	3471	844.50	12-4	1,211.60	
12-7	3472	1,426.80	12-8	2,365.10	
12-4	3475	1,640.70	12-16	2,672.70	
12-8	3476	1,300.00	12-21	2,945.00	
12-10	3477	2,130.00	12-26	2,567.30	
12-15	3479	3,080.00	12-29	2,836.00	
12-27	3480	600.00	12-30	1,025.00	
12-30	3482	475.50	Total	$18,152.90	
12-29	3483	1,140.00			
12-31	3485	540.80			
	Total	$15,438.70			

The cash records per books for December showed the following:

Cash Payments Journal

Date	Number	Amount	Date	Number	Amount
12-1	3475	$1,640.70	12-20	3482	$ 475.50
12-2	3476	1,300.00	12-22	3483	1,140.00
12-2	3477	2,130.00	12-23	3484	832.00
12-4	3478	538.20	12-24	3485	450.80
12-8	3479	3,080.00	12-30	3486	1,389.50
12-10	3480	600.00	Total		$14,384.10
12-17	3481	807.40			

Cash Receipts Journal

Date	Amount
12-3	$ 1,211.60
12-7	2,365.10
12-15	2,672.70
12-20	2,954.00
12-25	2,567.30
12-28	2,836.00
12-30	1,025.00
12-31	1,190.40
Total	$16,822.10

The bank statement contained two memoranda:

1. A credit of $3,145 for the collection of a $3,000 note for Kona Company plus interest of $160 and less a collection fee of $15.00. Kona Company has not accrued any interest on the note.
2. A debit of $647.10 for an NSF check written by A. Jordan, a customer. At December 31 the check had not been redeposited in the bank.

At December 31 the cash balance per books was $13,034.30, and the cash balance per bank statement was $19,580.00. The bank did not make any errors, but two errors were made by Kona Company.

Instructions

(a) Using the four steps in the reconciliation procedure described on pages 312–313, prepare a bank reconciliation at December 31.
(b) Prepare the adjusting entries based on the reconciliation. [*Note:* The correction of any errors pertaining to recording checks should be made to Accounts Payable. The correction of any errors relating to recording cash receipts should be made to Accounts Receivable.]

P7-5B Ag-Tech Company of Peoria, Illinois, provides liquid fertilizer and herbicides to regional farmers. On July 31, 2001, the company's cash account per its general ledger showed a balance of $5,815.30.

Prepare a bank reconciliation and adjusting entries. (SO 4)

The bank statement from Castle National Bank on that date showed the following balance:

CASTLE NATIONAL BANK

Checks and Debits	Deposits and Credits	Daily Balance
XXX	XXX	7-31 7,075.80

A comparison of the details on the bank statement with the details in the cash account revealed the following facts:

1. The bank service charge for July was $25.
2. The bank collected a note receivable of $1,200 for Ag-Tech Company on July 15, plus $48 of interest. The bank made a $10 charge for the collection. Ag-Tech has not accrued any interest on the note.
3. The July 31 receipts of $1,819.60 were not included in the bank deposits for July. These receipts were deposited by the company in a night deposit vault on July 31.
4. Company check No. 2480 issued to G. Shumway, a creditor, for $492 that cleared the bank in July was incorrectly entered in the cash payments journal on July 10 for $429.
5. Checks outstanding on July 31 totaled $2,480.10.
6. On July 31, the bank statement showed an NSF charge of $550 for a check received by the company from B.N. Dette, a customer, on account.

Instructions

(a) Prepare the bank reconciliation as of July 31, 2001.
(b) Prepare the necessary adjusting entries at July 31, 2001.

P7-6B Hawkeye Company prepares monthly cash budgets. Here are relevant data from operating budgets for 2001:

Prepare cash budget for two months. (SO 7)

	January	February
Sales	$370,000	$420,000
Direct materials purchases	120,000	130,000
Direct labor	80,000	95,000
Manufacturing overhead	70,000	75,000
Selling and administrative expenses	79,000	86,000

All sales are on account. Collections are expected to be 50% in the month of sale, 40% in the first month following the sale, and 10% in the second month following the sale. Fifty percent (50%) of direct materials purchases are paid in cash in the month of purchase, and the balance due is paid in the month following the purchase. All other items above are paid in the month incurred except for selling and administrative expenses that include $1,000 of depreciation per month.

Other data are listed here:
1. Credit sales—November 2000, $260,000; December 2000, $300,000.
2. Purchases of direct materials—December 2000, $100,000.
3. Other receipts—January: collection of December 31, 2000, notes receivable $10,000; February: proceeds from sale of securities $6,000.
4. Other disbursements—February: $8,000 cash dividend.
The company's cash balance on January 1, 2001, is expected to be $60,000. Hawkeye wants to maintain a minimum cash balance of $60,000.

Instructions
(a) Prepare schedules for (1) expected collections from customers and (2) expected payments for direct materials purchases.
(b) Prepare a cash budget for January and February.

Prepare comprehensive bank reconciliation with theft and internal control deficiencies.
(SO 1, 2, 3, 4)

P7-7B Giant Company is a very profitable small business. It has not, however, given much consideration to internal control. For example, in an attempt to keep clerical and office expenses to a minimum, the company has combined the jobs of cashier and bookkeeper. As a result, K. Kilgora handles all cash receipts, keeps the accounting records, and prepares the monthly bank reconciliations.

The balance per the bank statement on October 31, 2001, was $13,230. Outstanding checks were: No. 62 for $126.75, No. 183 for $150, No. 284 for $253.25, No. 862 for $190.71, No. 863 for $226.80, and No. 864 for $165.28. Included with the statement was a credit memorandum of $950 indicating the collection of a note receivable for Giant Company by the bank on October 25. This memorandum has not been recorded by Giant Company.

The company's ledger showed one cash account with a balance of $16,392.72. The balance included undeposited cash on hand. Because of the lack of internal controls, Kilgora took for personal use all of the undeposited receipts in excess of $2,695.51. He then prepared the following bank reconciliation in an effort to conceal his theft of cash.

Cash balance per books, October 31		$16,392.72
Add: Outstanding checks		
No. 862	$190.71	
No. 863	226.80	
No. 864	165.28	482.79
		16,875.51
Less: Undeposited receipts		2,695.51
Unadjusted balance per bank, October 31		14,180.00
Less: Bank credit memorandum		950.00
Cash balance per bank statement, October 31		$13,230.00

Instructions
(a) Prepare a correct bank reconciliation. (*Hint:* Deduct the amount of the theft from the adjusted balance per books.)
(b) Indicate the three ways that Kilgora attempted to conceal the theft and the dollar amount pertaining to each method.
(c) What principles of internal control were violated in this case?

FINANCIAL REPORTING AND ANALYSIS

FINANCIAL REPORTING PROBLEM: *Tootsie Roll Industries, Inc.*

BYP7-1 The financial statements of **Tootsie Roll** are presented in Appendix A of this book, together with an auditor's report—Report of Independent Auditors.

Instructions

Using the financial statements and reports, answer these questions about Tootsie Roll's internal controls and cash:

(a) What comments, if any, are made about cash in the report of the independent auditors?

(b) What data about cash and cash equivalents are shown in the consolidated balance sheet (statement of financial condition)?

(c) What activities are identified in the consolidated statement of cash flows as being responsible for the changes in cash during 1998?

(d) How are cash equivalents defined in the Notes to Consolidated Financial Statements?

COMPARATIVE ANALYSIS PROBLEM: *Tootsie Roll vs. Hershey Foods*

BYP7-2 The financial statements of **Hershey Foods** are presented in Appendix B, following the financial statements for **Tootsie Roll** in Appendix A.

Instructions

Answer the following questions for each company:

(a) What is the balance in cash and cash equivalents at December 31, 1998?

(b) How much cash was provided by operating activities during 1998?

(c) Calculate the ratio of cash to daily cash expenses.

(d) Calculate free cash flow.

(e) What conclusions regarding the ability to generate cash and the companies' cash management can be made from the comparison of these results?

RESEARCH CASE

BYP7-3 The September 20, 1999, issue of *Business Week* includes an article entitled "Dirty Money Goes Digital," by G. Silverman et al.

Instructions

Read the article and answer the following questions:

(a) What is money laundering?

(b) What are the money laundering steps illustrated in the article for the Moscow gangster?

(c) How has technology changed the practice of money laundering?

(d) What possible ways could the pace of money laundering be slowed? What potential dilemmas do these solutions present?

INTERPRETING FINANCIAL STATEMENTS

BYP7-4 **Microsoft** is the leading developer of software in the world. To continue to be successful Microsoft must generate new products, and generating new products requires significant amounts of cash. Shown on the following page is the current assets section of Microsoft's June 30, 1998, balance sheet (in millions) and excerpts from a footnote describing the first item listed in the balance sheet, "Cash, cash equivalent, and short-term investments." Following the Microsoft data is the current assets section for **Oracle** (in millions), another major software developer.

Microsoft

MICROSOFT, INC. Balance Sheets (partial) As of June 30		
	1997	1998
Current assets		
Cash, cash equivalents, and short-term		
investments	$ 8,966	$13,927
Accounts receivable	980	1,460
Other	427	502
Total current assets	$10,373	$15,889
Total current liabilities	$ 3,610	$ 5,730

ORACLE

ORACLE Balance Sheets (partial) As of May 31		
	1997	1998
Current assets		
Cash and cash equivalents	$ 890	$1,274
Short-term investments	323	646
Receivables	1,540	1,857
Other current assets	518	546
Total current assets	$3,271	$4,323
Current liabilities	$1,922	$2,484

Instructions
(a) What is the definition of a cash equivalent? Give some examples of cash equivalents. How do cash equivalents differ from other types of short-term investments?
(b) Comment on Microsoft's presentation of cash in its balance sheet.
(c) What problems might this presentation of cash pose for a user of Microsoft's financial statements?
(d) Calculate (1) the current ratio and (2) working capital for each company for 1998 and discuss your results.
(e) Is it possible to have too many liquid assets?

A GLOBAL FOCUS

BYP7-5   The international accounting firm **KPMG** recently performed a global survey on fraud. The following exercise reviews that survey.

Address: http://www.kpmg.com (or go to www.wiley.com/college/kimmel)

Steps: 1. At the KPMG site, choose **Virtual Library**.
2. Choose **Search Page**.
3. Type **"fraud survey."**

4. Choose the **"International May 1996 Fraud Survey."**

5. Choose **Full Text** to download the survey. (Your computer will need to be equipped with Adobe Acrobat Reader. Directions for downloading are provided.)

Instructions

Answer the following questions:

(a) Overall, what percentage of respondents stated that they felt that fraud was a major problem for their business? What percentage of South African respondents said that fraud was a problem for their business? What percentage of French respondents said that fraud was *not* a problem for their business?

(b) Overall, what percentage of frauds that were detected were detected by internal control?

(c) In which industries was fraud most likely to occur?

(d) When asked about "red flags" that might have forewarned the company of the fraud, 57% said that there were no early warning signs. What explanation does the study give for why so many companies said there were no early warning signals?

FINANCIAL ANALYSIS ON THE WEB

BYP7-6   The **Financial Accounting Standards Board** (FASB) is a private organization established to improve accounting standards and financial reporting. The FASB conducts extensive research before issuing a "Statement of Financial Accounting Standards," which represents an authoritative expression of generally accepted accounting principles.

Address: http://www.rutgers.edu/accounting/raw (or go to www.wiley.com/college/kimmel)

Steps: 1. Choose FASB.
2. Choose FASB Facts.

Instructions

Answer the following questions:

(a) What is the mission of the FASB?

(b) How are topics added to the FASB technical agenda?

(c) What characteristics make the FASB's procedures an "open" decision-making process?

BYP7-7   All organizations should have systems of internal control. Universities are no exception. This site discusses the basics of internal control in a university setting.

Address: http://www.bc.edu/bc_org/fvp/ia/ic/intro.html (or go to www.wiley.com/college/kimmel)

Steps: Go to the site shown above.

Instructions

The opening page of this site provides links to pages that answer six critical questions. Use these links to answer the following questions:

(a) In a university setting who has responsibility for evaluating the adequacy of the system of internal control?

(b) What do reconciliations ensure in the university setting? Who should review the reconciliation?

(c) What are some examples of physical controls?

(d) What are two ways to accomplish inventory counts?

CRITICAL THINKING

GROUP DECISION CASE

BYP7-8   Alternative Distributor Corp., a distributor of groceries and related products, is headquartered in Medford, Massachusetts.

During a recent audit, Alternative Distributor Corp. was advised that existing internal controls necessary for the company to develop reliable financial statements were inadequate. The audit report stated that the current system of accounting for sales, receivables, and cash receipts constituted a material weakness. Among other items, the report focused on nontimely deposit of cash receipts, exposing Alternative Distributor to potential loss or misappropriation, excessive past due accounts receivable due to lack of collection efforts, disregard of advantages offered by vendors for prompt payment of invoices, absence of appropriate segregation of duties by personnel consistent with appropriate control objectives, inadequate procedures for applying accounting principles, lack of qualified management personnel, lack of supervision by an outside board of directors, and overall poor recordkeeping.

Instructions
With the class divided into groups, do the following:
Identify the principles of internal control violated by Alternative Distributor Corporation.

COMMUNICATION ACTIVITY

BYP7-9 As a new auditor for the CPA firm of Rawls, Keoto, and Landry, you have been assigned to review the internal controls over mail cash receipts of Adirondack Company. Your review reveals that checks are promptly endorsed "For Deposit Only," but no list of the checks is prepared by the person opening the mail. The mail is opened either by the cashier or by the employee who maintains the accounts receivable records. Mail receipts are deposited in the bank weekly by the cashier.

Instructions
Write a letter to L. S. Osman, owner of the Adirondack Company, explaining the weaknesses in internal control and your recommendations for improving the system.

ETHICS CASE

BYP7-10 As noted in the chapter, banks charge fees of up to $30 for "bounced" checks—that is, checks that exceed the balance in the account. It has been estimated that processing bounced checks costs a bank roughly $1.50 per check. Thus, the profit margin on bounced checks is very high. Recognizing this, some banks have started to process checks from largest to smallest. By doing this, they maximize the number of checks that bounce if a customer overdraws an account. For example, **NationsBank** projected a $14 million increase in fee revenue as a result of processing largest checks first. In response to criticism, banks have responded that their customers prefer to have large checks processed first, because those tend to be the most important. At the other extreme, some banks will cover their customers' bounced checks, effectively extending them an interest-free loan while their account is overdrawn.

Instructions
Answer each of the following questions.
(a) Antonio Freeman had a balance of $1,500 in his checking account at First National Bank on a day when the bank received the following five checks for processing against his account.

Check Number	Amount		Check Number	Amount
3150	$ 35		3165	$550
3158	1,510		3169	180
3162	400			

Assuming a $30 fee assessed by the bank for each bounced check, how much fee revenue would the bank generate if it processed checks (1) from largest to smallest, (2) from smallest to largest, and (3) in order of check number?

(b) Do you think that processing checks from largest to smallest is an ethical business practice?

(c) In addition to ethical issues, what other issues must a bank consider in deciding whether to process checks from largest to smallest?

(d) If you were managing a bank, what policy would you adopt on bounced checks?

Answers to Self-Study Questions

1. a 2. c 3. b 4. b 5. d 6. a 7. c 8. c 9. d 10. c
*11. a

Answer to Tootsie Roll Review It Question 3, p. 322.

At December 31, 1998, Tootsie Roll reported cash and cash equivalents of $80,744,000. It reported no restricted cash. In Note 1 to its financial statements it defines cash equivalents as "temporary cash investments with an original maturity of three months or less."

CHAPTER 8

Reporting and Analyzing Receivables

◆ **STUDY OBJECTIVES**

After studying this chapter, you should be able to:

1 Identify the different types of receivables.

2 Explain how accounts receivable are recognized in the accounts.

3 Describe the methods used to account for bad debts.

4 Compute the maturity date of and interest on notes receivable.

5 Describe the entries to record the disposition of notes receivable.

6 Explain the statement presentation of receivables.

7 Describe the principles of sound accounts receivable management.

8 Identify ratios to analyze a company's receivables.

9 Describe methods to accelerate the receipt of cash from receivables.

◆ **HOW DO YOU SPELL RELIEF?**

Fred Tarter believes that in every problem lies an opportunity— and sometimes that opportunity can mean a big profit. For example, today fewer people pay cash for their prescriptions; instead, pharmacies bill a customer's health plan for some or all of the prescription's cost. Consequently pharmacies must spend a lot of time and energy collecting cash from these health plans. This procedure is a headache for pharmacies because there are 4,500 different health plans in the United States. Also, it often leaves pharmacies with too many receivables and not enough cash. Their suppliers want to be paid within 15 days, but their receivables are outstanding for 30 and often 60 days.

Enter Fred Tarter. Having recently sold his advertising agency, Fred had some spare time and money on his hands. While reading a pharmacy trade journal, he learned of the pharmacies' headache. To Fred this problem spelled opportunity.

Fred found out that 56,000 pharmacies are connected by computer to a claims processing business. Fred's idea was this:

Taking advantage of this network, he would purchase pharmacy receivables, charging a fee of 1.4% to 2%. Pharmacies would be willing to pay this because they would get their cash sooner and save the headache of having to collect the accounts. Fred would then use these receivables as backing to raise new money so he could buy more receivables.

Based on this idea, Fred started a company called the Pharmacy Fund. Over 500 small pharmacies sell their receivables to his company. The Pharmacy

Fund establishes a computer link with each pharmacy, which allows it to buy the receivables at the end of each day and credit the pharmacy's account immediately. Thus, rather than having to wait weeks to receive its cash from insurance companies, the pharmacy gets its cash the same day as the sale. The Pharmacy Fund's customers say that this has solved their cash-flow problems, reduced their overhead costs, and allowed them to automate their billing and record-keeping.

Other investors are interested in getting in on this action. Nursing home receivables or home health care receivables have been mentioned as other possibilities. Fred Tarter has already identified his next opportunity—a target some would say is a "natural" for him: dentistry receivables. (Get it? Tarter—dentistry. We'll stick to accounting jokes from now on!)

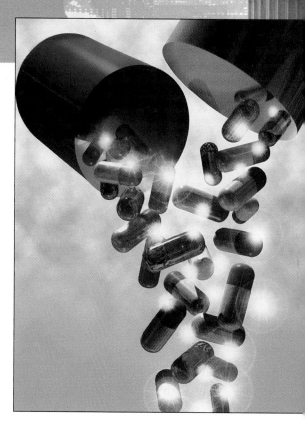

In this chapter we discuss some of the decisions related to reporting and analyzing receivables. As indicated in the opening story, receivables are a significant asset on the books of many pharmacies. Receivables are significant to companies in other industries as well, because a significant portion of sales are done on credit in the United States. As a consequence, companies must pay close attention to their receivables balances and manage them carefully.

The organization and content of the chapter are as follows:

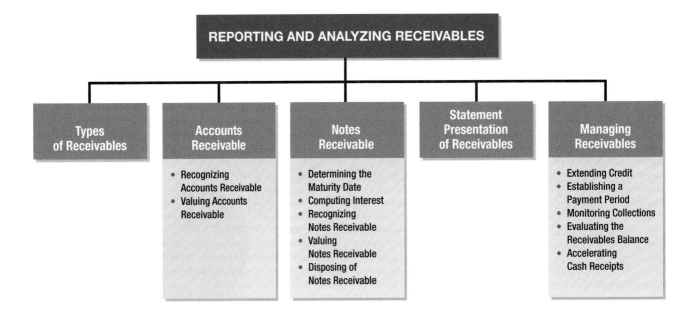

TYPES OF RECEIVABLES

STUDY OBJECTIVE

1

Identify the different types of receivables.

The term **receivables** refers to amounts due from individuals and companies. Receivables are claims that are expected to be collected in cash. The management of receivables is a very important activity for any company that sells goods on credit. Receivables are important because they represent one of a company's most liquid assets. For many companies receivables are also one of the largest assets. For example, receivables represented 20% of the current assets of pharmacy giant Rite Aid in 1999. Illustration 8-1 lists receivables as a percentage of total assets for five other well-known companies in a recent year.

Illustration 8-1 Receivables as a percentage of assets

Company	Receivables as a Percentage of Total Assets
Ford Motor Company	57%
General Mills	10%
Minnesota Mining and Manufacturing Company (3M)	6%
General Electric	43%
Intel Corporation	18%

The relative significance of a company's receivables as a percentage of its assets differs depending on its industry, the time of year, whether it extends long-term financing, and its credit policies. To reflect important differences among receivables, they are frequently classified as (1) accounts, (2) notes, and (3) other.

Accounts receivable are amounts owed by customers on account. They result from the sale of goods and services. These receivables generally are expected to be collected within 30 to 60 days. They are usually the most significant type of claim held by a company.

Notes receivable represent claims for which formal instruments of credit are issued as evidence of the debt. The credit instrument normally requires the debtor to pay interest and extends for time periods of 60–90 days or longer. Notes and accounts receivable that result from sales transactions are often called trade receivables.

Other receivables include nontrade receivables such as interest receivable, loans to company officers, advances to employees, and income taxes refundable. These are unusual; therefore, they are generally classified and reported as separate items in the balance sheet.

ACCOUNTS RECEIVABLE

Two accounting problems associated with accounts receivable are:

1. Recognizing accounts receivable.
2. Valuing accounts receivable.

A third issue, accelerating cash receipts from receivables, is discussed later in the chapter.

RECOGNIZING ACCOUNTS RECEIVABLE

STUDY OBJECTIVE
2
Explain how accounts receivable are recognized in the accounts.

Initial recognition of accounts receivable is relatively straightforward. For a service organization, a receivable is recorded when service is provided on account. For a merchandiser, accounts receivable are recorded at the point of sale of merchandise on account. When a merchandiser sells goods, both Accounts Receivable and Sales are increased.

Receivables also are reduced as a result of sales discounts and sales returns. The seller may offer terms that encourage early payment by providing a discount. For example, terms of 2/10, n/30 provide the buyer with a 2% discount if paid within 10 days. If the buyer chooses to pay within the discount period, the seller's accounts receivable is reduced. Also, the buyer might find some of the goods unacceptable and choose to return the unwanted goods. For example, if merchandise with a selling price of $100 is returned, the seller reduces Accounts Receivable by $100 upon receipt of the returned merchandise.

BUSINESS INSIGHT
Management Perspective

Sometimes returns can be very significant. Recently pharmacy giant Rite Aid sent out return notices to nearly all of its suppliers and reduced the amount it paid each accordingly. In most cases it provided no evidence that the goods were defective—and it did not return the goods, but instead often said that they had been destroyed. In some cases the returns represented 16% of the total goods the supplier had sold to Rite Aid. Analysts suggested that, since the move came immediately before the company's accounting year-end, Rite Aid was simply trying to increase its reported net income. Interestingly, in the subsequent year, in the face of lawsuits and threats by suppliers that they would no longer sell to Rite Aid, the company repaid nearly all of the suppliers for the amounts it had deducted.

Illustration 8-2 contains an excerpt from the notes to the financial statements of pharmaceutical manufacturer Del Laboratories that describes its revenue recognition procedures.

Illustration 8-2
Disclosure of revenue recognition policy

DEL LABORATORIES
Notes to the Financial Statements

Revenues are recognized and product discounts are recorded when merchandise is shipped. Net sales are comprised of gross revenues less returns, trade discounts, and customer allowances. Merchandise returns are accrued at the earlier of customer deduction or receipt of goods.

STUDY OBJECTIVE

3

Describe the methods used to account for bad debts.

VALUING ACCOUNTS RECEIVABLE

Once receivables are recorded in the accounts, the next question is: How should receivables be reported in the financial statements? They are reported on the balance sheet as an asset, but determining the **amount** to report is sometimes difficult because some receivables will become uncollectible.

Although each customer must satisfy the credit requirements of the seller before the credit sale is approved, inevitably some accounts receivable become uncollectible. For example, one of your customers may not be able to pay because it experienced a decline in sales due to a downturn in the economy. Similarly, individuals may be laid off from their jobs or be faced with unexpected hospital bills. Credit losses are debited to **Bad Debts Expense** (or Uncollectible Accounts Expense). Such losses are considered a normal and necessary risk of doing business on a credit basis.

Two methods are used in accounting for uncollectible accounts: (1) the direct write-off method and (2) the allowance method. Each of these methods is explained in the following sections.

Direct Write-off Method for Uncollectible Accounts

Under the **direct write-off method**, when a particular account is determined to be uncollectible, the loss is charged to Bad Debts Expense. Assume, for example, that Warden Co. writes off M. E. Doran's $200 balance as uncollectible on December 12. The entry is:

A	=	L	+	SE
−200				−200

Dec. 12	Bad Debts Expense	200	
	Accounts Receivable—M. E. Doran		200
	(To record write-off of M. E. Doran account)		

When this method is used, bad debts expense will show only **actual losses** from uncollectibles. Accounts receivable will be reported at its gross amount.

Use of the direct write-off method can reduce the usefulness of both the income statement and balance sheet. Consider the following example. In 2001, Quick Buck Computer Company decided it could increase its revenues by offering computers to college students without requiring any money down, and with no credit-approval process. It went on campuses across the country and distributed 1,000,000 computers with a selling price of $800 each. This increased Quick Buck's revenues and receivables by $800,000,000. The promotion was a huge success! The 2001 balance sheet and income statement looked wonderful. Unfortunately, during 2002, nearly 40% of the college student customers defaulted on their loans. This made the year 2002 income statement and balance sheet look terrible. Illustration 8-3 shows the effect of these events on the financial statements if the direct write-off method is used.

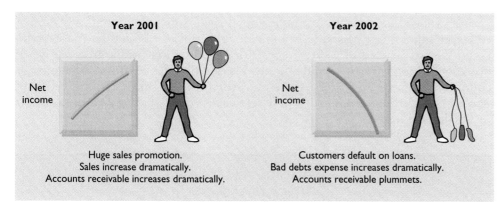

Illustration 8-3 Effects of direct write-off method

Under the direct write-off method, bad debts expense is often recorded in a period different from the period in which the revenue was recorded. Thus, no attempt is made to match bad debts expense to sales revenues in the income statement or to show accounts receivable in the balance sheet at the amount actually expected to be received. **Consequently, unless bad debts losses are insignificant, the direct write-off method is not acceptable for financial reporting purposes**.

Allowance Method for Uncollectible Accounts

The allowance method of accounting for bad debts involves estimating uncollectible accounts at the end of each period. This provides better matching on the income statement and ensures that receivables are stated at their cash (net) realizable value on the balance sheet. Cash (net) realizable value is the net amount expected to be received in cash; it excludes amounts that the company estimates it will not collect. Receivables are therefore reduced by estimated uncollectible receivables on the balance sheet through use of the allowance method.

The allowance method is required for financial reporting purposes when bad debts are material in amount. It has three essential features:

> **Helpful Hint** In this context, *material* means significant or important to financial statement users.

1. Uncollectible accounts receivable are **estimated** and **matched against sales** in the same accounting period in which the sales occurred.
2. Estimated uncollectibles are recorded as an increase (a debit) to Bad Debts Expense and an increase (a credit) to Allowance for Doubtful Accounts (a contra asset account) through an adjusting entry at the end of each period.
3. Actual uncollectibles are debited to Allowance for Doubtful Accounts and credited to Accounts Receivable at the time the specific account is written off as uncollectible.

Recording Estimated Uncollectibles. To illustrate the allowance method, assume that Hampson Furniture has credit sales of $1,200,000 in 2001, of which $200,000 remains uncollected at December 31. The credit manager estimates that $12,000 of these sales will prove uncollectible. The adjusting entry to record the estimated uncollectibles is:

Dec. 31	Bad Debts Expense	12,000	
	Allowance for Doubtful Accounts		12,000
	(To record estimate of uncollectible accounts)		

A	=	L	+	SE
−12,000				−12,000

Bad Debts Expense is reported in the income statement as an operating expense (usually as a selling expense). Thus, the estimated uncollectibles are matched with sales in 2001 because the expense is recorded in the same year the sales are made.

Allowance for Doubtful Accounts shows the estimated amount of claims on customers that are expected to become uncollectible in the future. A contra account is used instead of a direct credit to Accounts Receivable because we do not know which customers will not pay. The credit balance in the allowance account will absorb the specific write-offs when they occur. It is deducted from Accounts Receivable in the current asset section of the balance sheet as shown in Illustration 8-4.

Illustration 8-4 Presentation of allowance for doubtful accounts

HAMPSON FURNITURE Balance Sheet (partial)		
Current assets		
Cash		$ 14,800
Accounts receivable	$200,000	
Less: Allowance for doubtful accounts	12,000	188,000
Merchandise inventory		310,000
Prepaid expense		25,000
Total current assets		$537,800

The amount of $188,000 in Illustration 8-4 represents the expected **cash realizable value** of the accounts receivable at the statement date. **Allowance for Doubtful Accounts is not closed at the end of the fiscal year.**

Recording the Write-off of an Uncollectible Account.   Companies use various methods of collecting past-due accounts, such as letters, calls, and legal action. When all means of collecting a past-due account have been exhausted and collection appears impossible, the account should be written off. In the credit card industry it is standard practice to write off accounts that are 210 days past due. To prevent premature or unauthorized write-offs, each write-off should be formally approved in writing by authorized management personnel. To maintain good internal control, authorization to write off accounts should not be given to someone who also has daily responsibilities related to cash or receivables.

To illustrate a receivables write-off, assume that the vice-president of finance of Hampson Furniture authorizes a write-off of the $500 balance owed by R. A. Ware on March 1, 2002. The entry to record the write-off is:

A	=	L	+	SE
+500				
−500				

Mar. 1	Allowance for Doubtful Accounts	500	
	Accounts Receivable—R. A. Ware		500
	(Write-off of R. A. Ware account)		

Bad Debts Expense is not increased when the write-off occurs. **Under the allowance method, every bad debt write-off is debited to the allowance account and not to Bad Debts Expense**. A debit to Bad Debts Expense would be incorrect because the expense has already been recognized, when the adjusting entry was made for estimated bad debts. Instead, the entry to record the write-off of an uncollectible account reduces both Accounts Receivable and the Allowance for Doubtful Accounts. After posting, the general ledger accounts will appear as in Illustration 8-5.

Accounts Receivable		Allowance for Doubtful Accounts	
Jan. 1 Bal. 200,000	Mar. 1 **500**	Mar. 1 **500**	Jan. 1 Bal. 12,000
Mar. 1 Bal. 199,500			Mar. 1 Bal. 11,500

Illustration 8-5 General ledger balances after write-off

A write-off affects only balance sheet accounts. Cash realizable value in the balance sheet, therefore, remains the same, as shown in Illustration 8-6.

	Before Write-off	After Write-off
Accounts receivable	$ 200,000	$ 199,500
Allowance for doubtful accounts	12,000	11,500
Cash realizable value	**$188,000**	**$188,000**

Illustration 8-6 Cash realizable value comparison

BUSINESS INSIGHT
International Perspective

Many investors are eager to buy shares of Chinese companies. Analysts advise caution, however, because tight credit in China is making it hard for many companies to collect their receivables. Thus, a significant number of transactions booked as sales will never be collected. Under Chinese accounting practices, bad debt write-offs are rare, and so some companies have two-year-old receivables on their books. Even those Chinese companies that follow international standards are not required to write off an account until it is one year old.

Recovery of an Uncollectible Account. Occasionally, a company collects from a customer after the account has been written off as uncollectible. Two entries are required to record the recovery of a bad debt: (1) The entry made in writing off the account is reversed to reinstate the customer's account. (2) The collection is journalized in the usual manner. To illustrate, assume that on July 1, R. A. Ware pays the $500 amount that had been written off on March 1. These are the entries:

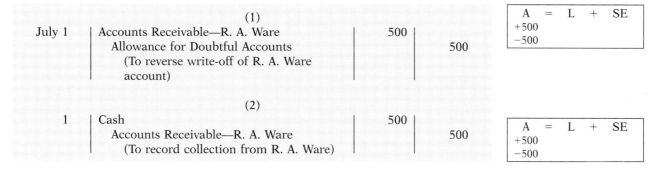

	(1)		
July 1	Accounts Receivable—R. A. Ware	500	
	Allowance for Doubtful Accounts		500
	(To reverse write-off of R. A. Ware account)		

A = L + SE
+500
−500

	(2)		
1	Cash	500	
	Accounts Receivable—R. A. Ware		500
	(To record collection from R. A. Ware)		

A = L + SE
+500
−500

Note that the recovery of a bad debt, like the write-off of a bad debt, affects only balance sheet accounts. The net effect of the two entries above is an increase in Cash and an increase in Allowance for Doubtful Accounts for $500. Accounts Receivable and the Allowance for Doubtful Accounts both increase in entry (1) for two reasons: First, the company made an error in judgment when it wrote off the account receivable. Second, R. A. Ware did pay, and therefore the Accounts Receivable account should show this collection for possible future credit purposes.

Helpful Hint Like the write-off, a recovery does not involve the income statement.

Estimating the Allowance. For Hampson Furniture in Illustration 8-4, the amount of the expected uncollectibles was given. However, in "real life," companies must estimate that amount if they use the allowance method. Frequently the allowance is estimated as a percentage of the outstanding receivables.

Under the percentage of receivables basis, management establishes a percentage relationship between the amount of receivables and expected losses from uncollectible accounts. A schedule is prepared in which customer balances are classified by the length of time they have been unpaid. Because of its emphasis on time, this schedule is often called an **aging schedule**, and the analysis of it is often called aging the accounts receivable.

After the accounts are arranged by age, the expected bad debt losses are determined by applying percentages based on past experience to the totals of each category. The longer a receivable is past due, the less likely it is to be collected. As a result, the estimated percentage of uncollectible debts increases as the number of days past due increases. An aging schedule for Dart Company is shown in Illustration 8-7. Note the increasing uncollectible percentages from 2% to 40%.

Illustration 8-7 Aging schedule

Customer	Total	Not Yet Due	Number of Days Past Due			
			1–30	31–60	61–90	Over 90
T. E. Adert	$ 600		$ 300		$ 200	$ 100
R. C. Bortz	300	$ 300				
B. A. Carl	450		200	$ 250		
O. L. Diker	700	500			200	
T. O. Ebbet	600			300		300
Others	36,950	26,200	5,200	2,450	1,600	1,500
	$39,600	$27,000	$5,700	$3,000	$2,000	$1,900
Estimated percentage uncollectible			2%	4%	10%	20%	40%
Total estimated bad debts	$ 2,228	$ 540	$ 228	$ 300	$ 400	$ 760

Total estimated bad debts for Dart Company ($2,228) represent the existing customer claims expected to become uncollectible in the future. Thus, this amount represents the **required balance** in Allowance for Doubtful Accounts at the balance sheet date. Accordingly, **the amount of the bad debts adjusting entry is the difference between the required balance and the existing balance in the allowance account**. If the trial balance shows Allowance for Doubtful Accounts with a credit balance of $528, then an adjusting entry for $1,700 ($2,228 − $528) is necessary:

A	=	L	+	SE
−1,700				−1,700

Dec. 31	Bad Debts Expense	1,700	
	Allowance for Doubtful Accounts		1,700
	(To adjust allowance account to total estimated uncollectibles)		

After the adjusting entry is posted, the accounts of Dart Company will appear as in Illustration 8-8.

Illustration 8-8 Bad debts accounts after posting

Bad Debts Expense		Allowance for Doubtful Accounts	
Dec. 31 Adj. **1,700**			Bal. 528
			Dec. 31 Adj. **1,700**
			Bal. 2,228

An important aspect of accounts receivable management is simply maintaining a close watch on the accounts. Studies have shown that accounts more than 60 days past due lose approximately 50% of their value if no payment activity occurs within the next 30 days. For each additional 30 days that pass, the collectible value halves once again.

Occasionally the allowance account will have a **debit balance** prior to adjustment because write-offs during the year have **exceeded** previous provisions for bad debts. In such a case, **the debit balance is added to the required balance** when the adjusting entry is made. Thus, if there had been a $500 debit balance in the allowance account before adjustment, the adjusting entry would have been for $2,728 ($2,228 + $500) to arrive at a credit balance of $2,228.

The percentage of receivables basis provides an estimate of the cash realizable value of the receivables. It also provides a reasonable matching of expense to revenue.

BUSINESS INSIGHT

Investor Perspective

Nearly half of the goods sold by Sears are purchased with a Sears credit card. This means that how Sears accounts for its uncollectible accounts can have a very significant effect on Sears' net income. In one quarter in 1998 Sears reduced its bad debts expense by 61% compared to the same quarter in the previous year. In so doing, Sears was able to report earnings that slightly exceeded analysts' forecasts. Some analysts expressed concern that, because the number of delinquent accounts receivable had actually increased, Sears should probably have *increased* its bad debts expense, rather than reduced it. While Sears management defended its actions, analysts appeared to be unimpressed, and Sears' stock price declined on the news.

DECISION TOOLKIT

Decision Checkpoints	Info Needed for Decision	Tool to Use for Decision	How to Evaluate Results
Is the amount of past due accounts increasing? Which accounts require management's attention?	List of outstanding receivables and their due dates	Prepare an aging schedule showing the receivables in various stages: outstanding 0–30 days, 30–60 days, 60–90 days, and over 90 days.	Accounts in the older categories require follow-up: letters, phone calls, and possible renegotiation of terms.

BEFORE YOU GO ON...

◆ Review It

1. What type of receivables does Tootsie Roll report on its balance sheet? Does it use the allowance method or the direct write-off method to account for uncollectibles? The answer to these questions is provided on page 395.

2. To maintain adequate internal controls over receivables, who should authorize receivables write-offs?

3. What are the essential features of the allowance method?

4. What is the primary criticism of the direct write-off method?

◆ Do It

Brule Corporation has been in business for 5 years. The ledger at the end of the current year shows: Accounts Receivable $30,000; Sales $180,000; and Allowance for Doubtful Accounts with a debit balance of $2,000. Bad debts are estimated to be 10% of accounts receivable. Prepare the entry necessary to adjust the Allowance for Doubtful Accounts.

Helpful Hint The debit to Bad Debts Expense is calculated as follows:

Allowance for Doubtful Accounts

2,000	**5,000**
	3,000

Reasoning: Receivables are to be reported at their cash (net) realizable value—that is, the amount the company expects to collect in cash. This amount excludes any amount the company does not expect it will collect. The estimated uncollectible amount should be recorded in an allowance account.

Solution: The following entry should be made to bring the balance in the Allowance for Doubtful Accounts up to a balance of $3,000 (.1 × $30,000):

Bad Debts Expense	5,000	
Allowance for Doubtful Accounts		5,000
(To record estimate of		
uncollectible accounts)		

NOTES RECEIVABLE

Credit may also be granted in exchange for a formal credit instrument known as a promissory note. A **promissory note** is a written promise to pay a specified amount of money on demand or at a definite time. Promissory notes may be used (1) when individuals and companies lend or borrow money, (2) when the amount of the transaction and the credit period exceed normal limits, and (3) in settlement of accounts receivable.

In a promissory note, the party making the promise to pay is called the **maker**; the party to whom payment is to be made is called the **payee**. The payee may be specifically identified by name or may be designated simply as the bearer of the note.

In the note shown in Illustration 8-9, Brent Company is the maker and Wilma Company is the payee. To the Wilma Company, the promissory note is a note receivable; to the Brent Company, the note is a note payable.

Illustration 8-9
Promissory note

Helpful Hint Who are the two key parties to a note, and what entry does each party make when the note is issued?
Answer:
1. The maker, Brent Company, credits Notes Payable.
2. The payee, Wilma Company, debits Notes Receivable.

Notes receivable give the holder a stronger legal claim to assets than accounts receivable. Like accounts receivable, notes receivable can be readily sold to another party. Promissory notes are negotiable instruments (as are checks), which means that, when sold, they can be transferred to another party by endorsement.

Notes receivable are frequently accepted from customers who need to extend the payment of an outstanding account receivable and are often required from high-risk customers. In some industries (e.g., the pleasure and sport boat industry) all credit sales are supported by notes. The majority of notes, however, originate from lending transactions. There are three basic issues in accounting for notes receivable:

1. **Recognizing** notes receivable.
2. **Valuing** notes receivable.
3. **Disposing** of notes receivable.

We will look at each of these issues, but first we need to consider two issues that did not apply to accounts receivable: determining the maturity date and computing interest.

DETERMINING THE MATURITY DATE

When the life of a note is expressed in terms of months, the due date is found by counting the months from the date of issue. For example, the maturity date of a three-month note dated May 1 is August 1. A note drawn on the last day of a month matures on the last day of a subsequent month; that is, a July 31 note due in two months matures on September 30. When the due date is stated in terms of days, it is necessary to count the exact number of days to determine the maturity date. In counting, **the date the note is issued is omitted but the due date is included**. For example, the maturity date of a 60-day note dated July 17 is September 15, computed as in Illustration 8-10.

STUDY OBJECTIVE

◆ 4 ◆

Compute the maturity date of and interest on notes receivable.

Term of note		60 days
July (31 − 17)	14	
August	31	45
Maturity date, September		15

Illustration 8-10 Computation of maturity date

The due date (maturity date) of a promissory note may be stated in one of three ways: on a specific date ("July 23, 2001"), at the end of a stated period ("one year from the date of the note"), or "on demand."

COMPUTING INTEREST

The basic formula for computing interest on an interest-bearing note is given in Illustration 8-11.

Illustration 8-11 Formula for computing interest

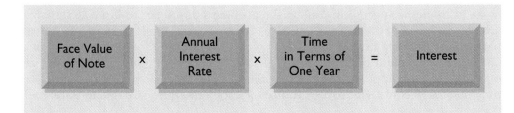

| Face Value of Note | × | Annual Interest Rate | × | Time in Terms of One Year | = | Interest |

The interest rate specified on the note is an **annual** rate of interest. The time factor in the computation expresses the fraction of a year that the note is outstanding. When the maturity date is stated in days, the time factor is frequently the number of days divided by 360. When the due date is stated in months, the time factor is the number of months divided by 12. The computation of interest is shown in Illustration 8-12.

Illustration 8-12
Computation of interest

Terms of Note	Interest Computation				
	Face	× Rate ×	Time	= Interest	
$ 730, 18%, 120 days	$ 730 × 18% ×	120/360	= $ 43.80	
$1,000, 15%, 6 months	$1,000 × 15% ×	6/12	= $ 75.00	
$2,000, 12%, 1 year	$2,000 × 12% ×	1/1	= $240.00	

There are different ways to calculate interest. For example, the computation in Illustration 8-12 assumed 360 days for the year. Many financial institutions use 365 days to compute interest. (For homework problems, assume 360 days.)

RECOGNIZING NOTES RECEIVABLE

To illustrate the basic entry for notes receivable, we will use Brent Company's $1,000, two-month, 12% promissory note dated May 1. Assuming that the note was written to settle an open account, we record this entry for the receipt of the note by Wilma Company:

A = L + SE
+1,000
−1,000

May 1	Notes Receivable	1,000	
	Accounts Receivable—Brent Company		1,000
	(To record acceptance of Brent Company note)		

The note receivable is recorded at its **face value**, the value shown on the face of the note. No interest revenue is reported when the note is accepted because the revenue recognition principle does not recognize revenue until earned. Interest is earned (accrued) as time passes.

If a note is exchanged for cash, the entry is a debit to Notes Receivable and a credit to Cash in the amount of the loan.

VALUING NOTES RECEIVABLE

Like accounts receivable, short-term notes receivable are reported at their **cash (net) realizable value**. The notes receivable allowance account is Allowance for Doubtful Accounts. Valuing short-term notes receivable is the same as valuing accounts receivable. The computations and estimations involved in determining cash realizable value and in recording the proper amount of bad debts expense and related allowance are similar.

Long-term notes receivable, however, pose additional estimation problems. As an example, we need only look at the problems a number of large U.S. banks are having in collecting their receivables. Loans to less-developed countries are particularly worrisome. Developing countries need loans for development but often find repayment difficult. U.S. loans (notes) to less-developed countries at one time totaled approximately $135 billion. In Brazil alone, Citibank at one time had loans equivalent to 80% of its stockholders' equity; Chemical Bank had

77% of its equity lent out in Mexico. Determining the proper allowance is understandably difficult for these types of long-term receivables.

DISPOSING OF NOTES RECEIVABLE

STUDY OBJECTIVE

◆5◆

Describe the entries to record the disposition of notes receivable.

Notes may be held to their maturity date, at which time the face value plus accrued interest is due. In some situations, the maker of the note defaults and appropriate adjustment must be made. In other situations, similar to accounts receivable, the holder of the note speeds up the conversion to cash by selling the receivables. The entries for honoring and dishonoring notes are illustrated next.

Honor of Notes Receivable

A note is **honored** when it is paid in full at its maturity date. For each interest-bearing note, the amount due at maturity is the face value of the note plus interest for the length of time specified on the note.

To illustrate, assume that Wolder Co. lends Higley Inc. $10,000 on June 1, accepting a four-month, 9% interest note. In this situation, interest is $300 ($10,000 × 9% × $\frac{4}{12}$); the amount due, the maturity value, is $10,300. To obtain payment, Wolder (the payee) must present the note either to Higley Inc. (the maker) or to the maker's agent, such as a bank. If Wolder presents the note to Higley Inc. on October 1, the maturity date, the entry by Wolder to record the collection is:

Helpful Hint How many days of interest should be accrued at September 30 for a 90-day note issued on August 16? *Answer:* 45 days (15 days in August plus 30 days in September).

Oct. 1	Cash	10,300	
	Notes Receivable		10,000
	Interest Revenue		300
	(To record collection of Higley Inc. note and interest)		

A	=	L	+	SE
+10,300				+300
−10,000				

If Wolder Co. prepares financial statements as of September 30, it is necessary to accrue interest. In this case, the adjusting entry by Wolder is for four months, or $300, as shown below:

Sept. 30	Interest Receivable	300	
	Interest Revenue		300
	(To accrue 4 months' interest on Higley note)		

A	=	L	+	SE
+300				+300

When interest has been accrued, it is necessary to credit Interest Receivable at maturity. The entry by Wolder to record the honoring of the Higley note on October 1 is:

Oct. 1	Cash	10,300	
	Notes Receivable		10,000
	Interest Receivable		300
	(To record collection of Higley Inc. note and interest)		

A	=	L	+	SE
+10,300				
−10,000				
−300				

In this case, Interest Receivable is credited because the receivable was established in the adjusting entry.

BUSINESS INSIGHT

International Perspective

Varied plans have been proposed to alleviate international debt problems. These plans range from encouraging more lending to reducing or forgiving the debt. At one time, this debt burden to banks worldwide exceeded $1.3 trillion. (As an aside, a trillion is a lot of money—enough money to give every man, woman, and child in the world approximately $250 each.) Why were these loans made in the first place? The reasons are numerous, but the three major ones are: (1) to provide stability to these governments and thereby increase trade, (2) the belief that governments would never default on payment, and (3) the desire by banks to increase their income by lending to these countries.

Dishonor of Notes Receivable

A **dishonored note** is a note that is not paid in full at maturity. A dishonored note receivable is no longer negotiable; however, the payee still has a claim against the maker of the note. Therefore, the Notes Receivable account is usually transferred to an Account Receivable.

To illustrate, assume that Higley Inc. on October 1 indicates that it cannot pay at the present time. The entry to record the dishonor of the note depends on whether eventual collection is expected. If Wolder Co. expects eventual collection, the amount due (face value and interest) on the note is recorded as an increase (a debit) to Accounts Receivable. Wolder Co. would make the following entry at the time the note is dishonored (assuming no previous accrual of interest):

A	=	L	+	SE
+10,300				+300
−10,000				

Oct. 1	Accounts Receivable	10,300	
	Notes Receivable		10,000
	Interest Revenue		300
	(To record the dishonor of the note)		

If there is no hope of collection, the face value of the note should be written off by decreasing (debiting) the Allowance for Doubtful Accounts. No interest revenue would be recorded because collection will not occur.

BEFORE YOU GO ON...

◆ **Review It**

1. What is the basic formula for computing interest?
2. At what value are notes receivable reported on the balance sheet?
3. Explain the difference between honoring and dishonoring a note receivable.

◆ **Do It**

Gambit Stores accepts from Leonard Co. a $3,400, 90-day, 12% note dated May 10 in settlement of Leonard's overdue open account. What is the maturity date of the note? What entry is made by Gambit at the maturity date, assuming Leonard pays the note and interest in full at that time?

Reasoning: When the due date is stated in terms of days, it is necessary to count the exact number of days to determine the maturity date. The date the note is issued is omitted from the count, but the due date is included. The entry to record interest at maturity in this solution assumes that no interest is previously accrued on this note.

Solution: The maturity date is August 8, computed as follows:

Term of note		90 days
May (31 − 10)	21	
June	30	
July	31	82
Maturity date, August		8

The interest payable at maturity date is $102, computed as follows:

$$\text{Face} \times \text{Rate} \times \text{Time} = \text{Interest}$$
$$\$3,400 \times 12\% \times \frac{90}{360} = \$102$$

This entry is recorded by Gambit Stores at the maturity date:

Cash	3,502	
Notes Receivable		3,400
Interest Revenue		102
(To record collection of Leonard note and interest)		

FINANCIAL STATEMENT PRESENTATION OF RECEIVABLES

Each of the major types of receivables should be identified in the balance sheet or in the notes to the financial statements. Short-term receivables are reported in the current assets section of the balance sheet below temporary investments. Temporary investments appear before short-term receivables because these investments are nearer to cash. Both the gross amount of receivables and the allowance for doubtful accounts should be reported. Illustration 8-13 shows the current assets presentation of receivables for CPC International Inc. for a recent year. Note that notes receivable are listed before accounts receivable because notes are more easily converted to cash.

STUDY OBJECTIVE

6

Explain the statement presentation of receivables.

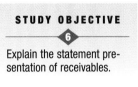

Illustration 8-13
Balance sheet presentation of receivables

CPC INTERNATIONAL INC. Balance Sheet (partial) (in millions)	
Receivables	
Notes receivable	$ 16.6
Accounts receivable	375.1
Other receivables	60.7
Total receivables	452.4
Less: Allowance for doubtful accounts	10.5
Net receivables	$441.9

In the income statement, bad debts expense is reported under Selling Expenses in the operating expenses section. Interest revenue is shown under Other Revenues and Gains in the nonoperating section of the income statement.

If a company has significant risk of uncollectible accounts or other problems with its receivables, it is required to discuss this possibility in the notes to the financial statements.

BEFORE YOU GO ON...

◆ Review It

1. Explain where receivables are reported on the balance sheet and in what order.
2. Where are bad debts expense and interest revenue reported on the income statement?

MANAGING RECEIVABLES

STUDY OBJECTIVE

7

Describe the principles of sound accounts receivable management.

Managing accounts receivable involves five steps:

1. Determine to whom to extend credit.
2. Establish a payment period.
3. Monitor collections.
4. Evaluate the receivables balance.
5. Accelerate cash receipts from receivables when necessary.

EXTENDING CREDIT

Determine to whom to extend credit

A critical part of managing receivables is determining who should be extended credit and who should not. Many companies increase sales by being generous with their credit policy, but they may end up extending credit to risky customers who do not pay. If the credit policy is too tight, you will lose sales; if it is too loose, you may sell to "deadbeats" who will pay either very late or not at all. One CEO noted that prior to getting his credit and collection department in order, his salespeople had 300 square feet of office space per person, while the people in credit and collections had six people crammed into a single 300-square-foot space. Although this arrangement boosted sales, it had very expensive consequences in bad debts expense.

Certain steps can be taken to help minimize losses as credit standards are relaxed. Risky customers might be required to provide letters of credit or bank guarantees. Then if the customer does not pay, the bank that provided the guarantee will. Particularly risky customers might be required to pay cash on delivery. In addition, you should ask potential customers for references from banks and suppliers to determine their payment history. It is important to check these references on potential new customers as well as periodically to check the financial health of continuing customers. Many resources are available for investigating customers. For example, *The Dun & Bradstreet Reference Book of American Business* lists millions of companies and provides credit ratings for many of them.

BUSINESS INSIGHT
Management Perspective

Give the man credit. Like most of us, John Galbreath receives piles of unsolicited, "preapproved" credit card applications in the mail. Galbreath doesn't just toss them out, though. He once filled out a credit card application on which he stated he was 97 years old and had no income, no telephone, and no Social Security number. In a space inviting him to let the credit card company pay off his other credit card balances, Galbreath said he owed money to the Mafia.

Back came a credit card and a letter welcoming John to the fold with a $1,500 credit limit. Galbreath had requested the card under a false name, John C. Reath, an alias under which he had received two other credit cards—earning exemplary credit. John C. Reath might be a bit "long in the tooth," but it seems he paid his bills on time.

Source: "Forbes Informer," edited by Kate Bohner Lewis, *Forbes,* August 14, 1995, p. 19. Reprinted by permission of FORBES Magazine © 1999 Forbes 1995.

ESTABLISHING A PAYMENT PERIOD

Companies that extend credit should determine a required payment period and communicate that policy to their customers. It is important to make sure that your company's payment period is consistent with that of your competitors. For example, if you decide to require payment within 15 days, but your competitors require payment within 45 days, you may lose sales to your competitor. However, as noted in Chapter 5, you might allow up to 45 days to pay but offer a sales discount for people paying within 15 days to match competitors' terms but encourage prompt payment of accounts.

Determine a payment period

MONITORING COLLECTIONS

One initial step that can be taken to monitor receivables is to calculate a company's **credit risk ratio**, which is found by dividing the Allowance for Doubtful Accounts by Accounts Receivable, as shown in Illustration 8-14:

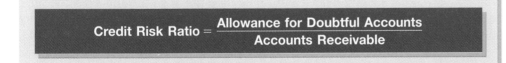

$$\text{Credit Risk Ratio} = \frac{\text{Allowance for Doubtful Accounts}}{\text{Accounts Receivable}}$$

Illustration 8-14   Credit risk ratio

Changes in this ratio over time may suggest that a company's overall credit risk is increasing or decreasing, and differences across companies may suggest differences in each company's overall credit risk. A high credit risk ratio may indicate that a company is extending credit to questionable customers.

To illustrate the use of the credit risk ratio, we will evaluate the receivables of McKesson HBOC. McKesson provides health-care supplies to pharmacies across the country. It has grown very rapidly in recent years, with total sales more than doubling during a four-year period. When evaluating a rapidly growing company, one concern would be whether the company has lowered its credit standards to increase sales. The following data are available for McKesson:

(in millions)	3/31/99	3/31/98
Accounts receivable (gross)	$2,765.2	$2,043.7
Allowance for doubtful accounts	181.5	83.7

The credit risk ratio for McKesson and comparative industry data are shown in Illustration 8-15.

Illustration 8-15 Credit risk ratio comparison

($ in millions)	1999	1998
McKesson HBOC	$\dfrac{\$181.5}{\$2,765.2} = 6.6\%$	$\dfrac{\$83.7}{\$2,043.7} = 4.1\%$
Industry average	3.5%	3.8%

McKesson's credit risk ratio increased substantially from 4.1% in fiscal 1998 to 6.6% in fiscal 1999. We also note that in both years its credit risk ratio is substantially higher than the industry average, especially in 1999. This would be of concern to analysts because it might suggest that McKesson's growth is being fueled by overly aggressive credit-granting practices. Since McKesson's growth was in part due to some major acquisitions and mergers, we might also question the quality of the receivables practices of the acquired companies.

Monitor collections

Preparation of the accounts receivable aging schedule was discussed on page 360. An accounts receivable aging schedule should be prepared at least monthly. In addition to estimating the allowance for bad debts, the aging schedule has other uses to management. It aids estimation of the timing of future cash inflows, which is very important to the treasurer's efforts to prepare a cash budget. It provides information about the overall collection experience of the company and identifies problem accounts. Problem accounts need to be pursued with phone calls, letters, and occasionally legal action. Sometimes special arrangements must be made with problem accounts. For example, it was recently reported that Intel Corporation (a major manufacturer of computer chips) required that Packard Bell (one of the largest U.S. sellers of personal computers) give Intel an interest-bearing note receivable in exchange for its past-due account receivable owed to Intel. This was cause for concern within the investment community, first because it suggested that Packard Bell was in trouble, and second because of the impact on Intel's accounts receivable, since Packard Bell is one of its largest customers.

BUSINESS INSIGHT
Investor Perspective

Changes in bad debts expense can be big news for investors. When Bank of New York announced a $350 million increase in its allowance for bad debts, the stock market reacted by sending the bank's stock price down by nearly 5%. Small investors were very angry because the news was first reported to a group of 90 large investors in a conference call before the market closed for the day, and then it was reported in a press release to the general public after the market closed. Share prices of many other large banks also declined that day because the market was anticipating that they too would soon announce increases in their allowance for bad debts.

DECISION TOOLKIT

Decision Checkpoints	Info Needed for Decision	Tool to Use for Decision	How to Evaluate Results
Is the company's credit risk increasing?	Allowance for doubtful accounts and accounts receivable	Credit risk ratio = $\dfrac{\text{Allowance for doubtful accounts}}{\text{Accounts receivable}}$	Increase in ratio may suggest increased credit risk, requiring evaluation of credit policies.

If a company has significant concentrations of credit risk, it is required to discuss this risk in the notes to its financial statements. A concentration of credit risk is a threat of nonpayment from a single customer or class of customers that could adversely affect the financial health of the company. An excerpt from the credit risk note from the 1998 annual report of McKesson HBOC is shown in Illustration 8-16.

McKESSON HBOC
Notes to the Financial Statements

Concentrations of Credit Risk: Trade receivables subject the Company to a concentration of credit risk with customers in the retail and institutional sectors. This risk is spread over a large number of geographically dispersed customers.

Illustration 8-16   Note on concentration of credit risk

This note to McKesson HBOC's financial statements suggests that, although the company extends significant amounts of credit, its exposure to any individual customer or group of customers is limited.

DECISION TOOLKIT

Decision Checkpoints	Info Needed for Decision	Tool to Use for Decision	How to Evaluate Results
Does the company have significant concentrations of credit risk?	Note to the financial statements on concentrations of credit risk	If risky credit customers are identified, the financial health of those customers should be evaluated to gain an independent assessment of the potential for a material credit loss.	If a material loss appears likely, the potential negative impact of that loss on the company should be carefully evaluated, along with the adequacy of the allowance for doubtful accounts.

EVALUATING THE RECEIVABLES BALANCE

STUDY OBJECTIVE
8
Identify ratios to analyze a company's receivables.

Investors and managers keep a watchful eye on the relationship among sales, accounts receivable, and cash collections. If sales increase, then accounts receivable are also expected to increase. But a disproportionate increase in accounts receivable might signal trouble. Perhaps the company increased its sales by loosening its credit policy, and these receivables may be difficult or impossible to collect. Such receivables are considered less liquid. Recall that liquidity is measured by how quickly certain assets can be converted to cash. The ratio used to assess the liquidity of the receivables is the receivables turnover ratio. This ratio measures the number of times, on average, receivables are collected during the period. The receivables turnover ratio is computed by dividing net credit sales (net sales less cash sales) by the average net receivables during the

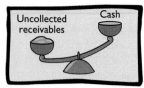

Evaluate the receivables balance

year. Unless seasonal factors are significant, **average** receivables outstanding can be computed from the beginning and ending balances of the net receivables.[1]

A popular variant of the receivables turnover ratio is to convert it into an average collection period in terms of days. This is done by dividing the receivables turnover ratio into 365 days. The average collection period is frequently used to assess the effectiveness of a company's credit and collection policies. The general rule is that the collection period should not greatly exceed the credit term period (i.e., the time allowed for payment). The following data (in millions) are available for McKesson HBOC:

	For the year ended March 31,	
	1999	**1998**
Sales	$30,382	$22,419
Accounts receivable	2,584	1,960

Illustration 8-17 Receivables turnover and average collection period

The receivables turnover ratio and average collection period for McKesson HBOC are shown in Illustration 8-17 along with comparative industry data.

$$\text{Receivables Turnover Ratio} = \frac{\text{Net Credit Sales}}{\text{Average Net Receivables}}$$

$$\text{Average Collection Period} = \frac{365}{\text{Receivables Turnover Ratio}}$$

($ in millions)		1999	1998
McKesson	Receivables turnover	$\frac{\$30,382}{(\$2,584 + \$1,960)/2} = 13.4$ times	$\frac{\$22,419}{(\$1,960 + \$1,612)/2*} = 12.6$ times
	Average collection period	$\frac{365}{13.4} = 27.2$ days	$\frac{365}{12.6} = 29.0$ days
Industry average	Receivables turnover	10.5 times	10.1 times
	Average collection period	34.8 days	36.1 days

*The net receivables balance at March 31, 1997, was $1,612 million.

These calculations assume that all sales were credit sales.

McKesson's receivables turnover was 13.4 times in 1999, with a corresponding average collection period of 27.2 days. This was an improvement over its 1998 collection period of 29 days. It also compares very favorably with the industry average collection period of 34.8 days. What this means is that McKesson is able to turn the receivables into cash more quickly than most of its competitors. McKesson is also more liquid, meaning that it has a better likelihood of paying its current obligations than a company with a slower receivables turnover.

---

[1]If seasonal factors are significant, the average receivables balance might be determined by using monthly amounts.

Management Perspective

In some cases, receivables turnover may be misleading. Some companies, especially large retail chains, encourage credit and revolving charge sales, and they slow collections in order to earn a healthy return on the outstanding receivables in the form of interest at rates of 18% to 22%. This may explain why J. C. Penney's turnover is only 4.1 times (an average collection period of 89 days), for example. In general, however, the faster the turnover, the greater the reliance that can be placed on the current ratio for assessing liquidity.

DECISION TOOLKIT

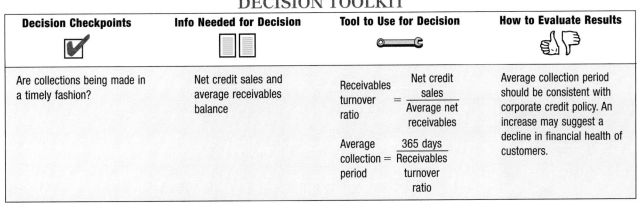

Decision Checkpoints	Info Needed for Decision	Tool to Use for Decision	How to Evaluate Results
Are collections being made in a timely fashion?	Net credit sales and average receivables balance	Receivables turnover ratio $= \dfrac{\text{Net credit sales}}{\text{Average net receivables}}$ Average collection period $= \dfrac{365 \text{ days}}{\text{Receivables turnover ratio}}$	Average collection period should be consistent with corporate credit policy. An increase may suggest a decline in financial health of customers.

ACCELERATING CASH RECEIPTS

In the normal course of events, accounts receivable are collected in cash and removed from the books. However, as credit sales and receivables have grown in size and significance, the "normal course of events" has changed. Two common expressions apply to the collection of receivables: (1) Time is money—that is, waiting for the normal collection process costs money. (2) A bird in the hand is worth two in the bush—that is, getting the cash now is better than getting it later or not at all. Therefore, in order to accelerate the receipt of cash from receivables, companies frequently sell their receivables to another company for cash, thereby shortening the cash-to-cash operating cycle.

There are three reasons for the sale of receivables. The first is their size. In recent years, **for competitive reasons, sellers (retailers, wholesalers, and manufacturers) often have provided financing to purchasers of their goods**. For example, many major companies in the automobile, truck, industrial and farm equipment, computer, and appliance industries have created companies that accept responsibility for accounts receivable financing. General Motors has General Motors Acceptance Corp. (GMAC), Sears has Sears Roebuck Acceptance Corp. (SRAC), and Ford has Ford Motor Credit Corp. (FMCC). These companies are referred to as **captive finance companies** because they are wholly owned by the company making the product. The purpose of captive finance companies is to encourage the sale of their product by assuring financing to buyers. However, the parent companies involved do not necessarily want to hold large amounts of receivables.

Second, **receivables may be sold because they may be the only reasonable source of cash**. When money is tight, companies may not be able to borrow money in the usual credit markets. If money is available, the cost of borrowing may be prohibitive.

9

Describe methods to accelerate the receipt of cash from receivables.

Accelerate cash receipts from receivables

A final reason for selling receivables is that **billing and collection are often time-consuming and costly**. As a result, it is often easier for a retailer to sell the receivables to another party that has expertise in billing and collection matters. Credit card companies such as MasterCard, VISA, American Express, and Diners Club specialize in billing and collecting accounts receivable.

Sale of Receivables to a Factor

A common way to accelerate receivables collection is a sale to a factor. A *factor* is a finance company or bank that buys receivables from businesses for a fee and then collects the payments directly from the customers. Factoring was traditionally associated with the textiles, apparel, footwear, furniture, and home furnishing industries. As you learned in the opening story, it has now spread to other types of businesses and is a multibillion dollar business. For example, Sears, Roebuck & Co. once sold $14.8 billion of customer accounts receivable. McKesson sold accounts receivable of $299.9 million at March 31, 1999, and $147.7 million at the previous year-end. McKesson's sale of receivables may explain why its receivables turnover ratio exceeds the industry average.

BUSINESS INSIGHT
Management Perspective

In 1996 JWA Security Services was cited by *Inc.* magazine as one of America's fastest growing businesses. However, in 1999 it filed for bankruptcy. Its failure was largely due to an inability to manage its receivables. JWA's largest contract, the state of California, often didn't pay JWA until nine months after the service had been performed. While it waited for this payment, the company still had to pay its bills. To make up for the cash shortfall that this time lag created, JWA factored its receivables with Imperial Bank in Los Angeles—an expensive source of cash that bit heavily into JWA's profits. JWA suffered a severe blow in 1999 when it lost the California contract, but according to company officials, the final blow actually occurred when Imperial Bank would no longer factor JWA's receivables. Suddenly JWA couldn't pay its bills, even though it still had $1.6 million in receivables.

Source: J.C. Dalton, "Flawed Safeguard Sinks Security Company," *Inc.*, September 1999, p. 27.

Factoring arrangements vary widely, but typically the factor charges a commission. It ranges from 1% to 3% of the amount of receivables purchased. To illustrate, assume that Hendredon Furniture factors $600,000 of receivables to Federal Factors, Inc. Federal Factors assesses a service charge of 2% of the amount of receivables sold. The following journal entry records the sale by Hendredon Furniture:

A	=	L	+	SE
+588,000				−12,000
−600,000				

Cash	588,000	
Service Charge Expense (2% × $600,000)	12,000	
Accounts Receivable		600,000
(To record the sale of accounts receivable)		

If the company usually sells its receivables, the service charge expense incurred by Hendredon Furniture is recorded as selling expense. If receivables are sold infrequently, this amount may be reported under Other Expenses and Losses in the income statement.

National Credit Card Sales

Approximately one billion credit cards were estimated to be in use recently—more than three credit cards for every man, woman, and child in this country. A common type of credit card is a national credit card such as VISA, Master-Card, and American Express. Three parties are involved when national credit cards are used in making retail sales: (1) the credit card issuer, who is independent of the retailer, (2) the retailer, and (3) the customer. **A retailer's acceptance of a national credit card is another form of selling—factoring—the receivable by the retailer**.

The use of national credit cards translates to more sales with zero bad debts for the retailer. Both are powerful reasons for a retailer to accept such cards. The major advantages of national credit cards to the retailer are shown in Illustration 8-18. In exchange for these advantages, the retailer pays the credit card issuer a fee of 2% to 6% of the invoice price for its services.

Issuer does credit investigation of customer

Credit card issuer   Customer   Retailer

Issuer maintains customer accounts

Issuer undertakes collection process and absorbs any losses

Retailer receives cash more quickly from credit card issuer

Illustration 8-18 Advantages of credit cards to the retailer

BUSINESS INSIGHT
Management Perspective

Between 1989 and 1998, nonmortgage consumer debt increased from $762 billion to $1,266 billion. This massive increase in borrowing resulted in personal bankruptcy filings at a record high of 1.3 million filings in 1998. In response, credit card issuers have cracked down on some consumers who file for bankruptcy to avoid paying their credit card debts. If a creditor can demonstrate that a person filed for bankruptcy fraudulently (that is, if the person actually had the ability to pay his or her debts but filed for bankruptcy to avoid bills), a creditor can sue the person and demand repayment. Of the 85,000 AT&T credit cardholders who filed for personal bankruptcy in 1996, AT&T sued 2,700 of them. In addition, lenders are lobbying Congress to change bankruptcy laws to make filing for bankruptcy less appealing to individuals.

VISA and MasterCard Sales. Sales resulting from the use of VISA and Master-Card are considered cash sales by the retailer. These cards are issued by banks. Upon receipt of credit card sales slips from a retailer, the bank immediately adds the amount to the seller's bank balance. These credit card sales slips are therefore recorded in the same manner as checks deposited from a cash sale. The banks that issue these cards generally charge a fee of 2% to 4% of the credit card sales slips for this service. To illustrate, Anita Ferreri purchases $1,000 of compact discs for her restaurant from Karen Kerr Music Co., and she charges this amount on her VISA First Bank Card. The service fee that First Bank charges Karen Kerr Music is 3%. The entry by Karen Kerr Music to record this transaction is:

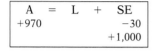

A	=	L	+	SE
+970				−30
				+1,000

Cash	970	
Service Charge Expense	30	
Sales		1,000
(To record VISA credit card sales)		

The basic principles of managing accounts receivable are summarized in Illustration 8-19.

Illustration 8-19
Managing receivables

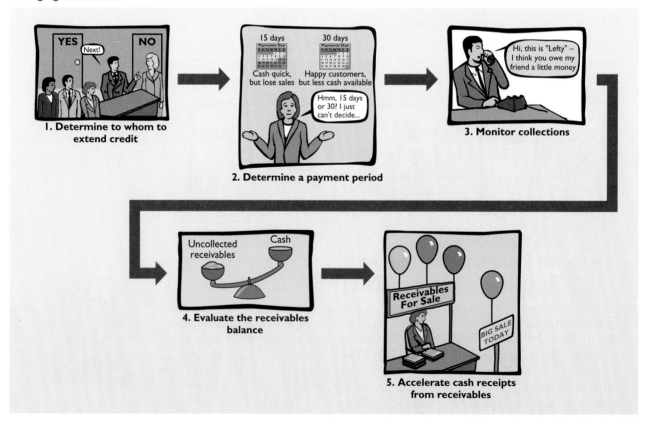

BEFORE YOU GO ON...

◆ Review It

1. What is meant by a concentration of credit risk?
2. What is the interpretation of the receivables turnover ratio and the average collection period?
3. Why do companies sell their receivables?
4. For whom is the service charge on a credit card sale an expense?

◆ Do It

Peter M. Dell Wholesalers Co. has been expanding faster than it can raise capital. According to its local banker, the company has reached its debt ceiling. Dell's customers are slow in paying (60–90 days), but its suppliers (creditors) are demanding 30-day payment. Dell has a cash flow problem.

Dell needs to raise $120,000 in cash to safely cover next Friday's employee payroll. Dell's present balance of outstanding receivables totals $750,000. What might Dell do to alleviate this cash crunch? Record the entry that Dell would make when it raises the needed cash.

Reasoning: One source of immediate cash at a competitive cost is the sale of receivables to a factor. Rather than waiting until it can collect receivables, Dell may raise immediate cash by selling its receivables. The last thing Dell (or any employer) wants to do is miss a payroll.

Solution: If Dell Co. factors $125,000 of its accounts receivable at a 1% service charge, this entry would be made:

Cash	123,750	
Service Charge Expense	1,250	
Accounts Receivable		125,000
(To record sale of receivables to factor)		

*U*SING THE DECISION TOOLKIT

The following information was taken from the December 31, 1998, financial statements of Del Laboratories. Similar to McKesson HBOC, Del Laboratories manufactures and distributes pharmaceuticals. Del Labs is, however, much smaller than McKesson, and it has not enjoyed the phenomenal growth of McKesson.

DEL LABORATORIES
Selected Financial Information
(in thousands)

	1998		1997	
Sales		$274,862		$263,010
Current assets				
Cash and cash equivalents		$ 3,731		$ 14,979
Accounts receivable	$48,416		$32,008	
Allowance for doubtful accounts	1,300		1,300	
Net accounts receivable		47,116		30,708
Inventories		55,620		47,687
Other current assets		6,624		3,985
Total current assets		$113,091		$ 97,359
Total current liabilities		$ 50,363		$ 43,783

Instructions

Comment on Del Laboratories' accounts receivable management and liquidity relative to that of McKesson, with consideration given to (1) the credit risk ratio, (2) the current ratio, and (3) the receivables turnover ratio and average collection period. McKesson's current ratio was 1.35:1. The other ratio values for McKesson were calculated earlier in the chapter.

Solution

(McKesson HBOC figures in millions, Del Labs figures in thousands)

1. Here are the credit risk ratios of McKesson and Del Laboratories:

McKesson	**Del Labs**
$\dfrac{\$181.5}{\$2,765.2} = 6.6\%$	$\dfrac{\$1,300}{\$48,416} = 2.7\%$

McKesson's note on credit risk (Illustration 8-16) does not suggest significant exposure to any troubled customers, even though its credit risk ratio is more than double that of Del Laboratories.

2. Here is the current ratio (Current assets ÷ Current liabilities) for each company:

McKesson	**Del Labs**
$\dfrac{\$6,499,000}{\$4,800,100} = 1.35:1$	$\dfrac{\$113,091}{\$50,363} = 2.25:1$

This suggests that Del Labs is substantially more liquid than McKesson.

3. The receivables turnover ratio and average collection period for each company are:

	McKesson	**Del Labs**
Receivables turnover ratio	13.4 times	$\dfrac{\$274,862}{(\$47,116 + \$30,708)\,/\,2} = 7.1$ times
Average collection period	27.2 days	$\dfrac{365}{7.1} = 51.4$ days

McKesson's receivables turnover ratio of 13.4 compared to Del Laboratories' 7.1, and its average collection days of 27.2 days versus Del Labs' 51.4 days, suggest that McKesson is able to collect from its customers much more rapidly. McKesson's more rapid collection of receivables may compensate in part for its lower current ratio. That is, since it can turn its receivables into cash more quickly, its receivables appear to be more liquid than those of Del Labs.

SUMMARY OF STUDY OBJECTIVES

1 Identify the different types of receivables. Receivables are frequently classified as accounts, notes, and other. Accounts receivable are amounts owed by customers on account. Notes receivable represent claims that are evidenced by formal instruments of credit. Other receivables include nontrade receivables such as interest receivable, loans to company officers, advances to employees, and income taxes refundable.

2 Explain how accounts receivable are recognized in the accounts. Accounts receivable are recorded at invoice price. They are reduced by sales returns and allowances. Cash discounts reduce the amount received on accounts receivable.

3 Describe the methods used to account for bad debts. The two methods of accounting for uncollectible accounts are the allowance method and the direct write-off method. The percentage of receivables basis is used to estimate uncollectible accounts in the allowance method. It emphasizes the cash realizable value of the accounts receivable. An aging schedule is frequently used with this basis.

4 Compute the maturity date of and interest on notes receivable. The maturity date of a note must be computed unless the due date is specified or the note is payable on demand. For a note stated in months, the maturity date is found by counting the months from the date of issue. For a note stated in days, the number of days is counted, omitting the issue date and including the due date. The formula for computing interest is: Face value × Interest rate × Time.

5 Describe the entries to record the disposition of notes receivable. Notes can be held to maturity, at which time the face value plus accrued interest is due and the note is removed from the accounts. In many cases, however, similar to accounts receivable, the holder of the note speeds up the conversion by selling the receivable to another party. In some situations, the maker of the note dishonors the note (defaults), and the note is written off.

6 Explain the statement presentation of receivables. Each major type of receivable should be identified in the balance sheet or in the notes to the financial statements. Short-term receivables are considered current assets. The gross amount of receivables and allowance for doubtful accounts should be reported. Bad debts and service charge expenses are reported in the income statement as operating (selling) expenses, and interest revenue is shown as other revenues and gains in the nonoperating section of the statement.

7 Describe the principles of sound accounts receivable management. To properly manage receivables, management must (a) determine to whom to extend credit, (b) determine a payment period, (c) monitor collections, (d) evaluate the receivables balance, and (e) accelerate cash receipts from receivables when necessary.

8 Identify ratios to analyze a company's receivables. The receivables turnover ratio and the average collection period both are useful in analyzing management's effectiveness in managing receivables. The accounts receivable aging schedule also provides useful information.

9 Describe methods to accelerate the receipt of cash from receivables. If the company needs additional cash, management can accelerate the collection of cash from receivables by selling (factoring) its receivables or by allowing customers to pay with bank credit cards.

DECISION TOOLKIT—A SUMMARY

Decision Checkpoints	Info Needed for Decision	Tool to Use for Decision	How to Evaluate Results
Is the amount of past due accounts increasing? Which accounts require management's attention?	List of outstanding receivables and their due dates	Prepare an aging schedule showing the receivables in various stages: outstanding 0–30 days, 30–60 days, 60–90 days, and over 90 days.	Accounts in the older categories require follow-up: letters, phone calls, and possible renegotiation of terms.
Is the company's credit risk increasing?	Allowance for doubtful accounts and accounts receivable	$$\text{Credit risk ratio} = \frac{\text{Allowance for doubtful accounts}}{\text{Accounts receivable}}$$	Increase in ratio may suggest increased credit risk, requiring evaluation of credit policies.
Does the company have significant concentrations of credit risk?	Note to the financial statements on concentrations of credit risk	If risky credit customers are identified, the financial health of those customers should be evaluated to gain an independent assessment of the potential for a material credit loss.	If a material loss appears likely, the potential negative impact of that loss on the company should be carefully evaluated, along with the adequacy of the allowance for doubtful accounts.
Are collections being made in a timely fashion?	Net credit sales and average receivables balance	$$\text{Receivables turnover ratio} = \frac{\text{Net credit sales}}{\text{Average net receivables}}$$ $$\text{Average collection period} = \frac{365 \text{ days}}{\text{Receivables turnover ratio}}$$	Average collection period should be consistent with corporate credit policy. An increase may suggest a decline in financial health of customers.

GLOSSARY

Accounts receivable Amounts owed by customers on account. (p. 355)

Aging the accounts receivable The analysis of customer balances by the length of time they have been unpaid. (p. 360)

Allowance method A method of accounting for bad debts that involves estimating uncollectible accounts at the end of each period. (p. 357)

Average collection period The average amount of time that a receivable is outstanding, calculated by dividing 365 days by the receivables turnover ratio. (p. 372)

Bad debts expense An expense account to record uncollectible receivables. (p. 356)

Cash (net) realizable value The net amount expected to be received in cash. (p. 357)

Concentration of credit risk The threat of nonpayment from a single customer or class of customers that could adversely affect the financial health of the company. (p. 371)

Credit risk ratio A measure of the risk that a company's customers may not pay their accounts, calculated as the Allowance for Doubtful Accounts divided by Accounts Receivable. (p. 369)

Direct write-off method A method of accounting for bad debts that involves expensing accounts at the time they are determined to be uncollectible. (p. 356)

Dishonored note A note that is not paid in full at maturity. (p. 366)

Factor A finance company or bank that buys receivables from businesses for a fee and then collects the payments directly from the customers. (p. 374)

Maker The party in a promissory note who is making the promise to pay. (p. 362)

Notes receivable Claims for which formal instruments of credit are issued as evidence of the debt. (p. 355)

Payee The party to whom payment of a promissory note is to be made. (p. 362)

Percentage of receivables basis Management establishes a percentage relationship between the amount of receivables and the expected losses from uncollectible accounts. (p. 360)

Promissory note A written promise to pay a specified amount of money on demand or at a definite time. (p. 362)

Receivables Amounts due from individuals and companies that are expected to be collected in cash. (p. 354)

Receivables turnover ratio A measure of the liquidity of receivables, computed by dividing net credit sales by average net receivables. (p. 371)

Trade receivables Notes and accounts receivable that result from sales transactions. (p. 355)

DEMONSTRATION PROBLEM

Presented here are selected transactions related to B. Dylan Corp:

Mar.	1	Sold $20,000 of merchandise to Potter Company, terms 2/10, n/30.
	11	Received payment in full from Potter Company for balance due.
	12	Accepted Juno Company's $20,000, 6-month, 12% note for balance due.
	13	Made B. Dylan Corp. credit card sales for $13,200.
	15	Made VISA credit sales totaling $6,700. A 5% service fee is charged by VISA.
Apr.	11	Sold accounts receivable of $8,000 to Harcot Factor. Harcot Factor assesses a service charge of 2% of the amount of receivables sold.
	13	Received collections of $8,200 on B. Dylan Corp. credit card sales.
May	10	Wrote off as uncollectible $16,000 of accounts receivable. B. Dylan Corp. uses the percentage of receivables basis to estimate bad debts.
June	30	The balance in accounts receivable at the end of the first 6 months is $200,000 and the bad debt percentage is 10%. At June 30 the credit balance in the allowance account prior to adjustment is $3,500.
July	16	One of the accounts receivable written off in May pays the amount due, $4,000, in full.

Instructions
Prepare the journal entries for the transactions.

Solution to Demonstration Problem

Mar.	1	Accounts Receivable—Potter Company	20,000	
		Sales		20,000
		(To record sales on account)		
	11	Cash	19,600	
		Sales Discounts (2% × $20,000)	400	
		Accounts Receivable—Potter Company		20,000
		(To record collection of accounts receivable)		
	12	Notes Receivable	20,000	
		Accounts Receivable—Juno Company		20,000
		(To record acceptance of Juno Company note)		
	13	Accounts Receivable	13,200	
		Sales		13,200
		(To record company credit card sales)		
	15	Cash	6,365	
		Service Charge Expense (5% × $6,700)	335	
		Sales		6,700
		(To record credit card sales)		

Problem-Solving Strategies

1. Accounts receivable are generally recorded at invoice price.
2. Sales returns and allowances and cash discounts reduce the amount received on accounts receivable.
3. When accounts receivable are sold, a service charge expense is incurred by the seller.
4. Bad debts expense is an adjusting entry.
5. The percentage of receivables basis considers any existing balance in the allowance account.
6. Write-offs of accounts receivable affect only balance sheet accounts.

Apr.	11	Cash	7,840	
		Service Charge Expense (2% × $8,000)	160	
		Accounts Receivable		8,000
		(To record sale of receivables to factor)		
	13	Cash	8,200	
		Accounts Receivable		8,200
		(To record collection of accounts receivable)		
May	10	Allowance for Doubtful Accounts	16,000	
		Accounts Receivable		16,000
		(To record write-off of accounts receivable)		
June	30	Bad Debts Expense	16,500	
		Allowance for Doubtful Accounts		16,500
		[($200,000 × 10%) − $3,500]		
		(To record estimate of uncollectible accounts)		
July	16	Accounts Receivable	4,000	
		Allowance for Doubtful Accounts		4,000
		(To reverse write-off of accounts receivable)		
		Cash	4,000	
		Accounts Receivable		4,000
		(To record collection of accounts receivable)		

SELF-STUDY QUESTIONS

Answers are at the end of the chapter.

(SO 2) 1. Jones Company on June 15 sells merchandise on account to Bullock Co. for $1,000, terms 2/10, n/30. On June 20 Bullock Co. returns merchandise worth $300 to Jones Company. On June 24 payment is received from Bullock Co. for the balance due. What is the amount of cash received?

(a) $700.   (c) $686.
(b) $680.   (d) None of the above.

(SO 3) 2. Net credit sales for the month are $800,000. The accounts receivable balance is $160,000. The allowance is calculated as 7.5% of the receivables balance using the percentage of receivables basis. If the Allowance for Doubtful Accounts has a credit balance of $5,000 before adjustment, what is the balance after adjustment?

(a) $12,000.   (c) $17,000.
(b) $7,000.   (d) $31,000.

(SO 3) 3. In 2001 D. H. Lawrence Company had net credit sales of $750,000. On January 1, 2001, Allowance for Doubtful Accounts had a credit balance of $18,000. During 2001, $30,000 of uncollectible accounts receivable were written off. Past experience indicates that the allowance should be 10% of the balance in receivables (percentage of receivables basis). If the accounts receivable balance at December 31 was $200,000, what is the required adjustment to the Allowance for Doubtful Accounts at December 31, 2001?

(a) $20,000.   (c) $32,000.
(b) $75,000.   (d) $30,000.

(SO 3) 4. An analysis and aging of the accounts receivable of Machiavelli Company at December 31 reveal these data:

Accounts receivable	$800,000
Allowance for doubtful accounts per	
books before adjustment (credit)	50,000
Amounts expected to become	
uncollectible	65,000

What is the cash realizable value of the accounts receivable at December 31, after adjustment?
(a) $685,000.   (c) $800,000.
(b) $750,000.   (d) $735,000.

(SO 4) 5. Which of these statements about promissory notes is *incorrect*?
(a) The party making the promise to pay is called the maker.
(b) The party to whom payment is to be made is called the payee.
(c) A promissory note is not a negotiable instrument.
(d) A promissory note is more liquid than an account receivable.

(SO 4) 6. Sorenson Co. accepts a $1,000, 3-month, 12% promissory note in settlement of an account with Parton Co. The entry to record this transaction is:

(a) Notes Receivable	1,030	
Accounts		
Receivable		1,030
(b) Notes Receivable	1,000	
Accounts		
Receivable		1,000
(c) Notes Receivable	1,000	
Sales		1,000
(d) Notes Receivable	1,020	
Accounts		
Receivable		1,020

(SO 5) 7. Schlicht Co. holds Osgrove Inc.'s $10,000, 120-day, 9% note. The entry made by Schlicht Co. when the note is collected, assuming no interest has previously been accrued, is:

| (a) Cash | 10,300 | |
| Notes Receivable | | 10,300 |

(b) Cash	10,000	
Notes Receivable		10,000
(c) Accounts Receivable	10,300	
Notes Receivable		10,000
Interest Revenue		300
(d) Cash	10,300	
Notes Receivable		10,000
Interest Revenue		300

8. Moore Corporation had net credit (SO 8) sales during the year of $800,000 and cost of goods sold of $500,000. The balance in receivables at the beginning of the year was $100,000 and at the end of the year was $150,000. What was the receivables turnover ratio?
(a) 6.4   (b) 8.0   (c) 5.3   (d) 4.0

9. Hoffman Corporation sells its goods (SO 8) on terms of 2/10, n/30. It has a receivables turnover ratio of 7. What is its average collection period (days)?
(a) 2,555   (b) 30   (c) 52   (d) 210

10. Which of these statements about VISA credit (SO 9) card sales is *incorrect*?
(a) The credit card issuer conducts the credit investigation of the customer.
(b) The retailer is not involved in the collection process.
(c) The retailer must wait to receive payment from the issuer.
(d) The retailer receives cash more quickly than it would from individual customers.

11. Morgan Retailers accepted $50,000 of Citibank (SO 9) VISA credit card charges for merchandise sold on July 1. Citibank charges 4% for its credit card use. The entry to record this transaction by Morgan Retailers will include a credit to Sales of $50,000 and a debit(s) to:
(a) Cash $48,000 and Service Charge Expense $2,000.
(b) Accounts Receivable $48,000 and Service Charge Expense $2,000.
(c) Cash $50,000.
(d) Accounts Receivable $50,000.

QUESTIONS

1. What is the difference between an account receivable and a note receivable?

2. What are some common types of receivables other than accounts receivable or notes receivable?

3. What are the essential features of the allowance method of accounting for bad debts?

4. Soo Eng cannot understand why the cash realizable value does not decrease when an uncollectible account is written off under the allowance method. Clarify this point for Soo Eng.

5. Kersee Company has a credit balance of $3,200 in Allowance for Doubtful Accounts before adjustment. The

estimated uncollectibles under the percentage of receivables basis is $5,800. Prepare the adjusting entry.

6. How are bad debts accounted for under the direct write-off method? What are the disadvantages of this method?

7. Your roommate is uncertain about the advantages of a promissory note. Compare the advantages of a note receivable with those of an accounts receivable.

8. How may the maturity date of a promissory note be stated?

9. Indicate the maturity date of each of the following promissory notes:

Date of Note	Terms
(a) March 13	One year after date of note
(b) May 4	3 months after date
(c) June 10	30 days after date
(d) July 2	60 days after date

10. Compute the missing amounts for each of the following notes:

Principal	Annual Interest Rate	Time	Total Interest
(a)	9%	120 days	$ 360
$30,000	10%	3 years	(d)
$60,000	(b)	5 months	$2,500
$50,000	11%	(c)	$1,375

11. May Company dishonors a note at maturity. What actions by May may occur with the dishonoring of the note?

12. **General Motors Company** has accounts receivable and notes receivable. How should the receivables be reported on the balance sheet?

13. What are the steps to good receivables management?

14. How might a company monitor the risk related to its accounts receivable?

15. What is meant by a concentration of credit risk?

16. **The Coca-Cola Company's** receivables turnover ratio was 11.38 in 1998 and its average net receivables during the period was $1,652.5 million. What is the amount of its net credit sales for the period? What is the average collection period in days?

17. **J. C. Penney Company** accepts both its own credit cards and national credit cards. What are the advantages of accepting both types of cards?

18. An article recently appeared in *The Wall Street Journal* indicating that companies are selling their receivables at a record rate. Why are companies selling their receivables?

19. Southern Textiles decides to sell $700,000 of its accounts receivable to First Central Factors Inc. First Central Factors assesses a service charge of 2% of the amount of receivables sold. Prepare the journal entry that Southern Textiles makes to record this sale.

BRIEF EXERCISES

Identify different types of receivables.
(SO 1)

BE8-1 Presented below are three receivables transactions. Indicate whether these receivables are reported as accounts receivable, notes receivable, or other receivables on a balance sheet.
(a) Advanced $10,000 to an employee
(b) Received a promissory note of $57,000 for services performed
(c) Sold merchandise on account for $60,000 to a customer

Record basic accounts receivable transactions.
(SO 2)

BE8-2 Record the following transactions on the books of Essex Co.:
(a) On July 1 Essex Co. sold merchandise on account to Cambridge Inc. for $14,000, terms 2/10, n/30.
(b) On July 8 Cambridge Inc. returned merchandise worth $3,800 to Essex Co.
(c) On July 11 Cambridge Inc. paid for the merchandise.

Prepare entry for write-off, and determine cash realizable value.
(SO 3)

BE8-3 At the end of 2001, Searcy Co. has accounts receivable of $700,000 and an allowance for doubtful accounts of $54,000. On January 24, 2002, it is learned that the company's receivable from Hutley Inc. is not collectible and therefore management authorizes a write-off of $8,000.
(a) Prepare the journal entry to record the write-off.
(b) What is the cash realizable value of the accounts receivable (1) before the write-off and (2) after the write-off?

Prepare entries for collection of bad debt write-off.
(SO 3)

BE8-4 Assume the same information as BE8-3 and that on March 4, 2002, Searcy Co. receives payment of $8,000 in full from Hutley Co. Prepare the journal entries to record this transaction.

Prepare entry using percentage of receivables method.
(SO 3)

BE8-5 Massey Co. uses the percentage of receivables basis to record bad debts expense and concludes that 1% of accounts receivable will become uncollectible. Accounts receivable are $500,000 at the end of the year, and the allowance for doubtful accounts has a credit balance of $3,000.
(a) Prepare the adjusting journal entry to record bad debts expense for the year.
(b) If the allowance for doubtful accounts had a debit balance of $800 instead of a credit balance of $3,000, determine the amount to be reported for bad debts expense.

BE8-6 Presented below are three promissory notes. Determine the missing amounts.

Compute maturity date and interest on note.
(SO 4)

Date of Note	Terms	Maturity Date	Principal	Annual Interest Rate	Total Interest
April 1	60 days	(a)	$900,000	10%	(e)
July 2	30 days	(b)	79,000	(d)	$592.50
March 7	6 months	(c)	56,000	12%	(f)

BE8-7 On January 10, 2001, Raja Co. sold merchandise on account to R. Opal for $12,000, terms n/30. On February 9 R. Opal gave Raja Co. a 10% promissory note in settlement of this account. Prepare the journal entry to record the sale and the settlement of the accounts receivable.

Prepare entry for note receivable exchanged for accounts receivable.
(SO 4)

BE8-8 During its first year of operations, Wendy Company had credit sales of $3,000,000, of which $600,000 remained uncollected at year-end. The credit manager estimates that $40,000 of these receivables will become uncollectible.
(a) Prepare the journal entry to record the estimated uncollectibles. (Assume an unadjusted balance of zero.)
(b) Prepare the current assets section of the balance sheet for Wendy Company, assuming that in addition to the receivables it has cash of $90,000, merchandise inventory of $130,000, and prepaid expenses of $13,000.
(c) Calculate the credit risk ratio, receivables turnover ratio, and average collection period. Assume that average net receivables were $530,000.

Prepare entry for estimated uncollectibles and classifications, and compute ratios.
(SO 3, 6, 7, 8)

BE8-9 The 1998 financial statements of **Minnesota Mining and Manufacturing Company (3M)** report net sales of $15.0 billion. Accounts receivable are $2.5 billion at the beginning of the year and $2.8 billion at the end of the year. Compute 3M's receivables turnover ratio. Compute 3M's average collection period for accounts receivable in days.

Analyze accounts receivable.
(SO 8)

BE8-10 Consider these transactions:
(a) St. Pierre Restaurant accepted a VISA card in payment of a $100 lunch bill. The bank charges a 3% fee. What entry should St. Pierre make?
(b) Mayfield Company sold its accounts receivable of $70,000. What entry should Mayfield make, given a service charge of 3% on the amount of receivables sold?

Prepare entries for credit card sale and sale of accounts receivable.
(SO 9)

EXERCISES

E8-1 On January 6 Peas Co. sells merchandise on account to Beans Inc. for $4,000, terms 2/10, n/30. On January 16 Beans pays the amount due.

Instructions
Prepare the entries on Peas Co.'s books to record the sale and related collection.

Prepare entries for recognizing accounts receivable.
(SO 2)

E8-2 On January 10 Elaine Stahl uses her Salizar Co. credit card to purchase merchandise from Salizar Co. for $1,300. On February 10 Stahl is billed for the amount due of $1,300. On February 12 Stahl pays $800 on the balance due. On March 10 Stahl is billed for the amount due, including interest at 1% per month on the unpaid balance as of February 12.

Instructions
Prepare the entries on Salizar Co.'s books related to the transactions that occurred on January 10, February 12, and March 10.

Prepare entries for recognizing accounts receivable.
(SO 2)

E8-3 The ledger of Patillo Company at the end of the current year shows Accounts Receivable $90,000; Credit Sales $840,000; and Sales Returns and Allowances $40,000.

Instructions
(a) If Allowance for Doubtful Accounts has a credit balance of $800 in the trial balance, journalize the adjusting entry at December 31, assuming bad debts are expected to be 10% of accounts receivable.
(b) If Allowance for Doubtful Accounts has a debit balance of $500 in the trial balance, journalize the adjusting entry at December 31, assuming bad debts are expected to be 8% of accounts receivable.

Prepare entries to record allowance for doubtful accounts.
(SO 3)

E8-4 Garcia Company has accounts receivable of $92,500 at March 31, 2001. An analysis of the accounts shows these amounts:

	Balance, March 31	
Month of Sale	**2001**	**2000**
March	$65,000	$75,000
February	12,600	8,000
December and January	8,500	2,400
November and October	6,400	1,100
	$92,500	$86,500

Credit terms are 2/10, n/30. At March 31, 2001, there is a $1,600 credit balance in Allowance for Doubtful Accounts prior to adjustment. The company uses the percentage of receivables basis for estimating uncollectible accounts. The company's estimates of bad debts are as follows:

Age of Accounts	**Estimated Percentage Uncollectible**
Current	2.0%
1–30 days past due	5.0
31–90 days past due	30.0
Over 90 days	50.0

Instructions
(a) Determine the total estimated uncollectibles.
(b) Prepare the adjusting entry at March 31, 2001, to record bad debts expense.
(c) Discuss the implications of the changes in the aging schedule from 2000 to 2001.

E8-5 On December 31, 2001, when its Allowance for Doubtful Accounts had a debit balance of $1,000, Lisa Ceja Co. estimates that 12% of its accounts receivable balance of $60,000 will become uncollectible and records the necessary adjustment to the Allowance for Doubtful Accounts. On May 11, 2002, Lisa Ceja Co. determined that Robert Worthy's account was uncollectible and wrote off $900. On June 12, 2002, Worthy paid the amount previously written off.

Instructions
Prepare the journal entries on December 31, 2001, May 11, 2002, and June 12, 2002.

E8-6 Northridge Supply Co. has the following transactions related to notes receivable during the last 2 months of the year:

Nov. 1 Loaned $30,000 cash to R. Stone on a 1-year, 8% note.
Dec. 11 Sold goods to W. Kimball, Inc., receiving a $3,600, 90-day, 12% note.
16 Received a $6,000, 6-month, 12% note on account from J. Bell.
31 Accrued interest revenue on all notes receivable.

Instructions
Journalize the transactions for Northridge Supply Co.

E8-7 These transactions took place for Guard Dog Co.:

2000

May 1 Received a $7,000, 1-year, 12% note on account from T. Jones.
Dec. 31 Accrued interest revenue on the T. Jones note.

2001

May 1 Received principal plus interest on the T. Jones note. (No interest has been accrued in 2001.)

Instructions
Record the transactions in the general journal.

E8-8 On May 2 Gore Company lends $4,000 to Global Inc., issuing a 6-month, 6% note. At the maturity date, November 2, Global indicates that it cannot pay.

Instructions
(a) Prepare the entry to record the dishonor of the note, assuming that Gore Company expects collection will occur.
(b) Prepare the entry to record the dishonor of the note, assuming that Gore Company does not expect collection in the future.

E8-9   Deere and Company had the following balances in receivable accounts at October 31, 1998 (in millions): Allowance for Doubtful Accounts $31; Accounts Receivable $2,907; Other Receivables $228; Notes Receivable $955.

Prepare a balance sheet presentation of receivables.
(SO 6)

Instructions
Prepare the balance sheet presentation of Deere and Company's receivables in good form.

E8-10   The following is a list of activities that companies perform in relation to their receivables.
1. Selling receivables to a factor.
2. Reviewing company ratings in *The Dun and Bradstreet Reference Book of American Business*.
3. Collecting information on competitors' payment period policies
4. Preparing accounts receivable aging schedule and calculating the credit risk ratio.
5. Calculating the receivables turnover ratio and average collection period.

Identify the principles of receivables management.
(SO 7)

Instructions
Match each of the activites listed above with a purpose of the activity listed below.
(a) Determine to whom to extend credit.
(b) Establish a payment period.
(c) Monitor collections.
(d) Evaluate the receivables balance.
(e) Accelerate cash receipts from receivables when necessary.

E8-11   The following information was taken from the 1998 financial statements of **The Scotts Company**

Compute ratios to evaluate a company's receivables balance.
(SO 7, 8)

(in millions)	1998	1997
Accounts receivable	$ 146.6	$ 104.3
Allowance for uncollectible accounts	6.3	5.7
Sales	1,113.0	899.3
Total current assets	367.2	285.8

Instructions
Answer each of the following questions.
(a) Calculate the receivables turnover ratio and average collection period for 1998 for the company.
(b) Calculate the 1998 credit risk ratio for the company.
(c) Is accounts receivable a material component of the company's total current assets?

E8-12   On March 3 Virtual Appliances sells $900,000 of its receivables to Fundamental Factors Inc. Fundamental Factors Inc. assesses a finance charge of 4% of the amount of receivables sold.

Prepare entry for sale of accounts receivable.
(SO 9)

Instructions
Prepare the entry on Virtual Appliances' books to record the sale of the receivables.

E8-13   On May 10 Cheng Company sold merchandise for $4,000 and accepted the customer's First Business Bank MasterCard. At the end of the day, the First Business Bank MasterCard receipts were deposited in the company's bank account. First Business Bank charges a 3% service charge for credit card sales.

Prepare entry for credit card sale.
(SO 9)

Instructions
Prepare the entry on Cheng Company's books to record the sale of merchandise.

E8-14   On July 4 Harry's Restaurant accepts a VISA card for a $200 dinner bill. VISA charges a 4% service fee.

Prepare entry for credit card sale.
(SO 9)

Instructions
Prepare the entries on Harry's books related to the transaction.

PROBLEMS: SET A

Prepare journal entries related to bad debt expense, and compute ratios.
(SO 2, 3, 8)

P8-1A   At December 31, 2001, Muzzillo Imports reported this information on its balance sheet:

Accounts receivable	$1,000,000
Less: Allowance for doubtful accounts	60,000

During 2002 the company had the following transactions related to receivables:

1. Sales on account	$2,600,000
2. Sales returns and allowances	40,000
3. Collections of accounts receivable	2,300,000
4. Write-offs of accounts receivable deemed uncollectible	65,000
5. Recovery of bad debts previously written off as uncollectible	25,000

Instructions

(a) Prepare the journal entries to record each of these five transactions. Assume that no cash discounts were taken on the collections of accounts receivable.

(b) Enter the January 1, 2002, balances in Accounts Receivable and Allowance for Doubtful Accounts, post the entries to the two accounts (use T accounts), and determine the balances.

(c) Prepare the journal entry to record bad debts expense for 2002, assuming that aging the accounts receivable indicates that estimated bad debts are $70,000.

(d) Compute the receivables turnover ratio and average collection period.

Journalize transactions related to bad debts.
(SO 2, 3)

P8-2A   This is an aging schedule for Cain Company:

Customer	Total	Not Yet Due	Number of Days Past Due			
			1–30	**31–60**	**61–90**	**Over 90**
Aber	$ 20,000		$ 9,000	$11,000		
Bohr	30,000	$ 30,000				
Case	50,000	15,000	5,000		$30,000	
Datz	38,000					$38,000
Others	120,000	92,000	15,000	13,000		
	$258,000	$137,000	$29,000	$24,000	$30,000	$38,000
Estimated percentage uncollectible		3%	6%	12%	24%	50%
Total estimated bad debts	$ 34,930	$ 4,110	$ 1,740	$ 2,880	$ 7,200	$19,000

At December 31, 2001, the unadjusted balance in Allowance for Doubtful Accounts is a credit of $10,000.

Instructions

(a) Journalize and post the adjusting entry for bad debts at December 31, 2001. (Use T accounts.)

(b) Journalize and post to the allowance account these 2002 events and transactions:
   1. March 1, a $600 customer balance originating in 2001 is judged uncollectible.
   2. May 1, a check for $600 is received from the customer whose account was written off as uncollectible on March 1.

(c) Journalize the adjusting entry for bad debts at December 31, 2002, assuming that the unadjusted balance in Allowance for Doubtful Accounts is a debit of $1,100 and the aging schedule indicates that total estimated bad debts will be $29,100.

Compute bad debt amounts.
(SO 3)

P8-3A   Here is information related to Tisinai Company for 2001:

Total credit sales	$1,500,000
Accounts receivable at December 31	600,000
Bad debts written off	24,000

Instructions

(a) What amount of bad debts expense will Tisinai Company report if it uses the direct write-off method of accounting for bad debts?

(b) Assume that Tisinai Company decides to estimate its bad debts expense based on 3% of accounts receivable. What amount of bad debts expense will the company record if Allowance for Doubtful Accounts has a credit balance of $3,000?

(c) Assume the same facts as in part (b), except that there is a $2,000 debit balance in Allowance for Doubtful Accounts. What amount of bad debts expense will Tisinai record?

(d) ▭▭▭▷ What is the weakness of the direct write-off method of reporting bad debts expense?

P8-4A At December 31, 2001, the trial balance of John Gleason Company contained the following amounts before adjustment:

Journalize entries to record transactions related to bad debts.
(SO 2, 3)

	Debits	Credits
Accounts Receivable	$350,000	
Allowance for Doubtful Accounts		$ 1,500
Sales		875,000

Instructions

(a) Prepare the adjusting entry at December 31, 2001, to record bad debt expense assuming that the aging schedule indicates that $16,750 of accounts receivable will be uncollectible.

(b) Repeat part (a) assuming that instead of a credit balance there is a $1,500 debit balance in the Allowance for Doubtful Accounts.

(c) During the next month, January 2002, a $4,500 account receivable is written off as uncollectible. Prepare the journal entry to record the write-off.

(d) Repeat part (c) assuming that John Gleason Company uses the direct write-off method instead of the allowance method in accounting for uncollectible accounts receivable.

(e) ▭▭▭▷ What are the advantages of using the allowance method in accounting for uncollectible accounts as compared to the direct write-off method?

P8-5A On January 1, 2001, Elam Company had Accounts Receivable $54,200 and Allowance for Doubtful Accounts $4,700. Elam Company prepares financial statements annually. During the year the following selected transactions occurred:

Journalize various receivables transactions.
(SO 1, 2, 4, 5)

Jan.	5	Sold $6,000 of merchandise to Garth Brooks Company, terms n/30.
Feb.	2	Accepted a $6,000, 4-month, 12% promissory note from Garth Brooks Company for balance due.
	12	Sold $7,800 of merchandise to Gage Company and accepted Gage's $7,800, 2-month, 10% note for the balance due.
	26	Sold $4,000 of merchandise to Mathias Co., terms n/10.
Apr.	5	Accepted a $4,000, 3-month, 8% note from Mathias Co. for balance due.
	12	Collected Gage Company note in full.
June	2	Collected Garth Brooks Company note in full.
July	5	Mathias Co. dishonors its note of April 5. It is expected that Mathias will eventually pay the amount owed.
	15	Sold $3,000 of merchandise to Tritt Inc. and accepted Tritt's $3,000, 3-month, 12% note for the amount due.
Oct.	15	The Tritt Inc. note was dishonored. Tritt Inc. is bankrupt, and there is no hope of future settlement.

Instructions
Journalize the transactions.

P8-6A Kolzow Company closes its books on July 31. On June 30 the Interest Receivable balance is $132.80, and the Notes Receivable account balance is $20,800. Notes Receivable include the following:

Prepare entries for various credit card and notes receivable transactions.
(SO 2, 4, 5, 6, 9)

Date	Maker	Face Value	Term	Interest Rate
May 21	Alder Inc.	$ 6,000	60 days	12%
May 25	Dorn Co.	4,800	60 days	11%
June 30	MJH Corp.	10,000	6 months	9%

During July the following transactions were completed:

> July 5 Made sales of $6,200 on Kolzow credit cards.
>
> 14 Made sales of $700 on VISA credit cards. The credit card service charge is 3%.
>
> 20 Received payment in full from Alder Inc. on the amount due.
>
> 25 Received notice that Dorn Co. note has been dishonored. (Assume that Dorn Co. is expected to pay in the future.)

Instructions

(a) Journalize the July transactions and the July 31 adjusting entry for accrued interest receivable. (Interest is computed using 360 days.)

(b) Enter the balances at July 1 in the receivable accounts and post the entries to all of the receivable accounts. (Use T accounts.)

(c) Show the balance sheet presentation of the receivable accounts at July 31.

Calculate and interpret various ratios.
(SO 7, 8)

P8-7A Presented here is basic financial information (in millions) from the 1998 annual reports of **Nike** and **Reebok**:

	Nike	Reebok
Sales	$9,553.1	$3,224.6
Allowance for doubtful accounts, Jan. 1	57.2	44.0
Allowance for doubtful accounts, Dec. 31	71.4	47.4
Accounts receivable balance (gross), Jan. 1	1,811.3	605.7
Accounts receivable balance (gross), Dec. 31	1,745.8	565.2

Instructions

(a) Calculate the receivables turnover ratio and average collection period for both companies. Comment on the difference in their collection experiences.

(b) Calculate the January 1 and December 31 ratio of allowance for doubtful accounts to gross accounts receivable (credit risk ratio) for each company. Comment on any apparent differences in their credit-granting practices.

PROBLEMS: SET B

Prepare journal entries related to bad debt expense, and compute ratios.
(SO 2, 3, 8)

P8-1B At December 31, 2001, Cellular Ten Inc. reported this information on its balance sheet:

Accounts receivable	$960,000
Less: Allowance for doubtful accounts	70,000

During 2002 the company had the following transactions related to receivables:

1. Sales on account	$3,800,000
2. Sales returns and allowances	50,000
3. Collections of accounts receivable	2,800,000
4. Write-offs of accounts receivable deemed uncollectible	90,000
5. Recovery of bad debts previously written off as uncollectible	25,000

Instructions

(a) Prepare the journal entries to record each of these five transactions. Assume that no cash discounts were taken on the collections of accounts receivable.

(b) Enter the January 1, 2002, balances in Accounts Receivable and Allowance for Doubtful Accounts, post the entries to the two accounts (use T accounts), and determine the balances.

(c) Prepare the journal entry to record bad debts expense for 2002, assuming that aging the accounts receivable indicates that expected bad debts are $100,000.

(d) Compute the receivables turnover ratio and average collection period.

Journalize transactions related to bad debts.
(SO 2, 3)

P8-2B Presented here is an aging schedule for Case Western Company:

Customer	Total	Not Yet Due	Number of Days Past Due			
			1–30	31–60	61–90	Over 90
Anita	$ 22,000		$10,000	$12,000		
Barry	40,000	$ 40,000				
Chagnon	57,000	16,000	6,000		$35,000	
David	34,000					$34,000
Others	126,000	96,000	16,000	14,000		
	$279,000	$152,000	$32,000	$26,000	$35,000	$34,000
Estimated percentage uncollectible		4%	7%	13%	25%	50%
Total estimated bad debts	$ 37,450	$ 6,080	$ 2,240	$ 3,380	$ 8,750	$17,000

At December 31, 2001, the unadjusted balance in Allowance for Doubtful Accounts is a credit of $12,000.

Instructions

(a) Journalize and post the adjusting entry for bad debts at December 31, 2001. (Use T accounts.)

(b) Journalize and post to the allowance account these 2002 events and transactions:
1. March 31, a $500 customer balance originating in 2001 is judged uncollectible.
2. May 31, a check for $500 is received from the customer whose account was written off as uncollectible on March 31.

(c) Journalize the adjusting entry for bad debts on December 31, 2002, assuming that the unadjusted balance in Allowance for Doubtful Accounts is a debit of $800 and the aging schedule indicates that total estimated bad debts will be $30,300.

P8-3B   Here is information related to Hohenberger Company for 2001:

Compute bad debt amounts.
(SO 3)

Total credit sales	$2,000,000
Accounts receivable at December 31	800,000
Bad debts written off	36,000

Instructions

(a) What amount of bad debts expense will Hohenberger Company report if it uses the direct write-off method of accounting for bad debts?

(b) Assume that Hohenberger Company decides to estimate its bad debts expense based on 3% of accounts receivable. What amount of bad debts expense will the company record if it has an Allowance for Doubtful Accounts credit balance of $4,000?

(c) Assume the same facts as in part (b), except that there is a $3,000 debit balance in Allowance for Doubtful Accounts. What amount of bad debts expense will Hohenberger record?

(d) What is the weakness of the direct write-off method of reporting bad debts expense?

P8-4B   At December 31, 2001, the trial balance of Lexington Company contained the following amounts before adjustment:

Journalize entries to record transactions related to bad debts.
(SO 2, 3)

	Debits	**Credits**
Accounts Receivable	$400,000	
Allowance for Doubtful Accounts		$ 1,000
Sales		950,000

Instructions

(a) Based on the information given, which method of accounting for bad debts is Lexington Company using—the direct write-off method or the allowance method? How can you tell?

(b) Prepare the adjusting entry at December 31, 2001, for bad debts expense assuming that the aging schedule indicates that $11,750 of accounts receivable will be uncollectible.

(c) Repeat part (b) assuming that instead of a credit balance there is a $1,000 debit balance in the Allowance for Doubtful Accounts.

(d) During the next month, January 2002, a $5,000 account receivable is written off as uncollectible. Prepare the journal entry to record the write-off.

(e) Repeat part (d) assuming that Lexington uses the direct write-off method instead of the allowance method in accounting for uncollectible accounts receivable.

(f) ◻▱▭▭⟹ What type of account is the allowance for doubtful accounts? How does it affect how accounts receivable is reported on the balance sheet at the end of the accounting period?

Journalize various receivables transactions. (SO 1, 2, 4, 5)

P8-5B On January 1, 2001, Diego Company had Accounts Receivable $146,000; Notes Receivable $15,000; and Allowance for Doubtful Accounts $13,200. The note receivable is from Annabelle Company. It is a 4-month, 12% note dated December 31, 2000. Diego Company prepares financial statements annually. During the year the following selected transactions occurred:

Jan. 5 Sold $16,000 of merchandise to George Company, terms n/15.
20 Accepted George Company's $16,000, 3-month, 9% note for balance due.
Feb. 18 Sold $8,000 of merchandise to Swaim Company and accepted Swaim's $8,000, 6-month, 10% note for the amount due.
Apr. 20 Collected George Company note in full.
30 Received payment in full from Annabelle Company on the amount due.
May 25 Accepted Avery Inc.'s $6,000, 3-month, 8% note in settlement of a past-due balance on account.
Aug. 18 Received payment in full from Swaim Company on note due.
25 The Avery Inc. note was dishonored. Avery Inc. is not bankrupt and future payment is anticipated.
Sept. 1 Sold $10,000 of merchandise to Young Company and accepted a $10,000, 6-month, 10% note for the amount due.

Instructions
Journalize the transactions.

Prepare entries for various credit card and notes receivable transactions. (SO 2, 4, 5, 6, 9)

P8-6B Zimpher Company closes its books on October 31. On September 30 the balance in Interest Receivable is $182.40, and the Notes Receivable account balance is $23,400. Notes Receivable include the following:

Date	Maker	Face Value	Term	Interest Rate
Aug. 16	Foran Inc.	$ 8,000	60 days	12%
Aug. 25	Drexler Co.	5,200	2 months	10%
Sept. 30	MGH Corp.	10,200	6 months	8%

Interest is computed using a 360-day year. During October the following transactions were completed:

Oct. 7 Made sales of $6,900 on Zimpher Credit cards.
12 Made sales of $750 on VISA credit cards. The credit card service charge is 4%.
15 Received payment in full from Foran Inc. on the amount due.
25 Received notice that Drexler Co. note has been dishonored. (Assume that Drexler Co. is expected to pay in future.)

Instructions
(a) Journalize the October transactions and the October 31 adjusting entry for accrued interest receivable.
(b) Enter the balances at October 1 in the receivable accounts and post the entries to all of the receivable accounts. (Use T accounts.)
(c) Show the balance sheet presentation of the receivable accounts at October 31.

Calculate and interpret various ratios. (SO 7, 8)

P8-7B Presented here is basic financial information from the 1998 annual reports of **Intel** and **Advanced Micro Devices (AMD)**, the two primary manufacturers of silicon chips for personal computers.

(in millions)	Intel	AMD
Sales	$26,273	$2,542.0
Allowance for doubtful accounts, Jan. 1	65	11.2
Allowance for doubtful accounts, Dec. 31	62	12.7
Accounts receivable balance (gross), Jan. 1	3,503	340.3
Accounts receivable balance (gross), Dec. 31	3,589	428.2

Instructions
(a) Calculate the receivables turnover ratio and average collection period for both companies. Comment on the difference in their collection experiences.
(b) Calculate the January 1 and December 31 ratio of allowance for doubtful accounts to gross accounts receivable (credit risk ratio) for each company. Comment on any apparent differences in their credit-granting practices.

FINANCIAL REPORTING AND ANALYSIS

FINANCIAL REPORTING PROBLEM: *Tootsie Roll Industries*

BYP8-1   Refer to the financial statements of Tootsie Roll Industries and the accompanying notes to its financial statements in Appendix A.

Instructions
(a) Calculate the receivables turnover ratio and average collection period for 1998.
(b) Calculate the credit risk ratio for 1998 and 1997.
(c) Did Tootsie Roll have any potentially significant credit risks in 1998? (Hint: Review Note 11 to the financial statements.)
(d) What conclusions can you draw from the information in parts (a)–(c)?

COMPARATIVE ANALYSIS PROBLEM: *Tootsie Roll vs. Hershey Foods*

BYP8-2   The financial statements of Hershey Foods are presented in Appendix B, following the financial statements for Tootsie Roll in Appendix A.

Instructions
(a) Based on the information contained in these financial statements, compute the following 1998 values for each company:
  (1) Receivables turnover ratio. (Assume all sales were credit sales.)
  (2) Average collection period for receivables.
  (3) Credit risk ratio. (Hint: Hershey's note 14 provides allowances and discounts combined.)
(b) What conclusions concerning the management of accounts receivable can be drawn from these data?

RESEARCH CASE

BYP8-3   The March 31, 1999, issue of *The Wall Street Journal* includes an article by Mark Maremont entitled "Store Markdowns: Leaning on Suppliers, Rite Aid Deducts Cash at Bill-Paying Time." The September 9, 1999, issue includes another article by the same writer entitled "Rite Aid Repays Some Disputed Deductions from Vendors' Bills."

Instructions
Read the articles and answer the following questions:
(a) What reasons did Rite Aid give for reducing the amount it paid its suppliers?
(b) Other than its stated reason for reducing its payments, what other incentives might Rite Aid have had for reducing the amount paid to its suppliers?
(c) What are the implications of Rite Aid's actions for the suppliers? What are the suppliers' possible courses of action?
(d) Why do you suppose Rite Aid eventually chose to repay these bills?

INTERPRETING FINANCIAL STATEMENTS

BYP8-4   Sears is one of the world's largest retailers. It is also a huge provider of credit through its Sears credit card. Revenue generated from credit operations was $4.6 billion in 1998 from 30 million Sears cardholders. The rate of interest Sears earns on outstanding receivables varies from 10% to 21% in the United States to up to 28% in Canada. In some instances, to acquire cash when needed, the company will sell its receivables. At December 31, 1998, Sears had sold $6.63 billion of its receivables.
   The following information (in millions) was available in Sears' 1998 financial statements:

	1998	1997	1996
Accounts receivable (gross)	$18,946	$20,956	$22,371
Allowance for doubtful accounts	974	1,113	808
Merchandise sales	36,704	36,371	33,751
Credit revenues	4,618	4,925	4,313
Bad debts expense	1,287	1,532	971

Instructions
(a) Discuss whether the sale of receivables by Sears represents a significant portion of its receivables. Why might Sears have sold these receivables? As an investor, what concerns might you have about these sales?
(b) Calculate and discuss the receivables turnover ratio and average collection period for Sears for 1998 and 1997.
(c) Do you think Sears provided credit as a revenue-generating activity or as a convenience for its customers?
(d) Compute the ratio of bad debts expense to merchandise sales for 1998 and 1997. Did this ratio improve or worsen? What considerations should Sears make in deciding whether it wants to have liberal or conservative credit-granting policies?

A GLOBAL FOCUS

BYP8-5 **Art World Industries, Inc.,** was incorporated in 1986 in Delaware, although it is located in Los Angeles. The company prints, publishes, and sells limited-edition graphics and reproductive prints in the wholesale market.

The company's balance sheet at the end of a recent year showed an allowance for doubtful accounts of $175,477. The allowance was set up against certain Japanese accounts receivable that average more than one year in age. The Japanese acknowledge the amount due, but with the slow economy in Japan lack the resources to pay at this time.

Instructions
(a) Which method of accounting for uncollectible accounts does Art World Industries use?
(b) Explain the difference between the direct write-off and percentage of receivables methods. Based on Art World's disclosure above, what important factor would you have to consider in arriving at appropriate percentages to apply for the percentage of receivables method?
(c) What are the implications for a company's receivables management of selling its products internationally?

FINANCIAL ANALYSIS ON THE WEB

BYP8-6 *Purpose:* The Security Exchange Act of 1934 requires any firm that is listed on one of the national exchanges to file annual reports (form 10-K), financial statements, and quarterly reports (form 10-Q) with the SEC. This exercise demonstrates how to search and access available SEC filings through the Internet.

Address: http://biz.yahoo.com/i (or go to www.wiley.com/college/kimmel)

Steps:
1. Type in a company's name, or use index to find a company name.
2. Choose **profile**.
3. Choose **SEC Filings**.

Instructions
Answer the following questions:
(a) Which SEC filings were available for the company you selected?
(b) In the company's quarterly report (SEC form 10-Q), what was one key point discussed in the "Management's Discussion and Analysis of Results of Operations and Financial Condition"?
(c) What was the net income for the period selected?

CRITICAL THINKING

GROUP DECISION CASE

BYP8-7 Johanna and Jake Berkvom own Campus Fashions. From its inception Campus Fashions has sold merchandise on either a cash or credit basis, but no credit cards have been accepted. During the past several months, the Berkvoms have begun to question their credit-sales policies. First, they have lost some sales because of their refusal to accept credit cards. Second, representatives of two metropolitan banks have convinced them to accept their national credit cards. One bank, City National Bank, has stated that (1) its credit card fee is 4% and (2) it pays the retailer 96 cents on each $1 of sales within 3 days of receiving the credit card billings.

The Berkvoms decide that they should determine the cost of carrying their own credit sales. From the accounting records of the past 3 years they accumulate these data:

	2001	2000	1999
Net credit sales	$500,000	$600,000	$400,000
Collection agency fees for slow-paying customers	2,450	2,500	1,600
Salary of part-time accounts receivable clerk	3,800	3,800	3,800

Credit and collection expenses as a percentage of net credit sales are as follows: uncollectible accounts 1.6%, billing and mailing costs .5%, and credit investigation fee on new customers .15%.

Johanna and Jake also determine that the average accounts receivable balance outstanding during the year is 5% of net credit sales. The Berkvoms estimate that they could earn an average of 10% annually on cash invested in other business opportunities.

Instructions
With the class divided into groups, answer the following:
(a) Prepare a tabulation for each year showing total credit and collection expenses in dollars and as a percentage of net credit sales.
(b) Determine the net credit and collection expenses in dollars and as a percentage of sales after considering the revenue not earned from other investment opportunities. [*Note:* The income lost on the cash held by the bank for 3 days is considered to be immaterial.]
(c) Discuss both the financial and nonfinancial factors that are relevant to the decision.

COMMUNICATION ACTIVITY

BYP8-8 Sara Joy Corporation is a recently formed business selling the "World's Best Doormat." The corporation is selling doormats faster than Sara Joy can make them. It has been selling the product on a credit basis, telling customers to "pay when they can." Oddly, even though sales are tremendous, the company is having trouble paying its bills.

Instructions
Write a memo to the president of Sara Joy Corporation discussing these questions:
(a) What steps should be taken to improve the company's ability to pay its bills?
(b) What accounting steps should be taken to measure its success in improving collections, and in recording its collection success?
(c) If the corporation is still unable to pay its bills, what additional steps can be taken with its receivables to ease its liquidity problems?

ETHICS CASE

BYP8-9 The controller of Shirt Corporation believes that the company's yearly allowance for doubtful accounts should be 2% of net credit sales. The president of Shirt Corporation, nervous that the stockholders might expect the company to sustain its 10% growth rate, suggests that the controller increase the allowance for doubtful accounts to 4%. The president thinks that the lower net income, which reflects a 6% growth rate, will be a more sustainable rate for Shirt Corporation.

Instructions
(a) Who are the stakeholders in this case?
(b) Does the president's request pose an ethical dilemma for the controller?
(c) Should the controller be concerned with Shirt Corporation's growth rate in estimating the allowance? Explain your answer.

Answers to Self-Study Questions
1. c   2. a   3. c   4. d   5. c   6. b   7. d   8. a   9. c   10. c   11. a

Answer to Tootsie Roll Review It Question 1, p. 361
Tootsie Roll reports two types of receivables on its balance sheet: Accounts receivable trade; and Other receivables. Since Tootsie Roll's balance sheet reports allowance amounts for receivables, we know that Tootsie Roll uses the allowance method rather than the direct write-off method.

CHAPTER 9

Reporting and Analyzing Long-Lived Assets

◆ STUDY OBJECTIVES

After studying this chapter, you should be able to:

1. Describe how the cost principle applies to plant assets.

2. Explain the concept of depreciation.

3. Compute periodic depreciation using the straight-line method, and contrast its expense pattern with those of other methods.

4. Describe the procedure for revising periodic depreciation.

5. Explain how to account for the disposal of plant assets.

6. Describe methods for evaluating the use of plant assets.

7. Identify the basic issues related to reporting intangible assets.

8. Indicate how long-lived assets are reported on the balance sheet.

◆ A TALE OF TWO AIRLINES

So, you're interested in starting a new business. Have you given any thought to the airline industry? Your only experience with airlines is as a passenger? Don't let that stop you, advises Ray Novelli. Novelli's airline, Presidential Air, was one of 30 new airlines that entered the U.S. market in a recent 30-month period—one per month.

The impetus behind all these upstarts was the tremendous success of two discount, no-frills airlines: Southwest Airlines and Valujet. Valujet, which was started with a $3.4-million investment, grew to be worth $630 million in its first three years. What is interesting is the different approach

taken by these two airlines to arrive at their success. Southwest Airlines' fleet is composed of primarily sleek, new, highly efficient planes requiring little maintenance. The average age of its planes is 8.3 years, the lowest in the industry. To be able to afford new planes, Southwest had to be very patient in its growth goals. Over a 22-year period, Southwest has risen to the number eight spot in size for U.S. airlines—and to even higher rankings in on-time performance, customer service, and baggage handling.

Valujet, on the other hand, opted for old planes, known in the industry as Zombies, which are 25 to 30 years old and cost

less than a tenth of the purchase price of a new plane. This practice of buying older planes allowed Valujet to add one or two planes a month to its fleet—an unheard-of expansion. Valujet started with two planes and within a year and a half had 36 planes. By comparison, it took Southwest Airlines 10 years to acquire that many planes. For a while there was a surplus of these old planes on the market, until Valujet enjoyed such tremendous success that seemingly everyone wanted to buy or lease old planes to start an airline.

However, a terrible crash in May 1996 in Florida focused the spotlight on Valujet and called

into question the wisdom of relying on old planes. Although
the cause of the crash appears to
have been unrelated to the age
of its planes, in the aftermath of
the crash Valujet struggled to
survive under the weight of both
government scrutiny and lack of
customer confidence. The crash
heightened awareness of the age
of the U.S. fleet as well as the
importance of ongoing maintenance. Whether this spells the
end for new discount startups
remains to be seen.

In the face of continuing financial problems and customer
skepticism, Valujet merged with
AirWays Corp. and took the
name of its airline, AirTran Airways. Perhaps you should proceed with caution in planning
the startup of your own airline!

On the World Wide Web
Southwest Airlines:
http://www.southwest.com
Valujet: http://www.airtran.com

Was Valujet's approach to buying equipment really the "right formula," or was it a recipe for disaster? For airlines and many other companies, making the right decisions regarding long-lived assets is critical because these assets represent huge investments. Management must make many ongoing decisions—what to acquire and when, how to finance the assets, how to account for them, and when to dispose of them.

In this chapter we address these and other issues surrounding long-lived assets. Our discussion of long-lived assets is presented in two parts: plant assets and intangible assets. *Plant assets* are the property, plant, and equipment (physical assets) that commonly come to mind when we think of a company. However, companies also have many important *intangible assets.* These are assets such as copyrights and patents that lack physical substance but can be extremely valuable and vital to a company's success.

The content and organization of this chapter are as follows:

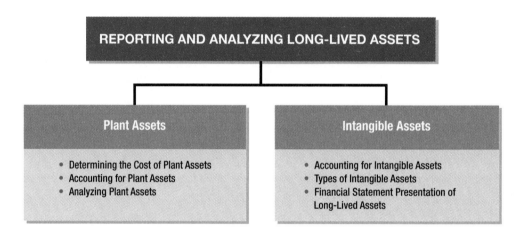

SECTION 1

PLANT ASSETS

Plant assets are resources that have physical substance (a definite size and shape), are used in the operations of a business, and are not intended for sale to customers. They are called various names—property, plant, and equipment; plant and equipment; and fixed assets. The term we use most often in this chapter is plant assets. By whatever name, these assets are generally long-lived and are expected to provide services to the company for a number of years. Except for land, plant assets decline in service potential (value) over their useful lives.

The acquisition of plant assets is critical to the success of nearly all businesses because these resources determine the company's capacity and therefore its ability to satisfy customers. With too few planes, for example, AirTran and Southwest Airlines will lose customers to their competitors, but with too many planes, they will be flying with empty seats. Management must constantly monitor its needs and acquire assets accordingly. Failure to do so results in lost business opportunities or inefficient use of existing assets and is likely to show up eventually in poor financial results, problems for management, and declining interest among investors.

It is also important for a business enterprise to (1) keep assets in good operating condition, (2) replace worn-out or outdated facilities, and (3) expand its productive resources as needed. The decline of rail travel in the United States can be traced in part to the failure of railroad companies to perform the first two of these functions. Conversely, the growth of air travel in this country can be attributed in part to the general willingness of airline companies to follow these essential guidelines.

Many companies have substantial investments in plant assets. In public utility companies, for example, plant assets often represent more than 75% of total assets. Recently plant assets were more than 80% of Consolidated Edison's total assets and 92% of Pennsylvania Power & Light Company's. Illustration 9-1 shows the percentages of plant assets in relation to total assets in some other companies.

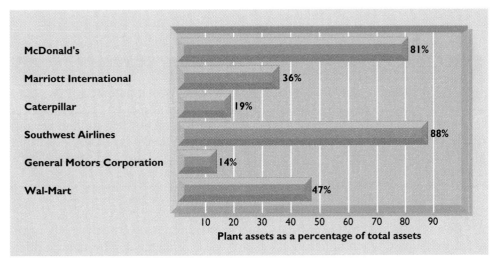

Illustration 9-1 Percentages of plant assets in relation to total assets

Plant assets are often subdivided into four classes:

1. Land, such as a building site.
2. Land improvements, such as driveways, parking lots, fences, and underground sprinkler systems.
3. Buildings, such as stores, offices, factories, and warehouses.
4. Equipment, such as store check-out counters, cash registers, coolers, office furniture, factory machinery, and delivery equipment.

DETERMINING THE COST OF PLANT ASSETS

Plant assets are recorded at cost in accordance with the **cost principle** of accounting. Thus, the planes at AirTran and Southwest Airlines are recorded at cost. **Cost consists of all expenditures necessary to acquire the asset and make it ready for its intended use**. For example, the purchase price, freight costs paid by the purchaser, and installation costs are all considered part of the cost of factory machinery.

STUDY OBJECTIVE

1

Describe how the cost principle applies to plant assets.

⊕ **International Note**

The United Kingdom is flexible regarding asset valuation. Companies revalue to fair value when they believe this information is more relevant. Switzerland and the Netherlands also permit revaluations.

Determining which costs to include in a plant asset account and which costs not to include is very important. If a cost is not included in a plant asset account, then it must be expensed immediately. Such costs are referred to as **revenue expenditures**. On the other hand, costs that are not expensed immediately but are instead included in a plant asset account are referred to as **capital expenditures**. This distinction is important because it has immediate, and often material, implications for the income statement. Some companies, in order to boost current income, have been known to improperly capitalize expenditures that should have been expensed. For example, suppose that $1,000 of maintenance costs incurred at the end of the year are improperly capitalized to a building account. (That is, they are included in the asset account Buildings rather than being expensed immediately.) If the cost of the building is being allocated as an expense (depreciated) over a 40-year life, then the maintenance cost of $1,000 will be incorrectly spread across 40 years instead of being expensed in the current year. Current-year expenses will be understated by $1,000, and current-year income will be overstated by $1,000. Thus, determining which costs to capitalize and which to expense is very important.

BUSINESS INSIGHT
Investor Perspective

Once a star on Wall Street, Chambers Development, a waste management company, saw its stock price plummet when it announced that its earnings over a five-year period were overstated by $362 million because it had improperly capitalized costs that should have been expensed. For example, Chambers had capitalized $162 million that it had paid in dumping fees at landfill sites.

Cost is measured by the cash paid in a cash transaction or by the **cash equivalent price** paid when noncash assets are used in payment. **The cash equivalent price is equal to the fair market value of the asset given up or the fair market value of the asset received**, **whichever is more clearly determinable**. Once cost is established, it becomes the basis of accounting for the plant asset over its useful life. Current market or replacement values are not used after acquisition. The application of the cost principle to each of the major classes of plant assets is explained in the following sections.

LAND

The cost of land includes (1) the cash purchase price, (2) closing costs such as title and attorney's fees, (3) real estate brokers' commissions, and (4) accrued property taxes and other liens on the land assumed by the purchaser. For example, if the cash price is $50,000 and the purchaser agrees to pay accrued taxes of $5,000, the cost of the land is $55,000.

All necessary costs incurred in making land **ready for its intended use** increase (debit) the Land account. When vacant land is acquired, its cost includes expenditures for clearing, draining, filling, and grading. If the land has a building on it that must be removed to make the site suitable for construction of a new building, all demolition and removal costs, less any proceeds from salvaged materials, are chargeable to the Land account.

To illustrate, assume that Hayes Manufacturing Company acquires real estate at a cash cost of $100,000. The property contains an old warehouse that is razed at a net cost of $6,000 ($7,500 in costs less $1,500 proceeds from salvaged materials). Additional expenditures are for the attorney's fee $1,000 and the real estate broker's commission $8,000. Given these factors, the cost of the land is $115,000, computed as shown in Illustration 9-2.

Illustration 9-2 Computation of cost of land

Land	
Cash price of property	$ 100,000
Net removal cost of warehouse	6,000
Attorney's fee	1,000
Real estate broker's commission	8,000
Cost of land	**$115,000**

When the acquisition is recorded, Land is debited for $115,000 and Cash is credited for $115,000.

LAND IMPROVEMENTS

The cost of land improvements includes all expenditures necessary to make the improvements ready for their intended use. For example, the cost of a new company parking lot includes the amount paid for paving, fencing, and lighting. These improvements have limited useful lives, and their maintenance and replacement are the responsibility of the company. Thus, these costs are debited to Land Improvements and are expensed over the useful lives of the improvements.

BUILDINGS

All necessary expenditures relating to the purchase or construction of a building are charged to the Buildings account. When a building is purchased, such costs include the purchase price, closing costs (attorney's fees, title insurance, etc.), and real estate broker's commission. Costs to make the building ready for its intended use consist of expenditures for remodeling rooms and offices and replacing or repairing the roof, floors, electrical wiring, and plumbing.

When a new building is constructed, its cost consists of the contract price plus payments made by the owner for architects' fees, building permits, and excavation costs. In addition, interest costs incurred to finance the project are included in the cost of the asset when a significant period of time is required to get the asset ready for use. In these circumstances, interest costs are considered as necessary as materials and labor. However, the inclusion of interest costs in the cost of a constructed building is **limited to the construction period**. When construction has been completed, subsequent interest payments on funds borrowed to finance the construction are recorded as increases (debits) to Interest Expense.

EQUIPMENT

The cost of equipment consists of the cash purchase price, sales taxes, freight charges, and insurance during transit paid by the purchaser. It also includes expenditures required in assembling, installing, and testing the unit. However, motor vehicle licenses and accident insurance on company trucks and cars are treated as expenses as they are incurred because they represent annual recurring expenditures and do not benefit future periods. Two criteria apply in determining the cost of equipment: (1) the frequency of the cost—one time or recurring, and (2) the benefit period—the life of the asset or one year.

To illustrate, assume that Lenard Company purchases a delivery truck at a cash price of $22,000. Related expenditures are for sales taxes $1,320, painting and lettering $500, motor vehicle license $80, and a 3-year accident insurance policy $1,600. The cost of the delivery truck is $23,820, computed as shown in Illustration 9-3.

Illustration 9-3 Computation of cost of delivery truck

Delivery Truck	
Cash price	$ 22,000
Sales taxes	1,320
Painting and lettering	500
Cost of delivery truck	**$23,820**

The cost of a motor vehicle license is treated as an expense, and the cost of an insurance policy is considered a prepaid asset. Thus, the entry to record the purchase of the truck and related expenditures is as follows:

A	=	L	+	SE
+23,820				−80
+1,600				
−25,500				

Delivery Truck	23,820	
License Expense	80	
Prepaid Insurance	1,600	
Cash		25,500
(To record purchase of delivery truck and related expenditures)		

For another example, assume Merten Company purchases factory machinery at a cash price of $50,000. Related expenditures are for sales taxes $3,000, insurance during shipping $500, and installation and testing $1,000. The cost of the factory machinery is $54,500, computed as in Illustration 9-4.

Illustration 9-4 Computation of cost of factory machinery

Factory Machinery	
Cash price	$ 50,000
Sales taxes	3,000
Insurance during shipping	500
Installation and testing	1,000
Cost of factory machinery	**$54,500**

Thus, the entry to record the purchase and related expenditures is as follows:

A	=	L	+	SE
+54,500				
−54,500				

Factory Machinery	54,500	
Cash		54,500
(To record purchase of factory machinery and related expenditures)		

TO BUY OR LEASE?

In this chapter we focus on assets that are purchased, but we want to expose you briefly to an alternative to purchasing—leasing. In a lease, a party that owns an asset (the lessor) agrees to allow another party (the lessee) to use the asset for an agreed period of time at an agreed price. Some advantages of leasing an asset versus purchasing it are:

1. **Reduced risk of obsolescence.** Frequently, lease terms allow the party using the asset (the lessee) to exchange the asset for a more modern one if it becomes outdated. This is much easier than trying to sell an obsolete asset.

2. **Little or no down payment.** To purchase an asset most companies must borrow money, which usually requires a down payment of at least 20%. Leasing an asset requires little or no down payment.

3. **Shared tax advantages.** Startup companies typically do not make much money in their early years, and so they have little need for the tax deductions available from owning an asset. In a lease, the lessor gets the tax advantage because it owns the asset. It often will pass these tax savings on to the lessee in the form of lower lease payments.

4. **Assets and liabilities not reported.** Many companies prefer to keep assets and especially liabilities off of their books. Certain types of leases, called operating leases, allow the lessee to account for the transaction as a rental with neither an asset nor a liability recorded.

Airlines often choose to lease many of their airplanes in long-term lease agreements. In its 1998 financial statements, Southwest Airlines stated that it leased 99 of its 280 planes under operating leases. Because operating leases are accounted for as a rental, these 99 planes did not show up on its balance sheet.

Under another type of lease, a capital lease, both the asset and the liability are shown on the balance sheet. For the lessee under a capital lease, long-term lease agreements are accounted for in a way that is very similar to purchases: On the lessee's balance sheet, the leased item is shown as an asset, and the obligation owed to the lessor is shown as a liability. The leased asset is depreciated by the lessee in a manner similar to purchased assets. About 5% of the planes that *are* listed as assets on Southwest Airlines' balance sheet are leased planes that are accounted for as capital leases. Additional discussion about leasing is presented in Chapter 10 on liabilities.

BUSINESS INSIGHT
Management Perspective

As an excellent example of the magnitude of leasing, leased planes account for nearly 40% of the U.S. fleet of commercial airlines. The reasons for leasing include favorable tax treatment, increased flexibility, and low airline income. As passenger volume is expected to double in the next 20 years, some industry analysts estimate that approximately $400 billion in airplanes will be needed, and it is anticipated that much of the financing will be done through leasing. Leasing is particularly attractive to lessors because airplanes have relatively long lives, a ready secondhand market, and a significant resale value. Or take the commercial truck fleet—over one-third of heavy-duty trucks are presently leased.

BEFORE YOU GO ON...

◆ Review It

1. What are plant assets? What are the major classes of plant assets? At what value should plant assets be recorded?
2. What are revenue expenditures? What are capital expenditures?
3. What are the primary advantages of leasing?

◆ Do It

Assume that a delivery truck is purchased for $15,000 cash plus sales taxes of $900 and delivery costs to the dealer of $500. The buyer also pays $200 for painting and lettering, $600 for an annual insurance policy, and $80 for a motor vehicle license. Explain how each of these costs is accounted for.

Reasoning: The cost principle applies to all expenditures made in order to get delivery equipment ready for its intended use. The principle does not apply to operating costs incurred during the useful life of the equipment, such as gas and oil, motor tuneups, licenses, and insurance.

Solution: The first four payments ($15,000, $900, $500, and $200) are considered to be expenditures necessary to make the truck ready for its intended use. Thus, the cost of the truck is $16,600. The payments for insurance and the license are considered to be operating expenses incurred during the useful life of the asset.

ACCOUNTING FOR PLANT ASSETS

DEPRECIATION

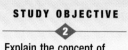

As explained in Chapter 4, depreciation **is the process of allocating to expense the cost of a plant asset over its useful (service) life in a rational and systematic manner.** Such cost allocation is designed to properly match expenses with revenues in accordance with the matching principle. (See Illustration 9-5.)

Illustration 9-5 Depreciation as an allocation concept

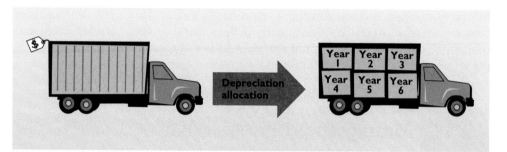

Helpful Hint Remember that depreciation is the process of allocating cost over the useful life of an asset. It is not a measure of value.

It is important to understand that **depreciation is a process of cost allocation, not a process of asset valuation.** No attempt is made to measure the change in an asset's market value during ownership because plant assets are not held for resale. Thus, the **book value**—cost less accumulated depreciation—of a plant asset may differ significantly from its **market value.** In fact, if an asset is fully depreciated, it can have zero book value but still have a significant market value.

Depreciation applies to three classes of plant assets: land improvements, buildings, and equipment. Each of these classes is considered to be a **depreciable asset** because the usefulness to the company and the revenue-producing ability of each class decline over the asset's useful life. Depreciation does not apply to land because its usefulness and revenue-producing ability generally remain intact as long as the land is owned. In fact, in many cases, the usefulness of land increases over time because of the scarcity of good sites. Thus, **land is not a depreciable asset.**

Helpful Hint Land does not depreciate because it does not wear out.

During a depreciable asset's useful life its revenue-producing ability declines because of **wear and tear.** A delivery truck that has been driven 100,000 miles will be less useful to a company than one driven only 800 miles. Similarly, trucks and cars exposed to snow and salt deteriorate faster than equipment that is not exposed to these elements.

A decline in revenue-producing ability may also occur because of **obsolescence.** Obsolescence is the process by which an asset becomes out of date before it physically wears out. The rerouting of major airlines from Chicago's Midway Airport to Chicago-O'Hare International Airport because Midway's runways were too short for jumbo jets is an example. Similarly, many companies have replaced their computers long before they had originally planned to do so because improvements in new computers made their old computers obsolete.

Recognizing depreciation for an asset does not result in the accumulation of cash for replacement of the asset. The balance in Accumulated Depreciation represents the total amount of the asset's cost that has been charged to expense to date; **it is not a cash fund**.

Factors in Computing Depreciation

Three factors affect the computation of depreciation, as shown in Illustration 9-6:

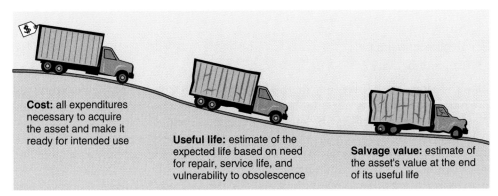

Illustration 9-6 Three factors in computing depreciation

Cost: all expenditures necessary to acquire the asset and make it ready for intended use

Useful life: estimate of the expected life based on need for repair, service life, and vulnerability to obsolescence

Salvage value: estimate of the asset's value at the end of its useful life

1. **Cost.** Considerations that affect the cost of a depreciable asset have been explained earlier in this chapter. Remember that plant assets are recorded at cost, in accordance with the cost principle.
2. **Useful life.** Useful life is an estimate of the expected productive life, also called service life, of the asset. Useful life may be expressed in terms of time, units of activity (such as machine hours), or units of output. Useful life is an estimate. In making the estimate, management considers such factors as the intended use of the asset, repair and maintenance policies, and vulnerability of the asset to obsolescence. The company's past experience with similar assets is often helpful in deciding on expected useful life.
3. **Salvage value.** Salvage value is an estimate of the asset's value at the end of its useful life. The value may be based on the asset's worth as scrap or salvage or on its expected trade-in value. Like useful life, salvage value is an estimate. In making the estimate, management considers how it plans to dispose of the asset and its experience with similar assets.

BUSINESS INSIGHT

Management Perspective

Willamette Industries, Inc., of Portland, Oregon, said in March 1999 that it would change its accounting estimates relating to depreciation of certain assets, beginning with the first quarter of 1999. The vertically integrated forest products company said the changes were due to advances in technology that have increased the service life on its equipment an extra five years. Willamette expected the accounting changes to increase its 1999 full-year earnings by about $57 milion, or $0.52 a share. Its 1998 earnings were $89 million, or $0.80 a share. Imagine a 65% improvement in earnings per share from a mere change in the estimated life of equipment!

BEFORE YOU GO ON...

◆ Review It

1. What is the relationship, if any, of depreciation to (a) cost allocation, (b) asset valuation, and (c) cash accumulation?
2. Explain the factors that affect the computation of depreciation.
3. What does Tootsie Roll use as the estimated useful life on its buildings? On its machinery and equipment? The answer to this question is provided on page 448.

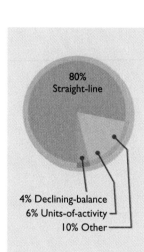

Illustration 9-7   Use of depreciation methods in major U.S. companies

Depreciation Methods

Depreciation is generally computed using one of these three methods:

1. Straight-line
2. Declining-balance
3. Units-of-activity

Like the alternative inventory methods discussed in Chapter 6, each of these depreciation methods is acceptable under generally accepted accounting principles. Management selects the method it believes best measures an asset's contribution to revenue over its useful life. Once a method is chosen, it should be applied consistently over the useful life of the asset. Consistency enhances the comparability of financial statements.

Depreciation affects the balance sheet through accumulated depreciation, which is reported as a deduction from plant assets. It affects the income statement through depreciation expense. Illustration 9-7 shows the distribution of the *primary* depreciation methods in 600 of the largest U.S. companies. Clearly, straight-line depreciation is the most widely used approach. In fact, because some companies use more than one method, **it can actually be said that straight-line depreciation is used for some or all of the depreciation taken by more than 90% of U.S. companies**. For this reason, we illustrate procedures for straight-line depreciation and discuss the alternative approaches only at a conceptual level. This coverage introduces you to the basic idea of depreciation as an allocation concept without entangling you in too much procedural detail. (Also, note that many hand-held calculators are preprogrammed to perform the basic depreciation methods.) Details on the alternative approaches are presented in the appendix to this chapter (page 428).

Our illustration of depreciation methods, both here and in the appendix, is based on the following data relating to a small delivery truck purchased by Bill's Pizzas on January 1, 2001:

Cost	$13,000
Expected salvage value	$1,000
Estimated useful life (in years)	5
Estimated useful life (in miles)	100,000

Straight-Line.   Under the straight-line method, depreciation is the same for each year of the asset's useful life. It is measured solely by the passage of time. Management must choose the useful life of an asset based on its own expectations and experience. To compute the annual depreciation expense, we need to determine depreciable cost, which represents the total amount subject to depreciation. Depreciable cost is calculated as the cost of the asset less its salvage value. Depreciable cost is then divided by the asset's useful life to determine **depreciation expense**. The computation of depreciation expense in the first year for Bill's Pizzas' delivery trucks is shown in Illustration 9-8.

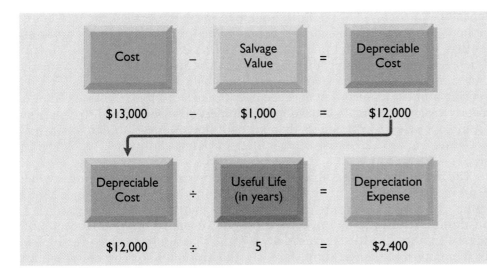

Illustration 9-8 Formula for straight-line method

Alternatively, we can compute an annual *rate* at which the delivery truck is being depreciated. In this case, the rate is 20% (100% ÷ 5 years). When an annual rate is used under the straight-line method, the percentage rate is applied to the depreciable cost of the asset, as shown in the **depreciation schedule** in Illustration 9-9.

Illustration 9-9 Straight-line depreciation schedule

	Computation			End of Year	
BILL'S PIZZAS					
Year	Depreciable Cost	× Depreciation Rate =	Annual Depreciation Expense	Accumulated Depreciation	Book Value
2001	$12,000	20%	$ 2,400	$ 2,400	$10,600*
2002	12,000	20	2,400	4,800	8,200
2003	12,000	20	2,400	7,200	5,800
2004	12,000	20	2,400	9,600	3,400
2005	12,000	20	2,400	12,000	**1,000**
		Total	$12,000		

*$13,000 − $2,400

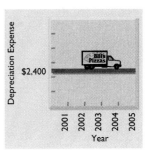

Note that the depreciation expense of $2,400 is the same each year, and that the book value at the end of the useful life is equal to the estimated $1,000 salvage value.

What happens when an asset is purchased **during** the year, rather than on January 1, as in our example? In that case, it is necessary to **prorate the annual depreciation** for the proportion of a year used. If Bill's Pizzas had purchased the delivery truck on April 1, 2001, the depreciation for 2001 would be $1,800 ($12,000 × 20% × $\frac{9}{12}$ of a year).

As indicated earlier, the straight-line method predominates in practice. For example, such large companies as Campbell Soup, Marriott International, and General Mills use the straight-line method. It is simple to apply, and it matches expenses with revenues appropriately when the use of the asset is reasonably uniform throughout the service life. The types of assets that give equal benefits over useful life generally are those for which daily use does not affect productivity. Examples are office furniture and fixtures, buildings, warehouses, and garages for motor vehicles.

Declining-Balance. The declining-balance method is called an "accelerated method" because it results in more depreciation in the early years of an asset's life than does the straight-line approach. However, because the total amount of depreciation (the depreciable cost) taken over an asset's life is the same no matter what approach is used, the declining-balance method produces a decreasing annual depreciation expense over the useful life of the asset. That is, in early years declining-balance depreciation expense will exceed straight-line, but in later years it will be less than straight-line. Managers might choose an accelerated approach if they think that an asset's utility will decline very quickly.

The declining-balance approach can be applied at different rates, which result in varying speeds of depreciation. A common declining-balance rate is double the straight-line rate. As a result, the method is often referred to as the **double-declining-balance method.** If we apply the double-declining-balance method to Bill's Pizzas' delivery truck, assuming a five-year life, we get the pattern of depreciation shown in Illustration 9-10. **The chapter's appendix, page 428, presents the computations behind these numbers.** Again, note that total depreciation over the life of the truck is $12,000, the depreciable cost.

Illustration 9-10
Declining-balance depreciation schedule

		BILL'S PIZZAS		
		Annual	End of Year	
		Depreciation	Accumulated	Book
	Year	Expense	Depreciation	Value
	2001	$ 5,200	$ 5,200	$7,800
	2002	3,120	8,320	4,680
	2003	1,872	10,192	2,808
	2004	1,123	11,315	1,685
	2005	685	12,000	1,000
	Total	$12,000		

Units-of-Activity. Under the units-of-activity method, instead of expressing the asset's life as a time period, useful life is expressed in terms of the total units of production or the use expected from the asset. The units-of-activity method is ideally suited to factory machinery: Production can be measured in terms of units of output or in terms of machine hours used in operating the machinery. It is also possible to use the method for such items as delivery equipment (miles driven) and airplanes (hours in use). The units-of-activity method is generally not suitable for such assets as buildings or furniture because depreciation for these assets is a function more of time than of use.

Applying the units-of-activity method to the delivery truck owned by Bill's Pizzas, we first must know some basic information. Bill's expects to be able to drive the truck a total of 100,000 miles. If we assume that the mileage occurs in the given pattern over the five-year life, depreciation in each year is shown in Illustration 9-11. **The computations used to arrive at these results are presented in the chapter's appendix, page 428.**

Illustration 9-11 Units-of-activity depreciation schedule

	Units of Activity (miles)	Annual Depreciation Expense	End of Year	
Year			Accumulated Depreciation	Book Value
2001	15,000	$ 1,800	$ 1,800	$11,200
2002	30,000	3,600	5,400	7,600
2003	20,000	2,400	7,800	5,200
2004	25,000	3,000	10,800	2,200
2005	10,000	1,200	12,000	1,000
Total	100,000	$12,000		

BILL'S PIZZAS

As the name implies, under units-of-activity depreciation, the amount of depreciation is proportional to the activity that took place during that period. For example, the delivery truck was driven twice as many miles in 2002 as in 2001, and depreciation was exactly twice as much in 2002 as it was in 2001.

Management's Choice: Comparison of Methods

Illustration 9-12 presents a comparison of annual and total depreciation expense for Bill's Pizzas under the three methods.

Illustration 9-12 Comparison of depreciation methods

Year	Straight-Line	Declining-Balance	Units-of-Activity
2001	$ 2,400	$ 5,200	$ 1,800
2002	2,400	3,120	3,600
2003	2,400	1,872	2,400
2004	2,400	1,123	3,000
2005	2,400	685	1,200
	$12,000	$12,000	$12,000

Periodic depreciation varies considerably among the methods, but total depreciation is the same for the five-year period. Each method is acceptable in accounting because each recognizes the decline in service potential of the asset in a rational and systematic manner. The depreciation expense pattern under each method is presented graphically in Illustration 9-13.

Illustration 9-13 Patterns of depreciation

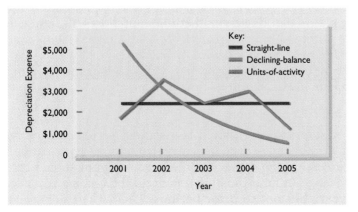

Depreciation and Income Taxes

The Internal Revenue Service (IRS) allows corporate taxpayers to deduct depreciation expense when computing taxable income. However, the tax regulations of the IRS do not require the taxpayer to use the same depreciation method on the tax return that is used in preparing financial statements. Consequently, many large corporations use straight-line depreciation in their financial statements in order to maximize net income, and at the same time they use a special accelerated-depreciation method on their tax returns in order to minimize their income taxes. For tax purposes, taxpayers must use on their tax returns either the straight-line method or a special accelerated-depreciation method called the **Modified Accelerated Cost Recovery System** (MACRS).

Depreciation Disclosure in the Notes

The choice of depreciation method must be disclosed in a company's financial statements or in related notes that accompany the statements. Illustration 9-14 shows the "Property and equipment" notes from the financial statements of Air-Tran and Southwest Airlines.

Illustration 9-14
Disclosure of depreciation policies

AIRTRAN
Notes to the Financial Statements

Property and equipment   Property and equipment is stated on the basis of cost. Flight equipment is depreciated to its salvage values, estimated at 5–40%, using the straight-line method over seven to ten years. Other property and equipment is depreciated over three to ten years.

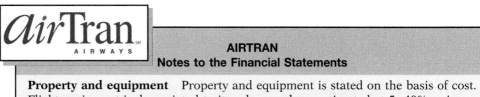

SOUTHWEST AIRLINES
Notes to the Financial Statements

Property and equipment   Depreciation is provided by the straight-line method to estimated residual values over periods ranging from 20 to 25 years for flight equipment and 3 to 30 years for ground property and equipment. Amortization of property under capital leases is on a straight-line basis over the lease term and is included in depreciation expense.

From these notes we learn that both companies use the straight-line method to depreciate their planes. Southwest Airlines also uses the straight-line method to depreciate planes that it leases rather than purchases. At first glance, AirTran would appear to be more conservative because it depreciates its planes over a 7- to 10-year life, whereas Southwest Airlines uses a 20- to 25-year life. Recall, however, that AirTran purchased primarily older planes, so it is not surprising that the company uses a shorter estimated life.

Revising Periodic Depreciation

Annual depreciation expense should be reviewed periodically by management. If wear and tear or obsolescence indicates that annual depreciation is either inadequate or excessive, the depreciation expense amount should be changed.

When a change in an estimate is required, the change is made in **current and future years but not to prior periods**. Thus, when a change is made, (1) there is no correction of previously recorded depreciation expense, and (2) depreciation expense for current and future years is revised. The rationale for this treatment is that continual restatement of prior periods would adversely affect users' confidence in financial statements.

Significant changes in estimates must be disclosed in the financial statements. Although a company may have a legitimate reason for changing an estimated life, financial statement users should be aware that some companies might change an estimate simply to achieve financial statement goals. For example, extending an asset's estimated life reduces depreciation expense and increases current period income.

Illustration 9-15 shows an example of changes in depreciation estimates that substantially increased income.

▲Delta AirLines

DELTA AIR LINES
Management Discussion and Analysis

Fiscal 1993 results were positively impacted by changes in two accounting estimates. Effective April 1, 1993, Delta revised its depreciation policy by increasing the estimated useful lives of substantially all of its flight equipment from 15 to 20 years and reducing residual values from 10% to 5% of cost. This change reduced depreciation expense by $34.3 million in fiscal 1993, and is expected to reduce depreciation expense by an estimated $126 million in fiscal 1994.

Illustration 9-15
Disclosure of changes in depreciation estimates

Delta Air Lines was operating at a loss at the time of these changes. Whether these changes are reasonable depends on the accuracy of the assumptions regarding these planes. Our opening story suggests that although many planes are lasting a long time, safety concerns might ground many old planes.

BEFORE YOU GO ON...

◆ Review It

1. Why is depreciation an allocation concept rather than a valuation concept?
2. What is the formula for computing annual depreciation under the straight-line method?
3. How do the depreciation methods differ in their effects on annual depreciation over the useful life of an asset?
4. Are revisions of periodic depreciation made to prior periods? Explain.

◆ Do It

On January 1, 2001, Iron Mountain Ski Corporation purchased a new snow grooming machine for $50,000. The machine is estimated to have a 10-year life with a $2,000 salvage value. What journal entry would Iron Mountain Ski Corporation make at December 31, 2001, if it uses the straight-line method of depreciation?

Reasoning: Depreciation is an allocation concept. Under straight-line depreciation an equal amount of the depreciable cost is allocated to each period.

Solution:

$$\text{Depreciation expense} = \frac{\text{Cost} - \text{Salvage value}}{\text{Useful life}} = \frac{\$50,000 - \$2,000}{10} = \$4,800$$

The entry to record the first year's depreciation would be:

Dec. 31	Depreciation Expense	4,800	
	Accumulated Depreciation		4,800
	(To record annual depreciation on snow		
	grooming machine)		

EXPENDITURES DURING USEFUL LIFE

During the useful life of a plant asset, a company may incur costs for ordinary repairs, additions, and improvements. Ordinary repairs are expenditures to maintain the operating efficiency and expected productive life of the unit. They usually are fairly small amounts that occur frequently throughout the service life. Motor tune-ups and oil changes, the painting of buildings, and the replacing of worn-out gears on factory machinery are examples. They are debited to Repair (or Maintenance) Expense as incurred. Because they are immediately charged against revenues as an expense, these costs are **revenue expenditures**.

Helpful Hint These expenditures occur after all costs have been incurred to make the asset ready for its intended use when it was acquired.

Additions and improvements are costs incurred to increase the operating efficiency, productive capacity, or expected useful life of the plant asset. These expenditures are usually material in amount and occur infrequently during the period of ownership. Expenditures for additions and improvements increase the company's investment in productive facilities and are generally debited to the plant asset affected. Accordingly, they are **capital expenditures**. The accounting for capital expenditures varies depending on the nature of the expenditure.

Northwest Airlines recently spent $120 million to spruce up 40 DC9-30 jets. The improvements were designed to extend the lives of the planes, meet stricter government noise limits, and save money. The capital expenditure was expected to extend the life of the jets by 10 to 15 years and save about $560 million over the cost of buying new planes. The DC9 jets are, on average, 24 years old.

IMPAIRMENTS

As noted earlier, the book value of plant assets is rarely the same as the market value. In instances where the market value of a plant asset declines substantially, its market value may be materially below book value. This may happen because a machine has become obsolete, or the market for the product made by the machine has dried up or has become very competitive. A **permanent decline** in the market value of an asset is referred to as an impairment. In order that the asset is not overstated on the books, it is written down to its new market value during the year in which the decline in value occurs.

In the past, some companies delayed recording losses on impairments until a year when it was "convenient" to do so—when the impact on the firm's reported results was minimized. For example, if a firm has record profits in one year, it can then afford to write down some of its bad assets without hurting its reported results too much. The practice of timing the recognition of gains and losses to achieve certain income results is known as **earnings management**. A recent FASB standard requires immediate recognition of these write-downs in order to reduce the practice of earnings management.

Write-downs can create problems for users of financial statements. Critics of write-downs note that after a company writes down assets, its depreciation expense will be lower in all subsequent periods. Some companies intentionally write down assets in bad years, when they are going to report low results anyway. Then in subsequent years, when the company recovers, its results will look even better because of lower depreciation expense.

BUSINESS INSIGHT
Investor Perspective

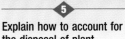

In recent years companies such as IBM, 3M, Westinghouse, and Digital Equipment Corporation have reported huge write-downs. These companies are quick to emphasize that these are "nonrecurring events"; that is, they are one-time charges and thus do not represent a recurring drag on future earnings. However, a number of large companies have reported large write-downs in multiple years, which makes analysts suspicious. After one of IBM's recent write-downs, one analyst recommended not buying IBM stock because, with such frequent write-downs, "What confidence do we have the same will not happen again?"

PLANT ASSET DISPOSALS

Companies dispose of plant assets that are no longer useful to them. Illustration 9-16 shows the three ways in which plant asset disposals are made.

STUDY OBJECTIVE
5
Explain how to account for the disposal of plant assets.

Sale	Retirement	Exchange
Equipment is sold to another party.	Equipment is scrapped or discarded.	Existing equipment is traded for new equipment.

Illustration 9-16
Methods of plant asset disposal

Whatever the disposal method, the company must determine the book value of the plant asset at the time of disposal. Recall that the book value is the difference between the cost of the plant asset and the accumulated depreciation to date. If the disposal occurs at any time during the year, depreciation for the fraction of the year to the date of disposal must be recorded. The book value is then eliminated by reducing (debiting) Accumulated Depreciation for the total depreciation associated with that asset to the date of disposal and reducing (crediting) the asset account for the cost of the asset.

Sale of Plant Assets

In a disposal by sale, the book value of the asset is compared with the proceeds received from the sale. If the proceeds from the sale exceed the book value of the plant asset, a **gain on disposal** occurs. If the proceeds from the sale are less than the book value of the plant asset sold, a **loss on disposal** occurs.

Only by coincidence will the book value and the fair market value of the asset be the same at the time the asset is sold. Gains and losses on sales of plant assets are therefore quite common. As an example, Delta Air Lines reported a $94,343,000 gain on the sale of five Boeing B-727-200 aircraft and five Lockheed L-1011-1 aircraft.

Gain on Sale. To illustrate a gain on sale of plant assets, assume that on July 1, 2001, Wright Company sells office furniture for $16,000 cash. The office furniture originally cost $60,000 and as of January 1, 2001, had accumulated depreciation of $41,000. Depreciation for the first six months of 2001 is $8,000. The entry to record depreciation expense and update accumulated depreciation to July 1 is as follows:

A = L + SE
−8,000   −8,000

July 1	Depreciation Expense	8,000	
	Accumulated Depreciation—Office Furniture		8,000
	(To record depreciation expense for the first 6 months of 2001)		

After the accumulated depreciation balance is updated, a gain on disposal of $5,000 is computed as shown in Illustration 9-17.

Illustration 9-17
Computation of gain on disposal

Cost of office furniture	$60,000
Less: Accumulated depreciation ($41,000 + $8,000)	49,000
Book value at date of disposal	11,000
Proceeds from sale	16,000
Gain on disposal of plant asset	**$ 5,000**

The entry to record the sale and the gain on sale of the plant asset is as follows:

A = L + SE
+16,000   +5,000
+49,000
−60,000

July 1	Cash	16,000	
	Accumulated Depreciation—Office Furniture	49,000	
	Office Furniture		60,000
	Gain on Disposal		5,000
	(To record sale of office furniture at a gain)		

The gain on disposal of the plant asset is reported in the Other Revenues and Gains section of the income statement.

Loss on Sale. Assume that instead of selling the office furniture for $16,000, Wright sells it for $9,000. In this case, a loss of $2,000 is computed as in Illustration 9-18.

Illustration 9-18
Computation of loss on disposal

Cost of office furniture	$60,000
Less: Accumulated depreciation	49,000
Book value at date of disposal	11,000
Proceeds from sale	9,000
Loss on disposal of plant asset	**$ 2,000**

The entry to record the sale and the loss on sale of the plant asset is as follows:

					A = L + SE
July 1	Cash	9,000			+9,000 −2,000
	Accumulated Depreciation—Office Furniture	49,000			+49,000
	Loss on Disposal	2,000			−60,000
	Office Furniture		60,000		
	(To record sale of office furniture at a loss)				

The loss on disposal of the plant asset is reported in the Other Expenses and Losses section of the income statement.

Retirement of Plant Assets

Some assets are simply retired by the company at the end of their useful life rather than sold. For example, some productive assets used in manufacturing may have very specific uses and consequently have no ready market when the company no longer needs them. In this case the asset is simply retired.

Retirement of an asset is recorded as a special case of a sale where no cash is received. Accumulated Depreciation is decreased (debited) for the full amount of depreciation taken over the life of the asset. The asset account is reduced (credited) for the original cost of the asset. The loss (a gain is not possible on a retirement) is equal to the asset's book value on the date of retirement.[1]

BEFORE YOU GO ON...

◆ Review It

1. What is the difference between an ordinary repair and an addition or improvement? Why is this distinction important to financial reporting?
2. What is an impairment? In what way do critics suggest that companies manage their earnings through the write-downs associated with impairments?
3. What is the proper accounting for sales and retirements of plant assets?

◆ Do It

Overland Trucking has an old truck that cost $30,000 and has accumulated depreciation of $16,000. Assume two different situations: (1) The company sells the old truck for $17,000 cash. (2) The truck is worthless, so the company simply retires it. What entry should Overland use to record each scenario?

Reasoning: Gains and losses on the sale or retirement of plant assets are determined by the difference between the book value and the fair market value of the company's asset.

Solution:

1. Sale of truck for cash:

Cash	17,000	
Accumulated Depreciation—Truck	16,000	
Truck		30,000
Gain on Disposal [$17,000 − ($30,000 − $16,000)]		3,000
(To record sale of truck at a gain)		

---

[1]The accounting for exchanges, the third method of plant asset disposal, is discussed in more advanced courses.

2. Retirement of truck:

Accumulated Depreciation—Truck	16,000	
Loss on Disposal	14,000	
Truck		30,000
(To record retirement of truck at a loss)		

Analyzing Plant Assets

STUDY OBJECTIVE

6

Describe methods for evaluating the use of plant assets.

The presentation of financial statement information about plant assets enables decision makers to analyze the company's use of its plant assets. We will use three measures to analyze plant assets: average useful life, average age of plant assets, and asset turnover ratio.

AVERAGE USEFUL LIFE

By selecting a longer estimated useful life, a company spreads the cost of its plant assets over a longer period of time. As a result, the amount of depreciation expense reported in each period is lower and net income is higher. A more conservative company will choose a shorter estimated useful life and will have a lower reported net income.

In the notes to financial statements, many companies are not very precise about the estimated useful life of specific assets. For example, a common disclosure might read, "Plant assets are depreciated using the straight-line method over estimated useful lives ranging from 5 to 40 years." This statement makes it difficult to determine whether a company is using a conservative approach for depreciation. It is unclear, for example, how many assets are being depreciated using short lives and how many using long lives. To overcome this problem, we can estimate the average useful life of plant assets for a company and compare it to that of its competitors. The average useful life is estimated by dividing the average cost of plant assets (property, plant, and equipment) by the depreciation expense. The following data are for AirTran and Southwest Airlines:

(in millions)	AirTran	Southwest
Total cost of plant assets—1998	$329	$4,709
Total cost of plant assets—1997	287	3,987
Depreciation expense—1998	28	225

Illustration 9-19 presents a computation of the average useful life used by AirTran and by Southwest Airlines.

Illustration 9-19
Average useful life of plant assets

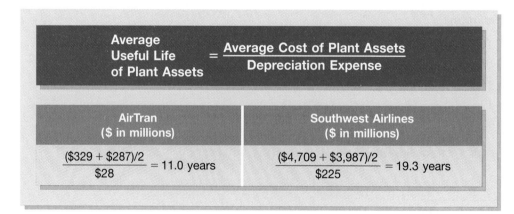

We estimate an average useful life of 11.0 years for AirTran and 19.3 years for Southwest. These estimates are consistent with the information published in their notes. Although both airlines depreciate some assets over a three-year life, the majority of their assets are depreciated over longer lives. Also, since AirTran purchases used equipment, we would expect AirTran to use a shorter useful life than Southwest. We recommend that, when analyzing a company, you use the estimate of the average useful life only as a check on the company's published depreciable lives. It is a rough approximation at best, but it can be useful when a company does not provide detailed disclosures for specific assets.

Helpful Hint Illustration 9-14 shows that AirTran depreciates its planes over 7 to 10 years, and Southwest uses a 20- to 25-year life. Also, AirTran depreciates its other property and equipment over a 3- to 10-year period, while Southwest uses a range of 3 to 30 years.

DECISION TOOLKIT

Decision Checkpoints	Info Needed for Decision	Tool to Use for Decision	How to Evaluate Results
Is the company's estimated useful life for depreciation reasonable?	Estimated useful life of assets from notes to financial statements of this company and its competitors; or cost of plant assets and depreciation expense.	If not provided in notes, average useful life can be estimated as: $$\text{Average useful life} = \frac{\text{Average cost of plant assets}}{\text{Depreciation expense}}$$	Too high an estimated useful life will result in understating depreciation expense and overstating net income.

AVERAGE AGE OF PLANT ASSETS

Consider the importance of new equipment to a hospital or new planes to an airline. Not only are newer planes more fuel efficient, but they also require less maintenance and they are safer—key features for an airline. Comparing the average age of plant assets gives an indication of the potential effectiveness of a company's plant assets relative to others in the industry. Both AirTran and Southwest report the average age of their planes in reports filed with the Securities and Exchange Commission. However, most companies do not report the age of their assets. But because most companies use straight-line depreciation in their financial reporting, the average age of plant assets can be approximated by dividing accumulated depreciation by depreciation expense. For example, if XYZ Co. has accumulated depreciation of $30,000 and depreciation expense of $10,000, the average age of plant assets is 3 years ($30,000 ÷ $10,000). The following 1998 data are for AirTran and Southwest:

(in millions)	AirTran	Southwest
Accumulated depreciation	$98	$1,601
Depreciation expense	28	225

The average age of plant assets for AirTran and for Southwest is estimated in Illustration 9-20.

Illustration 9-20
Average age of plant assets

$$\text{Average Age of Plant Assets} = \frac{\text{Accumulated Depreciation}}{\text{Depreciation Expense}}$$

AirTran ($ in millions)	Southwest Airlines ($ in millions)
$\dfrac{\$98}{\$28} = 3.5$ years	$\dfrac{\$1,601}{\$225} = 7.1$ years

Neither airline provides information by major class of asset for depreciation; as a consequence, we cannot refine our estimates. If, for example, they provided information on planes and buildings separately, we could calculate each and have a more precise estimate of the average age of planes and of buildings. Given the information available, we can calculate only the average age of plant assets in general. These numbers suggest that the average age of an AirTran plane is 3.5 years, and the average age of a Southwest Airlines plane is 7.1 years. From this we might conclude that AirTran planes are substantially newer than those of Southwest. But we know from the opening story that AirTran has one of the oldest fleets of any major airline—with an average plane age of 28 years—whereas Southwest has the newest fleet. So what is wrong with our estimate?

Our estimate of average age is wrong because this ratio does not work when a company purchases *used* assets. The figure of 3.5 years tells us that AirTran has **owned** its assets for 3.5 years. If they had been purchased new, they would be 3.5 years old. However, if they were 24.5 years old when purchased, they would now be 28 years old. This is an important lesson: **Never use ratios unless you fully understand their strengths and weaknesses.** Ratios can be very informative but also very misleading.

DECISION TOOLKIT

Decision Checkpoints	Info Needed for Decision	Tool to Use for Decision	How to Evaluate Results
Are the company's plant assets outdated or in need of replacement?	Depreciation expense and accumulated depreciation	$\text{Average age of plant assets} = \dfrac{\text{Accumulated depreciation}}{\text{Depreciation expense}}$	A high average age relative to competitors might suggest that the company's assets are not as efficient, or that they may be in need of replacement.

ASSET TURNOVER RATIO

The asset turnover ratio indicates how efficiently a company uses its assets—that is, how many dollars of sales are generated by each dollar invested in assets. It is calculated by dividing net sales by average total assets. When we compare two companies in the same industry, the one with the higher asset turnover ratio is operating more efficiently; it is generating more sales per dollar invested in assets. The following data are for AirTran and Southwest:

(in millions)	AirTran	Southwest
Total assets—1998	$376	$4,716
Total assets—1997	434	4,246
Net sales—1998	439	4,164

The asset turnover ratios for AirTran and Southwest Airlines for 1998 are computed in Illustration 9-21.

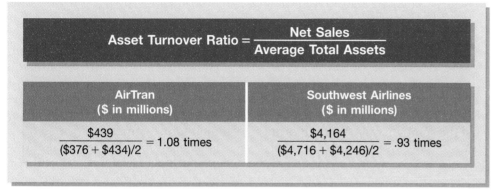

Illustration 9-21   Asset turnover ratio

The asset turnover ratios tell us that for each dollar invested in assets, AirTran generates sales of $1.08 and Southwest $.93. AirTran is more successful in generating sales per dollar invested in assets, perhaps due in part to its decision to buy older planes. The average asset turnover ratio for the airline industry is 1.01 times.

For a more complete picture, one would want to also look at the companies' profit margin ratios. As a result of AirTran's decision to use old planes, it probably incurs more costs per dollar of sales for things like repairs and additional fuel, which would result in lower profit per dollar of sales, as measured by the profit margin ratio.

Asset turnover ratios vary considerably across industries. The average asset turnover for utility companies is .45, and the grocery store industry has an average asset turnover of 3.49. Asset turnover ratios, therefore, are only comparable within—not between—industries.

DECISION TOOLKIT

Decision Checkpoints	Info Needed for Decision	Tool to Use for Decision	How to Evaluate Results
How effective is the company at generating sales from its assets?	Net sales and average total assets	Asset turnover ratio = Net sales / Average total assets	Indicates the sales dollars generated per dollar of assets. A high value suggests the company is effective in using its resources to generate sales.

BEFORE YOU GO ON...

◆ Review It

1. What is the purpose of the computation of the average age of plant assets? How is it calculated?
2. What is the purpose of the asset turnover ratio? How is it computed?

INTANGIBLE ASSETS

Intangible assets are rights, privileges, and competitive advantages that result from ownership of long-lived assets that do not possess physical substance. Many companies' most valuable assets are intangible. Some widely known intangibles are the patents of Polaroid, the franchises of McDonald's, the trade name iMac, and Nike's trademark "swoosh."

As you will learn in this section, although financial statements do report many intangibles, many other financially significant intangibles are not reported. To give an example, according to its 1998 financial statements, Microsoft had a net book value of $16.6 billion. But its *market* value—the total market price of all its shares on that same date—was roughly $465.4 billion. Thus, its actual market value was more than $448.8 billion greater than what its balance sheet said the company was worth. It is not uncommon for a company's reported book value to differ from its market value, because balance sheets are reported at historical cost. But such an extreme difference seriously diminishes the usefulness of the balance sheet to decision makers. In the case of Microsoft, the difference is due to unrecorded intangibles. For many high-tech or so-called intellectual property companies, most of their value is from intangibles, many of which are not reported under current accounting rules.

Intangibles may be evidenced by contracts, licenses, and other documents. Intangibles may arise from these sources:

1. Government grants such as patents, copyrights, franchises, trademarks, and trade names.
2. Acquisition of another business in which the purchase price includes a payment for goodwill.
3. Private monopolistic arrangements arising from contractual agreements, such as franchises and leases.

ACCOUNTING FOR INTANGIBLE ASSETS

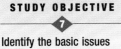

STUDY OBJECTIVE

7

Identify the basic issues related to reporting intangible assets.

Intangible assets are recorded at cost, and this cost is expensed **over the useful life of the intangible asset in a rational and systematic manner**. The term used to describe the allocation of the cost of an intangible asset to expense is amortization, rather than *depreciation*. To record amortization of an intangible, amortization expense is increased (debited) and the specific intangible asset account is decreased (credited). (Unlike depreciation, no contra account, such as Accumulated Amortization, is used.) Amortization expense is classified as an **operating expense** in the income statement. At disposal, the book value of the intangible asset is eliminated, and a gain or loss, if any, is recorded.

The amortization period of an intangible asset cannot be longer than 40 years. Even if the useful life of an intangible is 60 years, for example, it must be written off over 40 years. Conversely, if the useful life is less than 40 years, the useful life is used as the amortization period. This rule helps ensure that all intangibles, especially those with indeterminable lives, will be written off in a reasonable time.

Intangible assets are typically amortized on a straight-line basis. For example, the legal life of a patent is 20 years. **The cost of a patent should be amortized over its 20-year life or its useful life, whichever is shorter**. To illustrate the computation of patent amortization, assume that National Labs purchases a patent at a cost of $60,000. If the useful life of the patent is estimated to be eight years, the annual amortization expense is $7,500 ($60,000 ÷ 8). The following entry records the annual amortization:

Dec. 31	Patent Expense	7,500	
	Patent		7,500
	(To record patent amortization)		

A	=	L	+	SE
−7,500				−7,500

When analyzing a company that has significant intangibles, the reasonableness of the estimated useful life should be evaluated. In determining useful life, the company should consider obsolescence, inadequacy, and other factors. These may cause a patent or other intangible to become economically ineffective before the end of its legal life. For example, suppose a computer hardware manufacturer obtained a patent on a new computer chip that it had developed. The legal life of the patent is 20 years. From experience, however, we know that the useful life of a computer chip patent is rarely more than five years. Because new superior chips are developed so rapidly, existing chips become obsolete. Consequently, we would question the amortization expense of a company if it amortized its patent on a computer chip for longer than a five-year period. Amortizing an intangible over a period that is too long will understate amortization expense, overstate the company's net income, and overstate its assets.

DECISION TOOLKIT

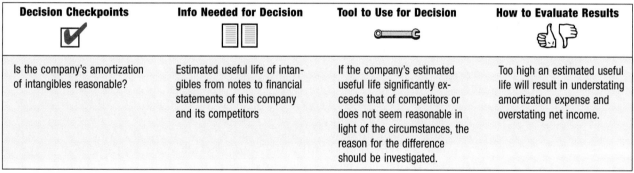

Decision Checkpoints	Info Needed for Decision	Tool to Use for Decision	How to Evaluate Results
Is the company's amortization of intangibles reasonable?	Estimated useful life of intangibles from notes to financial statements of this company and its competitors	If the company's estimated useful life significantly exceeds that of competitors or does not seem reasonable in light of the circumstances, the reason for the difference should be investigated.	Too high an estimated useful life will result in understating amortization expense and overstating net income.

TYPES OF INTANGIBLE ASSETS

PATENTS

A **patent** is an exclusive right issued by the United States Patent Office that enables the recipient to manufacture, sell, or otherwise control an invention for a period of 20 years from the date of the grant. **The initial cost of a patent is the cash or cash equivalent price paid to acquire the patent**.

The saying "A patent is only as good as the money you're prepared to spend defending it" is very true. Most patents are subject to some type of litigation by competitors. A well-known example is the patent infringement suit won by Polaroid against Eastman Kodak in protecting its patent on instant cameras. If the owner incurs legal costs in successfully defending the patent in an infringement suit, such costs are considered necessary to establish the validity of the patent. Thus, **they are added to the Patent account and amortized over the remaining life of the patent**.

Helpful Hint Patent infringement suits are expensive. One recent estimate of median cost of a patent case for each side was $280,000 through discovery and $580,000 through trial.

RESEARCH AND DEVELOPMENT COSTS

Helpful Hint Research and development costs are not intangible costs, but because these expenditures may lead to patents and copyrights, we discuss them in this section.

Research and development costs are expenditures that may lead to patents, copyrights, new processes, and new products. Many companies spend considerable sums of money on research and development in an ongoing effort to develop new products or processes. For example, in a recent year IBM spent over $2.5 billion on research and development. There are uncertainties in identifying the extent and timing of the future benefits of these expenditures. As a result, research and development costs are **usually recorded as an expense when incurred**, whether the research and development is successful or not.

To illustrate, assume that Laser Scanner Company spent $3 million on research and development that resulted in two highly successful patents. The R&D costs, however, cannot be included in the cost of the patents. Rather, they are recorded as an expense when incurred.

Many disagree with this accounting approach. They argue that to expense these costs leads to understated assets and net income. Others, however, argue that capitalizing these costs would lead to highly speculative assets on the balance sheet. Who is right is difficult to determine.

🌐 **International Note**
Many factors, including differences in accounting treatment of R&D, contribute to differences in R&D expenditures across nations. R&D as a percentage of gross domestic product in a recent year was 2.6% in the United States, 2.4% in France, 2.5% in Germany, 3% in Japan, and 1.8% in Korea.

COPYRIGHTS

Copyrights are granted by the federal government, giving the owner the exclusive right to reproduce and sell an artistic or published work. Copyrights extend for the life of the creator plus 50 years. The cost of the copyright consists of the **cost of acquiring and defending it**. The cost may be only the $10 fee paid to the U.S. Copyright Office, or it may amount to a great deal more if a copyright infringement suit is involved. The useful life of a copyright generally is significantly shorter than its legal life.

TRADEMARKS AND TRADE NAMES

A **trademark** or **trade name** is a word, phrase, jingle, or symbol that distinguishes or identifies a particular enterprise or product. Trade names like Wheaties, Trivial Pursuit, Sunkist, Kleenex, Coca-Cola, Big Mac, and Jeep create immediate product identification and generally enhance the sale of the product. The creator or original user may obtain the exclusive legal right to the trademark or trade name by registering it with the U.S. Patent Office. Such registration provides 20 years' protection and may be renewed indefinitely as long as the trademark or trade name is in use.

If the trademark or trade name is purchased, the cost is the purchase price. If it is developed by the enterprise itself, the cost includes attorney's fees, registration fees, design costs, successful legal defense costs, and other expenditures directly related to securing it.

As with other intangibles, the cost of trademarks and trade names must be amortized over the shorter of its useful life or 40 years. Because of the uncertainty involved in estimating the useful life, the cost is frequently amortized over a much shorter period.

FRANCHISES AND LICENSES

When you drive down the street in your RAV4 purchased from a Toyota dealer, fill up your tank at the corner Exxon station, eat lunch at Wendy's, and make plans to vacation at a Club Med resort, you are dealing with franchises. A **franchise** is a contractual arrangement under which the franchisor grants the franchisee the right to sell certain products, to render specific services, or to use certain trademarks or trade names, usually within a designated geographic area.

Another type of franchise, granted by a governmental body, permits the enterprise to use public property in performing its services. Examples are the use of city streets for a bus line or taxi service; the use of public land for telephone, electric, and cable television lines; and the use of airwaves for radio or TV broadcasting. Such operating rights are referred to as licenses.

Franchises and licenses may be granted for a definite period of time, an indefinite period, or perpetual. **When costs can be identified with the acquisition of the franchise or license, an intangible asset should be recognized**. Annual payments made under a franchise agreement should be recorded as **operating expenses** in the period in which they are incurred. In the case of a limited life, the cost of a franchise (or license) should be amortized as operating expense over the useful life. If the life is indefinite or perpetual, the cost may be amortized over a reasonable period not to exceed 40 years.

BUSINESS INSIGHT
Investor Perspective

King World's most valuable asset is the right to license television shows such as "Wheel of Fortune," "Jeopardy," "The Oprah Winfrey Show," and "Inside Edition." 88% of its $683.8 million in 1998 revenue came from the fees associated with the rights to license agreements on these intangible assets.

GOODWILL

Usually the largest intangible asset that appears on a company's balance sheet is goodwill. Goodwill represents the value of all favorable attributes that relate to a business enterprise. These include exceptional management, desirable location, good customer relations, skilled employees, high-quality products, fair pricing policies, and harmonious relations with labor unions. Goodwill is therefore unusual: Unlike other assets such as investments, plant assets, and even other intangibles, which can be sold *individually* in the marketplace, goodwill can be identified only with the business *as a whole*.

If goodwill can be identified only with the business as a whole, how can it be determined? Certainly, many business enterprises have many of the factors cited above (exceptional management, desirable location, and so on). However, to determine the amount of goodwill in these situations would be difficult and very subjective. In other words, to recognize goodwill without an exchange transaction that puts a value on the goodwill would lead to subjective valuations that do not contribute to the reliability of financial statements. **Therefore, goodwill is recorded only when there is an exchange transaction that involves the purchase of an entire business. When an entire business is purchased, goodwill is the excess of cost over the fair market value of the net assets (assets less liabilities) acquired**.

In recording the purchase of a business, the net assets are shown at their fair market values, cash is credited for the purchase price, and the difference is recorded as the cost of goodwill. The FASB is currently considering reducing the maximum amortization period for goodwill from a 40-year life down to a 20-year life.

BUSINESS INSIGHT
International Perspective

Does the amortization requirement for goodwill create a disadvantage for U.S. companies? Many think so. British companies, for example, can avoid amortizing goodwill against earnings, which made Pillsbury a more attractive purchase for Grand Met, a British firm, than for many domestic companies. Many complained that U.S. companies were reluctant to bid for Pillsbury because they would have to record a large amount of goodwill, which would substantially depress income in the future. What should be done when accounting practices are different among countries and perhaps give one country a competitive edge?

FINANCIAL STATEMENT PRESENTATION OF LONG-LIVED ASSETS

STUDY OBJECTIVE

8

Indicate how long-lived assets are reported on the balance sheet.

Usually plant assets are shown in the financial statements under Property, Plant, and Equipment, and intangibles are shown separately under Intangible Assets. Illustration 9-22 is adapted from The Coca-Cola Company's 1998 balance sheet.

Illustration 9-22
Presentation of property, plant, and equipment and intangible assets

THE COCA-COLA COMPANY Balance Sheet (partial) (in millions)		
Property, plant, and equipment		
Land		$ 199
Buildings and improvements	$1,507	
Machinery and equipment	3,855	
Containers	124	
Less: Accumulated depreciation	2,016	3,470
Intangibles		
Goodwill		547
Total		$4,216

Intangibles do not usually use a contra asset account like the contra asset account Accumulated Depreciation used for plant assets. Instead, amortization of these accounts is recorded as a direct decrease (credit) to the asset account.

Either within the balance sheet or in the notes, there should be disclosure of the balances of the major classes of assets, such as land, buildings, and equipment, and of accumulated depreciation by major classes or in total. In addition, the depreciation and amortization methods used should be described and the amount of depreciation and amortization expense for the period disclosed.

BEFORE YOU GO ON...

◆ **Review It**

1. Identify the major types of intangible assets and the proper accounting for them.
2. Explain the accounting for research and development costs.
3. How are intangible assets presented on the balance sheet?

USING THE DECISION TOOLKIT

Roberts Pharmaceuticals Corporation, a publicly traded company since 1990, has its headquarters in Eatontown, New Jersey. It is a rapidly growing company that acquires, develops, and markets pharmaceuticals. In 1998 it reported a substantial increase in net income, after reporting a loss in 1996 and a small profit in 1997. The company has acquired, rather than developed internally, a number of existing products from other companies. It reports significant intangible assets related to these acquisitions. Suppose you noticed the improvement in Roberts' operating results and were considering investing in Roberts.

Instructions

Review the excerpts shown below and on the following page from the company's 1998 annual report, and consider the company's sensitivity to the amortization of its intangibles and how that might affect your decision on whether to invest. Then answer these questions:

1. What percentage of total assets are intangibles as of December 31, 1998?
2. What method does the company use to amortize intangibles, and over what period are they amortized?
3. Calculate the average useful life that the company is using to amortize its intangible assets.
4. Comment on whether, in your opinion, the company's intangibles amortization policy is reasonable.
5. What would 1998 income have been if the company had used a 15-year useful life for amortization? [*Hint:* Base your calculation on the *average* intangible assets in 1998.]

ROBERTS PHARMACEUTICALS CORPORATION
Consolidated Balance Sheets (Assets Only)
(in thousands)

Assets	Dec. 31, 1998	Dec. 31, 1997
Total current assets	$157,234	$137,987
Plant assets and other	53,137	39,144
Intangible assets	315,865	190,724
Total assets	$526,236	$367,855

ROBERTS PHARMACEUTICALS CORPORATION
Consolidated Statement of Operations
Years Ended December 31
(in thousands)

	1998	1997
Total sales and revenue	$175,445	$122,508
Total operating costs and expenses	148,067	123,270
Operating income (loss)	27,378	(762)
Other revenues, (expenses), gains, and (losses)	(10,591)	3,279
Net income (loss)	$ 16,787	$ 2,517

ROBERTS PHARMACEUTICALS CORPORATION
Selected Notes to the Financial Statements

Summary of Significant Accounting Policies

Intangible assets: Intangible assets are stated at cost less accumulated amortization. Amortization is determined using the straight-line method over the estimated useful lives of the related assets which are estimated to range from five to forty years. It is the Company's policy to review periodically and evaluate whether there has been an impairment in the value of intangibles. In the fourth quarter of 1996, the Company recorded a charge to earnings for an impairment of intangible assets and to expense purchased development products totaling $25.4 million.

Intangible Assets

Intangible assets consist of (in thousands):

	Dec. 31	
	1998	1997
Product rights acquired	$349,282	$217,919
Less: Accumulated amortization	33,417	27,195
	$315,865	$190,724

Notes

Amortization expense for the years ended December 31, 1996, 1997, and 1998, was $6,692, $6,159, and $9,815, respectively.

Solution

1. As a percentage of the company's total assets, intangibles represented 60% in 1998 ($315,865,000 ÷ $526,236,000).

2. The company uses the straight-line method to amortize intangibles. The notes state that they are amortized over a 5- to 40-year period.

3. The average useful life being used to amortize intangible assets can be estimated by dividing the average cost of the intangible assets by the amortization expense.

$$\frac{(\$349,282,000 + \$217,919,000) \div 2}{\$9,815,000} = 28.9 \text{ years}$$

4. This is a matter of opinion. However, one factor to consider is that Roberts is purchasing the rights to existing products, so part of their useful life may already be gone. Additionally, because of rapidly changing technology, new drugs appear to be developed at a relatively rapid rate; thus, it seems unlikely that on average drugs would have a useful life of 40 years. Also, the notes state that the company took a $25.4 million write-down in 1996 due to the impairment of its intangibles. This suggests its intangibles were not being amortized fast enough. A 15-year life would seem more appropriate.

5. In order to estimate amortization expense using a 15-year life, we would first need to calculate average intangibles for the year to approximate the amortization:

$$\text{Average intangibles} = \frac{\$349,282,000 + \$217,919,000}{2} = \$283,600,500$$

Amortization over a 15-year period would be:

$$\frac{\$283,600,500}{15} = \$18,906,700$$

The reduction in income from the increased amortization (revised amortization minus actual amortization) would be:

$$\$18,906,700 - \$9,815,000 = \$9,091,700$$

Therefore, with amortization over a 15-year period, the resulting income (reported income minus increase in amortization) for the year would be:

$$\$16,787,000 - \$9,091,700 = \$7,695,300$$

Conclusion: These calculations make it clear the company's income is very sensitive to the assumed useful life. Therefore, before investing, you would want to investigate further the reasonableness of the 5–40-year assumption currently being used.

SUMMARY OF STUDY OBJECTIVES

1 Describe how the cost principle applies to plant assets. The cost of plant assets includes all expenditures necessary to acquire the asset and make it ready for its intended use. Cost is measured by the cash or cash equivalent price paid.

2 Explain the concept of depreciation. Depreciation is the process of allocating to expense the cost of a plant asset over its useful (service) life in a rational and systematic manner. Depreciation is not a process of valuation, and it is not a process that results in an accumulation of cash. Depreciation is caused by wear and tear and by obsolescence.

3 Compute periodic depreciation using the straight-line method, and contrast its expense pattern with those of other methods. The formula for straight-line depreciation is:

$$\frac{\text{Cost} - \text{Salvage value}}{\text{Useful life (in years)}}$$

The expense patterns of the three depreciation methods are as follows:

Method	Annual Depreciation Pattern
Straight-line	Constant amount
Declining-balance	Decreasing amount
Units-of-activity	Varying amount

4 Describe the procedure for revising periodic depreciation. Revisions of periodic depreciation are made in present and future periods, not retroactively. The new annual depreciation is determined by dividing the depreciable cost at the time of the revision by the remaining useful life.

5 Explain how to account for the disposal of plant assets. The procedure for accounting for the disposal of a plant asset through sale or retirement is: (a) Eliminate the book value of the plant asset at the date of disposal. (b) Record cash proceeds, if any. (c) Account for the difference between the book value and the cash proceeds as a gain or a loss on disposal.

6 Describe methods for evaluating the use of plant assets. Plant assets may be analyzed using average useful life, average age, and asset turnover ratio.

7 Identify the basic issues related to reporting intangible assets. Intangible assets are reported at their cost less any amounts amortized. Amortization is done over the shortest of the useful life, legal life, or 40 years—usually on a straight-line basis.

8 Indicate how long-lived assets are reported on the balance sheet. Plant assets are usually shown under Property, Plant, and Equipment; intangibles are shown separately under Intangible Assets. Either within the balance sheet or in the notes, the balances of the major classes of assets, such as land, buildings, and equipment, and accumulated depreciation by major classes or in total are disclosed. The depreciation and amortization methods used should be described, and the amount of depreciation and amortization expense for the period should be disclosed.

DECISION TOOLKIT—A SUMMARY

Decision Checkpoints	Info Needed for Decision	Tool to Use for Decision	How to Evaluate Results
Is the company's estimated useful life for depreciation reasonable?	Estimated useful life of assets from notes to financial statements of this company and its competitors; or cost of plant assets and depreciation expense	If not provided in notes, average useful life can be estimated as: $$\text{Average useful life} = \frac{\text{Average cost of plant assets}}{\text{Depreciation expense}}$$	Too high an estimated useful life will result in understating depreciation expense and overstating net income.
Are the company's plant assets outdated or in need of replacement?	Depreciation expense and accumulated depreciation	$$\text{Average age of plant assets} = \frac{\text{Accumulated depreciation}}{\text{Depreciation expense}}$$	A high average age relative to competitors might suggest that the company's assets are not as efficient, or that they may be in need of replacement.
How effective is the company at generating sales from its assets?	Net sales and average total assets	$$\text{Asset turnover ratio} = \frac{\text{Net sales}}{\text{Average total assets}}$$	Indicates the sales dollars generated per dollar of assets. A high value suggests the company is effective in using its resources to generate sales.
Is the company's amortization of intangibles reasonable?	Estimated useful life of intangibles from notes to financial statements of this company and its competitors	If the company's estimated useful life significantly exceeds that of competitors or does not seem reasonable in light of the circumstances, the reason for the difference should be investigated.	Too high an estimated useful life will result in understating amortization expense and overstating net income.

APPENDIX

CALCULATION OF DEPRECIATION USING OTHER METHODS

In this appendix we show the calculations of the depreciation expense amounts used in the chapter for the declining-balance and units-of-activity methods.

STUDY OBJECTIVE

9

Compute periodic depreciation using the declining-balance method and the units-of-activity method.

DECLINING-BALANCE

The **declining-balance method** produces a decreasing annual depreciation expense over the useful life of the asset. The method is so named because the computation of periodic depreciation is based on a **declining book value** (cost less accumulated depreciation) of the asset. Annual depreciation expense is computed by multiplying the book value at the beginning of the year by the declining-balance depreciation rate. **The depreciation rate remains constant from year to year, but the book value to which the rate is applied declines each year**.

Book value for the first year is the cost of the asset because the balance in accumulated depreciation at the beginning of the asset's useful life is zero. In subsequent years, book value is the difference between cost and accumulated depreciation at the beginning of the year. **Unlike other depreciation methods, salvage value is ignored in determining the amount to which the declining-balance rate is applied.** Salvage value, however, does limit the total depreciation that can be taken. Depreciation stops when the asset's book value equals its expected salvage value.

As noted in the chapter, a common declining-balance rate is double the straight-line rate—a method often referred to as the **double-declining-balance method.** If Bill's Pizzas uses the double-declining-balance method, the depreciation rate is 40% (2 × the straight-line rate of 20%). Illustration 9A-1 presents the formula and computation of depreciation for the first year on the delivery truck.

Helpful Hint The straight-line rate is approximated as 1 ÷ Estimated life. In this case it is 1 ÷ 5 = 20%.

Illustration 9A-1
Formula for declining-balance method

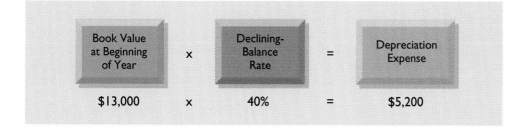

The depreciation schedule under this method is given in Illustration 9A-2.

Illustration 9A-2
Double-declining-balance depreciation schedule

| | | **BILL'S PIZZAS** | | | |
| | Computation | | Annual | End of Year | |
Year	Book Value Beginning of Year	× Depreciation Rate	= Depreciation Expense	Accumulated Depreciation	Book Value
2001	$13,000	40%	$5,200	$ 5,200	$7,800*
2002	7,800	40	3,120	8,320	4,680
2003	4,680	40	1,872	10,192	2,808
2004	2,808	40	1,123	11,315	1,685
2005	1,685	40	685**	12,000	1,000

* $13,000 − $5,200
**Computation of $674 ($1,685 × 40%) is adjusted to $685 in order for book value to equal salvage value.

Helpful Hint Depreciation stops when the asset's book value equals its expected salvage value.

You can see that the delivery equipment is 69% depreciated ($8,320 ÷ $12,000) at the end of the second year. Under the straight-line method it would be depreciated 40% ($4,800 ÷ $12,000) at that time. Because the declining-balance method produces higher depreciation expense in the early years than in the later years, it is considered an accelerated-depreciation method. The declining-balance method is compatible with the matching principle. The higher depreciation expense in early years is matched with the higher benefits received in these years. Conversely, lower depreciation expense is recognized in later years when the asset's contribution to revenue is less. Also, some assets lose their usefulness rapidly because of obsolescence. In these cases, the declining-balance method provides a more appropriate depreciation amount.

Helpful Hint The method to be used for an asset that is expected to be more productive in the first half of its useful life is the declining-balance method.

When an asset is purchased during the year, it is necessary to prorate the declining-balance depreciation in the first year on a time basis. For example, if Bill's Pizzas had purchased the delivery equipment on April 1, 2001, depreciation for 2001 would be $3,900 ($13,000 × 40% × $\frac{9}{12}$). The book value for computing depreciation in 2002 then becomes $9,100 ($13,000 − $3,900), and the 2002 depreciation is $3,640 ($9,100 × 40%).

UNITS-OF-ACTIVITY

Alternative Terminology
Another term often used is the **units-of-production method**.

Under the **units-of-activity method**, useful life is expressed in terms of the total units of production or use expected from the asset. The units-of-activity method is ideally suited to equipment whose activity can be measured in units of output, miles driven, or hours in use. The units-of-activity method is generally not suitable for assets for which depreciation is a function more of time than of use.

To use this method, the total units of activity for the entire useful life are estimated and that amount is divided into the depreciable cost to determine the depreciation cost per unit. The depreciation cost per unit is then multiplied by the units of activity during the year to give the annual depreciation for that year. To illustrate, assume that the delivery truck of Bill's Pizzas is driven 15,000 miles in the first year. Illustration 9A-3 presents the formula and computation of depreciation expense in the first year.

Illustration 9A-3
Formula for units-of-activity method

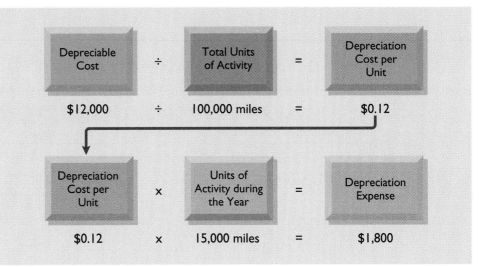

The depreciation schedule, using assumed mileage data, is shown in Illustration 9A-4.

Illustration 9A-4   Units-of-activity depreciation schedule

Helpful Hint Depreciation stops when the asset's book value equals its expected salvage value.

	Computation			Annual	End of Year	
Year	Units of Activity	×	Depreciation Cost/Unit	= Depreciation Expense	Accumulated Depreciation	Book Value
BILL'S PIZZAS						
2001	15,000		$.12	**$1,800**	$ 1,800	$11,200*
2002	30,000		.12	**3,600**	5,400	7,600
2003	20,000		.12	**2,400**	7,800	5,200
2004	25,000		.12	**3,000**	10,800	2,200
2005	10,000		.12	**1,200**	12,000	1,000

*$13,000 − $1,800

The units-of-activity method is not nearly as popular as the straight-line method, primarily because it is often difficult to make a reasonable estimate of total activity. However, this method is used by some very large companies, such as Standard Oil Company of California and Boise Cascade Corporation. When the productivity of the asset varies significantly from one period to another, the units-of-activity method results in the best matching of expenses with revenues. This method is easy to apply when assets are purchased during the year. In such a case, the productivity of the asset for the partial year is used in computing the depreciation.

SUMMARY OF STUDY OBJECTIVE FOR APPENDIX

9 *Compute periodic depreciation using the declining-balance method and the units-of-activity method.* The calculation for each of these methods is shown here:

Declining-balance:

$$\begin{array}{c}\text{Book value at}\\\text{beginning of year}\end{array} \times \begin{array}{c}\text{Declining-balance}\\\text{rate}\end{array}$$

Units-of-activity:

$$\begin{array}{c}\text{Depreciable}\\\text{cost}\end{array} \div \begin{array}{c}\text{Total units}\\\text{of activity}\end{array} = \begin{array}{c}\text{Depreciation}\\\text{cost per unit}\end{array}$$

$$\begin{array}{c}\text{Depreciation cost}\\\text{per unit}\end{array} \times \begin{array}{c}\text{Units of activity}\\\text{during year}\end{array}$$

GLOSSARY

Accelerated-depreciation method A depreciation method that produces higher depreciation expense in the early years than in the later years. (p. 429)

Additions and improvements Costs incurred to increase the operating efficiency, productive capacity, or expected useful life of a plant asset. (p. 412)

Amortization The allocation of the cost of an intangible asset to expense. (p. 420)

Asset turnover ratio Measure of sales volume, calculated as net sales divided by average total assets. (p. 418)

Average age of plant assets Measure of the age of a company's plant assets, calculated as accumulated depreciation divided by depreciation expense. (p. 417)

Average useful life A comparative measure of plant assets, calculated as the average cost of plant assets divided by depreciation expense. (p. 416)

Capital expenditures Expenditures that increase the company's investment in productive facilities. (p. 400)

Capital lease A long-term agreement allowing one party (the lessee) to use another party's asset (the lessor). The arrangement is accounted for like a purchase. (p. 403)

Cash equivalent price An amount equal to the fair market value of the asset given up or the fair market value of the asset received, whichever is more clearly determinable. (p. 400)

Copyright An exclusive right granted by the federal government allowing the owner to reproduce and sell an artistic or published work. (p. 422)

Declining-balance method A depreciation method that applies a constant rate to the declining book value of the asset and produces a decreasing annual depreciation expense over the useful life of the asset. (p. 408)

Depreciable cost The cost of a plant asset less its salvage value. (p. 406)

Depreciation The process of allocating to expense the cost of a plant asset over its useful life in a rational and systematic manner. (p. 404)

Franchise A contractual arrangement under which the franchisor grants the franchisee the right to sell certain products, to render specific services, or to use certain trademarks or trade names, usually within a designated geographic area. (p. 422)

Goodwill The value of all favorable attributes that relate to a business enterprise. (p. 423)

Impairment A permanent decline in the market value of an asset. (p. 412)

Intangible assets Rights, privileges, and competitive advantages that result from the ownership of long-lived assets that do not possess physical substance. (p. 420)

Lessee A party that has made contractual arrangements to use another party's asset without purchasing it. (p. 402)

Lessor A party that has agreed contractually to let another party use its asset. (p. 402)

Licenses Operating rights to use public property, granted by a governmental agency to a business enterprise. (p. 423)

Operating lease An arrangement allowing one party (the lessee) to use the asset of another party (the lessor). The arrangement is accounted for as a rental. (p. 403)

Ordinary repairs Expenditures to maintain the operating efficiency and expected productive life of the asset. (p. 412)

Patent An exclusive right issued by the U.S. Patent Office that enables the recipient to manufacture, sell, or otherwise control an invention for a period of 20 years from the date of the grant. (p. 421)

Plant assets Tangible resources that have physical substance, are used in the operations of the business, and are not intended for sale to customers. (p. 398)

Research and development costs Expenditures that may lead to patents, copyrights, new processes, and new products. (p. 422)

Revenue expenditures Expenditures that are immediately charged against revenues as an expense. (p. 400)

Straight-line method A method in which periodic depreciation is the same for each year of the asset's useful life. (p. 406)

Trademark (trade name) A word, phrase, jingle, or symbol that distinguishes or identifies a particular enterprise or product. (p. 422)

Units-of-activity method A depreciation method in which useful life is expressed in terms of the total units of production or use expected from the asset. (p. 408)

DEMONSTRATION PROBLEM 1

DuPage Company purchased a factory machine at a cost of $18,000 on January 1, 2001. The machine was expected to have a salvage value of $2,000 at the end of its 4-year useful life.

Instructions

Prepare a depreciation schedule using the straight-line method.

Solution to Demonstration Problem

Problem-Solving Strategy
Under the straight-line method, the depreciation rate is applied to depreciable cost.

DUPAGE COMPANY
Depreciation Schedule—Straight-Line Method

| | Computation | | | | Annual | End of Year | |
Year	Depreciable Cost	×	Depreciation Rate	=	Depreciation Expense	Accumulated Depreciation	Book Value
2001	$16,000		25%		$4,000	$ 4,000	$14,000*
2002	16,000		25		4,000	8,000	10,000
2003	16,000		25		4,000	12,000	6,000
2004	16,000		25		4,000	16,000	2,000

*$18,000 − $4,000

DEMONSTRATION PROBLEM 2

On January 1, 1998, Skyline Limousine Co. purchased a limousine at an acquisition cost of $28,000. The vehicle has been depreciated by the straight-line method using a 4-year service life and a $4,000 salvage value. The company's fiscal year ends on December 31.

Instructions

Prepare the journal entry or entries to record the disposal of the limousine assuming that it was:
(a) Retired and scrapped with no salvage value on January 1, 2002.
(b) Sold for $5,000 on July 1, 2001.

Solution to Demonstration Problem

(a)	Jan. 1, 2002	Accumulated Depreciation—Limousine	24,000	
		Loss on Disposal	4,000	
		Limousine		28,000
		(To record retirement of limousine)		
(b)	July 1, 2001	Depreciation Expense	3,000	
		Accumulated Depreciation—Limousine		3,000
		(To record depreciation to date of disposal)		
		Cash	5,000	
		Accumulated Depreciation—Limousine	21,000	
		Loss on Disposal	2,000	
		Limousine		28,000
		(To record sale of limousine)		

Problem-Solving Strategy
Accumulated depreciation is equal to depreciation expense per year times the number of years of use.

Note: All Questions, Exercises, and Problems marked with an asterisk relate to material in the appendix to the chapter.

SELF-STUDY QUESTIONS

Answers are at the end of the chapter.

(SO 1) 1. Corrieten Company purchased equipment and these costs were incurred:

Cash price	$24,000
Sales taxes	1,200
Insurance during transit	200
Installation and testing	400
Total costs	$25,800

What amount should be recorded as the cost of the equipment?
(a) $24,000.   (c) $25,400.
(b) $25,200.   (d) $25,800.

(SO 1) 2. ◖▬▬◗ Harrington Corporation recently leased a number of trucks from Andre Corporation. In inspecting the books of Harrington Corporation, you notice that the trucks have not been recorded as assets on its balance sheet. From this you can conclude that Harrington is accounting for this transaction as a/an:
(a) operating lease.   (c) purchase.
(b) capital lease.   (d) None of the above

(SO 2) 3. Depreciation is a process of:
(a) valuation.   (c) cash accumulation.
(b) cost allocation.   (d) appraisal.

(SO 3) 4. Cuso Company purchased equipment on January 1, 2000, at a total invoice cost of $400,000. The equipment has an estimated salvage value of $10,000 and an estimated useful life of 5 years. What is the amount of accumulated depreciation at December 31, 2001, if the straight-line method of depreciation is used?
(a) $80,000.   (c) $78,000.
(b) $160,000.   (d) $156,000.

(SO 3) 5. ◖▬▬◗ A company would minimize its depreciation expense in the first year of owning an asset if it used:
(a) a high estimated life, a high salvage value, and declining-balance depreciation.
(b) a low estimated life, a high salvage value, and straight-line depreciation.
(c) a high estimated life, a high salvage value, and straight-line depreciation.
(d) a low estimated life, a low salvage value, and declining-balance depreciation.

(SO 4) 6. When there is a change in estimated depreciation:
(a) previous depreciation should be corrected.
(b) current and future years' depreciation should be revised.
(c) only future years' depreciation should be revised.
(d) None of the above.

(SO 5) 7. Additions to plant assets:
(a) are revenue expenditures.
(b) increase a Repair Expense account.
(c) increase a Purchases account.
(d) are capital expenditures.

(SO 6) 8. Which of the following measures provides an indication of how efficient a company is in employing its assets?
(a) Current ratio.
(b) Average useful life.
(c) Average age of plant assets.
(d) Asset turnover ratio.

(SO 7) 9. Pierce Company incurred $150,000 of research and development costs in its laboratory to develop a new product. It spent $20,000 in legal fees for a patent granted on January 2, 2001.

On July 31, 2001, Pierce paid $15,000 for legal fees in a successful defense of the patent. What is the total amount that should be debited to Patents through July 31, 2001?
(a) $150,000.   (c) $185,000.
(b) $35,000.   (d) Some other amount.

(SO 7) 10. Indicate which one of these statements is *true*.
(a) Since intangible assets lack physical substance, they need to be disclosed only in the notes to the financial statements.
(b) Goodwill should be reported as a contra account in the Stockholders' Equity section.
(c) Totals of major classes of assets can be shown in the balance sheet, with asset details disclosed in the notes to the financial statements.
(d) Intangible assets are typically combined with plant assets and natural resources and then shown in the Property, Plant, and Equipment section.

(SO 7) 11. If a company reports goodwill as an intangible asset on its books, what is the one thing you know with certainty?

(a) The company is a valuable company worth investing in.
(b) The company has a well-established brand name.
(c) The company purchased another company.
(d) The goodwill will generate a lot of positive business for the company for many years to come.

*12. Kant Enterprises purchased a truck for $11,000 on January 1, 2000. The truck will have an estimated salvage value of $1,000 at the end of 5 years. If you use the units-of-activity method, the balance in accumulated depreciation at December 31, 2001, can be computed by the following formula: (SO 9)
(a) ($11,000 ÷ Total estimated activity) × Units of activity for 2001.
(b) ($10,000 ÷ Total estimated activity) × Units of activity for 2001.
(c) ($11,000 ÷ Total estimated activity) × Units of activity for 2000 and 2001.
(d) ($10,000 ÷ Total estimated activity) × Units of activity for 2000 and 2001.

QUESTIONS

1. Susan Day is uncertain about how the cost principle applies to plant assets. Explain the principle to Susan.
2. How is the cost for a plant asset measured in a cash transaction? In a noncash transaction?
3. What are the primary advantages of leasing?
4. Jamie Company acquires the land and building owned by Smitt Company. What types of costs may be incurred to make the asset ready for its intended use if Jamie Company wants to use only the land? Both the land and the building?
5. In a recent newspaper release, the president of Lawsuit Company asserted that something has to be done about depreciation. The president said, "Depreciation does not come close to accumulating the cash needed to replace the asset at the end of its useful life." What is your response to the president?
6. Cecile is studying for the next accounting examination. She asks your help on two questions: (a) What is salvage value? (b) How is salvage value used in determining depreciable cost under the straight-line method? Answer Cecile's questions.
7. ▭▭▭ Contrast the straight-line method and the units-of-activity method in relation to (a) useful life and (b) the pattern of periodic depreciation over useful life.
8. ▭▭▭ Contrast the effects of the three depreciation methods on annual depreciation expense.
9. In the fourth year of an asset's 5-year useful life, the company decides that the asset will have a 6-year service life. How should the revision of depreciation be recorded? Why?
10. Distinguish between revenue expenditures and capital expenditures during an asset's useful life.
11. How is a gain or a loss on the sale of a plant asset computed?
12. Ewing Corporation owns a machine that is fully depreciated but is still being used. How should Ewing account for this asset and report it in the financial statements?
13. What are the similarities and differences between depreciation and amortization?
14. Heflin Company hires an accounting intern who says that intangible assets should always be amortized over their legal lives. Is the intern correct? Explain.
15. Goodwill has been defined as the value of all favorable attributes that relate to a business enterprise. What types of attributes could result in goodwill?
16. Bob Leno, a business major, is working on a case problem for one of his classes. In this case problem, the company needs to raise cash to market a new product it developed. Saul Cain, an engineering major, takes one look at the company's balance sheet and says, "This company has an awful lot of goodwill. Why don't you recommend that they sell some of it to raise cash?" How should Bob respond to Saul?
17. Under what conditions is goodwill recorded?

18. Often research and development costs provide companies with benefits that last a number of years. (For example, these costs can lead to the development of a patent that will increase the company's income for many years.) However, generally accepted accounting principles require that such costs be recorded as an expense when incurred. Why?

19. In 1998 **Ben & Jerry's** reported average total assets of $148 million and net sales of $209 million. What was Ben & Jerry's asset turnover ratio?

20. Give an example of an industry that would be characterized by (a) a high asset turnover ratio and a low profit margin ratio, and (b) a low asset turnover ratio and a high profit margin ratio.

21. Morgan Corporation and Fairchild Corporation both operate in the same industry. Morgan uses the straight-line method to account for depreciation, whereas Fairchild uses an accelerated method. Explain what complications might arise in trying to compare the results of these two companies.

22. Lucille Corporation uses straight-line depreciation for financial reporting purposes but an accelerated method for tax purposes. Is it acceptable to use different methods for the two purposes? What is Lucille Corporation's motivation for doing this?

23. You are comparing two companies in the same industry. You have determined that Betty Corp. depreciates its plant assets over a 40-year life, whereas Herb Corp. depreciates its plant assets over a 20-year life. Discuss the implications this has for comparing the results of the two companies.

BRIEF EXERCISES

BE9-1 These expenditures were incurred by Gene Shumway Company in purchasing land: cash price $50,000; accrued taxes $7,000; attorney's fees $2,500; real estate broker's commission $2,000; and clearing and grading $3,500. What is the cost of the land?

Determine the cost of land.
(SO 1)

BE9-2 Shirley Basler Company incurs these expenditures in purchasing a truck: cash price $18,000; accident insurance (during use) $2,000; sales taxes $900; motor vehicle license $300; and painting and lettering $600. What is the cost of the truck?

Determine the cost of a truck.
(SO 1)

BE9-3 Joy Cunningham Company acquires a delivery truck at a cost of $22,000 on January 1, 2001. The truck is expected to have a salvage value of $2,000 at the end of its 6-year useful life. Compute annual depreciation for the first and second years using the straight-line method.

Compute straight-line depreciation.
(SO 3)

BE9-4 On January 1, 2001, the Asler Company ledger shows Equipment $32,000 and Accumulated Depreciation $12,000. The depreciation resulted from using the straight-line method with a useful life of 10 years and a salvage value of $2,000. On this date the company concludes that the equipment has a remaining useful life of only 2 years with the same salvage value. Compute the revised annual depreciation.

Compute revised depreciation.
(SO 4)

BE9-5 Prepare journal entries to record these transactions: (a) Ruiz Company retires its delivery equipment, which cost $41,000. Accumulated depreciation is also $41,000 on this delivery equipment. No salvage value is received. (b) Assume the same information as in part (a), except that accumulated depreciation for Ruiz Company is $35,000 instead of $41,000.

Journalize entries for disposal of plant assets.
(SO 5)

BE9-6 Wiley Company sells office equipment on September 30, 2001, for $21,000 cash. The office equipment originally cost $72,000 and as of January 1, 2001, had accumulated depreciation of $42,000. Depreciation for the first 9 months of 2001 is $6,250. Prepare the journal entries to (a) update depreciation to September 30, 2001, and (b) record the sale of the equipment.

Journalize entries for sale of plant assets.
(SO 5)

BE9-7 Popper Company purchases a patent for $180,000 on January 2, 2001. Its estimated useful life is 10 years.
(a) Prepare the journal entry to record patent expense for the first year.
(b) Show how this patent is reported on the balance sheet at the end of the first year.

Account for intangibles—patents.
(SO 7)

BE9-8 In its 1998 annual report, **McDonald's Corporation** reports beginning total assets of $18.2 billion; ending total assets of $19.8 billion; beginning property, plant, and equipment (at cost) of $20.1 billion; ending property, plant, and equipment (at cost) $21.8 billion; ending accumulated depreciation of $5.7 billion; depreciation expense of $808 million; and net sales of $12.4 billion.

Compute average life, average age of long-lived assets, and asset turnover ratio.
(SO 6)

(a) Compute the average useful life of McDonald's property, plant, and equipment.
(b) Compute the average age of McDonald's property, plant, and equipment.
(c) Compute McDonald's asset turnover ratio.

Classification of long-lived assets on balance sheet.
(SO 8)

BE9-9   Nike, Inc. reported the following plant assets and intangible assets for the year ended May 31, 1998 (in millions): leasehold improvements $887.4; land $93; patents and trademarks (at cost) $220.7; machinery and equipment $887.4; buildings $585.5; goodwill (at cost) $321.0; accumulated amortization $105.9; accumulated depreciation $666.5. Prepare a partial balance sheet for Nike for these items.

Compute declining-balance depreciation.
(SO 9)

*BE9-10   Depreciation information for Joy Cunningham Company is given in BE9-3. Assuming the declining-balance depreciation rate is double the straight-line rate, compute annual depreciation for the first and second years under the declining-balance method.

Compute depreciation using units-of-activity method.
(SO 9)

*BE9-11   Jerry Englehart Taxi Service uses the units-of-activity method in computing depreciation on its taxicabs. Each cab is expected to be driven 120,000 miles. Taxi 10 cost $24,500 and is expected to have a salvage value of $500. Taxi 10 was driven 30,000 miles in 2000 and 20,000 miles in 2001. Compute the depreciation for each year.

EXERCISES

Determine cost of plant acquisitions.
(SO 1)

E9-1   The following expenditures relating to plant assets were made by Salvador Company during the first 2 months of 2001:

1. Paid $5,000 of accrued taxes at time plant site was acquired.
2. Paid $200 insurance to cover possible accident loss on new factory machinery while the machinery was in transit.
3. Paid $850 sales taxes on new delivery truck.
4. Paid $17,500 for parking lots and driveways on new plant site.
5. Paid $250 to have company name and advertising slogan painted on new delivery truck.
6. Paid $8,000 for installation of new factory machinery.
7. Paid $900 for a 1-year accident insurance policy on new delivery truck.
8. Paid $75 motor vehicle license fee on new truck.

Instructions
(a) ▱▱▱▭▶ Explain the application of the cost principle in determining the acquisition cost of plant assets.
(b) List the numbers of the foregoing transactions, and opposite each indicate the account title to which each expenditure should be debited.

Determine acquisition costs of land.
(SO 1)

E9-2   On March 1, 2001, Neil Young Company acquired real estate, on which it planned to construct a small office building, by paying $90,000 in cash. An old warehouse on the property was demolished at a cost of $6,600; the salvaged materials were sold for $1,700. Additional expenditures before construction began included $1,100 attorney's fee for work concerning the land purchase, $4,000 real estate broker's fee, $7,800 architect's fee, and $14,000 to put in driveways and a parking lot.

Instructions
(a) Determine the amount to be reported as the cost of the land.
(b) For each cost not used in part (a), indicate the account to be debited.

Determine straight-line depreciation for partial period.
(SO 3)

E9-3   Tory Amos Company purchased a new machine on October 1, 2001, at a cost of $96,000. The company estimated that the machine has a salvage value of $12,000. The machine is expected to be used for 70,000 working hours during its 5-year life.

Instructions
Compute the depreciation expense under the straight-line method for 2001 and 2002 assuming a December 31 year-end.

E9-4 Bill Simpson, the new controller of Bellingham Company, has reviewed the expected useful lives and salvage values of selected depreciable assets at the beginning of 2001. Here are his findings:

Compute revised annual depreciation.
(SO 3,4)

Type of Asset	Date Acquired	Cost	Accumulated Depreciation, Jan. 1, 2001	Useful Life (in years) Old	Proposed	Salvage Value Old	Proposed
Building	Jan. 1, 1995	$800,000	$114,000	40	50	$40,000	$48,000
Warehouse	Jan. 1, 1998	100,000	11,400	25	20	5,000	3,600

All assets are depreciated by the straight-line method. Bellingham Company uses a calendar year in preparing annual financial statements. After discussion, management has agreed to accept Bill's proposed changes. (The "Proposed" useful life is total life, not remaining life.)

Instructions
(a) Compute the revised annual depreciation on each asset in 2001. (Show computations.)
(b) Prepare the entry (or entries) to record depreciation on the building in 2001.

E9-5 Presented here are selected transactions for Chen Company for 2001:

Journalize entries for disposal of plant assets.
(SO 5)

Jan. 1 — Retired a piece of machinery that was purchased on January 1, 1991. The machine cost $62,000 on that date and had a useful life of 10 years with no salvage value.

June 30 — Sold a computer that was purchased on January 1, 1998. The computer cost $35,000 and had a useful life of 7 years with no salvage value. The computer was sold for $25,000.

Dec. 31 — Discarded a delivery truck that was purchased on January 1, 1997. The truck cost $27,000 and was depreciated based on an 8-year useful life with a $3,000 salvage value.

Instructions
Journalize all entries required on the above dates, including entries to update depreciation, where applicable, on assets disposed of. Chen Company uses straight-line depreciation. (Assume depreciation is up to date as of December 31, 2000.)

E9-6 During 1998 **Federal Express** reported the following information (in millions): net sales of $13,255, net income of $421, and depreciation expense of $845. Its balance sheet also showed total assets at the beginning of the year of $7,625 and total assets at the end of the year of $8,433; beginning plant assets (at cost) of $9,819, ending plant assets (at cost) of $11,064, and accumulated depreciation at year-end of $5,863.

Calculate average useful life, average age of plant assets, and asset turnover ratio.
(SO 6)

Instructions
Calculate (a) average useful life of plant assets, (b) average age of plant assets, and (c) asset turnover ratio.

E9-7 These are selected 2001 transactions for Hingis Corporation:

Prepare adjusting entries for amortization.
(SO 7)

Jan. 1 — Purchased a small company and recorded goodwill of $140,000. The goodwill has a useful life of 55 years.

May 1 — Purchased a patent with an estimated useful life of 5 years and a legal life of 20 years for $30,000.

Instructions
Prepare all adjusting entries at December 31 to record amortization required by the events.

E9-8 Collins Company, organized in 2001, has these transactions related to intangible assets in that year:

Prepare entries to set up appropriate accounts for different intangibles; calculate amortization.
(SO 7)

Jan. 2 — Purchased patent (7-year life), $420,000.
Apr. 1 — Goodwill purchased (indefinite life), $360,000.
July 1 — Acquired 10-year franchise; expiration date July 1, 2011, $450,000.
Sept. 1 — Research and development costs, $185,000.

Instructions

Prepare the necessary entries to record these intangibles. All costs incurred were for cash. Make the entries as of December 31, 2001, recording any necessary amortization and indicating what the balances should be on December 31, 2001.

Discuss implications of amortization period.
(SO 7)

E9-9 **SoftKey International Inc.**, headquartered in Cambridge, Massachusetts, noted in its 1994 annual report that, beginning that year, it changed the estimated life of its computer software for amortization purposes from a 3-year life to a 12-year life.

Instructions

Write a short memo explaining the implications this has for the analysis of Softkey's results. Also, discuss whether this estimated life seems reasonable.

E9-10 The questions listed below are independent of one another.

Answer questions on depreciation and intangibles.
(SO 2, 7)

Instructions

Provide a brief answer to each question.

(a) Why should a company depreciate its buildings?
(b) How can a company have a building that has a zero reported book value but substantial market value?
(c) What are some examples of intangibles that you might find on your college campus?
(d) Give some examples of company or product trademarks or trade names. Are trade names and trademarks reported on a company's balance sheet?

Compute depreciation under units-of-activity method.
(SO 9)

*E9-11 Galactic Bus Lines uses the units-of-activity method in depreciating its buses. One bus was purchased on January 1, 2001, at a cost of $108,000. Over its 4-year useful life, the bus is expected to be driven 100,000 miles. Salvage value is expected to be $8,000.

Instructions

(a) Compute the depreciation cost per unit.
(b) Prepare a depreciation schedule assuming actual mileage was: 2001, 26,000; 2002, 32,000; 2003, 25,000; and 2004, 17,000.

Compute declining-balance and units-of-activity depreciation.
(SO 9)

*E9-12 Basic information relating to a new machine purchased by Tory Amos Company is presented in E9-3.

Instructions

Using the facts presented in E9-3, compute depreciation using the following methods in the year indicated:
(a) Declining-balance using double the straight-line rate for 2001 and 2002.
(b) Units-of-activity for 2001, assuming machine usage was 1,700 hours.

PROBLEMS: SET A

Determine acquisition costs of land and building.
(SO 1)

P9-1A Hootie and the Blowfish Company was organized on January 1. During the first year of operations, the following plant asset expenditures and receipts were recorded in random order:

Debits

1. Cost of real estate purchased as a plant site (land $235,000 and building $25,000)	$260,000
2. Installation cost of fences around property	6,750
3. Cost of demolishing building to make land suitable for construction of new building	19,000
4. Excavation costs for new building	23,000
5. Accrued real estate taxes paid at time of purchase of real estate	2,179
6. Cost of parking lots and driveways	29,000
7. Architect's fees on building plans	40,000
8. Real estate taxes paid for the current year on land	6,500
9. Full payment to building contractor	600,000
	$986,429

Credits

10. Proceeds from salvage of demolished building	$5,000

Instructions

Analyze the foregoing transactions using the following table column headings. Enter the number of each transaction in the Item column, and enter the amounts in the appropriate columns. For amounts in the Other Accounts column, also indicate the account title.

Item	Land	Building	Other Accounts

P9-2A At December 31, 2001, Jerry Hamsmith Corporation reported these plant assets:

Journalize equipment transactions related to purchase, sale, retirement, and depreciation.
(SO 5, 8)

Land		$ 3,000,000
Buildings	$26,500,000	
Less: Accumulated depreciation—buildings	12,100,000	14,400,000
Equipment	40,000,000	
Less: Accumulated depreciation—equipment	5,000,000	35,000,000
Total plant assets		$52,400,000

During 2002, the following selected cash transactions occurred:

Apr. 1   Purchased land for $2,200,000.
May 1   Sold equipment that cost $600,000 when purchased on January 1, 1998. The equipment was sold for $360,000.
June 1   Sold land for $1,800,000. The land cost $500,000.
July 1   Purchased equipment for $1,400,000.
Dec. 31   Retired equipment that cost $500,000 when purchased on December 31, 1992. No salvage value was received.

Instructions

(a) Journalize the transactions. [*Hint:*   You may wish to set up T accounts, post beginning balances, and then post 2002 transactions.] Hamsmith uses straight-line depreciation for buildings and equipment. The buildings are estimated to have a 40-year useful life and no salvage value; the equipment is estimated to have a 10-year useful life and no salvage value. Update depreciation on assets disposed of at the time of sale or retirement.
(b) Record adjusting entries for depreciation for 2002.
(c) Prepare the plant assets section of Hamsmith's balance sheet at December 31, 2002.

P9-3A   Ghani Co. has delivery equipment that cost $50,000 and has been depreciated $20,000.

Journalize transactions related to disposals of plant assets.
(SO 5)

Instructions

Record entries for the disposal under the following assumptions:
(a) It was scrapped as having no value.
(b) It was sold for $31,000.
(c) It was sold for $18,000.

P9-4A   The intangible assets section of El-Gazzar Corporation's balance sheet at December 31, 2001, is presented here:

Prepare entries to record transactions related to acquisition and amortization of intangibles; prepare the intangible assets section and notes.
(SO 7, 8)

Patent ($60,000 cost less $6,000 amortization)	$54,000
Copyright ($36,000 cost less $14,400 amortization)	21,600
Total	$75,600

The patent was acquired in January 2001 and has a useful life of 10 years. The copyright was acquired in January 1998 and also has a useful life of 10 years. The following cash transactions may have affected intangible assets during 2002:

Jan. 2   Paid $18,000 legal costs to successfully defend the patent against infringement by another company.
Jan.–June   Developed a new product, incurring $140,000 in research and development costs. A patent was granted for the product on July 1, and its useful life is equal to its legal life.

Sept. 1	Paid $60,000 to a quarterback to appear in commercials advertising the company's products. The commercials will air in September and October.
Oct. 1	Acquired a copyright for $180,000. The copyright has a useful life of 50 years.

Instructions
(a) Prepare journal entries to record the transactions.
(b) Prepare journal entries to record the 2002 amortization expense for intangible assets.
(c) Prepare the intangible assets section of the balance sheet at December 31, 2002.
(d) Prepare the note to the financial statements on El-Gazzar Corporation's intangible assets as of December 31, 2002.

Prepare entries to correct errors in recording and amortizing intangible assets.
(SO 7)

P9-5A   Due to rapid employee turnover in the accounting department, the following transactions involving intangible assets were improperly recorded by Baird Corporation in 2001:
1. Baird developed a new manufacturing process, incurring research and development costs of $85,000. The company also purchased a patent for $37,400. In early January Baird capitalized $122,400 as the cost of the patents. Patent amortization expense of $6,120 was recorded based on a 20-year useful life.
2. On July 1, 2001, Baird purchased a small company and as a result acquired goodwill of $60,000. Baird recorded a half-year's amortization in 2001, based on a 50-year life ($600 amortization).

Instructions
Prepare all journal entries necessary to correct any errors made during 2001. Assume the books have not yet been closed for 2001.

Calculate and comment on average age, average useful life of plant assets, and asset turnover ratio.
(SO 6)

P9-6A   Croix Corporation and Marais Corporation, two companies of roughly the same size, are both involved in the manufacture of canoes and sea kayaks. Each company depreciates its plant assets using the straight-line approach. An investigation of their financial statements reveals this information:

	Croix Corp.	Marais Corp.
Net income	$ 400,000	$ 600,000
Sales	1,400,000	1,200,000
Total assets (average)	3,200,000	2,500,000
Plant assets (average)	2,400,000	1,800,000
Accumulated depreciation	300,000	625,000
Depreciation expense	50,000	20,000
Intangible assets (goodwill)	300,000	0
Amortization expense	60,000	0

Instructions
(a) For each company, calculate these values:
   (1) Average age of plant assets.
   (2) Average useful life.
   (3) Asset turnover ratio.
(b) Based on your calculations in part (a), comment on the relative effectiveness of the two companies in using their assets to generate sales. What factors complicate your ability to compare the two companies?

Compute depreciation under different methods.
(SO 3, 9)

*P9-7A   In recent years Erie Company has purchased three machines. Because of frequent employee turnover in the accounting department, a different accountant was in charge of selecting the depreciation method for each machine, and various methods have been used. Information concerning the machines is summarized in the table:

Machine	Acquired	Cost	Salvage Value	Useful Life (in years)	Depreciation Method
1	Jan. 1, 1998	$96,000	$ 6,000	10	Straight-line
2	Jan. 1, 1999	80,000	10,000	8	Declining-balance
3	Nov. 1, 1999	78,000	6,000	6	Units-of-activity

For the declining-balance method, Erie Company uses the double-declining rate. For the units-of-activity method, total machine hours are expected to be 24,000. Actual hours of use in the first 3 years were: 1999, 4,000; 2000, 4,500; and 2001, 5,000.

Instructions

(a) Compute the amount of accumulated depreciation on each machine at December 31, 2001.

(b) If machine 2 was purchased on April 1 instead of January 1, what would be the depreciation expense for this machine in 1999? In 2000?

*P9-8A   Rose Corporation purchased machinery on January 1, 2001, at a cost of $200,000. The estimated useful life of the machinery is 4 years, with an estimated residual value at the end of that period of $20,000. The company is considering different depreciation methods that could be used for financial reporting purposes.

Compute depreciation under different methods.
(SO 3, 9)

Instructions

(a) Prepare separate depreciation schedules for the machinery using the straight-line method, and the declining-balance method using double the straight-line rate. Round to the nearest dollar.

(b) Which method would result in the higher reported 2001 income? In the highest total reported income over the 4-year period?

(c) Which method would result in the lower reported 2001 income? In the lowest total reported income over the 4-year period?

Problems: Set B

P9-1B   Earth, Wind, and Fire Company was organized on January 1. During the first year of operations, the following plant asset expenditures and receipts were recorded in random order:

Determine acquisition costs of land and building.
(SO 1)

Debits

1. Cost of real estate purchased as a plant site (land $180,000 and building $70,000)	$ 250,000
2. Accrued real estate taxes paid at time of purchase of real estate	3,123
3. Cost of demolishing building to make land suitable for construction of new building	21,000
4. Cost of filling and grading the land	7,270
5. Excavation costs for new building	21,900
6. Architect's fees on building plans	55,000
7. Full payment to building contractor	629,500
8. Cost of parking lots and driveways	31,800
9. Real estate taxes paid for the current year on land	5,320
	$1,024,913

Credits

10. Proceeds for salvage of demolished building	$12,700

Instructions

Analyze the transactions using the table column headings provided here. Enter the number of each transaction in the Item column, and enter the amounts in the appropriate columns. For amounts in the Other Accounts column, also indicate the account titles.

Item	Land	Building	Other Accounts

*Journalize equipment trans-
actions related to purchase,
sale, retirement, and depreciation.*
(SO 5, 8)

P9-2B At December 31, 2001, Los Alamos Corporation reported these plant assets:

Land		$ 4,000,000
Buildings	$28,500,000	
Less: Accumulated depreciation—buildings	12,100,000	16,400,000
Equipment	48,000,000	
Less: Accumulated depreciation—equipment	5,000,000	43,000,000
Total plant assets		$63,400,000

During 2002, the following selected cash transactions occurred:

Apr. 1   Purchased land for $2,630,000.

May 1   Sold equipment that cost $600,000 when purchased on January 1, 1998. The equipment was sold for $350,000.

June 1   Sold land purchased on June 1, 1992, for $1,800,000. The land cost $200,000.

July 1   Purchased equipment for $1,000,000.

Dec. 31   Retired equipment that cost $500,000 when purchased on December 31, 1992. No salvage value was received.

Instructions

(a) Journalize the transactions. [*Hint:* You may wish to set up T accounts, post beginning balances, and then post 2002 transactions.] Los Alamos uses straight-line depreciation for buildings and equipment. The buildings are estimated to have a 40-year life and no salvage value; the equipment is estimated to have a 10-year useful life and no salvage value. Update depreciation on assets disposed of at the time of sale or retirement.

(b) Record adjusting entries for depreciation for 2002.

(c) Prepare the plant asset section of Los Alamos' balance sheet at December 31, 2002.

*Journalize transactions
related to disposals of plant
assets.*
(SO 5)

P9-3B Chon Co. has office furniture that cost $80,000 and has been depreciated $48,000.

Instructions

Record entries for the disposal under these assumptions:

(a) It was scrapped as having no value.

(b) It was sold for $21,000.

(c) It was sold for $61,000.

*Prepare entries to record
transactions related to
acquisition and amortization
of intangibles; prepare the
intangible assets section
and note.*
(SO 7, 8)

P9-4B The intangible assets section of the balance sheet for De Paul Company at December 31, 2001, is presented here:

Patent ($70,000 cost less $7,000 amortization)	$63,000
Copyright ($48,000 cost less $19,200 amortization)	28,800
Total	$91,800

The patent was acquired in January 2001 and has a useful life of 10 years. The copyright was acquired in January 1998 and also has a useful life of 10 years. The following cash transactions may have affected intangible assets during 2002:

Jan. 2   Paid $18,000 legal costs to successfully defend the patent against infringement by another company.

Jan.–June   Developed a new product, incurring $140,000 in research and development costs. A patent was granted for the product on July 1, and its useful life is equal to its legal life.

Sept. 1   Paid $80,000 to an extremely large defensive lineman to appear in commercials advertising the company's products. The commercials will air in September and October.

Oct. 1   Acquired a copyright for $160,000. The copyright has a useful life of 50 years.

Instructions
(a) Prepare journal entries to record the transactions.
(b) Prepare journal entries to record the 2002 amortization expense.
(c) Prepare the intangible assets section of the balance sheet at December 31, 2002.
(d) Prepare the notes to the financial statements on De Paul Company's intangible assets as of December 31, 2002.

P9-5B   Due to rapid employee turnover in the accounting department, the following transactions involving intangible assets were improperly recorded by the Coker Company in 2001:

Prepare entries to correct errors in recording and amortizing intangible assets.
(SO 7)

1. Coker developed a new manufacturing process, incurring research and development costs of $153,000. The company also purchased a patent for $39,100. In early January Coker capitalized $192,100 as the cost of the patents. Patent amortization expense of $9,605 was recorded based on a 20-year useful life.
2. On July 1, 2001, Coker purchased a small company and as a result acquired goodwill of $76,000. Coker recorded a half-year's amortization in 2001 based on a 50-year life ($760 amortization).

Instructions
Prepare all journal entries necessary to correct any errors made during 2001. Assume the books have not yet been closed for 2001.

P9-6B   Reggie Corporation and Baxter Corporation, two corporations of roughly the same size, are both involved in the manufacture of in-line skates. Each company depreciates its plant assets using the straight-line approach. An investigation of their financial statements reveals the information:

Calculate and comment on average age, average useful life of plant assets, and asset turnover ratio.
(SO 6)

	Reggie Corp.	Baxter Corp.
Net income	$ 800,000	$1,000,000
Sales	1,600,000	1,300,000
Total assets (average)	2,500,000	1,700,000
Plant assets (average)	1,400,000	1,200,000
Accumulated depreciation	500,000	825,000
Depreciation expense	120,000	31,250
Intangible assets (goodwill)	600,000	0
Amortization expense	60,000	0

Instructions
(a) For each company, calculate these values:
    (1) Average age of plant assets.
    (2) Average useful life.
    (3) Asset turnover ratio.
(b) [icon] Based on your calculations in part (a), comment on the relative effectiveness of the two companies in using their assets to generate sales. What factors complicate your ability to compare the two companies?

*P9-7B   In recent years Lakeshore Transportation purchased three used buses. Because of frequent employee turnover in the accounting department, a different accountant selected the depreciation method for each bus, and various methods have been used. Information concerning the buses is summarized in the table:

Compute depreciation under different methods.
(SO 3, 9)

Bus	Acquired	Cost	Salvage Value	Useful Life (in years)	Depreciation Method
1	Jan. 1, 1999	$ 86,000	$ 6,000	5	Straight-line
2	Jan. 1, 1999	140,000	10,000	4	Declining-balance
3	Jan. 1, 1999	80,000	8,000	5	Units-of-activity

For the declining-balance method, Lakeshore Transportation uses the double-declining rate. For the units-of-activity method, total miles are expected to be 120,000. Actual miles of use in the first 3 years were: 1999, 24,000; 2000, 34,000; and 2001, 30,000.

Instructions
(a) Compute the amount of accumulated depreciation on each bus at December 31, 2001.
(b) If Bus 2 was purchased on April 1 instead of January 1, what would be the depreciation expense for this bus in 1999? In 2000?

Compute depreciation under different methods.
(SO 3, 9)

*P9-8B Axel Corporation purchased machinery on January 1, 2001, at a cost of $202,000. The estimated useful life of the machinery is 5 years, with an estimated residual value at the end of that period of $12,000. The company is considering different depreciation methods that could be used for financial reporting purposes.

Instructions
(a) Prepare separate depreciation schedules for the machinery using the straight-line method, and the declining-balance method using double the straight-line rate.
(b) Which method would result in the higher reported 2001 income? In the highest total reported income over the 5-year period?
(c) Which method would result in the lower reported 2001 income? In the lowest total reported income over the 5-year period?

◆ B R O A D E N I N G   Y O U R   P E R S P E C T I V E

*F*INANCIAL REPORTING AND ANALYSIS

FINANCIAL REPORTING PROBLEM: *Tootsie Roll Industries, Inc.*

BYP9-1 Refer to the financial statements and the Notes to Consolidated Financial Statements of **Tootsie Roll Industries** in Appendix A.

Instructions
Answer the following questions:
(a) What were the total cost and book value of property, plant, and equipment at December 31, 1998?
(b) What method or methods of depreciation are used by Tootsie Roll for financial reporting purposes?
(c) What was the amount of depreciation and amortization expense for each of the 3 years 1996–1998? (Hint—use statement of cash flows.)
(d) Using the statement of cash flows, what are the amounts of property, plant, and equipment purchased (capital expenditures) in 1998 and 1997?
(e) Read Tootsie Roll's note 8 on commitments. Does the company primarily engage in capital leases or operating leases? What are the implications for analysis of its financial statements?

COMPARATIVE ANALYSIS PROBLEM: *Tootsie Roll vs. Hershey Foods*

BYP9-2 The financial statements of **Hershey Foods** are presented in Appendix B, following the financial statements for **Tootsie Roll Industries** in Appendix A.

Instructions
(a) Based on the information in these financial statements and the accompanying notes and schedules, compute the following values for each company in 1998:
  (1) Average useful life of plant assets.
  (2) Average age of plant assets.
  (3) Asset turnover ratio.
(b) What conclusions concerning the management of plant assets can be drawn from these data?

RESEARCH CASE

BYP9-3   The April 5, 1999, issue of *The Wall Street Journal* includes an article by Tara Parker-Pope entitled "Stopping Diaper Leaks Can Be Nasty Business, P&G Shows Its Rivals."

Instructions
Read the article and answer the following questions:
(a) How much money does the article say that **Procter & Gamble** and **Kimberly-Clark** receive in royalty payments from the sale of every package of diapers sold by competitors?
(b) How many patents are held on diaper-related inventions?
(c) How did Kimberly-Clark and Procter & Gamble resolve their long-running patent lawsuit? Why do you suppose they chose to resolve it this way?
(d) What were the results of **Paragon Trade Brands'** decision to fight Procter & Gamble, rather than pay a royalty payment? What impact do royalty payments have on the profit margins of small diaper manufacturers?
(e) What would have been the accounting implications had Procter & Gamble lost its patent infringement lawsuit with Paragon? That is, what accounting entry or adjustments might have been required?

INTERPRETING FINANCIAL STATEMENTS

BYP9-4   **Merck & Co., Inc.,** and **Johnson & Johnson** are two leading producers of health care products. Each has considerable assets, and each expends considerable funds each year toward the development of new products. The development of a new health care product is often very expensive and risky. New products frequently must undergo considerable testing before they are approved for distribution to the public. For example, it took Johnson & Johnson 4 years and $200 million to develop its 1-DAY ACUVUE contact lenses. Here are some basic data compiled from the 1998 financial statements of these two companies:

($ in millions)	Johnson & Johnson	Merck
Total assets	$26,211	$31,853
Total revenue	23,657	26,898
Net income	3,059	5,248
Research and development expense	2,433	1,821
Intangible assets	7,209	8,287

Instructions
(a) What kinds of intangible assets might a health care products company have? Does the composition of these intangible assets matter to investors? That is, would Merck be perceived differently if all of its intangibles were goodwill than if all of its intangibles were patents?
(b) Using the asset turnover ratio, determine which company is using its assets more effectively. [*Note:*   In 1997 total assets were $25,736 million for Merck and $21,453 million for Johnson & Johnson.]
(c) Suppose the president of Merck has come to you for advice. He has noted that by eliminating research and development expenditures, the company could have reported $1.8 billion more in net income in 1998. He is frustrated because much of the research never results in a product, or the products take years to develop. He says shareholders are eager for higher returns, so he is considering eliminating research and development expenditures for at least a couple of years. What would you advise?
(d) The notes to Merck's financial statements indicate that Merck has goodwill of $4.3 billion. Where does recorded goodwill come from? Is it necessarily a good thing to have a lot of goodwill on your books?

BYP9-5   **Boeing** and **McDonnell Douglas** were two leaders in the manufacture of aircraft. In 1996 Boeing announced intentions to acquire McDonnell Douglas and create one huge corporation. Competitors, primarily Airbus of Europe, are very concerned that they will not be able to compete with such a huge rival. In addition, customers are concerned that this merger will reduce the number of suppliers to a point where Boeing will be able to dictate prices. Provided below are figures taken from the 1995 financial statements of Boeing and McDonnell Douglas, which allow a comparison of the operations of the two corporations prior to their proposed merger.

($ in millions)	Boeing	McDonnell Douglas
Total revenue	$19,515	$14,322
Net income (loss)	393	(416)
Total assets (average)	22,098	10,466
Land (average)	404	91
Buildings and fixtures	5,791	1,647
Machinery and equipment	7,251	2,161
Average property, plant, and equipment (at cost)	13,744	3,899
Accumulated depreciation	7,288	2,541
Depreciation expense	976	196

Instructions

(a) Which company had older assets?
(b) Which company used a longer average estimated useful life for its assets?
(c) Based on the asset turnover ratio, which company used its assets more effectively to generate sales?
(d) Besides an increase in size, what other factors might have motivated this merger?

A GLOBAL FOCUS

BYP9-6 As noted in the chapter, the accounting for goodwill differs in countries around the world. The following discussion of a change in goodwill accounting practices was taken from the notes to the financial statements of **J Sainsbury Plc**, one of the world's leading retailers. Headquartered in the United Kingdom, it serves 15 million customers a week.

J Sainsbury plc

J SAINSBURY PLC
Notes to the Financial Statements

Accounting Policies

Goodwill arising in connection with the acquisition of shares in subsidiaries and associated undertakings is calculated as the excess of the purchase price over the fair value of the net tangible assets acquired. In prior years goodwill has been deducted from reserves in the period of acquisition. FRS 10 is applicable in the current financial year, and in accordance with the standard acquired goodwill is now shown as an asset on the Group's Balance Sheet. As permitted by FRS 10, goodwill written off to reserves in prior periods has not been restated as an asset.

Goodwill is treated as having an indefinite economic life where it is considered that the acquired business has strong customer loyalty built up over a long period of time, based on advantageous store locations and a commitment to maintain the marketing advantage of the retail brand. The carrying value of the goodwill will be reviewed annually for impairment and adjusted to its recoverable amount if required. Where goodwill is considered to have a finite life, amortisation will be applied over that period.

For amounts stated as goodwill which are considered to have indefinite life, no amortisation is charged to the Profit and Loss Account.

Instructions

Answer the following questions:

(a) How does the initial determination and recording of goodwill compare with that in the United States? That is, is goodwill initially recorded in the same circumstances, and is the calculation of amount the same in both the United Kingdom and the United States?

(b) Prior to adoption of the new accounting standard (FRS 10), how did the company account for goodwill? What were the implications for the income statement?

(c) Under the new accounting standard, how does the company account for its goodwill? Is it possible, under the new standard, for a company to avoid charging goodwill amortization to net income?

(d) In what ways is the new standard similar to U.S. standards, and in what ways is it different?

FINANCIAL ANALYSIS ON THE WEB

BYP9-7 *Purpose:* Use an annual report to identify a company's plant assets and the depreciation method used.

Address: http://www.reportgallery.com (or go to www.wiley.com/college/kimmel)

Steps:

1. From Report Gallery Homepage, choose **Report Listings**.
2. Select a particular company.
3. Choose **Annual Report**.
4. Follow instructions below.

Instructions

Answer the following questions:

(a) What is the name of the company?
(b) What is the Internet address of the annual report?
(c) At fiscal year-end, what is the net amount of its plant assets?
(d) What is the accumulated depreciation?
(e) Which method of depreciation does the company use?

CRITICAL THINKING

GROUP DECISION CASE

BYP9-8 Tammy Company and Hamline Company are two companies that are similar in many respects except that Tammy Company uses the straight-line method and Hamline Company uses the declining-balance method at double the straight-line rate. On January 2, 1999, both companies acquired identical depreciable assets listed in the table below.

Asset	Cost	Salvage Value	Useful Life
Building	$320,000	$20,000	40 years
Equipment	110,000	10,000	10 years

Hamline's depreciation expense was $38,000 in 1999, $32,800 in 2000, and $28,520 in 2001. Including the appropriate depreciation charges, annual net income for the companies in the years 1999, 2000, and 2001 and total income for the 3 years were as follows:

	1999	2000	2001	Total
Tammy Company	$84,000	$88,400	$90,000	$262,400
Hamline Company	68,000	76,000	85,000	229,000

At December 31, 2001, the balance sheets of the two companies are similar except that Hamline Company has more cash than Tammy Company.

Dawna Tucci is interested in investing in one of the companies, and she comes to you for advice.

Instructions

With the class divided into groups, answer the following:

(a) Determine the annual and total depreciation recorded by Tammy during the 3 years.

(b) Assuming that Hamline Company also uses the straight-line method of depreciation instead of the declining-balance method (that is, Hamline's depreciation expense would equal Tammy's), prepare comparative income data for the 3 years.

(c) Which company should Dawna Tucci invest in? Why?

COMMUNICATION ACTIVITY

BYP9-9   The chapter presented some concerns regarding the current accounting standards for research and development expenditures.

Instructions

Pretend that you are either (a) the president of a company that is very dependent on ongoing research and development, writing a memo to the FASB complaining about the current accounting standards regarding research and development, or (b) the FASB member defending the current standards regarding research and development. Your letter should address these questions:

1. By requiring expensing of R&D, do you think companies will spend less on R&D? Why or why not? What are the possible implications for the competitiveness of U.S. companies?

2. If a company makes a commitment to spend money for R&D, it must believe it has future benefits. Shouldn't these costs therefore be capitalized just like the purchase of any long-lived asset that you believe will have future benefits?

ETHICS CASE

BYP9-10   Imporia Container Company is suffering declining sales of its principal product, nonbiodegradable plastic cartons. The president, Benny Benson, instructs his controller, John Straight, to lengthen asset lives to reduce depreciation expense. A processing line of automated plastic extruding equipment, purchased for $2.7 million in January 2001, was originally estimated to have a useful life of 8 years and a salvage value of $300,000. Depreciation has been recorded for 2 years on that basis. Benny wants the estimated life changed to 12 years total and the straight-line method continued. John is hesitant to make the change, believing it is unethical to increase net income in this manner. Benny says, "Hey, the life is only an estimate, and I've heard that our competition uses a 12-year life on their production equipment."

Instructions

(a) Who are the stakeholders in this situation?

(b) Is the proposed change in asset life unethical, or is it simply a good business practice by an astute president?

(c) What is the effect of Benny Benson's proposed change on income before taxes in the year of change?

Answers to Self-Study Questions
1. d   2. a   3. b   4. d   5. c   6. b   7. d   8. d   9. b   10. c
11. c   *12. d

Answer to Tootsie Roll Review It Question 3, p. 406
Tootsie Roll depreciates its buildings over 20 to 35 years and its machinery and equipment over 12 to 20 years.

Reporting and Analyzing Liabilities

◆ STUDY OBJECTIVES

After studying this chapter, you should be able to:

1 Explain a current liability and identify the major types of current liabilities.

2 Describe the accounting for notes payable.

3 Explain the accounting for other current liabilities.

4 Identify the requirements for the financial statement presentation and analysis of current liabilities.

5 Explain why bonds are issued and identify the types of bonds.

6 Prepare the entries for the issuance of bonds and interest expense.

7 Describe the entries when bonds are redeemed.

8 Identify the requirements for the financial statement presentation and analysis of long-term liabilities.

◆ AND THEN THERE WERE TWO

Debt can help a company acquire the things it needs to grow, but it is often the very thing that kills a company. A brief history of Maxwell Car Company illustrates the role of debt in the U.S. auto industry. In 1920 Maxwell Car Company was on the brink of financial ruin. Because it was axle-deep in debt and unable to pay its bills, its creditors stepped in and took over. A former General Motors executive named Walter Chrysler was hired to reorganize the company. By 1925 he had taken over the company and renamed it Chrysler. By 1933 Chrysler was booming,

with sales surpassing even those of Ford.

But the next few decades saw Chrysler make a series of blunders. During the 1940s, while its competitors were making yearly design changes to boost customer interest, Chrysler made no changes. During the 1960s, when customers wanted large cars, Chrysler produced small cars. During the 1970s, when customers wanted small cars, Chrysler offered big "boats." By 1980, with its creditors pounding at the gates, Chrysler was again on the brink of financial ruin.

At that point Chrysler brought in a former Ford executive named Lee Iacocca to save the company. Iacocca, considered by many as good a politician as a businessman, argued that the United States could not afford to let Chrysler fail because of the loss of jobs. He convinced the federal government to grant loan guarantees—promises that if Chrysler failed to pay its creditors, the government would pay them. Iacocca then streamlined operations and brought out some profitable products. Chrysler repaid all of its government-guaranteed loans by 1983, seven years ahead of the scheduled final payment.

What has happened since? In the 1990s Chrysler knew both feast and famine: In 1991 it operated in the red, with Iacocca leaving the company under pressure in 1992. By 1995 Chrysler was the most profitable U.S.-based car manufacturer and the envy of the entire industry. But to compete in today's global vehicle market, you must be big—really big. So in 1998 Chrysler merged with German automaker Daimler-Benz, to form Daimler-Chrysler. This left just two U.S.-based auto manufacturers—General Motors and Ford.

These companies are giants. In comparison with other U.S. corporations, General Motors and Ford rank, respectively, number one and two in total sales. But General Motors and Ford have accumulated a truckload of debt on their way to get-ting this big. Combined, they have *$457 billion* in total outstanding liabilities. Although debt has made it possible to get so big, the Chrysler story makes it clear that debt can also threaten a company's survival.

On the World Wide Web
DaimlerChrysler:
    http://www.daimlerchrysler.com
Ford: http://www.ford.com
General Motors: http://www.gm.com

The opening story suggests that General Motors and Ford have tremendous amounts of debt. It is unlikely that they could have grown so large without this debt, but at times this debt threatens their very existence. Given this risk, why do companies borrow money? Why do they sometimes borrow short-term and other times long-term? Besides bank borrowings, what other kinds of debts does a company incur? In this chapter we address these issues.

The content and organization of the chapter are as follows:

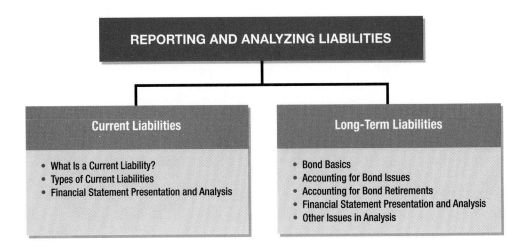

REPORTING AND ANALYZING LIABILITIES

Current Liabilities
- What Is a Current Liability?
- Types of Current Liabilities
- Financial Statement Presentation and Analysis

Long-Term Liabilities
- Bond Basics
- Accounting for Bond Issues
- Accounting for Bond Retirements
- Financial Statement Presentation and Analysis
- Other Issues in Analysis

SECTION 1
CURRENT LIABILITIES

WHAT IS A CURRENT LIABILITY?

STUDY OBJECTIVE

1

Explain a current liability and identify the major types of current liabilities.

You have learned that liabilities are defined as "creditors' claims on total assets" and as "existing debts and obligations." These claims, debts, and obligations must be settled or paid at some time in the future by the transfer of assets or services. The future date on which they are due or payable (the maturity date) is a significant feature of liabilities.

As explained in Chapter 2, a current liability is a debt that can reasonably be expected to be paid (1) from existing current assets or through the creation of other current liabilities, and (2) within one year or the operating cycle, whichever is longer. Debts that do not meet both criteria are classified as **long-term liabilities**.

Financial statement users want to know whether a company's obligations are current or long-term. A company, for example, that has more current liabilities than current assets often lacks liquidity, or short-term debt-paying ability. In addition, users want to know the types of liabilities a company has. If a company declares bankruptcy, a specific, predetermined order of payment to creditors exists. Thus, the amount and type of liabilities are of critical importance.

TYPES OF CURRENT LIABILITIES

The different types of current liabilities include notes payable, accounts payable, unearned revenues, and accrued liabilities such as taxes, salaries and wages, and interest. In this section we discuss a few of the common and more important types of current liabilities. All current liabilities that are material should be reported in a company's balance sheet.

Helpful Hint The entries for accounts payable and the adjusting entries for some current liabilities have been explained in previous chapters.

NOTES PAYABLE

Obligations in the form of written notes are recorded as **notes payable**. Notes payable are often used instead of accounts payable because they give the lender written documentation of the obligation in case legal remedies are needed to collect the debt. Notes payable usually require the borrower to pay interest and frequently are issued to meet short-term financing needs.

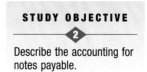

STUDY OBJECTIVE

2

Describe the accounting for notes payable.

Notes are issued for varying periods of time. **Those due for payment within one year of the balance sheet date are usually classified as current liabilities**. For example, General Motors recently reported $1.25 billion of notes payable. Most notes are interest-bearing.

To illustrate the accounting for notes payable, assume that First National Bank agrees to lend $100,000 on March 1, 2001, if Cole Williams Co. signs a $100,000, 12%, four-month note. With an interest-bearing note, the amount of assets received when the note is issued generally equals the note's face value. Cole Williams Co. therefore will receive $100,000 cash and will make the following journal entry:

Mar. 1	Cash	100,000	
	Notes Payable		100,000
	(To record issuance of 12%, 4-month note to First National Bank)		

A	=	L	+	SE
+100,000		+100,000		

Interest accrues over the life of the note and must be recorded periodically. If Cole Williams Co. prepares financial statements semiannually, an adjusting entry is required to recognize interest expense and interest payable of $4,000 ($100,000 \times 12\% \times \frac{4}{12}$) at June 30. The adjusting entry is:

June 30	Interest Expense	4,000	
	Interest Payable		4,000
	(To accrue interest for 4 months on First National Bank note)		

A	=	L	+	SE
		+4,000		−4,000

In the June 30 financial statements, the current liabilities section of the balance sheet will show notes payable $100,000 and interest payable $4,000. In addition, interest expense of $4,000 will be reported under Other Expenses and Losses in the income statement. If Cole Williams Co. prepared financial statements monthly, the adjusting entry at the end of each month would have been $1,000 ($100,000 \times 12\% \times \frac{1}{12}$).

At maturity (July 1), Cole Williams Co. must pay the face value of the note ($100,000) plus $4,000 interest ($100,000 × 12% × $\frac{4}{12}$). The entry to record payment of the note and accrued interest is:

A	=	L	+	SE
−104,000		−100,000		
		−4,000		

July 1	Notes Payable		100,000	
	Interest Payable		4,000	
	Cash			104,000
	(To record payment of First National			
	Bank interest-bearing note and			
	accrued interest at maturity)			

SALES TAXES PAYABLE

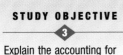

STUDY OBJECTIVE
3
Explain the accounting for other current liabilities.

As consumers, we are well aware that many of the products we purchase at retail stores are subject to sales taxes. The tax is expressed as a percentage of the sales price. The retailer (or selling company) collects the tax from the customer when the sale occurs and periodically (usually monthly) remits the collections to the state's department of revenue.

Helpful Hint Watch how sales are rung up at local retailers to see whether the sales tax is computed separately.

Under most state laws, the amount of the sale and the amount of the sales tax collected must be rung up separately on the cash register. (Gasoline sales are a major exception.) The cash register readings are then used to credit Sales and Sales Taxes Payable. For example, if the March 25 cash register readings for Cooley Grocery show sales of $10,000 and sales taxes of $600 (sales tax rate of 6%), the journal entry is:

A	=	L	+	SE
+10,600		+600		+10,000

Mar. 25	Cash		10,600	
	Sales			10,000
	Sales Taxes Payable			600
	(To record daily sales and sales taxes)			

When the taxes are remitted to the taxing agency, Sales Taxes Payable is decreased (debited) and Cash is decreased (credited). The company does not report sales taxes as an expense; it simply forwards the amount paid by the customer to the government. Thus, Cooley Grocery serves only as a **collection agent** for the taxing authority.

When sales taxes are not rung up separately on the cash register, total receipts are divided by 100% plus the sales tax percentage to determine sales. To illustrate, assume in our example that Cooley Grocery "rings up" total receipts of $10,600. Because the amount received from the sale is equal to the sales price 100% plus 6% of sales, or 1.06 times the sales total, we can compute sales as follows: $10,600 ÷ 1.06 = $10,000. Thus, the sales tax amount of $600 is found by either (1) subtracting sales from total receipts ($10,600 − $10,000) or (2) multiplying sales by the sales tax rate ($10,000 × 6%).

BUSINESS INSIGHT
Management Perspective

If you buy a book at a bookstore, you pay sales tax. If you buy the same book over the Internet, you don't pay a sales tax (in most cases). This is one reason why e-commerce, as it has come to be called, is growing exponentially and why Web sites like Amazon.com have become so popular. A recent study suggested that Internet sales would fall by 30 percent if sales tax were applied. Partly as a result of this study, the Clinton administration and Congress agreed to a three-year moratorium on Internet taxation. Most people in Washington expect that after the moratorium runs out in 2001, some kind of sales tax will be imposed on e-commerce. The idea is that by then the e-commerce model will have "matured" and thus can serve as a veritable gold mine for federal, state, and local taxation.

Source: John Ellis, "The Tax Consequences of Commerce on the Internet," *Boston Globe*, April 10, 1999, p. A23.

PAYROLL AND PAYROLL TAXES PAYABLE

Every employer incurs liabilities relating to employees' salaries and wages. One is the amount of wages and salaries owed to employees—**wages and salaries payable**. Another is the amount required by law to be withheld from employees' gross pay. Until these **withholding taxes**—federal and state income taxes and Social Security (FICA) taxes—are remitted to governmental taxing authorities, they are recorded as increases (credited) to appropriate liability accounts. For example, accrual and payment of a $100,000 payroll on which a corporation withholds taxes from its employees' wages and salaries would be recorded as follows:

Mar. 7	Salaries and Wages Expense	100,000	
	FICA Taxes Payable[1]		7,250
	Federal Income Taxes Payable		21,864
	State Income Taxes Payable		2,922
	Salaries and Wages Payable		67,964
	(To record payroll and withholding taxes for the week ending March 7)		

A	=	L	+	SE
		+7,250		−100,000
		+21,864		
		+2,922		
		+67,964		

	Salaries and Wages Payable	67,964	
	Cash		67,964
	(To record payment of the March 7 payroll)		

A	=	L	+	SE
−67,964		−67,964		

Illustration 10-1 (page 456) summarizes the types of payroll deductions that normally occur.

Also, with every payroll, the employer incurs liabilities to pay various **payroll taxes** levied upon the employer. These payroll taxes include the employer's share of Social Security (FICA) taxes and state and federal unemployment taxes. Based on the $100,000 payroll in our example, the following entry would be made to record the employer's expense and liability for these payroll taxes:

Mar. 7	Payroll Tax Expense	13,450	
	FICA Taxes Payable		7,250
	Federal Unemployment Taxes Payable		800
	State Unemployment Taxes Payable		5,400
	(To record employer's payroll taxes on March 7 payroll)		

A	=	L	+	SE
		+7,250		−13,450
		+800		
		+5,400		

[1]Social Security taxes are commonly referred to as FICA taxes. In 1937 Congress enacted the Federal Insurance Contribution Act (FICA). As can be seen in this journal entry and the payroll tax journal entry, the employee and employer must make equal contributions to Social Security.

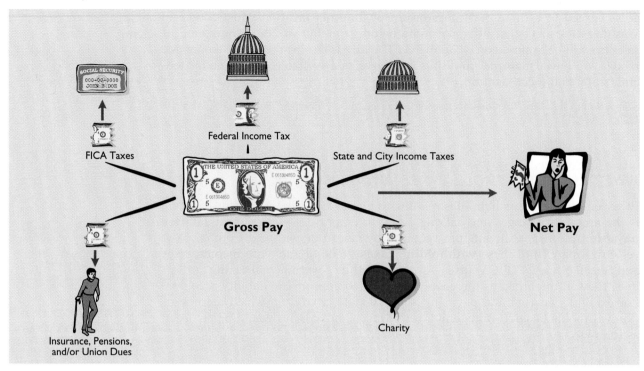

Illustration 10-1 Payroll deductions

The payroll and payroll tax liability accounts are classified as current liabilities because they must be paid to employees or remitted to taxing authorities periodically and in the near term. Taxing authorities impose substantial fines and penalties on employers if the withholding and payroll taxes are not computed correctly and paid on time.

UNEARNED REVENUES

A magazine publisher such as Sports Illustrated may receive a customer's check when magazines are ordered, and an airline company such as American Airlines often receives cash when it sells tickets for future flights. How do these companies account for unearned revenues that are received before goods are delivered or services are rendered?

1. When the advance is received, Cash is increased (debited), and a current liability account identifying the source of the unearned revenue is also increased (credited).
2. When the revenue is earned, the unearned revenue account is decreased (debited), and an earned revenue account is increased (credited).

To illustrate, assume that Superior University sells 10,000 season football tickets at $50 each for its five-game home schedule. The entry for the sales of season tickets is:

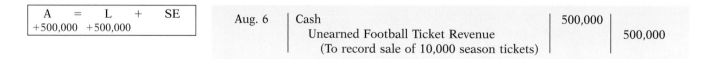

A	=	L	+	SE
+500,000		+500,000		

Aug. 6	Cash	500,000	
	Unearned Football Ticket Revenue		500,000
	(To record sale of 10,000 season tickets)		

As each game is completed, this entry is made:

Sept. 7	Unearned Football Ticket Revenue	100,000	
	Football Ticket Revenue		100,000
	(To record football ticket revenues earned)		

A	=	L	+	SE
		−100,000		+100,000

The account Unearned Football Ticket Revenue represents unearned revenue and is reported as a current liability in the balance sheet. As revenue is earned, a transfer from unearned revenue to earned revenue occurs. Unearned revenue is material for some companies: In the airline industry, tickets sold for future flights represent almost 50% of total current liabilities. At United Airlines, unearned ticket revenue is the largest current liability, recently amounting to more than $1 billion.

Illustration 10-2 shows specific unearned and earned revenue accounts used in selected types of businesses.

Type of Business	Account Title	
	Unearned Revenue	**Earned Revenue**
Airline	Unearned Passenger Ticket Revenue	Passenger Ticket Revenue
Magazine publisher	Unearned Subscription Revenue	Subscription Revenue
Hotel	Unearned Rental Revenue	Rental Revenue

Illustration 10-2
Unearned and earned revenue accounts

CURRENT MATURITIES OF LONG-TERM DEBT

Companies often have a portion of long-term debt that comes due in the current year. As an example, assume that Wendy Construction issues a five-year, interest-bearing $25,000 note on January 1, 2001. This note specifies that each January 1, starting January 1, 2002, $5,000 of the note should be paid. When financial statements are prepared on December 31, 2001, $5,000 should be reported as a current liability and $20,000 as a long-term liability. Current maturities of long-term debt are often identified on the balance sheet as **long-term debt due within one year.** Illustration 10-3 (on page 459) shows that at December 31, 1998, General Motors had $273 million of such debt.

It is not necessary to prepare an adjusting entry to recognize the current maturity of long-term debt. The proper statement classification of each balance sheet account is recognized when the balance sheet is prepared.

BEFORE YOU GO ON...

◆ Review It

1. What are the two criteria for classifying a debt as a current liability?
2. What are some examples of current liabilities?
3. What are three items generally withheld from employees' wages or salaries?
4. Identify three examples of unearned revenues.

◆ Do It

A local not-for-profit organization has asked you to act as its treasurer. Each fall the club holds a fund-raiser at which it offers space to craftspeople who bring their wares for sale. The organization charges these vendors a commission on sales and uses these collections to raise scholarship money to donate to local colleges. The organization acts as a collection agent for state sales taxes. The cash register total of $256,000 for the four-day event includes sales taxes. The state tax rate is 6.25%, and there are no city sales taxes. Assuming that all sales were taxable, what amount of sales taxes must the organization collect from the vendors and remit to the state? How should you, as treasurer, show that tax liability in the organization's financial statements?

Reasoning: To answer the first question, you must separate the sales taxes from the total sales amount. To answer the second question, you must know how sales taxes are reported in the financial statements and whether statements will be issued before you pay the sales taxes.

Solution: First divide the total proceeds by 100% plus the sales tax percentage to find the sales amount. Then, to determine the sales taxes, subtract the sales amount from the total proceeds, *or* multiply the sales amount by the tax rate:

$$\text{Sales amount} = \$256{,}000 \div 1.0625 = \$240{,}941.18$$
$$\text{Sales taxes due} = \$256{,}000 - \$240{,}941.18 = \$15{,}058.82$$

or

$$= \$240{,}941.18 \times .0625 = \$15{,}058.82$$

If financial statements are issued before you remit the sales taxes payable, you should show sales taxes payable of $15,058.82 as a current liability. It is unlikely that you would show the sales tax liability, however, because the sales taxes should be remitted to the state as quickly as possible. You would not show the sales tax as an expense because your organization was simply a collection agent.

FINANCIAL STATEMENT PRESENTATION AND ANALYSIS

PRESENTATION

Current liabilities are the first category under Liabilities on the balance sheet. Each of the principal types of current liabilities is listed separately within the category. In addition, the terms of notes payable and other pertinent information concerning the individual items are disclosed in the notes to the financial statements.

Current liabilities are seldom listed in their order of maturity because of the varying maturity dates that may exist for specific obligations such as notes payable. A more common, and entirely satisfactory, method of presenting current liabilities is to list them by **order of magnitude**, with the largest obligations first. Many companies, as a matter of custom, show current maturities of long-term debt first, regardless of amount. The adapted balance sheet of the Automotive and Electronics Divisions of General Motors Corporation in Illustration 10-3 shows its presentation of current liabilities.

ANALYSIS

Liquidity ratios measure the short-term ability of a company to pay its maturing obligations and to meet unexpected needs for cash. Two measures of liquidity were examined in Chapter 2: working capital (Current assets − Current liabilities) and the current ratio (Current assets ÷ Current liabilities). In this section we add a third useful measure of liquidity, the acid-test ratio.

**GENERAL MOTORS CORPORATION—
AUTOMOTIVE AND ELECTRONICS DIVISIONS**
Balance Sheets
December 31, 1998 and 1997
(in millions)

Assets	1998	1997
Current assets		
Cash and cash equivalents	$ 10,723	$ 10,685
Short-term investments	407	3,826
Accounts receivable, net	5,599	5,440
Inventories	12,207	12,102
Other current assets	15,427	11,274
Total current assets	44,363	43,327
Noncurrent assets	81,275	80,341
Total assets	$125,638	$123,668
Liabilities and Stockholders' Equity		
Current liabilities		
Accounts payable	**$ 13,479**	**$ 12,461**
Notes payable	**1,253**	**29**
Current maturities of long-term debt	**273**	**627**
Accrued liabilities and expenses	**32,801**	**33,254**
Total current liabilities	47,806	46,371
Long-term debt	7,217	5,695
Accrued noncurrent employee benefits	44,666	42,659
Other noncurrent liabilities	20,267	19,294
Total liabilities	119,956	114,019
Total stockholders' equity	5,682	9,649
Total liabilities and stockholders' equity	$125,638	$123,668

Illustration 10-3
Balance sheets for
General Motors
Corporation

The current ratio is a frequently used ratio, but it can be misleading. Consider the current ratio's numerator, which can include some items in current assets that are not very liquid. For example, when a company is having a difficult time selling its merchandise, its inventory increases. This will cause its current ratio to increase, even though the company's liquidity has actually declined. Similarly, prepaid expenses are considered current assets, but generally cannot be sold and therefore do not contribute to liquidity. Consequently, the current ratio is often supplemented with the acid-test ratio.

The acid-test ratio is a measure of a company's immediate short-term liquidity. It is computed by dividing the sum of cash, short-term investments, and net receivables by current liabilities. Short-term investments, also called marketable securities, are investments that have a ready market and are intended to be sold within the next year. Cash, short-term investments, and net receivables are usually highly liquid compared to inventory and prepaid expenses. Thus, because it measures **immediate** liquidity, the acid-test ratio should be computed along with the current ratio. Working capital, current ratios, and acid-test ratios for General Motors are provided in Illustration 10-4 (page 460). Industry averages are provided where available.

General Motors' current assets nearly equal its current liabilities; thus, its current ratio was approximately 1 in both 1997 and 1998. Its working capital was actually negative in 1997 and 1998. The industry average current ratio for

Alternative Terminology The acid-test ratio is often referred to as the **quick ratio**.

manufacturers of cars and car parts is 1.58:1. Thus, General Motors appears to lack liquidity. This is confirmed by the acid-test ratio. The industry average for this ratio is 1.19:1, whereas in 1998 General Motors had an acid-test ratio of approximately .35:1.

Illustration 10-4
Liquidity measures

$$\text{Working Capital} = \text{Current Assets} - \text{Current Liabilities}$$

$$\text{Current Ratio} = \frac{\text{Current Assets}}{\text{Current Liabilities}}$$

$$\frac{\text{Acid-Test}}{\text{Ratio}} = \frac{\text{Cash} + \text{Short-term Investments} + \text{Net Receivables}}{\text{Current Liabilities}}$$

($ in millions)	General Motors		Industry Average
	1998	**1997**	**1998**
Working Capital	$44,363 − $47,806 = −$3,443	$43,327 − $46,371 = −$3,044	na
Current Ratio	$\dfrac{\$44,363}{\$47,806} = .93:1$	$\dfrac{\$43,327}{\$46,371} = .93:1$	1.58:1
Acid-Test Ratio	$\dfrac{\$10,723 + \$407 + \$5,599}{\$47,806} = .35:1$	$\dfrac{\$10,685 + \$3,826 + \$5,440}{\$46,371} = .43:1$	1.19:1

DECISION TOOLKIT

Decision Checkpoints	Info Needed for Decision	Tool to Use for Decision	How to Evaluate Results
Can the company meet its current obligations?	Cash, accounts receivable, short-term investments, and other highly liquid assets, and current liabilities	$\text{Acid-test ratio} = \dfrac{\text{Cash} + \text{Short-term investments} + \text{Net receivables}}{\text{Current liabilities}}$	Ratio should be compared to others in same industry. High ratio indicates good liquidity.

Many companies have reduced their liquid assets because they cost too much to hold. Companies that keep fewer liquid assets on hand must rely on other sources of liquidity. One such source is a bank **line of credit**. A line of credit is a prearranged agreement between a company and a lender that permits, should it be necessary, a company to borrow up to an agreed-upon amount. To the extent that its low amount of liquid assets causes a cash shortfall, a company may borrow money on its available short-term lines of credit. Given General Motors' relatively low liquidity, adequate short-term lines of credit are critical. The debt note to General Motors' 1998 financial statements discusses its line of credit agreements.

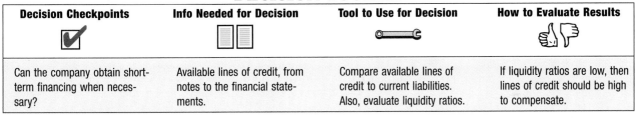

Illustration 10-5
Line of credit note

GM **General Motors**

GENERAL MOTORS CORPORATION
Notes to the Financial Statements

GM and its subsidiaries maintain substantial bank lines of credit with various banks that totaled $14.5 billion at December 31, 1998, of which $6.7 billion represented short-term credit facilities and $7.8 billion represented long-term credit facilities. . . . The unused short-term and long-term portions of the credit lines totaled $6.2 billion and $7.2 billion at December 31, 1998, compared with $2.5 billion and $4.8 billion at December 31, 1997. Certain bank lines of credit contain covenants with which the Corporation and applicable subsidiaries were in compliance during the year ended December 31, 1998.

General Motors' unused lines of credit, which total $13.4 billion ($6.2 + $7.2), are nearly equal to the sum of its existing cash, short-term investments, and net receivables. Thus, even though General Motors has lower liquidity ratios than the industry average, its available lines of credit appear adequate to meet any short-term cash deficiency it might experience.

DECISION TOOLKIT

Decision Checkpoints	Info Needed for Decision	Tool to Use for Decision	How to Evaluate Results
Can the company obtain short-term financing when necessary?	Available lines of credit, from notes to the financial statements.	Compare available lines of credit to current liabilities. Also, evaluate liquidity ratios.	If liquidity ratios are low, then lines of credit should be high to compensate.

BEFORE YOU GO ON...

◆ Review It

1. In what order are current liabilities usually presented?
2. Identify the liabilities classified as current by Tootsie Roll. The answer to this question is provided on page 507.
3. What does the acid-test ratio measure and how is it calculated?
4. What is a line of credit?

S E C T I O N   2

LONG-TERM LIABILITIES

Long-term liabilities are obligations that are expected to be paid after one year. In this section we explain the accounting for the principal types of obligations reported in the long-term liabilities section of the balance sheet. These obligations often are in the form of bonds or long-term notes.

*B*OND BASICS

Bonds are a form of interest-bearing note payable issued by corporations, universities, and governmental agencies. Bonds, like common stock, are sold in small denominations (usually $1,000 or multiples of $1,000). As a result, bonds attract many investors.

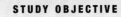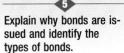

STUDY OBJECTIVE
5
Explain why bonds are issued and identify the types of bonds.

WHY ISSUE BONDS?

A corporation may use long-term financing other than bonds, such as notes payable and leasing. However, these other forms of financing involve an agreement between the corporation and one individual, one company, or a financial institution. Notes payable and leasing are therefore seldom sufficient to furnish the funds needed for plant expansion and major projects like new buildings. To obtain **large amounts of long-term capital**, corporate management usually must decide whether to issue bonds or to sell common stock.

From the standpoint of the corporation seeking long-term financing, bonds offer advantages over common stock as shown in Illustration 10-6.

Illustration 10-6   Advantages of bond financing over common stock

Bond Financing	Advantages
(Ballot Box)	1. **Stockholder control is not affected.** Bondholders do not have voting rights, so current owners (stockholders) retain full control of the company.
(Tax Bill)	2. **Tax savings result.** Bond interest is deductible for tax purposes; dividends on stock are not.
($/Stock)	3. **Earnings per share may be higher.** Although bond interest expense reduces net income, earnings per share often is higher under bond financing because no additional shares of common stock are issued.

⊕ International Note

The priority of bondholders' versus stockholders' rights varies across countries. In Japan, Germany, and France stockholders and employees are given priority, with liquidation of the firm to pay creditors seen as a last resort. In Britain creditors' interests are put first; the courts are quick to give control of the firm to creditors.

One commonly reported measure of corporate performance is **earnings per share**—Net income ÷ Average shares outstanding. We will discuss the pros and cons of earnings per share as a performance measure in Chapter 11. Now we focus on how earnings per share can be increased by the effective use of debt.

To illustrate the potential effect of debt on earnings per share, assume that Microsystems Inc. is considering two plans for financing the construction of a new $5 million plant: Plan A involves issuing 200,000 shares of common stock at the current market price of $25 per share. Plan B involves issuing $5 million, 12% bonds at face value. Income before interest and taxes on the new plant will be $1.5 million; income taxes are expected to be 30%. Microsystems currently has 100,000 shares of common stock outstanding. The alternative effects on earnings per share are shown in Illustration 10-7.

	Plan A: Issue stock	Plan B: Issue bonds
Income before interest and taxes	$1,500,000	$1,500,000
Interest (12% × $5,000,000)	—	600,000
Income before income taxes	1,500,000	900,000
Income tax expense (30%)	450,000	270,000
Net income	$1,050,000	$ 630,000
Outstanding shares	300,000	100,000
Earnings per share	$ 3.50	$ 6.30

Illustration 10-7   Effects on earnings per share—stocks vs. bonds

Note that with long-term debt financing (bonds) net income is $420,000 ($1,050,000 − $630,000) less. However, earnings per share is higher because there are 200,000 fewer shares of common stock outstanding.

The major disadvantage resulting from the use of bonds is that the company locks in fixed payments that must be made in good times and bad. Interest must be paid on a periodic basis, and the principal (face value) of the bonds must be paid at maturity. A company with fluctuating earnings and a relatively weak cash position may experience great difficulty in meeting interest requirements in periods of low earnings. In the extreme, this can result in bankruptcy. With common stock financing, on the other hand, the company can decide to pay low (or no) dividends if earnings are low.

TYPES OF BONDS

Bonds may have many different features. Some types of bonds commonly issued are described in the following sections.

Secured and Unsecured Bonds

Secured bonds have specific assets of the issuer pledged as collateral for the bonds. A bond secured by real estate, for example, is called a mortgage bond. A bond secured by specific assets set aside to retire the bonds is called a sinking fund bond.

Unsecured bonds are issued against the general credit of the borrower. These bonds, called debenture bonds, are used extensively by large corporations with good credit ratings. For example, in a recent annual report, DuPont reported more than $2 billion of debenture bonds outstanding.

Term and Serial Bonds

Bonds that are due for payment (mature) at a single specified future date are called term bonds. In contrast, bonds that mature in installments are called serial bonds. For example, Caterpillar Inc. debentures due in 2007 are term bonds, and their debentures due between 2000 and 2007 are serial bonds.

Convertible and Callable Bonds

Bonds that can be converted into common stock at the bondholder's option are called convertible bonds. Bonds subject to retirement at a stated dollar amount prior to maturity at the option of the issuer are known as callable bonds.

Convertible bonds have features that are attractive both to bondholders and to the issuer. The conversion often gives bondholders an opportunity to benefit if the market price of the common stock increases substantially. Furthermore, until conversion, the bondholder receives interest on the bond. For the issuer, the bonds sell at a higher price and pay a lower rate of interest than comparable debt securities that do not have a conversion option. Many corporations, such as USAir, USX Corp., and General Motors Corporation, have convertible bonds outstanding.

ISSUING PROCEDURES

State laws grant corporations the power to issue bonds. Within the corporation, formal approval by both the board of directors and the stockholders is usually required before bonds can be issued. **In authorizing the bond issue, the board of directors must stipulate the total number of bonds to be authorized, the**

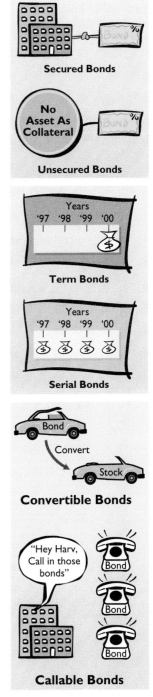

Secured Bonds

Unsecured Bonds

Term Bonds

Serial Bonds

Convertible Bonds

Callable Bonds

total face value, **and the contractual interest rate**. The total bond authorization often exceeds the number of bonds originally issued. This is done intentionally to help ensure that the corporation will have the flexibility it needs to meet future cash requirements by selling more bonds.

The face value is the amount of principal due at the maturity date. The **contractual interest rate** is the rate used to determine the amount of cash interest the borrower pays and the investor receives. Usually the contractual rate is stated as an annual rate, and interest is generally paid semiannually.

The terms of the bond issue are set forth in a legal document called a bond indenture. After the bond indenture is prepared, **bond certificates** are printed. The indenture and the certificate are separate documents. As shown in Illustration 10-8, a bond certificate provides information such as the name of the issuer, the face value of the bonds, the contractual interest rate, and the maturity date of the bonds. Bonds are generally sold through an investment company that specializes in selling securities. In most cases, the issue is **underwritten** by the investment company: The company sells the bonds to the investment company, which, in turn, sells the bonds to individual investors.

Alternative Terminology The contractual rate is often referred to as the **stated rate**.

Helpful Hint Do not confuse the terms *indenture* and *debenture*. Indenture refers to the formal bond document (contract). Debenture bonds are unsecured bonds.

Illustration 10-8 Bond certificate

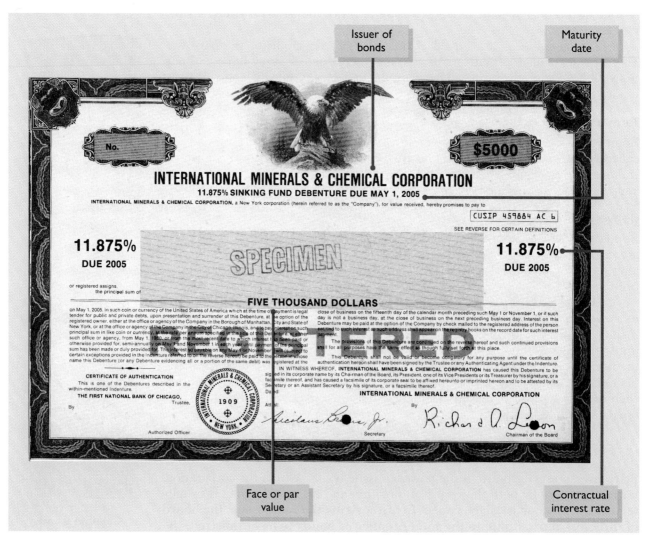

Although bonds are generally secured by solid, substantial assets like land, buildings, and equipment, exceptions occur. For example, Trans World Airlines Inc. (TWA) at one time decided to issue $300 million of high-yielding five-year bonds, secured by a grab-bag of assets—including some durable spare parts but also a lot of disposable items that TWA had in its warehouses, such as light bulbs and gaskets. Some called the planned TWA bonds "light bulb bonds." As one financial expert noted: "You've got to admit that some security is better than none." However, noted another, "They're digging pretty far down the barrel."

Source: The Wall Street Journal, June 2, 1989.

DETERMINING THE MARKET VALUE OF BONDS

If you were an investor interested in purchasing a bond, how would you determine how much to pay? To be more specific, assume that Coronet, Inc., issues a zero-interest bond (pays no interest) with a face value of $1,000,000 due in 20 years. For this bond, the only cash you receive is $1 million at the end of 20 years. Would you pay $1 million for this bond? We hope not, because $1 million received 20 years from now is not the same as $1 million received today. The reason you should not pay $1 million relates to what is called the **time value of money.** If you had $1 million today, you would invest it and earn interest such that at the end of 20 years, your investment would be worth much more than $1 million. Thus, if someone is going to pay you $1 million 20 years from now, you would want to find its equivalent today, or its present value. In other words, you would want to determine how much must be invested today at current interest rates to have $1 million in 20 years.

The current market value (present value) of a bond is therefore a function of three factors: (1) the dollar amounts to be received, (2) the length of time until the amounts are received, and (3) the market rate of interest. The market interest rate is the rate investors demand for loaning funds to the corporation. The process of finding the present value is referred to as **discounting** the future amounts.

To illustrate, assume that Acropolis Company on January 1, 2001, issues $100,000 of 9% bonds, due in five years, with interest payable annually at year-end. The purchaser of the bonds would receive the following two cash payments: (1) **principal** of $100,000 to be paid at maturity, and (2) five $9,000 **interest payments** ($100,000 × 9%) over the term of the bonds. A time diagram depicting both cash flows is shown in Illustration 10-9.

Same dollars at different times are not equal.

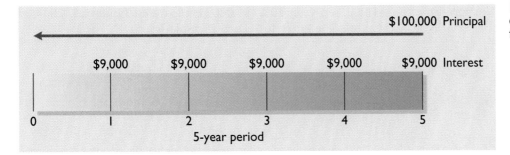

Illustration 10-9 Time diagram depicting cash flows

The current market value of a bond is equal to the present value of all the future cash payments promised by the bond. The present values of these amounts are listed in Illustration 10-10.

Illustration 10-10 Computing the market price of bonds

Present value of $100,000 received in 5 years	$ 64,993
Present value of $9,000 received annually for 5 years	35,007
Market price of bonds	**$100,000**

Tables are available to provide the present value numbers to be used, or these values can be determined mathematically.[2] Further discussion of the concepts and the mechanics of the time value of money computations is provided in Appendix C near the end of the book.

BEFORE YOU GO ON...

◆ Review It

1. What are the advantages of bond versus stock financing?
2. What are secured versus unsecured bonds, term versus serial bonds, and callable versus convertible bonds?
3. Explain the terms *face value, contractual interest rate,* and *bond indenture.*
4. Explain why you would prefer to receive $1 million today rather than five years from now.

ACCOUNTING FOR BOND ISSUES

A corporation receives payment for its bonds (and makes journal entries to record their sale) only when it issues or buys back bonds, and when bondholders convert bonds into common stock. If a bondholder sells a bond to another investor, the issuing firm receives no further money on the transaction, **nor is the transaction journalized by the issuing corporation** (although it does keep records of the names of bondholders in some cases).

Bonds may be issued at face value, below face value (discount), or above face value (premium). Bond prices for both new issues and existing bonds are quoted as **a percentage of the face value of the bond, which is usually $1,000**. Thus, a $1,000 bond with a quoted price of 97 means that the selling price of the bond is 97% of face value, or $970 in this case.

ISSUING BONDS AT FACE VALUE

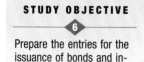

STUDY OBJECTIVE

6

Prepare the entries for the issuance of bonds and interest expense.

To illustrate the accounting for its bonds issued at face value, assume that Devor Corporation issues 1,000, ten-year, 10%, $1,000 bonds dated January 1, 2001, at 100 (100% of face value). The entry to record the sale is:

Jan. 1	Cash		1,000,000	
	Bonds Payable			1,000,000
	(To record sale of bonds at face value)			

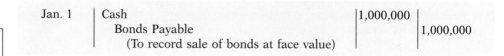

A	=	L	+	SE
+1,000,000		+1,000,000		

---

[2] For those knowledgeable in the use of present value tables, the computations in this example are: $100,000 × .64993 = $64,993 and $9,000 × 3.88965 = $35,007 (rounded).

Bonds payable are reported in the long-term liabilities section of the balance sheet because the maturity date is January 1, 2011 (more than one year away).

Over the term (life) of the bonds, entries are required for bond interest. Interest on bonds payable is computed in the same manner as interest on notes payable, as explained earlier. If it is assumed that interest is payable semiannually on January 1 and July 1 on the bonds described above, interest of $50,000 ($1,000,000 $\times$ 10% $\times \frac{6}{12}$) must be paid on July 1, 2001. The entry for the payment, assuming no previous accrual of interest, is:

July 1	Bond Interest Expense	50,000	
	Cash		50,000
	(To record payment of bond interest)		

A	=	L	+	SE
−50,000				−50,000

At December 31 an adjusting entry is required to recognize the $50,000 of interest expense incurred since July 1. The entry is:

Dec. 31	Bond Interest Expense	50,000	
	Bond Interest Payable		50,000
	(To accrue bond interest)		

A	=	L	+	SE
		+50,000		−50,000

Bond interest payable is classified as a current liability because it is scheduled for payment within the next year. When the interest is paid on January 1, 2002, Bond Interest Payable is decreased (debited) and Cash also is decreased (credited) for $50,000.

DISCOUNT OR PREMIUM ON BONDS

The previous illustrations assumed that the interest rates paid on bonds, often referred to as the contractual (stated) interest rate and the market (effective) interest rate, were the same. Recall that the contractual interest rate is the rate applied to the face (par) value to arrive at the interest paid in a year. The market interest rate is the rate investors demand for loaning funds to the corporation. When the contractual interest rate and the market interest rate are the same, bonds sell at face value, as illustrated above.

However, market interest rates change daily. They are influenced by the type of bond issued, the state of the economy, current industry conditions, and the company's individual performance. As a result, the contractual and market interest rates often differ, and therefore bonds sell below or above face value.

To illustrate, suppose that investors have one of two options: Purchase bonds that have a market rate of interest of 12% or purchase bonds that have a contractual rate of interest of 10%. Assuming that the bonds are of equal risk, investors will select the 12% investment. To make the investments equal, investors will demand a rate of return higher than the contractual interest rate on the 10% bonds. But the contractual interest rate cannot be changed, so investors will make up the difference by paying less than the face value for the bonds. In these cases, **bonds sell at a** discount. Without this discount, bonds with a contractual rate of 10% would not be marketable until the market rate of interest fell to that level.

Conversely, if the market rate of interest is **lower** than the contractual interest rate, investors will have to pay more than face value for the bonds. That is, if the market rate of interest is 8% but the contractual interest rate on the bonds is 10%, the issuer will require more funds from the investor. In these cases, **bonds sell at a** premium. These relationships are shown graphically in Illustration 10-11 (page 468).

⊕ **International Note**
The use of debt financing varies considerably across countries. The amount of debt borrowed by governments can affect a country's ability to borrow funds. One measure of the degree of debt financing is the ratio of national debt to gross national product. In a recent survey, this ratio was 49.7%, 13%, 106.2%, and 17.1% in the United States, Australia, Belgium, and Brazil, respectively.

Helpful Hint Bond prices vary inversely with changes in the market interest rate. As market interest rates decline, bond prices will increase. When a bond is issued, if the market interest rate is below the contractual rate, the price will be higher than the face value. In the example at left, the market rate is greater than the 8% bond rate and therefore the bonds sell at a discount.

Illustration 10-11 Interest rates and bond prices

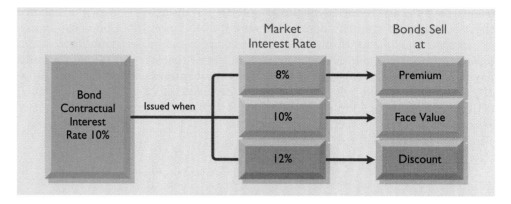

Helpful Hint Some bonds are sold at a discount by design. "Zero-coupon" bonds, which pay no interest, sell at a deep discount to face value.

Issuance of bonds at an amount different from face value is quite common. By the time a company prints the bond certificates and markets the bonds, it will be a coincidence if the market rate and the contractual rate are the same. Thus, the issuance of bonds at a discount does not mean that the financial strength of the issuer is suspect. Conversely, the sale of bonds at a premium does not indicate that the financial strength of the issuer is exceptional.

ISSUING BONDS AT A DISCOUNT

To illustrate the issuance of bonds at a discount, assume that on January 1, 2001, Candlestick Inc. sells $1 million, five-year, 10% bonds at 98 (98% of face value) with interest payable on July 1 and January 1. The entry to record the issuance is:

```
A    =    L    +    SE
+980,000    −20,000
            +1,000,000
```

Jan. 1	Cash	980,000	
	Discount on Bonds Payable	20,000	
	Bonds Payable		1,000,000
	(To record sale of bonds at a discount)		

Although Discount on Bonds Payable has a debit balance, **it is not an asset**. Rather it is a **contra account**, which is **deducted from bonds payable** on the balance sheet as in Illustration 10-12.

Illustration 10-12 Statement presentation of discount on bonds payable

> **CANDLESTICK INC.**
> **Balance Sheet (partial)**
>
> Long-term liabilities
>   Bonds payable $1,000,000
>   **Less: Discount on bonds payable**   20,000 $980,000

Helpful Hint The carrying value (book value) of bonds issued at a discount is determined by subtracting the balance of the discount account from the balance of the Bonds Payable account.

The $980,000 represents the **carrying (or book) value** of the bonds. On the date of issue this amount equals the market price of the bonds.

The issuance of bonds below face value causes the total cost of borrowing to differ from the bond interest paid. That is, the issuing corporation must pay not only the contractual interest rate over the term of the bonds but also at maturity the face value (rather than the issuance price). Therefore, the difference between the issuance price and the face value of the bonds—the discount—is an **additional cost of borrowing** that should be recorded as **bond interest expense** over the life of the bonds. The total cost of borrowing $980,000 for Candlestick Inc. is $520,000, computed as in Illustration 10-13.

Bonds Issued at a Discount

Semiannual interest payments		
($1,000,000 × 10% × $\frac{1}{2}$ = $50,000; $50,000 × 10)		$ 500,000
Add: Bond discount ($1,000,000 − $980,000)		20,000
Total cost of borrowing		**$520,000**

Illustration 10-13   Computation of total cost of borrowing—bonds issued at discount

Alternatively, the total cost of borrowing can be determined as in Illustration 10-14.

Bonds Issued at a Discount

Principal at maturity	$1,000,000
Semiannual interest payments ($50,000 × 10)	500,000
Cash to be paid to bondholders	1,500,000
Cash received from bondholders	980,000
Total cost of borrowing	**$ 520,000**

Illustration 10-14 Alternative computation of total cost of borrowing—bonds issued at discount

AMORTIZING BOND DISCOUNT

To comply with the matching principle, bond discount should be allocated systematically to each accounting period that benefits from the use of the cash proceeds. The **straight-line method of amortization** allocates the same amount to interest expense in each interest period. The amount is determined as shown in Illustration 10-15.

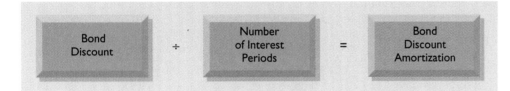

Illustration 10-15 Formula for straight-line method of bond discount amortization

In this example, the bond discount amortization is $2,000 ($20,000 ÷ 10) for each of the ten amortization periods (5 years × 2 payments per year). The entry to record the payment of bond interest and the amortization of bond discount on the first interest date (July 1, 2001) is:

July 1	Bond Interest Expense	52,000	
	Discount on Bonds Payable		2,000
	Cash		50,000
	(To record payment of bond interest and amortization of bond discount)		

A	=	L	+	SE
−50,000		+2,000		−52,000

At December 31, the adjusting entry is:

Dec. 31	Bond Interest Expense	52,000	
	Discount on Bonds Payable		2,000
	Bond Interest Payable		50,000
	(To record accrued bond interest and amortization of bond discount)		

A	=	L	+	SE
		+2,000		−52,000
		+50,000		

Over the term of the bonds, the balance in Discount on Bonds Payable will decrease annually by the same amount until it has a zero balance at the maturity

Alternative Terminology The amount in the Discount on Bonds Payable account is often referred to as **Unamortized Discount on Bonds Payable**.

date of the bonds. Thus, the carrying value of the bonds at maturity will be equal to the face value of the bonds.

Preparing a bond discount amortization schedule, as shown in Illustration 10-16, is useful to determine interest expense, discount amortization, and the carrying value of the bond. As indicated, the interest expense recorded each period is $52,000. Also note that the carrying value of the bond increases $2,000 each period until it reaches its face value $1,000,000 at the end of period 10.

Illustration 10-16   Bond discount amortization schedule

Semiannual Interest Periods	**(A)** Interest To Be Paid (5% × $1,000,000)	**(B)** Interest Expense To Be Recorded (A) + (C)	**(C)** Discount Amortization ($20,000 ÷ 10)	**(D)** Unamortized Discount (D) − (C)	**(E)** Bond Carrying Value ($1,000,000 − D)
Issue date				$20,000	$ 980,000
1	$ 50,000	$ 52,000	$ 2,000	18,000	982,000
2	50,000	52,000	2,000	16,000	984,000
3	50,000	52,000	2,000	14,000	986,000
4	50,000	52,000	2,000	12,000	988,000
5	50,000	52,000	2,000	10,000	990,000
6	50,000	52,000	2,000	8,000	992,000
7	50,000	52,000	2,000	6,000	994,000
8	50,000	52,000	2,000	4,000	996,000
9	50,000	52,000	2,000	2,000	998,000
10	50,000	52,000	2,000	0	1,000,000
	$500,000	$520,000	$20,000		

Column **(A)** remains constant because the face value of the bonds ($1,000,000) is multiplied by the semiannual contractual interest rate (5%) each period.
Column **(B)** is computed as the interest paid (Column A) plus the discount amortization (Column C).
Column **(C)** indicates the discount amortization each period.
Column **(D)** decreases each period by the same amount until it reaches zero at maturity.
Column **(E)** increases each period by the amount of discount amortization until it equals the face value at maturity.

ISSUING BONDS AT A PREMIUM

Helpful Hint Both a discount and a premium account are valuation accounts. A valuation account is one that is needed to value properly the item to which it relates.

The issuance of bonds at a premium can be illustrated by assuming the Candlestick Inc. bonds described above are sold at 102 (102% of face value) rather than at 98. The entry to record the sale is:

A	=	L	+	SE
+1,020,000		+1,000,000		
		+20,000		

Jan. 1	Cash	1,020,000	
	Bonds Payable		1,000,000
	Premium on Bonds Payable		20,000
	(To record sale of bonds at a premium)		

Premium on bonds payable is **added to bonds payable** on the balance sheet, as shown in Illustration 10-17.

Illustration 10-17   Statement presentation of bond premium

CANDLESTICK INC.
Balance Sheet (partial)

Long-term liabilities		
Bonds payable	$1,000,000	
Add: Premium on bonds payable	20,000	$1,020,000

The sale of bonds above face value causes the total cost of borrowing to be **less than the bond interest paid** because the borrower is not required to pay the bond premium at the maturity date of the bonds. Thus, the premium is considered to be **a reduction in the cost of borrowing** that reduces bond interest expense over the life of the bonds. The total cost of borrowing $1,020,000 for Candlestick Inc. is $480,000, computed as in Illustration 10-18.

Bonds Issued at a Premium

Semiannual interest payments	
($1,000,000 × 10% × ½ = $50,000; $50,000 × 10)	$ 500,000
Less: Bond premium ($1,020,000 − $1,000,000)	20,000
Total cost of borrowing	**$480,000**

Illustration 10-18
Computation of total cost of borrowing—bonds issued at a premium

Alternatively, the cost of borrowing can be computed as in Illustration 10-19.

Bonds Issued at a Premium

Principal at maturity	$1,000,000
Semiannual interest payments ($50,000 × 10)	500,000
Cash to be paid to bondholders	1,500,000
Cash received from bondholders	1,020,000
Total cost of borrowing	**$ 480,000**

Illustration 10-19 Alternative computation of total cost of borrowing—bonds issued at a premium

AMORTIZING BOND PREMIUM

The formula for determining bond premium amortization under the straight-line method is presented in Illustration 10-20.

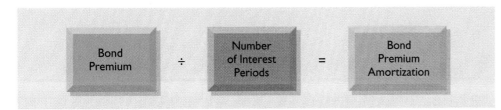

Illustration 10-20
Formula for straight-line method of bond premium amortization

Thus, in our example, the premium amortization for each interest period is $2,000 ($20,000 ÷ 10). The entry to record the first payment of interest on July 1 is:

July 1	Bond Interest Expense	48,000	
	Premium on Bonds Payable	2,000	
	Cash		50,000
	(To record payment of bond interest and		
	amortization of bond premium)		

A	=	L	+	SE
−50,000		−2,000		−48,000

At December 31, the adjusting entry is:

Dec. 31	Bond Interest Expense	48,000	
	Premium on Bonds Payable	2,000	
	Bond Interest Payable		50,000
	(To record accrued bond interest and		
	amortization of bond premium)		

A	=	L	+	SE
		−2,000		−48,000
		+50,000		

Over the term of the bonds, the balance in Premium on Bonds Payable will decrease annually by the same amount until it has a zero balance at maturity.

Preparing a bond premium amortization schedule, as shown in Illustration 10-21, is useful to determine interest expense, premium amortization, and the carrying value of the bond. As indicated, the interest expense recorded each period is $48,000. Also note that the carrying value of the bond decreases $2,000 each period until it reaches its face value $1,000,000 at the end of period 10.

Illustration 10-21 Bond premium amortization schedule

Semiannual Interest Periods	(A) Interest To Be Paid (5% × $1,000,000)	(B) Interest Expense To Be Recorded (A) – (C)	(C) Premium Amortization ($20,000 ÷ 10)	(D) Unamortized Premium (D) – (C)	(E) Bond Carrying Value ($1,000,000 + D)
Issue date				$20,000	$1,020,000
1	$ 50,000	$ 48,000	$ 2,000	18,000	1,018,000
2	50,000	48,000	2,000	16,000	1,016,000
3	50,000	48,000	2,000	14,000	1,014,000
4	50,000	48,000	2,000	12,000	1,012,000
5	50,000	48,000	2,000	10,000	1,010,000
6	50,000	48,000	2,000	8,000	1,008,000
7	50,000	48,000	2,000	6,000	1,006,000
8	50,000	48,000	2,000	4,000	1,004,000
9	50,000	48,000	2,000	2,000	1,002,000
10	50,000	48,000	2,000	0	1,000,000
	$500,000	$480,000	$20,000		

Column **(A)** remains constant because the face value of the bonds ($1,000,000) is multiplied by the semiannual contractual interest rate (5%) each period.
Column **(B)** is computed as the interest paid (Column A) less the premium amortization (Column C).
Column **(C)** indicates the premium amortization each period.
Column **(D)** decreases each period by the same amount until it reaches zero at maturity.
Column **(E)** decreases each period by the amount of premium amortization until it equals the face value at maturity.

ACCOUNTING FOR BOND RETIREMENTS

Bonds are retired when they are purchased (redeemed) by the issuing corporation. The appropriate entries for these transactions are explained next.

REDEEMING BONDS AT MATURITY

STUDY OBJECTIVE

7

Describe the entries when bonds are redeemed.

Regardless of the issue price of bonds, the book value of the bonds at maturity will equal their face value. Assuming that the interest for the last interest period is paid and recorded separately, the entry to record the redemption of the Candlestick bonds at maturity is:

A = L + SE
−1,000,000 −1,000,000

Bonds Payable	1,000,000	
Cash		1,000,000
(To record redemption of bonds at maturity)		

Helpful Hint If a bond is redeemed prior to its maturity date and its carrying value exceeds its redemption price, will the retirement result in a gain or a loss on redemption? Answer: Gain.

REDEEMING BONDS BEFORE MATURITY

Bonds may be redeemed before maturity. A company may decide to retire bonds before maturity to reduce interest cost and remove debt from its balance sheet. A company should retire debt early only if it has sufficient cash resources. When bonds are retired before maturity, it is necessary to: (1) eliminate the carrying value of the bonds at the redemption date, (2) record the cash paid, and (3) recognize the gain or loss on redemption. The carrying value of the bonds is the face value of the bonds less unamortized bond discount or plus unamortized bond premium at the redemption date.

To illustrate, assume at the end of the eighth period Candlestick Inc., having sold its bonds at a premium, retires its bonds at 103 after paying the semiannual interest. The carrying value of the bonds at the redemption date is $1,004,000. (The calculation of this value is shown in Illustration 10-21.) The entry to record the redemption at the end of the eighth interest period (January 1, 2005) is:

Jan. 1	Bonds Payable	1,000,000	
	Premium on Bonds Payable	4,000	
	Loss on Bond Redemption	26,000	
	Cash		1,030,000
	(To record redemption of bonds at 103)		

A	=	L	+	SE
−1,030,000		−1,000,000		−26,000
		−4,000		

Note that the loss of $26,000 is the difference between the cash paid of $1,030,000 and the carrying value of the bonds of $1,004,000. Losses (gains) on bond redemption are reported in a special line item at the bottom of the income statement referred to as *Extraordinary Items*. The significance of this classification is discussed in Chapter 14.

BUSINESS INSIGHT
International Perspective

A dramatic example of the importance of bond financing—which literally changed the course of history—is seen in Britain's struggle for supremacy in the 18th and 19th centuries. With only a fraction of the population and wealth of France, Britain ultimately humbled its mightier foe through the use of bonds. Because of its effective central bank and a fair system of collecting taxes, Britain developed the capital markets that enabled its government to issue bonds. Britain was able to borrow money at almost half the cost paid by France and was able to incur more debt as a proportion of the economy than could France. Britain thus could more than match the French navy, raise an army of its own, and lavishly subsidize other armies, eventually destroying Napoleon and his threat to Europe.

Source: "How British Bonds Beat Back Bigger France," *Forbes,* March 13, 1995.

BEFORE YOU GO ON...

◆ **Review It**

1. What entry is made to record the issuance of bonds payable of $1 million at 100? At 96? At 102?
2. Why do bonds sell at a discount? At a premium? At face value?
3. Explain the accounting for redemption of bonds at maturity and before maturity by payment in cash.

◆ **Do It**

A bond amortization table shows (a) interest to be paid $50,000, (b) interest expense to be recorded $52,000, and (c) amortization $2,000. Answer the following questions: (1) Were the bonds sold at a premium or a discount? (2) After recording the interest expense, will the bond carrying value increase or decrease?

Reasoning: To answer the questions you need to know the effects that the amortization of bond discount and bond premium have on bond interest expense and on the carrying value of the bonds. Bond discount amortization increases both bond interest expense and the carrying value of the bonds. Bond premium amortization has the reverse effect.

Solution: The bond amortization table indicates that interest expense is $2,000 greater than the interest paid. This difference is equal to the amortization amount. Thus, the bonds were sold at a discount. The interest entry will decrease Discount on Bonds Payable and increase the carrying value of the bonds.

FINANCIAL STATEMENT PRESENTATION AND ANALYSIS

STUDY OBJECTIVE

8

Identify the requirements for the financial statement presentation and analysis of long-term liabilities.

PRESENTATION

Long-term liabilities are reported in a separate section of the balance sheet immediately following Current Liabilities. An example is shown in Illustration 10-22.

Illustration 10-22 Balance sheet presentation of long-term liabilities

ANY COMPANY Balance Sheet (partial)		
Long-term liabilities		
Bonds payable 10% due in 2009	$1,000,000	
Less: Discount on bonds payable	80,000	$ 920,000
Notes payable, 11%, due in 2015		
and secured by plant assets		500,000
Lease liability		540,000
Total long-term liabilities		$1,960,000

Alternatively, summary data may be presented in the balance sheet with detailed data (such as interest rates, maturity dates, conversion privileges, and assets pledged as collateral) shown in a supporting schedule. The current maturities of long-term debt should be reported as current liabilities if they are to be paid from current assets. This is evident on the General Motors balance sheets in Illustration 10-3 (page 459).

ANALYSIS

Solvency ratios measure the ability of a company to survive over a long period of time. The opening story in this chapter mentioned that although there once were many U.S. automobile manufacturers, only two U.S.-based companies remain today. Many of the others went bankrupt. This highlights the fact that when making a long-term loan or purchasing a company's stock, you must give consideration to a company's solvency.

To reduce the risks associated with having a large amount of debt during an economic downturn, U.S. automobile manufacturers have taken two precautionary steps. First, they have built up large balances of cash and cash equivalents to avoid a cash crisis. Second, recently, they have been reluctant to build new plants or hire new workers to meet their production needs. Instead, they have asked existing workers to put in overtime, or they "outsource" work to other companies. In this way, if an economic downturn follows, they avoid having to make debt payments on idle production plants, and they minimize layoffs.

In an earlier chapter you learned that one measure of a company's solvency is the debt to total assets ratio. This ratio indicates the extent to which a company's debt could be repaid by liquidating its assets. Other measures can also be useful. One such measure is the times interest earned ratio, which provides an indication of a company's ability to meet interest payments as they come due. It is computed by dividing income before interest expense and income taxes by interest expense. It uses income before interest expense and taxes because this number best represents the amount available to pay interest.

We can use the balance sheet information in Illustration 10-3 and the additional information below to calculate solvency ratios for the Automotive and Electronics Divisions of General Motors and the auto industry.

($ in millions)	1998	1997
Net income	$1,534	$5,380
Interest expense	1,050	863
Tax expense	845	155

The debt to total assets ratios and times interest earned ratios for General Motors and averages for the industry are shown in Illustration 10-23.

Illustration 10-23
Solvency ratios

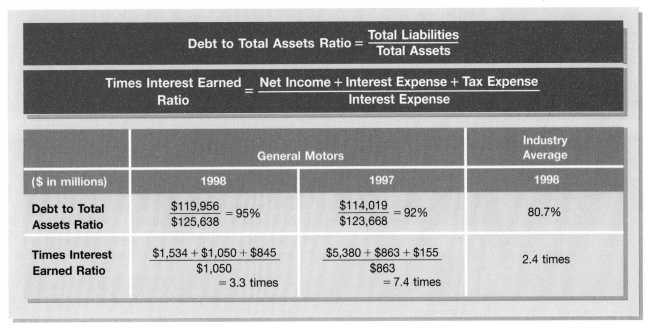

Debt to Total Assets Ratio = $\dfrac{\text{Total Liabilities}}{\text{Total Assets}}$
Times Interest Earned Ratio $= \dfrac{\text{Net Income} + \text{Interest Expense} + \text{Tax Expense}}{\text{Interest Expense}}$

	General Motors		Industry Average
($ in millions)	1998	1997	1998
Debt to Total Assets Ratio	$\dfrac{\$119,956}{\$125,638} = 95\%$	$\dfrac{\$114,019}{\$123,668} = 92\%$	80.7%
Times Interest Earned Ratio	$\dfrac{\$1,534 + \$1,050 + \$845}{\$1,050}$ $= 3.3$ times	$\dfrac{\$5,380 + \$863 + \$155}{\$863}$ $= 7.4$ times	2.4 times

The debt to total assets ratio varies across industries because different capital structures are appropriate for different industries. The debt to assets ratio for all manufacturers of cars and car parts is 80.7%. General Motors' ratio remained relatively constant over this two-year period, which indicates it did not change its mix between debt and equity financing. Its 1998 measure of 95% is higher than the industry average for this measure. General Motors' times interest earned ratio declined from 7.4 times in 1997 to 3.3 times in 1998. This decline was due to a drop in net income without an equivalent drop in interest expense. Even at its 1998 level, however, General Motors is well above the industry average for the times interest earned ratio of 2.4. Thus, this decline should not be a concern to investors at this time.

DECISION TOOLKIT

Decision Checkpoints	Info Needed for Decision	Tool to Use for Decision	How to Evaluate Results
Can the company meet its obligations in the long term?	Interest expense and net income before interest and taxes	Times interest earned ratio $= \dfrac{\text{Net income} + \text{Interest expense} + \text{Tax expense}}{\text{Interest expense}}$	High ratio indicates ability to meet interest payments as scheduled.

OTHER ISSUES IN ANALYSIS

CONTINGENT LIABILITIES

Contingencies are events with uncertain outcomes. For users of financial statements, contingencies are often very important to understanding a company's financial position. A common type of contingency is lawsuits. Suppose, for example, that you were analyzing the financial statements of a cigarette manufacturer and did not consider the possible negative implications of existing unsettled lawsuits. Your analysis of the company's financial position would certainly be misleading. Other common types of contingencies are product warranties and environmental problems.

Accounting rules require that contingencies be disclosed in the notes, and in some cases they must be accrued as liabilities. For example, suppose that Waterford Inc. is sued by a customer for $1 million due to an injury sustained by a defective product. If at December 31 (the company's year-end) the lawsuit had not yet been resolved, how should the company account for this event? If the company can determine **a reasonable estimate** of the expected loss and if it is **probable** it will lose the suit, then the company should accrue for the loss. The loss is recorded by increasing (debiting) a loss account and increasing (crediting) a liability such as Lawsuit Liability. If *both* of these conditions are not met, then the company discloses the basic facts regarding this suit in the notes to its financial statements.

The liabilities associated with contingencies can be material. For example, Procter & Gamble is phasing out its long-time use of promotional coupons, saying that the cost was too high; Exxon was ordered to pay billions of dollars as a result of an Alaskan oil spill; cigarette companies have been trying to negotiate a settlement of all their lawsuits with total payments of hundreds of billions of dollars. The notes to recent financial statements of cigarette manufacturer Phillip Morris contained four and one-half pages of discussion regarding litigation. Illustration 10-24 is an excerpt from the contingency note from the financial statements of General Motors.

GM General Motors

GENERAL MOTORS CORPORATION
Notes to the Financial Statements

GM is subject to potential liability under government regulations and various claims and legal actions which are pending or may be asserted against them. Some of the pending actions purport to be class actions. The aggregate ultimate liability of GM under these government regulations and under these claims and actions was not determinable at December 31, 1998. After discussion with counsel, it is the opinion of management that such liability is not expected to have a material adverse effect on the Corporation's consolidated financial statements.

Illustration 10-24
Contingency note
disclosure

The note suggests that at this time General Motors does not have any outstanding litigation requiring accrual or disclosure. Sometimes analysts make adjustments to the financial statements for unrecorded contingencies that they feel should have been reported as liabilities on the balance sheet.

BUSINESS INSIGHT
Management Perspective

The threat of huge potential liabilities from lawsuits arising from year 2000 (Y2K) computer problems was significantly reduced when Congress and the White House agreed in 1999 on legislation that would limit corporate liability as long as a company had put forth a good effort to eliminate its Y2K problems. This does not mean that companies won't still incur costs related to Y2K failures, or even that some companies won't be sued because they were negligent. The measure was strongly supported by business but was vehemently opposed by trial lawyers.

DECISION TOOLKIT

Decision Checkpoints	Info Needed for Decision	Tool to Use for Decision	How to Evaluate Results
Does the company have any contingent liabilities?	Knowledge of events with uncertain negative outcomes	Notes to financial statements and financial statements	If negative outcomes are possible, determine the probability, the amount of loss, and the potential impact on financial statements.

LEASE LIABILITIES

In most lease contracts, a periodic payment is made by the lessee and is recorded as rent expense in the income statement. The renting of an apartment and the rental of a car at an airport are examples of these types of leases, often referred to as **operating leases. In an operating lease the intent is temporary use of the property by the lessee with continued ownership of the property by the lessor. In some cases, however, the lease contract transfers substantially all the benefits and risks of ownership to the lessee, so that the lease is in**

effect a purchase of the property. This type of lease is called a capital lease because the fair value of the leased asset is *capitalized* by the lessee by recording it on its balance sheet.

Accounting standards have precise criteria that determine whether a lease should be accounted for as a capital lease. The thrust of these criteria is to determine whether the lease transaction more closely resembles a purchase transaction or a rental transaction. This is determined by asking these questions:

- Is it likely that the lessee will end up with the asset at the end of the lease?
- Will the lessee use the asset for most of its useful life?
- Will the payments made by the lessee be approximately the same as the payments it would have made if it had purchased the asset?

If the answer to any of these questions is yes, then the lease should be accounted for as a capital lease. That is, the lessee must record the asset on its books and a related liability for the lease payments. Otherwise, the lessee can account for the transaction as an operating lease, meaning that neither an asset nor liability is shown on its books.

Most lessees do not like to report leases on their balance sheets because the lease liability increases the company's total liabilities. This, in turn, may make it more difficult for the company to obtain needed funds from lenders. **As a result, companies attempt to keep leased assets and lease liabilities off the balance sheet by structuring the lease agreement to avoid meeting the criteria of a capital lease**. Then they account for most of their leases as operating leases. Recall from Chapter 9, for example, that Southwest Airlines leased about a third of its planes, and nearly all of these were accounted for as operating leases. Consequently, a third of the planes used by Southwest Airlines do not show up on its balance sheet, nor do the liabilities related to those planes. This procedure of keeping liabilities off the balance sheet is often referred to as off–balance sheet financing.

Critics of off–balance sheet financing contend that many operating leases represent unavoidable obligations that meet the definition of a liability, and therefore they should be reported as liabilities on the balance sheet. To reduce these concerns, companies are required to report their operating lease obligations for subsequent years in a note. This allows analysts and other financial statement users to adjust a company's financial statements by adding leased assets and lease liabilities if they feel that this treatment is more appropriate. The financial statement note describing General Motors' obligations under operating leases in 1998 is presented in Illustration 10-25.

Illustration 10-25
Operating
lease note

GM General Motors

GENERAL MOTORS CORPORATION
Notes to the Financial Statements

GM had the following minimum commitments under noncancelable operating leases having terms in excess of one year primarily for real property: 1999—$688 million; 2000—$668 million; 2001—$640 million; 2002—$620 million; 2003—$473 million; and $758 million in 2004 and thereafter. Certain of the leases contain escalation clauses and renewal or purchase options. Rental expenses under operating leases were $930 million in 1998, $925 million in 1997, and $853 million in 1996.

If the time value of money is ignored, the total increase in liabilities that would result if these leases were recorded on the balance sheet is $3.8 billion. However, this amount is immaterial relative to General Motors' total liabilities of nearly $120 billion. Thus, the potential unrecorded off-balance sheet liabilities resulting from General Motors' leases do not appear to be a concern.

DECISION TOOLKIT

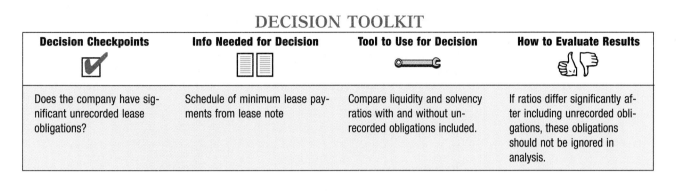

Decision Checkpoints	Info Needed for Decision	Tool to Use for Decision	How to Evaluate Results
Does the company have significant unrecorded lease obligations?	Schedule of minimum lease payments from lease note	Compare liquidity and solvency ratios with and without unrecorded obligations included.	If ratios differ significantly after including unrecorded obligations, these obligations should not be ignored in analysis.

BEFORE YOU GO ON...

◆ Review It

1. What is meant by solvency?
2. What information does the times interest earned ratio provide, and how is the ratio calculated?
3. Where should long-term capital lease obligations be reported in the balance sheet?
4. What are contingent liabilities?

*U*SING THE DECISION TOOLKIT

Ford Motor Company has enjoyed some tremendous successes, including its popular Taurus and Explorer vehicles. Yet observers are looking for the next big hit. Hopes are high for the Excursion, a giant sport utility vehicle designed to compete with General Motors' large sport utility vehicles. Development of a new vehicle costs billions. A flop is financially devastating, and the financial effect is magnified if the company has large amounts of outstanding debt.

The balance sheet provides financial information for the Automotive Division of Ford Motor Company as of December 31, 1998 and 1997. We have chosen to analyze only the Automotive Division rather than the total corporation, which includes Ford's giant financing division. In an actual analysis you would want to analyze the major divisions individually as well as the combined corporation as a whole.

Instructions

1. Evaluate Ford's liquidity using appropriate ratios and compare to those of General Motors and to industry averages.
2. Evaluate Ford's solvency using appropriate ratios and compare to those of General Motors and to industry averages.
3. Comment on Ford's available lines of credit.

**FORD MOTOR COMPANY—
AUTOMOTIVE DIVISION**
Balance Sheets
December 31, 1998 and 1997
(in millions)

Assets	1998	1997
Cash and cash equivalents	$ 3,685	$ 6,316
Short-term investments	20,120	14,519
Accounts receivable, net	2,604	3,097
Inventories	5,656	5,468
Other current assets	6,644	7,447
Total current assets	38,709	36,847
Noncurrent assets	50,035	48,232
Total assets	$88,744	$85,079

Liabilities and Shareholders' Equity		
Current liabilities		
Accounts payable	$13,368	$11,997
Other payables	2,825	2,557
Accrued liabilities	16,925	16,250
Income taxes payable	1,404	1,358
Current maturities of long-term debt	1,121	1,129
Total current liabilities	35,643	33,291
Long-term debt	8,713	7,047
Other noncurrent liabilities	31,702	30,109
Total liabilities	76,058	70,447
Total shareholders' equity	12,686	14,632
Total liabilities and shareholders' equity	$88,744	$85,079

Other Information		
Net income	$22,071	$ 6,920
Tax expense	3,176	3,741
Interest expense	829	788
Available lines of credit (Automotive Division)	8,346	

Solution

1. Ford's liquidity can be measured using the current ratio and acid-test ratio:

	1998	1997
Current ratio	$\dfrac{\$38,709}{\$35,643} = 1.09:1$	$\dfrac{\$36,847}{\$33,291} = 1.11:1$
Acid-test ratio	$\dfrac{\$3,685 + \$20,120 + \$2,604}{\$35,643}$ $= .74:1$	$\dfrac{\$6,316 + \$14,519 + \$3,097}{\$33,291}$ $= .72:1$

Like General Motors', Ford's current ratio hovers right around 1.0:1. These are increasingly common levels for large companies that have reduced the amount of cash, inventory, and receivables they hold. Due to a build-up of short-term investments, Ford's acid-test ratio is nearly as high as its current ratio. As noted earlier, these low current ratios are not necessarily cause for concern, but they do require more careful monitoring. Ford must also make sure to have other short-term financing options available, such as lines of credit.

2. Ford's solvency can be measured with the debt to total assets ratio and the times interest earned ratio:

	1998	**1997**
Debt to total assets ratio	$\dfrac{\$76,058}{\$88,744} = 86\%$	$\dfrac{\$70,447}{\$85,079} = 83\%$
Times interest earned ratio	$\dfrac{\$22,071 + \$829 + \$3,176}{\$829}$	$\dfrac{\$6,920 + \$788 + \$3,741}{\$788}$
	$= 31.5$ times	$= 14.5$ times

The debt to total assets ratio suggests that Ford, like General Motors, relies heavily on debt financing. But its high value for the times interest earned ratio indicates that this debt financing in no way threatens its solvency. It is worth noting that when the automotive and financing divisions of Ford are combined, its debt to total assets ratio increases only slightly to 90%.

3. Ford has available lines of credit of $8.346 billion. This significantly improves its liquidity. The company has tremendous resources available to it, should it face a liquidity crunch.

SUMMARY OF STUDY OBJECTIVES

❶ Explain a current liability and identify the major types of current liabilities. A current liability is a debt that can reasonably be expected to be paid (a) from existing current assets or through the creation of other current liabilities, and (b) within one year or the operating cycle, whichever is longer. The major types of current liabilities are notes payable, accounts payable, sales taxes payable, unearned revenues, and accrued liabilities such as taxes, salaries and wages, and interest payable.

❷ Describe the accounting for notes payable. When a promissory note is interest-bearing, the amount of assets received upon the issuance of the note is generally equal to the face value of the note, and interest expense is accrued over the life of the note. At maturity, the amount paid is equal to the face value of the note plus accrued interest.

❸ Explain the accounting for other current liabilities. Sales taxes payable are recorded at the time the related sales occur. The company serves as a collection agent for the taxing authority. Sales taxes are not an expense to the company. Until employee withholding taxes are remitted to the governmental taxing authorities, they are credited to appropriate liability accounts. Unearned revenues are initially recorded in an unearned revenue account. As the revenue is earned, a transfer from un-

earned revenue to earned revenue occurs. The current maturities of long-term debt should be reported as a current liability in the balance sheet.

❹ Identify the requirements for the financial statement presentation and analysis of current liabilities. The nature and amount of each current liability should be reported in the balance sheet or in schedules in the notes accompanying the statements. The liquidity of a company may be analyzed by computing working capital, the current ratio, and the acid-test ratio.

❺ Explain why bonds are issued and identify the types of bonds. Bonds may be sold to many investors, and they offer the following advantages over common stock: (a) stockholder control is not affected, (b) tax savings result, and (c) earnings per share of common stock may be higher. The following different types of bonds may be issued: secured and unsecured bonds, term and serial bonds, and convertible and callable bonds.

❻ Prepare the entries for the issuance of bonds and interest expense. When bonds are issued, Cash is debited for the cash proceeds and Bonds Payable is credited for the face value of the bonds. In addition, the accounts Premium on Bonds Payable and Discount on Bonds Payable are used to show the bond premium and bond discount, respectively. Bond discount and bond premium are amortized over the life of the bond.

7 *Describe the entries when bonds are redeemed.* When bonds are redeemed at maturity, Cash is credited and Bonds Payable is debited for the face value of the bonds. When bonds are redeemed before maturity, it is necessary to (a) eliminate the carrying value of the bonds at the redemption date, (b) record the cash paid, and (c) recognize the gain or loss on redemption.

8 *Identify the requirements for the financial statement presentation and analysis of long-term liabilities.*

The nature and amount of each long-term debt should be reported in the balance sheet or in schedules in the notes accompanying the statements. The long-run solvency of a company may be analyzed by computing the debt to total assets ratio and the times interest earned ratio. Other factors to consider are contingent liabilities and lease obligations.

DECISION TOOLKIT—A SUMMARY

Decision Checkpoints	Info Needed for Decision	Tool to Use for Decision	How to Evaluate Results
Can the company meet its current obligations?	Cash, accounts receivable, short-term investments, and other highly liquid assets, and current liabilities	$$\text{Acid-test ratio} = \frac{\text{Cash} + \text{Short-term investments} + \text{Net receivables}}{\text{Current liabilities}}$$	Ratio should be compared to others in same industry. High ratio indicates good liquidity.
Can the company obtain short-term financing when necessary?	Available lines of credit, from notes to the financial statements	Compare available lines of credit to current liabilities. Also, evaluate liquidity ratios.	If liquidity ratios are low, then lines of credit should be high to compensate.
Can the company meet its obligations in the long term?	Interest expense and net income before interest and taxes	$$\text{Times interest earned ratio} = \frac{\text{Net income} + \text{Interest expense} + \text{Tax expense}}{\text{Interest expense}}$$	High ratio indicates ability to meet interest payments as scheduled.
Does the company have any contingent liabilities?	Knowledge of events with uncertain negative outcomes	Notes to financial statements and financial statements	If negative outcomes are possible, determine the probability, the amount of loss, and the potential impact on financial statements.
Does the company have significant unrecorded lease obligations?	Schedule of minimum lease payments from lease note	Compare liquidity and solvency ratios with and without unrecorded obligations included.	If ratios differ significantly after including unrecorded obligations, these obligations should not be ignored in analysis.

APPENDIX 10A
EFFECTIVE-INTEREST AMORTIZATION

STUDY OBJECTIVE

9

Contrast the effects of the straight-line and effective-interest methods of amortizing bond discount and bond premium.

The straight-line method of amortization that you studied in the chapter has a conceptual deficiency: It does not completely satisfy the matching principle. Under the straight-line method, interest expense as a percentage of the carrying value of the bonds varies each interest period. This can be seen by using data from the first three interest periods of the bond amortization schedule that was shown in Illustration 10-16:

Semiannual Interest Period	Interest Expense to be Recorded (A)	Bond Carrying Value (B)	Interest Expense as a Percentage of Carrying Value (A) ÷ (B)
1	$52,000	$980,000	5.31%
2	52,000	982,000	5.30%
3	52,000	984,000	5.28%
10	52,000	998,000	5.21%

Illustration 10A-1
Interest percentage rates under straight-line method

Note that interest expense as a percentage of carrying value declines in each interest period. However, to completely comply with the matching principle, interest expense as a percentage of carrying value should not change over the life of the bonds. This percentage, referred to as the effective-interest rate, is established when the bonds are issued and remains constant in each interest period. The effective-interest method of amortization accomplishes this result.

Under the effective-interest method, the amortization of bond discount or bond premium results in periodic interest expense equal to a constant percentage of the carrying value of the bonds. The effective-interest method results in varying amounts of amortization and interest expense per period but a constant percentage rate. The straight-line method results in constant amounts of amortization and interest expense per period but a varying percentage rate.

The following steps are required under the effective-interest method:

1. Compute the **bond interest expense** by multiplying the carrying value of the bonds at the beginning of the interest period by the effective-interest rate.
2. Compute the **bond interest paid** (or accrued) by multiplying the face value of the bonds by the contractual interest rate.
3. Compute the **amortization amount** by determining the difference between the amounts computed in steps (1) and (2).

These steps are graphically depicted in Illustration 10A-2.

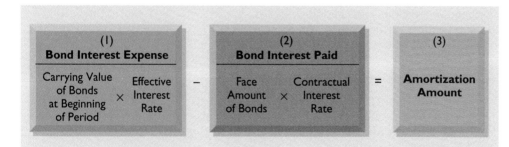

Illustration 10A-2
Computation of amortization using effective-interest method

Helpful Hint Note that the amount of periodic interest expense increases over the life of the bonds when the effective-interest method is used for bonds issued at a discount. The reason is that a constant percentage is applied to an increasing bond carrying value to compute interest expense. The carrying value is increasing because of the amortization of the discount.

Both the straight-line and effective-interest methods of amortization result in the same total amount of interest expense over the term of the bonds. Furthermore, interest expense each interest period is generally comparable in amount. However, **when the amounts are materially different, the effective-interest method is required under generally accepted accounting principles (GAAP).**

AMORTIZING BOND DISCOUNT

To illustrate the effective-interest method of bond discount amortization, assume that Wrightway Corporation issues $100,000 of 10%, five-year bonds on January 1, 2001, with interest payable each July 1 and January 1. The bonds sell for $92,639

(92.639% of face value), which results in bond discount of $7,361 ($100,000 − $92,639) and an effective-interest rate of 12%. (Note that the $92,639 can be proven as shown in Appendix C at the end of this book.) Preparing a bond discount amortization schedule as shown in Illustration 10A-3 facilitates the recording of interest expense and the discount amortization. Note that interest expense as a percentage of carrying value remains constant at 6%.

Illustration 10A-3 Bond discount amortization schedule

| | | (B)
Interest Expense
to Be Recorded | (C)
Discount | (D)
Unamortized | (E)
Bond |
Semiannual Interest Periods	(A) Interest to Be Paid (5% × $100,000)	(6% × Preceding Bond Carrying Value)	Amortization (B) − (A)	Discount (D) − (C)	Carrying Value ($100,000 − D)
Issue date				$7,361	$ 92,639
1	$ 5,000	$ 5,558 (6% × $92,639)	$ 558	6,803	93,197
2	5,000	5,592 (6% × $93,197)	592	6,211	93,789
3	5,000	5,627 (6% × $93,789)	627	5,584	94,416
4	5,000	5,665 (6% × $94,416)	665	4,919	95,081
5	5,000	5,705 (6% × $95,081)	705	4,214	95,786
6	5,000	5,747 (6% × $95,786)	747	3,467	96,533
7	5,000	5,792 (6% × $96,533)	792	2,675	97,325
8	5,000	5,840 (6% × $97,325)	840	1,835	98,165
9	5,000	5,890 (6% × $98,165)	890	945	99,055
10	5,000	5,945* (6% × $99,055)	945	–0–	100,000
	$50,000	$57,361	$7,361		

Column (A) remains constant because the face value of the bonds ($100,000) is multiplied by the semiannual contractual interest rate (5%) each period.
Column (B) is computed as the preceding bond carrying value times the semiannual effective-interest rate (6%).
Column (C) indicates the discount amortization each period.
Column (D) decreases each period until it reaches zero at maturity.
Column (E) increases each period until it equals face value at maturity.

*$2 difference due to rounding.

For the first interest period, the computations of bond interest expense and the bond discount amortization are as follows:

Illustration 10A-4 Computation of bond discount amortization

Bond interest expense ($92,639 × 6%)	$5,558
Bond interest paid ($100,000 × 5%)	5,000
Bond discount amortization	**$ 558**

As a result, the entry to record the payment of interest and amortization of bond discount by Wrightway Corporation on July 1, 2001, is:

A	=	L	+	SE
−5,000		+558		−5,558

July 1	Bond Interest Expense		5,558	
	Discount on Bonds Payable			558
	Cash			5,000
	(To record payment of bond interest and amortization of bond discount)			

For the second interest period, bond interest expense will be $5,592 ($93,197 × 6%), and the discount amortization will be $592. At December 31, the following adjusting entry is made:

Dec. 31	Bond Interest Expense	5,592	
	Discount on Bonds Payable		592
	Bond Interest Payable		5,000
	(To record accrued interest and		
	amortization of bond discount)		

```
A   =   L   +   SE
       +592    −5,592
       +5,000
```

Total bond interest expense for 2001 is $11,150 ($5,558 + $5,592). On January 1, payment of the interest is recorded by a debit to Bond Interest Payable and a credit to Cash.

AMORTIZING BOND PREMIUM

The amortization of bond premium by the effective-interest method is similar to the procedures described for bond discount. As an example, assume that Wrightway Corporation issues $100,000, 10%, five-year bonds on January 1, 2001, with interest payable on July 1 and January 1. In this case, the bonds sell for $108,111, which results in bond premium of $8,111 and an effective-interest rate of 8%. The bond premium amortization schedule is shown in Illustration 10A-5.

Helpful Hint When a bond sells for $108,111, it is quoted as 108.111% of face value. Note that $108,111 can be proven as shown in Appendix C.

Illustration 10A-5 Bond premium amortization schedule

WRIGHTWAY CORPORATION
Bond Premium Amortization
Effective-Interest Method—Semiannual Interest Payments
10% Bonds Issued at 8%

Semiannual Interest Periods	(A) Interest to Be Paid (5% × $100,000)	(B) Interest Expense to Be Recorded (4% × Preceding Bond Carry Value)	(C) Premium Amortization (A) − (B)	(D) Unamortized Premium (D) − (C)	(E) Bond Carrying Value ($100,000 + D)
Issue date				$8,111	$108,111
1	$ 5,000	$ 4,324 (4% × $108,111)	$ 676	7,435	107,435
2	5,000	4,297 (4% × $107,435)	703	6,732	106,732
3	5,000	4,269 (4% × $106,732)	731	6,001	106,001
4	5,000	4,240 (4% × $106,001)	760	5,241	105,241
5	5,000	4,210 (4% × $105,241)	790	4,451	104,451
6	5,000	4,178 (4% × $104,451)	822	3,629	103,629
7	5,000	4,145 (4% × $103,629)	855	2,774	102,774
8	5,000	4,111 (4% × $102,774)	889	1,885	101,885
9	5,000	4,075 (4% × $101,885)	925	960	100,960
10	5,000	4,040* (4% × $100,960)	960	–0–	100,000
	$50,000	$41,889	$8,111		

Column (**A**) remains constant because the face value of the bonds ($100,000) is multiplied by the semiannual contractual interest rate (5%) each period.
Column (**B**) is computed as the carrying value of the bonds times the semiannual effective-interest rate (4%).
Column (**C**) indicates the premium amortization each period.
Column (**D**) decreases each period until it reaches zero at maturity.
Column (**E**) decreases each period until it equals face value at maturity.

*$2 difference due to rounding.

For the first interest period, the computations of bond interest expense and the bond premium amortization are:

Illustration 10A-6
Computation of bond premium amortization

Bond interest paid ($100,000 × 5%)	$5,000
Bond interest expense ($108,111 × 4%)	4,324
Bond premium amortization	**$ 676**

The entry on the first interest date is:

A	=	L	+	SE
−5,000		−676		−4,324

July 1	Bond Interest Expense	4,324	
	Premium on Bonds Payable	676	
	Cash		5,000
	(To record payment of bond interest and amortization of bond premium)		

For the second interest period, interest expense will be $4,297, and the premium amortization will be $703. Total bond interest expense for 2001 is $8,621 ($4,324 + $4,297). Note that the amount of periodic interest expense decreases over the life of the bond when the effective-interest method is applied to bonds issued at a premium. The reason is that a constant percentage is applied to a decreasing bond carrying value to compute interest expense. The carrying value is decreasing because of the amortization of the premium.

SUMMARY OF STUDY OBJECTIVE FOR APPENDIX 10A

9 Contrast the effects of the straight-line and effective-interest methods of amortizing bond discount and bond premium. The straight-line method of amortization results in a constant amount of amortization and interest expense per period but a varying percentage rate. In contrast, the effective-interest method results in varying amounts of amortization and interest expense per period but a constant percentage rate of interest. The effective-interest method generally results in a better matching of expenses with revenues. When the difference between the straight-line and effective-interest method is material, the use of the effective-interest method is required under GAAP.

DEMONSTRATION PROBLEM FOR APPENDIX 10A

Problem-Solving Strategies
1. Bond carrying value at beginning of period times effective-interest rate equals interest expense.
2. Credit to cash (or bond interest payable) is computed by multiplying the face value of the bonds by the contractual interest rate.
3. Bond premium or discount amortization is the difference between (1) and (2).
4. Interest expense increases when the effective-interest method is used for bonds issued at a discount. The reason is that a constant percentage is applied to an increasing book value to compute interest expense.

Gardner Corporation issues $1,750,000, 10-year, 12% bonds on January 1, 2001, at $1,970,000 to yield 10%. The bonds pay semiannual interest July 1 and January 1. Gardner uses the effective-interest method of amortization.

Instructions

(a) Prepare the journal entry to record the issuance of the bonds.
(b) Prepare the journal entry to record the payment of interest on July 1, 2001.

Solution to Demonstration Problem for Appendix 10A

(a) 2001
Jan. 1	Cash	1,970,000	
	Bonds Payable		1,750,000
	Premium on Bonds Payable		220,000
	(To record issuance of bonds at a premium)		

(b) 2001
July 1	Bond Interest Expense	98,500*	
	Premium on Bonds Payable	6,500**	
	Cash		105,000
	To record payment of semiannual interest and amortization of bond premium)		
	*($1,970,000 × 5%)		
	**($105,000 − $98,500)		

ACCOUNTING FOR LONG-TERM NOTES PAYABLE

The use of notes payable in long-term debt financing is quite common. Long-term notes payable are similar to short-term interest-bearing notes payable except that the terms of the notes exceed one year. In periods of unstable interest rates, the interest rate on long-term notes may be tied to changes in the market rate for comparable loans. Examples are the 8.03% adjustable rate notes issued by General Motors and the floating-rate notes issued by American Express Company.

A long-term note may be secured by a document called a **mortgage** that pledges title to specific assets as security for a loan. Mortgage notes payable are widely used in the purchase of homes by individuals and in the acquisition of plant assets by many small and some large companies. For example, approximately 18% of McDonalds' long-term debt relates to mortgage notes on land, buildings, and improvements. Like other long-term notes payable, the mortgage loan terms may stipulate either a fixed or an adjustable interest rate. Typically, the terms require the borrower to make installment payments over the term of the loan. Each payment consists of (1) interest on the unpaid balance of the loan, and (2) a reduction of loan principal. The interest decreases each period, while the portion applied to the loan principal increases.

Mortgage notes payable are recorded initially at face value, and entries are required subsequently for each installment payment. To illustrate, assume that Porter Technology Inc. issues a $500,000, 12%, 20-year mortgage note on December 31, 2001, to obtain needed financing for the construction of a new research laboratory. The terms provide for semiannual installment payments of $33,231 (not including real estate taxes and insurance). The installment payment schedule for the first two years is as follows:

STUDY OBJECTIVE

10

Describe the accounting for long-term notes payable.

Helpful Hint Electronic spreadsheet programs can create a schedule of installment loan payments. This allows you to put in the data for your own mortgage loan and get an illustration that really hits home.

Illustration 10B-1
Mortgage installment payment schedule

Semiannual Interest Period	(A) Cash Payment	(B) Interest Expense (D) × 6%	(C) Reduction of Principal (A) − (B)	(D) Principal Balance (D) − (C)
Issue date				$500,000
1	$33,231	$30,000	$3,231	496,769
2	33,231	29,806	3,425	493,344
3	33,231	29,601	3,630	489,714
4	33,231	29,383	3,848	485,866

The entries to record the mortgage loan and first installment payment are as follows:

Dec. 31	Cash	500,000	
	Mortgage Notes Payable		500,000
	(To record mortgage loan)		

A	=	L	+	SE
+500,000		+500,000		

June 30	Interest Expense	30,000	
	Mortgage Notes Payable	3,231	
	Cash		33,231
	(To record semiannual payment on mortgage)		

A	=	L	+	SE
−33,231		−3,231		−30,000

In the balance sheet, the reduction in principal for the next year is reported as a current liability, and the remaining unpaid principal balance is classified as a long-term liability. At December 31, 2002, the total liability is $493,344, of which $7,478 ($3,630 + $3,848) is current, and $485,866 ($493,344 − $7,478) is long-term.

Summary of Study Objective for Appendix 10B

10 ▸ Describe the accounting for long-term notes payable. Each payment consists of (1) interest on the unpaid balance of the loan, and (2) a reduction of loan principal. The interest decreases each period, while the portion applied to the loan principal increases each period.

Glossary

Acid-test (quick) ratio A measure of a company's immediate short-term liquidity, calculated by dividing the sum of cash, marketable securities, and net receivables by current liabilities. (p. 459)

Bond certificate A legal document that indicates the name of the issuer, the face value of the bonds, and such other data as the contractual interest rate and the maturity date of the bonds. (p. 464)

Bond indenture A legal document that sets forth the terms of the bond issue. (p. 464)

Bonds A form of interest-bearing notes payable issued by corporations, universities, and governmental entities. (p. 461)

Callable bonds Bonds that are subject to retirement at a stated dollar amount prior to maturity at the option of the issuer. (p. 463)

Capital lease A type of lease whose characteristics make it similar to a debt-financed purchase and that is consequently accounted for in that fashion. (p. 478)

Contingencies Events with uncertain outcomes, such as a potential liability that may become an actual liability sometime in the future. (p. 476)

Contractual interest rate Rate used to determine the amount of interest the borrower pays and the investor receives. (p. 464)

Convertible bonds Bonds that permit bondholders to convert them into common stock at their option. (p. 463)

Current liability A debt that can reasonably be expected to be paid (1) from existing current assets or through the creation of other current liabilities, and (2) within one year or the operating cycle, whichever is longer. (p. 452)

Debenture bonds Bonds issued against the general credit of the borrower; also called unsecured bonds. (p. 463)

Discount (on a bond) The difference between the face value of a bond and its selling price, when a bond is sold for less than its face value. (p. 467)

Effective-interest method of amortization A method of amortizing bond discount or bond premium that results in periodic interest expense equal to a constant percentage of the carrying value of the bonds. (p. 483)

Effective-interest rate Rate established when bonds are issued that remains constant in each interest period. (p. 483)

Face value Amount of principal due at the maturity date of the bond. (p. 464)

Line of credit A prearranged agreement between a company and a lender that allows a company to borrow up to an agreed-upon amount. (p. 460)

Long-term liabilities Obligations expected to be paid more than one year in the future. (p. 461)

Market interest rate The rate investors demand for loaning funds to the corporation. (p. 465)

Mortgage bond A bond secured by real estate. (p. 463)

Mortgage note payable A long-term note secured by a mortgage that pledges title to specific units of property as security for the loan. (p. 487)

Notes payable An obligation in the form of a written promissory note. (p. 453)

Off–balance sheet financing The intentional effort by a company to structure its financing arrangements so as to avoid showing liabilities on its books. (p. 478)

Operating lease A contractual arrangement giving the lessee temporary use of the property with continued ownership of the property by the lessor. Accounted for as a rental. (p. 477)

Premium (on a bond) The difference between the selling price and the face value of a bond when a bond is sold for more than its face value. (p. 467)

Present value The value today of an amount to be received at some date in the future after taking into account current interest rates. (p. 465)

Secured bonds Bonds that have specific assets of the issuer pledged as collateral. (p. 463)

Serial bonds Bonds that mature in installments. (p. 463)

Sinking fund bonds Bonds secured by specific assets set aside to retire them. (p. 463)

Straight-line method of amortization A method of amortizing bond discount or bond premium that allocates the same amount to interest expense in each interest period. (p. 469)

Term bonds Bonds that mature at a single specified future date. (p. 463)

Times interest earned ratio A measure of a company's solvency, calculated by dividing income before interest expense and taxes by interest expense. (p. 475)

Unsecured bonds Bonds issued against the general credit of the borrower; also called debenture bonds. (p. 463)

DEMONSTRATION PROBLEM

Snyder Software Inc. successfully developed a new spreadsheet program. However, to produce and market the program, the company needed $2.0 million of additional financing. On January 1, 2001, Snyder borrowed money as follows:

1. Snyder issued $500,000, 11%, 10-year bonds. The bonds sold at face value and pay semiannual interest on January 1 and July 1.
2. Snyder issued $1.0 million, 10%, 10-year bonds for $885,301. Interest is payable semiannually on January 1 and July 1. Snyder uses the straight-line method of amortization.

Instructions

(a) For the 11% bonds, prepare journal entries for these items:
    (1) The issuance of the bonds on January 1, 2001.
    (2) Interest expense on July 1 and December 31, 2001.
    (3) The payment of interest on January 1, 2002.
(b) For the 10-year, 10% bonds:
    (1) Journalize the issuance of the bonds on January 1, 2001.
    (2) Prepare the entry for the redemption of the bonds at 101 on January 1, 2004, after paying the interest due on this date. The carrying value of the bonds at the redemption date was $919,711.

Solution to Demonstration Problem

(a) (1) 2001

Jan. 1	Cash	500,000	
	Bonds Payable		500,000
	(To record issue of 11%, 10-year bonds at face value)		

(2) 2001

July 1	Bond Interest Expense	27,500	
	Cash ($500,000 × .055)		27,500
	(To record payment of semiannual interest)		
Dec. 31	Bond Interest Expense	27,500	
	Bond Interest Payable		27,500
	(To record accrual of semiannual bond interest)		

Problem-Solving Strategy
Interest expense decreases each period because the principal is decreasing each period.

(3) 2002

Jan. 1	Bond Interest Payable	27,500	
	Cash		27,500
	(To record payment of accrued interest)		

(b) (1) 2001

Jan. 1	Cash	885,301	
	Discount on Bonds Payable	114,699	
	Bonds Payable		1,000,000
	(To record issuance of bonds at a discount)		

	(2) 2004			
Jan. 1	Bonds Payable		1,000,000	
	Loss on Bond Redemption		90,289*	
	Discount on Bonds Payable			80,289
	Cash			1,010,000
	(To record redemption of bonds at 101)			
	*($1,010,000 − $919,711)			

Note: All Questions, Exercises, and Problems marked with an asterisk relate to material in the appendixes to the chapter.

SELF-STUDY QUESTIONS

Answers are at the end of the chapter.

(SO 1) 1. The time period for classifying a liability as current is one year or the operating cycle, whichever is:
(a) longer.　(c) probable.
(b) shorter.　(d) possible.

(SO 1) 2. To be classified as a current liability, a debt must be expected to be paid:
(a) out of existing current assets.
(b) by creating other current liabilities.
(c) within 2 years.
(d) Either (a) or (b)

(SO 2) 3. Julie Gilbert Company borrows $88,500 on September 1, 2001, from Sandwich State Bank by signing an $88,500, 12%, one-year note. What is the accrued interest at December 31, 2001?
(a) $2,655.　(c) $4,425.
(b) $3,540.　(d) $10,620.

(SO 3) 4. Reeves Company has total proceeds from sales of $4,515. If the proceeds include sales taxes of 5%, what is the amount to be credited to Sales?
(a) $4,000.
(b) $4,300.
(c) $4,289.25.
(d) The correct answer is not given.

(SO 4) 5. Which of the following would *not* be included in the numerator of the acid-test ratio?
(a) Accounts receivable.
(b) Cash.
(c) Short-term investments.
(d) Inventory.

(SO 4) 6. Which of the following is *not* a measure of liquidity?
(a) Debt to total assets ratio.
(b) Working capital.
(c) Current ratio.
(d) Acid-test ratio.

(SO 5) 7. What term is used for bonds that are unsecured?
(a) *Callable* bonds.
(b) *Indenture* bonds.

(c) *Debenture* bonds.
(d) *Sinking fund* bonds.

(SO 6) 8. Karson Inc. issues 10-year bonds with a maturity value of $200,000. If the bonds are issued at a premium, this indicates that:
(a) the contractual interest rate exceeds the market interest rate.
(b) the market interest rate exceeds the contractual interest rate.
(c) the contractual interest rate and the market interest rate are the same.
(d) no relationship exists between the two rates.

(SO 6) 9. On January 1 Hurley Corporation issues $500,000, 5-year, 12% bonds at 96 with interest payable on July 1 and January 1. The entry on July 1 to record payment of bond interest and the amortization of bond discount using the straight-line method will include a:
(a) debit to Interest Expense, $30,000.
(b) debit to Interest Expense, $60,000.
(c) credit to Discount on Bonds Payable, $4,000.
(d) credit to Discount on Bonds Payable, $2,000.

(SO 6) 10. For the bonds issued in question 9, what is the carrying value of the bonds at the end of the third interest period?
(a) $486,000.　(c) $472,000.
(b) $488,000.　(d) $464,000.

(SO 7) 11. Gester Corporation retires its $100,000 face value bonds at 105 on January 1, following the payment of semiannual interest. The carrying value of the bonds at the redemption date is $103,745. The entry to record the redemption will include a:
(a) credit of $3,745 to Loss on Bond Redemption.
(b) debit of $3,745 to Premium on Bonds Payable.
(c) credit of $1,255 to Gain on Bond Redemption.
(d) debit of $5,000 to Premium on Bonds Payable.

(SO 8) 12. In a recent year Kennedy Corporation had net income of $150,000, interest expense of $30,000, and tax expense of $20,000. What was Kennedy Corporation's times interest earned ratio for the year?

(a) 5.00.   (c) 6.66.

(b) 4.00.   (d) 7.50.

(SO 9) *13. On January 1, Jean Loptein Inc. issued $1,000,000, 9% bonds for $939,000. The market rate of interest for these bonds is 10%. Interest is payable annually on December 31. Jean Loptein uses the effective-interest method of amortizing bond discount. At the end of the first year, Jean Loptein should report unamortized bond discount of:

(a) $54,900.   (c) $51,610.

(b) $57,100.   (d) $51,000.

*14. On January 1, Cleopatra Corporation issued   (SO 9) $1,000,000, 14%, 5-year bonds with interest payable on July 1 and January 1. The bonds sold for $1,098,540. The market rate of interest for these bonds was 12%. On the first interest date, using the effective-interest method, the debit entry to Bond Interest Expense is for:

(a) $60,000.   (c) $65,912.

(b) $76,898.   (d) $131,825.

QUESTIONS

1. Li Feng believes a current liability is a debt that can be expected to be paid in one year. Is Li correct? Explain.

2. Rio Grande Company obtains $25,000 in cash by signing a 9%, 6-month, $25,000 note payable to First Bank on July 1. Rio Grande's fiscal year ends on September 30. What information should be reported for the note payable in the annual financial statements?

3. (a) Your roommate says, "Sales taxes are reported as an expense in the income statement." Do you agree? Explain.

   (b) Hard Walk Cafe has cash proceeds from sales of $10,400. This amount includes $400 of sales taxes. Give the entry to record the proceeds.

4. Aurora University sold 10,000 season football tickets at $90 each for its five-game home schedule. What entries should be made (a) when the tickets are sold and (b) after each game?

5. Identify three taxes commonly withheld by the employer from an employee's gross pay.

6. (a) Identify three taxes commonly paid by employers on employees' salaries and wages.

   (b) Where in the financial statements does the employer report taxes withheld from employees' pay?

7. (a) What are long-term liabilities? Give two examples.

   (b) What is a bond?

8. (a) As a source of long-term financing, what are the major advantages of bonds over common stock?

   (b) What are the major disadvantages in using bonds for long-term financing?

9. Contrast these types of bonds:

   (a) Secured and unsecured.

   (b) Term and serial.

   (c) Convertible and callable.

10. Explain each of these important terms in issuing bonds:

   (a) Face value.

   (b) Contractual interest rate.

   (c) Bond indenture.

   (d) Bond certificate.

11. (a) What is a convertible bond?

   (b) Discuss the advantages of a convertible bond from the standpoint of the bondholders and of the issuing corporation.

12. Describe the two major obligations incurred by a company when bonds are issued.

13. Assume that Stoney Inc. sold bonds with a par value of $100,000 for $104,000. Was the market interest rate equal to, less than, or greater than the bonds' contractual interest rate? Explain.

14. Barbara Secord and Jack Dalton are discussing how the market price of a bond is determined. Barbara believes that the market price of a bond is solely a function of the amount of the principal payment at the end of the term of a bond. Is she right? Discuss.

15. If a 10%, 10-year, $600,000 bond is issued at par and interest is paid semiannually, what is the amount of the interest payment at the end of the first semiannual period?

16. If the Bonds Payable account has a balance of $900,000 and the Discount on Bonds Payable account has a balance of $40,000, what is the carrying value of the bonds?

17. Which accounts are debited and which are credited if a bond issue originally sold at a premium is redeemed before maturity at 97 immediately following the payment of interest?

18. Explain the straight-line method of amortizing discount and premium on bonds payable.

19. Jennifer Brent Corporation issues $200,000 of 8%, 5-year bonds on January 1, 2001, at 104. Assuming that the straight-line method is used to amortize the premium, what is the total amount of interest expense for 2001?

20. ⊙━━━━C

   (a) In general, what are the requirements for the financial statement presentation of long-term liabilities?

   (b) What ratios may be computed to evaluate a company's liquidity and solvency?

21. Michael Feldman says that liquidity and solvency are the same thing. Is he correct? If not, how do they differ?

22. Tom Dodge needs a few new trucks for his business. He is considering buying the trucks but is concerned that the additional debt he will need to borrow will make his liquidity and solvency ratios look bad. What options does he have other than purchasing the trucks, and how will these options affect his financial statements?

23. Lincoln Corporation has a current ratio of 1.1. Joe Investor has always been told that a corporation's current ratio should exceed 2.0. Lincoln argues that its ratio is low because it has a minimal amount of inventory on hand so as to reduce operating costs. Lincoln also points out that it has significant available lines of credit. Is Joe still correct? What other measures might he check?

24. What criteria must be met before a contingency must be recorded as a liability? How should the contingency be disclosed if the criteria are not met?

25. What is the primary difference between the nature of an operating lease and a capital lease? What is the difference in how they are recorded?

26. What are the implications for analysis if a company has significant operating leases?

*27. Kate Winslet is discussing the advantages of the effective-interest method of bond amortization with her accounting staff. What do you think Kate is saying?

*28. Summit Corporation issues $400,000 of 9%, 5-year bonds on January 1, 2001, at 104. If Summit uses the effective-interest method in amortizing the premium, will the annual interest expense increase or decrease over the life of the bonds? Explain.

BRIEF EXERCISES

Identify whether obligations are current liabilities.
(SO 1)

BE10-1 Fresno Company has these obligations at December 31: (a) a note payable for $100,000 due in 2 years, (b) a 10-year mortgage payable of $200,000 payable in ten $20,000 annual payments, (c) interest payable of $15,000 on the mortgage, and (d) accounts payable of $60,000. For each obligation, indicate whether it should be classified as a current liability.

Prepare entries for an interest-bearing note payable.
(SO 2)

BE10-2 Romez Company borrows $60,000 on July 1 from the bank by signing a $60,000, 10%, 1-year note payable. Prepare the journal entries to record (a) the proceeds of the note and (b) accrued interest at December 31, assuming adjusting entries are made only at the end of the year.

Compute and record sales taxes payable.
(SO 3)

BE10-3 Grandy Auto Supply does not segregate sales and sales taxes at the time of sale. The register total for March 16 is $9,975. All sales are subject to a 5% sales tax. Compute sales taxes payable and make the entry to record sales taxes payable and sales.

Prepare entries for unearned revenues.
(SO 3)

BE10-4 Outstanding University sells 3,000 season basketball tickets at $60 each for its 12-game home schedule. Give the entry to record (a) the sale of the season tickets and (b) the revenue earned by playing the first home game.

Compare bond financing to stock financing.
(SO 5)

BE10-5 Olga Inc. is considering these two alternatives to finance its construction of a new $2 million plant:
(a) Issuance of 200,000 shares of common stock at the market price of $10 per share.
(b) Issuance of $2 million, 8% bonds at face value.
Complete the table and indicate which alternative is preferable.

	Issue Stock	**Issue Bond**
Income before interest and taxes	$1,000,000	$1,000,000
Interest expense from bonds	_____	_____
Income before income taxes		
Income tax expense (30%)	_____	_____
Net income	$_____	$_____
Outstanding shares	_____	700,000
Earnings per share	$_____	$_____

BE10-6 Keystone Corporation issued 1,000 9%, 5-year, $1,000 bonds dated January 1, 2001, at 100.

(a) Prepare the journal entry to record the sale of these bonds on January 1, 2001.

(b) Prepare the journal entry to record the first interest payment on July 1, 2001 (interest payable semiannually), assuming no previous accrual of interest.

(c) Prepare the adjusting journal entry on December 31, 2001, to record interest expense.

Prepare journal entries for bonds issued at face value.
(SO 6)

BE10-7 The balance sheet for Hathaway Company reports the following information on July 1, 2001:

Prepare journal entry for redemption of bonds.
(SO 7)

HATHAWAY COMPANY
Balance Sheet (partial)

Long-term liabilities		
Bonds payable	$1,000,000	
Less: Discount on bonds payable	60,000	$940,000

Hathaway decides to redeem these bonds at 102 after paying semiannual interest. Prepare the journal entry to record the redemption on July 1, 2001.

BE10-8 Dominic Company issues $2 million, 10-year, 9% bonds at 98, with interest payable on July 1 and January 1. The straight-line method is used to amortize bond discount.

(a) Prepare the journal entry to record the sale of these bonds on January 1, 2001.

(b) Prepare the journal entry to record interest expense and bond discount amortization on July 1, 2001, assuming no previous accrual of interest.

Prepare journal entries for bonds issued at a discount.
(SO 6)

BE10-9 Hercules Inc. issues $5 million, 5-year, 10% bonds at 103, with interest payable on July 1 and January 1. The straight-line method is used to amortize bond premium.

(a) Prepare the journal entry to record the sale of these bonds on January 1, 2001.

(b) Prepare the journal entry to record interest expense and bond premium amortization on July 1, 2001, assuming no previous accrual of interest.

Prepare journal entries for bonds issued at a premium.
(SO 6)

BE10-10 Presented here are long-term liability items for Warner Company at December 31, 2001. Prepare the long-term liabilities section of the balance sheet for Warner Company.

Prepare statement presentation of long-term liabilities.
(SO 8)

Bonds payable, due 2005	$900,000
Notes payable, due 2003	80,000
Discount on bonds payable	45,000

BE10-11 The 1998 **Reebok** financial statements contain the following selected data (in millions):

Analyze liquidity and solvency.
(SO 4, 8)

Current assets	$1,362	Interest expense	$61
Total assets	1,740	Income taxes	12
Current liabilities	612	Net income	24
Total liabilities	1,216		
Cash	180		
Short-term investments	0		
Accounts receivable	518		

Compute these values:

(a) Working capital.   (d) Debt to total assets ratio.

(b) Current ratio.   (e) Times interest earned ratio.

(c) Acid-test ratio.

BE10-12 At December 31, 1998, **Southwest Airlines** reported $3,006,092,000 in required payments on operating leases. If these assets had been purchased with debt, assets and liabilities would rise by approximately $1,500,000,000. Southwest's total assets in this year were $4,715,996,000, and total liabilities were $2,318,078,000.

(a) Calculate Southwest's debt to assets ratio, first using the figures as reported, and then after increasing assets and liabilities for the unrecorded operating leases.

Calculate debt to total assets ratio; discuss effect of operating leases on solvency.
(SO 8)

(b) Discuss the potential effect of these operating leases on your assessment of Southwest's solvency.

*Use effective-interest method
of bond amortization.
(SO 9)*

***BE10-13** Presented below is the partial bond discount amortization schedule for Closet Corp., which uses the effective-interest method of amortization.

Semiannual Interest Periods	Interest to Be Paid	Interest Expense to Be Recorded	Discount Amortization	Unamortized Discount	Bond Carrying Value
Issue date				$62,311	$937,689
1	$45,000	$46,884	$1,884	60,427	939,573
2	45,000	46,979	1,979	58,448	941,552

Instructions
(a) Prepare the journal entry to record the payment of interest and the discount amortization at the end of period 1.
(b) [icon] Explain why interest expense is greater than interest paid.
(c) [icon] Explain why interest expense will increase each period.

EXERCISES

*Prepare entries for interest-bearing notes.
(SO 2)*

E10-1 Jim Eakins and Tom Zedek borrowed $15,000 on an 8-month, 8% note from Garden State Bank to open their business, EZ's Coffee House. The money was borrowed on May 1, 2001.

Instructions
(a) Prepare the entry to record the receipt of the funds from the loan.
(b) Prepare the entry to accrue the interest on May 31.
(c) Assuming adjusting entries are made at the end of each month, determine the balance relating to this note in the interest payable account at December 31, 2001.
(d) Prepare the entry required on January 1, 2002, when the loan is paid back.

*Prepare entries for interest-bearing notes.
(SO 2)*

E10-2 On May 15, Maranga's Outback Clothiers borrowed some money on a 4-month note to provide cash during the slow season of the year. The interest rate on the note was 7%. At the time the note was due, the amount of interest owed was $294.

Instructions
(a) Determine the amount borrowed by Maranga's.
(b) Assume the amount borrowed was $18,500. What was the interest rate if the amount of interest owed was $740?
(c) Prepare the entry for the initial borrowing and the repayment for the facts in part (a).

*Journalize sales and related taxes.
(SO 3)*

E10-3 In providing accounting services to small businesses, you encounter the following situations pertaining to cash sales:
1. Chan Company rings up sales and sales taxes separately on its cash register. On April 10 the register totals are sales $25,000 and sales taxes $1,800.
2. Dragon Company does not segregate sales and sales taxes. Its register total for April 15 is $13,780, which includes a 6% sales tax.

Instructions
Prepare the entries to record the sales transactions and related taxes for (a) Chan Company and (b) Dragon Company.

*Journalize payroll entries.
(SO 3)*

E10-4 During the month of March, WaterBabies Company's employees earned wages of $70,000. Withholdings related to these wages were $4,500 for Social Security (FICA), $7,500 for federal income tax, $2,200 for state income tax, and $500 for union dues. The company incurred no cost related to these earnings for federal unemployment tax, but incurred $700 for state unemployment tax.

Instructions
Prepare the following journal entries.
(a) Prepare the necessary March 31 journal entry to record wages expense and wages payable. Assume that wages earned during March will be paid during April.
(b) Prepare the entry to record the company's payroll tax expense.

E10-5   The Bundoora Desert Cats' season tickets are priced at $230 and include 23 games. Revenue is recognized after each game is played. When the season began, the amount credited to Unearned Season Ticket Revenue was $1,023,500. By the end of October, $756,500 of the Unearned Season Ticket Revenue had been recorded as earned.

Journalize unearned revenue transactions.
(SO 3)

Instructions
(a) How many season tickets did Bundoora sell?
(b) How many home games had Bundoora played by the end of October?
(c) Prepare the entry for the initial recording of the Unearned Season Ticket Revenue.
(d) Prepare the entry to recognize the revenue after the first home game had been played.

E10-6   Flypaper Airlines is considering these two alternatives for financing the purchase of a fleet of airplanes:
1. Issue 60,000 shares of common stock at $45 per share. (Cash dividends have not been paid nor is the payment of any contemplated.)
2. Issue 13%, 10-year bonds at face value for $2,700,000.

Compare issuance of stock financing to issuance of bond financing.
(SO 5)

It is estimated that the company will earn $800,000 before interest and taxes as a result of this purchase. The company has an estimated tax rate of 30% and has 90,000 shares of common stock outstanding prior to the new financing.

Instructions
Determine the effect on net income and earnings per share for (a) issuing stock and (b) issuing bonds.

E10-7   On January 1 Montana Company issued $100,000, 10%, 10-year bonds at face value. Interest is payable semiannually on July 1 and January 1. Interest is not accrued on June 30.

Prepare journal entries for issuance of bonds and payment and accrual of interest.
(SO 6)

Instructions
Prepare journal entries to record these events:
(a) The issuance of the bonds.
(b) The payment of interest on July 1.
(c) The accrual of interest on December 31.

E10-8   Whitewater Company issued $300,000, 9%, 20-year bonds on January 1, 2001, at 103. Interest is payable semiannually on July 1 and January 1. Whitewater uses straight-line amortization for bond premium or discount. Interest is not accrued on June 30.

Prepare journal entries to record issuance of bonds, payment of interest, amortization of premium, and redemption at maturity.
(SO 6, 7)

Instructions
Prepare the journal entries to record these events:
(a) The issuance of the bonds.
(b) The payment of interest and the premium amortization on July 1, 2001.
(c) The accrual of interest and the premium amortization on December 31, 2001.
(d) The redemption of the bonds at maturity, assuming interest for the last interest period has been paid and recorded.

E10-9   Teacher Company issued $220,000, 11%, 10-year bonds on December 31, 2000, for $210,000. Interest is payable semiannually on June 30 and December 31. Teacher uses the straight-line method to amortize bond premium or discount.

Prepare journal entries to record issuance of bonds, payment of interest, amortization of discount, and redemption at maturity.
(SO 6, 7)

Instructions
Prepare the journal entries to record these events:
(a) The issuance of the bonds.
(b) The payment of interest and the discount amortization on June 30, 2001.
(c) The payment of interest and the discount amortization on December 31, 2001.
(d) The redemption of the bonds at maturity, assuming interest for the last interest period has been paid and recorded.

Prepare journal entries for redemption of bonds.
(SO 7)

E10-10 The situations presented here are independent.

Instructions

For each situation prepare the appropriate journal entry for the redemption of the bonds.

(a) Price Corporation retired $130,000 face value, 12% bonds on June 30, 2001, at 102. The carrying value of the bonds at the redemption date was $122,500. The bonds pay semiannual interest, and the interest payment due on June 30, 2001, has been made and recorded.

(b) Coopers, Inc., retired $180,000 face value, 12.5% bonds on June 30, 2001, at 98. The carrying value of the bonds at the redemption date was $183,000. The bonds pay semiannual interest, and the interest payment due on June 30, 2001, has been made and recorded.

Prepare statement presentation of long-term liabilities.
(SO 8)

E10-11 The adjusted trial balance for Montreal Corporation at the end of the current year contained these accounts:

Bond Interest Payable	$ 9,000
Note Payable, due 2005	59,500
Bonds Payable, due 2010	160,000
Premium on Bonds Payable	41,000

Instructions

(a) Prepare the long-term liabilities section of the balance sheet.

(b) Indicate the proper balance sheet classification for the account(s) listed above that do not belong in the long-term liabilities section.

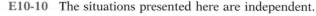

Calculate liquidity and solvency ratios; discuss impact of unrecorded obligations on liquidity and solvency.
(SO 4, 8)

E10-12 **McDonald's** 1998 financial statements contain the following selected data (in millions):

Current assets	$ 1,309	Interest expense	$ 414
Total assets	19,784	Income taxes	757
Current liabilities	2,497	Net income	1,550
Total liabilities	10,260		
Cash	299		
Accounts receivable	609		
Short-term investments	0		

Instructions

(a) Compute these values:

  (1) Working capital.   (4) Debt to total assets ratio.

  (2) Current ratio.   (5) Times interest earned ratio.

  (3) Acid-test ratio.

(b) The notes to McDonald's financial statements show that subsequent to 1998 the company will have future minimum lease payments under operating leases of $7,366.9 million. Discuss the implications of these unrecorded obligations for the analysis of McDonald's liquidity and solvency.

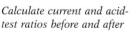

Calculate current and acid-test ratios before and after paying accounts payable.
(SO 4)

E10-13 The following financial data were reported by **Minnesota Mining and Manufacturing (3M)** for 1998 and 1997 ($ in millions):

MINNESOTA MINING AND MANUFACTURING
Balance Sheet (partial)

	1998	1997
Current assets		
Cash and cash equivalents	$ 211	$ 230
Short-term investments	237	247
Accounts receivable, net	2,666	2,434
Inventories	2,219	2,399
Other current assets	985	858
Total current assets	6,318	6,168
Current liabilities	4,386	3,983

Instructions

(a) Calculate the current and acid-test ratios for 3M for 1998 and 1997.

(b) Suppose that at the end of 1998 3M management used $200 million cash to pay off $200 million of accounts payable. How would its current ratio and acid-test ratio change?

*E10-14   Quebec Corporation issued $260,000, 9%, 10-year bonds on January 1, 2001, for $243,799. This price resulted in an effective interest rate of 10% on the bonds. Interest is payable semiannually on July 1 and January 1. Quebec uses the effective-interest method to amortize bond premium or discount. Interest is not accrued on June 30.

Prepare journal entries for issuance of bonds, payment of interest, and amortization of discount using effective-interest method.
(SO 9)

Instructions
Prepare the journal entries to record (round to the nearest dollar):
(a) The issuance of the bonds.
(b) The payment of interest and the discount amortization on July 1, 2001.
(c) The accrual of interest and the discount amortization on December 31, 2001.

*E10-15   Detroit Company issued $180,000, 11%, 10-year bonds on January 1, 2001, for $191,216. This price resulted in an effective interest rate of 10% on the bonds. Interest is payable semiannually on July 1 and January 1. Detroit uses the effective-interest method to amortize bond premium or discount. Interest is not accrued on June 30.

Prepare journal entries for issuance of bonds, payment of interest, and amortization of premium using effective-interest method.
(SO 9)

Instructions
Prepare the journal entries (rounded to the nearest dollar) to record:
(a) The issuance of the bonds.
(b) The payment of interest and the premium amortization on July 1, 2001.
(c) The accrual of interest and the premium amortization on December 31, 2001.

*E10-16   Peyton Co. receives $110,000 when it issues a $110,000, 10%, mortgage note payable to finance the construction of a building at December 31, 2001. The terms provide for semiannual installment payments of $7,500 on June 30 and December 31.

Prepare journal entries to record mortgage note and installment payments.
(SO 10)

Instructions
Prepare the journal entries to record the mortgage loan and the first two installment payments.

PROBLEMS: SET A

P10-1A   On January 1, 2001, the ledger of Malaga Company contained these liability accounts:

Prepare current liability entries, adjusting entries, and current liability section.
(SO 1, 2, 3)

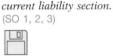

Accounts Payable	$42,500
Sales Taxes Payable	6,600
Unearned Service Revenue	19,000

During January the following selected transactions occurred:

Jan.   1   Borrowed $15,000 in cash from Midland Bank on a 4-month, 8%, $15,000 note.
      5   Sold merchandise for cash totaling $7,800, which includes 4% sales taxes.
      12   Provided services for customers who had made advance payments of $10,000. (Credit Service Revenue.)
      14   Paid state treasurer's department for sales taxes collected in December 2000, $6,600.
      20   Sold 500 units of a new product on credit at $52 per unit, plus 4% sales tax.

During January the company's employees earned wages of $60,000. Withholdings related to these wages were $4,000 for Social Security (FICA), $5,000 for federal income tax, and $1,500 for state income tax. The company owed no money related to these earnings for federal or state unemployment tax. Assume that wages earned during January will be paid during February. No entry had been recorded for wages or payroll tax expense as of January 31.

Instructions
(a) Journalize the January transactions.
(b) Journalize the adjusting entries at January 31 for the outstanding note payable and for wages expense and payroll tax expense.
(c) Prepare the current liability section of the balance sheet at January 31, 2001. Assume no change in Accounts Payable.

P10-2A   Cling-on Company sells rock-climbing products and also operates an indoor climbing facility for climbing enthusiasts. During the last part of 2001, Cling-on had the following transactions related to notes payable:

Journalize and post note transactions; show balance sheet presentation.
(SO 2, 4)

Sept. 1 Issued a $16,000 note to Black Diamond to purchase inventory. The note payable bears interest of 9% and is due in 3 months.

Sept. 30 Recorded accrued interest for the Black Diamond note.

Oct. 1 Issued a $10,000, 12%, 2-month note to Montpelier Bank to finance the building of a new climbing area for advanced climbers.

Oct. 31 Recorded accrued interest for the Black Diamond note and the Montpelier Bank note.

Nov. 1 Issued an $18,000 note and paid $8,000 cash to purchase a vehicle to transport clients to nearby climbing sites as part of a new series of climbing classes. This note bears interest of 14% and matures in 12 months.

Nov. 30 Recorded accrued interest for the Black Diamond note, the Montpelier Bank note, and the vehicle note.

Dec. 1 Paid principal and interest on the Black Diamond note.

Dec. 31 Recorded accrued interest for the Montpelier Bank note and the vehicle note.

Instructions

(a) Prepare journal entries for the transactions noted above.

(b) Post the above entries to the Notes Payable, Interest Payable, and Interest Expense accounts. (Use T accounts.)

(c) Show the balance sheet presentation of notes payable and interest payable at December 31.

(d) How much interest expense relating to notes payable did Cling-on Company incur during the year?

Prepare journal entries to record interest payments, discount amortization, and redemption of bonds.
(SO 6, 7)

P10-3A The following section is taken from Jamaica Corp.'s balance sheet at December 31, 2001:

Current liabilities		
Bond interest payable (for 6 months		
from July 1 to December 31)		$ 132,000
Long-term liabilities		
Bonds payable, 11%, due January 1, 2012	$2,400,000	
Less: Discount on bonds payable	42,000	2,358,000

Interest is payable semiannually on January 1 and July 1. The bonds are callable on any semiannual interest date. Jamaica uses straight-line amortization for any bond premium or discount. From December 31, 2001, the bonds will be outstanding for an additional 10 years (120 months). Assume no interest is accrued on June 30.

Instructions

(Round all computations to the nearest dollar.)

(a) Journalize the payment of bond interest on January 1, 2002.

(b) Prepare the entry to amortize bond discount and to pay the interest due on July 1, 2002.

(c) Assume on July 1, 2002, after paying interest, that Jamaica Corp. calls bonds having a face value of $800,000. The call price is 104. Record the redemption of the bonds.

(d) Prepare the adjusting entry at December 31, 2002, to amortize bond discount and to accrue interest on the remaining bonds.

Prepare journal entries to record issuance of bonds, interest, and amortization of bond premium and discount.
(SO 6, 8)

P10-4A Durango Corporation sold $1,500,000, 8%, 10-year bonds on January 1, 2001. The bonds were dated January 1, 2001, and pay interest on July 1 and January 1. Durango Corporation uses the straight-line method to amortize bond premium or discount. Assume no interest is accrued on June 30.

Instructions

(a) Prepare all the necessary journal entries to record the issuance of the bonds and bond interest expense for 2001, assuming that the bonds sold at 104.

(b) Prepare journal entries as in part (a) assuming that the bonds sold at 98.

(c) Show the balance sheet presentation for the bond issue at December 31, 2001 using (1) the 104 selling price, and then (2) the 98 selling price.

P10-5A J. Downey Co. sold $5,000,000, 9%, 5-year bonds on January 1, 2001. The bonds were dated January 1, 2001, and pay interest on July 1 and January 1. The company uses straight-line amortization on bond premiums and discounts. Financial statements are prepared annually.

Prepare journal entries to record issuance of bonds, interest, and amortization of bond premium and discount.
(SO 6, 7, 8)

Instructions
(a) Prepare the journal entries to record the issuance of the bonds assuming they sold at:
   (1) 103.
   (2) 98.
(b) Prepare amortization tables for both assumed sales for the first three interest payments.
(c) Prepare the journal entries to record interest expense for 2001 under both assumed sales.
(d) Show the balance sheet presentation for both assumed sales at December 31, 2001.

P10-6A Thompson Company sold $4,000,000, 9%, 20-year bonds on January 1, 2001. The bonds were dated January 1, 2001, and pay interest on June 30 and December 31. The bonds were sold at 96. Assume no interest is accrued on June 30.

Prepare journal entries to record issuance of bonds, show balance sheet presentation, and record bond redemption.
(SO 6, 8)

Instructions
(a) Prepare the journal entry to record the issuance of the bonds on January 1, 2001.
(b) At December 31, 2001, $8,000 of the bond discount had been amortized. Show the balance sheet presentation of the bond liability at December 31, 2001. (Assume that interest has been paid.)
(c) At December 31, 2002, when the carrying value of the bonds was $3,856,000, the company redeemed the bonds at 102. Record the redemption of the bonds assuming that interest for the year had already been paid.

*P10-7A On July 1, 2001, Global Satellites Corporation issued $1,200,000 face value, 9%, 10-year bonds at $1,125,227. This price resulted in an effective-interest rate of 10% on the bonds. Global uses the effective-interest method to amortize bond premium or discount. The bonds pay semiannual interest July 1 and January 1.

Prepare journal entries to record issuance of bonds, payment of interest, and amortization of bond discount using effective-interest method.
(SO 9)

Instructions
(Round all computations to the nearest dollar.)
(a) Prepare the journal entry to record the issuance of the bonds on July 1, 2001.
(b) Prepare an amortization table through December 31, 2002 (three interest periods) for this bond issue.
(c) Prepare the journal entry to record the accrual of interest and the amortization of the discount on December 31, 2001.
(d) Prepare the journal entry to record the payment of interest and the amortization of the discount on July 1, 2002.
(e) Prepare the journal entry to record the accrual of interest and the amortization of the discount on December 31, 2002.

*P10-8A On July 1, 2001, Amoco Imperial Company issued $2,000,000 face value, 12%, 10-year bonds at $2,249,245. This price resulted in a 10% effective-interest rate on the bonds. Amoco Imperial uses the effective-interest method to amortize bond premium or discount. The bonds pay semiannual interest on each July 1 and January 1.

Prepare journal entries to record issuance of bonds, payment of interest, and amortization of premium using effective-interest method. In addition, answer questions.
(SO 9)

Instructions
(a) Prepare the journal entries to record the following transactions:
   (1) The issuance of the bonds on July 1, 2001.
   (2) The accrual of interest and the amortization of the premium on December 31, 2001.
   (3) The payment of interest and the amortization of the premium on July 1, 2002.
   (4) The accrual of interest and the amortization of the premium on December 31, 2002.
(b) Show the proper balance sheet presentation for the liability for bonds payable on the December 31, 2002, balance sheet.
(c) ▭▭▭▷ Provide the answers to the following questions in letter form.
   (1) What amount of interest expense is reported for 2002?

(2) Would the bond interest expense reported in 2002 be the same as, greater than, or less than the amount that would be reported if the straight-line method of amortization were used?

Prepare journal entries for issuance of bonds and interest; prepare installment payments schedule and journal entries for a mortgage note payable.
(SO 6, 7, 8, 10)

*P10-9A Atwater Corporation is building a new, state-of-the-art production and assembly facility for $10,000,000. To finance the facility it is using $2,000,000 it received from the issuance of shares of common stock, and the balance is being funded from the issuance of bonds. The $8,000,000, 11%, 5-year bonds were sold on August 1, 2001. They were dated August 1, 2001, and pay interest August 1 and February 1. Atwater uses the straight-line method to amortize bond premium or discount. Assume no interest is accrued on January 31 or July 31.

Atwater also purchased a new piece of equipment to be used in its new facility. The $550,000 piece of equipment was purchased with a $50,000 down payment and with cash received through the issuance of a $500,000, 8%, 3-year mortgage note payable issued on October 1, 2001. The terms provide for quarterly installment payments of $47,280 on December 31, March 31, June 30, and September 30.

Instructions
(Round all computations to the nearest dollar.)
(a) Prepare all necessary journal entries to record the issuance of the bonds and bond interest expense for 2001, assuming the bonds sold at 101.
(b) Prepare an installment payments schedule for the first five payments of the notes payable.
(c) Prepare all necessary journal entries related to the notes payable for December 31, 2001.
(d) Show balance sheet presentation for these obligations for December 31, 2001. (*Hint:* Be sure to distinguish between the current and long-term portions of the note.)

PROBLEMS: SET B

Prepare current liability entries, adjusting entries, and current liability section.
(SO 1, 2, 3)

P10-1B On January 1, 2001, the ledger of Burlington Company contained these liability accounts:

Accounts Payable	$52,000
Sales Taxes Payable	8,500
Unearned Service Revenue	14,000

During January the following selected transactions occurred:

Jan. 5 Sold merchandise for cash totaling $16,642, which includes 6% sales taxes.
12 Provided services for customers who had made advance payments of $5,000. (Credit Service Revenue.)
14 Paid state revenue department for sales taxes collected in December 2000 ($8,500).
20 Sold 500 units of a new product on credit at $50 per unit, plus 8% sales tax.
21 Borrowed $18,000 from Midland Bank on a 3-month, 10%, $18,000 note.

During January the company's employees earned wages of $40,000. Withholdings related to these wages were $2,800 for Social Security (FICA), $3,800 for federal income tax, and $1,100 for state income tax. The company owed no money related to these earnings for federal or state unemployment tax. Assume that wages earned during January will be paid during February. No entry had been recorded for wages or payroll tax expense as of January 31.

Instructions
(a) Journalize the January transactions.
(b) Journalize the adjusting entries at January 31 for the outstanding notes payable and for wages expense and payroll tax expense.
(c) Prepare the current liability section of the balance sheet at January 31, 2001. Assume no change in accounts payable.

Journalize and post note transactions; show balance sheet presentation.
(SO 2, 4)

P10-2B MileHi Mountain Bikes markets mountain-bike tours to clients vacationing in various locations in the mountains of Colorado. In preparation for the upcoming summer biking season, MileHi entered into the following transactions related to notes payable.

Mar. 1 Purchased Mongoose bikes for use as rentals by issuing an $8,000, 9% note payable that is due in 3 months.

Mar. 31 Recorded accrued interest for the Mongoose note.

Apr. 1 Issued a $20,000 note for the purchase of mountain property on which to build bike trails. The note bears 12% interest and is due in 9 months.

Apr. 30 Recorded accrued interest for the Mongoose note and the land note.

May 1 Issued a note to Telluride National Bank for $15,000 at 6%. The funds will be used for working capital for the beginning of the season; the note is due in 4 months.

May 31 Recorded accrued interest for all three notes.

June 1 Paid principal and interest on the Mongoose note.

June 30 Recorded accrued interest for the land note and the Telluride Bank note.

Instructions

(a) Prepare journal entries for the transactions noted above.

(b) Post the above entries to the Notes Payable, Interest Payable, and Interest Expense accounts. (Use T accounts.)

(c) Assuming that MileHi's year-end is June 30, show the balance sheet presentation of notes payable and interest payable at that date.

(d) How much interest expense relating to notes payable did MileHi incur during the year?

P10-3B The following section is taken from Sandy Oil Company's balance sheet at December 31, 2001:

Prepare journal entries to record interest payments, premium amortization, and redemption of bonds.
(SO 6, 7)

Current liabilities		
Bond interest payable (for 6 months		
from July 1 to December 31)		$ 216,000
Long-term liabilities		
Bonds payable, 12% due January 1, 2012	$3,600,000	
Add: Premium on bonds payable	400,000	4,000,000

Interest is payable semiannually on January 1 and July 1. The bonds are callable on any semiannual interest date. Sandy uses straight-line amortization for any bond premium or discount. From December 31, 2001, the bonds will be outstanding for an additional 10 years (120 months). Assume no interest is accrued on June 30.

Instructions

(Round all computations to the nearest dollar.)

(a) Journalize the payment of bond interest on January 1, 2002.

(b) Prepare the entry to amortize bond premium and to pay the interest due on July 1, 2002.

(c) Assume on July 1, 2002, after paying interest, that Sandy Company calls bonds having a face value of $1,800,000. The call price is 103. Record the redemption of the bonds.

(d) Prepare the adjusting entry at December 31, 2002, to amortize bond premium and to accrue interest on the remaining bonds.

P10-4B Pompeii Company sold $1,500,000, 12%, 10-year bonds on July 1, 2001. The bonds were dated July 1, 2001, and pay interest on July 1 and January 1. Pompeii Company uses the straight-line method to amortize bond premium or discount. Assume no interest is accrued on June 30.

Prepare journal entries to record issuance of bonds, interest, and amortization of bond premium and discount.
(SO 6, 8)

Instructions

(a) Prepare all the necessary journal entries to record the issuance of the bonds and bond interest expense for 2001, assuming that the bonds sold at 103.

(b) Prepare journal entries as in part (a) assuming that the bonds sold at 95.

(c) Show the balance sheet presentation for the bond issue at December 31, 2001, using (1) the 103 selling price, and then (2) the 95 selling price.

P10-5B Chula Vista Corporation sold $3,500,000, 7%, 20-year bonds on June 30, 2001. The bonds were dated June 30, 2001, and pay interest on June 30 and December 31. The company uses straight-line amortization for premiums and discounts. Financial statements are prepared annually.

Prepare journal entries to record issuance of bonds, interest, and amortization of bond premium and discount.
(SO 6, 7, 8)

Instructions

(a) Prepare the journal entry to record the issuance of the bonds assuming they sold at:
   (1) 96 1/2.
   (2) 104.
(b) Prepare amortization tables for both of the assumed sales for the first three interest payments.
(c) Prepare the journal entries to record interest expense for the first two interest payments under both assumed sales.
(d) Show the balance sheet presentation for both assumed sales at December 31, 2001.

Prepare journal entries to record issuance of bonds, show balance sheet presentation, and record bond redemption.
(SO 6, 8)

P10-6B Carlsbad Electric sold $3,000,000, 10%, 20-year bonds on January 1, 2001. The bonds were dated January 1 and pay interest on July 1 and January 1. The bonds were sold at 102. Assume no interest is accrued on June 30.

Instructions

(a) Prepare the journal entry to record the issuance of the bonds on January 1, 2001.
(b) At December 31, 2001, $3,000 of the bond premium had been amortized. Show the balance sheet presentation of the bond liability at December 31, 2001. (Assume that interest has been paid.)
(c) At December 31, 2002, when the carrying value of the bonds was $3,054,000, the company redeemed the bonds at 104. Record the redemption of the bonds assuming that interest for the year had already been paid.

Prepare journal entries to record issuance of bonds, payment of interest, and amortization of bond premium using effective-interest method.
(SO 9)

*P10-7B On July 1, 2001, Cleopatra Corporation issued $1,500,000 face value, 12%, 10-year bonds at $1,686,934. This price resulted in an effective-interest rate of 10% on the bonds. Cleopatra uses the effective-interest method to amortize bond premium or discount. The bonds pay semiannual interest July 1 and January 1.

Instructions

(Round all computations to the nearest dollar.)
(a) Prepare the journal entry to record the issuance of the bonds on July 1, 2001.
(b) Prepare an amortization table through December 31, 2002 (three interest periods) for this bond issue.
(c) Prepare the journal entry to record the accrual of interest and the amortization of the premium on December 31, 2001.
(d) Prepare the journal entry to record the payment of interest and the amortization of the premium on July 1, 2002.
(e) Prepare the journal entry to record the accrual of interest and the amortization of the premium on December 31, 2002.

Prepare journal entries to record issuance of bonds, payment of interest, and amortization of discount using effective-interest method. In addition, answer questions.
(SO 5, 9)

*P10-8B On July 1, 2001, Waubonsee Company issued $2,200,000 face value, 10%, 10-year bonds at $1,947,661. This price resulted in an effective-interest rate of 12% on the bonds. Waubonsee uses the effective-interest method to amortize bond premium or discount. The bonds pay semiannual interest July 1 and January 1.

Instructions

(a) Prepare the journal entries to record the following transactions.
   (1) The issuance of the bonds on July 1, 2001.
   (2) The accrual of interest and the amortization of the discount on December 31, 2001.
   (3) The payment of interest and the amortization of the discount on July 1, 2002.
   (4) The accrual of interest and the amortization of the discount on December 31, 2002.
(b) Show the proper balance sheet presentation for the liability for bonds payable on the December 31, 2002, balance sheet.
(c) ▯▭▭▷ Provide the answers to the following questions in letter form.
   (1) What amount of interest expense is reported for 2002?
   (2) Would the bond interest expense reported in 2002 be the same as, greater than, or less than the amount that would be reported if the straight-line method of amortization were used?
   (3) Determine the total cost of borrowing over the life of the bond.
   (4) Would the total bond interest expense be greater than, the same as, or less than the total interest expense that would be reported if the straight-line method of amortization were used?

*P10-9B   Myron Corporation is building a new, state-of-the-art production and assembly facility for $15,000,000. To finance the facility it is using $3,000,000 it received from the issuance of shares of common stock, and the balance is being funded from the issuance of bonds. The $12,000,000, 9%, 10-year bonds were sold on August 1, 2001. They were dated August 1, 2001, and pay interest August 1 and February 1. Myron uses the straight-line method to amortize bond premium or discount. Assume no interest is accrued on January 31 or July 31.

Myron also purchased a new piece of equipment to be used in its new facility. The $750,000 piece of equipment was purchased with a $50,000 down payment and with cash received through the issuance of a $700,000, 6%, 4-year mortgage note payable issued on October 1, 2001. The terms provide for quarterly installment payments of $49,536 on December 31, March 31, June 30, and September 30.

Prepare journal entries for issuance of bonds and interest; prepare installment payments schedule and journal entries for a mortgage note payable.
(SO 6, 7, 8, 10)

Instructions

(Round all computations to the nearest dollar.)

(a) Prepare all necessary journal entries to record the issuance of the bonds and bond interest expense for 2001, assuming the bonds sold at 98.

(b) Prepare an installment payments schedule for the first five payments of the notes payable.

(c) Prepare all necessary journal entries related to the notes payable for December 31, 2001.

(d) Show balance sheet presentation for these obligations for December 31, 2001. (*Hint:* Be sure to distinguish between the current and long-term portions of the note.)

◆ BROADENING YOUR PERSPECTIVE

*F*INANCIAL REPORTING AND ANALYSIS

FINANCIAL REPORTING PROBLEM: *Tootsie Roll Industries*

BYP10-1   Refer to the financial statements of Tootsie Roll Industries and the Notes to Consolidated Financial Statements in Appendix A.

Instructions

Answer the following questions about current and contingent liabilities and payroll costs.

(a) What were Tootsie Roll's total current liabilities at December 31, 1998? What was the increase/decrease in Tootsie Roll's total current liabilities from the prior year?

(b) How much were the accounts payable at December 31, 1998?

(c) What were the components of total current liabilities on December 31, 1998 (other than accounts payable already discussed above)?

COMPARATIVE ANALYSIS PROBLEM: *Tootsie Roll vs. Hershey Foods*

BYP10-2   The financial statements of Hershey Foods are presented in Appendix B, following the financial statements for Tootsie Roll Industries in Appendix A.

Instructions

(a) Based on the information contained in these financial statements, compute the following 1998 ratios for each company:

(1) Current ratio.

(2) Acid-test ratio.

What conclusions concerning the companies' liquidity can be drawn from these ratios?

(b) Based on the information contained in these financial statements, compute the following 1998 ratios for each company:

(1) Debt to total assets.

(2) Times interest earned.

What conclusions concerning the companies' long-run solvency can be drawn from these ratios?

RESEARCH CASE

BYP10-3 The September 1999 edition of *Inc.* magazine contains an article by Jill Andresky Fraser entitled "Money Talk: Communicating with Your Banker Is Never Easy. But There Is a Smart Way to Do It."

Instructions

Read the article and answer these questions:

(a) List the five steps to better bank communication described in the article, and provide a brief description of each.

(b) What four criteria does the author suggest for deciding what news needs to be communicated to your banker? Briefly describe each of the criteria.

INTERPRETING FINANCIAL STATEMENTS

BYP10-4 **Hechinger Co.** and **Home Depot** are two home improvement retailers. Compared to Hechinger, which was founded in the early 1900s, Home Depot is a relative newcomer. But, in recent years, while Home Depot was reporting an average increase in net income of 28% per year between 1995 and 1998, Hechinger was reporting increasingly large net losses. Finally, in 1999, largely due to competition from newcomer Home Depot, Hechinger was forced to file for bankruptcy.

Here is financial data for both companies at their most recent year-ends (in millions).

	Hechinger 10/3/98	Home Depot 1/31/99
Cash	$ 21	$ 62
Short-term investments	0	0
Receivables	0	469
Total current assets	1,153	4,933
Beginning total assets	1,668	11,229
Ending total assets	1,577	13,465
Beginning current liabilities	935	2,456
Ending current liabilities	938	2,857
Beginning total liabilities	1,392	4,015
Ending total liabilities	1,339	4,716
Interest expense	67	37
Income tax expense	3	1,040
Cash provided (used) by operations	(257)	1,917
Net income	(93)	1,614
Net sales	3,444	30,219

Instructions

Using the data, perform the following analysis.

(a) Calculate working capital, the current ratio, the acid-test ratio, and the current cash debt coverage ratio for each company. Discuss their relative liquidity.

(b) Calculate the debt to total assets ratio, times interest earned, and cash debt coverage ratio for each company. Discuss their relative solvency.

(c) Calculate the return on assets ratio and profit margin ratio for each company. Comment on their relative profitability.

(d) The notes to Home Depot's financial statements indicate that it leases many of its facilities using operating leases. If these assets had instead been purchased with debt, assets and liabilities would have increased by approximately $2,347 million. Calculate the company's debt to total assets ratio employing this adjustment. Discuss the implications.

A GLOBAL FOCUS

BYP10-5   Many multinational companies find it beneficial to have their shares listed on stock exchanges in foreign countries. In order to do this, they must comply with the securities laws of those countries. Some of these laws relate to the form of financial disclosure the company must provide, including disclosures related to contingent liabilities. This exercise investigates the **Tokyo Stock Exchange**, the largest stock exchange in Japan.

Address: www.tse.or.jp/eindex.html (or go to www.wiley.com/college/kimmel)

Steps:
1. Choose **K-square**. Answer questions (a) and (b).
2. Choose **Investor Info**.
3. Choose **Listing guide for foreign corporations**.
4. Choose **Disclosure after listing**. Answer questions (c) and (d).

Instructions
Answer the following questions:
(a) When was the first stock exchange opened in Japan? How many exchanges does Japan have today?
(b) What event caused trading to stop for a period of time in Japan?
(c) What are four examples of decisions by corporations that must be disclosed at the time of their occurrence?
(d) What are four examples of "occurrence of material fact" that must be disclosed at the time of their occurrence?

FINANCIAL ANALYSIS ON THE WEB

BYP10-6   *Purpose:*   Bond or debt securities pay a stated rate of interest. This rate of interest is dependent on the risk associated with the investment. Moody's Investment Service provides ratings for companies that issue debt securities.

Address: http://www.moodys.com/index.shtml (or go to www.wiley.com/college/kimmel)

Steps: From Moody's homepage choose **SiteMap**.

Instructions
Answer the following questions:
(a) What year did Moody's introduce the first bond rating?
(b) List three basic principles Moody's uses in rating bonds.
(c) What is the definition of Moody's Aaa rating on long-term taxable debt?

BYP10-7   *Purpose:*   To illustrate the time value of money. If you want to see how long it will take to reach your financial goals, try using "Investing for Kids Java Goals Calculator." (Don't be put off by the title, it's a rather interesting site.)

Address: http://tqd.advanced.org/3096/3goal.htm (or go to www.wiley.com/college/kimmel)

Steps: Go to the site shown above.

Instructions
Your goal is to acquire $35,000 for a down payment on a house. You currently have $2,000 to invest and can contribute an additional $175 per month to reach your goal. Compare

the length of time it would take to reach your goal and your net investment gain using the following returns:

(a) 3% (bank deposit)   (d) 11% (common stock)
(b) 5% (T-bill)   (e) 15% (growth stock)
(c) 7% (T-bond)

CRITICAL THINKING

GROUP DECISION CASE

BYP10-8 On January 1, 1999, Jerry Mall Corporation issued $1,200,000 of 5-year, 8% bonds at 97; the bonds pay interest semiannually on July 1 and January 1. By January 1, 2001, the market rate of interest for bonds of risk similar to those of Jerry Mall Corporation had risen. As a result the market value of these bonds was $1,000,000 on January 1, 2001—below their carrying value.

Jerry Mall, president of the company, suggests repurchasing all of these bonds in the open market at the $1,000,000 price. But to do so the company will have to issue $1,000,000 (face value) of new 10-year, 12% bonds at par. The president asks you as controller: "What is the feasibility of my proposed repurchase plan?"

Instructions
With the class divided into groups, answer the following:
(a) What is the carrying value of the outstanding Jerry Mall Corporation 5-year bonds on January 1, 2001? (Assume straight-line amortization.)
(b) Prepare the journal entry to retire the 5-year bonds on January 1, 2001. Prepare the journal entry to issue the new 10-year bonds.
(c) Prepare a short memo to the president in response to his request for advice. List the economic factors that you believe should be considered for his repurchase proposal.

COMMUNICATION ACTIVITY

BYP10-9 Finn Berge, president of the Blue Marlin, is considering the issuance of bonds to finance an expansion of his business. He has asked you to (1) discuss the advantages of bonds over common stock financing, (2) indicate the type of bonds he might issue, and (3) explain the issuing procedures used in bond transactions.

Instructions
Write a memorandum to the president, answering his request.

ETHICS CASE

BYP10-10 The July 1998 issue of *Inc.* magazine includes an article by Jeffrey L. Seglin entitled "Would You Lie to Save Your Company?" It recounts the following true situation:

A Chief Executive Officer (CEO) of a $20-million company that repairs aircraft engines received notice from a number of its customers that engines that it had recently repaired had failed, and that the company's parts were to blame. The CEO had not yet determined whether his company's parts were, in fact, the cause of the problem. The Federal Aviation Administration (FAA) had been notified and was investigating the matter.

What complicated the situation was that the company was in the midst of its year-end audit. As part of the audit, the CEO was required to sign a letter saying that he was not aware of any significant outstanding circumstances that could negatively impact the company—in accounting terms, of any contingent liabilities. The auditor was not aware of the customer complaints or the FAA investigation.

The company relied heavily on short-term loans from eight banks. The CEO feared that if these lenders learned of the situation, they would pull their loans. The loss of these loans would force the company into bankruptcy, leaving hundreds of people without jobs. Prior to this problem, the company had a stellar performance record.

Instructions

Answer the following questions:

(a) Who are the stakeholders in this situation?

(b) What are the CEO's possible courses of action? What are the potential results of each course of action? (Your response should take into account the two alternative outcomes: the FAA determines the company was not at fault, and the FAA determines the company was at fault.)

(c) What would you do, and why?

(d) Suppose the CEO decides to conceal the situation, and that during the next year the company is found to be at fault and is forced into bankruptcy. What losses are incurred by the stakeholders in this situation? Do you think the CEO should suffer legal consequences if he decides to conceal the situation?

Answer to Tootsie Roll Review It Question 2, p. 461

The liabilities that Tootsie Roll has identified as current are: Accounts Payable, Dividends Payable, Accrued Liabilities, and Income Taxes Payable.

Reporting and Analyzing Stockholders' Equity

◆ STUDY OBJECTIVES

After studying this chapter, you should be able to:

1 Identify and discuss the major characteristics of a corporation.

2 Record the issuance of common stock.

3 Explain the accounting for the purchase of treasury stock.

4 Differentiate preferred stock from common stock.

5 Prepare the entries for cash dividends and stock dividends.

6 Identify the items that affect retained earnings.

7 Prepare a comprehensive stockholders' equity section.

8 Evaluate a corporation's dividend and earnings performance from a stockholder's perspective.

◆ WHAT'S COOKING?

What major U.S. corporation got its start 28 years ago with a waffle iron? Hint: It doesn't sell food. Another hint: Swoosh. Another hint: "Just do it." That's right, Nike. In 1971 Nike cofounder Bill Bowerman put a piece of rubber into a kitchen waffle iron, and the trademark waffle sole was born. It seems fair to say that at Nike, "They don't make 'em like they used to."

Nike was cofounded by Bowerman and Phil Knight, a member of Bowerman's University of Oregon track team. Each began in the shoe business indepen-

dently during the early 1960s. Bowerman got his start by making hand-crafted running shoes for his University of Oregon track team. Knight, after completing graduate school, started a small business importing low-cost, high-quality shoes from Japan. In 1964 the two joined forces, each contributing $500, and formed Blue Ribbon Sports, a partnership. At first they marketed Japanese shoes. It wasn't until 1971 that the company began manufacturing its own line of shoes. With the new shoes came a new corporate name—Nike—the Greek goddess of vic-

tory. It is hard to imagine that the company that now boasts a stable full of world-class athletes as promoters at one time had part-time employees selling shoes out of car trunks at track meets. Nike's success has been achieved through relentless innovation combined with unbridled promotion.

By 1980 Nike was sufficiently established that it was able to issue its first stock to the public. In that same year it also created a stock ownership program for its employees, allowing them to share in the company's success. Since then Nike has enjoyed phenomenal growth, with 1998 sales reaching $9.5 billion—fully $3 billion over 1996 sales. Its dividend per share to stockholders has increased every year for the last 11 years.

Nike is not alone in its quest for the top of the sport shoe world. Reebok pushes Nike every step of the way. However, Nike's recent success has resulted in sales that are three times those of Reebok.

Is the race over? Probably not. The shoe market is fickle, with new styles becoming popular almost daily and vast international markets still lying untapped. Reebok's unwillingness to give up the race was boldly stated in its recent ad campaign: "This is my planet." Whether one of these two giants does eventually take control of the planet remains to be seen. Meanwhile the shareholders sit anxiously in the stands as this Olympic-size drama unfolds.

just do it.

you will never be slammed, tackled, or bruised by another player,
but there is no ice pack for the mind.

On the World Wide Web
Nike: http://www.nike.com
Reebok: http://www.reebok.com

Corporations like Nike and Reebok have substantial resources at their disposal. In fact, the corporation is the dominant form of business organization in the United States in terms of sales, earnings, and number of employees. All of the 500 largest U.S. companies are corporations. In this chapter we look at the essential features of a corporation and explain the accounting for a corporation's capital stock transactions.

The content and organization of the chapter are as follows:

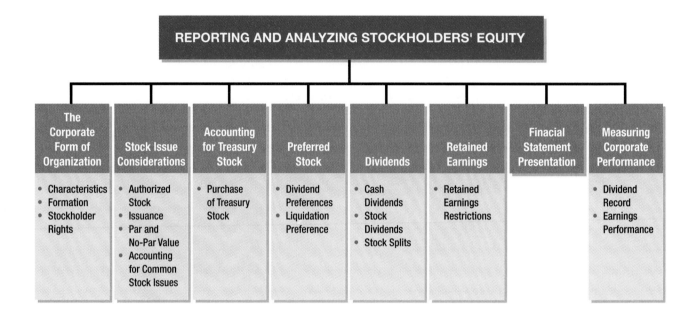

THE CORPORATE FORM OF ORGANIZATION

A corporation is created by law. As a legal entity, a **corporation** has most of the rights and privileges of a person. The major exceptions relate to privileges that can be exercised only by a living person, such as the right to vote or to hold public office. Similarly, a corporation is subject to the same duties and responsibilities as a person; for example, it must abide by the laws and it must pay taxes.

Corporations may be classified in a variety of ways. Two common classifications are **by purpose** and **by ownership**. A corporation may be organized for the purpose of making a profit (such as Nike or General Motors), or it may be a nonprofit charitable, medical, or educational corporation (such as the Salvation Army or the American Cancer Society).

Classification by ownership differentiates publicly held and privately held corporations. A **publicly held corporation** may have thousands of stockholders, and its stock is regularly traded on a national securities market such as the New York Stock Exchange. Examples are IBM, Caterpillar, and General Electric. In contrast, a **privately held corporation**, often referred to as a closely held corporation, usually has only a few stockholders, and it does not offer its stock for sale to the general public. Privately held companies are generally much smaller than publicly held companies, although some notable exceptions exist.

Cargill Inc., a private corporation that trades in grain and other commodities, is one of the largest companies in the United States.

CHARACTERISTICS OF A CORPORATION

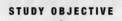

STUDY OBJECTIVE

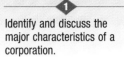

Identify and discuss the major characteristics of a corporation.

In 1964, when Nike's founders, Knight and Bowerman, were just getting started in the running shoe business, they formed their original organization as a partnership. In 1968 they reorganized the company as a corporation. A number of characteristics distinguish a corporation from proprietorships and partnerships. The most important of these characteristics are explained below.

Separate Legal Existence

As an entity separate and distinct from its owners, the corporation acts under its own name rather than in the name of its stockholders. Nike, for example, may buy, own, and sell property, borrow money, and enter into legally binding contracts in its own name. It may also sue or be sued, and it pays its own taxes.

In contrast to a partnership, in which the acts of the owners (partners) bind the partnership, the acts of the owners (stockholders) do not bind the corporation unless such owners are agents of the corporation. For example, if you owned shares of Nike stock, you would not have the right to purchase inventory for the company unless you were designated as an agent of the corporation.

Limited Liability of Stockholders

Since a corporation is a separate legal entity, creditors ordinarily have recourse only to corporate assets to satisfy their claims. The liability of stockholders is normally limited to their investment in the corporation, and creditors have no legal claim on the personal assets of the stockholders unless fraud has occurred. Thus, even in the event of bankruptcy of the corporation, stockholders' losses are generally limited to the amount of capital they have invested in the corporation.

Transferable Ownership Rights

Ownership of a corporation is shown in shares of capital stock, which are transferable units. Stockholders may dispose of part or all of their interest in a corporation simply by selling their stock. In contrast to the transfer of an ownership interest in a partnership, which requires the consent of each partner, the transfer of stock is entirely at the discretion of the stockholder. It does not require the approval of either the corporation or other stockholders.

The transfer of ownership rights among stockholders normally has no effect on the operating activities of the corporation or on a corporation's assets, liabilities, and total stockholders' equity. That is, the company does not participate in the transfer of these ownership rights after the original sale of the capital stock.

Stockholders
Legal existence separate from owners

Stockholders
Limited liability of stockholders

Transferable ownership rights

Ability to Acquire Capital

It generally is relatively easy for a corporation to obtain capital through the issuance of stock. Buying stock in a corporation is often more attractive to an investor than investing in a partnership because a stockholder has limited liability and because shares of stock are readily transferable. Moreover, individuals can become stockholders by investing small amounts of money. In sum, the ability of a successful corporation to obtain capital is virtually unlimited.

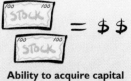

Ability to acquire capital

Continuous Life

The life of a corporation is stated in its charter; it may be perpetual or it may be limited to a specific number of years. If it is limited, the period of existence can be extended through renewal of the charter. Since a corporation is a sepa-

Continuous life

rate legal entity, the life of a corporation as a going concern is separate from its owners; it is not affected by the withdrawal, death, or incapacity of a stockholder, employee, or officer. As a result, a successful corporation can have a continuous and perpetual life.

Corporation Management

Although stockholders legally own the corporation, they manage it indirectly through a board of directors they elect. Philip Knight is the chairman of Nike's board of directors. Nike's board, in turn, formulates the operating policies for the company and selects officers, such as a president and one or more vice-presidents, to execute policy and to perform daily management functions.

A typical organization chart showing the delegation of responsibility is shown in Illustration 11-1.

Illustration 11-1 Corporation organization chart

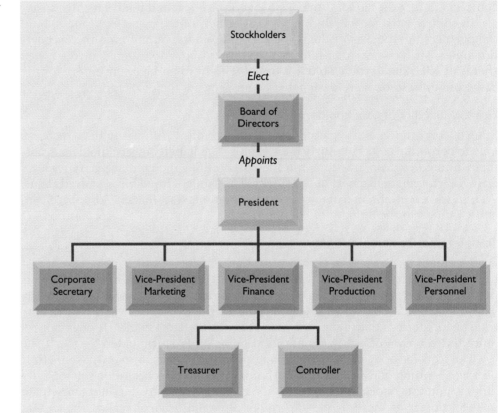

The **president** is the chief executive officer (CEO) with direct responsibility for managing the business. As the organization chart shows, the president delegates responsibility to other officers. The chief accounting officer is the **controller**. The controller's responsibilities include maintaining the accounting records and an adequate system of internal control, and preparing financial statements, tax returns, and internal reports. The **treasurer** has custody of the corporation's funds and is responsible for maintaining the company's cash position.

The organizational structure of a corporation enables a company to hire professional managers to run the business. On the other hand, some view this separation as a weakness. The separation of ownership and management prevents owners from having an active role in managing the company, which some owners like to have.

Government Regulations

A corporation is subject to numerous state and federal regulations. For example, state laws usually prescribe the requirements for issuing stock, the distributions of earnings permitted to stockholders, and the effects of retiring stock. Similarly, federal securities laws govern the sale of capital stock to the general public. Also, most publicly held corporations are required to make extensive disclosure of their financial affairs to the Securities and Exchange Commission through quarterly and annual reports. In addition, when a corporate stock is listed and traded on organized securities markets, the corporation must comply with the reporting requirements of these exchanges.

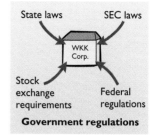

Government regulations

Additional Taxes

For proprietorships and partnerships, the owner's share of earnings is reported on his or her personal income tax return. Taxes are then paid by the individual on this amount. Corporations, on the other hand, must pay federal and state income taxes as a separate legal entity. These taxes are substantial: They can amount to as much as 40% of taxable income.

Additional taxes

In addition, stockholders are required to pay taxes on cash dividends. Thus, many argue that corporate income is **taxed twice (double taxation)**: once at the corporate level and again at the individual level.

The advantages and disadvantages of a corporation compared to a proprietorship and partnership are shown in Illustration 11-2.

Advantages	Disadvantages
• Separate legal existence	• Corporation management—separation of ownership and management
• Limited liability of stockholders	• Government regulations
• Transferable ownership rights	• Additional taxes
• Ability to acquire capital	
• Continuous life	
• Corporation management—professional managers	

Illustration 11-2   Advantages and disadvantages of a corporation

BUSINESS INSIGHT

Management Perspective

Sometimes you can have your cake, and eat it too. One type of corporate form, called an S corporation, allows for legal treatment as a corporation, but tax treatment as a partnership—that is, no double taxation. The rules regarding S corporation treatment were recently changed, making it possible for more small- and medium-sized businesses to qualify. One of the primary criteria is that the company cannot have more than 75 shareholders.

DECISION TOOLKIT

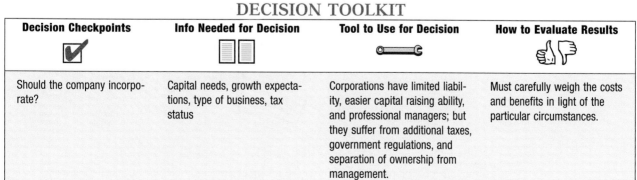

Decision Checkpoints	Info Needed for Decision	Tool to Use for Decision	How to Evaluate Results
Should the company incorporate?	Capital needs, growth expectations, type of business, tax status	Corporations have limited liability, easier capital raising ability, and professional managers; but they suffer from additional taxes, government regulations, and separation of ownership from management.	Must carefully weigh the costs and benefits in light of the particular circumstances.

FORMING A CORPORATION

A corporation is formed by grant of a state charter. Regardless of the number of states in which a corporation has operating divisions, it is incorporated in only one state. It is to the company's advantage to incorporate in a state whose laws are favorable to the corporate form of business organization. For example, although General Motors has its headquarters in Michigan, it is incorporated in New Jersey. In fact, more and more corporations have been incorporating in states with rules that favor existing management. For example, Gulf Oil changed its state of incorporation to Delaware to thwart possible unfriendly takeovers. There, certain defensive tactics against takeovers can be approved by the board of directors alone, without a vote by shareholders.

Upon receipt of its charter from the state of incorporation, the corporation establishes by-laws for conducting its affairs. Corporations engaged in interstate commerce must also obtain a license from each state in which they do business. The license subjects the corporation's operating activities to the general corporation laws of the state.

STOCKHOLDER RIGHTS

When chartered, the corporation may begin selling ownership rights in the form of shares of stock. When a corporation has only one class of stock, it is identified as **common stock.** Each share of common stock gives the stockholder the ownership rights pictured in Illustration 11-3. The ownership rights of a share of stock are stated in the articles of incorporation or in the by-laws.

Illustration 11-3
Ownership rights of stockholders

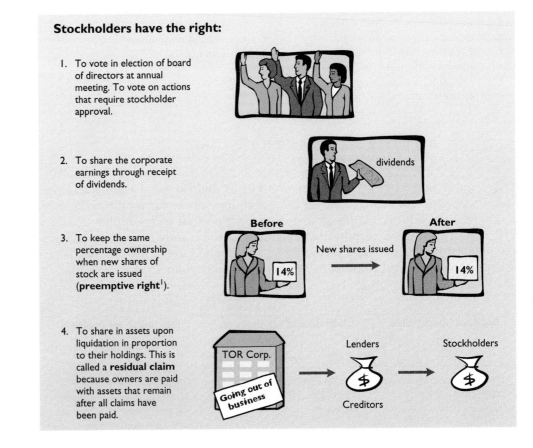

Stockholders have the right:

1. To vote in election of board of directors at annual meeting. To vote on actions that require stockholder approval.

2. To share the corporate earnings through receipt of dividends.

3. To keep the same percentage ownership when new shares of stock are issued (**preemptive right**[1]).

4. To share in assets upon liquidation in proportion to their holdings. This is called a **residual claim** because owners are paid with assets that remain after all claims have been paid.

---

[1]A number of companies have eliminated the preemptive right because they believe it makes an unnecessary and cumbersome demand on management. For example, IBM, by stockholder approval, has dropped its preemptive right for stockholders.

BUSINESS INSIGHT
International Perspective

In Japan, stockholders are considered to be far less important to a corporation than employees, customers, and suppliers. Stockholders are rarely asked to vote on an issue, and the notion of bending corporate policy to favor stockholders borders on heresy. This attitude toward stockholders appears to be slowly changing, however, as influential Japanese are advocating listening to investors, raising the extremely low dividends paid by Japanese corporations, and improving disclosure of financial information.

Proof of stock ownership is evidenced by a printed or engraved form known as a **stock certificate**. As shown in Illustration 11-4, the face of the certificate shows the name of the corporation, the stockholder's name, the class and special features of the stock, the number of shares owned, and the signatures of authorized corporate officials. Certificates are prenumbered to facilitate their accountability; they may be issued for any quantity of shares.

Illustration 11-4   A stock certificate

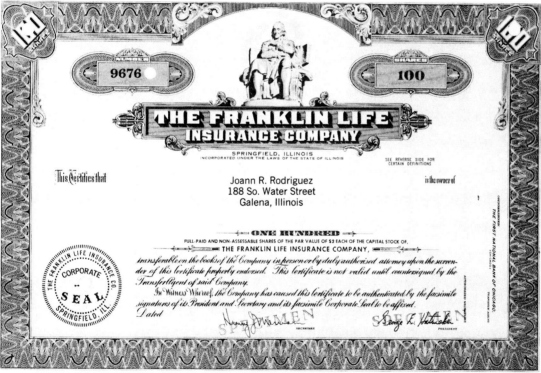

BEFORE YOU GO ON...

◆ **Review It**

1. What are the advantages and disadvantages of a corporation compared to a proprietorship and a partnership?
2. Identify the principal steps in forming a corporation.
3. What rights are inherent in owning a share of stock in a corporation?

STOCK ISSUE CONSIDERATIONS

Although Nike incorporated in 1968, it did not sell stock to the public until 1980. At that time Nike evidently decided it would benefit from the infusion of cash that a public sale of its shares would bring. When a corporation decides to issue stock, it must resolve a number of basic questions: How many shares should be authorized for sale? How should the stock be issued? At what price should the shares be issued? What value should be assigned to the stock? These questions are answered in the following sections.

AUTHORIZED STOCK

The amount of stock that a corporation is authorized to sell is indicated in its charter. If all authorized stock is sold, then a corporation must obtain consent of the state to amend its charter before it can issue additional shares.

The authorization of common stock does not result in a formal accounting entry because the event has no immediate effect on either corporate assets or stockholders' equity. However, disclosure of the number of shares authorized is required in the stockholders' equity section of the balance sheet.

ISSUANCE OF STOCK

International Note

U.S. and U.K. corporations raise most of their capital through millions of outside shareholders and bondholders. In contrast, companies in Germany, France, and Japan acquire financing from large banks or other institutions. Consequently, in the latter environment, shareholders are less important, and external reporting and auditing receive less emphasis.

A corporation has the choice of issuing common stock directly to investors or indirectly through an investment banking firm that specializes in bringing securities to the attention of prospective investors. Direct issue is typical in closely held companies, whereas indirect issue is customary for a publicly held corporation. New issues of stock may be offered for sale to the public through various organized U.S. securities exchanges: the New York Stock Exchange, the American Stock Exchange, and 13 regional exchanges. Stock may also be traded on the NASDAQ national market.

How does a corporation set the price for a new issue of stock? Among the factors to be considered are (1) the company's anticipated future earnings, (2) its expected dividend rate per share, (3) its current financial position, (4) the current state of the economy, and (5) the current state of the securities market. The calculation can be complex and is properly the subject of a finance course.

PAR AND NO-PAR VALUE STOCKS

Par value stock is capital stock that has been assigned a value per share in the corporate charter. The par value may be any amount selected by the corporation. Generally, the par value is quite low because states often levy a tax on the corporation based on its par value. For example, Reebok has a par of 1 cent, IBM has a par of $1.25, Ford Motor Company $1 par, General Motors Corporation $1.67, and PepsiCo $1\frac{2}{3}$ cents.

The significance of par value is a legal matter. Par value represents the legal capital per share that must be retained in the business for the protection of corporate creditors; that is, it is not available for withdrawal by stockholders. Thus, in the past, most states required the corporation to sell its shares at par or above. Today many states do not require a par value. Its usefulness as a protective device to creditors was questionable because par value was often immaterial relative to the value of the company's stock—even at the time of issue. For example, Reebok's par value is $.01 per share, yet a new issue in 1999 would have sold at a **market value** in the $11 per share range. Thus, par has no relationship with market value and in the vast majority of cases is an immaterial amount.

No-par value stock is capital stock that has not been assigned a value in the corporate charter. No-par value stock is often issued because some confusion still exists concerning par value and fair market value. If shares have no par value, then the questionable treatment of using par value as a basis for fair market value never arises. The major disadvantage of no-par stock is that some states levy a high tax on the shares issued.

No-par value stock is quite common today. For example, Nike, Procter & Gamble, and North American Van Lines all have no-par stock. In many states the board of directors is permitted to assign a stated value to the no-par shares, which then becomes the legal capital per share. The stated value of no-par stock may be changed at any time by action of the directors. Stated value, like par value, does not indicate or correspond to the market value of the stock. When there is no assigned stated value, the **entire proceeds received upon issuance of the stock is considered to be legal capital**.

The key point to remember is that legal capital per share always establishes the credit to the Common Stock account. The relationship of par and no-par value to legal capital is summarized in Illustration 11-5.

Stock	Legal Capital Per Share
Par value —————————→	Par value
No-par value with stated value ————→	Stated value
No-par value without stated value ——→	Entire proceeds

Illustration 11-5 Relationship of par and no-par value stock to legal capital

As will be explained later, the Common Stock account is credited for the legal capital per share each time stock is issued.

ACCOUNTING FOR COMMON STOCK ISSUES

The stockholders' equity section of a corporation's balance sheet includes: (1) **paid-in (contributed) capital** and (2) **retained earnings (earned capital)**. The distinction between paid-in capital and retained earnings is important from both a legal and an economic point of view. Paid-in capital is the amount paid in to the corporation by stockholders in exchange for shares of ownership. *Retained earnings* is earned capital held for future use in the business. In this section we discuss the accounting for paid-in capital. In a later section we discuss retained earnings.

Let's now look at how to account for new issues of common stock. The primary objectives in accounting for the issuance of common stock are to (1) identify the specific sources of paid-in capital and (2) maintain the distinction between paid-in capital and retained earnings. As shown below, **the issuance of common stock affects only paid-in capital accounts**.

As discussed earlier, par value does not indicate a stock's market value. The cash proceeds from issuing par value stock may be equal to, greater than, or less than par value. When the issuance of common stock for cash is recorded, the par value of the shares is credited to Common Stock, and the portion of the proceeds that is above or below par value is recorded in a separate paid-in capital account.

To illustrate, assume that Hydro-Slide, Inc., issues 1,000 shares of $1 par value common stock at par for cash. The entry to record this transaction is:

STUDY OBJECTIVE

2

Record the issuance of common stock.

Helpful Hint Stock is sometimes issued in exchange for services (payment to attorneys or consultants, for example) or other noncash assets (land or buildings). The accounting for such stock issues is beyond the scope of this book. Here we look at only the issuance of par value common stock in exchange for cash.

Cash	1,000	
Common Stock		1,000
(To record issuance of 1,000 shares of $1 par common stock at par)		

A	=	L	+	SE
+1,000				+1,000

If Hydro-Slide, Inc., issues an additional 1,000 shares of the $1 par value common stock for cash at $5 per share, the entry is:

A	=	L	+	SE
+5,000				+1,000
				+4,000

Cash	5,000	
Common Stock		1,000
Paid-in Capital in Excess of Par Value		4,000
(To record issuance of 1,000 shares of common		
stock in excess of par)		

The total paid-in capital from these two transactions is $6,000, and the legal capital is $2,000. If Hydro-Slide, Inc., has retained earnings of $27,000, the stockholders' equity section of the balance sheet is as shown in Illustration 11-6.

Illustration 11-6 Stockholders' equity—paid-in capital in excess of par value

HYDRO-SLIDE, INC.
Balance Sheet (partial)

Stockholders' equity	
Paid-in capital	
Common stock	$ 2,000
Paid-in capital in excess of par value	**4,000**
Total paid-in capital	6,000
Retained earnings	27,000
Total stockholders' equity	$33,000

Some companies issue no-par stock with a stated value. For accounting purposes, the stated value is treated in the same fashion as the par value. For example, if in our Hydro-Slide example above the stock was no-par stock with a stated value of $1, the entries would be the same as those presented for the par stock except the term "Par Value" would be replaced with "Stated Value." If a company issues no-par stock that does not have a stated value, then the full amount received is credited to the Common Stock account. In this case, there is no need for the Paid-in Capital in Excess of Stated Value account.

BUSINESS INSIGHT
Investor Perspective

The stock of publicly held companies is traded on organized exchanges at dollar prices per share established by the interaction between buyers and sellers. For each listed security the financial press reports the high and low prices of the stock during the year, the total volume of stock traded on a given day, the high and low prices for the day, and the closing market price, with the net change for the day. Nike is listed on the New York Stock Exchange. Here is a recent listing for Nike:

	52 Weeks						
Stock	High	Low	Volume	High	Low	Close	Net change
Nike	$66\frac{15}{16}$	$34\frac{7}{8}$	13905	$56\frac{13}{16}$	$54\frac{1}{4}$	$56\frac{3}{8}$	$+2\frac{9}{16}$

These numbers indicate that the high and low market prices for the last 52 weeks have been $66\frac{15}{16}$ and $34\frac{7}{8}$; the trading volume for the previous day was 1,390,500 shares; the high, low, and closing prices for that date were $56\frac{13}{16}$, $54\frac{1}{4}$, and $56\frac{3}{8}$, respectively; and the net change for the day was an increase of $2\frac{9}{16}$ or $2.5625 per share.

The trading of common stock on securities exchanges involves the transfer of already issued shares from an existing stockholder to another investor. Consequently, these transactions have no impact on a corporation's stockholders' equity section.

BEFORE YOU GO ON...

◆ Review It

1. Of what significance to a corporation is the amount of authorized stock?
2. What alternative approaches may a corporation use to sell new shares to investors?
3. Distinguish between par value and market value.
4. Explain the accounting for par and no-par common stock issued for cash.

◆ Do It

Cayman Corporation begins operations on March 1 by issuing 100,000 shares of $10 par value common stock for cash at $12 per share. Journalize the issuance of the shares.

Reasoning: In issuing shares for cash, common stock is credited for par value per share and any additional proceeds are credited to a separate paid-in capital account.

Solution:

Mar. 1	Cash	1,200,000	
	Common Stock		1,000,000
	Paid-in Capital in Excess of Par Value		200,000
	(To record issuance of 100,000 shares at $12 per share)		

ACCOUNTING FOR TREASURY STOCK

Treasury stock is a corporation's own stock that has been issued, fully paid for, reacquired by the corporation and held in its treasury for future use. A corporation may acquire treasury stock to meet any of these objectives:

1. Reissue the shares to officers and employees under bonus and stock compensation plans.
2. Increase trading of the company's stock in the securities market in the hopes of enhancing its market value.
3. Have additional shares available for use in the acquisition of other companies.
4. Reduce the number of shares outstanding and thereby increase earnings per share.

Another infrequent reason for purchasing treasury shares is that management may want to eliminate hostile shareholders by buying them out.

Many corporations have treasury stock. For example, one survey of 600 companies in the United States found that 64% have treasury stock.[2] Specifically, in

STUDY OBJECTIVE

3

Explain the accounting for the purchase of treasury stock.

Helpful Hint Treasury stock is so named because the company often holds the shares in its treasury for safekeeping.

---

[2]*Accounting Trends & Techniques 1998* (New York: American Institute of Certified Public Accountants).

1998 Reebok purchased 36.7 million treasury shares, PepsiCo 255 million shares, and Phillip Morris Company 380.5 million shares. Recent stock repurchases have been so substantial that a 1999 study by two Federal Reserve economists suggested that a sharp reduction in corporate purchases of treasury shares might result in as much as a 38% drop in the value of the U.S. stock market.

BUSINESS INSIGHT
Management Perspective

In a bold (and some would say very risky) move in late 1996, Reebok bought back nearly a *third* of its shares. This decision was risky because the repurchase of shares dramatically reduced Reebok's available cash. In fact, the company borrowed significant funds to accomplish the repurchase. In a press release, management stated that it was repurchasing the shares because it believed that the stock was severely underpriced. The repurchase of so many shares was meant to signal management's belief in good future earnings. Skeptics, however, suggest that Reebok's management was repurchasing shares to make it less likely that the company will be taken over by a different company (in which case Reebok's top managers would likely lose their jobs). By depleting its cash Reebok is less likely to be acquired because acquiring companies like to purchase companies with large cash reserves so they can pay off debt used in the acquisition. Time will tell whether the Reebok investors who chose to hold on to their shares benefit, or whether the cash strain caused by the repurchase only magnifies Reebok's troubles.

PURCHASE OF TREASURY STOCK

The purchase of treasury stock is generally accounted for by the **cost method**. This method derives its name from the fact that the Treasury Stock account is maintained at the cost of shares purchased. None of the values (par, stated, or legal) is involved in recording treasury stock transactions. Under the cost method, **Treasury Stock is increased (debited) by the price paid to reacquire the shares**; **Treasury Stock decreases by the same amount when the shares are later sold**.

To illustrate, assume that on January 1, 2001, the stockholders' equity section for Mead, Inc., has 100,000 shares of $5 par value common stock outstanding (all issued at par value) and Retained Earnings of $200,000. The stockholders' equity section of the balance sheet before purchase of treasury stock is as shown in Illustration 11-7.

Illustration 11-7   Stockholders' equity with no treasury stock

MEAD, INC. Balance Sheet (partial)	
Stockholders' equity	
Paid-in capital	
Common stock, $5 par value, 100,000 shares	
issued and outstanding	$500,000
Retained earnings	200,000
Total stockholders' equity	$700,000

On February 1, 2001, Mead acquires 4,000 shares of its stock at $8 per share. The entry is:

Feb. 1	Treasury Stock	32,000	
	Cash		32,000
	(To record purchase of 4,000 shares of		
	treasury stock at $8 per share)		

A	=	L	+	SE
−32,000				−32,000

The Treasury Stock account would increase by the cost of the shares purchased ($32,000). The original paid-in capital account, Common Stock, would not be affected because **the number of issued shares does not change**. Treasury stock is deducted from total paid-in capital and retained earnings in the stockholders' equity section of the balance sheet, as shown in Illustration 11-8 for Mead, Inc. Thus, the acquisition of treasury stock reduces stockholders' equity.

Helpful Hint Treasury Stock is a contra stockholders' equity account.

MEAD, INC.
Balance Sheet (partial)

Stockholders' equity	
Paid-in capital	
Common stock, $5 par value, 100,000 shares	
issued and 96,000 shares outstanding	$500,000
Retained earnings	200,000
Total paid-in capital and retained earnings	700,000
Less: Treasury stock (4,000 shares)	32,000
Total stockholders' equity	$668,000

Illustration 11-8
Stockholders' equity with treasury stock

Both the number of shares issued (100,000) and the number in the treasury (4,000) are disclosed. The difference is the number of shares of stock outstanding (96,000). The term outstanding stock means the number of shares of issued stock that are being held by stockholders.

Some maintain that treasury stock should be reported as an asset because it can be sold for cash. Under this reasoning, unissued stock (stock that has been authorized but not issued) should also be shown as an asset, clearly an erroneous conclusion. Rather than being an asset, treasury stock reduces stockholder claims on corporate assets. This effect is correctly shown by reporting treasury stock as a deduction from total paid-in capital and retained earnings.

BEFORE YOU GO ON...

◆ Review It

1. What is treasury stock, and why do companies acquire it?
2. How is treasury stock recorded?
3. Where is treasury stock reported in the financial statements?

◆ Do It

Santa Anita Inc. purchases 3,000 shares of its $50 par value common stock for $180,000 cash on July 1. The shares are to be held in the treasury until resold. Journalize the treasury stock transaction.

Reasoning: The purchase of treasury stock is recorded at cost.

Solution:

July 1	Treasury Stock		180,000	
	Cash			180,000
	(To record the purchase of 3,000 shares at $60 per share)			

PREFERRED STOCK

To appeal to a larger segment of potential investors, a corporation may issue a class of stock in addition to common stock, called preferred stock. Preferred stock has contractual provisions that give it preference or priority over common stock in certain areas. Typically, preferred stockholders have a priority in relation to (1) dividends and (2) assets in the event of liquidation. However, they often do not have voting rights. Reebok has no outstanding preferred stock, while Nike has a very minor amount outstanding. A recent survey of 600 companies indicated that 25% have one or more classes of preferred stock.

Like common stock, preferred stock may be issued for cash or for noncash consideration. The entries for these transactions are similar to the entries for common stock. When a corporation has more than one class of stock, each paid-in capital account title should identify the stock to which it relates (e.g., Preferred Stock, Common Stock, Paid-in Capital in Excess of Par Value—Preferred Stock, and Paid-in Capital in Excess of Par Value—Common Stock). Assume that Stine Corporation issues 10,000 shares of $10 par value preferred stock for $12 cash per share. The entry to record the issuance is:

A = L + SE
+120,000   +100,000
+20,000

Cash		120,000	
Preferred Stock			100,000
Paid-in Capital in Excess of Par Value—Preferred Stock			20,000
(To record the issuance of 10,000 shares of $10 par value preferred stock)			

Preferred stock may have either a par value or no-par value. In the stockholders' equity section of the balance sheet, preferred stock is shown first because of its dividend and liquidation preferences over common stock.

DIVIDEND PREFERENCES

As indicated before, **preferred stockholders have the right to share in the distribution of corporate income before common stockholders**. For example, if the dividend rate on preferred stock is $5 per share, common shareholders will not receive any dividends in the current year until preferred stockholders have received $5 per share. The first claim to dividends does not, however, **guarantee** dividends. Dividends depend on many factors, such as adequate retained earnings and availability of cash.

For preferred stock, the per share dividend amount is stated as a percentage of the par value of the stock or as a specified amount. For example, Kmart Corporation specifies a $7\frac{3}{4}$% dividend on its $50 par value preferred ($50 × $7\frac{3}{4}$% = $3.875 per share), whereas Nike pays 10 cents per share on its $1 par preferred stock.

Cumulative Dividend

Preferred stock contracts often contain a cumulative dividend feature. This right means that preferred stockholders must be paid both current-year dividends and any unpaid prior-year dividends before common stockholders receive dividends. When preferred stock is cumulative, preferred dividends not declared in a given period are called dividends in arrears. To illustrate, assume that Scientific-Leasing has 5,000 shares of 7%, $100 par value cumulative preferred stock outstanding. The annual dividend is $35,000 (5,000 × $7 per share). If dividends are two years in arrears, preferred stockholders are entitled to receive the dividends as shown in Illustration 11-9 in the current year before any distribution may be made to common stockholders.

Dividends in arrears ($35,000 × 2)	$ 70,000
Current-year dividends	35,000
Total preferred dividends	**$105,000**

Illustration 11-9   Computation of total dividends to preferred stock

Dividends in arrears are not considered a liability. **No obligation exists until a dividend is declared by the board of directors**. However, the amount of dividends in arrears should be disclosed in the notes to the financial statements. Doing so enables investors to assess the potential impact of this commitment on the corporation's financial position.

Dividends cannot be paid on common stock while any dividend on preferred stock is in arrears. The cumulative feature is often critical in selling a preferred stock issue to investors. When preferred stock is noncumulative, a dividend passed in any year is lost forever. Companies that are unable to meet their dividend obligations are not looked upon favorably by the investment community. As a financial officer noted in discussing one company's failure to pay its cumulative preferred dividend for a period of time, "Not meeting your obligations on something like that is a major black mark on your record."

BUSINESS INSIGHT
Investor Perspective

Dividends in arrears can extend for fairly long periods of time. Long Island Lighting Company's directors voted at one time to make up some $390 million in preferred dividends that had been in arrears for nearly ten years and to resume normal quarterly preferred payments. The announcement resulted from an agreement between the company and New York State to abandon a nuclear power plant in exchange for sizable rate increases over the next ten years.

LIQUIDATION PREFERENCE

Most preferred stocks have a preference on corporate assets if the corporation fails. This feature provides security for the preferred stockholder. The preference to assets may be for the par value of the shares or for a specified liquidating value. For example, Commonwealth Edison issued preferred stock that entitles the holders to receive $31.80 per share, plus accrued and unpaid dividends, in the event of involuntary liquidation. The liquidation preference is used in litigation pertaining to bankruptcy lawsuits involving the respective claims of creditors and preferred stockholders.

DIVIDENDS

STUDY OBJECTIVE

5

Prepare the entries for cash dividends and stock dividends.

As noted earlier, a dividend **is a distribution by a corporation to its stockholders on a pro rata basis.** *Pro rata* means that if you own, say, 10% of the common shares, you will receive 10% of the dividend. Dividends can take four forms: cash, property, script (promissory note to pay cash), or stock. Cash dividends, which predominate in practice, and stock dividends, which are declared with some frequency, are the focus of our discussion.

Investors are very interested in a company's dividend practices. In the financial press, **dividends are generally reported quarterly as a dollar amount per share**, although sometimes they are reported on an annual basis. For example, Nike's **quarterly** dividend rate in the fourth quarter of 1998 was 12 cents per share, whereas the dividend rate for that quarter for J.C. Penney Company was 54.5 cents, and for PepsiCo it was 13 cents.

CASH DIVIDENDS

A cash dividend is a pro rata distribution of cash to stockholders. For a corporation to pay a cash dividend, it must have the following:

1. **Retained earnings.** In many states, payment of dividends from legal capital is illegal. Payment of dividends from paid-in capital in excess of par is legal in some states. **Payment of dividends from retained earnings is legal in all states.** In addition, companies are frequently constrained by agreements with their lenders to pay dividends only from retained earnings.

2. **Adequate cash.** Recently Nike had a balance in retained earnings of $3,043 million but a cash balance of only $109 million. Thus, in order to pay a dividend equal to its retained earnings, Nike would have to raise $2,934 million more in cash. It is unlikely it would do this because a dividend of this size would not be sustainable in the future (that is, Nike would not be able to pay this much in dividends in future years). In addition, such a dividend would completely deplete Nike's balance in retained earnings, so it would not be able to pay a dividend in the next year unless it had positive net income.

3. **Declared dividends.** The board of directors has full authority to determine the amount of income to be distributed in the form of dividends and the amount to be retained in the business. Dividends do not accrue like interest on a note payable, and they are not a liability until declared.

The amount and timing of a dividend are important issues for management to consider. The payment of a large cash dividend could lead to liquidity problems for the enterprise. Conversely, a small dividend or a missed dividend may cause unhappiness among stockholders who expect to receive a reasonable cash payment from the company on a periodic basis. Many companies declare and pay cash dividends quarterly. On the other hand, a number of high-growth companies pay no dividends, preferring to retain earnings and use them to finance capital expenditures.

In order to remain in business, companies must honor their interest payments to creditors, bankers, and bondholders. But the payment of dividends to stockholders is another matter. Many companies can survive, and even thrive, without such payouts. "Why give money to those strangers?" is the response of one company president. Investors must keep an eye on the company's dividend policy and understand what it may mean. For most companies, for example, regular dividend boosts in the face of irregular earnings can be a warning signal. Companies with high dividends and rising debt may be borrowing money to pay shareholders. On the other hand, low dividends may not be a negative sign because they may mean high returns through market appreciation. Presumably, investors for whom regular dividends are important tend to buy stock in companies that pay periodic dividends, and those for whom growth in the stock price (capital gains) is more important tend to buy stock in companies that retain earnings.

Entries for Cash Dividends

Three dates are important in connection with dividends: (1) the declaration date, (2) the record date, and (3) the payment date. Normally there is a time span of two to four weeks between each date. Accounting entries are required on two of the dates: the declaration date and the payment date.

On the **declaration date**, the board of directors formally declares (authorizes) the cash dividend and announces it to stockholders. The declaration of a cash dividend **commits the corporation to a binding legal obligation** that cannot be rescinded. Thus, an entry is required to recognize the decrease in retained earnings and the increase in the liability Dividends Payable. To illustrate, assume that on December 1, 2001, the directors of Media General declare a $.50 per share cash dividend on 100,000 shares of $10 par value common stock. The dividend is $50,000 (100,000 × $.50), and the entry to record the declaration is:

Declaration Date

Dec. 1	Retained Earnings (or Cash Dividends Declared)	50,000	
	Dividends Payable		50,000
	(To record declaration of cash dividend)		

A	=	L	+	SE
		+50,000		−50,000

Dividends Payable is a current liability because it will normally be paid within the next several months. You may recall that in Chapter 3, instead of decreasing Retained Earnings, the account Dividends was used. This account provides additional information in the ledger. For example, a company may have separate dividend accounts for each class of stock or each type of dividend. When a separate dividend account is used, its balance is transferred to Retained Earnings at the end of the year by a closing entry. Consequently, the effect of the declaration is the same: Retained earnings is decreased and a current liability is increased. To avoid additional detail, we have chosen to use the Retained Earnings account. For homework problems, you should use the Retained Earnings account for recording dividend declarations.

The **record date** marks the time when ownership of the outstanding shares is determined for dividend purposes. The stockholders' records maintained by the corporation supply this information. The time interval between the declaration date and the record date enables the corporation to update its stock ownership records. Between the declaration date and the record date, the number of shares outstanding should remain the same. Thus, the purpose of the record date is to identify the persons or entities that will receive the dividend, not to determine the amount of the dividend liability. For Media General, the record date is December 22. No entry is required on this date because the corporation's liability recognized on the declaration date is unchanged:

Helpful Hint The record date is important in determining the dividend to be paid to each stockholder but not the total dividend.

Record Date

Dec. 22			
	No entry necessary		

On the payment date, dividend checks are mailed to the stockholders and the payment of the dividend is recorded. If January 20 is the payment date for Media General, the entry on that date is:

Payment Date

$A = L + SE$
$-50,000 \ -50,000$
	Jan. 20	Dividends Payable
		    Cash
		       (To record payment of cash dividend)
			50,000
			
				50,000

Note that payment of the dividend reduces both current assets and current liabilities but has no effect on stockholders' equity. The cumulative effect of the **declaration and payment** of a cash dividend on a company's financial statements is to **decrease both stockholders' equity and total assets**.

STOCK DIVIDENDS

A stock dividend is a pro rata distribution of the corporation's own stock to stockholders. Whereas a cash dividend is paid in cash, a stock dividend is paid in stock. **A stock dividend results in a decrease in retained earnings and an increase in paid-in capital**. Unlike a cash dividend, a stock dividend does not decrease total stockholders' equity or total assets.

Because a stock dividend does not result in a distribution of assets, many view it as nothing more than a publicity gesture. Stock dividends are often issued by companies that do not have adequate cash to issue a cash dividend. These companies may not want to announce that they are not going to be issuing a dividend at their normal time to do so. By issuing a stock dividend they "save face" by giving the appearance of distributing a dividend. Note that since a stock dividend neither increases nor decreases the assets in the company, investors are not receiving anything they didn't already own. In a sense it is like ordering two pieces of pie and having the host take one piece of pie and cut it into two smaller pieces. You are not better off, but you got your two pieces of pie.

To illustrate a stock dividend, assume that you have a 2% ownership interest in Cetus Inc. by virtue of owning 20 of its 1,000 shares of common stock. In a 10% stock dividend, 100 shares (1,000 × 10%) of stock would be issued. You would receive two shares (2% × 100), but your ownership interest would remain at 2% (22 ÷ 1,100). **You now own more shares of stock, but your ownership interest has not changed**. Moreover, no cash is disbursed, and no liabilities have been assumed by the corporation.

What then are the purposes and benefits of a stock dividend? Corporations generally issue stock dividends for one of the following reasons:

Helpful Hint Because of its effects, a stock dividend is also referred to as capitalizing retained earnings.

1. To satisfy stockholders' dividend expectations without spending cash.
2. To increase the marketability of its stock by increasing the number of shares outstanding and thereby decreasing the market price per share. Decreasing the market price of the stock makes it easier for smaller investors to purchase the shares.
3. To emphasize that a portion of stockholders' equity has been permanently reinvested in the business and therefore is unavailable for cash dividends.

The size of the stock dividend and the value to be assigned to each dividend share are determined by the board of directors when the dividend is declared. The per share amount must be at least equal to the par or stated value in order to meet legal requirements.

The accounting profession distinguishes between a **small stock dividend** (less than 20%–25% of the corporation's issued stock) and a **large stock dividend** (greater than 20%–25%). It recommends that the directors assign the **fair**

market value per share for small stock dividends. The recommendation is based on the assumption that a small stock dividend will have little effect on the market price of the shares previously outstanding. Thus, many stockholders consider small stock dividends to be distributions of earnings equal to the fair market value of the shares distributed. The amount to be assigned for a large stock dividend is not specified by the accounting profession; however, **par or stated value per share** is normally assigned. Small stock dividends predominate in practice. Thus, we illustrate only the entries for small stock dividends.

Entries for Stock Dividends

To illustrate the accounting for stock dividends, assume that Medland Corporation has a balance of $300,000 in retained earnings and declares a 10% stock dividend on its 50,000 shares of $10 par value common stock. The current fair market value of its stock is $15 per share. The number of shares to be issued is 5,000 (10% × 50,000), and the total amount to be debited to Retained Earnings is $75,000 (5,000 × $15). The entry to record this transaction at the declaration date is:

Retained Earnings (or Stock Dividends Declared)	75,000	
Common Stock Dividends Distributable		50,000
Paid-in Capital in Excess of Par Value		25,000
(To record declaration of 10% stock dividend)		

```
A   =   L   +   SE
              -75,000
              +50,000
              +25,000
```

Note that at the declaration date Retained Earnings is decreased (debited) for the fair market value of the stock issued; Common Stock Dividends Distributable is increased (credited) for the par value of the dividend shares (5,000 × $10); and the excess over par (5,000 × $5) is credited to an additional paid-in capital account.

Common Stock Dividends Distributable is a stockholders' equity account; it is not a liability because assets will not be used to pay the dividend. If a balance sheet is prepared before the dividend shares are issued, the distributable account is reported in paid-in capital as an addition to common stock issued, as shown in Illustration 11-10.

MEDLAND CORPORATION		
Balance Sheet (partial)		
Paid-in capital		
Common stock	$500,000	
Common stock dividends distributable	50,000	$550,000

Illustration 11-10 Statement presentation of common stock dividends distributable

When the dividend shares are issued, Common Stock Dividends Distributable is decreased and Common Stock is increased as follows:

Helpful Hint Note that the dividend account title is *distributable*, not *payable*.

Common Stock Dividends Distributable	50,000	
Common Stock		50,000
(To record issuance of 5,000 shares in a stock dividend)		

```
A   =   L   +   SE
              -50,000
              +50,000
```

Effects of Stock Dividends

How do stock dividends affect stockholders' equity? They **change the composition of stockholders' equity** because a portion of retained earnings is transferred to paid-in capital. However, **total stockholders' equity remains the same**. Stock dividends also have no effect on the par or stated value per share, but the number of shares outstanding increases. These effects are shown in Illustration 11-11 (page 528) for Medland Corporation.

Illustration 11-11   Stock dividend effects

	Before Dividend	After Dividend
Stockholders' equity		
Paid-in capital		
Common stock, $10 par	$ 500,000	$ 550,000
Paid-in capital in excess of par value	—	25,000
Total paid-in capital	500,000	575,000
Retained earnings	300,000	225,000
Total stockholders' equity	**$800,000**	**$800,000**
Outstanding shares	**50,000**	**55,000**

In this example, total paid-in capital is increased by $75,000 and retained earnings is decreased by the same amount. Note also that total stockholders' equity remains unchanged at $800,000.

STOCK SPLITS

A stock split, like a stock dividend, involves the issuance of additional shares of stock to stockholders according to their percentage ownership. However, **a stock split results in a reduction in the par or stated value per share**. The purpose of a stock split is to increase the marketability of the stock by lowering its market value per share. This, in turn, makes it easier for the corporation to issue additional stock.

The effect of a split on market value is generally inversely proportional to the size of the split. For example, after a 4-for-1 stock split, the market value of IBM stock fell from $284 to approximately $71. In announcing the split, the chief executive of IBM said, "We want to make our stock more attractive to the small investor." Similarly, on September 9, 1995, Nike announced a 2-for-1 stock split. The record date was October 9, 1995, and the distribution date was October 30, 1995. Nike's stock was trading at $111 just prior to the split and at roughly $55 after the split.

Helpful Hint A stock split changes the par value per share but does not affect any balances in stockholders' equity.

In a stock split, the number of shares is increased in the same proportion that the par or stated value per share is decreased. For example, in a 2-for-1 split, one share of $10 par value stock is exchanged for two shares of $5 par value stock. **A stock split does not have any effect on paid-in capital**, **retained earnings, and total stockholders' equity**. However, the number of shares outstanding increases. These effects are shown in Illustration 11-12, assuming that instead of issuing a 10% stock dividend, Medland splits its 50,000 shares of common stock on a 2-for-1 basis.

Illustration 11-12   Stock split effects

	Before Stock Split	After Stock Split
Stockholders' equity		
Paid-in capital		
Common stock	$ 500,000	$ 500,000
Paid-in capital in excess of par value	0	0
Total paid-in capital	500,000	500,000
Retained earnings	300,000	300,000
Total stockholders' equity	**$800,000**	**$800,000**
Outstanding shares	**50,000**	**100,000**

Because a stock split does not affect the balances in any stockholders' equity accounts, **it is not necessary to journalize a stock split**. The differences between the effects of stock splits and stock dividends are shown in Illustration 11-13.

Item	Stock Split	Stock Dividend
Total paid-in capital	No change	Increase
Total retained earnings	No change	Decrease
Total par value (common stock)	No change	Increase
Par value per share	Decrease	No change

Illustration 11-13
Effects of stock splits and stock dividends differentiated

BUSINESS INSIGHT

Management Perspective

A handful of U.S. companies have no intention of keeping their stock trading in a range accessible to mere mortals. These companies never split their stock, no matter how high their stock price gets. The king of these is investment company Berkshire Hathaway's Class A stock, which goes for a pricey $58,000—per share! The company's Class B stock is a relative bargain at roughly $2,000 per share. Other "premium" stocks are A.D. Makepeace at $12,700 and Mechanics Bank of Richmond, California, at $12,000.

BEFORE YOU GO ON...

◆ Review It

1. What factors affect the size of a company's cash dividend?
2. Why do companies issue stock dividends? Why do companies declare stock splits?
3. Distinguish between a small and a large stock dividend and indicate the basis for valuing each kind of dividend.
4. Contrast the effects of a small stock dividend and a 2-for-1 stock split on (a) stockholders' equity and (b) outstanding shares.

◆ Do It

Due to five years of record earnings at Sing CD Corporation, the market price of its 500,000 shares of $2 par value common stock tripled from $15 per share to $45. During this period, paid-in capital remained the same at $2,000,000, but retained earnings increased from $1,500,000 to $10,000,000. President Joan Elbert is considering either a 10% stock dividend or a 2-for-1 stock split. She asks you to show the before and after effects of each option on retained earnings.

Reasoning: A stock dividend decreases retained earnings and increases paid-in capital, but total stockholders' equity remains the same. A stock split changes only par value per share and the number of shares outstanding. Thus, a stock split has no effect on the retained earnings balance.

Solution: The stock dividend amount is $2,250,000 [(500,000 × 10%) × $45]. The new balance in retained earnings is $7,750,000 ($10,000,000 − $2,250,000). The retained earnings balance after the stock split is the same as it was before the split: $10,000,000. The effects in the stockholders' equity accounts are as follows:

	Original Balances	After Dividend	After Split
Paid-in capital	$ 2,000,000	$ 4,250,000	$ 2,000,000
Retained earnings	10,000,000	7,750,000	10,000,000
Total stockholders' equity	$12,000,000	$12,000,000	$12,000,000
Shares outstanding	500,000	550,000	1,000,000

RETAINED EARNINGS

STUDY OBJECTIVE

6

Identify the items that affect retained earnings.

Retained earnings is net income that is retained in the business. The balance in retained earnings is part of the stockholders' claim on the total assets of the corporation. It does not, however, represent a claim on any specific asset. Nor can the amount of retained earnings be associated with the balance of any asset account. For example, a $100,000 balance in retained earnings does not mean that there should be $100,000 in cash. The reason is that the cash resulting from the excess of revenues over expenses may have been used to purchase buildings, equipment, and other assets. Illustration 11-14 shows recent amounts of retained earnings and cash in selected companies.

Illustration 11-14
Retained earnings and cash balances

	(in millions)	
Company	Retained Earnings	Cash
Circuit City Stores, Inc.	$1,267	$266
Nike, Inc.	2,996	109
Starbucks Coffee Company	205	124
Amazon.com	(160)	373

When expenses exceed revenues, a **net loss** results. In contrast to net income, a net loss decreases retained earnings. In closing entries a net loss is debited to the Retained Earnings account. **Net losses are not debited to paid-in capital accounts.** To do so would destroy the distinction between paid-in and earned capital. If cumulative losses exceed cumulative income over a company's life, a debit balance in Retained Earnings results. A debit balance in retained earnings, such as that of Amazon.com in 1998, is identified as a deficit and is reported as a deduction in the stockholders' equity section of the balance sheet, as shown in Illustration 11-15.

Illustration 11-15
Stockholders' equity with deficit

Amazon.com

AMAZON.COM Balance Sheet (partial) December 31, 1998 (in thousands)	
Stockholders' equity	
Paid-in capital	
Common stock	$ 1,593
Paid-in capital in excess of par value	299,212
Total paid-in capital	300,805
Accumulated deficit	**(162,060)**
Total stockholders' equity	$138,745

RETAINED EARNINGS RESTRICTIONS

The balance in retained earnings is generally available for dividend declarations. Some companies state this fact. In some cases, however, there may be **retained earnings restrictions** that make a portion of the balance currently unavailable for dividends. Restrictions result from one or more of these causes: legal, contractual, or voluntary. Retained earnings restrictions are generally disclosed in the notes to the financial statements. For example, Tektronix Inc., a manufacturer of electronic measurement devices, included the note in Illustration 11-16 in its 1998 financial statements.

Illustration 11-16
Disclosure of retained earnings restriction

TEKTRONIX INC. **Notes to the Financial Statements**
Certain of the Company's debt agreements require the maintenance of specified interest rate coverage ratios and a minimum consolidated tangible net worth. At May 30, 1998, the Company had unrestricted retained earnings of $156.9 million after meeting those requirements.

Financial Statement Presentation of Stockholders' Equity

In the stockholders' equity section of the balance sheet, paid-in capital and retained earnings are reported, and the specific sources of paid-in capital are identified. Within paid-in capital, two classifications are recognized:

STUDY OBJECTIVE

7

Prepare a comprehensive stockholders' equity section.

1. **Capital stock**, which consists of preferred and common stock. Preferred stock is shown before common stock because of its preferential rights. Information about the par value, shares authorized, shares issued, and shares outstanding is reported for each class of stock.

2. **Additional paid-in capital**, which includes the excess of amounts paid in over par or stated value and paid-in capital from treasury stock.

The stockholders' equity section of the balance sheet of Graber Inc. is presented in Illustration 11-17 (page 532). Note that Common Stock Dividends Distributable is shown under Capital Stock in the Paid-in Capital category, and a retained earnings restriction is disclosed.

The stockholders' equity section for Graber Inc. includes most of the accounts discussed in this chapter. The disclosures pertaining to Graber's common stock indicate that 400,000 shares are issued, 100,000 shares are unissued (500,000 authorized less 400,000 issued), and 390,000 shares are outstanding (400,000 issued less 10,000 shares in treasury).

Illustration 11-17 Comprehensive stockholders' equity section

International Note

In Switzerland, there are no specific disclosure requirements for shareholders' equity. However, companies typically disclose separate categories of capital on the balance sheet.

GRABER INC. Balance Sheet (partial)			
Stockholders' equity			
Paid-in capital			
Capital stock			
9% Preferred stock, $100 par value, cumulative, callable at $120, 10,000 shares authorized, 6,000 shares issued and outstanding			$ 600,000
Common stock, no par, $5 stated value, 500,000 shares authorized, 400,000 shares issued, and 390,000 outstanding		$2,000,000	
Common stock dividends distributable		50,000	2,050,000
Total capital stock			2,650,000
Additional paid-in capital			
In excess of par value—preferred stock		30,000	
In excess of stated value—common stock		1,050,000	
Total additional paid-in capital			1,080,000
Total paid-in capital			3,730,000
Retained earnings (see Note R)			1,160,000
Total paid-in capital and retained earnings			4,890,000
Less: Treasury stock—common (10,000 shares)			(80,000)
Total stockholders' equity			$4,810,000

Note R: Retained earnings is restricted for the cost of treasury stock, $80,000.

In published annual reports, subclassifications within the stockholders' equity section are seldom presented. Moreover, the individual sources of additional paid-in capital are often combined and reported as a single amount, as shown by the excerpts from Kmart's 1998 balance sheet in Illustration 11-18.

Illustration 11-18 Stockholders' equity section

KMART INC. Balance Sheet (partial) (in millions)	
Stockholders' equity	
Common stock, $.1 par value; 1,500,000,000 shares authorized; 493,358,504 shares issued	$ 493
Capital in excess of par value	1,667
Retained earnings	3,819
Total stockholders' equity	$5,979

BEFORE YOU GO ON...

◆ Review It

1. Identify the classifications within the paid-in capital section and the totals that are stated in the stockholders' equity section of a balance sheet.
2. How are stock dividends distributable reported in the stockholders' equity section?

3. What was the total cost of Tootsie Roll's treasury stock in 1998? What was the total value of the 1998 cash dividend? What was the total charge to retained earnings of the 1998 stock dividend? The answer to these questions is provided on p. 557.

MEASURING CORPORATE PERFORMANCE

Investors are interested in both a company's dividend record and its earnings performance. Although they are often parallel, that is not always the case. Thus, each should be investigated separately.

DIVIDEND RECORD

One way that companies reward stock investors for their investment is to pay them dividends. The payout ratio measures the percentage of earnings distributed in the form of cash dividends to common stockholders. It is computed by **dividing total cash dividends declared to common shareholders by net income**. Another measure, the dividend yield, reports the rate of return an investor earned from dividends during the year. It is computed by **dividing cash dividends declared per share of common stock during the year by the stock price at the end of the year**. From the information shown below, the payout ratios and dividend yields for Nike in 1997 and 1998 are calculated in Illustration 11-19.

STUDY OBJECTIVE

8

Evaluate a corporation's dividend and earnings performance from a stockholder's perspective.

	1998	**1997**
Dividends (in millions)	$132.9	$108.2
Dividends per share	.46	.38
Net income (in millions)	399.6	795.8
Stock price at end of year	46.0	57.5

Illustration 11-19 Nike dividend ratios

$$\text{Payout Ratio} = \frac{\text{Cash Dividends Declared on Common Stock}}{\text{Net Income}}$$

$$\text{Dividend Yield} = \frac{\text{Cash Dividends Declared per Share}}{\text{Stock Price at Year-End}}$$

($ in millions except per share data)	1998	1997
Payout Ratio	$\dfrac{\$132.9}{\$399.6} = 33.3\%$	$\dfrac{\$108.2}{\$795.8} = 13.6\%$
Dividend Yield	$\dfrac{\$.46}{\$46} = 1.0\%$	$\dfrac{\$.38}{\$57.5} = 0.7\%$

Companies that have high growth rates are characterized by low payout ratios and dividend yields because they reinvest most of their net income in the business. Thus, a low payout ratio or dividend yield is not necessarily bad news. Companies, such as Nike and Reebok, that believe they have many good opportunities for growth will reinvest those funds in the company rather than pay high dividends. In fact, dividend payout ratios and dividend yields for the 500 largest U.S. companies are at all-time lows. However, low dividend payments, or a cut in dividend payments, might signal that a company has liquidity or solvency problems and is trying to free up cash by not paying dividends. Thus, the reason for low dividend payments should be investigated.

Listed in Illustration 11-20 are dividend ratios in recent years of four well-known companies.

Illustration 11-20 Variability of dividend ratios among companies

Company	Payout Ratio	Dividend Yield
Microsoft	0%	0%
Kellogg	82.6%	2.7%
Sears	32.3%	3.1%
Johnson & Johnson	41.6%	1.2%

DECISION TOOLKIT

Decision Checkpoints	Info Needed for Decision	Tool to Use for Decision	How to Evaluate Results
What portion of its earnings does the company pay out in dividends?	Net income and total cash dividends paid on common stock	$\text{Payout ratio} = \dfrac{\text{Cash dividends declared on common stock}}{\text{Net income}}$	A low ratio suggests that the company is retaining its earnings for investment in future growth.
What level of return can be earned on the company's dividends?	Market price of stock and dividends paid per share on common stock	$\text{Dividend yield} = \dfrac{\text{Cash dividends declared per share}}{\text{Stock price at year-end}}$	A high yield is attractive to investors looking for a steady investment income stream rather than stock price appreciation.

EARNINGS PERFORMANCE

Earnings per share measures the net income earned on each share of common stock. It is computed by dividing **net income** by the **average number of common shares outstanding during the year**. Stockholders usually think in terms of the number of shares they own or plan to buy or sell, so reducing net income earned to a per share amount provides a useful perspective for determining the investment return. Advanced accounting courses present more refined techniques for calculating earnings per share. For now, a basic approach is to divide earnings available to common stockholders (Net income − Preferred stock dividends) by average common shares outstanding during the year. By comparing earnings per share of a single company over time, one can evaluate its relative earnings performance from the perspective of a shareholder—that is, on a per share basis.

It is very important to note that comparisons of earnings per share across companies are **not meaningful** because of the wide variations in the numbers of shares of outstanding stock among companies and in the stock prices. Instead, in order to make a meaningful comparison of earnings across firms, we calculate the price-earnings ratio. The price-earnings ratio is an oft-quoted statistic that measures **the ratio of the market price of each share of common stock to the earnings per share**. It is computed by dividing the market price per share of stock by earnings per share. The price-earnings (P-E) ratio reflects the investors' assessment of a company's future earnings. The ratio of price to earnings will be higher if investors think that current earnings levels will persist or increase than it will be if investors think that earnings will decline. A high price-earnings ratio might also indicate that a stock is priced too high and is likely to come down. From the information presented below, the earnings per share and price-earnings ratios for Nike in 1997 and 1998 are calculated in Illustration 11-21. (Note that to simplify our calculations, we assumed that any change in shares for Nike occurred in the middle of the year.)

(in thousands except per share data)	1998	1997
Net income	$399,600	$795,800
Preferred stock dividends	$30	$30
Shares outstanding at beginning of year	287,000	287,200
Shares outstanding at end of year	289,300	287,000
Market price of stock at end of year	$46.0	$57.5

$$\text{Earnings per Share} = \frac{\text{Net Income} - \text{Preferred Stock Dividends}}{\text{Average Common Shares Outstanding}}$$

$$\text{Price-Earnings Ratio} = \frac{\text{Stock Price per Share}}{\text{Earnings per Share}}$$

($ in thousands)	1998	1997
Earnings per Share	$\frac{\$399,600 - \$30}{(289,300 + 287,000)/2} = \$1.39$	$\frac{\$795,800 - \$30}{(287,000 + 287,200)/2} = \$2.77$
Price-Earnings Ratio	$\frac{\$46.0}{\$1.39} = 33.1 \text{ times}$	$\frac{\$57.5}{\$2.77} = 20.8 \text{ times}$

Illustration 11-21
Nike earnings per share and price-earnings ratio

From 1997 to 1998, Nike's earnings per share decreased substantially, on approximately the same number of shares. Its price-earnings ratio increased. This increase might reflect a belief that Nike will be able to return to its usual profitability and growth.

As noted, earnings per share cannot be meaningfully compared across companies. Price-earnings ratios, however, can be compared. Illustration 11-22 lists five companies and their earnings per share and price-earnings ratios for 1998 (calculated at the end of each company's fiscal year). Note the dramatic difference between General Motors and Yahoo!

Company	Earnings Per Share	Price-Earnings Ratio
Microsoft	$ .92	55.7
Kellogg	1.23	30.8
Sears	2.70	14.3
General Motors	4.26	9.0
Yahoo!	.14	1,240.0

Illustration 11-22
Variability of earnings performance ratios among companies

DECISION TOOLKIT

Decision Checkpoints	Info Needed for Decision	Tool to Use for Decision	How to Evaluate Results
How does the company's earnings performance compare with that of previous years?	Net income available to common shareholders and average common shares outstanding	$\text{Earnings per share} = \dfrac{\text{Net income} - \text{Preferred stock dividends}}{\text{Average common shares outstanding}}$	A higher measure suggests improved performance, although the number is subject to manipulation. Values should not be compared across companies.
How does the market perceive the company's prospects for future earnings?	Earnings per share and market price per share	$\text{Price-earnings ratio} = \dfrac{\text{Stock price per share}}{\text{Earnings per share}}$	A high ratio suggests the market has favorable expectations, although it also may suggest stock is overpriced.

Another widely used ratio that measures profitability from the common stockholders' viewpoint is **return on common stockholders' equity**. This ratio shows how many dollars of net income were earned for each dollar invested by common stockholders. It is computed by dividing net income available to common stockholders (Net income − Preferred stock dividends) by average common stockholders' equity. From the additional information presented below, Nike's return on common stockholders' equity ratios are calculated for 1997 and 1998 in Illustration 11-23.

Illustration 11-23 Nike return on common stockholders' equity

(in thousands)	1998	1997	1996
Net income	$ 399,600	$ 795,800	$ 553,200
Preferred stock dividends	30	30	30
Common stockholders' equity	3,261,600	3,155,900	2,431,400

$$\text{Return on Common Stockholders' Equity Ratio} = \frac{\text{Net Income} - \text{Preferred Stock Dividends}}{\text{Average Common Stockholders' Equity}}$$

($ in thousands)	1998	1997
Return on Common Stockholders' Equity Ratio	$\dfrac{\$399,600 - \$30}{(\$3,261,600 + \$3,155,900)/2} = 12.5\%$	$\dfrac{\$795,800 - \$30}{(\$3,155,900 + \$2,431,400)/2} = 28.5\%$

From 1997 to 1998, Nike's return on common shareholders' equity decreased from 28.5% to 12.5%. As a company grows larger it becomes increasingly hard to sustain a high return. In Nike's case, since many believe the U.S. market for expensive sports shoes is saturated, it will need to grow either along new product lines, such as hiking shoes, or in new markets, such as Europe and Asia. We will talk more about factors that affect the return on common shareholders' equity in Chapter 14.

DECISION TOOLKIT

Decision Checkpoints	Info Needed for Decision	Tool to Use for Decision		How to Evaluate Results
What is the company's return on common stockholders' investment?	Earnings available to common stockholders and average common stockholders' equity	Return on common stockholders' equity ratio	$= \dfrac{\text{Net income} - \text{Preferred stock dividends}}{\text{Average common stockholders' equity}}$	A high measure suggests strong earnings performance from common stockholders' perspective.

BUSINESS INSIGHT
Management Perspective

Nike's advertising success, envied throughout the business world, was recently spoofed in the humor magazine *The Onion*. The article blared, "Nike to Cease Manufacturing Products: 'From now on, we'll focus on just making ads,' says a spokesman." Another "quote" attributed to Phil Knight, Nike cofounder and CEO, was "The last few years, it became impossible to maintain our high standards of advertising while faced with the daily distractions of making sneakers. By discontinuing our entire product line, we will ensure that Nike remains the world's leader in the field of incredibly cool TV commercials well into the 21st century." Based on your understanding of accounting, how would this strategy affect Nike's return on common shareholders' equity?

Source: "Nike to Cease Manufacturing Products," *The Onion*, September 11, 1996, p. 1 (www.TheOnion.com).

BEFORE YOU GO ON...

◆ **Review It**

1. What measures can be used to evaluate a company's dividend record, and how are they calculated?
2. Why should earnings per share not be compared across companies?
3. What does a high price-earnings ratio suggest about a company's future earnings potential?

USING THE DECISION TOOLKIT

During 1998 Reebok hit difficult times in which both its profits and market share declined. As a result, its stock price sagged and investors became impatient.

Instructions

The following facts are available for Reebok. Using this information, evaluate its (1) dividend record and (2) earnings performance, and contrast them with those for Nike for 1997 and 1998:

(in thousands except per share data)	1998	1997	1996
Dividends declared	0	0	$ 15,180
Dividends declared per share	0	0	$ 0.164
Net income	$ 23,927	$135,119	$138,950
Preferred stock dividends	0	0	0
Shares outstanding at end of year	56,590	56,400	55,840
Stock price at end of year	$ 14.88	$ 28.81	$ 42.00
Common stockholders' equity	$524,377	$507,157	$381,234

Solution

1. *Dividend record:* Two measures to evaluate dividend record are the payout ratio and the dividend yield. For Reebok, these measures in 1997 and 1998 are calculated as shown here:

	1998	**1997**
Payout ratio	$\dfrac{\$0}{\$23,927} = 0\%$	$\dfrac{\$0}{\$135,119} = 0\%$
Dividend yield	$\dfrac{\$0}{\$14.88} = 0\%$	$\dfrac{\$0}{\$28.81} = 0\%$

Nike's dividends paid per share increased 8 cents from 1997 to 1998, while Reebok's went from $.164 in 1996 to zero in 1997 and 1998. Elimination of a dividend is generally perceived as very bad news about a company's future prospects.

2. *Earnings performance:* There are many measures of earnings performance. Those presented in the chapter were earnings per share, the price-earnings ratio, and the return on common stockholders' equity ratio. These measures for Reebok in 1998 and 1997 are calculated as shown here:

	1998	**1997**
Earnings per share	$\dfrac{\$23,927 - 0}{(56,590 + 56,400)/2} = \$.42$	$\dfrac{\$135,119 - 0}{(56,400 + 55,840)/2} = \$2.41$
Price-earnings ratio	$\dfrac{\$14.88}{\$.42} = 35.4$	$\dfrac{\$28.81}{\$2.41} = 11.95$
Return on common stockholders' equity ratio	$\dfrac{\$23,927 - 0}{(\$524,377 + \$507,157)/2} = 4.6\%$	$\dfrac{\$135,119 - 0}{(\$507,157 + \$381,234)/2} = 30.4\%$

From 1997 to 1998 Reebok's earnings declined on both a total and per share basis. This decline was very significant and would be of obvious concern to both management and shareholders. Like Nike, Reebok's price-earnings ratio increased, perhaps hinting that investors believe earnings will rebound somewhat in coming years. Compared to Nike's P-E ratio of 33.1, Reebok seems to be slightly higher-priced; that is, Reebok's shareholders are paying more per dollar of earnings than are Nike's.

Reebok's return on common stockholders' equity declined from 30.4% to 4.6%. This is an alarming drop, which would be of great concern to shareholders.

SUMMARY OF STUDY OBJECTIVES

1 *Identify and discuss the major characteristics of a corporation.* The major characteristics of a corporation are separate legal existence, limited liability of stockholders, transferable ownership rights, ability to acquire capital, continuous life, corporation management, government regulations, and additional taxes.

2 *Record the issuance of common stock.* When the issuance of common stock for cash is recorded, the par value of the shares is credited to Common Stock and the portion of the proceeds that is above or below par value is recorded in a separate paid-in capital account. When no-par common stock has a stated value, the entries are similar to those for par value stock. When no-par common stock does not have a stated value, the entire proceeds from the issue become legal capital and are credited to Common Stock.

3 *Explain the accounting for the purchase of treasury stock.* The cost method is generally used in accounting for treasury stock. Under this approach, Treasury Stock is debited at the price paid to reacquire the shares.

4 *Differentiate preferred stock from common stock.* Preferred stock has contractual provisions that give it priority over common stock in certain areas. Typically, preferred stockholders have a preference as to (a) dividends and (b) assets in the event of liquidation. However, they often do not have voting rights.

5 *Prepare the entries for cash dividends and stock dividends.* Entries for both cash and stock dividends are required at the declaration date and the payment date. At the declaration date the entries are as follows: For a *cash dividend*—debit Retained Earnings and credit Dividends Payable; for a *small stock dividend*—debit Retained Earnings, credit Paid-in Capital in Excess of Par (or Stated) Value, and credit Common Stock Dividends Distributable. At the payment date, the entries for cash and

stock dividends, respectively, are debit Dividends Payable and credit Cash, and debit Common Stock Dividends Distributable and credit Common Stock.

6 *Identify the items that affect retained earnings.* Additions to retained earnings consist of net income. Deductions consist of net loss and cash and stock dividends. In some instances, portions of retained earnings are restricted, making that portion unavailable for the payment of dividends.

7 *Prepare a comprehensive stockholders' equity section.* In the stockholders' equity section of the balance sheet, paid-in capital and retained earnings are reported and specific sources of paid-in capital are identified. Within paid-in capital, two classifications are shown: capital stock and additional paid-in capital. If a corporation has treasury stock, the cost of treasury stock is deducted from total paid-in capital and retained earnings to obtain total stockholders' equity.

8 *Evaluate a corporation's dividend and earnings performance from a stockholder's perspective.* A company's dividend record can be evaluated by looking at what percentage of net income it chooses to pay out in dividends, as measured by the dividend payout ratio (dividends divided by net income), or it can be evaluated from the perspective of a rate of return on stockholders' investment through the dividend yield (dividends divided by stock price). Earnings performance is measured with earnings per share (net income available to common shareholders divided by average number of shares). In order to compare the relative amounts that investors are currently paying per dollar of reported earnings, the price-earnings ratio is calculated (share price divided by earnings per share). Another measure of earnings performance is the return on common stockholders' equity ratio (income available to common shareholders divided by average common shareholders' equity).

DECISION TOOLKIT—A SUMMARY

Decision Checkpoints	Info Needed for Decision	Tool to Use for Decision	How to Evaluate Results
Should the company incorporate?	Capital needs, growth expectations, type of business, tax status	Corporations have limited liability, easier capital raising ability, and professional managers; but they suffer from additional taxes, government regulations, and separation of ownership from management.	Must carefully weigh the costs and benefits in light of the particular circumstances.
What portion of its earnings does the company pay out in dividends?	Net income and total cash dividends paid on common stock	$\text{Payout ratio} = \dfrac{\text{Cash dividends declared on common stock}}{\text{Net income}}$	A low ratio suggests that the company is retaining its earnings for investment in future growth.
What level of return can be earned on the company's dividends?	Market price of stock and dividends paid per share on common stock	$\text{Dividend yield} = \dfrac{\text{Cash dividends declared per share}}{\text{Stock price at year-end}}$	A high yield is attractive to investors looking for a steady investment income stream rather than stock price appreciation.
How does the company's earnings performance compare with that of previous years?	Net income available to common shareholders and average common shares outstanding	$\text{Earnings per share} = \dfrac{\text{Net income} - \text{Preferred stock dividends}}{\text{Average common shares outstanding}}$	A higher measure suggests improved performance, although the number is subject to manipulation. Values should not be compared across companies.
How does the market perceive the company's prospects for future earnings?	Earnings per share and market price per share	$\text{Price-earnings ratio} = \dfrac{\text{Stock price per share}}{\text{Earnings per share}}$	A high ratio suggests the market has favorable expectations, although it also may suggest stock is overpriced.
What is the company's return on common stockholders' investment?	Earnings available to common stockholders and average common stockholders' equity	$\text{Return on common stockholders' equity ratio} = \dfrac{\text{Net income} - \text{Preferred stock dividends}}{\text{Average common stockholders' equity}}$	A high measure suggests strong earnings performance from common stockholders' perspective.

GLOSSARY

Authorized stock   The amount of stock that a corporation is authorized to sell as indicated in its charter. (p. 516)

Cash dividend   A pro rata distribution of cash to stockholders. (p. 524)

Corporation   A company organized as a separate legal entity, with most of the rights and privileges of a person. Evidence of ownership is shares of stock. (p. 510)

Cumulative dividend A feature of preferred stock entitling the stockholder to receive current and unpaid prior-year dividends before common stockholders receive any dividends. (p. 523)

Declaration date The date the board of directors formally declares the dividend and announces it to stockholders. (p. 525)

Deficit A debit balance in retained earnings. (p. 530)

Dividend A distribution by a corporation to its stockholders on a pro rata (equal) basis. (p. 524)

Dividend yield A measure of the rate of return an investor earned from dividends during the year. (p. 533)

Dividends in arrears Preferred dividends that were scheduled to be declared but were not declared during a given period. (p. 523)

Earnings per share A measure of the net income earned on each share of common stock; computed by dividing net income minus preferred stock dividends by the average number of common shares outstanding during the year. (p. 534)

Legal capital The amount per share of stock that must be retained in the business for the protection of corporate creditors. (p. 516)

No-par value stock Capital stock that has not been assigned a value in the corporate charter. (p. 517)

Outstanding stock Capital stock that has been issued and is being held by stockholders. (p. 521)

Paid-in capital The amount paid in to the corporation by stockholders in exchange for shares of ownership. (p. 517)

Par value stock Capital stock that has been assigned a value per share in the corporate charter. (p. 516)

Payment date The date dividend checks are mailed to stockholders. (p. 526)

Payout ratio A measure of the percentage of earnings distributed in the form of cash dividends to common stockholders. (p. 533)

Preferred stock Capital stock that has contractual preferences over common stock in certain areas. (p. 522)

Price-earnings ratio A measure of the ratio of the market price of each share of common stock to the earnings per share; it reflects the stock market's belief about a company's future earnings potential. (p. 535)

Privately held corporation A corporation that has only a few stockholders and whose stock is not available for sale to the general public. (p. 510)

Publicly held corporation A corporation that may have thousands of stockholders and whose stock is regularly traded on a national securities market. (p. 510)

Record date The date when ownership of outstanding shares is determined for dividend purposes. (p. 525)

Retained earnings Net income that is retained in the business. (p. 530)

Retained earnings restrictions Circumstances that make a portion of retained earnings currently unavailable for dividends. (p. 531)

Return on common stockholders' equity ratio A measure of profitability from the stockholders' point of view; computed by dividing net income minus preferred stock dividends by average common stockholders' equity. (p. 536)

Stated value The amount per share assigned by the board of directors to no-par stock that becomes legal capital per share. (p. 517)

Stock dividend A pro rata distribution of the corporation's own stock to stockholders. (p. 526)

Stock split The issuance of additional shares of stock to stockholders accompanied by a reduction in the par or stated value per share. (p. 528)

Treasury stock A corporation's own stock that has been issued, fully paid for, and reacquired by the corporation but not retired. (p. 519)

DEMONSTRATION PROBLEM

Rolman Corporation is authorized to issue 1,000,000 shares of $5 par value common stock. In its first year the company has these stock transactions:

Jan. 10 Issued 400,000 shares of stock at $8 per share.
Sept. 1 Purchased 10,000 shares of common stock for the treasury at $9 per share.
Dec. 24 Declared a cash dividend of 10 cents per share.

Instructions

(a) Journalize the transactions.
(b) Prepare the stockholders' equity section of the balance sheet assuming the company had retained earnings of $150,600 at December 31.

Problem-Solving Strategies

1. When common stock has a par value, Common Stock is always credited for par value.
2. The Treasury Stock account is debited at cost.

Solution to Demonstration Problem

(a)

Jan. 10	Cash		3,200,000	
	Common Stock			2,000,000
	Paid-in Capital in Excess of Par Value			1,200,000
	(To record issuance of 400,000 shares of $5 par value stock)			
Sept. 1	Treasury Stock		90,000	
	Cash			90,000
	(To record purchase of 10,000 shares of treasury stock at cost)			
Dec. 24	Retained Earnings		39,000	
	Dividends Payable			39,000
	(To record declaration of 10 cents per share cash dividend)			

ROLMAN CORPORATION
Balance Sheet (partial)

(b) Stockholders' equity

Paid-in capital	
Capital stock	
Common stock, $5 par value, 1,000,000 shares authorized, 400,000 shares issued, 390,000 outstanding	$2,000,000
Additional paid-in capital in excess of par value	1,200,000
Total paid-in capital	3,200,000
Retained earnings	150,600
Total paid-in capital and retained earnings	3,350,600
Less: Treasury stock (10,000 shares)	90,000
Total stockholders' equity	$3,260,600

SELF-STUDY QUESTIONS

Answers are at the end of the chapter.

(SO 1) 1. Which of these is *not* a major advantage of a corporation?
(a) Separate legal existence.
(b) Continuous life.
(c) Government regulations.
(d) Transferable ownership rights.

(SO 1) 2. A major disadvantage of a corporation is:
(a) limited liability of stockholders.
(b) additional taxes.
(c) transferable ownership rights.
(d) None of the above.

(SO 1) 3. Which of these statements is *false*?
(a) Ownership of common stock gives the owner a voting right.
(b) The stockholders' equity section begins with paid-in capital.
(c) The authorization of capital stock does not result in a formal accounting entry.
(d) Legal capital per share applies to par value stock but not to no-par value stock.

(SO 2) 4. ABC Corporation issues 1,000 shares of $10 par value common stock at $12 per share. When the transaction is recorded, credits are made to:
(a) Common Stock $10,000 and Paid-in Capital in Excess of Stated Value $2,000.
(b) Common Stock $12,000.
(c) Common Stock $10,000 and Paid-in Capital in Excess of Par Value $2,000.
(d) Common Stock $10,000 and Retained Earnings $2,000.

(SO 4) 5. Preferred stock may have priority over common stock *except* in:
(a) dividends.
(b) assets in the event of liquidation.
(c) conversion.
(d) voting.

(SO 5) 6. Entries for cash dividends are required on the:
(a) declaration date and the record date.
(b) record date and the payment date.
(c) declaration date, record date, and payment date.
(d) declaration date and the payment date.

(SO 5) 7. Which of these statements about small stock dividends is *true*?
(a) A debit should be made to Retained Earnings for the par value of the shares issued.
(b) Market value per share should be assigned to the dividend shares.
(c) A stock dividend decreases total stockholders' equity.
(d) A stock dividend ordinarily will increase total stockholders' equity.

(SO 7) 8. In the stockholders' equity section, the cost of treasury stock is deducted from:
(a) total paid-in capital and retained earnings.
(b) retained earnings.
(c) total stockholders' equity.
(d) common stock in paid-in capital.

9. A high price-earnings ratio indicates: (SO 8)
(a) a company has strong future earnings potential.
(b) a company's stock is priced too high and is likely to come down.
(c) either (a) or (b).
(d) neither (a) nor (b).

10. Herb Fischer is nearing retirement (SO 8) and would like to invest in a stock that will provide a good steady income supply. Herb should choose a stock with a:
(a) high current ratio.
(b) high dividend yield.
(c) high earnings per share.
(d) high price-earnings ratio.

QUESTIONS

1. Pat Kabza, a student, asks your help in understanding some characteristics of a corporation. Explain each of these to Pat:
(a) Separate legal existence.
(b) Limited liability of stockholders.
(c) Transferable ownership rights.

2. (a) Your friend T. R. Cedras cannot understand how the characteristic of corporation management is both an advantage and a disadvantage. Clarify this problem for T. R.
(b) Identify and explain two other disadvantages of a corporation.

3. Cary Brant believes a corporation must be incorporated in the state in which its headquarters office is located. Is Cary correct? Explain.

4. What are the basic ownership rights of common stockholders in the absence of restrictive provisions?

5. A corporation has been defined as an entity separate and distinct from its owners. In what ways is a corporation a separate legal entity?

6. What are the two principal components of stockholders' equity?

7. The corporate charter of Letterman Corporation allows the issuance of a maximum of 100,000 shares of common stock. During its first 2 years of operation, Letterman sold 60,000 shares to shareholders and reacquired 7,000 of these shares. After these transactions, how many shares are authorized, issued, and outstanding?

8. Which is the better investment—common stock with a par value of $5 per share or common stock with a par value of $20 per share?

9. What factors help determine the market value of stock?

10. Why is common stock usually not issued at a price that is less than par value?

11. For what reasons might a company like IBM repurchase some of its stock (treasury stock)?

12. Wilmor, Inc., purchases 1,000 shares of its own previously issued $5 par common stock for $11,000. Assuming the shares are held in the treasury, what effect does this transaction have on (a) net income, (b) total assets, (c) total paid-in capital, and (d) total stockholders' equity?

13. (a) What are the principal differences between common stock and preferred stock?
(b) Preferred stock may be cumulative. Discuss this feature.
(c) How are dividends in arrears presented in the financial statements?

14. Identify the events that result in credits and debits to retained earnings.

15. Indicate how each of these accounts should be classified in the stockholders' equity section of the balance sheet:
(a) Common stock.
(b) Paid-in capital in excess of par value.
(c) Retained earnings.
(d) Treasury stock.
(e) Paid-in capital in excess of stated value.
(f) Preferred stock.

16. What three conditions must be met before a cash dividend is paid?

17. Three dates associated with Galena Company's cash dividend are May 1, May 15, and May 31. Discuss the significance of each date and give the entry at each date.

18. Contrast the effects of a cash dividend and a stock dividend on a corporation's balance sheet.

19. Jill Sims asks, "Since stock dividends don't change anything, why declare them?" What is your answer to Jill?

20. Bella Corporation has 10,000 shares of $15 par value common stock outstanding when it announces a 2-for-1 split. Before the split, the stock had a market

price of $140 per share. After the split, how many shares of stock will be outstanding, and what will be the approximate market price per share?

21. The board of directors is considering a stock split or a stock dividend. They understand that total stockholders' equity will remain the same under either action. However, they are not sure of the different effects of the two actions on other aspects of stockholders' equity. Explain the differences to the directors.

22. (a) What is the purpose of a retained earnings restriction?
    (b) Identify the possible causes of retained earnings restrictions.

23. WAT Inc.'s common stock has a par value of $1 and a current market value of $15. Explain why these amounts are different.

24. What is the formula for the dividend yield and the payout ratio, and what does each indicate?

25. Matthew Dodge notes that TID Industries has an earnings per share that is double that of Derauf Inc. Therefore, he concludes that TID is a better investment. Is he correct?

26. Why do some investors like to buy stocks that have low price-earnings ratios?

BRIEF EXERCISES

Cite advantages and disadvantages of a corporation.
(SO 1)

BE11-1 Tracy Bono is studying for her accounting midterm examination. Identify for Tracy the advantages and disadvantages of the corporate form of business organization.

Journalize issuance of par value common stock.
(SO 2)

BE11-2 On May 10 Armada Corporation issues 1,000 shares of $10 par value common stock for cash at $14 per share. Journalize the issuance of the stock.

Journalize issuance of no-par common stock.
(SO 2)

BE11-3 On June 1 Eagle Inc. issues 2,000 shares of no-par common stock at a cash price of $7 per share. Journalize the issuance of the shares.

Journalize issuance of preferred stock.
(SO 4)

BE11-4 Ozark Inc. issues 5,000 shares of $100 par value preferred stock for cash at $112 per share. Journalize the issuance of the preferred stock.

Prepare entries for a cash dividend.
(SO 5)

BE11-5 The Seabee Corporation has 10,000 shares of common stock outstanding. It declares a $1 per share cash dividend on November 1 to stockholders of record on December 1. The dividend is paid on December 31. Prepare the entries on the appropriate dates to record the declaration and payment of the cash dividend.

Prepare entries for a stock dividend.
(SO 5)

BE11-6 Satina Corporation has 100,000 shares of $10 par value common stock outstanding. It declares a 10% stock dividend on December 1 when the market value per share is $12. The dividend shares are issued on December 31. Prepare the entries for the declaration and payment of the stock dividend.

Show before and after effects of a stock dividend.
(SO 5)

BE11-7 The stockholders' equity section of Desi Corporation's balance sheet consists of common stock ($10 par) $1,000,000 and retained earnings $400,000. A 10% stock dividend (10,000 shares) is declared when the market value per share is $12. Show the before and after effects of the dividend on (a) the components of stockholders' equity and (b) the shares outstanding.

Prepare a stockholders' equity section.
(SO 7)

BE11-8 Anita Corporation has these accounts at December 31: Common Stock, $10 par, 5,000 shares issued, $50,000; Paid-in Capital in Excess of Par Value $10,000; Retained Earnings $29,000; and Treasury Stock—Common, 500 shares, $7,000. Prepare the stockholders' equity section of the balance sheet.

Calculate dividend yield at beginning and end of year; comment on implications.
(SO 8)

BE11-9 Abdella Corporation had a stock price of $25 per share at the beginning of the year and $20 per share at the end of the year. Its dividend has remained a constant $1 per share for the last 3 years. Calculate the dividend yield at the beginning and end of the year and comment on its implications for an investor interested in dividend income.

BE11-10 Paul Schwartz, president of Schwartz Corporation, believes that it is a good practice to maintain a constant payout of dividends relative to its earnings. Last year net income was $500,000, and the corporation paid $200,000 in dividends. This year, due to some unusual circumstances, the corporation had income of $2,000,000. Paul expects next year's net income to be about $600,000. What was Schwartz Corporation's payout ratio last year? If it is to maintain the same payout ratio, what amount of dividends would it pay this year? Is this necessarily a good idea—that is, what are the pros and cons of maintaining a constant payout ratio in this scenario?

Evaluate a company's dividend record.
(SO 8)

EXERCISES

E11-1 During its first year of operations, Chile Corporation had these transactions pertaining to its common stock:

Journalize issuance of common stock.
(SO 2)

> Jan. 10 Issued 90,000 shares for cash at $5 per share.
> July 1 Issued 30,000 shares for cash at $8 per share.

Instructions

(a) Journalize the transactions, assuming that the common stock has a par value of $5 per share.

(b) Journalize the transactions, assuming that the common stock is no-par with a stated value of $1 per share.

E11-2 Walters Co. had these transactions during the current period:

Journalize issuance of common stock and preferred stock and purchase of treasury stock.
(SO 2, 3, 4)

June 12 Issued 60,000 shares of $1 par value common stock for cash of $275,000.
July 11 Issued 1,000 shares of $100 par value preferred stock for cash at $110 per share.
Nov. 28 Purchased 2,000 shares of treasury stock for $80,000.

Instructions

Prepare the journal entries for the transactions.

E11-3 Ricky Martin Corporation is authorized to issue both preferred and common stock. The par value of the preferred is $50. During the first year of operations, the company had the following events and transactions pertaining to its preferred stock:

Journalize preferred stock transactions and indicate statement presentation.
(SO 4, 7)

> Feb. 1 Issued 30,000 shares for cash at $51 per share.
> July 1 Issued 20,000 shares for cash at $55 per share.

Instructions

(a) Journalize the transactions.

(b) Post to the stockholders' equity accounts. (Use T accounts.)

(c) Discuss the statement presentation of the accounts.

E11-4 The stockholders' equity section of Henning Corporation's balance sheet at December 31 is presented here:

Answer questions about stockholders' equity section.
(SO 2, 3, 4, 7)

HENNING CORPORATION
Balance Sheet (partial)

Stockholders' equity	
Paid-in capital	
Preferred stock, cumulative, 10,000 shares authorized,	
6,000 shares issued and outstanding	$ 900,000
Common stock, no par, 750,000 shares authorized,	
600,000 shares issued	1,800,000
Total paid-in capital	2,700,000
Retained earnings	1,158,000
Total paid-in capital and retained earnings	3,858,000
Less: Treasury stock (10,000 common shares)	(64,000)
Total stockholders' equity	$3,794,000

Instructions

From a review of the stockholders' equity section, answer these questions:

(a) How many shares of common stock are outstanding?

(b) Assuming there is a stated value, what is the stated value of the common stock?

(c) What is the par value of the preferred stock?

(d) If the annual dividend on preferred stock is $45,000, what is the dividend rate on preferred stock?

(e) If dividends of $90,000 were in arrears on preferred stock, what would be the balance reported for retained earnings?

Prepare correct entries for capital stock transactions.
(SO 2, 3, 4)

E11-5 Castle Corporation recently hired a new accountant with extensive experience in accounting for partnerships. Because of the pressure of the new job, the accountant was unable to review what he had learned earlier about corporation accounting. During the first month, he made the following entries for the corporation's capital stock:

May 2	Cash		120,000	
	Capital Stock			120,000
	(Issued 10,000 shares of $5 par value			
	common stock at $12 per share)			
10	Cash		600,000	
	Capital Stock			600,000
	(Issued 10,000 shares of $50 par value			
	preferred stock at $60 per share)			
15	Capital Stock		12,000	
	Cash			12,000
	(Purchased 1,000 shares of common			
	stock for the treasury at $12 per share)			

Instructions

On the basis of the explanation for each entry, prepare the entries that should have been made for the capital stock transactions.

Journalize cash dividends and indicate statement presentation.
(SO 5)

E11-6 On January 1 Hinckley Corporation had 75,000 shares of no-par common stock issued and outstanding. The stock has a stated value of $5 per share. During the year, the following transactions occurred:

Apr. 1   Issued 5,000 additional shares of common stock for $11 per share.
June 15 Declared a cash dividend of $1.50 per share to stockholders of record on June 30.
July 10 Paid the $1.50 cash dividend.
Dec. 1   Issued 3,000 additional shares of common stock for $13 per share.
    15   Declared a cash dividend on outstanding shares of $1.80 per share to stockholders of record on December 31.

Instructions

(a) Prepare the entries, if any, on each of the three dates that involved dividends.

(b) How are dividends and dividends payable reported in the financial statements prepared at December 31?

Journalize stock dividends.
(SO 5)

E11-7 On January 1, 2001, Remmers Corporation had $1,500,000 of common stock outstanding that was issued at par and retained earnings of $750,000. The company issued 50,000 shares of common stock at par on July 1 and earned net income of $400,000 for the year.

Instructions

Journalize the declaration of a 10% stock dividend on December 10, 2001, for these two independent assumptions:

(a) Par value is $10 and market value is $12.

(b) Par value is $5 and market value is $18.

Compare effects of a stock dividend and a stock split.
(SO 5)

E11-8 On October 31 the stockholders' equity section of Sanders Company's balance sheet consists of common stock $800,000 and retained earnings $400,000. Sanders is considering the following two courses of action: (1) declaring a 5% stock dividend on the 80,000 $10 par value shares outstanding or (2) effecting a 2-for-1 stock split that will reduce par value to $5 per share. The current market price is $15 per share.

Instructions

Prepare a tabular summary of the effects of the alternative actions on the company's stockholders' equity, outstanding shares, and book value per share. Use these column headings: **Before Action**, **After Stock Dividend**, and **After Stock Split**.

E11-9 Before preparing financial statements for the current year, the chief accountant for Tanner Company discovered the following errors in the accounts:

Prepare correcting entries for dividends and a stock split.
(SO 5)

1. The declaration and payment of a $15,000 cash dividend were recorded as a debit to Interest Expense $15,000 and a credit to Cash $15,000.
2. A 10% stock dividend (1,000 shares) was declared on the $10 par value stock when the market value per share was $17. The only entry made was: Retained Earnings (Dr.) $10,000 and Dividend Payable (Cr.) $10,000. The shares have not been issued.
3. A 4-for-1 stock split involving the issue of 400,000 shares of $5 par value common stock for 100,000 shares of $20 par value common stock was recorded as a debit to Retained Earnings $2,000,000 and a credit to Common Stock $2,000,000.

Instructions
Prepare the correcting entries at December 31.

E11-10 The ledger of Jerry Springer Corporation contains these accounts: Common Stock, Preferred Stock, Treasury Stock—Common, Paid-in Capital in Excess of Par Value—Preferred Stock, Paid-in Capital in Excess of Stated Value—Common Stock, and Retained Earnings.

Classify stockholders' equity accounts.
(SO 7)

Instructions
Classify each account using the table column headings shown here:

	Paid-in Capital			
Account	Capital Stock	Additional	Retained Earnings	Other

E11-11 The following accounts appear in the ledger of Helen Hunt Inc. after the books are closed at December 31:

Prepare a stockholders' equity section.
(SO 7)

Common Stock (no-par, $1 stated value, 400,000 shares authorized, 200,000 shares issued)	$ 200,000
Common Stock Dividends Distributable	75,000
Paid-in Capital in Excess of Stated Value—Common Stock	1,200,000
Preferred Stock ($5 par value, 8%, 40,000 shares authorized, 30,000 shares issued)	150,000
Retained Earnings	900,000
Treasury Stock (10,000 common shares)	50,000
Paid-in Capital in Excess of Par Value—Preferred Stock	344,000

Instructions
Prepare the stockholders' equity section at December 31, assuming $100,000 of retained earnings is restricted for plant expansion.

E11-12 The following financial information is available for **Eskimo Pie Corporation**:

Calculate ratios to evaluate dividend and earnings performance.
(SO 8)

(in thousands, except per share data)	1998	1997
Average common stockholders' equity	$22,154	$44,551
Dividends declared for common stockholders	691	692
Dividends declared for preferred stockholders	0	0
Net income	795	108
Market price of common stock	13.25	11.5
Dividends declared per share	.20	.20

The average number of shares of common stock outstanding was 3,453,000 for 1997 and 3,458,500 for 1998.

Instructions
Calculate the dividend yield, payout ratio, earnings per share, price-earnings ratio, and return on common stockholders' equity ratio for 1998 and 1997. Comment on your findings.

Calculate ratios to evaluate dividend and earnings performance.

(SO 8)

E11-13 The following financial information is available for **Walgreen Company**:

(in millions, except per share data)	1998	1997
Average common stockholders' equity	$2,611	$2,208
Dividends declared for common stockholders	124	118
Dividends declared for preferred stockholders	0	0
Net income	511	436
Market price of common stock	38.50	26.94
Dividends declared per share	.25	.24

The average number of shares of common stock outstanding was 493,036,000 for 1997 and 496,017,000 for 1998.

Instructions
Calculate the dividend yield, payout ratio, earnings per share, price-earnings ratio, and return on common stockholders' equity ratio for 1998 and 1997.

PROBLEMS: SET A

Journalize stock transactions, post, and prepare paid-in capital section.

(SO 2, 4, 7)

P11-1A Hassan Corporation was organized on January 1, 2001. It is authorized to issue 20,000 shares of 6%, $50 par value preferred stock and 500,000 shares of no-par common stock with a stated value of $1 per share. The following stock transactions were completed during the first year:

Jan. 10	Issued 100,000 shares of common stock for cash at $4 per share.
Mar. 1	Issued 10,000 shares of preferred stock for cash at $51 per share.
May 1	Issued 150,000 shares of common stock for cash at $4 per share.
Sept. 1	Issued 5,000 shares of common stock for cash at $6 per share.
Nov. 1	Issued 2,000 shares of preferred stock for cash at $63 per share.

Instructions
(a) Journalize the transactions.
(b) Post to the stockholders' equity accounts. (Use T accounts.)
(c) Prepare the paid-in capital portion of the stockholders' equity section at December 31, 2001.

Journalize transactions, post, and prepare a stockholders' equity section; calculate ratios.

(SO 2, 3, 5, 7, 8)

P11-2A The stockholders' equity accounts of Ogilvy Corporation on January 1, 2001, were as follows:

Preferred Stock (10%, $100 par noncumulative, 5,000 shares authorized)	$ 400,000
Common Stock ($5 stated value, 300,000 shares authorized)	1,000,000
Paid-in Capital in Excess of Par Value—Preferred Stock	15,000
Paid-in Capital in Excess of Stated Value—Common Stock	400,000
Retained Earnings	488,000
Treasury Stock—Common (5,000 shares)	40,000

During 2001 the corporation had these transactions and events pertaining to its stockholders' equity:

Feb.	1	Issued 4,000 shares of common stock for $25,000.
Mar.	20	Purchased 1,000 additional shares of common treasury stock at $9 per share.
Oct.	1	Declared a 10% cash dividend on preferred stock, payable November 1.
Dec.	1	Declared a $.40 per share cash dividend to common stockholders of record on December 15, payable December 31, 2001.
	31	Determined that net income for the year was $265,000. At December 31 the market price of the common stock was $10 per share.

Instructions
(a) Journalize the transactions. (Include entries to close net income to Retained Earnings.)
(b) Enter the beginning balances in the accounts and post the journal entries to the stockholders' equity accounts. (Use T accounts.)
(c) Prepare the stockholders' equity section of the balance sheet at December 31, 2001.
(d) Calculate the dividend yield, payout ratio, earnings per share, price-earnings ratio, and return on common stockholders' equity ratio. (*Note:* Use the common shares outstanding on January 1 and December 31 to determine the average shares outstanding.)

P11-3A   On December 31, 2000, Sanibel Company had 1,500,000 shares of $5 par common stock issued and outstanding. The stockholders' equity accounts at December 31, 2000, had the balances listed here:

Prepare a stockholders' equity section.
(SO 7)

Common Stock	$7,500,000
Additional Paid-in Capital	1,500,000
Retained Earnings	1,200,000

Transactions during 2001 and other information related to stockholders' equity accounts were as follows:
1. On January 10, 2001, issued at $110 per share 100,000 shares of $100 par value, 8% cumulative preferred stock.
2. On February 8, 2001, reacquired 10,000 shares of its common stock for $16 per share.
3. On June 8, 2001, declared a cash dividend of $1.20 per share on the common stock outstanding, payable on July 10, 2001, to stockholders of record on July 1, 2001.
4. On December 9, 2001, declared the yearly cash dividend on preferred stock, payable January 10, 2002, to stockholders of record on December 15, 2001.
5. Net income for the year was $3,600,000. At December 31, 2001, the market price of the common stock was $18 per share.

Instructions
Prepare the stockholders' equity section of Sanibel's balance sheet at December 31, 2001.

P11-4A   The ledger of Nixon Corporation at December 31, 2001, after the books have been closed, contains the following stockholders' equity accounts:

Reproduce retained earnings account, and prepare a stockholders' equity section.
(SO 5, 6, 7)

Preferred Stock (10,000 shares issued)	$1,000,000
Common Stock (400,000 shares issued)	2,000,000
Paid-in Capital in Excess of Par Value—Preferred Stock	200,000
Paid-in Capital in Excess of Stated Value—Common Stock	1,200,000
Common Stock Dividends Distributable	100,000
Retained Earnings	2,840,000

A review of the accounting records reveals this information:
1. Preferred stock is 10%, $100 par value, noncumulative, and callable at $125. Since January 1, 2000, 10,000 shares have been outstanding; 20,000 shares are authorized.
2. Common stock is no-par with a stated value of $5 per share; 600,000 shares are authorized.
3. The January 1, 2001, balance in Retained Earnings was $2,500,000.
4. On October 1, 100,000 shares of common stock were sold for cash at $9 per share.
5. A cash dividend of $400,000 was declared and properly allocated to preferred and common stock on November 1. No dividends were paid to preferred stockholders in 2000.
6. On December 31 a 5% common stock dividend was declared out of retained earnings on common stock when the market price per share was $7.
7. Net income for the year was $880,000.
8. On December 31, 2001, the directors authorized disclosure of a $130,000 restriction of retained earnings for plant expansion. (Use Note A.)

Instructions
(a) Reproduce the retained earnings account (T account) for the year.
(b) Prepare the stockholders' equity section of the balance sheet at December 31.

P11-5A   Cattrall Corporation has been authorized to issue 20,000 shares of $100 par value, 10%, noncumulative preferred stock and 1,000,000 shares of no-par common stock. The corporation assigned a $5 stated value to the common stock. At December 31, 2001, the ledger contained the following balances pertaining to stockholders' equity:

Prepare entries for stock transactions, and prepare a stockholders' equity section.
(SO 2, 3, 4, 7)

Preferred Stock	$ 120,000
Paid-in Capital in Excess of Par Value—Preferred Stock	24,000
Common Stock	2,000,000
Paid-in Capital in Excess of Stated Value—Common Stock	1,850,000
Treasury Stock—Common (1,000 shares)	32,000
Retained Earnings	82,000

The preferred stock was issued for $144,000 cash. All common stock issued was for cash. In November 1,000 shares of common stock were purchased for the treasury at a per share cost of $32. No dividends were declared in 2001.

Instructions

(a) Prepare the journal entries for the:
   (1) Issuance of preferred stock for cash.
   (2) Issuance of common stock for cash.
   (3) Purchase of common treasury stock for cash.
(b) Prepare the stockholders' equity section of the balance sheet at December 31, 2001.

Prepare dividend entries, prepare a stockholders' equity section, and calculate ratios.
(SO 5, 7, 8)

P11-6A On January 1, 2001, Wirth Corporation had these stockholders' equity accounts:

Common Stock ($10 par value, 60,000 shares issued and outstanding)	$600,000
Paid-in Capital in Excess of Par Value	200,000
Retained Earnings	540,000

During the year, the following transactions occurred:

Jan.	15	Declared a $0.50 cash dividend per share to stockholders of record on January 31, payable February 15.
Feb.	15	Paid the dividend declared in January.
Apr.	15	Declared a 10% stock dividend to stockholders of record on April 30, distributable May 15. On April 15 the market price of the stock was $13 per share.
May	15	Issued the shares for the stock dividend.
Dec.	1	Declared a $0.75 per share cash dividend to stockholders of record on December 15, payable January 10, 2002.
	31	Determined that net income for the year was $370,000. On December 31 the market price of the stock was $15 per share.

Instructions

(a) Journalize the transactions. (Include entries to close net income to Retained Earnings.)
(b) Enter the beginning balances and post the entries to the stockholders' equity T accounts. [*Note:* Open additional stockholders' equity accounts as needed.]
(c) Prepare the stockholders' equity section of the balance sheet at December 31.
(d) Calculate the dividend yield, payout ratio, earnings per share, price-earnings ratio, and return on common stockholders' equity ratio. (*Hint:* Use the common shares outstanding on January 1 and December 31 to determine average shares outstanding.)

Prepare a stockholders' equity section.
(SO 7)

P11-7A The following stockholders' equity accounts, arranged alphabetically, are in the ledger of Dublin Corporation at December 31, 2001:

Common Stock ($10 stated value)	$1,500,000
Paid-in Capital in Excess of Par Value—Preferred Stock	280,000
Paid-in Capital in Excess of Stated Value—Common Stock	900,000
Preferred Stock (8%, $100 par, noncumulative)	400,000
Retained Earnings	1,134,000
Treasury Stock—Common (8,000 shares)	88,000

Instructions

Prepare the stockholders' equity section of the balance sheet at December 31, 2001.

Prepare a stockholders' equity section.
(SO 7)

P11-8A On January 1, 2001, Cedeno Inc. had these stockholders' equity balances:

Common Stock (500,000 shares issued)	$1,000,000
Paid-in Capital in Excess of Par Value	500,000
Stock Dividends Distributable	100,000
Retained Earnings	600,000

During 2001, the following transactions and events occurred:

1. Issued 50,000 shares of $2 par value common stock as a result of a 10% stock dividend declared on December 15, 2000.
2. Issued 30,000 shares of common stock for cash at $5 per share.
3. Purchased 20,000 shares of common stock for the treasury at $6 per share.
4. Declared and paid a cash dividend of $100,000.
5. Earned net income of $300,000.

Instructions

Prepare the stockholders' equity section of the balance sheet at December 31, 2001.

PROBLEMS: SET B

P11-1B   Cranium Corporation was organized on January 1, 2001. It is authorized to is-sue 10,000 shares of 8%, $100 par value preferred stock and 500,000 shares of no-par common stock with a stated value of $3 per share. The following stock transactions were completed during the first year:

Journalize stock transactions, post, and prepare paid-in capital section.
(SO 2, 4, 7)

Jan. 10   Issued 80,000 shares of common stock for cash at $3 per share.
Mar. 1   Issued 5,000 shares of preferred stock for cash at $104 per share.
May 1   Issued 80,000 shares of common stock for cash at $4 per share.
Sept. 1   Issued 10,000 shares of common stock for cash at $5 per share.
Nov. 1   Issued 1,000 shares of preferred stock for cash at $109 per share.

Instructions
(a) Journalize the transactions.
(b) Post to the stockholders' equity accounts. (Use T accounts.)
(c) Prepare the paid-in capital section of stockholders' equity at December 31, 2001.

P11-2B   The stockholders' equity accounts of Austin C.C. Corporation on January 1, 2001, were as follows:

Journalize transactions, post, and prepare a stockholders' equity section; calculate ratios.
(SO 2, 3, 5, 7, 8)

Preferred Stock (12%, $50 par cumulative, 10,000 shares authorized)	$ 400,000
Common Stock ($1 stated value, 2,000,000 shares authorized)	1,000,000
Paid-in Capital in Excess of Par Value—Preferred Stock	80,000
Paid-in Capital in Excess of Stated Value—Common Stock	1,400,000
Retained Earnings	1,716,000
Treasury Stock—Common (10,000 shares)	40,000

During 2001 the corporation had these transactions and events pertaining to its stock-holders' equity:

Feb. 1   Issued 20,000 shares of common stock for $100,000.
Nov. 10   Purchased 2,000 shares of common stock for the treasury at a cost of $6,000.
Nov. 15   Declared a 12% cash dividend on preferred stock, payable December 15.
Dec. 1   Declared a $0.30 per share cash dividend to stockholders of record on Decem-ber 15, payable December 31, 2001.
     31   Determined that net income for the year was $408,000. The market price of the common stock on this date was $9 per share.

Instructions
(a) Journalize the transactions. (Include entries to close net income to Retained Earnings.)
(b) Enter the beginning balances in the accounts, and post the journal entries to the stockholders' equity accounts. (Use T accounts.)
(c) Prepare the stockholders' equity section of the balance sheet at December 31, 2001, including the disclosure of the preferred dividends in arrears.
(d) Calculate the dividend yield, payout ratio, earnings per share, price-earnings ratio, and return on common stockholders' equity ratio. (*Hint:*   Use the common shares outstanding on January 1 and December 31 to determine average shares outstanding.)

P11-3B   On December 31, 2000, Claremont Company had 1,000,000 shares of $1 par common stock issued and outstanding. The stockholders' equity accounts at December 31, 2000, had the balances listed here:

Prepare a stockholders' equity section.
(SO 7)

Common Stock	$1,000,000
Additional Paid-in Capital	500,000
Retained Earnings	900,000

Transactions during 2001 and other information related to stockholders' equity accounts were as follows:

1. On January 9, 2001, issued at $7 per share 100,000 shares of $5 par value, 9% cumu-lative preferred stock.
2. On February 8, 2001, reacquired 10,000 shares of its common stock for $9 per share.
3. On June 10, 2001, declared a cash dividend of $1 per share on the common stock outstanding, payable on July 10, 2001, to stockholders of record on July 1, 2001.

4. On December 15, 2001, declared the yearly cash dividend on preferred stock, payable December 28, 2001, to stockholders of record on December 15, 2001.
5. Net income for the year is $2,400,000. At December 31, 2001, the market price of the common stock was $15 per share.

Instructions
Prepare the stockholders' equity section of Claremont's balance sheet at December 31, 2001.

Reproduce retained earnings account, and prepare a stockholders' equity section.
(SO 5, 6, 7)

P11-4B The post-closing trial balance of Conway Corporation at December 31, 2001, contains these stockholders' equity accounts:

Preferred Stock (15,000 shares issued)	$ 750,000
Common Stock (250,000 shares issued)	2,500,000
Paid-in Capital in Excess of Par Value—Preferred Stock	250,000
Paid-in Capital in Excess of Par Value—Common Stock	700,000
Common Stock Dividends Distributable	200,000
Retained Earnings	885,000

A review of the accounting records reveals this information:
1. Preferred stock is $50 par, 10%, and cumulative; 15,000 shares have been outstanding since January 1, 2000.
2. Authorized stock is 20,000 shares of preferred and 500,000 shares of common with a $10 par value.
3. The January 1, 2001, balance in Retained Earnings was $1,020,000.
4. On July 1, 20,000 shares of common stock were sold for cash at $16 per share.
5. A cash dividend of $250,000 was declared and properly allocated to preferred and common stock on October 1. No dividends were paid to preferred stockholders in 2000.
6. On December 31 an 8% common stock dividend was declared out of retained earnings on common stock when the market price per share was $16.
7. Net income for the year was $435,000.
8. On December 31, 2001, the directors authorized disclosure of a $150,000 restriction of retained earnings for plant expansion. (Use Note X.)

Instructions
(a) Reproduce the retained earnings account for the year.
(b) Prepare the stockholders' equity section of the balance sheet at December 31.

Prepare a stockholders' equity section.
(SO 7)

P11-5B The following stockholders' equity accounts, arranged alphabetically, are in the ledger of Elbe Corporation at December 31, 2001:

Common Stock ($5 stated value)	$2,800,000
Paid-in Capital in Excess of Par Value—Preferred Stock	783,000
Paid-in Capital in Excess of Stated Value—Common Stock	1,500,000
Preferred Stock (8%, $50 par, noncumulative)	800,000
Retained Earnings	1,958,000
Treasury Stock—Common (10,000 shares)	90,000

Instructions
Prepare the stockholders' equity section of the balance sheet at December 31, 2001.

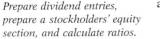

Prepare dividend entries, prepare a stockholders' equity section, and calculate ratios.
(SO 5, 7, 8)

P11-6B On January 1, 2001, Casey Stengel Corporation had these stockholders' equity accounts:

Common Stock ($20 par value, 60,000 shares issued and outstanding)	$1,200,000
Paid-in Capital in Excess of Par Value	200,000
Retained Earnings	600,000

During the year, the following transactions occurred:

Feb. 1 Declared an $.80 cash dividend per share to stockholders of record on February 15, payable March 1.
Mar. 1 Paid the dividend declared in February.

July 1 Declared a 5% stock dividend to stockholders of record on July 15, distributable July 31. On July 1 the market price of the stock was $30 per share.
     31 Issued the shares for the stock dividend.
Dec. 1 Declared a $1 per share dividend to stockholders of record on December 15, payable January 5, 2002.
     31 Determined that net income for the year was $390,000. The market price of the common stock on this date was $48.

Instructions

(a) Journalize the transactions. (Include entries to close net income to Retained Earnings.)
(b) Enter the beginning balances and post the entries to the stockholders' equity T accounts. [*Note:* Open additional stockholders' equity accounts as needed.]
(c) Prepare the stockholders' equity section of the balance sheet at December 31.
(d) Calculate the dividend yield, payout ratio, earnings per share, price-earnings ratio, and return on common stockholders' equity ratio. (*Hint:* Use the common shares outstanding on January 1 and December 31 to determine average shares outstanding.)

◆ BROADENING YOUR PERSPECTIVE

*F*INANCIAL REPORTING AND ANALYSIS

FINANCIAL REPORTING PROBLEM: *Tootsie Roll Industries, Inc.*

BYP11-1 The stockholders' equity section of **Tootsie Roll Industries'** balance sheet is shown in the Consolidated Balance Sheet in Appendix A. You will also find data relative to this problem on other pages of the appendix. (Note that Tootsie Roll has two classes of common stock. To answer the following questions, add the two classes of stock together.)

Instructions

Answer these questions:
(a) What is the par or stated value per share of Tootsie Roll's common stock?
(b) What percentage of Tootsie Roll's authorized common stock was issued at December 31, 1998? (Round to the nearest full percent.)
(c) How many shares of common stock were outstanding at December 31, 1997, and at December 31, 1998?
(d) Calculate the dividend yield, payout ratio, earnings per share, price-earnings ratio, and return on common stockholders' equity ratio for 1998. Tootsie Roll's stock price at December 31, 1998, was $37.985. (*Hint:* Use the common shares outstanding on January 1 and December 31 to determine average shares outstanding.)

COMPARATIVE ANALYSIS PROBLEM: *Tootsie Roll vs. Hershey Foods*

BYP11-2 The financial statements of **Hershey Foods** are presented in Appendix B, following the financial statements for **Tootsie Roll** in Appendix A.

Instructions

(a) Based on the information in these financial statements, compute the 1998 return on common stockholders' equity ratio for each company.
(b) What conclusions concerning the companies' profitability can be drawn from this ratio?

RESEARCH CASE

BYP11-3 The June 1999 issue of *Money* includes an article by David Futrelle entitled "Stock Splits: How the Dumb Get Rich."

Instructions
Read the article and answer the following questions:
(a) What is a stock split?
(b) How do anxious traders and investors obtain timely information about stock splits?
(c) What are the statistics relative to market price reactions for stocks of companies that have split their stocks?
(d) Is there a downside to buying the stock of companies that announce stock splits?

INTERPRETING FINANCIAL STATEMENTS

BYP11-4 **Kellogg Company** is the world's leading producer of ready-to-eat cereal products. In recent years the company has taken numerous steps aimed at improving its profitability and earnings per share. Included in these steps was the layoff of 2,000 employees—roughly 13% of Kellogg's workforce. In addition, Kellogg repurchased large amounts of its own shares: 5,684,864 in 1995; 6,194,500 in 1994; and 9,487,508 in 1993. It announced plans for significant additional repurchases in the coming year. The expenditures for share repurchases were $380 million in 1995, $327 million in 1994, and $548 million in 1993—that's nearly $1.3 billion dollars over a 3-year period. The total amount expended for new property during this same period was $1.1 billion; thus, the company spent more money repurchasing stock than building the company. Also during this period the company issued $400 million in new debt. The table presents some basic facts for Kellogg Company:

	($ in millions)	
	1995	**1994**
Net sales	$7,003	$6,562
Net income	490	705
Total assets	3,801	4,467
Total liabilities	2,824	2,659
Common stock, $.25 par value	78	78
Capital in excess of par value	105	69
Retained earnings	3,963	3,801
Treasury stock, at cost	2,361	1,981
Preferred stock	0	0

The number of shares outstanding was 222,000,000 on December 31, 1994, and 217,000,000 on December 31, 1995.

Instructions
(a) What are some of the reasons that management purchases its own stock?
(b) What was the approximate impact on earnings per share of the common stock repurchases during this 3-year period? That is, calculate earnings per share after the share repurchases and before the repurchases for 1995. (Use the total repurchases during the 3-year period—21,366,872 shares—rounded to 21 million.)
(c) Calculate the debt to total assets ratios for 1994 and 1995 and discuss the implications of the change.

BYP11-5 In 1993 Marriott Corporation split into two companies: **Host Marriott Corporation** and **Marriott International**. Host Marriott retained ownership of the corporation's vast hotel and other properties, while Marriott International, rather than owning hotels, managed them. The purpose of this split was to free Marriott International from the "baggage" associated with Host Marriott, thus allowing it to be more aggressive in its pursuit of growth. The following information is provided for each corporation for their first full year operating as independent companies:

	($ in millions)	
	Host Marriott	**Marriott International**
Sales	$1,501	$8,415
Net income	(25)	200
Total assets	3,822	3,207
Total liabilities	3,112	2,440
Stockholders' equity	710	767

Instructions

(a) The two companies were split by the issuance of shares of Marriott International to all shareholders of the previous combined company. Discuss the nature of this transaction.

(b) Calculate the debt to total assets ratio for each company.

(c) Calculate the return on assets and return on common stockholders' equity ratios for each company.

(d) The company's debtholders were fiercely opposed to the original plan to split the two companies because the original plan had Host Marriott absorbing the majority of the company's debt. They relented only when Marriott International agreed to absorb a larger share of the debt. Discuss the possible reasons the debtholders were opposed to the plan to split the company.

A GLOBAL FOCUS

BYP11-6 Investors with less than a controlling interest in a company are considered minority stockholders. The September 13, 1999, issue of *The Wall Street Journal* included an article by Namju Cho entitled "Minority Shareholders Lag in Emerging Markets."

Instructions

Read the article and answer the following questions:

(a) What are three weaknesses of many companies in emerging markets that contribute to those companies' lack of response to stockholders?

(b) What approach is Edward Schneider taking to try to improve the treatment of stockholders in Latin America?

(c) Why is it in the interest of emerging markets to react to stockholder concerns?

FINANCIAL ANALYSIS ON THE WEB

BYP11-7 *Purpose:* Use the stockholders' equity section of an annual report and identify the major components.

Address: http://www.reportgallery.com (or go to www.wiley.com/college/kimmel)

Steps:

1. From Report Gallery Homepage, choose **Viewing Library**.
2. Select a particular company.
3. Choose **Annual Report**.
4. Follow instructions below.

Instructions

Answer the following questions:

(a) What is the company's name?

(b) What classes of capital stock has the company issued?

(c) For each class of stock:
   (1) How many shares are authorized, issued, and/or outstanding?
   (2) What is the par value?

(d) What are the company's retained earnings?

(e) Has the company acquired treasury stock? How many shares?

CRITICAL THINKING

GROUP DECISION CASE

BYP11-8 The stockholders' meeting for Mantle Corporation has been in progress for some time. The chief financial officer for Mantle is presently reviewing the company's financial statements and is explaining the items that make up the stockholders' equity section of the balance sheet for the current year. The stockholders' equity section for Mantle Corporation at December 31, 2001, is presented here:

MANTLE CORPORATION
Balance Sheet (partial)

Stockholders' equity
  Paid-in capital
    Capital stock
      Preferred stock, authorized 1,000,000 shares

cumulative, $100 par value, $8 per share, 6,000		
shares issued and outstanding		$ 600,000
Common stock, authorized 5,000,000 shares, $1		
par value, 3,000,000 shares issued and 2,700,000		
outstanding		3,000,000
Total capital stock		3,600,000
Additional paid-in capital		
In excess of par value—preferred stock	$ 50,000	
In excess of par value—common stock	25,000,000	
Total additional paid-in capital		25,050,000
Total paid-in capital		28,650,000
Retained earnings		900,000
Total paid-in capital and retained earnings		29,550,000
Less: Common treasury stock (300,000 shares)		9,300,000
Total stockholders' equity		$20,250,000

A number of questions regarding the stockholders' equity section of Mantle Corporation's balance sheet have been raised at the meeting.

Instructions
With the class divided into groups, answer the following questions as if your group were the chief financial officer for Mantle Corporation:
(a) "What does the cumulative provision related to the preferred stock mean?"
(b) "I thought the common stock was presently selling at $29.75, and yet the company has the stock stated at $1 per share. How can that be?"
(c) "Why is the company buying back its common stock? Furthermore, the treasury stock has a debit balance because it is subtracted from stockholders' equity. Why is treasury stock not reported as an asset if it has a debit balance?"
(d) "Why is it necessary to show additional paid-in capital? Why not just show common stock at the total amount paid in?"

COMMUNICATION ACTIVITY

BYP11-9   Louis P. Brady, your uncle, is an inventor who has decided to incorporate. Uncle Lou knows that you are an accounting major at U.N.O. In a recent letter to you, he ends with the question, "I'm filling out a state incorporation application. Can you tell me the difference among the following terms: (1) authorized stock, (2) issued stock, (3) outstanding stock, and (4) preferred stock?"

Instructions
In a brief note, differentiate for Uncle Lou the four different stock terms. Write the letter to be friendly, yet professional.

ETHICS CASES

BYP11-10   The R&D division of Simplex Chemical Corp. has just developed a chemical for sterilizing the vicious Brazilian "killer bees" which are invading Mexico and the southern United States. The president of Simplex is anxious to get the chemical on the market because Simplex's profits need a boost—and his job is in jeopardy because of decreasing sales and profits. Simplex has an opportunity to sell this chemical in Central American countries, where the laws are much more relaxed than in the United States.

    The director of Simplex's R&D division strongly recommends further research in the laboratory to test the side effects of this chemical on other insects, birds, animals, plants, and even humans. He cautions the president, "We could be sued from all sides if the chemical has tragic side effects that we didn't even test for in the lab." The president answers, "We can't wait an additional year for your lab tests. We can avoid losses from such lawsuits by establishing a separate wholly owned corporation to shield Simplex Chemical Corp. from such lawsuits. We can't lose any more than our investment in the new corporation, and we'll invest just the patent covering this chemical. We'll reap the benefits if the chemical works and is safe, and avoid the losses from lawsuits if it's a disaster." The following week Simplex creates a new wholly owned corporation called Zoebee Inc., sells the chemical patent to it for $10, and watches the spraying begin.

Instructions
(a) Who are the stakeholders in this situation?
(b) Are the president's motives and actions ethical?
(c) Can Simplex shield itself against losses of Zoebee Inc.?

BYP11-11   Flambeau Corporation has paid 60 consecutive quarterly cash dividends (15 years). The last 6 months have been a real cash drain on the company, however, as profit margins have been greatly narrowed by increasing competition. With a cash balance sufficient to meet only day-to-day operating needs, the president, Vince Ramsey, has decided that a stock dividend instead of a cash dividend should be declared. He tells Flambeau's financial vice-president, Janice Rahn, to issue a press release stating that the company is extending its consecutive dividend record with the issuance of a 5% stock dividend. "Write the press release convincing the stockholders that the stock dividend is just as good as a cash dividend," he orders. "Just watch our stock rise when we announce the stock dividend; it must be a good thing if that happens."

Instructions
(a) Who are the stakeholders in this situation?
(b) Is there anything unethical about president Ramsey's intentions or actions?
(c) What is the effect of a stock dividend on a corporation's stockholders' equity accounts? Which would you rather receive as a stockholder—a cash dividend or a stock dividend? Why?

Reporting and Analyzing Investments

◆ IS THERE ANYTHING ELSE WE CAN BUY?

In a rapidly changing world you must change rapidly or suffer the consequences. In business, change requires investment. A case in point is found in the entertainment industry. Technology is bringing about new innovations so quickly that it is nearly impossible to guess which technologies will last and which will soon fade away. For example, will both satellite TV and cable TV survive, or will just one succeed, or will both be replaced by something else? If you guess (and invest) wrong, you lose. Or consider the publishing industry. Will paper newspapers and magazines be replaced by online

news via the World Wide Web? If you are a publisher, you have to make your best guess about what the future holds and invest accordingly.

Time Warner Inc. lives at the center of this arena. It is not an environment for the timid, and Time Warner's philosophy is anything but timid. It might be characterized as "If we can't beat you, we will buy you." Its mantra is "invest, invest, invest." An abbreviated list of Time Warner's holdings gives an idea of its reach. Magazines: *People, Time, Life, Sports Illustrated, Fortune.* Book publishers: Time-Life Books, Book-of-the Month Club, Little,

Brown & Co., Sunset Books. Music: Warner Bros. Records, Reprise, Atlantic, Rhino, Elektra, Asylum, representing such artists as Hootie and the Blowfish, Tori Amos, Eric Clapton, and Madonna. Television and movies: Warner Bros. ("ER" and "Friends"), HBO, and movies like *Batman Forever.* And, in 1996 Time Warner merged with Turner Broadcasting, so it now owns TNT, CNN, and Turner's incredible library of thousands of classic movies (e.g., *Gone with the Wind, The Wizard of Oz, Casablanca*). Even before the Turner merger, Time Warner owned more information and entertainment copy-

rights and brands than any other company in the world.

So what has Time Warner's aggressive acquisition spree meant for the bottom line? It has left Time Warner with huge debts and massive interest costs. In addition, some of the acquisitions have not come cheap, resulting in large amounts of reported goodwill and goodwill amortization. As a consequence, since the merger of Time and Warner in 1988, the combined corporation has reported positive net income in only three years through 1998, and analysts predict that its losses will continue for some time longer. With so much investing by Time Warner and so little profit to show for it, one is reminded of one more of its companies, Looney Tunes cartoons—"That's all, folks."

On the World Wide Web
Time Warner Inc.:
http://www.timewarner.com
America Online: http://www.aol.com

Postscript:

This just out: At the time this book went to press, America Online (AOL) and Time Warner announced plans to merge into a single company. The new company, which will be called AOL Time Warner Inc., will combine AOL's more than 20 million subscribers with Time Warner's extensive media content, including 13 million cable television subscribers. While it is being billed as a marriage of equals, it is AOL's phenomenal growth and astronomical stock price that made this merger possible. It appears that in many respects, AOL is in the driver's seat of this deal. This demonstrates that, in the corporate acquisition food chain, no company is too large to be devoured. Because this is the largest merger (to date) in U.S. history, the deal will require approval by the federal government.

Time Warner's management believes in a policy of aggressive growth through investing in the stock of existing companies. In addition to purchasing stock, companies also purchase other securities such as debt securities issued by corporations or by governments. Investments can be purchased for a short or long period of time, as a passive investment, or with the intent to control another company. As you will see later in the chapter, the way in which a company accounts for its investments is determined by a number of factors.

The content and organization of this chapter are as follows:

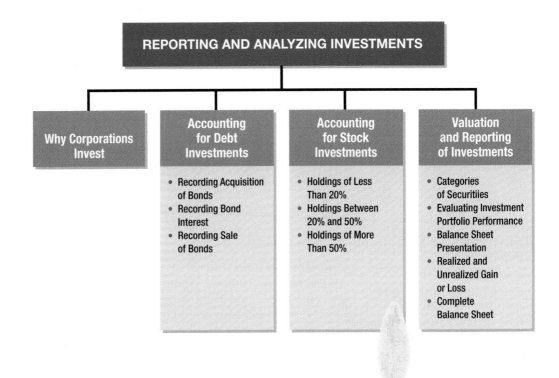

REPORTING AND ANALYZING INVESTMENTS

Why Corporations Invest	Accounting for Debt Investments	Accounting for Stock Investments	Valuation and Reporting of Investments
	• Recording Acquisition of Bonds • Recording Bond Interest • Recording Sale of Bonds	• Holdings of Less Than 20% • Holdings Between 20% and 50% • Holdings of More Than 50%	• Categories of Securitiies • Evaluating Investment Portfolio Performance • Balance Sheet Presentation • Realized and Unrealized Gain or Loss • Complete Balance Sheet

WHY CORPORATIONS INVEST

STUDY OBJECTIVE

1

Identify the reasons corporations invest in stocks and debt securities.

Corporations purchase investments in debt or equity securities generally for one of three reasons. First, a corporation may **have excess cash** that it does not need for the immediate purchase of operating assets. For example, many companies experience seasonal fluctuations in sales. A Cape Cod marina has more sales in the spring and summer than in the fall and winter, whereas the reverse is true for an Aspen ski shop. Thus, at the end of an operating cycle, many companies may have cash on hand that is temporarily idle pending the start of another operating cycle. Until the cash is needed, these companies may invest the excess funds to earn, through interest and dividends, a greater return than they would get by just holding the funds in the bank. The role played by such temporary investments in the operating cycle is depicted in Illustration 12-1.

Excess cash may also result from economic cycles. For example, when the economy is booming, General Motors generates considerable excess cash. Although it uses some of this cash to purchase new plant and equipment and pays out some of the cash in dividends, it may also invest excess cash in liq-

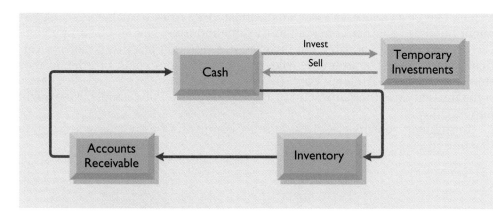

Illustration 12-1 Temporary investments and the operating cycle

uid assets in anticipation of a future downturn in the economy. It can then liquidate these investments during a recession, when sales slow down and cash is scarce.

When investing excess cash for short periods of time, corporations invest in low-risk, highly liquid securities—most often short-term government securities. It is generally not wise to invest short-term excess cash in shares of common stock because stock investments can experience rapid price changes. If you did invest your short-term excess cash in stock and the price of the stock declined significantly just before you needed cash again, you would be forced to sell your stock investment at a loss.

A second reason some companies such as banks purchase investments is because they generate a **significant portion of their earnings from investment income**. Although banks make most of their earnings by lending money, they also generate earnings by investing in debt and equity securities. Banks purchase investment securities because loan demand varies both seasonally and with changes in the economic climate. Thus, when loan demand is low, a bank must find other uses for its cash. Investing in securities also allows banks to diversify some of their risk. Bank regulators severely limit the ability of banks to invest in common stock; therefore, most investments held by banks are debt securities.

Pension funds and mutual funds are corporations that also regularly invest to generate earnings. However, they do so for *speculative reasons;* that is, they are speculating that the investment will increase in value and thus result in positive returns. Therefore, they invest primarily in the common stock of other corporations. These investments are passive in nature; the pension fund or mutual fund does not usually take an active role in controlling the affairs of the companies in which they invest.

A third reason why companies invest is for **strategic reasons**. A company may purchase a noncontrolling interest in another company in a related industry in which it wishes to establish a presence. For example, Time Warner initially purchased an interest of less than 20% in Turner Broadcasting to have a stake in Turner's expanding business opportunities. Similarly, Canadian giant Seagram purchased a significant interest in Time Warner. (Thus, not even a huge corporation like Time Warner is at the top of the corporate "food chain.") Alternatively, a company can exercise some influence over one of its customers or suppliers by purchasing a significant, but not controlling, interest in that company.

A corporation may also choose to purchase a controlling interest in another company. This might be done to enter a new industry without incurring the tremendous costs and risks associated with starting from scratch. Or a company might purchase another company in its same industry. The purchase of a company that is in your industry, but involved in a different activity, is called a **vertical acquisition**. For example, Nike might purchase a chain of athletic shoe stores, such as The Athlete's Foot. In a **horizontal acquisition** you purchase a company that does the same activity as your company. For example, Nike might purchase Reebok.

In summary, businesses invest in other companies for the reasons shown in Illustration 12-2.

Illustration 12-2 Why corporations invest

Reason	Typical Investment
To house excess cash until needed	Low-risk, high-liquidity, short-term securities such as government-issued securities
To generate earnings I need 1,000 Treasury bills by tonight	Debt securities (banks and other financial institutions); and stock securities (mutual funds and pension funds)
To meet strategic goals	Stocks of companies in a related industry or in an unrelated industry that the company wishes to enter

BUSINESS INSIGHT
Investor Perspective

In the two months prior to approval by the federal government of the Time Warner/Turner deal, as approval appeared more certain, Time Warner's stock price increased by 30%. Although investors were applauding the strength of the combined entity, many analysts were very concerned about the mega-corporation's ability to control costs. The Time Warner deal and other acquisitions resulted in a $17.5 billion mountain of debt on Time Warner's balance sheet.

Observers were also interested to see how the two corporate cultures would merge. Ted Turner had been openly critical of Time Warner's management for running a loose ship, with far too much being spent on unnecessary extravagances such as corporate jets. Time Warner executives privately responded that if Mr. Turner was really concerned, he might consider taking a cut in his salary of $10 million a year.

STUDY OBJECTIVE

2

Explain the accounting for debt investments.

ACCOUNTING FOR DEBT INVESTMENTS

Debt investments are investments in government and corporation bonds. In accounting for debt investments, entries are required to record (1) the acquisition, (2) the interest revenue, and (3) the sale.

RECORDING ACQUISITION OF BONDS

At acquisition, the cost principle applies. Cost includes all expenditures necessary to acquire these investments, such as the price paid plus brokerage fees (commissions), if any. Assume that Kuhl Corporation acquires 50 Doan Inc. 12%, 10-year, $1,000 bonds on January 1, 2001, for $54,000, including brokerage fees of $1,000. The entry to record the investment is:

Jan. 1	Debt Investments	54,000	
	Cash		54,000
	(To record purchase of 50 Doan Inc. bonds)		

A	=	L	+	SE
+54,000				
−54,000				

BUSINESS INSIGHT

Investor Perspective

Corporate bonds, like capital stock, are traded on national securities exchanges. They can be bought and sold by investors at any time at the current market price. Bond prices and trading activity are published daily in newspapers and the financial press, in the form shown below.

Bonds	Current Yield	Volume	Close	Net Change
Kmart $8\frac{3}{8}$ 17	8.4	35	$100\frac{1}{4}$	$+\frac{7}{8}$

This information indicates that Kmart Corporation has outstanding $8\frac{3}{8}\%$, $1,000 bonds maturing in 2017 and currently yielding an 8.4% return. In addition, 35 bonds were traded on this day; at the close of trading, the price was $100\frac{1}{4}\%$ of face value, or $1,002.50. The Net Change column indicates the difference between the day's closing price and the previous day's closing price. A slightly different format is used for quotations on government-issued bonds.

RECORDING BOND INTEREST

The Doan Inc. bonds pay interest of $3,000 semiannually on July 1 and January 1 ($50,000 × 12% × $\frac{1}{2}$). The entry for the receipt of interest on July 1 is:

July 1	Cash	3,000	
	Interest Revenue		3,000
	(To record receipt of interest on Doan Inc. bonds)		

A	=	L	+	SE
+3,000				+3,000

If Kuhl Corporation's fiscal year ends on December 31, it is necessary to accrue the interest of $3,000 earned since July 1. The adjusting entry is:

Dec. 31	Interest Receivable	3,000	
	Interest Revenue		3,000
	(To accrue interest on Doan Inc. bonds)		

A	=	L	+	SE
+3,000				+3,000

Interest Receivable is reported as a current asset in the balance sheet; Interest Revenue is reported under Other Revenues and Gains in the income statement. When the interest is received on January 1, the entry is:

A	=	L	+	SE
+3,000				
−3,000				

Jan. 1	Cash		3,000	
	Interest Receivable			3,000
	(To record receipt of accrued interest)			

A credit to Interest Revenue at this time is incorrect because the interest revenue was earned and accrued in the preceding accounting period.

RECORDING SALE OF BONDS

Helpful Hint The accounting for short-term debt investments and long-term debt investments is similar. Any exceptions are discussed in more advanced courses.

When a bondholder sells bonds, it is necessary to decrease the investment account by the amount of the cost of the bonds. Any difference between the net proceeds from sale (sales price less brokerage fees) and the cost of the bonds is recorded as a gain or loss. Assume, for example, that Kuhl Corporation receives net proceeds of $58,000 on the sale of the Doan Inc. bonds on January 1, 2002, after receiving the interest due. Since the securities cost $54,000, a gain of $4,000 has been realized. The entry to record the sale is:

A	=	L	+	SE
+58,000				+4,000
−54,000				

Jan. 1	Cash		58,000	
	Debt Investments			54,000
	Gain on Sale of Debt Investments			4,000
	(To record sale of Doan Inc. bonds)			

The gain on the sale of debt investments is reported under Other Revenues and Gains in the income statement.

BEFORE YOU GO ON...

◆ Review It

1. What are the reasons corporations invest in securities?
2. What entries are required in accounting for debt investments?

◆ Do It

Waldo Corporation had these transactions pertaining to debt investments:

Jan. 1   Purchased 30 10%, $1,000 Hillary Co. bonds for $30,000 plus brokerage fees of $900. Interest is payable semiannually on July 1 and January 1.
July 1   Received semiannual interest on Hillary Co. bonds.
July 1   Sold 15 Hillary Co. bonds for $15,000 less $400 brokerage fees.

(a) Journalize the transactions.
(b) Prepare the adjusting entry for the accrual of interest on December 31.

Reasoning: Bond investments are recorded at cost. Interest is recorded when received, accrued, or both. When bonds are sold, the investment account is credited for the cost of the bonds. Any difference between the cost and the net proceeds is recorded as a gain or loss.

Solution:

(a)	Jan. 1	Debt Investments		30,900	
		Cash			30,900
		(To record purchase of 30 Hillary Co. bonds)			

July 1	Cash	1,500	
	Interest Revenue ($30,000 \times .10 \times \frac{6}{12}$)		1,500
	(To record receipt of interest on Hillary Co. bonds)		

July 1	Cash	14,600	
	Loss on Sale of Debt Investments	850	
	Debt Investments ($30,900 \times \frac{15}{30}$)		15,450
	(To record sale of 15 Hillary Co. bonds)		

(b) Dec. 31	Interest Receivable	750	
	Interest Revenue ($15,000 \times .10 \times \frac{6}{12}$)		750
	(To accrue interest on Hillary Co. bonds)		

ACCOUNTING FOR STOCK INVESTMENTS

Stock investments are investments in the capital stock of corporations. When a company holds stock (and/or debt) of several different corporations, the group of securities is identified as an **investment portfolio**. The accounting for investments in common stock is based on the extent of the investor's influence over the operating and financial affairs of the issuing corporation (the **investee**) as shown in Illustration 12-3. In some cases, depending on the degree of investor influence, net income of the investee is considered to be income to the investor.

STUDY OBJECTIVE

3

Explain the accounting for stock investments.

Illustration 12-3
Accounting guidelines for stock investments

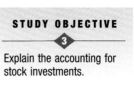

Investor's Ownership Interest in Investee's Common Stock	Presumed Influence on Investee	Accounting Guidelines
Less than 20%	Insignificant	Cost method
Between 20% and 50%	Significant	Equity method
More than 50%	Controlling	Consolidated financial statements

The presumed influence may be negated by extenuating circumstances. For example, a company that acquires a 25% interest in another company in a "hostile" takeover may not have any significant influence over the investee.[1] In other words, companies are required to use judgment instead of blindly following the guidelines. We explain and illustrate the application of each guideline next.

---

[1] Among the factors that should be considered in determining an investor's influence are whether (1) the investor has representation on the investee's board of directors, (2) the investor participates in the investee's policy-making process, (3) there are material transactions between the investor and the investee, and (4) the common stock held by other stockholders is concentrated or dispersed.

HOLDINGS OF LESS THAN 20%

In the accounting for stock investments of less than 20%, the cost method is used. Under the cost method, the investment is recorded at cost, and revenue is recognized only when cash dividends are received.

Recording Acquisition of Stock

At acquisition, the cost principle applies. Cost includes all expenditures necessary to acquire these investments, such as the price paid plus brokerage fees (commissions), if any. Assume, for example, that on July 1, 2001, Sanchez Corporation acquires 1,000 shares (10% ownership) of Beal Corporation common stock at $40 per share plus brokerage fees of $500. The entry for the purchase is:

A = L + SE
+40,500
−40,500

July 1	Stock Investments	40,500	
	Cash		40,500
	(To record purchase of 1,000 shares of Beal common stock)		

Recording Dividends

During the time the stock is held, entries are required for any cash dividends received. Thus, if a $2.00 per share dividend is received by Sanchez Corporation on December 31, the entry is:

A = L + SE
+2,000   +2,000

Dec. 31	Cash (1,000 × $2)	2,000	
	Dividend Revenue		2,000
	(To record receipt of a cash dividend)		

Dividend Revenue is reported under Other Revenues and Gains in the income statement.

Recording Sale of Stock

When stock is sold, the difference between the net proceeds from the sale (sales price less brokerage fees) and the cost of the stock is recognized as a gain or a loss. Assume, for instance, that Sanchez Corporation receives net proceeds of $39,500 on the sale of its Beal Corporation stock on February 10, 2002. Because the stock cost $40,500, a loss of $1,000 has been incurred. The entry to record the sale is:

A = L + SE
+39,500   −1,000
−40,500

Feb. 10	Cash	39,500	
	Loss on Sale of Stock Investments	1,000	
	Stock Investments		40,500
	(To record sale of Beal common stock)		

The loss account is reported under Other Expenses and Losses in the income statement, whereas a gain on sale is shown under Other Revenues and Gains.

HOLDINGS BETWEEN 20% AND 50%

When an investor company owns only a small portion of the shares of stock of another company (the investee), the investor cannot exercise control over the company. When an investor owns between 20% and 50% of the common stock of a corporation, however, it is generally presumed that the investor has significant influence over the financial and operating activities of the investee. The investor probably has a representative on the investee's board of directors. With a representative on the board, the investor begins to exercise some control over the investee—and the investee company in some sense really becomes part of the investor company.

For example, even prior to purchasing all of Turner Broadcasting, Time Warner owned 20% of Turner. Because it exercised significant control over major decisions made by Turner, Time Warner used an approach called the equity method. Under the equity method, **the investor records its share of the net income of the investee in the year when it is earned**. To delay recognizing the investor's share of net income until a cash dividend is declared ignores the fact that the investor and investee are, in some sense, one company, so the investor is better off by the investee's earned income.

Under the equity method, the investment in common stock is initially recorded at cost, and the investment account is **adjusted annually** to show the investor's equity in the investee. Each year, the investor (1) increases (debits) the investment account and increases (credits) revenue for its share of the investee's net income,[2] and (2) decreases (credits) the investment account for the amount of dividends received. The investment account is reduced for dividends received because the net assets of the investee are decreased when a dividend is paid.

Recording Acquisition of Stock

Assume that Milar Corporation acquires 30% of the common stock of Beck Company for $120,000 on January 1, 2001. The entry to record this transaction is:

Jan. 1	Stock Investments	120,000	
	Cash		120,000
	(To record purchase of Beck common stock)		

A	=	L	+	SE
+120,000				
−120,000				

Recording Revenue and Dividends

For 2001 Beck reports net income of $100,000 and declares and pays a $40,000 cash dividend. Milar is required to record (1) its share of Beck's income, $30,000 (30% × $100,000), and (2) the reduction in the investment account for the dividends received, $12,000 ($40,000 × 30%). The entries are:

(1)

Dec. 31	Stock Investments	30,000	
	Revenue from Investment in Beck Company		30,000
	(To record 30% equity in Beck's 2001 net income)		

A	=	L	+	SE
+30,000				+30,000

(2)

Dec. 31	Cash	12,000	
	Stock Investments		12,000
	(To record dividends received)		

A	=	L	+	SE
+12,000				
−12,000				

---

[2]Conversely, the investor increases (debits) a loss account and decreases (credits) the investment account for its share of the investee's net loss.

After the transactions for the year are posted, the investment and revenue accounts are as shown in Illustration 12-4.

Illustration 12-4
Investment and revenue
accounts after posting

Stock Investments			Revenue from Investment in Beck Company	
Jan. 1 120,000	Dec. 31 12,000			Dec. 31 30,000
Dec. 31 **30,000**				
Dec. 31 Bal. 138,000				

During the year, the investment account has increased by $18,000. This $18,000 is Milar's 30% equity in the $60,000 increase in Beck's retained earnings ($100,000 − $40,000). In addition, Milar reports $30,000 of revenue from its investment, which is 30% of Beck's net income of $100,000. Note that the difference between reported income under the cost method and reported revenue under the equity method can be significant. For example, Milar would report only $12,000 of dividend revenue (30% × $40,000) if the cost method were used.

HOLDINGS OF MORE THAN 50%

STUDY OBJECTIVE

4

Describe the purpose and usefulness of consolidated financial statements.

A company that owns more than 50% of the common stock of another entity is known as the parent company. The entity whose stock is owned by the parent company is called the subsidiary (affiliated) company. Because of its stock ownership, the parent company has a controlling interest in the subsidiary company.

When a company owns more than 50% of the common stock of another company, consolidated financial statements are usually prepared. Consolidated financial statements present the assets and liabilities controlled by the parent company and the aggregate profitability of the affiliated companies. They are prepared **in addition to** the financial statements for each of the individual parent and subsidiary companies. As noted earlier, prior to acquiring all of Turner Broadcasting, Time Warner accounted for its investment in Turner using the equity method. Time Warner's net investment in Turner was reported in a single line item—Other Investments. After the merger, Time Warner instead consolidated Turner's results with its own. Under this approach, the individual assets and liabilities of Turner are included with those of Time Warner; its plant and equipment are added to Time Warner's plant and equipment, its receivables are added to Time Warner's receivables, and so on.

Helpful Hint If the parent (A) has three wholly owned subsidiaries (B, C, and D), there are four separate legal entities but only one economic entity from the viewpoint of the shareholders of the parent company.

Consolidated statements are especially useful to the stockholders, board of directors, and management of the parent company. Moreover, consolidated statements inform creditors, prospective investors, and regulatory agencies as to the magnitude and scope of operations of the companies under common control. For example, regulators and the courts undoubtedly used the consolidated statements of AT&T to determine whether a breakup of AT&T was in the public interest. Listed here are three companies that prepare consolidated statements and some of the companies they have owned. Note that one, Disney, is Time Warner's arch rival.

Beatrice Foods	**American Brands, Inc.**	**The Walt Disney Company**
Tropicana Frozen Juices	American Tobacco Company	Capital Cities/ABC, Inc.
Switzer Candy Company	Master Lock Company	Disneyland, Disney World
Samsonite Corporation	Pinkerton's Security Service	Mighty Ducks
Dannon Yogurt Company	Titleist Golf Company	Anaheim Angels
		ESPN

BUSINESS INSIGHT

Management Perspective

Time Warner, Inc., owns 100% of the common stock of Home Box Office (HBO) Corporation. The common stockholders of Time Warner elect the board of directors of the company, who, in turn, select the officers and managers of the company. The board of directors controls the property owned by the corporation, which includes the common stock of HBO. Thus, they are in a position to elect the board of directors of HBO and, in effect, control its operations. These relationships are graphically illustrated here:

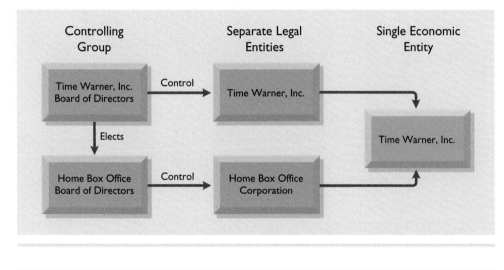

BEFORE YOU GO ON...

◆ Review It

1. What are the accounting entries for investments in stock with ownership of less than 20%?
2. What entries are made under the equity method when (a) the investor receives a cash dividend from the investee and (b) the investee reports net income for the year?
3. What is the purpose of consolidated financial statements?

◆ Do It

These are two independent situations:

1. Rho Jean Inc. acquired 5% of the 400,000 shares of common stock of Stillwater Corp. at a total cost of $6 per share on May 18, 2001. On August 30 Stillwater declared and paid a $75,000 dividend. On December 31 Stillwater reported net income of $244,000 for the year.

2. Debbie, Inc., obtained significant influence over North Sails by buying 40% of North Sails' 60,000 outstanding shares of common stock at a cost of $12 per share on January 1, 2001. On April 15 North Sails declared and paid a cash dividend of $45,000. On December 31 North Sails reported net income of $120,000 for the year.

Prepare all necessary journal entries for 2001 for (a) Rho Jean Inc. and (b) Debbie, Inc.

Reasoning: When an investor owns less than 20% of the common stock of another corporation, it is presumed that the investor has relatively little influence over the investee. As a result, net income earned by the investee is not considered a proper basis for recognizing income from the investment by the investor. For investments of 20%–50%, significant influence is presumed, and therefore the investor's share of the net income of the investee should be recorded.

Solution:

(a)	May 18	Stock Investments (20,000 × $6) 　　Cash 　　　(To record purchase of 20,000 shares of 　　　Stillwater stock)	120,000	120,000
	Aug. 30	Cash 　　Dividend Revenue ($75,000 × 5%) 　　　(To record receipt of cash dividend)	3,750	3,750
(b)	Jan. 1	Stock Investments (60,000 × 40% × $12) 　　Cash 　　　(To record purchase of 24,000 shares of 　　　North Sails stock)	288,000	288,000
	Apr. 15	Cash 　　Stock Investments ($45,000 × 40%) 　　　(To record receipt of cash dividend)	18,000	18,000
	Dec. 31	Stock Investments ($120,000 × 40%) 　　Revenue from Investment in North Sails 　　　(To record 40% equity in North Sails' net 　　　income)	48,000	48,000

VALUATION AND REPORTING OF INVESTMENTS

STUDY OBJECTIVE

5

Indicate how debt and stock investments are valued and reported in the financial statements.

The value of debt and stock investments may fluctuate greatly during the time they are held. For example, in one 12-month period, the stock of Digital Equipment Corporation hit a high of $76\frac{1}{2}$ and a low of $28\frac{3}{8}$. In light of such price fluctuations, how should investments be valued at the balance sheet date? Valuation could be at cost, at fair value (market value), or at the lower of cost or market value. Many people argue that fair value offers the best approach because it represents the expected cash realizable value of securities. Fair value is the amount for which a security could be sold in a normal market. Others counter that, unless a security is going to be sold soon, the fair value is not relevant because the price of the security will likely change again.

CATEGORIES OF SECURITIES

For purposes of valuation and reporting at a financial statement date, debt and stock investments are classified into three categories of securities:

1. Trading securities are securities bought and held primarily for sale in the near term to generate income on short-term price differences.
2. Available-for-sale securities are securities that may be sold in the future.

3. **Held-to-maturity securities** are debt securities that the investor has the intent and ability to hold to maturity.[3]

The valuation guidelines for these securities are shown in Illustration 12-5. These guidelines apply to all debt securities and all stock investments in which the holdings are less than 20%.

Illustration 12-5
Valuation guidelines

Trading	Available-for-sale	Held-to-maturity[3]
"We'll sell within ten days."	"We'll hold the stock for a while to see how it performs."	"We intend to hold until maturity."
At fair value with changes reported in net income	At fair value with changes reported in the stockholders' equity section	At amortized cost

Trading Securities

Trading securities are held with the intention of selling them in a short period of time (generally less than a month). *Trading* means frequent buying and selling. As indicated in Illustration 12-5, trading securities are reported at fair value, referred to as mark-to-market accounting, and changes from cost are reported **as part of net income**. The changes are reported as **unrealized gains or losses** because the securities have not been sold. The unrealized gain or loss is the difference between the **total cost** of the securities in the category and their **total fair value**.

As an example, Illustration 12-6 shows the costs and fair values for investments classified as trading securities for Pace Corporation on December 31, 2001.

Investments	Cost	Fair Value	Unrealized Gain (Loss)
Yorkville Company bonds	$ 50,000	$ 48,000	$(2,000)
Kodak Company stock	90,000	99,000	9,000
Total	$140,000	$147,000	$ 7,000

Illustration 12-6   Valuation of trading securities

Pace Corporation has an unrealized gain of $7,000 because total fair value ($147,000) is $7,000 greater than total cost ($140,000). The fact that trading securities are a short-term investment increases the likelihood that they will be sold at fair value (the company may not be able to time their sale) and the likelihood that there will be an unrealized gain or loss. Fair value and unrealized gain or loss are recorded through an adjusting entry at the time financial statements are prepared. In the entry a valuation allowance account, Market Adjustment—Trading, is used to record the difference between the total cost and the total fair value of the securities. The adjusting entry for Pace Corporation is:

Helpful Hint An unrealized gain or loss is reported in the income statement because of the likelihood that the securities will be sold at fair value since they are a short-term investment.

---

[3]This category is provided for completeness. The accounting and valuation issues related to held-to-maturity securities are discussed in more advanced accounting courses.

A	=	L	+	SE
+7,000				+7,000

Dec. 31	Market Adjustment—Trading	7,000	
	Unrealized Gain—Income		7,000
	(To record unrealized gain on trading securities)		

The use of the Market Adjustment—Trading account enables the company to maintain a record of the investment cost. Actual cost is needed to determine the gain or loss realized when the securities are sold. The Market Adjustment—Trading balance is added to the cost of the investments to arrive at a fair value for the trading securities.

The fair value of the securities is the amount reported on the balance sheet. The unrealized gain is reported on the income statement under Other Revenues and Gains. The term income is used in the account title to indicate that the gain affects net income. If the total cost of the trading securities is greater than total fair value, an unrealized loss has occurred. In such a case, the adjusting entry is a debit to Unrealized Loss—Income and a credit to Market Adjustment—Trading. The unrealized loss is reported under Other Expenses and Losses in the income statement.

The market adjustment account is carried forward into future accounting periods. No entries are made to this account during the period. At the end of each reporting period, the balance in the account is adjusted to the difference between cost and fair value at that time. The Unrealized Gain or Loss—Income account is closed at the end of the reporting period.

Available-for-Sale Securities

As indicated earlier, available-for-sale securities are held with the intent of selling them sometime in the future. If the intent is to sell the securities within the next year or operating cycle, the securities are classified as current assets in the balance sheet. Otherwise, they are classified as long-term assets in the investments section of the balance sheet.

Available-for-sale securities are also reported at fair value. The procedure for determining fair value and unrealized gain or loss for these securities is the same as that for trading securities. To illustrate, assume that Elbert Corporation has two securities that are classified as available-for-sale. Illustration 12-7 provides information on the cost, fair value, and amount of the unrealized gain or loss on December 31, 2001.

Illustration 12-7 Valuation of available-for-sale securities

Investments	Cost	Fair Value	Unrealized Gain (Loss)
Campbell Soup Corporation			
8% bonds	$ 93,537	$103,600	$10,063
Hershey Foods stock	200,000	180,400	(19,600)
Total	$293,537	$284,000	$(9,537)

For Elbert Corporation, there is an unrealized loss of $9,537 because total cost ($293,537) is $9,537 more than total fair value ($284,000). Both the adjusting entry and the reporting of the unrealized gain or loss from available-for-sale securities differ from those illustrated for trading securities. The differences result because these securities are not going to be sold in the near term. Thus, prior to actual sale there is a much greater likelihood of changes in fair value that may reverse either unrealized gains or losses. Accordingly, an unrealized gain or loss is not reported in the income statement. Instead, it is reported as

a separate component of stockholders' equity, referred to as a **contra equity account**. In the adjusting entry, the market adjustment account is identified with available-for-sale securities, and the unrealized gain or loss account is identified with stockholders' equity. The adjusting entry for Elbert Corporation to record the unrealized loss of $9,537 is:

Helpful Hint The entry is the same regardless of whether the securities are considered short-term or long-term.

Dec. 31	Unrealized Loss—Equity	9,537	
	Market Adjustment—Available-for-Sale		9,537
	(To record unrealized loss on available-for-sale securities)		

A	=	L	+	SE
−9,537				−9,537

If total fair value exceeds total cost, the adjusting entry would be recorded as an increase (debit) to the market adjustment account and an increase (a credit) to an unrealized gain account.

For available-for-sale securities, the unrealized gain or loss account is carried forward to future periods. At each future balance sheet date, it is adjusted with the market adjustment account to show the difference between cost and fair value at that time.

EVALUATING INVESTMENT PORTFOLIO PERFORMANCE

The latest accounting standards for reporting investments in debt securities and equity investments of less than 20% were introduced in 1993. These new rules were intended to improve the information provided about the performance of a company's investment portfolio. Unfortunately, even under these new standards, companies can "window-dress" their reported earnings results—that is, make net income look better than it really was.

Companies can choose which of the three categories of securities to use for an investment. Recall that gains and losses on investments classified as available-for-sale are not included in income, but rather are recorded as an adjustment to equity. If a company wanted to manage its reported income, it could simply sell those available-for-sale investments that have unrealized gains, and not sell those available-for-sale investments that have unrealized losses. By doing this, the company is deferring the losses until a later period. For example, refer back to Illustration 12-7. If Elbert Corporation wanted to increase its reported income, it could sell its investment in Campbell Soup and realize a gain of $10,063. It would then report an unrealized loss of $19,600 in the equity section of its balance sheet.

Sometimes unrealized losses on available-for-sale securities can be material. For example, in a recent year KeyCorp, a bank holding company headquartered in Cleveland, Ohio, reported net income of $853 million. However, the reduction to shareholders' equity for unrealized holding losses on available-for-sale securities was $115 million. That is, if these securities had been sold before year-end, income would have declined by $115 million. This potential loss represented 13% of net income. Similarly, in a recent year Bank of America reported a reduction to shareholders' equity of $326 million, when net income for the year was $2,176 million. Clearly, it is important to consider the potential impact of these unrealized losses on current and future income when evaluating the performance of the company's investment portfolio.

Helpful Hint Note that even though gains and losses on held-to-maturity securities also are not reported in income until realized, a company is less likely to window-dress with these securities because penalties are associated with selling these securities prior to maturity.

DECISION TOOLKIT

Decision Checkpoints	Info Needed for Decision	Tool to Use for Decision	How to Evaluate Results
Is the company window-dressing its results by manipulating its available-for-sale portfolio?	Balance of unrealized gains and unrealized losses	Unrealized gains and losses on available-for-sale securities are not run through net income but are recorded as adjustments to stockholders' equity. A company can window-dress by selling winners and holding losers to increase reported income, or do the opposite to reduce reported income.	Window-dressing is not easy to spot: It is difficult for an outsider to determine why companies chose to either sell or hold a security. A user should evaluate a company's earnings as reported, including any unrealized gains and losses, to see total potential variation.

BEFORE YOU GO ON...

◆ Review It

1. What are the three categories of investment securities?
2. What are the proper valuation and reporting for each of the three categories of investment securities?
3. Explain why unrealized gains and losses on trading securities are run through the income statement, while unrealized gains and losses on available-for-sale securities are not.
4. How might a company window-dress its reported earnings using its available-for-sale securities portfolio?

BALANCE SHEET PRESENTATION OF INVESTMENTS

For balance sheet presentation, investments must be classified as either short-term or long-term.

STUDY OBJECTIVE

6

Distinguish between short-term and long-term investments.

Short-Term Investments

Short-term investments (also called **marketable securities**) are securities held by a company that are (1) **readily marketable** and (2) **intended to be converted into cash** within the next year or operating cycle, whichever is longer. Investments that do not meet **both criteria** are classified as long-term investments. In a recent survey of 600 large U.S. companies, 401 reported short-term investments.

Helpful Hint Trading securities are always classified as short-term. Available-for-sale securities can be either short-term or long-term.

Readily Marketable.   An investment is readily marketable when it can be sold easily whenever the need for cash arises. Short-term paper[4] meets this criterion because it can be sold readily to other investors. Stocks and bonds traded on organized securities markets, such as the New York Stock Exchange, are readily marketable because they can be bought and sold daily. In contrast, there may be only a limited market for the securities issued by small corporations and no market for the securities of a privately held company.

---

[4]Short-term paper includes (1) certificates of deposits (CDs) issued by banks, (2) money market certificates issued by banks and savings and loan associations, (3) Treasury bills issued by the U.S. government, and (4) commercial paper issued by corporations with good credit ratings.

Intent to Convert. **Intent to convert means that management intends to sell the investment within the next year or operating cycle, whichever is longer.** Generally, this criterion is satisfied when the investment is considered a resource that will be used whenever the need for cash arises. For example, a ski resort may invest idle cash during the summer months with the intent to sell the securities to buy supplies and equipment shortly before the next winter season. This investment is considered short-term even if lack of snow cancels the next ski season and eliminates the need to convert the securities into cash as intended.

Because of their high liquidity, short-term investments are listed immediately below Cash in the current assets section of the balance sheet. Short-term investments are reported at fair value. For example, Pace Corporation would report its trading securities as shown in Illustration 12-8.

PACE CORPORATION Balance Sheet (partial)	
Current assets	
Cash	$21,000
Short-term investments, at fair value	60,000

Illustration 12-8
Presentation of temporary investments

Long-Term Investments

Long-term investments are generally reported in a separate section of the balance sheet immediately below Current Assets, as shown later in Illustration 12-11 (page 577). Long-term investments in available-for-sale securities are reported at fair value, and investments in common stock accounted for under the equity method are reported at equity.

PRESENTATION OF REALIZED AND UNREALIZED GAIN OR LOSS

Gains and losses on investments, whether realized or unrealized, must be presented in the financial statements. In the income statement, gains and losses, as well as interest and dividend revenue, are reported in the nonoperating section under the categories listed in Illustration 12-9.

Other Revenue and Gains	Other Expenses and Losses
Interest Revenue	Loss on Sale of Investments
Dividend Revenue	Unrealized Loss—Income
Gain on Sale of Investments	
Unrealized Gain—Income	

Illustration 12-9
Nonoperating items related to investments

As indicated earlier, an unrealized gain or loss on available-for-sale securities is reported as a separate component of stockholders' equity. To illustrate, assume that Dawson Inc. has common stock of $3,000,000, retained earnings of $1,500,000, and an unrealized loss on available-for-sale securities of $100,000. The financial statement presentation of the unrealized loss is shown in Illustration 12-10.

Illustration 12-10
Unrealized loss in stock-
holders' equity section

DAWSON INC. Balance Sheet (partial)	
Stockholders' equity	
Common stock	$3,000,000
Retained earnings	1,500,000
Total paid-in capital and retained earnings	4,500,000
Less: **Unrealized loss on available-for-sale securities**	(100,000)
Total stockholders' equity	$4,400,000

Note that the presentation of the loss is similar to the presentation of the cost of treasury stock in the stockholders' equity section. An unrealized gain is added in this section. Reporting the unrealized gain or loss in the stockholders' equity section serves two important purposes: (1) It reduces the volatility of net income due to fluctuations in fair value, and (2) it informs the financial statement user of the gain or loss that would occur if the securities were sold at fair value.

A new accounting standard requires that items such as this, which affect stockholders' equity but are not included in the calculation of net income, must be reported as part of a more inclusive measure called *comprehensive income*. For example, in Tootsie Roll Industries' balance sheet, stockholders' equity is reduced by "accumulated other comprehensive earnings" of negative $10,523,000. Note 9 to Tootsie Roll's financial statements shows that one component of this amount was unrealized gains and losses on investment securities. Comprehensive income is discussed more fully in Chapter 14.

COMPLETE BALANCE SHEET

Many sections of classified balance sheets have been presented in this and preceding chapters. The balance sheet in Illustration 12-11 (on the next page) includes such topics from previous chapters as the issuance of par value common stock, restrictions of retained earnings, issuance of long-term bonds, and bond sinking funds. From this chapter, the statement includes (highlighted in red) short-term and long-term investments. We have assumed the short-term investments are trading securities; the long-term investments in stock of less than 20% owned companies are assumed to be available-for-sale securities. Illustration 12-11 also includes a long-term investment reported at equity, descriptive notations within the statement such as the basis for valuing merchandise, and two notes to the statement.

Illustration 12-11
Complete balance sheet

PACE CORPORATION
Balance Sheet
December 31, 2001

Assets

Current assets

Cash			$ 21,000
Short-term investments, at fair value			60,000
Accounts receivable		$ 84,000	
Less: Allowance for doubtful accounts		4,000	80,000
Merchandise inventory, at FIFO cost			130,000
Prepaid insurance			23,000
Total current assets			314,000

Investments

Bond sinking fund		100,000	
Investments in stock of less than 20% owned companies, at fair value		50,000	
Investment in stock of 20%–50% owned company, at equity		150,000	
Total investments			300,000

Property, plant, and equipment

Land			200,000
Buildings	$800,000		
Less: Accumulated depreciation	200,000	600,000	
Equipment	180,000		
Less: Accumulated depreciation	54,000	126,000	
Total property, plant, and equipment			926,000

Intangible assets

Goodwill (Note 1)		170,000	
Total intangible assets			170,000
Total assets			$1,710,000

Liabilities and Stockholders' Equity

Current liabilities

Accounts payable			$ 185,000
Bond interest payable			10,000
Federal income taxes payable			60,000
Total current liabilities			255,000

Long-term liabilities

Bonds payable, 10%, due 2013		$ 300,000	
Less: Discount on bonds		10,000	
Total long-term liabilities			290,000
Total liabilities			545,000

Stockholders' equity

Paid-in capital

Common stock, $10 par value, 200,000 shares authorized, 80,000 shares issued and outstanding		800,000	
Paid-in capital in excess of par value		100,000	
Total paid-in capital		900,000	
Retained earnings (Note 2)		255,000	
Total paid-in capital and retained earnings		1,155,000	
Add: Unrealized gain on available-for-sale securities		10,000	
Total stockholders' equity			1,165,000
Total liabilities and stockholders' equity			$1,710,000

Note 1. Goodwill is amortized by the straight-line method over 40 years.
Note 2. Retained earnings of $100,000 is restricted for plant expansion.

BEFORE YOU GO ON...

◆ **Review It**

1. Explain where short-term and long-term investments are reported on a balance sheet.
2. Where are unrealized gains and losses from trading securities reported? Where are unrealized gains and losses from available-for-sale securities reported?

3. What was the amount of Tootsie Roll's investments that were classified as current? What amount was noncurrent? What percentage of total assets was investments? The answer to this question is provided on page 595.

USING THE DECISION TOOLKIT

KeyCorp is an Ohio bank holding company (a corporation that owns banks). It manages $80 billion in assets, the largest of which is its loan portfolio of $62 billion. In addition to its loan portfolio, however, like other banks it has significant debt and stock investments. The nature of these investments varies from short-term to long-term and as a consequence, consistent with accounting rules, KeyCorp reports its investments in three different categories: trading, available-for-sale, and held-to-maturity. The following facts are from KeyCorp's 1998 annual report:

($ in millions)	Amortized Cost	Gross Unrealized Gains	Gross Unrealized Losses	Fair Value
Trading securities	—	—	—	$1,974
Available-for-sale securities	$5,228	$75	$25	5,278
Held-to-maturity securities	976	28	0	1,004

Net income: $996 million

Instructions

Answer these questions:

1. Why do you suppose KeyCorp purchases investments rather than only making loans? Why does it purchase investments that vary in terms of both their maturities and their type (debt versus stock)?
2. How must KeyCorp account for its investments in each of the three categories? In what ways does classifying investments into three different categories assist investors in evaluating the profitability of a company like KeyCorp?
3. Suppose that the management of KeyCorp was not happy with its 1998 net income. What step could it have taken with its investment portfolio that definitely would have increased 1998 reported profit? How much could it have increased reported profit? Why do you suppose it chose not to do this?

Solution

1. Although banks are primarily in the business of lending money, they also need to balance their portfolios by investing in other assets. For example,

a bank may have excess cash that it has not yet loaned, which it wants to invest in very short-term liquid assets. Or it may believe that it can earn a higher rate of interest by buying long-term bonds than it can currently earn by making new loans. Or it may purchase investments for short-term speculation because it believes these investments will appreciate in value.

2. Trading securities are shown on the balance sheet at their current market value, and any unrealized gains and losses resulting from marking them to their market value are reported in income. Available-for-sale securities are reported on the balance sheet at their market value, and any unrealized gains and losses resulting from marking them to their market values are reported as a separate component of stockholders' equity on the balance sheet. Held-to-maturity securities are reported at their amortized cost; that is, they are not marked to market.

   Securities are reported in three different categories to reflect the likelihood that any unrealized gains and losses will eventually be realized by the company. Trading securities are held for a short period; thus, if the bank has an unrealized gain on its trading security portfolio, it is likely that these securities will be sold soon and the gain will be realized. On the other hand, held-to-maturity securities are not going to be sold for a long time; thus, unrealized gains on these securities may never be realized. If securities were all grouped into a single category, the investor would not be aware of these differences in the probability of realization of unrealized gains and losses.

3. The answer involves selling "winner" stocks in the available-for-sale portfolio at year-end. KeyCorp could have increased reported net income by $75 million (a material amount when total reported income was $996 million). Managers chose not to sell these securities because at the time (a) they felt that the securities had additional room for price appreciation, or (b) they didn't want to pay the additional taxes associated with a sale at a gain, or (c) they wanted to hold the securities because they were needed to provide the proper asset balance in their total asset portfolio, or (d) they preferred to report the gains in the next year.

SUMMARY OF STUDY OBJECTIVES

1 *Identify the reasons corporations invest in stocks and debt securities.* Corporations invest for three common reasons: (a) They have excess cash either because of their operating cycle or because of economic swings; (b) they view investments as a significant revenue source; (c) they have strategic goals such as gaining control of a competitor or moving into a new line of business.

2 *Explain the accounting for debt investments.* Entries for investments in debt securities are required when the bonds are purchased, interest is received or accrued, and the bonds are sold.

3 *Explain the accounting for stock investments.* Entries for investments in common stock are required when the stock is purchased, dividends are received, and stock is sold. When ownership is less than 20%, the cost

method is used—the investment is recorded at cost. When ownership is between 20% and 50%, the equity method should be used—the investor records its share of the net income of the investee in the year it is earned. When ownership is more than 50%, consolidated financial statements should be prepared.

4 *Describe the purpose and usefulness of consolidated financial statements.* When a company owns more than 50% of the common stock of another company, consolidated financial statements are usually prepared. These statements are especially useful to the stockholders, board of directors, and management of the parent company.

5 *Indicate how debt and stock investments are valued and reported in the financial statements.* Investments in debt and stock securities are classified as trading, available-for-sale, or held-to-maturity securities for valuation and reporting purposes. Trading securities are reported as current assets at fair value, with changes from cost reported in net income. Available-for-sale securities are also reported at fair value, with the changes from cost reported in stockholders' equity. Available-for-sale securities are classified as short-term or long-term depending on their expected realization.

6 *Distinguish between short-term and long-term investments.* Short-term investments are securities held by a company that are readily marketable and intended to be converted to cash within the next year or operating cycle, whichever is longer. Investments that do not meet both criteria are classified as long-term investments.

DECISION TOOLKIT—A SUMMARY

Decision Checkpoints	Info Needed for Decision	Tool to Use for Decision	How to Evaluate Results
Is the company window-dressing its results by manipulating its available-for-sale portfolio?	Balance of unrealized gains and unrealized losses	Unrealized gains and losses on available-for-sale securities are not run through net income but are recorded as adjustments to stockholders' equity. A company can window-dress by selling winners and holding losers to increase reported income, or do the opposite to reduce reported income.	Window-dressing is not easy to spot: It is difficult for an outsider to determine why companies chose to either sell or hold a security. A user should evaluate a company's earnings as reported, including any unrealized gains and losses, to see total potential variation.

GLOSSARY

Available-for-sale securities Securities that may be sold in the future. (p. 570)

Consolidated financial statements Financial statements that present the assets and liabilities controlled by the parent company and the aggregate profitability of the affiliated companies. (p. 568)

Controlling interest Ownership of more than 50% of the common stock of another entity. (p. 568)

Cost method An accounting method in which the investment in common stock is recorded at cost and revenue is recognized only when cash dividends are received. (p. 566)

Debt investments Investments in government and corporation bonds. (p. 562)

Equity method An accounting method in which the investment in common stock is initially recorded at cost, and the investment account is then adjusted annually to show the investor's equity in the investee. (p. 567)

Fair value Amount for which a security could be sold in a normal market. (p. 570)

Held-to-maturity securities Debt securities that the investor has the intent and ability to hold to their maturity date. (p. 571)

Long-term investments Investments that are not readily marketable or that management does not intend to convert into cash within the next year or operating cycle, whichever is longer. (p. 574)

Mark-to-market A method of accounting for certain investments that requires that they be adjusted to their fair value at the end of each period. (p. 571)

Parent company A company that owns more than 50% of the common stock of another entity. (p. 568)

Short-term investments (marketable securities) Investments that are readily marketable and intended to be converted into cash within the next year or operating cycle, whichever is longer. (p. 574)

Stock investments Investments in the capital stock of corporations. (p. 565)

Subsidiary (affiliated) company A company in which more than 50% of its stock is owned by another company. (p. 568)

Trading securities Securities bought and held primarily for sale in the near term to generate income on short-term price differences. (p. 570)

DEMONSTRATION PROBLEM

In its first year of operations, DeMarco Company had these selected transactions in stock investments that are considered **trading securities**:

June 1 Purchased for cash 600 shares of Sanburg common stock at $24 per share plus $300 brokerage fees.

July 1 Purchased for cash 800 shares of Cey common stock at $33 per share plus $600 brokerage fees.

Sept. 1 Received a $1 per share cash dividend from Cey Corporation.

Nov. 1 Sold 200 shares of Sanburg common stock for cash at $27 per share less $150 brokerage fees.

Dec. 15 Received a $.50 per share cash dividend on Sanburg common stock.

Instructions

(a) Journalize the transactions.
(b) Prepare the adjusting entry at December 31 to report the securities at fair value. At December 31 the fair values per share were: Sanburg $25 and Cey $30.

Solution to Demonstration Problem

(a) June 1	Stock Investments	14,700	
	Cash [(600 × $24) + $300]		14,700
	(To record purchase of 600 shares of Sanburg common stock)		

July 1	Stock Investments	27,000	
	Cash [(800 × $33) + $600]		27,000
	(To record purchase of 800 shares of Cey common stock)		

Sept. 1	Cash	800	
	Dividend Revenue		800
	(To record receipt of $1 per share cash dividend from Cey)		

Nov. 1	Cash [(200 × $27) − $150]	5,250	
	Stock Investments (200 × $24.50)		4,900
	Gain on Sale of Stock Investments		350
	(To record sale of 200 shares of Sanburg common stock)		

Dec. 15	Cash [(600 − 200) × $.50]	200	
	Dividend Revenue		200
	(To record receipt of $.50 per share dividend from Sanburg)		

(b) Dec. 31	Unrealized Loss—Income	2,800	
	Market Adjustment—Trading		2,800
	(To record unrealized loss on trading securities)		

Investment	Cost	Fair Value	Unrealized Gain (Loss)
Sanburg common stock	$ 9,800	$10,000	$ 200
Cey common stock	27,000	24,000	(3,000)
Total	$36,800	$34,000	$(2,800)

Problem-Solving Strategies

1. Cost includes the price paid plus brokerage fees.

2. Gain or loss on sales is determined by the difference between net selling price and the cost of the securities.

3. The adjustment to fair value is based on the total difference between cost and fair value of the securities.

SELF-STUDY QUESTIONS

Answers are at the end of the chapter.

(SO 2) 1. Debt investments are initially recorded at:
   (a) cost.
   (b) cost plus accrued interest.
   (c) fair value.
   (d) None of the above

(SO 2) 2. Hanes Company sells debt investments costing $26,000 for $28,000 plus accrued interest that has been recorded. In journalizing the sale, credits are:
   (a) Debt Investments and Loss on Sale of Debt Investments.
   (b) Debt Investments, Gain on Sale of Debt Investments, and Bond Interest Receivable.
   (c) Stock Investments and Bond Interest Receivable.
   (d) The correct answer is not given.

(SO 3) 3. Pryor Company receives net proceeds of $42,000 on the sale of stock investments that cost $39,500. This transaction will result in reporting in the income statement a:
   (a) loss of $2,500 under Other Expenses and Losses.
   (b) loss of $2,500 under Operating Expenses.
   (c) gain of $2,500 under Other Revenues and Gains.
   (d) gain of $2,500 under Operating Revenues.

(SO 3) 4. The equity method of accounting for long-term investments in stock should be used when the investor has significant influence over an investee and owns:
   (a) between 20% and 50% of the investee's common stock.
   (b) 20% or more of the investee's common stock.
   (c) more than 50% of the investee's common stock.
   (d) less than 20% of the investee's common stock.

(SO 4) 5. Which of these statements is *not* true?

   Consolidated financial statements are useful to:
   (a) determine the profitability of specific subsidiaries.
   (b) determine the aggregate profitability of enterprises under common control.
   (c) determine the breadth of a parent company's operations.

   (d) determine the full extent of aggregate obligations of enterprises under common control.

(SO 5) 6. At the end of the first year of operations, the total cost of the trading securities portfolio is $120,000 and the total fair value is $115,000. What should the financial statements show?
   (a) A reduction of an asset of $5,000 and a realized loss of $5,000.
   (b) A reduction of an asset of $5,000 and an unrealized loss of $5,000 in the stockholders' equity section.
   (c) A reduction of an asset of $5,000 in the current assets section and an unrealized loss of $5,000 under Other Expenses and Losses.
   (d) A reduction of an asset of $5,000 in the current assets section and a realized loss of $5,000 under Other Expenses and Losses.

(SO 5) 7. In the balance sheet, Unrealized Loss—Equity is reported as a:
   (a) contra asset account.
   (b) contra stockholders' equity account.
   (c) loss in the income statement.
   (d) loss in the retained earnings statement.

(SO 5) 8. ⬤▬▬◖ If a company wants to increase its reported income by manipulating its investment accounts, which should it do?
   (a) Sell its "winner" trading securities and hold its "loser" trading securities.
   (b) Hold its "winner" trading securities and sell its "loser" trading securities.
   (c) Sell its "winner" available-for-sale securities and hold its "loser" available-for-sale securities.
   (d) Hold its "winner" available-for-sale securities and sell its "loser" available-for-sale securities.

(SO 6) 9. To be classified as short-term investments, debt investments must be readily marketable and be expected to be sold within:
   (a) 3 months from the date of purchase.
   (b) the next year or operating cycle, whichever is shorter.
   (c) the next year or operating cycle, whichever is longer.
   (d) the operating cycle.

QUESTIONS

1. What are the reasons that corporations invest in securities?

2. (a) What is the cost of an investment in bonds?
   (b) When is interest on bonds recorded?

3. Ann Adler is confused about losses and gains on the sale of debt investments. Explain these issues to Ann:

   (a) How the gain or loss is computed.
   (b) The statement presentation of gains and losses.

4. Clio Company sells Cross's bonds that cost $40,000 for $45,000, including $3,000 of accrued interest. In recording the sale, Clio books a $5,000 gain. Is this correct? Explain.

5. What is the cost of an investment in stock?

6. To acquire Mega Corporation stock, R. L. Duran pays $65,000 in cash plus $1,500 broker's fees. What entry should be made for this investment, assuming the stock is readily marketable?

7. (a) When should a long-term investment in common stock be accounted for by the equity method?
   (b) When is revenue recognized under the equity method?

8. Malon Corporation uses the equity method to account for its ownership of 35% of the common stock of Flynn Packing. During 2001 Flynn reported a net income of $80,000 and declares and pays cash dividends of $10,000. What recognition should Malon Corporation give to these events?

9. What constitutes "significant influence" when an investor's financial interest is less than 50%?

10. Distinguish between the cost and equity methods of accounting for investments in stocks.

11. What are consolidated financial statements?

12. What are the valuation guidelines for investments at a balance sheet date?

13. Wendy Walner is the controller of G-Products, Inc. At December 31 the company's investments in trading securities cost $74,000 and have a fair value of $70,000. Indicate how Wendy would report these data in the financial statements prepared on December 31.

14. Using the data in question 13, how would Wendy report the data if the investment were long-term and the securities were classified as available-for-sale?

15. Reo Company's investments in available-for-sale securities at December 31 show total cost of $192,000 and total fair value of $210,000. Prepare the adjusting entry.

16. Using the data in question 15, prepare the adjusting entry assuming the securities are classified as trading securities.

17. What is the proper statement presentation of the account Unrealized Loss—Equity?

18. What purposes are served by reporting Unrealized Gains (Losses)—Equity in the stockholders' equity section?

19. Kirk Wholesale Supply owns stock in Xerox Corporation, which it intends to hold indefinitely because of some negative tax consequences if sold. Should the investment in Xerox be classified as a short-term investment? Why?

*B*RIEF EXERCISES

BE12-1 Phelps Corporation purchased debt investments for $41,500 on January 1, 2001. On July 1, 2001, Phelps received cash interest of $2,075. Journalize the purchase and the receipt of interest. Assume no interest has been accrued.

Journalize entries for debt investments.
(SO 2)

BE12-2 On August 1 McLain Company buys 1,000 shares of ABC common stock for $35,000 cash plus brokerage fees of $600. On December 1 the stock investments are sold for $38,000 in cash. Journalize the purchase and sale of the common stock.

Journalize entries for stock investments.
(SO 3)

BE12-3 Harmon Company owns 30% of Hook Company. For the current year Hook reports net income of $150,000 and declares and pays a $50,000 cash dividend. Record Harmon's equity in Hook's net income and the receipt of dividends from Hook.

Journalize transactions under the equity method.
(SO 3)

BE12-4 Cost and fair value data for the trading securities of Michele Company at December 31, 2001, are $62,000 and $59,000, respectively. Prepare the adjusting entry to record the securities at fair value.

Prepare adjusting entry using fair value.
(SO 5)

BE12-5 For the data presented in BE12-4, show the financial statement presentation of the trading securities and related accounts.

Indicate statement presentation using fair value.
(SO 6)

BE12-6 In its first year of operations Duggen Corporation purchased available-for-sale stock securities costing $72,000 as a long-term investment. At December 31, 2001, the fair value of the securities is $65,000. Prepare the adjusting entry to record the securities at fair value.

Prepare adjusting entry using fair value.
(SO 5)

BE12-7 For the data presented in BE12-6, show the financial statement presentation of the available-for-sale securities and related accounts. Assume the available-for-sale securities are noncurrent.

Indicate statement presentation using fair value.
(SO 6)

BE12-8 Saber Corporation has these long-term investments: common stock of Sword Co. (10% ownership) held as available-for-sale securities, cost $108,000, fair value $113,000; common stock of Epee Inc. (30% ownership), cost $210,000, equity $250,000; and a bond sinking fund of $150,000. Prepare the investments section of the balance sheet.

Prepare investments section of balance sheet.
(SO 6)

EXERCISES

Journalize debt investment transactions, and accrue interest.
(SO 2)

E12-1 Greer Corporation had these transactions pertaining to debt investments:

Jan. 1   Purchased 90 10%, $1,000 Ford Co. bonds for $90,000 cash plus brokerage fees of $900. Interest is payable semiannually on July 1 and January 1.

July 1   Received semiannual interest on Ford Co. bonds.

July 1   Sold 40 Ford Co. bonds for $44,000 less $400 brokerage fees.

Instructions
(a) Journalize the transactions.
(b) Prepare the adjusting entry for the accrual of interest at December 31.

Journalize stock investment transactions, and explain income statement presentation.
(SO 3)

E12-2 Puff Daddy Company had these transactions pertaining to stock investments:

Feb. 1   Purchased 800 shares of GET common stock (2%) for $9,000 cash plus brokerage fees of $200.

July 1   Received cash dividends of $1 per share on GET common stock.

Sept. 1   Sold 400 shares of GET common stock for $5,500 less brokerage fees of $100.

Dec. 1   Received cash dividends of $1 per share on GET common stock.

Instructions
(a) Journalize the transactions.
(b) Explain how dividend revenue and the gain (loss) on sale should be reported in the income statement.

Journalize transactions for investments in stock.
(SO 3)

E12-3 Grosby Inc. had these transactions pertaining to investments in common stock:

Jan. 1   Purchased 1,000 shares of Hannah Corporation common stock (5%) for $70,000 cash plus $1,400 broker's commission.

July 1   Received a cash dividend of $7 per share.

Dec. 1   Sold 500 shares of Hannah Corporation common stock for $32,000 cash less $800 broker's commission.

    31   Received a cash dividend of $7 per share.

Instructions
Journalize the transactions.

Journalize and post transactions under the equity method.
(SO 3)

E12-4 On January 1 Howell Corporation purchased a 30% equity investment in Bellingham Corporation for $150,000. At December 31 Bellingham declared and paid a $70,000 cash dividend and reported net income of $250,000.

Instructions
(a) Journalize the transactions.
(b) Determine the amount to be reported as an investment in Bellingham stock at December 31.

Journalize entries under cost and equity methods.
(SO 3)

E12-5 These are two independent situations:

1. Ritter Cosmetics acquired 10% of the 200,000 shares of common stock of Mai Fashion at a total cost of $13 per share on March 18, 2001. On June 30 Mai declared and paid a $75,000 dividend. On December 31 Mai reported net income of $122,000 for the year. At December 31 the market price of Mai Fashion was $16 per share. The stock is classified as available-for-sale.

2. Somer Inc. obtained significant influence over Ortiz Corporation by buying 40% of Ortiz's 30,000 outstanding shares of common stock at a total cost of $9 per share on January 1, 2001. On June 15 Ortiz declared and paid a cash dividend of $35,000. On December 31 Ortiz reported a net income of $90,000 for the year.

Instructions
Prepare all the necessary journal entries for 2001 for (a) Ritter Cosmetics and (b) Somer Inc.

E12-6 At December 31, 2001, the trading securities for Yanik, Inc., are as follows:

Prepare adjusting entry to record fair value, and indicate statement presentation.
(SO 5, 6)

Security	Cost	Fair Value
A	$17,500	$16,000
B	12,500	14,000
C	23,000	19,000
Total	$53,000	$49,000

Instructions
(a) Prepare the adjusting entry at December 31, 2001, to report the securities at fair value.
(b) Show the balance sheet and income statement presentation at December 31, 2001, after adjustment to fair value.

E12-7 Data for investments in stock classified as trading securities are presented in E12-6. Assume instead that the investments are classified as available-for-sale securities with the same cost and fair value data. The securities are considered to be a long-term investment.

Prepare adjusting entry to record fair value, and indicate statement presentation.
(SO 5, 6)

Instructions
(a) Prepare the adjusting entry at December 31, 2001, to report the securities at fair value.
(b) Show the statement presentation at December 31, 2001, after adjustment to fair value.
(c) M. Wise, a member of the board of directors, does not understand the reporting of the unrealized gains or losses. Write a letter to Mr. Wise explaining the reporting and the purposes it serves.

E12-8 Bill Bradley Company has these data at December 31, 2001:

Prepare adjusting entries for fair value, and indicate statement presentation for two classes of securities.
(SO 5, 6)

Securities	Cost	Fair Value
Trading	$120,000	$128,000
Available-for-sale	100,000	94,000

The available-for-sale securities are held as a long-term investment.

Instructions
(a) Prepare the adjusting entries to report each class of securities at fair value.
(b) Indicate the statement presentation of each class of securities and the related unrealized gain (loss) accounts.

PROBLEMS: SET A

P12-1A Marvel Davis Farms is a grower of hybrid seed corn for DeKalb Genetics Corporation. It has had two exceptionally good years and has elected to invest its excess funds in bonds. The following selected transactions relate to bonds acquired as an investment by Marvel Davis Farms, whose fiscal year ends on December 31.

Journalize debt investment transactions and show financial statement presentation.
(SO 2, 5, 6)

2001
Jan. 1 Purchased at par $1,000,000 of Sycamore Corporation 10-year, 9% bonds dated January 1, 2001, directly from the issuing corporation.
July 1 Received the semiannual interest on the Sycamore bonds.
Dec. 31 Accrual of interest at year-end on the Sycamore bonds.

(Assume that all intervening transactions and adjustments have been properly recorded and the number of bonds owned has not changed from December 31, 2001, to December 31, 2003.)

2004
Jan. 1 Received the semiannual interest on the Sycamore bonds.
Jan. 1 Sold $500,000 Sycamore bonds at 114. The broker deducted $7,000 for commissions and fees on the sale.
July 1 Received the semiannual interest on the Sycamore bonds.
Dec. 31 Accrual of interest at year-end on the Sycamore bonds.

Instructions

(a) Journalize the listed transactions for the years 2001 and 2004.

(b) Assume that the fair value of the bonds at December 31, 2001, was $960,000. These bonds are classified as available-for-sale securities. Prepare the adjusting entry to record these bonds at fair value.

(c) Show the balance sheet presentation of the bonds and interest receivable at December 31, 2001. Assume the investments are considered long-term. Indicate where any unrealized gain or loss is reported in the financial statements.

Journalize investment transactions, prepare adjusting entry, and show financial statement presentation.
(SO 2, 3, 6)

P12-2A   In January 2001 the management of Mann Company concludes that it has sufficient cash to purchase some short-term investments in debt and stock securities. During the year, these transactions occurred:

Feb. 1   Purchased 800 shares of SRI common stock for $40,000 plus brokerage fees of $800.

Mar. 1   Purchased 500 shares of FGH common stock for $18,000 plus brokerage fees of $500.

Apr. 1   Purchased 70 $1,000, 12% CRT bonds for $70,000 plus $1,200 brokerage fees. Interest is payable semiannually on April 1 and October 1.

July 1   Received a cash dividend of $.60 per share on the SRI common stock.

Aug. 1   Sold 200 shares of SRI common stock at $42 per share less brokerage fees of $350.

Sept. 1   Received $1 per share cash dividend on the FGH common stock.

Oct. 1   Received the semiannual interest on the CRT bonds.

Oct. 1   Sold the CRT bonds for $68,000 less $1,000 brokerage fees.

At December 31 the fair values of the SRI and FGH common stocks were $39 and $30 per share, respectively.

Instructions

(a) Journalize the transactions and post to the accounts Debt Investments and Stock Investments. (Use the T account form.)

(b) Prepare the adjusting entry at December 31, 2001, to report the investments at fair value. All securities are considered to be trading securities.

(c) Show the balance sheet presentation of investment securities at December 31, 2001.

(d) Identify the income statement accounts and give the statement classification of each account.

Journalize transactions, prepare adjusting entry for stock investments, and show balance sheet presentation.
(SO 3, 5, 6)

P12-3A   On December 31, 2000, Kern Associates owned the following securities that are held as long-term investments:

Common Stock	Shares	Cost
A Co.	1,000	$60,000
B Co.	6,000	36,000
C Co.	1,200	24,000

On this date the total fair value of the securities was equal to its cost. The securities are not held for influence or control over the investees. In 2001 these transactions occurred:

July 1   Received $1.50 per share semiannual cash dividend on B Co. common stock.

Aug. 1   Received $.50 per share cash dividend on A Co. common stock.

Sept. 1   Sold 500 shares of B Co. common stock for cash at $7 per share less brokerage fees of $100.

Oct. 1   Sold 400 shares of A Co. common stock for cash at $56 per share less brokerage fees of $600.

Nov. 1   Received $1 per share cash dividend on C Co. common stock.

Dec. 15   Received $.50 per share cash dividend on A Co. common stock.

     31   Received $1.50 per share semiannual cash dividend on B Co. common stock.

At December 31 the fair values per share of the common stocks were: A Co. $47, B Co. $6, and C Co. $19.

Instructions

(a) Journalize the 2001 transactions and post to the account Stock Investments. (Use the T account form.)

(b) Prepare the adjusting entry at December 31, 2001, to show the securities at fair value. The stock should be classified as available-for-sale securities.

(c) Show the balance sheet presentation of the investments and the unrealized gain (loss) at December 31, 2001. At this date Kern Associates has common stock $2,000,000 and retained earnings $1,200,000.

P12-4A   Wet Concrete acquired 20% of the outstanding common stock of Hawes Inc. on January 1, 2001, by paying $1,200,000 for 50,000 shares. Hawes declared and paid a $.60 per share cash dividend on June 30 and again on December 31, 2001. Hawes reported net income of $800,000 for the year.

Prepare entries under cost and equity methods, and prepare memorandum.
(SO 3)

Instructions

(a) Prepare the journal entries for Wet Concrete for 2001 assuming Wet cannot exercise significant influence over Hawes. (Use the cost method.)

(b) Prepare the journal entries for Wet Concrete for 2001 assuming Wet can exercise significant influence over Hawes. (Use the equity method.)

(c) The board of directors of Wet Concrete is confused about the differences between the cost and equity methods. Prepare a memorandum for the board that explains each method and shows in tabular form the account balances under each method at December 31, 2001.

P12-5A   Here is Sammy Sosa Company's portfolio of long-term available-for-sale securities at December 31, 2000:

Journalize stock transactions, and show balance sheet presentation.
(SO 3, 5, 6)

	Cost
1,000 shares of McGwire Inc. common stock	$52,000
1,400 shares of B. Ruth Corporation common stock	84,000
800 shares of H. Aaron Corporation preferred stock	33,600

On December 31 the total cost of the portfolio equaled the total fair value. Sosa had these transactions related to the securities during 2001:

Jan. 20   Sold 1,000 shares of McGwire Inc. common stock at $56 per share less brokerage fees of $600.

   28   Purchased 400 shares of $10 par value common stock of M. Mantle Corporation at $78 per share plus brokerage fees of $480.

   30   Received a cash dividend of $1.15 per share on B. Ruth Corporation common stock.

Feb. 8   Received cash dividends of $.40 per share on H. Aaron Corporation preferred stock.

   18   Sold all 800 shares of H. Aaron preferred stock at $30 per share less brokerage fees of $360.

July 30   Received a cash dividend of $1 per share on B. Ruth Corporation common stock.

Sept. 6   Purchased an additional 800 shares of the $10 par value common stock of M. Mantle Corporation at $82 per share plus brokerage fees of $800.

Dec. 1   Received a cash dividend of $1.50 per share on M. Mantle Corporation common stock.

At December 31, 2001, the fair values of the securities were:

B. Ruth Corporation common stock	$64 per share
M. Mantle Corporation common stock	$70 per share

Sosa uses separate account titles for each investment, such as Investment in B. Ruth Corporation Common Stock.

Instructions

(a) Prepare journal entries to record the transactions.

(b) Post to the investment accounts. (Use T accounts.)

(c) Prepare the adjusting entry at December 31, 2001, to report the portfolio at fair value.

(d) Show the balance sheet presentation at December 31, 2001.

Prepare a balance sheet.
(SO 6)

P12-6A The following data, presented in alphabetical order, are taken from the records of Jackson Corporation:

Accounts payable	$ 220,000
Accounts receivable	90,000
Accumulated depreciation—building	180,000
Accumulated depreciation—equipment	52,000
Allowance for doubtful accounts	6,000
Bond investments	400,000
Bonds payable (10%, due 2015)	400,000
Buildings	900,000
Cash	72,000
Common stock ($5 par value; 500,000 shares authorized, 300,000 shares issued)	1,500,000
Discount on bonds payable	20,000
Dividends payable	50,000
Equipment	275,000
Goodwill	220,000
Income taxes payable	70,000
Investment in Houston Inc. stock (30% ownership), at equity	240,000
Land	500,000
Merchandise inventory	170,000
Notes payable (due 2002)	70,000
Paid-in capital in excess of par value	200,000
Prepaid insurance	16,000
Retained earnings	340,000
Short-term stock investment, at fair value	185,000

Instructions
Prepare a balance sheet at December 31, 2001.

PROBLEMS: SET B

Journalize debt investment transactions and show financial statement presentation.
(SO 2, 5, 6)

P12-1B Willow Carecenters Inc. provides financing and capital to the health care industry, with a particular focus on nursing homes for the elderly. The following selected transactions relate to bonds acquired as an investment by Willow, whose fiscal year ends on December 31.

2001

Jan. 1 Purchased at par $5,000,000 of Friendship Nursing Centers, Inc., 10-year, 10% bonds dated January 1, 2001, directly from Friendship.
July 1 Received the semiannual interest on the Friendship bonds.
Dec. 31 Accrual of interest at year-end on the Friendship bonds.

(Assume that all intervening transactions and adjustments have been properly recorded and that the number of bonds owned has not changed from December 31, 2001, to December 31, 2003.)

2004

Jan. 1 Received the semiannual interest on the Friendship bonds.
Jan. 1 Sold $2,500,000 Friendship bonds at 106. The broker deducted $10,000 for commissions and fees on the sale.
July 1 Received the semiannual interest on the Friendship bonds.
Dec. 31 Accrual of interest at year-end on the Friendship bonds.

Instructions
(a) Journalize the listed transactions for the years 2001 and 2004.
(b) Assume that the fair value of the bonds at December 31, 2001, was $5,500,000. These bonds are classified as available-for-sale securities. Prepare the adjusting entry to record these bonds at fair value.

(c) Show the balance sheet presentation of the bonds and interest receivable at December 31, 2001. Assume the investments are considered long-term. Indicate where any unrealized gain or loss is reported in the financial statements.

P12-2B In January 2001 the management of Norris Company concludes that it has sufficient cash to permit some short-term investments in debt and stock securities. During the year these transactions occurred:

Journalize investment transactions, prepare adjusting entry, and show financial statement presentation.
(SO 2, 3, 6)

Feb. 1   Purchased 600 shares of Alpha common stock for $28,800 plus brokerage fees of $300.
Mar. 1   Purchased 800 shares of Omega common stock for $20,000 plus brokerage fees of $400.
Apr. 1   Purchased 60 $1,000, 12% Pep bonds for $60,000 plus $1,200 brokerage fees. Interest is payable semiannually on April 1 and October 1.
July 1   Received a cash dividend of $.60 per share on the Alpha common stock.
Aug. 1   Sold 200 shares of Alpha common stock at $56 per share less brokerage fees of $200.
Sept. 1   Received $1 per share cash dividend on the Omega common stock.
Oct. 1   Received the semiannual interest on the Pep bonds.
Oct. 1   Sold the Pep bonds for $65,000 less $1,000 brokerage fees.

At December 31 the fair values of the Alpha and Omega common stocks were $57 and $24 per share, respectively.

Instructions
(a) Journalize the transactions and post to the accounts Debt Investments and Stock Investments. (Use the T account form.)
(b) Prepare the adjusting entry at December 31, 2001, to report the investment securities at fair value. All securities are considered to be trading securities.
(c) Show the balance sheet presentation of investment securities at December 31, 2001.
(d) Identify the income statement accounts and give the statement classification of each account.

P12-3B On December 31, 2000, Milner Associates owned the following securities that are held as long-term investments. The securities are not held for influence or control over the investee.

Journalize transactions, prepare adjusting entry for stock investments, and show balance sheet presentation.
(SO 3, 5, 6)

Common Stock	Shares	Cost
D Co.	2,000	$90,000
E Co.	5,000	45,000
F Co.	1,500	30,000

On this date the total fair value of the securities was equal to its cost. In 2001 these transactions occurred:

July   1   Received $.80 per share semiannual cash dividend on E Co. common stock.
Aug.   1   Received $.50 per share cash dividend on D Co. common stock.
Sept. 1   Sold 700 shares of E Co. common stock for cash at $7 per share less brokerage fees of $200.
Oct.   1   Sold 500 shares of D Co. common stock for cash at $54 per share less brokerage fees of $500.
Nov.   1   Received $1 per share cash dividend on F Co. common stock.
Dec. 15   Received $.50 per share cash dividend on D Co. common stock.
      31   Received $.80 per share semiannual cash dividend on E Co. common stock.

At December 31 the fair values per share of the common stocks were: D Co. $48, E Co. $8, and F Co. $17.

Instructions
(a) Journalize the 2001 transactions and post to the account Stock Investments. (Use the T account form.)
(b) Prepare the adjusting entry at December 31, 2001, to show the securities at fair value. The stock should be classified as available-for-sale securities.

(c) Show the balance sheet presentation of the investments and the unrealized gain (loss) at December 31, 2001. At this date Milner Associates has common stock $1,700,000 and retained earnings $1,000,000.

Prepare entries under cost and equity methods, and tabulate differences.
(SO 3)

P12-4B Nayler Services acquired 30% of the outstanding common stock of Quinn Company on January 1, 2001, by paying $800,000 for the 40,000 shares. Quinn declared and paid $.40 per share cash dividends on March 15, June 15, September 15, and December 15, 2001. Quinn reported net income of $360,000 for the year.

Instructions
(a) Prepare the journal entries for Nayler Services for 2001 assuming Nayler cannot exercise significant influence over Quinn. (Use the cost method.)
(b) Prepare the journal entries for Nayler Services for 2001 assuming Nayler can exercise significant influence over Quinn. (Use the equity method.)
(c) In tabular form indicate the investment and income statement account balances at December 31, 2001, under each method of accounting.

Journalize stock transactions and show statement presentation.
(SO 3, 5, 6)

P12-5B The following are in Big Head Todd Company's portfolio of long-term available-for-sale securities at December 31, 2000:

	Cost
500 shares of Aglar Corporation common stock	$26,000
700 shares of BAL Corporation common stock	42,000
400 shares of Hicks Corporation preferred stock	16,800

On December 31, the total cost of the portfolio equaled total fair value. Big Head Todd had the following transactions related to the securities during 2001:

Jan. 7	Sold 500 shares of Aglar Corporation common stock at $56 per share less brokerage fees of $700.
10	Purchased 200 shares, $70 par value common stock of Miley Corporation at $78 per share, plus brokerage fees of $240.
26	Received a cash dividend of $1.15 per share on BAL Corporation common stock.
Feb. 2	Received cash dividends of $.40 per share on Hicks Corporation preferred stock.
10	Sold all 400 shares of Hicks Corporation preferred stock at $30.00 per share less brokerage fees of $180.
July 1	Received a cash dividend of $1.00 per share on BAL Corporation common stock.
Sept. 1	Purchased an additional 400 shares of the $70 par value common stock of Miley Corporation at $82 per share, plus brokerage fees of $400.
Dec. 15	Received a cash dividend of $1.50 per share on Miley Corporation common stock.

At December 31, 2001, the fair values of the securities were:

BAL Corporation common stock	$64 per share
Miley Corporation common stock	$72 per share

Big Head Todd Company uses separate account titles for each investment, such as Investment in BAL Corporation Common Stock.

Instructions
(a) Prepare journal entries to record the transactions.
(b) Post to the investment accounts. (Use T accounts.)
(c) Prepare the adjusting entry at December 31, 2001, to report the portfolio at fair value.
(d) Show the balance sheet presentation at December 31, 2001.

Prepare a balance sheet.
(SO 6)

P12-6B The following data, presented in alphabetical order, are taken from the records of Rothchild Corporation:

Accounts payable	$ 220,000
Accounts receivable	90,000
Accumulated depreciation—building	180,000
Accumulated depreciation—equipment	52,000
Allowance for doubtful accounts	6,000
Bond investments	250,000

Bonds payable (10%, due 2010)	500,000
Buildings	950,000
Cash	92,000
Common stock ($10 par value; 500,000 shares authorized, 150,000 shares issued)	1,500,000
Dividends payable	90,000
Equipment	275,000
Goodwill	250,000
Income taxes payable	110,000
Investment in Dodge common stock (10% ownership), at cost	278,000
Investment in Huston common stock (30% ownership), at equity	230,000
Land	400,000
Market adjustment—available-for-sale securities (Dr.)	8,000
Merchandise inventory	170,000
Notes payable (due 2002)	70,000
Paid-in capital in excess of par value	200,000
Premium on bonds payable	40,000
Prepaid insurance	16,000
Retained earnings	213,000
Short-term stock investment, at fair value	180,000
Unrealized gain—available-for-sale securities	8,000

The investment in Dodge common stock is considered to be a long-term available-for-sale security.

Instructions
Prepare a balance sheet at December 31, 2001.

◆ BROADENING YOUR PERSPECTIVE

*F*INANCIAL REPORTING AND ANALYSIS

FINANCIAL REPORTING PROBLEM: *Tootsie Roll Industries, Inc.*

BYP12-1   The annual report of **Tootsie Roll Industries** is presented in Appendix A.

Instructions
Answer these questions:
(a) What information about investments is reported in the consolidated balance sheet?
(b) Based on the information in Note 10 to Tootsie Roll's financial statements, what is the value of trading securities in 1998?
(c) What effect did interest income on investments have on Income Before Income Taxes in 1998?
(d) Judging from the statement of cash flows, did purchases of investment securities increase or decrease in 1998, and by how much?

COMPARATIVE ANALYSIS PROBLEM: *Tootsie Roll vs. Hershey Foods*

BYP12-2   The financial statements of **Hershey Foods** are presented in Appendix B, following the financial statements for **Tootsie Roll Industries** in Appendix A.

Instructions

Compare the investing activities sections of the statements of cash flows for the two companies for 1996, 1997, and 1998. What conclusions concerning the nature of investment activity can be drawn from these data?

RESEARCH CASE

BYP12-3 The January 9, 1999, issue of *The Economist* includes an article entitled "How to Make Mergers Work."

Instructions

Read the article and answer the following questions:

(a) What percentage of mergers actually added value to the combined company? Which investors tend to gain from the merger, and which tend to lose?

(b) The article suggests that mergers in the past tended to be undertaken to create diversified conglomerates, but that mergers of today tend to be defensive in nature. Give examples of motivations for defensive mergers and industries where they have taken place.

(c) What are some reasons why mergers often fail?

(d) What are some methods for increasing the likelihood of success?

INTERPRETING FINANCIAL STATEMENTS

BYP12-4 **Delta Air Lines, Inc.,** is based in Atlanta, Georgia, and is one of the world's largest air carriers. Besides carrying passengers, Delta also provides freight and mail transportation services.

Here is the assets section of a recent Delta balance sheet (excluding dollar amounts):

DELTA AIR LINES
Balance Sheet (partial)

Current assets
    Cash and cash equivalents
    Short-term investments
    Accounts receivable, net of allowance for uncollectible accounts
    Maintenance and operating supplies, at average cost
    Deferred income taxes
    Prepaid expenses and other
Property and equipment
    Flight equipment, less accumulated depreciation
    Flight equipment under capital leases, less accumulated amortization
    Ground property and equipment, less accumulated depreciation
    Advance payments for equipment
Other assets
    Marketable equity securities
    Deferred income taxes
    Investments in associated companies
    Cost in excess of net assets acquired, net of accumulated amortization
    Leasehold and operating rights, net of accumulated amortization
    Other

Delta also reported the following information concerning certain of its investments:

1. Investments in TransQuest Information Solutions (TransQuest), an information technology joint venture, are accounted for under the equity method.

2. Investments with an original maturity of 3 months or less are stated at cost, which approximates fair value.

3. Cost in excess of net assets acquired (goodwill), which is being amortized over 40 years, is related to the company's acquisition of Western Air Lines, Inc., on December 18, 1986.
4. The company's investments in Singapore Air Lines Limited are accounted for under the cost method and are classified as available-for-sale and carried at aggregate market value.
5. Cash in excess of operating requirements is invested in short-term, highly liquid investments. These investments are classified as available-for-sale and are stated at fair value.

Instructions
(a) For each item 1–5 above, determine where it should be shown on Delta's balance sheet, using the account titles listed earlier.
(b) Assume that item 2 includes an investment in IBM Corporation bonds consisting of ten bonds of $10,000 each. What accounting treatment is required for the following?
   (1) Singapore Air Lines Limited announces net income for the year of $3.15 per share. Assume that Delta holds 3,500 shares.
   (2) Western Air Lines announces a net loss of $18,000,000, or $.63 per share for the quarter.
   (3) IBM Corporation declares and pays a $.25 dividend per share.

BYP12-5   Firstar Inc. is a large bank holding company. In addition to making loans, it has significant trading activities. During 1998 the company reported net income of $430 million.

The following additional information was available regarding the company's available-for-sale portfolio:

(in millions)	Cost	Gross Unrealized Gains	Gross Unrealized Losses	Fair Value
1998	$6,064	$159.6	$2.5	$6,221

Instructions
Firstar has a significant available-for-sale portfolio. How much, and by what percentage, could the company have increased its 1998 income by selling its "winners" while holding its "losers"? Why do you suppose it chose not to do this?

A GLOBAL FOCUS

BYP12-6   Xerox Corporation has a 50% investment interest in a joint venture with the Japanese corporation Fuji, called **Fuji Xerox**. Xerox accounts for this investment using the equity method. The following additional information regarding this investment was taken from Xerox's 1998 annual report (in millions):

Investment in Fuji Xerox per balance sheet	$ 1,354
Fuji Xerox net income	108
Xerox total assets	30,024
Xerox total liabilities	25,167
Fuji Xerox total assets	6,279
Fuji Xerox total liabilities	3,757

Instructions
(a) What alternative approaches are available for accounting for long-term investments in stock? Discuss whether Xerox is correct in using the equity method to account for this investment.
(b) Under the equity method, how does Xerox report its investment in Fuji Xerox? If Xerox owned a majority of Fuji Xerox, it then would have to consolidate Fuji Xerox instead of using the equity method. Discuss how this would change Xerox's financial statements. That is, in what way and by how much would assets and liabilities change?
(c) The use of 50% joint ventures is becoming a fairly common practice. Why might companies like Xerox and Fuji prefer to participate in a joint venture rather than own a majority share?

FINANCIAL ANALYSIS ON THE WEB

BYP12-7 The **Securities and Exchange Commission (SEC)** is the primary regulatory agency of U.S. financial markets. Its job is to ensure that the markets remain fair for all investors. The following SEC site provides useful information for investors.

Address: http://www.sec.gov/consumer/weisktc.htm or go to
www.wiley.com/college/kimmel

Steps:
1. Go to the site shown above.
2. Choose **Glossary**.

Instructions
Using the glossary, find the definition of the following terms:
(a) Ask price.
(b) Margin account.
(c) Prospectus.
(d) Yield.

BYP12-8 Most publicly traded companies are analyzed by numerous analysts. These analysts often don't agree about a company's future prospects. In this exercise you will find analysts' ratings about companies and make comparisons over time and across companies in the same industry. You will also see to what extent the analysts experienced "earnings surprises." Earnings surprises can cause changes in stock prices.

Address: http://biz.yahoo.com/i or go to www.wiley.com/college/kimmel

Steps:
1. Choose a company.
2. Use the index to find the company's name.
3. Choose **Research**.

Instructions
Answer the following questions:
(a) How many brokers rated the company?
(b) What percentage rated it a strong buy?
(c) What was the average rating for the week?
(d) Did the average rating improve or decline relative to the previous week?
(e) How do the brokers rank this company among all the companies in its industry?
(f) What was the amount of the earnings surprise during the last quarter? (That is, to what extent were analysts' expectations of earnings incorrect?)
(g) Are earnings expected to increase or decrease this quarter compared to last?

CRITICAL THINKING

GROUP DECISION CASE

BYP12-9 At the beginning of the question and answer portion of the annual stockholders' meeting of Revell Corporation, stockholder Carol Finstrom asks, "Why did management sell the holdings in AHM Company at a loss when this company has been very profitable during the period its stock was held by Revell?"

Since President Larry Wisdom has just concluded his speech on the recent success and bright future of Revell, he is taken aback by this question and responds, "I remember we paid $1,100,000 for that stock some years ago, and I am sure we sold that stock at a much higher price. You must be mistaken."

Finstrom retorts, "Well, right here in footnote number 7 to the annual report it shows that 240,000 shares, a 30% interest in AHM, was sold on the last day of the year. Also, it states that AHM earned $550,000 this year and paid out $150,000 in cash dividends. Further, a summary statement indicates that in past years, while Revell held AHM stock, AHM earned $1,240,000 and paid out $440,000 in dividends. Finally, the income statement for this year shows a loss on the sale of AHM stock of $180,000. So, I doubt that I am mistaken."

Red-faced, President Wisdom turns to you.

Instructions

With the class divided into groups, answer the following:

Help out President Wisdom: What dollar amount did Revell receive upon the sale of the AHM stock? Explain why both Finstrom and Wisdom are correct.

COMMUNICATION ACTIVITY

BYP12-10   Chapperal Corporation has purchased two securities for its portfolio. The first is a stock investment in Sting Ray Corporation, one of its suppliers. Chapperal purchased 10% of Sting Ray with the intention of holding it for a number of years but has no intention of purchasing more shares. The second investment is a purchase of debt securities. Chapperal purchased the debt securities because its analysts believe that changes in market interest rates will cause these securities to increase in value in a short period of time. Chapperal intends to sell the securities as soon as they have increased in value.

Instructions

Write a memo to Gils Stiles, the chief financial officer, explaining how to account for each of these investments and the implications for reported income from this accounting treatment.

ETHICS CASE

BYP12-11   Scott Kreiter Financial Services Company holds a large portfolio of debt and stock securities as an investment. The total fair value of the portfolio at December 31, 2001, is greater than total cost, with some securities having increased in value and others having decreased. Vicki Lemke, the financial vice-president, and Ula Greenwood, the controller, are in the process of classifying for the first time the securities in the portfolio.

Lemke suggests classifying the securities that have increased in value as trading securities in order to increase net income for the year. She wants to classify the securities that have decreased in value as long-term available-for-sale securities so that the decreases in value will not affect 2001 net income.

Greenwood disagrees. She recommends classifying the securities that have decreased in value as trading securities and those that have increased in value as long-term available-for-sale securities. Greenwood argues that the company is having a good earnings year and that recognizing the losses now will help to smooth income for this year. Moreover, for future years, when the company may not be as profitable, the company will have built-in gains.

Instructions

(a) Will classifying the securities as Lemke and Greenwood suggest actually affect earnings as each says it will?

(b) Is there anything unethical in what Lemke and Greenwood propose? Who are the stakeholders affected by their proposals?

(c) Assume that Lemke and Greenwood properly classify the portfolio. Assume, at year-end, that Lemke proposes to sell the securities that will increase 2001 net income, and that Greenwood proposes to sell the securities that will decrease 2001 net income. Is this unethical?

Answers to Self-Study Questions

1. a   2. b   3. c   4. a   5. a   6. c   7. b   8. c   9. c

Answer to Tootsie Roll Review It Question 3, p. 578

Tootsie Roll had investments of $83,176,000 classified as current, and $59,252,000 classified as noncurrent. Investments represented 29.2% of total assets [($83,176,000 + $59,252,000) ÷ $487,423,000].

Statement of Cash Flows

After studying this chapter, you should be able to:

1 Indicate the primary purpose of the statement of cash flows.

2 Distinguish among operating, investing, and financing activities.

3 Explain the impact of the product life cycle on a company's cash flows.

4 Prepare a statement of cash flows using one of two approaches: (a) the indirect method or (b) the direct method.

5 Use the statement of cash flows to evaluate a company.

◆ **I'VE GOT $22 BILLION BURNING A HOLE IN MY POCKET!**

Imagine starting a company in a brand new industry and growing it into one of the biggest companies in the world—in just 24 years. Imagine you are one of the richest people on the planet at age 43. Now wake up! Bill Gates, founder of software maker Microsoft Corporation, accomplished all of this and more between 1975 and 1999. It all started with MS-DOS, a software package that Gates bought from a Seattle-based programmer for $50,000. Then MS-DOS was adopted by IBM as *the* operating system for all of its personal computers. Translation: Every IBM and IBM-compatible computer *in the world* needed a copy of MS-DOS to run. The rest is history.

Although MS-DOS got the Microsoft ball rolling, in an environment that changes as fast as the computer industry, it takes continual new products to survive and thrive. To develop new products it takes cash—lots and lots of cash. And to have lots and lots of cash when you are a young company requires great cash management and careful attention to cash flows.

During its early years, in order to ensure that it had enough cash to meet its needs, Microsoft employed many cash management techniques. For example, all of its employees received stock options, rather than cash, as a portion of their compensation. Stock options become valuable if Microsoft's stock price increases. By some estimates, more than 1,000 Microsoft employees have become millionaires because of these options.

These and other cash management practices enabled Microsoft to build up a "war chest" of cash and short-term investments. Its 1998 statement of cash flows reported cash provided by operations of approximately $4.5 billion. At its fiscal year-end of June 30, 1998, cash and short-term investments amounted to $13.9 billion—62% of its total assets. At March 31, 1999, this amount had grown to $22.8 billion. This might sound excessive, but it means that Microsoft can move quickly when it needs to—and in the computer industry speed is everything.

On the World Wide Web
Microsoft: http://www.microsoft.com

The balance sheet, income statement, and retained earnings statement do not always show the whole picture of the financial condition of a company or institution. In fact, looking at these three financial statements of some well-known companies, a thoughtful investor might ask questions like these: How did Eastman Kodak finance cash dividends of $649 million in a year in which it earned only $17 million? How could Delta Air Lines purchase new planes that cost $900 million in a year in which it reported a net loss of $86 million? How did the companies that were involved in the 7,000 mergers and acquisitions worth over $1 trillion in 1998 finance those deals? Answers to these and similar questions can be found in this chapter, which presents the statement of cash flows.

The content and organization of this chapter are as follows:

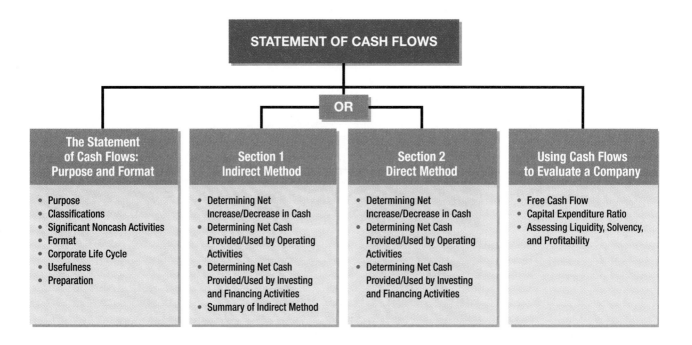

THE STATEMENT OF CASH FLOWS: PURPOSE AND FORMAT

The basic financial statements we have presented so far provide only limited information about a company's cash flows (cash receipts and cash payments). For example, comparative balance sheets show the increase in property, plant, and equipment during the year, but they do not show how the additions were financed or paid for. The income statement shows net income, but it does not indicate the amount of cash generated by operating activities. Similarly, the retained earnings statement shows cash dividends declared but not the cash dividends paid during the year. None of these statements presents a detailed summary of the **net change in cash** as a result of operating, investing, and financing activities during the period.

Helpful Hint Recall that the retained earnings statement is often presented in the statement of stockholders' equity.

PURPOSE OF THE STATEMENT OF CASH FLOWS

The primary purpose of the statement of cash flows is to provide information about cash receipts, cash payments, and the net change in cash resulting from the operating, investing, and financing activities of a company during the period. These activities involving cash are reported in a format that reconciles the beginning and ending cash balances.

Reporting the causes of changes in cash is useful because investors, creditors, and other interested parties want to know what is happening to a company's most liquid resource, its cash. As the opening story about Microsoft demonstrates, to understand a company's financial position it is essential to understand its cash flows. The statement of cash flows provides answers to these important questions about an enterprise:

Where did the cash come from during the period?

What was the cash used for during the period?

What was the change in the cash balance during the period?

The answers provide important clues about whether a dynamic company like Microsoft will be able to continue to thrive and invest in new opportunities. The statement of cash flows also provides clues about whether a struggling company will survive or perish.

STUDY OBJECTIVE

1

Indicate the primary purpose of the statement of cash flows.

CLASSIFICATION OF CASH FLOWS

The statement of cash flows classifies cash receipts and cash payments into operating, investing, and financing activities. Transactions within each activity are as follows:

1. **Operating activities** include the cash effects of transactions that create revenues and expenses and thus enter into the determination of net income.
2. **Investing activities** include (a) purchasing and disposing of investments and productive long-lived assets using cash and (b) lending money and collecting the loans.
3. **Financing activities** include (a) obtaining cash from issuing debt and repaying the amounts borrowed and (b) obtaining cash from stockholders and paying them dividends.

STUDY OBJECTIVE

2

Distinguish among operating, investing, and financing activities.

Operating activities is the most important category because it shows the cash provided or used by company operations. Ultimately a company must generate cash from its operating activities in order to continue as a going concern and to expand. Illustration 13-1 (page 600) lists typical cash receipts and cash payments within each of the three activities.

As you can see, some cash flows relating to investing or financing activities are classified as operating activities. For example, receipts of investment revenue (interest and dividends) and payments of interest to lenders are classified as operating activities because these items are reported in the income statement.

Note that, generally, **(1) operating activities involve income determination (income statement) items, (2) investing activities involve cash flows resulting from changes in investments and long-term asset items**, and **(3) financing activities involve cash flows resulting from changes in long-term liability and stockholders' equity items**.

SIGNIFICANT NONCASH ACTIVITIES

Not all of a company's significant activities involve cash. Here are four examples of significant noncash activities:

1. Issuance of common stock to purchase assets
2. Conversion of bonds into common stock
3. Issuance of debt to purchase assets
4. Exchanges of plant assets

Types of Cash Inflows and Outflows

Operating activities

Cash inflows:

From sale of goods or services

From interest received and dividends received

Cash outflows:

To suppliers for inventory

To employees for services

To government for taxes

To lenders for interest

To others for expenses

Investing activities

Cash inflows:

From sale of property, plant, and equipment

From sale of debt or equity securities of other entities

From collection of principal on loans to other entities

Cash outflows:

To purchase property, plant, and equipment

To purchase debt or equity securities of other entities

To make loans to other entities

Financing activities

Cash inflows:

From issuance of equity securities (company's own stock)

From issuance of debt (bonds and notes)

Cash outflows:

To stockholders as dividends

To redeem long-term debt or reacquire capital stock

Helpful Hint Operating activities generally relate to changes in current assets and current liabilities. Investing activities generally relate to changes in investments and noncurrent assets. Financing activities relate to changes in noncurrent liabilities and stockholders' equity accounts.

Helpful Hint Do not include noncash investing and financing activities in the body of the statement of cash flows. Report this information in a separate schedule at the bottom of the statement.

Significant financing and investing activities that do not affect cash are not reported in the body of the statement of cash flows. However, these activities are reported either in a separate schedule at the bottom of the statement of cash flows or in a separate note or supplementary schedule to the financial statements.

The reporting of these activities in a separate note or supplementary schedule satisfies the **full disclosure principle** because it identifies significant noncash investing and financing activities of the company. In doing homework assignments you should present significant noncash investing and financing activities in a separate schedule at the bottom of the statement of cash flows. (See the lower section of Illustration 13-2 for an example.)

FORMAT OF THE STATEMENT OF CASH FLOWS

The three activities discussed above—operating, investing, and financing—plus the significant noncash investing and financing activities make up the general format of the statement of cash flows. A widely used form of the statement of cash flows is shown in Illustration 13-2.

As illustrated, the section of cash flows from operating activities always appears first, followed by the investing activities and the financing activities sections. Also, **the individual inflows and outflows from investing and financ-**

COMPANY NAME
Statement of Cash Flows
Period Covered

Cash flows from operating activities
    (List of individual items)   XX
Net cash provided (used) by operating activities   XXX

Cash flows from investing activities
    (List of individual inflows and outflows)   XX
Net cash provided (used) by investing activities   XXX

Cash flows from financing activities
    (List of individual inflows and outflows)   XX
Net cash provided (used) by financing activities   XXX
Net increase (decrease) in cash   XXX
Cash at beginning of period   XXX
Cash at end of period   XXX

Noncash investing and financing activities
    (List of individual noncash transactions)   XXX

Illustration 13-2 Format of statement of cash flows

Helpful Hint Indicate the classification in the statement of cash flows for each of the following: (1) Proceeds from the sale of an investment. (2) Disbursement for the purchase of treasury stock. (3) Loan to another corporation. (4) Proceeds from an insurance policy because a building was destroyed by fire. (5) Proceeds from winning a lawsuit. (6) Receipt of interest from an investment in bonds. (7) Payment of dividends. (8) Sale of merchandise for cash.
Answers:

(1) Investing	(5) Operating
(2) Financing	(6) Operating
(3) Investing	(7) Financing
(4) Investing	(8) Operating

ing activities are reported separately. Thus, the cash outflow for the purchase of property, plant, and equipment is reported separately from the cash inflow from the sale of property, plant, and equipment. Similarly, the cash inflow from the issuance of debt securities is reported separately from the cash outflow for the retirement of debt. If a company did not report the inflows and outflows separately, it would obscure the investing and financing activities of the enterprise and thus make it more difficult for the user to assess future cash flows.

The reported operating, investing, and financing activities result in net cash either **provided or used** by each activity. The net cash provided or used by each activity is totaled to show the net increase (decrease) in cash for the period. The net increase (decrease) in cash for the period is then added to or subtracted from the beginning-of-period cash balance to obtain the end-of-period cash balance. Finally, any significant noncash investing and financing activities are reported in a separate schedule at the bottom of the statement.

BUSINESS INSIGHT
Investor Perspective

Net income is not the same as net cash generated by operations. The differences are illustrated by the following results from recent annual reports for 1998 ($ in millions):

Company	Net Income	Net Cash Provided by Operations
Kmart Corporation	$ 518	$1,237
Wal-Mart Stores, Inc.	4,430	7,580
J.C. Penney Company, Inc.	594	1,058
Sears, Roebuck & Co.	1,048	3,090
May Department Stores Company	849	1,505

Note the wide disparity among these companies that all engaged in similar types of retail merchandising.

1. What is the primary purpose of a statement of cash flows?
2. What are the major classifications of cash flows on the statement of cash flows?
3. What are some examples of significant noncash activities?

STUDY OBJECTIVE

3

Explain the impact of the product life cycle on a company's cash flows.

THE CORPORATE LIFE CYCLE

All products go through a series of phases called the product life cycle. The phases (in order of their occurrence) are often referred to as the **introductory phase**, **growth phase**, **maturity phase**, and **decline phase**. The introductory phase occurs at the beginning of a company's life, when the company is purchasing fixed assets and beginning to produce and sell products. During the growth phase, the company is striving to expand its production and sales. In the maturity phase, sales and production level off. And during the decline phase, sales of the product fall due to a weakening in consumer demand.

If a company had only one product and that product was, for example, nearing the end of its salable life, we would say that the company was in the decline phase. Companies generally have more than one product, however, and not all of a company's products are in the same phase of the product life cycle at the same time. We can still characterize a company as being in one of the four phases, however, because the majority of its products are in a particular phase.

Illustration 13-3 shows that the phase a company is in affects its cash flows. In the **introductory phase**, we expect that the company will not be generating positive cash from operations. That is, cash used in operations will exceed cash generated by operations during the introductory phase. Also, the company will be spending considerable amounts to purchase productive assets such as buildings and equipment. To support its asset purchases the company will have to issue stock or debt. Thus, during the introductory phase we expect cash from operations to be negative, cash from investing to be negative, and cash from financing to be positive.

Illustration 13-3 Impact of product life cycle on cash flows

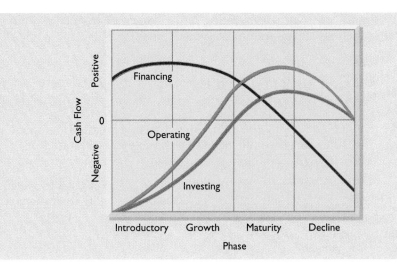

During the **growth phase**, we expect to see the company start to generate small amounts of cash from operations. Cash from operations will be less than net income during this phase. One reason income will exceed cash flow from operations during this period is explained by the difference between the cash paid for inventory and the amount expensed as cost of goods sold. Since sales are projected to be increasing, the size of inventory purchases must increase. Thus, less inventory will be expensed on an accrual basis than purchased on a cash basis in the growth phase. Also, collections on accounts receivable will lag behind sales, and because sales are growing, accrual sales during a period will exceed cash collections during that period. Cash needed for asset acquisitions will continue to exceed cash provided by operations, requiring that the company make up the deficiency by issuing new stock or debt. Thus, the company continues to show negative cash from investing and positive cash from financing in the growth phase.

During the **maturity phase**, cash from operations and net income are approximately the same. Cash generated from operations exceeds investing needs. Thus, in the maturity phase the company can actually start to retire debt or buy back stock.

Finally, during the **decline phase**, cash from operations decreases. Cash from investing might actually become positive as the company sells off excess assets, and cash from financing may be negative as the company buys back stock and retires debt.

Consider Microsoft: During its early years it had significant product development costs with little revenue. Microsoft was lucky in that its agreement with IBM to provide the operating system for IBM PCs gave it an early steady source of cash to support growth. As noted earlier, one way it conserved cash was to pay employees with stock options rather than cash. Today Microsoft could best be characterized as being between the growth and maturity phases. It continues to spend considerable amounts on research and development and investment in new assets. For the last three years, however, its cash from operations has exceeded its net income. Also, cash from operations over this period exceeded cash used for investing, and common stock repurchased exceeded common stock issued. For Microsoft, as for any large company, the challenge is to maintain its growth. In the software industry, where products become obsolete very quickly, the challenge is particularly great.

BUSINESS INSIGHT

Investor Perspective

Listed here are the net income and cash from operations, investing, and financing during 1998 for some well-known companies. The final column suggests their likely phase in the life cycle based on these figures.

Company ($ in millions)	Net Income	Cash Provided by Operations	Cash Provided (Used) by Investing	Cash Provided (Used) by Financing	Likely Phase in Life Cycle
Amazon.com	$(125)	$ 31	$(262)	$ 254	Introductory
Iomega	(54)	(3)	(103)	37	Introductory
Bethlehem Steel	120	444	(388)	(169)	Early decline
Kellogg	503	720	(398)	(358)	Late maturity
Southwest Airlines	433	886	(947)	(183)	Early maturity
Starbucks	68	142	(148)	(37)	Late growth

USEFULNESS OF THE STATEMENT OF CASH FLOWS

Many investors believe that "Cash is cash and everything else is accounting." That is, cash flow is less susceptible to management manipulation and fraud than traditional accounting measures such as net income. Although we suggest that reliance on cash flows to the exclusion of accrual accounting is inappropriate, comparing cash from operations to net income can reveal important information about the "quality" of reported net income—that is, the extent to which net income provides a good measure of actual performance.

The information in a statement of cash flows should help investors, creditors, and others evaluate these aspects of the company's financial position:

1. **The company's ability to generate future cash flows**. By examining relationships between sales and net cash provided by operating activities, or cash provided by operations and increases or decreases in cash, investors and others can predict the amounts, timing, and uncertainty of future cash flows better than with accrual-based data.

2. **The company's ability to pay dividends and meet obligations**. Simply put, if a company does not have adequate cash, it cannot pay employees, settle debts, or pay dividends. Employees, creditors, stockholders, and customers should be particularly interested in this statement because it alone shows the flows of cash in a business.

3. **The reasons for the difference between net income and net cash provided (used) by operating activities**. Net income is important because it provides information on the success or failure of a business enterprise. However, some analysts are critical of accrual-based net income because it requires many estimates; as a result, the reliability of net income is often challenged. Such is not the case with cash. Thus, many financial statement users investigate the reasons for the difference between net income and cash provided by operating activities. Then they can assess for themselves the reliability of the income number.

4. **The investing and financing transactions during the period**. By examining a company's investing activities and financing activities, a financial statement reader can better understand *why* assets and liabilities increased or decreased during the period.

In summary, the information in the statement of cash flows is useful in answering the following questions:

How did cash increase when there was a net loss for the period?

How were the proceeds of the bond issue used?

How was the expansion in the plant and equipment financed?

Why were dividends not increased?

How was the retirement of debt accomplished?

How much money was borrowed during the year?

Is cash flow greater or less than net income?

Helpful Hint Income from operations and cash flow from operating activities are different. Income from operations is based on accrual accounting; cash flow from operating activities is prepared on a cash basis.

BUSINESS INSIGHT
Investor Perspective

Analysts from investment houses such as Keefe Bruyette & Woods, J.P. Morgan, Goldman Sachs, and Credit Suisse First Boston say that they are using cash flow figures instead of, or in addition to, net income because they have lost faith in accrual accounting numbers. They suggest that accrual-basis net income is losing its usefulness because companies take advantage of accrual accounting rules to report net income figures that meet management's goals. Evidence of this shift toward cash flows is found in the fact that 72% of brokerage firm reports now use a cash-flow earnings multiple, and an increasing number of companies report a cash-earnings number as supplemental information in their annual report.

Source: Elizabeth MacDonald, "Analysts Increasingly Favor Using Cash Flow Over Reported Earnings in Stock Valuations," *The Wall Street Journal,* April 1, 1999, p. C1.

PREPARING THE STATEMENT OF CASH FLOWS

The statement of cash flows is prepared differently from the other basic financial statements. First, it is not prepared from an adjusted trial balance. Because the statement requires detailed information concerning the changes in account balances that occurred between two periods of time, an adjusted trial balance does not provide the data necessary for the statement. Second, the statement of cash flows deals with cash receipts and payments. As a result, **the accrual concept is not used in the preparation of a statement of cash flows**.

The information to prepare this statement usually comes from three sources:

1. **Comparative balance sheet.** Information in this statement indicates the amount of the changes in assets, liabilities, and stockholders' equities from the beginning to the end of the period.
2. **Current income statement.** Information in this statement helps the reader determine the amount of cash provided or used by operations during the period.
3. **Additional information.** Additional information includes transaction data that are needed to determine how cash was provided or used during the period.

Preparing the statement of cash flows from these data sources involves the three major steps explained in Illustration 13-4. First, to see where you are headed, start by identifying the change in cash during the period. Has cash increased or decreased during the year? Second, determine the net cash provided/used by operating activities. Third, determine the net cash provided/used by investing and financing activities.

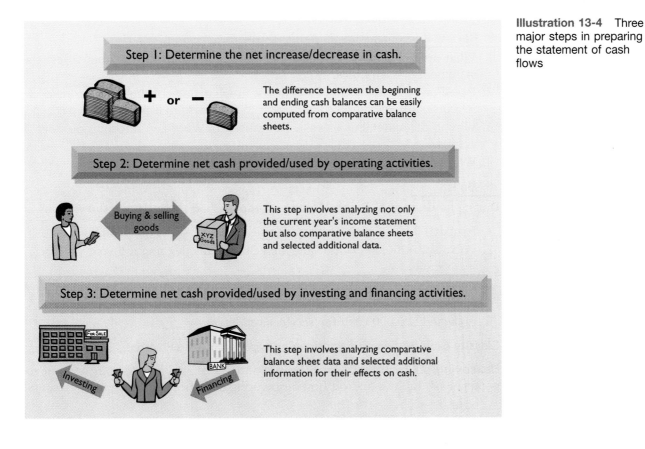

Illustration 13-4 Three major steps in preparing the statement of cash flows

Step 1: Determine the net increase/decrease in cash.

The difference between the beginning and ending cash balances can be easily computed from comparative balance sheets.

Step 2: Determine net cash provided/used by operating activities.

Buying & selling goods

This step involves analyzing not only the current year's income statement but also comparative balance sheets and selected additional data.

Step 3: Determine net cash provided/used by investing and financing activities.

This step involves analyzing comparative balance sheet data and selected additional information for their effects on cash.

Investing   Financing

Indirect and Direct Methods

In order to determine the cash provided/used by operating activities, **net income must be converted from an accrual basis to a cash basis**. This conversion may be done by either of two methods: indirect or direct. **Both methods arrive at the same total amount** for "Net cash provided by operating activities," but they differ in disclosing the items that make up the total amount. Note that the two different methods affect only the operating activities section; the investing activities and financing activities sections **are not affected by the choice of method**.

The indirect method is used extensively in practice—by about 98% of companies in a recent survey.[1] Companies favor the indirect method for three reasons: (1) It is easier to prepare, (2) it focuses on the differences between net income and net cash flow from operating activities, and (3) it tends to reveal less company information to competitors.

Others, however, favor the direct method, which is more consistent with the objective of a statement of cash flows because it shows operating cash receipts and payments. The FASB has expressed a preference for the direct method but allows the use of either method. However, when the direct method is used, the net cash flow from operating activities as computed using the indirect method must also be reported in a separate schedule.

On the following pages, in two separate sections, we describe the use of the two methods. Section 1 illustrates the indirect method, and Section 2 illustrates the direct method. These sections are independent of each other; *only one or the other* need be covered in order to understand and prepare the statement of cash flows. When you have finished the section assigned by your instructor, turn to the next topic on page 632—"Using Cash Flows to Evaluate a Company."

<hr>

BEFORE YOU GO ON...

◆ Review It

1. What are the phases of the product life cycle, and how do they affect the statement of cash flows?
2. Based on its statement of cash flows, in what stage of the product life cycle is Tootsie Roll Industries? The answer to this question is provided on page 663.
3. Why is the statement of cash flows useful? What key information does it convey?
4. What are the three major steps in the preparation of a statement of cash flows?

◆ Do It

During its first week, Plano Molding Company had these transactions:

1. Issued 100,000 shares of $5 par value common stock for $800,000 cash.
2. Borrowed $200,000 from Sandwich State Bank, signing a 5-year note bearing 8% interest.
3. Purchased two semi-trailer trucks for $170,000 cash.
4. Paid employees $12,000 for salaries and wages.
5. Collected $20,000 cash for services rendered.

Classify each of these transactions by type of cash flow activity.

Reasoning: All cash flows are classified into three activities for purposes of reporting cash inflows and outflows: operating activities, investing activities, and

⊕ **International Note**

International accounting requirements are quite similar with regard to the cash flow statement. Here are some interesting exceptions: In Japan operating and investing activities are combined, in Australia the direct method is mandatory, and in Spain the indirect method is mandatory. Also, in a number of European and Scandinavian countries a cash flow statement is not required at all, although in practice most publicly traded companies provide one.

[1]*Accounting Trends and Techniques—1998* (New York: American Institute of Certified Public Accountants, 1998).

financing activities. Operating activities include the cash effects of transactions that create revenues and expenses and thus enter into the determination of net income. Investing activities include (a) purchasing and disposing of investments and productive long-lived assets using cash and (b) lending money and collecting the loans. Financing activities include (a) obtaining cash from issuing debt and repaying the amounts borrowed and (b) obtaining cash from stockholders and providing them with a return on their investment.

Solution:

1. Financing activity   4. Operating activity
2. Financing activity   5. Operating activity
3. Investing activity

SECTION 1

STATEMENT OF CASH FLOWS— INDIRECT METHOD

To explain and illustrate the indirect method, we will use the transactions of Computer Services Company for two years: 2000 and 2001. Annual statements of cash flows will be prepared. Basic transactions will be used in the first year with additional transactions in the second year.

> **STUDY OBJECTIVE**
> **4a**
> Prepare a statement of cash flows using the indirect method.

FIRST YEAR OF OPERATIONS—2000

Computer Services Company started on January 1, 2000, when it issued 50,000 shares of $1 par value common stock for $50,000 cash. The company rented its office space and furniture and performed consulting services throughout the first year. The comparative balance sheet for the beginning and end of 2000, showing increases or decreases, appears in Illustration 13-5.

COMPUTER SERVICES COMPANY Comparative Balance Sheet			
Assets	Dec. 31, 2000	Jan. 1, 2000	Change Increase/Decrease
Cash	$34,000	$ -0-	$34,000 increase
Accounts receivable	30,000	-0-	30,000 increase
Equipment	10,000	-0-	10,000 increase
Total	$74,000	$ -0-	
Liabilities and Stockholders' Equity			
Accounts payable	$ 4,000	$ -0-	$ 4,000 increase
Common stock	50,000	-0-	50,000 increase
Retained earnings	20,000	-0-	20,000 increase
Total	$74,000	$ -0-	

Illustration 13-5 Comparative balance sheet, 2000, with increases and decreases

Helpful Hint Note that although each of the balance sheet items increased, their individual effects are not the same. Some of these increases are cash inflows, and some are cash outflows.

The income statement and additional information for Computer Services Company are shown in Illustration 13-6.

Illustration 13-6 Income statement and additional information, 2000

COMPUTER SERVICES COMPANY
Income Statement
For the Year Ended December 31, 2000

Revenues	$85,000
Operating expenses	40,000
Income before income taxes	45,000
Income tax expense	10,000
Net income	$35,000

Additional information:
(a) Examination of selected data indicates that a dividend of $15,000 was declared and paid during the year.
(b) The equipment was purchased at the end of 2000. No depreciation was taken in 2000.

DETERMINING THE NET INCREASE/DECREASE IN CASH (STEP 1)

Helpful Hint You may wish to insert the beginning and ending cash balances and the increase/decrease in cash necessitated by these balances immediately into the statement of cash flows. The net increase/decrease is the target amount. The net cash flows from the three activities must equal the target amount.

To prepare a statement of cash flows, the first step is to **determine the net increase or decrease in cash**. This is a simple computation. For example, Computer Services Company had no cash on hand at the beginning of 2000, but had $34,000 on hand at the end of the year. Thus, the change in cash for 2000 was an increase of $34,000.

DETERMINING NET CASH PROVIDED/USED BY OPERATING ACTIVITIES (STEP 2)

To determine net cash provided by operating activities under the indirect method, **net income is adjusted for items that did not affect cash**. A useful starting point in determining net cash provided by operating activities is to understand **why** net income must be converted. Under generally accepted accounting principles, most companies use the accrual basis of accounting. As you have learned, this basis requires that revenue be recorded when earned and that expenses be recorded when incurred. Earned revenues may include credit sales that have not been collected in cash, and expenses incurred may include costs that have not been paid in cash. Under the accrual basis of accounting, net income does not indicate the net cash provided by operating activities. Therefore, under the indirect method, net income must be adjusted to convert certain items to the cash basis.

The indirect method (or reconciliation method) starts with net income and converts it to net cash provided by operating activities. In other words, **the indirect method adjusts net income for items that affected reported net income but did not affect cash**, as shown in Illustration 13-7. That is, noncash charges in the income statement are added back to net income and noncash credits are deducted, to compute net cash provided by operating activities.

A useful starting point in identifying the adjustments to net income is the current asset and current liability accounts other than cash. Those accounts—receivables, payables, prepayments, and inventories—should be analyzed for their effects on cash. We do that next for various accounts.

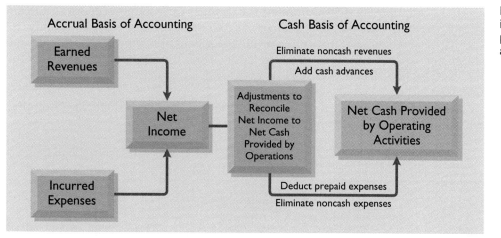

Increase in Accounts Receivable. When accounts receivable increase during the year, revenues on an accrual basis are higher than revenues on a cash basis. In other words, operations of the period led to revenues, **but not all of these revenues resulted in an increase in cash**; some of the revenues resulted in an increase in accounts receivable.

For example, Computer Services Company, in its first year of operations, had revenues of $85,000 but collected only $55,000 in cash. Thus, on an accrual basis revenue was $85,000, but on a cash basis we would record only the $55,000 received during the period. Illustration 13-8 shows that, to convert net income to net cash provided by operating activities, the increase of $30,000 in accounts receivable must be deducted from net income.

ACCOUNTS RECEIVABLE			
Jan. 1 Balance	0	**Receipts from customers**	**55,000**
Revenues	**85,000**		
Dec. 31 Balance	**30,000**		

Illustration 13-8 Analysis of accounts receivable

Increase in Accounts Payable. In the first year, operating expenses incurred on account were credited to Accounts Payable. When accounts payable increase during the year, operating expenses on an accrual basis are higher than they are on a cash basis. For Computer Services Company, operating expenses reported in the income statement were $40,000. However, since Accounts Payable increased $4,000, only $36,000 ($40,000 − $4,000) of the expenses were paid in cash. To convert net income to net cash provided by operating activities, the increase of $4,000 in accounts payable must be added to net income.

The T account analysis in Illustration 13-9 also indicates that payments to creditors are less than operating expenses.

ACCOUNTS PAYABLE			
Payments to creditors	**36,000**	Jan. 1 Balances	0
		Operating expenses	**40,000**
		Dec. 31 Balance	**4,000**

Illustration 13-9 Analysis of accounts payable

For Computer Services Company, the changes in accounts receivable and accounts payable were the only changes in current asset and current liability accounts. This means that any other revenues or expenses reported in the income statement were received or paid in cash. Thus, Computer Services' income tax expense of $10,000 was paid in cash, and no adjustment of net income is necessary.

The operating activities section of the statement of cash flows for Computer Services Company is shown in Illustration 13-10.

Illustration 13-10 Operating activities section, 2000—indirect method

COMPUTER SERVICES COMPANY		
Statement of Cash Flows—Indirect Method (partial)		
For the Year Ended December 31, 2000		
Cash flows from operating activities		
Net income		$35,000
Adjustments to reconcile net income to net cash		
provided by operating activities:		
Increase in accounts receivable	$(30,000)	
Increase in accounts payable	4,000	(26,000)
Net cash provided by operating activities		**$ 9,000**

DETERMINING NET CASH PROVIDED/USED BY INVESTING AND FINANCING ACTIVITIES (STEP 3)

The third and final step in preparing the statement of cash flows begins with a study of the balance sheet to determine changes in noncurrent accounts. The changes in each noncurrent account are then analyzed using selected transaction data to determine the effect, if any, the changes had on cash.

For Computer Services Company, the three noncurrent accounts are Equipment, Common Stock, and Retained Earnings, and all three have increased during the year. What caused these increases? No transaction data are given for the increases in Equipment of $10,000 and Common Stock of $50,000. When other explanations are lacking, we assume that any differences involve cash. Thus, the increase in equipment is assumed to be a purchase of equipment for $10,000 cash. This purchase is reported as a cash outflow in the investing activities section. The increase in common stock is assumed to result from the issuance of common stock for $50,000 cash. It is reported as an inflow of cash in the financing activities section of the statement of cash flows. In doing your homework, assume that **any unexplained differences in noncurrent accounts involve cash**.

The reasons for the net increase of $20,000 in the Retained Earnings account are determined by analysis. First, net income increased retained earnings by $35,000. Second, the additional information provided below the income statement in Illustration 13-6 indicates that a cash dividend of $15,000 was declared and paid. The $35,000 increase due to net income is reported in the operating activities section. The cash dividend paid is reported in the financing activities section.

This analysis can also be made directly from the Retained Earnings account in the ledger of Computer Services Company as shown in Illustration 13-11.

Illustration 13-11 Analysis of retained earnings

RETAINED EARNINGS			
Dec. 31 Cash dividend	15,000	Jan. 1 Balance	0
		Dec. 31 Net income	35,000
		Dec. 31 Balance	20,000

The $20,000 increase in Retained Earnings in 2000 is a **net** change. When a net change in a noncurrent balance sheet account has occurred during the year, it generally is necessary to report the causes of the net change separately in the statement of cash flows.

STATEMENT OF CASH FLOWS—2000

Having completed the three steps above, we can prepare the statement of cash flows by the indirect method. The statement starts with the operating activities section, followed by the investing activities section, and then the financing activities section. The 2000 statement of cash flows for Computer Services is shown in Illustration 13-12.

Illustration 13-12 Statement of cash flows, 2000—indirect method

COMPUTER SERVICES COMPANY
Statement of Cash Flows—Indirect Method
For the Year Ended December 31, 2000

Cash flows from operating activities		
Net income		$35,000
Adjustments to reconcile net income to net cash provided by operating activities:		
Increase in accounts receivable	$(30,000)	
Increase in accounts payable	4,000	(26,000)
Net cash provided by operating activities		9,000
Cash flows from investing activities		
Purchase of equipment	(10,000)	
Net cash used by investing activities		(10,000)
Cash flows from financing activities		
Issuance of common stock	50,000	
Payment of cash dividends	(15,000)	
Net cash provided by financing activities		35,000
Net increase in cash		34,000
Cash at beginning of period		0
Cash at end of period		$34,000

Computer Services Company's statement of cash flows for 2000 shows that operating activities **provided** $9,000 cash; investing activities **used** $10,000 cash; and financing activities **provided** $35,000 cash. The increase in cash of $34,000 reported in the statement of cash flows agrees with the increase of $34,000 shown as the change in the cash account in the comparative balance sheet.

SECOND YEAR OF OPERATIONS—2001

Presented in Illustrations 13-13 and 13-14 is information related to the second year of operations for Computer Services Company.

Illustration 13-13 Comparative balance sheet, 2001, with increases and decreases

COMPUTER SERVICES COMPANY
Comparative Balance Sheet
December 31

Assets	2001	2000	Change Increase/Decrease
Cash	$ 56,000	$34,000	$ 22,000 increase
Accounts receivable	20,000	30,000	10,000 decrease
Prepaid expenses	4,000	0	4,000 increase
Land	130,000	0	130,000 increase
Building	160,000	0	160,000 increase
Accumulated depreciation—building	(11,000)	0	11,000 increase
Equipment	27,000	10,000	17,000 increase
Accumulated depreciation—equipment	(3,000)	0	3,000 increase
Total	$383,000	$74,000	

Liabilities and Stockholders' Equity			
Accounts payable	$ 59,000	$ 4,000	$ 55,000 increase
Bonds payable	130,000	0	130,000 increase
Common stock	50,000	50,000	0
Retained earnings	144,000	20,000	124,000 increase
Total	$383,000	$74,000	

Illustration 13-14 Income statement and additional information, 2001

COMPUTER SERVICES COMPANY
Income Statement
For the Year Ended December 31, 2001

Revenues		$507,000
Operating expenses (excluding depreciation)	$261,000	
Depreciation expense	15,000	
Loss on sale of equipment	3,000	279,000
Income from operations		228,000
Income tax expense		89,000
Net income		$139,000

Additional information:
(a) In 2001 the company declared and paid a $15,000 cash dividend.
(b) The company obtained land through the issuance of $130,000 of long-term bonds.
(c) An office building costing $160,000 was purchased for cash; equipment costing $25,000 was also purchased for cash.
(d) During 2001 the company sold equipment with a book value of $7,000 (cost $8,000 less accumulated depreciation $1,000) for $4,000 cash.

DETERMINING THE NET INCREASE/DECREASE IN CASH (STEP 1)

To prepare a statement of cash flows from this information, the first step is to **determine the net increase or decrease in cash**. As indicated from the information presented, cash increased $22,000 ($56,000 − $34,000).

DETERMINING NET CASH PROVIDED/USED BY OPERATING ACTIVITIES (STEP 2)

As in step 2 in 2000, net income on an accrual basis must be adjusted to arrive at net cash provided/used by operating activities. Explanations for the adjustments to net income for Computer Services Company in 2001 are as follows:

Decrease in Accounts Receivable. Accounts receivable decreases during the period because cash receipts are higher than revenues reported on an accrual basis. To convert net income to net cash provided by operating activities, the decrease of $10,000 in accounts receivable must be added to net income.

Increase in Prepaid Expenses. Prepaid expenses increase during a period because cash paid for expenses is greater than expenses reported on an accrual basis. Cash payments have been made in the current period, but expenses (as charges to the income statement) have been deferred to future periods. To convert net income to net cash provided by operating activities, the increase of $4,000 in prepaid expenses must be deducted from net income. An increase in prepaid expenses results in a decrease in cash during the period.

Increase in Accounts Payable. Like the increase in 2000, the 2001 increase of $55,000 in accounts payable must be added to net income to convert to net cash provided by operating activities.

Depreciation Expense. During 2001 Computer Services Company reported depreciation expense of $15,000. Of this amount, $11,000 related to the building and $4,000 to the equipment. These two amounts were determined by analyzing the accumulated depreciation accounts as follows.

Increase in Accumulated Depreciation—Building. As shown in Illustration 13-13, this accumulated depreciation increased $11,000. This change represents the depreciation expense on the building for the year. **Because depreciation expense is a noncash charge, it is added back to net income** in order to arrive at net cash provided by operating activities.

Increase in Accumulated Depreciation—Equipment. The increase in the Accumulated Depreciation—Equipment account was $3,000. This amount does not represent the total depreciation expense for the year, though, because the additional information indicates that this account was decreased (debited $1,000) as a result of the sale of some equipment. Thus, depreciation expense for 2001 was $4,000 ($3,000 + $1,000). This amount is **added to net income** to determine net cash provided by operating activities. The T account in Illustration 13-15 provides information about the changes that occurred in this account in 2001.

Helpful Hint Whether the indirect or direct method (Section 2) is used, net cash provided by operating activities will be the same.

Helpful Hint Depreciation is similar to any other expense in that it reduces net income. It differs in that it does not involve a current cash outflow; that is why it must be added back to net income to arrive at cash provided by operations.

ACCUMULATED DEPRECIATION—EQUIPMENT			
Accumulated depreciation on equipment sold	1,000	Jan. 1 Balance	0
		Depreciation expense	**4,000**
		Dec. 31 Balance	3,000

Illustration 13-15 Analysis of accumulated depreciation—equipment

Depreciation expense of $11,000 on the building plus depreciation expense of $4,000 on the equipment equals the depreciation expense of $15,000 reported on the income statement.

Other charges to expense **that do not require the use of cash**, such as the amortization of intangible assets, are treated in the same manner as depreciation. Depreciation and similar noncash charges are frequently listed in the statement of cash flows as the first adjustments to net income.

Loss on Sale of Equipment. On the income statement, Computer Services Company reported a $3,000 loss on the sale of equipment (book value $7,000 less cash proceeds $4,000). The loss reduced net income but **did not reduce cash**. Thus, the loss is **added to net income** in determining net cash provided by operating activities.[2]

As a result of the previous adjustments, net cash provided by operating activities is $218,000, as computed in Illustration 13-16.

Illustration 13-16 Operating activities section, 2001—indirect method

COMPUTER SERVICES COMPANY		
Statement of Cash Flows—Indirect Method (partial)		
For the Year Ended December 31, 2001		
Cash flows from operating activities		
Net income		$ 139,000
Adjustments to reconcile net income to net cash		
provided by operating activities:		
Depreciation expense	$15,000	
Loss on sale of equipment	3,000	
Decrease in accounts receivable	10,000	
Increase in prepaid expenses	(4,000)	
Increase in accounts payable	55,000	79,000
Net cash provided by operating activities		$218,000

Helpful Hint By custom we use the label "depreciation expense," even though the expense causes an *increase* in accumulated depreciation and could also be described as "increase in accumulated depreciation."

DETERMINING NET CASH PROVIDED/USED BY INVESTING AND FINANCING ACTIVITIES (STEP 3)

After the determination of net cash provided by operating activities, the final step involves analyzing the remaining changes in balance sheet accounts to determine net cash provided/used by investing and financing activities.

Increase in Land. As indicated from the change in the land account, land of $130,000 was purchased through the issuance of long-term bonds. Although the issuance of bonds payable for land has no effect on cash, it is a significant noncash investing and financing activity that merits disclosure. As indicated earlier, these activities are disclosed in a separate schedule at the bottom of the statement of cash flows.

Increase in Building. As indicated in the additional information, an office building was acquired using cash of $160,000. This transaction is a cash outflow reported in the investing activities section.

Increase in Equipment. The equipment account increased $17,000. Based on the additional information, this was a net increase that resulted from two transactions: (1) a purchase of equipment for $25,000 and (2) the sale of equipment costing $8,000 for $4,000. These transactions are classified as investing activities, and each transaction should be reported separately. Thus, the purchase of equipment should be reported as an outflow of cash for $25,000, and the sale should be reported as an inflow of cash for $4,000. The T account in Illustration 13-17 shows the reasons for the change in this account during the year.

---

[2]If a gain on sale occurs, the treatment is the opposite: To allow a gain to flow through to net cash provided by operating activities would be double-counting the gain—once in net income and again in the investing activities section as part of the cash proceeds from sale. As a result, a gain is deducted from net income in reporting net cash provided by operating activities.

EQUIPMENT			
Jan. 1 Balance	10,000	Cost of equipment sold	8,000
Purchase of equipment	25,000		
Dec. 31 Balance	27,000		

Illustration 13-17
Analysis of equipment

Increase in Bonds Payable. The Bonds Payable account increased $130,000. As shown in the additional information, land was acquired through the issuance of these bonds. As indicated earlier, this noncash transaction is reported in a separate schedule at the bottom of the statement.

Increase in Retained Earnings. Retained Earnings increased $124,000 during the year. This increase can be explained by two factors: (1) Net income of $139,000 increased Retained Earnings and (2) dividends of $15,000 decreased Retained Earnings. Net income is converted to net cash provided by operating activities in the operating activities section. Payment of the dividends is a **cash outflow that is reported as a financing activity**.

Helpful Hint When stocks or bonds are issued for cash, it is the amount of the issuance price (proceeds) that appears on the statement of cash flows as a financing inflow—rather than the par value of the stocks or face value of bonds.

Helpful Hint It is the *payment* of dividends, not the declaration, that appears on the statement of cash flows.

STATEMENT OF CASH FLOWS—2001

Combining the previous items, we obtain a statement of cash flows for 2001 for Computer Services Company as presented in Illustration 13-18.

Illustration 13-18 Statement of cash flows, 2001—indirect method

COMPUTER SERVICES COMPANY Statement of Cash Flows—Indirect Method For the Year Ended December 31, 2001		
Cash flows from operating activities		
Net income		$139,000
Adjustments to reconcile net income to net cash provided by operating activities:		
Depreciation expense	$ 15,000	
Loss on sale of equipment	3,000	
Decrease in accounts receivable	10,000	
Increase in prepaid expenses	(4,000)	
Increase in accounts payable	55,000	79,000
Net cash provided by operating activities		218,000
Cash flows from investing activities		
Purchase of building	(160,000)	
Purchase of equipment	(25,000)	
Sale of equipment	4,000	
Net cash used by investing activities		(181,000)
Cash flows from financing activities		
Payment of cash dividends	(15,000)	
Net cash used by financing activities		(15,000)
Net increase in cash		22,000
Cash at beginning of period		34,000
Cash at end of period		$ 56,000
Noncash investing and financing activities		
Issuance of bonds payable to purchase land		$130,000

Helpful Hint Note that in the investing and financing activities sections, positive numbers indicate cash inflows (receipts) and negative numbers indicate cash outflows (payments).

SUMMARY OF CONVERSION TO NET CASH PROVIDED BY OPERATING ACTIVITIES—INDIRECT METHOD

As shown in the previous illustrations, the statement of cash flows prepared by the indirect method starts with net income and adds or deducts items not affecting cash, to arrive at net cash provided by operating activities. The additions and deductions consist of (1) changes in specific current assets and current liabilities and (2) noncash charges reported in the income statement. A summary of the adjustments for current assets and current liabilities is provided in Illustration 13-19.

Illustration 13-19
Adjustments for current assets and current liabilities

Current Assets and Current Liabilities	Add to Net Income	Deduct from Net Income
Accounts receivable	Decrease	Increase
Inventory	Decrease	Increase
Prepaid expenses	Decrease	Increase
Accounts payable	Increase	Decrease
Accrued expenses payable	Increase	Decrease

(Column heading: Adjustments to Convert Net Income to Net Cash Provided by Operating Activities)

Adjustments for the noncash charges reported in the income statement are made as shown in Illustration 13-20.

Illustration 13-20
Adjustments for noncash charges

Noncash Charges	Adjustments to Convert Net Income to Net Cash Provided by Operating Activities
Depreciation expense	Add
Patent amortization expense	Add
Loss on sale of asset	Add

BEFORE YOU GO ON...

◆ **Review It**

1. What is the format of the operating activities section of the statement of cash flows using the indirect method?
2. Where is depreciation expense shown on a statement of cash flows using the indirect method?
3. Where are significant noncash investing and financing activities shown in a statement of cash flows? Give some examples.

◆ **Do It**

The following information relates to Reynolds Company. Use it to prepare a statement of cash flows using the indirect method.

REYNOLDS COMPANY
Comparative Balance Sheet
December 31

Assets	2001	2000	Change Increase/Decrease
Cash	$ 54,000	$ 37,000	$ 17,000 increase
Accounts receivable	68,000	26,000	42,000 increase
Inventories	54,000	0	54,000 increase
Prepaid expenses	4,000	6,000	2,000 decrease
Land	45,000	70,000	25,000 decrease
Buildings	200,000	200,000	0
Accumulated depreciation—buildings	(21,000)	(11,000)	10,000 increase
Equipment	193,000	68,000	125,000 increase
Accumulated depreciation—equipment	(28,000)	(10,000)	18,000 increase
Totals	$569,000	$386,000	

Liabilities and Stockholders' Equity			
Accounts payable	$ 23,000	$ 40,000	$ 17,000 decrease
Accrued expenses payable	10,000	0	10,000 increase
Bonds payable	110,000	150,000	40,000 decrease
Common stock ($1 par)	220,000	60,000	160,000 increase
Retained earnings	206,000	136,000	70,000 increase
Total	$569,000	$386,000	

REYNOLDS COMPANY
Income Statement
For the Year Ended December 31, 2001

Revenues		$890,000
Cost of goods sold	$465,000	
Operating expenses	221,000	
Interest expense	12,000	
Loss on sale of equipment	2,000	700,000
Income from operations		190,000
Income tax expense		65,000
Net income		$125,000

Additional information:
(a) Operating expenses include depreciation expense of $33,000.
(b) Land was sold at its book value for cash.
(c) Cash dividends of $55,000 were declared and paid in 2001.
(d) Interest expense of $12,000 was paid in cash.
(e) Equipment with a cost of $166,000 was purchased for cash. Equipment with a cost of $41,000 and a book value of $36,000 was sold for $34,000 cash.
(f) Bonds of $10,000 were redeemed at their book value for cash; bonds of $30,000 were converted into common stock.
(g) Common stock ($1 par) of $130,000 was issued for cash.
(h) Accounts payable pertain to merchandise suppliers.

Reasoning: The balance sheet and the income statement are prepared from an adjusted trial balance of the general ledger. The statement of cash flows is prepared from an analysis of the content and changes in the balance sheet and the income statement.

Helpful Hint To prepare the statement of cash flows:

1. Determine the net increase/decrease in cash.
2. Determine net cash provided/used by operating activities.
3. Determine net cash provided/used by investing and financing activities.
4. Operating activities generally relate to changes in current assets and current liabilities.
5. Investing activities generally relate to changes in noncurrent assets.
6. Financing activities generally relate to changes in noncurrent liabilities and stockholders' equity accounts.

Solution:

REYNOLDS COMPANY Statement of Cash Flows—Indirect Method For the Year Ended December 31, 2001		
Cash flows from operating activities		
Net income		$125,000
Adjustments to reconcile net income to net cash		
provided by operating activities:		
Depreciation expense	$ 33,000	
Increase in accounts receivable	(42,000)	
Increase in inventories	(54,000)	
Decrease in prepaid expenses	2,000	
Decrease in accounts payable	(17,000)	
Increase in accrued expenses payable	10,000	
Loss on sale of equipment	2,000	(66,000)
Net cash provided by operating activities		59,000
Cash flows from investing activities		
Sale of land	25,000	
Sale of equipment	34,000	
Purchase of equipment	(166,000)	
Net cash used by investing activities		(107,000)
Cash flows from financing activities		
Redemption of bonds	(10,000)	
Sale of common stock	130,000	
Payment of dividends	(55,000)	
Net cash provided by financing activities		65,000
Net increase in cash		17,000
Cash at beginning of period		37,000
Cash at end of period		$ 54,000
Noncash investing and financing activities		
Conversion of bonds into common stock		$ 30,000

Note: This concludes Section 1 on preparation of the statement of cash flows using the indirect method. Unless your instructor assigns Section 2, you should turn to the concluding section of the chapter, "Using Cash Flows to Evaluate a Company," on page 632.

STATEMENT OF CASH FLOWS— DIRECT METHOD

To explain and illustrate the direct method, we will use the transactions of Juarez Company for two years: 2000 and 2001. Annual statements of cash flow will be prepared. Basic transactions will be used in the first year with additional transactions in the second year.

FIRST YEAR OF OPERATIONS—2000

Juarez Company began business on January 1, 2000, when it issued 300,000 shares of $1 par value common stock for $300,000 cash. The company rented office and sales space along with equipment. The comparative balance sheet at the beginning and end of 2000 and the changes in each account are shown in Illustration 13-21. The income statement and additional information for Juarez Company are shown in Illustration 13-22 on page 620.

STUDY OBJECTIVE

4b

Prepare a statement of cash flows using the direct method.

JUAREZ COMPANY
Comparative Balance Sheet

Assets	Dec. 31, 2000	Jan. 1, 2000	Change Increase/Decrease
Cash	$159,000	$-0-	$159,000 increase
Accounts receivable	15,000	-0-	15,000 increase
Inventory	160,000	-0-	160,000 increase
Prepaid expenses	8,000	-0-	8,000 increase
Land	80,000	-0-	80,000 increase
Total	$422,000	$-0-	
Liabilities and Stockholders' Equity			
Accounts payable	$ 60,000	$-0-	$ 60,000 increase
Accrued expenses payable	20,000	-0-	20,000 increase
Common stock	300,000	-0-	300,000 increase
Retained earnings	42,000	-0-	42,000 increase
Total	$422,000	$-0-	

Illustration 13-21 Comparative balance sheet, 2000, with increases and decreases

The three steps cited in Illustration 13-4 on page 605 for preparing the statement of cash flows are used in the direct method.

DETERMINING THE NET INCREASE/DECREASE IN CASH (STEP 1)

The comparative balance sheet for Juarez Company shows a zero cash balance at January 1, 2000, and a cash balance of $159,000 at December 31, 2000. Therefore, the change in cash for 2000 was a net increase of $159,000.

Illustration 13-22
Income statement and
additional information,
2000

JUAREZ COMPANY
Income Statement
For the Year Ended December 31, 2000

Revenues from sales	$780,000
Cost of goods sold	450,000
Gross profit	330,000
Operating expenses	170,000
Income before income taxes	160,000
Income tax expense	48,000
Net income	$112,000

Additional information:
(a) Dividends of $70,000 were declared and paid in cash.
(b) The accounts payable increase resulted from the purchase of merchandise.

DETERMINING NET CASH PROVIDED/USED BY OPERATING ACTIVITIES (STEP 2)

Under the **direct method**, net cash provided by operating activities is computed by **adjusting each item in the income statement** from the accrual basis to the cash basis. To simplify and condense the operating activities section, **only major classes of operating cash receipts and cash payments are reported**. The difference between these major classes of cash receipts and cash payments is the net cash provided by operating activities, as shown in Illustration 13-23.

Illustration 13-23 Major
classes of cash receipts
and payments

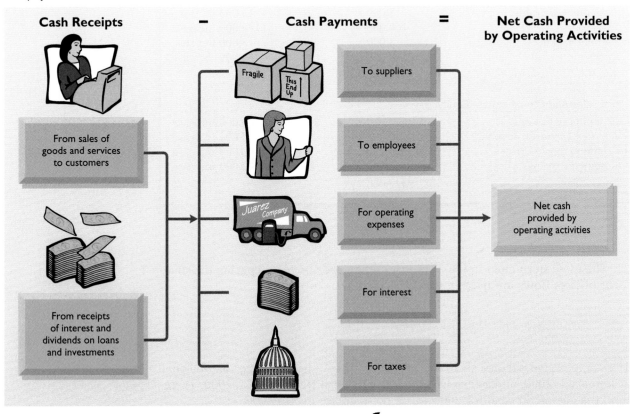

An efficient way to apply the direct method is to analyze the revenues and expenses reported in the income statement in the order in which they are listed and then determine cash receipts and cash payments related to these revenues and expenses. The direct method adjustments for Juarez Company in 2000 to determine net cash provided by operating activities are presented in the following sections.

Cash Receipts from Customers. The income statement for Juarez Company reported revenues from customers of $780,000. To determine cash receipts from customers, it is necessary to consider the change in accounts receivable during the year. When accounts receivable increase during the year, revenues on an accrual basis are higher than cash receipts from customers. In other words, operations led to increased revenues, but not all of these revenues resulted in cash receipts. To determine the amount of cash receipts, the increase in accounts receivable is deducted from sales revenues. Conversely, a decrease in accounts receivable is added to sales revenues because cash receipts from customers then exceed sales revenues.

For Juarez Company accounts receivable increased $15,000. Thus, cash receipts from customers were $765,000, computed as shown in Illustration 13-24.

Revenues from sales	$ 780,000
Deduct: Increase in accounts receivable	15,000
Cash receipts from customers	**$765,000**

Illustration 13-24   Computation of cash receipts from customers

Cash receipts from customers may also be determined from an analysis of the Accounts Receivable account, as shown in Illustration 13-25.

ACCOUNTS RECEIVABLE			
Jan. 1 Balance	0	**Receipts from customers**	**765,000**
Revenues from sales	780,000		
Dec. 31 Balance	15,000		

Illustration 13-25   Analysis of accounts receivable

Helpful Hint The T account shows that revenue less increase in receivables equals cash receipts.

The relationships among cash receipts from customers, revenues from sales, and changes in accounts receivable are shown in Illustration 13-26.

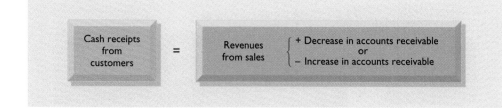

Illustration 13-26
Formula to compute cash receipts from customers—direct method

Cash Payments to Suppliers. Juarez Company reported cost of goods sold on its income statement of $450,000. To determine cash payments to suppliers, it is first necessary to find purchases for the year. To find purchases, cost of goods sold is adjusted for the change in inventory. When inventory increases during the year, it means that purchases this year exceed cost of goods sold. As a result, the increase in inventory is added to cost of goods sold to arrive at purchases.

In 2000 Juarez Company's inventory increased $160,000. Purchases, therefore, are computed as shown in Illustration 13-27.

Illustration 13-27
Computation of purchases

Cost of goods sold	$ 450,000
Add: Increase in inventory	160,000
Purchases	**$610,000**

After purchases are computed, cash payments to suppliers are determined by adjusting purchases for the change in accounts payable. When accounts payable increase during the year, purchases on an accrual basis are higher than they are on a cash basis. As a result, an increase in accounts payable is deducted from purchases to arrive at cash payments to suppliers. Conversely, a decrease in accounts payable is added to purchases because cash payments to suppliers exceed purchases. Cash payments to suppliers were $550,000, computed as in Illustration 13-28.

Illustration 13-28
Computation of cash payments to suppliers

Purchases	$ 610,000
Deduct: Increase in accounts payable	60,000
Cash payments to suppliers	**$550,000**

Cash payments to suppliers may also be determined from an analysis of the Accounts Payable account, as shown in Illustration 13-29.

Illustration 13-29   Analysis of accounts payable

ACCOUNTS PAYABLE			
Payments to suppliers	550,000	Jan. 1 Balance	0
		Purchases	610,000
		Dec. 31 Balance	60,000

Helpful Hint The T account shows that purchases less increase in accounts payable equals payments to suppliers.

The relationship between cash payments to suppliers, cost of goods sold, changes in inventory, and changes in accounts payable is shown in the formula in Illustration 13-30.

Illustration 13-30   Formula to compute cash payments to suppliers—direct method

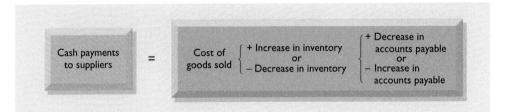

Cash Payments for Operating Expenses.   Operating expenses of $170,000 were reported on Juarez Company's income statement. To determine the cash paid for operating expenses, this amount must be adjusted for any changes in prepaid expenses and accrued expenses payable. For example, when prepaid expenses increased $8,000 during the year, cash paid for operating expenses was $8,000 higher than operating expenses reported on the income statement. To convert operating expenses to cash payments for operating expenses, the increase of $8,000 must be added to operating expenses. Conversely, if prepaid expenses decrease during the year, the decrease must be deducted from operating expenses.

Operating expenses must also be adjusted for changes in accrued expenses payable. When accrued expenses payable increase during the year, operating expenses on an accrual basis are higher than they are in a cash basis. As a result, an increase in accrued expenses payable is deducted from operating expenses to arrive at cash payments for operating expenses. Conversely, a decrease in accrued expenses payable is added to operating expenses because cash payments exceed operating expenses.

Juarez Company's cash payments for operating expenses were $158,000, computed as shown in Illustration 13-31.

Operating expenses	$ 170,000
Add: Increase in prepaid expenses	8,000
Deduct: Increase in accrued expenses payable	(20,000)
Cash payments for operating expenses	**$158,000**

> **Helpful Hint** **Decrease in accounts receivable**: Indicates that cash collections were greater than sales. **Increase in accounts receivable**: Indicates that sales were greater than cash collections. **Increase in prepaid expenses**: Indicates that the amount paid for the prepayments exceeded the amount that was recorded as an expense. **Decrease in prepaid expenses**: Indicates that the amount recorded as an expense exceeded the amount of cash paid for the prepayments. **Increase in accounts payable**: Indicates that expenses incurred exceed the cash paid for expenses that period.

Illustration 13-31
Computation of cash payments for operating expenses

The relationships among cash payments for operating expenses, changes in prepaid expenses, and changes in accrued expenses payable are shown in the formula in Illustration 13-32.

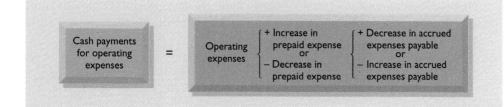

Illustration 13-32 Formula to compute cash payments for operating expenses—direct method

Cash Payments for Income Taxes. The income statement for Juarez Company shows income tax expense of $48,000. This amount equals the cash paid because the comparative balance sheet indicates no income taxes payable at either the beginning or end of the year.

All of the revenues and expenses in the 2000 income statement have now been adjusted to a cash basis. The operating activities section of the statement of cash flows is presented in Illustration 13-33.

Illustration 13-33
Operating activities section—direct method

JUAREZ COMPANY Statement of Cash Flows—Direct Method (partial) For the Year Ended December 31, 2000		
Cash flows from operating activities		
Cash receipts from customers		$765,000
Cash payments:		
To suppliers	$550,000	
For operating expenses	158,000	
For income taxes	48,000	756,000
Net cash provided by operating activities		**$ 9,000**

DETERMINING NET CASH PROVIDED/USED BY INVESTING AND FINANCING ACTIVITIES (STEP 3)

Preparing the investing and financing activities sections of the statement of cash flows begins with a determination of the changes in noncurrent accounts reported in the comparative balance sheet. The change in each account is then analyzed using the additional information to determine the effect, if any, the change had on cash.

Increase in Land.   No additional information is given for the increase in land. In such case, you should assume that the increase affected cash. You should make the same assumption in doing homework problems when the cause of a change in a noncurrent account is not explained. The purchase of land is an investing activity. Thus, an outflow of cash of $80,000 for the purchase of land should be reported in the investing activities section.

Increase in Common Stock.   As indicated earlier, 300,000 shares of $1 par value stock were sold for $300,000 cash. The issuance of common stock is a financing activity. Thus, a cash inflow of $300,000 from the issuance of common stock is reported in the financing activities section.

Helpful Hint It is the *payment* of dividends, not the declaration, that appears on the cash flow statement.

Increase in Retained Earnings.   For the Retained Earnings account, the reasons for the net increase of $42,000 are determined by analysis. First, net income increased retained earnings by $112,000. Second, the additional information indicates that a cash dividend of $70,000 was declared and paid. The adjustment of revenues and expenses to arrive at net cash provided by operations was done in step 2 earlier. The cash dividend paid is reported as an outflow of cash in the financing activities section.

This analysis can also be made directly from the Retained Earnings account in the ledger of Juarez Company, as shown in Illustration 13-34.

Illustration 13-34   Analysis of retained earnings

RETAINED EARNINGS			
Dec. 31 Cash dividend	70,000	Jan. 1 Balance	0
		Dec. 31 Net income	112,000
		Dec. 31 Balance	42,000

The $42,000 increase in Retained Earnings in 2000 is a net change. When a net change in a noncurrent balance sheet account has occurred during the year, it generally is necessary to report the individual items that cause the net change.

STATEMENT OF CASH FLOWS—2000

The statement of cash flows can now be prepared. The operating activities section is reported first, followed by the investing and financing activities sections. The statement of cash flows for Juarez Company for 2000 is presented in Illustration 13-35.

The statement of cash flows shows that operating activities **provided** $9,000 of the net increase in cash of $159,000. Financing activities **provided** $230,000 of cash, and investing activities **used** $80,000 of cash. The net increase in cash for the year of $159,000 agrees with the $159,000 increase in cash reported in the comparative balance sheet.

Illustration 13-35
Statement of cash flows,
2000—direct method

JUAREZ COMPANY
Statement of Cash Flows—Direct Method
For the Year Ended December 31, 2000

Cash flows from operating activities		
Cash receipts from customers		$765,000
Cash payments:		
To suppliers	$550,000	
For operating expenses	158,000	
For income taxes	48,000	756,000
Net cash provided by operating activities		9,000
Cash flows from investing activities		
Purchase of land	(80,000)	
Net cash used by investing activities		(80,000)
Cash flows from financing activities		
Issuance of common stock	300,000	
Payment of cash dividend	(70,000)	
Net cash provided by financing activities		230,000
Net increase in cash		159,000
Cash at beginning of period		0
Cash at end of period		$159,000

Helpful Hint Note that in the investing and financing activities sections, positive numbers indicate cash inflows (receipts) and negative numbers indicate cash outflows (payments).

SECOND YEAR OF OPERATIONS—2001

Illustrations 13-36 and 13-37 present the comparative balance sheet, the income statement, and additional information pertaining to the second year of operations for Juarez Company.

JUAREZ COMPANY
Comparative Balance Sheet
December 31

Assets	2001	2000	Change Increase/Decrease
Cash	$191,000	$159,000	$ 32,000 increase
Accounts receivable	12,000	15,000	3,000 decrease
Inventory	130,000	160,000	30,000 decrease
Prepaid expenses	6,000	8,000	2,000 decrease
Land	180,000	80,000	100,000 increase
Equipment	160,000	0	160,000 increase
Accumulated depreciation—equipment	(16,000)	0	16,000 increase
Total	$663,000	$422,000	
Liabilities and Stockholders' Equity			
Accounts payable	$ 52,000	$ 60,000	$ 8,000 decrease
Accrued expenses payable	15,000	20,000	5,000 decrease
Income taxes payable	12,000	0	12,000 increase
Bonds payable	90,000	0	90,000 increase
Common stock	400,000	300,000	100,000 increase
Retained earnings	94,000	42,000	52,000 increase
Total	$663,000	$422,000	

Illustration 13-37
Income statement and
additional information,
2001

JUAREZ COMPANY
Income Statement
For the Year Ended December 31, 2001

Revenues from sales		$975,000
Cost of goods sold	$660,000	
Operating expenses (excluding depreciation)	176,000	
Depreciation expense	18,000	
Loss on sale of store equipment	1,000	855,000
Income before income taxes		120,000
Income tax expense		36,000
Net income		$ 84,000

Additional information:
(a) In 2001 the company declared and paid a $32,000 cash dividend.
(b) Bonds were issued at face value for $90,000 in cash.
(c) Equipment costing $180,000 was purchased for cash.
(d) Equipment costing $20,000 was sold for $17,000 cash when the book value of the equipment was $18,000.
(e) Common stock of $100,000 was issued to acquire land.

DETERMINING THE NET INCREASE/DECREASE IN CASH (STEP 1)

The comparative balance sheet shows a beginning cash balance of $159,000 and an ending cash balance of $191,000. Thus, there was a net increase in cash in 2001 of $32,000.

DETERMINING NET CASH PROVIDED/USED BY OPERATING ACTIVITIES (STEP 2)

Cash Receipts from Customers. Revenues from sales were $975,000. Since accounts receivable decreased $3,000, cash receipts from customers were greater than sales revenues. Cash receipts from customers were $978,000, computed as shown in Illustration 13-38.

Illustration 13-38
Computation of cash
receipts from customers

Revenues from sales	$ 975,000
Add: Decrease in accounts receivable	3,000
Cash receipts from customers	**$978,000**

Cash Payments to Suppliers. The conversion of cost of goods sold to purchases and purchases to cash payments to suppliers is similar to the computations made in 2000. For 2001 purchases are computed using cost of goods sold of $660,000 from the income statement and the decrease in inventory of $30,000 from the comparative balance sheet. Purchases are then adjusted by the decrease in accounts payable of $8,000. Cash payments to suppliers were $638,000, computed as in Illustration 13-39.

Illustration 13-39
Computation of cash
payments to suppliers

Cost of goods sold	$ 660,000
Deduct: Decrease in inventory	30,000
Purchases	630,000
Add: Decrease in accounts payable	8,000
Cash payments to suppliers	**$638,000**

Cash Payments for Operating Expenses.   Operating expenses (exclusive of depreciation expense) for 2001 were reported at $176,000. This amount is then adjusted for changes in prepaid expenses and accrued expenses payable to arrive at cash payments for operating expenses.

As indicated from the comparative balance sheet, prepaid expenses decreased $2,000 during the year. This means that $2,000 was allocated to operating expenses (thereby increasing operating expenses), but cash payments did not increase by that amount. To arrive at cash payments for operating expenses, the decrease in prepaid expenses is deducted from operating expenses.

Accrued expenses payable decreased $5,000 during the period. As a result, cash payments were higher by $5,000 than the amount reported for operating expenses. The decrease in accrued expenses payable is added to operating expenses. Cash payments for operating expenses were $179,000, computed as shown in Illustration 13-40.

Operating expenses, exclusive of depreciation	$ 176,000
Deduct: Decrease in prepaid expenses	(2,000)
Add: Decrease in accrued expenses payable	5,000
Cash payments for operating expenses	**$179,000**

Illustration 13-40
Computation of cash payments for operating expenses

Depreciation Expense and Loss on Sale of Equipment.   Operating expenses are shown exclusive of depreciation. Depreciation expense in 2001 was $18,000. Depreciation expense is not shown on a statement of cash flows under the direct method because it is a noncash charge. If the amount for operating expenses includes depreciation expense, operating expenses must be reduced by the amount of depreciation to determine cash payments for operating expenses.

The loss on sale of store equipment of $1,000 is also a noncash charge. The loss on sale of equipment reduces net income, but it does not reduce cash. Thus, the loss on sale of equipment is not reported on a statement of cash flows prepared using the direct method.

Other charges to expense that do not require the use of cash, such as the amortization of intangible assets and depletion expense, are treated in the same manner as depreciation.

Cash Payments for Income Taxes.   Income tax expense reported on the income statement was $36,000. Income taxes payable, however, increased $12,000, which means that $12,000 of the income taxes have not been paid. As a result, income taxes paid were less than income taxes reported on the income statement. Cash payments for income taxes were therefore $24,000, as shown in Illustration 13-41.

Income tax expense	$36,000
Deduct: Increase in income taxes payable	12,000
Cash payments for income taxes	**$24,000**

Illustration 13-41
Computation of cash payments for income taxes

The relationships among cash payments for income taxes, income tax expense, and changes in income taxes payable are shown in the formula in Illustration 13-42.

Illustration 13-42 Formula to compute cash payments for income taxes—direct method

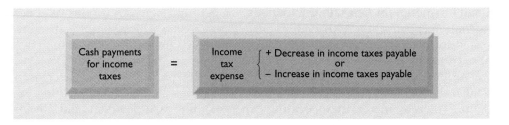

DETERMINING NET CASH PROVIDED/USED BY INVESTING AND FINANCING ACTIVITIES (STEP 3)

Increase in Land. Land increased $100,000. The additional information indicates that common stock was issued to purchase the land. Although the issuance of common stock for land has no effect on cash, it is a **significant noncash investing and financing transaction**. This transaction requires disclosure in a separate schedule at the bottom of the statement of cash flows.

Increase in Equipment. The comparative balance sheet shows that equipment increased $160,000 in 2001. The additional information in Illustration 13-37 indicates that the increase resulted from two investing transactions: (1) Equipment costing $180,000 was purchased for cash, and (2) equipment costing $20,000 was sold for $17,000 cash when its book value was $18,000. The relevant data for the statement of cash flows are the cash paid for the purchase and the cash proceeds from the sale. For Juarez Company the investing activities section will show: Purchase of equipment $180,000 as an outflow of cash, and sale of equipment $17,000 as an inflow of cash. The two amounts **should not be netted**; **both flows should be shown**.

The analysis of the changes in equipment should include the related Accumulated Depreciation account. These two accounts for Juarez Company are shown in Illustration 13-43.

Illustration 13-43 Analysis of equipment and related accumulated depreciation

EQUIPMENT				
Jan. 1 Balance	0	Cost of equipment sold	20,000
Cash purchase	180,000		
Dec. 31 Balance	160,000		

ACCUMULATED DEPRECIATION—EQUIPMENT				
Sale of equipment	2,000	Jan. 1 Balance	0
		Depreciation expense	18,000
		Dec. 31 Balance	16,000

Increase in Bonds Payable. Bonds Payable increased $90,000. The additional information in Illustration 13-37 indicates that bonds with a face value of $90,000 were issued for $90,000 cash. The issuance of bonds is a financing activity. For Juarez Company, there is an inflow of cash of $90,000 from the issuance of bonds payable.

Increase in Common Stock.   The Common Stock account increased $100,000. As indicated in the additional information, land was acquired from the issuance of common stock. This transaction is a **significant noncash investing and financing transaction** that should be reported in a separate schedule at the bottom of the statement.

Increase in Retained Earnings.   The net increase in Retained Earnings of $52,000 resulted from net income of $84,000 and the declaration and payment of a cash dividend of $32,000. **Net income is not reported in the statement of cash flows under the direct method**. Cash dividends paid of $32,000 are reported in the financing activities section as an outflow of cash.

STATEMENT OF CASH FLOWS—2001

The statement of cash flows for Juarez Company is shown in Illustration 13-44.

Illustration 13-44   Statement of cash flows, 2001—direct method

JUAREZ COMPANY Statement of Cash Flows—Direct Method For the Year Ended December 31, 2001		
Cash flows from operating activities		
Cash receipts from customers		$978,000
Cash payments:		
To suppliers	$638,000	
For operating expenses	179,000	
For income taxes	24,000	841,000
Net cash provided by operating activities		137,000
Cash flows from investing activities		
Purchase of equipment	(180,000)	
Sale of equipment	17,000	
Net cash used by investing activities		(163,000)
Cash flows from financing activities		
Issuance of bonds payable	90,000	
Payment of cash dividends	(32,000)	
Net cash provided by financing activities		58,000
Net increase in cash		32,000
Cash at beginning of period		159,000
Cash at end of period		$191,000
Noncash investing and financing activities		
Issuance of common stock to purchase land		$100,000

BEFORE YOU GO ON...

◆ Review It

1. What is the format of the operating activities section of the statement of cash flows using the direct method?

2. Where is depreciation expense shown on a statement of cash flows using the direct method?

3. Where are significant noncash investing and financing activities shown on a statement of cash flows? Give some examples.

◆ Do It

The following information relates to Reynolds Company. Use it to prepare a statement of cash flows using the direct method.

REYNOLDS COMPANY
Comparative Balance Sheet
December 31

Assets	2001	2000	Change Increase/Decrease
Cash	$ 54,000	$ 37,000	$ 17,000 increase
Accounts receivable	68,000	26,000	42,000 increase
Inventories	54,000	0	54,000 increase
Prepaid expenses	4,000	6,000	2,000 decrease
Land	45,000	70,000	25,000 decrease
Buildings	200,000	200,000	0
Accumulated depreciation—buildings	(21,000)	(11,000)	10,000 increase
Equipment	193,000	68,000	125,000 increase
Accumulated depreciation—equipment	(28,000)	(10,000)	18,000 increase
Total	$569,000	$386,000	

Liabilities and Stockholders' Equity			
Accounts payable	$ 23,000	$ 40,000	$ 17,000 decrease
Accrued expenses payable	10,000	0	10,000 increase
Bonds payable	110,000	150,000	40,000 decrease
Common stock ($1 par)	220,000	60,000	160,000 increase
Retained earnings	206,000	136,000	70,000 increase
Total	$569,000	$386,000	

REYNOLDS COMPANY
Income Statement
For the Year Ended December 31, 2001

Revenues		$890,000
Cost of goods sold	$465,000	
Operating expenses	221,000	
Interest expense	12,000	
Loss on sale of equipment	2,000	700,000
Income from operations		190,000
Income tax expense		65,000
Net income		$125,000

Additional information:
(a) Operating expenses include depreciation expense of $33,000 and charges from prepaid expenses of $2,000.
(b) Land was sold at its book value for cash.
(c) Cash dividends of $55,000 were declared and paid in 2001.
(d) Interest expense of $12,000 was paid in cash.
(e) Equipment with a cost of $166,000 was purchased for cash. Equipment with a cost of $41,000 and a book value of $36,000 was sold for $34,000 cash.
(f) Bonds of $10,000 were redeemed at their book value for cash; bonds of $30,000 were converted into common stock.
(g) Common stock ($1 par) of $130,000 was issued for cash.
(h) Accounts payable pertain to merchandise suppliers.

Reasoning: The direct method reports cash receipts less cash payments to arrive at net cash provided by operating activities.

Solution:

REYNOLDS COMPANY
Statement of Cash Flows—Direct Method
For the Year Ended December 31, 2001

Cash flows from operating activities		
Cash receipts from customers		$848,000[a]
Cash payments:		
To suppliers	$536,000[b]	
For operating expenses	176,000[c]	
For interest expense	12,000	
For income taxes	65,000	789,000
Net cash provided by operating activities		59,000
Cash flows from investing activities		
Sale of land	25,000	
Sale of equipment	34,000	
Purchase of equipment	(166,000)	
Net cash used by investing activities		(107,000)
Cash flows from financing activities		
Redemption of bonds	(10,000)	
Sale of common stock	130,000	
Payment of dividends	(55,000)	
Net cash provided by financing activities		65,000
Net increase in cash		17,000
Cash at beginning of period		37,000
Cash at end of period		$ 54,000
Noncash investing and financing activities		
Conversion of bonds into common stock		$ 30,000

Computations:
[a]$848,000 = $890,000 − $42,000
[b]$536,000 = $465,000 + $54,000 + $17,000
[c]$176,000 = $221,000 − $33,000 − $2,000 − $10,000
Technically, an additional schedule reconciling net income to net cash provided by operating activities should be presented as part of the statement of cash flows when using the direct method.

Helpful Hint To prepare the statement of cash flows:

1. Determine the net increase/decrease in cash.
2. Determine net cash provided/used by operating activities.
3. Determine net cash provided/used by investing and financing activities.
4. Operating activities generally relate to changes in current assets and current liabilities.
5. Investing activities generally relate to changes in noncurrent assets.
6. Financing activities generally relate to changes in noncurrent liabilities and stockholders' equity accounts.

Note: This concludes Section 2 on preparation of the statement of cash flows using the direct method. You should now turn to the next—and concluding—section of the chapter, "Using Cash Flows to Evaluate a Company."

USING CASH FLOWS TO EVALUATE A COMPANY

STUDY OBJECTIVE

5

Use the statement of cash flows to evaluate a company.

Traditionally, the ratios most commonly used by investors and creditors have been based on accrual accounting. In previous chapters we introduced cash-based ratios that are gaining increased acceptance among analysts. In this section we review those measures and introduce new ones.

FREE CASH FLOW

In the statement of cash flows, cash provided by operating activities is intended to indicate the cash-generating capability of the company. Analysts have noted, however, that **cash provided by operating activities fails to take into account that a company must invest in new fixed assets** just to maintain its current level of operations, and it must at least **maintain dividends at current levels** to satisfy investors. As discussed in Chapter 7, free cash flow is the term used to describe the cash remaining from operations after adjustment for capital expenditures and dividends.

Consider the following example: Suppose that MPC produced and sold 10,000 personal computers this year. It reported cash provided by operating activities of $100,000. In order to maintain production at 10,000 computers, MPC invested $15,000 in equipment. It chose to pay $5,000 in dividends. Its free cash flow was then $80,000 ($100,000 − $15,000 − $5,000). The company could use this $80,000 either to purchase new assets to expand the business or to pay an $80,000 dividend and continue to produce 10,000 computers. In practice, free cash flow is often calculated with the formula in Illustration 13-45. Alternative definitions also exist.

Illustration 13-45
Free cash flow

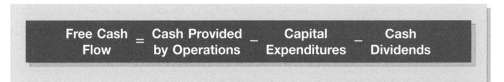

$$\text{Free Cash Flow} = \text{Cash Provided by Operations} - \text{Capital Expenditures} - \text{Cash Dividends}$$

Illustration 13-46 provides basic information excerpted from the 1998 statement of cash flows of Microsoft Corporation.

Illustration 13-46
Microsoft cash flow information ($ in millions)

MICROSOFT CORPORATION Statement of Cash Flows (partial) 1998		
Cash provided by operations		$6,880
Cash flows from investing activities		
Additions to property, plant, and equipment	$ 656	
Other assets and investments	1,788	
Short-term investments	4,828	
Cash used by investing activities		(7,272)
Cash paid for dividends on preferred stock		(28)

Microsoft's free cash flow is calculated as shown in Illustration 13-47.

Cash provided by operating activities	$6,880
Less: Expenditures on property, plant, and equipment	656
Dividends paid	28
Free cash flow	$6,196

Illustration 13-47   Calculation of Microsoft's free cash flow ($ in millions)

This is a tremendous amount of cash generated in a single year. It is available for the acquisition of new assets, the retirement of stock or debt, or the payment of dividends. It should also be noted that this amount far exceeds Microsoft's 1998 net income of $4,490 million. This lends additional credibility to Microsoft's income number as an indicator of potential future performance. If anything, Microsoft's net income might understate its actual performance.

Oracle Corporation is the world's largest seller of database software and information management services. Like Microsoft, its success depends on continuing to improve its existing products while developing new products to keep pace with rapid changes in technology. Oracle's free cash flow for 1998 was $1,287 million. This is impressive, but significantly less than Microsoft's amazing ability to generate cash.

DECISION TOOLKIT

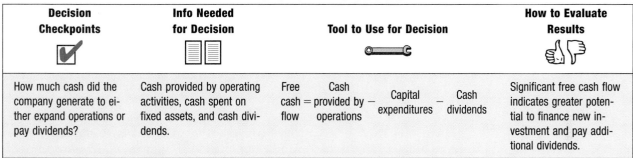

Decision Checkpoints	Info Needed for Decision	Tool to Use for Decision	How to Evaluate Results
How much cash did the company generate to either expand operations or pay dividends?	Cash provided by operating activities, cash spent on fixed assets, and cash dividends.	Free cash flow = Cash provided by operations − Capital expenditures − Cash dividends	Significant free cash flow indicates greater potential to finance new investment and pay additional dividends.

BUSINESS INSIGHT
Investor Perspective

Managers in some industries have long suggested that accrual-based income measures understate the true long-term potential of their companies because of what they suggest are excessive depreciation charges. For example, cable companies frequently suggested that, once they had installed a cable, it would require minimal maintenance and would guarantee the company returns for a long time to come. As a consequence, cable companies, which reported strong operating cash flows but low net income, had high stock prices because investors focused more on their cash flows from operations than on their net income. A recent *Wall Street Journal* article suggested, however, that investors have grown impatient with the cable companies and have lost faith in cash flow from operations as an indicator of cable company performance. As it turns out, cable companies have had to make many expensive upgrades to previously installed cable systems. Today, after cable stock prices have fallen dramatically, cable industry analysts emphasize that either free cash flows or net income is a better indicator of a cable TV company's long-term potential than cash provided by operating activities.

Source: Susan Pulliam and Mark Robichaux, "Heard on the Street: Cash Flow Stops Propping Cable Stock," *The Wall Street Journal*, January 9, 1997, p. C1.

CAPITAL EXPENDITURE RATIO

Capital expenditures are purchases of fixed assets. In addition to free cash flows, another indicator of a company's ability to generate sufficient cash to finance new fixed assets is the capital expenditure ratio: cash provided by operating activities divided by capital expenditures. This measure is similar to free cash flow, except that free cash flow reveals the amount of cash available for discretionary use by management, whereas the capital expenditure ratio provides a *relative measure* of cash provided by operations compared to cash used for the purchase of productive assets. Amounts spent on capital expenditures are listed in the investing activities section of the statement of cash flows. Using the Microsoft information in Illustration 13-46, we can calculate its capital expenditure ratio as shown in Illustration 13-48.

Illustration 13-48
Capital expenditure ratio for Microsoft

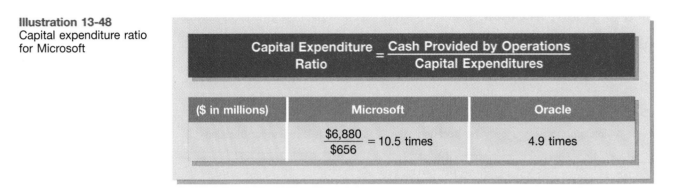

Microsoft's ratio of 10.5 times suggests that it could have purchased 10.5 times as much property, plant, and equipment as it did *without requiring any additional outside financing.* In comparison, Oracle's capital expenditure ratio for 1998 was 4.9 times. This provides additional evidence of Microsoft's superior cash-generating capability. It is important to note that this ratio will vary across industries depending on the capital intensity of the industry. That is, we would expect a manufacturing company to have a lower ratio (because by necessity it has higher capital expenditures) than a software company, which spends less of its money on fixed assets and more of its money on "intellectual" capital. This difference is evident in the Using the Decision Toolkit exercise at the end of this chapter where we evaluate two computer chip manufacturers.

DECISION TOOLKIT

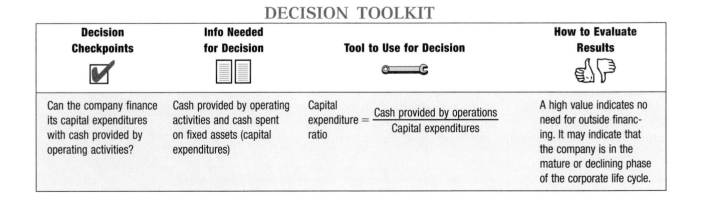

Decision Checkpoints	Info Needed for Decision	Tool to Use for Decision	How to Evaluate Results
Can the company finance its capital expenditures with cash provided by operating activities?	Cash provided by operating activities and cash spent on fixed assets (capital expenditures)	$\text{Capital expenditure ratio} = \dfrac{\text{Cash provided by operations}}{\text{Capital expenditures}}$	A high value indicates no need for outside financing. It may indicate that the company is in the mature or declining phase of the corporate life cycle.

ASSESSING LIQUIDITY, SOLVENCY, AND PROFITABILITY USING CASH FLOWS

Previous chapters have presented ratios used to analyze a company's liquidity, solvency, and profitability. Many of those ratios used accrual-based numbers from the income statement and balance sheet. In this section we focus on ratios that are *cash-based* rather than accrual-based; that is, instead of using numbers from the income statement, these ratios use numbers from the statement of cash flows.

As discussed earlier, many analysts are critical of accrual-based numbers because they feel that the adjustment process allows too much management discretion. These analysts like to supplement accrual-based analysis with measures that use the cash flow statement. One disadvantage of these measures is that, unlike the more commonly employed accrual-based measures, there are no readily available industry averages for comparison. In the following discussion we use cash flow–based ratios to analyze Microsoft. In addition to the cash flow information provided in Illustration 13-46, we need the following information related to Microsoft:

($ in millions)	1998	1997
Current liabilities	$ 5,730	$ 3,610
Total liabilities	5,730	3,610
Sales	14,484	11,358

Liquidity

Liquidity is the ability of a business to meet its immediate obligations. You learned that one measure of liquidity is the *current ratio*: current assets divided by current liabilities. A disadvantage of the current ratio is that it uses year-end balances of current asset and current liability accounts, and these year-end balances may not be representative of the company's position during most of the year.

A ratio that partially corrects this problem is the current cash debt coverage ratio: cash provided by operating activities divided by average current liabilities. Because cash provided by operating activities involves the entire year rather than a balance at one point in time, it is often considered a better representation of liquidity on the average day. The ratio is calculated as shown in Illustration 13-49, with the ratio computed for Microsoft Corporation and comparative numbers given for Oracle. We have also provided each company's current ratio for comparative purposes.

Illustration 13-49 Current cash debt coverage ratio

	Current Cash Debt Coverage Ratio	$=$	Cash Provided by Operations / Average Current Liabilities

($ in millions)	Current cash debt coverage ratio	Current ratio
Microsoft	$\dfrac{\$6,880}{(\$5,730 + \$3,610)/2} = 1.47$ times	2.77:1
Oracle	.73 times	1.74:1

Microsoft's net cash provided by operating activities is nearly two times its average current liabilities. Oracle's ratio of .73 times, though not a cause for concern, is substantially lower than that of Microsoft. Keep in mind that Microsoft's cash position is extraordinary. For example, many large companies now have current ratios in the range of 1.0. By this standard, Oracle's current ratio of 1.74 : 1 is respectable, but Microsoft's current ratio of 2.77 : 1 is very strong.

DECISION TOOLKIT

Decision Checkpoints	Info Needed for Decision	Tool to Use for Decision	How to Evaluate Results
Is the company generating sufficient cash provided by operating activities to meet its current obligations?	Cash provided by operating activities and average current liabilities	Current cash debt coverage ratio = $\dfrac{\text{Cash provided by operations}}{\text{Average current liabilities}}$	A high value suggests good liquidity. Since the numerator contains a "flow" measure, it provides a good supplement to the current ratio.

Solvency

Solvency is the ability of a company to survive over the long term. A measure of solvency that uses cash figures is the **cash debt coverage ratio**: the ratio of cash provided by operating activities to total debt as represented by average total liabilities. This ratio indicates a company's ability to repay its liabilities from cash generated from operations—that is, without having to liquidate productive assets such as property, plant, and equipment. The cash debt coverage ratios for Microsoft and Oracle for 1998 are given in Illustration 13-50. The debt to total assets ratios for each company are also provided for comparative purposes.

Illustration 13-50   Cash debt coverage ratio

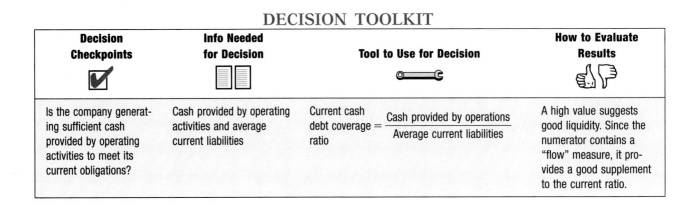

$\dfrac{\text{Cash Debt Coverage}}{\text{Ratio}} = \dfrac{\text{Cash Provided by Operations}}{\text{Average Total Liabilities}}$		
($ in millions)	Cash debt coverage ratio	Debt to total assets ratio
Microsoft	$\dfrac{\$6,880}{(\$5,730 + \$3,610)/2} = 1.47$ times	26%
Oracle	.63 times	49%

Microsoft has very low long-term obligations; thus, its cash debt coverage ratio is nearly identical to its current cash debt coverage ratio. Obviously, Microsoft is very solvent. Oracle has some long-term debt, but like Microsoft its cash debt coverage ratio suggests that its long-term financial health is strong. Neither the cash nor accrual measures suggest any cause for concern for either company.

DECISION TOOLKIT

Decision Checkpoints	Info Needed for Decision	Tool to Use for Decision	How to Evaluate Results
Is the company generating sufficient cash provided by operating activities to meet its long-term obligations?	Cash provided by operating activities and average total liabilities	Cash debt coverage ratio $=\dfrac{\text{Cash provided by operations}}{\text{Average total liabilities}}$	A high value suggests the company is solvent; that is, it will meet its obligations in the long term.

Profitability

Profitability refers to a company's ability to generate a reasonable return. Earlier chapters introduced accrual-based ratios that measure profitability, such as gross profit rate, profit margin, and return on assets. In measures of profitability the potential differences between cash accounting and accrual accounting are most pronounced. Although some differences are expected because of the difference in the timing of revenue and expense recognition under cash versus accrual accounting, significant differences should be investigated. A cash-based measure of performance is the cash return on sales ratio.

The cash return on sales ratio is cash provided by operating activities divided by net sales. This ratio indicates the company's ability to turn sales into dollars. A low cash return on sales ratio should be investigated because it might indicate that the company is recognizing sales that are not really sales—that is, sales it will never collect. The cash return on sales ratios for Microsoft and Oracle for 1998 are presented in Illustration 13-51. The profit margin ratio is also presented for comparison.

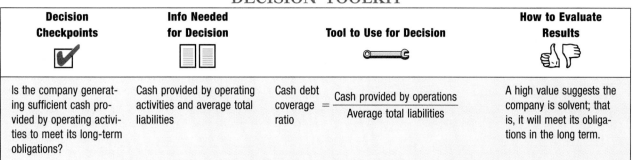

Illustration 13-51   Cash return on sales ratio

$$\text{Cash Return on Sales Ratio} = \frac{\text{Cash Provided by Operations}}{\text{Net Sales}}$$

($ in millions)	Cash return on sales ratio	Profit margin ratio
Microsoft	$\dfrac{\$6,880}{\$14,484} = 48\%$	31%
Oracle	23%	11%

Oracle's cash return on sales ratio of 23% is substantially less than Microsoft's of 48%. This indicates that Microsoft is more efficient in turning sales into cash. The cash return on sales ratio of both companies exceeds their profit margins. This is the result of timing differences between cash-basis and accrual-basis accounting. It suggests that both companies employ conservative accounting practices that result in lower reported net income.

DECISION TOOLKIT

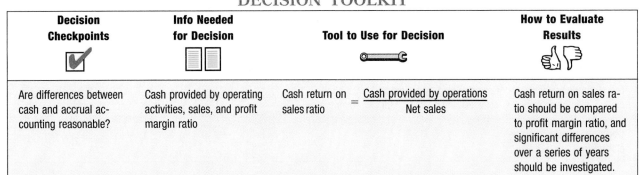

Decision Checkpoints	Info Needed for Decision	Tool to Use for Decision	How to Evaluate Results
Are differences between cash and accrual accounting reasonable?	Cash provided by operating activities, sales, and profit margin ratio	$$\text{Cash return on sales ratio} = \frac{\text{Cash provided by operations}}{\text{Net sales}}$$	Cash return on sales ratio should be compared to profit margin ratio, and significant differences over a series of years should be investigated.

BUSINESS INSIGHT
Management Perspective

A recent *Wall Street Journal* article noted that while Microsoft's cash position is enviable, it does present some challenges; management can't find enough ways to spend the cash. For example, unlike computer chip manufacturer Intel Corporation (another huge generator of cash), Microsoft has few manufacturing costs, so it cannot spend huge sums on new plant and equipment. Microsoft's management would like to purchase other major software companies, but the federal government won't let it, for fear that it will reduce competition. (For example, the Justice Department blocked Microsoft's proposed purchase of software maker Intuit.) Instead, Microsoft is constrained to purchasing small software makers with promising new products. Ironically, even this does not use much of its cash because, first of all, the companies are small, and second, the owners of these small companies prefer to be paid with Microsoft stock rather than cash.

Microsoft's huge holdings of liquid assets could eventually hurt its stock performance. Liquid assets typically provide about a 5% return, whereas Microsoft investors are accustomed to 30% returns. If Microsoft's performance starts to decline because it can't find enough good investment projects, it should distribute cash to its common stockholders in the form of dividends. One big problem: Bill Gates owns roughly 20% of Microsoft, and the last thing he wants to do is pay personal income tax on billions of dollars of dividend income. In the early years Microsoft did not pay dividends because it wanted to conserve cash. Today it is drowning in cash but still doesn't pay a dividend on its common stock.

Source: David Bank, "Microsoft's Problem Is What Many Firms Just Wish They Had," *The Wall Street Journal,* January 17, 1997, p. A9.

BEFORE YOU GO ON...

◆ Review It

1. What is the difference between cash from operations and free cash flow?
2. What does it mean if a company has negative free cash flow?
3. Why might an analyst want to supplement accrual-based ratios with cash-based ratios? What are some cash-based ratios?

USING THE DECISION TOOLKIT

Intel Corporation is the leading producer of computer chips for personal computers. It makes the hugely successful Pentium chip. Its primary competitor is AMD (formerly Advanced Micro Devices). The two are vicious competitors, with frequent lawsuits filed between them. Financial statement data for Intel are provided below.

Instructions

Calculate the following cash-based measures for Intel, and compare them with those provided on page 640 for AMD.

1. Free cash flow.
2. Capital expenditure ratio.
3. Current cash debt coverage ratio.
4. Cash debt coverage ratio.
5. Cash return on sales ratio.

INTEL CORPORATION
Balance Sheet
December 31, 1998 and 1997
(in millions)

	1998	1997
Assets		
Current assets	$13,475	$15,867
Noncurrent assets	17,996	13,013
Total assets	$31,471	$28,880
Liabilities and Stockholders' Equity		
Current liabilities	$ 5,804	$ 6,020
Long-term liabilities	2,089	1,524
Total liabilities	7,893	7,544
Stockholders' equity	23,578	21,336
Total liabilities and stockholders' equity	$31,471	$28,880

INTEL CORPORATION
Income Statement
For the Years Ended December 31, 1998 and 1997
(in millions)

	1998	1997
Net revenues	$26,273	$25,070
Expenses	20,205	18,125
Net income	$ 6,068	$ 6,945

INTEL CORPORATION
Statement of Cash Flows
For the Years Ended December 31, 1998 and 1997
(in millions)

	1998	1997
Net cash provided by operating activities	$ 9,191	$10,008
Net cash used for investing activities (see note 1)	(6,506)	(6,859)
Net cash used for financing activities	(4,749)	(3,212)
Net increase (decrease) in cash and cash equivalents	$(2,064)	$ (63)

Note 1. Cash spent on property, plant, and equipment in 1998 was $3,557. Cash paid for dividends was $217.

Here are the comparative data for AMD:

1. Free cash flow   ($852 million)
2. Capital expenditure ratio   .14 times
3. Current cash debt coverage ratio   .18 times
4. Cash debt coverage ratio   .08 times
5. Cash return on sales ratio   6%

Solution

1. Intel's free cash flow is $5,417 million ($9,191 − $3,557 − $217), and AMD's is actually a negative $852 million. This gives Intel a huge advantage in the ability to move quickly to invest in new projects.

2. Intel's capital expenditure ratio is 2.58 times ($9,191 ÷ $3,557), and AMD's is .14 times. This is a useful supplement to the free cash flow measure. It provides further evidence of Intel's superior cash-generating ability. Note that these values are well below those of Oracle and Microsoft. Manufacturing computer chips is very capital intensive, so we would expect these measures to be lower than those for software producers.

3. The current cash debt coverage ratio for Intel is calculated as:

$$\frac{\$9,191}{(\$5,804 + \$6,020)/2} = 1.55 \text{ times}$$

Compared to AMD's value of .18 times, Intel appears to be significantly more liquid.

4. The cash debt coverage ratio for Intel is calculated as:

$$\frac{\$9,191}{(\$7,893 + \$7,544)/2} = 1.19 \text{ times}$$

Compared to AMD's value of .08 times, Intel appears to be significantly more solvent.

5. The cash return on sales ratio for Intel is calculated as:

$$\frac{\$9,191}{\$26,273} = 35\%$$

AMD's cash return on sales ratio is 6%. Thus, Intel was far more successful in its ability to generate cash from sales.

SUMMARY OF STUDY OBJECTIVES

1 *Indicate the primary purpose of the statement of cash flows.* The statement of cash flows provides information about the cash receipts and cash payments of an entity during a period. A secondary objective is to provide information about the operating, investing, and financing activities of the entity during the period.

2 *Distinguish among operating, investing, and financing activities.* Operating activities include the cash effects of transactions that enter into the determination of net income. Investing activities involve cash flows resulting from changes in investments and long-term asset items. Financing activities involve cash flows resulting from changes in long-term liability and stockholders' equity items.

3 *Explain the impact of the product life cycle on a company's cash flows.* During the introductory stage, cash provided by operating activities and cash from investing are negative, whereas cash from financing is positive. During the growth stage, cash provided by operating activities becomes positive. During the maturity stage, cash provided by operating activities exceeds investing needs, so the company begins to retire debt. During the decline stage, cash provided by operating activities is reduced, cash from investing becomes positive, and cash from financing becomes more negative.

4a *Prepare a statement of cash flows using the indirect method.* The preparation of a statement of cash flows involves three major steps: (a) determine the net increase or decrease in cash, (b) determine net cash provided (used) by operating activities, and (c) determine net cash provided (used) by investing and financing activities. Under the indirect method, accrual-basis net income is adjusted to net cash provided by operating activities.

4b *Prepare a statement of cash flows using the direct method.* The preparation of the statement of cash flows involves three major steps: (a) determine the net increase or decrease in cash, (b) determine net cash provided (used) by operating activities, and (c) determine net cash provided (used) by investing and financing activities. The direct method reports cash receipts less cash payments to arrive at net cash provided by operating activities.

5 *Use the statement of cash flows to evaluate a company.* A number of measures can be derived by using information from the statement of cash flows as well as the other required financial statements. Free cash flow indicates the amount of cash a company generated during the current year that is available for the payment of dividends or for expansion. The capital expenditure ratio, cash provided by operating activities divided by capital expenditures, complements free cash flow by giving a relative indicator of the sufficiency of cash from operations to fund capital expenditures. Liquidity can be measured with the current cash debt coverage ratio (cash provided by operating activities divided by average current liabilities), solvency by the cash debt coverage ratio (cash provided by operating activities divided by average total liabilities), and profitability by the cash return on sales ratio (cash provided by operating activities divided by net sales).

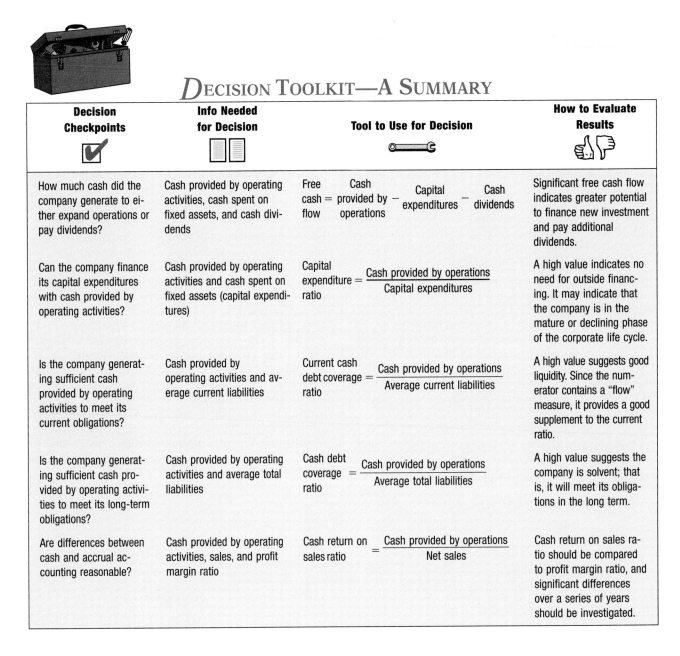

DECISION TOOLKIT—A SUMMARY

Decision Checkpoints	Info Needed for Decision	Tool to Use for Decision	How to Evaluate Results
How much cash did the company generate to either expand operations or pay dividends?	Cash provided by operating activities, cash spent on fixed assets, and cash dividends	$$\text{Free cash flow} = \text{Cash provided by operations} - \text{Capital expenditures} - \text{Cash dividends}$$	Significant free cash flow indicates greater potential to finance new investment and pay additional dividends.
Can the company finance its capital expenditures with cash provided by operating activities?	Cash provided by operating activities and cash spent on fixed assets (capital expenditures)	$$\text{Capital expenditure ratio} = \frac{\text{Cash provided by operations}}{\text{Capital expenditures}}$$	A high value indicates no need for outside financing. It may indicate that the company is in the mature or declining phase of the corporate life cycle.
Is the company generating sufficient cash provided by operating activities to meet its current obligations?	Cash provided by operating activities and average current liabilities	$$\text{Current cash debt coverage ratio} = \frac{\text{Cash provided by operations}}{\text{Average current liabilities}}$$	A high value suggests good liquidity. Since the numerator contains a "flow" measure, it provides a good supplement to the current ratio.
Is the company generating sufficient cash provided by operating activities to meet its long-term obligations?	Cash provided by operating activities and average total liabilities	$$\text{Cash debt coverage ratio} = \frac{\text{Cash provided by operations}}{\text{Average total liabilities}}$$	A high value suggests the company is solvent; that is, it will meet its obligations in the long term.
Are differences between cash and accrual accounting reasonable?	Cash provided by operating activities, sales, and profit margin ratio	$$\text{Cash return on sales ratio} = \frac{\text{Cash provided by operations}}{\text{Net sales}}$$	Cash return on sales ratio should be compared to profit margin ratio, and significant differences over a series of years should be investigated.

GLOSSARY

Capital expenditure ratio   A cash-based ratio that indicates the extent to which cash provided by operating activities was sufficient to fund capital expenditure (fixed asset) purchases during the year. (p. 634)

Cash debt coverage ratio   A cash-basis ratio used to evaluate solvency, calculated as cash provided by operating activities divided by average total liabilities. (p. 636)

Cash return on sales ratio   A cash-basis ratio used to evaluate profitability by dividing cash provided by operations by net sales. (p. 637)

Current cash debt coverage ratio   A cash-basis ratio used to evaluate liquidity, calculated as cash provided by operations divided by average current liabilities. (p. 635)

Direct method   A method of determining net cash provided by operating activities by adjusting each item in the income statement from the accrual basis to the cash basis. (p. 620)

Financing activities   Cash flow activities that include (a) obtaining cash from issuing debt and repaying the amounts borrowed and (b) obtaining cash from stockholders and providing them with a return on their investment. (p. 599)

Free cash flow   Cash provided by operating activities adjusted for capital expenditures and dividends paid. (p. 632)

Indirect method   A method of preparing a statement of

cash flows in which net income is adjusted for items that do not affect cash, to determine net cash provided by operating activities. (p. 608)

Investing activities   Cash flow activities that include (a) purchasing and disposing of investments and productive long-lived assets using cash and (b) lending money and collecting on those loans. (p. 599)

Operating activities   Cash flow activities that include the cash effects of transactions that create revenues and expenses and thus enter into the determination of net income. (p. 599)

Product life cycle   A series of phases in a product's sales and cash flows over time; these phases, in order of occurrence, are introductory, growth, maturity, and decline. (p. 602)

Statement of cash flows   A basic financial statement that provides information about the cash receipts and cash payments of an entity during a period, classified as operating, investing, and financing activities, in a format that reconciles the beginning and ending cash balances. (p. 598)

DEMONSTRATION PROBLEM

The income statement for John Kosinski Manufacturing Company contains the following condensed information:

JOHN KOSINSKI MANUFACTURING COMPANY
Income Statement
For the Year Ended December 31, 2001

Revenues		$6,583,000
Operating expenses, excluding depreciation	$4,920,000	
Depreciation expense	880,000	5,800,000
Income before income taxes		783,000
Income tax expense		353,000
Net income		$ 430,000

Included in operating expenses is a $24,000 loss resulting from the sale of machinery for $270,000 cash. Machinery was purchased at a cost of $750,000. The following balances are reported on Kosinski's comparative balance sheet at December 31:

	2001	2000
Cash	$672,000	$130,000
Accounts receivable	775,000	610,000
Inventories	834,000	867,000
Accounts payable	521,000	501,000

Income tax expense of $353,000 represents the amount paid in 2001. Dividends declared and paid in 2001 totaled $200,000.

Instructions

(a) Prepare the statement of cash flows using the indirect method.
(b) Prepare the statement of cash flows using the direct method.

Solution to Demonstration Problem

(a)
JOHN KOSINSKI MANUFACTURING COMPANY
Statement of Cash Flows—Indirect Method
For the Year Ended December 31, 2001

Cash flows from operating activities		
Net income		$ 430,000
Adjustments to reconcile net income to net cash provided by operating activities:		
Depreciation expense	$880,000	

Problem-Solving Strategy

This demonstration problem illustrates both the direct and indirect methods using the same basic data. Note the similarities and the differences between the two methods. Both methods report the same information in the investing and financing activities sections. The cash flow from operating activities section reports different information, but the amount—net cash provided by operating activities—is the same for both methods.

Loss on sale of machinery	24,000	
Increase in accounts receivable	(165,000)	
Decrease in inventories	33,000	
Increase in accounts payable	20,000	792,000
Net cash provided by operating activities		1,222,000
Cash flows from investing activities		
Sale of machinery	270,000	
Purchase of machinery	(750,000)	
Net cash used by investing activities		(480,000)
Cash flows from financing activities		
Payment of cash dividends	(200,000)	
Net cash used by financing activities		(200,000)
Net increase in cash		542,000
Cash at beginning of period		130,000
Cash at end of period		$ 672,000

(b)

JOHN KOSINSKI MANUFACTURING COMPANY
Statement of Cash Flows—Direct Method
For the Year Ended December 31, 2001

Cash flows from operating activities		
Cash collections from customers		$6,418,000[*]
Cash payments:		
For operating expenses	$4,843,000[**]	
For income taxes	353,000	5,196,000
Net cash provided by operating activities		1,222,000
Cash flows from investing activities		
Sale of machinery	270,000	
Purchase of machinery	(750,000)	
Net cash used by investing activities		(480,000)
Cash flows from financing activities		
Payment of cash dividends	(200,000)	
Net cash used by financing activities		(200,000)
Net increase in cash		542,000
Cash at beginning of period		130,000
Cash at end of period		$ 672,000

Direct Method Computations:

[*]Computation of cash collections from customers:

Revenues per the income statement	$6,583,000
Deduct: Increase in accounts receivable	(165,000)
Cash collections from customers	$6,418,000

[**]Computation of cash payments for operating expenses:

Operating expenses per the income statement	$4,920,000
Deduct: Loss from sale of machinery	(24,000)
Deduct: Decrease in inventories	(33,000)
Deduct: Increase in accounts payable	(20,000)
Cash payments for operating expenses	$4,843,000

SELF-STUDY QUESTIONS

Answers are at the end of the chapter.

(SO 1) 1. Which of the following is *incorrect* about the statement of cash flows?
(a) It is a fourth basic financial statement.
(b) It provides information about cash receipts and cash payments of an entity during a period.
(c) It reconciles the ending cash account balance to the balance per the bank statement.
(d) It provides information about the operating, investing, and financing activities of the business.

(SO 2) 2. The statement of cash flows classifies cash receipts and cash payments by these activities:
(a) operating and nonoperating.
(b) investing, financing, and operating.
(c) financing, operating, and nonoperating.
(d) investing, financing, and nonoperating.

(SO 2) 3. Which is an example of a cash flow from an operating activity?
(a) Payment of cash to lenders for interest.
(b) Receipt of cash from the sale of capital stock.
(c) Payment of cash dividends to the company's stockholders.
(d) None of the above.

(SO 2) 4. Which is an example of a cash flow from an investing activity?
(a) Receipt of cash from the issuance of bonds payable.
(b) Payment of cash to repurchase outstanding capital stock.
(c) Receipt of cash from the sale of equipment.
(d) Payment of cash to suppliers for inventory.

(SO 2) 5. Cash dividends paid to stockholders are classified on the statement of cash flows as:
(a) operating activities.
(b) investing activities.
(c) a combination of (a) and (b).
(d) financing activities.

(SO 2) 6. Which is an example of a cash flow from a financing activity?
(a) Receipt of cash from sale of land.
(b) Issuance of debt for cash.
(c) Purchase of equipment for cash.
(d) None of the above

(SO 2) 7. Which of the following is *incorrect* about the statement of cash flows?
(a) The direct method may be used to report cash provided by operations.
(b) The statement shows the cash provided (used) for three categories of activity.
(c) The operating section is the last section of the statement.
(d) The indirect method may be used to report cash provided by operations.

(SO 3) 8. During the introductory phase of a company's life cycle, one would normally expect to see:
(a) negative cash from operations, negative cash from investing, and positive cash from financing.
(b) negative cash from operations, positive cash from investing, and positive cash from financing.
(c) positive cash from operations, negative cash from investing, and negative cash from financing.
(d) positive cash from operations, negative cash from investing, and positive cash from financing.

Questions 9 and 10 apply only to the indirect method.

(SO 4a) 9. Net income is $132,000, accounts payable increased $10,000 during the year, inventory decreased $6,000 during the year, and accounts receivable increased $12,000 during the year. Under the indirect method, what is net cash provided by operations?
(a) $102,000.   (c) $124,000.
(b) $112,000.   (d) $136,000.

(SO 4a) 10. Noncash charges that are added back to net income in determining cash provided by operations under the indirect method do *not* include:
(a) depreciation expense.
(b) an increase in inventory.
(c) amortization expense.
(d) loss on sale of equipment.

Questions 11 and 12 apply only to the direct method.

(SO 4b) 11. The beginning balance in accounts receivable is $44,000, the ending balance is $42,000, and sales during the period are $129,000. What are cash receipts from customers?
(a) $127,000.   (c) $131,000.
(b) $129,000.   (d) $141,000.

(SO 4b) 12. Which of the following items is reported on a cash flow statement prepared by the direct method?
(a) Loss on sale of building.
(b) Increase in accounts receivable.
(c) Depreciation expense.
(d) Cash payments to suppliers.

(SO 5) 13. The statement of cash flows should *not* be used to evaluate an entity's ability to:
(a) earn net income.
(b) generate future cash flows.
(c) pay dividends.
(d) meet obligations.

(SO 5) 14. ⊙▭⊂ Free cash flow provides an indication of a company's ability to:
(a) generate net income.
(b) generate cash to pay dividends.
(c) generate cash to invest in new capital expenditures.
(d) both (b) and (c).

15. ⊙▭⊂ Which of the following ratios provides a useful comparison to the profit margin ratio? (SO 5)
(a) Capital expenditure ratio.
(b) Cash return on sales ratio.
(c) Cash debt coverage ratio.
(d) Current cash debt coverage ratio.

QUESTIONS

1. (a) What is a statement of cash flows?
   (b) Alice Weiseman maintains that the statement of cash flows is an optional financial statement. Do you agree? Explain.

2. What questions about cash are answered by the statement of cash flows?

3. Distinguish among the three activities reported in the statement of cash flows.

4. (a) What are the major sources (inflows) of cash in a statement of cash flows?
   (b) What are the major uses (outflows) of cash?

5. Why is it important to disclose certain noncash transactions? How should they be disclosed?

6. Wilma Flintstone and Barny Kublestone were discussing the format of the statement of cash flows of Rock Candy Co. At the bottom of Rock Candy's statement of cash flows was a separate section entitled "Noncash investing and financing activities." Give three examples of significant noncash transactions that would be reported in this section.

7. Why is it necessary to use comparative balance sheets, a current income statement, and certain transaction data in preparing a statement of cash flows?

8. ⊙▭⊂
   (a) What are the phases of the corporate life cycle?
   (b) What effect does each phase have on the numbers reported in a statement of cash flows?

9. Contrast the advantages and disadvantages of the direct and indirect methods of preparing the statement of cash flows. Are both methods acceptable? Which method is preferred by the FASB? Which method is more popular?

10. When the total cash inflows exceed the total cash outflows in the statement of cash flows, how and where is this excess identified?

11. Describe the indirect method for determining net cash provided (used) by operating activities.

12. Why is it necessary to convert accrual-based net income to cash-basis income when preparing a statement of cash flows?

13. ⊙▭⊂ The president of Aerosmith Company is puzzled. During the last year, the company experienced a net loss of $800,000, yet its cash increased $300,000 during the same period of time. Explain to the president how this could occur.

14. Identify five items that are adjustments to convert net income to net cash provided by operating activities under the indirect method.

15. Why and how is depreciation expense reported in a statement prepared using the indirect method?

16. Why is the statement of cash flows useful?

17. During 2001 Johnny Carson Company converted $1,700,000 of its total $2,000,000 of bonds payable into common stock. Indicate how the transaction would be reported on a statement of cash flows, if at all.

18. Describe the direct method for determining net cash provided by operating activities.

19. Give the formulas under the direct method for computing (a) cash receipts from customers and (b) cash payments to suppliers.

20. Cindy Crawford Inc. reported sales of $2 million for 2001. Accounts receivable decreased $100,000 and accounts payable increased $300,000. Compute cash receipts from customers, assuming that the receivable and payable transactions related to operations.

21. In the direct method, why is depreciation expense not reported in the cash flows from operating activities section?

22. ⊙▭⊂ Give an example of one accrual-based ratio and one cash-based ratio to measure these characteristics of a company:
    (a) Liquidity.
    (b) Solvency.
    (c) Profitability.

BRIEF EXERCISES

BE13-1   Each of these items must be considered in preparing a statement of cash flows for Murphy Co. for the year ended December 31, 2001. For each item, state how it should be shown in the statement of cash flows for 2001.
(a) Issued bonds for $200,000 cash.
(b) Purchased equipment for $150,000 cash.
(c) Sold land costing $20,000 for $20,000 cash.
(d) Declared and paid a $50,000 cash dividend.

Indicate statement presentation of selected transactions.
(SO 2)

BE13-2   Classify each item as an operating, investing, or financing activity. Assume all items involve cash unless there is information to the contrary.
(a) Purchase of equipment.   (d) Depreciation.
(b) Sale of building.   (e) Payment of dividends.
(c) Redemption of bonds.   (f) Issuance of capital stock.

Classify items by activities.
(SO 2)

BE13-3   The following T account is a summary of the cash account of Anita Baker Company:

Identify financing activity transactions.
(SO 2)

Cash (Summary Form)

Balance, Jan. 1	8,000		
Receipts from customers	364,000	Payments for goods	200,000
Dividends on stock investments	6,000	Payments for operating expenses	140,000
Proceeds from sale of equipment	36,000	Interest paid	10,000
Proceeds from issuance of		Taxes paid	8,000
bonds payable	100,000	Dividends paid	40,000
Balance, Dec. 31	116,000		

What amount of net cash provided (used) by financing activities should be reported in the statement of cash flows?

BE13-4
(a) Why is cash from operations likely to be lower than reported net income during the growth phase?
(b) Why is cash from investing often positive during the late maturity phase and during the decline phase?

Answer questions related to the phases of product life cycle.
(SO 3)

BE13-5   Crystal, Inc., reported net income of $2.5 million in 2001. Depreciation for the year was $260,000, accounts receivable decreased $350,000, and accounts payable decreased $310,000. Compute net cash provided by operating activities using the indirect approach.

Compute cash provided by operating activities—indirect method.
(SO 4a)

BE13-6   The net income for Sterling Engineering Co. for 2001 was $280,000. For 2001 depreciation on plant assets was $60,000, and the company incurred a loss on sale of plant assets of $9,000. Compute net cash provided by operating activities under the indirect method.

Compute cash provided by operating activities—indirect method.
(SO 4a)

BE13-7   The comparative balance sheet for Nolex Company shows these changes in non-cash current asset accounts: accounts receivable decrease $80,000, prepaid expenses increase $12,000, and inventories increase $30,000. Compute net cash provided by operating activities using the indirect method assuming that net income is $200,000.

Compute net cash provided by operating activities—indirect method.
(SO 4a)

BE13-8   The T accounts for Equipment and the related Accumulated Depreciation for Cindy Trevis Company at the end of 2001 are shown here:

Determine cash received from sale of equipment.
(SO 4a, 4b)

Equipment				**Accumulated Depreciation**			
Beg. bal.	80,000	Disposals	22,000	Disposals	5,500	Beg. bal.	44,500
Acquisitions	41,600					Depr. exp.	12,000
End. bal.	99,600					End. bal.	51,000

In addition, Cindy Trevis Company's income statement reported a loss on the sale of equipment of $6,700. What amount was reported on the statement of cash flows as "cash flow from sale of equipment"?

Compute receipts from customers—direct method.
(SO 4b)

BE13-9 **Columbia Sportswear Company** had accounts receivable of $76,086,000 at January 1, 1998, and $105,967,000 at December 31, 1998. Sales revenues were $427,278,000 for the year 1998. What is the amount of cash receipts from customers in 1998?

Compute cash payments for income taxes—direct method.
(SO 4b)

BE13-10 **Boeing Corporation** reported income taxes of $277,000,000 on its 1998 income statement and income taxes payable of $298,000,000 at December 31, 1997, and $569,000,000 at December 31, 1998. What amount of cash payments were made for income taxes during 1998? (Ignore deferred taxes.)

Compute cash payments for operating expenses—direct method.
(SO 4b)

BE13-11 Excel Corporation reports operating expenses of $90,000 excluding depreciation expense of $15,000 for 2001. During the year prepaid expenses decreased $6,600 and accrued expenses payable increased $4,400. Compute the cash payments for operating expenses in 2001.

Calculate cash-based ratios.
(SO 5)

BE13-12 During 1998 **Cypress Semiconductor Corporation** reported cash provided by operations of $99,907,000, cash used in investing of $60,338,000, and cash used in financing of $57,522,000. In addition, cash spent for fixed assets during the period was $82,205,000. Average current liabilities were $96,331,000, and average total liabilities were $289,996,000. No dividends were paid. Calculate these values:
(a) Free cash flow.
(b) Capital expenditure ratio.
(c) Current cash debt coverage ratio.

EXERCISES

Classify transactions by type of activity.
(SO 2)

E13-1 Depeche Mode Corporation had these transactions during 2001:
(a) Issued $50,000 par value common stock for cash.
(b) Purchased a machine for $30,000, giving a long-term note in exchange.
(c) Issued $200,000 par value common stock upon conversion of bonds having a face value of $200,000.
(d) Declared and paid a cash dividend of $25,000.
(e) Sold a long-term investment with a cost of $15,000 for $15,000 cash.
(f) Collected $16,000 of accounts receivable.
(g) Paid $18,000 on accounts payable.

Instructions
Analyze the transactions and indicate whether each transaction resulted in a cash flow from operating activities, investing activities, financing activities, or noncash investing and financing activities.

Classify transactions by type of activity.
(SO 2)

E13-2 An analysis of comparative balance sheets, the current year's income statement, and the general ledger accounts of Green Day Corp. uncovered the following items. Assume all items involve cash unless there is information to the contrary.

(a) Payment of interest on notes payable.
(b) Exchange of land for patent.
(c) Sale of building at book value.
(d) Payment of dividends.
(e) Depreciation.
(f) Receipt of dividends on investment in stock.
(g) Receipt of interest on notes receivable.
(h) Issuance of capital stock.
(i) Amortization of patent.
(j) Issuance of bonds for land.

(k) Purchase of land.
(l) Conversion of bonds into common stock.
(m) Loss on sale of land.
(n) Retirement of bonds.

Instructions
Indicate how each item should be classified in the statement of cash flows using these four major classifications: operating activity (indirect method), investing activity, financing activity, and significant noncash investing and financing activity.

E13-3 The information in the table is from the statement of cash flows for a company at four different points in time (A, B, C, and D). Negative values are presented in parentheses.

Identify phases of product life cycle.
(SO 3)

| | Point in Time | | | |
	A	B	C	D
Cash provided by operations	($ 60,000)	$30,000	$100,000	($ 10,000)
Cash provided by investing	(100,000)	25,000	30,000	(40,000)
Cash provided by financing	70,000	(110,000)	(50,000)	120,000
Net income	(40,000)	10,000	100,000	(5,000)

Instructions
For each point in time, state whether the company is most likely characterized as being in the introductory phase, growth phase, maturity phase, or decline phase. In each case explain your choice.

E13-4 Hugh Grant Company reported net income of $195,000 for 2001. Grant also reported depreciation expense of $45,000 and a loss of $5,000 on the sale of equipment. The comparative balance sheet shows a decrease in accounts receivable of $15,000 for the year, a $10,000 increase in accounts payable, and a $4,000 decrease in prepaid expenses.

Prepare the operating activities section—indirect method.
(SO 4a)

Instructions
Prepare the operating activities section of the statement of cash flows for 2001. Use the indirect method.

E13-5 The current sections of 2nd II None Inc.'s balance sheets at December 31, 2000 and 2001, are presented here:

Prepare the operating activities section—indirect method.
(SO 4a)

	2001	2000
Current assets		
Cash	$105,000	$ 99,000
Accounts receivable	120,000	89,000
Inventory	161,000	186,000
Prepaid expenses	27,000	22,000
Total current assets	$413,000	$396,000
Current liabilities		
Accrued expenses payable	$ 15,000	$ 5,000
Accounts payable	85,000	92,000
Total current liabilities	$100,000	$ 97,000

2nd II None's net income for 2001 was $153,000. Depreciation expense was $19,000.

Instructions
Prepare the net cash provided by operating activities section of the company's statement of cash flows for the year ended December 31, 2001, using the indirect method.

E13-6 These three accounts appear in the general ledger of Z.Z. Top Corp. during 2001:

Prepare partial statement of cash flows—indirect method.
(SO 4a)

Equipment

Date		Debit	Credit	Balance
Jan. 1	Balance			160,000
July 31	Purchase of equipment	70,000		230,000

Sept. 2	Cost of equipment constructed	53,000		283,000
Nov. 10	Cost of equipment sold		35,000	248,000

Accumulated Depreciation—Equipment

Date		Debit	Credit	Balance
Jan. 1	Balance			71,000
Nov. 10	Accumulated depreciation on equipment sold	30,000		41,000
Dec. 31	Depreciation for year		28,000	69,000

Retained Earnings

Date		Debit	Credit	Balance
Jan. 1	Balance			105,000
Aug. 23	Dividends (cash)	14,000		91,000
Dec. 31	Net income		67,000	158,000

Instructions

From the postings in the accounts, indicate how the information is reported on a statement of cash flows using the indirect method. The loss on sale of equipment was $3,000. [*Hint:* Purchase of equipment is reported in the investing activities section as a decrease in cash of $70,000.]

Prepare a statement of cash flows—indirect method, and compute cash-based ratios.
(SO 4a, 5)

E13-7 Here is a comparative balance sheet for New Radicals Company:

NEW RADICALS COMPANY
Comparative Balance Sheet
December 31

Assets	2001	2000
Cash	$ 63,000	$ 22,000
Accounts receivable	85,000	76,000
Inventories	170,000	189,000
Land	75,000	100,000
Equipment	270,000	200,000
Accumulated depreciation	(66,000)	(32,000)
Total	$597,000	$555,000

Liabilities and Stockholders' Equity	2001	2000
Accounts payable	$ 39,000	$ 47,000
Bonds payable	150,000	200,000
Common stock ($1 par)	209,000	174,000
Retained earnings	199,000	134,000
Total	$597,000	$555,000

Additional information:
1. Net income for 2001 was $105,000.
2. Cash dividends of $40,000 were declared and paid.
3. Bonds payable amounting to $50,000 were redeemed for cash $50,000.
4. Common stock was issued for $35,000 cash.
5. Sales for 2001 were $978,000.

Instructions
(a) Prepare a statement of cash flows for 2001 using the indirect method.
(b) Compute these cash-basis ratios:
   (1) Current cash debt coverage.
   (2) Cash return on sales.
   (3) Cash debt coverage.

Compute cash provided by operating activities—direct method.
(SO 4b)

E13-8 Beth Orton Company completed its first year of operations on December 31, 2001. Its initial income statement showed that Beth Orton had revenues of $182,000 and operating expenses of $78,000. Accounts receivable and accounts payable at year end were $52,000 and $21,000, respectively. Assume that accounts payable related to operating expenses. Ignore income taxes.

Instructions

Compute net cash provided by operating activities using the direct method.

E13-9 The 1998 income statement for **Ben & Jerry's Homemade** shows cost of goods sold $136,225,000 and operating expenses (including depreciation expense of $8,181,000) $63,895,000. The comparative balance sheet for the year shows that inventory increased $1,968,000, prepaid expenses increased $501,000, accounts payable (merchandise suppliers) increased $791,000, and accrued expenses payable increased $4,605,000.

Compute cash payments—direct method.
(SO 4b)

Instructions

Using the direct method, compute (a) cash payments to suppliers and (b) cash payments for operating expenses.

E13-10 The 2001 accounting records of Cattle Car Airlines reveal these transactions and events:

Compute cash flow from operating activities—direct method.
(SO 4b)

Payment of interest	$10,000	Collection of accounts receivable	$192,000
Cash sales	48,000	Payment of salaries and wages	53,000
Receipt of dividend revenue	14,000	Depreciation expense	16,000
Payment of income taxes	12,000	Proceeds from sale of aircraft	812,000
Net income	38,000	Purchase of equipment for cash	22,000
Payment of accounts payable		Loss on sale of aircraft	3,000
for merchandise	90,000	Payment of dividends	14,000
Payment for land	74,000	Payment of operating expenses	28,000

Instructions

Prepare the cash flows from operating activities section using the direct method. (Not all of the items will be used.)

E13-11 The following information is taken from the 2001 general ledger of Sound Garden Company:

Calculate cash flows—direct method.
(SO 4b)

Rent	Rent expense	$ 31,000
	Prepaid rent, January 1	5,900
	Prepaid rent, December 31	9,000
Salaries	Salaries expense	$ 54,000
	Salaries payable, January 1	10,000
	Salaries payable, December 31	8,000
Sales	Revenue from sales	$180,000
	Accounts receivable, January 1	12,000
	Accounts receivable, December 31	7,000

Instructions

In each case, compute the amount that should be reported in the operating activities section of the statement of cash flows under the direct method.

E13-12 Presented here is 1998 information for **PepsiCo, Inc.** and **The Coca-Cola Company:**

Compare two companies by using cash-based ratios.
(SO 5)

($ in millions)	PepsiCo	Coca-Cola
Cash provided by operations	$ 3,211	$ 3,433
Average current liabilities	6,085	6,175
Average total liabilities	14,712	10,175
Net income	1,993	3,533
Sales	22,348	18,813

Instructions

Using the cash-based ratios presented in this chapter, compare the (a) liquidity, (b) solvency, and (c) profitability of the two companies.

Problems: Set A

Prepare the operating activities section—indirect method.
(SO 4a)

P13-1A The income statement of Afghan Whigs Company is presented here:

AFGHAN WHIGS COMPANY
Income Statement
For the Year Ended November 30, 2001

Sales		$7,200,000
Cost of goods sold		
Beginning inventory	$1,900,000	
Purchases	4,400,000	
Goods available for sale	6,300,000	
Ending inventory	1,400,000	
Total cost of goods sold		4,900,000
Gross profit		2,300,000
Operating expenses		
Selling expenses	450,000	
Administrative expenses	600,000	1,050,000
Net income		$1,250,000

Additional information:
1. Accounts receivable increased $200,000 during the year.
2. Prepaid expenses increased $150,000 during the year.
3. Accounts payable to suppliers of merchandise decreased $300,000 during the year.
4. Accrued expenses payable decreased $100,000 during the year.
5. Administrative expenses include depreciation expense of $90,000.

Instructions
Prepare the operating activities section of the statement of cash flows for the year ended November 30, 2001, for Afghan Whigs Company, using the indirect method.

Prepare the operating activities section—direct method.
(SO 4b)

P13-2A Data for Afghan Whigs Company are presented in P13–1A.

Instructions
Prepare the operating activities section of the statement of cash flows using the direct method.

Prepare the operating activities section—direct method.
(SO 4b)

P13-3A Counting Crows Company's income statement contained the condensed information below:

COUNTING CROWS COMPANY
Income Statement
For the Year Ended December 31, 2001

Revenues		$970,000
Operating expenses, excluding depreciation	$624,000	
Depreciation expense	60,000	
Loss on sale of equipment	12,000	696,000
Income before income taxes		274,000
Income tax expense		40,000
Net income		$234,000

Counting Crow's balance sheet contained these comparative data at December 31:

	2001	2000
Accounts receivable	$67,000	$55,000
Accounts payable	41,000	33,000
Income taxes payable	11,000	9,000

Accounts payable pertain to operating expenses.

Instructions
Prepare the operating activities section of the statement of cash flows using the direct method.

P13-4A   Data for Counting Crows Company are presented in P13-3A.

Prepare the operating activities section—indirect method.
(SO 4a)

Instructions

Prepare the operating activities section of the statement of cash flows using the indirect method.

P13-5A   These are the financial statements of Korn Company:

Prepare a statement of cash flows—indirect method, and compute cash-based ratios.
(SO 4a, 5)

KORN COMPANY
Comparative Balance Sheet
December 31

Assets	2001	2000
Cash	$ 29,000	$ 20,000
Accounts receivable	38,000	14,000
Merchandise inventory	27,000	20,000
Property, plant, and equipment	60,000	78,000
Accumulated depreciation	(30,000)	(24,000)
Total	$124,000	$108,000

Liabilities and Stockholders' Equity		
Accounts payable	$ 29,000	$ 15,000
Income taxes payable	7,000	8,000
Bonds payable	27,000	33,000
Common stock	18,000	14,000
Retained earnings	43,000	38,000
Total	$124,000	$108,000

KORN COMPANY
Income Statement
For the Year Ended December 31, 2001

Sales		$242,000
Cost of goods sold		180,000
Gross profit		62,000
Selling expenses	$18,000	
Administrative expenses	6,000	24,000
Income from operations		38,000
Interest expense		2,000
Income before income taxes		36,000
Income tax expense		4,000
Net income		$ 32,000

The following additional data were provided:
1. Dividends declared and paid were $27,000.
2. During the year equipment was sold for $8,500 cash. This equipment cost $18,000 originally and had a book value of $8,500 at the time of sale.
3. All depreciation expense is in the selling expense category.
4. All sales and purchases are on account.

Instructions

(a) Prepare a statement of cash flows using the indirect method.
(b) Compute these cash-basis measures:
   (1) Current cash debt coverage ratio.
   (2) Cash return on sales ratio.
   (3) Cash debt coverage ratio.
   (4) Free cash flow.

P13-6A   Data for Korn Company are presented in P13-5A. Further analysis reveals the following:
1. Accounts payable pertain to merchandise suppliers.
2. All operating expenses except for depreciation were paid in cash.

Prepare a statement of cash flows—direct method, and compute cash-based ratios.
(SO 4b, 5)

Instructions

(a) Prepare a statement of cash flows for Korn Company using the direct method.

(b) Compute these cash-basis measures:

    (1) Current cash debt coverage ratio.

    (2) Cash return on sales ratio.

    (3) Cash debt coverage ratio.

    (4) Free cash flow.

Prepare a statement of cash flows—indirect method.
(SO 4a)

P13-7A Condensed financial data of Ramones Inc. follow.

RAMONES INC.
Comparative Balance Sheet
December 31

Assets	2001	2000
Cash	$ 97,800	$ 48,400
Accounts receivable	95,800	33,000
Inventories	112,500	102,850
Prepaid expenses	18,400	6,000
Investments	113,000	94,000
Plant assets	270,000	242,500
Accumulated depreciation	(50,000)	(52,000)
Total	$657,500	$474,750

Liabilities and Stockholders' Equity		
Accounts payable	$102,000	$ 67,300
Accrued expenses payable	16,500	17,000
Bonds payable	85,000	110,000
Common stock	220,000	175,000
Retained earnings	234,000	105,450
Total	$657,500	$474,750

RAMONES INC.
Income Statement Data
For the Year Ended December 31, 2001

Sales		$392,780
Less:		
Cost of goods sold	$135,460	
Operating expenses, excluding		
depreciation	12,410	
Depreciation expense	46,500	
Income taxes	7,280	
Interest expense	4,730	
Loss on sale of plant assets	7,500	213,880
Net income		$178,900

Additional information:

1. New plant assets costing $85,000 were purchased for cash during the year.
2. Old plant assets having an original cost of $57,500 were sold for $1,500 cash.
3. Bonds matured and were paid off at face value for cash.
4. A cash dividend of $50,350 was declared and paid during the year.

Instructions

Prepare a statement of cash flows using the indirect method.

Prepare a statement of cash flows—direct method.
(SO 4b)

P13-8A Data for Ramones Inc. are presented in P13–7A. Further analysis reveals that accounts payable pertain to merchandise creditors.

Instructions

Prepare a statement of cash flows for Ramones Inc. using the direct method.

Prepare a statement of cash flows—indirect method.
(SO 4a)

P13-9A This comparative balance sheet is for Oleander Company as of December 31:

OLEANDER COMPANY
Comparative Balance Sheet
December 31

Assets	2001	2000
Cash	$ 81,000	$ 45,000
Accounts receivable	47,500	62,000
Inventory	151,450	142,000
Prepaid expenses	16,780	21,000
Land	90,000	130,000
Equipment	228,000	155,000
Accumulated depreciation—equipment	(45,000)	(35,000)
Building	200,000	200,000
Accumulated depreciation—building	(60,000)	(40,000)
Total	$709,730	$680,000

Liabilities and Stockholders' Equity		
Accounts payable	$ 63,730	$ 40,000
Bonds payable	260,000	300,000
Common stock, $1 par	200,000	160,000
Retained earnings	186,000	180,000
Total	$709,730	$680,000

Additional information:
1. Operating expenses include depreciation expense of $42,000 and charges from prepaid expenses of $4,220.
2. Land was sold for cash at book value.
3. Cash dividends of $32,000 were paid.
4. Net income for 2001 was $38,000.
5. Equipment was purchased for $95,000 cash. In addition, equipment costing $22,000 with a book value of $10,000 was sold for $8,100 cash.
6. Bonds were converted at face value by issuing 40,000 shares of $1 par value common stock.

Instructions
Prepare a statement of cash flows for the year ended December 31, 2001, using the indirect method.

PROBLEMS: SET B

P13-1B   The income statement of Dishwalla Company is presented here:

Prepare the operating activities section—indirect method.
(SO 4a)

DISHWALLA COMPANY
Income Statement
For the Year Ended December 31, 2001

Sales		$5,400,000
Cost of goods sold		
Beginning inventory	$1,700,000	
Purchases	3,430,000	
Goods available for sale	5,130,000	
Ending inventory	1,920,000	
Total cost of goods sold		3,210,000
Gross profit		2,190,000
Operating expenses		
Selling expenses	400,000	
Administrative expense	525,000	
Depreciation expense	125,000	
Amortization expense	30,000	1,080,000
Net income		$1,110,000

Additional information:
1. Accounts receivable decreased $510,000 during the year.
2. Prepaid expenses increased $170,000 during the year.
3. Accounts payable to merchandise suppliers increased $50,000 during the year.
4. Accrued expenses payable increased $180,000 during the year.

Instructions
Prepare the operating activities section of the statement of cash flows for the year ended December 31, 2001, for Dishwalla Company, using the indirect method.

Prepare the operating activities section—direct method.
(SO 4b)

P13-2B Data for Dishwalla Company are presented in P13-1B.

Instructions
Prepare the operating activities section of the statement of cash flows using the direct method.

Prepare the operating activities section—direct method.
(SO 4b)

P13-3B The income statement of Wilco Inc. reported the following condensed information:

WILCO INC.
Income Statement
For the Year Ended December 31, 2001

Revenues	$545,000
Operating expenses	370,000
Income from operations	175,000
Income tax expense	47,000
Net income	$128,000

Wilco's balance sheet contained these comparative data at December 31:

	2001	2000
Accounts receivable	$50,000	$60,000
Accounts payable	30,000	41,000
Income taxes payable	8,000	4,000

Wilco has no depreciable assets. Accounts payable pertain to operating expenses.

Instructions
Prepare the operating activities section of the statement of cash flows using the direct method.

Prepare the operating activities section—indirect method.
(SO 4a)

P13-4B Data for Wilco are presented in P13-3B.

Instructions
Prepare the operating activities section of the statement of cash flows using the indirect method.

Prepare a statement of cash flows—indirect method, and compute cash-based ratios.
(SO 4a, 5)

P13-5B Here are the financial statements of 2 PAC Company:

2 PAC COMPANY
Comparative Balance Sheet
December 31

Assets		2001		2000
Cash		$ 26,000		$ 33,000
Accounts receivable		28,000		14,000
Merchandise inventory		38,000		25,000
Property, plant, and equipment	$70,000		$78,000	
Less accumulated depreciation	(30,000)	40,000	(24,000)	54,000
Total		$132,000		$126,000

Liabilities and Stockholders' Equity		2001		2000
Accounts payable		$ 29,000		$ 43,000
Income taxes payable		25,000		20,000
Bonds payable		20,000		10,000
Common stock		25,000		25,000
Retained earnings		33,000		28,000
Total		$132,000		$126,000

2 PAC COMPANY
Income Statement
For the Year Ended December 31, 2001

Sales		$286,000
Cost of goods sold		194,000
Gross profit		92,000
Selling expenses	$28,000	
Administrative expenses	6,000	34,000
Income from operations		58,000
Interest expense		7,000
Income before income taxes		51,000
Income tax expense		7,000
Net income		$ 44,000

The following additional data were provided:
1. Dividends of $39,000 were declared and paid.
2. During the year equipment was sold for $10,000 cash. This equipment cost $15,000 originally and had a book value of $10,000 at the time of sale.
3. All depreciation expense, $11,000, is in the selling expense category.
4. All sales and purchases are on account.
5. Additional equipment was purchased for $7,000 cash.

Instructions
(a) Prepare a statement of cash flows using the indirect method.
(b) Compute these cash-basis measures:
 (1) Current cash debt coverage ratio.
 (2) Cash return on sales ratio.
 (3) Cash debt coverage ratio.
 (4) Free cash flow.

P13-6B   Data for 2 PAC Company are presented in P13-5B. Further analysis reveals the following:

Prepare a statement of cash flows—direct method, and compute cash-based ratios.
(SO 4b, 5)

1. Accounts payable pertains to merchandise creditors.
2. All operating expenses except for depreciation are paid in cash.

Instructions
(a) Prepare a statement of cash flows using the direct method.
(b) Compute these cash-basis measures:
 (1) Current cash debt coverage ratio.
 (2) Cash return on sales ratio.
 (3) Cash debt coverage ratio.
 (4) Free cash flow.

P13-7B   Condensed financial data of Dru Hill Company follow.

Prepare a statement of cash flows—indirect method.
(SO 4a)

DRU HILL COMPANY
Comparative Balance Sheet
December 31

Assets	2001	2000
Cash	$ 92,700	$ 47,250
Accounts receivable	90,800	37,000
Inventories	121,900	102,650
Investments	84,500	107,000
Plant assets	290,000	205,000
Accumulated depreciation	(49,500)	(40,000)
Total	$630,400	$458,900

Liabilities and Stockholders' Equity		
Accounts payable	$ 52,700	$ 48,280
Accrued expenses payable	12,100	18,830
Bonds payable	140,000	70,000
Common stock	250,000	200,000
Retained earnings	175,600	121,790
Total	$630,400	$458,900

DRU HILL COMPANY
Income Statement Data
For the Year Ended December 31, 2001

Sales		$297,500
Gain on sale of plant assets		8,750
		306,250
Less:		
Cost of goods sold	$99,460	
Operating expenses, excluding		
depreciation expense	14,670	
Depreciation expense	58,700	
Income taxes	7,270	
Interest expense	2,940	183,040
Net income		$123,210

Additional information:
1. New plant assets costing $141,000 were purchased for cash during the year.
2. Investments were sold at cost.
3. Plant assets costing $56,000 were sold for $15,550, resulting in a gain of $8,750.
4. A cash dividend of $69,400 was declared and paid during the year.

Instructions
Prepare a statement of cash flows using the indirect method.

Prepare a statement of cash flows—direct method.
(SO 4b)

P13-8B   Data for Dru Hill Company are presented in P13-7B. Further analysis reveals that accounts payable pertain to merchandise creditors.

Instructions
Prepare a statement of cash flows for Dru Hill Company using the direct method.

Prepare a statement of cash flows—indirect method.
(SO 4a)

P13-9B   Presented here is the comparative balance sheet for MXPX Company at December 31:

MXPX COMPANY
Comparative Balance Sheet
December 31

Assets	2001	2000
Cash	$ 30,000	$ 57,000
Accounts receivable	77,000	64,000
Inventory	192,000	140,000
Prepaid expenses	12,140	16,540
Land	105,000	150,000
Equipment	200,000	175,000
Accumulated depreciation—equipment	(60,000)	(42,000)
Building	250,000	250,000
Accumulated depreciation—building	(75,000)	(50,000)
Total	$731,140	$760,540

Liabilities and Stockholders' Equity	2001	2000
Accounts payable	$ 63,000	$ 45,000
Bonds payable	235,000	265,000
Common stock, $1 par	280,000	250,000
Retained earnings	153,140	200,540
Total	$731,140	$760,540

Additional information:
1. Operating expenses include depreciation expense $70,000 and charges from prepaid expenses of $4,400.
2. Land was sold for cash at cost.
3. Cash dividends of $74,290 were paid.
4. Net income for 2001 was $26,890.

5. Equipment was purchased for $65,000 cash. In addition, equipment costing $40,000 with a book value of $13,000 was sold for $14,000 cash.
6. Bonds were converted at face value by issuing 30,000 shares of $1 par value common stock.

Instructions
Prepare a statement of cash flows for 2001 using the indirect method.

◆ BROADENING YOUR PERSPECTIVE

FINANCIAL REPORTING AND ANALYSIS

FINANCIAL REPORTING PROBLEM: *Tootsie Roll Industries, Inc.*

BYP13-1 The financial statements of **Tootsie Roll Industries** are presented in Appendix A.

Instructions
Answer these questions:

(a) What was the amount of net cash provided by operating activities for 1998? For 1997? What were the primary causes of any significant changes in cash from operations between 1997 and 1998?
(b) What was the amount of increase or decrease in cash and cash equivalents for the year ended December 31, 1998?
(c) Which method of computing net cash provided by operating activities does Tootsie Roll use?
(d) From your analysis of the 1998 statement of cash flows, was the change in accounts receivable a decrease or an increase? Was the change in inventories a decrease or an increase? Was the change in accounts payable a decrease or an increase?
(e) What was the total net cash used for investing activities for 1998?
(f) What was the amount of interest paid in 1998? What was the amount of income taxes paid in 1998?

COMPARATIVE ANALYSIS PROBLEM: *Tootsie Roll vs. Hershey Foods*

BYP13-2 The financial statements of **Hershey Foods** are presented in Appendix B, following the financial statements for **Tootsie Roll Industries** in Appendix A.

Instructions
(a) Based on the information in these financial statements, compute these 1998 ratios for each company:
    (1) Current cash debt coverage.
    (2) Cash return on sales.
    (3) Cash debt coverage.
(b) What conclusions concerning the management of cash can be drawn from these data?

RESEARCH CASE

BYP13-3 The March 21, 1997, issue of *The Wall Street Journal* contains an article by Greg Ip entitled "Cash Flow Rise Could Be Prop to Stock Prices."

Instructions
Read the article and answer the following questions:

(a) How is "free cash flow" defined in the article?
(b) What was the recent trend in free cash flow relative to earnings in the 1990s?
(c) How are stock prices related to companies' cash flows?
(d) Are there any negatives related to large free cash flows?

INTERPRETING FINANCIAL STATEMENTS

BYP13-4 The incredible growth of **Amazon.com** has put fear into the hearts of traditional retailers. Amazon.com's stock price has soared to amazing levels. However, it is often pointed out in the financial press that the company has never reported a profit. The following financial information is taken from the 1998 financial statements of Amazon.com.

($ in thousands)	1998	1997
Current assets	$424,254	$137,709
Total assets	648,460	149,844
Current liabilities	161,575	44,551
Total liabilities	509,715	121,253
Cash provided by operations	31,035	687
Capital expenditures	28,333	7,603
Dividends paid	0	0
Net loss	(124,546)	(31,020)
Sales	609,996	147,787

Instructions

(a) Calculate the current ratio and current cash debt coverage ratio for Amazon.com for 1998 and discuss its liquidity.

(b) Calculate the cash debt coverage ratio and the debt to total assets ratio for Amazon.com for 1998 and discuss its solvency.

(c) Calculate free cash flow and the capital expenditure ratio for Amazon.com for 1998 and discuss its ability to finance expansion from internally generated cash. Thus far Amazon.com has avoided purchasing large warehouses; instead, it has used those of others. It is possible, however, that in order to increase customer satisfaction the company may have to build its own warehouses. If this happens, how might your impression of its ability to finance expansion change?

(d) Discuss any potential implications of the change in Amazon.com's cash provided by operations, and its net loss from 1997 to 1998.

(e) Based on your findings in parts (a) through (d), can you conclude whether or not Amazon.com's amazing stock price is justified?

A GLOBAL FOCUS

BYP13-5 The statement of cash flows has become a commonly provided financial statement by companies throughout the world. It is interesting to note, however, that its format does vary across countries. The following statement of cash flows is from the 1998 financial statements of French building materials manufacturer **Saint-Gobain Group**

SAINT-GOBAIN

SAINT-GOBAIN GROUP Consolidated Statements of Cash Flows		
(in millions of euro)	1998	1997
Cash flow from operating activities		
Net operating income	1,096	920
Profit on sale of non-current assets	(394)	(307)
Depreciation and amortization (note 14)	1,136	1,037
Dividends from associated companies	74	43
Sources from operations	**1,912**	**1,693**
(Increase) decrease in stocks	(174)	(41)
(Increase) decrease in trade accounts receivable	(59)	(241)
Increase (decrease) in trade accounts payable	79	79
Changes in income taxes payable and deferred taxes	14	3
Change in provisions	(48)	4
Cash provided by operating activities	**1,724**	**1,497**

Cash flow from investing activities		
Acquisition of fixed assets	**(1,288)**	**(1,353)**
Investments in consolidated companies (note 2)	(1,349)	(850)
Investments in unconsolidated companies	(382)	(244)
Total expenditure on fixed assets and investments	**(3,019)**	**(2,447)**
Cash (debt) acquired (note 2)	(19)	(17)
Acquisition of treasury stock	(344)	(3)
Disposal of fixed and intangible assets	25	55
Disposal of investments	1,107	814
(Cash) debt disposed of (note 2)	3	(125)
(Increase) decrease in deferred charges and other intangible assets	(68)	(48)
(Increase) decrease in deposits, long term receivables	9	31
(Increase) decrease in receivables related to investing activities	(124)	37
Cash used for investing activities	**(2,430)**	**(1,703)**
Cash flow from financing activities		
Issue of share capital	105	265
Minority interests in share capital increases of subsidiaries	4	4
(Decrease) increase in long term debt	132	541
Dividends paid	(248)	(221)
Dividends paid to minority shareholders of consolidated subsidiaries	(44)	(82)
Cash provided by (used for) financing activities	**(51)**	**507**
Net effect of exchange rate fluctuations on cash and cash equivalents	(9)	(39)
Increase (decrease) in cash and cash equivalents (net)	**(766)**	**262**
Net cash and cash equivalents at the beginning of the year	(92)	(354)
Net cash and cash equivalents at the end of the year	**(858)**	**(92)**

Instructions

(a) What similarities to U.S. cash flow statements do you notice in terms of general format, as well as terminology?

(b) What differences do you notice in terms of general format, as well as terminology?

(c) Using the data provided in the statement of cash flows, compute (1) free cash flow and (2) capital expenditure ratio. Does the difference in the format of the statement or the terminology complicate your efforts to calculate these measures?

FINANCIAL ANALYSIS ON THE WEB

BYP13-6 *Purpose:* Locate SEC filing in Edgar Database.

Address: http://www.sec.gov/index.html or go to www.wiley.com/college/kimmel

Steps:

1. From the SEC homepage, choose **Edgar Database**.
2. Choose **Search the Edgar Database**.
3. Choose **Current Event Analysis**.
4. Select a company from the Edgar Daily Report.

Instructions
Answer the following questions:
(a) What form type did you retrieve?
(b) What is the company's name?
(c) What is the Standard Industrial Classification?
(d) What period does this report cover?
(e) In what state or jurisidiction is the organization?

BYP13-7 *Purpose:* Use the Internet to view SEC filings.

Address: http://www.yahoo.com or go to www.wiley.com/college/kimmel

Steps:

1. From the Yahoo homepage, choose **Stock Quotes**.
2. Enter a company's stock symbol or use "Symbol Lookup."
3. Choose **Get Quotes**.
4. Choose **SEC filings** (this will take you to Yahoo-Edgar Online).

Instructions
Answer the following questions:
(a) What company did you select?
(b) What is its stock symbol?
(c) What other recent SEC filings are available for your viewing?
(d) Which filing is the most recent? What is the date?

CRITICAL THINKING

GROUP DECISION CASE

BYP13-8 Greg Rhoda and Debra Sondgeroth are examining the following statement of cash flows for K.K. Bean Trading Company for the year ended January 31, 2001:

K.K. BEAN TRADING COMPANY
Statement of Cash Flows
For the Year Ended January 31, 2001

Sources of cash	
From sales of merchandise	$370,000
From sale of capital stock	420,000
From sale of investment (purchased below)	80,000
From depreciation	55,000
From issuance of note for truck	20,000
From interest on investments	6,000
Total sources of cash	951,000
Uses of cash	
For purchase of fixtures and equipment	340,000
For merchandise purchased for resale	258,000
For operating expenses (including depreciation)	160,000
For purchase of investment	75,000
For purchase of truck by issuance of note	20,000
For purchase of treasury stock	10,000
For interest on note payable	3,000
Total uses of cash	866,000
Net increase in cash	$ 85,000

Greg claims that K.K. Bean's statement of cash flows is an excellent portrayal of a superb first year with cash increasing $85,000. Debra replies that it was not a superb first year—but, rather, that the year was an operating failure, that the statement is presented incorrectly, and that $85,000 is not the actual increase in cash. The cash balance at the beginning of the year was $140,000.

Instructions
With the class divided into groups, answer the following:
(a) With whom do you agree, Greg or Debra? Explain your position.
(b) Using the data provided, prepare a statement of cash flows in proper form using the indirect method. The only noncash items in the income statement are depreciation and the gain from the sale of the investment.

COMMUNICATION ACTIVITY

BYP13-9 Arnold Byte, the owner-president of Computer Services Company, is unfamiliar with the statement of cash flows that you, as his accountant, prepared. He asks for further explanation.

Instructions
Write him a brief memo explaining the form and content of the statement of cash flows as shown in Illustration 13-12.

ETHICS CASE

BYP13-10 Puebla Corporation is a medium-sized wholesaler of automotive parts. It has ten stockholders who have been paid a total of $1 million in cash dividends for 8 consecutive years. The board of directors' policy requires that in order for this dividend to be declared, net cash provided by operating activities as reported in Puebla's current year's statement of cash flows must exceed $1 million. President and CEO Phil Monat's job is secure so long as he produces annual operating cash flows to support the usual dividend.

At the end of the current year, controller Rick Rodgers presents president Monat with some disappointing news: The net cash provided by operating activities is calculated by the indirect method to be only $970,000. The president says to Rick, "We must get that amount above $1 million. Isn't there some way to increase operating cash flow by another $30,000?" Rick answers, "These figures were prepared by my assistant. I'll go back to my office and see what I can do." The president replies, "I know you won't let me down, Rick."

Upon close scrutiny of the statement of cash flows, Rick concludes that he can get the operating cash flows above $1 million by reclassifying a $60,000, 2-year note payable listed in the financing activities section as Proceeds from bank loan—$60,000." He will report the note instead as "Increase in payables—$60,000" and treat it as an adjustment of net income in the operating activities section. He returns to the president, saying, "You can tell the board to declare their usual dividend. Our net cash flow provided by operating activities is $1,030,000." "Good man, Rick! I knew I could count on you," exults the president.

Instructions
(a) Who are the stakeholders in this situation?
(b) Was there anything unethical about the president's actions? Was there anything unethical about the controller's actions?
(c) Are the board members or anyone else likely to discover the misclassification?

Answers to Self-Study Questions
1. c   2. b   3. a   4. c   5. d   6. b   7. c   8. a   9. d
10. b   11. c   12. d   13. a   14. d   15. b

Answer to Tootsie Roll Review It Question 2, p. 606
Tootsie Roll has positive cash from operations that exceeds its net income. Its cash from operations far exceeded its investment needs, so it used its excess cash to retire debt and repurchase stock. Therefore, Tootsie Roll appears to be in the middle to late maturity phase.

14

Financial Analysis: The Big Picture

◆ STUDY OBJECTIVES

After studying this chapter, you should be able to:

1 Understand the concept of earning power and indicate how irregular items are presented.

2 Discuss the need for comparative analysis and identify the tools of financial statement analysis.

3 Explain and apply horizontal analysis.

4 Describe and apply vertical analysis.

5 Identify and compute ratios and describe their purpose and use in analyzing a company's liquidity, solvency, and profitability.

6 Discuss the limitations of financial statement analysis.

◆ **"FOLLOW THAT STOCK!"**

If you thought cab drivers with cell phones were scary, how about a cab driver with a trading desk in the front seat?

When a stoplight turns red or traffic backs up, New York City cabby Carlos Rubino morphs into a day trader, scanning real-time quotes of his favorite stocks as they spew across a PalmPilot mounted next to the steering wheel. "It's kind of stressful," he says. "But I like it."

Itching to know how a particular stock is doing? Mr. Rubino is happy to look up quotes for passengers. Yahoo!, Amazon.com, and America Online are the most requested ones. He even lets customers use his Hitachi Traveler laptop to send urgent e-mails from the back

seat. Aware of a new local law prohibiting cabbies from using cell phones while they're driving, Mr. Rubino extends that rule to his trading. "I stop the cab at the side of the road if I have to make a trade," he says. "Safety first."

Originally from São Paulo, Brazil, Mr. Rubino has been driving his cab since 1987, and started trading stocks a few years ago. His curiosity grew as he began to educate himself by reading business publications. The Wall Street brokers he picks up are usually impressed with his knowledge, he says. But the feeling generally isn't mutual. Some of them "don't know much," he says. "They buy what people tell them to buy—they're like a toll collector."

Mr. Rubino is an enigma to his fellow cab drivers. A lot of his colleagues say they want to trade too. "But cab drivers are a little cheap," he says. "The [real-time] quotes cost $100 a month. The wireless Internet access is $54 a month."

Will he give up his brokerage firm on wheels for a stationary job? Not likely. Though he claims a 70% return on his investments in recent months, he says he makes $1,300 and up a week driving his cab—more than he does trading. Besides, he adds, "Why go somewhere and have a boss?"

Source: Excerpted from Barbara Boydston, "With this Cab, People Jump in and Shout, "Follow that Stock!", *The Wall Street Journal,* August 18, 1999, p. C1.

An important lesson can be learned from the opening story: Experience is the best teacher. By now you have learned a significant amount about financial reporting by U.S. corporations. Using some of the basic decision tools presented in this book, you can perform a rudimentary analysis on any U.S. company and draw basic conclusions about its financial health. Although it would not be wise for you to bet your life savings on a company's stock relying solely on your current level of knowledge, we strongly encourage you to practice your new skills wherever possible. Only with practice will you improve your ability to interpret financial numbers.

Before unleashing you on the world of high finance, we will present a few more important concepts and techniques, as well as provide you with one last comprehensive review of corporate financial statements. We use all of the decision tools presented in this text to analyze a single company—Kellogg Company, the world's leading producer of ready-to-eat cereal products.

The content and organization of this chapter are as follows:

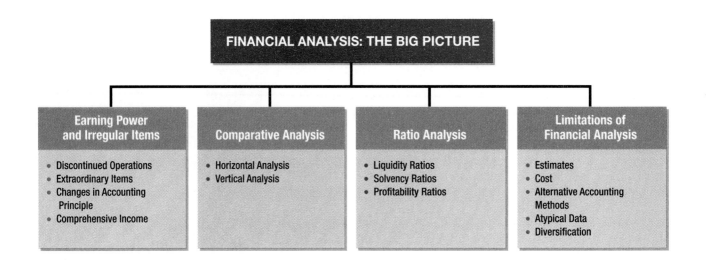

FINANCIAL ANALYSIS: THE BIG PICTURE

Earning Power and Irregular Items	Comparative Analysis	Ratio Analysis	Limitations of Financial Analysis
• Discontinued Operations • Extraordinary Items • Changes in Accounting Principle • Comprehensive Income	• Horizontal Analysis • Vertical Analysis	• Liquidity Ratios • Solvency Ratios • Profitability Ratios	• Estimates • Cost • Alternative Accounting Methods • Atypical Data • Diversification

*E*ARNING POWER AND IRREGULAR ITEMS

STUDY OBJECTIVE

1

Understand the concept of earning power and indicate how irregular items are presented.

Ultimately, the value of a company is a function of its future cash flows. When analysts use this year's net income to estimate future cash flows, they must make sure that this year's net income does not include irregular revenues, expenses, gains, or losses. Net income adjusted for irregular items is referred to as **earning power**. **Earning power is the most likely level of income to be obtained in the future**. Earning power differs from actual net income by the amount of irregular revenues, expenses, gains, and losses included in this year's net income.

Users are interested in earning power because it helps them derive an estimate of future earnings without the "noise" of irregular items. For example, suppose Rye Corporation reports that this year's net income is $500,000 but included in that amount is a once-in-a-lifetime gain of $400,000. In estimating next year's net income for Rye Corporation, we would likely ignore this $400,000 gain and estimate that next year's net income will be in the neighborhood of $100,000.

That is, based on this year's results, the company's earning power is roughly $100,000. Therefore, identifying irregular items is important if you are going to use reported earnings to estimate a company's value.

As an aid in the determination of earning power (or regular income), irregular items are identified by type on the income statement. Three types of irregular items are reported:

1. Discontinued operations
2. Extraordinary items
3. Changes in accounting principle

All these irregular items are reported net of income taxes; that is, the applicable income tax expense or tax savings is shown for income before income taxes and for each of the listed irregular items. The general concept is "Let the tax follow income or loss."

DISCONTINUED OPERATIONS

To downsize its operations, General Dynamics Corp. sold its missile business to Hughes Aircraft Co. for $450 million. In its income statement, General Dynamics was required to report the sale in a separate section entitled "Discontinued operations." **Discontinued operations** refer to the disposal of a significant segment of a business, such as the elimination of a major class of customers or an entire activity. Thus, the decision by Singer Co. to end its manufacture and sale of computers and the decision to close all overseas offices and terminate all foreign sales were both reported as discontinued operations. The phasing out of a model or part of a line of business, however, is *not* considered to be a disposal of a segment.

When the disposal of a significant segment occurs, the income statement should report both income from continuing operations and income (or loss) from discontinued operations. **The income (loss) from discontinued operations consists of the income (loss) from operations and the gain (loss) on disposal of the segment**. To illustrate, assume that Rozek Inc. has revenues of $2.5 million and expenses of $1.7 million from continuing operations in 2001. The company therefore has income before income taxes of $800,000. During 2001 the company discontinued and sold its unprofitable chemical division. The loss in 2001 from chemical operations (net of $60,000 taxes) was $140,000, and the loss on disposal of the chemical division (net of $30,000 taxes) was $70,000. Assuming a 30% tax rate on income before income taxes, we show the income statement presentation in Illustration 14-1.

ROZEK INC. Income Statement (partial) For the Year Ended December 31, 2001		
Income before income taxes		$800,000
Income tax expense		240,000
Income from continuing operations		560,000
Discontinued operations		
Loss from operations of chemical division,		
net of $60,000 income tax saving	$140,000	
Loss from disposal of chemical division, net of		
$30,000 income tax saving	70,000	(210,000)
Net income		$350,000

Illustration 14-1 Statement presentation of discontinued operations

Note that the caption "Income from continuing operations" is used and the section "Discontinued operations" is added. **Within the new section, both the operating loss and the loss on disposal are reported net of applicable income taxes.** This presentation clearly indicates the separate effects of continuing operations and discontinued operations on net income.

DECISION TOOLKIT

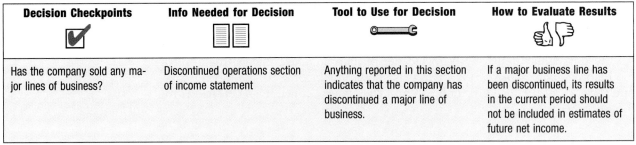

Decision Checkpoints	Info Needed for Decision	Tool to Use for Decision	How to Evaluate Results
Has the company sold any major lines of business?	Discontinued operations section of income statement	Anything reported in this section indicates that the company has discontinued a major line of business.	If a major business line has been discontinued, its results in the current period should not be included in estimates of future net income.

EXTRAORDINARY ITEMS

Extraordinary items are events and transactions that meet two conditions: They are **unusual in nature** and **infrequent in occurrence**. To be considered *unusual,* the item should be abnormal and only incidentally related to the customary activities of the entity. To be regarded as *infrequent,* the event or transaction should not be reasonably expected to recur in the foreseeable future. Both criteria must be evaluated in terms of the environment in which the entity operates. Thus, Weyerhaeuser Co. reported the $36 million in damages to its timberland caused by the eruption of Mount St. Helens as an extraordinary item because the event was both unusual and infrequent. In contrast, Florida Citrus Company does not report frost damage to its citrus crop as an extraordinary item because frost damage is not viewed as infrequent.

Helpful Hint Ordinary gains and losses are reported at pretax amounts in arriving at income before income taxes.

Extraordinary items are reported net of taxes in a separate section of the income statement immediately below discontinued operations. To illustrate, assume that in 2001 a revolutionary foreign government expropriated property held as an investment by Rozek Inc. If the loss is $70,000 before applicable income taxes of $21,000, the income statement presentation will show a deduction of $49,000, as in Illustration 14-2.

Illustration 14-2 Statement presentation of extraordinary items

ROZEK INC. Income Statement (partial) For the Year Ended December 31, 2001		
Income before income taxes		$800,000
Income tax expense		240,000
Income from continuing operations		560,000
Discontinued operations		
Loss from operations of chemical division, net of $60,000 income tax saving	$140,000	
Loss from disposal of chemical division, net of $30,000 income tax saving	70,000	(210,000)
Income before extraordinary item		350,000
Extraordinary item		
Expropriation of investment, net of $21,000 income tax saving		(49,000)
Net income		$301,000

As illustrated, the caption "Income before extraordinary item" is added immediately before the listing of extraordinary items. This presentation clearly indicates the effect of the extraordinary item on net income. If there were no discontinued operations, the third line of the income statement in Illustration 14-2 would be "Income before extraordinary item."

If a transaction or event meets one, but not both, of the criteria for an extraordinary item, it should be reported in a separate line item in the upper half of the income statement, rather than being reported in the bottom half as an extraordinary item. Usually these items are reported under either "Other revenues and gains" or "Other expenses and losses" at their gross amount (not net of tax). This is true, for example, of gains (losses) resulting from the sale of property, plant, and equipment, as explained in Chapter 9. Illustration 14-3 shows the appropriate classification of extraordinary and ordinary items.

Illustration 14-3 Classification of extraordinary and ordinary items

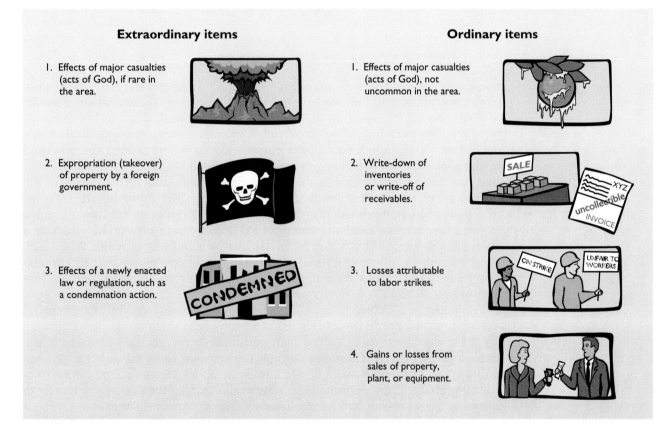

Extraordinary items

1. Effects of major casualties (acts of God), if rare in the area.

2. Expropriation (takeover) of property by a foreign government.

3. Effects of a newly enacted law or regulation, such as a condemnation action.

Ordinary items

1. Effects of major casualties (acts of God), not uncommon in the area.

2. Write-down of inventories or write-off of receivables.

3. Losses attributable to labor strikes.

4. Gains or losses from sales of property, plant, or equipment.

Kellogg, for example, did not report any extraordinary items in its 1997 or 1998 income statements. It did, however, incur significant charges as the result of "restructuring" efforts to reduce costs. These restructuring charges did not meet the criteria required for extraordinary item classification. Instead, Kellogg reported them as "Nonrecurring charges"—of $184.1 million in 1997 and $70.5 million in 1998—in the upper half (income from operations section) of its income statement. The title "nonrecurring" suggests that the charges occur infrequently. In analyzing Kellogg's results, we must decide whether to use its income as reported, or instead to assume that these charges are, in fact, not representative of the company's future earning power. If we assume they are not representative of the company's earning power, we would add them back to net income (after consideration of their tax impact) to estimate next year's income. Further investigation reveals that the company has had "nonrecurring charges" in every year except one since 1993. We therefore conclude that these charges are not as "infrequent" as the name "nonrecurring" might imply. As a consequence, we use net income as it was reported by the company for all subsequent analysis.

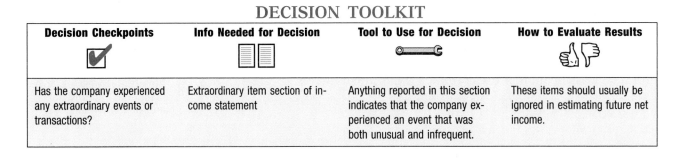

DECISION TOOLKIT

Decision Checkpoints	Info Needed for Decision	Tool to Use for Decision	How to Evaluate Results
Has the company experienced any extraordinary events or transactions?	Extraordinary item section of income statement	Anything reported in this section indicates that the company experienced an event that was both unusual and infrequent.	These items should usually be ignored in estimating future net income.

CHANGES IN ACCOUNTING PRINCIPLE

For ease of comparison, financial statements are expected to be prepared on a basis **consistent** with that used for the preceding period. That is, where a choice of accounting principles is available, the principle initially chosen should be applied consistently from period to period. A change in accounting principle occurs when the principle used in the current year is different from the one used in the preceding year. A change is permitted, when (1) management can show that the new principle is preferable to the old principle and (2) the effects of the change are clearly disclosed in the income statement. Two examples are a change in depreciation methods (such as declining-balance to straight-line) and a change in inventory costing methods (such as FIFO to average cost). The effect of a change in an accounting principle on net income can be significant. When U.S. West, one of the six regional Bell telephone companies, changed the depreciation method for its telecommunications equipment, it posted a $3.2 billion loss (net of tax).

Sometimes a change in accounting principle is mandated by the Financial Accounting Standards Board (FASB). An example is the change in accounting for postretirement benefits other than pensions. In its income statement in the change period, Owens-Corning Fiberglas Corporation reported a charge of $227 million, net of income taxes of $117 million, under "Cumulative effect of accounting change." An accompanying note explained that the charge resulted from adopting the new standard for its domestic postretirement plans.

A change in an accounting principle affects reporting in two ways:

1. The new principle should be used in reporting the results of operations of the current year.
2. The cumulative effect of the change on all prior-year income statements should be disclosed net of applicable taxes in a special section immediately preceding Net Income.

To illustrate, we will assume that at the beginning of 2001, Rozek Inc. changes from the straight-line method to the declining-balance method for equipment that was purchased on January 1, 1998. The cumulative effect on prior-year income statements (statements for 1998–2000) is to increase depreciation expense and decrease income before income taxes by $24,000. If there is a 30% tax rate, the net-of-tax effect of the change is $16,800 ($24,000 × 70%). The income statement presentation is shown in Illustration 14-4.

ROZEK INC. Income Statement (partial) For the Year Ended December 31, 2001		
Income before income taxes		$800,000
Income tax expense		240,000
Income from continuing operations		560,000
Discontinued operations		
Loss from operations of chemical division, net of $60,000 income tax saving	$140,000	
Loss from disposal of chemical division, net of $30,000 income tax saving	70,000	(210,000)
Income before extraordinary item and cumulative effect of change in accounting principle		350,000
Extraordinary item		
Expropriation of investment, net of $21,000 income tax saving		(49,000)
Cumulative effect of change in accounting principle		
Effect on prior years of change in depreciation method, net of $7,200 income tax saving		**(16,800)**
Net income		$284,200

Illustration 14-4 Statement presentation of a change in accounting principle

The income statement for Rozek will also show depreciation expense for the current year. The amount is based on the new depreciation method. In this case the caption "Income before extraordinary item and cumulative effect of change in accounting principle" is inserted immediately following the section on discontinued operations. This presentation clearly indicates the cumulative effect of the change on prior years' income. If a company has neither discontinued operations nor extraordinary items, the caption "Income before cumulative effect of change in accounting principle" is used in place of "Income from continuing operations." A complete income statement showing all material items not typical of regular operations is presented in the Demonstration Problem on page 701.

In 1997 Kellogg reported an $18 million reduction in net income due to the cumulative effect of a change in the way it accounted for business process reengineering costs. In analyzing a company, we suggest eliminating any effect from a change in accounting principle (that is, using the amount of income before the change in accounting principle). So, in our subsequent analysis of Kellogg, we will eliminate this $18 million item.

In summary, in evaluating a company, it generally makes sense to eliminate all irregular items in estimating future earning power. In some cases you must decide whether certain information reported in the top half of the income statement should be ignored for analysis purposes, such as Kellogg's "nonrecurring" items.

DECISION TOOLKIT

Decision Checkpoints	Info Needed for Decision	Tool to Use for Decision	How to Evaluate Results
✔	▤▤	⌐━━━C	👍👎
Has the company changed any of its accounting policies?	Cumulative effect of change in accounting principle section of income statement	Anything reported in this section indicates that the company has changed an accounting policy during the current year.	The cumulative effect should be ignored in estimating the future net income.

COMPREHENSIVE INCOME

Most revenues, expenses, gains, and losses recognized during the period are included in income. However, over time, specific exceptions to this general practice have developed so that certain items now bypass income and are reported directly in stockholders' equity. For example, in Chapter 12 you learned that unrealized gains and losses on available-for-sale securities are not included in income, but rather are reported in the balance sheet as adjustments to stockholders' equity.

Why are these gains and losses on available-for-sale securities excluded from net income? Because disclosing them separately (1) reduces the volatility of net income due to fluctuations in fair value, yet (2) informs the financial statement user of the gain or loss that would be incurred if the securities were sold at fair value.

Many analysts have expressed concern that the number of items that bypass the income statement has increased significantly. They feel that this has reduced the usefulness of the income statement. To address this concern, the FASB now requires that, in addition to reporting net income, a company must also report comprehensive income. **Comprehensive income** includes all changes in stockholders' equity during a period except those resulting from investments by stockholders and distributions to stockholders. A number of alternative formats for reporting comprehensive income are allowed. The income statement of Tootsie Roll Industries in Appendix A provides an example of one format. These formats are discussed in advanced accounting courses.

BEFORE YOU GO ON...

◆ **Review It**

1. What is earning power?
2. What are irregular items and what effect might they have on the estimation of future earnings and future cash flows?
3. What amount did Tootsie Roll Industries report as "Other comprehensive earnings" in 1998? What was the percentage increase of Tootsie Roll's "Comprehensive earnings" over its "Net earnings"? The answer to this question is provided on page 723.

COMPARATIVE ANALYSIS

STUDY OBJECTIVE

2

Discuss the need for comparative analysis and identify the tools of financial statement analysis.

Any item reported in a financial statement has significance: Its inclusion indicates that the item exists at a given time and in a certain quantity. For example, when Kellogg Company reports $136.4 million of cash on its balance sheet, we know that Kellogg did have cash and that the quantity was $136.4 million. But whether that represents an increase over prior years, or whether it is adequate in relation to the company's needs, cannot be determined from the amount alone. The amount must be compared with other financial data to provide more information.

Throughout this book we have relied on three types of comparisons to improve the decision usefulness of financial information:

1. **Intracompany basis.** Comparisons within a company are often useful to detect changes in financial relationships and significant trends. For example, a comparison of Kellogg's current year's cash amount with the prior year's cash amount shows either an increase or a decrease. Likewise, a comparison of Kellogg's year-end cash amount with the amount of its total assets at year-end shows the proportion of total assets in the form of cash.

2. **Intercompany basis**.   Comparisons with other companies provide insight into a company's competitive position. For example, Kellogg's total sales for the year can be compared with the total sales of its competitors in the breakfast cereal area, such as Quaker Oats and General Mills.

3. **Industry averages**.   Comparisons with industry averages provide information about a company's relative position within the industry. For example, Kellogg's financial data can be compared with the averages for its industry compiled by financial ratings organizations such as Dun & Bradstreet, Moody's, and Standard & Poor's, or with information provided on the Internet by organizations such as Yahoo! on its financial site.

Three basic tools are used in financial statement analysis to highlight the significance of financial statement data:

1. Horizontal analysis
2. Vertical analysis
3. Ratio analysis

In previous chapters we relied primarily on ratio analysis, supplemented with some basic horizontal and vertical analysis. In the remainder of this section, we introduce more formal forms of horizontal and vertical analysis. In the next section we review ratio analysis in some detail.

HORIZONTAL ANALYSIS

Horizontal analysis, also known as trend analysis, is a technique for evaluating a series of financial statement data over a period of time. Its purpose is to determine the increase or decrease that has taken place, expressed as either an amount or a percentage. For example, here are recent net sales figures (in millions) of Kellogg Company:

1998	1997	1996	1995	1994
$6,762.1	$6,830.1	$6,676.6	$7,003.7	$6,562.0

If we assume that 1994 is the base year, we can measure all percentage increases or decreases relative to this base-period amount with the formula shown in Illustration 14-5.

$$\text{Change Since Base Period} = \frac{\text{Current-Year Amount} - \text{Base-Year Amount}}{\text{Base-Year Amount}}$$

For example, we can determine that net sales for Kellogg Company increased approximately 6.7% [($7,003.7 − $6,562.0) ÷ $6,562.0] from 1994 to 1995. Similarly, we can also determine that net sales increased by 3.0% [($6,762.1 − $6,562.0) ÷ $6,562.0] from 1994 to 1998.

Alternatively, we can express current-year sales as a percentage of the base period. To do so, we would divide the current-year amount by the base-year amount, as shown in Illustration 14-6.

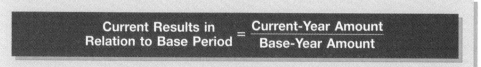

$$\text{Current Results in Relation to Base Period} = \frac{\text{Current-Year Amount}}{\text{Base-Year Amount}}$$

STUDY OBJECTIVE

3

Explain and apply horizontal analysis.

Alternative Terminology Horizontal analysis is also often referred to as **trend analysis.**

Illustration 14-5
Horizontal analysis computation of changes since base period

Illustration 14-6
Horizontal analysis computation of current year in relation to base year

Current-period sales expressed as a percentage of the base period for each of the five years, using 1994 as the base period, are shown in Illustration 14-7.

Illustration 14-7
Horizontal analysis of net sales

KELLOGG COMPANY Net Sales (in millions) Base Period 1994				
1998	1997	1996	1995	1994
$6,762.1	$6,830.1	$6,676.6	$7,003.7	$6,562.0
103.0%	104.1%	101.7%	106.7%	100%

To further illustrate horizontal analysis, we use the financial statements of Kellogg Company. Its two-year condensed balance sheets for 1998 and 1997 showing dollar and percentage changes are presented in Illustration 14-8.

Illustration 14-8
Horizontal analysis of a balance sheet

Helpful Hint It is difficult to comprehend the significance of a change when only the dollar amount of change is examined. When the change is expressed in percentage form, it is easier to grasp the true magnitude of the change.

KELLOGG COMPANY, INC. Condensed Balance Sheets December 31 (in millions)			Increase (Decrease) during 1998	
	1998	1997	Amount	Percent
Assets				
Current assets	$1,496.5	$1,467.7	$ 28.8	2.0
Property assets (net)	2,888.8	2,773.3	115.5	4.2
Other assets	666.2	636.6	29.6	4.6
Total assets	$5,051.5	$4,877.6	$173.9	3.6
Liabilities and Stockholders' Equity				
Current liabilities	$1,718.5	$1,657.3	$ 61.2	3.7
Long-term liabilities	2,443.2	2,222.8	220.4	9.9
Total liabilities	4,161.7	3,880.1	281.6	7.3
Stockholders' equity				
Common stock	208.8	196.3	12.5	6.4
Retained earnings and other	1,075.3	958.5	116.8	12.2
Treasury stock (cost)	(394.3)	(157.3)	(237.0)	150.7
Total stockholders' equity	889.8	997.5	(107.7)	(10.8)
Total liabilities and stockholders' equity	$5,051.5	$4,877.6	$173.9	3.6

The comparative balance sheet shows that a number of changes occurred in Kellogg's financial position from 1997 to 1998. In the assets section, current assets increased $28.8 million, or 2.0% ($28.8 ÷ $1,467.7), and property assets (net) increased $115.5 million, or 4.2%. In the liabilities section, current liabilities increased $61.2 million, or 3.7%, while long-term liabilities increased $220.4 million, or 9.9%. In the stockholders' equity section, we find that retained earnings increased $116.8 million, or 12.2%. This suggests that the company expanded its asset base during 1998 and financed this expansion primarily by retaining income in the business and assuming additional long-term debt. In addition, the company reduced its stockholders' equity 10.8% by purchasing treasury stock.

Presented in Illustration 14-9 is a two-year comparative income statement of Kellogg Company for 1998 and 1997 in a condensed format.

Illustration 14-9
Horizontal analysis of an income statement

KELLOGG COMPANY, INC. Condensed Income Statements For the Years Ended December 31 (in millions)			Increase (Decrease) during 1998	
	1998	1997	Amount	Percent
Net sales	$6,762.1	$6,830.1	$(68.0)	(1.0)
Cost of goods sold	3,282.6	3,270.1	12.5	0.4
Gross profit	3,479.5	3,560.0	(80.5)	(2.3)
Selling and administrative expenses	2,513.9	2,366.8	147.1	6.2
Nonrecurring charges	70.5	184.1	(113.6)	(61.7)
Income from operations	895.1	1,009.1	(114.0)	(11.3)
Interest expense	119.5	108.3	11.2	10.3
Other income (expense), net	6.9	3.7	3.2	86.5
Income before income taxes	782.5	904.5	(122.0)	(13.5)
Income tax expense	279.9	340.5	(60.6)	(17.8)
Net income	$ 502.6	$ 564.0	$(61.4)	(10.9)

Helpful Hint Note that, in a horizontal analysis, while the amount column is additive (the total is negative $61.4 million), the percentage column is not additive (10.9% is **not** a total).

Horizontal analysis of the income statements shows the following changes: Net sales decreased $68.0 million, or 1.0% ($68.0 ÷ $6,830.1). Cost of goods sold increased $12.5 million, or 0.4% ($12.5 ÷ $3,270.1). Selling and administrative expenses increased $147.1 million, or 6.2% ($147.1 ÷ $2,366.8). Overall, gross profit decreased 2.3% and net income decreased 10.9%. The decrease in net income can be attributed to the increase in selling and administrative expenses and the decline in sales.

The measurement of changes from period to period in percentages is relatively straightforward and quite useful. However, complications can result in making the computations. If an item has no value in a base year or preceding year and a value in the next year, no percentage change can be computed. And if a negative amount appears in the base or preceding period and a positive amount exists the following year, no percentage change can be computed.

Helpful Hint When using horizontal analysis, both dollar amount changes and percentage changes need to be examined. It is not necessarily bad if a company's earnings are growing at a declining rate. The **amount** of increase may be the same as or more than the base year, but the **percentage** change may be less because the base is greater each year.

DECISION TOOLKIT

Decision Checkpoints	Info Needed for Decision	Tool to Use for Decision	How to Evaluate Results
How do the company's financial position and operating results compare with those of previous period?	Income statement and balance sheet	Comparative financial statements should be prepared over at least two years, with the first year reported being the base year. Changes in each line item relative to the base year should be presented both by amount and by percentage. This is called horizontal analysis.	Significant changes should be investigated to determine the reason for the change.

VERTICAL ANALYSIS

STUDY OBJECTIVE

◆4◆

Describe and apply vertical analysis.

Alternative Terminology Vertical analysis is sometimes referred to as **common-size analysis**.

Vertical analysis, also called common-size analysis, is a technique for evaluating financial statement data that expresses each item in a financial statement as a percent of a base amount. For example, on a balance sheet we might say that current assets are 22% of total assets (total assets being the base amount). Or on an income statement we might say that selling expenses are 16% of net sales (net sales being the base amount).

Presented in Illustration 14-10 is the comparative balance sheet of Kellogg for 1998 and 1997, analyzed vertically. The base for the asset items is **total assets**, and the base for the liability and stockholders' equity items is **total liabilities and stockholders' equity**.

Illustration 14-10
Vertical analysis of a
balance sheet

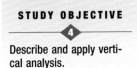

KELLOGG COMPANY, INC.
Condensed Balance Sheets
December 31
(in millions)

	1998		1997	
Assets	Amount	Percent*	Amount	Percent*
Current assets	$1,496.5	29.6	$1,467.7	30.1
Property assets (net)	2,888.8	57.2	2,773.3	56.9
Other assets	666.2	13.2	636.6	13.0
Total assets	$5,051.5	100.0	$4,877.6	100.0
Liabilities and Stockholders' Equity				
Current liabilities	$1,718.5	34.0	$1,657.3	34.0
Long-term liabilities	2,443.2	48.4	2,222.8	45.5
Total liabilities	4,161.7	82.4	3,880.1	79.5
Stockholders' equity				
Common stock	208.8	4.1	196.3	4.0
Retained earnings and other	1,075.3	21.3	958.5	19.7
Treasury stock (cost)	(394.3)	(7.8)	(157.3)	(3.2)
Total stockholders' equity	889.8	17.6	997.5	20.5
Total liabilities and stockholders' equity	$5,051.5	100.0	$4,877.6	100.0

*Numbers have been rounded to total 100%.

In addition to showing the relative size of each category on the balance sheet, vertical analysis may show the percentage change in the individual asset, liability, and stockholders' equity items. In this case, even though current assets increased $28.8 million from 1997 to 1998, they decreased from 30.1% to 29.6% of total assets. Property assets (net) increased from 56.9% to 57.2% of total assets. Also, even though retained earnings increased by $116.8 million from 1997 to 1998, total stockholders' equity decreased from 20.5% to 17.6% of total liabilities and stockholders' equity. This switch to a higher percentage of debt financing has two causes: First, long-term liabilities increased by $220.4 million, going from 45.5% to 48.4% of total liabilities and stockholders' equity. Second, treasury stock increased by $237.0 million, going from 3.2% to 7.8% of total liabilities and stockholders' equity. Thus, the company shifted toward a heavier reliance on debt financing both by using more long-term debt and by reducing the amount of outstanding equity.

Vertical analysis of the comparative income statements of Kellogg, shown in Illustration 14-11 below, reveals that cost of goods sold **as a percentage of net sales** increased from 47.9% to 48.6%, and selling and administrative expenses increased from 34.6% to 37.2%. Net income as a percent of net sales decreased from 8.3% to 7.4%. Kellogg's decline in net income as a percentage of sales is due primarily to the increase in both cost of goods sold and selling and administrative expenses as a percent of sales. The drop in nonrecurring charges was not sufficient to offset the increase in these costs.

KELLOGG COMPANY, INC.
Condensed Income Statements
For the Years Ended December 31
(in millions)

	1998 Amount	1998 Percent*	1997 Amount	1997 Percent*
Net sales	$6,762.1	100.0	$6,830.1	100.0
Cost of goods sold	3,282.6	48.6	3,270.1	47.9
Gross profit	3,479.5	51.4	3,560.0	52.1
Selling and administrative expenses	2,513.9	37.2	2,366.8	34.6
Nonrecurring charges	70.5	1.0	184.1	2.7
Income from operations	895.1	13.2	1,009.1	14.8
Interest expense	119.5	1.8	108.3	1.6
Other income (expense), net	6.9	0.1	3.7	0.1
Income before income taxes	782.5	11.5	904.5	13.3
Income tax expense	279.9	4.1	340.5	5.0
Net income	$ 502.6	7.4	$ 564.0	8.3

*Numbers have been rounded to total 100%.

Illustration 14-11
Vertical analysis of an income statement

Vertical analysis also enables you to compare companies of different sizes. For example, one of Kellogg's main competitors is The Quaker Oats Company. Using vertical analysis, we can more meaningfully compare the condensed income statements of Kellogg and Quaker Oats, as shown in Illustration 14-12.

Illustration 14-12 Intercompany comparison by vertical analysis

CONDENSED INCOME STATEMENTS
For the Year Ended December 31, 1998
(in millions)

	Kellogg Company, Inc. Amount	Kellogg Company, Inc. Percent*	The Quaker Oats Company Amount	The Quaker Oats Company Percent*
Net sales	$6,762.1	100.0	$4,842.5	100.0
Cost of goods sold	3,282.6	48.6	2,374.4	49.0
Gross profit	3,479.5	51.4	2,468.1	51.0
Selling and administrative expenses	2,513.9	37.2	1,872.5	38.7
Nonrecurring charges	70.5	1.0	128.5	2.6
Income from operations	895.1	13.2	467.1	9.7
Other expenses and revenues (including income taxes)	392.5	5.8	182.6	3.8
Net income	$ 502.6	7.4	$ 284.5	5.9

*Numbers have been rounded to total 100%.

Although Kellogg's net sales are 40% greater than the net sales of Quaker Oats, vertical analysis eliminates the impact of this size difference for our analysis. Kellogg's income from operations as a percentage of net sales is 13.2%, compared to 9.7% for Quaker Oats. This difference can be attributed both to Kellogg's relative superiority in maintaining its gross profit margin (Kellogg's gross profit rate of 51.4% vs. Quaker Oats' rate of 51%) and to Kellogg's lower selling and administrative expense percentage (37.2% vs. 38.7%). In one area Quaker Oats was better: Kellogg's other expenses were 5.8% of net sales compared to only 3.8% for Quaker Oats. However, given that these items are usually not very predictable over time, Kellogg's profitability picture appears more positive than that of Quaker Oats.

DECISION TOOLKIT

Decision Checkpoints	Info Needed for Decision	Tool to Use for Decision	How to Evaluate Results
How do the relationships between items in this year's financial statements compare with those of last year or those of competitors?	Income statement and balance sheet	Each line item on the income statement should be presented as a percentage of net sales, and each line item on the balance sheet should be presented as a percentage of total assets or total liabilities and stockholders' equity. These percentages should be investigated for differences either across years in the same company or in the same year across different companies. This is called vertical analysis.	Any differences either across years or between companies should be investigated to determine the cause.

BEFORE YOU GO ON...

◆ Review It

1. What different bases can be used to compare financial information?
2. What is horizontal analysis?
3. What is vertical analysis?

RATIO ANALYSIS

STUDY OBJECTIVE

5

Identify and compute ratios and describe their purpose and use in analyzing a company's liquidity, solvency, and profitability.

In previous chapters we presented many ratios used for evaluating the financial health and performance of a company. In this section we provide a comprehensive review of those ratios and discuss some important relationships among the ratios. Since earlier chapters demonstrated the calculation of each of these ratios, in this chapter we instead focus on their interpretation. Page references to prior discussions are provided if you feel you need to review any individual ratios.

The financial information in Illustrations 14-13 through 14-16 (pages 679 and 680) was used to calculate Kellogg's 1998 ratios. You can use these data to review the computations.

KELLOGG'S

Illustration 14-13
Kellogg Company's
balance sheet

KELLOGG COMPANY, INC.
Balance Sheets
December 31
(in millions)

Assets	1998	1997
Current assets		
Cash and short-term investments	$ 136.4	$ 173.2
Accounts receivable (net)	693.0	587.5
Inventories	451.4	434.3
Prepaid expenses and other current assets	215.7	272.7
Total current assets	1,496.5	1,467.7
Property assets (net)	2,888.8	2,773.3
Intangibles and other assets	666.2	636.6
Total assets	$5,051.5	$4,877.6
Liabilities and Stockholders' Equity		
Current liabilities	$1,718.5	$1,657.3
Long-term liabilities	2,443.2	2,222.8
Stockholders' equity—common	889.8	997.5
Total liabilities and stockholders' equity	$5,051.5	$4,877.6

Illustration 14-14
Kellogg Company's
income statement

KELLOGG COMPANY, INC.
Condensed Income Statements
For the Years Ended December 31
(in millions)

	1998	1997
Net sales	$6,762.1	$6,830.1
Cost of goods sold	3,282.6	3,270.1
Gross profit	3,479.5	3,560.0
Selling and administrative expenses	2,513.9	2,366.8
Nonrecurring charges	70.5	184.1
Income from operations	895.1	1,009.1
Interest expense	119.5	108.3
Other income (expense), net	6.9	3.7
Income before income taxes	782.5	904.5
Income tax expense	279.9	340.5
Net income	$ 502.6	$ 564.0

Illustration 14-15
Kellogg Company's
statement of cash flows

KELLOGG COMPANY, INC.
Condensed Statements of Cash Flows
For the Years Ended December 31
(in millions)

	1998	1997
Cash flows from operating activities		
Cash receipts from operating activities	$6,656.6	$6,834.9
Cash payments for operating activities	5,936.9	5,955.1
Net cash provided by operating activities	719.7	879.8
Cash flows from investing activities		
Purchases of property, plant, and equipment	(373.9)	(312.4)
Other investing activities	(24.1)	(16.9)
Net cash used in operating activities	(398.0)	(329.3)
Cash flows from financing activities		
Issuance of common stock	15.2	70.7
Issuance of debt	605.5	1,004.8
Reductions of debt	(364.0)	(896.7)
Reductions of common stock	(239.7)	(426.0)
Payment of dividends	(375.3)	(360.1)
Net cash used in financing activities	(358.3)	(607.3)
Other	(.2)	(13.8)
Increase (decrease) in cash and cash equivalents	(36.8)	(70.6)
Cash and cash equivalents at beginning of year	173.2	243.8
Cash and cash equivalents at end of year	$ 136.4	$ 173.2

Illustration 14-16
Additional information for
Kellogg Company

Additional information

	1998	1997
Average number of shares (millions)	408.6	414.7
Stock price at year-end	$34.1	$49.6

For analysis of the primary financial statements, ratios can be classified into three types:

1. **Liquidity ratios**: measures of the short-term ability of the enterprise to pay its maturing obligations and to meet unexpected needs for cash.

2. **Solvency ratios**: measures of the ability of the enterprise to survive over a long period of time.

3. **Profitability ratios**: measures of the income or operating success of an enterprise for a given period of time.

As a tool of analysis, ratios can provide clues to underlying conditions that may not be apparent from an inspection of the individual components of a particular ratio. But a single ratio by itself is not very meaningful. Accordingly, in this discussion we use the following comparisons:

1. **Intracompany comparisons** covering two years for Kellogg Company (using comparative financial information from Illustrations 14-10 and 14-11).
2. **Intercompany comparisons** using The Quaker Oats Company as one of Kellogg's principal competitors.
3. **Industry average comparisons** based on Robert Morris Associates' median ratios for manufacturers of flour and other grain mill products and comparisons with other sources. For some of the ratios that we use, industry comparisons are not available. (These are denoted "na.")

LIQUIDITY RATIOS

Liquidity ratios measure the short-term ability of the enterprise to pay its maturing obligations and to meet unexpected needs for cash. Short-term creditors such as bankers and suppliers are particularly interested in assessing liquidity. The measures that can be used to determine the enterprise's short-term debt-paying ability are the current ratio, the acid-test ratio, the current cash debt coverage ratio, the receivables turnover ratio, the average collection period, the inventory turnover ratio, and average days in inventory.

1. **Current ratio.** The current ratio expresses the relationship of current assets to current liabilities, computed by dividing current assets by current liabilities. It is widely used for evaluating a company's liquidity and short-term debt-paying ability. The 1998 and 1997 current ratios for Kellogg and comparative data are shown in Illustration 14-17.

Illustration 14-17
Current ratio

Ratio	Formula	Indicates:	Kellogg 1998	Kellogg 1997	Quaker Oats 1998	Industry 1998	Page in book
Current ratio	Current assets / Current liabilities	Short-term debt-paying ability	.87	.89	1.10	1.27	64

What do the measures tell us? Kellogg's 1998 current ratio of .87 means that for every dollar of current liabilities, Kellogg has $.87 of current assets. We sometimes state such ratios as .87 : 1 to reinforce this interpretation. Kellogg's current ratio—and therefore its liquidity—decreased slightly in 1998. It is well below the industry average and also below that of Quaker Oats.

The current ratio is only one measure of liquidity. It does not take into account the composition of current assets. For example, a satisfactory current ratio could conceal the fact that a portion of current assets may be tied up in slow-moving inventory. The current ratio does not take into account the fact that a dollar of cash is more readily available to pay the bills than is a dollar's worth of slow-moving inventory. These weaknesses are addressed by the next ratio.

BUSINESS INSIGHT
Investor Perspective

The apparent simplicity of the current ratio can have real-world limitations because adding equal amounts to both the numerator and the denominator causes the ratio to decrease. Assume, for example, that a company has $2,000,000 of current assets and $1,000,000 of current liabilities; its current ratio is 2:1. If it purchases $1,000,000 of inventory on account, it will have $3,000,000 of current assets and $2,000,000 of current liabilities; its current ratio decreases to 1.5:1. If, instead, the company pays off $500,000 of its current liabilities, it will have $1,500,000 of current assets and $500,000 of current liabilities; its current ratio increases to 3:1. Thus, any trend analysis should be done with care because the ratio is susceptible to quick changes and is easily influenced by management.

2. **Acid-test ratio.** The acid-test or quick ratio is a measure of a company's immediate short-term liquidity. It is computed by dividing the sum of cash, short-term investments, and net receivables by current liabilities. Thus, it is an important complement to the current ratio. Note that it does not include inventory or prepaid expenses. Cash, short-term investments, and receivables (net) are much more liquid than inventory and prepaid expenses. The inventory may not be readily salable, and the prepaid expenses may not be transferable to others. The acid-test ratio for Kellogg is shown in Illustration 14-18.

Illustration 14-18
Acid-test ratio

Ratio	Formula	Indicates:	Kellogg 1998	Kellogg 1997	Quaker Oats 1998	Industry 1998	Page in book
Acid-test or quick ratio	$\dfrac{\text{Cash} + \text{Short-term investments} + \text{Net receivables}}{\text{Current liabilities}}$	Immediate short-term liquidity	.48	.46	.63	.64	459

The 1998 and 1997 acid-test ratios for Kellogg again suggest low liquidity. Is Kellogg's 1998 acid-test ratio of .48:1 adequate? Unlike its current ratio, its acid-test ratio increased slightly in 1998. However, when compared with the industry average of .64:1 and Quaker Oats' .63:1, Kellogg's acid-test ratio seems to require additional investigation.

3. **Current cash debt coverage ratio.** A disadvantage of the current and acid-test ratios is that they use year-end balances of current asset and current liability accounts. These year-end balances may not be representative of the company's current position during most of the year. A ratio that partially corrects for this problem is the ratio of cash provided by operating activities to average current liabilities, called the current cash debt coverage ratio. Because it uses cash provided by operating activities rather than a balance at one point in time, it may provide a better representation of liquidity. Kellogg's current cash debt coverage ratio is shown in Illustration 14-19.

Illustration 14-19
Current cash debt coverage ratio

Ratio	Formula	Indicates:	Kellogg 1998	Kellogg 1997	Quaker Oats 1998	Industry 1998	Page in book
Current cash debt coverage ratio	$\dfrac{\text{Cash provided by operations}}{\text{Average current liabilities}}$	Short-term debt-paying ability (cash basis)	.43	.46	.53	na	68

Like the current ratio, this ratio decreased in 1998 for Kellogg. Is the coverage adequate? Probably so. Even though Kellogg's operating cash flow coverage of average current liabilities is less than Quaker Oats', it exceeds a commonly accepted threshold of .40. No industry comparison is available.

4. **Receivables turnover ratio.** Liquidity may be measured by how quickly certain assets can be converted to cash. Low values of the previous ratios can sometimes be compensated for if some of the company's current assets are highly liquid. How liquid, for example, are the receivables? The ratio used to assess the liquidity of the receivables is the receivables turnover ratio, which measures the number of times, on average, receivables are collected during the period. The receivables turnover ratio is computed by dividing net credit sales (net sales less cash sales) by average net receivables during the year. The receivables turnover ratio for Kellogg is shown in Illustration 14-20.

Illustration 14-20
Receivables turnover ratio

Ratio	Formula	Indicates:	Kellogg 1998	Kellogg 1997	Quaker Oats 1998	Industry 1998	Page in book
Receivables turnover ratio	Net credit sales / Average net receivables	Liquidity of receivables	10.6	11.6	16.4	11.4	371

We have assumed that all Kellogg's sales are credit sales. The receivables turnover ratio for Kellogg declined in 1998. However, the turnover of 10.6 times compares favorably with the industry median of 11.4, even though it is well below that of 16.4 times for Quaker Oats.

BUSINESS INSIGHT
Investor Perspective

In some cases, the receivables turnover ratio may be misleading. Some companies, especially large retail chains, issue their own credit cards. They encourage customers to use these cards, and they slow their collections in order to earn a healthy return on the outstanding receivables in the form of interest at rates of 18% to 22%. In general, however, the faster the turnover, the greater the reliance that can be placed on the current and acid-test ratios for assessing liquidity.

5. **Average collection period.** A popular variant of the receivables turnover ratio converts it into an average collection period in days. This is done by dividing the receivables turnover ratio into 365 days. The average collection period for Kellogg is shown in Illustration 14-21.

Illustration 14-21
Average collection period

Ratio	Formula	Indicates:	Kellogg 1998	Kellogg 1997	Quaker Oats 1998	Industry 1998	Page in book
Average collection period	365 days / Receivables turnover ratio	Liquidity of receivables and collection success	34.4	31.5	22.3	32	372

Kellogg's 1998 receivables turnover of 10.6 times is divided into 365 days to obtain approximately 34.4 days. This means that the average collection period for receivables is 34 days. Analysts frequently use the average collection period to assess the effectiveness of a company's credit and collection policies. The general rule is that the collection period should not greatly exceed the credit term period (i.e., the time allowed for payment). It is interesting to note that Quaker Oats' average collection period is significantly shorter than those of Kellogg and the industry. This difference may be due to more aggressive collection practices, but it is more likely due to a difference in credit terms granted. Quaker Oats might grant more generous discounts for early payment than others in the industry.

6. **Inventory turnover ratio.** The inventory turnover ratio measures the number of times on average the inventory is sold during the period. Its purpose is to measure the liquidity of the inventory. The inventory turnover ratio is computed by dividing the cost of goods sold by the average inventory during the period. Unless seasonal factors are significant, average inventory can be computed from the beginning and ending inventory balances. Kellogg's inventory turnover ratio is shown in Illustration 14-22.

Illustration 14-22
Inventory turnover ratio

| | | | Kellogg | | Quaker Oats | Industry | Page in |
Ratio	Formula	Indicates:	1998	1997	1998	1998	book
Inventory turnover ratio	Cost of goods sold / Average inventory	Liquidity of inventory	7.4	7.6	9.2	6.7	264

Kellogg's inventory turnover ratio declined slightly in 1998. The turnover ratio of 7.4 times is higher than the industry average of 6.7 but significantly lower than Quaker Oats' 9.2. Generally, the faster the inventory turnover, the less cash is tied up in inventory and the less the chance of inventory becoming obsolete. Of course, a downside of high inventory turnover is that the company can run out of inventory when it is needed.

7. **Days in inventory.** A variant of the inventory turnover ratio is the days in inventory, which measures the average number of days it takes to sell the inventory. The days in inventory for Kellogg is shown in Illustration 14-23.

Illustration 14-23
Days in inventory

| | | | Kellogg | | Quaker Oats | Industry | Page in |
Ratio	Formula	Indicates:	1998	1997	1998	1998	book
Days in inventory	365 days / Inventory turnover ratio	Liquidity of inventory and inventory management	49.3	48	39.7	54.5	264

Kellogg's 1998 inventory turnover ratio of 7.4 divided into 365 is approximately 49.3 days. An average selling time of 49 days is faster than the industry average but significantly slower than that of Quaker Oats. Some of this difference might be explained by differences in product lines across the two companies, although in many ways the types of products of these two companies are quite similar.

Inventory turnover ratios vary considerably among industries. For example, grocery store chains have a turnover of 10 times and an average selling period of 37 days. In contrast, jewelry stores have an average turnover of 1.3 times and an average selling period of 281 days. Within a company there may even be significant differences in inventory turnover among different types of products. Thus, in a grocery store the turnover of perishable items such as produce, meats, and dairy products is faster than the turnover of soaps and detergents.

To conclude, nearly all of these liquidity measures suggest that Kellogg's liquidity declined during 1998. However, its liquidity appears acceptable when compared both to that of Quaker Oats and to the industry as a whole.

SOLVENCY RATIOS

Solvency ratios measure the ability of the enterprise to survive over a long period of time. Long-term creditors and stockholders are interested in a company's long-run solvency, particularly its ability to pay interest as it comes due and to repay the face value of debt at maturity. The debt to total assets ratio, the times interest earned ratio, and the cash debt coverage ratio provide information about debt-paying ability. In addition, free cash flow provides information about the company's solvency and its ability to pay additional dividends or invest in new projects.

8. **Debt to total assets ratio.** The debt to total assets ratio measures the percentage of the total assets provided by creditors. It is computed by dividing total liabilities (both current and long-term) by total assets. This ratio indicates the degree of financial leveraging; it provides some indication of the company's ability to withstand losses without impairing the interests of its creditors. The higher the percentage of debt to total assets, the greater the risk that the company may be unable to meet its maturing obligations. The lower the ratio, the more equity "buffer" is available to creditors if the company becomes insolvent. Thus, from the creditors' point of view, a low ratio of debt to total assets is desirable. Kellogg's debt to total assets ratio is shown in Illustration 14-24.

Illustration 14-24   Debt to total assets ratio

Ratio	Formula	Indicates:	Kellogg 1998	Kellogg 1997	Quaker Oats 1998	Industry 1998	Page in book
Debt to total assets ratio	Total liabilities Total assets	Percentage of total assets provided by creditors	.82	.80	.94	.73	65

Kellogg's 1998 ratio of .82 means that creditors have provided financing sufficient to cover 82% of the company's total assets. Alternatively, it says that Kellogg would have to liquidate 82% of its assets at their book value in order to pay off all of its debts. Kellogg's 82% is above the industry average of 73% but below the 94% ratio of Quaker Oats. Kellogg's solvency declined during the year. In that time, Kellogg's use of debt financing changed in two ways: First, Kellogg increased its use of long-term debt, and second, it repurchased a considerable amount of its own stock. Both these factors reduced its solvency.

The adequacy of this ratio is often judged in light of the company's earnings. Generally, companies with relatively stable earnings, such as public utilities, have higher debt to total assets ratios than cyclical companies with widely fluctuating earnings, such as many high-tech companies.

Another ratio with a similar meaning is the **debt to equity ratio**. It shows the relative use of borrowed funds (total liabilities) compared with resources invested by the owners. Because this ratio can be computed in several ways, care should be taken when making comparisons. Debt may be defined to include only the noncurrent portion of liabilities, and intangible assets may be excluded from stockholders' equity (which would equal tangible net worth). If debt and assets are defined as above (all liabilities and all assets), then when the debt to total assets ratio equals 50%, the debt to equity ratio is 1:1.

9. **Times interest earned ratio.** The times interest earned ratio (also called interest coverage) indicates the company's ability to meet interest payments as they come due. It is computed by dividing income before interest expense and income taxes by interest expense. Note that this ratio uses income before interest expense and income taxes because this amount represents what is available to cover interest. Kellogg's times interest earned ratio is shown in Illustration 14-25.

Illustration 14-25   Times interest earned ratio

Ratio	Formula	Indicates:	Kellogg 1998	Kellogg 1997	Quaker Oats 1998	Industry 1998	Page in book
Times interest earned ratio	$\dfrac{\text{Net income} + \text{Interest expense} + \text{Tax expense}}{\text{Interest expense}}$	Ability to meet interest payments as they come due	7.5	9.4	6.7	6.0	475

For Kellogg the 1998 coverage was 7.5, which indicates that income before interest and taxes was 7.5 times the amount needed for interest expense. This exceeds both the rate for Quaker Oats and the average rate for the industry. Thus, although the debt to assets ratio suggests that Kellogg relies heavily on debt financing, the times interest earned ratio suggests that the company can easily service its debt.

10. **Cash debt coverage ratio.** The ratio of cash provided by operating activities to average total liabilities, called the cash debt coverage ratio, is a cash-basis measure of solvency. This ratio indicates a company's ability to repay its liabilities from cash generated from operating activities without having to liquidate the assets used in its operations. Illustration 14-26 shows Kellogg's cash debt coverage ratio.

Illustration 14-26   Cash debt coverage ratio

Ratio	Formula	Indicates:	Kellogg 1998	Kellogg 1997	Quaker Oats 1998	Industry 1998	Page in book
Cash debt coverage ratio	$\dfrac{\text{Cash provided by operations}}{\text{Average total liabilities}}$	Long-term debt-paying ability (cash basis)	.18	.23	.21	na	68

An industry average for this measure is not available. Kellogg's .18 is less than Quaker Oats' .21, and it did decline from .23 in 1997. One way of interpreting this ratio is to say that net cash generated from one year of operations would be sufficient to pay off 18% of Kellogg's total liabilities. If 18% of this year's liabilities were retired each year, it would take approximately five years to retire all of its debt. It would also take Quaker Oats approximately five years to do so. A general rule of thumb is that a measure above .20 is acceptable.

11. **Free cash flow**.   One indication of a company's solvency, as well as of its ability to pay dividends or expand operations, is the amount of excess cash it generated after investing to maintain its current productive capacity and paying dividends. This amount is referred to as *free cash flow*. For example, if you generate $100,000 of cash from operations but you spend $30,000 to maintain and replace your productive facilities at their current levels and pay $10,000 in dividends, you have $60,000 to use either to expand operations or to pay additional dividends.

Kellogg's free cash flow is shown in Illustration 14-27.

Illustration 14-27
Free cash flow

Ratio	Formula			Indicates:	Kellogg		Quaker Oats 1998	Industry 1998	Page in book
					1998	1997			
Free cash flow	Cash provided by operations	− Capital expenditures	− Cash dividends	Cash available for paying dividends or expanding operations	−$29.5 (in millions)	$207.3	$149.1 (in millions)	na	323

Kellogg's free cash flow declined considerably from 1997 to 1998. In fact, it was negative in 1998. Both Kellogg and Quaker Oats have used a large portion of free cash flow in recent years to repurchase their own stock.

PROFITABILITY RATIOS

Profitability ratios measure the income or operating success of an enterprise for a given period of time. A company's income, or the lack of it, affects its ability to obtain debt and equity financing, its liquidity position, and its ability to grow. As a consequence, creditors and investors alike are interested in evaluating profitability. Profitability is frequently used as the ultimate test of management's operating effectiveness. Some commonly used measures of profitability are discussed in the following pages.

Throughout this book we have introduced numerous measures of profitability. The relationships among these measures are very important. Understanding them can help management determine where to focus its efforts to improve profitability. Illustration 14-28 diagrams these relationships. Our discussion of Kellogg's profitability is structured around this diagram.

Illustration 14-28
Relationships among profitability measures

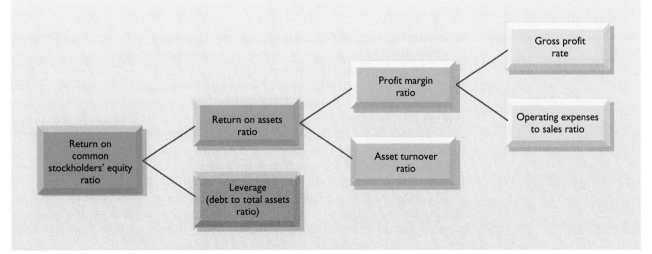

12. **Return on common stockholders' equity ratio.**   A widely used measure of profitability from the common stockholder's viewpoint is the return on common stockholders' equity ratio. This ratio shows how many dollars of net income were earned for each dollar invested by the owners. It is computed by dividing net income minus any preferred stock dividends—that is, income available to common stockholders—by average common stockholders' equity. The return on common stockholders' equity for Kellogg is shown in Illustration 14-29.

Illustration 14-29
Return on common stockholders' equity ratio

Ratio	Formula	Indicates:	Kellogg 1998	Kellogg 1997	Quaker Oats 1998	Industry 1998	Page in book
Return on common stockholders' equity ratio	$\dfrac{\text{Net income} - \text{Preferred stock dividends}}{\text{Average common stockholders' equity}}$	Profitability of common stockholders' investment	.53	.49	1.48	.39	536

Kellogg's 1998 rate of return on common stockholders' equity is unusually high at 53%, considering an industry average of 39%. Quaker Oats' return of 148% is extraordinary. In the subsequent sections we investigate the causes of these high returns.

13. **Return on assets ratio.**   The return on common stockholders' equity ratio is affected by two factors: the return on assets ratio and the degree of leverage. The return on assets ratio measures the overall profitability of assets in terms of the income earned on each dollar invested in assets. It is computed by dividing net income by average total assets. Kellogg's return on assets ratio is shown in Illustration 14-30.

Illustration 14-30
Return on assets ratio

Ratio	Formula	Indicates:	Kellogg 1998	Kellogg 1997	Quaker Oats 1998	Industry 1998	Page in book
Return on assets ratio	$\dfrac{\text{Net income}}{\text{Average total assets}}$	Overall profitability of assets	.10	.11	.11	.09	60

Kellogg had a 10% return on assets in 1998 and 11% in 1997. This rate is slightly lower than that of Quaker Oats, but exceeds the industry average.

Note that Kellogg's rate of return on stockholders' equity (53%) is substantially higher than its rate of return on assets (10%). The reason is that Kellogg has made effective use of **leverage**. Leveraging or trading on the equity at a gain means that the company has borrowed money at a lower rate of interest than the rate of return it earns on the assets it purchased with the borrowed funds. Leverage enables management to use money supplied by nonowners to increase the return to owners.

A comparison of the rate of return on assets with the rate of interest paid for borrowed money indicates the profitability of trading on the equity. If you borrow money at 8% and your rate of return on assets is 11%, you are trading on the equity at a gain. Note, however, that trading on the equity is a two-way street: for example, if you borrow money at 11% and earn only 8% on it, you are trading on the equity at a loss.

Kellogg earns more on its borrowed funds than it has to pay in interest. The notes to Kellogg's financial statements disclose that it pays interest rates of between 5% and 8% on outstanding debts, yet, as noted above, it earns 10% on each dollar invested in assets. Thus, the return to stockholders exceeds the return on the assets because of the positive benefit of leverage. Recall from our earlier discussion that Kellogg's percentage of debt financing as measured by the ratio of debt to total assets (or debt to equity) increased in 1998. It appears that Kellogg's high return on stockholders' equity is largely a function of its significant use of leverage.

14. **Profit margin ratio.** The return on assets ratio is affected by two factors, the first of which is the profit margin ratio. The profit margin ratio, or rate of return on sales, is a measure of the percentage of each dollar of sales that results in net income. It is computed by dividing net income by net sales for the period. Kellogg's profit margin ratio is shown in Illustration 14-31.

Illustration 14-31 Profit margin ratio

Ratio	Formula	Indicates:	Kellogg 1998	Kellogg 1997	Quaker Oats 1998	Industry 1998	Page in book
Profit margin ratio	$\dfrac{\text{Net income}}{\text{Net sales}}$	Net income generated by each dollar of sales	.07	.08	.06	.06	60

Kellogg experienced a decline in its profit margin ratio from 1997 to 1998 of 8% to 7%. Its profit margin ratio exceeds the industry average of 6% and Quaker Oats' 6%.

High-volume (high inventory turnover) enterprises such as grocery stores and pharmacy chains generally have low profit margins, whereas low-volume enterprises such as jewelry stores and airplane manufacturers have high profit margins.

15. **Asset turnover ratio.** The other factor that affects the return on assets ratio is the asset turnover ratio. The asset turnover ratio measures how efficiently a company uses its assets to generate sales. It is determined by dividing net sales by average total assets for the period. The resulting number shows the dollars of sales produced by each dollar invested in assets. Illustration 14-32 shows the asset turnover ratio for Kellogg.

Illustration 14-32 Asset turnover ratio

Ratio	Formula	Indicates:	Kellogg 1998	Kellogg 1997	Quaker Oats 1998	Industry 1998	Page in book
Asset turnover ratio	$\dfrac{\text{Net sales}}{\text{Average total assets}}$	How efficiently assets are used to generate sales	1.36	1.38	1.86	1.61	418

The asset turnover ratio shows that in 1998 Kellogg generated sales of $1.36 for each dollar it had invested in assets. The ratio declined a bit from 1997 to 1998. Kellogg's asset turnover ratio is below the industry average of 1.61 times and well below Quaker Oats' ratio of 1.86.

Asset turnover ratios vary considerably among industries. The average asset turnover for utility companies is .45, for example, while the grocery store industry has an average asset turnover of 3.49.

In summary, Kellogg's return on assets ratio declined from 11% in 1997 to 10% in 1998. Underlying this decline was a decreased profitability on each dollar of sales, as measured by the profit margin ratio, and a decline in the sales-generating efficiency of its assets, as measured by the asset turnover ratio. The combined effects of profit margin and asset turnover on return on assets for Kellogg can be analyzed as shown in Illustration 14-33.

Illustration 14-33
Composition of return on assets ratio

Ratios:	Profit Margin × $\dfrac{\text{Net Income}}{\text{Net Sales}}$	×	Asset Turnover $\dfrac{\text{Net Sales}}{\text{Average Total Assets}}$	=	Return on Assets $\dfrac{\text{Net Income}}{\text{Average Total Assets}}$
Kellogg					
1998	7%	×	1.36 times	=	10%
1997	8%	×	1.38 times	=	11%

16. **Gross profit rate.**   Two factors strongly influence the profit margin ratio. One is the gross profit rate. The gross profit rate is determined by dividing gross profit (net sales less cost of goods sold) by net sales. This rate indicates a company's ability to maintain an adequate selling price above its cost of goods sold. As an industry becomes more competitive, this ratio declines. For example, in the early years of the personal computer industry, gross profit rates were quite high. Today, because of increased competition and a belief that most brands of personal computers are similar in quality, gross profit rates have become thin. Gross profit rates should be closely monitored over time. Illustration 14-34 shows Kellogg's gross profit rate.

Illustration 14-34
Gross profit rate

			Kellogg		Quaker Oats	Industry	Page in
Ratio	Formula	Indicates:	1998	1997	1998	1998	book
Gross profit rate	$\dfrac{\text{Gross profit}}{\text{Net sales}}$	Margin between selling price and cost of goods sold	.51	.52	.51	.40	221

Kellogg's gross profit rate declined slightly from 1997 to 1998 in the face of cuts in the selling price of cereal by many of its competitors. Discussion in the financial press has often noted that Kellogg is somewhat slow to respond to price cuts but eventually also drops its prices.

17. **Operating expenses to sales ratio.**   This is the other factor that directly affects the profit margin ratio. Management can influence a company's profitability by maintaining adequate prices, cutting expenses, or both. The operating expenses to sales ratio measures the costs incurred to support each dollar of sales. It is computed by dividing operating expenses (selling and administrative expenses) by net sales. The operating expenses to sales ratio for Kellogg is shown in Illustration 14-35.

Illustration 14-35
Operating expenses to
sales ratio

Ratio	Formula	Indicates:	Kellogg		Quaker Oats 1998	Industry 1998	Page in book
			1998	1997			
Operating expenses to sales ratio	Operating expenses / Net sales	The costs incurred to support each dollar of sales	.37	.35	.39	na	222

In recent years the financial press has frequently carried stories about the cereal industry's efforts to "restructure" operations and cut expenses. This is necessary because cereal sales have leveled off, and so the only way to increase net income is to cut costs. Kellogg's operating expenses to sales ratio actually increased from 35% to 37% during this two-year period.

18. **Cash return on sales ratio**.   The profit margin ratio discussed earlier is an accrual-based ratio using net income as a numerator. The cash-basis counterpart to that ratio is the **cash return on sales ratio**, which uses cash provided by operating activities as the numerator and net sales as the denominator. The difference between these two ratios should be explainable as differences between accrual accounting and cash-basis accounting, such as differences in the timing of revenue and expense recognition. The cash return on sales ratio for Kellogg is shown in Illustration 14-36.

Illustration 14-36   Cash
return on sales ratio

Ratio	Formula	Indicates:	Kellogg		Quaker Oats 1998	Industry 1998	Page in book
			1998	1997			
Cash return on sales ratio	Cash provided by operations / Net sales	Net cash flow generated by each dollar of sales	.11	.13	.11	na	637

19. **Earnings per share (EPS)**.   Stockholders usually think in terms of the number of shares they own or plan to buy or sell. Expressing net income earned on a per share basis provides a useful perspective for determining profitability. **Earnings per share** is a measure of the net income earned on each share of common stock. It is computed by dividing net income by the average number of common shares outstanding during the year. When we use "net income per share" or "earnings per share," it refers to the amount of net income applicable to each share of *common stock*. Therefore, when we compute earnings per share, if there are preferred dividends declared for the period, they must be deducted from net income to arrive at income available to the common stockholders. Kellogg's earnings per share is shown in Illustration 14-37.

Illustration 14-37
Earnings per share

Ratio	Formula	Indicates:	Kellogg		Quaker Oats 1998	Industry 1998	Page in book
			1998	1997			
Earnings per share (EPS)	Net income − Preferred stock dividends / Average common shares outstanding	Net income earned on each share of common stock	$1.23	$1.36	$2.04	na	534

Note that no industry average is presented in Illustration 14-37. Industry data for earnings per share are not reported, and in fact the Kellogg and Quaker Oats ratios should not be compared. Such comparisons are not meaningful because of the wide variations in the number of shares of outstanding stock among companies. Kellogg's earnings per share decreased 13 cents per share in 1998. This represents a 9.6% decrease from the 1997 EPS of $1.36.

20. **Price-earnings ratio.** The price-earnings ratio is an oft-quoted statistic that measures the ratio of the market price of each share of common stock to the earnings per share. The price-earnings (P-E) ratio is a reflection of investors' assessments of a company's future earnings. It is computed by dividing the market price per share of the stock by earnings per share. Kellogg's price-earnings ratio is shown in Illustration 14-38.

Illustration 14-38
Price-earnings ratio

| | | | Kellogg | | Quaker Oats | Industry | Page in |
| | | | | | | | |
Ratio	Formula	Indicates:	1998	1997	1998	1998	book
Price-earnings ratio	Stock price per share / Earnings per share	Relationship between market price per share and earnings per share	27.7	36.5	28.9	26	535

At the end of 1998 and 1997 the market price of Kellogg's stock was $34\frac{1}{8}$ and $49\frac{5}{8}$, respectively. Quaker Oats' stock was selling for $59 at the end of 1998.

In 1998 each share of Kellogg's stock sold for 27.7 times the amount that was earned on each share. Kellogg's price-earnings ratio is higher than the industry average of 26 times but significantly lower than its previous year's ratio of 36.5 and lower than Quaker Oats' ratio of 28.9. These higher P-E ratios suggest that the market is more optimistic about Kellogg and Quaker Oats than about the other companies in the industry. However, it might also signal that their stock is overpriced. The average price-earnings ratio for the stocks that constitute the Standard and Poor's Composite 500 Company Index in October 1999 was an unusually high 36 times.

21. **Payout ratio.** The payout ratio measures the percentage of earnings distributed in the form of cash dividends. It is computed by dividing cash dividends declared on common stock by net income. Companies that have high growth rates are characterized by low payout ratios because they reinvest most of their net income in the business. The payout ratio for Kellogg is shown in Illustration 14-39.

Illustration 14-39
Payout ratio

| | | | Kellogg | | Quaker Oats | Industry | Page in |
| | | | | | | | |
Ratio	Formula	Indicates:	1998	1997	1998	1998	book
Payout ratio	Cash dividends declared on common stock / Net income	Percentage of earnings distributed in the form of cash dividends	.75	.64	.57	.43	533

The 1998 and 1997 payout ratios for Kellogg and Quaker Oats are comparatively high in relation to the industry average of .43.

Management has some control over the amount of dividends paid each year, and companies are generally reluctant to reduce a dividend below the amount paid in a previous year. Therefore, the payout ratio will actually increase if a company's net income declines but the company keeps its total dividend payment the same. Of course, unless the company returns to its previous level of profitability, maintaining this higher dividend payout ratio is probably not possible over the long run. Before drawing any conclusions regarding Kellogg's dividend payout ratio, we should calculate this ratio over a longer period of time to evaluate any trends, and also try to find out whether management's philosophy regarding dividends has changed recently. The "Selected financial data" section of Kellogg's Management Discussion and Analysis shows that over a 10-year period earnings per share have grown 2% per year, while dividends per share have grown 9% per year. Unless earnings growth improves, this rapid dividend growth is not sustainable over the long term.

BUSINESS INSIGHT
Management Perspective

Generally, companies with stable earnings have high payout ratios. For example, a utility such as Potomac Electric Company had an 86% payout ratio over a recent five-year period, and Amoco Corporation had a 63% payout ratio over the same period. Conversely, companies that are expanding rapidly, such as Toys 'R' Us and Microsoft, have never paid a cash dividend.

In terms of the types of financial information available and the ratios used by various industries, what can be practically covered in this textbook gives you only the "Titanic approach": You are seeing only the tip of the iceberg compared to the vast databases and types of ratio analysis that are available on computers. The availability of information is not a problem. The real trick is to be discriminating enough to perform relevant analysis and select pertinent comparative data.

BEFORE YOU GO ON...

◆ Review It

1. What are liquidity ratios? Explain the current ratio, acid-test ratio, receivables turnover ratio, inventory turnover ratio, and current cash debt coverage ratio.
2. What are solvency ratios? Explain the debt to total assets ratio, the times interest earned ratio, and the cash debt coverage ratio.
3. What are profitability ratios? Explain the return on common stockholders' equity ratio, return on assets ratio, asset turnover ratio, cash return on sales, earnings per share, price-earnings ratio, and payout ratio.

LIMITATIONS OF FINANCIAL ANALYSIS

Significant business decisions are frequently made using one or more of the three analytical tools presented in this chapter: horizontal, vertical, and ratio analysis. You should be aware of some of the limitations of these tools and of the financial statements on which they are based.

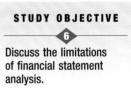

STUDY OBJECTIVE
6

Discuss the limitations of financial statement analysis.

ESTIMATES

Financial statements contain numerous estimates. Estimates are used, for example, in determining the allowance for uncollectible receivables, periodic depreciation, the costs of warranties, and contingent losses. To the extent that these estimates are inaccurate, the financial ratios and percentages are also inaccurate.

COST

Traditional financial statements are based on cost and are not adjusted for price-level changes. Comparisons of unadjusted financial data from different periods may be rendered invalid by significant inflation or deflation. For example, a five-year comparison of Kellogg's revenues shows a growth of 5%. But if, for example, the general price level also increased by 5%, the company's real growth would be zero. Also, some assets such as property, plant, and equipment might be many years old. The historical cost at which they are shown on the balance sheet might be significantly lower than what they could currently be sold for.

ALTERNATIVE ACCOUNTING METHODS

Variations among companies in the application of generally accepted accounting principles may hamper comparability. For example, one company may use the FIFO method of inventory costing, while another company in the same industry may use LIFO. If inventory is a significant asset to both companies, it is unlikely that their current ratios are comparable. For example, if General Motors Corporation had used FIFO instead of LIFO in valuing its inventories, its inventories would have been 26% higher, which significantly affects the current ratio (and other ratios as well).

In addition to differences in inventory costing methods, differences also exist in reporting such items as depreciation, depletion, and amortization. Although these differences in accounting methods might be detectable from reading the notes to the financial statements, adjusting the financial data to compensate for the different methods is difficult, if not impossible, in some cases.

ATYPICAL DATA

Fiscal year-end data may not be typical of a company's financial condition during the year. Companies frequently establish a fiscal year-end that coincides with the low point in their operating activity or inventory levels. Therefore, certain account balances (cash, receivables, payables, and inventories) may not be representative of the balances in the accounts during the year.

DIVERSIFICATION

Diversification in American industry also limits the usefulness of financial analysis. Many companies today are so diversified that they cannot be classified by industry. Others appear to be comparable but are not. You might think that PepsiCo, Inc., and The Coca-Cola Company would be comparable as soft drink industry competitors. But are they comparable when until recently, PepsiCo, in addition to producing Pepsi-Cola, owned Pizza Hut, Kentucky Fried Chicken, Taco Bell, and Frito-Lay; and Coca-Cola, in addition to producing Coke, owns Hi-C (fruit drinks), Minute Maid (frozen juice concentrate), and Columbia Pictures (motion pictures, TV shows, and commercials)? Or, we might like to compare Kellogg to Post Cereals, another of its competitors. But since Post is owned by Phillip Morris, and Phillip Morris generates most of its profits from cigarette sales, and a lot of the rest of its profits from nongrain-related products, comparisons are difficult. As a consequence, deciding what industry a company is in is actually one of the main challenges to effective evaluation of its results.

When companies have significant operations in different lines of business, they are required to report additional disclosures in a segmental data note to their financial statements. Segmental data include total sales, total identifiable assets, operating profit, depreciation expense, and capital expenditures by business segment. Many analysts say that the segmental information is the most important data in the financial statements because, without it, comparison of diversified companies is very difficult.

DECISION TOOLKIT

Decision Checkpoints	Info Needed for Decision	Tool to Use for Decision	How to Evaluate Results
Are efforts to evaluate the company significantly hampered by any of the common limitations of financial analysis?	Financial statements as well as a general understanding of the company and its business	The primary limitations of financial analysis are estimates, cost, alternative accounting methods, atypical data, and diversification.	If any of these factors is significant, the analysis should be relied upon with caution.

BEFORE YOU GO ON...

◆ Review It

1. What are some of the limitations of financial analysis?
2. What are the required disclosures in segmental data notes?

*U*SING THE *D*ECISION *T*OOLKIT

In analyzing a company, you should always investigate an extended period of time in order to determine whether the condition and performance of the company are changing. The condensed financial statements of Kellogg Company for 1996 and 1995 are presented here:

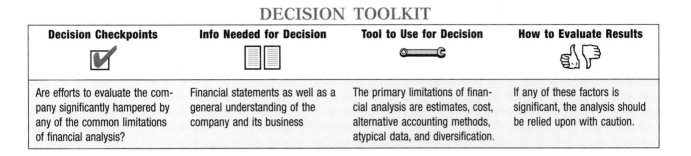

KELLOGG COMPANY, INC.
Balance Sheets
December 31
(in millions)

Assets	1996	1995
Current assets		
Cash and short-term investments	$ 243.8	$ 221.9
Accounts receivable (net)	592.3	590.1
Inventories	424.9	376.7
Prepaid expenses and other current assets	267.6	240.1
Total current assets	1,528.6	1,428.8
Property assets (net)	2,932.9	2,784.8
Intangibles and other assets	588.5	201.0
Total assets	$5,050.0	$4,414.6
Liabilities and Stockholders' Equity		
Current liabilities	$2,199.0	$1,265.4
Long-term liabilities	1,568.6	1,558.3
Stockholders' equity—common	1,282.4	1,590.9
Total liabilities and stockholders' equity	$5,050.0	$4,414.6

KELLOGG COMPANY, INC.
Condensed Income Statements
For the Years Ended December 31
(in millions)

	1996	1995
Net sales	$6,676.6	$7,003.7
Cost of goods sold	3,122.9	3,177.7
Gross profit	3,553.7	3,826.0
Selling and administrative expenses	2,458.7	2,566.7
Nonrecurring charges	136.1	421.8
Income from operations	958.9	837.5
Interest expense	65.6	62.6
Other income (expense), net	(33.4)	21.1
Income before income taxes	859.9	796.0
Income tax expense	328.9	305.7
Net income	$ 531.0	$ 490.3

Instructions

Compute the following ratios for Kellogg for 1996 and 1995, and comment on each relative to the amounts reported in the chapter.

1. Liquidity:
   (a) Current ratio.
   (b) Inventory turnover ratio. (Inventory on December 31, 1994, was $396.3 million.)
2. Solvency:
   (a) Debt to total assets ratio.
   (b) Times interest earned ratio.
3. Profitability:
   (a) Return on common stockholders' equity ratio. (Equity on December 31, 1994, was $1,807.5 million.)
   (b) Return on assets ratio. (Assets on December 31, 1994, were $4,467.3 million.)
   (c) Profit margin ratio.

Solution

1. Liquidity
   (a) Current ratio:

$$1996: \quad \frac{\$1,528.6}{\$2,199.0} = .70:1$$

$$1995: \quad \frac{\$1,428.8}{\$1,265.4} = 1.13:1$$

   (b) Inventory turnover ratio:

$$1996: \quad \frac{\$3,122.9}{(\$424.9 + \$376.7)/2} = 7.8 \text{ times}$$

$$1995: \quad \frac{\$3,177.7}{(\$376.7 + \$396.3)/2} = 8.2 \text{ times}$$

In the chapter we noted that Kellogg's liquidity as measured by the current ratio declined slightly in 1998. We see that between 1995 and 1996 the current ratio declined sharply. Countering this decline in the current ratio, however, is the fact that the inventory turnover ratio has stayed consistently high since 1995. The faster that inventory turns over (is sold), the more liquid it is; that is, the company can accept a lower current ratio if it can turn over its inventory (and receivables) more quickly.

2. Solvency
   (a) Debt to total assets ratio:

   $$1996: \quad \frac{\$3,767.6}{\$5,050.0} = 75\%$$

   $$1995: \quad \frac{\$2,823.7}{\$4,414.6} = 64\%$$

   (b) Times interest earned ratio:

   $$1996: \quad \frac{\$531.0 + \$328.9 + \$65.6}{\$65.6} = 14.1 \text{ times}$$

   $$1995: \quad \frac{\$490.3 + \$305.7 + \$62.6}{\$62.6} = 13.7 \text{ times}$$

Kellogg's solvency as measured by the debt to total assets ratio declined in 1997 and 1998 relative to its level in 1995 and 1996. We can also see from the 1995 and 1996 measures that the times interest earned ratio has also declined during this period, but remains relatively high. This consistently high times interest earned measure gives us confidence that Kellogg can meet its debt payments when due.

3. Profitability
   (a) Return on common stockholders' equity ratio:

   $$1996: \quad \frac{\$531.0}{(\$1,282.4 + \$1,590.9)/2} = 37\%$$

   $$1995: \quad \frac{\$490.3}{(\$1,590.9 + \$1,807.5)/2} = 29\%$$

   (b) Return on assets ratio:

   $$1996: \quad \frac{\$531.0}{(\$5,050.0 + \$4,414.6)/2} = 11\%$$

   $$1995: \quad \frac{\$490.3}{(\$4,414.6 + \$4,467.3)/2} = 11\%$$

   (c) Profit margin ratio:

   $$1996: \quad \frac{\$531.0}{\$6,676.6} = 8\%$$

   $$1995: \quad \frac{\$490.3}{\$7,003.7} = 7\%$$

We noted in the chapter that Kellogg's return on common stockholders' equity ratio was unusually high. We suggested that in 1998 Kellogg reached this high measure by increasing its leverage—that is, by trading on the equity. Note that its return on common stockholders' equity ratio was not nearly as high back in 1995 and 1996. Its profit margin ratio and return on assets have been relatively unchanged during this period. By increasing its leverage, Kellogg has been able to increase its return on common stockholders' equity ratio, but, as we noted in the chapter, higher leverage means higher risk. That is, with higher leverage, if the company's sales turn sour, its profitability could really be hurt.

SUMMARY OF STUDY OBJECTIVES

1 *Understand the concept of earning power and indicate how irregular items are presented.* Earning power refers to a company's ability to sustain its profits from operations. Irregular items—discontinued operations, extraordinary items, and changes in accounting principles—are presented on the income statement net of tax below "Income from continuing operations" to highlight their unusual nature.

2 *Discuss the need for comparative analysis and identify the tools of financial statement analysis.* Comparative analysis is performed to evaluate a company's short-term liquidity, profitability, and long-term solvency. Comparisons can detect changes in financial relationships and significant trends, and provide insight into a company's competitive position and relative position in its industry. Financial statements may be analyzed horizontally, vertically, and with ratios.

3 *Explain and apply horizontal analysis.* Horizontal analysis is a technique for evaluating a series of data over a period of time to determine the increase or decrease that has taken place, expressed as either an amount or a percentage.

4 *Describe and apply vertical analysis.* Vertical analysis is a technique that expresses each item in a financial statement as a percentage of a relevant total or a base amount.

5 *Identify and compute ratios and describe their purpose and use in analyzing a company's liquidity, solvency, and profitability.* Financial ratios are provided in Illustrations 14-17 through 14-23 (liquidity), Illustrations 14-24 through 14-27 (solvency), and Illustrations 14-29 through 14-39 (profitability).

6 *Discuss the limitations of financial statement analysis.* The usefulness of analytical tools is limited by the use of estimates, the cost basis, the application of alternative accounting methods, atypical data at year-end, and the diversification of companies.

*D*ECISION *T*OOLKIT—*A* *S*UMMARY

Decision Checkpoints	Info Needed for Decision	Tool to Use for Decision	How to Evaluate Results
Has the company sold any major lines of business?	Discontinued operations section of income statement	Anything reported in this section indicates that the company has discontinued a major line of business.	If a major business line has been discontinued, its results in the current period should not be included in estimates of future net income.
Has the company experienced any extraordinary events or transactions?	Extraordinary item section of income statement	Anything reported in this section indicates that the company experienced an event that was both unusual and infrequent.	These items should usually be ignored in estimating future net income.
Has the company changed any of its accounting policies?	Cumulative effect of change in accounting principle section of income statement	Anything reported in this section indicates that the company has changed an accounting policy during the current year.	The cumulative effect should be ignored in estimating the future net income.
How do the company's financial position and operating results compare with those of previous period?	Income statement and balance sheet	Comparative financial statements should be prepared over at least two years, with the first year reported being the base year. Changes in each line item relative to the base year should be presented both by amount and by percentage. This is called horizontal analysis.	Significant changes should be investigated to determine the reason for the change.
How do the relationships between items in this year's financial statements compare with those of last year or those of competitors?	Income statement and balance sheet	Each line item on the income statement should be presented as a percentage of net sales, and each line item on the balance sheet should be presented as a percentage of total assets or total liabilities and stockholders' equity. These percentages should be investigated for differences either across years in the same company or in the same year across different companies. This is called vertical analysis.	Any differences either across years or between companies should be investigated to determine the cause.
Are efforts to evaluate the company significantly hampered by any of the common limitations of financial analysis?	Financial statements as well as a general understanding of the company and its business	The primary limitations of financial analysis are estimates, cost, alternative accounting methods, atypical data, and diversification.	If any of these factors is significant, the analysis should be relied upon with caution.

GLOSSARY

Acid-test (quick) ratio A measure of a company's immediate short-term liquidity, computed as the sum of cash, short-term investments, and net receivables divided by current liabilities. (p. 682)

Asset turnover ratio A measure of how efficiently a company uses its assets to generate sales, computed as net sales divided by average total assets. (p. 689)

Average collection period The average number of days that receivables are outstanding, calculated as receivables turnover divided into 365 days. (p. 683)

Cash debt coverage ratio A cash-basis measure used to evaluate solvency, computed as cash from operations divided by average total liabilities. (p. 686)

Cash return on sales ratio The cash-basis measure of net income generated by each dollar of sales, computed as net cash from operations divided by net sales. (p. 691)

Change in accounting principle Use of an accounting principle in the current year different from the one used in the preceding year. (p. 670)

Comprehensive income Includes all changes in stockholders' equity during a period except those resulting from investments by stockholders and distributions to stockholders. (p. 672)

Current cash debt coverage ratio A cash-basis measure of short-term debt-paying ability, computed as cash provided by operations divided by average current liabilities. (p. 682)

Current ratio A measure that expresses the relationship of current assets to current liabilities, calculated as current assets divided by current liabilities. (p. 681)

Days in inventory A measure of the average number of days it takes to sell the inventory, computed as inventory turnover divided into 365 days. (p. 684)

Debt to total assets ratio A measure of the percentage of total assets provided by creditors, computed as total debt divided by total assets. (p. 685)

Discontinued operations The disposal of a significant segment of a business. (p. 667)

Earnings per share The net income earned by each share of common stock, computed as net income divided by the average common shares outstanding. (p. 691)

Extraordinary items Events and transactions that meet two conditions: (1) unusual in nature and (2) infrequent in occurrence. (p. 668)

Free cash flow The amount of cash from operations after adjusting for capital expenditures and cash dividends paid. (p. 687)

Gross profit rate An indicator of a company's ability to maintain an adequate selling price of goods above their cost, computed as gross profit divided by net sales. (p. 690)

Horizontal analysis A technique for evaluating a series of financial statement data over a period of time to determine the increase (decrease) that has taken place, expressed as either an amount or a percentage. (p. 673)

Inventory turnover ratio A measure of the liquidity of inventory, computed as cost of goods sold divided by average inventory. (p. 684)

Leveraging Borrowing money at a lower rate of interest than can be earned by using the borrowed money; also referred to as trading on the equity. (p. 688)

Liquidity ratios Measures of the short-term ability of the enterprise to pay its maturing obligations and to meet unexpected needs for cash. (p. 680)

Operating expenses to sales ratio A measure of the costs incurred to support each dollar of sales, computed as operating expenses divided by net sales. (p. 690)

Payout ratio A measure of the percentage of earnings distributed in the form of cash dividends, calculated as cash dividends divided by net income. (p. 692)

Price-earnings ratio A comparison of the market price of each share of common stock to the earnings per share, computed as the market price of the stock divided by earnings per share. (p. 692)

Profit margin ratio A measure of the net income generated by each dollar of sales, computed as net income divided by net sales. (p. 689)

Profitability ratios Measures of the income or operating success of an enterprise for a given period of time. (p. 680)

Quick ratio Another name for the acid-test ratio. (p. 682)

Receivables turnover ratio A measure of the liquidity of receivables, computed as net credit sales divided by average net receivables. (p. 683)

Return on assets ratio An overall measure of profitability, calculated as net income divided by average total assets. (p. 688)

Return on common stockholders' equity ratio A measure of the dollars of net income earned for each dollar invested by the owners, computed as income available to common stockholders divided by average common stockholders' equity. (p. 688)

Segmental data A required note disclosure for diversified companies in which the company reports sales, operating profit, identifiable assets, depreciation expense, and capital expenditures by major business segment. (p. 694)

Solvency ratios Measures of the ability of the enterprise to survive over a long period of time. (p. 680)

Times interest earned ratio A measure of a company's ability to meet interest payments as they come due, calculated as income before interest expense and income taxes divided by interest expense. (p. 686)

Trading on the equity Same as leveraging. (p. 688)

Vertical analysis A technique for evaluating financial statement data that expresses each item in a financial statement as a percent of a base amount. (p. 676)

DEMONSTRATION PROBLEM

The events and transactions of Dever Corporation for the year ending December 31, 2001, resulted in these data:

Cost of goods sold	$2,600,000
Net sales	4,400,000
Other expenses and losses	9,600
Other revenues and gains	5,600
Selling and administrative expenses	1,100,000
Income from operations of plastics division	70,000
Gain on sale of plastics division	500,000
Loss from tornado disaster (extraordinary loss)	600,000
Cumulative effect of changing from straight-line depreciation to double-declining-balance (increase in depreciation expense)	300,000

Analysis reveals:

1. All items are before the applicable income tax rate of 30%.
2. The plastics division was sold on July 1.
3. All operating data for the plastics division have been segregated.

Instructions

Prepare an income statement for the year, excluding the presentation of earnings per share.

Solution to Demonstration Problem

Problem-Solving Strategies

1. Remember that material items not typical of operations are reported in separate sections net of taxes.
2. Income taxes should be associated with the item that affects the taxes.
3. A corporation income statement has income tax expense when there is income before income tax.
4. All data presented in determining income before income taxes are the same as for unincorporated companies.

DEVER CORPORATION
Income Statement
For the Year Ended December 31, 2001

Net sales		$4,400,000
Cost of goods sold		2,600,000
Gross profit		1,800,000
Selling and administrative expenses		1,100,000
Income from operations		700,000
Other revenues and gains	$ 5,600	
Other expenses and losses	9,600	4,000
Income before income taxes		696,000
Income tax expense ($696,000 × 30%)		208,800
Income from continuing operations		487,200
Discontinued operations		
Income from operations of plastics division, net of $21,000 income taxes ($70,000 × 30%)	49,000	
Gain on sale of plastics division, net of $150,000 income taxes ($500,000 × 30%)	350,000	399,000
Income before extraordinary item and cumulative effect of change in accounting principle		886,200
Extraordinary item		
Tornado loss, net of income tax saving $180,000 ($600,000 × 30%)		(420,000)
Cumulative effect of change in accounting principle		
Effect on prior years of change in depreciation method, net of $90,000 income tax saving ($300,000 × 30%)		(210,000)
Net income		$ 256,200

SELF-STUDY QUESTIONS

Answers are at the end of the chapter.

All of the Self-Study Questions in this chapter employ decision tools.

(SO 1) 1. In reporting discontinued operations, the income statement should show in a special section:
   (a) gains and losses on the disposal of the discontinued segment.
   (b) gains and losses from operations of the discontinued segment.
   (c) Neither (a) nor (b).
   (d) Both (a) and (b).

(SO 1) 2. The Candy Stick Corporation has income before taxes of $400,000 and an extraordinary loss of $100,000. If the income tax rate is 25% on all items, the income statement should show income before extraordinary items, and extraordinary items, respectively, of
   (a) $325,000 and $100,000.
   (b) $325,000 and $75,000.
   (c) $300,000 and $100,000.
   (d) $300,000 and $75,000.

(SO 2) 3. Comparisons of data within a company are an example of the following comparative basis:
   (a) industry averages.
   (b) intracompany.
   (c) intercompany.
   (d) Both (b) and (c).

(SO 3) 4. In horizontal analysis, each item is expressed as a percentage of the:
   (a) net income amount.
   (b) stockholders' equity amount.
   (c) total assets amount.
   (d) base-year amount.

(SO 3) 5. Leland Corporation reported net sales of $300,000, $330,000, and $360,000 in the years 1999, 2000, and 2001, respectively. If 1999 is the base year, what is the trend percentage for 2001?
   (a) 77%.
   (b) 108%.
   (c) 120%.
   (d) 130%.

(SO 4) 6. The following schedule is a display of what type of analysis?

	Amount	Percent
Current assets	$200,000	25%
Property, plant, and equipment	600,000	75%
Total assets	$800,000	

   (a) Horizontal analysis.
   (b) Differential analysis.

   (c) Vertical analysis.
   (d) Ratio analysis.

(SO 4) 7. In vertical analysis, the base amount for depreciation expense is generally:
   (a) net sales.
   (b) depreciation expense in a previous year.
   (c) gross profit.
   (d) fixed assets.

(SO 5) 8. Which measure is an evaluation of a company's ability to pay current liabilities?
   (a) Acid-test ratio.
   (b) Current ratio.
   (c) Both (a) and (b).
   (d) None of the above.

(SO 5) 9. Which measure is useful in evaluating the efficiency in managing inventories?
   (a) Inventory turnover ratio.
   (b) Days in inventory.
   (c) Both (a) and (b).
   (d) None of the above.

(SO 5) 10. Which of these is *not* a liquidity ratio?
   (a) Current ratio.
   (b) Asset turnover ratio.
   (c) Inventory turnover ratio.
   (d) Receivables turnover ratio.

(SO 5) 11. Plano Corporation reported net income $24,000; net sales $400,000; and average assets $600,000 for 2001. What is the 2001 profit margin?
   (a) 6%.
   (b) 12%.
   (c) 40%.
   (d) 200%.

(SO 6) 12. Which of the following is generally *not* considered to be a limitation of financial analysis?
   (a) Use of ratio analysis.
   (b) Use of estimates.
   (c) Use of cost.
   (d) Use of alternative accounting methods.

QUESTIONS

⊙━━━━C All of the Questions in this chapter employ decision tools.

1. Explain earning power. What relationship does this concept have to the treatment of irregular items on the income statement?

2. Indicate which of the following items would be reported as an extraordinary item on Fine & Fancy Food Corporation's income statement.
   (a) Loss from damages caused by a volcano eruption.
   (b) Loss from the sale of short-term investments.
   (c) Loss attributable to a labor strike.
   (d) Loss caused when the Food and Drug Administration prohibited the manufacture and sale of a product line.
   (e) Loss of inventory from flood damage because a warehouse is located on a flood plain that floods every 5 to 10 years.
   (f) Loss on the write-down of outdated inventory.
   (g) Loss from a foreign government's expropriation of a production facility.
   (h) Loss from damage to a warehouse in southern California from a minor earthquake.

3. Iron Ingots Inc. reported 2000 earnings per share of $3.26 and had no extraordinary items. In 2001 earnings per share on income before extraordinary items was $2.99, and earnings per share on net income was $3.49. Do you consider this trend to be favorable? Why or why not?

4. Rodger Robotics Inc. has been in operation for 3 years. All of its manufacturing equipment, which has a useful life of 10 to 12 years, has been depreciated on a straight-line basis. During the fourth year, Rodger Robotics changes to an accelerated depreciation method for all of its equipment.
   (a) Will Rodger Robotics post a gain or a loss on this change?
   (b) How will this change be reported?

5. (a) Tia Kim believes that the analysis of financial statements is directed at two characteristics of a company: liquidity and profitability. Is Tia correct? Explain.
   (b) Are short-term creditors, long-term creditors, and stockholders interested in primarily the same characteristics of a company? Explain.

6. (a) Distinguish among the following bases of comparison: intracompany, industry averages, and intercompany.
   (b) Give the principal value of using each of the three bases of comparison.

7. Two popular methods of financial statement analysis are horizontal analysis and vertical analysis. Explain the difference between these two methods.

8. (a) If Roe Company had net income of $540,000 in 2000 and it experienced a 24.5% increase in net income for 2001, what is its net income for 2001?
   (b) If six cents of every dollar of Roe's revenue is net income in 2000, what is the dollar amount of 2000 revenue?

9. Name the major ratios useful in assessing (a) liquidity and (b) solvency.

10. Tony Robins is puzzled. His company had a profit margin of 10% in 2001. He feels that this is an indication that the company is doing well. Joan Graham, his accountant, says that more information is needed to determine the company's financial well-being. Who is correct? Why?

11. What does each type of ratio measure?
    (a) Liquidity ratios.
    (b) Solvency ratios.
    (c) Profitability ratios.

12. What is the difference between the current ratio and the acid-test ratio?

13. Gerry Bullock Company, a retail store, has a receivables turnover ratio of 4.5 times. The industry average is 12.5 times. Does Bullock have a collection problem with its receivables?

14. Which ratios should be used to help answer each of these questions?
    (a) How efficient is a company in using its assets to produce sales?
    (b) How near to sale is the inventory on hand?
    (c) How many dollars of net income were earned for each dollar invested by the owners?
    (d) How able is a company to meet interest charges as they fall due?

15. In October 1999 the price-earnings ratio of **General Motors** was 7, and the price-earnings ratio of **Microsoft** was 61. Which company did the stock market favor? Explain.

16. What is the formula for computing the payout ratio? Do you expect this ratio to be high or low for a growth company?

17. Holding all other factors constant, indicate whether each of the following changes generally signals good or bad news about a company:
    (a) Increase in profit margin ratio.
    (b) Decrease in inventory turnover ratio.
    (c) Increase in current ratio.
    (d) Decrease in earnings per share.
    (e) Increase in price-earnings ratio.
    (f) Increase in debt to total assets ratio.
    (g) Decrease in times interest earned ratio.

18. The return on assets for Windsor Corporation is 7.6%. During the same year Windsor's return on common stockholders' equity is 12.8%. What is the explanation for the difference in the two rates?

19. Which two ratios do you think should be of greatest interest in each of the following cases?
    (a) A pension fund considering the purchase of 20-year bonds.

(b) A bank contemplating a short-term loan.

(c) A common stockholder.

20. (a) What is meant by trading on the equity?

(b) How would you determine the profitability of trading on the equity?

21. Khris Inc. has net income of $270,000, average shares of common stock outstanding of 50,000 and preferred dividends for the period of $40,000. What is Khris's earnings per share of common stock? Phil Remmers, the president of Khris Inc., believes that the computed EPS of the company is high. Comment.

22. Identify and briefly explain five limitations of financial analysis.

23. Explain how the choice of one of the following accounting methods over the other raises or lowers a company's net income during a period of continuing inflation.

(a) Use of FIFO instead of LIFO for inventory costing.

(b) Use of a 6-year life for machinery instead of a 9-year life.

(c) Use of straight-line depreciation instead of accelerated declining-balance depreciation.

BRIEF EXERCISES

All of the Brief Exercises in this chapter employ decision tools.

Prepare a discontinued operations section of an income statement.
(SO 1)

BE14-1 On June 30 Osborn Corporation discontinued its operations in Mexico. During the year, the operating loss was $400,000 before taxes. On September 1 Osborn disposed of the Mexico facility at a pretax loss of $150,000. The applicable tax rate is 30%. Show the discontinued operations section of Osborn's income statement.

Prepare a corrected income statement with an extraordinary item.
(SO 1)

BE14-2 An inexperienced accountant for Lima Corporation showed the following in Lima's 2001 income statement: Income before income taxes, $300,000; Income tax expense, $72,000; Extraordinary loss from flood (before taxes), $60,000; and Net income, $168,000. The extraordinary loss and taxable income are both subject to a 30% tax rate. Prepare a corrected income statement beginning with "Income before income taxes."

Prepare a change in accounting principles section of an income statement.
(SO 1)

BE14-3 On January 1, 2001, Shirli Inc. changed from the straight-line method of depreciation to the declining-balance method. The cumulative effect of the change was to increase the prior years' depreciation by $40,000 and 2001 depreciation by $8,000. Show the change in accounting principle section of the 2001 income statement, assuming the tax rate is 30%.

Prepare horizontal analysis.
(SO 3)

BE14-4 Using these data from the comparative balance sheet of All-State Company, perform horizontal analysis.

	December 31, 2001	December 31, 2000
Accounts receivable	$ 600,000	$ 400,000
Inventory	780,000	600,000
Total assets	3,220,000	2,800,000

Prepare vertical analysis.
(SO 4)

BE14-5 Using the data presented in BE14-4 for All-State Company, perform vertical analysis.

Calculate percentage of change.
(SO 3)

BE14-6 Net income was $500,000 in 1999, $420,000 in 2000, and $504,000 in 2001. What is the percentage of change from (a) 1999 to 2000 and (b) 2000 to 2001? Is the change an increase or a decrease?

Calculate net income.
(SO 3)

BE14-7 If Cavalier Company had net income of $672,300 in 2001 and it experienced a 25% increase in net income over 2000, what was its 2000 net income?

Calculate change in net income.
(SO 4)

BE14-8 Vertical analysis (common-size) percentages for Waubons Company's sales, cost of goods sold, and expenses are listed here:

Vertical Analysis	2001	2000	1999
Sales	100.0%	100.0%	100.0%
Cost of goods sold	59.2	62.4	64.5
Expenses	25.0	26.6	29.5

Did Waubons' net income as a percent of sales increase, decrease, or remain unchanged over the 3-year period? Provide numerical support for your answer.

BE14-9   Horizontal analysis (trend analysis) percentages for Tilden Company's sales, cost of goods sold, and expenses are listed here:

Calculate change in net income.
(SO 3)

Horizontal Analysis	2001	2000	1999
Sales	96.2%	106.8%	100.0%
Cost of goods sold	102.0	97.0	100.0
Expenses	110.6	95.4	100.0

Explain whether Tilden's net income increased, decreased, or remained unchanged over the 3-year period.

BE14-10   These selected condensed data are taken from a recent balance sheet of **Bob Evans Farms**:

Calculate liquidity ratios.
(SO 5)

Cash	$ 8,241,000
Marketable securities	1,947,000
Accounts receivable	12,545,000
Inventories	14,814,000
Other current assets	5,371,000
Total current assets	$42,918,000
Total current liabilities	$44,844,000

What are the (a) current ratio and (b) acid-test ratio?

BE14-11   The following data are taken from the financial statements of Diet-Mite Company:

Evaluate collection of accounts receivable.
(SO 5)

	2001	2000
Accounts receivable (net), end of year	$ 560,000	$ 540,000
Net sales on account	5,500,000	4,100,000
Terms for all sales are 1/10, n/45.		

Compute for each year (a) the receivables turnover ratio and (b) the average collection period. What conclusions about the management of accounts receivable can be drawn from these data? At the end of 1999, accounts receivable (net) was $490,000.

BE14-12   The following data were taken from the income statements of Linda Shumway Company:

Evaluate management of inventory.
(SO 5)

	2001	2000
Sales revenue	$6,420,000	$6,240,000
Beginning inventory	980,000	837,000
Purchases	4,640,000	4,661,000
Ending inventory	1,020,000	980,000

Compute for each year (a) the inventory turnover ratio and (b) days in inventory. What conclusions concerning the management of the inventory can be drawn from these data?

BE14-13   **Staples, Inc.** is one of the largest suppliers of office products in the United States. It had net income of $185.3 million and net revenue of $7,123 million in 1998. Its total assets were $2,639 million at the beginning of the year and $3,179 million at the end of the year. What is Staples, Inc.'s (a) asset turnover ratio and (b) profit margin ratio? (Round to two decimals.)

Calculate profitability ratios.
(SO 5)

BE14-14   Haymark Products Company has stockholders' equity of $400,000 and net income of $50,000. It has a payout ratio of 20% and a rate of return on assets of 16%. How much did Haymark Products pay in cash dividends, and what were its average assets?

Calculate profitability ratios.
(SO 5)

BE14-15   Selected data taken from the 1998 financial statements of trading card company **Topps Company, Inc.** are as follows (in thousands):

Calculate cash-basis liquidity, profitability, and solvency ratios.
(SO 5)

Net sales for 1998	$229,414
Current liabilities, January 1, 1998	80,964
Current liabilities, December 31, 1998	68,619
Net cash provided by operating activities	29,522
Total liabilities, January 1, 1998	86,858
Total liabilities, December 31, 1998	116,797

Compute these ratios at December 31, 1998: (a) current cash debt coverage ratio, (b) cash return on sales ratio, and (c) cash debt coverage ratio.

EXERCISES

⊙━━━⊙   All of the Exercises in this chapter employ decision tools.

Prepare irregular items portion of an income statement.
(SO 1)

E14-1   The Davis Company has income from continuing operations of $240,000 for the year ended December 31, 2001. It also has the following items (before considering income taxes): (1) an extraordinary fire loss of $60,000, (2) a gain of $40,000 from the discontinuance of a division, which includes a $110,000 gain from the operation of the division and a $70,000 loss on its disposal, and (3) a cumulative change in accounting principle that resulted in an increase in the prior year's depreciation of $30,000. Assume all items are subject to income taxes at a 30% tax rate.

Instructions
Prepare Davis Company's income statement for 2001, beginning with "Income from continuing operations."

Evaluate the effects of unusual or irregular items.
(SO 1, 5, 6)

E14-2   *The Wall Street Journal* routinely publishes summaries of corporate quarterly and annual earnings reports in a feature called the "Earnings Digest." A typical "digest" report takes the following form:

ENERGY ENTERPRISES (A)

	Quarter ending July 31	
	2001	**2000**
Revenues	$2,049,000,000	$1,754,000,000
Net income	97,000,000	(a) 68,750,000
EPS: Net income	1.31	.93

	9 months ending July 31	
	2001	**2000**
Revenues	$5,578,500,000	$5,065,300,000
Extraordinary item	(b) 1,900,000	
Net income	102,700,000	(a) 33,250,000
EPS: Net income	1.39	.45

(a) Includes a net charge of $26,000,000 from loss on the sale of electrical equipment
(b) Extraordinary gain on Middle East property expropriation

The letter in parentheses following the company name indicates the exchange on which Energy Enterprises' stock is traded—in this case, the American Stock Exchange.

Instructions
Answer these questions:
(a) How was the loss on the electrical equipment reported on the income statement? Was it reported in the third quarter of 2000? How can you tell?
(b) Why did *The Wall Street Journal* list the extraordinary item separately?
(c) What is the extraordinary item? Was it included in income for the third quarter? How can you tell?
(d) Did Energy Enterprises have an operating loss in any quarter of 2000? Of 2001? How do you know?
(e) Approximately how many shares of stock were outstanding in 2001? Did the number of outstanding shares change from July 31, 2000 to July 31, 2001?
(f) As an investor, what numbers should you use to determine Energy Enterprises' profit margin ratio? Calculate the 9-month profit margin ratio for 2000 and 2001 that you consider most useful. Explain your decision.

E14-3 Here is financial information for Merchandise Inc.:

Prepare horizontal analysis.
(SO 3)

	December 31, 2001	December 31, 2000
Current assets	$120,000	$100,000
Plant assets (net)	400,000	330,000
Current liabilities	91,000	70,000
Long-term liabilities	144,000	95,000
Common stock, $1 par	150,000	115,000
Retained earnings	135,000	150,000

Instructions

Prepare a schedule showing a horizontal analysis for 2001 using 2000 as the base year.

E14-4 Operating data for Fleetwood Corporation are presented here:

Prepare vertical analysis.
(SO 4)

	2001	2000
Sales	$800,000	$600,000
Cost of goods sold	472,000	390,000
Selling expenses	120,000	72,000
Administrative expenses	80,000	54,000
Income tax expense	38,400	25,200
Net income	89,600	58,800

Instructions

Prepare a schedule showing a vertical analysis for 2001 and 2000.

E14-5 The comparative balance sheets of **Philip Morris Companies, Inc.**, are presented here:

Prepare horizontal and vertical analyses.
(SO 3, 4)

PHILIP MORRIS COMPANIES
Comparative Balance Sheets
December 31
($ in millions)

Assets	1998	1997
Current assets	$20,230	$17,440
Property, plant, and equipment (net)	12,335	11,621
Other assets	27,355	26,886
Total assets	$59,920	$55,947

Liabilities and Stockholders' Equity		
Current liabilities	$16,379	$15,071
Long-term liabilities	27,344	25,956
Stockholders' equity	16,197	14,920
Total liabilities and stockholders' equity	$59,920	$55,947

Instructions

(a) Prepare a horizontal analysis of the balance sheet data for Philip Morris using 1997 as a base. (Show the amount of increase or decrease as well.)

(b) Prepare a vertical analysis of the balance sheet data for Philip Morris for 1998.

E14-6 Here are the comparative income statements of Olympic Corporation:

Prepare horizontal and vertical analyses.
(SO 3, 4)

OLYMPIC CORPORATION
Comparative Income Statements
For the Years Ended December 31

	2001	2000
Net sales	$550,000	$550,000
Cost of goods sold	440,000	450,000
Gross profit	$110,000	$100,000
Operating expenses	57,200	54,000
Net income	$ 52,800	$ 46,000

Instructions

(a) Prepare a horizontal analysis of the income statement data for Olympic Corporation using 2000 as a base. (Show the amounts of increase or decrease.)

(b) Prepare a vertical analysis of the income statement data for Olympic Corporation for both years.

Compute liquidity ratios and compare results.
(SO 5)

E14-7 **Nordstrom, Inc.,** operates department stores in numerous states. Selected financial statement data (in millions) for 1998 are presented here:

	End of Year	Beginning of Year
Cash and cash equivalents	$ 241.4	$ 24.8
Receivables (net)	587.1	664.4
Merchandise inventory	750.3	826.0
Other current assets	101.6	79.7
Total current assets	$1,680.4	$1,594.9
Total current liabilities	$ 768.5	$ 942.6

For the year, net credit sales were $5,135.0 million, cost of goods sold was $3,164.8 million, and cash from operations was $600.8 million.

Instructions

Compute the current ratio, acid-test ratio, current cash debt coverage ratio, receivables turnover ratio, average collection period, inventory turnover ratio, and days in inventory at the end of the current year.

Perform current and acid-test ratio analysis.
(SO 5)

E14-8 **Firpo Incorporated** had the following transactions involving current assets and current liabilities during February 2001:

Feb.	3	Collected accounts receivable of $15,000.
	7	Purchased equipment for $25,000 cash.
	11	Paid $3,000 for a 3-year insurance policy.
	14	Paid accounts payable of $14,000.
	18	Declared cash dividends, $6,000.

Additional information:

1. As of February 1, 2001, current assets were $140,000 and current liabilities were $50,000.
2. As of February 1, 2001, current assets included $15,000 of inventory and $5,000 of prepaid expenses.

Instructions

(a) Compute the current ratio as of the beginning of the month and after each transaction.

(b) Compute the acid-test ratio as of the beginning of the month and after each transaction.

Compute selected ratios.
(SO 5)

E14-9 **Georgette Company** has these comparative balance sheet data:

GEORGETTE COMPANY
Balance Sheets
December 31

	2001	2000
Cash	$ 20,000	$ 30,000
Receivables (net)	65,000	60,000
Inventories	60,000	50,000
Plant assets (net)	200,000	180,000
	$345,000	$320,000
Accounts payable	$ 50,000	$ 60,000
Mortgage payable (15%)	100,000	100,000
Common stock, $10 par	140,000	120,000
Retained earnings	55,000	40,000
	$345,000	$320,000

Additional information for 2001:
1. Net income was $25,000.
2. Sales on account were $420,000. Sales returns and allowances amounted to $20,000.
3. Cost of goods sold was $198,000.
4. Net cash provided by operating activities was $44,000.

Instructions
Compute the following ratios at December 31, 2001:

(a) Current.
(b) Acid-test.
(c) Receivables turnover.
(d) Average collection period.
(e) Inventory turnover.

(f) Days in inventory.
(g) Cash return on sales.
(h) Cash debt coverage.
(i) Current cash debt coverage.

E14-10   Selected comparative statement data for the giant bookseller **Barnes & Noble** are presented here. All balance sheet data are as of December 31 (in millions).

Compute selected ratios.
(SO 5)

	1998	1997
Net sales	$3,005.6	$2,796.9
Cost of goods sold	2,142.7	2,019.3
Interest expense	25.4	38.1
Net income	92.4	53.2
Accounts receivable	57.5	43.9
Inventory	945.1	852.1
Total assets	1,807.6	1,591.2
Total common stockholders' equity	678.8	531.8
Cash provided by operating activities	181.1	169.2

Instructions
Compute the following ratios for 1998:

(a) Profit margin.
(b) Asset turnover.
(c) Return on assets.

(d) Return on common stockholders' equity.
(e) Cash return on sales.
(f) Gross profit rate.

E14-11   Here is the income statement for Jean LeFay, Inc:

Compute selected ratios.
(SO 5)

JEAN LEFAY, INC.
Income Statement
For the Year Ended December 31, 2001

Sales	$400,000
Cost of goods sold	230,000
Gross profit	170,000
Expenses (including $20,000 interest and $24,000 income taxes)	100,000
Net income	$ 70,000

Additional information:
1. Common stock outstanding January 1, 2001, was 30,000 shares. On July 1, 2001, 10,000 more shares were issued.
2. The market price of Jean LeFay, Inc., stock was $15 in 2001.
3. Cash dividends of $21,000 were paid, $5,000 of which were to preferred stockholders.
4. Cash provided by operating activities was $98,000.

Instructions
Compute the following measures for 2001:

(a) Earnings per share.
(b) Price-earnings ratio.
(c) Payout ratio.

(d) Times interest earned ratio.
(e) Cash return on sales ratio.

E14-12   Shaker Corporation experienced a fire on December 31, 2001, in which its financial records were partially destroyed. It has been able to salvage some of the records and has ascertained the following balances:

Compute amounts from ratios.
(SO 5)

	December 31, 2001	December 31, 2000
Cash	$ 30,000	$ 10,000
Receivables (net)	72,500	126,000
Inventory	200,000	180,000
Accounts payable	50,000	10,000
Notes payable	30,000	20,000
Common stock, $100 par	400,000	400,000
Retained earnings	113,500	101,000

Additional information:
1. The inventory turnover is 3.6 times.
2. The return on common stockholders' equity is 22%. The company had no additional paid-in capital.
3. The receivables turnover is 9.4 times.
4. The return on assets is 16%.
5. Total assets at December 31, 2000, were $605,000.

Instructions
Compute the following for Shaker Corporation:
(a) Cost of goods sold for 2001.
(b) Net sales for 2001.
(c) Net income for 2001.
(d) Total assets at December 31, 2001.

PROBLEMS: SET A

All of the Problems in this chapter employ decision tools.

Prepare vertical analysis and comment on profitability.
(SO 4, 5)

P14-1A Here are comparative statement data for Catchem Company and Eatum Company, two competitors. All balance sheet data are as of December 31, 2001, and December 31, 2000.

	Catchum Company		Eatum Company	
	2001	**2000**	**2001**	**2000**
Net sales	$1,849,035		$539,038	
Cost of goods sold	1,080,490		238,006	
Operating expenses	302,275		79,000	
Interest expense	6,800		1,252	
Income tax expense	51,030		6,650	
Current assets	325,975	$312,410	83,336	$ 79,467
Plant assets (net)	521,310	500,000	139,728	125,812
Current liabilities	66,325	75,815	35,348	30,281
Long-term liabilities	108,500	90,000	29,620	25,000
Common stock, $10 par	500,000	500,000	120,000	120,000
Retained earnings	172,460	146,595	38,096	29,998

Instructions
(a) Prepare a vertical analysis of the 2001 income statement data for Catchem Company and Eatum Company.
(b) Comment on the relative profitability of the companies by computing the 2001 return on assets and the return on common stockholders' equity ratios for both companies.

P14-2A   The comparative statements of Harry Connick, Jr., Company are presented here: *Compute ratios from balance sheet and income statement.*
(SO 5)

HARRY CONNICK, JR., COMPANY
Income Statements
For the Years Ended December 31

	2001	2000
Net sales	$1,918,500	$1,750,500
Cost of goods sold	1,005,500	996,000
Gross profit	913,000	754,500
Selling and administrative expenses	506,000	479,000
Income from operations	407,000	275,500
Other expenses and losses		
Interest expense	28,000	19,000
Income before income taxes	379,000	256,500
Income tax expense	86,700	77,000
Net income	$ 292,300	$ 179,500

HARRY CONNICK, JR., COMPANY
Balance Sheets
December 31

	2001	2000
Assets		
Current assets		
Cash	$ 60,100	$ 64,200
Short-term investments	54,000	50,000
Accounts receivable (net)	107,800	102,800
Inventory	143,000	115,500
Total current assets	364,900	332,500
Plant assets (net)	625,300	520,300
Total assets	$990,200	$852,800
Liabilities and Stockholders' Equity		
Current liabilities		
Accounts payable	$170,000	$145,400
Income taxes payable	43,500	42,000
Total current liabilities	213,500	187,400
Bonds payable	210,000	200,000
Total liabilities	423,500	387,400
Stockholders' equity		
Common stock ($5 par)	280,000	300,000
Retained earnings	286,700	165,400
Total stockholders' equity	566,700	465,400
Total liabilities and stockholders' equity	$990,200	$852,800

On July 1, 2001, 4,000 shares were repurchased and canceled. All sales were on account.
Net cash provided by operating activities for 2001 was $280,000.

Instructions
Compute the following ratios for 2001:
(a) Earnings per share.
(b) Return on common stockholders' equity.
(c) Return on assets.
(d) Current ratio.

(e) Acid-test.

(f) Receivables turnover.

(g) Average collection period.

(h) Inventory turnover.

(i) Days in inventory.

(j) Times interest earned.

(k) Asset turnover.

(l) Debt to total assets.

(m) Current cash debt coverage.

(n) Cash return on sales.

(o) Cash debt coverage.

Perform ratio analysis.
(SO 5)

P14-3A Condensed balance sheet and income statement data for Midnight Oil Corporation are presented here:

MIDNIGHT OIL CORPORATION
Balance Sheets
December 31

	2001	2000	1999
Cash	$ 25,000	$ 20,000	$ 18,000
Receivables (net)	50,000	45,000	48,000
Other current assets	90,000	85,000	64,000
Investments	55,000	70,000	45,000
Plant and equipment (net)	500,000	370,000	258,000
	$720,000	$590,000	$433,000
Current liabilities	$ 75,000	$ 80,000	$ 30,000
Long-term debt	160,000	85,000	20,000
Common stock, $10 par	340,000	300,000	300,000
Retained earnings	145,000	125,000	83,000
	$720,000	$590,000	$433,000

MIDNIGHT OIL CORPORATION
Income Statements
For the Years Ended December 31

	2001	2000
Sales	$640,000	$500,000
Less: Sales returns and allowances	40,000	50,000
Net sales	600,000	450,000
Cost of goods sold	420,000	300,000
Gross profit	180,000	150,000
Operating expenses (including income taxes)	126,000	88,000
Net income	$ 54,000	$ 62,000

Additional information:

1. The market price of Midnight Oil's common stock was $4.00, $6.00, and $7.95 for 1999, 2000, and 2001, respectively.

2. You must compute dividends paid. All dividends were paid in cash.

3. On July 1, 2001, 4,000 shares of common stock were issued.

Instructions

(a) Compute the following ratios for 2000 and 2001:

   (1) Profit margin.

   (2) Gross profit.

   (3) Asset turnover.

   (4) Earnings per share.

   (5) Price-earnings.

   (6) Payout.

   (7) Debt to total assets.

(b) Based on the ratios calculated, discuss briefly the improvement or lack thereof in the financial position and operating results from 2000 to 2001 of Midnight Oil Corporation.

P14-4A   This financial information is for Semisonic Company:

SEMISONIC COMPANY
Balance Sheets
December 31

	2001	2000
Assets		
Cash	$ 70,000	$ 65,000
Short-term investments	45,000	40,000
Receivables (net)	94,000	90,000
Inventories	230,000	125,000
Prepaid expenses	25,000	23,000
Land	130,000	130,000
Building and equipment (net)	290,000	175,000
Total assets	$884,000	$648,000
Liabilities and Stockholders' Equity		
Notes payable	$200,000	$100,000
Accounts payable	45,000	42,000
Accrued liabilities	40,000	40,000
Bonds payable, due 2003	250,000	150,000
Common stock, $10 par	200,000	200,000
Retained earnings	149,000	116,000
Total liabilities and stockholders' equity	$884,000	$648,000

SEMISONIC COMPANY
Income Statements
For the Years Ended December 31

	2001	2000
Sales	$850,000	$790,000
Cost of goods sold	620,000	575,000
Gross profit	230,000	215,000
Operating expenses	194,000	180,000
Net income	$ 36,000	$ 35,000

Additional information:
1. Inventory at the beginning of 2000 was $115,000.
2. Receivables at the beginning of 2000 were $88,000.
3. Total assets at the beginning of 2000 were $630,000.
4. No common stock transactions occurred during 2000 or 2001.
5. All sales were on account.

Instructions
(a) Indicate, by using ratios, the change in liquidity and profitability of Semisonic Company from 2000 to 2001. [*Note:*   Not all profitability ratios can be computed nor can cash-basis ratios be computed.]
(b) Given below are three independent situations and a ratio that may be affected. For each situation, compute the affected ratio (1) as of December 31, 2001, and (2) as of December 31, 2002, after giving effect to the situation. Net income for 2002 was $40,000. Total assets on December 31, 2002, were $900,000.

Situation	Ratio
1. 18,000 shares of common stock were sold at par on July 1, 2002.	Return on common stockholders' equity
2. All of the notes payable were paid in 2002.	Debt to total assets
3. The market price of common stock was $9 and $12.80 on December 31, 2001 and 2002, respectively.	Price-earnings

Compute selected ratios, and compare liquidity, profitability, and solvency for two companies.
(SO 5)

P14-5A Selected financial data of **Kmart** and **Wal-Mart** for 1998 are presented here (in millions):

	Kmart Corporation	Wal-Mart Stores, Inc.
	Income Statement Data for Year	
Net sales	$33,674	$137,634
Cost of goods sold	26,319	108,725
Selling and administrative expenses	6,245	22,363
Interest expense	343	797
Other income (expense)	(19)	1,421
Income tax expense	230	2,740
Net income	$ 518	$ 4,430
	Balance Sheet Data (End of Year)	
Current assets	$ 7,830	$ 21,132
Noncurrent assets	6,336	28,864
Total assets	$14,166	$ 49,996
Current liabilities	$ 3,691	$ 16,762
Long-term debt	4,496	12,122
Total stockholders' equity	5,979	21,112
Total liabilities and stockholders' equity	$14,166	$ 49,996
	Beginning-of-Year Balances	
Total assets	$13,558	$ 45,384
Total stockholders' equity	5,434	18,503
Current liabilities	3,274	14,460
Total liabilities	8,124	26,881
	Other Data	
Average net receivables	–0–	$ 1,047
Average inventory	$ 6,452	16,787
Net cash provided by operating activities	1,237	7,580

Instructions
(a) For each company, compute the following ratios:

(1) Current.
(2) Receivables turnover.
(3) Average collection period.
(4) Inventory turnover.
(5) Days in inventory.
(6) Profit margin.
(7) Asset turnover.

(8) Return on assets.
(9) Return on common stockholders' equity.
(10) Debt to total assets.
(11) Times interest earned.
(12) Current cash debt coverage.
(13) Cash return on sales.
(14) Cash debt coverage.

(b) Compare the liquidity, solvency, and profitability of the two companies.

PROBLEMS: SET B

Prepare vertical analysis and comment on profitability.
(SO 4, 5)

P14-1B Here are comparative statement data for Jimmy Paige Company and Robert Plant Company, two competitors. All balance sheet data are as of December 31, 2001, and December 31, 2000.

	Jimmy Paige Company		Robert Plant Company	
	2001	**2000**	**2001**	**2000**
Net sales	$350,000		$1,400,000	
Cost of goods sold	180,000		720,000	
Operating expenses	51,000		272,000	

	Jimmy Paige Company		Robert Plant Company	
	2001	**2000**	**2001**	**2000**
Interest expense	3,000		10,000	
Income tax expense	11,000		65,000	
Current assets	130,000	$110,000	700,000	$650,000
Plant assets (net)	405,000	270,000	1,000,000	750,000
Current liabilities	60,000	52,000	250,000	275,000
Long-term liabilities	50,000	68,000	200,000	150,000
Common stock	360,000	210,000	950,000	700,000
Retained earnings	65,000	50,000	300,000	275,000

Instructions
(a) Prepare a vertical analysis of the 2001 income statement data for Paige Company and Plant Company.
(b) Comment on the relative profitability of the companies by computing the return on assets and the return on common stockholders' equity ratios for both companies.

P14-2B The comparative statements of Monster Magnet Company are presented here:

Compute ratios from balance sheet and income statement. (SO 5)

MONSTER MAGNET COMPANY
Income Statements
For the Years Ended December 31

	2001	2000
Net sales	$780,000	$624,000
Cost of goods sold	440,000	405,600
Gross profit	340,000	218,400
Selling and administrative expense	143,880	149,760
Income from operations	196,120	68,640
Other expenses and losses		
Interest expense	9,920	7,200
Income before income taxes	186,200	61,440
Income tax expense	25,300	24,000
Net income	$160,900	$ 37,440

MONSTER MAGNET COMPANY
Balance Sheets
December 31

Assets	2001	2000
Current assets		
Cash	$ 23,100	$ 21,600
Short-term investments	34,800	33,000
Accounts receivable (net)	106,200	93,800
Inventory	122,400	64,000
Total current assets	286,500	212,400
Plant assets (net)	465,300	459,600
Total assets	$751,800	$672,000
Liabilities and Stockholders' Equity		
Current liabilities		
Accounts payable	$184,200	$132,000
Income taxes payable	25,300	24,000
Total current liabilities	209,500	156,000
Bonds payable	132,000	120,000
Total liabilities	341,500	276,000
Stockholders' equity		
Common stock ($10 par)	140,000	150,000
Retained earnings	270,300	246,000
Total stockholders' equity	410,300	396,000
Total liabilities and stockholders' equity	$751,800	$672,000

On July 1, 2001, 1,000 shares were repurchased and canceled. All sales were on account. Net cash provided by operating activities was $36,000.

Instructions
Compute the following ratios for 2001:

(a) Earnings per share.
(b) Return on common stockholders' equity.
(c) Return on assets.
(d) Current.
(e) Acid-test.
(f) Receivables turnover.
(g) Average collection period.
(h) Inventory turnover.

(i) Days in inventory.
(j) Times interest earned.
(k) Asset turnover.
(l) Debt to total assets.
(m) Current cash debt coverage.
(n) Cash return on sales.
(o) Cash debt coverage.

Perform ratio analysis.
(SO 5)

P14-3B   These are condensed balance sheet and income statement data for Vicente Fernandez Corporation:

VICENTE FERNANDEZ CORPORATION
Balance Sheets
December 31

	2001	2000	1999
Cash	$ 40,000	$ 24,000	$ 20,000
Receivables (net)	120,000	45,000	48,000
Other current assets	80,000	75,000	62,000
Investments	90,000	70,000	50,000
Plant and equipment (net)	650,000	400,000	360,000
	$980,000	$614,000	$540,000
Current liabilities	$ 98,000	$ 75,000	$ 70,000
Long-term debt	297,000	75,000	65,000
Common stock, $10 par	400,000	340,000	300,000
Retained earnings	185,000	124,000	105,000
	$980,000	$614,000	$540,000

VICENTE FERNANDEZ CORPORATION
Income Statements
For the Years Ended December 31

	2001	2000
Sales	$800,000	$750,000
Less: Sales returns and allowances	40,000	50,000
Net sales	760,000	700,000
Cost of goods sold	420,000	400,000
Gross profit	340,000	300,000
Operating expenses (including income taxes)	194,000	237,000
Net income	$146,000	$ 63,000

Additional information:
1. The market price of Vicente Fernandez's common stock was $5.00, $3.50, and $2.30 for 1999, 2000, and 2001, respectively.
2. You must compute dividends paid. All dividends were paid in cash.
3. On July 1, 2000, 4,000 shares of common stock were issued, and on July 1, 2001, 6,000 shares were issued.

Instructions
(a) Compute the following ratios for 2000 and 2001:
    (1) Profit margin.
    (2) Gross profit rate.
    (3) Asset turnover.
    (4) Earnings per share.
    (5) Price-earnings.
    (6) Payout.
    (7) Debt to total assets.

(b) Based on the ratios calculated, discuss briefly the improvement or lack thereof in the financial position and operating results from 2000 to 2001 of Vicente Fernandez Corporation.

P14-4B Financial information for Dwight Yoakam Company is presented here:

Compute ratios; comment on overall liquidity and profitability.
(SO 5)

DWIGHT YOAKAM COMPANY
Balance Sheets
December 31

	2001	2000
Assets		
Cash	$ 50,000	$ 42,000
Short-term investments	80,000	50,000
Receivables (net)	100,000	87,000
Inventories	440,000	300,000
Prepaid expenses	25,000	31,000
Land	75,000	75,000
Building and equipment (net)	570,000	400,000
Total assets	$1,340,000	$985,000
Liabilities and Stockholders' Equity		
Notes payable	$ 125,000	$ 25,000
Accounts payable	160,000	90,000
Accrued liabilities	50,000	50,000
Bonds payable, due 2003	200,000	100,000
Common stock, $5 par	500,000	500,000
Retained earnings	305,000	220,000
Total liabilities and stockholders' equity	$1,340,000	$985,000

DWIGHT YOAKAM COMPANY
Income Statements
For the Years Ended December 31

	2001	2000
Sales	$1,000,000	$940,000
Cost of goods sold	650,000	635,000
Gross profit	350,000	305,000
Operating expenses	235,000	215,000
Net income	$ 115,000	$ 90,000

Additional information:
1. Inventory at the beginning of 2000 was $350,000
2. Receivables at the beginning of 2000 were $80,000.
3. Total assets at the beginning of 2000 were $1,175,000.
4. No common stock transactions occurred during 2000 or 2001.
5. All sales were on account.

Instructions
(a) Indicate, by using ratios, the change in liquidity and profitability of Dwight Yoakam Company from 2000 to 2001. [*Note:* Not all profitability ratios can be computed nor can cash-basis ratios be computed.]
(b) Given below are three independent situations and a ratio that may be affected. For each situation, compute the affected ratio (1) as of December 31, 2001, and (2) as of December 31, 2002, after giving effect to the situation. Net income for 2002 was $125,000. Total assets on December 31, 2002, were $1,500,000.

Situation	Ratio
1. 65,000 shares of common stock were sold at par on July 1, 2002.	Returns on common stockholders' equity
2. All of the notes payable were paid in 2002.	Debt to total assets
3. The market price of common stock on December 31, 2002, was $6.25. The market price on December 31, 2001, was $5.	Price-earnings

Compute selected ratios, and compare liquidity, profitability, and solvency for two companies.
(SO 5)

P14-5B Selected financial data for **Bethlehem Steel** and **USX** are presented here (in millions):

	Bethlehem Steel Corporation	USX Corporation
	Income Statement Data for Year	
Net sales	$4,477.8	$28,310
Cost of goods sold	3,883.2	20,712
Selling and administrative expenses	370.1	5,839
Interest expense	62.4	279
Other income (expense)	(18.0)	(491)
Income tax expense	24.0	315
Net income	$ 120.1	$ 674

	Bethlehem Steel Corporation	USX Corporation
	Balance Sheet Data (End of Year)	
Current assets	$1,494.8	$ 4,206
Property, plant, and equipment (net)	2,655.7	12,929
Other assets	1,471.0	3,998
Total assets	$5,621.5	$21,133
Current liabilities	$985.2	$3,619
Long-term debt	3,160.6	11,112
Total stockholders' equity	1,475.7	6,402
Total liabilities and stockholders' equity	$5,621.5	$21,133

	Bethlehem Steel Corporation	USX Corporation
	Beginning-of-Year Balances	
Total assets	$4,802.6	$17,284
Total stockholders' equity	1,201.1	5,397
Current liabilities	910.8	3,523
Total liabilities	3,601.5	11,887

	Bethlehem Steel Corporation	USX Corporation
	Other Data	
Average net receivables	$ 307	$ 1,540
Average inventory	967	1,847
Net cash provided by operating activities	444	1,803

Instructions

(a) For each company, compute the following ratios:

(1) Current ratio.		(8) Return on assets.	
(2) Receivables turnover.		(9) Return on common stockholders' equity.	
(3) Average collection period.		(10) Debt to total assets.	
(4) Inventory turnover.		(11) Times interest earned.	
(5) Days in inventory.		(12) Current cash debt coverage.	
(6) Profit margin.		(13) Cash return on sales.	
(7) Asset turnover.		(14) Cash debt coverage.	

(b) Compare the liquidity, solvency, and profitability of the two companies.

FINANCIAL REPORTING AND ANALYSIS

FINANCIAL REPORTING PROBLEM: *Tootsie Roll Industries, Inc.*

BYP14-1   Your parents are considering investing in Tootsie Roll Industries common stock. They ask you, as an accounting expert, to make an analysis of the company for them. Fortunately, excerpts from a recent annual report of Tootsie Roll are presented in Appendix A of this textbook.

Instructions
(a) Make a 5-year trend analysis, using 1994 as the base year, of (1) net revenues and (2) net earnings. Comment on the significance of the trend results.
(b) Compute for 1998 and 1997 the (1) debt to total assets ratio and (2) times interest earned ratio. How would you evaluate Tootsie Roll's long-term solvency?
(c) Compute for 1998 and 1997 the (1) profit margin ratio, (2) asset turnover ratio, (3) return on assets ratio, and (4) return on common stockholders' equity ratio. How would you evaluate Tootsie Roll's profitability? Total assets at December 31, 1996, were $391,456,000, and total stockholders' equity at December 31, 1996, was $312,881,000.
(d) What information outside the annual report may also be useful to your parents in making a decision about Tootsie Roll?

COMPARATIVE ANALYSIS PROBLEM: *Tootsie Roll vs. Hershey Foods*

BYP14-2   The financial statements of Hershey Foods are presented in Appendix B, following the financial statements for Tootsie Roll Industries in Appendix A.

Instructions
(a) Based on the information in the financial statements, determine each of the following for each company:
   (1) The percentage increase in net sales and in net income from 1997 to 1998.
   (2) The percentage increase in total assets and in total stockholders' equity from 1997 to 1998.
   (3) The earnings per share for 1998.
(b) What conclusions concerning the two companies can be drawn from these data?

RESEARCH CASE

BYP14-3   The chapter stresses the importance of comparing an individual company's financial ratios to industry norms. Robert Morris Associates (RMA), a national association of bank loan and credit officers, publishes industry-specific financial data in its *Annual Statement Studies*. This publication includes vertical analysis financial statements and various ratios classified by four-digit SIC code. [*Note:*   An alternative source is Dun & Bradstreet's *Industry Norms and Key Business Ratios*.]

   Obtain the most recent edition of *Annual Statement Studies* and the most recent annual report of Wal-Mart Stores, Inc.

Instructions
(a) Prepare a vertical analysis balance sheet and income statement for Wal-Mart.
(b) Calculate those ratios for Wal-Mart that are covered by RMA. [*Note:*   The specific ratio definitions used by RMA are described in the beginning of the book. Use ending values for balance sheet items.]
(c) What is Wal-Mart's SIC code? Use your answers from parts (a) and (b) to compare Wal-Mart to the appropriate current industry data. How does Wal-Mart compare to

its competitors? [*Note:* RMA sorts current-year data by firm assets and sales, while 5 years of historical data are presented on an aggregate basis.]

(d) How many sets of financial statements did RMA use in compiling the current industry data sorted by sales?

INTERPRETING FINANCIAL STATEMENTS

BYP14-4 **The Coca-Cola Company** and **PepsiCo, Inc.** provide refreshments to every corner of the world. Selected data from the 1998 consolidated financial statements for The Coca-Cola Company and for PepsiCo, Inc., are presented here (in millions):

	Coca-Cola	PepsiCo
Total current assets (including cash, accounts receivable, and short-term investments totaling $3,473 for Coke and $2,847 for Pepsi)	$6,380	$4,362
Total current liabilities	8,640	7,914
Net sales	18,813	22,348
Cost of goods sold	5,562	9,330
Net income	3,533	1,993
Average receivables for the year	1,653	2,302
Average inventories for the year	925	874
Average total assets	18,013	21,381
Average common stockholders' equity	7,839	6,669
Average current liabilities	8,010	6,086
Average total liabilities	10,225	14,712
Total assets	19,145	22,660
Total liabilities	10,742	16,259
Income taxes	1,665	270
Interest expense	277	395
Cash provided by operating activities	3,433	3,211

Instructions

(a) Compute the following liquidity ratios for 1998 for Coca-Cola and for PepsiCo and comment on the relative liquidity of the two competitors:
  (1) Current ratio.
  (2) Acid-test.
  (3) Receivables turnover.
  (4) Average collection period.
  (5) Inventory turnover.
  (6) Days in inventory.
  (7) Current cash debt coverage.

(b) Compute the following solvency ratios for the two companies and comment on the relative solvency of the two competitors:
  (1) Debt to total assets ratio.
  (2) Times interest earned.
  (3) Cash debt coverage ratio.

(c) Compute the following profitability ratios for the two companies and comment on the relative profitability of the two competitors:
  (1) Profit margin.
  (2) Cash return on sales.
  (3) Asset turnover.
  (4) Return on assets.
  (5) Return on common stockholders' equity.

A GLOBAL FOCUS

BYP14-5 The use of railroad transportation has changed dramatically around the world. Attitudes about railroads and railroad usage differ across countries. In England, the railroads were run by the government until recently. Five years ago, **Railtrack Group PLC** became a publicly traded company. The largest railroad company in the United States is **Burlington Northern Railroad Company**. The following data were taken from the 1998 financial statements of each company.

Financial Highlights	Railtrack Group (pounds in millions)		Burlington Northern (dollars in millions)	
	1998	1997	1998	1997
Cash and short-term investments	£ 380	£ 26	$ 95	$ -0-
Accounts receivable	434	402	676	632
Total current assets	909	521	1,357	1,197
Total assets	7,095	5,760	22,725	21,199
Current liabilities	1,128	1,209	2,175	2,089
Total liabilities	3,882	2,888	14,497	14,176
Total stockholders' equity	3,213	2,872	8,228	7,023
Sales	2,573		8,936	
Operating costs	2,102		6,781	
Interest expense	93		293	
Income tax expense	3		733	
Net income	425		1,206	
Cash provided by operations	988		2,107	

Instructions

(a) Calculate the following 1998 liquidity ratios and discuss the relative liquidity of the two companies:
   (1) Current ratio.
   (2) Acid-test.
   (3) Current cash debt coverage.
   (4) Receivables turnover.
(b) Calculate the following 1998 solvency ratios and discuss the relative solvency of the two companies:
   (1) Debt to total assets.
   (2) Times interest earned.
   (3) Cash debt coverage.
(c) Calculate the following 1998 profitability ratios and discuss the relative profitability of the two companies:
   (1) Asset turnover.
   (2) Profit margin.
   (3) Return on assets.
   (4) Return on common stockholders' equity.
(d) What other issues must you consider when comparing these two companies?

FINANCIAL ANALYSIS ON THE WEB

BYP14-6 **Purpose:** To use the Management Discussion and Analysis (MD&A) section of an annual report to evaluate corporate performance for the year.

Addresses: http://www.ibm.com/financialguide,
http://www.ge.com/investor/finance.htm,
(or go to www.wiley.com/college/kimmel)

Steps:

1. From IBM's Financial Guide, choose Guides Contents.
2. Choose **Anatomy of an Annual Report**.
3. Follow instruction (a).
4. From General Electric's website, choose the most recent annual report, then choose financial section, and then choose management discussion.
5. Follow instructions (b)–(c), below.

Instructions

(a) Using IBM's Financial Guide, describe the contents of the "Management Discussion."
(b) Compare current-year earnings with the previous year's earnings.
(c) What were some of management's explanations for the change in net earnings?

BYP14-7 *Purpose:* To employ comparative data and industry data to evaluate a company's performance and financial position.

Address: http://www.biz.yahoo.com/i (or go to www.wiley.com/college/kimmel)

Steps:

(1) Identify two competing companies.
(2) Go to the above address.
(3) Type in the first company's name and choose **Search**.
(4) Choose **Profile**.
(5) Choose **Ratio Comparisons**.
(6) Print out the results.
(7) Repeat steps 3–6 for the competitor.

Instructions
Answer the following questions:

(a) Evaluate the company's liquidity relative to the industry averages and to the competitor that you chose.
(b) Evaluate the company's solvency relative to the industry averages and to the competitor that you chose.
(c) Evaluate the company's profitability relative to the industry averages and to the competitor that you chose.

CRITICAL THINKING

GROUP DECISION CASE

BYP14-8 You are a loan officer for Second State Bank of Port Washington. Ted Worth, president of T. Worth Corporation, has just left your office. He is interested in an 8-year loan to expand the company's operations. The borrowed funds would be used to purchase new equipment. As evidence of the company's debt-worthiness, Worth provided you with the following facts:

	2001	2000
Current ratio	3.1	2.1
Acid-test ratio	.8	1.4
Asset turnover ratio	2.8	2.2
Cash debt coverage ratio	.1	.2
Net income	Up 32%	Down 8%
Earnings per share	$3.30	$2.50

Ted Worth is a very insistent (some would say pushy) man. When you told him that you would need additional information before making your decision, he acted offended, and said, "What more could you possibly want to know?" You responded that, at a minimum, you would need complete, audited financial statements.

Instructions
With the class divided into groups, answer the following:

(a) Explain why you would want the financial statements to be audited.
(b) Discuss the implications of the ratios provided for the lending decision you are to make. That is, does the information paint a favorable picture? Are these ratios relevant to the decision?
(c) List three other ratios that you would want to calculate for this company, and explain why you would use each.
(d) What are the limitations of ratio analysis for credit and investing decisions?

COMMUNICATION ACTIVITY

BYP14-9 L. R. Stanton is the chief executive officer of Hi-Tech Electronics. Stanton is an expert engineer but a novice in accounting. Stanton asks you, as an accounting major, to explain (a) the bases for comparison in analyzing Hi-Tech's financial statements and (b) the limitations, if any, in financial statement analysis.

Instructions

Write a memo to L. R. Stanton that explains the basis for comparison and the limitations of financial statement analysis.

ETHICS CASE

BYP14-10 Vern Fairly, president of Fairly Industries, wishes to issue a press release to bolster his company's image and maybe even its stock price, which has been gradually falling. As controller, you have been asked to provide a list of 20 financial ratios along with some other operating statistics relative to Fairly Industries' first-quarter financials and operations.

Two days after you provide the ratios and data requested, you are asked by Roberta Sanchez, the public relations director of Fairly, to prove the accuracy of the financial and operating data contained in the press release written by the president and edited by Roberta. In the news release, the president highlights the sales increase of 25% over last year's first quarter and the positive change in the current ratio from 1.5:1 last year to 3:1 this year. He also emphasizes that production was up 50% over the prior year's first quarter. You note that the release contains only positive or improved ratios and none of the negative or deteriorated ratios. For instance, no mention is made that the debt to total assets ratio has increased from 35% to 55%, that inventories are up 89%, and that although the current ratio improved, the acid-test ratio fell from 1:1 to .5:1. Nor is there any mention that the reported profit for the quarter would have been a loss had not the estimated lives of Fairly's plant and machinery been increased by 30%. Roberta emphasized, "The Pres wants this release by early this afternoon."

Instructions

(a) Who are the stakeholders in this situation?
(b) Is there anything unethical in president Fairly's actions?
(c) Should you as controller remain silent? Does Roberta have any responsibility?

Answer to Tootsie Roll Review It Question 3, p. 672
Tootsie Roll reported "Other comprehensive earnings" of $946,000,000 in 1998. "Comprehensive earnings" exceeded "Net earnings" by 1.4% [($68,472 − $67,526) ÷ $67,526].

APPENDIX A

Specimen Financial Statements: Tootsie Roll Industries, Inc.

THE ANNUAL REPORT

Once each year a corporation communicates to its stockholders and other interested parties by issuing a complete set of audited financial statements. The **annual report**, as this communication is called, summarizes the financial results of the company's operations for the year and its plans for the future. Many annual reports are attractive, multicolored, glossy public relations ad pieces containing pictures of corporate officers and directors as well as photos and descriptions of new products and new buildings. Yet the basic function of every annual report is to report financial information, almost all of which is a product of the corporation's accounting system.

The content and organization of corporate annual reports have become fairly standardized. Excluding the public relations part of the report (pictures, products, and propaganda), the following items are the traditional financial portions of the annual report:

    Financial Highlights
    Letter to the Stockholders
    Management's Discussion and Analysis
    Financial Statements
    Notes to the Financial Statements
    Auditor's Report
    Supplementary Financial Information

In this appendix we illustrate current financial reporting with a comprehensive set of corporate financial statements that are prepared in accordance with generally accepted accounting principles and audited by an international independent certified public accounting firm. We are grateful for permission to use the actual financial statements and other accompanying financial information from the annual report of a large, publicly held company, Tootsie Roll Industries, Inc.

FINANCIAL HIGHLIGHTS

The financial highlights section is usually presented inside the front cover or on the first two pages of the annual report. This section generally reports the total or per share amounts for five to ten financial items for the current year and one or more previous years. Financial items from the income statement and the balance sheet that typically are presented are sales, income from continuing operations, net income, net income per share, dividends per common share, and the amount of capital expenditures. The financial highlights section from **Tootsie Roll Industries' Annual Report** is shown on page A-2. We have also included Tootsie Roll's discussion of its corporate principles and corporate profile.

Financial Highlights

	December 31,	
	1998	1997
	(in thousands except per share data)	
Net Sales	$388,659	$375,594
Net Earnings.	67,526	60,682
Working Capital	175,155	153,355
Net Property, Plant and Equipment	83,024	78,364
Shareholders' Equity.	396,457	351,163
Average Shares Outstanding*.	48,051	48,294
Per Share Items*		
Net Earnings.	$1.41	$1.26
Shareholders' Equity	8.29	7.29
Cash Dividends Paid.	.20	.16

*Based on average shares outstanding adjusted for stock dividends and 2-for-1 stock split.

Corporate Principles

We believe that the differences among companies are attributable to the caliber of their people, and therefore we strive to attract and retain superior people for each job.

We believe that an open family atmosphere at work combined with professional management fosters cooperation and enables each individual to maximize his or her contribution to the company and realize the corresponding rewards.

We do not jeopardize long-term growth for immediate, short-term results.

We maintain a conservative financial posture in the deployment and management of our assets.

We run a trim operation and continually strive to eliminate waste, minimize cost and implement performance improvements.

We invest in the latest and most productive equipment to deliver the best quality product to our customers at the lowest cost.

We seek to outsource functions where appropriate and to vertically integrate operations where it is financially advantageous to do so.

We view our well known brands as prized assets to be aggressively advertised and promoted to each new generation of consumers.

Melvin J. Gordon, Chairman and Chief Executive Officer and Ellen R. Gordon, President and Chief Operating Officer.

Corporate Profile

Tootsie Roll Industries, Inc. has been engaged in the manufacture and sale of candy for 102 years. Our products are primarily sold under the familiar brand names, Tootsie Roll, Tootsie Roll Pops, Caramel Apple Pops, Child's Play, Charms, Blow Pop, Blue Razz, Cella's, Mason Dots, Mason Crows, Junior Mints, Charleston Chew, Sugar Daddy and Sugar Babies.

LETTER TO THE STOCKHOLDERS

Nearly every annual report contains a letter to the stockholders from the Chairman of the Board or the President (or both). This letter typically discusses the company's accomplishments during the past year and highlights significant events such as mergers and acquisitions, new products, operating achievements, business philosophy, changes in officers or directors, financing commitments, expansion plans, and future prospects. The letter to the stockholders signed by Melvin J. Gordon, Chairman of the Board and Chief Executive Officer, and Ellen R. Gordon, President and Chief Operating Officer, of Tootsie Roll Industries is shown below. The letter is followed by a discussion referred to as the "Operating Report" by Tootsie Roll.

To Our Shareholders

We are once again pleased to report another year of record operating performance for Tootsie Roll Industries. Sales in 1998 reached $389 million, a $13 million or 3.5% increase over 1997. This was our twenty-second consecutive year of record sales results.

Sales increases were attributable to another strong Halloween season and effective, ongoing promotional programs. Gains were seen in all major domestic brands and trade classes, as movement of our basic product lines continues to be strong at the retail level.

This growth in our base business was supplemented by strength in several new products and line extensions that have been introduced in the past few years. Domestic sales growth more than offset a decline in Mexico, where results were adversely affected by currency devaluations and increased local competitive pressure.

Net Income rose to $67 million, a $7 million or 11.3% increase over 1997. On a per share basis, net income was up by an even larger 11.9% due to share repurchases that were made throughout the year. As a percent of sales, our net income rose to 17.4% from 16.2% in the prior year.

Net income gains were due to increased sales, improved manufacturing productivity, lower costs for packaging and certain commodities, increased investment income

and ongoing efforts within the company to control expenses. 1998 represents the seventeenth consecutive year the company has achieved record earnings.

Our financial position has been further strengthened by these successful operating results. Cash and investments in marketable securities at year end increased over 1997. These financial assets place us in a position to respond to growth and investment opportunities as they arise. In this regard, we continue our pursuit of appropriate, strategic acquisitions.

Capital expenditures for the year were $15 million, representing capacity additions, efficiency improvements and infrastructure enhancements needed to support our growth into the new millennium.

Our thirty-fourth consecutive 3% stock dividend was distributed in April. Cash dividends, which have been paid for fifty-six consecutive years, were increased in July, the same month in which a two-for-one stock split was distributed.

During 1998 Tootsie Roll established a presence on the internet with the launch of "tootsie.com" The introduction of this interactive web site was immediately met with a positive response and received widespread press coverage. The company also received favorable coverage in Forbes magazine and in numerous other publications throughout the year.

We have taken appropriate steps to review our computer systems, ensuring that they are "Y2K compliant." We have begun testing to confirm that all systems will function in the new millennium and are confident that final testing will be completed by mid 1999.

We have also invested heavily in preparing our company to function in the next century. Since building niche brands is one of our primary goals, we have focused on increasing the market penetration of our well-known brands. Accordingly, we are encouraged by the continued growth of Tootsie Rolls, Tootsie Pops, Blow Pops, Junior Mints, Dots and other established products, as well as by Child's Play, Caramel Apple Pops, Super Blow Pops and other more recently introduced items.

To efficiently meet growing demand for these products, we have increased our production capacity and implemented the latest manufacturing technology, enabling us to produce the highest quality at the lowest cost. Consequently, sufficient blending, cooking, forming, cut and wrap and bagging capacity, as well as the infrastructure to support it, is either in place or on the drawing board to carry us into the next century.

Our distribution systems have been tailored to meet the evolving shipping patterns our customers require and tuned to handle each order with maximum efficiency. Through the use of advanced technology, we are able to precisely track inventory quantities to minimize out-of-stock situations. In 1998 our order fulfillment rate reached a record level.

Likewise, we have upgraded our EDP systems to handle the vast data requirements we foresee as both we and the companies we do business with move forward in the "information age." Our financial and accounting systems utilize state-of-the-art software and provide extensive capability for future growth.

These past investments, along with those that we will make in the years to come, are essential as we strive to continue providing good, branded values for our consumers in the new millennium and beyond.

We wish to thank our customers, suppliers, sales brokers and employees for their contributions to the success of the company in 1998 and years prior, and for helping to make Tootsie Roll Industries an attractive investment for our shareholders.

As we look forward to further profitable growth in the new millennium, we welcome the above mentioned constituencies to the business opportunities we anticipate there.

Melvin J. Gordon

Melvin J. Gordon
Chairman of the Board and Chief Executive Officer

Ellen R. Gordon

Ellen R. Gordon
President and Chief Operating Officer

"Tootsie Caramel Apple Pops—so good, only the stick will remain."

Operating Report

Marketing and Sales

Sales reached a new record high in 1998, driven by continued growth in our core brands. These increases resulted from successfully targeted promotions such as shipper displays, combo packs and bonus bags.

Sales growth was also realized from a shift to larger sized bags which reflect a continuing trend in the trade toward a higher "ring" or selling price per item. This trend meshes well with our products which continue to offer quality, branded confections that are attractive values.

Another trend that emerged recently is the popularity of multi-packs which feature popular bars or boxed goods in 5 and 10 count lay-down packs. Incremental sales were realized by launching snack-size Tootsie Roll and Charleston Chew bars and mini-boxes of Junior Mints and Dots in this new format. We also extended our popular Caramel Apple Pop to several new pack configurations, including a unique bulk display that incorporates a real wooden apple basket!

As is customary for our company, the third quarter was again our highest selling period due to Halloween and back-to-school programs. Halloween was led by continuing strength in our bagged goods, particularly in the larger sized assortments that have become well established consumer favorites during the past several years. We also experienced Halloween growth from the introduction of several new and larger pack sizes for existing items that we felt could become even more popular among trick-or-treaters.

New product growth included Wicked Red-berry Blow Pop, a mouth-watering strawberry-kiwi flavored Blow Pop in a bold, eye catching wrapper and Caramel-A-Lot, a blend of luscious caramel and chewy nougat wrapped in chocolaty goodness. In addition, several promising new items were developed for introduction in early 1999.

Advertising and Public Relations

Television was again the chief medium used to advertise our products to broad audiences of children and adults in 1998. Numerous placements in selected spot and cable markets featured our classic "How Many Licks?" theme, as well as two new commercials that were developed and introduced during the year.

The first of these new commercials, "Caramel Apple Pops," tempts consumers with the message that this remarkable pop is "so good only the stick will remain," while "Chocolate Attack" encourages mothers to quell their youngsters' chocolate cravings with delicious, low-fat Tootsie Rolls and Tootsie Pops. Both of these messages were economically delivered in ten and fifteen second formats on popular talk, game and adventure shows to maximize their reach.

Also in 1998 we launched the company's first web site on the internet. Both children and adults can now enhance their cyber travels by visiting "tootsie.com" to learn interesting facts about Tootsie Roll Industries, its history and its products in an enjoyable, user friendly environment. Whether curious about Clara Hirshfield (the original "Tootsie"), looking for our latest financial release or seeking an answer to the famous question "How many licks does it take to get to the Tootsie Roll center of a Tootsie Pop?," "tootsie.com" has something of interest for every Tootsie Roll fan.

The introduction of our web site was but one of the many positive mentions we received in the press and on television news programs last year. The company was also favorably reviewed in Forbes' Annual Report on American Industry.

We again received thousands of positive letters from our loyal consumers during the year. These serve as a constant reminder that each of the millions of Tootsie Rolls, Tootsie Pops and other popular confections we produce each day can make a life-long impression.

Manufacturing and Distribution

Continuing capital investments and operating improvements were made throughout the company in 1998 to support growth, increase efficiency or improve quality.

We added production capacity to meet growing demand for the products we make in Chicago, Illinois and Covington, Tennessee. We also reengineered several key processes at these plants to increase efficiency and reduce cost, and began the first of several infrastructure enhancements that are needed to support expanding production.

Also in support of our continued growth, we acquired land adjacent to our Covington, Tennessee plant and have commenced construction of a new regional distribution center there. This center will incorporate the automated inventory tracking systems that we have successfully implemented in Chicago, utilizing advanced technology to maximize control and minimize out of stock situations.

Purchasing

Markets for the key commodities and ingredients we use remained stable or declined slightly in 1998 as adverse economic conditions in many markets continued to dampen world-wide demand. Further, our ongoing hedging program and fixed price contracts helped to insulate us from those price fluctuations that did occur in spot markets.

The cost of the various packaging materials we use remained stable during the year. Also, leveraging the high volume of annual purchases we make of these

items, competitive bidding was again successfully utilized to further control cost.

Information Technology

During 1998 we completed an extensive review of the information systems we utilize throughout the company and determined that the vast majority of these systems—indeed those most critical to our operations—are "Y2K" compliant by design. Our initial testing has confirmed this, and final testing is scheduled for completion by the middle of 1999.

Y2K issues were identified in our systems in Mexico and the necessary corrective programming changes have been written and implemented. Final testing of these changes is scheduled to be completed by mid year, as are the other minor program corrections that were identified in several secondary domestic systems.

We view information technology as an indispensable tool with which we can streamline an ever-expanding variety of functions and tasks. In this regard, during 1998 we completed the initial phases of automating a number of operations that had previously been handled manually. Completion of the final phases of these projects is scheduled for 1999, and we expect that these and other information technology applications will yield ongoing efficiencies.

International

Our Canadian subsidiary reported increased sales and profits in 1998, both due to growth in seasonal sales at Halloween and to distribution gains throughout the year. Also, the Super Blow Pop was introduced in that market during the year with promising results.

Our Mexican operations had a difficult year due to currency devaluations and increased competitive pressures on top of generally soft local market conditions for confectionery. On the positive side, the latest phase of our plant modernization program was completed there, which will increase productivity and enhance our competitive position in Mexico. These improvements will enable us to respond more quickly to local competition with efficiently produced, high quality products. Our Tutsi Pop still remains the local favorite.

Sales trends in other international markets were positive as we continue to export our well known items to many markets throughout the world.

"Oh-oh, another chocolate attack! Better reach for a Tootsie Roll or chocolatey center Tootsie Pop! Delicious and always low in fat."

MANAGEMENT DISCUSSION AND ANALYSIS

The management discussion and analysis (MD&A) section covers three financial aspects of a company: its results of operations, its ability to pay near-term obligations, and its ability to fund operations and expansion. Management must highlight favorable or unfavorable trends and identify significant events and uncertainties that affect these three factors. This discussion obviously involves a number of subjective estimates and opinions. The MD&A section of Tootsie Roll's annual report is presented below.

Management's Discussion and Analysis of Financial Condition and Results of Operations

(in thousands except per share, percentage and ratio figures)

NET SALES
Millions of dollars

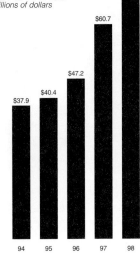

NET EARNINGS
Millions of dollars

FINANCIAL REVIEW

This financial review discusses the company's financial condition, results of operations, liquidity and capital resources. It should be read in conjunction with the Consolidated Financial Statements and related footnotes that follow this discussion.

FINANCIAL CONDITION

The sound financial condition in which we entered 1998 was further strengthened by our record operating results for the year. Net earnings for the year increased by 11.3% to a record $67,526. Shareholders' equity increased by 12.9% to $396,457 and cash and investments increased by $41,154 to $223,172, the result of continued strong cash flow from operating activities.

Cash flow from operating activities was also used to fund capital expenditures of $14,878, share repurchases of $13,445 and cash dividends of $9,150. The cash dividend rate was increased by 31% during 1998, the fifty-sixth consecutive year in which cash dividends have been paid.

A 3% stock dividend was also distributed to shareholders during the year. This was the thirty-fourth consecutive year that a stock dividend has been distributed.

As a consequence of the successful operations of this past year, our financial position remains such that we can respond to future growth opportunities

that may arise with internally generated funds. In this regard, we continue to reinvest in our own operations as well as to pursue acquisitions that would complement those operations.

Our financial position in 1998, versus 1997, measured by commonly used financial ratios, is as follows: the current ratio rose from 3.9:1 to 4.3:1 due to increased cash and equivalents at the end of 1998. Current liabilities to net worth declined from 15.3% to 13.5% and debt to equity fell from 2.1% to 1.9%, both due to the increase in the company's net worth during the year.

These statistics reflect both the company's history of successful operations and its conservative financial posture.

RESULTS OF OPERATIONS
1998 vs. 1997

1998 represented the company's twenty-second consecutive year of record sales. Sales reached $388,659, an increase of 3.5% over 1997 sales of $375,594. Increases were seen in each quarter, and the third quarter, which was driven by another successful Halloween season, continued to be our largest selling period.

Sales throughout the year were favorably impacted by successful promotional programs. Increases were seen in all major trade classes and in all major domestic brands. Line extensions, new products and seasonal packs that have been introduced in recent years also contributed to sales gains.

Domestic sales growth was partially offset by declines in the sales of our Mexican subsidiary due to currency devaluations and difficult local market conditions. Sales in our Canadian operation increased due to distribution gains, seasonal sales growth at Halloween and a new product introduction. These increases were also partially offset by the effects of adverse currency translation.

Cost of goods sold, as a percentage of sales, decreased from 50.1% to 48.3%. This reflected favorable ingredient costs and increased operating efficiencies associated with higher production volumes, coupled with stable packaging and labor costs. Consequently, gross margin, which was $201,042 or 7.3% higher than in 1997, improved as a percentage of sales from 49.9% to 51.7%.

Gross margin as a percent of sales has historically been lower in the third and fourth quarters of the year due to the seasonal nature of our business and the product mix sold at that time of year. This occurred again in 1998.

Selling, marketing and administrative expenses, as a percent of sales were 25.0% in 1998, a decrease of .2% versus 1997. This improvement is due to effective expense control programs aimed at keeping costs in check. Earnings from operations were $101,265 or 26.1% of sales versus 24.0% in 1997, reflecting the combined effects of an increased gross margin percentage and lower operating costs as a percent of sales.

Other income decreased to $4,798, due to exchange losses from Mexico, partially offset by higher investment income. Inasmuch as most of this investment income is not subject to federal income taxes, the effective tax rate declined from 36.4% in 1997 to 36.3% in 1998.

Consolidated net earnings rose 11.9% to a new company record of $1.41 per share, or $67,526, from the previous record of $1.26, or $60,682, in 1997. This represents an improvement in earnings as a percent of sales to 17.4% and the seventeenth consecutive year of record earnings for the company.

"Comprehensive earnings" is a newly required disclosure whereby traditionally reported net earnings must be adjusted by items that are normally recorded directly to the equity accounts. By this measure, our 1998 earnings were $68,472 or 13.7% higher than in 1997.

1997 vs. 1996

1997 was our twenty-first consecutive year of record sales achievement. Sales of $375,594 were up 10.2% over 1996 sales of $340,909 and increases were seen in each quarter. The third quarter, driven by Halloween sales, continued to be our largest selling period. Halloween sales also carried over and drove a double digit sales increase in the fourth quarter.

Throughout the year, sales were favorably impacted by successful promotional programs as we continued to broaden distribution in mass merchandisers and other select trade classes with our core product offerings. Line extensions, new products and seasonal packs all contributed to added sales.

Sales growth occurred in our two most significant foreign operations as well. In Mexico, the introduction of a new assortment complemented the already strong business we have developed for the Christmas holiday season in that market.

Sales growth in our Canadian operation was attributable to further distribution gains in the mass merchandiser and grocery trade classes and to a successful new product introduction.

Cost of goods sold, as a percentage of sales, decreased from 52.4% to 50.1%. This improvement reflected lower costs for certain packaging and ingredients as well as higher production efficiencies associated with increased volumes in relation to fixed costs.

Gross margin dollars grew by 15.3% to $187,281, and increased as a percent of sales from 47.6% to 49.9%, due to the factors cited above. Gross margins in the third and fourth quarters continued to be somewhat lower due to the seasonal nature of our business and to the product mix sold in those quarters.

Selling, marketing and administrative

GROSS MARGIN
Millions of dollars

$141 — 94
$146 — 95
$162 — 96
$187 — 97
$201 — 98

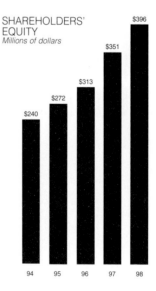

SHAREHOLDERS' EQUITY
Millions of dollars

$240 — 94
$272 — 95
$313 — 96
$351 — 97
$396 — 98

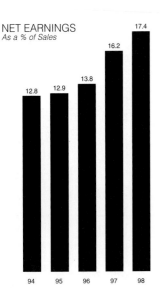

NET EARNINGS
As a % of Sales

12.8 12.9 13.8 16.2 17.4
94   95   96   97   98

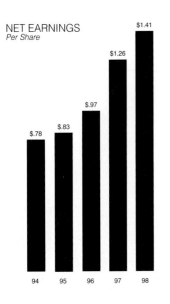

NET EARNINGS
Per Share

$1.41
$1.26
$.97
$.78 $.83
94   95   96   97   98

expenses, as a percent of sales, declined from 25.9% to 25.2%. This improvement was due to distribution and warehousing efficiencies and to effective expense control programs aimed at holding down costs. Earnings from operations increased by 25.9% to $90,087, or 24.0% of sales, as a result of favorable gross margins and operating expenses.

Other income increased by $1,708 to $5,274, primarily reflecting lower interest expense and higher interest income due to lower average borrowings and increased investments in marketable securities, respectively. As a majority of our interest income is not subject to federal income tax, the effective tax rate declined from 37.1% to 36.4%.

Consolidated net earnings rose to a new company record of $60,682. Earnings per share increased 30% to $1.26 from the previous record of $.97 reached in 1996. Our net earnings as a percent of sales increased to 16.2% from 13.8%. 1997 was the sixteenth consecutive year of record earnings achievement for the company.

Liquidity and Capital Resources

Cash flows from operating activities increased to $77,735 in 1998 from $68,176 in 1997 and $76,710 in 1996. The increase in 1998 is attributable to higher net earnings augmented by other receivables, inventory, deferred compensation and other liabilities and income taxes payable and deferred, partially offset by accounts receivable and accounts payable and accrued liabilities.

Cash flows from investing activities reflect net increases in marketable securities of $19,951, $23,087 and $42,573, as well as capital expenditures of $14,878, $8,611 and $9,791 in 1998, 1997 and 1996, respectively.

Cash flows from financing activities in 1998 reflect a short-term borrowing and the subsequent repayment thereof during the year as well as share repurchases of $13,445 and $14,401 in 1998 and 1997, respectively. Cash dividends of $9,150 were paid in 1998, the fifty-sixth in which we have paid cash dividends.

Year 2000 Conversion

The company recognizes the need to ensure that its operations will not be adversely impacted by software failures arising from calculations using the year 2000 date. Accordingly, we have established a process for evaluating and managing the risks and costs associated with this problem.

We have completed an internal review of our financial and operational systems and have begun final testing of these systems to ensure that they are Year 2000 compliant. Likewise, we have surveyed significant vendors and customers to determine the status of their systems with respect to this issue. We believe that the risks and costs of year 2000 compliance will be minimal for the systems we use, and do not expect this issue to have a material impact on the company or its operations.

The results of these operations and our financial condition are expressed in the following financial statements.

*F*INANCIAL STATEMENTS AND ACCOMPANYING NOTES

The standard set of financial statements consists of : (1) a comparative income statement for three years, (2) a comparative balance sheet for two years, (3) a comparative statement of cash flows for three years, (4) a statement of retained earnings (or stockholders' equity) for three years, and (5) a set of accompanying notes that are considered an integral part of the financial statements. The auditor's report, unless stated otherwise, covers the financial statements and the accompanying notes. The financial statements and accompanying notes plus some supplementary data and analyses for Tootsie Roll Industries follow.

CONSOLIDATED STATEMENT OF

Earnings, Comprehensive Earnings and Retained Earnings

TOOTSIE ROLL INDUSTRIES, INC. AND SUBSIDIARIES   (in thousands except per share data)

	For the year ended December 31,		
	1998	1997	1996
Net sales	$388,659	$375,594	$340,909
Cost of goods sold	187,617	188,313	178,489
Gross margin	201,042	187,281	162,420
Selling, marketing and administrative expenses	97,071	94,488	88,182
Amortization of intangible assets	2,706	2,706	2,706
Earnings from operations	101,265	90,087	71,532
Other income, net	4,798	5,274	3,566
Earnings before income taxes	106,063	95,361	75,098
Provision for income taxes	38,537	34,679	27,891
Net earnings	$ 67,526	$ 60,682	$ 47,207
Net earnings	$ 67,526	$ 60,682	$ 47,207
Other comprehensive earnings, net of tax			
Unrealized gains (losses) on securities	976	(417)	
Foreign currency translation adjustments	(30)	(17)	(57)
Other comprehensive earnings	946	(434)	(57)
Comprehensive earnings	$ 68,472	$ 60,248	$ 47,150
Retained earnings at beginning of year	$159,124	$136,352	$121,477
Net earnings	67,526	60,682	47,207
Cash dividends ($.20, $.16 and $.13 per share)	(9,484)	(7,472)	(6,372)
Stock dividends	(52,514)	(30,438)	(25,960)
Retained earnings at end of year	$164,652	$159,124	$136,352
Earnings per share	$1.41	$1.26	$.97
Average common and class B common shares outstanding	48,051	48,294	48,442

(The accompanying notes are an integral part of these statements.)

CONSOLIDATED STATEMENT OF

Financial Position

TOOTSIE ROLL INDUSTRIES, INC. AND SUBSIDIARIES   (in thousands)

Assets   December 31,

	1998	1997
CURRENT ASSETS:		
Cash and cash equivalents	$ 80,744	$ 60,433
Investments	83,176	81,847
Accounts receivable trade, less allowances of $2,184 and $2,085	19,110	18,636
Other receivables	3,324	4,683
Inventories:		
Finished goods and work-in-process	21,395	22,938
Raw materials and supplies	15,125	13,721
Prepaid expenses	3,081	2,910
Deferred income taxes	2,584	1,793
Total current assets	228,539	206,961
PROPERTY, PLANT AND EQUIPMENT, at cost:		
Land	7,774	6,895
Buildings	22,226	22,100
Machinery and equipment	133,601	122,430
	163,601	151,425
Less—Accumulated depreciation	80,577	73,061
	83,024	78,364
OTHER ASSETS:		
Intangible assets, net of accumulated amortization of $20,791 and $18,085	87,843	90,549
Investments	59,252	39,738
Cash surrender value of life insurance and other assets	28,765	21,130
	175,860	151,417
	$487,423	$436,742

(The accompanying notes are an integral part of these statements.)

(in thousands except per share data)

Liabilities and Shareholders' Equity   December 31,

	1998	1997
CURRENT LIABILITIES:		
Accounts payable	$12,450	$ 11,624
Dividends payable	2,514	1,930
Accrued liabilities	31,297	32,793
Income taxes payable	7,123	7,259
Total current liabilities	53,384	53,606
NONCURRENT LIABILITIES:		
Deferred income taxes	9,014	8,650
Postretirement health care and life insurance benefits	6,145	5,904
Industrial development bonds	7,500	7,500
Deferred compensation and other liabilities	14,923	9,919
Total noncurrent liabilities	37,582	31,973
SHAREHOLDERS' EQUITY:		
Common stock, $.69-4/9 par value—		
50,000 shares authorized—		
32,439 and 15,851, respectively, issued	22,527	11,008
Class B common stock, $.69-4/9 par value—		
20,000 shares authorized—		
15,422 and 7,547, respectively, issued	10,710	5,241
Capital in excess of par value	210,064	187,259
Retained earnings, per accompanying statement	164,652	159,124
Accumulated other comprehensive earnings	(10,523)	(11,469)
Treasury stock (at cost)—		
25 shares and 0 shares, respectively	(973)	—
	396,457	351,163
	$487,423	$436,742

CONSOLIDATED STATEMENT OF

Cash Flows

TOOTSIE ROLL INDUSTRIES, INC. AND SUBSIDIARIES   (in thousands)

	For the year ended December 31,		
	1998	1997	1996
CASH FLOWS FROM OPERATING ACTIVITIES:			
Net earnings	$67,526	$60,682	$47,207
Adjustments to reconcile net earnings to net cash provided by operating activities:			
Depreciation and amortization	12,807	12,819	12,068
Loss on retirement of fixed assets	118	26	714
Changes in operating assets and liabilities:			
Accounts receivable	(915)	199	2,355
Other receivables	1,358	(2,526)	(41)
Inventories	(106)	(6,463)	1,879
Prepaid expenses and other assets	(7,723)	(6,622)	(4,253)
Accounts payable and accrued liabilities	(596)	9,624	9,362
Income taxes payable and deferred	(625)	(2,049)	3,718
Postretirement health care and life insurance benefits	241	269	250
Deferred compensation and other liabilities	5,004	1,932	3,460
Other	646	285	(9)
Net cash provided by operating activities	77,735	68,176	76,710
CASH FLOWS FROM INVESTING ACTIVITIES:			
Capital expenditures	(14,878)	(8,611)	(9,791)
Purchase of held to maturity securities	(259,112)	(68,982)	(47,221)
Maturity of held to maturity securities	240,195	27,473	16,523
Purchase of available for sale and trading securities	(217,799)	(304,910)	(35,883)
Sale and maturity of available for sale and trading securities	216,765	323,332	24,008
Net cash used in investing activities	(34,829)	(31,698)	(52,364)
CASH FLOWS FROM FINANCING ACTIVITIES:			
Issuance of notes payable	7,000	—	—
Repayments of notes payable	(7,000)	—	(20,000)
Treasury stock purchases	(973)	—	—
Shares repurchased and retired	(12,472)	(14,401)	—
Dividends paid in cash	(9,150)	(7,303)	(6,211)
Net cash used in financing activities	(22,595)	(21,704)	(26,211)
Increase (decrease) in cash and cash equivalents	20,311	14,774	(1,865)
Cash and cash equivalents at beginning of year	60,433	45,659	47,524
Cash and cash equivalents at end of year	$80,744	$60,433	$45,659
Supplemental cash flow information:			
Income taxes paid	$40,000	$36,716	$23,969
Interest paid	$ 803	$ 389	$ 1,015

(The accompanying notes are an integral part of these statements.)

Notes to Consolidated Financial Statements

TOOTSIE ROLL INDUSTRIES, INC. AND SUBSIDIARIES
($ in thousands except per share data)

NOTE 1—SIGNIFICANT ACCOUNTING POLICIES:

Basis of consolidation:

The consolidated financial statements include the accounts of Tootsie Roll Industries, Inc. and its wholly-owned subsidiaries (the company), which are primarily engaged in the manufacture and sale of candy products. All significant intercompany transactions have been eliminated.

The preparation of financial statements in conformity with generally accepted accounting principles requires management to make estimates and assumptions that affect the reported amounts of assets and liabilities and disclosure of contingent assets and liabilities at the date of the financial statements and the reported amounts of revenues and expenses during the reporting period. Actual results could differ from those estimates.

Revenue recognition:

Revenues are recognized when products are shipped. Accounts receivable are unsecured.

Cash and cash equivalents:

The company considers temporary cash investments with an original maturity of three months or less to be cash equivalents.

Investments:

Investments consist of various marketable securities with maturities of generally less than one year. In accordance with Statement of Financial Accounting Standards (SFAS) No. 115, "Accounting For Certain Investments in Debt and Equity Securities," the company's debt and equity securities are considered as either held to maturity, available for sale or trading. Held to maturity securities represent those securities that the company has both the positive intent and ability to hold to maturity and are carried at amortized cost. Available for sale securities represent those securities that do not meet the classification of held to maturity, are not actively traded and are carried at fair value. Unrealized gains and losses on these securities, where material, are excluded from earnings and are reported as a separate component of shareholders' equity, net of applicable taxes, until realized. Trading securities relate to deferred compensation arrangements and are carried at fair value.

Inventories:

Inventories are stated at cost, not in excess of market. The cost of domestic inventories ($31,307 and $30,530 at December 31, 1998 and 1997, respectively) has been determined by the last-in, first-out (LIFO) method. The excess of current cost over LIFO cost of inventories approximates $5,016 and $4,918 at December 31, 1998 and 1997, respectively. The cost of foreign inventories ($5,213 and $6,129 at December 31, 1998 and 1997, respectively) has been determined by the first-in, first-out (FIFO) method.

From time to time, the company enters into commodity futures and option contracts in order to fix the future price of certain key ingredients which may be subject to price volatility (primarily sugar and corn syrup). Gains or losses, if any, resulting from these contracts are considered as a component of the cost of the ingredients being hedged. At December 31, 1998 the company had open contracts to purchase approximately eighteen months of its expected sugar usage.

Property, plant and equipment:

Depreciation is computed for financial reporting purposes by use of both the straight-line and accelerated methods based on useful lives of 20 to 35 years for buildings and 12 to 20 years for machinery and equipment. For income tax purposes the company uses accelerated methods on all properties. Depreciation expense was $10,101, $9,947 and $9,839 in 1998, 1997 and 1996, respectively.

Carrying value of long-lived assets:

In the event that facts and circumstances indicate that the company's long-lived assets may be impaired, an evaluation of recoverability would be performed. Such an evaluation entails comparing the estimated future undiscounted cash flows associated with the asset to the asset's carrying amount to determine if a write down to market value or discounted cash flow value is required. The company considers that no circumstances exist that would require such an evaluation.

Postretirement health care and life insurance benefits:

The company provides certain postretirement health care and life insurance benefits. The cost of these postretirement benefits is accrued during employees' working careers.

Income taxes:

The company uses the liability method of computing deferred income taxes.

Intangible assets:

Intangible assets represent the excess of cost over the acquired net tangible assets of operating companies and is amortized on a straight-line basis over a 40 year period. The company assesses the recoverability of its intangible assets using undiscounted future cash flows.

Foreign currency translation:

Prior to January 1, 1997, management designated the local currency as the functional currency for the company's Mexican operations. Accordingly, the net effect of translating the Mexican operations' financial statements was reported in a separate component of shareholders' equity. During 1997, management determined that the Mexican economy was hyper-inflationary. Accordingly, the US dollar is now used as the functional currency, and translation gains and losses are included in the determination of 1997 and 1998 earnings.

Comprehensive earnings

Effective January 1, 1998, the company adopted SFAS No. 130, "Reporting Comprehensive Income." Accordingly, net income, foreign currency translation adjustments and unrealized gains/losses on marketable securities are presented in the accompanying Statement of Earnings, Comprehensive Earnings and Retained Earnings. The adoption of SFAS No. 130 had no impact on shareholders' equity and prior year financial statements have been reclassified to conform to its requirements.

Earnings per share:

On December 31, 1997, the company adopted SFAS No. 128, "Earnings per Share." A dual presentation of basic and diluted earnings per share is not required due to the lack of potentially dilutive securities under the company's simple capital structure. Therefore, all earnings per share amounts represent basic earnings per share.

NOTE 2—ACCRUED LIABILITIES:

Accrued liabilities are comprised of the following:

	December 31,	
	1998	1997
Compensation	**$ 8,433**	$ 6,114
Other employee benefits	**4,143**	5,490
Taxes, other than income	**2,460**	2,494
Advertising and promotions	**8,451**	6,939
Other	**7,810**	11,756
	$31,297	$32,793

NOTE 10—DISCLOSURES ABOUT THE FAIR VALUE OF FINANCIAL INSTRUMENTS:

Carrying amount and fair value:

The carrying amount approximates fair value of cash and cash equivalents because of the short maturity of those instruments. The fair values of investments are estimated based on quoted market prices. The fair value of the company's industrial development bonds approximates their carrying value because they have a floating interest rate. The carrying amount and estimated fair values of the company's financial instruments are as follows:

	1998		1997	
	Carrying Amount	Fair Value	Carrying Amount	Fair Value
Cash and cash equivalents	$ 80,744	$ 80,744	$60,433	$60,433
Investments held to maturity	106,415	109,182	95,086	97,000
Investments available for sale	28,214	28,214	22,010	22,010
Investments in trading securities	7,799	7,799	4,489	4,489
Industrial development bonds	7,500	7,500	7,500	7,500

A summary of the aggregate fair value, gross unrealized gains, gross unrealized losses and amortized cost basis of the company's investment portfolio by major security type is as follows:

			December 31, 1998	
			Unrealized	
Held to Maturity:	Amortized Cost	Fair Value	Gains	Losses
Unit investment trusts of preferred stocks	$ 3,626	$ 5,978	$2,352	$ —
Tax-free commercial paper	8,250	8,250	—	—
Municipal bonds	96,828	97,266	438	—
Unit investment trusts of municipal bonds	979	956	—	(23)
US gov't/gov't agency obligations	—	—	—	—
Private export funding securities	4,982	4,982	—	—
	$114,665	$117,432	$2,790	$ (23)
Available for Sale:				
Municipal bonds	$ 39,397	$ 39,264	$ —	$ (133)
Mutual funds	3,007	4,028	1,021	—
	$ 42,404	$ 43,292	$1,021	$ (133)

			December 31, 1997	
			Unrealized	
Held to Maturity:	Amortized Cost	Fair Value	Gains	Losses
Unit investment trusts of preferred stocks	$ 4,724	$ 6,794	$2,070	$ —
Tax-free commercial paper	15,300	15,300	—	—
Municipal bonds	87,456	87,218	—	(238)
Unit investment trusts of municipal bonds	1,103	1,484	381	—
US gov't/gov't agency obligations	1,803	1,803	—	—
	$110,386	$112,599	$2,451	$ (238)
Available for Sale:				
Municipal bonds	$ 37,587	$ 37,484	$ —	$ (103)
Mutual funds	3,307	2,993	—	(314)
	$ 40,894	$ 40,477	$ —	$ (417)

Held to maturity securities of $8,250 and $15,300 and available for sale securities of $15,078 and $18,467 were included in cash and cash equivalents, and held to maturity securities greater than one year were $51,453 and $35,249 at December 31, 1998 and 1997, respectively. There were no securities with maturities greater than three years and gross realized gains and losses on the sale of available for sale securities in 1998 and 1997 were not significant.

NOTE 11—GEOGRAPHIC AREA AND SALES INFORMATION:

Summary of sales, net earnings and assets by geographic area

	1998			1997			1996		
	United States	Mexico and Canada	Consolidated	United States	Mexico and Canada	Consolidated	United States	Mexico and Canada	Consolidated
Sales to unaffiliated customers	$363,569	$25,090	$388,659	$346,487	$29,107	$375,594	$315,131	$25,778	$340,909
Sales between geographic areas	2,339	4,374		1,694	3,314		1,888	3,152	
	$365,908	$29,464		$348,181	$32,421		$317,019	$28,930	
Net earnings	$ 68,270	$ (744)	$ 67,526	$ 58,898	$ 1,784	$ 60,682	$ 44,946	$ 2,261	$ 47,207
Total assets	$467,265	$20,158	$487,423	$414,629	$22,113	$436,742	$373,925	$17,531	$391,456
Net assets	$379,106	$17,351	$396,457	$332,410	$18,753	$351,163	$298,565	$14,316	$312,881

Total assets are those assets associated with or used directly in the respective geographic area, excluding intercompany advances and investments.

Major customer

Revenues from a major customer aggregated approximately 17.2%, 15.9% and 16.2% of total net sales during the years ended December 31, 1998, 1997 and 1996, respectively.

AUDITOR'S REPORT

All publicly held corporations, as well as many other enterprises and organizations (both profit and not-for-profit, large and small) engage the services of independent certified public accountants for the purpose of obtaining an objective, expert report on their financial statements. Based on a comprehensive examination of the company's accounting system and records, and the financial statements, the outside CPA issues the auditor's report.

The standard auditor's report consists of three paragraphs: (1) an introductory paragraph, (2) a scope paragraph, and (3) the opinion paragraph. In the introductory paragraph, the auditor identifies who and what was audited and indicates the responsibilities of management and the auditor relative to the financial statements. In the scope paragraph the auditor states that the audit was conducted in accordance with generally accepted auditing standards and discusses the nature and limitations of the audit. In the opinion paragraph, the auditor expresses an informed opinion as to (1) the fairness of the financial statements and (2) their conformity with generally accepted accounting principles. The Report of PricewaterhouseCoopers LLP appearing in Tootsie Roll's Annual Report is shown below.

Report of Independent Accountants

To the Board of Directors and Shareholders of Tootsie Roll Industries, Inc.

In our opinion, the accompanying consolidated statement of financial position and the related consolidated statement of earnings, comprehensive earnings and retained earnings and of cash flows present fairly, in all material respects, the financial position of Tootsie Roll Industries, Inc. and its subsidiaries at December 31, 1998 and 1997, and the results of their operations and their cash flows for each of the three years in the period ended December 31, 1998, in conformity with generally accepted accounting principles. These financial statements are the responsibility of the Company's management; our responsibility is to express an opinion on these financial statements based on our audits. We conducted our audits of these statements in accordance with generally accepted auditing standards which require that we plan and perform the audit to obtain reasonable assurance about whether the financial statements are free of material misstatement. An audit includes examining, on a test basis, evidence supporting the amounts and disclosures in the financial statements, assessing the accounting principles used and significant estimates made by management, and evaluating the overall financial statement presentation. We believe that our audits provide a reasonable basis for the opinion expressed above.

PricewaterhouseCoopers LLP

Chicago, Illinois
February 9, 1999

Supplementary Financial Information

In addition to the financial statements and the accompanying notes, supplementary financial information is often presented. Tootsie Roll has provided quarterly financial data, stock performance information, and a five-year summary of earnings and financial highlights.

Quarterly Financial Data

TOOTSIE ROLL INDUSTRIES, INC. AND SUBSIDIARIES

		(Thousands of dollars except per share data)			
1998	First	Second	Third	Fourth	Total
Net sales	$69,701	$85,931	$144,230	$88,797	$388,659
Gross margin.	36,966	45,133	73,251	45,692	201,042
Net earnings	11,217	13,910	27,216	15,183	67,526
Net earnings per share	.23	.29	.57	.32	1.41
1997					
Net sales	$66,258	$82,287	$140,645	$86,404	$375,594
Gross margin.	33,323	41,382	69,746	42,830	187,281
Net earnings	9,751	12,507	24,695	13,729	60,682
Net earnings per share	.20	.26	.51	.29	1.26
1996					
Net sales	$63,265	$72,511	$128,658	$76,475	$340,909
Gross margin.	30,687	35,292	60,415	36,026	162,420
Net earnings	8,118	9,327	19,143	10,619	47,207
Net earnings per share	.17	.19	.39	.22	.97

Net earnings per share is based upon average outstanding shares as adjusted for 3% stock dividends issued during the second quarter of each year and the 2-for-1 stock split effective July 13, 1998.

1998-1997 QUARTERLY SUMMARY OF TOOTSIE ROLL INDUSTRIES, INC. STOCK PRICE AND DIVIDENDS PER SHARE

STOCK PRICES*

	1998		1997	
	High	Low	High	Low
1st Qtr	38-13/32	29-27/32	23-3/8	18-7/8
2nd Qtr	40-3/4	34-31/32	24-15/16	22-1/4
3rd Qtr	47-1/4	33-3/4	25-7/16	22-7/8
4th Qtr	42-7/8	34-1/8	32-7/16	25-1/2

*NYSE—Composite Quotations adjusted for the 2-for-1 stock split effective July 13,1998
Estimated Number of shareholders at 12/31/98 9,500

DIVIDENDS**

	1998	1997
1st Qtr	$.0401	$.0344
2nd Qtr	$.0525	$.0402
3rd Qtr	$.0525	$.0402
4th Qtr.	$.0525	$.0401

NOTE: In addition to the above cash dividends, a 3% stock dividend was issued on 4/22/98 and 4/22/97.

**Cash dividends are restated to reflect 3% stock dividends and the 2-for-1 stock split.

Five Year Summary of Earnings and Financial Highlights

TOOTSIE ROLL INDUSTRIES, INC. AND SUBSIDIARIES

(Thousands of dollars except per share, percentage and ratio figures)

(See Management's Comments starting on page A-6)

	1998	1997	1996	1995	1994
Sales and Earnings Data					
Net sales	$388,659	$375,594	$340,909	$312,660	$296,932
Gross margin	201,042	187,281	162,420	145,922	141,367
Interest expense	756	483	1,498	1,515	1,649
Provision for income taxes	38,537	34,679	27,891	23,670	23,236
Net earnings	67,526	60,682	47,207	40,368	37,931
% of sales	17.4%	16.2%	13.8%	12.9%	12.8%
% of shareholders' equity	17.0%	17.3%	15.1%	14.8%	15.8%
Per Common Share Data (1)					
Net sales	$ 8.09	$ 7.78	$ 7.04	$ 6.45	$ 6.13
Net earnings	1.41	1.26	.97	.83	.78
Shareholders' equity	8.29	7.29	6.46	5.62	4.96
Cash dividends declared	.20	.16	.13	.11	.09
Stock dividends	3%	3%	3%	3%	3%
Additional Financial Data					
Working capital	$175,155	$153,355	$153,329	$109,643	$ 92,626
Current ratio	4.3	3.9	4.2	3.0	4.5
Net cash provided by operating activities	77,735	68,176	76,710	50,851	40,495
Net cash used in (provided by) investing activities	34,829	31,698	52,364	14,544	(1,077)
Net cash used in financing activities	22,595	21,704	26,211	5,292	27,049
Property, plant & equipment additions	14,878	8,611	9,791	4,640	8,179
Net property, plant & equipment	83,024	78,364	81,687	81,999	85,648
Total assets	487,423	436,742	391,456	353,816	310,083
Long term debt	7,500	7,500	7,500	7,500	27,500
Shareholders' equity	396,457	351,163	312,881	272,186	240,461
Average shares outstanding (1)	48,051	48,294	48,442	48,442	48,442

(1) Adjusted for annual 3% stock dividends and the 2-for-1 stock splits effective July 13, 1998 and July 11, 1995.

Specimen Financial Statements: Hershey Foods Corporation

HERSHEY FOODS CORPORATION

MANAGEMENT'S DISCUSSION AND ANALYSIS

OPERATING RESULTS

The Corporation achieved record sales and income levels in 1998, following a record performance in 1997. Results over the two-year period reflected a strategic acquisition and several divestitures, along with a significant contribution from the introduction of new confectionery products and solid growth from existing confectionery and grocery brands. Sales increases during the period were offset somewhat by lower sales of pasta products, a higher level of confectionery unsalables and the impact of currency exchange rates in the Canadian and Mexican markets.

Net sales during the two-year period increased at a compound annual rate of 5% and net income also increased at a compound annual rate of 5%, excluding the loss on disposal of businesses in 1996. The increase in net income over the period reflected the growth in sales, partially offset by lower gross margin and higher selling, marketing and administrative expenses.

The following acquisition and divestitures occurred during the period:

- December 1996—The acquisition from an affiliate of Huhtamäki Oy (Huhtamaki), the international foods company based in Finland, of Huhtamaki's Leaf North America (Leaf) confectionery operations for $437.2 million, plus the assumption of $17.0 million in debt. In addition, the parties entered into a trademark and technology license agreement under which the Corporation will manufacture and/or market and distribute in North, Central and South America Huhtamaki's confectionery brands including *Good & Plenty, Heath, Jolly Rancher, Milk Duds, PayDay* and *Whoppers.*

- December 1998—The announcement that the Corporation had signed a definitive agreement providing for the sale of a 94% majority interest of its U.S. pasta business to New World Pasta, LLC. The transaction was completed in January 1999 and included the *American Beauty, Ideal by San Giorgio, Light 'n Fluffy, Mrs. Weiss, P&R, Ronzoni, San Giorgio* and *Skinner* pasta brands along with six manufacturing plants. In the first quarter of 1999, the Corporation received cash proceeds of $450.0 million, retained a 6% minority interest and recorded an after-tax gain of approximately $165.0 million or $1.13 per share—diluted as a result of the transaction.

- December 1996—The sale to Huhtamaki of the outstanding shares of Gubor Holding GmbH (Gubor) and Sperlari S.r.l. (Sperlari). Gubor manufactures and markets high-quality assorted pralines and seasonal chocolate products in Germany, and Sperlari manufactures and markets various confectionery and grocery products in Italy. The sale resulted in an after-tax loss of $35.4 million, since no tax benefit associated with the transaction was recorded. Combined net sales for Gubor and Sperlari were $216.6 million in 1996.

- January 1996—The sale of the assets of Hershey Canada, Inc.'s *Planters* nut (Planters) business to Johnvince Foods Group and the *Life Savers* and *Breath Savers* hard candy and *Beech-Nut* cough drops (Life Savers) business to Beta Brands Inc. Both transactions were part of a restructuring program announced by the Corporation in late 1994.

Net Sales

Net sales rose $133.4 million or 3% in 1998 and $312.9 million in 1997, an increase of 8%. The increase in 1998 was primarily a result of incremental sales from the introduction of new confectionery products and increased sales volume for existing confectionery and grocery products in North America. These increases were offset somewhat by a decline in sales in the Corporation's Asian and Russian markets and the impact of currency exchange rates in the Canadian and Mexican markets, in addition to higher levels of confectionery unsalables and lower sales of pasta products. The increase in

1997 was primarily due to incremental sales from the Leaf acquisition, increased sales of existing confectionery items and the introduction of new confectionery products. These increases were offset somewhat by lower sales resulting from the divestiture of the Gubor and Sperlari businesses and a decline in sales of pasta and grocery products.

Costs and Expenses

Cost of sales as a percent of net sales increased from 57.7% in 1996 to 57.9% in 1997, and to 59.2% in 1998. The decrease in gross margin in 1998 was principally the result of higher costs for certain major raw materials, primarily milk and cocoa, labor and overhead, higher shipping and distribution costs and the mix of non-chocolate and chocolate confectionery items sold in 1998 compared to 1997. These cost increases were partially offset by lower costs for certain raw materials and improved manufacturing efficiencies, including significant improvements in plants acquired with the Leaf business. The decrease in gross margin in 1997 was primarily the result of the lower margin associated with the Leaf business and higher costs associated with certain new products and seasonal items, partially offset by lower costs for certain major raw materials, primarily milk and semolina, and the favorable impact of the Gubor and Sperlari divestitures.

Selling, marketing and administrative costs decreased by 1% in 1998, as reduced marketing expenses for existing brands, lower selling expenses in international markets and lower administrative expenses were only partially offset by higher marketing expenses associated with the introduction of new products. Selling, marketing and administrative expenses increased by 5% in 1997, as a result of incremental expenses associated with the Leaf business and increased marketing expenses related to the introduction of new products, partially offset by decreases resulting from the Gubor and Sperlari divestitures and reduced marketing spending for existing brands.

Interest Expense, Net

Net interest expense in 1998 exceeded the prior year by $9.4 million, primarily as a result of increased borrowings associated with the purchase of Common Stock from the Hershey Trust Company, as Trustee for the benefit of Milton Hershey School (Milton Hershey School Trust), partially offset by lower interest expense reflecting reduced average short-term borrowings.

Net interest expense in 1997 was $28.2 million above prior year, primarily as a result of incremental borrowings associated with the Leaf acquisition and the purchase of Common Stock from the Milton Hershey School Trust. Fixed interest expense increased as a result of the issuance of $150 million of 6.95% Notes due 2007 in March 1997 and $150 million of 6.95% Notes due 2012 and $250 million of 7.2% Debentures due 2027 in August 1997.

Provision for Income Taxes

The Corporation's effective income tax rate was 43.1%, 39.3% and 38.8% in 1996, 1997 and 1998, respectively. The rate decreased from 39.3% in 1997 to 38.8% in 1998 primarily due to changes in the mix of the Corporation's income among various tax jurisdictions. The rate decreased in 1997 compared to 1996 primarily due to the lack of any tax benefit associated with the 1996 loss on disposal of businesses and the lower 1997 effective state income tax rate.

Net Income

Net income increased $4.6 million or 1% in 1998, following an increase of $63.1 million or 23% in 1997. Excluding the loss on the disposal of the Gubor and Sperlari businesses in 1996, 1997 income increased $27.7 million or 9%. Net income as a percent of net sales was 7.7% in 1998, 7.8% in 1997 and 6.8% in 1996. Income as a percent of net sales excluding the loss on the sale of the Gubor and Sperlari businesses was 7.7% in 1996.

FINANCIAL POSITION

The Corporation's financial position remained strong during 1998. The capitalization ratio (total short-term and long-term debt as a percent of stockholders' equity, short-term and long-term debt) was 54% as of December 31, 1998, and 60% as of December 31, 1997. The higher capitalization ratio in 1997 primarily reflected the additional borrowings to finance the purchase of Common Stock and the related decrease in stockholders' equity as a result of the additional treasury stock. The ratio of current assets to current liabilities was 1.4:1 as of December 31, 1998, and 1.3:1 as of December 31, 1997.

Assets

Total assets increased $112.9 million or 3% as of December 31, 1998, primarily as a result of increases in accounts receivable and other current and non-current assets.

Current assets increased by $99.2 million or 10% reflecting increased accounts receivable and higher prepaid expenses and other current assets. The increase in accounts receivable was primarily the result of the timing and payment terms associated with sales occurring toward the end of the year and the increase in prepaid expenses and other current assets was principally associated with commodities transactions. These increases were offset somewhat by lower deferred income taxes and reduced inventory levels.

Property, plant and equipment was slightly lower than the prior year as capital additions of $161.3 million were more than offset by depreciation expense of $138.5 million and the retirement and translation of fixed assets of $23.0 million. The increase in other non-current assets was primarily associated with the capitalization of software.

Liabilities

Total liabilities decreased by $76.6 million or 3% as of December 31, 1998, primarily due to a decrease in debt and lower accrued liabilities, partially offset by higher deferred income taxes. The increase in short-term debt of $113.5 million reflected the reclassification of commercial paper borrowings of $150.0 million which were classified as long-term debt as of December 31, 1997, partially offset by a reduction in short-term borrowings of $36.5 million in 1998. As of December 31, 1997, $150.0 million of commercial paper borrowings were reclassified as long-term debt in accordance with the Corporation's intent and ability to refinance such obligations on a long-term basis. A similar reclassification was not recorded as of December 31, 1998, because the Corporation intends to reduce commercial paper borrowings during 1999. Accrued liabilities decreased by $77.1 million primarily reflecting commodities transactions and reduced accruals for marketing programs and integration costs related to the Leaf acquisition.

Stockholders' Equity

Total stockholders' equity increased by 22% in 1998, as net income exceeded dividends paid. Total stockholders' equity has increased at a compound annual rate of less than 1% over the past ten years reflecting the $1.3 billion of Common Stock repurchased since 1993.

Capital Structure

The Corporation has two classes of stock outstanding, Common Stock and Class B Common Stock (Class B Stock). Holders of the Common Stock and the Class B Stock generally vote together without regard to class on matters submitted to stockholders, including the election of directors, with the Common Stock having one vote per share and the Class B Stock having ten votes per share. However, the Common Stock, voting separately as a class, is entitled to elect one-sixth of the Board of Directors. With respect to dividend rights, the Common Stock is entitled to cash dividends 10% higher than those declared and paid on the Class B Stock.

LIQUIDITY

Historically, the Corporation's major source of financing has been cash generated from operations. The Corporation's income and, consequently, cash provided from operations during the year are affected by seasonal sales patterns, the timing of new product introductions, business acquisitions and divestitures, and price increases. Chocolate, confectionery and grocery seasonal and holiday-related sales have typically been highest during the third and fourth quarters of the year, representing the principal seasonal effect. Generally, seasonal working capital needs peak during the summer months and have been met by issuing commercial paper.

Over the past three years, cash requirements for share repurchases, capital expenditures, capitalized software additions, business acquisitions and dividend payments exceeded cash provided from operating activities and proceeds from business divestitures by $449.5 million. Total debt, including debt assumed, increased during the period by $454.4 million. Cash and cash equivalents increased by $6.7 million during the period.

The Corporation anticipates that capital expenditures will be in the range of $150 million to $170 million per annum during the next several years as a result of continued modernization of existing facilities and capacity expansion to support new products and line extensions. As of December 31, 1998, the Corporation's principal capital commitments included manufacturing capacity expansion and modernization.

In August 1996, the Corporation's Board of Directors declared a two-for-one split of the Common Stock and Class B Common Stock effective September 13, 1996, to stockholders of record August 23, 1996. The split was effected as a stock dividend by distributing one additional share for each share held. Unless otherwise indicated, all shares and per share information have been restated to reflect the stock split.

Under share repurchase programs which began in 1993, a total of 9,861,119 shares of Common Stock have been repurchased for approximately $287.5 million. Of the shares repurchased, 528,000 shares were retired, 529,498 shares were reissued to satisfy stock options obligations and the remaining 8,803,621 shares were held as Treasury Stock as of December 31, 1998. Additionally, the Corporation has purchased a total of 28,000,536 shares of its Common Stock to be held as Treasury Stock from the Milton Hershey School Trust for $1.0 billion. As of December 31, 1998, a total of 36,804,157 shares were held as Treasury Stock and $112.5 million remained available for repurchases of Common Stock under a program approved by the Corporation's Board of Directors in February 1996. In February 1999, the Corporation purchased approximately 2.0 million shares, completing the 1996 repurchase program. Also in February, the Corporation's Board of Directors approved an additional share repurchase program authorizing the repurchase of up to $230 million of the Corporation's Common Stock of which $100.0 million was used to purchase approximately 1.6 million shares of Common Stock from the Milton Hershey School Trust.

In March 1997, the Corporation issued $150 million of 6.95% Notes due 2007 under a Form S-3 Registration Statement which was declared effective in November 1993. Proceeds from the debt issuance were used to repay a portion of the commercial paper borrowings associated with the Leaf acquisition.

In August 1997, the Corporation filed another Form S-3 Registration Statement under which it could offer, on a delayed or continuous basis, up to $500 million of additional debt securities. Also in August 1997, the Corporation issued $150 million of 6.95% Notes due 2012 and $250 million of 7.2% Debentures due 2027 under the November 1993 and August 1997 Registration Statements. Proceeds from the debt issuance were used to repay a portion of the short-term borrowings associated with the purchase of Common Stock from the Milton Hershey School Trust. As of December 31, 1998, $250 million of debt securities remained available for issuance under the August 1997 Registration

Statement. Proceeds from any offering of the $250 million of debt securities available under the shelf registration may be used for general corporate requirements which include reducing existing commercial paper borrowings, financing capital additions, and funding future business acquisitions and working capital requirements.

In December 1995, the Corporation entered into committed credit facility agreements with a syndicate of banks under which it could borrow up to $600 million with options to increase borrowings by $1.0 billion with the concurrence of the banks. Lines of credit previously maintained by the Corporation were significantly reduced when the credit facility agreements became effective. Of the total committed credit facility, $200 million was for a renewable 364-day term and $400 million was effective for a five-year term. In December 1998, the short-term credit facility agreement was renewed for a total of $177 million. The long-term committed credit facility agreement was amended and renewed in December 1997 and will expire in December 2002. The credit facilities may be used to fund general corporate requirements, to support commercial paper borrowings and, in certain instances, to finance future business acquisitions. The Corporation also had lines of credit with domestic and international commercial banks of $23.0 million and $20.7 million as of December 31, 1998 and 1997, respectively.

Cash Flow Activities

Cash provided from operating activities totaled $1.4 billion during the past three years. Over this period, cash used by or provided from accounts receivable and inventories has tended to fluctuate as a result of sales during December and inventory management practices. The change in cash required for or provided from other assets and liabilities between the years was primarily related to commodities transactions, the timing of payments for accrued liabilities, including income taxes, and variations in the funding status of pension plans.

Investing activities included capital additions and business acquisitions and divestitures. Capital additions during the past three years included the purchase of manufacturing equipment, and expansion and modernization of existing facilities. In 1996, the Leaf business was acquired, and the Gubor, Sperlari, Planters and Life Savers businesses were sold. Cash used for the Leaf acquisition represented the purchase price paid and consisted of the current assets, property, plant and equipment, intangibles and other assets acquired, net of liabilities assumed.

Financing activities included debt borrowings and repayments, payment of dividends, the exercise of stock options, incentive plan transactions and the repurchase of Common Stock. During the past three years, short-term borrowings in the form of commercial paper or bank borrowings were used to fund seasonal working capital requirements, business acquisitions, share repurchase programs and purchases of Common Stock from the Milton Hershey School Trust. The proceeds from the issuance of long-term debt were used to reduce short-term borrowings. During the past three years, a total of 11,909,849 shares of Common Stock has been repurchased for $589.9 million. Cash requirements for incentive plan transactions were $103.2 million during the past three years, partially offset by cash received from the exercise of stock options of $55.8 million.

MARKET PRICES AND DIVIDENDS

Cash dividends paid on the Corporation's Common Stock and Class B Stock were $129.0 million in 1998 and $121.5 million in 1997. The annual dividend rate on the Common Stock was $.96 per share, an increase of 9% over the 1997 rate of $.88 per share. The 1998 dividend represented the 24th consecutive year of Common Stock dividend increases.

On February 10, 1999, the Corporation's Board of Directors declared a quarterly dividend of $.24 per share of Common Stock payable on March 15, 1999, to stockholders of record as of February 24, 1999. It is the Corporation's 277th consecutive Common Stock dividend. A quarterly dividend of $.2175 per share of Class B Stock also was declared.

Hershey Foods Corporation's Common Stock is listed and traded principally on the New York Stock Exchange (NYSE) under the ticker symbol "HSY." Approximately 79.0 million shares of the Corporation's Common Stock were traded during 1998. The Class B Stock is not publicly traded.

The closing price of the Common Stock on December 31, 1998, was $62³⁄₁₆. There were 44,364 stockholders of record of the Common Stock and the Class B Stock as of December 31, 1998.

The following table shows the dividends paid per share of Common Stock and Class B Stock and the price range of the Common Stock for each quarter of the past two years:

	Dividends Paid Per Share		Common Stock Price Range*	
	Common Stock	Class B Stock	High	Low
1998				
1st Quarter	$ .22	$ .2000	$73⅜	$59¹¹⁄₁₆
2nd Quarter	.22	.2000	76⅜	67³⁄₁₆
3rd Quarter	.24	.2175	72⁵⁄₁₆	60½
4th Quarter	.24	.2175	75¹³⁄₁₆	60¾
Total	$ .92	$ .8350		
1997				
1st Quarter	$ .20	$ .1800	$52⅞	$42⅛
2nd Quarter	.20	.1800	58⅝	48⅜
3rd Quarter	.22	.2000	59¹⁵⁄₁₆	51⅞
4th Quarter	.22	.2000	63⅞	50⅝
Total	$ .84	$ .7600		

* NYSE-Composite Quotations for Common Stock by calendar quarter.

RETURN MEASURES

Operating Return on Average Stockholders' Equity

The Corporation's operating return on average stockholders' equity was 36.0% in 1998. Over the most recent five-year period, the return has ranged from 18.5% in 1994 to 36.0% in 1998. For the purpose of calculating operating return on average stockholders' equity, earnings is defined as net income, excluding the after-tax restructuring activities in 1994 and 1995, and the after-tax loss on the disposal of businesses in 1996.

Operating Return on Average Invested Capital

The Corporation's operating return on average invested capital was 17.4% in 1998. Over the most recent five-year period, the return has ranged from 15.6% in 1994 to 17.8% in 1996. Average invested capital consists of the annual average of beginning and ending balances of long-term debt, deferred income taxes and stockholders' equity. For the purpose of calculating operating return on average invested capital, earnings is defined as net income, excluding the after-tax restructuring activities in 1994 and 1995, the after-tax loss on disposal of businesses in 1996, and the after-tax effect of interest on long-term debt.

YEAR 2000 ISSUES

Year 2000 issues associated with information systems relate to the way dates are recorded and computed in many computer systems. These year 2000 issues could have an impact upon the Corporation's information technology (IT) and non-IT systems. Non-IT systems include embedded technology such as microcontrollers which are integral to the operation of most machinery and equipment. Additionally, year 2000 issues could have a similar impact on the Corporation's major business partners, including both customers and suppliers. While it is not currently possible to estimate the total impact of a failure of either the Corporation or its major business partners or suppliers to complete their year 2000 remediation in a timely manner, the Corporation has determined that it could suffer significant adverse financial consequences as a result of such failure.

Awareness and assessment of year 2000 issues regarding major business applications software and other significant IT systems began in 1990. A formal program to address year 2000 issues associated with IT systems was established in late 1995. In early 1998, a team was established with representatives from all major functional areas of the Corporation which assumed overall responsibility for ensuring that remediation of both IT and non-IT systems will be completed in time to prevent material adverse consequences to the Corporation's business, operations or financial condition. The Corporation expects that remediation of these systems will be essentially completed by the third quarter of 1999.

In late 1996, the Corporation approved a project to implement an enterprise-wide integrated information system to improve process efficiencies in all of the major functional areas of the Corporation, enabling the Corporation to provide better service to its customers. This system will replace most of the transaction systems and applications supporting operations of the Corporation. In addition to improving efficiency and customer service, another benefit of this system is that it is year 2000 compliant and will address year 2000 issues for approximately 80% of the Corporation's business applications software. As of December 31, 1998, approximately $62.1 million of capitalized software and hardware and $6.9 million of expenses have been incurred for this project. As of December 31, 1998, spending for implementation of this system was approximately 65% complete, with full implementation expected by the third quarter of 1999. Total commitments for this system and subsequently identified enhancements are expected to be approximately $110 million which will be financed with cash provided from operations and short-term borrowings.

The Corporation's mainframe, network and desktop hardware and software have recently been upgraded and are substantially year 2000 compliant. The Corporation is in the process of remediating year 2000 compliance issues associated with legacy information systems not being replaced by the integrated information system project, including process automation and factory management systems. During late 1998, the Corporation undertook an extensive review of its year 2000 remediation program. As a result of this review, the Corporation has undertaken additional testing to confirm its year 2000 compliance, but is otherwise maintaining its current program of remediation. As of December 31, 1998, remediation of both IT and non-IT systems was approximately 60% complete, reflecting the latest estimate of testing and work requirements to be performed. The total cost of remediation of IT and non-IT systems is expected to be in the range of $6.0 million to $8.0 million.

The Corporation is also in the process of assessing year 2000 remediation issues relating to its major business partners. All of the Corporation's major customers have been contacted regarding year 2000 issues related to electronic data interchange. The Corporation is also in the process of contacting its major suppliers of ingredients, packaging, facilities, logistics and financial services with regard to year 2000 issues. Because of the uncertainties associated with assessing the ability of major business partners to complete the remediation of their systems in time to prevent operational difficulties, the Corporation will continue to contact and/or visit major customers and suppliers to gain assurances that no significant adverse consequences will result due to their failure to complete remediation of their systems.

Year 2000 remediation, conversion, validation and implementation is continuing and, at the present time, it is expected that remediation to both the Corporation's IT and non-IT systems and those of major business partners will be completed in time to prevent material adverse consequences to the Corporation's business, operations or financial condition. However, contingency plans are being developed, including possible increases in raw material and finished goods inventory levels, and the identification of alternate vendors and suppliers. Additional contingency plans, to the extent feasible, will be developed for any potential failures resulting from year 2000 issues.

FORWARD LOOKING INFORMATION

The nature of the Corporation's operations and the environment in which it operates subject it to changing economic, competitive, regulatory and technological conditions, risks and uncertainties. In connection with the "safe harbor" provisions of the Private Securities Litigation Reform Act of 1995, the Corporation notes the following factors which, among others, could cause future results to differ materially from the forward-looking statements, expectations and assumptions expressed or implied herein. Many of the forward-looking statements contained in this document may be identified by the use of forward-looking words such as "believe," "expect," "anticipate," "should," "planned," "estimated," and "potential" among others. Factors which could cause results to differ include, but are not limited to: changes in the confectionery and grocery business environment, including actions of competitors and changes in consumer preferences; changes in governmental laws and regulations, including income taxes; market demand for new and existing products; and raw material pricing.

Based upon preliminary information, potential financial results for the first quarter of 1999 may not compare favorably to the prior year's first quarter. Net sales are expected to be lower than in the prior year primarily reflecting the divestiture of the Corporation's pasta business in January 1999. Additionally, the timing of sales for seasonal and promoted items may result in lower confectionery and grocery sales compared to the first quarter of 1998. The divestiture of the Corporation's pasta business, higher amortization of capitalized software associated with the enterprise-wide integrated information system and an emphasis on expanding the distribution of the Corporation's products in new international markets will make the earnings comparison more difficult, considering a very strong first quarter of 1998.

HERSHEY FOODS CORPORATION
CONSOLIDATED STATEMENTS OF INCOME

For the years ended December 31,	1998	1997	1996
In thousands of dollars except per share amounts			
Net Sales	**$ 4,435,615**	$ 4,302,236	$ 3,989,308
Costs and Expenses:			
Cost of sales	**2,625,057**	2,488,896	2,302,089
Selling, marketing and administrative	**1,167,895**	1,183,130	1,124,087
Loss on disposal of businesses	**—**	—	35,352
Total costs and expenses	**3,792,952**	3,672,026	3,461,528
Income before Interest and Income Taxes	**642,663**	630,210	527,780
Interest expense, net	**85,657**	76,255	48,043
Income before Income Taxes	**557,006**	553,955	479,737
Provision for income taxes	**216,118**	217,704	206,551
Net Income	**$ 340,888**	$ 336,251	$ 273,186
Net Income Per Share—Basic	**$ 2.38**	$ 2.25	$ 1.77
Net Income Per Share—Diluted	**$ 2.34**	$ 2.23	$ 1.75
Cash Dividends Paid Per Share:			
Common Stock	**$ .920**	$ .840	$ .760
Class B Common Stock	**.835**	.760	.685

The notes to consolidated financial statements are an integral part of these statements.

HERSHEY FOODS CORPORATION
CONSOLIDATED BALANCE SHEETS

December 31,	1998	1997
In thousands of dollars		
ASSETS		
Current Assets:		
Cash and cash equivalents	$ **39,024**	$ 54,237
Accounts receivable—trade	**451,324**	360,831
Inventories	**493,249**	505,525
Deferred income taxes	**58,505**	84,024
Prepaid expenses and other	**91,864**	30,197
Total current assets	**1,133,966**	1,034,814
Property, Plant and Equipment, Net	**1,648,058**	1,648,237
Intangibles Resulting from Business Acquisitions	**530,464**	551,849
Other Assets	**91,610**	56,336
Total assets	**$ 3,404,098**	$ 3,291,236
LIABILITIES AND STOCKHOLDERS' EQUITY		
Current Liabilities:		
Accounts payable	$ **156,937**	$ 146,932
Accrued liabilities	**294,415**	371,545
Accrued income taxes	**17,475**	19,692
Short-term debt	**345,908**	232,451
Current portion of long-term debt	**89**	25,095
Total current liabilities	**814,824**	795,715
Long-term Debt	**879,103**	1,029,136
Other Long-term Liabilities	**346,769**	346,500
Deferred Income Taxes	**321,101**	267,079
Total liabilities	**2,361,797**	2,438,430
Stockholders' Equity:		
Preferred Stock, shares issued: none in 1998 and 1997	**—**	—
Common Stock, shares issued: 149,502,964 in 1998 and 149,484,964 in 1997	**149,503**	149,485
Class B Common Stock, shares issued: 30,447,908 in 1998 and 30,465,908 in 1997	**30,447**	30,465
Additional paid-in capital	**29,995**	33,852
Unearned ESOP compensation	**(25,548)**	(28,741)
Retained earnings	**2,189,693**	1,977,849
Treasury—Common Stock shares, at cost: 36,804,157 in 1998 and 37,018,566 in 1997	**(1,267,422)**	(1,267,861)
Accumulated other comprehensive loss	**(64,367)**	(42,243)
Total stockholders' equity	**1,042,301**	852,806
Total liabilities and stockholders' equity	**$ 3,404,098**	$ 3,291,236

The notes to consolidated financial statements are an integral part of these balance sheets.

HERSHEY FOODS CORPORATION

CONSOLIDATED STATEMENTS OF CASH FLOWS

For the years ended December 31,	1998	1997	1996
In thousands of dollars			
Cash Flows Provided from (Used by)			
Operating Activities			
Net income	**$ 340,888**	$ 336,251	$ 273,186
Adjustments to reconcile net income to net cash provided from operations:			
Depreciation and amortization	**158,161**	152,750	133,476
Deferred income taxes	**82,241**	16,915	22,863
Loss on disposal of businesses	**—**	—	35,352
Changes in assets and liabilities, net of effects from business acquisitions and divestitures:			
Accounts receivable—trade	**(90,493)**	(68,479)	5,159
Inventories	**12,276**	(33,538)	(41,038)
Accounts payable	**10,005**	12,967	14,032
Other assets and liabilities	**(124,118)**	85,074	15,120
Other, net	**745**	4,018	5,593
Net Cash Provided from Operating Activities	**389,705**	505,958	463,743
Cash Flows Provided from (Used by)			
Investing Activities			
Capital additions	**(161,328)**	(172,939)	(159,433)
Capitalized software additions	**(42,859)**	(29,100)	—
Business acquisitions	**—**	—	(437,195)
Proceeds from divestitures	**—**	—	149,222
Other, net	**9,284**	21,368	9,333
Net Cash (Used by) Investing Activities	**(194,903)**	(180,671)	(438,073)
Cash Flows Provided from (Used by)			
Financing Activities			
Net change in short-term borrowings partially classified as long-term debt	**(36,543)**	(217,018)	210,929
Long-term borrowings	**—**	550,000	—
Repayment of long-term debt	**(25,187)**	(15,588)	(3,103)
Cash dividends paid	**(129,044)**	(121,546)	(114,763)
Exercise of stock options	**19,368**	14,397	22,049
Incentive plan transactions	**(22,458)**	(35,063)	(45,634)
Repurchase of Common Stock	**(16,151)**	(507,654)	(66,072)
Net Cash (Used by) Provided from Financing Activities	**(210,015)**	(332,472)	3,406
Increase (Decrease) in Cash and Cash Equivalents	**(15,213)**	(7,185)	29,076
Cash and Cash Equivalents as of January 1	**54,237**	61,422	32,346
Cash and Cash Equivalents as of December 31	**$ 39,024**	$ 54,237	$ 61,422
Interest Paid	**$ 89,001**	$ 64,937	$ 52,143
Income Taxes Paid	**123,970**	181,377	180,347

The notes to consolidated financial statements are an integral part of these statements.

HERSHEY FOODS CORPORATION

CONSOLIDATED STATEMENTS OF STOCKHOLDERS' EQUITY

In thousands of dollars	Preferred Stock	Common Stock	Class B Common Stock	Additional Paid-in Capital	Unearned ESOP Compensation	Retained Earnings	Treasury Common Stock	Accumulated Other Comprehensive Loss	Total Stockholders' Equity
Balance as of January 1, 1996	$—	$ 74,734	$ 15,241	$ 47,732	$ (35,128)	$1,694,696	$ (685,076)	$ (29,240)	$ 1,082,959
Comprehensive income (loss)									
Net income						273,186			273,186
Other comprehensive income (loss):									
Foreign currency translation adjustments								(3,635)	(3,635)
Comprehensive income									269,551
Dividends:									
Common Stock, $.76 per share						(93,884)			(93,884)
Class B Common Stock, $.685 per share						(20,879)			(20,879)
Two-for-one stock split		74,736	15,239			(89,975)			—
Conversion of Class B Common Stock into Common Stock		2	(2)						
Incentive plan transactions				(426)					(426)
Exercise of stock options				(5,391)			(8,547)		(13,938)
Employee stock ownership trust transactions				517	3,193				3,710
Repurchase of Common Stock							(66,072)		(66,072)
Balance as of December 31, 1996	—	149,472	30,478	42,432	(31,935)	1,763,144	(759,695)	(32,875)	1,161,021
Comprehensive income (loss)									
Net income						336,251			336,251
Other comprehensive income (loss):									
Foreign currency translation adjustments								(9,368)	(9,368)
Comprehensive income									326,883
Dividends:									
Common Stock, $.84 per share						(98,390)			(98,390)
Class B Common Stock, $.76 per share						(23,156)			(23,156)
Conversion of Class B Common Stock into Common Stock		13	(13)						
Incentive plan transactions				(879)					(879)
Exercise of stock options				(8,200)			(512)		(8,712)
Employee stock ownership trust transactions				499	3,194				3,693
Repurchase of Common Stock							(507,654)		(507,654)
Balance as of December 31, 1997	—	149,485	30,465	33,852	(28,741)	1,977,849	(1,267,861)	(42,243)	852,806
Comprehensive income (loss)									
Net income						340,888			340,888
Other comprehensive income (loss):									
Foreign currency translation adjustments								(18,073)	(18,073)
Minimum pension liability adjustments, net of tax benefit								(4,051)	(4,051)
Comprehensive income									318,764
Dividends:									
Common Stock, $.92 per share						(103,616)			(103,616)
Class B Common Stock, $.835 per share						(25,428)			(25,428)
Conversion of Class B Common Stock into Common Stock		18	(18)						
Incentive Plan transactions				(985)					(985)
Exercise of stock options				(3,375)			16,590		13,215
Employee stock ownership trust transactions				503	3,193				3,696
Repurchase of Common Stock							(16,151)		(16,151)
Balance as of December 31, 1998	$—	$149,503	$30,447	$29,995	$(25,548)	$2,189,693	$(1,267,422)	$(64,367)	$1,042,301

The notes to consolidated financial statements are an integral part of these statements.

HERSHEY FOODS CORPORATION
NOTES TO CONSOLIDATED FINANCIAL STATEMENTS

1. SUMMARY OF SIGNIFICANT ACCOUNTING POLICIES

Significant accounting policies employed by the Corporation are discussed below and in other notes to the consolidated financial statements. Certain reclassifications have been made to prior year amounts to conform to the 1998 presentation. Unless otherwise indicated, all shares and per share information have been restated for the two-for-one stock split effective September 13, 1996.

Principles of Consolidation

The consolidated financial statements include the accounts of the Corporation and its subsidiaries after elimination of intercompany accounts and transactions.

Use of Estimates

The preparation of financial statements in conformity with generally accepted accounting principles requires management to make estimates and assumptions that affect the reported amounts of assets and liabilities, the disclosure of contingent assets and liabilities at the date of the financial statements and the reported amounts of revenues and expenses during the reporting period. Actual results could differ from those estimates, particularly for accounts receivable and certain current and long-term liabilities.

Cash Equivalents

All highly liquid debt instruments purchased with a maturity of three months or less are classified as cash equivalents.

Commodities Futures and Options Contracts

In connection with the purchasing of cocoa, sugar, corn sweeteners, natural gas and certain dairy products for anticipated manufacturing requirements, the Corporation enters into commodities futures and options contracts as deemed appropriate to reduce the effect of price fluctuations. In accordance with Statement of Financial Accounting Standards No. 80 "Accounting for Futures Contracts," these futures and options contracts meet the hedge criteria and are accounted for as hedges. Accordingly, gains and losses are deferred and recognized in cost of sales as part of the product cost.

Property, Plant and Equipment

Property, plant and equipment are stated at cost. Depreciation of buildings, machinery and equipment is computed using the straight-line method over the estimated useful lives.

Intangibles Resulting from Business Acquisitions

Intangible assets resulting from business acquisitions principally consist of the excess of the acquisition cost over the fair value of the net assets of businesses acquired (goodwill). Goodwill was $508.0 million and $527.6 million as of December 31, 1998 and 1997, respectively. Goodwill is amortized on a straight-line basis over 40 years. Other intangible assets are amortized on a straight-line basis over the estimated useful lives. The Corporation periodically evaluates whether events or circumstances have occurred indicating that the carrying amount of goodwill may not be recoverable. When factors indicate that goodwill should be evaluated for possible impairment, the Corporation uses an estimate of the acquired business' undiscounted future cash flows compared to the related carrying amount of net assets, including goodwill, to determine if an impairment loss should be recognized.

Accumulated amortization of intangible assets resulting from business acquisitions was $132.3 million and $116.5 million as of December 31, 1998 and 1997, respectively.

Comprehensive Income

In June 1997, the Financial Accounting Standards Board issued Statement of Financial Accounting Standards No. 130, Reporting Comprehensive Income (SFAS No. 130). SFAS No. 130 establishes standards for reporting and display of comprehensive income and its components. SFAS No. 130 requires that an enterprise (a) classify items of other comprehensive income by their nature in a financial statement and (b) display the accumulated balance of other comprehensive income separately from retained earnings and additional paid-in capital in the equity section of a statement of financial position. SFAS No. 130 is effective for the Corporation's 1998 financial statements.

Results of operations for foreign entities are translated using the average exchange rates during the period. For foreign entities, assets and liabilities are translated to U.S. dollars using the exchange rates in effect at the balance sheet date. Resulting translation adjustments are recorded as a component of other comprehensive income (loss), "Foreign Currency Translation Adjustments."

A minimum pension liability adjustment is required when the actuarial present value of accumulated pension plan benefits exceeds plan assets and accrued pension liabilities, less allowable intangible assets. Minimum pension liability adjustments, net of income taxes, are recorded as a component of other comprehensive income (loss), "Minimum Pension Liability Adjustments."

Comprehensive income (loss) is reported on the Consolidated Statements of Stockholders' Equity and accumulated other comprehensive income (loss) is reported on the Consolidated Balance Sheets.

Foreign Exchange Contracts

The Corporation enters into foreign exchange forward and options contracts to hedge transactions primarily related to firm commitments to purchase equipment, certain raw materials and finished goods denominated in foreign currencies, and to hedge payment of intercompany transactions with its non-domestic subsidiaries. These contracts reduce currency risk from exchange rate movements.

Foreign exchange forward contracts are intended and effective as hedges of firm, identifiable, foreign currency commitments and foreign exchange options contracts meet required hedge criteria for anticipated transactions. Accordingly, gains and losses are deferred and accounted for as part of the underlying transactions. Gains and losses on terminated derivatives designated as hedges are accounted for as part of the originally hedged transaction. Gains and losses on derivatives designated as hedges of items which mature, are sold or terminated, or of anticipated transactions which are no longer likely to occur, are recorded currently in income. In entering into these contracts the Corporation has assumed the risk which might arise from the possible inability of counterparties to meet the terms of their contracts. The Corporation does not expect any losses as a result of counterparty defaults.

License Agreements

The Corporation has entered into license agreements under which it has access to certain trademarks and proprietary technology, and manufactures and/or markets and distributes certain products. The rights under these agreements are extendible on a long-term basis at the Corporation's option subject to certain conditions, including minimum sales levels, which the Corporation has met. License fees and royalties, payable under the terms of the agreements, are expensed as incurred.

Research and Development

The Corporation expenses research and development costs as incurred. Research and development expense was $28.6 million, $27.5 million and $26.1 million in 1998, 1997 and 1996, respectively.

Advertising

The Corporation expenses advertising costs as incurred. Advertising expense was $187.5 million, $202.4 million and $174.2 million in 1998, 1997 and 1996, respectively. Prepaid advertising as of December 31, 1998 and 1997, was $12.1 million and $2.0 million, respectively.

Computer Software

In 1997, the Corporation began capitalizing certain costs of computer software developed or obtained for internal use. The amount capitalized as of December 31, 1998 and 1997, was $69.3 million and $29.1 million, respectively. If such costs were capitalized in prior years, the effect would not have been material. Software assets are classified as other non-current assets and are amortized over periods up to five years. Accumulated amortization of capitalized software was $2.8 million and $.2 million as of December 31, 1998 and 1997, respectively.

2. ACQUISITION AND DIVESTITURES

In December 1996, the Corporation acquired from an affiliate of Huhtamäki Oy (Huhtamaki), the international foods company based in Finland, Huhtamaki's Leaf North America (Leaf) confectionery operations for $437.2 million, plus the assumption of $17.0 million in debt. In addition, the parties entered into a trademark and technology license agreement under which the Corporation will manufacture and/or market and distribute in North, Central and South America Huhtamaki's confectionery brands including *Good & Plenty, Heath, Jolly Rancher, Milk Duds, PayDay* and *Whoppers.* Leaf's principal manufacturing facilities are located in Denver, Colorado; Memphis, Tennessee; and Robinson, Illinois.

In accordance with the purchase method of accounting, the purchase price of the Leaf acquisition was allocated on a preliminary basis to the underlying assets and liabilities at the date of acquisition based on their estimated respective fair values, which were revised and finalized by the anniversary date of the acquisition. Total liabilities assumed, including debt, were $138.0 million in 1996. Results subsequent to the date of the acquisition are included in the consolidated financial statements.

Had the acquisition of Leaf occurred at the beginning of 1996, pro forma consolidated results would have been as follows:

For the year ended December 31,	1996
In thousands of dollars except per share amounts	(unaudited)
Net sales	$4,473,950
Net income	234,000
Net income per share—Basic	1.52
Net income per share—Diluted	1.50

The pro forma results are based on historical financial information provided by Huhtamaki, including a business restructuring charge recorded by Huhtamaki in 1996, and adjusted to give effect to certain costs and expenses, including fees under the trademark and technology license agreement, goodwill amortization, interest expense and income taxes which would have been incurred by the Corporation if it had owned and operated the Leaf confectionery business throughout 1996. These results are not necessarily reflective of the actual results which would have occurred if the acquisition had been completed at the beginning of the year, nor are they necessarily indicative of future combined financial results.

In December 1998, the Corporation announced that it had signed a definitive agreement providing for the sale of a 94% majority interest of its U.S. pasta business to New World Pasta, LLC. The transaction was completed in January 1999, and included the *American Beauty, Ideal by San Giorgio, Light 'n Fluffy, Mrs. Weiss, P&R, Ronzoni, San Giorgio* and *Skinner* pasta brands, along with six manufacturing plants. In the first quarter of 1999, the Corporation received cash proceeds of $450.0 million, retained a 6% minority interest and recorded an after-tax gain of approximately $165.0 million or $1.13 per share—diluted as a result of the transaction. Net sales for the pasta business were $373.1 million, $386.2 million and $407.4 million for 1998, 1997 and 1996, respectively. Net income for the pasta business was $25.9 million, $25.2 million and $18.7 million for 1998, 1997 and 1996, respectively.

In December 1996, the Corporation completed the sale to Huhtamaki of the outstanding shares of Gubor Holding GmbH (Gubor) and Sperlari S.r.l. (Sperlari). Gubor manufactures and markets high-quality assorted pralines and seasonal chocolate products in Germany and Sperlari manufactures and markets various confectionery and grocery products in Italy. The total proceeds from the sale of the Gubor and Sperlari businesses were $121.7 million. The transaction resulted in an after-tax loss of $35.4 million since no tax benefit associated with the transaction was recorded. Combined net sales for Gubor and Sperlari were $216.6 million in 1996. The sale of Gubor and Sperlari allowed the Corporation to place additional focus on its North American markets and improve financial returns.

In January 1996, the Corporation completed the sale of the assets of Hershey Canada, Inc.'s *Planters* nut (Planters) business to Johnvince Foods Group and the *Life Savers* and *Breath Savers* hard candy and *Beech-Nut* cough drops (Life Savers) business to Beta Brands Inc. Both transactions were part of a restructuring program announced by the Corporation in late 1994.

3.   RENTAL AND LEASE COMMITMENTS

Rent expense was $39.6 million, $31.8 million and $25.3 million for 1998, 1997 and 1996, respectively. Rent expense pertains to all operating leases, which were principally related to certain administrative buildings, distribution facilities and transportation equipment. Future minimum rental payments under non-cancelable operating leases with a remaining term in excess of one year as of December 31, 1998, were: 1999, $13.3 million; 2000, $13.0 million; 2001, $12.7 million; 2002, $12.2 million; 2003, $9.3 million; 2004 and beyond, $46.8 million.

4.   DERIVATIVE INSTRUMENTS AND HEDGING ACTIVITES

In June 1998, the Financial Accounting Standards Board issued Statement of Financial Accounting Standards No. 133, Accounting for Derivative Instruments and Hedging Activities (SFAS No. 133). SFAS No. 133 establishes accounting and reporting standards requiring that every derivative instrument be recorded in the balance sheet as either an asset or liability measured at its fair value. SFAS No. 133 requires that changes in the derivative's fair value be recognized currently in earnings unless specific hedge accounting criteria are met. Special accounting for qualifying hedges allows a derivative's gains and losses to offset related results on the hedged item in the income statement, and requires that a company must formally document, designate, and assess the effectiveness of transactions that receive hedge accounting.

SFAS No. 133 is effective for fiscal years beginning after June 15, 1999, but may be implemented as of the beginning of any fiscal quarter after issuance. Retroactive application is not permitted. SFAS No. 133 must be applied to (a) derivative instruments and (b) certain derivative instruments embedded in hybrid contracts that were issued, acquired, or substantively modified after December 31, 1997. Changes in accounting methods will be required for derivative instruments utilized by the Corporation to hedge commodity price, foreign currency exchange rate and interest rate risks. Such derivatives include commodity futures and options contracts, foreign exchange forward and options contracts and interest rate swaps.

The Corporation anticipates the adoption of SFAS No. 133 as of January 1, 2000. As of December 31, 1998, net deferred losses on derivatives of approximately $16.5 million after tax would have been reported as a component of other comprehensive loss and classified as accumulated other comprehensive loss on the consolidated balance sheets upon adoption of SFAS No. 133.

5. FINANCIAL INSTRUMENTS

The carrying amounts of financial instruments including cash and cash equivalents, accounts receivable, accounts payable and short-term debt approximated fair value as of December 31, 1998 and 1997, because of the relatively short maturity of these instruments. The carrying value of long-term debt, including the current portion, was $879.2 million as of December 31, 1998, compared to a fair value of $1.0 billion based on quoted market prices for the same or similar debt issues. The carrying value of long-term debt, including the current portion, was $904.2 million as of December 31, 1997, compared to a fair value of $961.0 million.

As of December 31, 1998, the Corporation had foreign exchange forward contracts maturing in 1999 and 2000 to purchase $10.5 million in foreign currency, primarily British sterling and Dutch gilders, and to sell $9.6 million in Japanese yen at contracted forward rates.

As of December 31, 1997, the Corporation had foreign exchange forward contracts maturing in 1998 and 1999 to purchase $19.2 million in foreign currency, primarily British sterling, and to sell $16.7 million in foreign currency, primarily Japanese yen and Canadian dollars, at contracted forward rates.

To hedge foreign currency exposure related to anticipated transactions associated with the purchase of certain raw materials and finished goods generally covering 3 to 24 months, the Corporation, from time to time, also purchases foreign exchange options which permit, but do not require, the Corporation to exchange foreign currencies at a future date with another party at a contracted exchange rate. No options were outstanding as of December 31, 1998. As of December 31, 1997, the Corporation had purchased foreign exchange options of $3.6 million, related to Swiss francs.

The fair value of foreign exchange forward contracts is estimated by obtaining quotes for future contracts with similar terms, adjusted where necessary for maturity differences, and the fair value of foreign exchange options is estimated using active market quotations. As of December 31, 1998 and 1997, the fair value of foreign exchange forward and options contracts approximated the contract value. The Corporation does not hold or issue financial instruments for trading purposes.

In order to minimize its financing costs and to manage interest rate exposure, the Corporation, from time to time, enters into interest rate swap agreements to effectively convert a portion of its floating rate debt to fixed rate debt. As of December 31, 1998 and 1997, the Corporation had agreements outstanding with an aggregate notional amount of $75.0 million and $150.0 million with maturities through September 1999 and September 1998, respectively. As of December 31, 1998 and 1997, interest rates payable were at a weighted average fixed rate of 6.3%. As of December 31, 1998 and 1997, interest rates receivable of 5.2% and 5.7%, respectively, were based on 30-day commercial paper composite rates. Any interest rate differential on interest rate swaps is recognized as an adjustment to interest expense over the term of each agreement. The Corporation's risk related to swap agreements is limited to the cost of replacing such agreements at prevailing market rates.

6.   INTEREST EXPENSE

Interest expense, net consisted of the following:

For the years ended December 31,	1998	1997	1996
In thousands of dollars			
Long-term debt and lease obligations	**$67,538**	$48,737	$30,818
Short-term debt	**23,657**	32,284	22,752
Capitalized interest	**(2,547)**	(1,883)	(1,534)
Interest expense, gross	**88,648**	79,138	52,036
Interest income	**(2,991)**	(2,883)	(3,993)
Interest expense, net	**$85,657**	$76,255	$48,043

7.   SHORT-TERM DEBT

Generally, the Corporation's short-term borrowings are in the form of commercial paper or bank loans with an original maturity of three months or less. In December 1995, the Corporation entered into committed credit facility agreements with a syndicate of banks under which it could borrow up to $600 million, with options to increase borrowings by $1.0 billion with the concurrence of the banks. Of the total committed credit facility, $200 million was for a renewable 364-day term and $400 million was effective for a five-year term. In December 1998, the short-term credit facility agreement was renewed for a total of $177 million. The long-term credit facility agreement was amended and renewed in December 1997 and will expire in December 2002. The credit facilities may be used to fund general corporate requirements, to support commercial paper borrowings and, in certain instances, to finance future business acquisitions. As of December 31, 1997, $150.0 million of commercial paper borrowings were reclassified as long-term debt in accordance with the Corporation's intent and ability to refinance such obligations on a long-term basis. A similar reclassification was not recorded as of December 31, 1998, because the Corporation intends to reduce commercial paper borrowings during 1999.

The Corporation also maintains lines of credit arrangements with domestic and international commercial banks, under which it could borrow in various currencies up to approximately $23.0 million and $20.7 million as of December 31, 1998 and 1997, respectively, at the lending banks' prime commercial interest rates or lower. The Corporation had combined domestic commercial paper borrowings, including the portion classified as long-term debt as of December 31, 1997, and short-term foreign bank loans against its credit facilities and lines of credit of $345.9 million as of December 31, 1998, and $382.5 million as of December 31, 1997. The weighted average interest rates on short-term borrowings outstanding as of December 31, 1998 and 1997, were 5.2% and 5.7%, respectively.

The credit facilities and lines of credit were supported by commitment fee arrangements. The average fee during 1998 was less than .1% per annum of the commitment. The Corporation's credit facility agreements contain a financial covenant which requires that a specified interest and fixed charge ratio be maintained. These agreements are also subject to other representations and covenants which do not materially restrict the Corporation's activities. The Corporation is in compliance with all covenants included in the credit facility agreements. There were no significant compensating balance agreements which legally restricted these funds.

As a result of maintaining a consolidated cash management system, the Corporation maintains overdraft positions at certain banks. Such overdrafts, which were included in accounts payable, were $57.0 million and $30.7 million as of December 31, 1998 and 1997, respectively.

8. LONG-TERM DEBT

Long-term debt consisted of the following:

December 31,	1998	1997
In thousands of dollars		
Commercial Paper at interest rates ranging from 5.64% to 6.55%	$ —	$ 150,000
Medium-term Notes, 8.875% due 1998	—	25,000
6.7% Notes due 2005	**200,000**	200,000
6.95% Notes due 2007	**150,000**	150,000
6.95% Notes due 2012	**150,000**	150,000
8.8% Debentures due 2021	**100,000**	100,000
7.2% Debentures due 2027	**250,000**	250,000
Other obligations, net of unamortized debt discount	**29,192**	29,231
Total long-term debt	**879,192**	1,054,231
Less—current portion	**89**	25,095
Long-term portion	**$879,103**	$1,029,136

As of December 31, 1997, $150.0 million of commercial paper borrowings were reclassified as long-term debt. A similar reclassification was not recorded as of December 31, 1998, because the Corporation intends to reduce commercial paper borrowings during 1999.

In March 1997, the Corporation issued $150 million of 6.95% Notes due 2007 under the November 1993 Form S-3 Registration Statement. Proceeds from the debt issuance were used to repay a portion of the commercial paper borrowings associated with the Leaf acquisition.

In August 1997, the Corporation issued $150 million of 6.95% Notes due 2012 and $250 million of 7.2% Debentures due 2027 under the November 1993 and August 1997 Registration Statements. Proceeds from the debt issuance were used to repay a portion of the short-term borrowings associated with the purchase of Common Stock from the Milton Hershey School Trust.

Aggregate annual maturities during the next five years are: 1999, $.1 million; 2000, $2.2 million; 2001, $.2 million; 2002, $.2 million; and 2003, $17.1 million. The Corporation's debt is principally unsecured and of equal priority. None of the debt is convertible into stock of the Corporation. The Corporation is in compliance with all covenants included in the related debt agreements.

9. INCOME TAXES

The provision for income taxes was as follows:

For the years ended December 31,	1998	1997	1996
In thousands of dollars			
Current:			
Federal	**$119,706**	$177,145	$158,040
State	**10,498**	20,252	23,288
Foreign	**3,673**	3,392	2,360
Current provision for income taxes	**133,877**	200,789	183,688
Deferred:			
Federal	**73,422**	9,370	12,952
State	**10,568**	5,103	8,134
Foreign	**(1,749)**	2,442	1,777
Deferred provision for income taxes	**82,241**	16,915	22,863
Total provision for income taxes	**$216,118**	$217,704	$206,551

The tax effects of the significant temporary differences which comprised the deferred tax assets and liabilities were as follows:

December 31,	1998	1997
In thousands of dollars		
Deferred tax assets:		
Post-retirement benefit obligations	**$ 87,954**	$ 91,706
Accrued expenses and other reserves	**96,843**	91,067
Accrued trade promotion reserves	**28,118**	30,905
Other	**21,530**	23,234
Total deferred tax assets	**234,445**	236,912
Deferred tax liabilities:		
Depreciation	**308,074**	302,675
Other	**188,967**	117,292
Total deferred tax liabilities	**497,041**	419,967
Net deferred tax liabilities	**$262,596**	$183,055
Included in:		
Current deferred tax assets, net	**$ 58,505**	$ 84,024
Non-current deferred tax liabilities, net	**321,101**	267,079
Net deferred tax liabilities	**$262,596**	$183,055

The following table reconciles the Federal statutory income tax rate with the Corporation's effective income tax rate:

For the years ended December 31,	1998	1997	1996
Federal statutory income tax rate	**35.0%**	35.0%	35.0%
Increase (reduction) resulting from:			
State income taxes, net of Federal income tax benefits	**3.0**	3.4	4.7
Non-deductible acquisition costs	**.9**	.9	.6
Loss on disposal of businesses for which no tax benefit was provided	**—**	—	2.6
Other, net	**(.1)**	—	.2
Effective income tax rate	**38.8%**	39.3%	43.1%

In January 1999, the Corporation received a Notice of Proposed Deficiency (Notice) from the Internal Revenue Service (IRS) related to the years 1989 through 1996. The most significant issue pertains to the Corporate Owned Life Insurance (COLI) program which was implemented by the Corporation in 1989. The IRS proposed the disallowance of interest expense deductions associated with the underlying life insurance policies. The Corporation believes that it has fully complied with the tax law as it relates to its COLI program. The Corporation expects to file a protest of the proposed deficiency with the Appeals section of the IRS in early 1999 and intends to vigorously defend its position on this matter.

10.   PENSION AND OTHER POST-RETIREMENT BENEFIT PLANS

The Corporation's policy is to fund domestic pension liabilities in accordance with the minimum and maximum limits imposed by the Employee Retirement Income Security Act of 1974 and Federal income tax laws, respectively. Non-domestic pension liabilities are funded in accordance with applicable local laws and regulations. Plan assets are invested in a broadly diversified portfolio consisting primarily of domestic and international common stocks and fixed income securities. Other benefits include health care and life insurance provided by the Corporation under two post-retirement benefit plans.

Effective December 31, 1998, the Corporation adopted Statement of Financial Accounting Standards No. 132, Employers' Disclosures about Pension and Other Post-Retirement Benefits (SFAS No. 132). The provisions of SFAS No. 132 revise employers' disclosures about pension and other post-retirement benefit plans. It does not change the measurement or recognition of these plans.

A summary of the changes in benefit obligations and plan assets as of December 31, 1998 and 1997 is presented below:

	Pension Benefits		Other Benefits	
December 31,	1998	1997	1998	1997
In thousands of dollars				
Change in benefits obligation				
Benefits obligation at beginning of year	**$602,081**	$503,528	**$ 206,695**	$ 176,301
Service cost	**27,621**	26,177	**4,452**	4,390
Interest cost	**41,855**	39,385	**13,524**	13,395
Amendments	**(440)**	9,840	**(17,427)**	967
Actuarial loss	**72,944**	32,325	**54,698**	18,332
Acquisition	**—**	26,560	**(1,799)**	1,677
Other	**(2,440)**	(1,587)	**(228)**	(154)
Benefits paid	**(49,199)**	(34,147)	**(8,875)**	(8,213)
Benefits obligation at end of year	**692,422**	602,081	**251,040**	206,695
Change in plan assets				
Fair value of plan assets at beginning of year	**566,810**	450,426	**—**	—
Actual return on plan assets	**91,338**	86,405	**—**	—
Acquisition	**—**	38,328	**—**	—
Employer contribution	**20,634**	26,855	**8,875**	8,213
Other	**(1,542)**	(1,057)	**—**	—
Benefits paid	**(49,199)**	(34,147)	**(8,875)**	(8,213)
Fair value of plan assets at end of year	**628,041**	566,810	**—**	—
Funded status	**(64,381)**	(35,271)	**(251,040)**	(206,695)
Unrecognized transition obligation	**(91)**	193	**—**	—
Unrecognized prior service cost	**35,854**	39,337	**(33,202)**	(25,685)
Unrecognized net actuarial loss (gain)	**6,164**	(27,318)	**59,589**	4,330
Intangible asset	**(1,261)**	(6,336)	**—**	—
Accumulated other comprehensive income	**(6,750)**	—	**—**	—
Prior service cost recognized due to curtailment	**—**	—	**12,991**	—
Unrecognized prior service cost due to amendment	**—**	—	**(6,924)**	—
(Accrued) benefits cost	**$ (30,465)**	$ (29,395)	**$(218,586)**	$(228,050)
Weighted-average assumptions				
Discount rate	**6.40%**	7.00%	**6.40%**	7.00%
Expected long-term rate of return on assets	**9.50**	9.50	**N/A**	N/A
Rate of increase in compensation levels	**4.80**	4.80	**N/A**	N/A

For measurement purposes, a 6% annual rate of increase in the per capita cost of covered health care benefits was assumed for 1999 and future years.

The Corporation's acquisition of the Leaf business in 1996 included its pension plan. The Leaf pension plan was merged into the Hershey Foods Corporation Retirement Plan as of December 31, 1997.

As of December 31, 1998, for pension plans with accumulated benefit obligations in excess of plan assets, the related projected benefit obligation, accumulated benefit obligation and the fair value of plan assets were $81.1 million, $66.9 million and $22.7 million, respectively.

As of December 31, 1997, for pension plans with accumulated benefit obligations in excess of plan assets, the related projected benefit obligation and accumulated benefit obligation were $36.4 million and $34.9 million, respectively. As of December 31, 1997, there were no funded pension plans with accumulated benefit obligations in excess of plan assets.

A summary of the components of net periodic benefits cost for the years ended December 31, 1998 and 1997 is presented below:

	Pension Benefits		Other Benefits	
For the years ended December 31,	**1998**	**1997**	**1998**	**1997**
In thousands of dollars				
Components of net periodic benefits cost				
Service cost	**$ 27,621**	$ 26,177	**$ 4,452**	$ 4,390
Interest cost	**41,855**	39,385	**13,524**	13,395
Expected return on plan assets	**(53,399)**	(42,700)	**—**	—
Amortization of prior service cost	**2,941**	190	**(2,986)**	(2,252)
Recognized net actuarial loss (gain)	**717**	(1,652)	**—**	—
Other	**—**	—	**9**	6
Corporate sponsored plans	**19,735**	21,400	**14,999**	15,539
Multi-employer plans	**1,571**	1,627	**—**	—
Administrative expenses	**796**	864	**—**	—
Net periodic benefits cost	**$ 22,102**	$ 23,891	**$14,999**	$15,539

The Corporation has two post-retirement benefit plans. The health care plan is contributory, with participants' contributions adjusted annually, and the life insurance plan is non-contributory. Effective December 1998, for all eligible employees under age 45, the Corporation will provide annual contributions into the Employee Savings Stock Investment and Ownership Plan (ESSIOP) instead of providing coverage under the current retiree medical plan. This change resulted in the immediate recognition of a $13.0 million pre-tax gain which is not included above as a component of net periodic benefits cost. The changes apply to all U.S. full-time salaried employees, and all non-union hourly plant employees working outside of Hershey, PA.

Assumed health care cost trend rates have a significant effect on the amounts reported for the health care plans. A one percentage point change in assumed health care cost trend rates would have the following effects:

	1 Percentage Point Increase	1 Percentage Point (Decrease)
In thousands of dollars		
Effect on total service and interest cost components	$ 940	$ (872)
Effect on post-retirement benefit obligation	12,935	(11,552)

A minimum pension liability adjustment is required when the actuarial present value of accumulated plan benefits exceeds plan assets and accrued pension liabilities. In 1998, a minimum liability adjustment of $4.1 million, less allowable intangible assets, net of a deferred tax benefit of $2.7 million, was recorded as a component of other comprehensive loss and reported in accumulated other comprehensive loss as a component of stockholders' equity.

11.   EMPLOYEE STOCK OWNERSHIP TRUST

The Corporation's employee stock ownership trust (ESOP) serves as the primary vehicle for contributions to its existing ESSIOP for participating domestic salaried and hourly employees. The ESOP was funded by a 15-year 7.75% loan of $47.9 million from the Corporation. During 1998 and 1997, the ESOP received a combination of dividends on unallocated shares and contributions from the Corporation equal to the amount required to meet its principal and interest payments under the loan. Simultaneously, the ESOP allocated to participants 159,176 shares of Common Stock each year. As of December 31, 1998, the ESOP held 927,863 allocated shares and 1,273,400 unallocated shares. All ESOP shares are considered outstanding for income per share computations.

The Corporation recognized net compensation expense equal to the shares allocated multiplied by the original cost of $20\frac{1}{16}$ per share less dividends received by the ESOP on unallocated shares. Compensation expense related to the ESOP for 1998, 1997 and 1996 was $1.0 million, $1.4 million and $1.8 million, respectively. Dividends paid on unallocated ESOP shares were $1.2 million in 1998 and $1.3 million in 1997 and 1996. The unearned ESOP compensation balance in stockholders' equity represented deferred compensation expense to be recognized by the Corporation in future years as additional shares are allocated to participants.

12. CAPITAL STOCK AND NET INCOME PER SHARE

As of December 31, 1998, the Corporation had 530,000,000 authorized shares of capital stock. Of this total, 450,000,000 shares were designated as Common Stock, 75,000,000 shares as Class B Common Stock (Class B Stock), and 5,000,000 shares as Preferred Stock, each class having a par value of one dollar per share. As of December 31, 1998, a combined total of 179,950,872 shares of both classes of common stock had been issued of which 143,146,715 shares were outstanding. No shares of the Preferred Stock were issued or outstanding during the three-year period ended December 31, 1998.

In August 1996, the Corporation's Board of Directors declared a two-for-one split of the Common Stock and Class B Common Stock effective September 13, 1996, to stockholders of record August 23, 1996. The split was effected as a stock dividend by distributing one additional share for each share held.

Holders of the Common Stock and the Class B Stock generally vote together without regard to class on matters submitted to stockholders, including the election of directors, with the Common Stock having one vote per share and the Class B Stock having ten votes per share. However, the Common Stock, voting separately as a class, is entitled to elect one-sixth of the Board of Directors. With respect to dividend rights, the Common Stock is entitled to cash dividends 10% higher than those declared and paid on the Class B Stock.

Class B Stock can be converted into Common Stock on a share-for-share basis at any time. During 1998, 1997 and 1996, a total of 18,000 shares, 13,000 shares and 2,000 shares, respectively, of Class B Stock were converted into Common Stock.

Hershey Trust Company, as Trustee for the benefit of Milton Hershey School (Milton Hershey School Trust), as institutional fiduciary for estates and trusts unrelated to Milton Hershey School, and as direct owner of investment shares, held a total of 14,531,294 shares of the Common Stock, and as Trustee for the benefit of Milton Hershey School, held 30,306,006 shares of the Class B Stock as of December 31, 1998, and was entitled to cast approximately 76% of the total votes of both classes of the Corporation's common stock. The Milton Hershey School Trust must approve the issuance of shares of Common Stock or any other action which would result in the Milton Hershey School Trust not continuing to have voting control of the Corporation.

A total of 9,861,119 shares of Common Stock have been repurchased for approximately $287.5 million under share repurchase programs which were approved by the Corporation's Board of Directors in 1993 and 1996. Of the shares repurchased, 528,000 shares were retired, 529,498 shares were reissued to satisfy stock options obligations and the remaining 8,803,621 shares were held as Treasury Stock as of December 31, 1998. In August 1997, the Corporation purchased an additional

9,900,990 shares of its Common Stock to be held as Treasury Stock from the Milton Hershey School Trust for $500.0 million. This was in addition to the 18,099,546 shares purchased from the Milton Hershey School Trust in August 1995 for $500.0 million. A total of 36,804,157 shares were held as Treasury Stock as of December 31, 1998.

Basic and Diluted Earnings per Share were computed based on the weighted average number of shares of the Common Stock and the Class B Stock outstanding as follows:

For the year ended December 31, 1998	Income (Numerator)	Shares (Denominator)	Per-Share Amount
In thousands of dollars except shares and per share amounts			
Net Income per Share—Basic			
Net income	**$340,888**	**143,446,421**	**$2.38**
Effect of Dilutive Securities			
Stock options	**—**	**2,008,355**	
Performance stock units	**—**	**106,968**	
Restricted stock units	**—**	**1,238**	
Net Income per Share—Diluted			
Net income and assumed conversions	**$340,888**	**145,562,982**	**$2.34**

For the year ended December 31, 1997	Income (Numerator)	Shares (Denominator)	Per-Share Amount
In thousands of dollars except shares and per share amounts			
Net Income per Share—Basic			
Net income	$336,251	149,173,558	$2.25
Effect of Dilutive Securities			
Stock options	—	1,726,761	
Performance stock units	—	112,649	
Restricted stock units	—	3,389	
Net Income per Share—Diluted			
Net income and assumed conversions	$336,251	151,016,357	$2.23

For the year ended December 31, 1996	Income (Numerator)	Shares (Denominator)	Per-Share Amount
In thousands of dollars except shares and per share amounts			
Net Income per Share—Basic			
Net income	$273,186	154,333,549	$1.77
Effect of Dilutive Securities			
Stock options	—	1,270,177	
Performance stock units	—	84,697	
Restricted stock units	—	1,528	
Net Income per Share—Diluted			
Net income and assumed conversions	$273,186	155,689,951	$1.75

13. STOCK COMPENSATION PLAN

The long-term portion of the Key Employee Incentive Plan (KEIP), provides for grants of stock-based compensation awards to senior executives and key employees of one or more of the following: non-qualified stock options (fixed stock options), performance stock units, stock appreciation rights and restricted stock units. The KEIP also provides for the deferral of performance stock unit awards by participants. As of December 31, 1998, 15.3 million shares were authorized for grants under the long-term portion of the KEIP.

In 1996, the Corporation's Board of Directors approved a world-wide, broad-based employee stock option program, called HSY Growth. HSY Growth provides all eligible employees with a one-time grant of 100 non-qualified stock options. Under HSY Growth, over 1.2 million shares were granted on January 7, 1997.

The Corporation applies Accounting Principles Board Opinion No. 25 "Accounting for Stock Issued to Employees," and related Interpretations in accounting for the KEIP and HSY Growth. Accordingly, no compensation cost has been recognized for its fixed stock option grants. Had compensation cost for the Corporation's stock-based compensation plans been determined based on the fair value at the grant dates for awards under the KEIP and HSY Growth consistent with the method of Statement of Financial Accounting Standards No. 123 "Accounting for Stock-Based Compensation," the Corporation's net income and net income per share would have been reduced to the pro forma amounts indicated below:

For the years ended December 31,		1998	1997	1996
In thousands of dollars except per share amounts				
Net income	As reported	**$340,888**	$336,251	$273,186
	Pro forma	**329,621**	330,710	266,517
Net income per share—Basic	As reported	**$ 2.38**	$ 2.25	$ 1.77
	Pro forma	**2.30**	2.22	1.73
Net income per share—Diluted	As reported	**$ 2.34**	$ 2.23	$ 1.75
	Pro forma	**2.26**	2.19	1.71

The fair value of each option grant is estimated on the date of grant using a Black-Scholes option-pricing model with the following weighted-average assumptions used for grants in 1998, 1997 and 1996, respectively: dividend yields of 1.6%, 1.9% and 2.4%, expected volatility of 21%, 20% and 20%, risk-free interest rates of 5.9%, 6.2% and 5.6%, and expected lives of 6.5, 5.7 and 7.5 years.

Fixed Stock Options

The exercise price of each option equals the market price of the Corporation's Common Stock on the date of grant. Under the KEIP, options are granted in January and generally vest at the end of the second year and have a maximum term of ten years. Options granted under the HSY Growth program vest at the end of the fifth year and have a term of ten years.

A summary of the status of the Corporation's fixed stock options as of December 31, 1998, 1997, and 1996, and changes during the years ending on those dates is presented below:

Fixed Options	1998		1997		1996	
	Shares	Weighted-Average Exercise Price	Shares	Weighted-Average Exercise Price	Shares	Weighted-Average Exercise Price
Outstanding at beginning of year	6,713,920	$31.73	5,902,220	$27.40	4,435,800	$22.54
Granted	1,739,050	$61.22	1,485,250	$44.64	2,619,200	$33.08
Exercised	(751,600)	$25.78	(656,350)	$21.94	(1,062,980)	$20.74
Forfeited	(36,100)	$52.61	(17,200)	$33.06	(89,800)	$31.92
Outstanding at end of year	7,665,270	$38.91	6,713,920	$31.73	5,902,220	$27.40
Options exercisable at year-end	4,480,670	$28.45	3,013,670	$24.38	3,670,020	$23.94
Weighted-average fair value of options granted during the year (per share)	$ 18.30		$ 11.66		$ 8.70	

The increase in the weighted-average fair value of options reflects higher grant prices and lower dividend yields.

The following table summarizes information about fixed stock options outstanding as of December 31, 1998:

Range of Exercise Prices	Options Outstanding			Options Exercisable	
	Number Outstanding as of 12/31/98	Weighted-Average Remaining Contractual Life in Years	Weighted-Average Exercise Price	Number Exercisable as of 12/31/98	Weighted-Average Exercise Price
$17¹¹⁄₁₆-26½	2,194,970	4.4	$23.63	2,194,970	$23.63
$33¹⁄₁₆-44½	3,728,050	7.4	$37.50	2,285,700	$33.07
$56¼-63¹¹⁄₁₆	1,742,250	9.0	$61.17	—	
$17¹¹⁄₁₆-63¹¹⁄₁₆	7,665,270	6.9	$38.91	4,480,670	$28.45

Performance Stock Units

Under the long-term portion of the KEIP, each January the Corporation grants selected executives and other key employees performance stock units whose vesting is contingent upon the achievement of certain performance objectives. If at the end of three-year performance cycles, targets for financial measures of earnings per share, economic value added and free cash flow are met, the full number of shares are awarded to the participants. The performance scores can range from 0% to 150% of the targeted amounts. The compensation cost charged against income for the performance-based plan was $6.6 million, $9.1 million and $5.8 million for 1998, 1997, and 1996, respectively. The compensation cost associated with the long-term portion of the KEIP is recognized ratably over the three-year term based on the year-end market value of the stock. Performance stock units and restricted stock units granted for potential future distribution were as follows:

For the years ended December 31,	1998	1997	1996
Shares granted	48,150	95,250	86,000
Weighted-average fair value at date of grant	$ 61.54	$ 45.17	$ 33.56

Deferred performance stock units, deferred directors' fees and accumulated dividend amounts totaled 373,933 shares as of December 31, 1998.

No stock appreciation rights were outstanding as of December 31, 1998.

14.   SUPPLEMENTAL BALANCE SHEET INFORMATION

Accounts Receivable—Trade

In the normal course of business, the Corporation extends credit to customers which satisfy pre-defined credit criteria. The Corporation believes that it has little concentration of credit risk due to the diversity of its customer base. Receivables, as shown on the consolidated balance sheets, were net of allowances and anticipated discounts of $19.9 million and $15.8 million as of December 31, 1998 and 1997, respectively.

Inventories

The Corporation values the majority of its inventories under the last-in, first-out (LIFO) method and the remaining inventories at the lower of first-in, first-out (FIFO) cost or market. LIFO cost of inventories valued using the LIFO method was $342.9 million and $372.7 million as of December 31, 1998 and 1997, respectively, and all inventories were stated at amounts that did not exceed realizable values. Total inventories were as follows:

December 31,	1998	1997
In thousands of dollars		
Raw materials	$ 205,111	$ 223,702
Goods in process	38,420	36,015
Finished goods	340,442	334,639
Inventories at FIFO	583,973	594,356
Adjustment to LIFO	(90,724)	(88,831)
Total inventories	$ 493,249	$ 505,525

Property, Plant and Equipment

Property, plant and equipment balances included construction in progress of $96.6 million and $144.0 million as of December 31, 1998 and 1997, respectively. Major classes of property, plant and equipment were as follows:

December 31,	1998	1997
In thousands of dollars		
Land	$ 30,871	$ 31,340
Buildings	541,181	540,729
Machinery and equipment	2,130,735	2,015,161
Property, plant and equipment, gross	2,702,787	2,587,230
Accumulated depreciation	(1,054,729)	(938,993)
Property, plant and equipment, net	$ 1,648,058	$ 1,648,237

Accrued Liabilities

Accrued liabilities were as follows:

December 31,	1998	1997
In thousands of dollars		
Payroll and other compensation	$ 87,666	$ 92,102
Advertising and promotion	67,916	86,184
Other	138,833	193,259
Total accrued liabilities	$ 294,415	$ 371,545

Other Long-term Liabilities

Other long-term liabilities were as follows:

December 31,	1998	1997
In thousands of dollars		
Accrued post-retirement benefits	$ 206,345	$ 216,901
Other	140,424	129,599
Total other long-term liabilities	$ 346,769	$ 346,500

15. SEGMENT INFORMATION

The Corporation operates in a single consumer foods line of business, encompassing the manufacture, distribution and sale of confectionery, grocery and pasta products. Consolidated net sales represented primarily sales of confectionery products. The Corporation's principal operations and markets are located in the United States. The Corporation also manufactures, markets, sells and distributes confectionery and grocery products in Canada and Mexico, imports and/or markets selected confectionery and grocery products in Japan, China and the Philippines, and markets confectionery products in over 90 countries worldwide.

Net sales and long-lived assets of businesses outside of the United States were not significant. Sales to Wal-Mart Stores, Inc. and Subsidiaries exceeded 10% of total net sales and amounted to approximately $619.1 million, $529.6 million and $471.3 million in 1998, 1997 and 1996, respectively.

RESPONSIBILITY FOR FINANCIAL STATEMENTS

Hershey Foods Corporation is responsible for the financial statements and other financial information contained in this report. The Corporation believes that the financial statements have been prepared in conformity with generally accepted accounting principles appropriate under the circumstances to reflect in all material respects the substance of applicable events and transactions. In preparing the financial statements, it is necessary that management make informed estimates and judgements. The other financial information in this annual report is consistent with the financial statements.

The Corporation maintains a system of internal accounting controls designed to provide reasonable assurance that financial records are reliable for purposes of preparing financial statements and that assets are properly accounted for and safeguarded. The concept of reasonable assurance is based on the recognition that the cost of the system must be related to the benefits to be derived. The Corporation believes its system provides an appropriate balance in this regard. The Corporation maintains an Internal Audit Department which reviews the adequacy and tests the application of internal accounting controls.

The financial statements have been audited by Arthur Andersen LLP, independent public accountants, whose appointment was ratified by stockholder vote at the stockholders' meeting held on April 28, 1998. Their report expresses an opinion that the Corporation's financial statements are fairly stated in conformity with generally accepted accounting principles, and they have indicated to us that their audit was performed in accordance with generally accepted auditing standards which are designed to obtain reasonable assurance about whether the financial statements are free of material misstatement.

The Audit Committee of the Board of Directors of the Corporation, consisting solely of non-management directors, meets regularly with the independent public accountants, internal auditors and management to discuss, among other things, the audit scopes and results. Arthur Andersen LLP and the internal auditors both have full and free access to the Audit Committee, with and without the presence of management.

REPORT OF INDEPENDENT PUBLIC ACCOUNTANTS

To the Stockholders and Board of Directors
of Hershey Foods Corporation:

We have audited the accompanying consolidated balance sheets of Hershey Foods Corporation (a Delaware Corporation) and subsidiaries as of December 31, 1998 and 1997, and the related consolidated statements of income, stockholders' equity and cash flows for each of the three years in the period ended December 31, 1998, appearing on pages [B-10 through B-29]. These financial statements are the responsibility of the Corporation's management. Our responsibility is to express an opinion on these financial staements based on our audits.

We conducted our audits in accordance with generally accepted auditing standards. Those standards require that we plan and perform the audit to obtain reasonable assurance about whether the financial statements are free of material misstatement. An audit includes examining, on a test basis, evidence supporting the amounts and disclosures in the financial statements. An audit also includes assessing the accouning principles used and significant estimates made by management, as well as evaluating the overall financial statement presentation. We believe that our audits provide a reasonable basis for our opinion.

In our opinion, the financial statements referred to above present fairly, in all material respects, the financial position of Hershey Foods Corporation and subsidiaries as of December 31, 1998 and 1997, and the results of their operations and their cash flows for each of the three years in the period ended December 31, 1998 in conformity with generally accepted accounting principles.

Arthur Andersen LLP

New York, New York
January 29, 1999

APPENDIX C

Time Value of Money

◆ **STUDY OBJECTIVES**

After studying this appendix, you should be able to:

1 Distinguish between simple and compound interest.

2 Solve for future value of a single amount.

3 Solve for future value of an annuity.

4 Identify the variables fundamental to solving present value problems.

5 Solve for present value of a single amount.

6 Solve for present value of an annuity.

7 Compute the present value of notes and bonds.

Would you rather receive $1,000 today or a year from now? You should prefer to receive the $1,000 today because you can invest the $1,000 and earn interest on it. As a result, you will have more than $1,000 a year from now. What this example illustrates is the concept of the **time value of money.** Everyone prefers to receive money today rather than in the future because of the interest factor.

Nature of Interest

Interest is payment for the use of another person's money. It is the difference between the amount borrowed or invested (called the **principal**) and the amount repaid or collected. The amount of interest to be paid or collected is usually stated as a rate over a specific period of time. The rate of interest is generally stated as an annual rate.

The amount of interest involved in any financing transaction is based on three elements:

STUDY OBJECTIVE

◆ **1** ◆

Distinguish between simple and compound interest.

1. **Principal (p):** The original amount borrowed or invested.
2. **Interest Rate (i):** An annual percentage of the principal.
3. **Time (n):** The number of years that the principal is borrowed or invested.

SIMPLE INTEREST

Simple interest is computed on the principal amount only. It is the return on the principal for one period. Simple interest is usually expressed as shown in Illustration C-1.

Illustration C-1 Interest computation

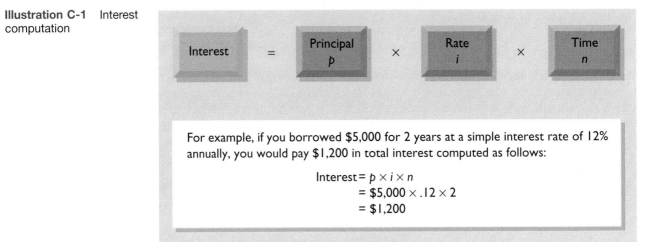

$$\text{Interest} = \text{Principal } p \times \text{Rate } i \times \text{Time } n$$

For example, if you borrowed \$5,000 for 2 years at a simple interest rate of 12% annually, you would pay \$1,200 in total interest computed as follows:

$$\text{Interest} = p \times i \times n$$
$$= \$5,000 \times .12 \times 2$$
$$= \$1,200$$

COMPOUND INTEREST

Compound interest is computed on principal **and** on any interest earned that has not been paid or withdrawn. It is the return on (or growth of) the principal for two or more time periods. Compounding computes interest not only on the principal but also on the interest earned to date on that principal, assuming the interest is left on deposit.

To illustrate the difference between simple and compound interest, assume that you deposit $1,000 in Bank Two, where it will earn simple interest of 9% per year, and you deposit another $1,000 in Citizens Bank, where it will earn compound interest of 9% per year compounded annually. Also assume that in both cases you will not withdraw any interest until 3 years from the date of deposit. The computation of interest to be received and the accumulated year-end balances are indicated in Illustration C-2.

Illustration C-2 Simple versus compound interest

Bank Two				Citizens Bank		
Simple Interest Calculation	Simple Interest	Accumulated Year-end Balance		Compound Interest Calculation	Compound Interest	Accumulated Year-end Balance
Year 1 $1,000.00 × 9%	$ 90.00	$1,090.00		Year 1 $1,000.00 × 9%	$ 90.00	$1,090.00
Year 2 $1,000.00 × 9%	90.00	$1,180.00		Year 2 $1,090.00 × 9%	98.10	$1,188.10
Year 3 $1,000.00 × 9%	90.00	$1,270.00		Year 3 $1,188.10 × 9%	106.93	$1,295.03
	$ 270.00		$25.03 Difference		$ 295.03	

Note in Illustration C-2 that simple interest uses the initial principal of $1,000 to compute the interest in all 3 years. Compound interest uses the accumulated balance (principal plus interest to date) at each year-end to compute interest in the succeeding year—which explains why your compound interest account is larger.

Obviously, if you had a choice between investing your money at simple interest or at compound interest, you would choose compound interest, all other things—especially risk—being equal. In the example, compounding provides $25.03 of additional interest income. For practical purposes, compounding assumes that unpaid interest earned becomes a part of the principal, and the accumulated balance at the end of each year becomes the new principal on which interest is earned during the next year.

As can be seen in Illustration C-2, you should invest your money at Citizens Bank, which compounds interest annually. Compound interest is used in most business situations. Simple interest is generally applicable only to short-term situations of one year or less.

SECTION 1

FUTURE VALUE CONCEPTS

FUTURE VALUE OF A SINGLE AMOUNT

The **future value of a single amount** is the value at a future date of a given amount invested, assuming compound interest. For example, in Illustration C-2, $1,295.03 is the future value of the $1,000 at the end of 3 years. The $1,295.03 could be determined more easily by using the following formula:

$$FV = p \times (1 + i)^n$$

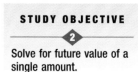

STUDY OBJECTIVE
2
Solve for future value of a single amount.

where:

$$FV = \text{Future value of a single amount}$$
$$p = \text{Principal (or present value)}$$
$$i = \text{Interest rate for one period}$$
$$n = \text{Number of periods}$$

The $1,295.03 is computed as follows:

$$FV = p \times (1 + i)^n$$
$$= \$1,000 \times (1 + i)^3$$
$$= \$1,000 \times 1.29503$$
$$= \$1,295.03$$

The 1.29503 is computed by multiplying $(1.09 \times 1.09 \times 1.09)$. The amounts in this example can be depicted in the time diagram shown in Illustration C-3.

Illustration C-3 Time diagram

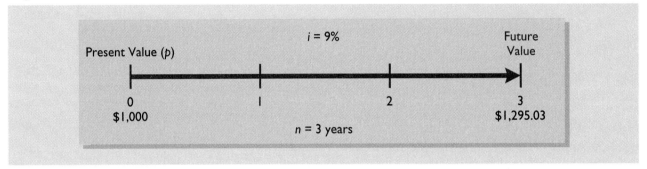

Another method that may be used to compute the future value of a single amount involves the use of a compound interest table. This table shows the future value of 1 for n periods. Table 1 is such a table.

TABLE 1   Future Value of 1

(n) Periods	4%	5%	6%	8%	9%	10%	11%	12%	15%
1	1.04000	1.05000	1.06000	1.08000	1.09000	1.10000	1.11000	1.12000	1.15000
2	1.08160	1.10250	1.12360	1.16640	1.18810	1.21000	1.23210	1.25440	1.32250
3	1.12486	1.15763	1.19102	1.25971	1.29503	1.33100	1.36763	1.40493	1.52088
4	1.16986	1.21551	1.26248	1.36049	1.41158	1.46410	1.51807	1.57352	1.74901
5	1.21665	1.27628	1.33823	1.46933	1.53862	1.61051	1.68506	1.76234	2.01136
6	1.26532	1.34010	1.41852	1.58687	1.67710	1.77156	1.87041	1.97382	2.31306
7	1.31593	1.40710	1.50363	1.71382	1.82804	1.94872	2.07616	2.21068	2.66002
8	1.36857	1.47746	1.59385	1.85093	1.99256	2.14359	2.30454	2.47596	3.05902
9	1.42331	1.55133	1.68948	1.99900	2.17189	2.35795	2.55803	2.77308	3.51788
10	1.48024	1.62889	1.79085	2.15892	2.36736	2.59374	2.83942	3.10585	4.04556
11	1.53945	1.71034	1.89830	2.33164	2.58043	2.85312	3.15176	3.47855	4.65239
12	1.60103	1.79586	2.01220	2.51817	2.81267	3.13843	3.49845	3.89598	5.35025
13	1.66507	1.88565	2.13293	2.71962	3.06581	3.45227	3.88328	4.36349	6.15279
14	1.73168	1.97993	2.26090	2.93719	3.34173	3.79750	4.31044	4.88711	7.07571
15	1.80094	2.07893	2.39656	3.17217	3.64248	4.17725	4.78459	5.47357	8.13706
16	1.87298	2.18287	2.54035	3.42594	3.97031	4.59497	5.31089	6.13039	9.35762
17	1.94790	2.29202	2.69277	3.70002	4.32763	5.05447	5.89509	6.86604	10.76126
18	2.02582	2.40662	2.85434	3.99602	4.71712	5.55992	6.54355	7.68997	12.37545
19	2.10685	2.52695	3.02560	4.31570	5.14166	6.11591	7.26334	8.61276	14.23177
20	2.19112	2.65330	3.20714	4.66096	5.60441	6.72750	8.06231	9.64629	16.36654

In Table 1, n is the number of compounding periods, the percentages are the periodic interest rates, and the 5-digit decimal numbers in the respective columns are the future value of 1 factors. In using Table 1, the principal amount is multiplied by the future value factor for the specified number of periods and interest rate. For example, the future value factor for 2 periods at 9% is 1.18810. Multiplying this factor by $1,000 equals $1,188.10, which is the accumulated balance at the end of year 2 in the Citizens Bank example in Illustration C-2. The $1,295.03 accumulated balance at the end of the third year can be calculated from Table 1 by multiplying the future value factor for 3 periods (1.29503) by the $1,000.

The demonstration problem in Illustration C-4 shows how to use Table 1.

Illustration C-4
Demonstration problem—
Using Table 1 for *FV* of 1

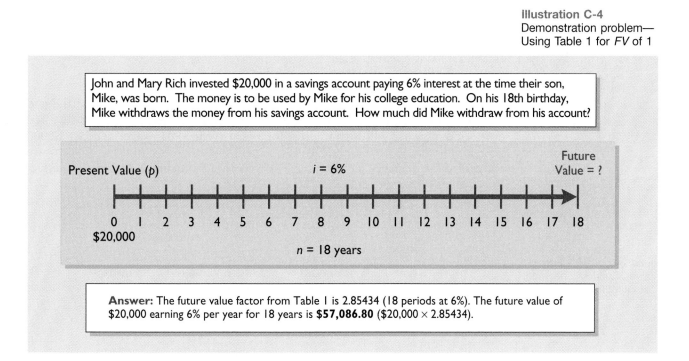

John and Mary Rich invested $20,000 in a savings account paying 6% interest at the time their son, Mike, was born. The money is to be used by Mike for his college education. On his 18th birthday, Mike withdraws the money from his savings account. How much did Mike withdraw from his account?

Answer: The future value factor from Table 1 is 2.85434 (18 periods at 6%). The future value of $20,000 earning 6% per year for 18 years is **$57,086.80** ($20,000 × 2.85434).

FUTURE VALUE OF AN ANNUITY

The preceding discussion involved the accumulation of only a single principal sum. Individuals and businesses frequently encounter situations in which a series of equal dollar amounts are to be paid or received periodically, such as loans or lease (rental) contracts. Such payments or receipts of equal dollar amounts are referred to as annuities. The future value of an annuity is the sum of all the payments (receipts) plus the accumulated compound interest on them. In computing the future value of an annuity, it is necessary to know (1) the interest rate, (2) the number of compounding periods, and (3) the amount of the periodic payments or receipts.

To illustrate the computation of the future value of an annuity, assume that you invest $2,000 at the end of each year for 3 years at 5% interest compounded annually. This situation is depicted in the time diagram in Illustration C-5.

STUDY OBJECTIVE

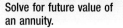

Solve for future value of an annuity.

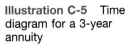

Illustration C-5 Time diagram for a 3-year annuity

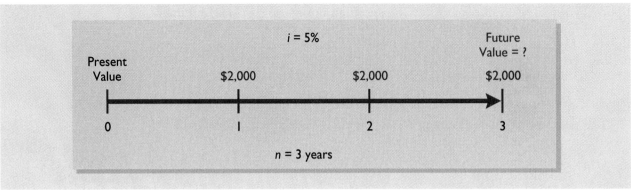

As can be seen from the preceding diagram, the $2,000 invested at the end of year 1 will earn interest for 2 years (years 2 and 3), and the $2,000 invested at the end of year 2 will earn interest for 1 year (year 3). However, the last $2,000 investment (made at the end of year 3) will not earn any interest. The future value of these periodic payments could be computed using the future value factors from Table 1, as shown in Illustration C-6.

Illustration C-6 Future value of periodic payment computation

Year Invested	Amount Invested	×	Future Value of 1 Factor at 5%	=	Future Value
1	$2,000	×	1.10250		$2,205
2	$2,000	×	1.05000		2,100
3	$2,000	×	1.00000		2,000
			3.15250		$6,305

The first $2,000 investment is multiplied by the future value factor for 2 periods (1.1025) because 2 years' interest will accumulate on it (in years 2 and 3). The second $2,000 investment will earn only 1 year's interest (in year 3) and therefore is multiplied by the future value factor for 1 year (1.0500). The final $2,000 investment is made at the end of the third year and will not earn any interest. Consequently, the future value of the last $2,000 invested is only $2,000 since it does not accumulate any interest.

Calculating the future value of each individual cash flow is required when the periodic payments or receipts are not equal in each period. However, when the periodic payments (receipts) are the same in each period, the future value can be computed by using a future value of an annuity of 1 table. Table 2 is such a table.

TABLE 2   Future Value of an Annuity of 1

(n) Periods	4%	5%	6%	8%	9%	10%	11%	12%	15%
1	1.00000	1.00000	1.00000	1.00000	1.00000	1.00000	1.00000	1.00000	1.00000
2	2.04000	2.05000	2.06000	2.08000	2.09000	2.10000	2.11000	2.12000	2.15000
3	3.12160	3.15250	3.18360	3.24640	3.27810	3.31000	3.34210	3.37440	3.47250
4	4.24646	4.31013	4.37462	4.50611	4.57313	4.64100	4.70973	4.77933	4.99338
5	5.41632	5.52563	5.63709	5.86660	5.98471	6.10510	6.22780	6.35285	6.74238
6	6.63298	6.80191	6.97532	7.33592	7.52334	7.71561	7.91286	8.11519	8.75374
7	7.89829	8.14201	8.39384	8.92280	9.20044	9.48717	9.78327	10.08901	11.06680
8	9.21423	9.54911	9.89747	10.63663	11.02847	11.43589	11.85943	12.29969	13.72682
9	10.58280	11.02656	11.49132	12.48756	13.02104	13.57948	14.16397	14.77566	16.78584
10	12.00611	12.57789	13.18079	14.48656	15.19293	15.93743	16.72201	17.54874	20.30372
11	13.48635	14.20679	14.97164	16.64549	17.56029	18.53117	19.56143	20.65458	24.34928
12	15.02581	15.91713	16.86994	18.97713	20.14072	21.38428	22.71319	24.13313	29.00167
13	16.62684	17.71298	18.88214	21.49530	22.95339	24.52271	26.21164	28.02911	34.35192
14	18.29191	19.59863	21.01507	24.21492	26.01919	27.97498	30.09492	32.39260	40.50471
15	20.02359	21.57856	23.27597	27.15211	29.36092	31.77248	34.40536	37.27972	47.58041
16	21.82453	23.65749	25.67253	30.32428	33.00340	35.94973	39.18995	42.75328	55.71747
17	23.69751	25.84037	28.21288	33.75023	36.97351	40.54470	44.50084	48.88367	65.07509
18	25.64541	28.13238	30.90565	37.45024	41.30134	45.59917	50.39593	55.74972	75.83636
19	27.67123	30.53900	33.75999	41.44626	46.01846	51.15909	56.93949	63.43968	88.21181
20	29.77808	33.06595	36.78559	45.76196	51.16012	57.27500	64.20283	72.05244	102.44358

Table 2 shows the future value of 1 to be received periodically for a given number of periods. From Table 2 it can be seen that the future value of an annuity of 1 factor for 3 periods at 5% is 3.15250. The future value factor is the total of the three individual future value factors as shown in Illustration C-6. Multiplying this amount by the annual investment of $2,000 produces a future value of $6,305.

The demonstration problem in Illustration C-7 (at the top of the next page) shows how to use Table 2.

Illustration C-7
Demonstration problem—
Using Table 2 for *FV* of
an annuity of 1

> John and Char Lewis' daughter, Debra, has just started high school. They decide to start a college fund for her and will invest $2,500 in a savings account at the end of each year she is in high school (4 payments total). The account will earn 6% interest compounded annually. How much will be in the college fund at the time Debra graduates from high school?

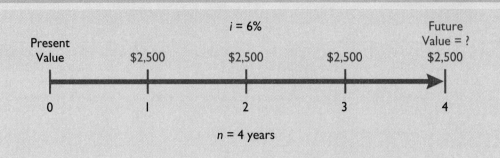

Answer: The future value factor from Table 2 is 4.37462 (4 periods at 6%). The future value of $2,500 invested each year for 4 years at 6% interest is **$10,936.55** ($2,500 × 4.37462).

SECTION 2

PRESENT VALUE CONCEPTS

PRESENT VALUE VARIABLES

STUDY OBJECTIVE

4

Identify the variables fundamental to solving present value problems.

The present value, like the future value, is based on three variables: (1) the dollar amount to be received (future amount), (2) the length of time until the amount is received (number of periods), and (3) the interest rate (the discount rate). The process of determining the present value is referred to as discounting the future amount.

In this textbook, present value computations are used in measuring several items. For example, in Chapter 10, to determine the market price of a bond, the present value of the principal and interest payments is computed. In addition, the determination of the amount to be reported for notes payable and lease liability involves present value computations.

Present Value of a Single Amount

PRESENT VALUE OF A SINGLE AMOUNT

To illustrate present value concepts, assume that you are willing to invest a sum of money that will yield $1,000 at the end of one year. In other words, what amount would you need to invest today to have $1,000 one year from now? If you want a 10% rate of return, the investment or present value is $909.09 ($1,000 ÷ 1.10). The computation of this amount is shown in Illustration C-8.

STUDY OBJECTIVE

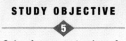

Solve for present value of a single amount.

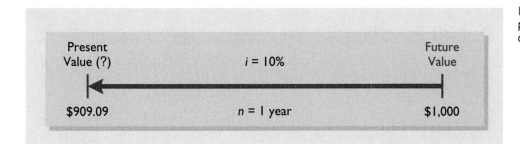

$$\text{Present Value} = \text{Future Value} \div (1 + i)^1$$
$$PV = FV \div (1 + 10\%)^1$$
$$PV = \$1,000 \div 1.10$$
$$PV = \$909.09$$

Illustration C-8 Present value computation—$1,000 discounted at 10% for 1 year

The future amount ($1,000), the discount rate (10%), and the number of periods (1) are known. The variables in this situation can be depicted in the time diagram in Illustration C-9.

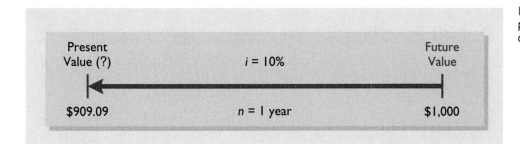

Illustration C-9 Finding present value if discounted for one period

If the single amount of $1,000 is to be received **in 2 years** and discounted at 10% [$PV = \$1,000 \div (1 + 10\%)^2$], its present value is $826.45 [($1,000 ÷ 1.10) ÷ 1.10], depicted as shown in Illustration C-10.

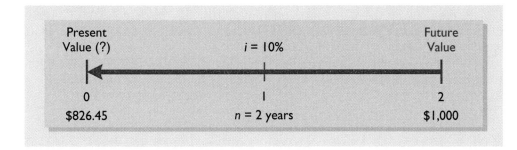

Illustration C-10 Finding present value if discounted for two periods

The present value of 1 may also be determined through tables that show the present value of 1 for n periods. In Table 3 (page C-10), n is the number of discounting periods involved. The percentages are the periodic interest rates or discount rates, and the 5-digit decimal numbers in the respective columns are the present value of 1 factors.

TABLE 3   Present Value of 1

(*n*) Periods	4%	5%	6%	8%	9%	10%	11%	12%	15%
1	.96154	.95238	.94340	.92593	.91743	.90909	.90090	.89286	.86957
2	.92456	.90703	.89000	.85734	.84168	.82645	.81162	.79719	.75614
3	.88900	.86384	.83962	.79383	.77218	.75132	.73119	.71178	.65752
4	.85480	.82270	.79209	.73503	.70843	.68301	.65873	.63552	.57175
5	.82193	.78353	.74726	.68058	.64993	.62092	.59345	.56743	.49718
6	.79031	.74622	.70496	.63017	.59627	.56447	.53464	.50663	.43233
7	.75992	.71068	.66506	.58349	.54703	.51316	.48166	.45235	.37594
8	.73069	.67684	.62741	.54027	.50187	.46651	.43393	.40388	.32690
9	.70259	.64461	.59190	.50025	.46043	.42410	.39092	.36061	.28426
10	.67556	.61391	.55839	.46319	.42241	.38554	.35218	.32197	.24719
11	.64958	.58468	.52679	.42888	.38753	.35049	.31728	.28748	.21494
12	.62460	.55684	.49697	.39711	.35554	.31863	.28584	.25668	.18691
13	.60057	.53032	.46884	.36770	.32618	.28966	.25751	.22917	.16253
14	.57748	.50507	.44230	.34046	.29925	.26333	.23199	.20462	.14133
15	.55526	.48102	.41727	.31524	.27454	.23939	.20900	.18270	.12289
16	.53391	.45811	.39365	.29189	.25187	.21763	.18829	.16312	.10687
17	.51337	.43630	.37136	.27027	.23107	.19785	.16963	.14564	.09293
18	.49363	.41552	.35034	.25025	.21199	.17986	.15282	.13004	.08081
19	.47464	.39573	.33051	.23171	.19449	.16351	.13768	.11611	.07027
20	.45639	.37689	.31180	.21455	.17843	.14864	.12403	.10367	.06110

When Table 3 is used, the future value is multiplied by the present value factor specified at the intersection of the number of periods and the discount rate. For example, the present value factor for 1 period at a discount rate of 10% is .90909, which equals the $909.09 ($1,000 × .90909) computed in Illustration C-8. For 2 periods at a discount rate of 10%, the present value factor is .82645, which equals the $826.45 ($1,000 × .82645) computed previously.

Note that a higher discount rate produces a smaller present value. For example, using a 15% discount rate, the present value of $1,000 due one year from now is $869.57 versus $909.09 at 10%. It should also be recognized that the further removed from the present the future value is, the smaller the present value. For example, using the same discount rate of 10%, the present value of $1,000 due in **five years** is $620.92 versus the present value of $1,000 due in **one year**, which is $909.09.

The following two demonstration problems (Illustrations C-11, C-12) illustrate how to use Table 3.

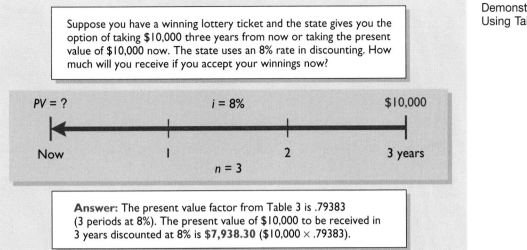

Illustration C-11
Demonstration problem—
Using Table 3 for *PV* of 1

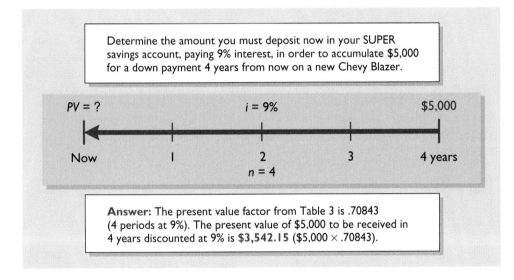

Illustration C-12
Demonstration problem—
Using Table 3 for *PV* of 1

PRESENT VALUE OF AN ANNUITY

The preceding discussion involved the discounting of only a single future amount. Businesses and individuals frequently engage in transactions in which a series of equal dollar amounts are to be received or paid periodically. Examples of a series of periodic receipts or payments are loan agreements, installment sales, mortgage notes, lease (rental) contracts, and pension obligations. These series of periodic receipts or payments are called **annuities.** In computing the present value of an annuity, it is necessary to know (1) the discount rate, (2) the number of discount periods, and (3) the amount of the periodic receipts or payments. To illustrate the computation of the present value of an annuity, assume that you will receive $1,000 cash annually for three years at a time when the discount rate is 10%. This situation is depicted in the time diagram in Illustration C-13.

STUDY OBJECTIVE

Solve for present value of an annuity.

Illustration C-13 Time diagram for a 3-year annuity

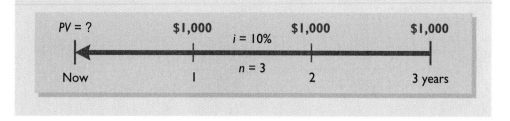

The present value in this situation may be computed as shown in Illustration C-14.

Illustration C-14
Present value of a series of future amounts computation

Future Amount	×	Present Value of 1 Factor at 10%	=	Present Value
$1,000 (One year away)		.90909		$ 909.09
1,000 (Two years away)		.82645		826.45
1,000 (Three years away)		.75132		751.32
		2.48686		$2,486.86

This method of calculation is required when the periodic cash flows are not uniform in each period. However, when the future receipts are the same in each period, there are two other ways to compute present value. First, the annual cash flow can be multiplied by the sum of the three present value factors. In the previous example, $1,000 × 2.48686 equals $2,486.86. Second, annuity tables may be used. As illustrated in Table 4 below, these tables show the present value of 1 to be received periodically for a given number of periods.

TABLE 4 Present Value of an Annuity of 1

(n) Periods	4%	5%	6%	8%	9%	10%	11%	12%	15%
1	.96154	.95238	.94340	.92593	.91743	.90909	.90090	.89286	.86957
2	1.88609	1.85941	1.83339	1.78326	1.75911	1.73554	1.71252	1.69005	1.62571
3	2.77509	2.72325	2.67301	2.57710	2.53130	2.48685	2.44371	2.40183	2.28323
4	3.62990	3.54595	3.46511	3.31213	3.23972	3.16986	3.10245	3.03735	2.85498
5	4.45182	4.32948	4.21236	3.99271	3.88965	3.79079	3.69590	3.60478	3.35216
6	5.24214	5.07569	4.91732	4.62288	4.48592	4.35526	4.23054	4.11141	3.78448
7	6.00205	5.78637	5.58238	5.20637	5.03295	4.86842	4.71220	4.56376	4.16042
8	6.73274	6.46321	6.20979	5.74664	5.53482	5.33493	5.14612	4.96764	4.48732
9	7.43533	7.10782	6.80169	6.24689	5.99525	5.75902	5.53705	5.32825	4.77158
10	8.11090	7.72173	7.36009	6.71008	6.41766	6.14457	5.88923	5.65022	5.01877
11	8.76048	8.30641	7.88687	7.13896	6.80519	6.49506	6.20652	5.93770	5.23371
12	9.38507	8.86325	8.38384	7.53608	7.16073	6.81369	6.49236	6.19437	5.42062
13	9.98565	9.39357	8.85268	7.90378	7.48690	7.10336	6.74987	6.42355	5.58315
14	10.56312	9.89864	9.29498	8.24424	7.78615	7.36669	6.98187	6.62817	5.72448
15	11.11839	10.37966	9.71225	8.55948	8.06069	7.60608	7.19087	6.81086	5.84737
16	11.65230	10.83777	10.10590	8.85137	8.31256	7.82371	7.37916	6.97399	5.95424
17	12.16567	11.27407	10.47726	9.12164	8.54363	8.02155	7.54879	7.11963	6.04716
18	12.65930	11.68959	10.82760	9.37189	8.75563	8.20141	7.70162	7.24967	6.12797
19	13.13394	12.08532	11.15812	9.60360	8.95012	8.36492	7.83929	7.36578	6.19823
20	13.59033	12.46221	11.46992	9.81815	9.12855	8.51356	7.96333	7.46944	6.25933

From Table 4 it can be seen that the present value of an annuity of 1 factor for three periods at 10% is 2.48685.[1] This present value factor is the total of the three individual present value factors, as shown in Illustration C-14. Applying this amount to the annual cash flow of $1,000 produces a present value of $2,486.85.

The following demonstration problem (Illustration C-15) illustrates how to use Table 4.

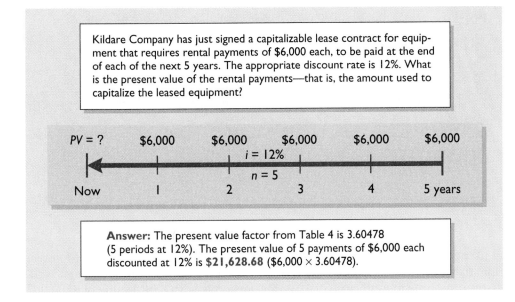

Illustration C-15
Demonstration problem—
Using Table 4 for *PV* of an annuity of 1

TIME PERIODS AND DISCOUNTING

In the preceding calculations, the discounting has been done on an annual basis using an annual interest rate. Discounting may also be done over shorter periods of time such as monthly, quarterly, or semiannually. When the time frame is less than one year, it is necessary to convert the annual interest rate to the applicable time frame. Assume, for example, that the investor in Illustration C-14 received $500 **semiannually** for three years instead of $1,000 annually. In this case, the number of periods becomes 6 (3 × 2), the discount rate is 5% (10% ÷ 2), the present value factor from Table 4 is 5.07569, and the present value of the future cash flows is $2,537.85 (5.07569 × $500). This amount is slightly higher than the $2,486.85 computed in Illustration C-14 because interest is computed twice during the same year; therefore interest is earned on the first half year's interest.

COMPUTING THE PRESENT VALUE OF A LONG-TERM NOTE OR BOND

The present value (or market price) of a long-term note or bond is a function of three variables: (1) the payment amounts, (2) the length of time until the amounts are paid, and (3) the discount rate. Our illustration uses a 5-year bond issue.

STUDY OBJECTIVE

Compute the present value of notes and bonds.

---
[1]The difference of .00001 between 2.48686 and 2.48685 is due to rounding.

The first variable (dollars to be paid) is made up of two elements: (1) a series of interest payments (an annuity) and (2) the principal amount (a single sum). To compute the present value of the bond, both the interest payments and the principal amount must be discounted—two different computations. The time diagrams for a bond due in 5 years are shown in Illustration C-16.

Illustration C-16
Present value of a bond
time diagram

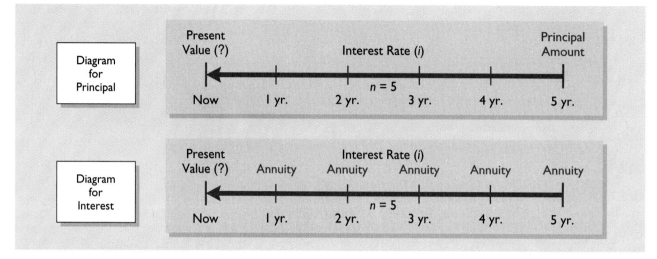

When the investor's discount rate is equal to the bond's contractual interest rate, the present value of the bonds will equal the face value of the bonds. To illustrate, assume a bond issue of 10%, 5-year bonds with a face value of $100,000 with interest payable **semiannually** on January 1 and July 1. If the discount rate is the same as the contractual rate, the bonds will sell at face value. In this case, the investor will receive (1) $100,000 at maturity and (2) a series of ten $5,000 interest payments [($100,000 × 10%) ÷ 2] over the term of the bonds. The length of time is expressed in terms of interest periods, in this case, 10, and the discount rate per interest period, 5%. The following time diagram (Illustration C-17) depicts the variables involved in this discounting situation.

Illustration C-17   Time
diagram for present
value of a 10%, 5-year
bond paying interest
semiannually

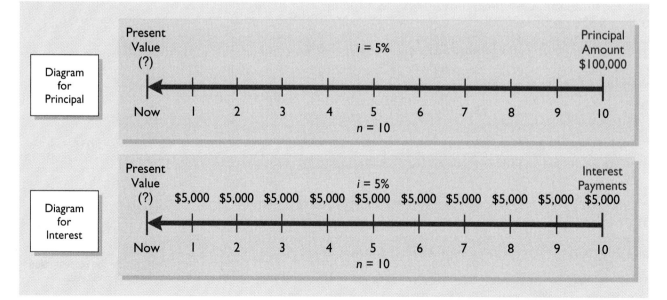

The computation of the present value of these bonds is shown in Illustration C-18.

Illustration C-18
Present value of principal
and interest (face value)

10% Contractual Rate—10% Discount Rate	
Present value of principal to be received at maturity	
$100,000 × *PV* of 1 due in 10 periods at 5%	
$100,000 × .61391 (Table 3)	$ 61,391
Present value of interest to be received periodically over the term of the bonds	
$5,000 × *PV* of 1 due periodically for 10 periods at 5%	
$5,000 × 7.72173 (Table 4)	38,609*
Present value of bonds	$100,000

*Rounded

Now assume that the investor's required rate of return is 12%, not 10%. The future amounts are again $100,000 and $5,000, respectively, but now a discount rate of 6% (12% ÷ 2) must be used. The present value of the bonds is $92,639, as computed in Illustration C-19.

Illustration C-19
Present value of principal
and interest (discount)

10% Contractual Rate—12% Discount Rate	
Present value of principal to be received at maturity	
$100,000 × .55839 (Table 3)	$ 55,839
Present value of interest to be received periodically over the term of the bonds	
$5,000 × 7.36009 (Table 4)	36,800
Present value of bonds	$92,639

Conversely, if the discount rate is 8% and the contractual rate is 10%, the present value of the bonds is $108,111, computed as shown in Illustration C-20.

Illustration C-20
Present value of principal
and interest (premium)

10% Contractual Rate—8% Discount Rate	
Present value of principal to be received at maturity	
$100,000 × .67556 (Table 3)	$ 67,556
Present value of interest to be received periodically over the term of the bonds	
$5,000 × 8.11090 (Table 4)	40,555
Present value of bonds	$108,111

The above discussion relied on present value tables in solving present value problems. Electronic hand-held calculators may also be used to compute present values without the use of these tables. Many calculators, especially the "business" calculators, have present value (*PV*) functions that allow you to calculate present values by merely inputting the proper amount, discount rate, periods, and pressing the PV key.

SUMMARY OF STUDY OBJECTIVES

1 *Distinguish between simple and compound interest.* Simple interest is computed on the principal only, while compound interest is computed on the principal and any interest earned that has not been withdrawn.

2 *Solve for future value of a single amount.* Prepare a time diagram of the problem. Identify the principal amount, the number of compounding periods, and the interest rate. Using the future value of 1 table, multiply the principal amount by the future value factor specified at the intersection of the number of periods and the interest rate.

3 *Solve for future value of an annuity.* Prepare a time diagram of the problem. Identify the amount of the periodic payments, the number of compounding periods, and the interest rate. Using the future value of an annuity of 1 table, multiply the amount of the payments by the future value factor specified at the intersection of the number of periods and the interest rate.

4 *Identify the variables fundamental to solving present value problems.* The following three variables are fundamental to solving present value problems: (1) the future amount, (2) the number of periods, and (3) the interest rate (the discount rate).

5 *Solve for present value of a single amount.* Prepare a time diagram of the problem. Identify the future amount, the number of discounting periods, and the discount (interest) rate. Using the present value of a single amount table, multiply the future amount by the present value factor specified at the intersection of the number of periods and the discount rate.

6 *Solve for present value of an annuity.* Prepare a time diagram of the problem. Identify the future amounts (annuities), the number of discounting periods, and the discount (interest) rate. Using the present value of an annuity of 1 table, multiply the amount of the annuity by the present value factor specified at the intersection of the number of periods and the interest rate.

7 *Compute the present value of notes and bonds.* Determine the present value of the principal amount: Multiply the principal amount (a single future amount) by the present value factor (from the present value of 1 table) intersecting at the number of periods (number of interest payments) and the discount rate. Determine the present value of the series of interest payments: Multiply the amount of the interest payment by the present value factor (from the present value of an annuity of 1 table) intersecting at the number of periods (number of interest payments) and the discount rate. Add the present value of the principal amount to the present value of the interest payments to arrive at the present value of the note or bond.

GLOSSARY

Annuity A series of equal dollar amounts to be paid or received periodically. (p. C-5)

Compound interest The interest computed on the principal and any interest earned that has not been paid or received. (p. C-2)

Discounting the future amount(s) The process of determining present value. (p. C-8)

Future value of a single amount The value at a future date of a given amount invested assuming compound interest. (p. C-3)

Future value of an annuity The sum of all the payments or receipts plus the accumulated compound interest on them. (p. C-5)

Interest Payment for the use of another's money. (p. C-2)

Present value The value now of a given amount to be invested or received in the future assuming compound interest. (p. C-8)

Present value of an annuity A series of future receipts or payments discounted to their value now assuming compound interest. (p. C-11)

Principal The amount borrowed or invested. (p. C-2)

Simple interest The interest computed on the principal only. (p. C-2)

BRIEF EXERCISES (USE TABLES TO SOLVE EXERCISES)

Compute the future value of a single amount.

BEC-1 Don Smith invested $5,000 at 8% annual interest, and left the money invested without withdrawing any of the interest for 12 years. At the end of the 12 years, Don withdrew the accumulated amount of money. (a) What amount did Don withdraw, assuming the investment earns simple interest? (b) What amount did Don withdraw, assuming the investment earns interest compounded annually?

BEC-2   For each of the following cases, indicate (a) to what interest rate columns and (b) to what number of periods you would refer in looking up the future value factor. *Use future value tables.*

(1) In Table 1 (future value of 1):

	Annual Rate	**Number of Years Invested**	**Compounded**
Case A	6%	5	Annually
Case B	5%	3	Semiannually

(2) In Table 2 (future value of an annuity of 1):

	Annual Rate	**Number of Years Invested**	**Compounded**
Case A	5%	10	Annually
Case B	4%	6	Semiannually

BEC-3   Porter Company signed a lease for an office building for a period of 8 years. Under the lease agreement, a security deposit of $10,000 is made. The deposit will be returned at the expiration of the lease with interest compounded at 6% per year. What amount will Porter receive at the time the lease expires? *Compute the future value of a single amount.*

BEC-4   Gordon Company issued $1,000,000, 10-year bonds and agreed to make annual sinking fund deposits of $60,000. The deposits are made at the end of each year into an account paying 5% annual interest. What amount will be in the sinking fund at the end of 10 years? *Compute the future value of an annuity.*

BEC-5   David and Kathy Hatcher invested $7,000 in a savings account paying 8% annual interest when their daughter, Sue, was born. They also deposited $1,000 on each of her birthdays until she was 18 (including her 18th birthday). How much was in the savings account on her 18th birthday (after the last deposit)? *Compute the future value of a single amount and of an annuity.*

BEC-6   Ron Watson borrowed $20,000 on July 1, 2001. This amount plus accrued interest at 9% compounded annually is to be repaid on July 1, 2006. How much will Ron have to repay on July 1, 2006? *Compute the future value of a single amount.*

BEC-7   For each of the following cases, indicate (a) to what interest rate columns and (b) to what number of periods you would refer in looking up the discount rate. *Use present value tables.*

(1) In Table 3 (present value of 1):

	Annual Rate	**Number of Years Involved**	**Discounts per Year**
Case A	12%	6	Annually
Case B	10%	15	Annually
Case C	8%	8	Semiannually

(2) In Table 4 (present value of an annuity of 1):

	Annual Rate	**Number of Years Involved**	**Number of Payments Involved**	**Frequency of Payments**
Case A	12%	20	20	Annually
Case B	10%	5	5	Annually
Case C	8%	4	8	Semiannually

BEC-8   (a) What is the present value of $10,000 due 8 periods from now, discounted at 10%? *Determine present values.*

(b) What is the present value of $10,000 to be received at the end of each of 6 periods, discounted at 8%?

BEC-9   Smolinski Company is considering an investment which will return a lump sum of $500,000 five years from now. What amount should Smolinski Company pay for this investment to earn a 12% return? *Compute the present value of a single amount investment.*

BEC-10   Pizzeria Company earns 15% on an investment that will return $875,000 eight years from now. What is the amount Pizzeria should invest now to earn this rate of return? *Compute the present value of a single amount investment.*

Compute the present value of an annuity investment.

BEC-11   Kilarny Company is considering investing in an annuity contract that will return $25,000 annually at the end of each year for 15 years. What amount should Kilarny Company pay for this investment if it earns a 6% return?

Compute the present value of an annuity investment.

BEC-12   Zarita Enterprises earns 9% on an investment that pays back $110,000 at the end of each of the next six years. What is the amount Zarita Enterprises invested to earn the 9% rate of return?

Compute the present value of bonds.

BEC-13   Hernandez Railroad Co. is about to issue $100,000 of 10-year bonds paying an 11% interest rate, with interest payable semiannually. The discount rate for such securities is 8%. How much can Hernandez expect to receive for the sale of these bonds?

Compute the present value of bonds.

BEC-14   Assume the same information as BEC-13 except that the discount rate was 12% instead of 8%. In this case, how much can Hernandez expect to receive from the sale of these bonds?

Compute the present value of a note.

BEC-15   Caledonian Taco Company receives a $50,000, 6-year note bearing interest of 8% (paid annually) from a customer at a time when the discount rate is 9%. What is the present value of the note received by Caledonian?

Compute the present value of bonds.

BEC-16   Galway Bay Enterprises issued 9%, 8-year, $2,000,000 par value bonds that pay interest semiannually on October 1 and April 1. The bonds are dated April 1, 2001, and are issued on that date. The discount rate of interest for such bonds on April 1, 2001, is 12%. What cash proceeds did Galway Bay receive from issuance of the bonds?

Compute the present value of a machine for purposes of making a purchase decision.

BEC-17   Barney Googal owns a garage and is contemplating purchasing a tire retreading machine for $16,100. After estimating costs and revenues, Barney projects a net cash flow from the retreading machine of $2,690 annually for 8 years. Barney hopes to earn a return of 11 percent on such investments. What is the present value of the retreading operation? Should Barney Googal purchase the retreading machine?

Compute the present value of a note.

BEC-18   Hung-Chao Yu Company issues a 10%, 5-year mortgage note on January 1, 2001 to obtain financing for new equipment. Land is used as collateral for the note. The terms provide for semiannual installment payments, of $112,825. What were the cash proceeds received from the issuance of the note?

Compute the maximum price to pay for a machine.

BEC-19   Ramos Company is considering purchasing equipment. The equipment will produce the following cash flows: Year 1, $35,000; Year 2, $45,000; Year 3, $55,000. Ramos requires a minimum rate of return of 15%. What is the maximum price Ramos should pay for this equipment?

Compute the interest rate on a single amount.

BEC-20   If Kerry Rodriguez invests $2,090 now and she will receive $10,000 at the end of 15 years, what annual rate of interest will Kerry earn on her investment? [*Hint:*   Use Table 3.]

Compute the number of periods of a single amount.

BEC-21   Maloney Cork has been offered the opportunity of investing $43,233 now. The investment will earn 15% per year and at the end of that time will return Maloney $100,000. How many years must Maloney wait to receive $100,000? [*Hint:*   Use Table 3.]

Compute the interest rate on an annuity.

BEC-22   Annie Dublin made an investment of $9,818.15. From this investment, she will receive $1,000 annually for the next 20 years starting one year from now. What rate of interest will Annie's investment be earning for her? [*Hint:*   Use Table 4.]

Compute the number of periods of an annuity.

BEC-23   Andy Sanchez invests $7,786.15 now for a series of $1,000 annual returns beginning one year from now. Andy will earn a return of 9% on the initial investment. How many annual payments of $1,000 will Andy receive? [*Hint:*   Use Table 4].

PHOTO CREDITS

Chapter 1

Opener: Courtesy Tootsie Roll Industries, Inc. Page 22: Peter Johnson/CORBIS.

Chapter 2

Opener: Jeanne Strongin. Page 50: SUPERSTOCK. Page 54 (top): Gary Holscher/Tony Stone Images/New York, Inc. Page 54 (bottom): Courtesy The Coca-Cola Company. Page 55 (top): Reproduced with permission of Yahoo! Inc. © 1999 by Yahoo! Inc. Yahoo! and the Yahoo! logo are trademarks of Yahoo! Inc. Page 55 (middle): Used with permission of Ben & Jerry's Homemade Holdings, Inc. 1999. Page 55 (bottom): Courtesy Morrow Snowboards Inc. Page 56 (top): Jonathan Elderfield/Gamma Liaison. Page 56 (bottom): Courtesy of Northwest Airlines, Inc. Page 61: Andy Caulfield/The Image Bank. Page 66: Vladimir Pcholkin/FPG International. Page 70: Courtesy Tweeter Home Entertainment Group. Page 75: Courtesy Circuit City. Page 90: Courtesy MoDo. Pages 59, 62, 63 & 67: James Schnepf/Gamma Liaison.

Chapter 3

Opener: Peter Poulides/Tony Stone Images/New York, Inc. Page 102: Courtesy Rhino Foods. Page 106: Vera R. Storman/Tony Stone Images/New York, Inc. Page 108: Peter Pawinski/CORBIS.

Chapter 4

Opener: James Porto/FPG International. Page 152: AP/Wide World Photos. Page 154: SUPERSTOCK. Page 157: Courtesy Proctor & Gamble/Saatchi & Saatchi. Page 161: Courtesy Microsoft. Page 175: Courtesy Wal-Mart Stores, Inc. Page 176: John Bleck/Lori Nowicki. Pages 177 & 178: Courtesy Humana, Inc. Page 200: Courtesy Case Corporation.

Chapter 5

Opener: George Kavanagh/Tony Stone Images/New York, Inc. Page 209: Courtesy Morrow Snowboards Inc. Page 212: Gregory Heisler/The Image Bank. Page 215: Grant V. Faint/The Image Bank. Page 217: Courtesy Wal-Mart Stores, Inc. Page 219: Gary Buss/FPG International. Page 222: R. Schneider/The Image Bank. Page 223: Courtesy Kmart Corporation.

Chapter 6

Opener: VCG/FPG International. Page 251: L.D. Gordon/The Image Bank. Page 261: Tim Flach/Tony Stone Images/New York, Inc. Page 262 (top): Logo used permission of The Quaker Oats Company. Page 262 (bottom): Bob Krist/Tony Stone Images/New York, Inc. Page 265: Richard T. Nowitz/Corbis Images. Page 266: Courtesy Caterpillar, Inc. Page 268: Courtesy

of The Manitowoc Company. Page 292: Courtesy Morrow Snowboards, Inc. Page 294: Courtesy Fujifilm. Page 295: Courtesy Eastman Kodak Company.

Chapter 7

Opener: Abrams/Lacagnina/The Image Bank. Page 301: Christian Michaels/FPG International. Pages 303, 306 & 311: SUPERSTOCK. Page 305: Reuters Newmedia Inc./Corbis Images. Page 308: R. Michael Stuckey/Comstock, Inc. Page 312: J.W. Burkey/Tony Stone Images/New York, Inc. Page 314: Salem Krieger/The Image Bank. Page 317: Courtesy Avis. Page 324: Courtesy Harley-Davidson Motor Company. Page 348 (top): Courtesy Microsoft Corporation. Page 348 (bottom): Courtesy Oracle Corporation. Oracle is a registered trademark of Oracle Corporation.

Chapter 8

Opener: William Whitehurst/The Stock Market. Page 355: Gary Gladstone/The Image Bank. Pages 356 & 378: Dennis Galante/Tony Stone Images/New York, Inc. Page 359 & 361: SUPERSTOCK. Page 366: Telegraph Colour Library/FPG International. Page 367: Courtesy CPC International, Inc. Page 369: Shaun Egan/Tony Stone Images/New York, Inc. Page 370: Bob Krist/Black Star. Page 371: Courtesy of McKesson HBOC, Inc. Page 374: Steve Edson/Photonica. Page 375: Randee Ladden.

Chapter 9

Opener: Photo by Mike Eller courtesy Southwest Airlines Co. Page 400: Michael Goodman/FPG International. Page 403: Etienne de Malgaive/Liaison Agency. Page 405: John M. Roberts/The Stock Market. Page 410 (top): Courtesy AirTran Airways. Page 410 (bottom): Courtesy Southwest Airlines Co. Page 411: Courtesy Delta Air Lines, Inc. Page 413: Peter Poulides/Tony Stone Images/New York, Inc. Page 423: © Schnepf/Gamma Liaison. Page 424 (top): Courtesy The Pillsbury Company. Page 424 (bottom): Courtesy The Coca-Cola Company. Pages 425 & 426: G. Watson/Photo Researchers. Page 446: Courtesy J Sainsbury, plc.

Chapter 10

Opener: Courtesy Chrysler Corporation. Page 454: Pamela Hamilton/The Image Bank. Pages 459, 461, 477 (top) & 478: © General Motors Corp. Used with permission. Page 465: Tony Stone Imaging/Tony Stone Images/New York, Inc. Page 473: AKG Photo, London/Archiv/Photo Researchers. Page 477 (bottom): Jeff Zaruba/The Stock Market. Page 480: Courtesy Ford Motor Company.

Chapter 11

Opener & pages 518 & 537: Courtesy Nike, Inc. Page 513: Darren Robb/Tony Stone Images/New York, Inc. Page 515: Greg Davis/The Stock Market. Page 520: Courtesy Reebok International, Ltd. Page 523: SUPERSTOCK. Page 529: Frank White/Gamma Liaison. Page 531: Courtesy Tektronix, Inc. Page 532: Courtesy Kmart Corporation.

Chapter 12

Opener: SUPERSTOCK. Page 562: Robert Maass/CORBIS. Page 563: Jonathan Kirn/Tony Stone Images/New York, Inc.

Chapter 13

Opener & pages 597 & 632: Courtesy Microsoft Corporation. Page 601: Lance Nelson/The Stock Market. Page 604: Vladimir Pcholkin/FPG International. Page 633: D. Redfearn/The Image Bank. Page 638: Index Stock. Pages 639–640: Courtesy Intel. Page 660: Courtesy Saint-Gobain.

Chapter 14

Opener: Mitchell Funk/The Image Bank. Pages 674, 676, 677, 679, 680, 695 & 696: Courtesy Kellogg Company. Page 682: SUPERSTOCK. Page 683: Courtesy JCPenney. Page 693: Courtesy Toys "Я" Us.

COMPANY INDEX

SUBJECT INDEX

Accelerated-depreciation method, 429, 431

Accountability, 302

Accounting: constraints in, 51–52; explanation of, 6, 28; varying standards for international, 50. *See also* Accrual accounting

Accounting cycle, 175–176

Accounting information: characteristics of useful, 49–51; external users of, 6–7; internal users of, 6. *See also* Financial statements

Accounting information system, 7; accounting transactions and, 97–103; accounts and, 103–109; explanation of, 96, 126; recording process and, 109–120; trial balance and, 121–122

Accounting transactions: analysis of, 97–102; explanation of, 97, 126; summary of, 102–103

Accounts: chart of, 113; debits and credits and, 104–108; elements of, 104; expanded basic equation and, 108–109; explanation of, 103, 126; stockholders' equity relationships and, 108

Accounts payable: explanation of, 8; statement of cash flows and, 609–610, 613, 622

Accounts receivable: aging the, 360, 370, 380; allowance method for uncollectible accounts and, 257; direct write-off method for uncollectible accounts and, 356–357; estimating allowance and, 360–361; explanation of, 355, 380; management of, 361; recognizing, 355–356; recording estimated uncollectibles and, 357–358; recording write-off of uncollectible accounts and, 358–359; recovery of uncollectible accounts and, 359; statement of cash flows and, 609, 613, 621

Accrual accounting: adjusting entries and, 154–169; adjusting trial balance and, 170; cash basis of accounting vs., 153–154; closing the books and, 171–174; financial statement preparation and, 171; summary of accounting cycle and, 175–176; timing issues and, 150–154; use of cash flows and, 604

Accrual basis accounting: cash basis vs., 153–154; explanation of, 153, 181

Accruals, 162–166

Accrued expenses, 168, 181

Accrued interest, 164–165

Accrued revenue: adjusting entries for, 163–164; explanation of, 168, 181

Accrued salaries, 165–166

Acid-test ratio: example of, 460; explanation of, 459, 488, 682, 700

Acquisition: horizontal, 562; of plant assets, 398–399; recording bond, 563; of stock, 566, 567; vertical, 562

Additions and improvements, 412, 431

Adjusted balance, 314, 315

Adjusted entries, 179–180

Adjusted trial balance: explanation of, 181, 300; financial statements and, 171; preparation of, 170; preparation of balance sheet from, 172

Adjusting entries: for accrued expenses, 162, 164–166; for accrued revenue, 162–164; explanation of, 154, 181; for prepaid expenses, 155–159; summary of, 167–169; types of, 155; for unearned revenue, 156, 159–160; use of, 154–155

Administrative expenses, 9, 219

Advertising costs, 157

Aging the accounts receivable: explanation of, 360, 380; uses of, 370

Airline industry, 396–397, 403

Allowance for doubtful accounts: credit risk ratio and, 369; explanation of, 357, 358

Allowance method: estimating allowance and, 360–361; explanation of, 357, 380; recording estimated uncollectibles and, 357–358; recording write-off of uncollectible accounts and, 358–359; recovery of uncollectible account and, 359

Allowances: purchase, 210–211; sales, 214–215

American Stock Exchange, 516

Amortization: bond discount, 482–485; bond premium, 485–486; explanation of, 431; of intangible assets, 420–421, 424; straight-line method of, 469–471, 482, 483

Annual reports: auditor's report and, 20, 21; elements of, A-1; explanation of, 18, 28, A-1; management discussion and analysis and, 19; notes to financial statements and, 20; for Tootsie Roll Industries, A-1–A-19

Annuities: explanation of, C-16; future value of, C-5–C-8; present value of, C-11–C-13

Assets: accountability for, 302; calculation of average, 59; current, 53–54, 73; debit/credit procedures and, 105–106; explanation of, 8, 28; fixed, 8; intangible, 20, 55, 73, 420–423; plant, 398–419. *See also* Intangible assets; Plant assets

Asset turnover ratio, 418–419, 431, 689–690, 700

Assumptions: economic entity, 21–22, 28; going concern, 22, 29; illustration of accounting, 23; monetary unit, 21, 29; time period, 22, 29

Auditors: explanation of, 20; internal, 304–305

Auditor's reports: explanation of, 20, 28; for Tootsie Roll Industries, 21, A-17

Authorized stock, 516, 540

Available-for-sale securities: comprehensive income and, 672; explanation of, 473, 570, 580; fair value and, 572, 672

Average age of plant assets, 417–418, 431

Average assets, 59

Average collection period, 372, 380, 683–684, 700

Average cost method, 258–259, 278

Average days in inventory, 684, 700

Average useful life, 416–417, 431

Bad debts expense, 356, 380

Balance sheets: adjusted trial balance and, 172; cash listed in, 316; classified, 52–57, 63–65; cost flow